History of Classical India
322 BCE to 550 BCE

Compiled by
Bailee Skeen

Scribbles

Year of Publication 2018

ISBN : 9789352979172

Book Published by

Scribbles

(An Imprint of Alpha Editions)

email - alphaedis@gmail.com

Produced by: PediaPress GmbH
Limburg an der Lahn
Germany
http://pediapress.com/

The content within this book was generated collaboratively by volunteers. Please be advised that nothing found here has necessarily been reviewed by people with the expertise required to provide you with complete, accurate or reliable information. Some information in this book may be misleading or simply wrong. Alpha Editions and PediaPress does not guarantee the validity of the information found here. If you need specific advice (for example, medical, legal, financial, or risk management) please seek a professional who is licensed or knowledgeable in that area.

Sources, licenses and contributors of the articles and images are listed in the section entitled "References". Parts of the books may be licensed under the GNU Free Documentation License. A copy of this license is included in the section entitled "GNU Free Documentation License"

The views and characters expressed in the book are those of the contributors and his/her imagination and do not represent the views of the Publisher.

Contents

Articles   **1**

Introduction   **1**
    Middle kingdoms of India 1

The North West   **41**
    Indo-Scythians 41
    Saka 74
    Indo-Greek Kingdom 87
    Yona 158
    Indo-Parthian Kingdom 170
    Pahlavas 183
    Western Satraps 186
    Kushan Empire 215
    Kushano-Sasanian Kingdom 249
    Huna people 257
    Hephthalite Empire 262
    Rai dynasty 278
    Gandhara 281
    Kambojas 316
    Karkoṭa Empire 324
    Kabul Shahi 326

The Gangetic Plains and Deccan — 343

- Satavahana dynasty 343
- Mahameghavahana dynasty 377
- Nagas of Padmavati 383
- Gupta Empire 388
- Vakataka dynasty 411
- Harsha 423
- Gurjar 428
- Vishnukundina dynasty 438
- Maitraka dynasty 445
- Gurjara-Pratihara dynasty 464
- Rajput 475
- Katoch 489
- Chauhan 491
- Chahamanas of Shakambhari 495
- Kachwaha 505
- Paramara dynasty 509
- Chaulukya dynasty 526
- Tomara dynasty 541
- Pala Empire 547
- Chandra dynasty 566
- Eastern Ganga dynasty 567
- Sena dynasty 573
- Varman dynasty 579

The Northeast — 585

- Kamarupa 585
- Mlechchha dynasty 595
- Pala dynasty (Kamarupa) 597
- Twipra Kingdom 599

The Deccan plateau and South	603
Sangam period	603
Chera dynasty	610
Kalabhra dynasty	632
Kadamba dynasty	636
Western Ganga dynasty	651
Chalukya dynasty	674
Pallava dynasty	697
Eastern Chalukyas	711
Pandyan dynasty	720
Rashtrakuta dynasty	743
Western Chalukya Empire	766
Seuna (Yadava) dynasty	791
Kakatiya dynasty	804
Kalachuri dynasty	821
Hoysala Empire	828
Chola dynasty	848

Appendix	883
References	883
Article Sources and Contributors	980
Image Sources, Licenses and Contributors	986

Article Licenses	1001

Index	1003

Introduction

Middle kingdoms of India

Human history
↑ **Prehistory**
Recorded history
Ancient
• Earliest records • Africa • Americas • Oceania • East Asia • South Asia • Southeast Asia • West Asia • Europe
Postclassical
• Africa • Americas • Oceania • East Asia • South Asia • Southeast Asia • West Asia • Europe
Modern
• Early modern • Late modern
See also
• Contemporary • Modernity • Futurology
↓ **Future**
• $\underline{v}$ • $\underline{t}$ • $\underline{e}^1$

The **Middle kingdoms of India** were the political entities in India from the 3rd century BCE to the 13th century CE. The period begins after the decline of the Maurya Empire, and the corresponding rise of the Satavahana dynasty, beginning with Simuka, from 230 BCE. The "Middle" period lasted for about 1500 years and ended in the 13th century, with the rise of the Delhi Sultanate, founded in 1206, and the end of the Later Cholas (Rajendra Chola III, who died in 1279 CE).

This period encompasses two eras: **Classical India**, from the Maurya Empire up until the end of the Gupta Empire in the 6th century CE, and early Medieval India from the 6th century onwards. It also encompasses the era of classical Hinduism, which is dated from 200 BCE to 1100 CE. From 1 CE until 1000 CE, India's economy is estimated to have been the largest in the world, having between one-third and one-quarter of the world's wealth. It is followed by the late Medieval period in the 13th century.

The Northwest

During the 2nd century BCE, the Maurya Empire became a collage of regional powers with overlapping boundaries. The whole northwest attracted a series of invaders between 200 BCE and 300 CE. The Puranas speak of many of these tribes as foreigners and impure barbarians (Mlecchas). First the Satavahana dynasty and then the Gupta Empire, both successor states to the Maurya Empire, attempt to contain the expansions of the successive before eventually crumbling internally due pressure exerted by these wars.

The invading tribes were influenced by Buddhism which continued to flourish under the patronage of both invaders and the Satavahanas and Guptas and provides a cultural bridge between the two cultures. Over time, the invaders became "Indianized" as they influenced society and philosophy across the Gangetic plains and were conversely influenced by it. This period is marked by both intellectual and artistic achievements inspired by cultural diffusion and syncretism as the new kingdoms straddle the Silk Road.

The Indo-Scythian Sakas

The Indo-Scythians are a branch of the Sakas who migrated from southern Siberia into Bactria, Sogdia, Arachosia, Gandhara, Kashmir, Punjab, and into parts of Western and Central India, Gujarat, Maharashtra and Rajasthan, from the middle of the 2nd century BCE to the 4th century CE. The first Saka king in India was Maues or Moga who established Saka power in Gandhara and gradually extended supremacy over north-western India. Indo-Scythian rule

Middle kingdoms of India

Figure 1: *Silver coin of the founder of the Indo-Greek Kingdom, Demetrius (r. c. 205–171 BC).*

in India ended with the last of the Western Satraps, Rudrasimha III, in 395 CE.

The invasion of India by Scythian tribes from Central Asia, often referred to as the "Indo-Scythian invasion", played a significant part in the history of India as well as nearby countries. In fact, the Indo-Scythian war is just one chapter in the events triggered by the nomadic flight of Central Asians from conflict with Chinese tribes which had lasting effects on Bactria, Kabul, Parthia and India as well as far off Rome in the west. The Scythian groups that invaded India and set up various kingdoms, included besides the Sakas[2] other allied tribes, such as the Medes,[3] WP:NOTRS Wikipedia:Citation needed Scythians,[4] Massagetae, Wikipedia:Citation needed Getae,[5] Parama Kamboja Kingdom, Avars, Wikipedia:Citation needed Bahlikas, Rishikas and Parada Kingdom.

The Indo-Greeks

The Indo-Greek Kingdom covered various parts of the Northwestern South Asia during the last two centuries BCE, and was ruled by more than 30 Hellenistic kings, often in conflict with each other.

The kingdom was founded when Demetrius I of Bactria invaded the Hindu Kush early in the 2nd century BCE. The Greeks in India were eventually divided from the Greco-Bactrian Kingdom centered in Bactria (now the border between Afghanistan and Uzbekistan).

The expression "Indo-Greek Kingdom" loosely describes a number of various dynastic polities. There were numerous cities, such as Taxila[6] Pakistan's Punjab, or Pushkalavati and Sagala.[7] These cities would house a number of dynasties in their times, and based on Ptolemy's *Geography* and the nomenclature of later kings, a certain Theophila in the south was also probably a satrapal or royal seat at some point.

Euthydemus I was, according to Polybius[8] a Magnesian Greek. His son, Demetrius, founder of the Indo-Greek kingdom, was therefore of Greek descent from his father at minimum. A marriage treaty was arranged for Demetrius with a daughter of Antiochus III the Great, who had partial Persian descent.[9] The ethnicity of later Indo-Greek rulers is less clear.[10] For example, Artemidoros Aniketos (80 BCE) may have been of Indo-Scythian descent. Intermarriage also occurred, as exemplified by Alexander the Great, who married Roxana of Bactria, or Seleucus I Nicator, who married Apama of Sogdia.

During the two centuries of their rule, the Indo-Greek kings combined the Greek and Indian languages and symbols, as seen on their coins, and blended Greek, Hindu and Buddhist religious practices, as seen in the archaeological remains of their cities and in the indications of their support of Buddhism, pointing to a rich fusion of Indian and Hellenistic influences.[11] The diffusion of Indo-Greek culture had consequences which are still felt today, particularly through the influence of Greco-Buddhist art. The Indo-Greeks ultimately disappeared as a political entity around 10 CE following the invasions of the Indo-Scythians, although pockets of Greek populations probably remained for several centuries longer under the subsequent rule of the Indo-Parthians and Kushan Empire.[12]

The Yavanas

The **Yavana** or **Yona** people, literally "Ionian" and meaning "Western foreigner", were described as living beyond Gandhara. Yavanas, Sakas, the Pahlavas and Hunas were sometimes described as *mlecchas*, "barbarians". Kambojas and the inhabitants of Madra, the Kekeya Kingdom, the Indus River region and Gandhara were sometimes also classified as *mlecchas*. This name was used to indicate their cultural differences with the culture of the Kuru Kingdom and Panchala.Wikipedia:Citation needed

The Indo-Parthians

The Indo-Parthian Kingdom was founded by Gondophares around 20 BCE. The kingdom lasted only briefly until its conquest by the Kushan Empire in the late 1st century CE and was a loose framework where many smaller dynasts maintained their independence.

The Pahlavas

The **Pahlavas** are a people mentioned in ancient Indian texts like the *Manusmṛti*, various Puranas, the *Ramayana*, the *Mahabharata*, and the *Brhatsamhita*. In some texts the Pahlavas are synonymous with the Pallava dynasty of South India. While the *Vayu Purana* distinguishes between *Pahlava* and *Pahnava*, the *Vamana Purana* and *Matsya Purana* refer to both as *Pallava*. The *Brahmanda Purana* and *Markendeya Purana* refer to both as *Pahlava* or *Pallava*. The *Bhishama Parava* of the Mahabharata does not distinguish between the Pahlavas and Pallavas. The Pahlavas are said to be same as the Parasikas, a Saka group. According to P. Carnegy,[13] the Pahlava are probably those people who spoke Paluvi or Pehlvi, the Parthian language. Buhler similarly suggests Pahlava is an Indic form of *Parthava* meaning "Parthian".[14] In a 4th-century BCE, the *Vartika* of Kātyāyana mentions the *Sakah-Parthavah*, demonstrating an awareness of these Saka-Parthians, probably by way of commerce.[15]

The Western Satraps

The Western Satraps (35-405 CE) were Saka rulers of the western and central part of India (Saurashtra and Malwa: modern Gujarat, southern Sindh, Maharashtra, Rajasthan and Madhya Pradesh states). Their state, or at least part of it, was called "Ariaca" according to the *Periplus of the Erythraean Sea*. They were successors to the Indo-Scythians and were contemporaneous with the Kushan Empire, which ruled the northern part of the Indian subcontinent and were possibly their overlords, and the Satavahana dynasty of Andhra who ruled in Central India. They are called "Western" in contrast to the "Northern" Indo-Scythian satraps who ruled in the area of Mathura, such as Rajuvula, and his successors under the Kushans, the "Great Satrap" Kharapallana and the "Satrap" Vanaspara.[16] Although they called themselves "Satraps" on their coins, leading to their modern designation of "Western Satraps", Ptolemy's *Geography* still called them "Indo-Scythians".[17] Altogether, there were 27 independent Western Satrap rulers during a period of about 350 years.

The Kushans

The Kushan Empire (c. 1st–3rd centuries) originally formed in Bactria on either side of the middle course of the Amu Darya in what is now northern Afghanistan, Tajikistan and Uzbekistan; during the 1st century CE, they expanded their territory to include the Punjab and much of the Ganges basin, conquering a number of kingdoms across the northern part of the Indian subcontinent in the process.[18,19] The Kushans conquered the central section of the main Silk Road and, therefore, had control of the overland trade between India, and China to the east, and the Roman Empire and Persia to the west.

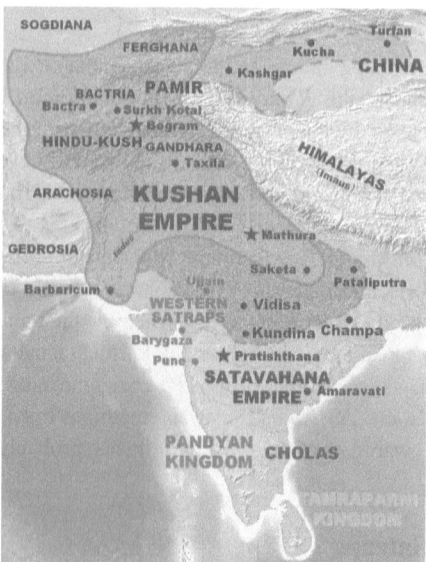

Figure 2: *Kushan Empire*

Emperor Kanishka was a great patron of Buddhism; however, as Kushans expanded southward toward the Indian subcontinent the deities of their later coinage came to reflect its new Hindu majority.

The Indo-Sasanians

The rise of new Persian power, the Sasanian Empire, saw them exert their influence into the Indus region and conquer lands from the Kushan Empire, setting up the Indo-Sasanians around 240 CE. They were to maintain their influence in the region until they were overthrown by the Rashidun Caliphate. Afterwards, they were displaced in 410 CE by the invasions of the Hephthalite Empire.

The Hephthalite Hunas

The Hephthalite Empire was another Central Asian nomadic group to invade. They are also linked to the Yuezhi who had founded the Kushan Empire. From their capital in Bamyan (present-day Afghanistan) they extended their rule across the Indus and North India, thereby causing the collapse of the Gupta Empire. They were eventually defeated by the Sasanian Empire allied with Turkic peoples.

Figure 3: *Billon drachma of the Huna King Napki Malka (Afghanistan or Gandhara, c. 475–576).*

The Rais

The Rai dynasty of Sindh were patrons of Buddhism even though they also established a huge temple of Shiva in Sukkur close to their capital, Aror.

The Gandharan Kambojas

The **Gandhara** Satrapy became an independent kingdom based from Afghanistan and vied with the Tang dynasty, Tibetan Empire, the Islamic Caliphate and Turkic tribes for domination in the region.

The Karkotas

The Karkota Empire was established around 625 CE. During the eighth century they consolidated their rule over Kashmir.[22] The most illustrious ruler of the dynasty was Lalitaditya Muktapida. According to Kalhana's *Rajatarangini*, he defeated the Tibetans and Yashovarman of Kanyakubja, and subsequently conquered eastern kingdoms of Magadha, Kamarupa, Gauda, and Kalinga. Kalhana also states that he extended his influence of Malwa and Gujarat and defeated Arabs at Sindh.[23,24] According to historians, Kalhana highly exaggerated the conquests of Lalitaditya.[20,21]

Figure 4: *Extent of the Karkota Empire during the reign of Lalitaditya Muktapida (8th century), according to Kalhana's Rajatarangini. Note that Kalhana highly exaggerated the conquests of Lalitaditya.*[20,21]

The Kabul Shahis

The Kabul Shahi dynasties ruled portions of the Kabul valley and Gandhara from the decline of the Kushan Empire in the 3rd century to the early 9th century.[25] The kingdom was known as the Kabul Shahan or Ratbelshahan from 565 CE-670 CE, when the capitals were located in Kapisa and Kabul, and later Udabhandapura, also known as Hund[26] for its new capital. In ancient time, the title Shahi appears to be a quite popular royal title in Afghanistan and the northwestern areas of the Indian subcontinent. Variants were used much more priorly in the Near East,[27] but as well later on by the Sakas, Kushans Hunas, Bactrians, by the rulers of Kapisa/Kabul and Gilgit.[28] In Persian form, the title appears as *Kshathiya, Kshathiya Kshathiyanam*, Shao of the Kushanas and the *Ssaha* of Mihirakula (Huna chief).[29] The Kushanas are stated to have adopted the title *Shah-in-shahi* (*"Shaonano shao"*) in imitation of Achaemenid practice.[30] The Shahis are generally split up into two eras—the Buddhist Shahis and the Hindu Shahis, with the change-over thought to have occurred sometime around 870 CE.

The Gangetic Plains and Deccan

Following the demise of the Mauryan Empires the Satavahanas rose as the successor state to check and contend with the influx of the Central Asian tribes from the Northwest. The Satavahanas straddling the Deccan plateau also provided a link for transmission of Buddhism and contact between the Northern Gangetic plains and the Southern regions even as the Upanishads were gaining ground. Eventually weakened both by contention with the northwestern invaders and internal strife they broke up and gave rise to several nations around Deccan and central India regions even as the Gupta Empire arose in the Indo-Gangetic Plain and ushered in a **"Golden Age"** and rebirth of empire as decentralized local administrative model and the spread of Indian culture until collapse under the Huna invasions. After the fall of Gupta Empire the Gangetic region broke up into several states temporarily reunited under Harsha then giving rise to the Rajput dynasties. In the Deccan, the Chalukyas arose forming a formidable nation marking the migration of the centers of cultural and military power long held in the Indo-Gangetic Plain to the new nations forming in the southern regions of India.

The Satavahana Empire

The **Sātavāhana dynasty** began as feudatories to the Maurya Empire but declared independence with its decline. They were the first Indic rulers to issue coins struck with their rulers embossed and are known for their patronage of Buddhism, resulting in Buddhist monuments from the Ellora Caves to Amaravathi village, Guntur district. They formed a cultural bridge and played a vital role in trade and the transfer of ideas and culture to and from the Gangetic plains to the southern tip of India.

The Sātavāhanas had to compete with the Shunga Empire and then the Kanva dynastys of Magadha to establish their rule. Later they had to contend in protecting their domain from the incursions of Sakas, Yonas and the Pahlavas. In particular their struggles with the Western Satraps weakened them and the empire split into smaller states.

The Mahameghavahana dynasty

The Mahameghavahana dynasty (c. 250s BCE-400s CE) was an ancient ruling dynasty of Kalinga after the decline of the Mauryan Empire. The third ruler of the dynasty, Khārabēḷa, conquered much of India in a series of campaigns at the beginning of the common era.[31] Kaḷingan military might was reinstated by Khārabēḷa: under Khārabēḷa's generalship, the Kaḷinga state had a formidable maritime reach with trade routes linking it to the then-Simhala

Figure 5: *Silver coin of the Gupta King Kumara Gupta I (414–455).*

(Sri Lanka), Burma (Myanmar), Siam (Thailand), Vietnam, Kamboja (Cambodia), Borneo, Bali, Samudra (Sumatra) and Jabadwipa (Java). Khārabēḷa led many successful campaigns against the states of Magadha, Anga, the Satavahanas and the South Indian regions ruled by the Pandyan dynasty (modern Andhra Pradesh) and expanded Kaḷinga as far as the Ganges and the Kaveri.

The Kharavelan state had a formidable maritime empire with trading routes linking it to Sri Lanka, Burma, Thailand, Vietnam, Cambodia, Borneo, Bali, Sumatra and Java. Colonists from Kalinga settled in Sri Lanka, Burma, as well as the Maldives and Maritime Southeast Asia. Even today Indians are referred to as Keling in Malaysia because of this.[32]

Although religiously tolerant, Khārabēḷa patronised Jainism, and was responsible for the propagation of Jainism in the Indian subcontinent but his importance is neglected in many accounts of Indian history. The main source of information about Khārabeḷa is his famous seventeen line rock-cut Hātigumphā inscription in the Udayagiri and Khandagiri Caves near Bhubaneswar, Odisha. According to the Hathigumpha inscription, he attacked Rajagriha in Magadha, thus inducing the Indo-Greek king Demetrius I of Bactria to retreat to Mathura.[33]

The Bharshiva dynasty

Before the rise of the Guptas, Bharshiva Kings ruled most of the Indo-Gangetic plains. They perform ten Ashvamedha sacrifices on the banks of Ganga River. Samudragupta mention Naga rulers in his Allahabad pillar.[34]

The Guptas

The **Classical Age** refers to the period when much of the Indian Subcontinent was reunited under the Gupta Empire (ca. 320 CE–550 CE).[35] This period is called the Golden Age of India and was marked by extensive achievements in science, technology, engineering, art, dialectic, literature, logic, mathematics, astronomy, religion and philosophy that crystallized the elements of what is generally known as Hindu culture.[36] The decimal numeral system, including the concept of zero, was invented in India during this period.Wikipedia:Citation needed The peace and prosperity created under Guptas leadership enabled the pursuit of scientific and artistic endeavors in India.[37]

The high points of this cultural creativity is seen in Gupta architecture, sculpture and painting.[38] The Gupta period produced scholars such as Kalidasa, Aryabhata, Varahamihira, Vishnu Sharma, and Vatsyayana who made advances in a variety of academic fields.[39] Science and political administration advanced during the Gupta era.Wikipedia:Citation neededWikipedia:Please clarify Trade ties made the region an important cultural center and set the region up as a base that would influence nearby kingdoms and regions in Burma, Sri Lanka, and both maritime and mainland Southeast Asia.

The Guptas performed Vedic sacrifices to legitimize their rule, but they also patronized Buddhism, which continued to provide an alternative to Brahmanical orthodoxy.Wikipedia:Citation needed The military exploits of the first three rulers - Chandragupta I (ca. 319–335), Samudragupta (ca. 335–376), and Chandragupta II (ca. 376–415) —brought much of India under their leadership.[40] They successfully resisted the North-Western Kingdoms until the arrival of the Hunas who established themselves in Afghanistan by the first half of the 5th century, with their capital at Bamiyan. Nevertheless, much of the Deccan and southern India were largely unaffected by this state of flux in the north.Wikipedia:Citation needed

The Vakatakas

The **Vakataka Empire** was the contemporaries of the Gupta Empire and the successor state of the Satavahanas they formed the southern boundaries of the north and ruled over today's modern-day states of Madhya Pradesh and Maharashtra during the 3rd and 5th centuries. The rock-cut Buddhist viharas and chaityas of Ajanta Caves (a UNESCO World Heritage Site), built under the patronage of the Vakataka rulers. They were eventually overrun by the Chalukyas.

Figure 6: *The rock-cut Buddhist viharas and chaityas of Ajanta Caves, built under the patronage of the Vakataka rulers.*

The Harsha Vardhana

After the collapse of the Gupta Empire, the gangetic plains fractured into numerous small nations. Harsha of Kannauj was able to briefly bind them together under his rulership as the Empire of Harsha. Only a defeat at the hands of the Chalukyas (Pulakeshin II) prevented him from expanding his reign south of the Narmada River. This unity did not last long beyond his reign and his empire fractured soon after his death in 647 AD.

The Gurjars

From 550 to 1018 AD, the **Gurjars** played a great part in history of Northern India nearly for 500 years.[41] Present day Rajasthan was under the rule of Gurjars for centuries with capital at Bhilmal (Bhinmal or Srimal), situated nearly 50 miles to the north west of Mount Abu. The Gurjars of Bhilmal conquered Kannuaj on the Ganges at the beginning of the 9th century and transferred their capital to Kannuaj and founded an empire which at its peak was bounded on the east by Bihar, on the west by the *lost river*, the Hakra, and the Arabian Sea, on the North By the Himalaya and Sutlaj, and on the South by the Jumna and Narmada. The region round Broach, which was offshoot of this kingdom, was also ruled by the Gurjaras of Nandipuri (or Nadol).

The Vishnukundinas

The **Vishnukundina Empire** was an Indian dynasty that ruled over the Deccan, Odisha and parts of South India during the 5th and 6th centuries carving land out from the Vakataka Empire. The Vishnukundin reign came to an end with the conquest of the eastern Deccan by the Chalukya, Pulakeshin II. Pulakeshin appointed his brother Kubja Vishnuvardhana as Viceroy to rule over the conquered lands. Eventually Vishnuvardhana declared his independence and started the Eastern Chalukya dynasty.

The Maitrakas

The **Maitraka Empire** ruled Gujarat in western India from the c. 475 to 767 CE. The founder of the dynasty, *Senapati* (general) Bhatarka, was a military governor of Saurashtra peninsula under Gupta Empire, who had established himself as the independent ruler of Gujarat approximately in the last quarter of the 5th century. The first two Maitraka rulers Bhatarka and Dharasena I used only the title of *Senapati* (general). The third ruler Dronasimha declared himself as the *Maharaja*.[42] King Guhasena stopped using the term *Paramabhattaraka Padanudhyata* along his name like his predecessors, which denotes the cessation of displaying of the nominal allegiance to the Gupta overlords. He was succeeded by his son Dharasena II, who used the title of *Mahadhiraja*. His son, the next ruler Siladitya I, Dharmaditya was described by Hiuen Tsang as a "monarch of great administrative ability and of rare kindness and compassion". Siladitya I was succeeded by his younger brother Kharagraha I.[43] Virdi copperplate grant (616 CE) of Kharagraha I proves that his territories included Ujjain.

The Gurjara Pratiharas

The **Gurjara Pratihara Empire** (Hindi: गुर्जर प्रतिहार) formed an Indian dynasty that ruled much of Northern India from the 6th to the 11th centuries. At its peak of prosperity and power (c. 836–910 CE), it rivaled the Gupta Empire in the extent of its territory.[44]

Pointing out the importance of the Gurjara Pratihara empire in the history of India Dr. R. C. Majumdar has observed, "the *Gurjara Pratihara Empire* which continued in full glory for nearly a century, was the last great empire in Northern India before the Muslim conquest." This honour is accorded to the empire of Harsha by many historians of repute but without any real justification, for the Pratihara empire was probably larger, certainly not less in extent rivalled the Gupta Empire and brought political unity and its attendant blessings upon a large part of Northern India. But its chief credit lies in its succecessful resistance to the foreign invasions from the west, from the days of Junaid. This was frankly recognised by the Arab writers themselves.

Historians of India, since the days of Eliphinstone, has wondered at slow progress of Muslim invaders in India compared to their rapid advance in other parts of the world. Arguments of doubtful validity have often been put forward to explain this unique phenomenon. Now there can be little doubt that it was the power of the Gurjara Pratihara army that effectively barred the progress of the Muslims beyond the confines of Sindh, their first conquest for nearly three hundred years. In the light of later events this might be regarded as the "chief contribution of the Gurjara Pratiharas to the history of India".

The Rajputs

The **Rajput** were a Hindu clan who rose to power across a region stretching from the gangaetic plains to the Afghan mountains, and refer to the various dynasties of the many kingdoms in the region in the wake of the collapse of the Sassanid Empire and Gupta Empire and marks the transition of Buddhist ruling dynasties to Hindu ruling dynasties.

Katoch Dynasty

The **Katoch** were a Hindu Rajput clan of the Chandravanshi lineage; with recent research suggests that Katoch may be one of the oldest royal dynasty in the world.[45]

The Chauhans

The **Chauhan dynasty** flourished from the 8th to 12th centuries CE. It was one of the three main Rajput dynasties of that era, the others being Pratiharas and Paramaras. Chauhan dynasties established themselves in several places in North India and in the state of Gujarat in Western India. They were also prominent at Sirohi in the southwest of Rajputana, and at Bundi and Kota in the east. Inscriptions also associate them with Sambhar, the salt lake area in the Amber (later Jaipur) district (the Sakhambari branch remained near lake Sambhar and married into the ruling Gurjara–Pratihara, who then ruled an empire in Northern India). Chauhans adopted a political policy that saw them indulge largely in campaigns against the Chalukyas and the invading Muslim hordes. In the 11th century, they founded the city of Ajayameru (Ajmer) in the southern part of their kingdom, and in the 12th century, the Chauhans captured Dhilika (the ancient name of Delhi) from the Tomaras and annexed some of their territory along the Yamuna River.

The **Chauhan Kingdom** became the leading state in Northern India under King Prithviraj III (1165–1192 CE), also known as **Prithvi Raj Chauhan** or

Middle kingdoms of India 15

Figure 7: *Statue of Prithvi Raj Chauhan at Ajmer*

Rai Pithora. Prithviraj III has become famous in folk tales and historical literature as the Chauhan king of Delhi who resisted and repelled the invasion by Mohammed of Ghor at the first Battle of Tarain in 1191. Armies from other Rajput kingdoms, including Mewar, assisted him. The Chauhan kingdom collapsed after Prithviraj and his armies fled[46,47] from Mohammed of Ghor in 1192 at the Second Battle of Tarain.

The Kachwaha

The **Kachwaha** originated as tributaries of the preceding powers of the region. Some scholars point out that it was only following the downfall, in the 8th-10th century, of Kannauj (the regional seat-of-power, following the break-up of Harsha's empire), that the Kacchapaghata state emerged as a principal power in the Chambal valley of present-day Madhya Pradesh.[48]

The Paramaras

The **Paramara dynasty** was an early medieval Indian dynasty who ruled over Malwa region in central India. This dynasty was founded by Upendra in c. 800 CE. The most significant ruler of this dynasty was Bhoja I who was a philosopher king and polymath. The seat of the Paramara kingdom was *Dhara Nagari* (the present day Dhar city in Madhya Pradesh state).[49]

Figure 8: *Modhera Sun Temple built by the Chaulukyas.*

Chalukyas

The **Chaulukyas** (also called Solankis) in vernacular literature) were Hindu. In Gujarat, Anhilwara (modern Siddhpur Patan) served as their capital. Gujarat was a major center of Indian Ocean trade, and Anhilwara was one of the largest cities in India, with population estimated at 100,000 in the year 1000. The Chaulukyas were patrons of the great seaside temple of Shiva at Somnath Patan in Kathiawar; Bhima Dev helped rebuild the temple after it was sacked by Mahmud of Ghazni in 1026. His son, Karna, conquered the Bhil king Ashapall or Ashaval, and after his victory established a city named Karnavati on the banks of the Sabarmati River, at the site of modern Ahmedabad.

Tomaras of Delhi

During 9th-12th century, the Tomaras of Delhi ruled parts of the present-day Delhi and Haryana.[50] Much of the information about this dynasty comes from bardic legends of little historical value, and therefore, the reconstruction of their history is difficult.[51] According to the bardic tradition, the dynasty's founder Anangpal Tuar (that is Anangapala I Tomara) founded Delhi in 736 CE.[52] However, the authenticity of this claim is doubtful.[51] The bardic legends also state that the last Tomara king (also named Anangpal) passed on the throne of Delhi to his maternal grandson Prithviraj Chauhan. This claim is

Figure 9: *Buddha and Bodhisattvas, 11th century, Pala Empire*

also inaccurate: historical evidence shows that Prithviraj inherited Delhi from his father Someshvara.[51] According to the Bijolia inscription of Someshvara, his brother Vigraharaja IV had captured Dhillika (Delhi) and Ashika (Hansi); he probably defeated a Tomara ruler.[53]

The Pratihars

Pratihars ruled from Mandore, near present day Jodhpur, they held the title of Rana before being defeated by Guhilots of Chittore.

The Palas

Pala Empire was a Buddhist dynasty that ruled from the north-eastern region of the Indian subcontinent. The name *Pala* (Modern Bengali: পাল *pal*) means *protector* and was used as an ending to the names of all Pala monarchs. The Palas were followers of the Mahayana and Tantric schools of Buddhism. Gopala was the first ruler from the dynasty. He came to power in 750 CE in Gaur by a democratic election. This event is recognized as one of the first democratic elections in South Asia since the time of the Mahā Janapadas. He reigned from 750-770 CE and consolidated his position by extending his control over all of Bengal. The Buddhist dynasty lasted for four centuries (750-1120 CE) and ushered in a period of stability and prosperity in Bengal. They created many temples and works of art as well as supported the Universities of Nalanda and Vikramashila. Somapura Mahavihara built by Dharmapala is the greatest Buddhist Vihara in the Indian Subcontinent.

The empire reached its peak under Dharmapala and Devapala. Dharmapala extended the empire into the northern parts of the Indian Subcontinent. This triggered once again the power struggle for the control of the subcontinent. Devapala, successor of Dharmapala, expanded the empire to cover much of South Asia and beyond. His empire stretched from Assam and Utkala in the east, Kamboja (modern-day Afghanistan) in the north-west and Deccan in the south. According to Pala copperplate inscription Devapala exterminated the Utkalas, conquered the Pragjyotisha (Assam), shattered the pride of the Huna, and humbled the lords of Pratiharas, Gurjara and the Dravidas.

The death of Devapala ended the period of ascendancy of the Pala Empire and several independent dynasties and kingdoms emerged during this time. However, Mahipala I rejuvenated the reign of the Palas. He recovered control over all of Bengal and expanded the empire. He survived the invasions of Rajendra Chola and the Chalukyas. After Mahipala I the Pala dynasty again saw its decline until Ramapala, the last great ruler of the dynasty, managed to retrieve the position of the dynasty to some extent. He crushed the Varendra rebellion and extended his empire farther to Kamarupa, Odisha and Northern India.

The Pala Empire can be considered as the golden era of Bengal. Palas were responsible for the introduction of Mahayana Buddhism in Tibet, Bhutan and Myanmar. The Palas had extensive trade as well as influence in south-east Asia. This can be seen in the sculptures and architectural style of the Sailendra Empire (present-day Malaya, Java, Sumatra).

The Candras

The **Candra Dynasty** who ruled over eastern Bengal and were contemporaries of the Palas.

The Eastern Gangas

The **Eastern Ganga dynasty** rulers reigned over Kalinga which consisted of the parts of the modern-day Indian states of Odisha, West Bengal, Jharkhand, Chhattisgarh, Madhya Pradesh and Andhra Pradesh from the 11th century to the early 15th century.[54] Their capital was known by the name Kalinganagar, which is the modern Srimukhalingam in Srikakulam District of Andhra Pradesh bordering Odisha. Today they are most remembered as the builders of the Konark Sun Temple a World Heritage site at Konark, Odisha. It was

Figure 10: *Konark Sun Temple at Konark, Odisha, built by King Narasimhadeva I (1236–1264 AD) also a World Heritage site.*

built by King Narasimhadeva I (1238–1264 CE). During their reign (1078-1434 CE) a new style of temple architecture came into being, commonly called as Indo-Aryan architecture. This dynasty was founded by King Anantavarma Chodaganga Deva (1078–1147 CE). He was a religious person and a patron of art and literature. He is credited for having built the famous Jagannath Temple of Puri in Odisha.

King Anantavarman Chodagangadeva was succeeded by a long line of illustrious rulers such as Narasimhadeva I (1238–1264 CE). The rulers of Eastern Ganga dynasty not only defended their kingdom from the constant attacks of the Muslim rulers from both northern and southern India but were perhaps one of the few empires to have successfully invaded and defeated their Muslim adversaries. The Eastern Ganga King Narasimha Deva I invaded the Muslim kingdom of Bengal and handed a heavy defeat to the Sultan. This ensured that Sultanate never encroached upon the domains of the Ganga Emperors for nearly a century. His military exploits still survive today as folklore in Odisha. This kingdom prospered through trade and commerce and the wealth was mostly used in the construction of temples. The rule of the dynasty came to end under the reign of King Bhanudeva IV (1414–1434 CE), in the early 15th century.

The Senas

The Palas were followed by the Sena dynasty who brought Bengal under one ruler during the 12th century. Vijay Sen the second ruler of this dynasty defeated the last Pala emperor Madanapala and established his reign. Ballal Sena introduced Kulīna System in Bengal and made Nabadwip the capital. The fourth king of this dynasty Lakshman Sen expanded the empire beyond Bengal to Bihar, Assam, northern Odisha and probably to Varanasi. Lakshman was later defeated by the Muslims and fled to eastern Bengal where he ruled few more years. The Sena dynasty brought a revival of Hinduism and cultivated Sanskrit literature in India.

The Varmans

The **Varman Dynasty** (not to be confused with the Varman dynasty of Kamarupa) ruled over eastern Bengal and were contemporaries of the Senas.

The Northeast

Kamarupa

The **Kāmarūpa**, also called **Pragjyotisha**, was one of the historical kingdoms of Assam alongside Davaka,[55] that existed from 350 to 1140 CE. Ruled by three dynasties from their capitals in present-day Guwahati, North Guwahati and Tezpur, it at its height covered the entire Brahmaputra Valley, North Bengal, Bhutan and parts of Bangladesh, and at times portions of West Bengal and Bihar.

The Varmans

The **Varman dynasty** (350-650 CE), the first historical rulers of Kamarupa; was established by Pushyavarman, a contemporary of Samudragupta.[56,57] This dynasty became vassals of the Gupta Empire, but as the power of the Guptas waned, Mahendravarman (470-494 CE) performed two horse sacrifices and threw off the imperial yoke.[58] The first of the three Kamarupa dynasties, the Varmans were followed by the Mlechchha and then the Pala dynasties.

The Mlechchhas

The **Mlechchha dynasty** succeeded the Varman dynasty and ruled to the end of the 10th century. They ruled from their capital in the vicinity of the Harrupeshwara (Tezpur). The rulers were aboriginals, with lineage from Narakasura. According to historical records, there were ten rulers in this dynasty. The Mlechchha dynasty in Kamarupa was followed by the Pala kings.

Figure 11:
9th-10th century lion sculpture representing powerful Kamarupa-Palas, Madan Kamdev

The Palas

The **Pala dynasty** of Kamarupa succeeded the Mlechchha dynasty, ruled from its capital at Durjaya (North Gauhati). Dynasty reigned till the end of the 12th century.

Brahma Pala (900-920 CE), was founder Pala dynasty (900–1100 CE) of Kamarupa. Dynasty ruled from its capital Durjaya, modern-day North Guwahati. The greatest of the Pala kings, Dharma Pala had his capital at Kamarupa Nagara, now identified with North Guwahati. Ratna Pala was another notable sovereign of this line. Records of his land-grants have been found at Bargaon and Sualkuchi, while a similar relic of Indra Pala, has been discovered at Guwahati. Pala dynasty come to end with Jaya Pala (1075-1100 CE).

The Twipra

The **Twipra Kingdom** ruled ancient Tripura. Kingdom was established around the confluence of the Brahmaputra river with the Meghna and Surma rivers in today's Central Bangladesh area. The capital was called Khorongma and was along the Meghna river in the Sylhet Division of present-day Bangladesh.

The Deccan plateau and South

In the first half of the millennium the South saw various smalled kingdoms rise and fall mostly independent to the turmoil in the Gangetic plains and the spread of the Buddhism and Jainism to the southern tip of India. During the second half of the millennium after the fall of the Gupta Empire we see a gradual shift of the balance of power both military and cultural from the northern states to the rise of large southern states.

In fact, from the Mid-Seventh to the mid-13th centuries, regionalism was the dominant theme of political or dynastic history of the Indian subcontinent. Three features commonly characterize the sociopolitical realities of this period.

- First, the spread of Brahmanical religions was a two-way process of Sanskritization of local cults and localization of Brahmanical social order.
- Second was the ascendancy of the Brahman priestly and landowning groups that later dominated regional institutions and political developments.
- Third, because of the seesawing of numerous dynasties that had a remarkable ability to survive perennial military attacks, regional kingdoms faced frequent defeats but seldom total annihilation.

Peninsular India was involved in an 8th-century tripartite power struggle among the Chalukyas (556–757 CE), the Pallavas (300–888 CE) of Kanchipuram, and the Pandyas. The Chalukya rulers were overthrown by their subordinates, the Rashtrakutas (753-973 CE). Although both the Pallava and Pandya kingdoms were enemies, the real struggle for political domination was between the Pallava and Chalukya realms.

The emergence of the Rashtrakutas heralded a new era in the history of South India. The idiom of a Pan-Indian empire had moved to south. South Indian kingdoms had hitherto ruled areas only up to and south of the Narmada River. It was the Rashtrakutas who first forged north to the Gangetic plains and successfully contested their might against the Palas of Bengal and the Rajput Pratiharas of Gujarat.

Despite interregional conflicts, local autonomy was preserved to a far greater degree in the south where it had prevailed for centuries. The absence of a highly centralized government was associated with a corresponding local autonomy in the administration of villages and districts. Extensive and well-documented overland and maritime trade flourished with the Arabs on the west coast and with Southeast Asia. Trade facilitated cultural diffusion in Southeast Asia, where local elites selectively but willingly adopted Indian art, architecture, literature, and social customs.

The interdynastic rivalry and seasonal raids into each other's territory notwithstanding, the rulers in the Deccan and South India patronized all three religions - Buddhism, Hinduism, and Jainism. The religions vied with each other for royal favor, expressed in land grants but more importantly in the creation of monumental temples, which remain architectural wonders. The cave temples of Elephanta Island (near Mumbai or Bombay, as it was known formerly), Ajanta, and Ellora (in Maharashtra), and structural temples of Pattadakal, Aihole, Badami in Karnataka and Mahaballipuram and Kanchipuram in Tamil Nadu are enduring legacies of otherwise warring regional rulers.

By the mid-7th century, Buddhism and Jainism began to decline as sectarian Hindu devotional cults of Shiva and Vishnu vigorously competed for popular support.

Although Sanskrit was the language of learning and theology in South India, as it was in the north, the growth of the bhakti (devotional) movements enhanced the crystallization of vernacular literature in Dravidian languages: Kannada and Tamil; they often borrowed themes and vocabulary from Sanskrit but preserved much local cultural lore. Examples of Tamil literature include two major poems, Cilappatikaram (The Jewelled Anklet) and Manimekalai (The Jewelled Belt); the body of devotional literature of Shaivism and Vaishnavism—Hindu devotional movements; and the reworking of the Ramayana by Kamban in the 12th century. A nationwide cultural synthesis had taken place with a minimum of common characteristics in the various regions of South Asia, but the process of cultural infusion and assimilation would continue to shape and influence India's history through the centuries.

The Sangam Era Kingdoms

Farther south were three ancient Tamil states — Chera (on the west), Chola (on the east), and Pandya (in the south). They were involved in internecine warfare seeking regional supremacy. They are mentioned in Greek and Ashokan sources as important Indian kingdoms beyond the Mauryan Empire. A corpus of ancient Tamil literature, known as Sangam (academy) works, provides much useful information about life in these kingdoms in the era 300 BCE to 200 CE.

Dravidian social order was based on different ecoregions rather than on the Aryan varna paradigm, although the Brahmans had a high status at a very early stage. Segments of society were characterized by matriarchy and matrilineal succession—which survived well into the 19th century—cross-cousin marriage, and strong regional identity. Tribal chieftains emerged as "kings" just as people moved from pastoralism toward agriculture sustained by irrigation based on rivers by small-scale water tanks (as man-made ponds are called in India) and wells, as well as maritime trade with Rome and Southeast Asia.

Discoveries of Roman gold coins in various sites attest to extensive South Indian links with the outside world. As with Pataliputra in the northeast and Taxila in the northwest (in modern Pakistan), the city of Madurai, the capital of the Pandyan Kingdom (in modern Tamil Nadu), was the center of intellectual and literary activity. Poets and bards assembled there under royal patronage at successive concourses to composed anthologies of poems and expositions on Tamil grammar. By the end of the 1st century BCE, South Asia was crisscrossed by overland trade routes, which facilitated the movements of Buddhist and Jain missionaries and other travelers and opened the area to a synthesis of many cultures.

The Cheras

From early pre-historic times, Tamil Nadu was the home of the four Tamil states of the Chera, Chola, Pandya and Pallavas. The oldest extant literature, dated between 300 BCE and 600 CE mentions the exploits of the kings and the princes, and of the poets who extolled them. Cherans, who spoke Tamil language ruled from the capital of Karur in the west and traded extensively with West Asian kingdoms.

An unknown dynasty called Kalabhras invaded and displaced the three Tamil kingdoms between the 4th and the 7th centuries. This is referred to as the Dark Age in Tamil history. They were eventually expelled by the Pallavas and the Pandyas.

The Kalabhras

Little of their origins or the time during which they ruled is known beyond that they ruled over the entirety of the southern tip of India during the 3rd to the 6th century, overcoming the Sangam era kingdoms. The appear to be patrons of Jainism and Buddhism as the only source of information on them is the scattered mentions in the many Buddhist and Jain literature of the time. They were contemporaries of the Kadambas and the Western Ganga Dynasty. They were overcome by the rise of the Pallavas and the resurgence of the Pandyan Kingdom.

The Kadambas

The **Kadamba Dynasty** (Kannada: ಕದಂಬರು) (345–525 CE) was an ancient royal family of Karnataka that ruled from Banavasi in present-day Uttara Kannada district. The dynasty later continued to rule as a feudatory of larger Kannada empires, the Chalukya and the Rashtrakuta empires for over five hundred years during which time they branched into Goa and Hanagal. At the peak of their power under King Kakushtavarma, they ruled large parts of Karnataka.

Figure 12: *Kadamba tower at Doddagaddavalli*

During the pre-Kadamba era the ruling families that controlled Karnataka, the Mauryas, Satavahanas and Chutus were not natives of the region and the nucleus of power resided outside present day Karnataka. The Kadambas were the first indigenous dynasty to use Kannada, the language of the soil at an administrative level. In the history of Karnataka, this era serves as a broad based historical starting point in the study of the development of region as an enduring geo-political entity and Kannada as an important regional language.

The dynasty was founded by Mayurasharma in 345 which at times showed the potential of developing into imperial proportions, an indication to which is provided by the titles and epithets assumed by its rulers. One of his successors, Kakusthavarma was a powerful ruler and even the kings of imperial Gupta Dynasty of northern India cultivated marital relationships with his family, giving a fair indication of the sovereign nature of their kingdom. Tiring of the endless battles and bloodshed, one of the later descendants, King Shivakoti adopted Jainism. The Kadambas were contemporaries of the Western Ganga Dynasty of Talakad and together they formed the earliest native kingdoms to rule the land with absolute autonomy.

Figure 13: *Statue of Bahubali as Gommateshvara built by the Western Ganga is one of the largest monolithic statues in the world.*

The Western Gangas

The **Western Ganga Dynasty** (350–1000 CE) (Kannada: ಪಶ್ಚಿಮ ಗಂಗ ಸಂಸ್ಥಾನ) was an important ruling dynasty of ancient Karnataka in India. They are known as **Western Gangas** to distinguish them from the Eastern Gangas, who in later centuries ruled over modern Odisha. The general belief is the Western Gangas began their rule during a time when multiple native clans asserted their freedom due to the weakening of the Pallava dynasty of South India, a geo-political event sometimes attributed to the southern conquests of Samudragupta. The Western Ganga sovereignty lasted from about 350 to 550 CE, initially ruling from Kolar and later moving their capital to Talakad on the banks of the Kaveri in modern Mysore district.

After the rise of the imperial Chalukya dynasty of Badami, the Gangas accepted Chalukya overlordship and fought for the cause of their overlords against the Pallavas of Kanchipuram. The Chalukyas were replaced by the Rashtrakutas of Manyakheta in 753 CE as the dominant power in the Deccan. After a century of struggle for autonomy, the Western Gangas finally accepted Rashtrakuta overlordship and successfully fought alongside them against their foes, the Chola dynasty of Tanjavur. In the late 10th century, north of Tungabhadra river, the Rashtrakutas were replaced by the emerging Western Chalukya

Empire and the Chola Dynasty saw renewed power south of the Kaveri. The defeat of the Western Gangas by Cholas around 1000 resulted in the end of Ganga influence over the region.

Though territorially a small kingdom, the Western Ganga contribution to polity, culture and literature of the modern south Karnataka region is considered important. The Western Ganga kings showed benevolent tolerance to all faiths but are most famous for their patronage towards Jainism resulting in the construction of monuments in places such as Shravanabelagola and Kambadahalli. The kings of this dynasty encouraged the fine arts due to which literature in Kannada and Sanskrit flourished. Chavundaraya's writing, *Chavundaraya Purana* of 978 CE, is an important work in Kannada prose. Many classics were written on subjects ranging from religious topics to elephant management.

The Badami Chalukyas

The **Chalukya Empire**, natives of the Aihole and Badami region in Karnataka, were at first a feudatory of the Kadambas.[59,60,61,62,63] They encouraged the use of Kannada in addition to the Sanskrit language in their administration.[64,65] In the middle of the 6th century the Chalukyas came into their own when Pulakeshin I made the hill fortress in Badami his center of power.[66] During the rule of Pulakeshin II a south Indian empire sent expeditions to the north past the Tapti River and Narmada River for the first time and successfully defied Harshavardhana, the King of Northern India (*Uttarapatheswara*). The Aihole inscription of Pulakeshin II, written in classical Sanskrit language and old Kannada script dated 634,[67,68] proclaims his victories against the Kingdoms of Kadambas, Western Gangas, Alupas of South Canara, Mauryas of Puri, Kingdom of Kosala, Malwa, Lata and Gurjaras of southern Rajasthan. The inscription describes how King Harsha of Kannauj lost his *Harsha* (joyful disposition) on seeing a large number of his war elephants die in battle against Pulakeshin II.[69,70,71,72,73]

These victories earned him the title *Dakshinapatha Prithviswamy* (lord of the south). Pulakeshin II continued his conquests in the east where he conquered all kingdoms in his way and reached the Bay of Bengal in present-day Odisha. A Chalukya viceroyalty was set up in Gujarat and Vengi (coastal Andhra) and princes from the Badami family were dispatched to rule them. Having subdued the Pallavas of Kanchipuram, he accepted tributes from the Pandyas of Madurai, Chola dynasty and Cheras of the Kerala region. Pulakeshin II thus became the master of India, south of the Narmada River.[74] Pulakeshin II is widely regarded as one of the great kings in Indian history.[75,76] Hiuen-Tsiang, a Chinese traveller visited the court of Pulakeshin II at this time and Persian emperor Khosrau II exchanged ambassadors.[77] However, the continuous wars with Pallavas took a turn for the worse in 642 when the Pallava

Figure 14: *Badami Cave Temples No 3. (Vishnu)*

king Narasimhavarman I avenged his father's defeat, conquered and plundered the capital of Pulakeshin II who may have died in battle.[78] A century later, Chalukya Vikramaditya II marched victoriously into Kanchipuram, the Pallava capital and occupied it on three occasions, the third time under the leadership of his son and crown prince Kirtivarman II. He thus avenged the earlier humiliation of the Chalukyas by the Pallavas and engraved a Kannada inscription on the victory pillar at the Kailasanatha Temple.[79,80,81,82] He later overran the other traditional kingdoms of Tamil country, the Pandyas, Cholas and Keralas in addition to subduing a Kalabhra ruler.[83]

The Kappe Arabhatta record from this period (700) in *tripadi* (three line) metre is considered the earliest available record in Kannada poetics. The most enduring legacy of the Chalukya dynasty is the architecture and art that they left behind.[84] More than one hundred and fifty monuments attributed to them, built between 450 and 700, have survived in the Malaprabha basin in Karnataka.[85] The constructions are centred in a relatively small area within the Chalukyan heartland. The structural temples at Pattadakal, a UNESCO World Heritage Site, the cave temples of Badami, the temples at Mahakuta and early experiments in temple building at Aihole are their most celebrated monuments. Two of the famous paintings at Ajanta cave no. 1, "The Temptation of the Buddha" and "The Persian Embassy" are also credited to them.[86] Further,

Figure 15: *Shore Temple in Mamallapuram built by the Pallavas. (c. eighth century CE)*

they influenced the architecture in far off places like Gujarat and Vengi as evidenced in the Nava Brahma temples at Alampur.[87]

The Pallavas

The 7th century Tamil Nadu saw the rise of the Pallavas under Mahendravarman I and his son *Mamalla* Narasimhavarman I. The Pallavas were not a recognised political power before the 2nd century.[88] It has been widely accepted by scholars that they were originally executive officers under the Satavahana Empire.[89] After the fall of the Satavahanas, they began to get control over parts of Andhra and the Tamil country. Later they had marital ties with the Vishnukundina who ruled over the Deccan. It was around 550 AD under King Simhavishnu that the Pallavas emerged into prominence. They subjugated the Cholas and reigned as far south as the Kaveri River. Pallavas ruled a large portion of South India with Kanchipuram as their capital. Dravidian architecture reached its peak during the Pallava rule.Wikipedia:Citation needed Narasimhavarman II built the Shore Temple which is a UNESCO World Heritage Site. Many sources describe Bodhidharma, the founder of the Zen school of Buddhism in China, as a prince of the Pallava dynasty.[90]

The Eastern Chalukyas

Eastern Chalukyas were a South Indian dynasty whose kingdom was located in the present day Andhra Pradesh. Their capital was Vengi and their dynasty lasted for around 500 years from the 7th century until c. 1130 CE when the Vengi kingdom merged with the Chola empire. The Vengi kingdom was continued to be ruled by Eastern Chalukyan kings under the protection of the Chola empire until 1189 CE, when the kingdom succumbed to the Hoysalas and the Yadavas. They had their capital originally at Vengi now (Pedavegi, Chinavegi and Denduluru) near Eluru of the West Godavari district end later changed to Rajamahendravaram (Rajamundry).

Eastern Chalukyas were closely related to the Chalukyas of Vatapi (Badami). Throughout their history they were the cause of many wars between the more powerful Cholas and Western Chalukyas over the control of the strategic Vengi country. The five centuries of the Eastern Chalukya rule of Vengi saw not only the consolidation of this region into a unified whole, but also saw the efflorescence of Telugu culture, literature, poetry and art during the later half of their rule. It can be said to be the golden period of Andhra history.

The Pandyas

Pallavas were replaced by the Pandyas in the 8th century. Their capital Madurai was in the deep south away from the coast. They had extensive trade links with the Southeast Asian maritime empires of Srivijaya and their successors. As well as contacts, even diplomatic, reaching as far as the Roman Empire. During the 13th century of the Christian era Marco Polo mentioned it as the richest empire in existence.Wikipedia:Citation needed Temples like Meenakshi Amman Temple at Madurai and Nellaiappar Temple at Tirunelveli are the best examples of Pandyan Temple architecture.[91,92] The Pandyas excelled in both trade as well as literature and they controlled the pearl fisheries along the South Indian coast, between Sri Lanka and India, which produced some of the finest pearls in the known ancient world.

The Rashtrakutas

In the middle of the 8th century the Chalukya rule was ended by their feudatory, the Rashtrakuta family rulers of Berar (in present-day Amravati district of Maharashtra). Sensing an opportunity during a weak period in the Chalukya rule, Dantidurga trounced the great Chalukyan "Karnatabala" (power of Karnata).[93,94] Having overthrown the Chalukyas, the Rashtrakutas made Manyakheta their capital (modern Malkhed in Gulbarga district).[95,96] Although the origins of the early Rashtrakuta ruling families in central India and the Deccan in the 6th and 7th centuries is controversial, during the eighth

Middle kingdoms of India

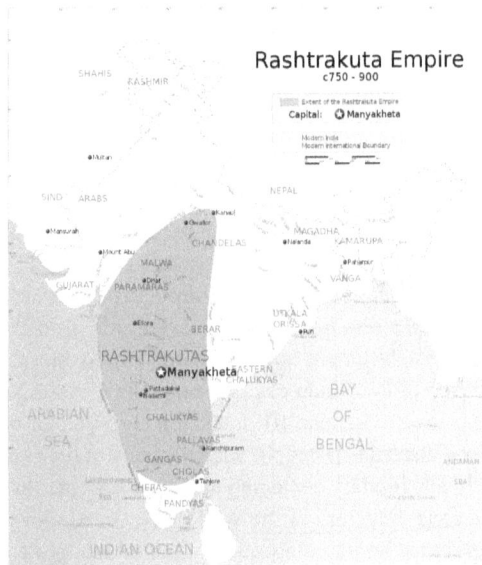

Figure 16: *Rashtrakuta Empire in 800 CE, 915 CE.*

Figure 17: *Kailash Temple in Ellora Caves*

through the 10th centuries they emphasised the importance of the Kannada language in conjunction with Sanskrit in their administration. Rashtrakuta inscriptions are in Kannada and Sanskrit only. They encouraged literature in both languages and thus literature flowered under their rule.[97,98,99,100]

The Rashtrakutas quickly became the most powerful Deccan empire, making their initial successful forays into the doab region of Ganges River and Jamuna River during the rule of Dhruva Dharavarsha.[101] The rule of his son Govinda III signaled a new era with Rashtrakuta victories against the Pala Dynasty of Bengal and Gurjara Pratihara of north western India resulting in the capture of Kannauj. The Rashtrakutas held Kannauj intermittently during a period of a tripartite struggle for the resources of the rich Gangetic plains.[102] Because of Govinda III's victories, historians have compared him to Alexander the Great and Pandava Arjuna of the Hindu epic Mahabharata.[103] The Sanjan inscription states the horses of Govinda III drank the icy water of the Himalayan stream and his war elephants tasted the sacred waters of the Ganges River.[104] Amoghavarsha I, eulogised by contemporary Arab traveller Sulaiman as one among the four great emperors of the world, succeeded Govinda III to the throne and ruled during an important cultural period that produced landmark writings in Kannada and Sanskrit.[105,106] The benevolent development of Jain religion was a hallmark of his rule. Because of his religious temperament, his interest in the arts and literature and his peace-loving nature,[107] he has been compared to emperor Ashoka.[108] The rule of Indra III in the 10th century enhanced the Rashtrakuta position as an imperial power as they conquered and held Kannauj again.[109] Krishna III followed Indra III to the throne in 939. A patron of Kannada literature and a powerful warrior, his reign marked the submission of the Paramara of Ujjain in the north and Cholas in the south.[110]

An Arabic writing *Silsilatuttavarikh* (851) called the Rashtrakutas one among the four principle empires of the world.[111] *Kitab-ul-Masalik-ul-Mumalik* (912) called them the "greatest kings of India" and there were many other contemporaneous books written in their praise.[112] The Rashtrakuta empire at its peak spread from Cape Comorin in the south to Kannauj in the north and from Banaras in the east to Broach (Bharuch) in the west.[113] While the Rashtrakutas built many fine monuments in the Deccan, the most extensive and sumptuous of their work is the monolithic Kailasanatha temple at Ellora, the temple being a splendid achievement.[114] In Karnataka their most famous temples are the Kashivishvanatha temple and the Jain Narayana temple at Pattadakal. All of the monuments are designated UNESCO World Heritage Sites.

The Western Chalukyas

In the late 10th century, the Western Chalukyas, also known as the Kalyani Chalukyas or 'Later' Chalukyas rose to power by overthrowing the Rashtrakutas under whom they had been serving as feudatories. Manyakheta was their capital early on before they moved it to Kalyani (modern Basavakalyan). Whether the kings of this empire belonged to the same family line as their namesakes, the Badami Chalukyas is still debated.[115,116] Whatever the Western Chalukya origins, Kannada remained their language of administration and the Kannada and Sanskrit literature of their time was prolific.[117,118,119,120] Tailapa II, a feudatory ruler from Tardavadi (modern Bijapur district), re-established the Chalukya rule by defeating the Rashtrakutas during the reign of Karka II. He timed his rebellion to coincide with the confusion caused by the invading Paramara of Central India to the Rashtrakutas capital in 973.[121,122,123] This era produced prolonged warfare with the Chola dynasty of Tamilakam for control of the resources of the Godavari River–Krishna River doab region in Vengi. Someshvara I, a brave Chalukyan king, successfully curtailed the growth of the Chola Empire to the south of the Tungabhadra River region despite suffering some defeats[124,125] while maintaining control over his feudatories in the Konkan, Gujarat, Malwa and Kalinga regions.[126] For approximately 100 years, beginning in the early 11th century, the Cholas occupied large areas of South Karnataka region (Gangavadi).[127]

In 1076 CE, the ascent of the most famous king of this Chalukya family, Vikramaditya VI, changed the balance of power in favour of the Chalukyas.[128] His fifty-year reign was an important period in Karnataka's history and is referred to as the "Chalukya Vikrama era".[129] His victories over the Cholas in the late 11th and early 12th centuries put an end to the Chola influence in the Vengi region permanently. Some of the well known contemporaneous feudatory families of the Deccan under Chalukya control were the Hoysalas, the Seuna Yadavas of Devagiri, the Kakatiya dynasty and the Southern Kalachuri.[130] At their peak, the Western Chalukyas ruled a vast empire stretching from the Narmada River in the north to the Kaveri River in the south. Vikramaditya VI is considered one of the most influential kings of Indian history.[131,132] Important architectural works were created by these Chalukyas, especially in the Tungabhadra river valley, that served as a conceptual link between the building idioms of the early Badami Chalukyas and the later Hoysalas.[133,134] With the weakening of the Chalukyas in the decades following the death of Vikramaditya VI in 1126, the feudatories of the Chalukyas gained their independence.

The Kalachuris of Karnataka, whose ancestors were immigrants into the southern deccan from central India, had ruled as a feudatory from Mangalavada (modern Mangalavedhe in Maharashtra).[135] Bijjala II, the most powerful ruler of this dynasty, was a commander (*mahamandaleswar*) during the reign of

Figure 18: *Gadag style pillars, Western Chalukya art.*

Chalukya Vikramaditya VI.[136] Seizing an opportune moment in the waning power of the Chalukyas, Bijjala II declared independence in 1157 and annexed their capital Kalyani.[137] His rule was cut short by his assassination in 1167 and the ensuing civil war caused by his sons fighting over the throne ended the dynasty as the last Chalukya scion regained control of Kalyani. This victory however, was short-lived as the Chalukyas were eventually driven out by the Seuna Yadavas.[138]

The Yadavas

The **Seuna**, *Sevuna* or **Yadava dynasty** (Marathi: देवगिरीचे यादव, Kannada: ಸೇವುಣರು) (c. 850–1334 CE) was an Indian dynasty, which at its peak ruled a kingdom stretching from the Tungabhadra to the Narmada rivers, including present-day Maharashtra, north Karnataka and parts of Madhya Pradesh, from its capital at Devagiri (present-day Daulatabad in Maharashtra). The Yadavas initially ruled as feudatories of the Western Chalukyas. Around the middle of the 12th century, they declared independence and established rule that reached its peak under Singhana II. The foundations of Marathi culture was laid by the Yadavas and the peculiarities of Maharashtra's social life developed during their rule.Wikipedia:Citation needed

Figure 19: *Sangamanatha temple at Kudalasangama, North Karnataka*

The Kakatiyas

The Kakatiya dynasty was a South Indian dynasty that ruled parts of what is now Telangana, India from 1083 to 1323 CE. They were one of the great Telugu kingdoms that lasted for centuries.

The Kalachuris

Kalachuri is this the name used by two kingdoms who had a succession of dynasties from the 10th-12th centuries, one ruling over areas in Central India (west Madhya Pradesh, Rajasthan) and were called Chedi or *Haihaya (Heyheya)* (northern branch) and the other southern Kalachuri who ruled over parts of Karnataka. They are disparately placed in time and space. Apart from the dynastic name and perhaps a belief in common ancestry, there is little in known sources to connect them.Wikipedia:Citation needed

The earliest known Kalachuri family (550–620 CE) ruled over northern Maharashtra, Malwa and western Deccan. Their capital was Mahismati situated in the Narmada river valley. There were three prominent members; Krishnaraja, Shankaragana and Buddharaja. They distributed coins and epigraphs around this area.[139]

Kalachuris of Kalyani or the southern Kalachuris (1130–1184 CE) at their peak ruled parts of the Deccan extending over regions of present-day North

Figure 20: *Shilabalika, Chennakeshava temple, Belur.*

Karnataka and parts of Maharashtra. This dynasty rose to power in the Deccan between 1156 and 1181 CE. They traced their origins to *Krishna* who was the conqueror of *Kalinjar* and Dahala in Madhya Pradesh. It is said that *Bijjala* a viceroy of this dynasty established the authority over Karnataka. He wrested power from the Chalukya king Taila III. Bijjala was succeeded by his sons Someshwara and Sangama but after 1181 CE, the Chalukyas gradually retrieved the territory. Their rule was a short and turbulent and yet very important from the socio-religious movement point of view; a new sect called the Lingayat or Virashaiva sect was founded during these times.

A unique and purely native form of Kannada literature-poetry called the *Vachanas* was also born during this time. The writers of *Vachanas* were called *Vachanakaras* (poets). Many other important works like Virupaksha Pandita's *Chennabasavapurana*, Dharani Pandita's *Bijjalarayacharite* and Chandrasagara Varni's *Bijjalarayapurana* were also written.

Kalachuris of Tripuri (Chedi) ruled in central India with its base at the ancient city of Tripuri (Tewar); it originated in the 8th century, expanded significantly in the 11th century, and declined in the 12th–13th centuries.

The Hoysalas

The Hoysalas had become a powerful force even during their rule from Belur in the 11th century as a feudatory of the Chalukyas (in the south Karnataka region).[140] In the early 12th century they successfully fought the Cholas in the south, convincingly defeating them in the battle of Talakad and moved their capital to nearby Halebidu.[141,142] Historians refer to the founders of the dynasty as natives of Malnad Karnataka, based on the numerous inscriptions calling them *Maleparolganda* or "Lord of the Male (hills) chiefs" (*Malepas*).[143,144,145,146,147] With the waning of the Western Chalukya power, the Hoysalas declared their independence in the late 12th century.

During this period of Hoysala control, distinctive Kannada literary metres such as *Ragale* (blank verse), *Sangatya* (meant to be sung to the accompaniment of a musical instrument), *Shatpadi* (seven line) etc. became widely accepted.[148,149,150] The Hoysalas expanded the Vesara architecture stemming from the Chalukyas,[151] culminating in the Hoysala architectural articulation and style as exemplified in the construction of the Chennakesava Temple at Belur and the Hoysaleswara temple at Halebidu.[152] Both these temples were built in commemoration of the victories of the Hoysala Vishnuvardhana against the Cholas in 1116.[153,154] Veera Ballala II, the most effective of the Hoysala rulers, defeated the aggressive Pandya when they invaded the Chola kingdom and assumed the titles "Establisher of the Chola Kingdom" (*Cholarajyapratishtacharya*), "Emperor of the south" (*Dakshina Chakravarthi*) and "Hoysala emperor" (*Hoysala Chakravarthi*).[155] The Hoysalas extended their foothold in areas known today as Tamil Nadu around 1225, making the city of Kannanur Kuppam near Srirangam a provincial capital. This gave them control over South Indian politics that began a period of Hoysala hegemony in the southern Deccan.[156,157]

In the early 13th century, with the Hoysala power remaining unchallenged, the first of the Muslim incursions into South India began. After over two decades of waging war against a foreign power, the Hoysala ruler at the time, Veera Ballala III, died in the battle of Madurai in 1343.[158] This resulted in the merger of the sovereign territories of the Hoysala empire with the areas administered by Harihara I, founder of the Vijayanagara Empire, located in the Tungabhadra region in present-day Karnataka. The new kingdom thrived for another two centuries with Vijayanagara as its capital.[159]

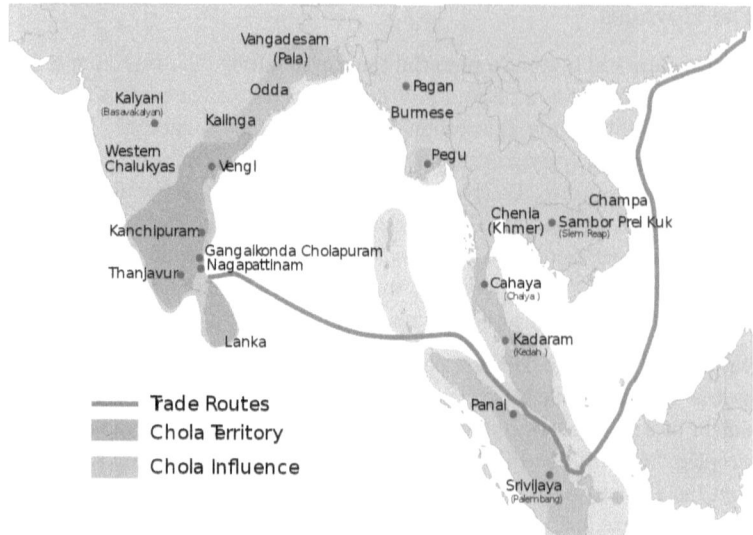

Figure 21: *Chola Empire under Rajendra Chola c. 1030 CE*

The Cholas

By the 9th century, under Rajaraja Chola and his son Rajendra Chola, the Cholas rose as a notable power in south Asia. The Chola Empire stretched as far as Bengal. At its peak, the empire spanned almost 3,600,000 km² (1,389,968 sq mi). Rajaraja Chola conquered all of peninsular South India and parts of the Sri Lanka. Rajendra Chola's navies went even further, occupying coasts from Burma (now Myanmar) to Vietnam, the Andaman and Nicobar Islands, Lakshadweep, Sumatra, Java, Malaya in South East Asia and Pegu islands. He defeated Mahipala, the king of the Bengal, and to commemorate his victory he built a new capital and named it Gangaikonda Cholapuram.Wikipedia:Citation needed

The Cholas excelled in building magnificent temples. Brihadeshwara Temple in Thanjavur is a classical example of the magnificent architecture of the Chola kingdom. Brihadshwara temple is an UNESCO Heritage Site under "Great Living Chola Temples."[160] Another example is the Chidambaram Temple in the heart of the temple town of Chidambaram.

References

Sources
<templatestyles src="Template:Refbegin/styles.css" />

Books
- Agarwala, V. S. (1954). *India as Known to Panini*.
- Barstow, A.E., *The Sikhs: An Ethnology*, Reprinted by B.R. Publishing Corporation, Delhi, India, 1985, first published in 1928.
- Alexander Cunningham (1888) *Coins of the Indo-Scythians, Sakas, and Kushans*, Reprint: Indological Book House, Varanasi, India, 1971.
- D. C. Ganguly (1981). R. S. Sharma, ed. *A Comprehensive History of India (A. D. 300-985)*[161]. 3, Part 1. Indian History Congress / Orient Longmans.
- Dilip Kumar Ganguly (1984). *History and Historians in Ancient India*[162]. Abhinav. ISBN 978-0-391-03250-7.
- Hill, John E. 2004. *The Peoples of the West from the Weilüe 魏略 by Yu Huan 魚豢 : A Third Century Chinese Account Composed between 239 and 265 CE*. Draft annotated English translation. Weilue: The Peoples of the West[163]
- Hill, John E. (2009) *Through the Jade Gate to Rome: A Study of the Silk Routes during the Later Han Dynasty, 1st to 2nd Centuries CE*. BookSurge, Charleston, South Carolina. ISBN 978-1-4392-2134-1.
- Latif, S.M., (1891) *History of the Panjab*, Reprinted by Progressive Books, Lahore, Pakistan, 1984.
- Chadurah, Haidar Malik (1991). *History of Kashmir*[164]. Bhavna Prakashan.
- Hasan, Mohibbul (1959). *Kashmir Under the Sultans*[165]. Aakar. ISBN 9788187879497.
- Sailendra Nath Sen (1999). *Ancient Indian History and Civilization*[166]. New Age. ISBN 9788122411980.
- Upinder Singh (2008). *A History of Ancient and Early Medieval India: From the Stone Age to the 12th Century*[167]. Pearson Education India. ISBN 978-81-317-1120-0.
- Bharatiya Vidya Bhavan (Bombay, Inde), Majumdar, R. C., Pusalker, A. D., & Majumdar, A. K. (1988). The history and culture of the Indian people: 3. (History and culture of the Indian people.) Bombay: Bharatiya Vidya Bhavan.

Website
- @ This article incorporates public domain material from the Library of Congress Country Studies website http://lcweb2.loc.gov/frd/cs/[168]. - India[169]

The North West

Indo-Scythians

Indo-Scythian Kingdom	
c. 150 BCE–400 CE	
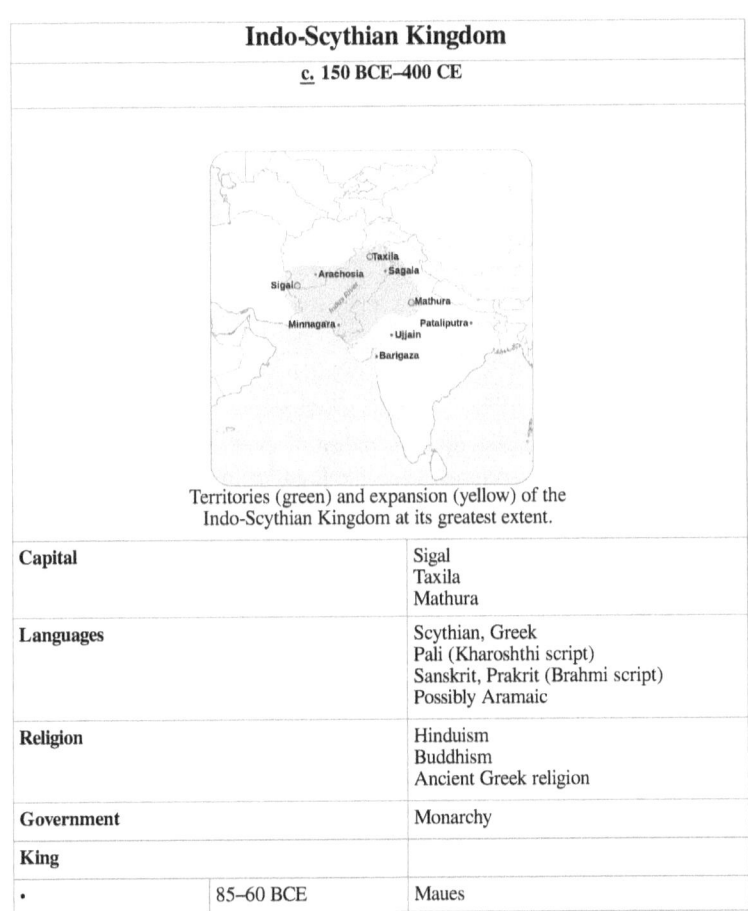 Territories (green) and expansion (yellow) of the Indo-Scythian Kingdom at its greatest extent.	
Capital	Sigal Taxila Mathura
Languages	Scythian, Greek Pali (Kharoshthi script) Sanskrit, Prakrit (Brahmi script) Possibly Aramaic
Religion	Hinduism Buddhism Ancient Greek religion
Government	Monarchy
King	
•	85–60 BCE	Maues

		10 CE	Hajatria
Historical era			Antiquity
•		Established	c. 150 BCE
•		Disestablished	400 CE
	Preceded by		Succeeded by
	Greco-Bactrian Kingdom		Kushan Empire
	Indo-Greek_Kingdom		Sassanid Empire
	Maurya Empire		Gupta Empire

Indo-Scythians is a term used to refer to Scythians (Sakas) who migrated into parts of central, northern and western South Asia (Sogdiana, Bactria, Arachosia, Gandhara, Sindh, Kashmir, Punjab, Haryana, Uttar Pradesh, Rajasthan, Gujarat and Maharashtra) from the middle of the 2nd century BC to the 4th century AD.

The first Saka king in South Asia was Maues/Moga (1st century BC) who established Saka power in Gandhara, and Indus Valley. The Indo-Scythians extended their supremacy over north-western India, conquering the Indo-Greeks and other local kingdoms. The Indo-Scythians were apparently subjugated by the Kushan Empire, by either Kujula Kadphises or Kanishka[170]. Yet the Saka continued to govern as satrapies[171], forming the Northern Satraps and Western Satraps. The power of the Saka rulers started to decline in the 2nd century CE after the Indo-Scythians were defeated by the Satavahana emperor Gautamiputra Satakarni.[172,173] Indo-Scythian rule in the northwestern Indian subcontinent ceased when the last Western Satrap Rudrasimha III was defeated by the Gupta emperor Chandragupta II in 395 CE.[174,175]

The invasion of northern regions of the Indian subcontinent by Scythian tribes from Central Asia, often referred to as the Indo-Scythian invasion, played a significant part in the history of the Indian subcontinent as well as nearby countries. In fact, the Indo-Scythian war is just one chapter in the events triggered by the nomadic flight of Central Asians from conflict with tribes such as the Xiongnu in the 2nd century AD, which had lasting effects on Bactria, Kabul, and the Indian subcontinent as well as far-off Rome in the west, and more nearby to the west in Parthia.

Ancient Roman historians including Arrian[176] and Claudius Ptolemy have mentioned that the ancient Sakas ('Sakai') were nomadic people.[177] However, Italo Ronca, in his detailed study of Ptolemy's chapter vi, states: "The land of the Sakai belongs to nomads, they have no towns but dwell in forests and caves" as spurious.[178]

Figure 22: *A Scythian horseman from the general area of the Ili River, Pazyryk, c 300 BC*

Origins

The ancestors of the Indo-Scythians are thought to be Sakas (Scythian) tribes.

> *"One group of Indo-European speakers that makes an early appearance on the Xinjiang stage is the Saka (Ch. Sai). Saka is more a generic term than a name for a specific state or ethnic group; Saka tribes were part of a cultural continuum of early nomads across Siberia and the Central Eurasian steppe lands from Xinjiang to the Black Sea. Like the Scythians whom Herodotus describes in book four of his History (Saka is an Iranian word equivalent to the Greek Scythes, and many scholars refer to them together as Saka-Scythian), Sakas were Iranian-speaking horse nomads who deployed chariots in battle, sacrificed horses, and buried their dead in barrows or mound tombs called kurgans."*[179]

According to their own origin myths, they claimed descent from Kushtana Maurya, the exiled son of the Indian Emperor Ashokavardhana Maurya who established the Kingdom of Khotan at Tarim Basin.[180]

Figure 23: *The treasure of the royal burial Tillya Tepe is attributed to 1st century BC Sakas in Bactria.*

Figure 24: *Bearded man with cap, probably Scythian, Bamiyan, 3rd–4th centuries.*

Figure 25: *Detail of one of the Orlat plaques seemingly representing Scythian soldiers.*

Yuezhi expansion

In the 2nd century BC, a fresh nomadic movement started among the Central Asian tribes, producing lasting effects on the history of Rome in Europe, Parthia in Western Asia, and Bactria, Kabul, and India in the east in Southern Asia.Wikipedia:Citation needed Recorded in the annals of the Han dynasty and other Chinese records, this great tribal movement began after the Yuezhi tribe was defeated by the Xiongnu, fleeing westwards after their defeat and creating a domino effect as they displaced other central Asian tribes in their path.

According to these ancient sources *Modu Shanyu* of the Xiongnu tribe of Mongolia attacked the Yuezhi (possibly related to the Tocharians who lived in eastern Tarim Basin area) and evicted them from their homeland between the Qilian Shan and Dunhuang around 175 BC.[181] Leaving behind a remnant of their number, most of the population moved westwards into the Ili River area. There, they displaced the Sakas, who migrated south into Ferghana and Sogdiana. According to the Chinese historical chronicles (who call the Sakas, "Sai" 塞): "[The Yuezhi] attacked the king of the Sai who moved a considerable distance to the south and the Yuezhi then occupied his lands."[182]

Sometime after 155 BC, the Yuezhi were again defeated by an alliance of the Wusun and the Xiongnu, and were forced to move south, again displacing the Scythians, who migrated south towards Bactria and present Afghanistan, and south-west closer towards Parthia.

The Sakas seem to have entered the territory of the Greco-Bactrian Kingdom around 145 BC, where they burnt to the ground the Greek city of Alexandria on the Oxus.Wikipedia:Citation needed The Yuezhi remained in Sogdiana on the northern bank of the Oxus, but they became suzerains of the Sakas in Bactrian territory, as described by the Chinese ambassador Zhang Qian who visited the region around 126 BC.Wikipedia:Citation needed

In Parthia, between 138–124 BC, the Sakas tribes of the Massagetae and Sacaraucae came into conflict with the Parthian Empire, winning several battles, and killing successively King Phraates II and King Artabanus I.

The Parthian king Mithridates II finally retook control of parts of Central Asia, first by defeating the Yuezhi in Sogdiana in 115 BC, and then defeating the Scythians in Parthia and Seistan around 100 BC.Wikipedia:Citation needed

After their defeat, the Yuezhi tribes migrated relatively far to the east into Bactria, which they were to control for several centuries,Wikipedia:Citation needed and from which they later conquered northern India to found the Kushan Empire.

Settlement in Sakastan

The Sakas settled in Drangiana, an area of Southern Afghanistan, western Pakistan and south Iran, which was then called after them as Sakastan or Sistan. From there, they progressively expanded into present day Iran as well as northern India, where they established various kingdoms, and where they are known as "Saka".Wikipedia:Citation needed

The Arsacid emperor Mithridates II (c. 123–88/87 BCE) had scored many successes against the Scythians and added many provinces to the Parthian Empire,[183] and apparently the Scythian hordes that came from Bactria were also conquered by him. A section of these people moved from Bactria to Lake Helmond in the wake of Yue-chi pressure and settled about Drangiana (Sigal), a region which later came to be called "Sakistana of the Skythian (Scythian) Sakai",[184] towards the end of 1st century BC.[185] The region is still known as Seistan.

The presence of the Sakas in Sakastan in the 1st century BC is mentioned by Isidore of Charax in his "Parthian stations". He explained that they were bordered at that time by Greek cities to the east (Alexandria of the Caucasus

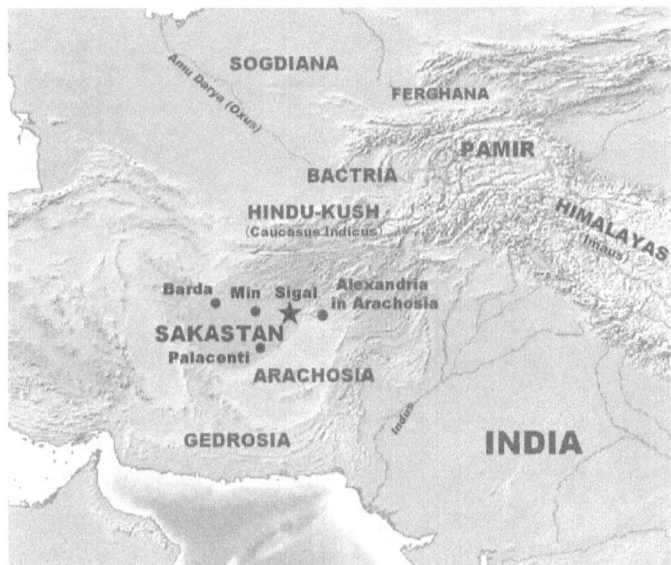

Figure 26: *Map of Sakastan around 100 BC*

and Alexandria of the Arachosians), and the Parthian-controlled territory of Arachosia to the south:

> "Beyond is Sacastana of the Scythian Sacae, which is also Paraetacena, 63 schoeni. There are the city of Barda and the city of Min and the city of Palacenti and the city of Sigal; in that place is the royal residence of the Sacae; and nearby is the city of Alexandria (Alexandria Arachosia), and six villages." Parthian stations, 18.

Indo-Scythian kingdoms

Abhira to Surastrene

The first Indo-Scythian kingdom in south western Asia was located in Pakistan in the areas from Abiria (Sindh) to Surastrene (Saurashtra, Gujarat), from around 110 to 80 BC. They moved progressively further north into Indo-Greek territory until the conquests of Maues, c. 80 BC.

The 1st century AD Periplus of the Erythraean Sea describes the Scythian territories there:

> "Beyond this region (Gedrosia), the continent making a wide curve from the east across the depths of the bays, there follows the coast district of

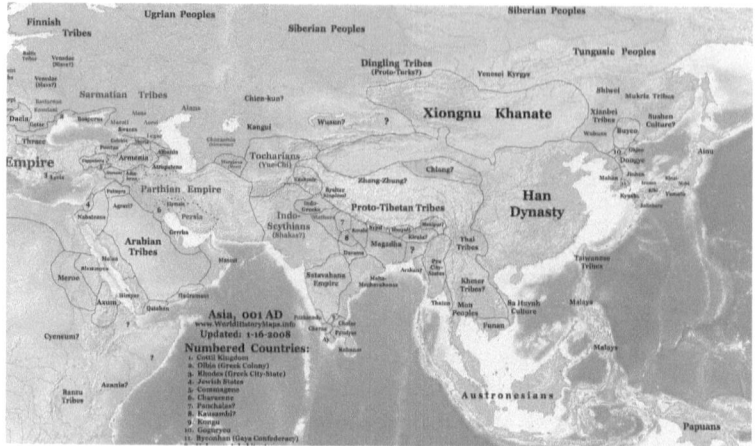

Figure 27: *Asia in 1 CE, showing the Indo-Scythians and their neighbors*

Figure 28: *Scythian devotee, Butkara Stupa*

Figure 29: *A coin of the Indo-Scythian king Azes*

Scythia, which lies above toward the north; the whole marshy; from which flows down the river Sinthus, the greatest of all the rivers that flow into the Erythraean Sea, bringing down an enormous volume of water (...) This river has seven mouths, very shallow and marshy, so that they are not navigable, except the one in the middle; at which by the shore, is the market-town, Barbaricum. Before it there lies a small island, and inland behind it is the metropolis of Scythia, Minnagara."

The Indo-Scythians ultimately established a kingdom in the northwest, based near Taxila, with two great Satraps, one in Mathura in the east, and one in Surastrene (Gujarat) in the southwest.

In the southeast, the Indo-Scythians invaded the area of Ujjain, but were subsequently repelled in 57 BC by the Malwa king Vikramaditya. To commemorate the event Vikramaditya established the Vikrama era, a specific Indian calendar starting in 57 BC. More than a century later, in AD 78, the Sakas would again invade Ujjain and establish the Saka era, marking the beginning of the long-lived Saka Western Satraps kingdom.[186]

Gandhara and Punjab

The presence of the Scythians in north-western India during the 1st century BCE was contemporary with that of the Indo-Greek Kingdoms there, and it seems they initially recognized the power of the local Greek rulers.

Maues first conquered Gandhara and Taxila around 80 BCE, but his kingdom disintegrated after his death. In the east, the Indian king Vikrama retook Ujjain from the Indo-Scythians, celebrating his victory by the creation of the Vikrama era (starting 58 BCE). Indo-Greek kings again ruled after Maues,

Figure 30: *A toilet tray of the type found in the Early Saka layer at Sirkap*

and prospered, as indicated by the profusion of coins from Kings Apollodotus II and Hippostratos. Not until Azes I, in 55 BC, did the Indo-Scythians take final control of northwestern India, with his victory over Hippostratos.

Sculpture

Several stone sculptures have been found in the Early Saka layer (Layer No4, corresponding to the period of Azes I, in which numerous coins of the latter were found) in the ruins of Sirkap, during the excavations organized by John Marshall.

Several of them are toilet trays (also called Stone palettes) roughly imitative of earlier, and finer, Hellenistic ones found in the earlier layers. Marshall comments that "we have a praiseworthy effort to copy a Hellenistic original but obviously without the appreciation of form and skill which were necessary for the task". From the same layer, several statuettes in the round are also known, in very rigid and frontal style.

Figure 31: *A bronze coin of the Indo-Scythian King Azes. Obverse: BASILEWS BASILEWN MEGALOU AZOU, Humped Brahman bull (zebu) walking right, Whitehead symbol 15 (Z in square) above; Reverse: Kharosthi "jha" to right / Kharosthi legend, Lion or leopard standing right, Whitehead symbol 26 above; Reference: Whitehead 259; BMC p. 86, 141.*

Figure 32: *The Bimaran casket, representing the Buddha surrounded by Brahma (left) and Śakra (right) was found inside a stupa with coins of Azes inside. British Museum.*

Figure 33: *Coin of Rajuvula (c. 10 CE), AE, Mathura*
Obv: *Bust of King Rajuvula, with Greek legend.*
Rev: *Pallas standing right (crude). Kharoshthi legend.*

Bimaran casket

Azes is connected to the Bimaran casket, one of the earliest representations of the Buddha. The casket was used for the dedication of a stupa in Bamiran, near Jalalabad in Afghanistan, and placed inside the stupa with several coins of Azes. This event may have happened during the reign of Azes (60–20 BCE), or slightly later. The Indo-Scythians are otherwise connected with Buddhism (see Mathura lion capital), and it is indeed possible they would have commended the work.

Mathura area ("Northern Satraps")

In northern India, the Indo-Scythians conquered the area of Mathura over Indian kings around 60 BCE. Some of their satraps were Hagamasha and Hagana, who were in turn followed by the Saca Great Satrap Rajuvula.

The Mathura lion capital, an Indo-Scythian sandstone capital in crude style, from Mathura in northern India, and dated to the 1st century CE, describes in kharoshthi the gift of a stupa with a relic of the Buddha, by Queen Nadasi Kasa, the wife of the Indo-Scythian ruler of Mathura, Rajuvula. The capital also mentions the genealogy of several Indo-Scythian satraps of Mathura.

Rajuvula apparently eliminated the last of the Indo-Greek kings Strato II around 10 CE, and took his capital city, Sagala.

The coinage of the period, such as that of Rajuvula, tends to become very crude and barbarized in style. It is also very much debased, the silver content becoming lower and lower, in exchange for a higher proportion of bronze, an alloying technique (billon) suggesting less than wealthy finances.

Figure 34: *The Mathura lion capital is an important Indo-Scythian monument dedicated to the Buddhist religion (British Museum).*

The Mathura lion capital inscriptions attest that Mathura fell under the control of the Sakas. The inscriptions contain references to Kharahostes and Queen Ayasia, the "chief queen of the Indo-Scythian ruler of Mathura, satrap Rajuvula." Kharahostes was the son of *Arta* as is attested by his own coins.[187] Arta is stated to be brother of King Moga or Maues.[188]

The Indo-Scythian satraps of Mathura are sometimes called the "Northern Satraps", in opposition to the "Western Satraps" ruling in Gujarat and Malwa. After Rajuvula, several successors are known to have ruled as vassals to the Kushans, such as the "Great Satrap" Kharapallana and the "Satrap" Vanaspara, who are known from an inscription discovered in Sarnath, and dated to the 3rd year of Kanishka (c. AD 130), in which they were paying allegiance to the Kushans.[189]

Pataliputra

The text of the Yuga Purana describes an invasion of Pataliputra by the Scythians sometimes during the 1st century BC, after seven great kings had ruled in succession in Saketa following the retreat of the Yavanas. The Yuga Purana explains that the king of the Sakas killed one fourth of the population, before he was himself slain by the Kalinga king Shata and a group of Sabalas (Sabaras or Bhillas).

Figure 35: *Silver coin of Vijayamitra in the name of Azes. Buddhist triratna symbol in the left field on the reverse.*

Figure 36: *Profile of the Indo-Scythian King Azes on one of his coins.*

Figure 37: *Coin of the Western Kshatrapa ruler Rudrasimha I (c. AD 175 to 197), a descendant of the Indo-Scythians*

Kushan and Indo-Parthian conquests

After the death of Azes, the rule of the Indo-Scythians in northwestern India was shattered with the rise of the Indo-Parthian ruler Gondophares in the last years of the 1st century BC. For the following decades, a number of minor Scythian leaders maintained themselves in local strongholds on the fringes of the loosely assembled Indo-Parthian empire, some of them paying formal allegiance to Gondophares I and his successors.

During the latter part of the 1st century AD, the Indo-Parthian overlordship was gradually replaced with that of the Kushans, one of the five tribes of the Yuezhi who had lived in Bactria for more than a century, and were now expanding into India to create a Kushan Empire. The Kushans ultimately regained northwestern India from around AD 75, and the area of Mathura from around AD 100, where they were to prosper for several centuries.Wikipedia:Citation needed

Western Kshatrapas legacy

Indo-Scythians continued to hold the area of Seistan until the reign of Bahram II (AD 276–293), and held several areas of India well into the 1st millennium: Kathiawar and Gujarat were under their rule until the 5th century under the designation of Western Kshatrapas, until they were eventually conquered by the Gupta emperor Chandragupta II (also called Vikramaditya).

Figure 38: *Silver tetradrachm of the Indo-Scythian king Maues (85–60 BC).*

Indo-Scythian coinage

Indo-Scythian coinage is generally of a high artistic quality, although it clearly deteriorates towards the disintegration of Indo-Scythian rule around AD 20 (coins of Rajuvula). A fairly high-quality but rather stereotypical coinage would continue in the Western Satraps until the 4th century.

Indo-Scythian coinage is generally quite realistic, artistically somewhere between Indo-Greek and Kushan coinage. It is often suggested Indo-Scythian coinage benefited from the help of Greek celators (Boppearachchi).

Indo-Scythian coins essentially continue the Indo-Greek tradition, by using the Greek language on the obverse and the Kharoshthi language on the reverse. The portrait of the king is never shown however, and is replaced by depictions of the king on horse (and sometimes on camel), or sometimes sitting cross-legged on a cushion. The reverse of their coins typically show Greek divinities.

Buddhist symbolism is present throughout Indo-Scythian coinage. In particular, they adopted the Indo-Greek practice since Menander I of showing divinities forming the vitarka mudra with their right hand (as for the mudra-forming Zeus on the coins of Maues or Azes II), or the presence of the Buddhist lion on the coins of the same two kings, or the triratana symbol on the coins of Zeionises.

Depiction of Indo-Scythians

Besides coinage, few works of art are known to indisputably represent Indo-Scythians. Indo-Scythian rulers are usually depicted on horseback in armour, but the coins of Azilises show the king in a simple, undecorated, tunic.Wikipedia:Citation needed

Figure 39: *Azilises on horse, wearing a tunic*

Several Gandharan sculptures also show foreigners in soft tunics, sometimes wearing the typical Scythian cap. They stand in contrast to representations of Kushan men, who seem to wear thick, rigid, tunics, and who are generally represented in a much more simplistic manner.[190]

Buner reliefs

Indo-Scythian soldiers in military attire are sometimes represented in Buddhist friezes in the art of Gandhara (particularly in Buner reliefs). They are depicted in ample tunics with trousers, and have heavy straight swords as weapons. They wear pointed hoods (the Scythian cap or bashlyk), which distinguishes them from the Indo-Parthians who only wore a simple fillet over their bushy hair,[191] and which is also systematically worn by Indo-Scythian rulers on their coins. With the right hand, some of them are forming the Karana mudra against evil spirits. In Gandhara, such friezes were used as decorations on the pedestals of Buddhist stupas. They are contemporary with other friezes representing people in purely Greek attire, hinting at an intermixing of Indo-Scythians (holding military power) and Indo-Greeks (confined, under Indo-Scythian rule, to civilian life).

Another relief is known where the same type of soldiers are playing musical instruments and dancing, activities which are widely represented elsewhere in Gandharan art: Indo-Scythians are typically shown as reveling devotees.

Figure 40: *One of the Buner reliefs showing Scythian soldiers dancing. Cleveland Museum of Art.*

Figure 41: *Indo-Scythians pushing along the Greek god Dionysos with Ariadne. UNIQ-ref-0-8c889858087207e6-QINU*

Figure 42: *Hunting scene.*

Figure 43: *Hunting scene.*

Stone palettes

Numerous stone palettes found in Gandhara are considered good representatives of Indo-Scythian art. These palettes combine Greek and Iranian influences, and are often realized in a simple, archaic style. Stone palettes have only been found in archaeological layers corresponding to Indo-Greek, Indo-Scythian and Indo-Parthian rule, and are essentially unknown in the preceding Mauryan layers or the succeeding Kushan layers.[192]

Very often these palettes represent people in Greek dress in mythological scenes, a few in Parthian dress (head-bands over bushy hair, crossed-over jacket on a bare chest, jewelry, belt, baggy trousers), and even fewer in Indo-Scythian dress (Phrygian hat, tunic and comparatively straight trousers). A palette found in Sirkap and now in the New Delhi Museum shows a winged Indo-Scythian horseman riding winged deer, and being attacked by a lion.

The Indo-Scythians and Buddhism

The Indo-Scythians seem to have been followers of Buddhism, and many of their practices apparently continued those of the Indo-Greeks.

Figure 44: *Gandhara stone palette with Scythians playing music.*

Royal dedications

Several Indo-Scythian kings after Azes are known for making Buddhist dedications in their name, on plaques or reliquaries:

- Patika Kusulaka (25 BCE – 10 CE) related his donation of a relic of the Buddha Shakyamuni to a Buddhist monastery, in the Taxila copper plate.
- Kharahostes (10 BCE – 10 CE) is mentioned on the Buddhist Mathura lion capital and on a reliquary.[194,195] His coins were also found in the Bimaran casket, a beautiful Buddhist gold reliquary with an early image of the Buddha, now in the British Museum. Some of his coins bear the Buddhist triratna symbol.
- Vijayamitra (ruled 12 BCE - 15 CE) personally dedicated in his name a Buddhist reliquary.[196,197] Some of his coins bear the Buddhist triratna symbol.
- Indravarman, while still a Prince, personally dedicated in 5-6 CE a Buddhist reliquary, the Bajaur casket, now in the Metropolitan Museum of Art.
- Zeionises and Aspavarma also used the Buddhist triratna symbol on their coins.
- Rajula erected the Mathura lion capital, which incorporates Buddhist symbols and relates the donations by his wife of relics to a stupa.

Figure 45: *The Bajaur casket was dedicated by Indravarman, Metropolitan Museum of Art.*[193]

Butkara Stupa

Excavations at the Butkara Stupa in Swat by an Italian archaeological team have yielded various Buddhist sculptures thought to belong to the Indo-Scythian period. In particular, an Indo-Corinthian capital representing a Buddhist devotee within foliage has been found which had a reliquary and coins of Azes buried at its base, securely dating the sculpture to around 20 BC.[200] A contemporary pilaster with the image of a Buddhist devotee in Greek dress has also been found at the same spot, again suggesting a mingling of the two populations.[201] Various reliefs at the same location show Indo-Scythians with their characteristic tunics and pointed hoods within a Buddhist context, and side-by-side with reliefs of standing Buddhas.[202]

Gandharan sculptures

Other reliefs have been found, which show Indo-Scythian men with their characteristic pointed cap pushing a cart on which is reclining the Greek god Dionysos with his consort Ariadne.Wikipedia:Citation needed

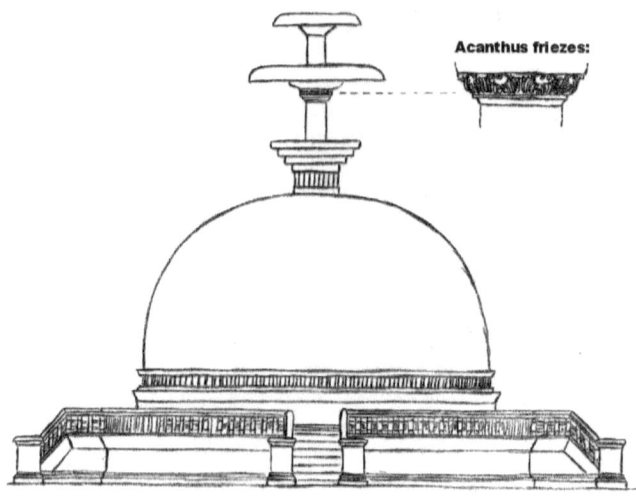

Figure 46: *Buddhist stupas during the late Indo-Greek/Indo-Scythian period were highly decorated structures with columns, flights of stairs, and decorative Acanthus leaf friezes. Butkara stupa, Swat, 1st century BC.*[198]

Figure 47: *Possible Scythian devotee couple (extreme left and right, often described as "Scytho-Parthian"),*[199] *around the Buddha, Brahma and Indra.*

Mathura lion capital

The Mathura lion capital, which associates many of the Indo-Scythian rulers from Maues to Rajuvula, mentions a dedication of a relic of the Buddha in a stupa. It also bears centrally the Buddhist symbol of the triratana, and is also filled with mentions of the bhagavat Buddha Sakyamuni, and characteristically Buddhist phrases such as:

"*sarvabudhana puya dhamasa puya saghasa puya*"

"Revere all the Buddhas, revere the dharma, revere the sangha"

(Mathura lion capital, inscription O1/O2)

Figure 48: *Indo-Corinthian capital from Butkara Stupa, dated to 20 BC, during the reign of Azes II. Turin City Museum of Ancient Art.*

Figure 49: *Dancing Indo-Scythians (top) and hunting scene (bottom). Buddhist relief from Swat, Gandhara.*

Figure 50: *Butkara doorjamb, with Indo-Scythians dancing and reveling. On the back side is a relief of a standing Buddha UNIQ-ref-1-8c889858087207e6-QINU*

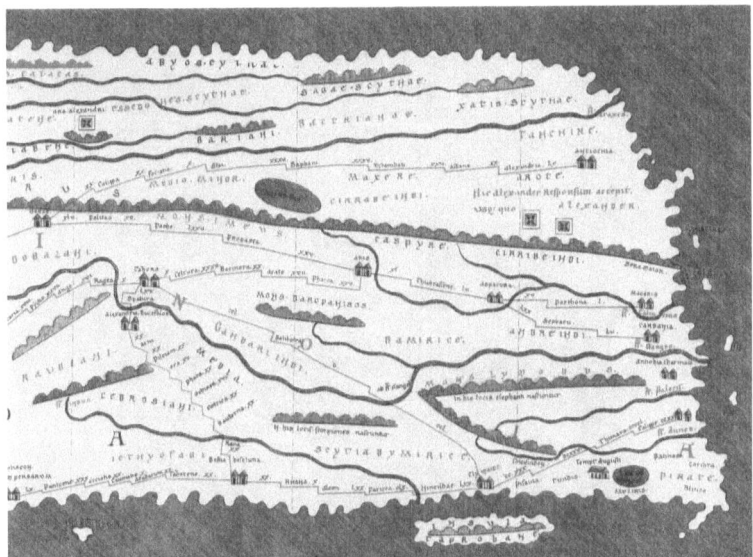

Figure 51: *"Scythia" appears around the mouth of the river Indus in the Roman period Tabula Peutingeriana.*

Indo-Scythians in Western sources

The country of Scythia in the area of Pakistan, and especially around the mouth of the Indus with its capital at Minnagara (modern day Karachi) is mentioned extensively in Western maps and travel descriptions of the period. The Ptolemy world map, as well as the Periplus of the Erythraean Sea mention prominently, the country of Scythia on the Indus Valley, as well as Roman Tabula Peutingeriana. The Periplus states that Minnagara was the capital of Scythia, and that Parthian Princes from within it were fighting for its control during the 1st century AD. It also distinguishes Scythia with Ariaca further east (centred in Gujarat and Malwa), over which ruled the Western Satrap king Nahapana.

Indo-Scythians in Indian literature

The Indo-Scythians were named "Shaka" in India, an extension on the name Saka used by the Persians to designate Scythians. From the time of the Mahabharata wars (400–150 BC roughlyWikipedia:Citation needed) Shakas receive numerous mentions in texts like the Puranas, the Manusmriti, the Ramayana, the Mahabharata, the Mahabhasiya of Patanjali, the Brhat Samhita of Vraha Mihira, the Kavyamimamsa, the Brihat-Katha-Manjari, the Katha-Saritsagara

Figure 52: *Coin of Azes, with king seated, holding a drawn sword and a whip.*

and several other old texts. They are described as part of an amalgam of other war-like tribes from the northwest.

Sai-Wang Scythian hordes of Chipin or Kipin

A section of the Central Asian Scythians (under Sai-Wang) is said to have taken southerly direction and after passing through the Pamirs it entered the Chipin or Kipin after crossing the Hasuna-tu (*Hanging Pass*) located above the valley of Kanda in Swat country.[203] Chipin has been identified by Pelliot, Bagchi, Raychaudhury and some others with Kashmir[204] while other scholars identify it with Kapisha (Kafirstan).[205,206] The Sai-Wang had established his kingdom in Kipin. S. Konow interprets the Sai-Wang as Saka Murunda of Indian literature, Murunda being equal to Wang i.e. king, master or lord,[207] but Bagchi who takes the word Wang in the sense of the king of the Scythians but he distinguishes the Sai Sakas from the Murunda Sakas.[208] There are reasons to believe that Sai Scythians were Kamboja Scythians and therefore *Sai-Wang* belonged to the *Scythianised Kambojas* (i.e. Parama-Kambojas) of the Transoxiana region and came back to settle among his own stock after being evicted from his ancestral land located in *Scythia* or *Shakadvipa*. King Moga or Maues could have belonged to this group of Scythians who had migrated from the *Sai* country (*Central Asia*) to Chipin.[209]

Figure 53: *Coin of Maues depicting Balarama, 1st century BC. British Museum.*

Establishment of Mlechcha Kingdoms in Northern India

The mixed Scythian hordes that migrated to Drangiana and surrounding regions later spread further into north and south-west India via the lower Indus valley. Their migration spread into Sovira, Gujarat, Rajasthan and northern India, including kingdoms in the Indian mainland.

There are important references to the warring *Mleccha* hordes of the Sakas, Yavanas, Kambojas and Pahlavas in the *Bala Kanda* of the Valmiki Ramayana. H. C. Raychadhury glimpses in these verses the struggles between the Hindus and the invading hordes of Mlechcha barbarians from the northwest. The time frame for these struggles is the 2nd century BC onwards. Raychadhury fixes the date of the present version of the Valmiki Ramayana around or after the 2nd century AD.[210]

Mahabharata too furnishes a veiled hint about the invasion of the mixed hordes from the northwest. *Vanaparava* by Mahabharata contains verses in the form of prophecy deploring that "......the Mlechha (barbaric) kings of the Shakas, Yavanas, Kambojas, Bahlikas, etc. shall rule the earth (i.e. India) un-righteously in Kaliyuga..."[211]

According to H. C. Ray Chaudhury, this is too clear a statement to be ignored or explained away.Wikipedia:Citation needed

Evidence about joint invasions

The Scythian groups that invaded India and set up various kingdoms included, besides the Sakas, other allied tribes, such as the Medii, Xanthii, and Massagetae. These peoples were all absorbed into the community of Kshatriyas of mainstream Indian society.[212]

The Shakas were formerly a people of the *trans-Hemodos* region—the *Shakadvipa* of the Puranas or the Scythia of the classical writings. *Isidor of Charax* (beginning of 1st century AD) attests them in Sakastana (modern Seistan). The *Periplus of the Erythraean Sea* (c. AD 70–80) also attests a Scythian district in lower Indus with Minnagra as its capital. Ptolemy (c. AD 140) also attests to an Indo-Scythia in south-western India which comprised the Patalene and Surastrene (Saurashtra) territories.

The 2nd century BC Scythian invasion of India, was in all probability carried out jointly by the Sakas, Pahlavas, Kambojas, Paradas, Rishikas and other allied tribes from the northwest.[213]

Main Indo-Scythian rulers

Khyber-Pakhtunkhwa and Eastern Pakistan

- Maues, c. 85–60 BC
- Vonones, c. 75–65 BC
- Spalahores, c. 75–65 BC, satrap and brother of King Vonones, and probably the later King Spalirises.
- Spalirises, c. 60–57 BC, king and brother of King Vonones.
- Spalagadames c. 50 BC, satrap, and son of Spalahores.
- Azilises, before 60 BC
- Azes I, c. 60–20 BC
- Zeionises, c. 10 BC – AD 10
- Kharahostes, c. 10 BC – AD 10
- Hajatria

Kshaharatas (Punjab, Pakistan and beyond)

- Liaka Kusuluka, satrap of Chuksa
- Kusulaka Patika, satrap of Chuksa and son of Liaka Kusuluka
- Bhumaka
- Nahapana (founder of the Western Satraps)

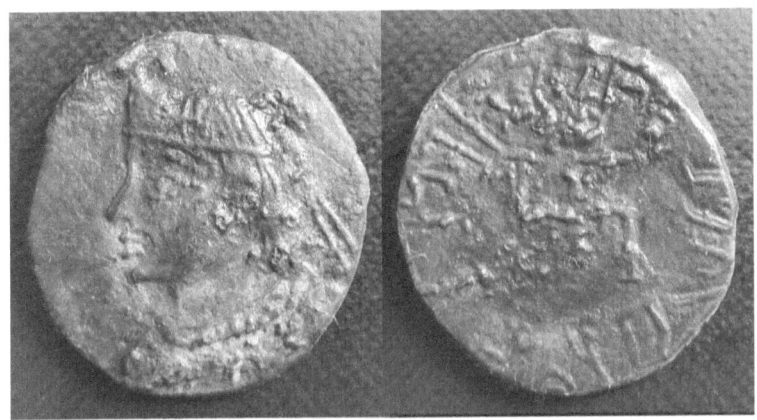

Figure 54: *Drachm of Parataraja Bhimarjuna.*
Obv: *Robed bust of Bhimarjuna left, wearing tiara-shaped diadem.*
Rev: *Swastika with legend surrounding.*
1.70g. Senior (Indo-Scythian) 286.1 (Bhimajhuna)

Aprācas (Bajaur, Khyber-Pakhtunkhwa, Pakistan)

- Vijayamitra (12 BC - AD 15), wife Rukhana
- Indravasu (c. AD 20), wife Vasumitra
- Vispavarman, wife Śiśirena
- Indravarman, wife Uttara
- Aspa (AD 15–45)[214] or Aspavarma (AD 15 - 45)
- Sasan[215]

Pāratas[216] (Balochistan, Pakistan)

- Yolamira, son of Bagareva (c. 125–150)
- Bagamira, son of Yolamira (c. 150)
- Arjuna, a second son of Yolamira (c. 150–160)
- Hvaramira, a third son of Yolamira (c. 160–175)
- Mirahvara, son of Hvaramira (c. 175–185)
- Miratakhma, another son of Hvaramira (c. 185–200)
- Kozana, son of Bagavharna (and perhaps grandson of Bagamira?) (c. 200–220)
- Bhimarjuna, son of Yolatakhma (and perhaps grandson of Arjuna?) (c. 220–235)
- Koziya, son of Kozana (c. 235–265)
- Datarvharna, son of Datayola I (possible grandson of Bhimarjuna) (c. 265–280)

- Datayola II, son of Datarvharna (c. 280–300)

"Northern Satraps" (Mathura area)

- Hagamasha (satrap, 1st century BC)
- Hagana (satrap, 1st century BC)
- Rajuvula, c. AD 10 (Great Satrap)
- Sodasa, son of Rajuvula
- "Great Satrap" Kharapallana (c. AD 130)
- "Satrap" Vanaspara (c. AD 130)

Minor local rulers

- Bhadayasa
- Mamvadi
- Arsakes

Western Satraps

- Nahapana (119–124)
- Chastana (c. 120), son of Ghsamotika
- Jayadaman, son of Chastana
- Rudradaman I (c. 130–150), son of Jayadaman
- Damajadasri I (170–175)
- Jivadaman (175 died 199)
- Rudrasimha I (175–188 died 197)
- Isvaradatta (188–191)
- Rudrasimha I (restored) (191–197)
- Jivadaman (restored) (197–199)
- Rudrasena I (200–222)
- Samghadaman (222–223)
- Damasena (223–232)
- Damajadasri II (232–239) with
- Viradaman (234–238)
- Yasodaman I (239)
- Vijayasena (239–250)
- Damajadasri III (251–255)
- Rudrasena II (255–277)
- Visvasimha (277–282)
- Bhratadarman (282–295) with
- Visvasena (293–304)
- Rudrasimha II, son of Lord (Svami) Jivadaman (304–348) with
- Yasodaman II (317–332)

- Rudradaman II (332–348)
- Rudrasena III (348–380)
- Simhasena (380– ?)
- Rudrasena IV (382–388)
- Rudrasimha III (388–395)

Descendants of the Indo-Scythians

Tadeusz Sulimirski notes that the Sacae also invaded parts of Northern India. Weer Rajendra Rishi, an Indian linguist[217] has identified linguistic affinities between Indian and Central Asian languages, which further lends credence to the possibility of historical Sacae influence in Northern India.

References

<templatestyles src="Template:Refbegin/styles.css" />

- Bailey, H. W. 1958. "Languages of the Saka." *Handbuch der Orientalistik*, I. Abt., 4. Bd., I. Absch., Leiden-Köln. 1958.
- Faccenna D., "Sculptures from the sacred area of Butkara I", Istituto Poligrafico Dello Stato, Libreria Dello Stato, Rome, 1964.
- Harmatta, János, ed., 1994. *History of civilizations of Central Asia, Volume II. The development of sedentary and nomadic civilizations: 700 B.C. to A.D. 250.* Paris, UNESCO Publishing.
- Hill, John E. 2004. *The Peoples of the West from the Weilue* 魏略 *by Yu Huan* 魚豢 *: A Third Century Chinese Account Composed between AD 239 and 265.* Draft annotated English translation.[218]
- Hill, John E. (2009) *Through the Jade Gate to Rome: A Study of the Silk Routes during the Later Han Dynasty, 1st to 2nd Centuries AD.* BookSurge, Charleston, South Carolina. ISBN 978-1-4392-2134-1.
- Hulsewé, A. F. P. and Loewe, M. A. N. 1979. *China in Central Asia: The Early Stage 125 BC – AD 23: an annotated translation of chapters 61 and 96 of the History of the Former Han Dynasty.* E. J. Brill, Leiden.
- Huet, Gerard (2010) *"Heritage du Sanskrit Dictionnaire, Sanskrit-Francais,"* p. 128.[219]
- Litvinsky, B. A., ed., 1996. *History of civilizations of Central Asia, Volume III. The crossroads of civilizations: A.D. 250 to 750.* Paris, UNESCO Publishing.
- Liu, Xinru 2001 "Migration and Settlement of the Yuezhi-Kushan: Interaction and Interdependence of Nomadic and Sedentary Societies." *Journal of World History*, Volume 12, No. 2, Fall 2001. University of Hawaii Press, pp 261–292.[220]

- *Bulletin of the Asia Institute: The Archaeology and Art of Central Asia. Studies From the Former Soviet Union.* New Series. Edited by B. A. Litvinskii and Carol Altman Bromberg. Translation directed by Mary Fleming Zirin. Vol. 8, (1994), pp 37–46.
- Millward, James A. (2007). *Eurasian Crossroads: A History of Xinjiang.* Columbia University Press, New York. ISBN 978-0-231-13924-3.
- Pulleyblank, Edwin G. 1970. "The Wu-sun and Sakas and the Yüeh-chih Migration." *Bulletin of the School of Oriental and African Studies 33* (1970), pp 154–160.
- Ptolemy (1932). *The Geography.* Translated and edited by Edward Luther Stevenson. 1991 unabridged reproduction. Dover Publications, Mineola, N. Y. ISBN 0-486-26896-9 (pbk)
- Puri, B. N. 1994. "The Sakas and Indo-Parthians." In: *History of civilizations of Central Asia, Volume II. The development of sedentary and nomadic civilizations: 700 B.C. to A.D. 250.* Harmatta, János, ed., 1994. Paris: UNESCO Publishing, pp 191–207.
- Ronca, Italo (1971). *Ptolemaios Geographie 6,9–21. Ostrian und Zentralasien, Teil I.* IsMEO — ROM.
- Watson, Burton. Trans. 1993. *Records of the Grand Historian of China: Han Dynasty II (Revised Edition).* Translated from the *Shih chi* of Ssuma Ch'ien. Chapter 123: The Account of Ta-yüan. Columbia University Press. ISBN 0-231-08167-7
- Wilcox, Peter and Angus McBride (1986). *Rome's Enemies (3): Parthians and Sassanid Persians (Men-at-Arms).* Osprey Publishing; illustrated edition. ISBN 978-0-85045-688-2.
- Yu, Taishan. 1998. *A Study of Saka History.* Sino-Platonic Papers No. 80. July 1998. Dept. of Asian and Middle Eastern Studies, University of Pennsylvania.
- Yu, Taishan. 2000. *A Hypothesis about the Source of the Sai Tribes.* Sino-Platonic Papers No. 106. September 2000. Dept. of Asian and Middle Eastern Studies, University of Pennsylvania.
- *Political History of Ancient India*, 1996, H. C. Raychaudhury
- *Hindu Polity, A Constitutional history of India in Hindu Times*, 1978, K. P. Jayswal
- *Geographical Data in Early Puranas*, 1972, M. R. Singh
- *India and Central Asia*, 1955, P. C. Bagchi.
- *Geography of Puranas*, 1973, S. M. Ali
- *Greeks in Bactria and India*, W. W. Tarn
- *Early History of North India*, S. Chattopadhyava
- *Sakas in Ancient India*, S. Chattopadhyava
- *Development of Kharoshthi script*, C. C. Dasgupta
- *Ancient India*, 1956, R. K. Mukerjee

- *Ancient India*, Vol III, T. L. Shah
- *Hellenism in Ancient India*, G. N. Banerjee
- *Manu and Yajnavalkya*, K. P. Jayswal
- Anabaseeos Alexanddrou, Arrian
- Mathura lion capital inscriptions
- *Corpus Inscriptionium Indicarum*, Vol II, Part I, S. Konow

External links

 Wikimedia Commons has media related to *Indo-Scythians*.

- "Indo-Scythian dynasties", R. C. Senior[221]
- Coins of the Indo-Scythians[222]
- Burner relief[223]
- History of Greco-India[224]

Saka

> **Part of a series on**
> **Indo-European topics**
>
> - v
> - t
> - e[225]

Saka, **Śaka**, **Shaka** or **Saca** (Persian: old *Sakā*, mod. ساکا; Sanskrit: Śaka; Ancient Greek: Σάκαι, *Sákai*; Latin: *Sacae*; Chinese: 塞, old **Sək*, mod. *Sāi*) is the name used in Middle Persian and Sanskrit sources for the Scythians, a large group of Eurasian nomads on the Eurasian Steppe speaking Eastern Iranian languages.[226,227,228] Modern scholars usually use the term Saka to refer to Iranians of the Eastern Steppe and the Tarim Basin.

René Grousset wrote that they formed a particular branch of the "Scytho-Sarmatian family" originating from nomadic Iranian peoples of the northwestern steppe in Eurasia. They migrated into Sogdia and Bactria in Central Asia and then to the northwest of the Indian subcontinent where they were known as the Indo-Scythians. In the Tarim Basin and Taklamakan Desert region of Northwest China, they settled in Khotan and Kashgar which were at various times vassals to greater powers, such as Han China and Tang China.

Usage of name

Modern debate about the identity of the "Saka" is partly from ambiguous usage of the word by ancient, non-Saka authorities. According to Herodotus, the Persians gave the name "Saka" to all Scythians.[229] However, Pliny the Elder (*Gaius Plinius Secundus*, AD 23–79) claims that the Persians gave the name Sakai only to the Scythian tribes "nearest to them".[230] The Scythians to the far north of Assyria were also called the *Saka suni* (Saka or Scythian sons) by the Persians.Wikipedia:Citation needed The Neo-Assyrian Empire of the

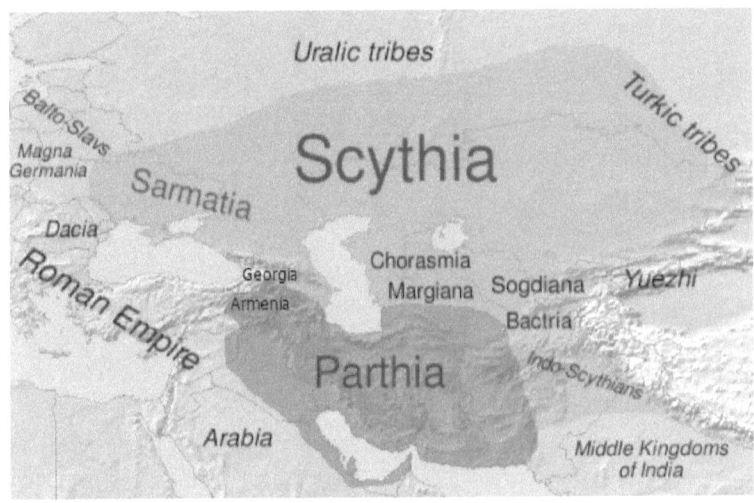

Figure 55: *Scythia and Parthia in about 170 BC (before the Yuezhi invaded Bactria).*

Figure 56: *Gold artifacts of the Saka in Bactria, at the site of Tillya Tepe, northern Afghanistan.*

Figure 57: *A cataphract-style parade armour of a Saka royal, also known as "The Golden Warrior", from the Issyk kurgan, a historical burial site near ex-capital city of Almaty, Kazakhstan*

time of Esarhaddon record campaigning against a people they called in the Akkadian the *Ashkuza* or *Ishhuza*. However, modern scholarly consensus is that the Eastern Iranian language ancestral to the Pamir languages in North India and the medieval Saka language of Xinjiang, was one of the Scythian languages.[231]

Another people, the *Gimirrai*, who were known to the ancient Greeks as the Cimmerians, were closely associated with the Sakas. In Biblical Hebrew, the *Ashkuz* (*Ashkenaz*) are considered to be a direct offshoot from the Gimirri (Gomer).[232]

The Saka were regarded by the Babylonians as synonymous with the *Gimirrai*; both names are used on the trilingual Behistun Inscription, carved in 515 BC on the order of Darius the Great.[233] (These people were reported to be mainly interested in settling in the kingdom of Urartu, later part of Armenia, and Shacusen in Uti Province derives its name from them.) The Behistun Inscription initially only gave one entry for saka, they were however further differentiated later into three groups:

- the *Sakā tigraxaudā* – "Saka with pointy hats/caps",

- the *Sakā haumavargā* – interpreted as "haoma-drinking saka" but there are other suggestions,
- the *Sakā paradraya* – "Saka beyond the sea", a name added after Darius' campaign into Western Scythia north of the Danube.

An additional term is found in two inscriptions elsewhere:

- the *Sakā para Sugdam* – "Saka beyond Sugda (Sogdia)", a term was used by Darius for the people who formed the limits of his empire at the opposite end to Kush (the Ethiopians), therefore should be located at the eastern edge of his empire.

The *Sakā paradraya* were the western Scythians (European Scythians) or Sarmatians. Both the *Sakā tigraxaudā* and *Sakā haumavargā* are thought to be located in Central Asia east of the Caspian Sea. *Sakā haumavargā* is considered to be the same as Amyrgians, the Saka tribe in closest proximity to Bactria and Sogdia. It has been suggested that the *Sakā haumavargā* may be the *Sakā para Sugdam*, therefore *Sakā haumavargā* is argued by some to be located further east than the *Sakā tigraxaudā*, perhaps at the Pamir Mountains or Xinjiang, although Syr Darya is considered to be their more likely location given that the name says "beyond Sogdia" rather than Bactria.

In the modern era, the archaeologist Hugo Winckler (1863–1913) was the first to associate the Sakas with the Scyths. John Manuel Cook, in *The Cambridge History of Iran*, states: "The Persians gave the single name Sakā both to the nomads whom they encountered between the Hunger steppe and the Caspian, and equally to those north of the Danube and Black Sea against whom Darius later campaigned; and the Greeks and Assyrians called all those who were known to them by the name Skuthai (Iškuzai). Sakā and Skuthai evidently constituted a generic name for the nomads on the northern frontiers." Persian sources often treat them as a single tribe called the Saka (*Sakai* or *Sakas*), but Greek and Latin texts suggest that the Scythians were composed of many sub-groups.[234] Modern scholars usually use the term Saka to refer to Iranian-speaking tribes who inhabited the Eastern Steppe and the Tarim Basin.

History

Greek and Persian reports

The Saka people were an Iranian people who spoke a language belonging to the Iranian branch of the Indo-European languages. They are known to the ancient Greeks as Scythians and are attested in historical and archaeological records dating to around the 8th century BC. In the Achaemenid-era Old Persian inscriptions found at Persepolis, dated to the reign of Darius I (r. 522-486

Figure 58: *Artifacts found the tombs 2 and 4 of Tillya Tepe and reconstitution of their use on the man and woman found in these tombs*

BC), the Saka are said to have lived just beyond the borders of Sogdia. Likewise an inscription dated to the reign of Xerxes I (r. 486-465 BC) has them coupled with the Dahae people of Central Asia. The contemporary Greek historian Herodotus noted that the Achaemenid Empire called all of Scythians as "Saka".

Greek historians wrote of the wars between the Saka and the Medes, as well as their wars against Cyrus the Great of the Persian Achaemenid Empire where Saka women were said to fight alongside their men. According to Herodotus, Cyrus the Great confronted the Massagetae, a people related to the Saka, while campaigning to the east of the Caspian Sea and was killed in the battle in 530 BC. Darius I also waged wars against the eastern Sakas, who fought him with three armies led by three kings according to Polyaenus. In 520–519 BC, Darius I defeated the *Sakā tigraxaudā* tribe and captured their king Skunkha (depicted as wearing a pointed hat in Behistun). The territories of Saka were absorbed into the Achaemenid Empire as part of Chorasmia that included much of the Amu Darya (Oxus) and the Syr Darya (Jaxartes), and the Saka then supplied the Achaemenid army with large number of mounted bowmen. They were also mentioned as among those who resisted Alexander the Great's incursions into Central Asia.

Figure 59: *Captured Saka king Skunkha, from Mount Behistun, Iran, Achaemenid stone relief from the reign of Darius I (r. 522-486 BC)*

Sakas in the Ili valley and Bactria

The Saka were known as the Sak or Sai (Chinese: 塞) in ancient Chinese records. These records indicate that they originally inhabited the Ili and Chu River valleys of modern Kyrgyzstan and Kazakhstan. In the *Book of Han*, the area was called the "land of the Sak", i.e. the Saka. The exact date of the Sakas' arrival in the valleys of the Ili and Chu in Central Asia is unclear, perhaps it was just before the reign of Darius I. Around 30 Saka tombs in the form of kurgans (burial mounds) have also been found in the Tian Shan area dated to between 550–250 BC. Indications of Saka presence have also been found in the Tarim Basin region, possibly as early as the 7th century BC.

The Saka were pushed out of the Ili and Chu River valleys by the Yuezhi, thought by some to be Tocharians. An account of the movement of these people is given in Sima Qian's *Records of the Grand Historian*. The Yuezhi, who originally lived between Tängri Tagh (Tian Shan) and Dunhuang of Gansu, China, were assaulted and forced to flee from the Hexi Corridor of Gansu by the forces of the Xiongnu ruler Modu Chanyu, who conquered the area in 177-176 BC.[235,236,237,238] In turn the Yuezhi were responsible for attacking and pushing the Sai (i.e. Saka) west into Sogdiana, where around 140 and 130

BC the latter crossed the Syr Darya into Bactria. The Saka also moved southwards towards to the Pamirs and northern India where they settled in Kashmir, and eastwards to settle in some of the oasis city-states of Tarim Basin sites like Yanqi (焉耆, Karasahr) and Qiuci (龜茲, Kucha).[239] The Yuezhi, themselves under attacks from another nomadic tribe the Wusun in 133-132 BC, moved again from the Ili and Chu valleys and occupied the country of Daxia (大夏, "Bactria").[240,241]

The ancient Greco-Roman geographer Strabo noted that the four tribes that took down the Bactrians in the Greek and Roman account – the *Asioi*, *Pasianoi*, *Tokharoi* and *Sakaraulai* – came from land north of the Syr Darya where the Ili and Chu valleys are located. Identification of these four tribes varies, but *Sakaraulai* may indicate an ancient Saka tribe, the *Tokharoi* is possibly the Yuezhi, and while the Asioi had been proposed to be groups such as the Wusun or Alans.

Grousset wrote of the migration of the Saka: "the Saka, under pressure from the Yueh-chih [Yuezhi], overran Sogdiana and then Bactria, there taking the place of the Greeks." Then, "Thrust back in the south by the Yueh-chih," the Saka occupied "the Saka country, Sakastana, whence the modern Persian Seistan." According to Harold Walter Bailey, the territory of Drangiana (now in Afghanistan and Pakistan) became known as "Land of the Sakas", and was called Sakastāna in the Persian language of contemporary Iran, in Armenian as Sakastan, with similar equivalents in Pahlavi, Greek, Sogdian, Syriac, Arabic, and the Middle Persian tongue used in Turfan, Xinjiang, China. This is attested in a contemporary Kharosthi inscription found on the Mathura lion capital belonging to the Saka kingdom of the Indo-Scythians (200 BC - 400 AD) in North India, roughly the same time the Chinese record that the Saka had invaded and settled the country of *Jibin* 罽賓 (i.e. Kashmir, of modern-day India and Pakistan).[242]

Migrations of the 2nd and 1st century BC have left traces in Sogdia and Bactria, but they cannot firmly be attributed to the Saka, similarly with the sites of Sirkap and Taxila in ancient India. The rich graves at Tillya Tepe in Afghanistan are seen as part of a population affected by the Saka.[243]

The Shakya clan of India, to which Gautama Buddha, called *Śākyamuni* "Sage of the Shakyas", belonged, has been suggested to be Sakas by Michael Witzel and Christopher I. Beckwith.

Figure 60: *Coin of Gurgamoya, king of Khotan. Khotan, first century. Obv: Kharosthi legend, "Of the great king of kings, king of Khotan, Gurgamoya. Rev: Chinese legend: "Twenty-four grain copper coin". British Museum*

Indo-Scythians

The region in modern Afghanistan and Pakistan where the Saka moved to become known as "land of the Saka" or Sakastan. The Sakas also captured Gandhara and Taxila, and migrated to North India. An Indo-Scythians kingdom was established in Mathura (200 BC - 400 AD). Weer Rajendra Rishi, an Indian linguist, identified linguistic affinities between Indian and Central Asian languages, which further lends credence to the possibility of historical Sakan influence in North India. According to historian Michael Mitchiner, the Abhira tribe were a Saka people cited in the Gunda inscription of the Western Satrap Rudrasimha I dated to 181 CE.

Kingdom of Khotan

The Kingdom of Khotan was a Saka city state in on the southern edge of the Tarim Basin. As a consequence of the Han–Xiongnu War spanning from 133 BCE to 89 CE, the Tarim Basin (now Xinjiang, Northwest China), including Khotan and Kashgar, fell under Han Chinese influence, beginning with the reign of Emperor Wu of Han (r. 141-87 BC).[244,245] The region once again came under Chinese suzerainty with the campaigns of conquest by Emperor Taizong of Tang (r. 626-649).[246] From the late eighth to ninth centuries, the region changed hands between the rival Tang and Tibetan Empires.[247,248] However, by the early 11th century the region fell to the Muslim Turkic peoples of the Kara-Khanid Khanate, which led to both the Turkification of the region as well as its conversion from Buddhism to Islam.

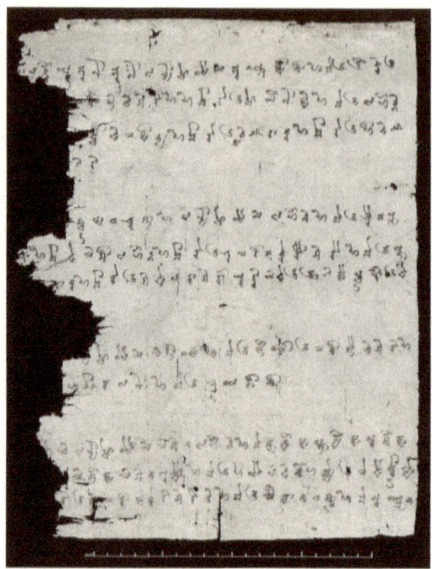

Figure 61: *A document from Khotan written in Khotanese Saka, part of the Eastern Iranian branch of the Indo-European languages, listing the animals of the Chinese zodiac in the cycle of predictions for people born in that year; ink on paper, early 9th century*

Archaeological evidence and documents from Khotan and other sites in the Tarim Basin provided information on the language spoken by the Saka. The official language of Khotan was initially Gandhari Prakrit written in Kharosthi, and coins from Khotan dated to the 1st century bear dual inscriptions in Chinese and Gandhari Prakrit, indicating links of Khotan to both India and China. Surviving documents however suggest that an Iranian language was used by the people of the kingdom for a long time Third-century AD documents in Prakrit from nearby Shanshan record the title for the king of Khotan as *hinajha* (i.e. "generalissimo"), a distinctively Iranian-based word equivalent to the Sanskrit title *senapati*, yet nearly identical to the Khotanese Saka *hīnāysa* attested in later Khotanese documents. This, along with the fact that the king's recorded regnal periods were given as the Khotanese *kṣuṇa*, "implies an established connection between the Iranian inhabitants and the royal power," according to the Professor of Iranian Studies Ronald E. Emmerick. He contended that Khotanese-Saka-language royal rescripts of Khotan dated to the 10th century "makes it likely that the ruler of Khotan was a speaker of Iranian." Furthermore, he argued that the early form of the name of Khotan, *hvatana*, is connected semantically with the name Saka.

Later Khotanese-Saka-language documents, ranging from medical texts to Buddhist literature, have been found in Khotan and Tumshuq (northeast of Kashgar). Similar documents in the Khotanese-Saka language dating mostly to the 10th century have been found in the Dunhuang manuscripts.

Although the ancient Chinese had called Khotan *Yutian* (于闐), another more native Iranian name occasionally used was *Jusadanna* (瞿薩旦那), derived from Indo-Iranian *Gostan* and *Gostana*, the names of the town and region around it, respectively.[249]

Shule Kingdom

Much like the neighboring people of the Kingdom of Khotan, people of Kashgar, the capital of Shule, spoke Saka, one of the Eastern Iranian languages.[250] According to the *Book of Han*, the Saka split and formed several states in the region. These Saka states may include two states to the northwest of Kashgar, and Tumshuq to its northeast, and Tushkurgan south in the Pamirs. Kashgar also conquered other states such as Yarkand and Kucha during the Han dynasty, but in its later history, Kashgar was controlled by various empires, including Tang China,[251,252] before it became part of the Turkic Kara-Khanid Khanate in the 10th century. In the 11th century, according to Mahmud al-Kashgari, some non-Turkic languages like the Kanchaki and Sogdian were still used in some areas in the vicinity of Kashgar, and Kanchaki is thought to belong to the Saka language group. It is believed that the Tarim Basin was linguistically Turkified before the 11th century ended.

Language

Attestations of the Saka language show that it was an Eastern Iranian language. The linguistic heartland of Saka was the Kingdom of Khotan, which had two varieties, corresponding to the major settlements at Khotan (now Hotan) and Tumshuq (now Tumxuk).[253,254] Both the Tumshuqese and Khotanese varieties of Saka contain many borrowings from the Middle Indo-Aryan Prakrit, but also share features with modern Wakhi and Pashto.

The Issyk inscription, a short fragment on a silver cup found in the Issyk kurgan (modern Kazakhstan) is believed to be an early example of Saka, constituting one of very few autochthonous epigraphic traces of that language.Wikipedia:Citation needed The inscription is in a variant of Kharosthi. Harmatta identifies the dialect as Khotanese Saka, tentatively translating its as: "The vessel should hold wine of grapes, added cooked food, so much, to the mortal, then added cooked fresh butter on".

The Saka heartland was gradually conquered during the Turkic expansion, beginning in the 4th century and the area was gradually Turkified linguistically under the Uyghurs.

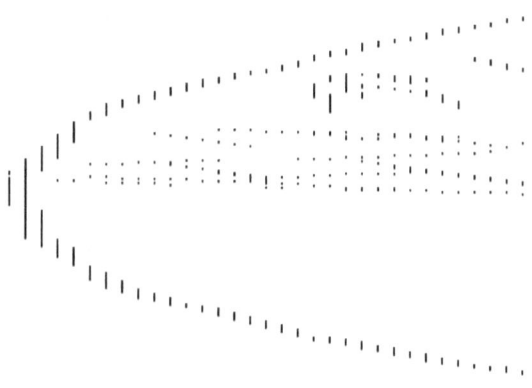

Figure 62: *Drawing of the Issyk inscription*

References

Bibliography

- Akiner (28 October 2013). *Cultural Change & Continuity In Central Asia*. Routledge. ISBN 978-1-136-15034-0.
- Bailey, H. W. 1958. "Languages of the Saka." *Handbuch der Orientalistik*, I. Abt., 4. Bd., I. Absch., Leiden-Köln. 1958.
- Bailey, H. W. (1979). *Dictionary of Khotan Saka*. Cambridge University Press. 1979. 1st Paperback edition 2010. ISBN 978-0-521-14250-2.
- Beckwith, Christopher. (1987). *The Tibetan Empire in Central Asia*. Princeton, NJ: Princeton University Press. ISBN 0-691-05494-0.
- Bernard, P. (1994). "The Greek Kingdoms of Central Asia". In Harmatta, János. *History of civilizations of Central Asia, Volume II. The development of sedentary and nomadic civilizations: 700 B.C. to A.D. 250.* Paris: UNESCO. pp. 96–126. ISBN 92-3-102846-4.
- Bailey, H.W. (1996) "Khotanese Saka Literature", in Ehsan Yarshater (ed), *The Cambridge History of Iran, Vol III: The Seleucid, Parthian, and Sasanian Periods, Part 2* (reprint edition), Cambridge: Cambridge University Press.

- Chang, Chun-shu. (2007). *The Rise of the Chinese Empire: Volume II; Frontier, Immigration, & Empire in Han China, 130 B.C. – A.D. 157.* Ann Arbor: University of Michigan Press, ISBN 978-0-472-11534-1.
- Davis-Kimball, Jeannine. 2002. *Warrior Women: An Archaeologist's Search for History's Hidden Heroines.* Warner Books, New York. 1st Trade printing, 2003. ISBN 0-446-67983-6 (pbk).
- Di Cosmo, Nicola. (2002). *Ancient China and Its Enemies: The Rise of Nomadic Power in East Asian History.* Cambridge: Cambridge University Press, ISBN 978-0-521-77064-4.
- *Bulletin of the Asia Institute: The Archaeology and Art of Central Asia.* Studies From the Former Soviet Union. New Series. Edited by B. A. Litvinskii and Carol Altman Bromberg. Translation directed by Mary Fleming Zirin. Vol. 8, (1994), pp. 37–46.
- Emmerick, R. E. (2003) "Iranian Settlement East of the Pamirs", in Ehsan Yarshater (ed), *The Cambridge History of Iran, Vol III: The Seleucid, Parthian, and Sasanian Periods, Part 1* (reprint edition) Cambridge: Cambridge University Press, pp 265–266.
- Hill, John E. (2009) *Through the Jade Gate to Rome: A Study of the Silk Routes during the Later Han Dynasty, 1st to 2nd Centuries CE.* John E. Hill. BookSurge, Charleston, South Carolina. ISBN 978-1-4392-2134-1.
- Hill, John E. 2004. *The Peoples of the West from the Weilue*[255] 魏略 *by Yu Huan* 魚豢 : *A Third Century Chinese Account Composed between 239 and 265 CE.* Draft annotated English translation.
- Kuz'mina, Elena E. (2007). *The Origin of the Indo Iranians.* Edited by J.P. Mallory. Leiden, Boston: Brill. ISBN 978-90-04-16054-5.
- Lebedynsky, Iaroslav. (2006). *Les Saces: Les <<Scythes>> d'Asie, VIIIe av. J.-C.-IVe siècle apr. J.-C.* Editions Errance, Paris. ISBN 2-87772-337-2 (in French).
- Loewe, Michael. (1986). "The Former Han Dynasty," in *The Cambridge History of China: Volume I: the Ch'in and Han Empires, 221 B.C. – A.D. 220, 103–222.* Edited by Denis Twitchett and Michael Loewe. Cambridge: Cambridge University Press. ISBN 978-0-521-24327-8.
- Millward, James A. (2007). *Eurasian Crossroads: A History of Xinjiang* (illustrated ed.). Columbia University Press. ISBN 0231139241.
- Pulleyblank, Edwin G. 1970. "The Wu-sun and Sakas and the Yüeh-chih Migration." *Bulletin of the School of Oriental and African Studies 33* (1970), pp. 154–160.
- Puri, B. N. 1994. "The Sakas and Indo-Parthians." In: *History of civilizations of Central Asia, Volume II. The development of sedentary and nomadic civilizations: 700 B.C. to A.D. 250.* Harmatta, János, ed., 1994. Paris: UNESCO Publishing, pp. 191–207.

- Sulimirski, Tadeusz (1970). *The Sarmatians. Volume 73 of Ancient peoples and places.* New York: Praeger. pp. 113–114. "The evidence of both the ancient authors and the archaeological remains point to a massive migration of Sacian (Sakas)/Massagetan tribes from the Syr Daria Delta (Central Asia) by the middle of the second century B.C. Some of the Syr Darian tribes; they also invaded North India."
- Theobald, Ulrich. (26 November 2011). " Chinese History - Sai 塞 The Saka People or Soghdians[256]." *ChinaKnowledge.de.* Accessed 2 September 2016.
- Thomas, F. W. 1906. "Sakastana." *Journal of the Royal Asiatic Society* (1906), pp. 181–216.
- Torday, Laszlo. (1997). *Mounted Archers: The Beginnings of Central Asian History.* Durham: The Durham Academic Press, ISBN 978-1-900838-03-0.
- Tremblay, Xavier (2007), "The Spread of Buddhism in Serindia: Buddhism Among Iranians, Tocharians and Turks before the 13th Century", in *The Spread of Buddhism*, eds Ann Heirman and Stephan Peter Bumbacker, Leiden: Koninklijke Brill.
- Xue, Zongzheng (薛宗正). (1992). *History of the Turks* (突厥史). Beijing: Zhongguo shehui kexue chubanshe. ISBN 978-7-5004-0432-3; OCLC 28622013.
- Yu, Taishan. 1998. *A Study of Saka History.* Sino-Platonic Papers No. 80. July, 1998. Dept. of Asian and Middle Eastern Studies, University of Pennsylvania.
- Yu, Taishan. 2000. *A Hypothesis about the Source of the Sai Tribes.* Sino-Platonic Papers No. 106. September, 2000. Dept. of Asian and Middle Eastern Studies, University of Pennsylvania.
- Yu, Taishan (June 2010), "The Earliest Tocharians in China" in Victor H. Mair (ed), *Sino-Platonic Papers*, Chinese Academy of Social Sciences, University of Pennsylvania Department of East Asian Languages and Civilizations.
- Yü, Ying-shih. (1986). "Han Foreign Relations," in *The Cambridge History of China: Volume I: the Ch'in and Han Empires, 221 B.C. – A.D. 220*, 377-462. Edited by Denis Twitchett and Michael Loewe. Cambridge: Cambridge University Press. ISBN 978-0-521-24327-8.
- Wechsler, Howard J.; Twitchett, Dennis C. (1979). Denis C. Twitchett; John K. Fairbank, eds. *The Cambridge History of China, Volume 3: Sui and T'ang China, 589–906, Part I.* Cambridge University Press. pp. 225–227. ISBN 978-0-521-21446-9.
- West, Barbara A. (January 1, 2009). *Encyclopedia of the Peoples of Asia and Oceania*[257]. Infobase Publishing. ISBN 1438119135. Retrieved January 18, 2015.

External links

- Scythians/Sacae[258] by Jona Lendering
- Article by Kivisild et al. on genetic heritage of early Indian settlers[259]
- Indian, Japanese and Chinese Emperors[260]Wikipedia:Link rot

Indo-Greek Kingdom

Indo-Greek Kingdom	
180 BC–AD 10	
Territory of the Indo-Greeks circa 100 BC.	
Capital	Alexandria in the Caucasus Sirkap/Taxila Chiniot Sagala/Sialkot Pushkalavati/Charsadda
Languages	Greek (Greek alphabet) Pali (Kharoshthi script) Sanskrit Prakrit (Brahmi script)
Religion	Hinduism Ancient Greek religion Buddhism Zoroastrianism
Government	Monarchy
King	
• 180–160 BC	Apollodotus I
• 25 BC – AD 10	Strato II & Strato III
Historical era	Antiquity
• Established	180 BC
• Disestablished	AD 10

Area	2,500,000 km² (970,000 sq mi)	
	Preceded by	**Succeeded by**
	Greco-Bactrian Kingdom	Arjunayanas Audumbaras Indo-Scythians Yaudheyas
Today part of	Pakistan Afghanistan India Turkmenistan	

Indo-Greek Kingdom
(200 BCE–10 CE)

200–190 BCE	Demetrius I
190–180 BCE	Agathocles, Pantaleon
185–170 BCE	Antimachus I
180–160 BCE	Apollodotus I
175–170 BCE	Demetrius II
160–155 BCE	Antimachus II
170–145 BCE	Eucratides
155–130 BCE	Menander I
130–120 BCE	Zoilos I, Agathokleia
155–130 BCE	Lysias, Strato I
110–100 BCE	Antialcidas, Heliokles II
100 BCE	Polyxenos, Demetrius III
100–95 BCE	Philoxenus
95–90 BCE	Diomedes, Amyntas, Epander
90 BCE	Theophilos, Peukolaos, Thraso
90–85 BCE	Nicias, Menander II, Artemidoros
90–70 BCE	Hermaeus, Archebius
75–70 BCE	Telephos, Apollodotus II
65–55 BCE	Hippostratos, Dionysios
55–35 BCE	Zoilos II
55–35 BCE	Apollophanes
25 BCE–10 CE	Strato II, Strato III

- v
- t
- e[261]

Indo-Greek Kingdom

Part of a series on the
Indo-Greek Kingdom

- History
  - Ancient sources
- Religion
- Art
- Legacy

- v
- t
- e[262]

The **Indo-Greek Kingdom** or **Graeco-Indian Kingdom**[263] was an Hellenistic kingdom covering various parts of Afghanistan and the northwest regions of the Indian subcontinent (parts of modern Pakistan and northwestern India), during the last two centuries BC and was ruled by more than thirty kings, often conflicting with one another.

The kingdom was founded when the Graeco-Bactrian king Demetrius invaded the subcontinent early in the 2nd century BC. The Greeks in the Indian Subcontinent were eventually divided from the Graeco-Bactrians centered in Bactria (now the border between Afghanistan and Uzbekistan), and the Indo-Greeks in the present-day north-western Indian Subcontinent. The most famous Indo-Greek ruler was Menander (Milinda). He had his capital at Sakala in the Punjab (present-day Sialkot).

The expression "Indo-Greek Kingdom" loosely describes a number of various dynastic polities, traditionally associated with a number of regional capitals like Taxila,[264] (modern Punjab (Pakistan)), Pushkalavati and Sagala.[265] Other potential centers are only hinted at; for instance, Ptolemy's *Geographia* and the nomenclature of later kings suggest that a certain Theophila in the south of the Indo-Greek sphere of influence may also have been a satrapal or royal seat at one time.

During the two centuries of their rule, the Indo-Greek kings combined the Greek and Indian languages and symbols, as seen on their coins, and blended Greek and Indian ideas, as seen in the archaeological remains.[266] The diffusion of Indo-Greek culture had consequences which are still felt today, particularly through the influence of Greco-Buddhist art.[267]. The ethnicity of the Indo-Greek may also have been hybrid to some degree. Euthydemus I was, according to Polybius,[268] a Magnesian Greek. His son, Demetrius I, founder of the Indo-Greek kingdom, was therefore of Greek ethnicity at least by his

Figure 63: *Pataliputra Palace capital, showing Greek and Persian influence, early Mauryan Empire period, 3rd century BC.*

father. A marriage treaty was arranged for the same Demetrius with a daughter of the Seleucid ruler Antiochus III (who had some Persian descent). The ethnicity of later Indo-Greek rulers is sometimes less clear.[269] For example, Artemidoros (80 BC) may have been of Indo-Scythian ascendency, although this is now disputed.[270]

Following the death of Menander, most of his empire splintered and Indo-Greek influence was considerably reduced. Many new kingdoms and republics east of the Ravi River began to mint new coinage depicting military victories.[271] The most prominent entities to form were the Yaudheya Republic, Arjunayanas, and the Audumbaras. The Yaudheyas and Arjunayanas both are said to have won "victory by the sword".[272] The Datta dynasty and Mitra dynasty soon followed in Mathura. The Indo-Greeks ultimately disappeared as a political entity around 10 AD following the invasions of the Indo-Scythians, although pockets of Greek populations probably remained for several centuries longer under the subsequent rule of the Indo-Parthians and Kushans.[273]

Background

Preliminary Greek presence in the Indian Subcontinent

In 326 BC, Alexander the Great conquered the northwestern part of the Indian subcontinent as far as the Hyphasis River, and established satrapies and founded several settlements, including Bucephala; he turned south when his troops refused to go further east.[274] The Indian satrapies of the Punjab were left to the rule of Porus and Taxiles, who were confirmed again at the Treaty of Triparadisus in 321 BC, and remaining Greek troops in these satrapies were left under the command of general Eudemus. After 321 BC Eudemus toppled Taxiles, until he left India in 316 BC. To the south, another general also ruled over the Greek colonies of the Indus: Peithon, son of Agenor,[275] until his departure for Babylon in 316 BC.

Around 322 BC, the Greeks (described as Yona or Yavana in Indian sources) may then have participated, together with other groups, in the armed uprising of Chandragupta Maurya against the Nanda Dynasty, and gone as far as Pataliputra for the capture of the city from the Nandas. The Mudrarakshasa of Visakhadutta as well as the Jaina work Parisishtaparvan talk of Chandragupta's alliance with the Himalayan king Parvatka, often identified with Porus,[276] and according to these accounts, this alliance gave Chandragupta a composite and powerful army made up of Yavanas (Greeks), Kambojas, Shakas (Scythians), Kiratas (Nepalese), Parasikas (Persians) and Bahlikas (Bactrians) who took Pataliputra.[277,278,279]

In 305 BC, Seleucus I led an army to the Indus, where he encountered Chandragupta. The confrontation ended with a peace treaty, and "an intermarriage agreement" (Epigamia, Greek: Ἐπιγαμία), meaning either a dynastic marriage or an agreement for intermarriage between Indians and Greeks. Accordingly, Seleucus ceded to Chandragupta his northwestern territories, possibly as far as Arachosia and received 500 war elephants (which played a key role in the victory of Seleucus at the Battle of Ipsus):[280]

> *The Indians occupy in part some of the countries situated along the Indus, which formerly belonged to the Persians: Alexander deprived the Ariani of them, and established there settlements of his own. But Seleucus Nicator gave them to Sandrocottus in consequence of a marriage contract, and received in return five hundred elephants.*
>
> *—Strabo 15.2.1(9)*

The details of the marriage agreement are not known,[281] but since the extensive sources available on Seleucus never mention an Indian princess, it is thought that the marital alliance went the other way, with Chandragupta himself or his son Bindusara marrying a Seleucid princess, in accordance with

Figure 64: *Kandahar Bilingual Rock Inscription (Greek and Aramaic) by king Ashoka, from Kandahar, Afghanistan.*[284]

contemporary Greek practices to form dynastic alliances. An Indian Puranic source, the Pratisarga Parva of the Bhavishya Purana, described the marriage of Chandragupta with a Greek ("Yavana") princess, daughter of Seleucus,[282] before accurately detailing early Mauryan genealogy:

> *"Chandragupta married with a daughter of Suluva, the Yavana king of Pausasa. Thus, he mixed the Buddhists and the Yavanas. He ruled for 60 years. From him, Vindusara was born and ruled for the same number of years as his father. His son was Ashoka."*
>
> —*Pratisarga Parva*[283]

Also several Greeks, such as the historian Megasthenes,[285] followed by Deimachus and Dionysius, were sent to reside at the Mauryan court.[286] Presents continued to be exchanged between the two rulers.[287] The intensity of these contacts is testified by the existence of a dedicated Mauryan state department for Greek (Yavana) and Persian foreigners,[288] or the remains of Hellenistic pottery that can be found throughout northern India.[289]

On these occasions, Greek populations apparently remained in the northwest of the Indian subcontinent under Mauryan rule. Chandragupta's grandson Ashoka, who had converted to the Buddhist faith declared in the Edicts of

Figure 65: *According to the Mahavamsa, the Great Stupa in Anuradhapura, Sri Lanka, was dedicated by a 30,000-strong "Yona" (Greek) delegation from "Alexandria" around 130 BC.*

Ashoka, set in stone, some of them written in Greek,[290,291] that Greek populations within his realm also had converted to Buddhism:[292]

> Here in the king's domain among the Greeks, the Kambojas, the Nabhakas, the Nabhapamkits, the Bhojas, the Pitinikas, the Andhras and the Palidas, everywhere people are following Beloved-of-the-Gods' instructions in Dharma.
>
> —*Rock Edict Nb13 (S. Dhammika).*

In his edicts, Ashoka mentions that he had sent Buddhist emissaries to Greek rulers as far as the Mediterranean (Edict No. 13),[293,294] and that he developed herbal medicine in their territories, for the welfare of humans and animals (Edict No. 2).[295]

The Greeks in India even seem to have played an active role in the propagation of Buddhism, as some of the emissaries of Ashoka such as Dharmaraksita,[296] or the teacher Mahadharmaraksita,[297] are described in Pali sources as leading Greek ("Yona", i.e., Ionian) Buddhist monks, active in Buddhist proselytism (the Mahavamsa, XII).[298] It is also thought that Greeks contributed to the sculptural work of the Pillars of Ashoka,[299] and more generally to the

Figure 66: *Greco-Bactrian statue of an old man or philosopher, Ai Khanoum, Bactria, 2nd century BC*

blossoming of Mauryan art.[300] Some Greeks (Yavanas) may have played an administrative role in the territories ruled by Ashoka: the Junagadh rock inscription of Rudradaman records that during the rule of Ashoka, a Yavana King/ Governor named Tushaspha was in charge in the area of Girnar, Gujarat, mentioning his role in the construction of a water reservoir.[301,302]

Again in 206 BC, the Seleucid emperor Antiochus led an army to the Kabul valley, where he received war elephants and presents from the local king Sophagasenus:[303]

> *He (Antiochus) crossed the Caucasus (the Caucasus Indicus or Paropamisus: mod. Hindú Kúsh) and descended into India; renewed his friendship with Sophagasenus the king of the Indians; received more elephants, until he had a hundred and fifty altogether; and having once more provisioned his troops, set out again personally with his army: leaving Androsthenes of Cyzicus the duty of taking home the treasure which this king had agreed to hand over to him.*
>
> —*Polybius, Histories 11.39*

Greek rule in Bactria

Alexander had also established several colonies in neighbouring Bactria, such as Alexandria on the Oxus (modern Ai-Khanoum) and Alexandria of the Caucasus (medieval Kapisa, modern Bagram). After Alexander's death in 323 BC, Bactria came under the control of Seleucus I Nicator, who founded the Seleucid Empire. The Greco-Bactrian Kingdom was founded when Diodotus I, the satrap of Bactria (and probably the surrounding provinces) seceded from the Seleucid Empire around 250 BC. The preserved ancient sources (see below) are somewhat contradictory and the exact date of Bactrian independence has not been settled. Somewhat simplified, there is a high chronology (c. 255 BC) and a low chronology (c. 246 BC) for Diodotos' secession.[304] The high chronology has the advantage of explaining why the Seleucid king Antiochus II issued very few coins in Bactria, as Diodotos would have become independent there early in Antiochus' reign.[305] On the other hand, the low chronology, from the mid-240s BC, has the advantage of connecting the secession of Diodotus I with the Third Syrian War, a catastrophic conflict for the Seleucid Empire.

> *Diodotus, the governor of the thousand cities of Bactria (Latin: Theodotus, mille urbium Bactrianarum praefectus), defected and proclaimed himself king; all the other people of the Orient followed his example and seceded from the Macedonians.*

—*(Justin, XLI,4[306])*

The new kingdom, highly urbanized and considered as one of the richest of the Orient (*opulentissimum illud mille urbium Bactrianum imperium* "The extremely prosperous Bactrian empire of the thousand cities" Justin, XLI,1[307]), was to further grow in power and engage into territorial expansion to the east and the west:

> *The Greeks who caused Bactria to revolt grew so powerful on account of the fertility of the country that they became masters, not only of Ariana, but also of India, as Apollodorus of Artemita says: and more tribes were subdued by them than by Alexander... Their cities were Bactra (also called Zariaspa, through which flows a river bearing the same name and emptying into the Oxus), and Darapsa, and several others. Among these was Eucratidia, which was named after its ruler.*

—*(Strabo, XI.XI.I[308])*

When the ruler of neighbouring Parthia, the former satrap and self-proclaimed king Andragoras, was eliminated by Arsaces, the rise of the Parthian Empire

Figure 67: *Corinthian capital, found at Ai-Khanoum, 2nd century BC*

cut off the Greco-Bactrians from direct contact with the Greek world. Overland trade continued at a reduced rate, while sea trade between Greek Egypt and Bactria developed.

Diodotus was succeeded by his son Diodotus II, who allied himself with the Parthian Arsaces in his fight against Seleucus II:

> *Soon after, relieved by the death of Diodotus, Arsaces made peace and concluded an alliance with his son, also by the name of Diodotus; some time later he fought against Seleucos who came to punish the rebels, and he prevailed: the Parthians celebrated this day as the one that marked the beginning of their freedom*
>
> —*(Justin, XLI,4)*[309]

Euthydemus, a Magnesian Greek according to Polybius[310] and possibly satrap of Sogdiana, overthrew Diodotus II around 230 BC and started his own dynasty. Euthydemus's control extended to Sogdiana, going beyond the city of Alexandria Eschate founded by Alexander the Great in Ferghana:

> *"And they also held Sogdiana, situated above Bactriana towards the east between the Oxus River, which forms the boundary between the Bactrians and the Sogdians, and the Iaxartes River. And the Iaxartes forms also the boundary between the Sogdians and the nomads.*

Indo-Greek Kingdom

Figure 68: *Coin depicting the Greco-Bactrian king Euthydemus 230–200 BC. The Greek inscription reads: ΒΑΣΙΛΕΩΣ ΕΥΘΥΔΗΜΟΥ – "(of) King Euthydemus".*

—*Strabo XI.11.2*[311]

Euthydemus was attacked by the Seleucid ruler Antiochus III around 210 BC. Although he commanded 10,000 horsemen, Euthydemus initially lost a battle on the Arius[312] and had to retreat. He then successfully resisted a three-year siege in the fortified city of Bactra (modern Balkh), before Antiochus finally decided to recognize the new ruler, and to offer one of his daughters to Euthydemus's son Demetrius around 206 BC.[313] Classical accounts also relate that Euthydemus negotiated peace with Antiochus III by suggesting that he deserved credit for overthrowing the original rebel Diodotus, and that he was protecting Central Asia from nomadic invasions thanks to his defensive efforts:

> ...for if he did not yield to this demand, neither of them would be safe: seeing that great hordes of Nomads were close at hand, who were a danger to both; and that if they admitted them into the country, it would certainly be utterly barbarised.
>
> —*(Polybius, 11.34)*

Following the departure of the Seleucid army, the Bactrian kingdom seems to have expanded. In the west, areas in north-eastern Iran may have been absorbed, possibly as far as into Parthia, whose ruler had been defeated by Antiochus the Great. These territories possibly are identical with the Bactrian satrapies of Tapuria and Traxiane.

To the north, Euthydemus also ruled Sogdiana and Ferghana, and there are indications that from Alexandria Eschate the Greco-Bactrians may have led expeditions as far as Kashgar and Ürümqi in Chinese Turkestan, leading to the

Figure 69: *Possible statuette of a Greek soldier, wearing a version of the Greek Phrygian helmet, from a 3rd-century BC burial site north of the Tian Shan, Xinjiang Region Museum, Urumqi.*

first known contacts between China and the West around 220 BC. The Greek historian Strabo too writes that:

> they extended their empire even as far as the Seres (Chinese) and the Phryni
>
> —(Strabo, XI.XI.1)

Several statuettes and representations of Greek soldiers have been found north of the Tien Shan, on the doorstep to China, and are today on display in the Xinjiang museum at Urumqi (Boardman[314]).

Greek influences on Chinese art have also been suggested (Hirth, Rostovtzeff). Designs with rosette flowers, geometric lines, and glass inlays, suggestive of Hellenistic influences,[315] can be found on some early Han dynasty bronze mirrors.[316]

Numismatics also suggest that some technology exchanges may have occurred on these occasions: the Greco-Bactrians were the first in the world to issue cupro-nickel (75/25 ratio) coins,[317] an alloy technology only known by the Chinese at the time under the name "White copper" (some weapons from the

Warring States period were in copper-nickel alloy[318]). The practice of exporting Chinese metals, in particular iron, for trade is attested around that period. Kings Euthydemus, Euthydemus II, Agathocles and Pantaleon made these coin issues around 170 BC and it has alternatively been suggested that a nickeliferous copper ore was the source from mines at Anarak.[319] Copper-nickel would not be used again in coinage until the 19th century.

The presence of Chinese people in the Indian subcontinent from ancient times is also suggested by the accounts of the "Ciñas" in the *Mahabharata* and the *Manu Smriti*.

The Han Dynasty explorer and ambassador Zhang Qian visited Bactria in 126 BC, and reported the presence of Chinese products in the Bactrian markets:

> "When I was in Bactria (Daxia)", Zhang Qian reported, "I saw bamboo canes from Qiong and cloth made in the province of Shu (territories of southwestern China). When I asked the people how they had gotten such articles, they replied, "Our merchants go buy them in the markets of Shendu (India)."
>
> —(Shiji 123, Sima Qian, trans. Burton Watson)

Upon his return, Zhang Qian informed the Chinese emperor Han Wudi of the level of sophistication of the urban civilizations of Ferghana, Bactria and Parthia, who became interested in developing commercial relationships with them:

> The Son of Heaven on hearing all this reasoned thus: Ferghana (Dayuan) and the possessions of Bactria (Daxia) and Parthia (Anxi) are large countries, full of rare things, with a population living in fixed abodes and given to occupations somewhat identical with those of the Chinese people, and placing great value on the rich produce of China
>
> —(Hanshu, Former Han History)

A number of Chinese envoys were then sent to Central Asia, triggering the development of the Silk Road from the end of the 2nd century BC.[320]

The Indian emperor Chandragupta, founder of the Mauryan dynasty, had reconquered northwestern India upon the death of Alexander the Great around 322 BC. However, contacts were kept with his Greek neighbours in the Seleucid Empire, a dynastic alliance or the recognition of intermarriage between Greeks and Indians were established (described as an agreement on Epigamia in Ancient sources), and several Greeks, such as the historian Megasthenes, resided at the Mauryan court. Subsequently, each Mauryan emperor had a Greek ambassador at his court.

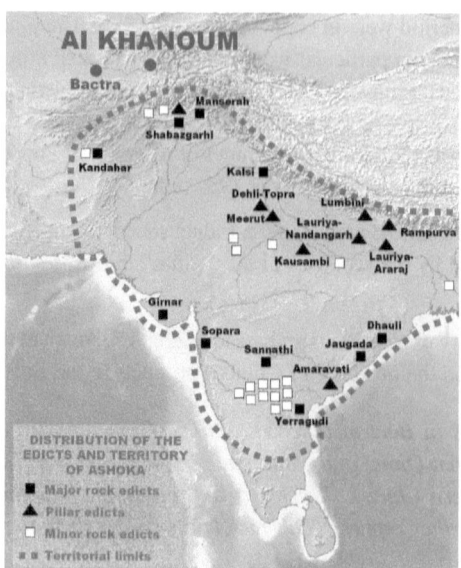

Figure 70: *Greco-Bactria and the city of Ai-Khanoum were located at the very doorstep of Mauryan India.*

Chandragupta's grandson Ashoka converted to the Buddhist faith and became a great proselytizer in the line of the traditional Pali canon of Theravada Buddhism, directing his efforts towards the Indian and the Hellenistic worlds from around 250 BC. According to the Edicts of Ashoka, set in stone, some of them written in Greek, he sent Buddhist emissaries to the Greek lands in Asia and as far as the Mediterranean. The edicts name each of the rulers of the Hellenistic world at the time.

> *The conquest by Dharma has been won here, on the borders, and even six hundred yojanas (4,000 miles) away, where the Greek king Antiochos rules, beyond there where the four kings named Ptolemy, Antigonos, Magas and Alexander rule, likewise in the south among the Cholas, the Pandyas, and as far as Tamraparni.*
>
> —*(Edicts of Ashoka, 13th Rock Edict, S. Dhammika)*

Some of the Greek populations that had remained in northwestern India apparently converted to Buddhism:

> *Here in the king's domain among the Greeks, the Kambojas, the Nabhakas, the Nabhapamkits, the Bhojas, the Pitinikas, the Andhras and the*

Indo-Greek Kingdom 101

Figure 71: *The Khalsi rock edict of Ashoka, which mentions the Greek kings Antiochus, Ptolemy, Antigonus, Magas and Alexander by name, as recipients of his teachings.*

> *Palidas, everywhere people are following Beloved-of-the-Gods' instructions in Dharma.*
>
> *—(Edicts of Ashoka, 13th Rock Edict, S. Dhammika)*

Furthermore, according to Pali sources, some of Ashoka's emissaries were Greek Buddhist monks, indicating close religious exchanges between the two cultures:

> *When the thera (elder) Moggaliputta, the illuminator of the religion of the Conqueror (Ashoka), had brought the (third) council to an end... he sent forth theras, one here and one there: ...and to Aparantaka (the "Western countries" corresponding to Gujarat and Sindh) he sent the Greek (Yona) named Dhammarakkhita... and the thera Maharakkhita he sent into the country of the Yona.*
>
> *—(Mahavamsa XII)*

Greco-Bactrians probably received these Buddhist emissaries (At least Maharakkhita, lit. "The Great Saved One", who was "sent to the country of the Yona") and somehow tolerated the Buddhist faith, although little proof remains. In the 2nd century AD, the Christian dogmatist Clement of Alexandria

Figure 72: *Shunga horseman, Bharhut.*

recognized the existence of Buddhist Sramanas among the Bactrians ("Bactrians" meaning "Oriental Greeks" in that period), and even their influence on Greek thought:

> *Thus philosophy, a thing of the highest utility, flourished in antiquity among the barbarians, shedding its light over the nations. And afterwards it came to Greece. First in its ranks were the prophets of the Egyptians; and the Chaldeans among the Assyrians; and the Druids among the Gauls; and the* **Sramanas** *among the Bactrians ("Σαρμαναίοι Βάκτρων"); and the philosophers of the Celts; and the Magi of the Persians, who foretold the Saviour's birth, and came into the land of Judea guided by a star. The Indian gymnosophists are also in the number, and the other barbarian philosophers. And of these there are two classes, some of them called* **Sramanas** *("Σαρμάναι"), and others Brahmins ("Βραφμαναι").*
>
> — *Clement of Alexandria, "The Stromata, or Miscellanies" Book I, Chapter XV*[321]

Rise of the Shungas (185 BC)

In India, the Maurya Dynasty was overthrown around 185 BC when Pushyamitra Shunga, the commander-in-chief of Mauryan Imperial forces and a

Brahmin, assassinated the last of the Mauryan emperors Brihadratha.[322,323] Pushyamitra Shunga then ascended the throne and established the Shunga Empire, which extended its control as far west as the Punjab.

Buddhist sources, such as the *Ashokavadana*, mention that Pushyamitra was hostile towards Buddhists and allegedly persecuted the Buddhist faith. A large number of Buddhist monasteries (viharas) were allegedly converted to Hindu temples, in such places as Nalanda, Bodhgaya, Sarnath or Mathura. While it is established by secular sources that Hinduism and Buddhism were in competition during this time, with the Shungas preferring the former to the latter, historians such as Etienne Lamotte[324] and Romila Thapar[325] argue that Buddhist accounts of persecution of Buddhists by Shungas are largely exaggerated. Some Puranic sources however also describe the resurgence of Brahmanism following the Maurya Dynasty, and the killing of millions of Buddhists, such as the *Pratisarga Parva* of the *Bhavishya Purana*:[326]

> "At this time [after the rule of Chandragupta, Bindusara and Ashoka] the best of the brahmanas, Kanyakubja, performed sacrifice on the top of a mountain named Arbuda. By the influence of Vedic mantras, four Kshatriyas appeared from the yajna (sacrifice). (...) They kept Ashoka under their control and annihilated all the Buddhists. It is said there were 4 million Buddhists and all of them were killed by uncommon weapons".
>
> —*Pratisarga Parva*[327]

History of the Indo-Greek kingdom

Nature and quality of the sources

Some narrative history has survived for most of the Hellenistic world, at least of the kings and the wars;[328] this is lacking for India. The main Greco-Roman source on the Indo-Greeks is Justin, who wrote an anthology drawn from the Roman historian Pompeius Trogus, who in turn wrote, from Greek sources, at the time of Augustus Caesar.[329] In addition to these dozen sentences, the geographer Strabo mentions India a few times in the course of his long dispute with Eratosthenes about the shape of Eurasia. Most of these are purely geographical claims, but he does mention that Eratosthenes' sources say that some of the Greek kings conquered further than Alexander; Strabo does not believe them on this, nor does he believe that Menander and Demetrius son of Euthydemus conquered more tribes than Alexander[330] There is half a story about Menander in one of the books of Polybius which has not come down to us intact.[331]

There are Indian literary sources, ranging from the Milinda Panha, a dialogue between a Buddhist sage Nagasena and Indianized names that may be related

Figure 73: *Apollodotus I (180–160 BC) the first king who ruled in the subcontinent only, and therefore the founder of the proper Indo-Greek kingdom.*

to Indo-Greek kings such as Menander I. Names in these sources are consistently Indianized, and there is some dispute whether, for example, *Dharmamitra* represents "Demetrius" or is an Indian prince with that name. There was also a Chinese expedition to Bactria by Chang-k'ien under the Emperor Wu of Han, recorded in the Records of the Grand Historian and Book of the Former Han, with additional evidence in the Book of the Later Han; the identification of places and peoples behind transcriptions into Chinese is difficult, and several alternate interpretations have been proposed.[332]Wikipedia:Citing sources#What information to include

Other evidence of the broader and longer influence of Indo-Greeks is possibly suggested by Yavanarajya inscription, dated to 1st-century BCE. It mentions Yavana, a term which literally implies "foreigner" and may mean Indo-Greeks or someone else.

Expansion of Demetrius into India

Demetrius I, the son of Euthydemus is generally considered as the Greco-Bactrian king who first launched the Greek expansion into India. He is therefore the founder of the Indo-Greek realm. The true intents of the Greek kings in occupying India are unknown, but it is thought that the elimination of the Maurya Empire by the Sunga greatly encouraged this expansion. The Indo-Greeks, in particular Menander I who is said in the *Milindapanha* to have converted to Buddhism, also possibly received the help of Indian Buddhists.[334]

There is an inscription from his father's reign already officially hailing Demetrius as victorious. He also has one of the few absolute dates in Indo-Greek history: after his father held off Antiochus III for two years, 208–6 BC,

Indo-Greek Kingdom

Figure 74: *Silver coin depicting Demetrius I of Bactria (reigned c. 200–180 BC), wearing an elephant scalp, symbol of his conquests of areas in Northwest Indian subcontinent, what is now Afghanistan and Pakistan.*[333]

the peace treaty included the offer of a marriage between Demetrius and Antiochus' daughter.[335] Coins of Demetrius I have been found in Arachosia and in the Kabul Valley; the latter would be the first entry of the Greeks into India, as they defined it. There is also literary evidence for a campaign eastward against the Seres and the Phryni; but the order and dating of these conquests is uncertain.[336]

Demetrius I seems to have conquered the Kabul valley, Arachosia and perhaps Gandhara;[337] he struck no Indian coins, so either his conquests did not penetrate that far into India or he died before he could consolidate them. On his coins, Demetrius I always carries the elephant-helmet worn by Alexander, which seems to be a token of his Indian conquests.[338] Bopearachchi believes that Demetrius received the title of "King of India" following his victories south of the Hindu Kush.[339] He was also given, though perhaps only posthumously, the title Ἀνίκητος ("Aniketos", lit. *Invincible*) a cult title of Heracles, which Alexander had assumed; the later Indo-Greek kings Lysias, Philoxenus, and Artemidorus also took it.[340] Finally, Demetrius may have been the founder of a newly discovered Yavana era, starting in 186/5 BC.[341]

Figure 75: *Kharoshthi legend on the reverse of a coin of Indo-Greek king Artemidoros Aniketos, reading "Rajatirajasa Moasa Putasa cha Artemidorasa".*

First bilingual monetary system

After the death of Demetrius, the Bactrian kings Pantaleon and Agathocles struck the first bilingual coins with Indian inscriptions found as far east as Taxila[342] so in their time (c. 185–170 BC) the Bactrian kingdom seems to have included Gandhara.[343] These first bilingual coins used the Brahmi script, whereas later kings would generally use Kharoshthi. They also went as far as incorporating Indian deities, such as goddess Lakshmi and Hindu deities, as well as various Indian devices (lion, elephant, zebu bull) and symbols, which can also be seen in the Post-Mauryan coinage of Gandhara.

The Hinduist coinage of Agathocles is few but spectacular. Six Indian-standard silver drachmas were discovered at Ai-Khanoum in 1970, which depict Hindu deities.[344] These are early Avatars of Vishnu: Balarama-Sankarshana with attributes consisting of the Gada mace and the plow, and Vasudeva-Krishna with the Vishnu attributes of the Shankha (a pear-shaped case or conch) and the Sudarshana Chakra wheel. These first attempts at incorporating Indian culture were only partly preserved by later kings: they all continued to struck bilingual coins, sometimes in addition to Attic coinage, but Greek deities remained prevalent. Indian animals however, such as the elephant, the bull or the lion, possibly with religious overtones, were used extensively in their Indian-standard square coinage.

Indo-Greek Kingdom

Figure 76: *Coin of Agathocles with Hindu deities: Balarama-Samkarshana (left) and Vasudeva-Krishna (right).*

Figure 77: *Menander I (155–130 BC) is one of the few Indo-Greek kings mentioned in both Graeco-Roman and Indian sources.*

Several Bactrian kings followed after Demetrius' death, and it seems likely that the civil wars between them made it possible for Apollodotus I (from c. 180/175 BC) to make himself independent as the first proper Indo-Greek king (who did not rule from Bactria). Large numbers of his coins have been found in India, and he seems to have reigned in Gandhara as well as western Punjab. Apollodotus I was succeeded by or ruled alongside Antimachus II, likely the son of the Bactrian king Antimachus I.[345]

Rule of Menander I

The Shiva Reh Inscription discovered in 1979 near Kausambi, was proposed to be related to Menander but now discredited.[346]

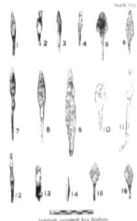

Indo-Greek arrowheads from Kausambi.

The next important Indo-Greek king was Menander (from c. 165/155 BC) who has been described as the greatest of the Indo-Greek Kings; his coins are found as far as eastern Punjab. Menander seems to have begun a second wave of conquests, and since he already ruled in India, it seems likely that the easternmost conquests were made by him.[347] Thus from 161 B.C. onwards Menander was the ruler of Punjab until his death in 130 B.C. Menander made Sagala his capital, and after conquering the Punjab region he subsequently made an expedition across northern India and reached the Mauryan capital of Patna. Soon after, Eucratides I king of the Greco-Bactrian Kingdom began warring with the Indo-Greeks in the north western frontier.

According to Apollodorus of Artemita, quoted by Strabo, the Indo-Greek territory for a while included the Indian coastal provinces of Sindh and possibly Gujarat.[348] With archaeological methods, the Indo-Greek territory can however only be confirmed from the Kabul Valley to the eastern Punjab, so Greek presence outside was probably short-lived or non-existent.

Some sources also claim that the Indo-Greeks may have reached the Shunga capital Pataliputra in northeastern India.[349,350,351] However, the nature of this expedition is a matter of controversy. One theory is that Indo-Greeks were invited to join a raid led by local Indian kings down the Ganges river. The other is that it was a campaign likely made by Menander. Irrespective it appears that Pataliputra, if at all captured, was not held as the expedition was forced to retreat, probably due to wars in their own territories.

Indo-Greek Kingdom

| Menander I became the most important of the Indo-Greek rulers.[352] | Eucratides I toppled the Greco-Bactrian Euthydemid dynasty, and attacked the Indo-Greeks from the west. |

The important Bactrian king Eucratides seems to have attacked the Indo-Greek kingdom during the mid 2nd century BC. A Demetrius, called "King of the Indians", seems to have confronted Eucratides in a four-month siege, reported by Justin, but he ultimately lost.[353]

In any case, Eucratides seems to have occupied territory as far as the Indus, between ca. 170 BC and 150 BC.[354] His advances were ultimately reclaimed by the Indo-Greek king Menander I,[355]

Menander is considered to have been probably the most successful Indo-Greek king, and the conqueror of the largest territory.[356] The finds of his coins are the most numerous and the most widespread of all the Indo-Greek kings. Menander is also remembered in Buddhist literature, where he is called Milinda, and is described in the Milinda Panha as a convert to Buddhism he became an arhat[357] whose relics were enshrined in a manner reminiscent of the Buddha.[358,359] He also introduced a new coin type, with Athena Alkidemos ("Protector of the people") on the reverse, which was adopted by most of his successors in the East.[360]

Following the death of Menander his empire was greatly reduced due to the emergence of new kingdoms and republics within his allotted territories within India.[361] The most eminent entities to splinter were the Yaudheya Republic and the Arjunayanas, which began to mint coins mentioning military victories. Along with numismatic evidence, the Junagadh rock inscription of Rudradaman details the conquests of the Saka King Rudradaman I of the Western Satraps over the Yaudheya Republic, reaffirming their independence from the Menanders Empire.[362]

From the mid-2nd century BC, the Scythians, in turn being pushed forward by the Yuezhi who were completing a long migration from the border of China, started to invade Bactria from the north.[363] Around 130 BC the last Greco-Bactrian king Heliocles was probably killed during the invasion and the Greco-Bactrian kingdom proper ceased to exist. The Parthians also probably played a role in the downfall of the Bactrian kingdom.

Figure 78: *King Hippostratos riding a horse, circa 100 BCE (coin detail).*

There are however no historical recordings of events in the Indo-Greek kingdom after Menander's death around 130 BC, since the Indo-Greeks had now become very isolated from the rest of the Graeco-Roman world. The later history of the Indo-Greek states, which lasted to around the shift BC/AD, is reconstructed almost entirely from archaeological and numismatical analyses.[364]

Western accounts

Greek presence in Arachosia, where Greek populations had been living since before the acquisition of the territory by Chandragupta from Seleucus, is mentioned by Isidore of Charax. He describes Greek cities there, one of them called Demetrias, probably in honour of the conqueror Demetrius.[365]

Apollodotus I (and Menander I) were mentioned by Pompeius Trogus as important Indo-Greek kings.[366] It is theorized that Greek advances temporarily went as far as the Shunga capital Pataliputra (today Patna) in eastern India. Senior considers that these conquests can only refer to Menander:[367] Against this, John Mitchener considers that the Greeks probably raided the Indian capital of Pataliputra during the time of Demetrius,[368] though Mitchener's analysis is not based on numismatic evidence.

Figure 79: *The Yavanarajya inscription discovered in Mathura, mentions its carving on "The last day of year 116 of Yavana hegemony" (Yavanarajya), or 116th year if the Yavana era, suggesting the Greeks ruled over Mathura as late as 60 BC. Mathura Museum.*

Of the eastern parts of India, then, there have become known to us all those parts which lie this side of the Hypanis, and also any parts beyond the Hypanis of which an account has been added by those who, after Alexander, advanced beyond the Hypanis, to the Ganges and Pataliputra.

—*Strabo, 15-1-27*[369]

The seriousness of the attack is in some doubt: Menander may merely have joined a raid led by Indian Kings down the Ganges,[370] as Indo-Greek presence has not been confirmed this far east.

To the south, the Greeks may have occupied the areas of the Sindh and Gujarat, including the strategic harbour of Barygaza (Bharuch),[371] conquests also attested by coins dating from the Indo-Greek ruler Apollodotus I and by several ancient writers (Strabo 11; Periplus of the Erythraean Sea, Chap. 41/47):[372]

The Greeks... took possession, not only of Patalene, but also, on the rest of the coast, of what is called the kingdom of Saraostus and Sigerdis.

—*Strabo 11.11.1*[373]

The *Periplus* further explains ancient Indo-Greek rule and continued circulation of Indo-Greek coinage in the region:

"To the present day ancient drachmae are current in Barygaza, coming from this country, bearing inscriptions in Greek letters, and the devices of those who reigned after Alexander, Apollodorus [sic] and Menander."

—*Periplus Chap. 47*[374]

Narain however dismisses the account of the Periplus as "just a sailor's story", and holds that coin finds are not necessarily indicators of occupation.[375] Coin hoards further suggest that in Central India, the area of Malwa may also have been conquered.[376]

Figure 80: *The Mathura Herakles. A statue of Herakles strangling the Nemean lion from Mathura.*[380] *Today in the Kolkota Indian Museum.*

Rule in Mathura

Slightly northwest of Mathura, numerous Indo-Greek coins were found in the city of Khokrakot (modern Rohtak), belonging to as many as 14 different Indo-Greek kings, as well as coin molds in Naurangabad,[377] suggesting Indo-Greek occupation of Haryana in the 2nd-1st centuries BCE.[378,379]

From numismatic, literary and epigraphic evidence, it seems that the Indo-Greeks also had control over Mathura at some time, especially during the rule of Menander I (165–135 BC).

An inscription in Mathura discovered in 1988,[381] the Yavanarajya inscription, mentions "The last day of year 116 of Yavana hegemony (*Yavanarajya*)". The "Yavanarajya" probably refers to the rule of the Indo-Greeks in Mathura as late as around 70-60 BC (year 116 of the Yavana era).[382] The extent of Indo-Greek rule in Mathura has been disputed, but it is also known that no remains of Sunga rule have been found in Mathura, and their territorial control is only proved as far as the central city of Ayodhya in northern central India, through the Dhanadeva-Ayodhya inscription.[383] Archeological excavations of cast die-struck coins have also revealed the presence of a Mitra dynasty (coin issuers who did not name themselves "kings" on their coins) in Mathura sometime between 150 BC to 20 BC. Additionally, coins belonging to a Datta dynasty have also been excavated in Mathura. Whether these dynasties ruled independently or as satraps to larger kingdoms is unknown.

Mathura may then have been conquered by the Mitra dynasty, or ruled independently by the Datta dynasty during the 1st century BCE.[384] In any case Mathura was under the control of the Indo-Scythian Northern Satraps from the 1st century CE.

Indian sources

Various Indian records describe *Yavana* attacks on Mathura, Panchala, Saketa, and Pataliputra. The term *Yavana* is thought to be a transliteration of "Ionians" and is known to have designated Hellenistic Greeks (starting with the Edicts of Ashoka, where Ashoka writes about "the *Yavana* king Antiochus"),[385] but may have sometimes referred to other foreigners as well after the 1st century AD.[386]

Patanjali, a grammarian and commentator on Pāṇini around 150 BC, describes in the *Mahābhāsya*, the invasion in two examples using the imperfect tense of Sanskrit, denoting a recent event:[387,388]

- *"Arunad Yavanah Sāketam"* ("The Yavanas (Greeks) were besieging Saketa")
- *"Arunad Yavano Madhyamikām"* ("The Yavanas were besieging Madhyamika" (the "Middle country")).

Also the Brahmanical text of the *Yuga Purana*, which describes Indian historical events in the form of a prophecy, but is thought to be likely historical,[389,390,391] relates the attack of the Indo-Greeks on the capital Pataliputra,[392] a magnificent fortified city with 570 towers and 64 gates according to Megasthenes,[393] and describes the ultimate destruction of the city's walls:[394]

> *Then, after having approached Saketa together with the Panchalas and the Mathuras, the Yavanas, valiant in battle, will reach Kusumadhvaja ('The town of the flower-standard", Pataliputra). Then, once Puspapura (another name of Pataliputra) has been reached and its celebrated mudwalls cast down, all the realm will be in disorder.*
>
> —*Yuga Purana, Paragraph 47–48, quoted in Mitchener, The Yuga Purana, 2002 edition*[395,396]

Accounts of battles between the Greeks and the Shunga in Central India are also found in the *Mālavikāgnimitram*, a play by Kālidāsa which is thought to describe an encounter between a Greek cavalry squadron and Vasumitra, the grandson of Pushyamitra, during the latter's reign, by the Sindh River or the Kali Sindh River.[398]

Figure 81: *Possible statue of a Yavana/ Indo-Greek warrior with boots and chiton, from the Rani Gumpha or "Cave of the Queen" in the Udayagiri Caves on the east coast of India, where the Hathigumpha inscription was also found. 2nd or 1st century BCE.*[397]

According to the Yuga Purana, the Yavanas thereafter retreated following internal conflicts:

> *'The Yavanas (Greeks) will command, the Kings will disappear. (But ultimately) the Yavanas, intoxicated with fighting, will not stay in Madhadesa (the Middle Country); there will be undoubtedly a civil war among them, arising in their own country (Bactria), there will be a terrible and ferocious war." (Gargi-Samhita, Yuga Purana chapter, No7).*

Earlier authors such as Tarn have suggested that the raid on Pataliputra was made by Demetrius.[399] According to Mitchener, the Hathigumpha inscription indicates the presence of the Greeks led by a "Demetrius" in eastern India (Magadha) during the 1st century BC,[400] although this interpretation was previously disputed by Narain.[401]

> *'Then in the eighth year, (Kharavela) with a large army having sacked Goradhagiri causes pressure on Rajagaha (Rajagriha). On account of the loud report of this act of valour, the Yavana (Greek) King Dimi[ta] retreated to Mathura having extricated his demoralized army."*

—Hathigumpha inscription, line 8, probably in the 1st century BCE. Original text is in Brahmi script.[402]

But while this inscription may be interpreted as an indication that Demetrius I was the king who made conquests in Punjab, it is still true that he never issued any Indian-standard coins, only numerous coins with elephant symbolism, and the restoration of his name in Kharosthi on the Hathigumpha inscription: *Di-Mi-Ta*, has been doubted.[403] The *"Di"* is a reconstruction, and it may be noted that the name of another Indo-Greek king, Amyntas, is spelt *A-Mi-Ta* in Kharosthi and may fit in.

Therefore, Menander remains the likeliest candidate for any advance east of Punjab.

Consolidation

| Menander I became the most important of the Indo-Greek rulers.[404] | Eucratides I toppled the Greco-Bactrian Euthydemid dynasty, and attacked the Indo-Greeks from the west. |

The important Bactrian king Eucratides seems to have attacked the Indo-Greek kingdom during the mid 2nd century BC. A Demetrius, called "King of the Indians", seems to have confronted Eucratides in a four-month siege, reported by Justin, but he ultimately lost.[405]

In any case, Eucratides seems to have occupied territory as far as the Indus, between ca. 170 BC and 150 BC.[406] His advances were ultimately checked by the Indo-Greek king Menander I,[407]

Menander is considered to have been probably the most successful Indo-Greek king, and the conqueror of the largest territory.[408] The finds of his coins are the most numerous and the most widespread of all the Indo-Greek kings. Menander is also remembered in Buddhist literature, where he is called Milinda, and is described in the Milinda Panha as a convert to Buddhism:[409] he became an arhat[410] whose relics were enshrined in a manner reminiscent of the Buddha.[411,412] He also introduced a new coin type, with Athena Alkidemos ("Protector of the people") on the reverse, which was adopted by most of his successors in the East.[413]

Figure 82: *Heliocles (145–130 BC) was the last Greek king in Bactria.*

Fall of Bactria and death of Menander

From the mid-2nd century BC, the Scythians, in turn being pushed forward by the Yuezhi who were completing a long migration from the border of China, started to invade Bactria from the north.[414] Around 130 BC the last Greco-Bactrian king Heliocles was probably killed during the invasion and the Greco-Bactrian kingdom proper ceased to exist. The Parthians also probably played a role in the downfall of the Bactrian kingdom.

Immediately after the fall of Bactria, the bronze coins of Indo-Greek king Zoilos I (130–120 BC), successor of Menander in the western part of the Indian territories, combined the club of Herakles with a Scythian-type bowcase and short recurve bow inside a victory wreath, illustrating interaction with horse-mounted people originating from the steppes, possibly either the Scythians (future Indo-Scythians), or the Yuezhi (future Kushans) who had invaded Greco-Bactria.[415] This bow can be contrasted to the traditional Hellenistic long bow depicted on the coins of the eastern Indo-Greek queen Agathokleia. It is now known that 50 years later, the Indo-Scythian Maues was in alliance with the Indo-Greek kings in Taxila, and one of those kings, Artemidoros seems to claim on his coins that he is the son of Maues,[416] although this is now disputed.[417]

Preservation of the Indo-Greek realm

The extant of Indo-Greek rule is still uncertain and disputed. Probable members of the dynasty of Menander include the ruling queen Agathokleia, her son Strato I, and Nicias, though it is uncertain whether they ruled directly after Menander.[418]

Indo-Greek Kingdom

Figure 83: *Coin of Antialcidas (105–95 BC).*

Figure 84: *Coin of Philoxenos (100–95 BC).*

Other kings emerged, usually in the western part of the Indo-Greek realm, such as Zoilos I, Lysias, Antialcidas and Philoxenos.[419] These rulers may have been relatives of either the Eucratid or the Euthydemid dynasties. The names of later kings were often new (members of Hellenistic dynasties usually inherited family names) but old reverses and titles were frequently repeated by the later rulers.

Immediately after the fall of Bactria, the bronze coins of Indo-Greek king Zoilos I (130–120 BC), successor of Menander in the western part of the Indian territories, combined the club of Herakles with a Scythian-type bowcase and short recurve bow inside a victory wreath, illustrating interaction with horse-mounted people originating from the steppes, possibly either the Scythians (future Indo-Scythians), or the Yuezhi (future Kushans) who had invaded Greco-Bactria.[420] This bow can be contrasted to the traditional Hellenistic long bow

Figure 85: *Coin of Zoilos I (130–120 BC) showing on the reverse the Heraklean club with the Scythian bow, inside a victory wreath.*

depicted on the coins of the eastern Indo-Greek queen Agathokleia. It is now known that 50 years later, the Indo-Scythian Maues was in alliance with the Indo-Greek kings in Taxila, and one of those kings, Artemidoros seems to claim on his coins that he is the son of Maues,[421] although this is now disputed.[422]

While all Indo-Greek kings after Apollodotus I mainly issued bilingual (Greek and Kharoshti) coins for circulation in their own territories, several of them also struck rare Greek coins which have been found in Bactria. The later kings probably struck these coins as some kind of payment to the Scythian or Yuezhi tribes who now ruled there, though if as tribute or payment for mercenaries remains unknown.[423] For some decades after the Bactrian invasion, relationships seem to have been peaceful between the Indo-Greeks and these relatively hellenised nomad tribes.

Interactions with Indian culture and religions

Indo-Greeks in the regions of Vidisha and Sanchi (115 BC)

Vidisha

It is around this time, in 115 BC, that the embassy of Heliodorus, from king Antialkidas to the court of the Sungas king Bhagabhadra in Vidisha, is recorded. In the Sunga capital, Heliodorus established the Heliodorus pillar in a dedication to Vāsudeva. This would indicate that relations between the Indo-Greeks and the Sungas had improved by that time, that people traveled between the two realms, and also that the Indo-Greeks readily followed Indian religions.[425]

Indo-Greek Kingdom

Figure 86: *The Heliodorus pillar, commissioned by Indo-Greek ambassador Heliodorus, is the first known inscription related to Vaishnavism in India.*[424] *Heliodurus was one of the earliest recorded Indo-Greek converts to Hinduism.*

Sanchi

Also around the same period, circa 115 BC, decorative reliefs were introduced for the first time at nearby Sanchi, 6 km away from Vidisha, by craftsmen from the northwest. These craftsmen left mason's marks in Kharoshthi, mainly used in the area around Gandhara, as opposed to the local Brahmi script. This seems to imply that these foreign workers were responsible for some of the earliest motifs and figures that can be found on the railings of the stupa.[426] These early reliefs at Sanchi, (those of Sanchi Stupa No.2), are dated to 115 BC, while the more extensive pillar carvings are dated to 80 BC.[427] These reliefs have been described as "the oldest extensive stupa decoration in existence".[428] They are considered as the origin of Jataka illustrations in India.[429]

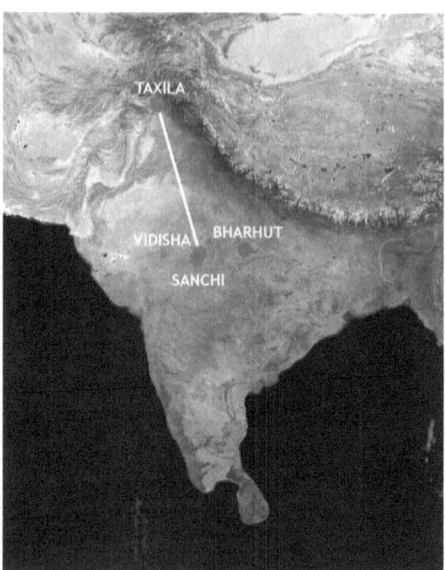

Figure 87: *Heliodorus travelled from Taxila to Vidisha as an ambassador of king Antialkidas, and erected the Heliodorus pillar.*

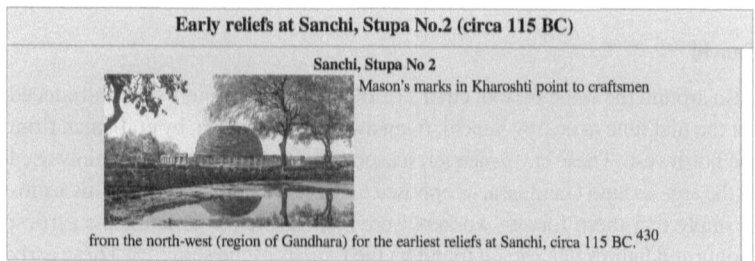

Early reliefs at Sanchi, Stupa No.2 (circa 115 BC)

Sanchi, Stupa No 2

Mason's marks in Kharoshti point to craftsmen from the north-west (region of Gandhara) for the earliest reliefs at Sanchi, circa 115 BC.[430]

Indo-Greek Kingdom

Figure 88: *Foreigner on a horse. The medallions are dated circa 115 BC.*[431]

Figure 89: *Lakshmi with lotus and two child attendants, probably derived from similar images of Venus*

Figure 90: *Lotus within Hellenistic beads and reels motif.*

Figure 91: *Floral motif.*

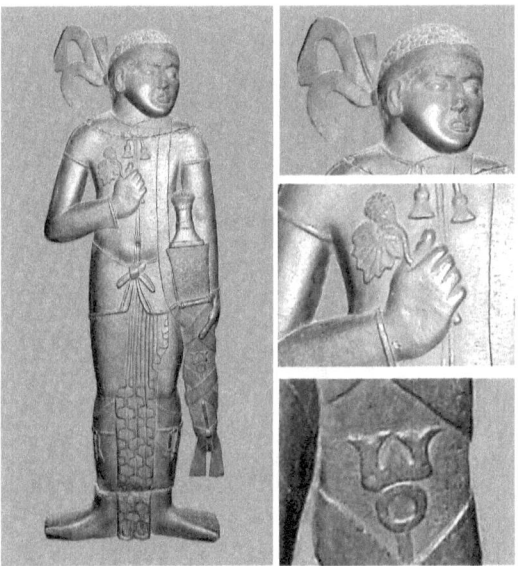

Figure 92: *The Bharhut Yavana, a possible Indian depiction of Menander, with the flowing head band of a Greek king, northern tunic with Hellenistic pleats, and Buddhist triratana symbol on his sword. Bharhut, 100 BC. Indian Museum, Calcutta.*[432,433,434]

Indo-Greeks and Bharhut (100-75 BC)

A warrior figure, the Bharhut Yavana, appeared prominently on a high relief on the railings of the stupa of Bharhut circa 100 BC.[435] The warrior has the flowing head band of a Greek king, a northern tunic with Hellenistic pleats, he hold a grape in his hand, and has a Buddhist triratana symbol on his sword. He has the role of a dvarapala, a Guardian of the entrance of the Stupa. The warrior has been described as a Greek,[436] Some have suggested that he might even represent king Menander.

Also around that time, craftsmen from the Gandhara area are known to have been involved in the construction of the Buddhist torana gateways at Bharhut, which are dated to 100-75 BC:[437] this is because mason's marks in Kharosthi have been found on several elements of the Bharhut remains, indicating that some of the builders at least came from the north, particularly from Gandhara where the Kharoshti script was in use.[438,439,440]

Cunningham explained that the Kharosthi letters were found on the ballusters between the architraves of the gateway, but none on the railings which all had Indian markings, summarizing that the gateways, which are artistically more

Figure 93: *At Bharhut, the gateways were made by northwestern (probably Gandharan) masons using Kharosthi marks 100-75 BC.*

Figure 94: *Foreigners on the Northern Gateway of Stupa I at Sanchi.*

refined, must have been made by artists from the North, whereas the railings were made by local artists.[441]

Sanchi Yavanas (50-0 BC)

Again in Sanchi, but this time dating to the period of Satavahana rule circa 50-0 BC, one frieze can be observed which shows devotees in Greek attire making a dedication to the Great Stupa of Sanchi.[442] The official notice at Sanchi describes "Foreigners worshiping Stupa". The men are depicted with short curly hair, often held together with a headband of the type commonly seen on Greek coins. The clothing too is Greek, complete with tunics, capes and sandals, typical of the Greek travelling costume.[443] The musical instruments are also quite characteristic, such as the double flute called aulos. Also visible are carnyx-like horns.[444] They are all celebrating at the entrance of the stupa.

The actual participation of Yavanas/Yonas (Greek donors) to the construction of Sanchi is known from three inscriptions made by self-declared Yavana donors:

- The clearest of these reads "*Setapathiyasa Yonasa danam*" ("Gift of the Yona of Setapatha"),[445,446] Setapatha being an uncertain city, possibly a location near Nasik,[447] a place where other dedications by Yavanas are known, in cave No.17 of the Nasik caves complex, and on the pillars of the Karla caves not far away.
- A second similar inscription on a pillar reads: *"[Sv]etapathasa (Yona?)sa danam"*, with probably the same meaning, ("Gift of the Yona of Setapatha").[448]
- The third inscription, on two adjacent pavement slabs reads *"Cuda yo[vana]kasa bo silayo"* ("Two slabs of Cuda, the Yonaka").[449]

Decline

King Philoxenus (100–95 BC) briefly occupied the whole Greek territory from the Paropamisadae to Western Punjab, after what the territories fragmented again between smaller Indo-Greek kings. Throughout the 1st century BC, the Indo-Greeks progressively lost ground to the Indians in the east, and the Scythians, the Yuezhi, and the Parthians in the West. About 20 Indo-Greek kings are known during this period,[450] down to the last known Indo-Greek rulers, Strato II and Strato III, who ruled in the Punjab region until around 10 AD.[451]

Loss of Hindu Kush territories (70 BC-)

Around eight "western" Indo-Greek kings are known; most of them are distinguished by their issues of Attic coins for circulation in the neighbouring region.

One of the last important kings in the Paropamisadae (part of the Hindu Kush) was Hermaeus, who ruled until around 80 BC; soon after his death the Yuezhi or Sakas took over his areas from neighbouring Bactria. When Hermaeus is depicted on his coins riding a horse, he is equipped with the recurve bow and bow-case of the steppes and RC Senior believes him to be of partly nomad

Figure 95: *Hermaeus (90–70 BC) was the last Indo-Greek king in the Western territories (Paropamisadae).*

Figure 96: *Hermaeus posthumous issue struck by Indo-Scythians near Kabul, circa 80–75 BCE.*

origin. The later king Hippostratus may however also have held territories in the Paropamisadae.

After the death of Hermaeus, the Yuezhi or Saka nomads became the new rulers of the Paropamisadae, and minted vast quantities of posthumous issues of Hermaeus up to around 40 AD, when they blend with the coinage of the Kushan king Kujula Kadphises.[452] The first documented Yuezhi prince, Sapadbizes, ruled around 20 BC, and minted in Greek and in the same style as the western Indo-Greek kings, probably depending on Greek mints and celators.

Indo-Greek Kingdom

Figure 97: *Tetradrachm of Hippostratos, reigned circa 65–55 BC, was the last Indo-Greek king in Western Punjab.*

Loss of Central territories (48/47 BC)

Around 80 BC, an Indo-Scythian king named Maues, possibly a general in the service of the Indo-Greeks, ruled for a few years in northwestern India before the Indo-Greeks again took control. He seems to have been married to an Indo-Greek princess named Machene.[453] King Hippostratus (65–55 BC) seems to have been one of the most successful subsequent Indo-Greek kings until he lost to the Indo-Scythian Azes I, who established an Indo-Scythian dynasty in 48/47 BC.[454] Various coins seem to suggest that some sort of alliance may have taken place between the Indo-Greeks and the Scythians.[455]

Although the Indo-Scythians clearly ruled militarily and politically, they remained surprisingly respectful of Greek and Indian cultures. Their coins were minted in Greek mints, continued using proper Greek and Kharoshthi legends, and incorporated depictions of Greek deities, particularly Zeus.[456] The Mathura lion capital inscription attests that they adopted the Buddhist faith, as do the depictions of deities forming the vitarka mudra on their coins. Greek communities, far from being exterminated, probably persisted under Indo-Scythian rule. There is a possibility that a fusion, rather than a confrontation, occurred between the Greeks and the Indo-Scythians: in a recently published coin, Artemidorus seems to present himself as "son of Maues"[457] (but this is now disputed), and the Buner reliefs show Indo-Greeks and Indo-Scythians reveling in a Buddhist context.

The last known mention of an Indo-Greek ruler is suggested by an inscription on a signet ring of the 1st century AD in the name of a king Theodamas, from the Bajaur area of Gandhara, in modern Pakistan. No coins of him are known,

Figure 98: *Hippostratos was replaced by the Indo-Scythian king Azes I (r. c. 35–12 BC).*

but the signet bears in kharoshthi script the inscription *"Su Theodamasa"*, *"Su"* being explained as the Greek transliteration of the ubiquitous Kushan royal title *"Shau"* ("Shah", "King").[458]

Loss of Eastern territories (10 AD)

The Indo-Greek kingdoms lost most of their eastern territories in the 1st century BCE following the death of Menander[459]. The Arjunayanas and the Yaudheya Republic mention military victories on their coins ("Victory of the Arjunayanas", "Victory of the Yaudheyas"). These entities would remain independamt until being conquered by the Saka King Rudradaman I of the Western Satraps.

> *Rudradaman (...) who by force destroyed the Yaudheyas who were loath to submit, rendered proud as they were by having manifested their' title of' heroes among all Kshatriyas.*
>
> —*Junagadh rock inscription of Rudradaman*

They would again win independence until being conquered by Samudragupta of the Gupta Empire, and would disintegrate soon after.

Indo-Greek Kingdom

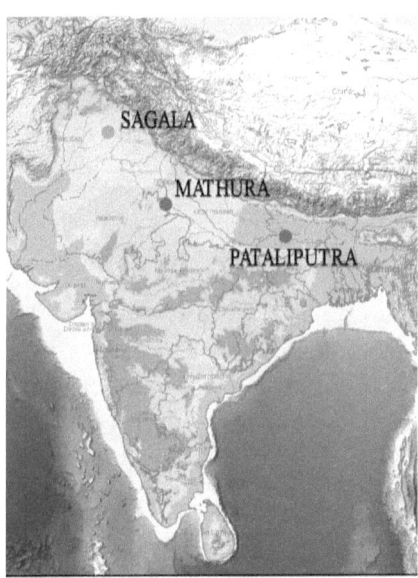

Figure 99: *Approximate region of East Punjab and Strato II's capital Sagala.*

Figure 100: *The last known Indo-Greek kings Strato II and Strato III, here on a joint coin (25 BC-10 AD), were the last Indo-Greek king in eartern territories of Eastern Punjab.*

Figure 101: *Pillar of the Great Chaitya at Karla Caves, mentioning its donation by a Yavana.*[468] *Below: detail of the word "Ya-va-na-sa" in old Brahmi script: , circa 120 CE.*

During the 1st century BC, the Trigartas, Audumbaras[460] and finally the Kunindas[461] also started to mint their own coins, usually in a style highly reminiscent of Indo-Greek coinage.[462,463,464]

The Yavanas may have ruled as far as the area of Mathura from the time of Menander I until the middle of the 1st century BC: the Maghera inscription, from a village near Mathura, records the dedication of a well "in the one hundred and sixteenth year of the reign of the Yavanas", which corresponds to circa 70 BC.[465] In the 1st century BC, however, they lost the area of Mathura, either to the Mitra rulers under the Shunga Empire or to the Datta dynasty[466].

Fleeing the Sakas in the west, the Indo-Greeks continued to rule a territory in the eastern Punjab. The kingdom of the last Indo-Greek kings Strato II and Strato III was conquered by the Northern Satrap Saka ruler Rajuvula around 10 AD.[467]

Later contributions

Some Greek nuclei may have continued to survive until the 2nd century AD.

Nahapana had at his court a Greek writer named Yavanesvara ("Lord of the Greeks"), who translated from Greek to Sanskrit the Yavanajataka ("Saying

Indo-Greek Kingdom

Figure 102: *The Buddhist symbols of the triratna and of the swastika (reversed) around the word "Ya-va-ṇa-sa" in Brahmi ( ). Shivneri Caves 1st century AD.*

of the Greeks"), an astrological treatise and India's earliest Sanskrit work in horoscopy.[469]

Buddhist caves

A large number of Buddhist caves in western India were artistically hewn between the 1st century BCE and the 2nd century CE. Numerous donors provided the funds for the building of these caves and left donatory inscriptions, including laity, members of the clergy, government officials. Foreigners, mostly self-declared *Yavanas*, represented about 8% of all inscriptions.[470]

Karla caves

Yavanas from the region of Nashik are mentioned as donors for six structural pillars in the Great Buddhist Chaitya of the Karla Caves built and dedicated by Western Satraps ruler Nahapana in 120 AD,[471] although they seem to have adopted Buddhist names.[472] In total, the Yavanas account for nearly half of the known dedicatory inscriptions on the pillars of the Great Chaitya.[473] To this day, Nasik is known as the wine capital of India, using grapes that were probably originally imported by the Greeks.

Shivneri caves

Two more Buddhist inscriptions by Yavanas were found in the Shivneri Caves.[474] One of the inscriptions mentions the donation of a tank by the Yavana named Irila, while the other mentions the gift of a refectory to the Sangha by the Yavana named Cita. On this second inscription, the Buddhist symbols of the triratna and of the swastika (reversed) are positionned on both sides of the first word "Yavana(sa)".

Pandavleni caves

One of the Buddhist caves (Cave No.17) in the Pandavleni caves complex near Nashik was built and dedicated by "Indragnidatta the son of the Yavana Dharmadeva, a northerner from Dattamittri", in the 2nd century CE.[475,476,477] The city of "Dattamittri" is thought to be the city of Demetrias in Arachosia, mentioned by Isidore of Charax.

> **The "Yavana cave", Cave No.17 of Pandavleni caves, near Nashik (2nd century AD)**
>
>
>
> **Figure 103:** *The "Yavana" inscription on the back wall of the veranda, Cave No.17, Nashik.*
>
> Cave No.17 has one inscription, mentioning the gift of the cave by Indragnidatta the son of the Yavana (i.e. Greek or Indo-Greek) Dharmadeva:
> "Success! (The gift) of Indragnidatta, son of Dhammadeva, the Yavana, a northerner from Dattamittri. By him, inspired by true religion, this cave has been caused to be excavated in mount Tiranhu, and inside the cave a Chaitya and cisterns. This cave made for the sake of his father and mother has been, in order to honor all Buddhas bestowed on the universal Samgha by monks together with his son Dhammarakhita."
> Inscription of Cave No.17, Nashik

Manmodi caves

In the Manmodi caves, near Junnar, an inscription by a Yavana donor appears on the façade of the main Chaitya, on the central flat surface of the lotus over the entrance: it mentions the erection of the hall-front (façade) for the Buddhist Samgha, by a Yavana donor named Chanda:

At the Manmodi caves, the facade of the Chaitya (left) was donated by a Yavana, according to the inscription on the central flat surface of the lotus (right). Detail of the "Ya-va-na-sa" inscription in old Brahmi script: ⏌ Δ ⏊ ⋎ , circa 120 CE.[478]

> '*yavanasa camdānam gabhadā[ra]* "
> '*The meritorious gift of the façade of the (gharba) hall by the Yavana Chanda*"

Figure 104: *Evolution of Zeus Nikephoros ("Zeus holding Nike") on Indo-Greek coinage: from the Classical motif of Nike handing the wreath of victory to Zeus himself (left, coin of Heliocles I 145–130 BC), then to a baby elephant (middle, coin of Antialcidas 115–95 BC), and then to the Wheel of the Law, symbol of Buddhism (right, coin of Menander II 90–85 BC).*

—*Inscription on the façade of the Manmodi Chaitya.*

These contributions seem to have ended when the Satavahana King Gautamiputra Satakarni vanquished the Western Satrap ruler Nahapana, who had ruled over the area where these inscriptions were made, circa 130 CE. This victory is known from the fact that Gautamiputra Satakarni restruck many of Nahapana's coins, and that he is claimed to have defeated a confederacy of Shakas (Western Kshatrapas), Pahlavas (Indo-Parthians), and Yavanas (Indo-Greeks), in the inscription of his mother Queen Gotami Balasiri at Cave No.3 of the Nasik caves:[479,480]

> ...Siri-Satakani Gotamiputa (....) who crushed down the pride and conceit of the Kshatriyas; who destroyed the Sakas, Yavanas and Palhavas; who rooted out the Khakharata race; who restored the glory of the Satavahana family...
>
> —*Nasik caves inscription of Queen Gotami Balasiri, circa 170 CE, Cave No.3*[481]

Ideology

Buddhism flourished under the Indo-Greek kings, and their rule, especially that of Menander, has been remembered as benevolent. It has been suggested, although direct evidence is lacking, that their invasion of India was intended to show their support for the Mauryan empire which may have had a long history of marital alliances,[486] exchange of presents,[487] demonstrations of friendship,[488] exchange of ambassadors[489] and religious missions[490] with

Figure 105: *Greek and Indian deities on the coinage of Agathokles (190-180 BCE)*[482]*: 1. Zeus standing with goddess Hecate.. Greek: "King Agathokles". 2. Unidentified deity wearing a long himation with a volume on the head, arm partly bent, and contrapposto pose. Greek: "King Agathokles".*[483]*. 3. Hindu god Balarama-Samkarshana with attributes. Greek: "King Agathokles".*[484]*. 4. Hindu god Vasudeva-Krishna with attributes.. Brahmi: "Rajane Agathuklayasa", "King Agathokles". 5. Goddess Lakshmi, holding a lotus in her right hand.*[485] *Brahmi: "Rajane Agathuklayasa", "King Agathokles".*

the Greeks. The historian Diodorus even wrote that the king of Pataliputra had "great love for the Greeks".[491,492]

The Greek expansion into Indian territory may have been intended to protect Greek populations in India,[493] and to protect the Buddhist faith from the religious persecutions of the Shungas.[494] The city of Sirkap founded by Demetrius combines Greek and Indian influences without signs of segregation between the two cultures.

The first Greek coins to be minted in India, those of Menander I and Apollodotus I bear the mention "Saviour king" (ΒΑΣΙΛΕΩΣ ΣΩΤΗΡΟΣ), a title with high value in the Greek world which indicated an important deflective victory. For instance, Ptolemy I had been *Soter* (saviour) because he had helped save Rhodes from Demetrius the Besieger, and Antiochus I because he had saved Asia Minor from the Gauls. The title was also inscribed in Pali as ("Tratarasa") on the reverse of their coins. Menander and Apollodotus may indeed have been saviours to the Greek populations residing in India, and to some of the Indians as well.[495]

Also, most of the coins of the Greek kings in India were bilingual, written in Greek on the front and in Pali on the back (in the Kharosthi script, derived from Aramaic, rather than the more eastern Brahmi, which was used only once on coins of Agathocles of Bactria), a tremendous concession to another culture never before made in the Hellenic world.[496] From the reign of Apollodotus II, around 80 BC, Kharosthi letters started to be used as mintmarks on coins in combination with Greek monograms and mintmarks, suggesting the participation of local technicians to the minting process.[497] Incidentally, these bilingual coins of the Indo-Greeks were the key in the decipherment of the Kharosthi script by James Prinsep (1799–1840).[498] Kharoshthi became extinct around the 3rd century AD.

In Indian literature, the Indo-Greeks are described as Yavanas (in Sanskrit),[499,500,501] or Yonas (in Pali)[502] both thought to be transliterations of "Ionians". In the Harivamsa the "Yavana" Indo-Greeks are qualified, together with the Sakas, Kambojas, Pahlavas and Paradas as *Kshatriya-pungava* i.e. foremost among the Warrior caste, or Kshatriyas. The Majjhima Nikaya explains that in the lands of the Yavanas and Kambojas, in contrast with the numerous Indian castes, there were only two classes of people, Aryas and Dasas (masters and slaves).

Religion

The Heliodorus pillar, commissioned by Indo-Greek ambassador Heliodorus, one of the earliest recorded Indo-Greek converts to Hinduism.

Menander I converted to Buddhism, as described in the Milinda Panha. After his conversion, he became noted for being a leading patron of Buddhism.[503]

In addition to the worship of the Classical pantheon of the Greek deities found on their coins (Zeus, Herakles, Athena, Apollo...), the Indo-Greeks were involved with local faiths, particularly with Buddhism, but also with Hinduism and Zoroastrianism.[506]

Figure 106: *Indo-Corinthian capital representing a man wearing a Graeco-Roman-style coat with fibula, and making a blessing gesture. Butkara Stupa, National Museum of Oriental Art, Rome.*

Figure 107: *Indian-standard coinage of Menander I.* **Obv** *ΒΑΣΙΛΕΩΣ ΣΩΤΗΡΟΣ ΜΕΝΑΝΔΡΟΥ "Of Saviour King Menander".* **Rev** *Palm of victory, Kharoshthi legend Māhārajasa trātadasa Menandrāsa, British Museum.*[504]

Indo-Greek Kingdom 137

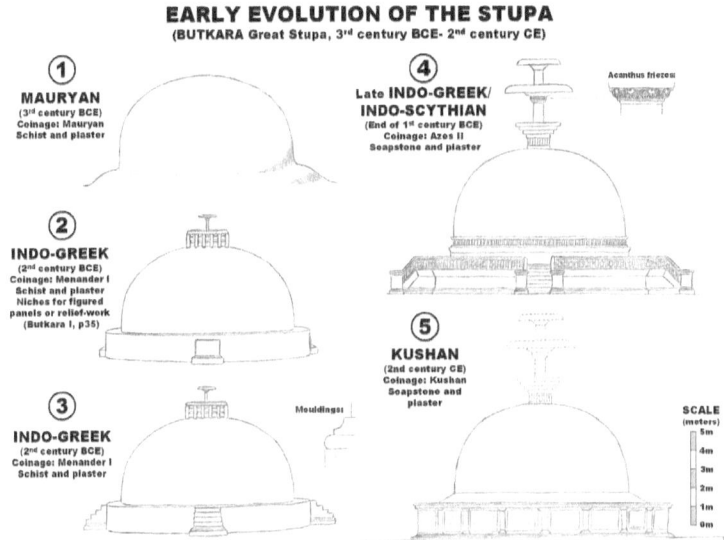

Figure 108: *Evolution of the Butkara stupa, a large part of which occurred during the Indo-Greek period, through the addition of Hellenistic architectural elements.*[505]

Interactions with Buddhism

Chandragupta Maurya, the founder of the Mauryan Empire, conquered the Greek satraps left by Alexander, which belonged to Seleucus I Nicator of the Seleucid Empire. The Mauryan Emperor Ashoka would then establish the largest empire in the Indian Subcontinent through an aggressive expansion. Ashoka converted to Buddhism following the destructive Kalinga War, abandoning further conquests in favor of humanitarian reforms.[507] Ashoka erected the Edicts of Ashoka to spread Buddhism and the 'Law of Piety' throughout his dominion. In one of his edicts, Ashoka claims to have converted his Greek population along with others to Buddhism.

> *Here in the king's domain among the Greeks, the Kambojas, the Nabhakas, the Nabhapamkits, the Bhojas, the Pitinikas, the Andhras and the Palidas, everywhere people are following Beloved-of-the-Gods' instructions in Dharma.*[508]

The last Mauryan Emperor Brihadratha was assassinated by Pushyamitra Shunga, the former senapati or "army lord" of the Mauryan Empire and founder of the Shunga Empire. Pushyamitra is alleged to have persecuted Buddhism in favor of brahmanism, likely in attempt to further remove the legacy of the Mauryan Empire[509].

> ... *Pushyamitra equipped a fourfold army, and intending to destroy the Buddhist religion, he went to the Kukkutarama (in Pataliputra). ... Pushyamitra therefore destroyed the sangharama, killed the monks there, and departed. ... After some time, he arrived in Sakala, and proclaimed that he would give a ... reward to whoever brought him the head of a Buddhist monk.*[510]

It is possible that Menander I Soter or the "Saviour king", choose Sakala as his capital due to the Buddhist presence there. Menander I, is stated to have converted to Buddhism[511] in the Milinda Panha, which records the dialogue between Menander and the Buddhist monk Nagasena. Meander is claimed to have obtained the title of an arhat.

> *And afterwards, taking delight in the wisdom of the Elder, he (Menander) handed over his kingdom to his son, and abandoning the household life for the house-less state, grew great in insight, and himself attained to Arahatship!*
>
> —*The Questions of King Milinda, Translation by T. W. Rhys Davids.*

The wheel he represented on some of his coins was most likely Buddhist Dharmachakra,[512].

Another Indian text, the *Stupavadana* of Ksemendra, mentions in the form of a prophecy that Menander will build a stupa in Pataliputra.[513]

Plutarch also presents Menander as an example of benevolent rule, and explains that upon his death, the honour of sharing his remains was claimed by the various cities under his rule, and they were enshrined in "monuments" (μνημεία, probably stupas), in a parallel with the historic Buddha:[514]

> *But when one Menander, who had reigned graciously over the Bactrians, died afterwards in the camp, the cities indeed by common consent celebrated his funerals; but coming to a contest about his relics, they were difficultly at last brought to this agreement, that his ashes being distributed, everyone should carry away an equal share, and they should all erect monuments to him.*
>
> —*Plutarch, "Political Precepts" Praec. reip. ger. 28, 6).*[515]

The Butkara stupa was "monumentalized" by the addition of Hellenistic architectural decorations during Indo-Greek rule in the 2nd century BC. A coin of Menander I was found in the second oldest stratum (GSt 2) of the Butkara stupa suggesting a period of additional constructions during the reign of Menander.[516] It is thought that Menander was the builder of the second oldest layer of the Butkara stupa, following its initial construction during the Mauryan Empire.[517]

Indo-Greek Kingdom

Figure 109: *Coin of Menander II (90–85 BCE). "King Menander, follower of the Dharma" in Kharoshthi script, with Zeus holding Nike, who holds a victory wreath over an Eight-spoked wheel.*

"Followers of the Dharma"

Several Indo-Greek kings use the title "Dharmikasa", i.e. "Follower of the Dharma", in the Kharoshti script on the obverse of their coins. The corresponding legend in Greek is "Dikaios" ("The Just"), a rather usual attribute on Greek coins. The expression "Follower of the Dharma" would of course resonate strongly with Indian subjects, used to this expression being employed by pious kings, especially since the time of Ashoka who advocated the Dharma in his inscriptions. The seven kings using "Dharmakasa", i.e. "Follower of the Dharma", are late Indo-Greek kings, from around 150 BCE, right after the reign of Menander I, and mainly associated with the area of Gandhara: Zoilos I (130–120 BCE), Strato (130–110 BCE), Heliokles II (95–80 BCE), Theophilos (130 or 90 BCE), Menander II (90–85 BCE), Archebios (90–80 BCE) and Peukolaos (c. 90 BCE).[518] The attribute of *Dhramika* was again used a century later by a known Buddhist practitioner, Indo-Scythian king Kharahostes, to extoll on his coins the virtues of his predecessor king Azes.[519]

Blessing gestures

From the time of Agathokleia and Strato I, circa 100 BCE, kings and divinities are regularly show on coins making blessing gestures,[520] which often seem similar to the Buddhist Vitarka mudra.[521] As centuries past, the exact shapes taken by the hand becomes less clear. This blessing gesture was also often adopted by the Indo-Scythians.

Figure 110: *Philoxenus (c. 100 BC), unarmed, making a blessing gesture.*

Figure 111: *Nicias making a blessing gesture.*

Indo-Greek Kingdom

Figure 112: *Strato I in combat gear, making a blessing gesture, circa 100 BCE.*

Figure 113: *Various blessing gestures: divinities (top), kings (bottom).*

Figure 114: *Greek Buddhist devotees, holding plantain leaves, in purely Hellenistic style, inside Corinthian columns, Buner relief, Victoria and Albert Museum.*

Bhagavata cult

The Heliodorus pillar is a stone column that was erected around 113 BCE in central IndiaWikipedia:Citation needed in Vidisha near modern Besnagar, by Heliodorus, a Greek ambassador of the Indo-Greek king Antialcidas to the court of the Shunga king Bhagabhadra. The pillar originally supported a statue of Garuda. In the dedication, the Indo-Greek ambassador explains he is a devotee of "Vāsudeva, the God of Gods". Historically, it is the first known inscription related to the Bhagavata cult in India.[424]

Art

In general, the art of the Indo-Greeks is poorly documented, and few works of art (apart from their coins and a few stone palettes) are directly attributed to them. The coinage of the Indo-Greeks however is generally considered as some of the most artistically brilliant of Antiquity.[522] The Hellenistic heritage (Ai-Khanoum) and artistic proficiency of the Indo-Greek world would suggest a rich sculptural tradition as well, but traditionally very few sculptural remains have been attributed to them. On the contrary, most Gandharan Hellenistic works of art are usually attributed to the direct successors of the Indo-Greeks in India in the 1st century AD, such as the nomadic Indo-Scythians, the Indo-Parthians and, in an already decadent state, the Kushans[523] In general, Gandharan sculpture cannot be dated exactly, leaving the exact chronology open to interpretation.

The possibility of a direct connection between the Indo-Greeks and Greco-Buddhist art has been reaffirmed recently as the dating of the rule of Indo-Greek kings has been extended to the first decades of the 1st century AD, with the reign of Strato II in the Punjab.[524] Also, Foucher, Tarn, and more recently,

Figure 115: *Hellenistic culture in the Indian subcontinent: Greek clothes, amphoras, wine and music (Detail of Chakhil-i-Ghoundi stupa, Hadda, Gandhara, 1st century AD).*

Boardman, Bussagli and McEvilley have taken the view that some of the most purely Hellenistic works of northwestern India and Afghanistan, may actually be wrongly attributed to later centuries, and instead belong to a period one or two centuries earlier, to the time of the Indo-Greeks in the 2nd–1st century BC.[525]

This is particularly the case of some purely Hellenistic works in Hadda, Afghanistan, an area which "might indeed be the cradle of incipient Buddhist sculpture in Indo-Greek style".[527] Referring to one of the Buddha triads in Hadda, in which the Buddha is sided by very Classical depictions of Herakles/Vajrapani and Tyche/Hariti, Boardman explains that both figures "might at first (and even second) glance, pass as, say, from Asia Minor or Syria of the first or second century BC (...) these are essentially Greek figures, executed by artists fully conversant with far more than the externals of the Classical style".[528]

Alternatively, it has been suggested that these works of art may have been executed by itinerant Greek artists during the time of maritime contacts with the West from the 1st to the 3rd century AD.[529]

Figure 116: *Standing Bodhisattva Gandhara at Guimet Museum, Paris, France. Ancient Greeks (Indo-Greeks) may have been the earliest features for the Buddhist culture in India.*[526]

The Greco-Buddhist art of Gandhara, beyond the omnipresence of Greek style and stylistic elements which might be simply considered as an enduring artistic tradition,[530] offers numerous depictions of people in Greek Classical realistic style, attitudes and fashion (clothes such as the chiton and the himation, similar in form and style to the 2nd century BC Greco-Bactrian statues of Ai-Khanoum, hairstyle), holding contraptions which are characteristic of Greek culture (amphoras, "kantaros" Greek drinking cups), in situations which can range from festive (such as Bacchanalian scenes) to Buddhist-devotional.[531,532]

Uncertainties in dating make it unclear whether these works of art actually depict Greeks of the period of Indo-Greek rule up to the 1st century BC, or remaining Greek communities under the rule of the Indo-Parthians or Kushans in the 1st and 2nd century AD. Benjamin Rowland thinks that the Indo-Greeks, rather than the Indo-Scythians or the Kushans, may have been the models for the Bodhisattva statues of Gandhara[533]

Figure 117: *Seated Boddhisatva, Gandhara, 2nd century (Ostasiatisches Museum, Berlin)*

Economy

Very little is known about the economy of the Indo-Greeks, although it seems to have been rather vibrant.[534,535]

Coinage

The abundance of their coins would tend to suggest large mining operations, particularly in the mountainous area of the Hindu-Kush, and an important monetary economy. The Indo-Greek did strike bilingual coins both in the Greek "round" standard and in the Indian "square" standard,[536] suggesting that monetary circulation extended to all parts of society. The adoption of Indo-Greek monetary conventions by neighbouring kingdoms, such as the Kunindas to the east and the Satavahanas to the south,[537] would also suggest that Indo-Greek coins were used extensively for cross-border trade.

Figure 118: *Stone palette depicting a mythological scene, 2nd–1st century BC.*

Tribute payments

It would also seem that some of the coins emitted by the Indo-Greek kings, particularly those in the monolingual Attic standard, may have been used to pay some form of tribute to the Yuezhi tribes north of the Hindu-Kush. This is indicated by the coins finds of the Qunduz hoard in northern Afghanistan, which have yielded quantities of Indo-Greek coins in the Hellenistic standard (Greek weights, Greek language), although none of the kings represented in the hoard are known to have ruled so far north.[538] Conversely, none of these coins have ever been found south of the Hindu-Kush.[539]

Trade with China

The Indo-Greek kings in Southern Asia issued the first known cupro-nickel coins, with Euthydemus II, dating from 180 to 170 BC, and his younger brothers Pantaleon and Agathocles around 170 BC. As only China was able to produce cupro-nickel at that time, and as the alloy ratios are exclusively similar, it has been suggested that the metal was the result of exchanges between China and Bactria.[540]

An indirect testimony by the Chinese explorer Zhang Qian, who visited Bactria around 128 BC, suggests that intense trade with Southern China was going through northern India. Zhang Qian explains that he found Chinese products

Figure 119: *Cupro-nickel coins of king Pantaleon point to a Chinese origin of the metal.*

in the Bactrian markets, and that they were transiting through northwestern India, which he incidentally describes as a civilization similar to that of Bactria:

> *"When I was in Bactria", Zhang Qian reported, "I saw bamboo canes from Qiong and cloth (silk?) made in the province of Shu. When I asked the people how they had gotten such articles, they replied: "Our merchants go buy them in the markets of Shendu (northwestern India). Shendu, they told me, lies several thousand li southeast of Bactria. The people cultivate land, and live much like the people of Bactria".*
>
> —*Sima Qian, "Records of the Great Historian", trans. Burton Watson, p. 236.*

Recent excavations at the burial site of China's first Emperor Qin Shi Huang, dating back to the 3rd century BCE, also suggest Greek influence in the artworks found there, including in the manufacture of the famous Terracotta army. It is also suggested that Greek artists may have come to China at that time to train local artisans in making sculptures.

Indian Ocean trade

Maritime relations across the Indian Ocean started in the 3rd century BC, and further developed during the time of the Indo-Greeks together with their territorial expansion along the western coast of India. The first contacts started when the Ptolemies constructed the Red Sea ports of Myos Hormos and Berenike, with destination the Indus delta, the Kathiawar peninsula or Muziris. Around 130 BC, Eudoxus of Cyzicus is reported (Strabo, *Geog.* II.3.4) to have made a successful voyage to India and returned with a cargo of perfumes and

Figure 120: *Athena in the art of Gandhara*

gemstones. By the time Indo-Greek rule was ending, up to 120 ships were setting sail every year from Myos Hormos to India (Strabo *Geog.* II.5.12).[541]

Armed forces

The coins of the Indo-Greeks provide rich clues on their uniforms and weapons. Typical Hellenistic uniforms are depicted, with helmets being either round in the Greco-Bactrian style, or the flat kausia of the Macedonians (coins of Apollodotus I).

Military technology

Their weapons were spears, swords, longbow (on the coins of Agathokleia) and arrows. Around 130 BC, the Central Asian recurve bow of the steppes with its gorytos box started to appear for the first time on the coins of Zoilos I, suggesting strong interactions (and apparently an alliance) with nomadic peoples, either the Yuezhi or the Scythians.[542] The recurve bow becomes a standard feature of Indo-Greek horsemen by 90 BC, as seen on some of the coins of Hermaeus.

Generally, Indo-Greek kings are often represented riding horses, as early as the reign of Antimachus II around 160 BC. The equestrian tradition probably goes

Indo-Greek Kingdom

back to the Greco-Bactrians, who are said by Polybius to have faced a Seleucid invasion in 210 BC with 10,000 horsemen. Although war elephants are never represented on coins, a harness plate (phalera) dated to the 3–2nd century BC, today in the Hermitage Museum, depicts a helmetted Greek combatant on an Indian war elephant.

The Milinda Panha, in the questions of Nagasena to king Menander, provides a rare glimpse of the military methods of the period:

> -(Nagasena) Has it ever happened to you, O king, that rival kings rose up against you as enemies and opponents?
>
> -(Menander) Yes, certainly.
>
> -Then you set to work, I suppose, to have moats dug, and ramparts thrown up, and watch towers erected, and strongholds built, and stores of food collected?
>
> -Not at all. All that had been prepared beforehand.
>
> -Or you had yourself trained in the management of war elephants, and in horsemanship, and in the use of the war chariot, and in archery and fencing?
>
> -Not at all. I had learnt all that before.
>
> -But why?
>
> -With the object of warding off future danger.
>
> —(Milinda Panha, Book III, Chap 7)

The Milinda Panha also describes the structure of Menander's army:

> Now one day Milinda the king proceeded forth out of the city to pass in review the innumerable host of his mighty army in its fourfold array (of elephants, cavalry, bowmen, and soldiers on foot).
>
> —(Milinda Panha, Book I)

Figure 121: *King Strato I in combat gear, making a blessing gesture, circa 100 BCE.*

Size of Indo-Greek armies

The armed forces of the Indo-Greeks engaged in battles with other Indian kingdoms. The ruler of Kalinga, King Kharavela, states in the Hathigumpha inscription that during the 8th year of his reign he led a large army in the direction of a Yavana King, and that he forced their demoralized army to retreat to Mathura.

> *'Then in the eighth year, (Kharavela) with a large army having sacked Goradhagiri causes pressure on Rajagaha (Rajagriha). On account of the loud report of this act of valour, the Yavana (Greek) King Dimi[ta] retreated to Mathura having extricated his demoralized army."*
>
> —*Hathigumpha inscription, lines 7-8, probably in the 1st century BCE. Original text is in Brahmi script.*[543]

The name of the Yavana king is not clear, but it contains three letters, and the middle letter can be read as *ma* or *mi*.[544] R. D. Banerji and K.P. Jayaswal read the name of the Yavana king as "Dimita", and identify him with Demetrius I of Bactria. However, according to Ramaprasad Chanda, this identification results in "chronological impossibilities". The Greek ambassador Megasthenes took

Figure 122: *The Indo-Scythian Taxila copper plate uses the Macedonian month of "Panemos" for calendrical purposes (British Museum).*[545]

special note of the military strength of Kalinga in his *Indica* in the middle of the 3rd century BC:

> *The royal city of the Calingae (Kalinga) is called Parthalis. Over their king 60,000 foot-soldiers, 1,000 horsemen, 700 elephants keep watch and ward in "procinct of war."*
>
> —*Megasthenes fragm. LVI. in Plin. Hist. Nat. VI. 21. 8–23. 11.*

An account by the Roman writer Justin gives another hint of the size of Indo-Greek armies, which, in the case of the conflict between the Greco-Bactrian Eucratides and the Indo-Greek Demetrius II, he numbers at 60,000 (although they allegedly lost to 300 Greco-Bactrians):

> *Eucratides led many wars with great courage, and, while weakened by them, was put under siege by Demetrius, king of the Indians. He made numerous sorties, and managed to vanquish 60,000 enemies with 300 soldiers, and thus liberated after four months, he put India under his rule*
>
> —*Justin, XLI,6*

The Indo-Greek armies would be conquered by Indo-Scythians, a nomadic tribe from Central Asia.

Legacy of the Indo-Greeks

From the 1st century AD, the Greek communities of central Asia and the northwestern Indian subcontinent lived under the control of the Kushan branch of the Yuezhi, apart from a short-lived invasion of the Indo-Parthian Kingdom.[546] The Kushans founded the Kushan Empire, which was to prosper for several centuries. In the south, the Greeks were under the rule of the Western Kshatrapas. The Kalash tribe of the Chitral Valley claim to be descendants of the Indo-Greeks; although this is disputed.

Figure 123: *Hellenistic couple from Taxila (IV)*

It is unclear how much longer the Greeks managed to maintain a distinct presence in the Indian sub-continent. The legacy of the Indo-Greeks was felt however for several centuries, from the usage of the Greek language and calendrical methods,[547] to the influences on the numismatics of the Indian subcontinent, traceable down to the period of the Gupta Empire in the 4th century.[548]

The Greeks may also have maintained a presence in their cities until quite late. Isidorus of Charax in his 1st century AD "Parthian stations" itinerary described an "Alexandropolis, the metropolis of Arachosia", thought to be Alexandria Arachosia, which he said was still Greek even at such a late time:

> *Beyond is Arachosia. And the Parthians call this White India; there are the city of Biyt and the city of Pharsana and the city of Chorochoad and the city of Demetrias; then Alexandropolis, the metropolis of Arachosia; it is Greek, and by it flows the river Arachotus. As far as this place the land is under the rule of the Parthians.*[549]

The Indo-Greeks may also have had some influence on the religious plane as well, especially in relation to the developing Mahayana Buddhism. Mahayana Buddhism has been described as "the form of Buddhism which (regardless of how Hinduized its later forms became) seems to have originated in the

Figure 124: *The story of the Trojan horse was depicted in the art of Gandhara. British Museum.*

Greco-Buddhist communities of India, through a conflation of the Greek Democritean–Sophistic–Skeptical tradition with the rudimentary and unformalized empirical and skeptical elements already present in early Buddhism".[550]

Indo-Greek kings: their coins, territories and chronology

Today 36 Indo-Greek kings are known. Several of them are also recorded in Western and Indian historical sources, but the majority are known through numismatic evidence only. The exact chronology and sequencing of their rule is still a matter of scholarly inquiry, with adjustments regular being made with new analysis and coin finds (overstrikes of one king over another's coins being the most critical element in establishing chronological sequences).

There is an important evolution of coin shape (round to square) and material (from gold to silver to brass) across the territories and the periods, and from Greek type to Indian type over a period of nearly 3 centuries. Also, the quality of coinage illustration decreases down to the 1st century CE. Coinage evolution is an important point of Indo-Greek history, and actually one of the most important since most of these kings are only known by their coins, and their chronology is mainly established by the evolution of the coin types.

The system used here is adapted from Osmund Bopearachchi, supplemented by the views of R C Senior and occasionally other authorities.[551]

Greco-Bactrian and Indo-Greek kings, their coins, territories and chronology
Based on Bopearachchi (1991)[552]

Territories/dates	Greco-Bactrian kings		Indo-Greek kings					
	West Bactria	East Bactria	Paropamisade	Arachosia	Gandhara	Western Punjab	Eastern Punjab	Mathura[553]
326–325 BCE	Campaigns of Alexander the Great in India							
312 BCE	Creation of the Seleucid Empire							
305 BCE	Seleucid Empire after Mauryan war							
280 BCE	Foundation of Ai-Khanoum							
255–239 BCE	Independence of the Greco-Bactrian kingdom Diodotus I							
239–223 BCE	Diodotus II							
230–200 BCE	Euthydemus I							
200–190 BCE		Demetrius I						
190–185 BCE	Euthydemus II							
190–180 BCE		Agathocles			Pantaleon			
185–170 BCE		Antimachus I						
180–160 BCE			Apollodotus I					
175–170 BCE		Demetrius II						
160–155 BCE			Antimachus II					
170–145 BCE		Eucratides						
155–130 BCE	Yuezhi occupation, loss of Ai-Khanoum	Eucratides II / Plato / Heliocles I			Menander I			
130–120 BCE	Yuezhi occupation		Zoilos I		Agathokleia			Yavanarajya inscription
120–110 BCE			Lysias		Strato I			

Indo-Greek Kingdom 155

110–100 BCE		Antialcidas		Heliokles II	
100 BCE		Polyxenos		Demetrius III	
100–95 BCE		Philoxenus			
95–90 BCE		Diomedes	Amyntas	Epander	
90 BCE		Theophilos	Peukolaos	Thraso	
90–85 BCE		Nicias	Menander II	Artemidoros	
90–70 BCE		Hermaeus	Archebius		
		Yuezhi occupation	Maues (Indo-Scythian)		
75–70 BCE			Telephos	Apollodotus II	
65–55 BCE				Hippostratos	Dionysios
55–35 BCE				Azes I (Indo-Scythian)	Zoilos II
55–35 BCE					Apollophanes
25 BCE – 10 CE					Strato II and Strato III
					Zoilos III/ Bhadayasa
					Rajuvula (Indo-Scythian)

References

Works cited

<templatestyles src="Template:Refbegin/styles.css" />

- Avari, Burjor (2007). *India: The ancient past. A history of the Indian sub-continent from c. 7000 BC to AD 1200*. Routledge. ISBN 0-415-35616-4.
- Banerjee, Gauranga Nath (1961). *Hellenism in ancient India*. Delhi: Munshi Ram Manohar Lal. OCLC 1837954 ISBN 0-8364-2910-9.
- Bernard, Paul (1994). "The Greek Kingdoms of Central Asia." In: *History of civilizations of Central Asia, Volume II. The development of sedentary and nomadic civilizations: 700 B.C. to A.D. 250*, pp. 99–129. Harmatta, János, ed., 1994. Paris: UNESCO Publishing. ISBN 92-3-102846-4.
- Boardman, John (1994). *The Diffusion of Classical Art in Antiquity*. Princeton, New Jersey: Princeton University Press. ISBN 0-691-03680-2.
- Bopearachchi, Osmund (1991). *Monnaies Gréco-Bactriennes et Indo-Grecques, Catalogue Raisonné* (in French). Bibliothèque Nationale de France. ISBN 2-7177-1825-7.
- Bopearachchi, Osmund (1998). *SNG 9*. New York: American Numismatic Society. ISBN 0-89722-273-3.
- Bopearachchi, Osmund (2003). *De l'Indus à l'Oxus, Archéologie de l'Asie Centrale* (in French). Lattes: Association imago-musée de Lattes. ISBN 2-9516679-2-2.
- Bopearachchi, Osmund (1993). *Indo-Greek, Indo-Scythian and Indo-Parthian coins in the Smithsonian Institution*. Washington: National Numismatic Collection, Smithsonian Institution. OCLC 36240864[554].
- Bussagli, Mario; Francine Tissot; Béatrice Arnal (1996). *L'art du Gandhara* (in French). Paris: Librairie générale française. ISBN 2-253-13055-9.
- Cambon, Pierre (2007). *Afghanistan, les trésors retrouvés* (in French). Musée Guimet. ISBN 978-2-7118-5218-5.
- Errington, Elizabeth; Joe Cribb; Maggie Claringbull; Ancient India and Iran Trust; Fitzwilliam Museum (1992). *The Crossroads of Asia: transformation in image and symbol in the art of ancient Afghanistan and Pakistan*. Cambridge: Ancient India and Iran Trust. ISBN 0-9518399-1-8.
- Faccenna, Domenico (1980). *Butkara I (Swāt, Pakistan) 1956–1962, Volume III 1*. Rome: IsMEO (Istituto Italiano Per Il Medio Ed Estremo Oriente).

- Foltz, Richard (2010). *Religions of the Silk Road: premodern patterns of globalization*. New York: Palgrave Macmillan. ISBN 978-0-230-62125-1.
- Keown, Damien (2003). *A Dictionary of Buddhism*. New York: Oxford University Press. ISBN 0-19-860560-9.
- Lowenstein, Tom (2002). *The vision of the Buddha: Buddhism, the path to spiritual enlightenment*. London: Duncan Baird. ISBN 1-903296-91-9.
- Marshall, Sir John Hubert (2000). *The Buddhist art of Gandhara: the story of the early school, its birth, growth, and decline*. New Delhi: Munshiram Manoharlal. ISBN 81-215-0967-X.
- Marshall, John (1956). *Taxila. An illustrated account of archaeological excavations carried out at Taxila (3 volumes)*. Delhi: Motilal Banarsidass.
- McEvilley, Thomas (2002). *The Shape of Ancient Thought. Comparative studies in Greek and Indian Philosophies*. Allworth Press and the School of Visual Arts. ISBN 1-58115-203-5.
- Mitchiner, John E.; Garga (1986). *The Yuga Purana: critically edited, with an English translation and a detailed introduction*. Calcutta, India: Asiatic Society. OCLC 15211914 ISBN 81-7236-124-6.
- Narain, A.K. (1957). *The Indo-Greeks*. Oxford: Clarendon Press.
  - reprinted by Oxford, 1962, 1967, 1980; reissued (2003), "revised and supplemented", by B. R. Publishing Corporation, New Delhi.
- Narain, A.K. (1976). *The coin types of the Indo-Greeks kings*. Chicago, USA: Ares Publishing. ISBN 0-89005-109-7.
- Puri, Baij Nath (2000). *Buddhism in Central Asia*. Delhi: Motilal Banarsidass. ISBN 81-208-0372-8.
- Rosenfield, John M. (1967). *The Dynastic Arts of the Kushans*. Berkeley, California: University of California Press. ISBN 81-215-0579-8.
- Salomon, Richard. "The "Avaca" Inscription and the Origin of the Vikrama Era". **102**.
- Seldeslachts, E. (2003). *The end of the road for the Indo-Greeks?*. (Also available online[555]): Iranica Antica, Vol XXXIX, 2004.
- Senior, R. C. (2006). *Indo-Scythian coins and history. Volume IV*. Classical Numismatic Group, Inc. ISBN 0-9709268-6-3.
- Tarn, W. W. (1938). *The Greeks in Bactria and India*. Cambridge University Press.
  - Second edition, with addenda and corrigenda, (1951). Reissued, with updating preface by Frank Lee Holt (1985), Ares Press, Chicago ISBN 0-89005-524-6
- *Afghanistan, ancien carrefour entre l'est et l'ouest* (in French and English). Belgium: Brepols. 2005. ISBN 2-503-51681-5.
- 東京国立博物館 (Tokyo Kokuritsu Hakubutsukan); 兵庫県立美術館 (Hyogo Kenritsu Bijutsukan) (2003). *Alexander the Great: East-West*

cultural contacts from Greece to Japan. Tokyo: 東京国立博物館 (Tokyo Kokuritsu Hakubutsukan). OCLC 53886263.
- Vassiliades, Demetrios (2000). *The Greeks in India – A Survey in Philosophical Understanding*. New Delhi: Munshiram Manoharlal Publishers Pvt Limited. ISBN 81-215-0921-1.

External links

 Wikimedia Commons has media related to *Indo-Greek Kingdom*.

- Indo-Greek history and coins[556]
- Ancient coinage of the Greco-Bactrian and Indo-Greek kingdoms[557]
- Text of Prof. Nicholas Sims-Williams (University of London) mentioning the arrival of the Kushans and the replacement of Greek Language.[558]
- Wargame reconstitution of Indo-Greek armies[559]
- Files dealing with Indo-Greeks & a genealogy of the Bactrian kings[560]
- The impact of Greco-Indian Culture on Western Civilisation[561]
- Some new hypotheses on the Greco-Bactrian and Indo-Greek kingdoms[562] by Antoine Simonin
- Greco-Bactrian and Indo-Greek Kingdoms in Ancient Texts[563]

Yona

The word **Yona** in Pali and the Prakrits, and the analogue **"Yavana"** in Sanskrit, are words used in Ancient India to designate Greek speakers. "Yona" and "Yavana" are transliterations of the Greek word for "Ionians" (Ancient Greek: Ἴωνες < Ἰάονες < *Ἰάϝονες), who were probably the first Greeks to be known in the East.

Both terms appear in ancient Sanskrit literature. *Yavana* appears for instance, in the *Mahabharata*, while *Yona* appears in texts such as the *Mahavamsa*.

The Yona are mentioned in the Ashoka inscriptions, along with the Kambojas, as two societies where there are only nobles and slaves.

Examples of direct association of these terms with the Greeks include:

- The mention of the "Yona king Aṃtiyoka" in the Edicts of Ashoka (280 BCE)
- The mention of the "Yona king Aṃtalikitasa" in the Heliodorus pillar in Vidisha (110 BCE)
- King Milinda and his bodyguard of "500 Yonas" in the Milinda Panha.

Figure 125: *The "Yona" Greek king of India Menander (160–135 BCE). Inscription in Greek: Βασιλέως Σωτῆρος Μενάνδρου, lit. "of Saviour King Menander".*

- The description of Greek astrology and Greek terminology in the *Yavanajātaka* "Nativity of the Yavanas" (150 CE).
- The mention of Alexandria on the Caucasus, "the city of the Yonas" in the *Mahavamsa*, Chapter 29 (4th century CE).

In general, the words "Yoṇa" or "Yoṇaka" were the current Greek Hellenistic forms, while the term "Yavana" was the Indian word to designate the Greeks or the Indo-Greeks.[564]

Comparable terms in the Ancient Mediterranean world

This usage was shared by many of the countries east of Greece, from the Mediterranean to Sindh:

- Egyptians used the word *j-w-n(-n)-'*.
- Assyrians used the word *Iawanu*.
- Persians used the word *Yauna*.
- Babylonians used the word *Yaman* and *Yamanaya*.
- In Biblical Hebrew, the word was *Yāvān* (and still is, in Modern Hebrew: (יוון

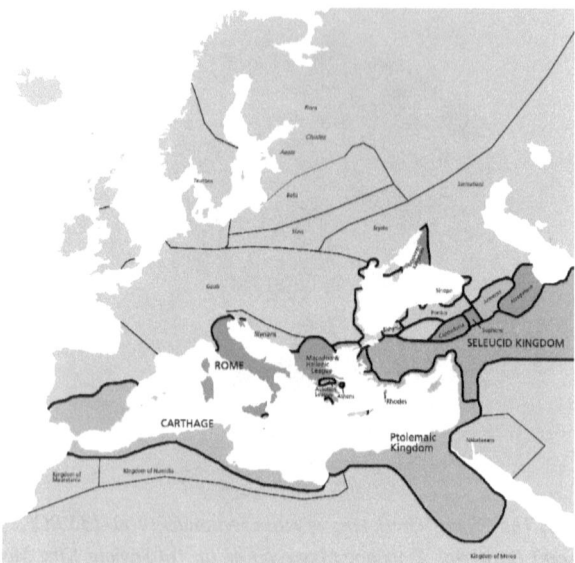

Figure 126: *The Mediterranean region in 220 BCE.*

- In modern Turkish, Persian, and Arabic it is *Yūnān*, derived from the same Old Persian word for designating the Greeks, namely "Yauna" (literally 'Ionians', as they were the first of the Greeks the Persians had firstly the most extensive encounters with)

History

The usage of "Yona" and "Yavana, or variants such as "Yauna", "Yonaka" and "Javana", appears repeatedly, and particularly in relation to the Greek kingdoms which neighbored or sometimes occupied the Punjab over a period of several centuries from the 4th century BCE to the first century CE, such as the Seleucid Empire, the Greco-Bactrian Kingdom and the Indo-Greek Kingdom.Wikipedia:Citation needed The Yavanas are mentioned in detail in Sangam literature epics such as *Paṭṭiṇappālai*, describing their brisk trade with the Early Cholas in the Sangam period.

After Alexander the Great's invasion, the Greek settlements had existed in eastern parts of Achaemenid Empire, northwest of India, as neighbors to the Kambojas.Wikipedia:Citation needed The references to the Yonas in the early Buddhist texts may be related to the same.Wikipedia:Citation needed

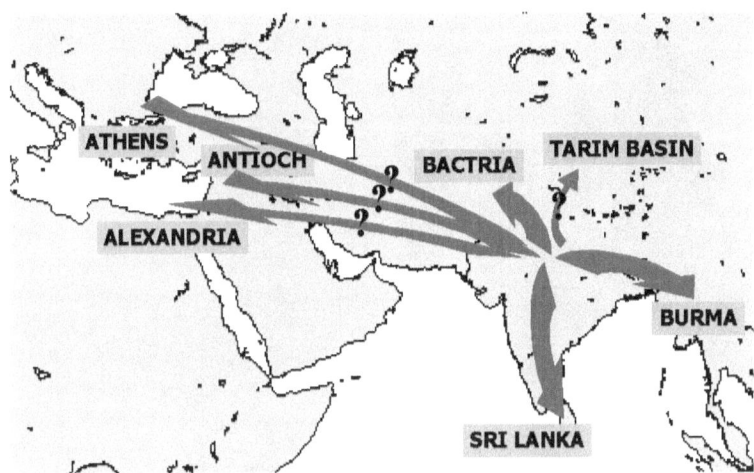

Figure 127: *Buddhist proselytism at the time of king Ashoka (260–218 BCE).*

Role in Buddhism

Edicts of Ashoka (250 BC)

Some of the better-known examples are those of the Edicts of Ashoka (c. 250 BCE), in which the Buddhist emperor Ashoka refers to the Greek populations under his rule. Rock Edicts V and XIII mention the Yonas (or the Greeks) along with the Kambojas and Gandharas as a subject people forming a frontier region of his empire and attest that he sent envoys to the Greek rulers in the West as far as the Mediterranean, faultlessly naming them one by one.

In the Gandhari original of Rock XIII, the Greek kings to the West are associated unambiguously with the term "Yona": Antiochus is referred as *"Amtiyoko nama Yonaraja"* (lit. "The Greek king by the name of Antiochus"), beyond whom live the four other kings: *"param ca tena Atiyokena cature 4 rajani Turamaye nama Amtikini nama Maka nama Alikasudaro nama"* (lit. "And beyond Antiochus, four kings by the name of Ptolemy, the name of Antigonos, the name of Magas, the name Alexander").

In Buddhist Texts

Other Buddhist texts such as the *Dipavamsa* and the 1861 *Sasana Vamsa* reveal that after the Third Buddhist council, the elder monk (*thero*) Maharakkhita was sent to the "Yona country" and he preached Buddhism among the Yonas and the Kambojas, and that at the same time the Yona elder monk (*thero*) Dharmaraksita was sent to the country of Aparantaka in Western India also.

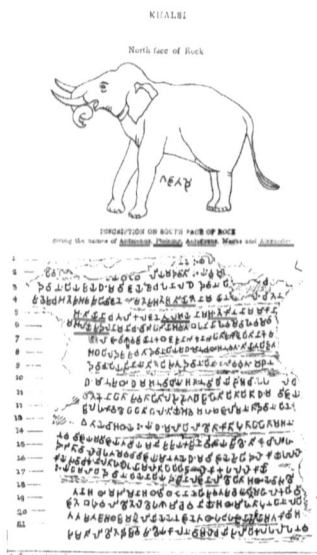

Figure 128: *The Khalsi rock edict of Ashoka, which mentions the Greek kings Antiochus, Ptolemy, Antigonus, Magas and Alexander by name (underlined in color). Here the Greek rulers are described as "Yona" (Brahmi: , third and fourth letters after the first occurrence of Antigonus in red).*

Ashoka's Rock Edict XIII also pairs the Yonas with the Kambojas (*Yonakambojesu*) and conveys that brahmans and śramaṇas are found everywhere in his empire except in the lands of the Yonas and the Kambojas.Wikipedia:Citation needed

Mahavamsa

The *Mahavamsa* or "Great Chronicle" of Sri Lanka refers to the thera Mahārakkhita being sent to preach to the Yona country, and also to the Yona thera Dhammarakkhita, who was sent to Aparanta ("the Western Ends").[565] It also mentions that Pandukabhaya of Anuradhapura set aside a part of his capital city of Anuradhapura for the Yonas.[566]

Another Yona thera, Mahādhammarakkhita, is mentioned as having come from Alexandria on the Caucasus in the country of the Yonas, to be present at the building of the Ruwanwelisaya.[567]

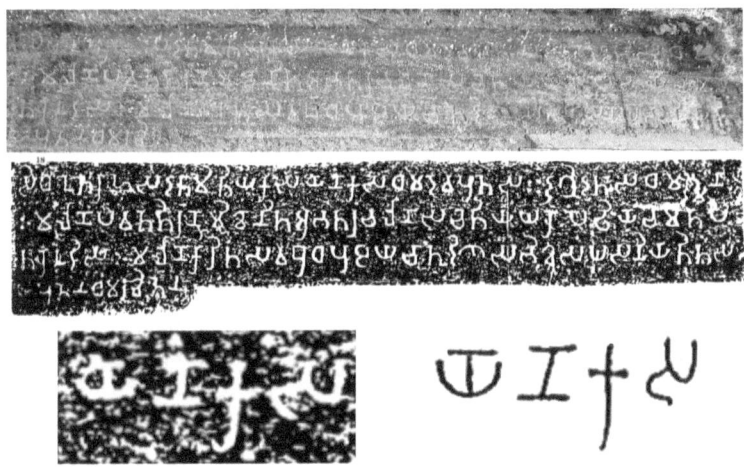

Figure 129: *Dedication by a man of Greek descent on a wall of Cave 17 in the Nasik caves (photograph and rubbing). Detail of the "Yo-ṇa-ka-sa" word (adjectival form of "Yoṇaka", Brahmi:), with Nasik/Karla-period Brahmi script for reference. Circa 120 CE.*

Milindapanha

Another example is that of the Milinda Panha (Chapter I), where "Yonaka" is used to refer to the great Indo-Greek king Menander (160–135 BC), and to the guard of "five hundred Greeks" that constantly accompanies him.

Invasion of India

The *Vanaparava* of Mahabharata contains prophecies that "Mleccha kings of the Shakas, Yavanas, Kambojas, Bahlikas etc. shall rule the earth unrighteously in Kaliyuga ...".[568] This reference apparently alludes to chaotic political scenario following the collapse of the Maurya and Shunga Empires in northern India and its subsequent occupation by foreign hordes such as of the Yonas, Kambojas, Sakas and Pahlavas.

There are important references to the warring Mleccha hordes of the Shakas, Yavanas, Kambojas, the Pahlavas and others in the *Bala Kanda* of Valmiki's *Ramayana*.Wikipedia:Citation needed

Indologists like Dr H. C. Raychadhury, Dr B. C. Law, Dr Satya Shrava and others see in these verses the clear glimpses of the struggles of the Hindus with the mixed invading hordes of the barbaric Sakas, Yavanas, Kambojas,

Pahlavas etc. from north-west.[569] The time frame for these struggles is 2nd century BCE downwards.[570]

The other Indian records prophecies the 180 BCE Yona attacks on Saket, Panchala, Mathura and Pataliputra, probably against the Shunga Empire, and possibly in defense of Buddhism: "After having conquered Saketa, the country of the Panchala and the Mathuras, the Yavanas, wicked and valiant, will reach Kusumadhvaja ("The town of the flower-standard", Pataliputra). The thick mud-fortifications at Pataliputra being reached, all the provinces will be in disorder, without doubt. Ultimately, a great battle will follow, with tree-like engines (siege engines)."[571] "The Yavanas (Greeks) will command, the Kings will disappear. (But ultimately) the Yavanas, intoxicated with fighting, will not stay in Madhadesa (the Middle Country); there will be undoubtedly a civil war among them, arising in their own country, there will be a terrible and ferocious war."[572] The "Anushasanaparava" of the *Mahabharata* affirms that the country of Majjhimadesa was invaded the Yavanas and the Kambojas who were later utterly defeated. The Yona invasion of Majjhimadesa ("middle country, midlands") was jointly carried out by the Yonas and the Kambojas. Majjhimadesa here means the middle of Greater India which then included Afghanistan, Pakistan and large parts of Central Asia.

Other references

On the 110 BCE Heliodorus pillar in Vidisha in Central India, the Indo-Greek king Antialcidas, who had sent an ambassador to the court of the Shunga emperor Bhagabhadra, was also qualified as "Yona".

The Mahavamsa also attests Yona settlement in Anuradhapura in ancient Sri Lanka, probably contributing to trade between East and West.

Buddhist texts like Sumangala Vilasini class the language of the Yavanas with the Milakkhabhasa i.e. *impure language*.

Roman traders in Tamilakkam were also considered Yavanas.

Sanchi

Some of the friezes of Sanchi also show devotees in Greek attire. The men are depicted with short curly hair, often held together with a headband of the type commonly seen on ancient Greek coinage. The clothing too is Greek, complete with tunics, capes and sandals. The musical instruments are also quite characteristic, such as the double flute called aulos. Also visible are carnyx-like horns. They are all celebrating at the entrance of the stupa. These men would be foreigners from north-west India visiting the stupa, possibly Mallas, Indo-Scythians or Indo-Greeks.[573]

Figure 130: *Foreigners on the Northern Gateway of Stupa I.*

Three inscriptions are known from Yavana (Greek) donors at Sanchi, the clearest of which reads "*Setapathiyasa Yonasa danam*" ("Gift of the Yona of Setapatha"), Setapatha being an uncertain city.

Buddhist caves of Western India

In the Great Chaitya of the Karla Caves built and dedicated by Western Satraps Nahapana in 120 CE,[575] there are six inscriptions made by self-described Yavana (Greek or Indo-Greek) donors, who donated six of the pillars, although their names are Buddhist names.[576] They account for nearly half of the known dedicatory inscriptions on the pillars of the Chaitya.[577]

- 3rd pillar of the left row:

  "(This) pillar (is) the gift of the Yavana Sihadhaya from Dhenukataka"[578,579]

- 4th pillar of the left row:

  "Of Dhamma, a Yavana from Dhenukakata"[580]

- 9th pillar of the left row:

  "(This) pillar (is) the gift of the Yavana Yasavadhana from Denukakata"[581]

- 5th pillar of the right row:

  "This pillar is the gift of the Yavana Vitasamghata from Umehanakata"[582]

- 13th pillar of the right row:

  "(This) pillar (is) the gift of the Yavana Dhamadhaya from Denukakata"[583]

- 15th pillar of the right row:

Figure 131: *Left pillar No.9 of the Great Chatya at Karla Caves. This pillar was donated by a Yavana circa 120 CE, like five other pillars. The inscription of this pillar reads: "Dhenukakata Yavanasa/ Yasavadhanana[m]/ thabo dana[m]" i.e. "(This) pillar (is) the gift of the Yavana Yasavadhana from Denukakata".[574] Below: detail of the word "Ya-va-na-sa" (adjectival form of "Yavana", old Brahmi script).*

"(This) pillar (is) the gift of the Yavana Chulayakha from Dhenukakata"[584]

The city of Dhenukakata is thought to be Danahu near the city of Karli. It is described by other donors in other inscriptions as a "vaniya-gama" (A community of merchants).

The Yavanas are also known for their donation of a complete cave at the Nasik caves (cave No.17), and for their donations with inscriptions at the Junnar caves.

The Yonas and other northwestern invaders in Indian literature

The Yavanas or Yonas are frequently found listed with the Kambojas, Sakas, Pahlavas and other northwestern tribes in numerous ancient Indian texts.

The Mahabharata groups the Yavanas with the Kambojas and the Chinas and calls them "Mlechchas" (Barbarians). In the Shanti Parva section, the Yavanas

Figure 132: *Vedika pillar with possible Greek warrior (headband of a king, tunic etc...) from Bharhut.*[585] *Bharhut, Madhya Pradesh, Shunga Period, c.100-80BC. Reddish brown sandstone.*[586] *Indian Museum, Calcutta.*

are grouped with the Kambojas, Kiratas, Sakas, and the Pahlavas etc. and are spoken of as living the life of Dasyus (slaves). In another chapter of the same Parva, the Yaunas, Kambojas, Gandharas etc. are spoken of as equal to the "Svapakas" and the "Grddhras".

Udyogaparva of Mahabharata[587] says that the composite army of the Kambojas, Yavanas and Sakas had participated in the Mahabharata war under the supreme command of Kamboja king Sudakshina. The epic numerously applauds this composite army as being very fierce and wrathful.

Balakanda of Ramayana also groups the Yavanas with the Kambojas, Sakas, Pahlavas etc. and refers to them as the military allies of sage Vishistha against Vedic king Vishwamitra[588] The Kishkindha Kanda of Ramayana locates the Sakas, Kambojas, Yavanas and Paradas in the extreme north-west beyond the Himavat (i.e. Hindukush).[589]

The Buddhist drama Mudrarakshasa by Visakhadutta as well as the Jaina works Parishishtaparvan refer to Chandragupta's alliance with Himalayan king Parvataka. This Himalayan alliance gave Chandragupta a powerful composite army made up of the frontier martial tribes of the Shakas, Kambojas, Yavanas, Parasikas, Bahlikas etc.[590] which he may have utilised to aid defeat the Greek successors of Alexander the Great and the Nanda rulers of Magadha, and thus establishing his Mauryan Empire in northern India.

Manusmriti[591] lists the Yavanas with the Kambojas, Sakas, Pahlavas, Paradas etc. and regards them as degraded Kshatriyas (Hindu caste). Anushasanaparva of Mahabharata[592] also views the Yavanas, Kambojas, Shakas etc. in the same light. Patanjali's Mahabhashya[593] regards the Yavanas and Sakas as Anirvasita (pure) Shudras. Gautama-Dharmasutra[594] regards the Yavanas or Greeks as having sprung from Shudra females and Kshatriya males.

The Assalayana Sutta of Majjhima Nikaya attests that in Yona and Kamboja nations, there were only two classes of people...Aryas and Dasas...the masters and slaves, and that the Arya could become Dasa and vice versa. The Vishnu Purana also indicates that the "Chaturvarna" or four class social system was absent in the lands of Kiratas in the East, and the Yavanas and Kambojas etc. in the West.

Numerous Puranic literature groups the Yavanas with the Sakas, Kambojas, Pahlavas and Paradas and refers to the peculiar hair styles of these people which were different from those of the Hindus. Ganapatha on Pāṇini attests that it was a practice among the Yavanas and the Kambojas to wear short-cropped hair (*Kamboja-mundah Yavana-mundah*).

Vartika of Katayayana informs us that the kings of the Shakas and the Yavanas, like those of the Kambojas, may also be addressed by their respective tribal names.

Brihatkathamanjari of Kshmendra[595] informs us that king Vikramaditya had unburdened the sacred earth of the Barbarians like the Shakas, Kambojas, Yavanas, Tusharas, Parasikas, Hunas etc. by annihilating these sinners completely.

The Brahmanda Purana[596] refers to the horses born in Yavana country.

The Mahaniddesa[597] speaks of Yona and Parama Yona, probably referring to Arachosia as the Yona and Bactria as the Parama Yona.

Later meanings

The terms "Yona", "Yonaka" or "Yavana" literally referred to the Greeks, however "mlechas" was also used probably due to their barbaric behaviour as invaders. Indian languages did not base a distinction on religion early on but after the arrival of Islam to the subcontinent, the term Yavana was used along with Turuka, Turuska, Tajik, and Arab more than Mussalaman or Muslim for invaders professing Islam as their religion.

Figure 133: *The façade of the Chaitya Hall at Manmodi caves was donated by a Yavana, according to the inscription on the central flat surface of the lotus. Detail of the "Ya-va-na-sa" circular inscription in old Brahmi script: , circa 120 CE.*[598]

The Chams of Champa referred to Đại Việt as "Yavana".

The Khmer word "Yuon" (yuôn) ឈួន /yuən/ is an ethnic slur for Vietnamese, derived from the Indian word for Greek, "Yavana". It can also be spelled as "Youn".

The Sinhalese term Yonaka referring to the Sri Lankan Moors, is thought to have been derived from the term Yona.

Contemporary usage

The word Yona, or one of its derivatives, is still used by some languages to designate contemporary Greece, such as in Arabic (يونان), in Hebrew (יוון), in Turkish ("Yunanistan"), in modern Aramaic (Yawnoye ܝܘܢܝܐ), or the Pashto, Hindi, Urdu, Malay and Indonesian languages ("Yunani").

References

- The shape of ancient thought. Comparative Studies in Greek and Indian philosophies, by Thomas Mc Evilly (Allworth Press, New York 2002) ISBN 1-58115-203-5

External links

- Pali dictionary definition of "Yona"[599]
- Yavana[600]

Indo-Parthian Kingdom

Indo-Parthian Kingdom	
12 BC–c. 130 AD	
Indo-Parthian Kingdom at its maximum extent.	
Capital	Taxila Kabul
Languages	Aramaic Greek (Greek alphabet) Pali (Kharoshthi script) Sanskrit, Prakrit (Brahmi script) Parthian (Parthian script)
Religion	Buddhism Zoroastrianism Ancient Greek religion
Government	Monarchy
King	
• 20 BC	Gondophares I
Historical era	Antiquity

•	Gondophares I	12 BC
•	Disestablished	c. 130 AD

Preceded by	Succeeded by
Parthian Empire	Kushan Empire

The **Indo-Parthian Kingdom** was ruled by the Gondopharid dynasty and other rulers who were a group of ancient kings from Central Asia that ruled parts of present-day Afghanistan, Pakistan and northwestern India, during or slightly before the 1st century AD. For most of their history, the leading Gondopharid kings held Taxila (in the present Punjab province of Pakistan) as their residence, but during their last few years of existence the capital shifted between Kabul and Peshawar. These kings have traditionally been referred to as Indo-Parthians, as their coinage was often inspired by the Arsacid dynasty, but they probably belonged to a wider group of Iranian tribes who lived east of Parthia proper, and there is no evidence that all the kings who assumed the title *Gondophares*, which means "Holder of Glory", were even related. The Indo-Parthians are noted for the construction of the Buddhist monastery Takht-i-Bahi (UNESCO World Heritage Site).

Gondophares I and his successors

Gondophares I originally seems to have been a ruler of Seistan in what is today eastern Iran, probably a vassal or relative of the Apracarajas. Around 20–10 BC,[602] he made conquests in the former Indo-Scythian kingdom, perhaps after the death of the important ruler Azes. Gondophares became the ruler of areas comprising Arachosia, Seistan, Sindh, Punjab, and the Kabul valley, but it does not seem as though he held territory beyond eastern Punjab.[603] Gondophares called himself "King of Kings", a Parthian title that in his case correctly reflects that the Indo-Parthian empire was only a loose framework: a number of smaller dynasts certainly maintained their positions during the Indo-Parthian period, likely in exchange for their recognition of Gondophares and his successors. These smaller dynasts included the Apracarajas themselves, and Indo-Scythian satraps such as Zeionises and Rajuvula, as well as anonymous Scythians who struck imitations of Azes coins. The Ksaharatas also held sway in Gujarat, perhaps just outside Gondophares' dominions.

After the death of Gondophares I, the empire started to fragment. The name or title *Gondophares* was adapted by Sarpedones, who become **Gondophares II** and was possibly son of the first Gondophares. Even though he claimed to be the main ruler, Sarpedones' rule was shaky and he issued a fragmented coinage

Figure 134: *Portrait of Gondophares, founder of the Indo-Parthian kingdom. He wears a headband, earrings, a necklace, and a cross-over jacket with round decorations.*

in Sind, eastern Punjab and Arachosia in southern Afghanistan. The most important successor was Abdagases, Gondophares' nephew, who ruled in Punjab and possibly in the homeland of Seistan. After a short reign, Sarpedones seems to have been succeeded by Orthagnes, who became **Gondophares III Gadana**. Orthagnes ruled mostly in Seistan and Arachosia, with Abdagases further east, during the first decades AD, and was briefly succeeded by his son Ubouzanes Coin[604]. After 20 AD, a king named Sases, a nephew of the Apracaraja ruler Aspavarma, took over Abdagases' territories and became **Gondophares IV Sases**. According to Senior, this is the Gondophares referred to in the Takht-i-Bahi inscription.[605]

There were other minor kings: Sanabares was an ephemeral usurper in Seistan, who called himself Great King of Kings, and there was also a second Abdagases Coin[606], a ruler named Agata in Sind, another ruler called Satavastres Coin[607], and an anonymous prince who claimed to be brother of the king Arsaces, in that case an actual member of the ruling dynasty in Parthia.

But the Indo-Parthians never regained the position of Gondophares I, and from the middle of the 1st century AD the Kushans under Kujula Kadphises began absorbing the northern Indian part of the kingdom. The last king Pacores (perhaps before 100 AD)[608] only ruled in Seistan and Kandahar.

Figure 135: *King Abdagases I being crowned by the Greek goddess Tyche, on the reverse of some of his coins.*[601]

Figure 136: *Ancient Buddhist monastery Takht-i-Bahi (a UNESCO World Heritage Site) constructed by the Indo-Parthian.*

Figure 137: *The Hellenistic temple with Ionic columns at Jandial, Taxila, is usually interpreted as a Zoroastrian fire temple from the period of the Indo-Parthians.*

Archaeology and sources

The city of Taxila is thought to have been a capital of the Indo-Parthians. Large strata were excavated by Sir John Marshall with a quantity of Parthian-style artifacts. The nearby temple of Jandial is usually interpreted as a Zoroastrian fire temple from the period of the Indo-Parthians.

Some ancient writings describe the presence of the Indo-Parthians in the area, such as the story of Saint Thomas the Apostle, who was recruited as a carpenter to serve at the court of king "Gudnaphar" (thought to be Gondophares) in India. The Acts of Thomas describes in chapter 17 Thomas' visit to king Gudnaphar in northern India; chapters 2 and 3 depict him as embarking on a sea voyage to India, thus connecting Thomas to the west coast of India.

As Senior points out,[609] this Gudnaphar has usually been identified with the first Gondophares, who has thus been dated after the advent of Christianity, but there is no evidence for this assumption, and Senior's research shows that Gondophares I could be dated even before 1 AD. If the account is even historical, Saint Thomas may have encountered one of the later kings who bore the same title.

The Greek philosopher Apollonius of Tyana is related by Philostratus in *Life of Apollonius Tyana* to have visited India, and specifically the city of Taxila around 46 AD. He describes constructions of the Greek type,[610] probably

Figure 138: *Gondophares on horse, from his coinage. He wears a short jacket and baggy trousers, rather typical of Parthian clothing.*

Figure 139: *Portrait on Gondophares on one of his coins.*

referring to Sirkap, and explains that the Indo-Parthian king of Taxila, named Phraotes, received a Greek education at the court of his father and spoke Greek fluently:

> "Tell me, O King, how you acquired such a command of the Greek tongue, and whence you derived all your philosophical attainments in this place?"[611]

> [...]-"My father, after a Greek education, brought me to the sages at an age somewhat too early perhaps, for I was only twelve at the time, but they brought me up like their own son; for any that they admit knowing the Greek tongue they are especially fond of, because they consider that in virtue of the similarity of his disposition he already belongs to themselves."[612]

The Periplus of the Erythraean Sea is a surviving 1st century guide to the routes commonly being used for navigating the Arabian Sea. It describes the presence of Parthian kings fighting with each other in the area of Sindh, a region traditionally known at that time as "Scythia" due to the previous rule of the Indo-Scythians there:

> "This river (Indus) has seven mouths, very shallow and marshy, so that they are not navigable, except the one in the middle; at which by the shore, is the market-town, Barbaricum. Before it there lies a small island, and inland behind it is the metropolis of Scythia, Minnagara; it is subject to Parthian princes who are constantly driving each other out." Periplus of the Erythraean Sea, Chap 38[613]

An inscription from Takht-i-Bahi bears two dates, one in the regnal year 26 of the Maharaja Guduvhara (again thought to be a Gondophares), and the year 103 of an unknown era.[614]

Religion of the Indo-Parthians

To the contrary of the Indo-Greeks or Indo-Scythians, there are no explicit records of Indo-Parthian rulers supporting Buddhism, such as religious dedications, inscriptions, or even legendary accounts. Also, although Indo-Parthian coins generally closely follow Greek numismatics, they never display the Buddhist triratna symbol (apart from the later Sases), nor do they ever use depictions of the elephant or the bull, possible religious symbols which were profusely used by their predecessors. They are thought to have retained Zoroastrianism, being of Iranian extraction themselves. This Iranian mythological system was inherited from them by the later Kushans who ruled from the Peshawar-Khyber-Pakhtunkhwa region of Pakistan.

Indo-Parthian Kingdom 177

Figure 140: *Devotees at Zoroastrian fire-altar.*

Representation of Indo-Parthian devotees

On their coins and in the art of Gandhara, Indo-Parthians are depicted with short crossover jackets and large baggy trousers, possibly supplemented by chap-like over-trousers.[615] Their jackets are adorned with rows of decorative rings or medals. Their hair is usually bushy and contained with a headband, a practise largely adopted by the Parthians from the 1st century AD.[616]

Individuals in Indo-Parthian attire are sometimes shown as actors in Buddhist devotional scenes. It is usually considered that most of the excavations that were done at Sirkap near Taxila by John Marshall relate to Indo-Parthian layers, although more recent scholarship sometimes relates them to the Indo-Greeks instead.[617] These archaeological researches provided a quantity of Hellenistic artifacts combined with elements of Buddhist worship (stupas). Some other temples, such as nearby Jandial may have been used as a Zoroastrian fire temple.

Buddhist sculptures

The statues found at Sirkap in the late Scythian to Parthian level (level 2, 1–60 AD) suggest an already developed state of Gandharan art at the time or even before Parthian rule. A multiplicity of statues, ranging from Hellenistic gods, to various Gandharan lay devotees, are combined with what are thought as

Figure 141: *Indo-Parthian King*

some of the early representations of the Buddha and Bodhisattvas. Today, it is still unclear when the Greco-Buddhist art of Gandhara exactly emerged, but the findings in Sirkap do indicate that this art was already highly developed before the advent of the Kushans.

Stone palettes

Numerous stone palettes found in Gandhara are considered as good representatives of Indo-Parthian art. These palettes combine Greek and Persian influences, together with a frontality in representations which is considered as characteristic of Parthian art. Such palettes have only been found in archaeological layers corresponding to Indo-Greek, Indo-Scythian and Indo-Parthian rule, and are essentially unknown the preceding Mauryan layers or the succeeding Kushan layers.[618]

Very often these palettes represent people in Greek dress in mythological scenes, but a few of them represent people in Parthian dress (head-bands over bushy hair, crossed-over jacket on a bare chest, jewelry, belt, baggy trousers). A palette from the Naprstek Museum in Prague shows an Indo-Parthian king seated crossed-legged on a large sofa, surrounded by two attendants also in Parthian dress. They are shown drinking and serving wine.

Indo-Parthian Kingdom

Figure 142: *Indo-Parthian man hunting.*

Figure 143: *Indo-Parthian revelers.*

180 Indo-Parthian Kingdom

Figure 145: *Gandhara Buddhist reliquary with content, including Indo-Parthian coins. 1st century AD.*

Figure 144: *Indo-Parthian couple.*

Indo-Parthian Kingdom

Figure 146: *Coins of the Indo-Parthian king Abdagases, in which his clothing is clearly apparent. He wears baggy trousers, rather typical of Parthian clothing.*

Silk Road transmission of Buddhism

Some pockets of Parthian rule remained in the East, even after the takeover by the Sassanids in 226. From the 2nd century several Central-Asian Buddhist missionaries appeared in the Chinese capital cities of Loyang and sometimes Nanjing, where they particularly distinguished themselves by their translation work. The first known translators of Buddhist texts into Chinese are actually Parthian missionaries, distinguished in Chinese by their Parthian surname "An", for "Anshi", "country of the Arsacids".

- An Shih Kao, was a Parthian prince, who made the first known translations of Hinayana Buddhist texts into Chinese (148–170).
- An Hsuan, was a Parthian merchant who became a monk in China 181 AD.
- Tan-ti (c. 254), a Parthian monk.
- An Fajin (281–306), a monk of Parthian origins.

Main Indo-Parthian rulers

- Gondophares I (c. 20 BC – first years AD) Coin[619]
- Gondophares II Sarpedones (first years AD – c. 20 AD) Coin[620]
- Abdagases I (first years AD – mid-1st century AD) Coin[621]
- Gondophares III Gudana, previously Orthagnes (c. 20 AD – 30 AD)
- Gondophares IV Sases, (mid-1st century AD)
- Ubouzanes, (late-1st century AD)
- Pacores (late 1st century AD) Coin[622]

Figure 147: *Coins of the Indo-Parthian king Abdagases, in which his clothing is clearly apparent. He wears baggy trousers and a crossover jacket.*

References

<templatestyles src="Template:Refbegin/styles.css" />

- "Les Palettes du Gandhara", Henri-Paul Francfort, Diffusion de Boccard, Paris, 1979
- "Reports on the campaigns 1956–1958 in Swat (Pakistan)", Domenico Faccenna
- "Sculptures from the sacred site of Butkara I", Domenico Faccena

External links

 Wikimedia Commons has media related to *Indo-Parthian*.

- Coins of the Indo-Parthians[623]
- History of Greco-India[624]

Pahlavas

The **Pahlavas** are a people mentioned in ancient Indian texts like the Manu Smriti, various Puranas, the Ramayana, the Mahabharata, and the Brhatsamhita. In some texts the Pahlavas are also mentioned as "Pallavas": While the Vayu Purana distinguishes between *Pahlava* and *Pahnava*, the Vamana Purana and Matsya Purana refer to both as *Pallava*. The Brahmanda Purana and Markendeya Purana refer to both as *Pahlava* or *Pallava*. *Bhishama Parava* Mahabharata 6.11.66 . of the Mahabharata also does not distinguish between the Pahlavas and Pallavas. The Pahlavas are said to be same as the Parasikas.Wikipedia:Citation needed According to P. Carnegy,[625] the Pahlava are probably those people who spoke Paluvi or Pehlvi, that is the Parthian language. Buhler similarly suggests Pahlava is an Indic form of *Parthava* meaning 'Parthian'.[626] In the 4th century BCE, Vartika of Katyayana mentions the *Sakah-Parthavah* demonstrating an awareness of these Saka-Parthians, probably by way of commerce.[627]

Literary references

In Puranic texts

Pahlavas are referenced in various Puranic texts like Vayu Purana, Brahmanda Purana, Markendeya Purana, Matsya Purana, Vamana Purana etc.

Kirfel's list of Uttarapatha countries of the *Bhuvanakosha* locates the Pahlavas along with the Tusharas, Chinas, Angalaukikas, Barbaras, Kambojas, Daradas, Bahlikas and other countries of the Udichya division of ancient India. e.g.:

ete desha udichyastu

Kambojashchaiva Dardashchaiva Barbarashcha Angaukikah ||

Chinashchaiva Tusharashcha **Pahlava**dhayata narah ||.[628]

The Vayu Purana, Brahamanda Purana and several other Puranas mention the Pahlavas with the tribes of Uttarapatha or north-west. The 6th century CE text Markendeya Purana[629] lists the Pahlavas, Kambojas, Daradas, Bahlikas, Barbaras, Tusharas, Daradas, Paradas, Chinas, Lampakas etc. as the countries of Udichya division i.e. Uttarapatha, but 58th chapter of the Markendeya Purana also refers to yet other settlements of the Pahlavas and the Kambojas and locates them both specifically in the south-west of India as neighbors to the Sindhu, Sauvira and Anarta (north Saurashtra) countries. Further the 6th century Brhatsamhita of Varaha Mihira also locates the Pahlavas and Kamboja kingdoms in south-west India i.e. around Gujarat/Saurashtra.[630]

Puranas like Vayu also state that the Udichyas including the Pahlavas, Paradas, Gandharas, Sakas, Yavanas, Tusharas, Kambojas, Khasas, Lampakas, Madhyadesis, Vindhyas, Aprantas, Dakshinatyas, Dravidas, Pulindas, Simhalas etc. would be proceeded against and annihilated by Kalki in Kaliyuga. And they are stated to have been annihilated by king Pramiti at the end of Kali age as per Puranic evidence.

According to Vayu Purana and Matsya Purana, river Chakshu (Oxus or Amu Darya) flowed through the countries of Pahlavas, Tusharas, Lampakas, Paradas and the Sakas etc.[631]

Pānca Ganahas or Five Hordes

Puranas associate the Pahlavas with the Kambojas, Sakas, Yavanas and Paradas and brands them together as *Panca-ganah* (fiver-hordes). These five hordes were military allies of the Haihaya or Taljunga Kshatriyas of Yadava line and were chiefly responsible for dethroning king Bahu of Kosala. Later, king Sagara, son of king Bahu, was able to defeat the Haihayas or Taljungas together with these five-hordes. According to Puranic accounts, king Sagara had divested the Paradas and other members of the well-known Pānca-gana (i.e. the Sakas, Yavanas, Kambojas and Pahlavas) of their Kshatriyahood and turned them into the Mlechchas. Before their defeat at the hands of king Sagara, these five-hordes were called Kshatriya-pungava (i.e. *foremost among the Kshatriyas*).

In the Ramayana

The Balakanda of the Ramayana groups the Pahlavas with the Sakas, Kambojas, Yavanas, Mlechhas and the Kiratas and refers to them as military allies of sage Vasishtha against Vedic sage king Vishwamitra.[632]

The Kiskindha Kanda of Ramayana associates the Pahlavas with the Yavanas, Shakas, Kambojas, Paradas (Varadas), Rishikas and the Uttarakurus etc. and locates them all in the trans-Himalayan territories i.e. in the Sakadvipa.[633]

In the Mahabharata

In the Uttarapatha

Mahabharata attests that Pandava-putra Nakula had defeated the Pahlavas in the course of his western expedition. The kings of Pahlava were also present at the Rajasuya sacrifice of king Yudhishtra.

The Mahabharata also associates the Pahlavas with the Sakas, Yavanas, Gandharas, Kambojas, Tusharas, Sabaras, Barbaras, etc. and addresses them all as the barbaric tribes of Uttarapatha.

In the Udyoga-Parva

But the Udyoga-Parva of Mahabharata groups the Pahlavas with the Sakas, Paradas and the Kambojas-Rishikas and locates them all in/around Anupa region in western India.

Mahabharata[634] reads: These kings of the Shakas, Pahlavas and Daradas (i.e. the Paradas) and the Kamboja Rshikas, these are in the western riverine (Anupa) area.

This epic reference implies that sections of the Pahlavas, Sakas, Paradas, Kambojas were also located in western India near Saurashtra/Maharashtra.

In Kurukshetra War

The Pahlavas along with the Sakas, Kiratas, Yavanas etc. joined Saradwat's son Kripacharya, the high-souled and mighty bowman, and took up their positions at the northern point of the army.[635,636]

In the Manusmriti

Manusmriti[637] states that the **Pahlavas** and several other tribes like the Sakas, Yavanas, Kambojas, Paradas, Daradas, Khasas, etc. were originally noble Kshatriyas, but later, due to their non-observance of valorous Kshatriya codes and neglect of chivalry, they had gradually sunken to the status of Mlechchas.

In the Mudrarakshas Drama

The Buddhist drama Mudrarakshas by Visakhadutta and the Jaina works Parishishtaparvan refer to Chandragupta's alliance with Himalayan king Parvatka. This Himalayan alliance gave Chandragupta a powerful composite army made up of the frontier martial tribes of the Shakas, Kambojas, Yavanas, Parasikas (Pahlavas), Bahlikas etc. (predominantly an Iranian army) which he utilised to defeat the Greek successors of Alexander and the Nanda rulers of Magadha, and thus establishing his Mauryan Empire in northern India.[638]

In the Brihat-Katha-Manjari

The Brihat-Katha-Manjari of the Kshmendra[639] relates that around 400, the Gupta king Vikramaditya (Chandragupta II) had "unburdened the sacred earth of the barbarians" like the Shakas, Mlecchas, Kambojas, Yavanas, Tusharas, Parasikas, Hunas, etc. by annihilating these "unrighteous people" completely.

In the Kavyamimamsa

The 10th century Kavyamimamsa[640] of Pt Raj Shekhar still lists the Sakas, Tusharas, Vokanas, Hunas, Kambojas, Bahlikas, Pahlavas, Tangana, Turukshas, etc. together and states them as the tribes located in the Uttarapatha division.

Western Satraps

Western Satraps (Ariaca)	
35–405	
Approximate territory of the Western Satraps (35–405).	
Capital	Ujjain Barygaza
Languages	Pali (Kharoshthi script) Sanskrit, Prakrit (Brahmi script) Possibly Greek (Greek alphabet)
Religion	Hinduism, Buddhism
Government	Monarchy
Satrap, King	
• c. 35	Abhiraka

• 388–395	Rudrasimha III	
Historical era	Antiquity	
• Established	35	
• Disestablished	405	
	Preceded by	Succeeded by
	Indo-Scythians	Gupta Empire
Today part of	India Pakistan	

The **Western Satraps**, **Western Kshatrapas**, or **Kshaharatas** (35–405 CE) were Indo-Scythian (Saka) rulers of the western and central part of India (Saurashtra and Malwa: modern Gujarat, Maharashtra, Rajasthan and Madhya Pradesh states). The Western Satraps were contemporaneous with the Kushans who ruled the northern part of the Indian subcontinent and were possibly their overlords, and the Satavahana (Andhra) who ruled in Central India. The power of the Saka rulers started to decline in the 2nd century CE after the Saka rulers were defeated by the south Indian Emperor Gautamiputra Satakarni of the Satavahana dynasty.[641] Later the Saka kingdom was completely destroyed by Chandragupta II of the Gupta Empire in the 4th century CE.[642]

Altogether, there were 27 independent Western Satrap rulers during a period of about 350 years.

Name

They are named Western Satraps in contrast to the "Northern Satraps" who ruled around East Punjab and the area of Mathura, such as Rajuvula, and his successors under the Kushans, the "Great Satrap" Kharapallana and the "Satrap" Vanaspara.[643]

Although they called themselves "Satraps" on their coins, leading to their modern designation of "Western Satraps", Ptolemy in his 2nd century "Geographia" still called them "Indo-Scythians".[644] The word *Kshatrapa* stands for *satrap*, itself descended from Old Persian and which means viceroy or governor of a province. According to John Marshall, the word "kshatrapa" means the viceroy of the "King of kings". The title of the "Mahakshatrapa" or the "Great Satrap" was given to the ruling Satrap, and the title of "kshatrapa" was given to the heir apparent. The western Kshatrapas were also known as Sakas to Indians. The Kshatrapas of western region were of foreign origin, and they were feudatories at first to the Scytho-Parthian, and later the Kushan Empire. In the eastern Malwa region, they appear on the scene only after the Kushan empire established itself, a few sculptures in the Kushan style during the reign of King Shahi Vasishka attesting to their presence in the region.

Figure 148: *Coin of Bhumaka (?–119).* **Obv:** *Arrow, pellet, and thunderbolt. Kharoshthi inscription Chaharasada Chatrapasa Bhumakasa: "Ksaharata Satrap Bhumaka".* **Rev:** *Capital of a pillar with seated lion with upraised paw, and wheel (dharmachakra). Brahmi inscription: Kshaharatasa Kshatrapasa Bhumakasa.*

First expansion: Kshaharata dynasty (1st century CE)

The Western Satraps are thought to have started with the rather short-lived *Kshaharata* dynasty (also called *Chaharada*, *Khaharata* or *Khakharata* depending on sources).[645] The term *Kshaharata* is also known from the 6 CE Taxila copper plate inscription, in which it qualifies the Indo-Scythian ruler Liaka Kusulaka. The Nasik inscription of the 19th year of Sri Pulamavi also mentions the *Khakharatavasa*, or *Kshaharata* race.[646]

The earliest Kshaharata for whom there is evidence is Abhiraka, whose rare coins are known. He was succeeded by Bhumaka, father of Nahapana, who only used on his coins the title of Satrap, and not that of *Raja* or *Raño* (king). Bhumaka was the father of the great ruler Nahapana, according to one of the latter's coins. His coins bear Buddhist symbols, such as the eight-spoked wheel (dharmachakra), or the lion seated on a capital, a representation of a pillar of Ashoka.

Figure 149: *Coin of Nahapana (119–124). British Museum.*

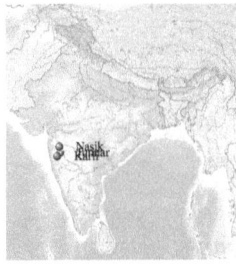

File:India relief location map.jpg

Location of Western Satrap inscriptions in Buddhist rock-cut caves, indicating the southern extent of their territory, circa 120 CE.

Nahapana succeeded him, and became a very powerful ruler. He occupied portions of the Satavahana empire in western and central India. Nahapana held sway over Malwa, Southern Gujarat, and Northern Konkan, from Bharuch to Sopara and the Nasik and Poona districts.[647] His son-in-law, the Saka Ushavadata (married to his daughter Dakshamitra), is known from inscriptions in Nasik and Karle and Junnar (Manmodi caves, inscription of the year 46) to have been viceroy of Nahapana, ruling over the southern part of his territory.[648]

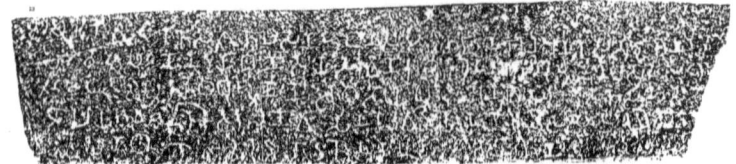

Figure 150: *Karla Caves, inscription of Nahapana.*

Nahapana established the silver coinage of the Kshatrapas.

Circa 120 CE, the Western Satraps are known to have allied with the Uttamabhadras in order to repulse an attack by the Malavas, whom they finally crushed.[649] The claim appears in an inscription at the Nashik Caves, made by the Nahapana's viceroy Ushavadata:

> ...And by order of the lord I went to release the chief of the Uttamabhadras, who had been besieged for the rainy season by the Malayas, and those Malayas fled at the mere roar (of my approaching) as it were, and were all made prisoners of the Uttamabhadra warriors.
>
> —Inscription in Cave No.10 of the Nashik Caves.[650]

Support of Indian religions

An important inscription related to Nahapana in the Great Chaitya at Karla Caves (Valukura is thought to be an ancient name for Karla Caves) shows his support of Buddhist as well as Brahmanical religions:

> Success!! By Ushabadata, the son of Dinaka and the son-in-law of the king, the Kshaharata, the Kshatrapa Nahapana, who gave three hundred thousand cows, who made gifts of gold and a tirtha on the river Banasa, who gave to the Devas and Brahmanas sixteen villages, who at the pure tirtha Prabhasa gave eight wives to the Brahmanas, and who also fed annually a hundred thousand Brahmanas- there has been given the village of Karajika for the support of the ascetics living in the caves at Valuraka without any distinction of sect or origin, for all who would keep the varsha.
>
> —Inscription of Nahapana, Karla Caves.[651]

Construction of Buddhist caves

The Western Satraps are known for the construction and dedication of numerous Buddhist caves in Central India, particularly in the areas of Maharashtra and Gujarat.[652] It is thought that Nahapana ruled at least 35 years in the region of Karla, Junnar and Nasik, giving him ample time for construction works there.

Numerous inscriptions in the caves are known, which were made by the family of Nahapana: six inscriptions in Nasik caves, one inscription at Karli caves, and one by Nahapana's minister in the Manmodi caves at Junnar.[653,654] At the same time, "Yavanas", Greeks or Indo-Greeks, also left donative inscriptions at the Nasik caves, Karla caves, Lenyadri and Manmodi caves.

Great Chaitya hall at Karla Caves

In particular, the chaitya cave complex of the Karla Caves, the largest in South Asia, was constructed and dedicated in 120 CE by the Western Satraps ruler Nahapana.[575,655,656]

Figure 151: *Hall of the Great Chaitya Cave at Karla (120 CE) UNIQ-ref-0-8c889858087207e6-QINU*

Figure 152: *Chaitya roof*

Figure 153: *Capitals*

Figure 154: *Donative inscription by a Yavana ("Indo-Greek") named Vitasamghata. UNIQ-ref-1-8c889858087207e6-QINU*

Cave No.10 of Nasik, the 'Nahapana Vihara'

Parts of the Nasik caves, also called Pandavleni Caves, were also carved during the time of Nahapana.

The inscriptions of cave no.10 in the Pandavleni Caves near Nasik, reveal that in 105-106 CE, Kshatrapas defeated the Satavahanas after which Kshatrapa Nahapana's son-in-law and Dinika's son- Ushavadata donated 3000 gold coins for this cave as well as for the food and clothing of the monks. Usabhdatta's wife (Nahapana's daughter), Dakshmitra also donated one cave for the Buddhist monks. Cave 10 - 'Nahapana Vihara' is spacious with 16 rooms.

Two inscriptions in Cave 10 mention the building and the gift of the whole cave to the Samgha by Ushavadata, the Saka[657] son-in-law and viceroy of Nahapana:

> *Success! Ushavadata, son of Dinika, son-in-law of king Nahapana, the Kshaharata Kshatrapa, (...) inspired by (true) religion, in the Trirasmi hills at Govardhana, has caused this cave to be made and these cisterns.*
>
> —*Inscription No.10 of Nahapana, Cave No.10, Nasik*[658]

Figure 155: *Nasik Cave inscription No.10. of Nahapana, Cave No.10.*

Figure 156: *One of the pillars built by Ushavadata, viceroy of Nahapana, circa 120 CE, Pandavleni Caves, cave No10.*

Success! In the year 42, in the month Vesakha, Ushavadata, son of Dinika, son-in-law of king Nahapana, the Kshaharata Kshatrapa, has bestowed this cave on the Samgha generally....

—*Inscription No.12 of Nahapana, Cave No.10, Nasik*[659]

According to the inscriptions, Ushavadata accomplished various charities and conquests on behalf of his father-in-law. He constructed rest-houses, gardens and tanks at Bharukachchha (Broach), Dashapura (Mandasor in Malva), Govardhana (near Nasik) and Shorparaga (Sopara in the Thana district).

Junnar dedication

A dedication in the Lenyadri complex of the Junnar caves (inscription No. 26 in Cave VI of the Bhimasankar group of caves), mentions a gift by Nahapana's prime minister Ayama in the "year 46":

The meritorious gift.... of Ayama of the Vachhasagotra, prime minister of the King Mahakshatrapa the lord Nahapana

—*Junnar inscription No. 26, 124 CE*[660]

This inscription, the last one of the reign of Nahapana, suggests that Nahapana may have become an independent ruler since he is described as a King.

International trade: the Periplus of the Erythraean Sea

Nahapana is mentioned in the Periplus of the Erythraean Sea under the name *Nambanus*,[661] as ruler of the area around Barigaza:

Beyond the gulf of Baraca is that of Barygaza and the coast of the country of Ariaca, which is the beginning of the Kingdom of Nambanus and of all India. That part of it lying inland and adjoining Scythia is called Abiria, but the coast is called Syrastrene. It is a fertile country, yielding wheat and rice and sesame oil and clarified butter, cotton and the Indian cloths made therefrom, of the coarser sorts. Very many cattle are pastured there, and the men are of great stature and black in color. The metropolis of this country is Minnagara, from which much cotton cloth is brought down to Barygaza.

—*Periplus of the Erythraean Sea, Chap. 41*[662]

Under the Western Satraps, Barigaza was one of the main centers of Roman trade with India. The Periplus describes the many goods exchanged:

There are imported into this market-town (Barigaza), wine, Italian preferred, also Laodicean and Arabian; copper, tin, and lead; coral and topaz; thin clothing and inferior sorts of all kinds; bright-colored girdles

Figure 157: *Nahapana coin hoard.*

a cubit wide; storax, sweet clover, flint glass, realgar, antimony, gold and silver coin, on which there is a profit when exchanged for the money of the country; and ointment, but not very costly and not much. And for the King there are brought into those places very costly vessels of silver, singing boys, beautiful maidens for the harem, fine wines, thin clothing of the finest weaves, and the choicest ointments. There are exported from these places spikenard, costus, bdellium, ivory, agate and carnelian, lycium, cotton cloth of all kinds, silk cloth, mallow cloth, yarn, long pepper and such other things as are brought here from the various market-towns. Those bound for this market-town from Egypt make the voyage favorably about the month of July, that is Epiphi.

—*Periplus of the Erythraean Sea, Chapter 49.*[663]

Goods were also brought down in quantity from Ujjain, the capital of the Western Satraps:

Inland from this place and to the east, is the city called Ozene, formerly a royal capital; from this place are brought down all things needed for the welfare of the country about Barygaza, and many things for our trade: agate and carnelian, Indian muslins and mallow cloth, and much ordinary cloth.

—*Periplus of the Erythraean Sea, Chapter 48.*

Some ships were also fitted out from Barigaza, to export goods westward across the Indian Ocean:

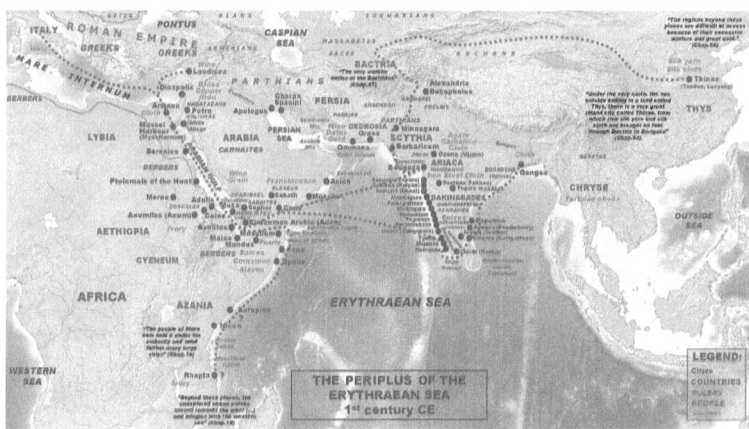

Figure 158: *The Western Satraps under Nahapana, with their harbour of Barigaza, were among the main actors of the 1st century CE international trade according to the Periplus of the Erythraean Sea.*

Ships are also customarily fitted out from the places across this sea, from Ariaca and Barygaza, bringing to these far-side market-towns the products of their own places; wheat, rice, clarified butter, sesame oil, cotton cloth (the monache and the sagmatogene), and girdles, and honey from the reed called sacchari. Some make the voyage especially to these market-towns, and others exchange their cargoes while sailing along the coast.

—*Periplus of the Erythraean Sea, Chapter 14.*

Defeat by Gautamiputra Satakarni

Nahapana and Ushavadata were ultimately defeated by the powerful Satavahana king Gautamiputra Satakarni. Gautamiputra drove the Sakas from Malwa and Western Maharashtra, forcing Nahapana west to Gujarat. His victory is known from the fact that Gautamiputra restruck many of Nahapana's coins, and that he claimed victory on them in an inscription at Cave No. 3 of the Pandavleni Caves in Nashik:

Gautamiputra Satakarni (...) who crushed down the pride and conceit of the Kshatriyas; who destroyed the Sakas (Western Satraps), Yavanas (Indo-Greeks) and Pahlavas (Indo-Parthians),... who rooted out the Khakharata family (the Kshaharata family of Nahapana); who restored the glory of the Satavahana race.

—*Inscription of Queen Mother Gautami Balashri at Cave No. 3 of the Pandavleni Caves in Nashik.*

Figure 159: *One of the many coins of Nahapana, re-struck by Gautamiputra Satakarni.*

Colonization of Java and Sumatra

It seems that the Indian colonization of the islands of Java and Sumatra took place during the time of the Western Satraps. People may have fled the subcontinent due to the conflicts there. Some foundation legends of Java describe the leader of the colonists as Aji Saka, a prince from Gujarat, at the beginning of the Shaka era (which is also the Java era).[664]

Kardamaka dynasty, family of Castana (1st–4th century)

A new dynasty, called the Bhadramukhas or Kardamaka dynasty, was established by the "Satrap" Castana. The date of Castana is not certain, but many believe his reign started in the year 78 CE, thus making him the founder of the Saka era.[665] This is consistent with the fact that his descendants (who we know used the Saka era on their coins and inscriptions) would use the date of their founder as their era. Castana was satrap of Ujjain during that period. A statue found in Mathura together with statues of the Kushan king Kanishka and Vima Taktu, and bearing the name "Shastana" is often attributed to Castana himself, and suggests Castana may have been a feudatory of the Kushans. Conversely,

Figure 160: *Coin of the Western Satrap Chastana (c. 130 CE). Obv: King in profile. The legend typically reads "PANNIΩ IAT-PAΠAC CIASTANCA" (corrupted Greek script), transliteration of the Prakrit Raño Kshatrapasa Castana: "King and Satrap Castana".*

the Rabatak inscription also claims Kushan dominion over Western Satrap territory (by mentioning Kushan control over the capital Ujjain) during the reign of Kanishka (c. 127–150 CE).

Territory under Chastana

The territory of the Western Satraps at the time of Chastana is described extensively by the geographer Ptolemy in his "Geographia", where he qualifies them as "Indo-Scythians". He describes this territory as starting from Patalene in the West, to Ujjain in the east ("Ozena-Regia Tiastani", "Ozene/Ujjain, capital of king Chastana"), and beyond Barigaza in the south.

> *Moreover the region which is next to the western part of India, is called Indoscythia. A part of this region around the (Indus) river mouth is Patalena, above which is Abiria. That which is about the mouth of the Indus and the Canthicolpus bay is called Syrastrena. (...) In the island formed by this river are the cities Pantala, Barbaria. (...) The Larica region of Indoscythia is located eastward from the swamp near the sea, in which on*

Figure 161: *Statue of Chastana, with costume details. The belt displays designs of horsemen and tritons/anguipeds, the coat has a highly ornate hem. Inscription "Chastana". Mathura Museum.*[666]

the west of the Namadus river is the interior city of Barygaza emporium. On the east side of the river (...) Ozena-Regia Tiastani (...) Minnagara.

—Ptolemy, Geographia, Book Seven, Chapter I

Rudradaman I (130-150 CE)

Victory against the Satavahanas

Around 130 CE, Rudradaman I, grandson of Chastana, took the title "Mahakshatrapa" ("Great Satrap"), and defended his kingdom from the Satavahanas. The conflict between Rudradaman and Satavahanas became so gruelling, that in order to contain the conflict, a matrimonial relationship was concluded by giving Rudradaman's daughter to the Satavahana king Vashishtiputra Satakarni. The inscription relating the marriage between Rudradaman's daughter and Vashishtiputra Satakarni appears in a cave at Kanheri:

Of the queen ... of the illustrious Satakarni Vasishthiputra, descended from the race of Karddamaka kings, (and) daughter of the Mahakshatrapa Ru(dra)....... ....of the confidential minister Sateraka, a water-cistern, the meritorious gift.

Figure 162: *Silver coin of Rudradaman I (130–150).* ***Obv:*** *Bust of Rudradaman, with corrupted Greek legend "OVONIΛOOCVΛCHΛNO".* ***Rev:*** *Three-arched hill or Chaitya with river, crescent and sun. Brahmi legend: Rajno Ksatrapasa Jayadamasaputrasa Rajno Mahaksatrapasa Rudradamasa: "King and Great Satrap Rudradaman, son of King and Satrap Jayadaman" 16mm, 2.0 grams.*

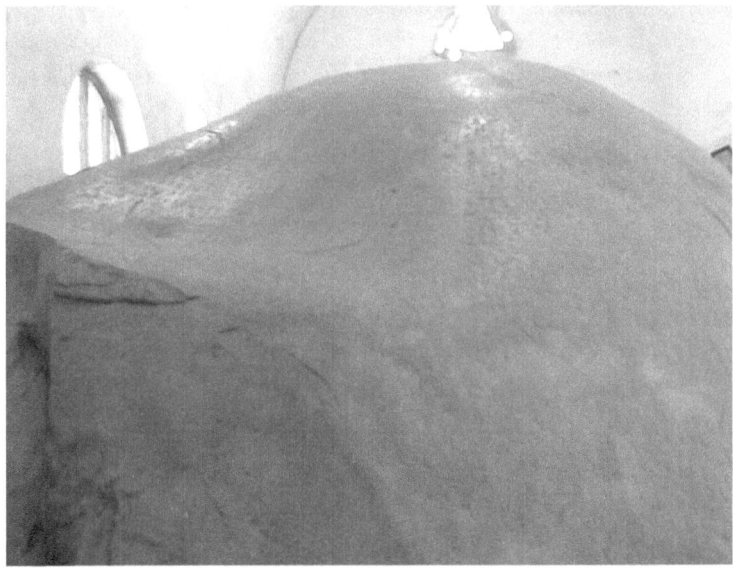

Figure 163: *The Junagadh rock contains inscriptions of Ashoka (fourteen of the Edicts of Ashoka), Rudradaman I (the Junagadh rock inscription of Rudradaman) and Skandagupta.*[667]

—*Kanheri inscription of Rudradaman I's daughter.*

The Satavahanas and the Western Satraps remained at war however, and Rudradaman I defeated the Satavahanas twice in these conflicts, only sparing the life of Vashishtiputra Satakarni due to their family alliance:

> *Rudradaman (...) who obtained good report because he, in spite of having twice in fair fight completely defeated Satakarni, the lord of Dakshinapatha, on account of the nearness of their connection did not destroy him.*
>
> —*Junagadh rock inscription of Rudradaman*[668]

Rudradaman regained all the previous territories held by Nahapana, probably with the exception of the southern areas of Poona and Nasik (epigraphical remains in these two areas at that time are exclusively Satavahana):

> *Rudradaman (...) who is the lord of the whole of eastern and western Akaravanti (Akara: East Malwa and Avanti: West Malwa), the Anupa country, Anarta, Surashtra, Svabhra (northern Gujarat), Maru (Marwar), Kachchha (Cutch), Sindhu-Sauvira (Sindh and Multan districts), Kukura (Eastern Rajputana), Aparanta ("Western Border" – Northern Konkan), Nishada (an aboriginal tribe, Malwa and parts of Central India) and other territories gained by his own valour, the towns, marts and rural parts of which are never troubled by robbers, snakes, wild beasts, diseases and the like, where all subjects are attached to him, (and) where through his might the objects of [religion], wealth and pleasure [are duly attained].*
>
> —*Junagadh rock inscription of Rudradaman. Geographical interpretations in parentheses from Rapson.*[669]

Victory against the Yaudheyas

Later, the Junagadh rock inscription (c. 150 CE) of Rudradaman I[670] acknowledged the military might of the Yaudheyas "who would not submit because they were proud of their title 'heroes among the Kshatriyas'", before explaining that they were ultimately vanquished by Rudradaman I.[671,672]

> *Rudradaman (...) who by force destroyed the Yaudheyas who were loath to submit, rendered proud as they were by having manifested their title of 'heroes among all Kshatriyas'.*
>
> —*Junagadh rock inscription of Rudradaman*

Recently discovered pillar inscriptions describe the presence of a Western Satrap named *Rupiamma* in the Bhandara district of the area of Vidarbha, in the extreme northeastern area of Maharashtra, where he erected the pillars.[673]

Figure 164: *A coin dated to the beginning of the first reign of Jivadaman, in the year 100 of the Saka Era (corresponding to 178 CE).*

Rudradarman is known for his sponsoring of the arts. He is known to have written poetry in the purest of Sanskrit, and made it his court language. His name is forever attached to the inscription by Sudharshini lake.

He had at his court a Greek writer named Yavanesvara ("Lord of the Greeks"), who translated from Greek to Sanskrit the Yavanajataka ("Saying of the Greeks"), an astrological treatise and India's earliest Sanskrit work in horoscopy.[674]

Jivadaman (178-181 CE, 197-198 CE)

King Jivadaman became king for the centenary of the Saka Era, in the year 100 (corresponding to 178 CE). His reign is otherwise undocumented, but he is the first Western Satrap ruler who started to print the minting date on his coins, using the Brāhmī numerals of the Brāhmī script behind the king's head.[675] This is of immense value to date precisely Western Satrap rulers, and to clarify perfectly the chronology and succession between them, as they also mention their predecessor on their coins. According to his coins, Jivadaman seems to have ruled two times, once between Saka Era 100 and 103 (178-181 CE), before the rule of Rudrasimha I, and once between Saka Era 119 and 120 (197-198 CE).

Rudrasimha I (180-197)

An inscription of Rudrasimha I (178-197) was recently found at Setkhedi in Shajapur district, dated to 107 Saka Era, that is 185 CE, confirming the expansion of the Western Satraps to the east at that date. There is also an earlier inscription related to Saka rule in Ujjain, as well as a later one, the Kanakerha inscription, related to Sala rule in the area of Vidisha, Sanchi and Eran in the early 4th century.

Figure 165: *Coin of the Western Kshatrapa ruler Rudrasimha I (178 to 197).*

Loss of southern territories to the Satavahanas (end of 2nd century CE)

The south Indian ruler Yajna Sri Satakarni (170-199 CE) of the Satavahana dynasty defeated the Western Satraps in the late 2nd century CE, thereby reconquering their southern regions in western and central India, which led to the decline of the Western Satraps.[676]

Yajna Sri Satakarni left inscriptions in Nasik caves, Kanheri and Guntur, testifying to the renewed extent of Satavahana territory. There are two inscriptions of Yajna Sri Satakarni at Kanheri, in cave No. 81, and in the Chaitya cave No. 3. In the Nasik caves, there is one inscription of Sri Yajna Satakarni, in the 7th year of his reign.

There is a possibility, however, that the areas of Poona and Nasik had remained in the hands of the Satavahanas since the time of Gautamiputra Satakarni after his victory over Nahapana, as there are no epigraphical records of the Kardamakas in this area.

Figure 166: *Rudrasena II (256-278 CE). Head right, wearing close-fitting cap / Three-arched hill; group of five pellets to right.*[677]

Rudrasena II (256–278)

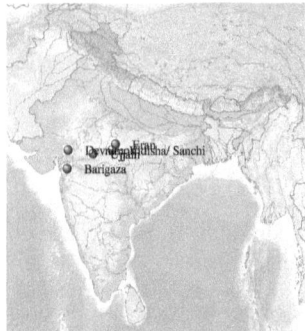

File:India relief location map.jpg

Western Satrap territory extended from the west coast of India to Vidisha/ Sanchi and Eran, from the time of Rudrasena II (256–278) well into the 4th century.

The Kshatrapa dynasty seems to have reached a high level of prosperity under the rule of Rudrasena II (256–278), 19th ruler of Kshatrapa.

The region of Sanchi-Vidisha was again captured from the Satavahanas during the rule of Rudrasena II (255-278 CE), as shown by finds of his coinage in the area.

The last Kshatrapa ruler of the Chastana family was Visvasena (Vishwasen), brother and successor to Bhartrdaman and son of Rudrasena II.

Figure 167: *Head of Buddha Shakyamuni, Devnimori, Gujarat (375-400). Derived from the Greco-Buddhist art of Gandhara, an example of the Western Indian art of the Western Satraps.*[678]

Rudrasimha II family (304-396 CE)

A new family took over, started by the rule of Rudrasimha II. He declared on his coins to be the son of a Lord (Svami) Jivadaman.[679]

His rule is partly coeval with that of other rulers, who were his sons as written on their coins, and may have been sub-kings: Yasodaman II (317–332) and Rudradaman II (332–348).

Contributions to Buddhism

Under Rudrasimha II, the Western Satraps are known to have maintained their presence in the Central Indian areas of Vidisha/Sanchi/Eran well into the 4th century: during his rule, in 319 CE, a Saka ruler inscribed the Kanakerha inscription,[680] on the hill of Sanchi mentioning the construction of a well by the Saka chief and "righteous conqueror" (*dharmaviyagi mahadandanayaka*) Sridharavarman (339-368 CE).[681] Another inscription of the same Sridhavarman with his military commander is known from Eran. These inscriptions point to the extent of Saka rule as of the time of Rudrasimha II.

The construction of Buddhist monuments in the area of Gujarat during the later part of Western Satrap rule is attested with the site of Devnimori, which

Figure 168: *Coin of the last Western Satrap ruler Rudrasimha III (388–395).*

incorporates viharas and a stupa. Coins of Rudrasimha were found inside the Buddhist stupa of Devnimori. The Buddha images in Devnimori clearly show the influence of the Greco-Buddhist art of Gandhara,[682] and have been described as examples of the Western Indian art of the Western Satraps. It has been suggested that the art of Devnimori represented a Western Indian artistic tradition that was anterior to the rise of Gupta Empire art, and that it may have influenced not only the latter, but also the art of the Ajanta Caves, Sarnath and other places from the 5th century onward.

Overall, the Western Satraps may have played a role in the transmission of the art of Gandhara to the western Deccan region.

Defeat by the Guptas (c. 400)

Rudrasimha III seems to have been the last of the Western Satrap rulers. A fragment from the Natya-darpana mentions that the Gupta king Ramagupta, the elder brother of Chandragupta II, decided to expand his kingdom by attacking the Western Satraps in Gujarat.

The campaign soon took a turn for the worse and the Gupta army was trapped. The Saka king, Rudrasimha III, demanded that Ramagupta hand over his wife Dhruvadevi in exchange for peace. To avoid the ignominy, the Guptas decided to send Madhavasena, a courtesan and a beloved of Chandragupta, disguised as the queen. However, Chandragupta changed the plan and himself went to the Saka King disguised as the queen. He then killed Rudrasimha and later his own brother, Ramagupta. Dhruvadevi was then married to Chandragupta.

The Western Satraps were eventually conquered by emperor Chandragupta II. Inscriptions of a victorious Chandragupta II in the year 412-413 CE can be found on the railing near the Eastern Gateway of the Great Stupa in Sanchi.[683]

Figure 169: *Coin of Damasena. The minting date, here 153 (100-50-3 in Brahmi script numerals) of the Saka era, therefore 232 CE, clearly appears behind the head of the king.*

The glorious Candragupta (II), (...) who proclaims in the world the good behaviour of the excellent people, namely, the dependents (of the king), and who has acquired banners of victory and fame in many battles

—*Sanchi inscription of Chandragupta II, 412-413 CE.*[684]

This brought an end to nearly four centuries of Saka rule on the subcontinent.

Coinage

The Kshatrapas have a very rich and interesting coinage. It was based on the coinage of the earlier Indo-Greek Kings, with Greek or pseudo-Greek legend and stylized profiles of royal busts on the obverse. The reverse of the coins, however, is original and typically depict a thunderbolt and an arrow, and later, a chaitya or three-arched hill and river symbol with a crescent and the sun, within a legend in Brahmi. These coins are very informative, since they record the name of the King, of his father, and the date of issue, and have helped clarify the early history of India.

Regnal dates

From the reigns of Jivadaman and Rudrasimha I, the date of minting of each coin, reckoned in the Saka era, is usually written on the obverse behind the king's head in Brahmi numerals, allowing for a quite precise datation of the rule of each king.[685] This is a rather uncommon case in Indian numismatics.

Figure 170: *Coin of the Western Kshatrapa ruler Rudrasimha I (178–197). **Obv:** Bust of Rudrasimha, with corrupted Greek legend "..OHIIOIH.." (Indo-Greek style).* ***Rev:*** *Three-arched hill or Chaitya, with river, crescent and sun, within Prakrit legend in Brahmi script:Rajno Mahaksatrapasa Rudradamnaputrasa Rajna Mahaksatrapasa Rudrasihasa "King and Great Satrap Rudrasimha, son of King and Great Satrap Rudradaman".*

Some, such as the numismat R.C Senior considered that these dates might correspond to the much earlier Azes era instead.

Also the father of each king is systematically mentioned in the reverse legends, which allows reconstruction of the regnal succession.

Languages

Kharoshthi, a script in use in more northern territories (area of Gandhara), is employed together with the Brahmi script and the Greek script on the first coins of the Western Satraps, but is finally abandoned from the time of Chastana.[686] From that time, only the Brahmi script would remain, together with the pseudo-Greek script on the facing, to write the Prakrit language employed by the Western satraps. Occasionally, the legends are in Sanskrit instead.

The coins of Nahapana bear the Greek script legend "PANNIΩ IAHAPATAC NAHAΠANAC", transliteration of the Prakrit "Raño Kshaharatasa Nahapanasa": "In the reign of Kshaharata Nahapana". The coins of Castana also have a readable legend "PANNIΩ IATPAΠAC CIASTANCA", transliteration of the Prakrit "Raño Kshatrapasa Castana": "In the reign of the Satrap Castana". After these two rulers, the legend in Greek script becomes denaturated, and seems to lose all signification, only retaining an esthetic value. By the 4th century, the coins of Rudrasimha II exhibit the following type of meaningless legend in corrupted Greek script: "...ΛΙΟΛVICIVIIIΛ...".[687]

Figure 171: *The Guptas imitated Western Satrap coins for their silver coinage. Here, a coin of the Gupta king Kumaragupta I (414–455) (Western territories).*

Influences

The coins of the Kshatrapas were also very influential and imitated by neighbouring or later dynasties, such as the Satavahanas, and the Guptas. Silver coins of the Gupta kings Chandragupta II and his son Kumaragupta I adopted the Western Satrap design (itself derived from the Indo-Greeks) with bust of the ruler and pseudo-Greek inscription on the obverse, and a royal eagle (Garuda, the dynastic symbol of the Guptas) replacing the chaitya hill with star and crescent on the reverse.[688]

The Western Satrap coin design was also adopted by the subsequent dynasty of the Traikutakas (388–456).

Monuments

Sudarshan Lake of the Satrap period is mentioned in major rock edicts of Junagadh but no trace of it remains. Six inscription-stones called *Lashti*s of 1st century were recovered from a hillock near Andhau village in the Khavda region of Kutch and were moved to the Kutch Museum in Bhuj. They are the earliest dated monuments of the Satrap period and were erected in the time of Rudradaman I.

The large number of stone inscriptions from Kutch and Saurastra as well as hundreds of coins throughout Gujarat are found belonging to the Satrap period. The earlier caves at Sana, Junagadh, Dhank, Talaja, Sidhasar, Prabhas Patan and Ranapar in the Barada Hills are mostly plain and austere in looks except some carvings in the Bava Pyara caves of Junagadh. They are comparable to Andhra-Satrap period caves in Deccan. As they have almost no carvings, the

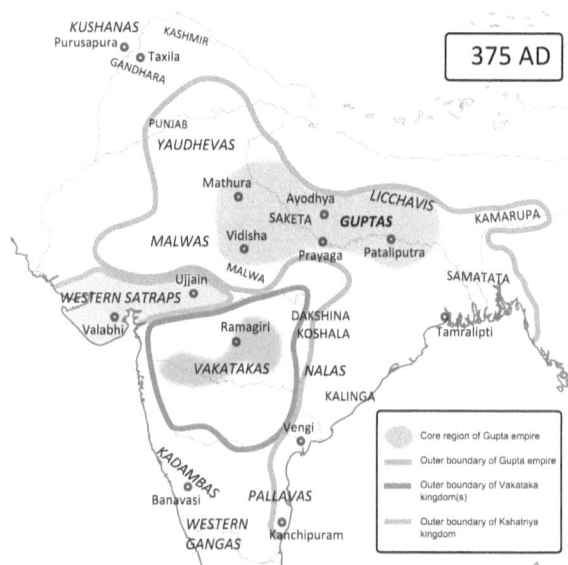

Figure 172: *Territories under Western Satraps in 375 AD*

determination of their date and chronology is difficult. The Uparkot Caves of Junagadh and the Khambhalida Caves belong to the later years of the Satraps. The *stupas* excavated at Boria and Intwa near Junagadh belonged to the Satrap period. The *stupa* excavated at Shamlaji probably belonged to this period or to the Gupta period.

Possible vassalage to the Kushans

It is still unclear whether the Western Satraps were independent rulers or vassals of the Kushans. The continued use of the word "Satrap" on their coin would suggest a recognized subjection to a higher ruler, possibly the Kushan emperor.[689]

Also, a statue of Chastana was found in Mathura at the Temple of Mat together with the famous statues of Vima Kadphises and Kanishka. This also would suggest at least alliance and friendship, if not vassalage. Finally Kanishka claims in the Rabatak inscription that his power extends to Ujjain, the classical capital of the Western Satrap realm. This combined with the presence of the Chastana statue side-by-side with Kanishka would also suggest Kushan alliance with the Western Satraps.

Figure 173: *Inscribed statue of King Chastana in Mathura. Kushan Period.*

Finally, following the period of the "Northern Satraps" who ruled in the area of Mathura, the "Great Satrap" Kharapallana and the "Satrap" Vanaspara are known from an inscription in Sarnath to have been feudatories of the Kushans.

Generally, the position taken by modern scholarship is that the Western Satraps were vassals of the Kushans, at least in the early period until Rudradaman I conquered the Yaudheyas, who are usually thought to be Kushan vassals. The question is not considered perfectly settled.

Main rulers

History of Gujarat

Kshaharata dynasty

- Yapirajaya
- Hospises
- Higaraka
- Abhiraka (Aubhirakes)
- Bhumaka (?–119)
- Nahapana (119–124)
  - Viceroy Ushavadata

Bhadramukhas or Kardamaka dynasty

Family of Chastana:

- Chastana (c. 78-130) , son of Zamotika
- Jayadaman, son of Chastana
- Rudradaman I (c. 130–150) , son of Jayadaman
- Damajadasri I (170–175)
- Jivadaman (178-181, d. 199)
- Rudrasimha I (180–188, d. 197)
- Rudrasimha I (restored) (191–197)
- Satyadaman (197-198)
- Jivadaman (restored) (197–199)
- Rudrasena I (200–222)
- Prthivisena (222)
- Samghadaman (222–223)
- Damasena (223–232)
- Damajadasri II (232–239) with
- Viradaman (234–238)
- Isvaradatta (236–239)
- Yasodaman I (239)
- Vijayasena (239–250)
- Damajadasri III (251–255)
- Rudrasena II (255–277)
- Visvasimha (277–282)
- Bhartrdaman (282–295)

- Visvasena (293–304)

Family of Rudrasimha II:

- Rudrasimha II (304–348) , son of Lord (Svami) Jivadaman, with
  - Yasodaman II (317–332)
  - Rudradaman II (332–348) *No coins known*
- Rudrasena III (348–380)
- Simhasena (380–384/5)
- Rudrasena IV (382–388)
- Rudrasimha III (388–395)

Notes

In foot note number 13 on Rupiamma, I would like to point out that he wasn't from the Kshahartha family or the Kardamaka family of Chashtana. Some rulers used the title Mahakshtrapa without belonging to these dynasties. There is an article in Journal of Epigraphic Society of India Vol 18 by H.S. Thosar that will tell us the history of this Rupiamma. The pillar inscriptions merely mentions his name Mahakshtrapa Rupiamma with a low relief sculpture. There is no date or any other record. Rupiamma should not be included in the Western Satrap history.

References

<templatestyles src="Template:Refbegin/styles.css" />

- Rapson, "A Catalogue of Indian coins in the British Museum. Andhras etc."
- John Rosenfield, "The dynastic art of the Kushans", 1976
- Claudius Ptolemy, "The geography", Translated and edited by Edward Luther Stevenson, Dover Publications Inc., New York, ISBN 0-486-26896-9

External links

- [691] History of the Andhras, Prasad 1988 With many references to Western Satrap rule
- Online catalogue of Western Kshatrapa coins[692]
- Coins of the Western Kshatrapas[693]
- The Kshatrapas in Nasik[694]
- The Origins of the Indian Coinage Tradition[695] at Academia.edu

Kushan Empire

	Kushan Empire
	Κυþανο (Bactrian) कुषाण साम्राज्य (Sanskrit) Βασιλεία Κοσσανῶν (Greek)
	Nomadic empire
	30–375
	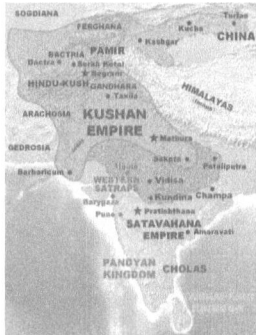 Kushan territories (full line) and maximum extent of Kushan dominions under Kanishka the Great (dotted line), according to the Rabatak inscription.[696]
Capital	Bagram (*Kapiśi*) Peshawar (*Puruṣapura*) Taxila (*Takṣaśilā*) Mathura (*Mathurā*)
Languages	Greek (official until ca. 127)[697] Bactrian[698] (official from ca. 127) Unofficial regional languages: Gurjari-Gandhari, Sogdian, Chorasmian, Tocharian, Saka dialects, Prakrit Liturgical language: Sanskrit
Religion	Hinduism[699] Buddhism[700] Bactrian religion Zoroastrianism[701]
Government	Monarchy
Emperor	
• 30–80	Kujula Kadphises
• 350–375	Kipunada
Historical era	Classical Antiquity
• Kujula Kadphises unites Yuezhi tribes into a confederation	30

• Subjugated by the Sasanians, Guptas, and Hepthalites	375
Area	3,800,000 km² (1,500,000 sq mi)
Currency	Kushan drachma

Preceded by	Succeeded by
	Sasanian Empire
Indo-Parthian Kingdom	Gupta Empire
Indo-Scythians	Hephthalite Empire
	Khasa kingdom

Today part of	Afghanistan China Kyrgyzstan India Nepal Pakistan Tajikistan Uzbekistan Turkmenistan

The **Kushan Empire** (Ancient Greek: Βασιλεία Κοσσανῶν; Bactrian: Κυþανο, *Kushano*; Sanskrit: कुषाण साम्राज्य *Kuṣāṇa Samrajya*; BHS: *Guṣāṇa-vaṃśa*; Chinese: 貴霜帝國 ; Parthian: Kušan-xšaθr[702]) was a syncretic empire, formed by the Yuezhi, in the Bactrian territories in the early 1st century. It spread to encompass much of Afghanistan,[703] present-day Pakistan and then the northern parts of India at least as far as Saketa and Sarnath near Varanasi (Benares), where inscriptions have been found dating to the era of the Kushan Emperor Kanishka the Great.[704] Kanishka was a great patron of Buddhism; however, as Kushans expanded southward toward the Indian subcontinent the deities of their later coinage came to reflect its new Hindu majority.

The Kushans were one of five branches of the Yuezhi confederation, a possibly Iranic or Tocharian,[705] Indo-European[706] nomadic people who migrated from Gansu and settled in ancient Bactria. The Kushans possibly used the Greek language initially for administrative purposes, but soon began to use Bactrian language.[698] Kanishka sent his armies north of the Karakoram mountains, capturing territories as far as Kashgar, Khotan and Yarkant, in the Tarim Basin of modern-day Xinjiang, China. A direct road from Gandhara to China remained under Kushan control for more than a century, encouraging travel across the Karakoram and facilitating the spread of Mahayana Buddhism to China.

The Kushan dynasty had diplomatic contacts with the Roman Empire, Sasanian Persia, the Aksumite Empire and Han Dynasty of China. While much philosophy, art, and science was created within its borders, the only textual record of the empire's history today comes from inscriptions and accounts in other languages, particularly Chinese.[707]

The Kushan empire fragmented into semi-independent kingdoms in the 3rd century AD, which fell to the Sasanians invading from the west, establishing the Kushano-Sasanian Kingdom in the areas of Sogdiana, Bactria and Gandhara. In the 4th century, the Guptas, an Indian dynasty also pressed from the east. The last of the Kushan and Kushano-Sasanian kingdoms were eventually overwhelmed by invaders from the north, known as the Kidarites, and then the Hepthalites.

Origins

Chinese sources describe the *Guishuang* (貴霜), *i.e.* the Kushans, as one of the five aristocratic tribes of the Yuezhi, with some people claiming they were a loose confederation of Indo-European peoples, though many scholars are still unconvinced that they originally spoke an Indo-European language. As the historian John E. Hill has put it: "For well over a century ... there have been many arguments about the ethnic and linguistic origins of the Great Yuezhi or Da Yuezhi (大月氏), Kushans (貴霜), and the Tochari, and still there is little consensus".[708]

The Yuezhi were described in the *Records of the Great Historian* 史記 and the *Book of Han* 漢書 as living in the grasslands of Gansu, in the northwest of modern-day China, until their King was beheaded by the Huns from Siberia (the Xiongnu 匈奴) who were also at war with China, which eventually forced them to migrate west in 176–160 BCE.[709] The five tribes constituting the Yuezhi are known in Chinese history as *Xiūmì* (休密), *Guìshuāng* (貴霜), *Shuāngmǐ* (雙靡), *Xìdùn* (肸頓), and *Dūmì* (都密).

The Yuezhi reached the Hellenic kingdom of Greco-Bactria (in northern Afghanistan and Uzbekistan) around 135 BC. The displaced Greek dynasties resettled to the southeast in areas of the Hindu Kush and the Indus basin (in present-day Afghanistan and Pakistan), occupying the western part of the Indo-Greek Kingdom.

Early Kushans

Some traces remain of the presence of the Kushans in the area of Bactria and Sogdiana. Archaeological structures are known in Takht-I-Sangin, Surkh Kotal (a monumental temple), and in the palace of Khalchayan. Various sculptures and friezes are known, representing horse-riding archers,[710] and, significantly, men with artificially deformed skulls, such as the Kushan prince of Khalchayan[711] (a practice well attested in nomadic Central Asia). The Chinese first referred to these people as the Yuezhi and said they established the Kushan Empire, although the relationship between the Yuezhi and the Kushans

Figure 174: *Head of a Kushan prince (Khalchayan palace, Uzbekistan)*

is still unclear. On the ruins of ancient Hellenistic cities such as Ai-Khanoum, the Kushans are known to have built fortresses.

The earliest documented ruler, and the first one to proclaim himself as a Kushan ruler, was Heraios. He calls himself a "tyrant" in Greek on his coins, and also exhibits skull deformation. He may have been an ally of the Greeks, and he shared the same style of coinage. Heraios may have been the father of the first Kushan emperor Kujula Kadphises.

Ban Gu's Book of Han tells us the Kushans (Kuei-shuang) divided up Bactria in 128 BC. Fan Ye's Book of the Later Han "relates how the chief of the Kushans, Ch'iu-shiu-ch'ueh (the Kujula Kadphises of coins), founded by means of the submission of the other Yueh-chih clans the Kushan Empire, known to the Greeks and Romans under the name of Empire of the Indo-Scythians."

The Chinese Hou Hanshu 後漢書 chronicles gives an account of the formation of the Kushan empire based on a report made by the Chinese general Ban Yong to the Chinese Emperor c. 125 AD:

> More than a hundred years later [than the conquest of Bactria by the Da Yuezhi], the prince [xihou] of Guishuang (Badakhshan) established himself as king, and his dynasty was called that of the Guishuang (Kushan)

Figure 175: *The first known Kushan king Heraios (1-30 CE)*

King. He invaded Anxi (Indo-Parthia), and took the Gaofu (Kabul) region. He also defeated the whole of the kingdoms of Puda (Paktiya) and Jibin (Kapisha and Gandhara). Qiujiuque (Kujula Kadphises) was more than eighty years old when he died. His son, Yangaozhen [probably Vema Tahk (tu) or, possibly, his brother Sadaṣkaṇa], became king in his place. He defeated Tianzhu [North-western India] and installed Generals to supervise and lead it. The Yuezhi then became extremely rich. All the kingdoms call [their king] the Guishuang [Kushan] king, but the Han call them by their original name, Da Yuezhi.

—*Hou Hanshu*[712,713]

Diverse cultural influences

In the 1st century BCE, the *Guishuang* (Ch: 貴霜) gained prominence over the other Yuezhi tribes, and welded them into a tight confederation under *yabgu* (Commander) Kujula Kadphises. The name *Guishuang* was adopted in the West and modified into *Kushan* to designate the confederation, although the Chinese continued to call them *Yuezhi*.

Gradually wresting control of the area from the Scythian tribes, the Kushans expanded south into the region traditionally known as Gandhara (an area

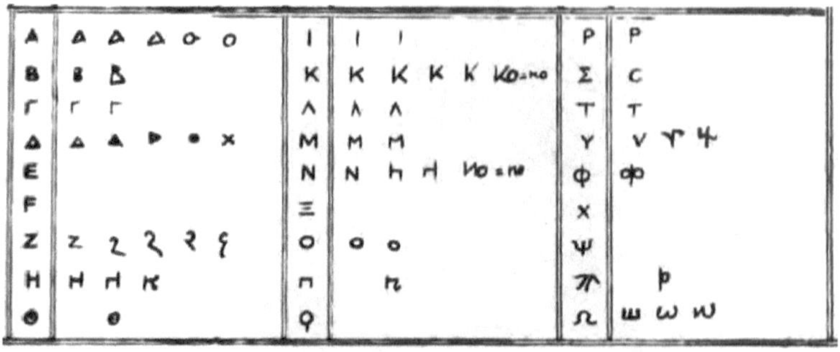

Figure 176: *Greek alphabet (narrow columns) with Kushan script (wide columns)*

Figure 177: *A Buddhist devotee in Kushan dress, Mathura, 2nd century. The Kushan dress is generally depicted as quite stiff, and it is thought it was often made of leather (Francine Tissot, "Gandhara").*

Figure 178: *The Kushan writing system used the Greek alphabet, with the addition of the letter Sho (associated with the Greek Sampi).*

primarily in Pakistan's Pothowar and Khyber Pakhtunkhwa region but going in an arc to include the Kabul valley and part of Qandahar in Afghanistan)Wikipedia:Citation needed and established twin capitals in Begram[714] and Peshawar, then known as Kapisa and Pushklavati respectively.

The Kushans adopted elements of the Hellenistic culture of Bactria. They adopted the Greek alphabet to suit their own language (with the additional development of the letter Þ "sh", as in "Kushan") and soon began minting coinage on the Greek model. On their coins they used Greek language legends combined with Pali legends (in the Kharoshthi script), until the first few years of the reign of Kanishka. After that date,Wikipedia:VaguenessWikipedia:Manual of Style/Dates and numbers#Chronological itemsWikipedia:Accuracy dispute#Disputed statement they used Kushan language legends (in an adapted Greek script), combined with legends in Greek (Greek script) and legends in Prakrit (Kharoshthi script).

The Kushans "adopted many local beliefs and customs, including Zoroastrianism and the two rising religions in the region, the Greek cults and Buddhism".[715] From the time of Vima Takto, many Kushans started adopting aspects of Buddhist culture, and like the Egyptians, they absorbed the strong remnants of the Greek culture of the Hellenistic Kingdoms, becoming at least partly Hellenised. The great Kushan emperor Vima Kadphises may have embraced Saivism (a sect of Hinduism), as surmised by coins minted during the

Figure 179: *Kushan king or prince, Greco-Buddhist art of Gandhara, 2nd-3rd century CE*

period. The following Kushan emperors represented a wide variety of faiths including Zoroastrianism, Buddhism, and possibly Saivism.

The rule of the Kushans linked the seagoing trade of the Indian Ocean with the commerce of the Silk Road through the long-civilized Indus Valley. At the height of the dynasty, the Kushans loosely ruled a territory that extended to the Aral Sea through present-day Uzbekistan, Afghanistan, and Pakistan into northern India.

The loose unity and comparative peace of such a vast expanse encouraged long-distance trade, brought Chinese silks to Rome, and created strings of flourishing urban centers.

Territorial expansion

Rosenfield notes that archaeological evidence of a Kushan rule of long duration is present in an area stretching from Surkh Kotal, Begram, the summer capital of the Kushans, Peshawar, the capital under Kanishka I, Taxila, and Mathura, the winter capital of the Kushans.[716]

Other areas of probable rule include Khwarezm, Kausambi (excavations of Allahabad University), Sanchi and Sarnath (inscriptions with names and dates of

Figure 180: *Remains of a Kushan fortress in Sirsukh, Pakistan*

Kushan kings), Malwa and Maharashtra,[717] and Odisha (imitation of Kushan coins, and large Kushan hoards).

Kushan invasions in the 1st century CE had been given as an explanation for the migration of Indians from the Indian Subcontinent toward Southeast Asia according to proponents of a Greater India theory by 20th-century Indian nationalists. However, there is no evidence to support this hypothesis.

The recently discovered Rabatak inscription confirms the account of the Hou Hanshu, Weilüe, and inscriptions dated early in the Kanishka era (incept probably 127 CE), that large Kushan dominions expanded into the heartland of northern India in the early 2nd century CE. Lines 4 to 7 of the inscription[718] describe the cities which were under the rule of Kanishka, among which six names are identifiable: Ujjain, Kundina, Saketa, Kausambi, Pataliputra, and Champa (although the text is not clear whether Champa was a possession of Kanishka or just beyond it).[719,720] The Kushan state was bounded to the south by the Pārata state of Balochistan, western Pakistan, Afghanistan, Kyrgyzstan, Tajikistan, Uzbekistan, and Turkmenistan. Turkmenistan was known for the kushan Buddhist city of Merv. As late as the 3rd century AD, decorated coins of Huvishka were dedicated at Bodh Gaya together with other gold offerings under the "Enlightenment Throne" of the Buddha, suggesting direct Kushan influence in the area during that period.[721]

Northward, in the 2nd century AD, the Kushans under Kanishka made various forays into the Tarim Basin, where they had various contacts with the

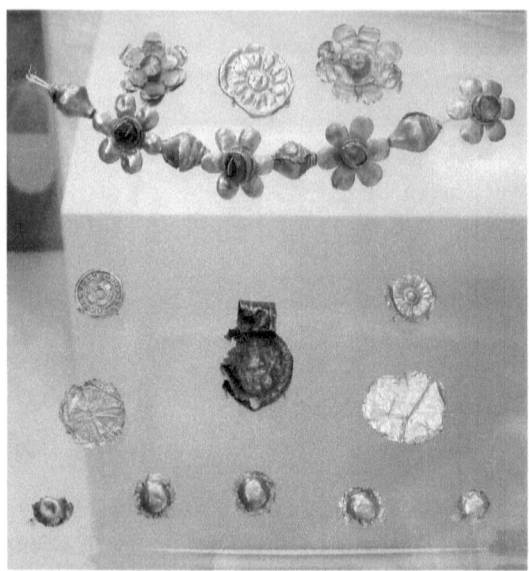

Figure 181: *Offerings found in Bodh Gaya under the "Enlightenment Throne of the Buddha", with an impression of an imitation of a coin of the Kushan emperor Huvishka, 2nd century CE. British Museum*

Chinese. Both archaeological findings and literary evidence suggest Kushan rule, in Kashgar, Yarkand, and Khotan.[722]

Main Kushan rulers

Kujula Kadphises (c. 30 – c. 80)

> ...the prince [elavoor] of Guishuang, named thilac [Kujula Kadphises], attacked and exterminated the four other xihou. He established himself as king, and his dynasty was called that of the Guishuang [Kushan] King. He invaded Anxi [Indo-Parthia] and took the Gaofu [Kabul] region. He also defeated the whole of the kingdoms of Puda [Paktiya] and Jibin [Kapisha and Gandhara]. Qiujiuque [Kujula Kadphises] was more than eighty years old when he died."
>
> —*Hou Hanshu*

These conquests probably took place sometime between 45 and 60 and laid the basis for the Kushan Empire which was rapidly expanded by his descendants.

Kujula issued an extensive series of coins and fathered at least two sons, Sadaṣkaṇa (who is known from only two inscriptions, especially the Rabatak inscription, and apparently never ruled), and seemingly Vima Takto.

Kujula Kadphises was the great-grandfather of Kanishka.

Vima Taktu or Sadashkana (c. 80 – c. 95)

Vima Takto (Ancient Chinese: 閻膏珍 *Yangaozhen*) is mentioned in the Rabatak inscription (another son, Sadashkana, is mentioned in an inscription of Senavarman, the King of Odi). He was the predecessor of Vima Kadphises, and Kanishka I. He expanded the Kushan Empire into the northwest of South Asia. The Hou Hanshu says:

> "*His son, Yangaozhen [probably Vema Tahk (tu) or, possibly, his brother Sadaṣkaṇa], became king in his place. He defeated Tianzhu [Northwestern India] and installed Generals to supervise and lead it. The Yuezhi then became extremely rich. All the kingdoms call [their king] the Guishuang [Kushan] king, but the Han call them by their original name, Da Yuezhi.*"

—*Hou Hanshu*

Vima Kadphises (c. 95 – c. 127)

Vima Kadphises (Kushan language: Οοημο Καδφισης) was a Kushan emperor from around 90–100 CE, the son of Sadashkana and the grandson of Kujula Kadphises, and the father of Kanishka I, as detailed by the Rabatak inscription.

Vima Kadphises added to the Kushan territory by his conquests in Afghanistan and north-west Pakistan. He issued an extensive series of coins and inscriptions. He issued gold coins in addition to the existing copper and silver coinage.

Kanishka I (c. 127 – c. 140)

The rule of Kanishka the Great, fifth Kushan king, lasted for about 13 years from c. 127. Upon his accession, Kanishka ruled a huge territory (virtually all of northern India), south to Ujjain and Kundina and east beyond Pataliputra, according to the Rabatak inscription:

> *In the year one, it has been proclaimed unto India, unto the whole realm of the governing class, including Koonadeano (Kaundiny, Kundina) and the city of Ozeno (Ozene, Ujjain) and the city of Zageda (Saketa) and the city of Kozambo (Kausambi) and the city of Palabotro (Pataliputra) and so long unto (i.e., as far as) the city of Ziri-tambo (Sri-Champa).*

Figure 182: *Kanishka, Mathura art, Mathura Museum*

Figure 183: *The Qila Mubarak fort at Bathinda, India was built by Kanishka the Great.*

—*Rabatak inscription, Lines 4–6*

His territory was administered from two capitals: Purushapura (now Peshawar in northwestern Pakistan) and Mathura, in northern India. He is also credited (along with Raja Dab) for building the massive, ancient Fort at Bathinda (Qila Mubarak), in the modern city of Bathinda, Indian Punjab.

The Kushans also had a summer capital in Bagram (then known as Kapisa), where the "Begram Treasure", comprising works of art from Greece to China, has been found. According to the Rabatak inscription, Kanishka was the son of Vima Kadphises, the grandson of Sadashkana, and the great-grandson of Kujula Kadphises. Kanishka's era is now generally accepted to have begun in 127 on the basis of Harry Falk's ground-breaking research.[723,724] Kanishka's era was used as a calendar reference by the Kushans for about a century, until the decline of the Kushan realm.

Vāsishka (c. 140 – c. 160)

Vāsishka was a Kushan emperor who seems to have had a 20-year reign following Kanishka. His rule is recorded as far south as Sanchi (near Vidisa), where several inscriptions in his name have been found, dated to the year 22 (the Sanchi inscription of "Vaksushana" – i.e., Vasishka Kushana) and year 28 (the Sanchi inscription of Vasaska – i.e., Vasishka) of the Kanishka era.

Huvishka (c. 160 – c. 190)

Huvishka (Kushan: Οοηþκι, "Ooishki") was a Kushan emperor from about 20 years after the death of Kanishka (assumed on the best evidence available to be in 140) until the succession of Vasudeva I about thirty years later. His rule was a period of retrenchment and consolidation for the Empire. In particular he devoted time and effort early in his reign to the exertion of greater control over the city of Mathura.

Vasudeva I (c. 190 – c. 230)

Vasudeva I (Kushan: Βαζοδηο "Bazodeo", Chinese: 波調 "Bodiao") was the last of the "Great Kushans". Named inscriptions dating from year 64 to 98 of Kanishka's era suggest his reign extended from at least 191 to 225 AD. He was the last great Kushan emperor, and the end of his rule coincides with the invasion of the Sasanians as far as northwestern India, and the establishment of the Indo-Sasanians or *Kushanshahs* in what is nowadays Afghanistan, Pakistan and northwestern India from around 240 AD.

Figure 184: *Kumara/Kartikeya with a Kushan devotee, 2nd century CE*

Kushan deities

The Kushan religious pantheon is extremely varied, as revealed by their coins that were made in gold, silver, and copper. These coins contained more than thirty different gods, belonging mainly to their own Iranic, Greek, and Indo-Aryan worlds as well. Kushan coins had images of Kushan Kings, Buddha, and figures from the Indo-Aryan and Iranian pantheons.[725] Greek deities, with Greek names are represented on early coins. During Kanishka's reign, the language of the coinage changes to Bactrian (though it remained in Greek script for all kings). After Huvishka, only two divinities appear on the coins: *Ardoxsho* and *Oesho* (see details below).

The Iranic entities depicted on coinage include:

- Αρδοχþο (*ardoxsho*, Ashi Vanghuhi)
- Αþαειχþο (*ashaeixsho*, Asha Vahishta)
- Αθþο (*athsho*, Atar)
- Φαρρο (*pharro*, Khwarenah)
- Λροοασπο (*lrooaspa*, Drvaspa)
- Μαναοβαγο, (*manaobago*, Vohu Manah)
- Μαο (*mao*, Mah)
- Μιθρο, Μιρο, Μιορο, Μιυρο (*mithro* and variants, Mithra)
- Μοζδοοανο (*mozdooano*, Mazda *vana "Mazda the victorious?")

Figure 185: *Kushan prince making a donation to a Boddhisattva*

- Νανα, Ναναια, Ναναþαο (variations of pan-Asiatic *nana*, Sogdian *nny*, Nana)
- Οαδο (*oado* Vata)
- Οαxþο (*oaxsho*, "Oxus")
- Οορομοζδο (*ooromozdo*, Ahura Mazda)
- Οραλαγνο (*orlagno*, Verethragna)
- Τιερο (*tiero*, Tir)

Representation of entities from Greek mythology and Hellenistic syncretism are:

- Ηλιος (Helios), Ηφαηστος (Hephaistos), Σαληνη (Selene), Ανημος (Anemos). Further, the coins of Huvishka also portray the demi-god *erakilo* Heracles, and the Egyptian god *sarapo* Sarapis

The Indic entities represented on coinage include:

- Βοδδο (*boddo*, Buddha)
- Μετραγο Βοδδο (*metrago boddo*, bodhisattava Maitreya)
- Μαασηνο (*maaseno*, Mahasena)
- Σκανδο κομαρο (*skando komaro*, Skanda Kumara)
- þακαμανο Βοδδο (*shakamano boddho*, Shakyamuni Buddha)
- Οηþο (*oesho*), long considered to represent Indic Shiva,[726,727,728] but also identified as Avestan Vayu conflated with Shiva.[729]

- Two copper coins of Huvishka bear a 'Ganesa' legend, but instead of depicting the typical theriomorphic figure of Ganesha, have a figure of an archer holding a full-length bow with string inwards and an arrow. This is typically a depiction of Rudra, but in the case of these two coins is generally assumed to represent Shiva.

Images of Kushan worshippers

Kushan worshipper with Zeus/Serapis/Ohrmazd, Bactria, 3rd century CE.[730]

Kushan worshipper with Pharro, Bactria, 3rd century AD.

Kushan worshipper with Shiva/Oesho, Bactria, 3rd century CE.

Deities on Kushan coinage

Mahasena on a coin of Huvishka

Four-faced Oesho

Rishti

Manaobago

Kushan Empire

Pharro

Ardochsho

Oesho or Shiva

Oesho or Shiva with bull

Skanda and Visakha

Gold coin of Kanishka the Great, with a depiction of the Buddha, with the legend "Boddo" in Greek script;Ahin Posh

Herakles.

Kushan Carnelian seal representing the "AΔÞO" (*adsho* Atar), with triratana symbol left, and Kanishka the Great's dynastic mark right

Buddha

Kushans and Buddhism

The Kushans inherited the Greco-Buddhist traditions of the Indo-Greek Kingdom they replaced, and their patronage of Buddhist institutions allowed them to grow as a commercial power.[732] Between the mid-1st century and the mid-3rd century, Buddhism, patronized by the Kushans, extended to China and other Asian countries through the Silk Road.

Kanishka is renowned in Buddhist tradition for having convened a great Buddhist council in Kashmir. Along with his predecessors in the region, the Indo-Greek king Menander I (Milinda) and the Indian emperors Ashoka and Harsha Vardhana, Kanishka is considered by Buddhism as one of its greatest benefactors.

During the 1st century AD, Buddhist books were being produced and carried by monks, and their trader patrons. Also, monasteries were being established along these land routes that went from China and other parts of Asia. With the development of Buddhist books, it caused a new written language called Gandhara. Gandhara consists of eastern Afghanistan and northern Pakistan. Scholars are said to have found many Buddhist scrolls that contained the Gandhari language.[733]

The reign of Huvishka corresponds to the first known epigraphic evidence of the Buddha Amitabha, on the bottom part of a 2nd-century statue which has been found in Govindo-Nagar, and now at the Mathura Museum. The statue is dated to "the 28th year of the reign of Huvishka", and dedicated to "Amitabha

Buddha" by a family of merchants. There is also some evidence that Huvishka himself was a follower of Mahāyāna Buddhism. A Sanskrit manuscript fragment in the Schøyen Collection describes Huvishka as one who has "set forth in the Mahāyāna."[734]

Kushan art

The art and culture of Gandhara, at the crossroads of the Kushan hegemony, continued the traditions of Greco-Buddhist art and are the best known expressions of Kushan influences to Westerners. Several direct depictions of Kushans are known from Gandhara, where they are represented with a tunic, belt and trousers and play the role of devotees to the Buddha, as well as the Bodhisattva and future Buddha Maitreya.

During the Kushan Empire, many images of Gandhara share a strong resemblance to the features of Greek, Syrian, Persian and Indian figures. These Western-looking stylistic signatures often include heavy drapery and curly hair, representing a composite (the Greeks, for example, often possessed curly hair).

In the iconography, they are never associated however with the very Hellenistic "Standing Buddha" statues, which might therefore correspond to an earlier historical period.

Contacts with Rome

Several Roman sources describe the visit of ambassadors from the Kings of Bactria and India during the 2nd century, probably referring to the Kushans.

Figure 186: *Kushan coins showing half-length bust of Vima Kadphises in various poses, holding mace-scepter or laurel branch in right hand; flames at shoulder, tamgha to right or left. On the other side of coin is a deity with a bull. Some consider the deity as Shiva because he is in ithyphallic state, holds a trident, and the Nandi bull is his mount, as in Hindu mythology.*[731] *Others suggest him as Oesho, Zoroastrian Vayu.*

Figure 187: *Kanishka the Great inaugurates Mahayana Buddhism. Illustration from 1910*

Figure 188: *Early Mahayana Buddhist triad. From left to right, a Kushan devotee, Maitreya, the Buddha, Avalokitesvara, and a Buddhist monk. 2nd–3rd century, Gandhara*

Historia Augusta, speaking of Emperor Hadrian (117–138) tells:

Reges Bactrianorum legatos ad eum, amicitiae petendae causa, supplices miserunt 'The kings of the Bactrians sent supplicant ambassadors to him, to seek his friendship.'

Also in 138, according to Aurelius Victor (*Epitome*, XV, 4), and Appian (*Praef.*, 7), Antoninus Pius, successor to Hadrian, received some Indian, Bactrian, and Hyrcanian ambassadors.

"Precious things from Da Qin [the Roman Empire] can be found there [in Tianzhu or Northwestern India], as well as fine cotton cloths, fine wool carpets, perfumes of all sorts, sugar candy, pepper, ginger, and black salt."

—*Hou Hanshu*[735]

The summer capital of the Kushan Empire in Begram has yielded a considerable amount of goods imported from the Roman Empire–in particular, various types of glassware.

Figure 189: *Standing Female, 1st century CE Terracotta. This lively female figure comes from an area of Pakistan where merchants from around the Mediterranean had long maintained trading posts. The area, known in antiquity as Gandhara, developed an unusual hybrid style of art and culture that was at once Hellenic and Indic. Brooklyn Museum*

Contacts with China

During the 1st and 2nd century, the Kushan Empire expanded militarily to the north and occupied parts of the Tarim Basin, their original grounds, putting them at the center of the profitable Central Asian commerce with the Roman Empire. They are related to have collaborated militarily with the Chinese against nomadic incursion, particularly when they collaborated with the Han Dynasty general Ban Chao against the Sogdians in 84, when the latter were trying to support a revolt by the king of Kashgar.[736] Around 85, they also assisted the Chinese general in an attack on Turpan, east of the Tarim Basin.

In recognition for their support to the Chinese, the Kushans requested a Han princess, but were denied,[737] even after they had sent presents to the Chinese court. In retaliation, they marched on Ban Chao in 86 with a force of 70,000, but were defeated by a smaller Chinese force. The Yuezhi retreated and paid tribute to the Chinese Empire during the reign of emperor He of Han (89–106).

Figure 190: *Greco-Roman gladiator on a glass vessel, Begram, 2nd century*

Figure 191: *Coin of the Roman Emperor Trajan, found together with coins of Kanishka the Great at the Ahin Posh Monastery*

Kushan Empire

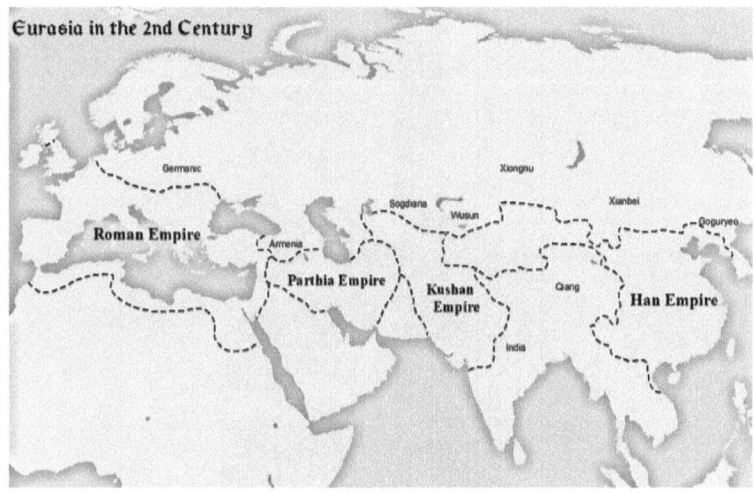

Figure 192: *Map showing the four empires of Eurasia in 2nd Century AD. Kushan shared a border with the Chinese empire of Han.*

Figure 193: *A bronze coin of Kanishka the Great found in Khotan, Tarim Basin*

Figure 194: *The Kushan Buddhist monk Lokaksema, first known translator of Buddhist Mahayana scriptures into Chinese, c. 170*

Later, around 116, the Kushans under Kanishka established a kingdom centered on Kashgar, also taking control of Khotan and Yarkand, which were Chinese dependencies in the Tarim Basin, modern Xinjiang. They introduced the Brahmi script, the Indian Prakrit language for administration, and expanded the influence of Greco-Buddhist art which developed into Serindian art.

The Kushans are again recorded to have sent presents to the Chinese court in 158–159 during the reign of emperor Huan of Han.

Following these interactions, cultural exchanges further increased, and Kushan Buddhist missionaries, such as Lokaksema, became active in the Chinese capital cities of Loyang and sometimes Nanjing, where they particularly distinguished themselves by their translation work. They were the first recorded promoters of Hinayana and Mahayana scriptures in China, greatly contributing to the Silk Road transmission of Buddhism.

Decline

After the death of Vasudeva I in 225, the Kushan empire split into western and eastern halves. The Western Kushans (in Afghanistan) were soon subjugated by the Persian Sasanian Empire and lost Sogdiana, Bactria, and Gandhara to them. The Sasanians deposed the Western dynasty and replaced them

Figure 195: *Eastern Han inscriptions on lead ingot, using barbarous Greek alphabet in the style of the Kushans, excavated in Shaanxi, 1st-2nd century CE.*[738]

Figure 196: *Hormizd I Kushanshah (277-286 CE), king of the Indo-Sasanians, maintained Sasanian rule in former Kushan territories of the northwest. Naqsh-e Rustam Bahram II panel.*

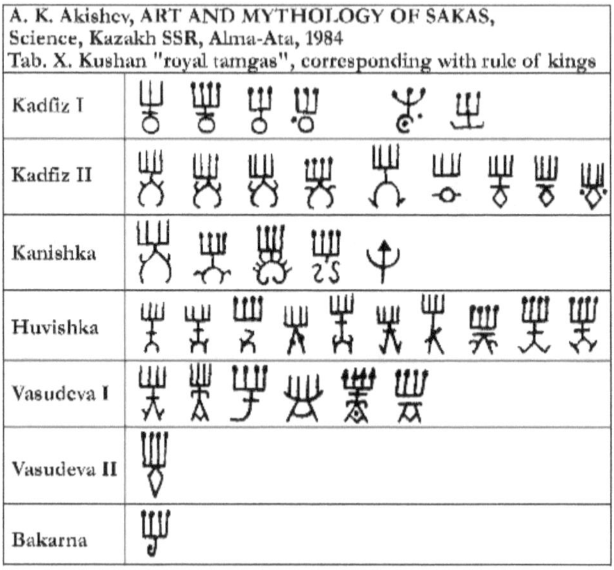

A. K. Akishev, ART AND MYTHOLOGY OF SAKAS, Science, Kazakh SSR, Alma-Ata, 1984 Tab. X. Kushan "royal tamgas", corresponding with rule of kings	
Kadfiz I	
Kadfiz II	
Kanishka	
Huvishka	
Vasudeva I	
Vasudeva II	
Bakarna	

Figure 197: *Listing of Kushan royal tamgas*

with Persian vassals known as the Kushanshas (also called Indo-Sasanians or Kushano-Sasanians).

The Eastern Kushan kingdom was based in the Punjab. Around 270 their territories on the Gangetic plain became independent under local dynasties such as the Yaudheyas. Then in the mid-4th century they were subjugated by the Gupta Empire under Samudragupta.

In 360 a Kidarite Hun named Kidara overthrew the Indo-Sasanians and remnants of the old Kushan dynasty, and established the Kidarite Kingdom. The Kushan style of Kidarite coins indicates they claimed Kushan heritage. The Kidarite seem to have been rather prosperous, although on a smaller scale than their Kushan predecessors.

These remnants of the Kushan empire were ultimately wiped out in the 5th century by the invasions of the Hephthalites, the Alchon Huns and the Nezak Huns in the northwest, and the rise of the Gupta Empire in the east.

Rulers

- Heraios (c. 1 – 30), first Kushan ruler, generally Kushan ruling period is disputed
- Kujula Kadphises (c. 30 – c. 80)

- Vima Takto (c. 80 – c. 95), alias Soter Megas or "Great Saviour."
- Vima Kadphises (c. 95 – c. 127) the first great Kushan emperor
- Kanishka the Great (127 – c. 140)
- Vāsishka (c. 140 – c. 160)
- Huvishka (c. 160 – c. 190)
- Vasudeva I (c. 190 – to at least 230), the last of the great Kushan emperors
- Kanishka II (c. 230 – 240)
- Vashishka (c. 240 – 250)
- Kanishka III (c. 250 – 275)
- Vasudeva II (c. 275 – 310)
  - Vasudeva III reported son of Vasudeva II, a King, uncertain.
  - Vasudeva IV reported possible child of Vasudeva III, ruling in Kandahar, uncertain.
  - Vasudeva V, or "Vasudeva of Kabul", reported possible child of Vasudeva IV, ruling in Kabul, uncertain.[739]
- Chhu (c. 310? – 325?)
- Shaka I (c. 325 – 345)
- Kipunada (c. 345 – 375)

Notes

- v
- t
- e⁷⁴⁰

Part of a series on the
History of Afghanistan

Timeline

Associated Historical Regions

- Arachosia
- Aria
- Ariana
- Bactria
- Gandhara
- Iran
- Kabulistan
- Khorasan
- Kushanshahr
- Paropamisadae
- Sejestan

- Book
- Category
- Portal

- v
- t
- e⁷⁴¹

Kushan Empire

Figure 198: *Kushan devotee, Mathura*

Part of a series on the
History of Tajikistan

- Early history
- Medieval history
- Early modern history
- Russian vassalage
- Soviet rule
- Since independence

Timeline

Tajikistan portal

- v
- t
- e[742]

References

<templatestyles src="Template:Refbegin/styles.css" />

- Avari, Burjor (2007). *India: The Ancient Past*. London: Routledge. ISBN 978-0-415-35616-9.
- Bopearachchi, Osmund (2003). *De l'Indus à l'Oxus, Archéologie de l'Asie Centrale* (in French). Lattes: Association imago-musée de Lattes. ISBN 2-9516679-2-2.
- Chavannes, Édouard (1906). *Trois Généraux Chinois de la dynastie des Han Orientaux. Pan Tch'ao (32–102 p.C.); – son fils Pan Yong; – Leang K'in (112 p.C.). Chapitre LXXVII du* Heou Han chou*"*. *T'oung pao* 7.
- Faccenna, Domenico (1980). Butkara I (Swāt, Pakistan) 1956–1962, Volume III 1 (in English). Rome: IsMEO (Istituto Italiano Per Il Medio Ed Estremo Oriente).
- Chavannes, Édouard (1907). *Les pays d'occident d'après le* Heou Han chou. *T'oung pao* 8. pp. 149–244.
- Enoki, K.; Koshelenko, G. A.; Haidary, Z. (1 January 1994). "The Yu'eh-chih and their migrations". In Harmatta, János. *History of Civilizations of Central Asia: The Development of Sedentary and Nomadic Civilizations, 700 B. C. to A. D. 250*[743]. UNESCO. pp. 171–191. ISBN 9231028464. Retrieved 29 May 2015.
- Falk, Harry. 1995–1996. *Silk Road Art and Archaeology IV*.
- Falk, Harry. 2001. "The yuga of Sphujiddhvaja and the era of the Kuṣāṇas." *Silk Road Art and Archaeology VII*, pp. 121–136.
- Falk, Harry. 2004. "The Kaniṣka era in Gupta records." Harry Falk. *Silk Road Art and Archaeology X*, pp. 167–176.
- Golden, Peter B. (1992). *An Introduction to the History of the Turkic Peoples*. Harrassowitz Verlag.
- Goyal, S. R. "Ancient Indian Inscriptions" Kusumanjali Book World, Jodhpur (India), 2005.
- Hill, John E. 2004. *The Peoples of the West from the Weilüe* 魏略 *by Yu Huan* 魚豢 *: A Third Century Chinese Account Composed between 239 and 265 CE*. Draft annotated English translation.[744]
- Hill, John E. (2009). *Through the Jade Gate to Rome: A Study of the Silk Routes during the Later Han Dynasty, First to Second Centuries CE*. BookSurge. ISBN 978-1-4392-2134-1.
- Lebedynsky, Iaroslav (2006). *Les Saces*. Paris: Editions Errance. ISBN 2-87772-337-2.
- Loewe, Michael; Shaughnessy, Edward L. (1999). *The Cambridge History of Ancient China: From the Origins of Civilization to 221 BC*[745]. Cambridge University Press. ISBN 0-5214-7030-7. Retrieved 2013-11-01.

- Mallory, J. P. (1989). *In Search of the Indo-Europeans: Language, Archaeology, and Myth*[746]. Thames and Hudson. ISBN 050005052X. Retrieved 29 May 2015.
- Mallory, J. P. (1997). *Encyclopedia of Indo-European Culture*[747]. Taylor & Francis. ISBN 1884964982. Retrieved 29 May 2015.
- Mallory, J. P.; Mair, Victor H. (2000). "The Tarim Mummies: Ancient China and the Mystery of the Earliest Peoples from the West". London: Thames & Hudson. ISBN 0-500-05101-1..
- Pulleyblank, Edwin G. (1966). *Chinese and Indo-Europeans*[748]. University of British Columbia, Department of Asian Studies. Retrieved February 14, 2015.
- Rosenfield, John M. (1993). *The Dynastic Art of the Kushans*. New Delhi: Munshiram Manoharlal. ISBN 81-215-0579-8.
- Sivaramamurti, C. (1976). *Śatarudrīya: Vibhūti of Śiva's Iconography*. Delhi: Abhinav Publications.
- Roux, Jean-Paul, *L'Asie Centrale, Histoire et Civilization* (French), Fayard, 1997, ISBN 978-2-213-59894-9
- "Red Sandstone Railing Pillar." *The British Museum Quarterly*, vol. 30, no. 1/2, 1965, pp. 64–64. www.jstor.org/stable/4422925.
- Masson, V. M. "The Forgotten Kushan Empire: New Discoveries at Zar-Tepe." *Archaeology*, vol. 37, no. 1, 1984, pp. 32–37. www.jstor.org/stable/41728802.
- Hoey, W. "The Word Kozola as Used of Kadphises on Ku̱shān Coins." *Journal of the Royal Asiatic Society of Great Britain and Ireland*, 1902, pp. 428–429. www.jstor.org/stable/25208419.
- West, Barbara A. (January 1, 2009). *Encyclopedia of the Peoples of Asia and Oceania*[749]. Infobase Publishing. ISBN 1438119135. Retrieved 2015-05-29.

Further reading

<templatestyles src="Template:Refbegin/styles.css" />

- Benjamin, Craig (2007). *The Yuezhi: Origin, Migration and the Conquest of Northern Bactria*[750]. ISD. ISBN 250352429X. Retrieved 29 May 2015.
- Dorn'eich, Chris M. (2008). *Chinese sources on the History of the Niusi-Wusi-Asi (oi)-Rishi (ka)-Arsi-Arshi-Ruzhi and their Kueishuang-Kushan Dynasty. Shiji 110/Hanshu 94A: The Xiongnu: Synopsis of Chinese original Text and several Western Translations with Extant Annotations*. Berlin. To read or download go to:[751]
- Foucher, M. A. 1901. "Notes sur la geographie ancienne du Gandhâra (commentaire à un chaptaire de Hiuen-Tsang)." *BEFEO* No. 4, Oct. 1901, pp. 322–369.

- Hargreaves, H. (1910–11): "Excavations at Shāh-jī-kī Dhērī"; *Archaeological Survey of India, 1910–11*, pp. 25–32.
- Iloliev, A. "King of Men: ʿAli ibn Abi Talib in Pamiri Folktales." Journal of Shi'a Islamic Studies, vol. 8 no. 3, 2015, pp. 307–323. Project MUSE, doi:10.1353/isl.2015.0036.
- Harmatta, János, ed., 1994. *History of civilizations of Central Asia, Volume II. The development of sedentary and nomadic civilizations: 700 B.C. to A.D. 250*. Paris, UNESCO Publishing.
- Kennedy, J. "The Later Kushans." *Journal of the Royal Asiatic Society of Great Britain and Ireland*, 1913, pp. 1054–1064. www.jstor.org/stable/25189078.
- Konow, Sten. Editor. 1929. *Kharoshthī Inscriptions with Exception of those of Asoka*. Corpus Inscriptionum Indicarum, Vol. II, Part I. Reprint: Indological Book House, Varanasi, 1969.
- Lerner, Martin (1984). The flame and the lotus: Indian and Southeast Asian art from the Kronos collections[752]. New York: The Metropolitan Museum of Art. ISBN 0-87099-374-7.
- Litvinsky, B. A., ed., 1996. *History of civilizations of Central Asia, Volume III. The crossroads of civilizations: A.D. 250 to 750*. Paris, UNESCO Publishing.
- Liu, Xinru 2001 "Migration and Settlement of the Yuezhi-Kushan: Interaction and Interdependence of Nomadic and Sedentary Societies." *Journal of World History*, Volume 12, No. 2, Fall 2001. University of Hawaii Press, pp. 261–292.[753]
- Rife, J. L. "The Making of Roman India by Grant Parker (review)." American Journal of Philology, vol. 135 no. 4, 2014, pp. 672–675. Project MUSE, doi:10.1353/ajp.2014.0046.
- Sarianidi, Viktor. 1985. *The Golden Hoard of Bactria: From the Tillya-tepe Excavations in Northern Afghanistan*. Harry N. Abrams, Inc. New York.
- Sims-Williams, Nicholas. 1998. "Further notes on the Bactrian inscription of Rabatak, with an Appendix on the names of Kujula Kadphises and Vima Taktu in Chinese." *Proceedings of the Third European Conference of Iranian Studies Part 1: Old and Middle Iranian Studies*. Edited by Nicholas Sims-Williams. Wiesbaden. 1998, pp. 79–93.
- Spooner, D. B. 1908–9. "Excavations at Shāh-jī-kī Dhērī."; *Archaeological Survey of India*, 1908–9, pp. 38–59.
- Watson, Burton. Trans. 1993. *Records of the Grand Historian of China: Han Dynasty II*. Translated from the *Shiji* of Sima Qian. Chapter 123: "The Account of Dayuan", Columbia University Press. Revised Edition. ISBN 0-231-08166-9; ISBN 0-231-08167-7 (pbk.)
- Zürcher, E. (1968). "The Yüeh-chih and Kaniṣka in the Chinese sources."

Papers on the Date of Kaniṣka. Basham, A. L., ed., 1968. Leiden: E. J. Brill. pp. 346–393.

External links

 Wikimedia Commons has media related to *Kushan Empire*.

- Kushan dynasty[754] in Encyclopædia Britannica
- Metropolitan Museum capsule history[755]
- New documents help fix controversial Kushan dating[756] at the Wayback Machine (archived 2005-02-04)
- Coins of the Kushans on wildwinds.com[757]
- Antique Indian Coins[758] at the Library of Congress Web Archives (archived 2013-02-07)
- Brief Guide to Kushan History[759]
- The CoinIndia Online Catalogue of Kushan Coins[760]
- Dedicated resource to study of Kushan Empire[759]

Template:Kushan Empire

Kushano-Sasanian Kingdom

The **Kushano-Sassanids** (also called **Kushanshas** or **Indo-Sassanians**) were a branch of the Sassanid Persians who established their rule in Bactria and in northwestern India (present day Pakistan) during the 3rd and 4th centuries at the expense of the declining Kushans. They captured the provinces of Sogdiana, Bactria and Gandhara from the Kushans in 225 CE. The Sasanians established governors for the Sasanian Empire, who minted their own coinage and took the title of Kushanshas, i.e. "Kings of the Kushans". They are sometimes considered as forming a "sub-kingdom" inside the Sasanian Empire.[761] This administration continued until 360-370 CE, when the Kushano-Sasanians lost their territories to the invading Kidarites Huns. Thereafter the limit of Sasanian territory was near Merv. Later, the Kidarites were in turn displaced by the Hephthalites.[762] The Sasanians were able to re-establish some authority after they destroyed the Hephthalites with the help of the Turks in 565, but their rule collapsed under Arab attacks in the mid 7th century.

The Kushanshas are mainly known through their coins. Their coins were minted at Kabul, Balkh, Herat, and Merv, attesting the extent of their realm.

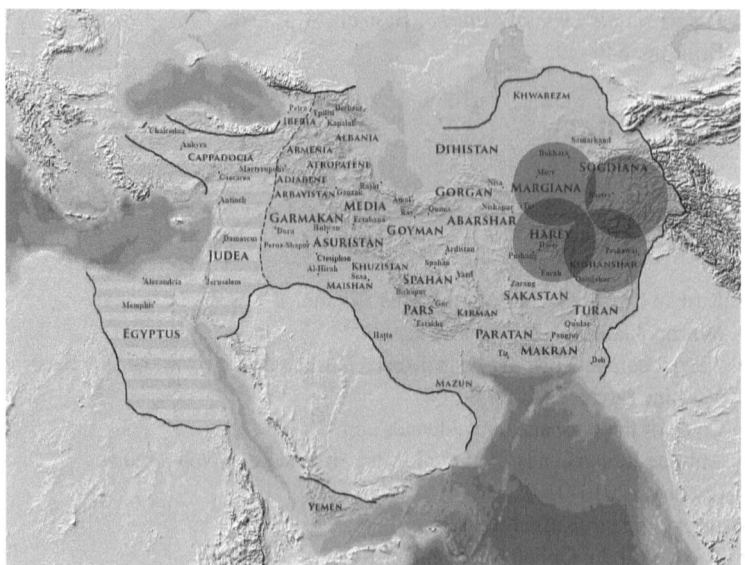

Figure 199: *Sasanian Empire (orange), and the Kushano-Sasanian realm (violet), centered on Kushanshahr, the province at the eastern edge of the Sasanian Empire. The four violet disks represent the four main areas where Kushano-Sasanian coins were minted (Kabul, Balkh, Herat, and Merv), attesting the extent of their realm.*

A rebellion of Hormizd I Kushanshah (277-286 CE), who issued coins with the title *Kushanshahanshah* ("King of kings of the Kushans"), seems to have occurred against contemporary emperor Bahram II (276-293 CE) of the Sasanian Empire, but failed.

History

First Kushano-Sassanid period

The Sassanids, shortly after victory over the Parthians, extended their dominion into Bactria during the reign of Ardashir I around 230 CE, then further to the eastern parts of their empire in western Pakistan during the reign of his son Shapur I (240–270). Thus the Kushans lost their western territory (including Bactria and Gandhara) to the rule of Sassanid nobles named Kushanshahs or "Kings of the Kushans".

The Kushano-Sasanians under Hormizd I Kushanshah seem to have led a rebellion against contemporary emperor Bahram II (276-293 CE) of the Sasanian Empire, but failed.[763] According to the *Panegyrici Latini* (3rd-4th century CE), there was a rebellion of a certain Ormis (Ormisdas) against his

Kushano-Sasanian Kingdom

Figure 200: *Portrait of Kushano-Sasanian ruler Hormizd I Kushanshah (c. 277-286 CE) in Kushan style.*

Figure 201: *Hormizd I Kushanshah on the Naqsh-e Rustam Bahram II panel.*

Figure 202: *Sasanian dignitary drinking wine, on ceiling of Cave 1, at Ajanta Caves, India, end of the 5th century.*[766]

brother Bahram II, and Ormis was supported the people of Saccis (Sakastan).[764] Hormizd I Kushanshah issued coins with the title *Kushanshahanshah* ("King of kings of the Kushans"),[765] probably in defiance of imperial Sasanian rule.

Around 325, Shapur II was directly in charge of the southern part of the territory, while in the north the Kushanshahs maintained their rule until the rise of the Kidarites.

The decline of the Kushans and their defeat by the Kushano-Sassanids led to the rise of the Kidarites and then the Hephthalites who conquered Bactria and Gandhara, thus replacing the Kushano-Sassanids, until the arrival of Islam to Pakistan.

Second Kushano-Sassanid period

The Hephthalites dominated the area until they were defeated in 565 AD by an alliance between the Gokturks and Sassanids, and some Indo-Sassanid authority was re-established. The Kushano-Hephthalites were able to set up rival states in Kapisa, Bamiyan, and Kabul. The 2nd Indo-Sassanid period ended with the collapse of Sassanids to the Rashidun Caliphate in the mid 7th century. Sind remained independent until the Arab invasions of India in the early

Figure 203: *Coin of the last Kushano-Sasanian ruler Bahram Kushanshah (circa 350-365 CE) in Kushan style. Obv: King Varhran I with characteristic head-dress. Rev: Shiva with bull Nandi, in Kushan style.*

8th century. The Kushano-Hephthalites or Turkshahis were replaced by the Shahi in the mid 8th century.

Religious influences

Coins depicting Shiva and the Nandi bull have been discovered, indicating a strong influence of Shaivite Hinduism.[767]

The prophet Mani (210–276 CE), founder of Manichaeism, followed the Sassanids' expansion to the east, which exposed him to the thriving Buddhist culture of Gandhara. He is said to have visited Bamiyan, where several religious painting are attributed to him, and is believed to have lived and taught for some time. He is also related to have sailed to the Indus valley area now in modern-day Pakistan in 240 or 241 CE, and to have converted a Buddhist King, the Turan Shah of India.[768]

On that occasion, various Buddhist influences seem to have permeated Manichaeism: "Buddhist influences were significant in the formation of Mani's religious thought. The transmigration of souls became a Manichaean belief, and the quadripartite structure of the Manichaean community, divided between male and female monks (the 'elect') and lay follower (the 'hearers') who supported them, appears to be based on that of the Buddhist sangha"

Figure 204: *Kushano-Sasanian ruler Ardashir I Kushanshah, circa 230-250 CE. Merv mint.*

Artistic influences

The Indo-Sassanids traded goods such as silverware and textiles depicting the Sassanid emperors engaged in hunting or administering justice. The example of Sassanid art was influential on Kushan art, and this influence remained active for several centuries in the northwest South Asia.

Main Kushano-Sassanid rulers

Based on coinage, a list of the Kushanshah rulers can be established:[769,770]

- Ardashir I Kushanshah (230-?)
- Ardashir II Kushanshah (?-245)
- Peroz I Kushanshah (245-270)
- Hormizd I Kushanshah (270-295), rebelled against Bahram II of Iran.
- Hormizd II Kushanshah (295-300)
- Peroz II Kushanshah (300-325)
- Varahran I Kushanshah (325-350), also named Bahram
- Varahran II Kushanshah (360)
- Peroz III Kushanshah (350-360) in Gandhara.[771]

Coinage

 Wikimedia Commons has media related to *Kushano-Sasanian Kingdom*.

The Kushano-Sassanids created an extensive coinage with legend in Brahmi, Pahlavi or Bactrian, sometimes inspired from Kushan coinage, and sometimes more clearly Sassanid.

The obverse of the coin usually depicts the ruler with elaborate headdress and on the reverse either a Zoroastrian fire altar, or Shiva with the bull Nandi.

Figure 205: *Ardashir I Kushanshah in the name of Kushan ruler Vasudeva I, circa 230-245 CE.*

Figure 206: *Indo-Sassanid coin.*

Figure 207: *A gold Indo-Sassanid coin.*

Figure 208: *Hormizd I Kushanshah with mention of Mazda and Anahita. Merv mint.*

Sources

- Vaissière, Étienne de La (2016). "Kushanshahs i. History". *Encyclopaedia Iranica*[772].
- Kia, Mehrdad (2016). *The Persian Empire: A Historical Encyclopedia [2 volumes]: A Historical Encyclopedia*[773]. ABC-CLIO. ISBN 978-1610693912.

External links
- Coins of the Kushano-Sassanids[774]

Huna people

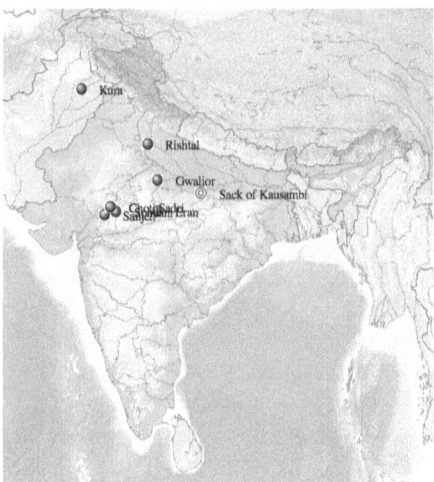

File:India relief location map.jpg

Find spots of inscriptions related to local control by the Alchon Huns (map of India)[775]

Hunas or **Huna** was the name given by the ancient Indians to a group of Central Asian tribes who, via the Khyber Pass, entered India at the end of the 5th or early 6th century. They occupied areas as far as Eran and Kausambi, greatly weakening the Gupta Empire. The Hunas were ultimately defeated by the Indian Gupta Empire and the Indian king Yasodharman.[776]

The Hunas are thought to have included the Xionite and/or Hephthalite, the Kidarites, the Alchon Huns (also known as the Alxon, Alakhana, Walxon etc) and the Nezak Huns. Such names, along with that of the Harahunas (also known as the Halahunas or Haraharas) mentioned in Hindu texts, have sometimes been used for the Hunas in general; while these groups appear to have been a component of the Hunas, such names were not necessarily synonymous.

The relationship, if any, of the Hunas to the Huns, a Central Asian people who invaded Europe during the same period, is also unclear.

In its farthest geographical extent in India, the territories controlled by the Hunas covered the region up to Malwa in central India.

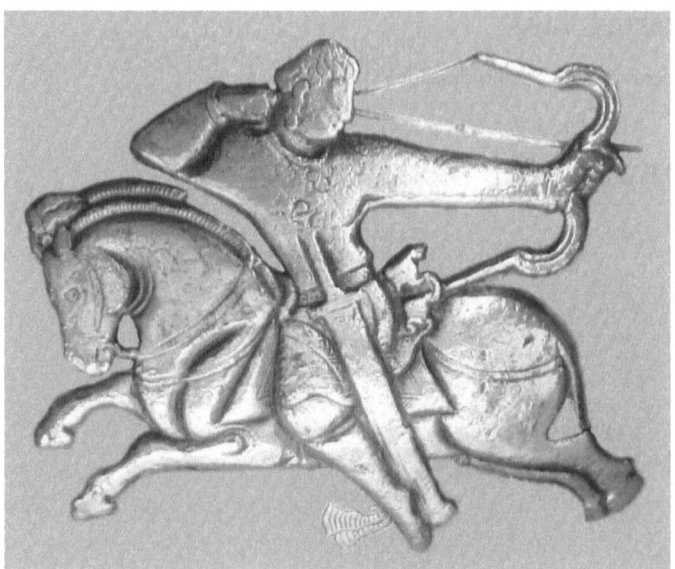

Figure 209: *Hephthalite horseman on British Museum bowl, 460–479 CE.*[780] *According to Procopius of Caesarea, they were of the same stock as European Huns "in fact as well as in name", but sedentary and white-skinned.*

Their repeated invasions and war losses were the main reason for the decline of the Gupta Empire.

History

The Mongolian-Tibetan historian de:Sumpa Yeshe Peljor (writing in the 18th century) lists the Hunas alongside other peoples found in Central Asia since antiquity, including the Yavanas (Greeks), Kambojas, Tukharas, Khasas and Daradas.[777,778]

Chinese sources link the Central Asian tribes comprising the Hunas to both the Xiongnu of north east Asia and the Huns who later invaded and settled in Europe.[779] Similarly, Gerald Larson suggests that the Hunas were a Turkic-Mongolian grouping from Central Asia. The works of Ptolemy (2nd century) are among the first European texts to mention the Huns, followed by the texts by Marcellinus and Priscus. They too suggest that the Huns were an inner Asian people.

The 6th-century Roman historian Procopius of Caesarea (Book I. ch. 3), related the Huns of Europe with the Hephthalites or "White Huns" who subjugated the Sassanids and invaded northwestern India, stating that they were of the same stock, "in fact as well as in name", although he contrasted the Huns with the Hephthalites, in that the Hephthalites were sedentary, white-skinned, and possessed "not ugly" features:[781,782]

> *The Ephthalitae Huns, who are called White Huns [...] The Ephthalitae are of the stock of the Huns in fact as well as in name, however they do not mingle with any of the Huns known to us, for they occupy a land neither adjoining nor even very near to them; but their territory lies immediately to the north of Persia [...] They are not nomads like the other Hunnic peoples, but for a long period have been established in a goodly land... They are the only ones among the Huns who have white bodies and countenances which are not ugly. It is also true that their manner of living is unlike that of their kinsmen, nor do they live a savage life as they do; but they are ruled by one king, and since they possess a lawful constitution, they observe right and justice in their dealings both with one another and with their neighbours, in no degree less than the Romans and the Persians*[783]

The Kidarites, who invaded Bactria in the second half of the 4th century,[784] are generally regarded as the first wave of Hunas to enter South Asia.

Religion

The religious beliefs of the Hunas is unknown, and believed to be a combination of ancestor worship, totemism and animism.

Song Yun and Hui Zheng, who visited the chief of the Hephthalite nomads at his summer residence in Badakshan and later in Gandhara, observed that they had no belief in the Buddhist law and served a large number of divinities."

Gallery

Figure 210: *Victory pillar of Yashodharman at Sondani, Mandsaur claiming victory over the Huns.*

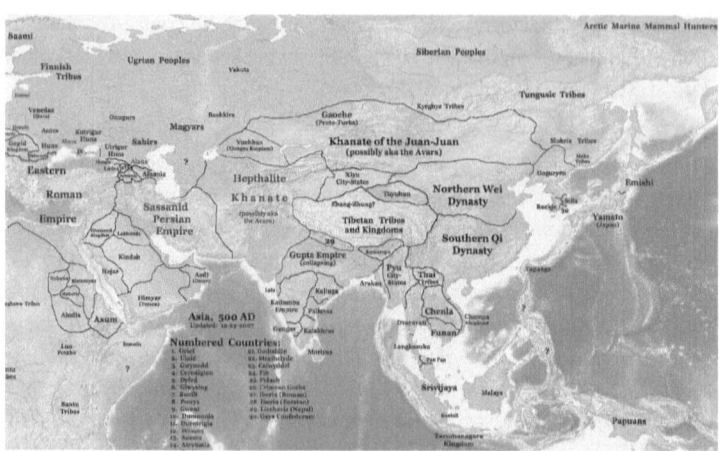

Figure 211: *Asia in 500 AD, showing the Huna domain at its greatest extent.*

Figure 212: *Alchon Huns king Khingila. UNIQ-ref-0-8c889858087207e6-QINU*

Figure 213: *Nezak Huns king Napki Malka.*

Figure 214: *The "Hephthalite bowl", NFP Pakistan, 5th or 6th century CE. British Museum. UNIQ-ref-1-8c889858087207e6-QINU*

References

- Iaroslav Lebedynsky, "Les Nomades", Paris 2007, ISBN 978-2-87772-346-6

Hephthalite Empire

	Hephthalite Empire	
	Nomadic empire	
	440s–670	
	⚒ ⚒ Tamga of the Hephthalites	
	The Hephthalites (green), c. 500.	
Capital	• Kunduz (*Walwalij*, *Drapsaka*, or *Badian*) • Balkh (*Pakhlo*)	
Languages	• Middle Bactrian • Gandhari (Gandhara) • Sogdian (Sogdiana) • Chorasmian • Sanskrit • Turkic	
Religion	• Hinduism[785] • Buddhism • Manichaeism • Zoroastrianism	
Political structure	Nomadic empire	
Historical era	Late Antiquity	
•	Established	440s
•	Disestablished	670

Preceded by	Succeeded by
Kushan Empire	Alchon Huns
Sassanid Empire	Nezak Huns
Gupta Empire	Kabul Shahi
Kangju	Göktürk Empire
Kidarites	Zunbils
	Principality of Chaghaniyan

Today part of	• Afghanistan • China • India • Kazakhstan • Kyrgyzstan • Pakistan • Tajikistan • Turkmenistan • Uzbekistan

The **Hephthalites** (or Ephthalites) were a people of Central Asia who were militarily important circa 450–560. They were based in Bactria and expanded east to the Tarim Basin, west to Sogdia and south through Afghanistan to northern India. They were a tribal confederation and included both nomadic and settled urban communities. They were part of the four major states known collectively as *Xyon* (Xionites) or *Huna*, being preceded by the Kidarites, and succeeded by the Alkhon and lastly the Nezak. All of these peoples have often been linked to the Huns who invaded Eastern Europe during the same period, and/or have been referred to as "Huns", but there is no consensus among scholars about such a connections, if they actually existed.

The *Sveta Huna* who invaded northern India are probably the Hephthalites, but the exact relation is not clear.

The stronghold of the Hephthalites was Tokharistan on the northern slopes of the Hindu Kush, in what is present-day northeastern Afghanistan. By 479, the Hephthalites had conquered Sogdia and driven the Kidarites westwards, and by 493 they had captured parts of present-day Dzungaria and the Tarim Basin in what is now Northwest China. They expanded into northwestern India as well.[786]

The sources for Hepthalite history are poor and historians' opinions differ. There is no king-list and historians are not sure how they arose or what language they spoke.

They seem to have called themselves *Ebodalo* (ηβοδαλο, hence *Hephthal*), often abbreviated *Eb* (ηβ), a name they wrote in the Bactrian script on some of their coins. The origin of the name "Hephthalites" is unknown, possibly from either a Khotanese word **Hitala*, itself borrowed from Uigur, meaning "Strong" or from postulated Middle Persian **haft āl* "the Seven".[787]

Territory

The Hephthalites formed in Bactria around 450, or sometime before. In 442 their tribes were fighting the Persians. Around 451 they pushed southeast to Gandhara. In 456 a Hephthalite embassy arrived in China. By 458 they were strong enough to intervene in Persia.

Figure 215: *Hephthalites chieftain circa 484–560.*[788]

Around 466 they probably took Transoxianan lands from the Kidarites with Persian help but soon took from Persia the area of Balkh and eastern Kushanshahr.

In the second half of the fifth century they controlled the deserts of Turkmenistan as far as the Caspian Sea and possibly Merv.[789]

By 500 they held the whole of Bactria and the Pamirs and parts of Afghanistan.

Probably in the late fifth century they took the western Tarim Basin (Kashgar and Khotan) and in 479 they took the east end (Turfan). In 497–509, they pushed north of Turfan to the Urumchi region. In 509 they took 'Sughd' (the capital of Sogdiana).

Around 565 their empire was destroyed by an alliance of the Göktürks and the Sasanians, but some of them remained as local rulers in the Afghan region for the next 150 years.

Figure 216: *Hephthalite king wearing the crown of Sasanian Emperor Peroz I. Late 5th century CE.*[790]

Figure 217: *Hephthalite coin with Sasanian-style bust imitating Khavadh I, whom the Hephthalites had helped to the Sasanian throne. Late 5th century CE.*

History

5th century: conflicts and alliances with the Sasanians

The most reliable information comes from Persian sources: from 442, Yazdegerd II (435–457) fought 'tribes of the Hephthalites', according to the Armenian Elisee Vardaped. In 453, Yazdegerd moved his court east to deal with the Hephthalites or related groups.

Support of Peroz I, then war

In 458, a Hephthalite king called Khushnavaz helped Sasanian Emperor Peroz I (458–484) gain the Persian throne from his brother.[791] The Hephthalites

Figure 218: *The "Hephthalite bowl", NFP Pakistan, 460–479 CE. British Museum.*[794,795]

may have also helped the Sasanians eliminate another Hunnic tribe, the Kidarites: by 467, Peroz I, with Hephthalite aid, reportedly managed to capture Balaam and put an end to Kidarite rule in Transoxiana once and for all.[792] The Kidarites, weakened, had to take refuge in the area of Gandhara.

Later however, Peroz I fought three wars with his former allies the Hephthalites. In the first two he was captured and ransomed himself.[793] In the third, at the Battle of Herat (484), he was killed, and for the next two years the Hephthalites plundered parts of Persia.

With the Sasanian Empire paying tribute to the Hephthalites, from 474, the Hephthalites themselves adopted the winged, triple-crescent crown of Peroz I to crown their effigy in their own coinage. They thus expressed symbolically that they had become the legitimate rulers of Iran.

Support of Kavadh I

From 484 until the middle of the sixth century, Persia paid tribute to the Hephthalites. In 488, Kavadh I (488–496, 498–531) made himself king of Persia with Hephthalite help. (He overthrew his uncle, the brother of Peroz). In 496–498, he was overthrown by the nobles and clergy, escaped and restored himself with a Hephthalite army. Hephthalite troops helped Kavadh at a siege of Edessa.

Figure 219: *A Hephthalite coin imitating the coinage of Khosrow II. Obverse: Hephthalite signature in Sogdian to the left and Tamgha symbol to the right. Susa mint. 7th century.*[798]

6th century and later

The period c. 498–555 is almost blank in the standard English sources. In 552, the Göktürks took over Mongolia, and by 558 reached the Volga. By 581 or before, the western part separated and became the Western Turkic Khaganate.

Circa 555–567,[796] the Turks and the Persians allied against the Hephthalites and defeated them after an eight-day battle near Qarshi, the Battle of Bukhara, perhaps in 557.[797] The allies then fought each other and c. 571 drew a border along the Oxus. After the battle, the Hephthalites withdrew to Bactria and replaced king Gatfar with Faganish, the ruler of Chaghaniyan. What happened in the Tarim Basin is not clear.

Invasion of the Sasanid Empire (7th century)

Circa 600, the Hephthalites were raiding the Sasanian Empire as far as Spahan in central Iran. The Hephthalites issued numerous coins imitating the coinage of Khosrow II, adding on the obverse a Hephthalite signature in Sogdian and Tamgha symbol. In ca. 606/607, Khosrow recalled Smbat IV Bagratuni from Persian Armenia and sent him to Iran to repel the Hephthalites. Smbat, with the aid of a Persian prince named Datoyean, repelled the Hephthalites from Persia, and plundered their domains in eastern Khorasan, where Smbat is said to have killed their king in single combat. Khosrow then gave Smbat the honorific title *Khosrow Shun* ("the Joy or Satisfaction of Khosrow"), while his son Varaztirots II Bagratuni received the honorific name *Javitean Khosrow* ("Eternal Khosrow").[799]

Figure 220: *Coin of the Hephthalites circa 350 CE, possibly from Bactria, imitating a coin of Shapur I.*

Small Hephthalite states remained, paying tribute either to the Turks or the Persians. They are reported in the Zarafshan valley, Chaghaniyan, Khuttal, Termez, Balkh, Badghis, Herat and Kabul.[800] Circa 651, during the Arab conquest, the ruler of Badghis was involved in the fall of the last Sassanian Shah Yazdegerd III. Circa 705, the Hephthalite rulers of Badghis and Chaghaniyan surrendered to the Arabs under Qutaiba ibn Muslim.

Ethnonyms

The name Hephthalites originated with Ancient Greek sources, which also referred to them as *Ephthalite*, *Abdel* or *Avdel*.

To the Armenians, the Hephthalites were *Haital*, to the Persians and Arabs, they were *Haytal* or *Hayatila* (هياطلة), while their Bactrian name was *Ebodalo* (ηβοδαλο).

In Chinese chronicles, the Hephthalites are usually called *Ye-ta-i-li-to* (or *Yediyiliduo*), or the more usual modern and abbreviated form *Yada* (嚈噠 *Yàdā*). The latter name has been given various Latinised renderings, including *Yeda*, *Ye-ta*, *Ye-Tha*; *Ye-dā* and *Yanda*. The corresponding Cantonese and Korean names *Yipdaat* and *Yeoptal* (Korean: 엽달), which preserve aspects of the Middle Chinese pronunciation (roughly *yep-daht*, [ʔjɛpdɑt]) better than the modern Mandarin pronunciation, are more consistent with the Greek *Hephthalite*. Some Chinese chroniclers suggest that the root *Hephtha-* (as in *Ye-ta-i-li-to* or *Yada*) was technically a title equivalent to "emperor", while *Hua* was the name of the dominant tribe.[801]

Figure 221: *Hephthalites chieftain late 5th century.*[803]

In Ancient India, names such as Hephthalite were unknown. The Hephthalites were apparently part of, or offshoots of, people known in India as *Hunas* or *Turushkas*,[802] although these names may have referred to broader groups or neighbouring peoples.

Ethnicity

There are several theories regarding the origins of the White Huns, with the Iranian[804,805,806] and Turkic[807,808] theories being the most prominent.

According to most specialist scholars, the spoken language of the Hephthalites was an Eastern Iranian language, but different from the Bactrian language written in the Greek alphabet that was used as their "official language" and minted on coins, as was done under the preceding Kushan Empire.[809,810,811]

According to Xavier Tremblay, one of the Hephthalite rulers was named "Khingila", which has the same root as the Sogdian word *xnγr* and the Wakhi word *xiŋgār*, meaning "sword". The name Mihirakula is thought to be derived from *mithra-kula* which is Iranian for "the Sun family", with *kula* having the same root as Pashto *kul*, "family". Toramāna, Mihirakula's father, is also considered to have an Iranian origin. In Sanskrit, *mihira-kula* would mean the *kul* "family" of *mihira* "Sun", although *mihira* is not purely Sanskrit but is a

Figure 222: *Hephthalite king wearing the crown of Sasanian Emperor Peroz I. Late 5th century CE.*

borrowing from Middle Iranian *mihr*.[812] Janos Harmatta gives the translation "Mithra's Begotten" and also supports the Iranian theory.[813]

For many years, however, scholars suggested that they were of Turkic stock. Some have claimed that some groups amongst the Hephthalites were Turkic-speakers. Today the Hephthalites are generally held to have been an Eastern Iranian people speaking an East Iranian language. The Hephthalites enscribed their coins in the Bactrian (Iranian) script, held Iranian titles, the names of Hephthalite rulers given in Ferdowsi's Shahnameh are Iranian, and gem inscriptions and other evidence shows that the official language of the Hephthalite elite was East Iranian. In 1959, Kazuo Enoki proposed that the Hephthalites were probably Indo-European (East) Iranians as some sources indicated that they were originally from Bactria, which is known to have been inhabited by Indo-Iranian people in antiquity. Richard Frye is cautiously accepting of Enoki's hypothesis, while at the same time stressing that the Hephthalites "were probably a mixed horde".[814] More recently Xavier Tremblay's detailed examination of surviving Hephthalite personal names has indicated that Enoki's hypothesis that they were East Iranian may well be correct, but the matter remains unresolved in academic circles.

According to the *Encyclopaedia Iranica* and *Encyclopaedia of Islam*, the Hephthalites possibly originated in what is today Afghanistan.[815,816] They appar-

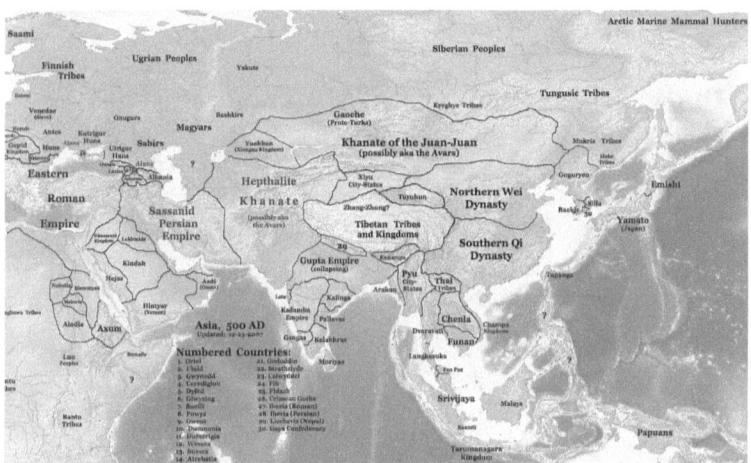

Figure 223: *Asia in 500, showing the Hephthalite Khanate at its greatest extent.*

ently had no direct connection with the European Huns, but may have been causally related with their movement. The tribes in question deliberately called themselves "Huns" in order to frighten their enemies.[817]

Some White Huns may have been a prominent tribe or clan of the Chionites. According to Richard Nelson Frye:

> *Just as later nomadic empires were confederations of many peoples, we may tentatively propose that the ruling groups of these invaders were, or at least included, Turkic-speaking tribesmen from the east and north. Although most probably the bulk of the people in the confederation of Chionites and then Hephhtalites spoke an Iranian language... this was the last time in the history of Central Asia that Iranian-speaking nomads played any role; hereafter all nomads would speak Turkic languages.*[818]

The 6th-century Byzantine historian Procopius of Caesarea (Book I. ch. 3), related them to the Huns in Europe:

> *The Ephtalitae Huns, who are called White Huns [...] The Ephtalitae are of the stock of the Huns in fact as well as in name, however they do not mingle with any of the Huns known to us, for they occupy a land neither adjoining nor even very near to them; but their territory lies immediately to the north of Persia [...] They are not nomads like the other Hunnic peoples, but for a long period have been established in a goodly land... They are the only ones among the Huns who have white bodies and countenances which are not ugly. It is also true that their manner of living is unlike that of their kinsmen, nor do they live a savage life as they do; but they*

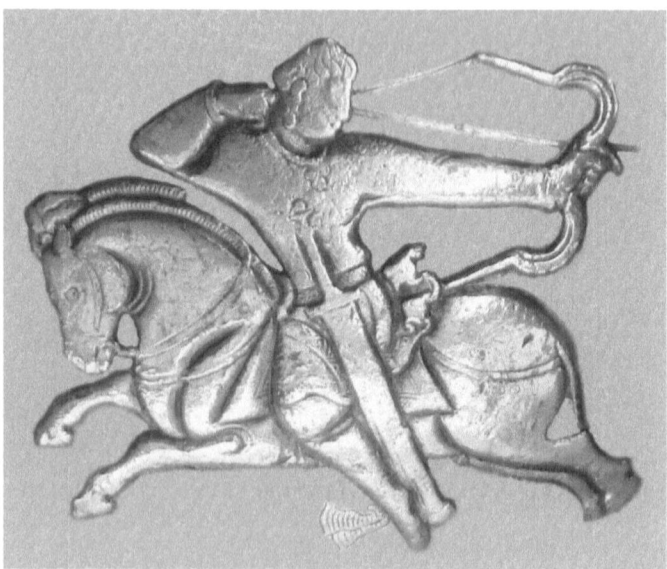

Figure 224: *Hephthalite horseman on British Museum bowl, 460–479 CE.*

are ruled by one king, and since they possess a lawful constitution, they observe right and justice in their dealings both with one another and with their neighbours, in no degree less than the Romans and the Persians[819]

As an illustration of how little we know of the Hephthalites, Kurbanov[820] surveyed the literature and found these opinions: They were named after a king Eftalan or Hephtal. They lived in the Eftali valley (location not given). They called themselves War or Jabula or Alkhon. They were a political rather than ethnic unit. They, the Xionites and Kidarites were the same people or three different peoples. They were the ruling class of the Xionites. They were not Xionites. They were not the White Huns. They were natives of Bactria, or the Pamirs, or the Kundu Kush. They began as the Hua who were subjects of the Rouran in the Turfan area. They were a branch of the Yuezhi in the Altai area who merged with the Dinglings, defeated the Yueban and moved south. They arose near the Aral Sea from a fusion of Massagetae and Alans and moved southeast under the name of Xionites. They were partly Tibetan or Mongol or Tokharian or Huns who returned east after the fall of Attila. Kurbanov gives a few other theories and makes no attempt to reconcile them.

Origins

Ancient Chinese chroniclers, as well as Procopius, wrote various theories about the origins of the people:

- They were descendants of the Yuezhi or Tocharian tribes who remained behind after the rest of the people fled the Xiongnu;
- They were descendants of the Kangju;
- They were a branch of the Tiele; or
- They were a branch of the Uar.

Older Chinese sources (c. 125) refer to them as *Hua* (滑 *Huá*) or *Hudun*, and describe the Hephthalites as a tribe living beyond the Great Wall, in Dzungaria.[821] Chinese chronicles state that they were originally a tribe of the Yuezhi, living to the north of the Great Wall, and subject to the Rouran (*Jwen-Jwen*), as were some Turkic peoples at the time. Their original name was **Hoa** or **Hoa-tun**; subsequently they named themselves **Ye-tha-i-li-to** (厌带夷栗陁 , or more briefly Ye-tha 嚈),[822] after their royal family, which descended from one of the five Yuezhi families which also included the Kushan.

The Hephthalite was a vassal state to the Rouran Khaganate until the beginning of the 5th century.[823] Between Hephthalites and Rourans were also close contacts, although they had different languages and cultures, and Hephthalites borrowed much of their political organization from Rourans.[824] In particular, the title "Khan", which according to McGovern was original to the Rourans, was borrowed by the Hephthalite rulers. The reason for the migration of the Hephthalites southeast was to avoid a pressure of the Rourans. Further, the Hephthalites defeated the Yuezhi in Bactria and their leader Kidara led the Yuezhi to the south.

Religion and culture

They were said to practice Polyandry and Artificial cranial deformation. Chinese sources said they worshiped 'foreign gods', 'demons', the 'heaven god' or the 'fire god'. The Gokturks told the Byzantines that they had walled cities. Some Chinese sources said that they had no cities and lived in tents. Litvinsky tries to resolve this by saying that they were nomads who moved into the cities they had conquered. There were some government officials but central control was weak and local dynasties paid tribute.[825]

According to Song Yun, the Chinese Buddhist monk who visited the Hephthalite territory in 540 and "provides accurate accounts of the people, their clothing, the empresses and court procedures and traditions of the people and he states the Hephthalites did not recognize the Buddhist religion and they preached pseudo gods, and killed animals for their meat." It is reported that

Figure 225: *Hephthalite successor kingdoms in 600.*

some Hephthalites often destroyed Buddhist monasteries but these were rebuilt by others. According to Xuanzang, the third Chinese pilgrim who visited the same areas as Song Yun about 100 years later, the capital of Chaghaniyan had five monasteries.

According to historian André Wink, "...in the Hephthalite dominion Buddhism was predominant but there was also a religious sediment of Zoroastrianism and Manichaeism."[826] Balkh had some 100 Buddhist monasteries and 30,000 monks. Outside the town was a large Buddhist monastery, later known as Naubahar.

White Huns in Southern Central Asia

It is not clear whether the people called **Sveta Huna** (*White Huns*) in Sanskrit were the Hephthalites or a related people, the Xionites. In the northwest of the Indian subcontinent, the Hephthalites were not distinguished from their immediate Chionite predecessors; both are known as *Huna* (Sanskrit: Sveta-Hūna, White Huns). In Ancient India, names such as Hephthalite were unknown. The Hephthalites were apparently part of, or offshoots of, people known in India as *Hunas* or *Turushkas*.

Historians such as Beckwith, referring to Étienne de la Vaissière, say that the Hephthalites were not necessarily one and the same as the White Huns (*Sveta*

Huna). According to de la Vaissiere, the Hephthalites are not directly identified in classical sources alongside that of the White Huns.

The *Huna* had already established themselves in Afghanistan and the modern province of Khyber Pakhtunkhwa of Pakistan by the first half of the 5th century, and the Gupta emperor Skandagupta had repelled a *Hūna* invasion in 455 before the Hephthalite clan came along. These attacks on the Guptas were therefore probably made by the predecessors of the Hephthalites, the Kidarites.

India was invaded during the 5th century by a people known in the Indian Subcontinent as the *Hunas* – including the Alchon Huns and possibly an alliance broader than the Hephthalites and/or Xionites. The *Hunas* were initially defeated by Emperor Skandagupta of the Gupta Empire.[827] By the end of the 5th century, however, the *Hunas* had overrun the part of the Gupta Empire that was to their southeast and had conquered Central and North India. Gupta Emperor Bhanugupta defeated the Hunas under Toramana in 510.[828,829] The *Hunas* were driven out of India by the kings Yasodharman and Narasimhagupta, during the early 6th century.[830,831]

The Hephthalites had their capital at *Badian*, modern Kunduz, but the emperor lived in the capital city for just three winter months, and for the rest of the year, the government seat would move from one locality to another like a camp. The Hephthalites continued the pressure on ancient India's northwest frontier and broke east by the end of the 5th century, hastening the disintegration of the Gupta Empire. They made their capital at the city of *Sakala*, modern Sialkot in Pakistan, under their Emperor Mihirakula. But later the Huns were defeated and driven out of India by the Indian kings Yasodharman and Narasimhagupta in the 6th century.

Possible descendants

A number of groups in Afghanistan and India may be partly descended from the Hephthalites.[832]

- Karluks: The 'Karluks' or Qarlughids reported from near Ghazni in the thirteenth century may have arisen from the Hephthalites. Others say they were Khalachs, the names being similar in Arabic.
- Khalachs: The Khalachs or Khalaj people are first mentioned in the 7th–9th centuries in the area of Kabul and Ghazni. They spoke Turkic, possibly arose from the Hephthalites and later probably merged into the Ghilzai Pashtuns. Their descendents may have founded the Khalji dynasty (1290) and the Lodi dynasty (1451) of the Delhi Sultanate.

- Abdal is a name associated with the Hephthalites. It is an alternate name for the Äynu people of the Tarim Basin and appears as a sub-tribe of the Chowdur Turkmen, Kazakhs and Volga Bulgars.
- Duranni: The Durrani of Afghanistan were called Abdali before 1747.
- Rajputs: The Rajputs may have begun as assimilation of Hephthalites in Indian society.

The Pashtuns began as a union of largely East-Iranian tribes which became the initial ethnic stratum of the Pashtun ethnogenesis, dates from the middle of the first millennium CE and is connected with the dissolution of the Epthalite (White Huns) confederacy. ... Of the contribution of the Epthalites (White Huns) to the ethnogenesis of the Pashtuns we find evidence in the ethnonym of the largest of the Pashtun tribe unions, the Abdali (Durrani after 1747) associated with the ethnic name of the Epthalites — Abdal. The Siah-posh, the Kafirs (Nuristanis) of the Hindu Kush, called all Pashtuns by a general name of Abdal still at the beginning of the 19th century.[833]

Sources

<templatestyles src="Template:Refbegin/styles.css" />

- B.A. Litvinsky, The Hephthalite Empire, 1996, in History of Civilizations in Central Asia, iii, p135-183
- Kurbanov, Aydogdy (2010). "The Hephthalites: Archaeological and Historical Analysis"[834] (PDF). Retrieved 11 January 2013.
- Grignaschi, M. (1980). "La Chute De L'Empire Hephthalite Dans Les Sources Byzantines et Perses et Le Probleme Des Avar". *Acta Antiqua Academiae Scientiarum Hungaricae, Tomus XXVIII*. Budapest: Akademiai Kiado.
- Haussig, Hans Wilhelm (1983). *Die Geschichte Zentralasiens und der Seidenstraße in vorislamischer Zeit*. Darmstadt: Wissenschaftliche Buchgesellschaft. ISBN 3-534-07869-1.
- Theophylaktos Simokates. P. Schreiner, ed. *Geschichte*.
- West, Barbara A. (January 1, 2009). *Encyclopedia of the Peoples of Asia and Oceania*[835]. Infobase Publishing. ISBN 1438119135. Retrieved January 18, 2015.
- Zeimal, E. V. (1996). "The Kidarite kingdom in Central Asia". *History of Civilizations of Central Asia, Volume III: The Crossroads of Civilizations: A.D. 250 to 750*.[836] Paris: UNESCO. pp. 119–135. ISBN 92-3-103211-9.

External links

 Wikimedia Commons has media related to *Hephthalites*.

- "The Ethnonym Apar in the Turkish Inscriptions of the VIII. Century and Armenian Manuscripts" Dr. Mehmet Tezcan.[837]
- The Anthropology of Yanda (Chinese)[838] pdf
- The Silkroad Foundation[839]
- Columbia Encyclopedia: Hephthalites[840]
- Hephthalite coins[841]
- Hephthalite History and Coins of the Kashmir Smast Kingdom- Waleed Ziad[842] at the Wayback Machine (archived 27 October 2009)
- The Hephthalites of Central Asia – by Richard Heli[843] (long article with a timeline)
- The Hephthalites[844] at the Wayback Machine (archived 9 February 2005) Article archived from the University of Washington's Silk Road exhibition – has a slightly adapted form of the Richard Heli timeline.
- (pdf)[837] The Ethnonym Apar in the Turkish Inscriptions of the VIII. Century and Armenian Manuscripts – Mehmet Tezcan
- iranicaonline hephthalites[845]

Rai dynasty

Rai dynasty	
راء	
524–632	
Capital	Aror
Religion	Buddhism[846] Hinduism
Government	Absolute Monarchy
Emperor	Rai Diwa
	Rai Sahiras
	Rai Sahasi I
	Rai Sahasi II
Historical era	Classical India
• Established	524
• Disestablished	632
Area	
• c. 600	1,553,993 km² (600,000 sq mi)
Succeeded by	
Brahmin dynasty	

Part of a series on the
History of Sindh

History of Pakistan

The **Rai Dynasty** (c. 524–632 CE) was a dynasty that ruled on the Indian subcontinent during the Classical period. Originating in the region of Sindh, in modern Pakistan,[846] the dynasty at its height of power ruled much of the Northwestern regions of the Indian subcontinent. The influence of the Rais extended from Kashmir in the east, Makran and Debal port (modern Karachi) in the west, Surat port in the south, and the Kandahar, Sulaiman, Ferdan and Kikanan hills in the north.[846] It ruled an area of over 600,000 square miles (1,553,993 km²), and the dynasty reigned a period of 143 years.[846]

The Battle of Rasil in 644 played a crucial role in their decline. The battle resulted in the Makran coast being annexed by Rashidun Caliphate.[847,848] The book *Chach Nama* chronicles the final demise of the Rai dynasty and the ascent of the Hindu Chach of Alor to the throne.

The emperors of this dynasty were great patrons of Buddhism. They established a formidable temple of Shiva in present-day Sukkur, Pakistan, close to their capital in Aror. This is consistent with the historical accounts from the times of Ashoka and Harsha, as numerous monarchs from the Indian Subcontinent never sponsored a state religion and usually patronised all Dharmic religions.

Origins

B. D. Mirchandani says, "Our knowledge of the Rai dynasty, which is not a great deal, is derived entirely from three Muslim chronicles of Sind."[849] The history of the Rai and Brahman dynasties is almost entirely dependent on the Muslim chronicles, especially the *Chachnama* and *Shahnama*.

Their rise to power in the time of shifting political scenes with the wane of the Sassanid influence in the wake of the Hepthalite (White Hun/Huna) invasions, and with the rulers issuing silver coins bearing their likeness by the 7th century.

The *Chachnama* describes that the Rai dynasty was an important Brahmin dynasty of that time and the extant of Rai Sahiras' domain:

> *The limits of his dominions extended on the east to the boundary of Kashmir, on the west to Makran, on the south to the coast of the sea and Debal, and on the north to the mountains of Kurdan and Kíkánán. He had appointed four Governors (Maliks) in his kingdom: one at Brahminabad; and the fort of Nerun and Debal, Luhánah, Lákhah. Sammah and the river were left under his management. Another at the town of Siwis-tán; and Ladhia, Chingán, the skirts of the hills of Rojhán up to the boundary of Makrán, were given into his charge. The third at the fort of Iskandah; and Báhíah, Stwárah, Jajhór, and the supplementary territories of Dhanód were given in his possession; and the fourth at the town of Multan; and the towns of Sikkah, Karnd, Ishthar and Kíh up to the boundary of Kashmir were en¬trusted to him. The king himself had his headquarters in the city of Aror, retaining Kurdán, Kíkánán, and Bar-hamas directly under his sway.*[850]

Demise

According to the *Chachnama*, the last Rai emperor, Rai Sahasi II, died through illness without any issue. By that time Chach was in complete control of the affairs of the kingdom. However, when Rai Sahasi II was near to death, Suhanadi explained to Chach that the kingdom would pass to other relatives of the dying king in absence of any direct heir to the kingdom. Consequently, they kept secret the news of the king's death until claimants to the throne were killed through conspiracy. Following this, Chach declared himself ruler and later married Suhandi. This ended the Rai Dynasty and began the dynasty of another Brahmin dynasties called Chach dynasty.[851]

Six months after death of Rai Sahasi his brother, Rana Maharath of Chittor, challenged Chach in combat, claiming to be rightful ruler of the Rai Dynasty. Chachnama states that Maharath was killed as the two engaged in a duel, in which it was forbidden to mount a horse or any other animal. During the duel Chach mounted a horse in order to kill his rival.[852]

Rulers

Andre Wink reports on the possibility of the corruption of the Sanskrit names and renders them as related in parenthesis in the following chronology of the Rai rulers of Sindh:

- Rai Diwa ji (Devaditya), a powerful chief who forged alliances and extended his rule east of Makran and west of Kashmir, south to the port of Karachi and north to KandaharWikipedia:Citation needed
- Rai Sahiras (Shri Harsha)
- Rai Sahasi (Sinhasena)
- Rai Sahiras II, died battling the King of Nimroz
- Rai Sahasi II, the last of the line

Notes

Preceded by **Ror Dynasty**	**Rai Dynasty** 489–690 AD	Succeeded by **Islamic Invasion / Chach of Alor**

Gandhara

Gandhāra c. 1500 BC–535 AD	
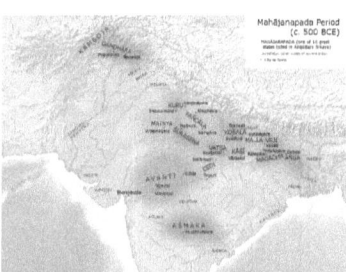 Gandhāra and other Mahajanapadas in the Post Vedic period.	
 Approximate boundaries of the Gandhara Mahajanapada, in present-day northwest Pakistan and northeast Afghanistan.	
Capital	Puṣkalavati (modern Charsadda) and Taxila, and later Peshawar (Puruṣapura)
Government	Monarchy
King	
• c. 750 BCE	Nagnajit
• c. 518 BCE	Pushkarasakti
Historical era	Ancient Era
• Established	c. 1500 BC
• Disestablished	535 AD
Succeeded by	
Achaemenid Empire	

Today part of	Afghanistan Pakistan

Part of a series on the
History of Pakistan

Timeline

- Category
- Portal

- v
- t
- e[853]

Gandhāra was an ancient kingdom situated along the Kabul and Swat rivers of Afghanistan and Pakistan. It was one of sixteen Mahajanapada of ancient India. During the Achaemenid period and Hellenistic period, its capital city was Charsadda,[854] but later the capital city was moved to Peshawar[855] by the Kushan emperor Kanishka the Great in about AD 127.

Gandhara existed since the time of the Rigveda (c. 1500–1200 BC), as well as the Zoroastrian Avesta, which mentions it as *Vaēkərəta*, the sixth most beautiful place on earth, created by Ahura Mazda. Gandhara was conquered by the Achaemenid Empire in the 6th century BC. Conquered by Alexander the Great in 327 BC, it subsequently became part of the Maurya Empire and then the Indo-Greek Kingdom. The region was a major center for Greco-Buddhism under the Indo-Greeks and Gandharan Buddhism under later dynasties. It was also a central location for the spread of Buddhism to Central Asia and East Asia.[856] It was also a center of Bactrian Zoroastrianism and Hinduism.[857] Famed for its local tradition of Gandhara (Greco-Buddhist) Art, Gandhara attained its height from the 1st century to the 5th century under the Kushan Empire. Gandhara "flourished at the crossroads of Asia," connecting trade routes and absorbing cultural influences from diverse civilizations; Buddhism thrived until 8th or 9th centuries, when Islam first began to gain sway in the region.[858] Pockets of Buddhism persisted in Pakistan's Swat valley until the 11th century.

The Persian term *Shahi* is used by historian Al-Biruni[859] to refer to the ruling dynasty[860] that took over from the *Kabul Shahi*[861] and ruled the region during the period prior to Muslim conquests of the 10th and 11th centuries. After it was conquered by Mahmud of Ghazni in 1001 AD, the name Gandhara disappeared. During the Muslim period, the area was administered from Lahore or from Kabul. During Mughal times, it was an independent district which included the Kabul province.

Etymology

Gandhara was known in Sanskrit as गन्धार *gandhāra*, in Avestan as *Vaēkərəta*, in Old Persian as *Para-upari-sena*, in Chinese as 犍陀罗 , and in Greek as Παροπαμισάδαι *Paropamisadae*.

The Gandhari people are a tribe mentioned in the Rigveda, the Atharvaveda, and later Vedic texts.[862] They are recorded in the Avestan-language of Zoroastrianism under the name *Vaēkərəta*. The name *Gāndhāra* occurs later in the classical Sanskrit of the epics. One proposed origin of the name is from the Sanskrit word *gandha*, meaning "perfume" and "referring to the spices and aromatic herbs which they [the inhabitants] traded and with which they anointed themselves.".[863,864]

A Persian form of the name, *Gandara*, appearing in the Behistun inscription of Emperor Darius I,[865] is also mentioned by Herodotus[866] in the context of the story of the Greek explorer Scylax of Caryanda, who sailed down the Indus River starting at the city of *Caspatyrus* in *Gandara* (Κασπάτυρος, πόλις Γανδαρική). Herodotus records that those Iranic tribes, which were adjacent to the city of Caspatyrus and the district of Pactyïce, had customs similar to the Bactrians, and are the most warlike amongst them. These are also the people who obtain gold from the ant-hills of the adjoining desert. On the identity of Caspatyrus, there have been two opinions, one equating it with Kabul, the other with the name of Kashmir (*Kasyapa pur*, condensed to *Kaspapur* as found in Hecataeus).[867]

Figure 226: *Female spouted figure, terracotta, Charsadda, Gandhara, 3rd to 1st century BC Victoria and Albert Museum*

Kandahar is sometimes etymologically associated with Gandhara. However, Kandahar was not part of the main territory of Gandhara.

Geography

The boundaries of Gandhara varied throughout history. Sometimes the *Peshawar* Valley and *Taxila* were collectively referred to as Gandhara; sometimes the Swat Valley (Sanskrit: *Suvāstu*) was also included. The heart of Gandhara, however, was always the Peshawar Valley. The kingdom was ruled from capitals at *Kapisa* (*Bagram*),[868] *Pushkalavati* (*Charsadda*), *Taxila*, *Puruṣapura* (*Peshawar*) and in its final days from *Udabhandapura* (*Hund*) on the River Indus.

Figure 227: *Mother Goddess (fertility divinity), possibly derived from the Indus Valley Civilization, terracotta, Sar Dheri, Gandhara, 1st century BC, Victoria and Albert Museum*

History

Stone age

Evidence of the Stone Age human inhabitants of Gandhara, including stone tools and burnt bones, was discovered at Sanghao near Mardan in area caves. The artifacts are approximately 15,000 years old. More recent excavations point to 30,000 years before the present.

Vedic Gandhara

Gandhara was an ancient kingdom of the Peshawar Valley, extending between the Swat valley and Potohar plateau regions of Pakistan as well as the Jalalabad district of northeastern Afghanistan. In an archaeological context, the Vedic period in Gandhara corresponds to the Gandhara grave culture.

The name of the Gandhāris is attested in the Rigveda (RV 1.126.7) and in ancient inscriptions dating back to Achaemenid Persia. The Behistun inscription listing the 23 territories of King Darius I (519 BC) includes Gandāra along with Bactria and Sattagydia (Θataguš). In the book *Histories* by Herodotus,

Gandhara is named as a source of tax collections for King Darius. The Gandhāris, along with the Balhika (Bactrians), Mūjavants, Angas, and the Magadhas, are also mentioned in the Atharvaveda (AV 5.22.14), as distant people. Gandharas are included in the Uttarapatha division of Puranic and Buddhistic traditions. The Aitareya Brahmana refers to King Nagnajit of Gandhara who was a contemporary of Janaka, king of Videha.[869]

Mahajanapada

Gandhara was one of sixteen Mahajanapada of ancient India. The primary cities of Gandhara were Puruṣapura (Peshawar), Takṣaśilā (Taxila), and Pushkalavati (Charsadda). The latter remained the capital of Gandhara down to the 2nd century AD, when the capital was moved to Peshawar. An important Buddhist shrine helped to make the city a centre of pilgrimage until the 7th century. Pushkalavati, in the Peshawar Valley, is situated at the confluence of the Swat and Kabul rivers, where three different branches of the River Kabul meet. That specific place is still called Prang (from Prayāga) and considered sacred; local people still bring their dead there for burial. Similar geographical characteristics are found at site of Prang in Kashmir and at the confluence of the Ganges and Yamuna, where the sacred city of Prayag is situated, west of Benares. There are some legendsWikipedia:Citation needed in which the two rivers are said to be joined here by the underground Sarasvati River, forming a triveṇī, a confluence of three rivers. However, Rigvedic texts, and modern research, suggest that the path of the Sarasvati River was very different. It ended in the ocean at Kachchh in modern Gujrat and not at Prayag. The Gandharan city of Taxila was an important Buddhist and Hindu centre of learning from the 5th century BC[870] to the 2nd century.

Gandhara is mentioned in the Hindu epics, the Mahabharata and the Ramayana, as a western kingdom. In Treta Yuga, before Lord Rama, during the reigns of Muchukunda, the kingdom of Gandhara was founded by the Druhyu prince Gandhara who was the son of King Angara of Druhyu Dynasty. During Ramayana time King Nagnajit(1) who was a contemporary of Lord Rama was defeated and killed by Rama's brother Bharata and Bharata's 1st son Taksha established Takshasila (Taxila) in Gandhara Kingdom on the banks of river Sindhu and Pushkara established Pushkaravati or Purushapura (Pushkar) in Gandharva tribe on the banks of river Saraswati after defeating and killing its king Sailusha who was the father-in-law of Vibhishana. In Dvapara Yuga, Gandhara prince Shakuni was the root of all the conspiracies of Duryodhana against the Pandavas, which finally resulted in the Kurukshetra War. Shakuni's sister was the wife of the Kuru king Dhritarashtra and was known as Gandhari. Gandhara was in modern Pakistan. Puskalavati, *Takshasila* (Taxila) and *Purushapura* (Peshawar) were cities in this Gandhara kingdom. Takshasila was founded by Raghava Rama's brother Bharata. Bharata's descendants ruled this kingdom afterwards. During epic period it was ruled by Shakuni's father *Suvala*, Shakuni and Shakuni's son. Arjuna defeated Shakuni's son during his post-war military campaign for Yudhishthira's Aswamedha Yagna.

Achaemenid Gandhara

The main Vedic tribes remaining in the Indus Valley by 550 BC were the *Kamboja, Sindhu, Taksas* of Gandhara, the *Madras* and *Kathas* of the River Chenab, *Mallas* of the River Ravi and *Tugras* of the River Sutlej. These several tribes and principalities fought against one another to such an extent that the Indus Valley no longer had one powerful Vedic tribal kingdom to defend against outsiders and to wield the warring tribes into one organized kingdom. The area was wealthy and fertile, yet infighting led misery and despair. King Pushkarasakti of Gandhara was engaged in power struggles against his local rivals and as such the Khyber Pass remained poorly defended. King Darius I of the Achaemenid Empire took advantage of the opportunity and planned for an invasion. The Indus Valley was fabled in Persia for its gold and fertile soil and conquering it had been a major objective of his predecessor Cyrus The Great.[871] In 542 BC, Cyrus had led his army and conquered the Makran coast in southern Balochistan. However, he is known to have campaigned beyond Makran (in the regions of Kalat, Khuzdar, Panjgur) and lost most of his army in the *Gedrosian Desert* (speculated today as the Kharan Desert).

In 518 BC, Darius led his army through the Khyber Pass and southwards in stages, eventually reaching the Arabian Sea coast in Sindh by 516 BC. Under Persian rule, a system of centralized administration, with a bureaucratic system, was introduced into the Indus Valley for the first time. Provinces or "satrapy" were established with provincial capitals:

Gandhara satrapy, established 518 BC with its capital at Pushkalavati (Charsadda).[872] Gandhara Satrapy was established in the general region of the old Gandhara grave culture, in what is today Khyber Pakhtunkhwa. During Achaemenid rule, the Kharosthi alphabet, derived from the one used for Aramaic (the official language of Achaemenids), developed here and remained the national script of Gandhara until 200 AD.

Gandhara Kingdom/Takshila in Punjab was conquered by the Achaemenid empire in 518 BC.[873] During this time, King Pushkarasakti, a contemporary of Emperor Bimbisara (558–491 BC) of the Magadha empire of Haryanka dynasty, was the king of Gandhara. King Pushkarasakti was engaged in power struggles against his local rivals. The Achaemenids under Darius penetrated to the region in 516 BC and annexed other parts of modern-day Punjab, Pakistan west to the Indus river and Sindh.

Figure 228: *Coin of Early Gandhara Janapada: AR Shatamana and one-eighth Shatamana (round), Taxila-Gandhara region, c. 600–300 BC*

The inscription on Darius' (521–486 BC) tomb at Naqsh-i-Rustam near Persepolis records Gadāra (Gandāra) along with Hindush (Həntuš, Sindh) in the list of *satrapies*. By about 380 BC the Persian hold on the region had weakened. Many small kingdoms sprang up in Gandhara. In 327 BC, Alexander the Great conquered Gandhara as well as the Indian *satrapies* of the Persian Empire. The expeditions of Alexander were recorded by his court historians and by Arrian (around AD 175) in his *Anabasis Alexandri* and by other chroniclers many centuries after the event.

Sir Mortimer Wheeler conducted some excavations there in 1962, and identified various Achaemenid remains.

Macedonian Gandhara

In the winter of 327 BC, Alexander invited all the chieftains in the remaining five Achaemenid satraps to submit to his authority. Ambhi, then ruler of Taxila in the former Hindush satrapy complied, but the remaining tribes and clans in the former satraps of Gandhara, Arachosia, Sattagydia and Gedrosia rejected Alexander's offer.

The first tribe they encountered were the Aspasioi tribe of the Kunar Valley, who initiated a fierce battle against Alexander, in which he himself was wounded in the shoulder by a dart. However, the Aspasioi eventually lost

Figure 229: *A monetary silver coin of the satrapy of Gandhara about 500–400 BC.* **Obv:** *Gandhara symbol representing 6 weapons with one point between two weapons; At the bottom of the point, a hollow moon.* **Rev:** *Empty.* **Dimensions:** *14 mm* **Weight:** *1.4 g.*

and 40,000 people were enslaved. Alexander then continued in a southwestern direction where he encountered the Assakenoi tribe of the Swat & Buner valleys in April 326 BC. The Assakenoi fought bravely and offered stubborn resistance to Alexander and his army in the cities of Ora, Bazira (Barikot) and Massaga. So enraged was Alexander about the resistance put up by the Assakenoi that he killed the entire population of Massaga and reduced its buildings to rubble. A similar slaughter then followed at Ora, another stronghold of the Assakenoi. The stories of these slaughters reached numerous Assakenians, who began fleeing to Aornos, a hill-fort located between Shangla and Kohistan. Alexander followed close behind their heels and besieged the strategic hill-fort, eventually capturing and destroying the fort and killing everyone inside. The remaining smaller tribes either surrendered or like the Astanenoi tribe of Pushkalavati(Charsadda) were quickly neutralized where 38,000 soldiers and 230,000 oxen were captured by Alexander.[874] Eventually Alexander's smaller force would meet with the larger force which had come through the Khyber Pass met at Attock. With the conquest of Gandhara complete, Alexander switched to strengthening his military supply line, which by now stretched dangerously vulnerable over the Hindu Kush back to Balkh in Bactria.

After conquering Gandhara and solidifying his supply line back to Bactria, Alexander combined his forces with the King Ambhi of Taxila and crossed the River Indus in July 326 BC to begin the Archosia (Punjab) campaign. Alexander founded several new settlements in Gandhara, Punjab and Sindh. and nominated officers as Satraps of the new provinces:

In Gandhara, Oxyartes was nominated to the position of Satrap by Alexander in 326 BC.

Maurya arrival to Gandhara

Chandragupta Maurya, the founder of the Mauryan dynasty, is said to have lived in Taxila when Alexander captured the city. According to tradition, he trained under Kautilya, who remained his chief adviser throughout his reign. Supposedly using Gandhara and Vahika as his base, Chandragupta led a rebellion against the Magadha Empire and ascended the throne at Pataliputra in 321 BC. However, there are no contemporary Indian records of Chandragupta Maurya and almost all that is known is based on the diaries of Megasthenes, the ambassador of Seleucus at Pataliputra, as recorded by Arrian in his *Indika*. Ambhi hastened to relieve Alexander of his apprehension and met him with valuable presents, placing himself and all of his forces at his disposal. Alexander not only returned Ambhi his title, and the gifts, but he also presented him with a wardrobe of: "Persian robes, gold and silver ornaments, 30 horses and 1000 talents in gold". Alexander was emboldened to divide his forces, and Ambhi assisted Hephaestion and Perdiccas in constructing a bridge over the Indus where it bends at Hund (Fox 1973), supplied their troops with provisions, and received Alexander himself, and his whole army, in his capital city of Taxila, with every demonstration of friendship and the most liberal hospitality.

On the subsequent advance of the Macedonian king, Taxiles accompanied him with a force of 5000 men and took part in the battle of the Hydaspes River. After that victory he was sent by Alexander in pursuit of Porus, to whom he was charged to offer favourable terms, but narrowly escaped losing his life at the hands of his old enemy. Subsequently, however, the two rivals were reconciled by the personal mediation of Alexander; and Taxiles, after having contributed zealously to the equipment of the fleet on the Hydaspes, was entrusted by the king with the government of the whole territory between that river and the Indus. A considerable accession of power was granted him after the death of Philip (son of Machatas); and he was allowed to retain his authority at the death of Alexander himself (323 BC), as well as in the subsequent partition of the provinces at Triparadisus, 321 BC. Later Ambhi was deposed and killed by Chandragupta Maurya, emperor of the Mauryan Empire. Gandhara was acquired from the Greeks by Chandragupta Maurya.

After a battle with Seleucus Nicator (Alexander's successor in Asia) in 305 BC, the Mauryan Emperor extended his domain up to and including present Southern Afghanistan. With the completion of the Empire's Grand Trunk Road, the

Figure 230: *Greco-Buddhist statue of standing Buddha, Gandhara (1st–2nd century), Tokyo National Museum*

region prospered as a center of trade. Gandhara remained a part of the Mauryan Empire for about a century and a half.

Ashoka, the grandson of Chandragupta, was one of the greatest Indian rulers. Like his grandfather, Ashoka also started his career in Gandhara as a governor. Later he supposedly became a Buddhist and promoted this religion in his empire. He built many *stupas* in Gandhara. Mauryan control over the northwestern frontier, including the Yonas, Kambojas, and the Gandharas, is attested from the Rock Edicts left by Ashoka. According to one school of scholars, the Gandharas and Kambojas were cognate people.[875,876,877] It is also contended that the Kurus, Kambojas, Gandharas and Bahlikas were cognate people and all had Iranian affinities,[878] or that the Gandhara and Kamboja were nothing but two provinces of one empire and hence influencing each other's language.[879] However, the local language of Gandhara is represented by Panini's conservative *bhāṣā* ("language"), which is entirely different from the Iranian (Late Avestan) language of the Kamboja that is indicated by Patanjali's quote of Kambojan śavati 'to go' (= Late Avestan šava(i)ti).[880]

Graeco-Bactrians, Sakas, and Indo-Parthians

The decline of the Empire left the sub-continent open to Greco-Bactrian invasions. Present-day southern Afghanistan was absorbed by Demetrius I of

Figure 231: *Marine deities, Gandhara.*

Bactria in 180 BC. Around about 185 BC, Demetrius invaded and conquered Gandhara and the Punjab. Later, wars between different groups of Bactrian Greeks resulted in the independence of Gandhara from Bactria and the formation of the Indo-Greek kingdom. Menander I was its most famous king. He ruled from Taxila and later from Sagala (Sialkot). He rebuilt Taxila (Sirkap) and Pushkalavati. He became a Buddhist and is remembered in Buddhist records for his discussions with the great Buddhist philosopher, Nāgasena, in the book *Milinda Panha*.

Around the time of Menander's death in 140 BC, the Central Asian Kushans overran Bactria and ended Greek rule there. Around 80 BC, the Sakas, diverted by their Parthian cousins from Iran, moved into Gandhara and other parts of Pakistan and Western India. The most famous king of the Sakas, Maues, established himself in Gandhara.

By 90 BC the Parthians had taken control of eastern Iran and, around 50 BC, they put an end to the last remnants of Greek rule in today's Afghanistan. Eventually an Indo-Parthian dynasty succeeded in taking control of Gandhara. The Parthians continued to support Greek artistic traditions. The start of the Gandharan Greco-Buddhist art is dated to about 75–50 BC. Links between Rome and the Indo-Parthian kingdoms existed.[881] There is archaeological evidence that building techniques were transmitted between the two realms. Christian records claim that around AD 40 Thomas the Apostle visited the Indian subcontinent and encountered the Indo-Parthian king Gondophares.[882]

Kushan Gandhara

The Parthian dynasty fell about 75 to another group from Central Asia. The Kushans, known as Yuezhi in China (argued by someWikipedia:Manual of Style/Words to watch#Unsupported attributions to be ethnically Asii) moved from Central Asia to Bactria, where they stayed for a century. Around 75, one

Figure 232: *Casket of Kanishka the Great, with Buddhist motifs*

of their tribes, the Kushan (Kuṣāṇa), under the leadership of Kujula Kadphises gained control of Gandhara and other parts of what is now Pakistan.

The Kushan period is considered the Golden Period of Gandhara. Peshawar Valley and Taxila are littered with ruins of *stupas* and monasteries of this period. Gandharan art flourished and produced some of the best pieces of sculpture from the Indian subcontinent. Many monuments were created to commemorate the Jatakas.

Gandhara's culture peaked during the reign of the great Kushan king Kanishka the Great (128–151). The cities of Taxila (Takṣaśilā) at Sirsukh and Peshawar were built. Peshawar became the capital of a great empire stretching from Gandhara to Central Asia. Kanishka was a great patron of the Buddhist faith; Buddhism spread to Central Asia and the Far East across Bactria and Sogdia, where his empire met the Han Empire of China. Buddhist art spread from Gandhara to other parts of Asia. Under Kanishka, Gandhara became a holy land of Buddhism and attracted Chinese pilgrims eager to view the monuments associated with many Jatakas.

In Gandhara, Mahayana Buddhism flourished and Buddha was represented in human form. Under the Kushans new Buddhists *stupas* were built and old ones were enlarged. Huge statues of the Buddha were erected in monasteries and carved into the hillsides. Kanishka also built a great 400-foot tower at

Figure 233: *Head of a bodhisattva, c. 4th century*

Figure 234: *The Seated Buddha, dating from 300 to 500 CE, was found near Jamal Garhi, and is now on display at the Asian Art Museum in San Francisco.*

Figure 235: *Gandhara fortified city depicted in a Buddhist relief*

Peshawar. This tower was reported by Chinese monks Faxian, Song Yun, and Xuanzang who visited the country. This structure was destroyed and rebuilt many times until it was finally destroyed by Mahmud of Ghazni in the 11th century.

Hepthalite Invasion

The Hephthalite Huns captured Gandhara around 451, and did not adopt Buddhism, but in fact "perpetrated frightful massacres." Mihirakula became a "terrible persecutor" of the religion. During their rule, Hinduism revived itself and the Buddhist Gandharan civilization declined.

The travel records of many Chinese Buddhist pilgrims record that Gandhara was going through a transformation during these centuries. Buddhism was declining, and Hinduism was rising. Faxian traveled around 400, when Prakrit was the language of the people, and Buddhism was flourishing. 100 years later, when Song Yun visited in 520, a different situation was described: the area had been destroyed by the White Huns and was ruled by Lae-Lih, who did not practice the laws of the Buddha. Xuanzang visited India around 644 and found Buddhism on the wane in Gandhara and Hinduism in the ascendant. Gandhara was ruled by a king from Kabul, who respected Buddha's law, but Taxila was in ruins, and Buddhist monasteries were deserted.

Figure 236: *Sharing of the Buddha's relics, above a Gandhara fortified city.*

Kabul Shahi

After the fall of the Sassanid Empire to the Arabs in 644, today's Afghanistan region and Gandhara came under pressure from Muslims. But they failed to extend their empire to Gandhara. Gandhara was first ruled by local kings who later expanded their kingdom onto an empire.

Gandhara was ruled from Kabul by Kabulshahi for next 200 years. Sometime in the 9th century the Kabul Shahi replaced the Shahi. Based on various Muslim records it is estimated this occurred in 870. According to Al-Biruni (973–1048), Kallar, a Brahmin minister of the Kabulshahi, founded the Shahi dynasty in 843. The dynasty ruled from Kabul, later moved their capital to Udabhandapura. They built great temples all over their kingdoms. Some of these buildings are still in good condition in the Salt Range of the Punjab.

Decline

Jayapala was the last great king of this dynasty. His empire extended from west of Kabul to the river Sutlej. However, this expansion of Gandhara kingdom coincided with the rise of the powerful Ghaznavid Empire under Sabuktigin. Defeated twice by Sabuktigin and then by Mahmud of Ghazni in the Kabul valley, Jayapala gave his life on a funeral pyre. Anandapala, a son of Jayapala, moved his capital near Nandana in the Salt Range. In 1021 the last king of this dynasty, Trilochanapala, was assassinated by his own troops which spelled the end of Gandhara. Subsequently, some Shahi princes moved to Kashmir and became active in local politics.

The city of Kandahar in Afghanistan is said to have been named after Gandhara. According to H.W. Bellow, an emigrant from Gandhara in the 5th century brought this name to modern Kandahar. Faxian reported that the Buddha's alms-bowl existed in Peshawar Valley when he visited around 400 (chapter XII). In 1872 Bellow saw this huge begging bowl (seven feet in diameter) preserved in the shrine of Sultan Wais outside Kandahar. When Olaf Caroe wrote his book in 1958 (Caroe, pp. 170–171), this relic was reported to be at Kabul Museum. The present status of this bowl is unknown.

Writing c. 1030, Al Biruni reported on the devastation caused during the conquest of Gandhara and much of northwest India by Mahmud of Ghazni following his defeat of Jayapala in the Battle of Peshawar at Peshawar in 1001:

Now in the following times no Muslim conqueror passed beyond the frontier of Kâbul and the river Sindh until the days of the Turks, when they seized the power in Ghazna under the Sâmânî dynasty, and the supreme power fell to the lot of Nâṣir-addaula Sabuktagin. This prince chose the holy war as his calling, and therefore called himself al-Ghâzî ("the warrior/invader"). In the interest of his successors he constructed, in order to weaken the Indian frontier, those roads on which afterwards his son Yamin-addaula Maḥmûd marched into India during a period of thirty years and more. God be merciful to both father and son! Maḥmûd utterly ruined the prosperity of the country, and performed there wonderful exploits, by which the Hindus became like atoms of dust scattered in all directions, and like a tale of old in the mouth of the people. Their scattered remains cherish, of course, the most inveterate aversion towards all Muslims. This is the reason, too, why Hindu sciences have retired far away from those parts of the country conquered by us, and have fled to places which our hand cannot yet reach, to Kashmir, Benares, and other places. And there the antagonism between them and all foreigners receives more and more nourishment both from political and religious sources.[883]

During the closing years of the tenth and the early years of the succeeding century of our era, Mahmud the first Sultan and Musalman of the Turk dynasty of kings who ruled at Ghazni, made a succession of inroads twelve or fourteen in number, into Gandhar – the present Peshwar valley – in the course of his proselytizing invasions of Hindustan.<

Fire and sword, havoc and destruction, marked his course everywhere. Gandhar which was styled the Garden of the North was left at his death a weird and desolate waste. Its rich fields and fruitful gardens, together with

Figure 237: *Many stupas, such as the Shingerdar stupa in Ghalegay, are scattered throughout the region near Peshawar.*

the canal which watered them (the course of which is still partially traceable in the western part of the plain), had all disappeared. Its numerous stone built cities, monasteries, and topes with their valuable and revered monuments and sculptures, were sacked, fired, razed to the ground, and utterly destroyed as habitations.

Rediscovery

By the time Gandhara had been absorbed into the empire of Mahmud of Ghazni, Buddhist buildings were already in ruins and Gandhara art had been forgotten. After Al-Biruni, the Kashmiri writer Kalhaṇa wrote his book *Rajatarangini* in 1151. He recorded some events that took place in Gandhara, and provided details about its last royal dynasty and capital Udabhandapura.

In the 19th century, British soldiers and administrators started taking an interest in the ancient history of the Indian Subcontinent. In the 1830s coins of the post-Ashoka period were discovered, and in the same period Chinese travelogues were translated. Charles Masson, James Prinsep, and Alexander Cunningham deciphered the Kharosthi script in 1838. Chinese records provided locations and site plans for Buddhist shrines. Along with the discovery of coins, these records provided clues necessary to piece together the history of Gandhara. In 1848 Cunningham found Gandhara sculptures north of Peshawar. He also identified the site of Taxila in the 1860s. From then on a large number of Buddhist statues were discovered in the Peshawar valley.

Archaeologist John Marshall excavated at Taxila between 1912 and 1934. He discovered separate Greek, Parthian, and Kushan cities and a large number of *stupas* and monasteries. These discoveries helped to piece together much more of the chronology of the history of Gandhara and its art.

After 1947 Ahmed Hassan Dani and the Archaeology Department at the University of Peshawar made a number of discoveries in the Peshawar and Swat Valley. Excavation of many of the sites of Gandhara Civilization are being done by researchers from Peshawar and several universities around the world.

Taliban destruction of Buddhist relics

Swat Valley in Pakistan has many Buddhist carvings, and *stupas*, and Jehanabad contains a Seated Buddha statue.[884] Kushan era Buddhist *stupas* and statues in Swat valley were demolished after two attempts by the Taliban and the Jehanabad Buddha's face was dynamited. Only the Buddhas of Bamiyan were larger than the carved giant Buddha statues in Swat near Manglore which the Taliban attacked. The government did nothing to safeguard the statue after the initial attempts to destroy the Buddha, which did not cause permanent harm. But when a second attack took place on the statue, the feet, shoulders, and face were demolished. Islamists such as the Taliban, and looters, destroyed many of Pakistan's Buddhist artifacts from the Buddhist Gandhara civilization especially in the Swat Valley. The Taliban deliberately targeted Gandhara Buddhist relics for destruction. The Christian Archbishop of Lahore, Lawrence John Saldanha, wrote a letter to Pakistan's government denouncing the Taliban's activities in Swat Valley including their destruction of Buddha statues and their attacks on Christians, Sikhs, and Hindus. Gandhara Buddhist artifacts were illegally looted by smugglers. A group of Italians helped repair the Buddha.

Language

The Gandharan Buddhist texts are both the earliest Buddhist as well as Asian manuscripts discovered so far. Most are written on birch bark and were found in labelled clay pots. Panini has mentioned both the Vedic form of Sanskrit as well as what seems to be Gandhari, a later form of Sanskrit, in his Ashtadhyayi.

Gandhara's language was a Prakrit or "Middle Indo-Aryan" dialect, usually called Gāndhārī. The language used the Kharosthi script, which died out about the 4th century. However, Punjabi, Hindko, and Kohistani, are derived from

Figure 238: *Maitreya Bodhisattva, Gautama Buddha, and Avalokiteśvara Bodhisattva. 2nd–3rd century AD, Gandhāra*

the Indo-Aryan Prakrits that were spoken in Gandhara and surrounding areas. However, a language shift occurred as the ancient Gandharan culture gave way to Iranian invaders from Central Asia.

Buddhism

Mahāyāna Buddhism

Mahāyāna Pure Land sūtras were brought from the Gandhāra region to China as early as AD 147, when the Kushan monk Lokakṣema began translating some of the first Buddhist sūtras into Chinese. The earliest of these translations show evidence of having been translated from the Gāndhārī language.[885] Lokakṣema translated important Mahāyāna sūtras such as the *Aṣṭasāhasrikā Prajñāpāramitā Sūtra*, as well as rare, early Mahāyāna sūtras on topics such as samādhi, and meditation on the buddha Akṣobhya. Lokaksema's translations continue to provide insight into the early period of Mahāyāna Buddhism. This corpus of texts often includes and emphasizes ascetic practices and forest dwelling, and absorption in states of meditative concentration:[886]

> Paul Harrison has worked on some of the texts that are arguably the earliest versions we have of the Mahāyāna sūtras, those translated into Chinese in the last half of the second century CE by the Indo-Scythian translator Lokakṣema. Harrison points to the enthusiasm in the Lokakṣema sūtra corpus for the extra ascetic practices, for dwelling in the forest, and above

Figure 239: *Bronze statue of Avalokiteśvara Bodhisattva. Fearlessness mudrā. 3rd century AD, Gandhāra*

all for states of meditative absorption (samādhi). Meditation and meditative states seem to have occupied a central place in early Mahāyāna, certainly because of their spiritual efficacy but also because they may have given access to fresh revelations and inspiration.

Some scholars believe that the Mahāyāna *Longer Sukhāvatīvyūha Sūtra* was compiled in the age of the Kushan Empire in the 1st and 2nd centuries AD, by an order of Mahīśāsaka bhikṣus which flourished in the Gandhāra region.[887,888] However, it is likely that the longer *Sukhāvatīvyūha* owes greatly to the Mahāsāṃghika-Lokottaravāda sect as well for its compilation, and in this sūtra there are many elements in common with the Lokottaravādin *Mahāvastu*. There are also images of Amitābha Buddha with the bodhisattvas Avalokiteśvara and Mahāsthāmaprāpta which were made in Gandhāra during the Kushan era.

The *Mañjuśrīmūlakalpa* records that Kaniṣka of the Kushan Empire presided over the establishment of the Mahāyāna Prajñāpāramitā teachings in the northwest.[889] Tāranātha wrote that in this region, 500 bodhisattvas attended the council at Jālandhra monastery during the time of Kaniṣka, suggesting some institutional strength for Mahāyāna in the northwest during this period. Edward Conze goes further to say that Prajñāpāramitā had great success in the northwest during the Kushan period, and may have been the "fortress and hearth" of early Mahāyāna, but not its origin, which he associates with the Mahāsāṃghika branch of Buddhism.[890]

Buddhist translators

Gandharan Buddhist missionaries were active, with other monks from Central Asia, from the 2nd century AD in the Han-dynasty (202 BC – 220 AD) at China's capital of Luoyang, and particularly distinguished themselves by their translation work. They promoted scriptures from Early Buddhist schools as well as those from the Mahāyāna. These translators included:

- Lokakṣema, a Kushan and the first to translate Mahāyāna scriptures into Chinese (167–186)
- Zhi Yao (c. 185), a Kushan monk, second generation of translators after Lokakṣema
- Zhi Qian (220–252), a Kushan monk whose grandfather had settled in China during 168–190
- Zhi Yue (c. 230), a Kushan monk who worked at Nanjing
- Dharmarakṣa (265–313), a Kushan whose family had lived for generations at Dunhuang
- Jñānagupta (561–592), a monk and translator from Gandhāra
- Śikṣānanda (652–710), a monk and translator from Oḍḍiyāna, Gandhāra
- Prajñā (c. 810), a monk and translator from Kabul, who educated the Japanese Kūkai in Sanskrit texts

Textual finds

The Chinese Buddhist monk Xuanzang visited a Lokottaravāda monastery in the 7th century, at Bamiyan, Afghanistan. The site of this monastery has since been rediscovered by archaeologists. Birchbark and palm leaf manuscripts of texts in this monastery's collection, including Mahāyāna sūtras, have been discovered at the site, and these are now located in the Schøyen Collection. Some manuscripts are in the Gāndhārī language and Kharoṣṭhī script, while others are in Sanskrit and written in forms of the Gupta script. Manuscripts and fragments that have survived from this monastery's collection include the following source texts:

- *Pratimokṣa Vibhaṅga* of the Mahāsāṃghika-Lokottaravāda (MS 2382/269)
- *Mahāparinirvāṇa Sūtra*, a sūtra from the Āgamas (MS 2179/44)
- *Caṃgī Sūtra*, a sūtra from the Āgamas (MS 2376)
- *Vajracchedikā Prajñāpāramitā Sūtra*, a Mahāyāna sūtra (MS 2385)
- *Bhaiṣajyaguru Sūtra*, a Mahāyāna sūtra (MS 2385)
- *Śrīmālādevī Siṃhanāda Sūtra*, a Mahāyāna sūtra (MS 2378)

Figure 240: *Greco-Buddhist Portraits from the site of Hadda, Gandhara, 3rd century, Guimet Museum*

- *Pravāraṇa Sūtra*, a Mahāyāna sūtra (MS 2378)
- *Sarvadharmapravṛttinirdeśa Sūtra*, a Mahāyāna sūtra (MS 2378)
- *Ajātaśatrukaukṛtyavinodana Sūtra*, a Mahāyāna sūtra (MS 2378)
- *Śāriputra Abhidharma Śāstra* (MS 2375/08)

A Sanskrit manuscript of the *Bhaiṣajyaguruvaiḍūryaprabhārāja Sūtra* was among the textual finds at Gilgit, Pakistan, attesting to the popularity of the Medicine Buddha in Gandhāra.[891] The manuscripts in this find are dated before the 7th century, and are written in the upright Gupta script.

Art

Gandhāra is noted for the distinctive **Gandhāra style** of Buddhist art, which developed from a merger of Greek, Syrian, Persian, and local artistic influences. This development began during the Parthian Period (50 BC – AD 75). The Gandhāran style flourished and achieved its peak during the Kushan period, from the 1st to the 5th centuries. It declined and was destroyed after the invasion of the White Huns in the 5th century.

Stucco as well as stone was widely used by sculptors in Gandhara for the decoration of monastic and cult buildings. Stucco provided the artist with a medium of great plasticity, enabling a high degree of expressiveness to be given to the sculpture. Sculpting in stucco was popular wherever Buddhism spread from Gandhara – Afghanistan, Pakistan, India, Central Asia, and China.

Figure 241: *Standing Bodhisattva (1st–2nd century)*

Figure 242: *Buddha head (2nd century)*

Figure 243: *Buddha head (4th–6th century)*

Figure 244: *Buddha in acanthus capital*

Figure 245: *The Greek god Atlas, supporting a Buddhist monument, Hadda*

Figure 246: *The Bodhisattva Maitreya (2nd century)*

Figure 247: *Wine-drinking and music, Hadda (1st–2nd century)*

Figure 248: *Maya's white elephant dream (2nd–3rd century)*

Figure 249: *The birth of Siddharta (2nd–3rd century)*

Figure 250: *The Great Departure from the Palace (2nd–3rd century)*

Figure 251: *The end of ascetism (2nd–3rd century)*

Figure 252: *The Buddha preaching at the Deer Park in Sarnath (2nd–3rd century)*

Figure 253: *Scene of the life of the Buddha (2nd–3rd century)*

Figure 254: *The death of the Buddha, or parinirvana (2nd–3rd century)*

Figure 255: *A sculpture from Hadda, (3rd century)*

Figure 256: *The Bodhisattva and Chandeka, Hadda (5th century)*

Figure 257: *The Buddha and Vajrapani under the guise of Herakles*

Figure 258: *Hellenistic decorative scrolls from Hadda, Afghanistan*

Figure 259: *Hellenistic scene, Gandhara (1st century)*

Figure 260: *A stone plate (1st century).*

Figure 261: *"Laughing boy" from Hadda*

Figure 262: *Bodhisattva seated in meditation*

Timeline

- c. 2300 – c. 1900 BC Indus Valley civilization
- c. 1900 – c. 520 BC No written records. Indo-Aryan migrations. Ramayana legend says Lord Rama's brother Bharat ruled from Gandhara.
- c. 1500 – c. 500 BC Gandhara grave culture
- c. 1200 – c. 800 BC Gandhari people mentioned in Rigveda and Atharvaveda.
- c. 520 – c. 326 BC Persian Empire. Under direct Persian control and/or local control under Achaemenid suzerainty.
- c. 326 – c. 305 BC Occupied by Alexander the Great and Macedonian generals
- c. 305 – c. 180 BC Controlled by the Maurya dynasty, founded by Chandragupta. Converted to Buddhism under King Ashoka (273–232 BC)
- c. 185 – c. 97 BC Under control of the Indo-Greek Kingdom, with some incursions of the Indo-Scythians from around 100 BC
- c. 97 BC – c. AD 7 Saka (Indo-Scythian) Rule
- c. 7 – c. 75 Parthian invasion and Indo-Parthian Kingdom, Rule of Commander Aspavarman?. Ambhi Kumar, king of Gandhara was a descendant of Lord Raghu and prince Bharat of Kosala Kingdom.
- c. 75 – c. 230 Kushan Empire

- c. 230 – c. 440 Kushanshas under Persian Sassanid suzerainty
- c. 450 – c. 565 White Huns (Hephthalites)
- c. 565 – c. 644 Nezak kingdom, ruled from Kapisa and Udabhandapura
- c. 650 – c. 870 Kabul Shahi, ruled from Kabul
- c. 870 – 1021 Hindu Shahi, ruled from Udabhandapura
- c. 1032 – 1350 Conquered and controlled by the empire of Mahmud of Ghazni.

Sources

<templatestyles src="Template:Refbegin/styles.css" />

- Beal, Samuel. 1884. *Si-Yu-Ki: Buddhist Records of the Western World, by Hiuen Tsiang*. 2 vols. Trans. by Samuel Beal. London. Reprint: Delhi. Oriental Books Reprint Corporation. 1969.
- Beal, Samuel. 1911. *The Life of Hiuen-Tsiang by the Shaman Hwui Li, with an Introduction containing an account of the Works of I-Tsing.* Trans. by Samuel Beal. London. 1911. Reprint: Munshiram Manoharlal, New Delhi. 1973.
- Bellew, H.W. *Kashmir and Kashgar*. London, 1875. Reprint: Sang-e-Meel Publications 1999 ISBN 969-35-0738-X
- Caroe, Sir Olaf, *The Pathans*, Oxford University Press, Karachi, 1958.
- Herodotus (1920). *Histories*[892] (in Greek and English). With an English translation by A. D. Godley. Cambridge: Harvard University Press.
- Hill, John E. 2003. "Annotated Translation of the Chapter on the Western Regions according to the *Hou Hanshu*"[893]. 2nd Edition: *Through the Jade Gate to Rome: A Study of the Silk Routes, 1st to 2nd Centuries CE*. 2015. John E. Hill. Volume I, ISBN 978-1500696702; Volume II, ISBN 978-1503384620. CreateSpace, North Charleston, S.C.
- Hussain, J. *An Illustrated History of Pakistan*, Oxford University Press, Karachi, 1983.
- Legge, James. Trans. and ed. 1886. *A Record of Buddhistic Kingdoms: being an account by the Chinese monk Fâ-hsien of his travels in India and Ceylon (A.D. 399–414) in search of the Buddhist Books of Discipline*. Reprint: Dover Publications, New York. 1965.
- Shaw, Isobel. *Pakistan Handbook*, The Guidebook Co., Hong Kong, 1989
- Watters, Thomas. 1904–5. *On Yuan Chwang's Travels in India (A.D. 629–645)*. Reprint: Mushiram Manoharlal Publishers, New Delhi. 1973.

Further reading

<templatestyles src="Template:Refbegin/styles.css" />

- Lerner, Martin (1984). *The flame and the lotus: Indian and Southeast Asian art from the Kronos collections*[894]. New York: The Metropolitan Museum of Art. ISBN 0-87099-374-7.

External links

 Wikimedia Commons has media related to *Gandhara*.

- Livius.org: Gandara[895]
- The Buddhist Manuscript project[896]
- University of Washington's Gandharan manuscript[897]
- Coins of Gandhara janapada[898]
- Gandhara Civilization[899]- National Fund for Cultural Heritage (Pakistan)

Coordinates: 33.7560°N 72.8291°E[900]

Kambojas

Kingdom of Kamboja	
c. 700 BCE–c. 300 BCE	
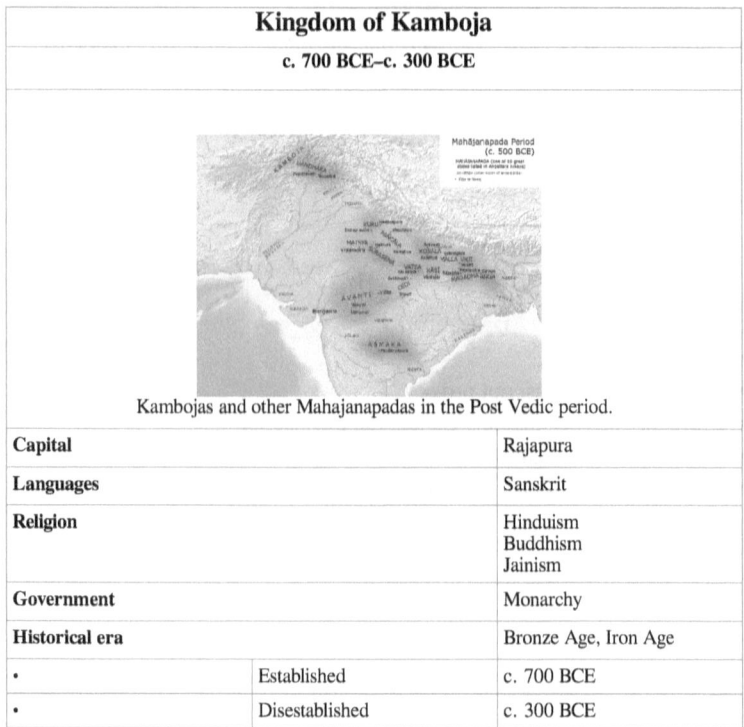	
Kambojas and other Mahajanapadas in the Post Vedic period.	
Capital	Rajapura
Languages	Sanskrit
Religion	Hinduism Buddhism Jainism
Government	Monarchy
Historical era	Bronze Age, Iron Age
• Established	c. 700 BCE
• Disestablished	c. 300 BCE

The **Kambojas** were a tribe of Iron Age India, frequently mentioned in Sanskrit and Pali literature. The tribe coalesced to become one of the *solasa* (sixteen) Mahajanapadas (great kingdoms) of ancient India mentioned in the *Anguttara Nikaya*.

Ethnicity and language

The ancient Kambojas were probably of Indo-Iranian origin.[901] They are, however, sometimes described as Indo-Aryans[902] Wikipedia:Citing sources[903] Wikipedia:Citing sources[904] and sometimes as having both Indian and Iranian affinities.[905,906,907] The Kambojas are also described as a royal clan of the Sakas.[908]

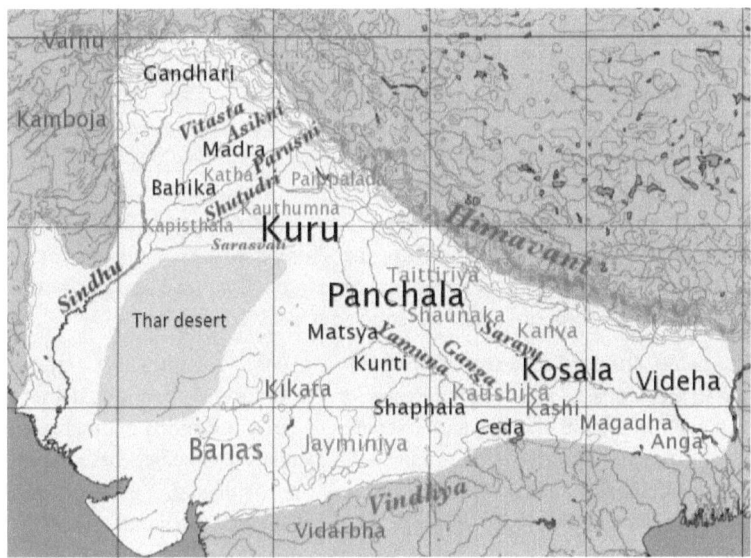

Figure 263: *Vedic period India, with the Kamboja on the northwest border*

Origins

The earliest reference to the Kambojas is in the works of Pāṇini, around the 5th century BCE. Other pre-Common Era references appear in the *Manusmriti* (2nd century) and the *Mahabharata* (10th century BCE), both of which described the Kambojas as former kshatriyas (Warriors caste) who had degraded through a failure to abide by Hindu sacred rituals.[909] Their territories were located beyond Gandhara, beyond Pakistan, Afghanistan laying in Tajikistan, Uzbekistan, Kyrgyzstan where Buddha statues were built in the name of king Maurya & Ashoka[910] and the 3rd century BCE *Edicts of Ashoka* refers to the area under Kamboja control as being independent of the Mauryan empire in which it was situated.

Some sections of the Kambojas crossed the Hindu Kush and planted Kamboja colonies in Paropamisadae and as far as Rajauri. The *Mahabharata* locates the Kambojas on the near side of the Hindu Kush as neighbors to the Daradas, and the Parama-Kambojas across the Hindu Kush as neighbors to the Rishikas (or Tukharas) of the Ferghana region.[911] Wikipedia:Citing sources[912,913]

The confederation of the Kambojas may have stretched from the valley of Rajauri in the south-western part of Kashmir to the Hindu Kush Range; in the south–west the borders extended probably as far as the regions of Kabul, Ghazni and Kandahar, with the nucleus in the area north-east of the present day Kabul, between the Hindu Kush Range and the Kunar river, including Kapisa[914,915] possibly extending from the Kabul valleys to Kandahar.[916]

Others locate the Kambojas and the Parama-Kambojas in the areas spanning Balkh, Badakshan, the Pamirs and Kafiristan.[917] D. C. Sircar supposed them to have lived "in various settlements in the wide area lying between Punjab, Iran, to the south of Balkh." and the Parama-Kamboja even farther north, in the Trans-Pamirian territories comprising the Zeravshan valley, towards the Farghana region, in the Scythia of the classical writers.Wikipedia:Citing sources[918,919] The mountainous region between the Oxus and Jaxartes is also suggested as the location of the ancient Kambojas.[920]

The name *Kamboja* may derive from (*Kam* + *bhoj* "Kamma+boja"), referring to the people of a country known as "Kum" or "Kam". The mountainous highlands where the Jaxartes and its confluents arise are called the highlands of the Komedes by Ptolemy. Ammianus Marcellinus also names these mountains as *Komedas*.[921,922,923] The *Kiu-mi-to* in the writings of Xuanzang have also been identified with the *Komudha-dvipa* of the Puranic literature and the Iranian Kambojas.[924,925]

The two Kamboja settlements on either side of the Hindu Kush are also substantiated from Ptolemy's Geography, which refers to the *Tambyzoi* located north of the Hindu Kush on the river Oxus in Bactria, and the *Ambautai* people on the southern side of Hindukush in the Paropamisadae.Wikipedia:Citation needed Scholars have identified both the Ptolemian *Tambyzoi* and *Ambautai* with Sanskrit *Kamboja*.[926,927,928,929]

Scholars, such as Ernst Herzfeld, have suggested etymological links between some Indo-Aryan ethnonyms and some geonyms used by Iranian-speaking peoples of the Caucasus Mountains and Caspian basin. In particular, Kamboja somewhat resembles the hydronym *Kambujiya* – the Iranian name for the Iori/Gabirri river (modern Georgia/Azerbaijan). *Kambujiya* is also the root of Cambysene (an archaic name for the Kakheti/Balakan regions of Georgia and Azerbaijan) and the Persian personal name Cambyses. (A similar link is suggested between the Kura River, which is near the Iori, and the name of the Kurus and Kaurava mentioned in vedic literature.)[930] Such etymologies have not, however, been universally accepted.Wikipedia:Citation needed

Kambojan States

The capital of Kamboja was probably Rajapura (modern Rajauri). The Kamboja Mahajanapada of Buddhist traditions refers to this branch.[931]

Kautiliya's *Arthashastra* and Ashoka's Edict No. XIII attest that the Kambojas followed a republican constitution. Pāṇini's Sutras tend to convey that the

Kamboja of Pāṇini was a "Kshatriya monarchy", but "the special rule and the exceptional form of derivative" he gives to denote the ruler of the Kambojas implies that the king of Kamboja was a titular head (*king consul*) only.[932] One king of Kamboja was King Srindra Varmana Kamboj.[933]

The Aśvakas

The Kambojas were famous in ancient times for their excellent breed of horses and as remarkable horsemen located in the *Uttarapatha* or north-west.[934,935] They were constituted into military *sanghas* and corporations to manage their political and military affairs.Wikipedia:Citation needed The Kamboja cavalry offered their military services to other nations as well. There are numerous references to Kamboja having been requisitioned as cavalry troopers in ancient wars by outside nations.[936,937]

It was on account of their supreme position in horse (*Ashva*) culture that the ancient Kambojas were also popularly known as *Ashvakas*, i.e. horsemen. Their clans in the Kunar and Swat valleys have been referred to as *Assakenoi* and *Aspasioi* in classical writings, and *Ashvakayanas* and *Ashvayanas* in Pāṇini's *Ashtadhyayi*.

> *The Kambojas were famous for their horses and as cavalry-men (aśva-yuddha-Kuśalah), Aśvakas, 'horsemen', was the term popularly applied to them... The Aśvakas inhabited Eastern Afghanistan, and were included within the more general term Kambojas.*
>
> —*K.P.Jayswal*

> *Elsewhere Kamboja is regularly mentioned as "the country of horses" (Asvanam ayatanam), and it was perhaps this well-established reputation that won for the horsebreeders of Bajaur and Swat the designation Aspasioi (from the Old Pali aspa) and assakenoi (from the Sanskrit asva "horse").*
>
> —*Etienne Lamotte*[938]

Conflict with Alexander

The Kambojas entered into conflict with Alexander the Great as he invaded Central Asia. The Macedonian conqueror made short shrift of the arrangements of Darius and after over-running the Achaemenid Empire he dashed into today's eastern Afghanistan and western Pakistan. There he encountered resistance from the Kamboja *Aspasioi* and *Assakenoi* tribes.[939,940]

The Ashvayans (Aspasioi) were also good cattle breeders and agriculturists. This is clear from the large number of bullocks that Alexander captured from them - 230,000 according to Arrian[941] - some of which were of a size and shape superior to what the Macedonians had known, and which Alexander decided to send to Macedonia for agriculture.[942,943]

Migrations

During the 2nd and 1st centuries BCE, clans of the Kambojas from Central Asia in alliance with the Sakas, Pahlavas and the Yavanas entered present Afghanistan and India, spread into Sindhu, Saurashtra, Malwa, Rajasthan, Punjab and Surasena, and set up independent principalities in western and southwestern India. Later, a branch of the same people took Gauda and Varendra territories from the Palas and established the Kamboja-Pala Dynasty of Bengal in Eastern India.[944,945,946]

There are references to the hordes of the Sakas, Yavanas, Kambojas, and Pahlavas in the Bala Kanda of the Valmiki Ramayana. In these verses one may see glimpses of the struggles of the Hindus with the invading hordes from the north-west.[947,948] The royal family of the Kamuias mentioned in the Mathura Lion Capital are believed to be linked to the royal house of Taxila in Gandhara.[949] In the medieval era, the Kambojas are known to have seized northwest Bengal (*Gauda* and *Radha*) from the Palas of Bengal and established their own Kamboja-Pala Dynasty. Indian texts like *Markandeya Purana*, *Vishnu Dharmottari Agni Purana*,[950]

Eastern Kambojas

A branch of Kambojas seems to have migrated eastwards towards Nepal and Tibet in the wake of Kushana (1st century) or else Huna (5th century) pressure and hence their notice in the chronicles of Tibet ("Kam-po-tsa, Kam-po-ce, Kam-po-ji") and Nepal (Kambojadesa).[951,952] The 5th-century *Brahma Purana* mentions the Kambojas around Pragjyotisha and Tamraliptika.[953,954,955,956] Wikipedia:Citing sources

> The Kambojas of ancient India are known to have been living in northwest, but in this period (9th century AD), they are known to have been

living in the north-east India also, and very probably, it was meant Tibet.[957]

The last Kambojas ruler of the Kamboja-Pala Dynasty Dharmapala was defeated by the south Indian Emperor Rajendra Chola I of the Chola dynasty in the 11th century.[958,959]

Mauryan period

The Kambojas find prominent mention as a unit in the 3rd-century BCE Edicts of Ashoka. Rock Edict XIII tells us that the Kambojas had enjoyed autonomy under the Mauryas.Wikipedia:Citing sources[960] The republics mentioned in Rock Edict V are the Yonas, Kambojas, Gandharas, Nabhakas and the Nabhapamkitas. They are designated as *araja. vishaya* in Rock Edict XIII, which means that they were kingless, i.e. republican polities. In other words, the Kambojas formed a self-governing political unit under the Maurya emperors.[961,962]

Ashoka sent missionaries to the Kambojas to convert them to Buddhism, and recorded this fact in his Rock Edict V.[963,964]

Bibliography

- Acharya, K. T. (2001) *A Historical Dictionary of Indian Food* (Oxford India Paperbacks). ISBN 978-0-19-565868-2
- Barnes, Ruth and David Parkin (eds.) (2002) *Ships and the Development of Maritime Technology on the Indian Ocean*. London: Curzon. ISBN 0-7007-1235-6
- Bhatia, Harbans Singh (1984) *Political, legal, and military history of India*. New Delhi: Deep & Deep Publications
- Bhattacharyya, Alakananda (2003) *The Mlechchhas in Ancient India*, Kolkata: Firma KLM. ISBN 81-7102-112-3
- Boardman, John and N. G. L. Hammond, D. M. Lewis, and M. Ostwald (1988) *The Cambridge Ancient History: Volume 4, Persia, Greece and the Western Mediterranean (c. 525 to 479 BC)*. Cambridge: Cambridge University Press. ISBN 0-521-22804-2
- Bongard-Levin, Grigoriĭ Maksimovich (1985) *Ancient Indian Civilization*. New Delhi: Arnold-Heinemann
- Bowman, John Stewart (2000) *Columbia chronologies of Asian history and culture*, New York; Chichester: Columbia University Press. ISBN 0-231-11004-9

- Boyce, Mary and Frantz Grenet (1991) *A History of Zoroastrianism*, Vol. 3, Zoroastrianism under Macedonian and Roman rule. Leiden: Brill. ISBN 90-04-09271-4
- Collins, Steven (1998) *Nirvana and Other Buddhist Felicities: Utopias of the Pali Imaginaire*. Cambridge: Cambridge University Press. ISBN 0-521-57054-9. ISBN 0-521-57842-6 ISBN 978-0-521-57842-4
- Drabu, V. N. (1986) *Kashmir Polity, c. 600-1200 A.D.* New Delhi: Bahri Publications. Series in Indian history, art, and culture; 2. ISBN 81-7034-004-7
- Ganguly, Dilip Kumar (1994) *Ancient India, History and Archaeology*. New Delhi: Abhinav Publications. ISBN 81-7017-304-3
- Dwivedi, R. K., (1977) "A Critical study of Changing Social Order at Yuganta: or the end of the Kali Age" in Lallanji Gopal, J.P. Singh, N. Ahmad and D. Malik (eds.) (1977) *D.D. Kosambi commemoration volume*. Varanasi: Banaras Hindu University.
- Jha, Jata Shankar (ed.) (1981) *K.P. Jayaswal commemoration volume*. Patna: K P Jayaswal Research Institute
- Jindal, Mangal Sen (1992) *History of Origin of Some Clans in India, with Special Reference to Jats*. New Delhi: Sarup & Sons. ISBN 81-85431-08-6
- Lamotte, Etienne (1988) *History of Indian Buddhism: From the Origins to the Saka Era*. Sara Webb-Boin and Jean Dantinne (transl.) Louvain-la-Neuve: Université Catholique de Louvain, Institut Orientaliste. ISBN 90-6831-100-X
- Mishra, Krishna Chandra (1987) *Tribes in the Mahabharata: A Socio-cultural Study*. New Delhi, India: National Pub. House. ISBN 81-214-0028-7
- Misra, Satiya Deva (ed.) (1987) *Modern Researches in Sanskrit: Dr. Veermani Pd. Upadhyaya Felicitation Volume*. Patna: Indira Prakashan
- Pande, Govind Chandra (1984) *Foundations of Indian Culture*, Delhi: Motilal Banarsidass ISBN 81-208-0712-X (1990 edition.)
- Pande, Ram (ed.) (1984) *Tribals Movement [proceedings of the National Seminar on Tribals of Rajasthan held on 9–10 April 1983 at Jaipur under the auspices of Shodhak in collaboration of Indian Council of Historical Research, New Delhi*. Jaipur: Shodhak
- Patton, Laurie L. and Edwin Bryant (eds.) (2005) *Indo-Aryan Controversy: Evidence and Inference in Indian History*, London: Routledge. ISBN 0-7007-1462-6 ISBN 0-7007-1463-4
- Rishi, Weer Rajendra (1982) *India & Russia: Linguistic & Cultural Affinity*. Chandigarh: Roma Publications
- Sathe, Shriram (1987) *Dates of the Buddha*. Hyderabad: Bharatiya Itihasa Sankalana Samiti Hyderabad

- Sethna, K. D. (2000) *Problems of Ancient India*, New Delhi: Aditya Prakashan. ISBN 81-7742-026-7
- Sethna, Kaikhushru Dhunjibhoy (1989) *Ancient India in a new light.* New Delhi: Aditya Prakashan. ISBN 81-85179-12-3
- Shastri, Biswanarayan (ed.) and Pratap Chandra Choudhury, (1982) *Abhinandana-Bhāratī: Professor Krishna Kanta Handiqui Felicitation Volume.* Gauhati: Kāmarūpa Anusandhāna Samiti
- Shrava, Satya (1981 [1947]) *The Śakas in India.* New Delhi: Pranava Prakashan
- Singh, Acharya Phool (2002) *Philosophy, religion and Vedic education*, Jaipur: Sublime. ISBN 81-85809-97-6
- Singh, G. P., Dhaneswar Kalita, V. Sudarsen and Mohammed Abdul Kalam (1990) *Kiratas in Ancient India: Displacement, Resettlement, Development.* India University Grants Commission, Indian Council of Social Science Research. New Delhi: Gian. ISBN 81-212-0329-5
- Singh, Gursharan (ed.) (1996) *Punjab history conference.* Punjabi University. ISBN 81-7380-220-3 ISBN 81-7380-221-1
- Talbert, Richard J.A. (ed.) (2000) *Barrington Atlas of the Greek and Roman World.* Princeton, N.J.: Princeton University Press. ISBN 978-0-691-04945-8
- Vogelsang, Willem (2001) *The Afghans.* Peoples of Asia Series. ISBN 978-1-4051-8243-0
- Walker, Andrew and Nicholas Tapp (2001) in *Tai World: A Digest of Articles from the Thai -Yunnan Project Newsletter.* Or in Scott Bamber (ed.) *Thai-Yunnan Project Newsletter.* Australian National University, Department of Anthropology, Research School of Pacific Studies. http://www.nectec.or.th/thai-yunnan/20.html. ISSN 1326-2777
- Witzel, M. (1999a) "Substrate Languages in Old Indo-Aryan (Rgvedic, Middle and Late Vedic)", *Electronic Journal of Vedic Studies*, 5:1 (September).
- Witzel, Michael (1980) "Early Eastern Iran and the Atharvaveda", *Persica* 9
- Witzel, Michael (1999b) "Aryan and non-Aryan Names in Vedic India. Data for the linguistic situation, c. 1900-500 B.C.", in J. Bronkhorst & M. Deshpande (eds.), *Aryans and Non-Non-Aryans, Evidence, Interpretation and Ideology.* Cambridge, Massachusetts: Dept. of Sanskrit and Indian Studies, Harvard University (Harvard Oriental Series, Opera Minora 3). ISBN 1-888789-04-2 pp. 337–404
- Witzel, Michael (2001) in *Electronic Journal of Vedic Studies* 7:3 (May 25), Article 9. ISSN 1084-7561
- Yar-Shater, Ehsan (ed.) (1983) The Cambridge History of Iran, Vol. 3: The Seleucid, Parthian and Sasanian periods. ISBN 0-521-20092-X

ISBN 0-521-24693-8 (v.3/2) ISBN 0-521-24699-7 (v.3/1-2)

External links
- Kamboj Society - Ancient Kamboja Country[965]

Karkoṭa Empire

Karkota Empire		
625 CE–885 CE		
Karkota territory at its maximum extent, according to Joseph E. Schwartzberg's *A Historical Atlas of South Asia*		
Capital		Srinagar (625-724) Parihaspore (724-760) Srinagar (760-885)Wikipedia:Citation needed
Religion		Hinduism
Government		Monarchy
Samraat (Emperor)		Durlabhvardhana
		Durlabahaka
•	724 CE–760 CE	Lalitaditya Muktapida
Historical era		Classical India
•	Established	625 CE
•	Disestablished	885 CE
Succeeded by		
Utpala dynasty		
Today part of		Afghanistan India Pakistan Bangladesh

Karkota Empire (c. 625 - 885 CE) was a major power from the Indian subcontinent; which originated in the region of Kashmir. It was founded by Durlabhvardhana during the lifetime of Harshavardhan. The dynasty marked the rise of Kashmir as a power in Northern India.[967] Avanti Varman ascended the throne of Kashmir on 855 A.D., establishing the Utpala dynasty and ending the rule of Karkota dynasty.

Lalitaditya Muktapida, the dynasty's strongest ruler captured parts of Central Asia, Afghanistan and Punjab with Chinese help.[968] According to Kalhana's *Rajatarangini*, Lalitaditya was able to extend the power of Kashmir beyond the normal mountain limits and in about 740 AD inflicted a defeat upon Yashovarman, the King of Kannauj. Lalitaditya was able to vanquish the Turks, Tibetans, Bhutias, Kambojas and others. According to some historians, Kalhana highly exaggerated the conquests of Lalitaditya.[969,970]

The Karkota emperors were primarily Hindu. They built spectacular Hindu temples in their capital Parihaspur. They however also allowed Buddhism to flourish under them. Stupa, Chaitya and Vihara can be found in the ruins of their capital. Martand Sun Temple in the Anantnag district were built by

Lalitaditya. It is the oldest known Sun temple in India and was also one of the biggest temple complexes at the time.

Notes

References

- Wink, André (2002), *Al-Hind, the Making of the Indo-Islamic World*[971], **1**, BRILL, ISBN 9780391041738
- Chadurah, Haidar Malik (1991), *History of Kashmir*[972], Bhavna Prakashan
- Hasan, Mohibbul (1959), *Kashmir Under the Sultans*[973], Aakar, ISBN 9788187879497

Kabul Shahi

Kabul Shahi		
काबुल शाही Kabul Shahi		
c. 500 CE–c.1026 CE		
The Kabul Shahi or Hindu Shahi in Asia in 800 CE.		
Capital		Kabul Waihind (870–1010)[974]
Languages		SanskritWikipedia:Citation needed
Religion		Buddhism Hinduism
Government		Monarchy
Kshayathiya Shah Shahanshah		
•	700s	Khingala of Kapisa
•	964–1001	Jayapala
•	1001–1010	Anandapala

Historical era		Early Medieval India
•	Established	c. 500 CE
•	Disestablished	c.1026 CE
	Preceded by	Succeeded by
	ﻭ Alchon Huns	
		Ghaznavids
	Nezak Huns	
Today part of		Afghanistan
		Pakistan

The **Kabul Shahi dynasties**[975,976] also called **Shahiya**[977,978] ruled the Kabul Valley (in eastern Afghanistan) and the old province of Gandhara (northern Pakistan) during the Classical Period of India from the decline of the Kushan Empire[979] in the 3rd century to the early 11th century.[25] They are split into two eras: the Buddhist Turk Shahi and the later Hindu-Shahis with the change-over occurring around 870 CE.

When Xuanzang visited the region early in the 7th century, the Kabul region was ruled by a Kshatriya king, who is identified as the *Shahi Khingal*, and whose name has been found in an inscription found in Gardez.

These Hindu kings of Kabul and Gandhara may have had links to some ruling families in neighboring Kashmir, Punjab and other areas to the east. The Shahis were rulers of predominantly Buddhist and Hindu populations and were thus patrons of numerous faiths, and various artifacts and coins from their rule have been found that display their multicultural domain. At the end period the last Shahi emperors Jayapala, Anandapala and Tirlochanpala fought the Muslim Turk Ghaznavids of Ghazna and were gradually defeated. Their remaining army were eventually exiled into northern India.

Origin

Xuanzang describes the ruler of Kapisa/Kabul, whom he had personally met, as a devout Buddhist and a Kshatriya. The 11th-century Persian Muslim scholar Alberuni recorded folklore concerning the early history of the Kabul Shahi rulers,[980] including beliefs that:

- the kings residing in Kabul, while they practised Hinduism, also belonged to a Turkic culture;
- they were also, however, Tibetan in origin, including the founder of the dynasty, Barahatakin;

Figure 264: *Coins of the Shahis, 8th century*

Figure 265: *Coin of Shahi Kings of Kabul and Gandhara: Samanta Deva, c. 850–1000 CE.* ***Obv****: Rider bearing lance on caparisoned horse facing right. Devnagari Legends: "bhi"* ***Rev****: Recumbent bull facing left, trishula on bull's rump, Devnagari Legends: Sri Samanta Deva.*

Figure 266: *The Amb Temples in Pakistan's Salt Range mountains were built between the 7th and 9th centuries CE.*

- when Barahatakin migrated from Tibet, he took up residence in a cave near Kabul and did not venture out in public for a few days, at which point local people regarded him and his Turkic clothing with curiosity, like a "new born baby", and honoured him as a being of miraculous birth, who was destined to be a king;
- in his lifetime Barahatakin came to rule the country, under the title "Shahiya of Kabul";
- the title remained among his descendants for about 60 generations and;
- the descendants of Barahatakin include one was Kanik (possibly the Kushan ruler Kanishka), who is said to have built a *vihara* called Kanika Caitya in Purushapura (Peshawar).[981]

Thus the folklore accounts recorded by Alberuni connect the earlier Shahis of Kabul/Kapisa to Turkish extraction and also claim their descent from Kanik (or Kanishaka of Kushana lineage). At the same time it is also claimed that 'their first king Barahatigin (Vrahitigin?) had originally come from Tibet and concealed in a narrow cave in Kabul area (and here is given a strange legend which we omit).' One can easily see the above account of Shahi origin as totally fanciful and fairy tale-like. These statements taken together are very confusing, inconsistent and bear the express marks of a folklore and vulgar tradition, hence unworthy of inspiring any confidence in the early history of

Shahis. The allegation that the first dynasty of Kabul was Turki is plainly based on the vulgar tradition, which Alberuni himself remarked was clearly absurd.

The historian V. A. Smith speculates – based on Alberuni – that the earlier Shahis were a cadet branch of the Kushanas who ruled both over Kabul and Gandhara until the rise of the Saffarids. H. M. Elliot relates the early Kabul Shahis to the Kators and further connects the Kators with the Kushanas. Charles Frederick Oldham also traces the Kabul Shahi lineage to the Kators—whom he identifies with the Kathas orTakkhas—Naga worshipping collective groups of Hinduism (*chandravanshi group*) lineage. He further speaks of the Urasas, Abhisaras, Daradas, Gandharas, Kambojas, et al. as allied tribal groups of the Takkhas belonging to the *Sun-worshiping* races of the north-west frontier.[982,983] D. B. Pandey traces the affinities of the early Kabul Shahis to the Hunas.

Other accounts suggest Punjabi Kshatriya origins for the Shahi dynasty. Xuanzang clearly describes the ruler of Kapisa/Kabul, whom he had personally met, as a devout Buddhist and a Kshatriya and not a Tu-kiue/Tu-kue (Turk).[984] The fact that Xuanzang (AD 644) specifically describes the ruler of Kapisa as *Kshatriya*,[985] and that of Zabul at this time being known as Shahi[986] casts serious doubt about the speculated connections of the first Shahis of Kabul/Kapisa to the Kushanas or the Hephthalites. Neither the Kushanas, the Hunas/Hephthalites nor the Turks (or Turushkas) have ever been designated or classified as Kshatriyas in any ancient Indian tradition. Therefore, the identification of the first line of Shahi kings of Kapisa/Kabul with the Kushanas, Hunas, or Turks obviously seems to be in gross error.[987]

It is very interesting that Alberuni calls the early Shahi rulers "Turks", but this should be interpreted to mean Turkicised, rather than Turkic in origin.[988]

Hindu origins and Turkic influences

The Shahi rulers of Kapisa/Kabul who ruled from the early 4th century until 870 CE were Hindu Brahmins.Wikipedia:Citation needed The Shahis of Afghanistan were discovered in 1874 to be connected to the Kamboja "race" by E. Vesey Westmacott.[989]

E. Vesey Westmacott,[990] Bishan Singh, K. S. Dardi, et al. connect the Kabul Shahis to the ancient Indian Kshatriya clans of the Kambojas/Gandharas. George Scott Robertson[991] writes that the Kators/Katirs of Kafiristan belong to the well known *Siyaposh* tribal group of the Kams, Kamoz and Kamtoz tribes.[992] But numerous scholars now also agree that the *Siyaposh* tribes of Hindukush are the modern representatives of the ancient Iranian cis-Hindukush Kambojas.[993]

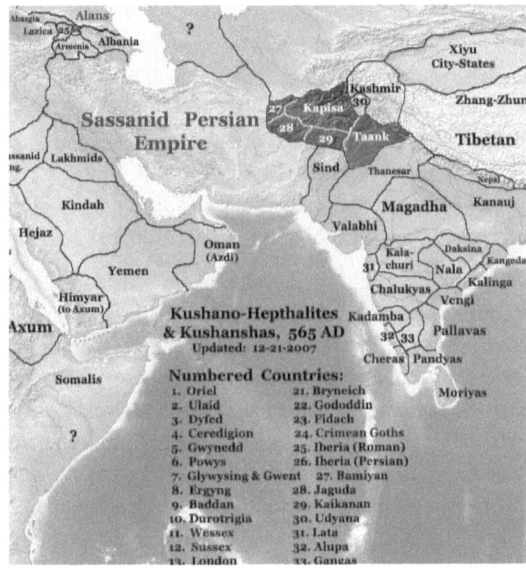

Figure 267: *Asia in AD 565, showing the Shahi kingdoms and their neighbours.*

The powerful evidence from Xuanzang (AD 644) attesting that the ruler of Kabul/Kapisa was a *devout Buddhist* and belonged to *Kshatriya* caste would rather connect this ruling dynasty either to the erstwhile Gandharas or more probably to Ashvaka clan of the Kambojas, the eminent *Kshatriya* clan of the Mauryan times from the neighbouring region in India.[994]

The name (*Katorman* or *Lagaturman*) of the last king of the so-called first Shahi line of Kabul/Kapisa simply reveals a trace of Tukhara cultural influence in the Kamboja (Kapisa) region, as hinted in the above discussion. Thus, the first ruling dynasty of Kapisa and Kabul, designated as a *Kshatriya* dynasty by Xuanzang had been a Kamboja dynasty from India.[995]

From the 2nd century BC onwards (much prior to the Huna ascendancy), the Tukharas had settled in considerable numbers in the ancient Kamboja land[996,997] and thus the culture of the Kambojas undoubtedly underwent some changes and due to the interaction of two cultures, the Kambojas of Kapisa were also substantially influenced by Tukharas[998,999] who remained for quite a time the ruling power in this region.

This fact is also verified by Xuanzang who records that the literature, customary rules, and currency of Bamiyan were same as those of Tukhara; the spoken language is only little different and in personal appearance the people closely resembled those of the Tukhara country. On the other hand, the literature and written language of Kapisa (=Kamboja) was like that of Tukharas but the social customs, colloquial idiom, rules of behavior (and their personal resemblance) differed somewhat from those of Tukhara country[1000] which means that the original and dominant community of Kapisa had imbibed the Tukharan culture and customs but to a limited extent and the penetration of the Tukharas in the Kapisa territory appears to have therefore been also limited. The Kambojas and the Tukharas (Turks) are mentioned as immediate neighbors in north-west as late as the 8th century AD as Rajatarangini of Kalhana demonstrates.[1001]

Evidence also exists that some medieval Muslim writers have confused the Kamboja clans of Pamirs/Hindukush with the Turks and invested the former with Turkic ethnicity. For example, 10th-century Arab geographer Al-Muqaddasi, refers to the *Kumiji* (=*Kamoji/Kamboja*) tribesmen of Buttaman mountains (Tajikistan),[1002] on upper Oxus, and calls them of Turkic race.[1003,1004,1005,1006,1007] Song Yun, the Chinese Ambassador to the Huna kingdom of Gandhara, in AD 520 writes that the Yethas (*Hephthalites*) had invaded Gandhara two generations prior to him and had completely destroyed this country. The then Yetha ruler was extremely cruel, vindictive, and anti-Buddhist and had engaged in a three years border war with the king of Ki-pin (Cophene or Kapisa), disputing the boundaries of that country.[1008] The Yetha king referred to by Song Yun may have been Mihirakula (AD 515-540/547) or his governor. This evidence also proves that the Kapisa kingdom was well established prior to the Huna/Hephthalite invasion of Gandhara (c. AD 477) and that it did not submit to the Yethas but had survived and continued to maintain its independence.

Once the political clout of the invaders like the Kushanas or the Hephthalites had declined, some native chieftain from the original dominant clans of this region seems to have attained ascendancy in political power and established an independent kingdom on the ruins of the Kushana and/or the Hephthalite empire.

Commenting on the rise of Shahi dynasty in Kabul/Kapisa, Charles Frederick Oldham observes: "Kabulistan must have passed through many vicissitudes during the troublous times which followed the overthrow of the great Persian empire by the Alexander. It no doubt fell for a time under the sway of foreign rulers (Yavanas, Kushanas, Hunas etc). The great mass of the population, however, remained Zoroastrian or Shamanic Polytheists. And probably too, the Kshatriya chiefs from India retained great shadow of authority, and conquered Kabulistan when the opportunity arose.".

Barhatigin is said to be the founder of the dynasty which is said to have ruled for 60 generations until AD 870. This, if true, would take Barhatigin and the founding of the early Shahi dynasty back about 20x60=1200 years, i.e., to about the 4th century BC if we take the average generation of 20 years; and

Figure 268: *Newly excavated Buddhist stupa at Mes Aynak in Logar Province. Similar stupas have been discovered in neighbouring Ghazni Province, including in the northern Samangan Province.*

to the 7th century BC if an average generation is taken as 25 years. It is well nigh impossible that a single dynasty could have ruled for 1200 (or 1500) years at a stretch. Moreover, King Kanik (if Kanishaka) ruled (AD 78 – 101) not over Kabul but over Purushapura/Gandhara and his descendants could not have ruled for almost 900 years as a single dynasty over Kapisa/Kabul especially in a frontier region called the gateway of India. Pre Islamic Hindu and Buddhist heritage of Afghanistan is well established in the Shahi coinage from Kabul of this period.

Based on fragmentary evidence of coins, there was one king named Vrahitigin (Barhatigin?) who belonged to pre-Christian times as Alberuni's accounts would tend to establish. If Kanik is same as Kanishaka of Kushana race as is often claimed, then the second claim that the ancestors of the early Shahis came from Tibet becomes incompatible to known facts of history.

According to Olaf Caroe, "the earlier Kabul Shahis in some sense were the inheritors of the Kushana chancery tradition and were staunch Hindus in character.[1009] The affinities of the early Shahis of Kapisa/Kabul are still speculative, and the inheritance of the Kushan-Hephthalite chancery tradition and political institutions by Kabul Shahis do not necessarily connect them to the preceding dynasty (i.e. the Kushanas or Hephthalites).

Figure 269: *Abbasid Shahi-inspired coin, Iraq 908–930. British Museum.*

It appears that from start of the 5th century till AD 793-94, the capital of the Kabul Shahis was Kapisa. As early as AD 424, the prince of Kapisa (*Ki-pin of the Chinese*) was known as Guna Varman.[1010] The name ending "Varman" is used after the name of a Ksahriya only.[1011,1012,1013,1014] Thus the line of rulers whom Xuanzang refers to in his chronicles appears to be an extension of the *Kshatriya* dynasty whom this Guna Varman of Ki-pin or Kapisa (AD 424) belonged. Thus this *Kshatriya* dynasty was already established prior to AD 424 and it was neither a Kushana nor a Hephthalite dynasty by any means.[1015]

It appears more than likely that, rather than the Kushanas or Hunas or the Turks, the Shahi rulers of Kabul/Kapisa and Gandhara had a descent Wikipedia:Citation needed from the neighbouring warlike Kshatriya clans of the Kambojas known as Ashvakas (q.v.), who in the 4th century BC, had offered stubborn and decisive resistance to Macedonian invader, Alexander, and later had helped Chandragupta Maurya found the Mauryan empire of India.[1016] They were the same bold and warlike people on whom king Ashoka Maurya had thought it wise and expedient to *bestow autonomous status*[1017] and to whom he gave eminent place in his Rock Edicts V and XIII. They were fiercely independent warlike people who had never easily yielded to any foreign overlord.[1018] They were the people who, in the 5th century AD, had formed the very neighbours of the Bactrian Ephthalites of Oxus and whom Chandragupta II of Gupta dynasty had campaigned against and had obtained tribute from about the start of the 5th century AD.[1019,1020] Dr V. A. Smith says that this epic verse is reminiscent of the times when the Hunas first came into contact with the Sassanian dynasty of Persia.[1021] Sata-pañcāśaddesa-vibhaga of the medieval era Tantra book *Saktisamgma Tantra*[1022] locates Kambojas (*Kabul Shahis*?) to the west of southwest Kashmir (or Pir-pañcāla), to the south of Bactria and to the east of *Maha-Mlechcha-desa* (=*Mohammadan countries* i.e Khorasan/Iran) and likewise, locates the Hunas (*Zabul Shahis*?) to the south of Kama valley (*or Jallalabad/Afghanistan*) and to the north of Marudesa (or Rajputana) towards western Punjab.[1023]

The Kavyamimasa of Rajshekhar also lists the *Sakas, Kekayas, Kambojas, Vanayujas, Bahlikas, Hunas, Pahlvas, Limpakas, Harahuras, Hansmaragas (Hunzas) etc*[1024] in the north-west. Since Rajshekhar (AD 880–920) was contemporary with Hindu Shahis, he identifies people called *Kambojas (Kabul/Kapisa), Vanayujas (Bannus), Limpakas (Lamghanis), Hunas (Zabul), Pahlvas (Persians—Maha-mlechchas), Harahuras (Red Hunas* located in Herat*)* etc almost exactly in the same localities which were occupied by *Kabul Shahi* and *Zabul Shahi* kingdoms respectively. The above referred to pieces of evidence again spotlight on the Kambojas and the Hunas together and places them near the environs of the Muslim Persians in north-west. During the 1st century AD and later in the 5th century (c. AD 477), the cis-Hindukush Kambojas and Gandharas partially came under the sway of foreign invaders like the Kushanas and the Hephthalites (Hunas). These warlike people were temporarily overpowered by the numerous hordes but they did not become extinct; and once the political tide of the foreign hordes ebbed, *someone from the native chieftains from the original dominant clans (i.e. the Ksatrya Ashvakas) of this region asserted his authority and attained ascendancy in political power and had established himself as Kshatriya overlord of an independent kingdom on the ruins of the erstwhile Kushana and/or the Hephthalites empire.*[1025]

The title of "Shahi"

In ancient time, the title Shahi appears to be a quite popular royal title in Afghanistan and the north-western areas of the Indian sub-continent. Sakas,[1026] Wikipedia:Citation needed Kushanas,[1027] Hunas,[1028] Bactrians,[1029] by the rulers of Kapisa/Kabul,[1030] and Gilgit used it.[1031] Wikipedia:Verifiability In Persian form, the title appears as *Kshathiya, Kshathiya Kshathiyanam*, Shao of the Kushanas and the *Ssaha* of Mihirakula (Huna chief).[1032] The Kushanas are stated to have adopted the title *Shah-in-shahi* (*"Shaonano shao"*) in imitation of Achaemenid practice.[1033]

An ancient Jaina work, *Kalakacarya-kathanaka*, says that the rulers of the Sakas who had invaded Ujjaini/Malwa in 62 BC also used the titles of *Sahi* and

Sahnusahi.[1034] Since the title *Shahi* was used by the rulers of *Kapisa/Kabul or Gandhara* also in imitation of Kushana "Shao", it has been speculated by some writers that the Shahi dynasty of Kapisa/Kabul or Gandhara was a *foreign* dynasty and had descended from the Kushans or Turks (*Turushkas*). However, the title has been used by several rulers irrespective of any racial connotations and this may refute the above speculation.

In addition, one ancient inscription and several ancient Buddhist manuscripts from the Gilgit area between upper Indus and river Kabul shed some light on the three kings who ruled in the Gilgit region in the 6th and 7th centuries AD. They also bore Shahi titles and their names are mentioned as *Patoladeva alias Navasurendradiyta Nandin*, *Srideva alias Surendra Vikrmadiyta Nandin* and *Patoladeva alias Vajraditya Nandin*. It is very relevant to mention here that each of the Shahi rulers mentioned in the above list of Gilgit rulers has Nandin as his surname or last name[1035] It is more than likely that the surname Nandin refers to their clan name. It is also very remarkable that the modern Kamboj tribe of northern Punjab still has *Nandan (Nandin)* as one of their important clan names. It is therefore very likely that these Gilgit rulers of upper Indus may also have belonged to the Kamboja lineage.[1036,1037] Furthermore, **"Shahi, Sahi, Shahiya"** as a septal name is still carried by a section of the Punjab Kambojs which appears to be a relic from the Shahi title of their Kabul/Kapisa princes.[1038]

Hindu and Buddhist culture

Alberuni's reference to the supplanting of the Kabul Shahi dynasty in about AD 870 by a Brahmin called Kallar actually implies only that the religious faith of the royal family had changed from Buddhism to Hinduism by about that date; it might not have actually involved any physical supplanting of the existing Kabul Shahi dynasty as is stated by Alberuni whose account of early Shahis is indeed based on telltale stories.[1039]

Archeological sites of the period, including a major Hindu Shahi temple north of Kabul and a chapel in Ghazni, contain both the pre-dominant Hindu and Buddhist statuary, suggesting that there was a close interaction between the two religions.

When the Chinese monk Xuanzang visited Kapisa (about 60 km north of modern Kabul) in the 7th century, the local ruler was a Kshatriya King Shahi Khingala. A Ganesha idol has been found near Gerdez that bears the name of this king, see Shahi Ganesha[1040].

Several 6th- or 7th-century AD Buddhist manuscripts were found from a stupa at Gilgit. One of the manuscripts reveals the name of a Shahi king *Srideva Sahi Surendra Vikramaditya Nanda*.[1041]

Figure 270: *6th-century "image of Hindu deity, Ganesha, consecrated by the Shahi King Khingala." (Gardez, Afghanistan)*

Invasions from the 7th century

In the wake of Muslim invasions of Kabul and Kapisa in second half of the 7th century (AD 664), the Kapisa/Kabul ruler called by Muslim writers Kabul Shah (*Shahi of Kabul*) made an appeal to the Kshatriyas of the Hind who had gathered there in large numbers for assistance and drove out the Muslim invaders as far as Bost.[1042] This king of Kapisa/Kabul who faced the Muslim invasion was undoubtedly a Kshatriya.[1043]

In AD 645, when Chinese pilgrim Xuanzang was passing through the Uttarapatha, *Udabhanda or Udabhandapura* was the place of residence or secondary capital of emperor of Kapisa which then dominated over 10 neighboring states comprising Lampaka, Nagara, Gandhara and Varna (Bannu) and probably also Jaguda. About Gandhara, the pilgrim says that its capital was Purushapura; the royal family was extinct and country was subject to Kapisa; the towns and villages were desolate and the inhabitants were very few. It seems that under pressure from Arabs in the southwest and the Turks in the north, the kings of Kapisa had left their western possessions in the hands of their viceroys and made Udabhanda their principal seat of residence. The reason why Udabhandapura was selected in preference to Peshawar is at present unknown but it is possible that the new city of Udabhanda was built by Kapisa rulers for strategic reasons.[1044]

In AD 671 Muslim armies seized Kabul and the capital was moved to Udabhandapura.[1045]

Move to Kabul; dynastic continuity

In subsequent years, the Muslim armies returned with large reinforcements and Kabul was swept when the Shahi ruler agreed to pay tribute to the conquerors. For strategical reasons, the Shahis, who continued to offer stubborn resistance to Muslim onslaughts, finally moved their capital from Kapisa to Kabul in about AD 794. Kabul Shahis remained in Kabul until AD 879 when Ya'qub-i Laith Saffari, the founder of the Saffarid dynasty, conquered the city. Kabul Shahis had built a defensive wall all around the Kabul city to protect it against the army of Muslim Saffarids. The remains of these walls are still visible over the mountains which are located inside the Kabul city.

The first Hindu Shahi dynasty was founded in AD 870 by Kallar (see above). Kallar is well documented to be a Brahmin. The kingdom was bounded on the north by the Hindu kingdom of Kashmir, on the east by Rajput kingdoms, on the south by the Muslim Emirates of Multan and Mansura, and on the west by the Abbasid Caliphate.

According to the confused accounts recorded by the Persian historian Al-Biruni which are chiefly based on folklore,[1046,1047,1048] the last king of the first Shahi dynasty, Lagaturman (*Katorman*) was overthrown and imprisoned by his Brahmin vizier Kallar, thus resulting in the change-over of dynasty.

The Hindu Shahi, a term used by Al-Biruni[1049] to refer to the ruling Hindu dynasty[1050] that took over from the *Turki Shahi* and ruled the region during the period prior to Muslim conquests of the 10th and 11th centuries.

The term *Hindu Shahi* was a royal title of this dynasty and not its actual clan or ethnological name. Al-Biruni used the title *Shah* for many other contemporary royal houses in his descriptions as well.[1051]

It is very remarkableWikipedia:Manual_of_Style/Words_to_watch#Unsupported_attributions that Kalhana (c. 12th century), the author of *Rajatarangini* (written in AD 1147–49), also refers to the Shahis and does not maintain any difference or distinction between the earlier Shahis (RT IV.143) and the later Shahis or does not refer to any supplanting of the dynasty at any stage as Alberuni does in his *Tarikh-al-Hind*.[1052] etc., unbroken to as far as or earlier than AD 730.[1053] It is also remarkableWikipedia:Manual_of_Style/Words_to_watch#Unsupported_attributions that Rajatrangini and all other sources refer to the Shahi rulers of Udabhandapura/Waihind as belonging to the Kshatriya lineage[1054,1055] in contrast to Alberuni who designates the earlier Shahi rulers as Turks and the later as Brahmins[1056]

Since the change of Shahi capital from Kabul to Waihind or Uddhabhandapura had also occurred precisely around this period, it is probable that the narrator of the folklore/tellatale to Alberuni had confused the "change of capital" issue with the "supplanting of Kabul Shahi dynasty" since the incidence of shift had occurred remotely about 200 years prior to Alberuni's writing (AD 1030). There is no doubt, as the scholars also admit, that the change in dynasty is effected by *"a common legend of eastern story"*, which surely bears the express mark of folklore for the previous history of Kabul Shahis, hence obviously speculative and not much worthy of serious history.[1057]

Retreat and dependence on Kashmir

The Hindu Shahis became engaged with the Yamini Turks of Ghazni[1058] over supremacy of the eastern regions of Afghanistan initially before it extended towards the Punjab region. They briefly recaptured the Kabul Valley from the Samanid successors of the Saffarids, until a general named Alptigin drove out the Samanid *wali* of Zabulistan and established the Ghaznavid dynasty at Ghazna.[1059] Under his general and successor Sabuktigin the Ghaznavids had begun to raid the provinces of Lamghan.[1060] and Multan. This precipitated an alliance first between the then King Jayapala and the Amirs of Multan, and then in a second battle in alliance with Delhi, Ajmer, Kalinjar, and Kannauj which saw the Hindu Shahi lose all lands west of the Indus River. His successor Anandapala arrived at a tributary arrangement with Sebuktigin's successor, Mahmud of Ghazni, before he was defeated and exiled to Kashmir in the early 11th century.

Al-Idirisi (AD 1100-1165/66) testifies that until as late as the 12th century, a contract of investiture for every Shahi king was performed at Kabul and that here he was obliged to agree to certain ancient conditions which completed the contract.[1061] Kalhana remarked: "To this day, the appellation Shahi throws its lustre on a numberless host of kshatriya abroad who trace their origin to that family".[1062]

The kings of Kashmir were related to the Shahis through marital and political alliance. Didda, a queen of Kashmir was a granddaughter of the Brahmin Shahi Bhima, who was married to Kshemagupta (r. 951–959). Bhima had visited Kashmir and built the temple Bhima Keshava.

Jayapal

The initial Hindu Shahi dynasty was the House of Kallar, but in AD 964 the rule was assumed from Bhima upon his death by Jayapala, son of Rai AsatapalaWikipedia:Citation needed .[1063] Epithets from the Bari Kot inscriptions record his full title as *"Parambhattaraka Maharajadhiraja Paramesvara Sri Jayapala deva"* the first Emperor of the Janjua Shahi phase.Wikipedia:Citation needed He is celebrated as a hero for his struggles in defending his kingdom from the Turkic rulers of Ghazni.

Emperor Jayapala was challenged by the armies of Sultan Sabuktigin in Battle of Peshawar (1001) and later by his son Sultan Mahmud of Ghazni. According to the *Minháj ad-Dīn* in his chronicle *Tabaqát-i Násiri*,[1064] he bears a testament to the political and powerful stature of Maharaja Jayapala Shah, *"Jayapála, who is the greatest of all the ráis (kings) of Hind..."* Misra wrote on Jaypala: *"(He) was perhaps the last Indian ruler to show such spirit of aggression, so sadly lacking in later Rajput kings."*[1065]

Anandpal

Prince Anandapala who ascended his father's throne (in about March/April AD 1002) already proved an able warrior and general in leading many battles prior to his ascension. According to 'Adáb al-Harb' (pp. 307–10) in about AD 990, it is written, *"the arrogant but ambitious Raja of Lahore Bharat, having put his father in confinement, marched on the country of Jayapála with the intention of conquering the districts of Nandana, Jailum (Jehlum) and Tákeshar"* (in an attempt to take advantage of Jayapala's concentrated effort with defence against the armies of Ghazni). *"Jayapala instructed Prince Anandapala to repel the opportunist Raja Bharat. Anandapala defeated Bharat and took him prisoner in the battle of Takeshar and marched on Lahore and captured the city and extended his father's kingdom yet further."*

However, during his reign as emperor many losses were inflicted on his kingdom by the Ghaznavids. During the battle of Chach between Mahmud and Anandapala, it is stated that *"a body of 30,000 Gakhars fought alongside as soldiers for the Shahi Emperor and incurred huge losses for the Ghaznavids"*. However, despite the heavy losses of the enemy, he lost the battle and suffered much financial and territorial loss. This was Anandapala's last stand against Sultan Mahmud of Ghazni. He eventually signed a treaty with the Ghaznavid Empire in AD 1010 and shortly a year later died a peaceful death. R.C Majumdar (D.V. *Potdar Commemoration Volume*, Poona 1950, p. 351) compared him ironically to his dynastic ancient famous ancestor *"King Porus, who bravely opposed Alexander but later submitted and helped in subduing other Indian rulers"*. And *Tahqíq Má li'l-Hind* (p. 351) finally revered him in his legacy as *"noble and courageous"* .

Trilochanpal

Prince Trilochanpála, the son of Anandapala, ascended the imperial throne in about AD 1011. Inheriting a reduced kingdom, he immediately set about expanding his kingdom into the Sivalik Hills, the domain of the *Rai of Sharwa*. His kingdom now extended from the River Indus to the upper Ganges valley. According to Al-Biruni, Tirlochanpála *"was well inclined towards the Muslims (Ghaznavids)"* and was honourable in his loyalty to his father's peace treaty to the Ghaznavids. He eventually rebelled against Sultan Mahmud and was later assassinated by some of his own mutinous troops in AD 1021–22, an assassination which was believed to have been instigated by the *Rai of Sharwa* who became his arch-enemy due to Tirlochanpala's expansion into the Sivalik ranges. He was romanticised in Punjabi folklore as *the Last Punjabi ruler of Punjab*.

Bheempal

Prince Bhímapála, son of Tirlochanpala, succeeded his father in AD 1021–22. He was referred to by Utbí as "Bhīm, the Fearless" due to his courage and valour. Considering his kingdom was at its lowest point, possibly only in control of Nandana, he admirably earned the title of "fearless" from his enemy's own chronicle writer. He is known to have commanded at the battle of Nandana personally and seriously wounded the commander of the Ghaznavid army Muhammad bin Ibrahim at-Tāī ('Utbi, vil.ii, p. 151.). He ruled only five years before meeting his death in AD 1026. He was final Shahi Emperor of the famed dynasty.

Kalhana, a 12th-century Kashmiri Brahmin, wrote of one campaign in the process that led to this collapse.

After the loss of empire

His sons Rudrapal, Diddapal, Kshempala, and Anangpala served as generals in Kashmir. They gained prominence in the Kashmiri royal court where they occupied influential positions and intermarried with the royal family. Hindu Kashmir had aided the Hindus Shahis against Mahmud of Ghazni. As a result after barely defeating the Hindu Shahis, Mahmud marched his men to Hindu Kashmir to take revenge for Kashmir's support of the Hindu Shahis. Al-Biruni was with Mahmud on these campaigns. They are mentioned frequently in Rajatarangini of Kalhana written during AD 1147–49. Rudrapal was mentioned by the writer Kalhana as a valiant general in the campaigns he led to quell resistance to the Kashmiri kings whom they served whilst in exile. His later descendants fell out of favour at the royal court and were exiled to the Siwalik Hills, retaining control of the Mandu fort. After a brief period, they rose again to take control of Mathura under Raja Dhrupet Dev in the 12th century before the campaigns of the Ghorid Empire.

The Janjua Rajputs of Punjab region claim to be the descendants of the Jayapala.[1066,1067]

Shahi rulers

- Khingala of Kapisa (7th century)
- Patoladeva alias Navasurendradiyta Nandin of Gilgit (6th–7th century)
- Srideva alias Surendra Vikrmadiyta Nandin of Gilgit (6th–7th century)
- Patoladeva alias Vajraditya Nandin of Gilgit (6th–7th century)
- Barha Tegin (?-680)
- Tegin Shah (680-739)
- Fromo Kesar/Phrom Gesar (739-?)
- Samantadeva Kallar alias Lalliya (c. 890–895) of Kabul
- Kamalavarmadeva/Kamaluka (895–921)
- Bhimadeva (921–964), son of Kamaluka
- Ishtthapala (?)
- Jayapala (964–1001)
- Anandapala (1001 - c. 1010), son of Jayapala
- Trilochanapala (ruled c. 1010 - 1021-22; assassinated by mutinous troops)
- Bhímapála (died in 1022–1026)

References

<templatestyles src="Template:Refbegin/styles.css" />

- Wink, André,*Al Hind: the Making of the Indo Islamic World*, Brill Academic Publishers, 1 Jan 1996, ISBN 90-04-09249-8
- Coinage of the Hindu Shahi period from Mardan, Pakistan[1068]. Treasures of Kashmir Smast.

Coordinates: 28°33′00″N 79°19′12″E[1069]

The Gangetic Plains and Deccan

Satavahana dynasty

<indicator name="pp-default"> 🔒 </indicator>

Satavahana Empire		
1st century BCE–2nd century CE		
Approximate extent of the Satavahana empire under Gautamiputra Satkarni		
Capital		Pratishthana, Amaravati
Languages		Prakrit, Telugu, Tamil[1070]
Religion		Hinduism, Buddhism
Government		Monarchy
Historical era		Antiquity
•	Established	1st century BCE

•	Disestablished	2nd century CE
	Preceded by	**Succeeded by**
	Maurya Empire Kanva dynasty	Western Kshatrapas Andhra Ikshvaku Chutu dynasty Pallava dynasty
Today part of		India

Satavahana Kings	
Simuka	(100-70 BCE)
Kanha	(70-60 BCE)
Satakarni	(1st BCE)
Sivasvati	(1st century CE)
Gautamiputra Satakarni	(2nd century CE)
Vasishthiputra Pulumavi	(2nd century CE)
Vashishtiputra Satakarni	(2nd century CE)
Shivaskanda Satakarni	(2nd century CE)
Yajna Sri Satakarni	(2nd century CE)
Vijaya	(2nd century CE)

The **Satavahanas** (IAST: *Sātavāhana*), also referred to as the **Andhras** in the Puranas, were an ancient Indian dynasty based in the Deccan region. Most modern scholars believe that the Satavahana rule began in the first century BCE and lasted until the second century CE, although some assign the beginning of their rule to as early as the 3rd century BCE. The Satavahana kingdom mainly comprised the present-day Telangana, Andhra Pradesh and Maharashtra. At different times, their rule extended to parts of modern Gujarat, Madhya Pradesh, and Karnataka. The dynasty had different capital cities at different times, including Pratishthana (Paithan) and Amaravati (Dharanikota).

The origin of the dynasty is uncertain, but according to the Puranas, their first king overthrew the Kanva dynasty. In the post-Maurya era, the Satavahanas established peace in the Deccan region, and resisted the onslaught of foreign invaders. In particular their struggles with the Saka Western Satraps went on for a long time. The dynasty reached its zenith under the rule of Gautamiputra Satakarni and his successor Vasisthiputra Pulamavi. The kingdom fragmented into smaller states by the early 3rd century CE.

The Satavahanas were early issuers of Indian state coinage struck with images of their rulers. They formed a cultural bridge and played a vital role in trade and the transfer of ideas and culture to and from the Indo-Gangetic Plain to the southern tip of India. They supported Brahmanism as well as Buddhism, and patronised Prakrit literature.

Origins

The date and place of origin of the Satavahanas, as well as the meaning of the dynasty's name, are a matter of debate among the historians. Some of these debates have happened in the context of regionalism, with the present-day Andhra Pradesh, Maharashtra, Karnataka and Telangana being variously claimed as the original homeland of the Satavahanas.[1071]

Etymology

According to one theory, the word "Satavahana" is a Prakrit form of the Sanskrit *Sapta-Vahana* ("driven by seven"; in Hindu mythology, the chariot of the sun god is drawn by seven horses). This would indicate that the Satavahanas originally claimed association with the legendary solar dynasty, as was common in ancient India.[1072] According to Inguva Kartikeya Sarma, the dynasty's name is derived from the words *sata* ("sharpened", "nimble" or "swift") and *vahana* ("vehicle"); the expression thus means "one who rides a nimble horse".[1073]

Another theory connects their name to the earlier Satiyaputa dynasty. Yet another theory derives their name from the Munda words *Sadam* ("horse") and *Harpan* ("son"), implying "son of the performer of a horse sacrifice".[1074] Several rulers of the dynasty bear the name or title "Satakarni". Satavahana, Satakarni, Satakani and Shalivahana appear to be variations of the same word. Damodar Dharmanand Kosambi theorized that the word "Satakarni" is derived from the Munda words *sada* ("horse") and *kon* ("son").[1075]

The Puranas use the name "Andhra" or "Andhra-Bhritya" for the Satavahanas. The term "Andhra" may refer to ethnicity or territory of the dynasty (see Original homeland below). It does not appear in the dynasty's own records.[1076]

Original homeland

The use of the name "Andhra" in the Puranas has led some scholars to believe that the dynasty originated in the eastern Deccan region (the historic Andhra region, present-day Andhra Pradesh and Telangana).[1077] At Kotilingala in Telangana, coins bearing the legend "Rano Siri Chimuka Satavahanasa" were found.[1078] Epigraphist and numismastist P. V. P. Sastry initially identified Chimuka with the dynasty's founder Simuka,[1079] because of which Kotilingala came to be known as the only place where coins attributed to Simuka were

Figure 271: *Cave No.19 of Satavahana king Kanha at the Nasik caves, 1st century BCE.*

Figure 272: *Krishna inscription of king Kanha in cave No.19, Nasik caves. This is the oldest known Satavahana inscription, circa 100-70 BCE.*[1071]

Figure 273: *Naneghat inscription. Dated to 70-60 BCE, in the reign of Satakarni I.*[1071]

found.[1080] Coins attributed to Simuka's successors Kanha and Satakarni I were also discovered at Kotilingla.[1081] Based on these discoveries, historians such as D. R. Reddy, S. Reddy and Shankar R. Goyal theorized that Kotlingala was the original home of the Satavahanas. However, the coin samples from Kotlingala are small, and it is not certain if these coins were minted there or reached there from somewhere else.[1082] Moreover, the identification of Chimuka of Kotilingala with the dynasty's founder Simuka has been contested by several scholars including P. L. Gupta and I. K. Sarma, who identified Chimuka as a later ruler.[1083,1084] P.V.P. Sastry also later changed his view, and stated that the two kings were different.[1079] As for the Puranas, these texts were compiled much later, during the Gupta period, and it is not certain if the Satavahanas were referred to as Andhras during their time.[1084]

Another section of scholars believe that the Satavahanas originated in western Deccan (present-day Maharashtra).[1077] All four extant inscriptions from the early Satavahana period (c. 1st century BCE) have been found in and around this region. The oldest known Satavahana inscription was found at Cave No.19 of the Pandavleni Caves in Nashik district, and was issued during the reign of Kanha (100-70 BCE). An inscription found at Naneghat was issued by Nayanika (or Naganika), the widow of Satakarni I; another inscription found at Naneghat has been dated to the same period on a paleographic basis. A slightly later inscription dated to the reign of Satakarni II has been found at Sanchi in Madhya Pradesh, located to the north of Maharashtra.[1071] The majority of the other Satavahana inscriptions have also been found in western Deccan.[1082] On the other hand, the epigraphic evidence from eastern Deccan does not mention the Satavahanas before the 4th century CE.[1084] At Nevasa, a seal and coins attributed to Kanha have been discovered.[1085] Coins attributed to Satakarni I have also been discovered at Nashik, Nevasa and Pauni in Maharashtra (besides places in eastern Deccan and present-day Madhya Pradesh).[1078] Based on this evidence, some historians argue that the Satavahanas initially came to power in the area around their capital Pratishthana (modern Paithan, Maharashtra) and then expanded their territory to eastern Deccan.[1086] Carla Sinopoli cautions that the inference about the western Deccan origin of the Satavahanas is "tentative at best" given the small sample of early inscriptions.[1087]

Kanha's Pandavleni mentions the term *maha-matra* (officer-in-charge), which indicates that the early Satavahanas followed the Mauryan administrative model.[1088] C. Margabandhu theorized that the Satavahanas were called Andhras because they were natives of eastern Deccan (the Andhra region), although they first established their empire in western Deccan after having served as Mauryan subordinates. Himanshu Prabha Ray (1986) opposes this theory, stating that the Andhra was originally an ethnic term, and did not come to denote the geographical region of eastern Deccan until well after the Satavahana period.[1071] According to Vidya Dehejia, the writers of the Puranas (which were compiled after the Satavahana period) mistook the Satavahana presence in eastern Deccan as evidence for their origin in that region, and wrongly labeled them as "Andhra".[1089]

Some scholars also suggest that the dynasty originated in present-day Karnataka, and initially owed allegiance to some Andhra rulers (because of which they were called Andhra-Bhrityas or "servants of the Andhras".[1090] V. S. Sukthankar theorized that the territorial division Satavahani-Satahani (Satavahanihara or Satahani-rattha), in present-day Bellary district, was the homeland of the Satavahana family.[1091] A stupa in Kanaganahalli village of Karnataka, dated between the first century BCE and first century CE, features limestone panels depicting portraits of Chimuka (Simuka), Satakani (Satakarni) and other Satavahana rulers.[1092]

History

Information about the Satavahanas comes from the Puranas, some Buddhist and Jain texts, the dynasty's inscriptions and coins, and foreign (Greek and Roman) accounts that focus on trade.[1093] The information provided by these

Figure 274: *Satavahana depiction of the city of Kushinagar in the War over the Buddha's Relics, South Gate, Stupa no. 1, Sanchi.*

sources is not sufficient to reconstruct the dynasty's history with absolute certainty. As a result, there are multiple theories about the Satavahana chronology.[1094]

Foundation

Simuka is mentioned as the first king in a list of royals in a Satavahana inscription at Naneghat. The various Puranas state that the first king of the dynasty ruled for 23 years, and mention his name variously as Sishuka, Sindhuka, Chhismaka, Shipraka, etc. These are believed to be corrupted spellings of Simuka, resulting from copying and re-copying of manuscripts.[1095] Simuka cannot be dated with certainty based on available evidence. Based on the following theories, the beginning of the Satavahana rule is dated variously from 271 BCE to 30 BCE.[1096]

- According to the Puranas, the first Andhra king overthrew the Kanva rule. D. C. Sircar dated this event to c. 30 BCE, a theory supported by many other scholars.[1094]
- The *Matsya Purana* mentions that the Andhra dynasty ruled for around 450 years. As the Satavahana rule ended in the early 3rd century, the beginning of their rule can be dated to the 3rd century BCE. The *Indica* of Megasthenes (350 – 290 BCE) mentions a powerful tribe named "Andarae", whose king maintained an army of 100,000 infantry, 2,000 cavalry and 1,000 elephants. If Andarae is identified with the Andhras, this can be considered additional evidence of Satavahana rule starting in the 3rd century BCE. The *Brahmanda Purana* states that "the four Kanvas will rule the earth for 45 years; *then* (it) will *again* go to the Andhras". Based on this statement, the proponents of this theory argue

that the Satavahana rule began immediately after the Maurya rule, followed by a Kanva interregnum, and then, a revival of the Satavahana rule. According to one version of the theory Simuka succeeded the Mauryans. A variation of the theory is that Simuka was the person who restored the Satavahana rule by overthrowing the Kanvas; the compiler of the Puranas confused him with the founder of the dynasty.[1097]

Most modern scholars believe that the Satavahana ruler began in the first century BCE and lasted until the second century CE. This theory is based on Puranic records as well as archaeological and numismatic evidence. The theory that dates their rule to an earlier period is now largely discredited because the various Puranas contradict each other, and are not fully supported by epigraphic or numismatic evidence.[1076]

Early expansion

Simuka was succeeded by his brother Kanha (also known as Krishna), who extended the kingdom up to Nashik in the west.[1098,1097] His successor Satakarni I conquered western Malwa, Anupa (Narmada valley) and Vidarbha, taking advantage of the turmoil caused by Greek invasions of northern India. He performed Vedic sacrifices including Ashvamedha and Rajasuya. Instead of the Buddhists, he patronised Brahmins and donated a substantial amount of wealth to them.[1074] The Hathigumpha inscription of the Kalinga king Kharavela mentions a king named "Satakani" or "Satakamini", who some[1099] identify with Satakarni I. The inscription describes dispatching of an army and Kharavela's threat to a city. Since the inscription is only partially legible, different scholars interpret the events described in the inscription differently. According to R. D. Banerji and Sailendra Nath Sen, Kharavela sent out an army against Satakarni.[1100] According to Bhagwal Lal, Satakarni wanted to avoid an invasion of his kingdom by Kharavela. So, he sent horses, elephants, chariots and men to Kharavela as a tribute. According to Sudhakar Chattopadhyaya, Kharavela's army diverted its course after failing to advance against Satakarni.[1101] According to Alain Daniélou, Kharavela was friendly with Satakarni, and only crossed his kingdom without any clashes.

Satakarni's successor Satakarni II ruled for 56 years, during which he captured eastern Malwa from the Shungas. He was succeeded by Lambodara. The coins of Lambodara's son and successor Apilaka have been found in eastern Madhya Pradesh.[1074]

Figure 275: *A coin of Nahapana restruck by the Satavahana king Gautamiputra Satakarni. Nahapana's profile and coin legend are still clearly visible.*

First Saka invasion

Little is known about Apilaka's successors, except cryptic references to one Kuntala Satakarni. The next well-known ruler of the dynasty was Hāla, who composed *Gaha Sattasai* in Maharashtri Prakrit. Like Hala, his four successors also ruled for very short periods (a total of 12 years), indicating troubled times for the Satavahanas.[1074]

Epigraphic and numismatic evidence suggests that the Satavahanas earlier controlled the northern Deccan plateau, the northern Konkan coastal plains, and the mountain passes connecting these two regions. During 15-40 CE, their northern neighbours - the Western Kshatrapas - extended their influence into these regions.[1102] The Western Kshatrapa ruler Nahapana is known to have ruled the former Satavahana territory, as attested by the inscriptions of his governor and son-in-law, Rishabhadatta.[1103]

First revival

The Satavahana power was revived by Gautamiputra Satakarni, who is considered the greatest of the Satavahana rulers.[1098] Charles Higham dates his reign c. 103 – c. 127 CE.[1098] S. Nagaraju dates it 106–130 CE. The king defeated by him appears to have been the Western Kshatrapa ruler Nahapana, as suggested

Figure 276: *Satavahana architecture at Cave No.3 of the Pandavleni Caves in Nashik. This cave was probably started during the reign of Gautamiputra Satakarni, and was finished and dedicated to the Buddhist Samgha during the reign of his son Vasishthiputra Pulumavi, circa 150 CE.*

by Nahapana's coins overstuck with names and titles of Gautamiputra.[1103] The Nashik *prashasti* inscription of Gautamiputra's mother Gautami Balashri, dated to the 20th year after his death, records his achievements. The most liberal interpretation of the inscription suggests that his kingdom extended from the present-day Rajasthan in the north to Krishna river in the south, and from Saurashtra in the west to Kalinga in the east. He assumed the titles *Raja-Raja* (King of Kings) and *Maharaja* (Great King), and was described as the Lord of Vindhya.[1074]

During the last years of his reign, his administration was apparently handled by his mother, which could have been a result of an illness or military preoccupation.[1074] According to the Nasik inscription made by his mother Gautami Balashri, he was the one ...[1104]

> ... who crushed down the pride and conceit of the Kshatriyas; who destroyed the Sakas (Western Satraps), Yavanas (Indo-Greeks) and Pahlavas (Indo-Parthians),... who rooted out the Khakharata family (the Kshaharata family of Nahapana); who restored the glory of the Satavahana race.

Figure 277: *Coin of Vashishtiputra Satakarni.*

—*Inscription of Queen Mother Gautami Balashri at Cave No.3 of the Pandavleni Caves in Nashik.*

Gautamiputra was succeeded by his son Vasisthiputra Sri Pulamavi (or Pulumayi). According to Sailendra Nath Sen, Pulumavi ruled from 96–119 CE.[1074] According to Charles Higham, he ascended the throne around 110 CE.[1098] Pulumavi features in a large number of Satavahana inscriptions and his coins have been found distributed over a wide area. This indicates that he maintained Gautamiputra's territory, and ruled a prosperous kingdom. He is believed to have added the Bellary region to Satakarni's kingdom. His coins featuring ships with double mast have been found on the Coromandel Coast, indicating involvement in maritime trade and naval power. The old stupa at Amaravati was renovated during his reign.[1074]

Second Saka invasion

Pulumavi's successor was his brother Vashishtiputra Satakarni. According to S. N. Sen he ruled during 120–149 CE;[1074] according to Charles Higham, his regnal years spanned 138–145 CE.[1098] He entered into a marriage alliance with the Western Satraps, marrying the daughter of Rudradaman I.[1074]

Figure 278: *Coin of Yajna Sri Satakarni, British Museum.*

The Junagadh inscription of Rudradaman I states that he defeated Satakarni, the lord of Dakshinapatha (Deccan), twice. It also states that he spared the life of the defeated ruler because of close relations:[1098]

> "*Rudradaman (...) who obtained good report because he, in spite of having twice in fair fight completely defeated Satakarni, the lord of Dakshinapatha, on account of the nearness of their connection did not destroy him.*"

—*Junagadh rock inscription*

According to D. R. Bhandarkar and Dineshchandra Sircar, the ruler defeated by Rudradaman was Gautamiputra Satakarni. However, E. J. Rapson believed that the defeated ruler was his son Vasishthiputra Pulumavi.[1105] Shailendra Nath Sen and Charles Higham believe that the defeated ruler was Vashishtiputra's successor Shivaskanda or Shiva Sri Pulumayi (or Pulumavi).[1098,1074]

As a result of his victories, Rudradaman regained all the former territories previously held by Nahapana, except for the extreme south territories of Pune and Nasik. Satavahana dominions were limited to their original base in the Deccan and eastern central India around Amaravati.

Second revival

Sri Yajna Sātakarni, the last person belonging to the main Satavahana dynastic line, briefly revived the Satavahana rule. According to S. N. Sen, he ruled during 170–199 CE.[1074] Charles Higham dates the end of his reign to 181 CE. His coins feature images of ships, which suggest naval and marine trade success.[1098] Wide distribution of his coins, and inscriptions at Nashik, Kanheri and Guntur indicate that his rule extended over both eastern and western parts of Deccan. He recovered much of the territory lost the Western Kshatrapas, and issued silver coinage, imitating them. During the last years of his reign, the Abhiras captured the northern parts of the kingdom, around Nashik region.[1074]

Decline

After Yajna Satakarni, the dynasty was soon extinguished following the rise of its feudatories, perhaps on account of a decline in central power.[1106] Yajna Sri was succeeded by Madhariputra Swami Isvarasena. The next king Vijaya ruled for 6 years. His son Vasishthiputra Sri Chadha Satakarni ruled for 10 years.[1074] Pulumavi IV, the last king of the main line, ruled until c. 225 CE. During his reign, several Buddhist monuments were constructed at Nagarjunakonda and Amaravati.[1098] Madhya Pradesh was also part of his kingdom.[1074]

After the death of Pulumavi IV, the Satavahana empire fragmented into five smaller kingdoms:[1074]

1. Northern part, ruled by a collateral branch of the Satavahanas (which ended in early 4th century[1098])
2. Western part around Nashik, ruled by the Abhiras
3. Eastern part (Krishna-Guntur region), ruled by the Andhra Ikshvakus
4. South-western parts (northern Karanataka), ruled by the Chutus of Banavasi
5. South-eastern part, ruled by the Pallavas

Territorial extent

The Satavahana territory included northern Deccan region, spanning the present-day Andhra Pradesh, Maharashtra and Telangana states. At times, their rule also extended to present-day Gujarat, Karnataka and Madhya Pradesh. The Nashik *prashasti* inscription issued by Gautami Balashri, the mother of Gautamiputra Satakarni, claims that her son ruled an extensive territory that stretched from Gujarat in the north to northern Karnataka in the south. It is not clear if Gautamiputra had effective control over these claimed territories. In any case, historical evidence suggests that his control over these territories did not last long.[1107] Moreover, this realm was not continuous:

Figure 279: *Ashoka with his Queens, at Sannati (Kanaganahalli Stupa), Satavahana period, 1st-3rd century CE. The inscription "Raya Asoko" ("King Ashoka") in Brahmi script is carved on the relief.*

many areas in this region remained under the control of the hunter-gatherers and other tribal communities.[1108]

The Satavahana capital kept shifting with time. The Nashik inscription describes Gautamiputra as the lord of Benakataka, suggesting that this was the name of his capital. Ptolemy (2nd century CE) mentioned Pratishthana (modern Paithan) as the capital of Pulumavi.[1107] At other times, the Satavahana capitals included Amaravati (Dharanikota) and Junnar. M. K. Dhavalikar theorized that the original Satavahana capital was located at Junnar, but had to be moved to Pratishthana because of Saka-Kushana incursions from the northwest.

Several Satavahana-era inscriptions record grants to religious monasteries. The settlements most frequently mentioned as the residences of donors in these inscriptions include the sea ports of Sopara, Kalyan, Bharucha, Kuda (unidentified), and Chaul. The most frequently mentioned inland settlements include Dhenukakata (unidentified), Junnar, Nashik, Paithan, and Karadh.[1107]

Other important Satavahana sites in western Deccan include Govardhana, Nevasa, Ter, and Vadgaon-Madhavpur. The ones in eastern Deccan include Amaravati, Dhulikatta, Kotalingala and Peddabankur.[1109]

Administration

The Satavahanas followed the administration guidelines of the Shastras. Their government was less top-heavy than that of the Mauryans, and featured several levels of feudatories:[1074]

- Rajan, the hereditary rulers
- Rajas, petty princes who struck coins in their own names
- Maharathis, hereditary lords who could grant villages in their own names and maintained matrimonial relations with the ruling family
- Mahabhojas
- Mahasenapati (civil administrator under Pulumavi II; governor of a janapada under Pulumavi IV)
- Mahatalavara ("great watchman")

The royal princes (*kumara*s) were appointed as viceroys of the provinces.[1074]

The *ahara* appears to have been the largest geographical subdivision of the Satavahana polity. Several inscriptions refer to *ahara*s named after the governors appointed to rule them (e.g. Govardhanahara, Mamalahara, Satavanihara and Kapurahara).[1107] This suggests that the Satavahanas attempted to build a formal administrative and revenue collection structure.[1110]

The inscriptions of Gautamiputra Satakarni suggest the existence of a bureaucratic structure, although it is not certain how stable and effective this structure was. For example, two inscriptions from Nashik Cave 11 record donations of agricultural land to ascetic communities. They state that the ascetics would enjoy tax exemption and non-interference from the royal officials. The first inscription states that the grant was approved by Gautamiputra's minister Sivagupta on the king's verbal orders, and preserved by the "great lords". The second inscription records a grant by Gautamiputra and his mother, and mentions Syamaka as the minister of the Govardhana *ahara*. It states that the charter was approved by a woman named Lota, who according to archaeologist James Burgess' interpretation, was the chief lady-in-waiting of Gautamiputra's mother.[1111]

The Satavahana-era inscriptions mention three types of settlements: *nagara* (city), *nigama* (market town) and *gama* (village).[1107]

Economy

The Satavahanas participated in (and benefited from) economic expansion through intensification of agriculture, increased production of other commodities, and trade within and beyond the Indian subcontinent.[1112]

Figure 280: *Indian ship on lead coin of Vasisthiputra Sri Pulamavi, testimony to the naval, seafaring and trading capabilities of the Satavahanas during the 1st–2nd century CE.*

During the Satavahana period, several large settlements emerged in the fertile areas, especially along the major rivers. The amount of land under agricultural use also expanded significantly, as a result of forest clearance and construction of irrigation reservoirs.[1110]

The exploitation of sites with mineral resources may have increased during the Satavahana period, leading to the emergence of new settlements in these areas. Such sites facilitated commerce and crafts (such as ceramic ware). The increased craft production during the Satavahana period is evident from archaeological discoveries at sites such as Kotalingala, as well as epigraphic references to artisans and guilds.[1110]

The Satavahanas controlled the Indian sea coast, and as a result, they dominated the growing Indian trade with the Roman Empire. The *Periplus of the Erythraean Sea* mentions two important Satavahana trade centres: Pratishthana and Tagara. Other important urban centres included Kondapur, Banavasi and Madhavpur. Nanaghat was the site of an important pass that linked the Satavahana capital Pratishthana to the sea.[1098]

Figure 281: *The Pompeii Lakshmi ivory statuette was found in the ruin of Pompeii (destroyed in an eruption of Mount Vesuvius in 79 CE). It is thought to have come from Bhokardan in the Satavahana realm in the first half of the 1st century CE. It testifies to Indo-Roman trade relations in the beginning of our era.*

Religion

The Satavahanas were Hindus and claimed Brahmanical status,[1113] although they also made generous donations to Buddhist monasteries.[1114] The lay people in the Satavahana period generally did not exclusively support a particular religious group .[1102]

The Naneghat inscription of Nayanika, recorded on the walls of a Buddhist monastic cave, mentions that her husband Satakarni I performed several Vedic sacrifices, including *ashvamedha* (horse sacrifice), *rajasuya* (royal consecration), and *agnyadheya* (fire ceremony).[1115] The inscription also records subsantial fees paid to Brahmin priests and attendees for these sacrifices. For example, 10,001 cows were granted for the *Bhagala-Dasaratra* sacrifice; and 24,400 coins were granted for another sacrifice, whose name is not clear.[1116]

In the Nashik inscription of Gautami Balashri, her son Gautamiputra Satakarni is called "ekabamhana", which is interpreted by some as "unrivaled Brahmana", thus indicating a Brahmin origin. However, R. G. Bhandarkar interprets this word as "the only protector of the Brahmins".[1117]

A number of Buddhist monastic sites emerged in the Deccan region during the Satavahana period. However, the exact relations between these monasteries and the Satavahana government is not clear.[1109] The Pandavleni Caves inscription issued during the reign of Kanha states that the cave was excavated by *maha-matra* (officer-in-charge) of the shramanas (non-Vedic ascetics). Based on this, Sudhakar Chattopadhyaya concludes that Kanha favoured Buddhism, and had an administrative department dedicated to the welfare of Buddhist monks.[1088]

However, Carla M. Sinopoli notes that although there are some records of donations to the Buddhist monasteries by the Satavahana royals, the vast majority of the donations were made by the non-royals. The most common among these donors were merchants, and many of the monasteries were located along the important trade routes.[1109] The merchants probably donated to the monasteries, because these sites facilitated trade by serving as rest houses, and possibly by directly participating in the trade.[1113] The monasteries appear to have been an important venue for displaying charitable donations, including the donations made to non-Buddhists (especially Brahmins).[1114]

Inscriptions

Several Brahmi script inscriptions are available from the Satavahana period, but most of these record donations to Buddhist institutions by individuals, and do not provide much information about the dynasty. The inscriptions issued by the Satavahana royals themselves also primarily concern religious donations, although some of them provide some information about the rulers and the imperial structure.[1070]

The earliest extant Satavahana inscription is from Nashik Cave 19, which states that the cave was commissioned by Mahamatra Saman of Nashik during the reign of king Kanha.[1071]

At Naneghat, an inscription issued by Nayanika, the widow of Satakarni I, has been found. It records Nayanika's lineage and mentions the Vedic sacrifices performed by the royal family.[1071] Another inscription at Naneghat comprises names of Satavahana royals, appearing as labels over their bas-relief portraits. The portraits are now completely eroded, but the inscription is believed to be contemporary to Nayanika's inscription on a paleographic basis.[1082]

The next oldest Satavahana-era inscription appears on a sculpted gateway element of Stupa 1 at Sanchi. It states that the element was donated by Ananda, who was the son of Siri Satakarni's foreman of artisans. This inscription is probably from the reign of Satakarni II.[1082]

Figure 282: *The inscription on the Southern Gateway at Sanchi mentioning "Gift of Ananda, the son of Vasithi, the foreman of the artisans of rajan Siri Satakarni" (the inscription is written in three lines over the dome of the stupa in this relief).*[1118] *Circa 50 BCE- 0 CE.*

Coinage

The Satavahanas are among the earliest Indian rulers to issue their own coins with portraits of their rulers, starting with king Gautamiputra Satakarni, a practice derived from that of the Western Kshatrapas he defeated, itself originating with the Indo-Greek kings to the northwest.

Thousands of lead, copper and potin Satavahana coins have been discovered in the Deccan region; a few gold and silver coins are also available. These coins do not feature uniform design or size, and suggest that multiple minting locations existed within the Satavahana territory, leading to regional differences in coinage.[1070]

The coin legends of the Satavahanas, in all areas and all periods, used a Prakrit dialect without exception. Some reverse coin legends are in Tamil, and Telugu languages.[1070]

Several coins carry titles or matronyms that were common to multiple rulers (e.g. Satavahana, Satakarni, and Pulumavi), so the number of rulers attested by coinage cannot be determined with certainty. The names of 16 to 20 rulers appear on the various coins. Some of these rulers appear to be local elites rather than the Satavahana monarchs.[1070]

The Satavahana coins give unique indications as to their chronology, language, and even facial features (curly hair, long ears and strong lips). They issued mainly lead and copper coins; their portrait-style silver coins were usually struck over coins of the Western Kshatrapa kings. The Satavahana coins also display various traditional symbols, such as elephants, lions, horses and chaityas (stupas), as well as the "Ujjain symbol", a cross with four circles at the end.

Figure 283: *Coin of Gautamiputra Yajna Satakarni ().*

Cultural achievements

The Satavahanas patronised the Prakrit language instead of Sanskrit.[1074] The Satavahana king Hāla is famous for compiling the collection of Maharashtri poems known as the *Gaha Sattasai* (Sanskrit: Gāthā Saptashatī), although from linguistic evidence it seems that the work now extant must have been re-edited in the succeeding century or two. Through this book, it was evident that agriculture was the main means of livelihood. Also many sorts of superstitions had prevailed. Additionally, Gunadhya, the minister of Hala, was the author of Brihatkatha.

Sculptures

Madhukar Keshav Dhavalikar writes that "The Satavahana sculptures unfortunately has never been recognized as an independent school in spite of the fact it has its own distinctive characteristic features. The earliest in point of time is that in the Bhaja Vihara cave which marks the beginning of sculptural art in the Satavahana dominion around 200BC. It is profusely decorated with

Figure 284: *The Great Chaitya in the Karla Caves, Maharashtra, India, c. 120 CE. The Satavahana rulers made grants for its construction.*

carvings, and even pillars have a lotus capital crowned with sphinx-like mythic animals."[1119] Dhavalikar also writes that in Chankama "the panel occurring on the west pillar of Northern Gateway portrays a very important event in Buddha's life. It depicts votaries, two each on either side of what looks like a ladder which actually is the promenade which Buddha is supposed to have walked. It is said that Buddha, after attaining Enlightenment, spent four weeks near the Bodhi tree. Of these, the third week he spent walking along the promenade (*chankama*) to and fro."[1120]

Along with some of the above major Satavahana sculptures some more sculptures existed—namely, *Dvarapala, Gajalaksmi, Shalabhanjikas*, Royal Procession, Decorative pillar, etc.[1121]

Bronze

Several metal figurines are found that could be attributed to the Satavahanas. A hoard of unique bronze objects were also found from Bramhapuri. Numerous articles obtained from there were Indian but also reflected Roman and Italian influence. A small statue of Poseidon, wine jugs, and a plaque depicting Perseus and Andromeda were also obtained from the house from where the objects were found. The fine elephant in the Ashmolean Museum, the Yaksi

Figure 285: *Royal earrings, Andhra Pradesh, 1st Century BCE.*

image in the British Museum, and the cornucopia found in Posheri, kept at Chhatrapati Shivaji Maharaj Vastu Sangrahalaya can also be attributed to the Satavahana period.

Architecture

Sculptures of Amravati represent the architectural development of the Satavahana periods. They built Buddhist stupas in Amravati (95 feet high). They also constructed a large number of stupas at Goli, Jaggiahpeta, Gantasala, Amravati Bhattiprolu, and Shri Parvatam. Caves IX and X, containing Ajanta paintings, were patronized by Satavahana, and the painting throughout the caves appear to have started with them. Ashokan Stupas were enlarged, the earlier bricks and wood works being replaced with stone works. The most famous of these monuments are the stupas, the most famous among them being the Amravati Stupa and the Nagarjunakonda Stupa.

Paintings

The Satavahana paintings are the earliest surviving specimens—excluding prehistoric—in India, and they are to be found only at the Ajanta. There were two phases of artistic activity of Ajanta: the first occurring in the 2nd to 1st centuries BC, when Hinayana caves were excavated during Satavahana rule; the later in the second half of the 5th century under the Vakatakas. Vagaries of nature and some vandalism have taken a heavy toll on the Ajanta Caves. Only a few fragments related to the Satavahanas have survived in Caves No. 9 and 10, both of which are chaitya-grihas with stupas.

The most important surviving painting of the Satavahana period at Ajanta is the *Chhadanta Jataka* in Cave No. 10, but that, too, is only fragmentary. It is a painting of an elephant named Bodhisattva with six tusks, related to a mythological story. The human figures, both male and female, are typically Satavahanas, almost identical with their counterparts on the Sanchi Gateways so far as their physiognomy, costumes, and jewellery are concerned. The only difference is that the Sanchi figures have shed some of their weight.[1122]

Art of Sanchi

The Satavahanas contributed greatly to the embellishment of the Buddhist stupa of Sanchi. It was heavily repaired under King Satakarni II. The gateways and the balustrade were built after 70 BCE, and appear to have been commissioned by the Satavahanas. An inscription on the Southern Gateway records that it was the work of Satakarni II's royal architect Ananda.[1123] An inscription records the gift of one of the top architraves of the Southern Gateway by the artisans of the Satavahana Emperor Satakarni:

Gift of Ananda, the son of Vasithi, the foreman of the artisans of rajan Siri Satakarni[1124]

Sanchi under the Satavahanas
1st century BCE/CE.

Figure 286: *The Miracle of Walking in the air at Savrasti.*

Figure 287: *Pipal tree.*

Figure 288: *Miracle of the Buddha walking on the River Nairanjana*

Figure 289: *Bimbisara with his royal cortege issuing from the city of Rajagriha to visit the Buddha.*

Figure 290: *Foreigners making a dedication to the Great Stupa at Sanchi.*

Figure 291: *Procession of king Suddhodana from Kapilavastu.*

Satavahana dynasty 369

Figure 292: *Architrave*

Figure 293: *Architrave*

Figure 294: *Yakshini.*

Figure 295: *Pillar capital.*

Figure 296: *Lion pillar capital.*

Art of Amaravati

The Satavahana rulers are also remarkable for their contributions to Buddhist art and architecture. They built great stupas in the Krishna River Valley, including the stupa at Amaravati in Andhra Pradesh. The stupas were decorated in marble slabs and sculpted with scenes from the life of the Buddha, portrayed in a characteristic slim and elegant style. The Amaravati style of sculpture also influenced the sculpture of Southeast Asia.[1125]

List of rulers

Multiple Puranas contain chronology of Satavahana kings. However, there are inconsistencies among the various Puranas over the number of kings in the dynasty, the names of the kings, and the length of their rule. In addition, some of the kings listed in the Puranas are not attested via archaeological and numismatic evidence. Similarly, there are some kings known from coins and inscriptions, whose names are not found in the Puranic lists.[1096,1097]

The reconstructions of the Satavahana kings by historians fall into two categories. According to the first one, 30 Satavahana kings ruled for around 450 years, starting from Simuka's rule immediately after the fall of the Mauryan empire. This view relies heavily on the Puranas, and is now largely discredited.

According to the second (and more widely accepted) category of reconstructions, the Satavahana rule started in around first century BCE. The chronologies in this category contain a smaller number of kings, and combine Puranic records with archaeological, numismatic and textual evidence.[1126]

Because of uncertainty regarding the establishment date of the Satavahana kingdom, it is difficult to give absolute dates for the reigns of the Satavahana kings.[1096] Therefore, many modern scholars do not assign absolute dates to the reigns of the historically attested Satavahana kings, and those who do vary greatly with each other.[1076]

Himanshu Prabha Ray provides the following chronology, based on archaeological and numismatic evidence:[1077]

- Simuka (before 100 BCE)
- Kanha (100–70 BCE)
- Satakarni I (70–60 BCE)
- Satakarni II (50–25 BCE)
- *Kshatrapa interregnum* with vassal Satavahana kings like Hāla
  - Nahapana (54-100 CE)
- Gautamiputra Satakarni (86–110 CE)
- Pulumavi (110–138 CE)
- Vashishtiputra Satakarni (138–145 CE)
- Shiva Shri Pulumavi (145–152 CE)
- Shiva Skanda Satakarni (145–152 CE)
- Yajna Shri Satakarni (152–181 CE)
- Vijaya Satakarni
- Regional rulers of south-eastern Deccan:[1112]
  - Chandra Shri
  - Pulumavi II
  - Abhira Isvasena
  - Madhariputra Sakasena
  - Haritiputra Satakarni

Puranic lists

The various Puranas give different lists of the Satavahana rulers. The *Matsya Purana* states that 30 Andhra kings ruled for 460 years, but some of its manuscripts name only 19 kings whose reigns add up to 448.5 years. The *Vayu Purana* also mentions that there were 30 Andhra kings, but its various manuscripts name only 17, 18, and 19 kings respectively; the reigns add up to 272.5, 300, and 411 years respectively. Many of these kings are not attested by historical evidence. On the other hand, some Satavahana kings attested by numismatic evidence (such as Rudra Satakarni) are not mentioned in the Puranas at all.[1127]

Different scholars have explained these anamolies in different ways. Scholars such as R. G. Bhandarkar, D. C. Sircar and H. C. Raychaudhuri theorized that the *Vayu Purana* mentions only the main imperial branch of the dynasty, while the *Matsya Purana* puts together princes of all its branches.[1127]

The names of the Andhra kings (in IAST), as mentioned in the various Puranas, are given below. These names vary across different manuscripts of the same Puranas, and some names are missing in some of the manuscripts. The list given below for each Purana contains the most exhaustive version. In the Puranas, Krishna (IAST: Kṛṣṇa) is described as brother of the first king, who overthrew the Kanva king Susharman. All other kings are described as sons of their predecessors. The first king of the Andhra-Bhrityas is also known as Shudraka or Suraka in the *Kumarika Khanda* of *Skanda Purana* (not present in the table below).

Puranic genealogy of Andhra dynasty[1128]

#	Ruler	Coins	Epigraphy	Bhagavata	Brahmanda	Matsya	Vayu	Vishnu	Reign (years)	Alternative names and reigns
1	Simuka	☐	☐	☐	☐	☐	☐	☐	23	Śiśuka (*Matsya*), Sindhuka (*Vayu*), Śipraka (*Vishnu*), Chhismaka (*Brahmanda*)
2	Kṛṣṇa (Kanha)	☐	☐	☐	☐	☐	☐	☐	18	
3	Śātakarṇi I	☐	☐	☐	☐	☐	☐	☐	10	Śantakarṇa (*Bhagavata*), Mallakarni - 10 or 18 years (*Matsya*), Śri Śatakarṇi (*Vishnu*)
4	Pūrṇotsanga			☐	☐	☐		☐	18	Paurṇamāsa (*Bhagavata*)
5	Skandastambhi				☐	☐			18	Śrivasvani (*Matsya*)
6	Śātakarṇi II	☐	☐	☐	☐	☐	☐	☐	56	
7	Lambodara			☐	☐	☐		☐	18	
8	Āpīlaka	☐		☐	☐	☐	☐	☐	12	Apītaka (*Matsya*), Ivīlaka (*Vishnu*), Hivilaka (*Bhagavata*)
9	Meghasvāti	☐		☐	☐	☐		☐	18	Saudāsa (*Brahmanda*)
10	Svāti (Śatakarṇi)			☐	☐	☐		☐	12	
11	Skandasvāti				☐	☐			7	Skandasvati - 28 years (*Brahmanda*)
12	Mṛgendra-Svātikarṇa				☐	☐			3	Mahendra Śatakarṇi (*Brahmanda*)
13	Kuntala-Svātikarṇa				☐	☐			8	
14	Svātikarṇa				☐	☐			1	

#	Name								Years	Notes
15	Pulomavi I	☐		☐		☐	☐	☐	24	Pulomavi - 36 years (*Matsya*), Aṭamāna (*Bhagavata*), Paṭimavi (*Vayu*), Paṭumat (*Vishnu*), Ābhi - *Brahmanda*
16	Gaurakṛṣṇa			☐		☐	☐	☐	25	Gorakṣāśvaśri (*Matsya*), Nemi Kṛṣṇa (*Vayu*), Arishṭakarman (*Vishnu*)
17	Hāla			☐		☐	☐	☐	5	Hāleya (*Bhagavata*); 1 year in one manuscript
18	Mandalaka			☐	☐	☐	☐	☐	5	Talaka (*Bhagavata*), Saptaka (*Vayu*), Pattalaka (*Vishnu*), Bhavaka (*Brahmanda*)
19	Purindrasena			☐	☐	☐	☐	☐	5	Purīṣabhiru (*Bhagavata*), Purikaṣena - 21 years (*Vayu*), Pravillasena (*Vishnu*), Pravillasena - 12 years (*Brahmanda*)
20	Sundara Śatakarṇi			☐	☐	☐	☐	☐	1	Sundara Svatikarṇa (*Matsya*), Sunandana (*Bhagavata*)
21	Cakora Śatakarṇi (Chakora)			☐	☐	☐	☐	☐	0.5	
22	Śivasvāti			☐	☐	☐	☐	☐	28	Svātisena - 1 year (*Brahmanda*), Śivasvāmi (*Vayu*)
23	Gautamīputra	☐	☐	☐	☐	☐	☐	☐	21	Yantramati - 34 years (*Brahmanda*), Gotamīputra (*Bhagavata* and *Vishnu*); 24 years according to inscriptions
24	Pulomavi II (Vashishtiputra)	☐	☐	☐		☐		☐	28	Purīmān (*Bhagavata*), Pulomat (*Matsya*), Pulimat (*Vishnu*). See also: Vashishtiputra Satakarni.
25	Śivaśri	☐	☐	☐	☐	☐		☐	7	Madaśīrā (*Bhagavata*)
26	Śivaskanda Śatakarṇi	☐	☐	☐	☐	☐		☐	7	
27	Yajñaśri	☐	☐	☐	☐	☐	☐	☐	29	Yajñaśri Śatakarṇi - 19 years (*Brahmanda*), Yajñaśri - 9, 20 or 29 years (*Matsya*)
28	Vijaya	☐	☐	☐		☐	☐	☐	6	
29	Candraśri (Chandrashri)	☐	☐	☐	☐	☐	☐	☐	3	Candravijaya (*Bhagavata*), Daṇḍaśri (*Brahmanda* and *Vayu*), Vada-Śri or Candra-Śri-Śatakarṇi - 10 years (*Matsya*)
30	Pulomavi III	☐	☐	☐	☐	☐	☐	☐	7	Sulomadhi (*Bhagavata*), Pulomavit (*Matsya*), Pulomarchis (*Vishnu*)

Purana-based lists

S. Nagaraju relies on the Puranic lists of 30 kings, and gives the following regnal dates:

1. Simuka (r. 228 – 205 BCE)
2. Krishna (r. 205 – 187 BCE)

3. Satakarni I (r. 187 – 177 BCE)
4. Purnotsanga (r. 177 – 159 BCE)
5. Skandhastambhi (r. 159 – 141 BCE)
6. Satakarni II (r. 141 – 85 BCE)
7. Lambodara (r. 85 – 67 BCE)
8. Apilaka (r. 67 – 55 BCE)
9. Meghasvati (r. 55 – 37 BCE)
10. Svati (r. 37 – 19 BCE)
11. Skandasvati (r. 19 – 12 BCE)
12. Mrigendra Satakarni (r. 12 – 9 BCE)
13. Kunatala Satakarni (r. 9 – 1 BCE)
14. Satakarni III (r. 1 BCE-1 CE)
15. Pulumavi I (r. 1 – 36 CE)
16. Gaura Krishna (r. 36 – 61 CE)
17. Hāla (r. 61 – 66 CE)
18. Mandalaka aka Puttalaka or Pulumavi II (r. 69 – 71 CE)
19. Purindrasena (r. 71 – 76 CE)
20. Sundara Satakarni (r. 76 – 77 CE)
21. Chakora Satakarni (r. 77 – 78 CE)
22. Shivasvati (r. 78 – 106 CE)
23. Gautamiputra Satkarni (r. 106 – 130 CE)
24. Vasisthiputra aka Pulumavi III (r. 130 – 158 CE)
25. Shiva Sri Satakarni (r. 158 – 165 CE)
26. Shivaskanda Satakarni (r. 165–172)
27. Sri Yajna Satakarni (r. 172 – 201 CE)
28. Vijaya Satakarni (r. 201 – 207 CE)
29. Chandra Sri Satakarni (r. 207 – 214 CE)
30. Pulumavi IV (r. 217 – 224 CE)

References

Bibliography

<templatestyles src="Template:Refbegin/styles.css" />

- Ajay Mitra Shastri (1999). *The Age of the Sātavāhanas*[1129]. Aryan. ISBN 978-81-7305-158-6.
- Ajay Mitra Shastri (1998). *The Sātavāhanas and the Western Kshatrapas: a historical framework*[1130]. Dattsons. ISBN 978-81-7192-031-0.
- Akira Shimada (9 November 2012). *Early Buddhist Architecture in Context*[1131]. BRILL. ISBN 90-04-23283-4.
- B. S. L. Hanumantha Rao (1976). *The Age of Satavahanas*[1132]. Andhra Pradesh Sahitya Akademi.

- Carla M. Sinopoli (2001). "On the edge of empire: form and substance in the Satavahana dynasty". In Susan E. Alcock. *Empires: Perspectives from Archaeology and History*[1133]. Cambridge University Press.
- Charles Higham (2009). *Encyclopedia of Ancient Asian Civilizations*[1134]. Infobase. ISBN 9781438109961.
- Damodar Dharmanand Kosambi (1975). *An Introduction to the Study of Indian History*[1135]. Popular Prakashan. ISBN 978-81-7154-038-9.
- G. Mannepalli (2013). "Courses towards Trade in Early Andhra"[1136] (PDF). *American International Journal of Research in Humanities, Arts and Social Sciences*. **4** (2): 107–113.
- Harry Falk (2009). "Two Dated Sātavāhana Epigraphs"[1137]. *Indo-Iranian Journal*. **52** (2): 197–206. doi: 10.1163/001972409X445924[1138]. ISSN 0019-7246[1139].
- Hemchandra Raychaudhuri (2006). *Political History of Ancient India: From the Accession of Parikshit to the Extinction of the Gupta Dynasty*[1140]. Cosmo Publications. ISBN 978-81-307-0291-9.
- Himanshu Prabha Ray (1986). *Monastery and guild: commerce under the Sātavāhanas*[1141]. Oxford University Press.
- I. K. Sarma (1980). *Coinage of the Satavahana Empire*[1142]. Agam.
- Mala Dutta (1990). *A Study of the Sātavāhana Coinage*[1143]. Harman. ISBN 978-81-85151-39-7.
- M. K. Dhavalikar (2004). *Satavahana Art*. Delhi: B.L Bansal, Sharada. ISBN 81-88934-04-6.
- M. K. Dhavalikar (1996). "Sātavāhana Chronology: A Re-examination". *Annals of the Bhandarkar Oriental Research Institute*. Bhandarkar Oriental Research Institute. **77** (1/4): 133–140. JSTOR 41702166[1144].
- P. Raghunadha Rao (1993). *Ancient and medieval history of Andhra Pradesh*[1145]. Sterling Publishers. ISBN 978-81-207-1495-3.
- R.C.C. Fynes (1995). "The Religious Patronage of the Satavahana Dynasty"[1146]. *South Asian Studies*. **11** (1): 43–50.
- Sailendra Nath Sen (1999). *Ancient Indian History and Civilization*[1147]. New Age International. ISBN 9788122411980.
- Sudhakar Chattopadhyaya (1974). *Some Early Dynasties of South India*[1148]. Motilal Banarsidass.
- Upinder Singh (2008). *A History of Ancient and Early Medieval India: From the Stone Age to the 12th Century*[1149]. Pearson Education India. ISBN 978-81-317-1120-0.
- Rao (1994), *History and Culture of Andhra pradesh: From the Earliest Times to the Present Day*, Sterling Publishers, ISBN 81-207-1719-8

- Joglekar, S. A. "SĀTAVĀHANA AND SĀTAKARṆI." Annals of the Bhandarkar Oriental Research Institute, vol. 27, no. 3/4, 1946, pp. 237–287. www.jstor.org/stable/41688591.

- Pradhan, Shruti S. "FROM THE SĀTAVĀHANAS TO THE ANDHRAS AND THE ANDHRA-BHRTYAS." Annals of the Bhandarkar Oriental Research Institute, vol. 75, no. 1/4, 1994, pp. 121–142. www.jstor.org/stable/41694410.

External links

 Wikimedia Commons has media related to *Satavahana*.

Mahameghavahana dynasty

Maha-Meghavahana Dynasty Mahāmēghabāhana	
c. 250s BC–c. 5th century CE	
Capital	Not specified
Religion	Jainism
Government	Monarchy
King	Vriddharaja
	Kharavela
	Kudepasiri
Historical era	Classical India
• Established	c. 250s BC
• Disestablished	c. 5th century CE
Preceded by	Succeeded by
Maurya Empire	Gupta Empire

The **Mahameghavahana dynasty** (*Mahā-Mēgha-Vāhana*, c. 250s BC to 5th century CEWikipedia:Citation needed) was an ancient ruling dynasty of Kalinga (modern-day Odisha state) after the decline of the Maurya Empire. The third ruler of the dynasty, Kharavela is known by his Hathigumpha inscription.

Kharavela patronised Jainism, but did not discriminate against other religions.

Architecture

Udayagiri and Khandagiri Caves is the most prominent example of Mahameghavahana dynasty work. These caves were built in 2nd Century BCE during the rule of King Kharavela. Udayagiri means "Sunrise Hill" and has 18 caves while Khandagiri has 15 caves. The Hathigumpha cave ("Elephant Cave") has the Hathigumpha inscription, written by Raja Kharavela, the king of Kalinga in India, during the 2nd century BCE. The Hathigumpha inscription consists of seventeen lines incised in deep cut Brahmi letters starting with Jain Namokar Mantra. In Udayagiri, *Hathigumpha* (cave 14) and *Ganeshagumpha* (cave 10) are especially well known due to art treasures of their sculptures and reliefs as well as due to their historical importance. *Rani ka Naur* (Queen's Palace cave, cave 1) is also an extensively carved cave and elaborately embellished with sculptural friezes. Khandagiri offers a fine view back over Bhubaneswar from its summit. The *Ananta cave* (cave 3) depicts carved figures of women, elephants, athletes, and geese carrying flowers.

Figure 297: *Udayagiri*

Figure 298: *Ganesha Gumpha (cave no-10), Udayagiri*

Figure 299: *Hathi Gumpha (cave no-14), Udayagiri*

Figure 300: *Hathigumpha inscription*

Figure 301: *Carving of Tirthankaras & Goddesses inside Navamuni Gumpha*

Figure 302: *Cave monastery in Khandagiri*

Figure 303: *Carving of Jain Tirthanakars*

Figure 304: *Sarpa Gumpha (cave no-13), Udayagiri*

External links

- Map of India depicting Maha-Meghavahana kingdom[1150]

Nagas of Padmavati

Nagas of Padmavati	
Empire	
early 3rd century–mid-4th century	
Capital	Padmavati
Languages	Sanskrit Prakrit
Religion	Hinduism
Government	Monarchy
History	
• Established	early 3rd century
• Disestablished	mid-4th century
Preceded by	Succeeded by
Kushan Empire	Gupta Empire
Today part of	India

The **Naga** (IAST: Nāga) dynasty ruled parts of north-central India during the 3rd and the 4th centuries, after the decline of the Kushan Empire and before the rise of the Gupta Empire. Its capital was located at Padmavati, which is identified with modern Pawaya in Madhya Pradesh. Modern historians identify it with the family that is called **Bharashiva** (IAST: Bhāraśiva) in the records of the Vakataka dynasty.

According to the Puranic texts as well as numismatic evidence, dynasties known as the Nagas also ruled at Padmavati, Vidisha, Kantipuri, and Mathura. All these Naga dynasties may have been different branches of a single family, or may have been a single family that ruled from different capitals at different times. No concrete conclusions can be drawn regarding this based on the available historical evidence.

Chronology

The Naga dynasty is known mainly from the coins issued by its rulers, and from brief mentions in literary texts and inscriptions of the other dynasties.[1151] According to the *Vayu* and the *Brahmanda* Puranas, nine Naga kings ruled Padmavati (or Champavati), and seven Naga kings ruled Mathura, before the Guptas. According to the *Vishnu Purana*, nine Naga kings ruled at Padmavati, Kantipuri, and Mathura.[1152,1153]

The Puranas state that only nine Naga kings ruled at Padmavati, but coins of twelve kings believed to be Naga kings by modern historians have been discovered.[1154] The coins of eleven of these rulers have been discovered at Padmavati (modern Pawaya): the only exception is Vyaghra, who is known from a single coin discovered at the nearby Narwar.[1155]

The inscriptions of the Vakataka dynasty (such as those from Chamak and Tirodi) state the mother of the Vakataka king Rudrasena was a daughter of the Bharashiva king Bhava-naga.[1156] This Bhava-naga has been identified with the Naga king of same name, whose coins have been discovered at Padmavati. Rudrasena's reign is dated to c. 335-355, therefore, his maternal grandfather Bhava-naga can be dated to the early 4th century CE. Historian H. V. Trivedi assumes that Bhava-naga ruled for around 25 years, based on the large number and variety of coins issued by him, dating his rule to c. 310-335 CE.[1154]

The Allahabad Pillar inscription of Samudragupta (r. c. 335–380) mentions Ganapati-naga as one of the kings defeated by him. Thus, Ganapati can be dated to the mid-4th cenury. The other Naga rulers cannot be dated with certainty, but H. V. Trivedi came up with the following tentative chronological list of Naga rulers, based on numismatic and palaeographic evidence:[1157,1154]

1. Vrisha-naga alias Vrisha-bhava or Vrishabha, possibly ruled at Vidisha in the late 2nd century
    - Vrishabha or Vrisha-bhava may also be the name of a distinct king who succeeded Vrisha-naga
2. Bhima-naga, r. c. 210-230 CE, probably the first king to rule from Padmavati
3. Skanda-naga
4. Vasu-naga
5. Brihaspati-naga
6. Vibhu-naga
7. Ravi-naga
8. Bhava-naga
9. Prabhakara-naga
10. Deva-naga
11. Vyaghra-naga
12. Ganapati-naga

Nagas of Kantipuri

Since the Nagas of Kantipuri are known only from a passing mention in the *Vishnu Purana*, it is possible that Kantipuri was a subsidiary capital of the dynasty.[1158] Historian K. P. Jayaswal attributed several coins to the Nagas of Kantipuri, reading the names on these coins as Haya-naga, Traya-naga,

Barhina-naga, Chharaja-naga, Bhava-naga, and Rudra-sena.[1159] However, other scholars, such as A. S. Altekar have disagreed with Jayaswal's reading of the coin legends, and disputed the attribution of these coins to the Nagas.[1160] According to Altekar, only one of the coins mentioned by Jayaswal *possibly* bears the legend "Traya-naga".[1161] Jayaswal identified Kantipuri as present-day Kantit in Mirzapur district, connecting the Bharashivas to the local Bhar kings. However, there is no evidence to support this identification.[1162] No Naga kings have been found at Kantit,[1163] and Kotwal (also Kutwal or Kutwar) in Morena district is a better candidate for the location of Kantipuri.[1164]

Origin

According to the Puranas, the Naga kings ruled at Padmavati (or Champavati), Kantipuri (or Kantipura), Mathura, and Vidisha (see Nagas of Vidisha).[1165] Based on the available information, it cannot be said with certainty if these Naga dynasties were different families, different branches of the same family, or a single family that ruled from all these locations at different times, moving its capital to a new location each time. H. V. Trivedi, the editor of the *Catalogue of the Coins of the Naga Kings of Padmavati*, theorized that the Naga dynasty probably originated at Vidisha, from where its members moved northwards to Padmavati, Kantipuri, and Mathura.[1151,1155]

Earlier, historian K. P. Jayaswal had theorized that the Naga dynasty was established by a 2nd century ruler named Nava-naga. Based on the misinterpretation of the word *nava* (which can mean "new" or "nine") in the Puranas as "new", he speculated that a king called Nava had established a new dynasty.[1155] According to him, the coins bearing the legend "Navasa" (or "Nevasa") were issued by this king.[1159] Jayaswal interpreted a symbol on this coin as a serpent (*nāga*) with raised hood.[1166] He further theorized that Nava-naga's successor was Virasena, whose coins have been discovered in present-day western Uttar Pradesh and eastern Punjab.[1167] According to Jayaswal, Virasena evicted the Kushan rulers from Mathura, and subsequently, the Naga dynasty was divided into three branches, which ruled from Mathura, Padmavati, and Kantipuri.[1159]

Jayaswal's theory has been disputed by other historians, based on the following points:

- The Puranic verse containing the word *nava* means that nine (not "new") Naga kings ruled at Padmavati; this interpretation is supported by the fact that the next verse mentions that seven Naga kings ruled at Mathura.[1159,1155]
- The coins bearing the legend "Navsasa" are not similar to the coins of the Nagas of Padmavati:[1166]

- they do not feature the suffix "-naga", which occurs on the Padmavati coins
- they weigh substantially more: 65 grains, as opposed to the Padmavati coins which weigh 9, 18, 36 and 50 grains
- they always feature a bull; the Padmavati coins occasionally feature a bull, which is often replaced by other symbols that do not occur on the Navasa coins)
- No Navasa coins have been discovered at Padmavati: these coins have been discovered around Kaushambi, and are similar to the other coins issued from that city, which suggests that the issuer was a king of Kaushambi.[1167]
- The purported serpent symbol on these coins appears to be a serpent only on a single specimen published by the Indian Museum, Kolkata: after examining the other specimens, historian A. S. Altekar concluded that the symbol cannot be interpreted as a serpent with certainty.[1166]
- Even if the coins featured a serpent symbol, this cannot be considered as the evidence for the issuer being a Naga king: none of the coins issued by the Nagas of Padmavati feature a serpent symbol. The serpent symbol occurs on the coins of several other rulers of northern India, none of whom were Nagas.[1166]
- Virasena's coins are rectangular unlike the circular coins issued by the Nagas of Padmavati, and feature different symbols.[1168] Also, they are much bigger than the Padmavati coins, and bear the legend "Virasenasa" without the suffix "-naga" which occurs on the Padmavati coins.[1169]
- Virasena's coins feature a vertical wavy line which Jayaswal interprted as a serpent (*naga*): however, the line actually represents the long stake of a lotus being held by the goddess Lakshmi.[1169]

Political history

The Nagas rose to power after the decline of the Kushan Empire in north-central India, in the early 3rd century.[1170] The Vakataka inscription that mentions the Bharashiva king Bhava-naga states that the Bharashivas performed ashvamedha (horse sacrifices) ten times. The ashvamedha ceremony was used by the Indian kings to prove their imperial sovereignty, and therefore, the identification of the Bharashivas with the Nagas has led to suggestions that the Nagas assumed a sovereign status after defeating the Kushan rulers.[1156,1151] However, there is no concrete evidence for this: several other powers, including the Yaudheyas and the Malavas, rose to prominence in this period, and the decline of the Kushan power in this region may be alternatively attributed to them.[1171] It is also possible that a confederation of these powers defeated the

Kushan rulers, or they independently, but simulatenously, took control of the Kushan territories.[1170]

Several Naga coins feature a bull (*vrisha* in Sanskrit), and Vrisha was also the name of a Naga king known from coinage. H. V. Trivedi theorized that Vrisha was the founder of the dynasty, and initially ruled at Vidisha, where several Naga coins have been discovered.[1172] The Vakataka inscription mentions that the Bharashiva family obtained the holy water of the Ganges for their coronation by the prowess of their arms. Therefore, Trivedi theorized that the Nagas (that is, the Bharashivas) subsequently migrated northwards (towards the Ganges), establishing their rule at Padmavati. From there, they advanced up to Kantipuri and Mathura in the process of invading the Kushan territory.[1173] Bhima-naga, whose coins bear the title *Maharaja*, may have been the dynasty's first king to rule from Padmavati.[1174]

The Allahabad Pillar inscription of the Gupta king Samudragupta states that he defeated Ganapati-naga. This suggests that Ganapati-naga was the last Naga king, and after his defeat, the Naga territory was annexed to the Gupta Empire. The inscription also mentions two other rulers - Nagadatta and Nagasena, whose identity is not certain. According to *Harsha-charita*, Nagasena was a Naga ruler of Padmavati, but neither of these kings are attested by any coins.[1154]

References

Bibliography

<templatestyles src="Template:Refbegin/styles.css" />

- Ashvini Agrawal (1989). *Rise and Fall of the Imperial Guptas*[1175]. Motilal Banarsidass. ISBN 978-81-208-0592-7.
- Dilip Kumar Ganguly (1984). *History and Historians in Ancient India*[1176]. Abhinav. ISBN 978-0-391-03250-7.
- H. V. Trivedi (1957). *Catalogue of the Coins of the Naga Kings of Padmavati*[1177]. Department of Archaeology & Museums, Madhya Pradesh.
- R. K. Sharma (2001). "Ancient history of the Naga tribe of Central India". In A. A. Abbasi. *Dimensions of Human Cultures in Central India: Professor S.K. Tiwari Felicitation Volume*[1178]. Sarup & Sons. ISBN 978-81-7625-186-0.
- Tej Ram Sharma (1989). *A Political History of the Imperial Guptas: From Gupta to Skandagupta*[1179]. Concept. ISBN 978-81-7022-251-4.

Gupta Empire

Gupta Empire
240 CE–590 CE
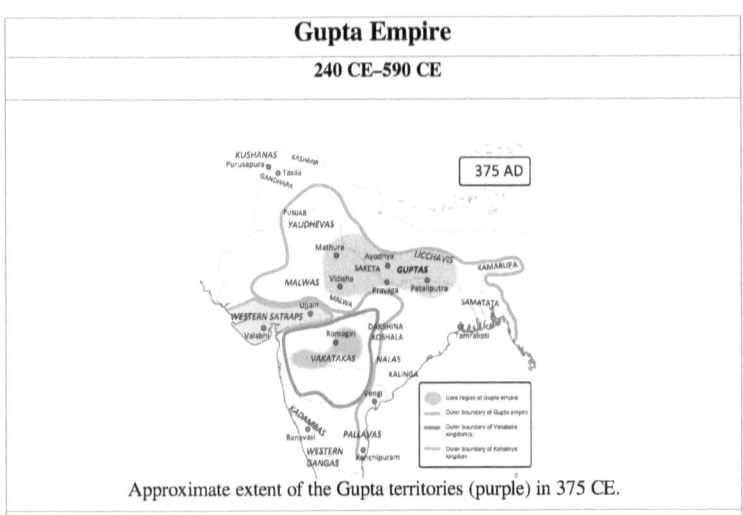 Approximate extent of the Gupta territories (purple) in 375 CE.
 Approximate extent of the Gupta territories (purple) in 450 CE.

Capital		Pataliputra
Languages		Sanskrit (literary and academic); Prakrit (vernacular)
Religion		• Hinduism • Buddhism • Jainism
Government		Monarchy
Maharajadhiraja		
•	240s–280s	Sri-Gupta
•	319–335	Chandragupta I
•	335-380	Samudragupta

•	380–415	Chandragupta II
•	540–550	Vishnu Gupta
Historical era		Ancient India
•	Established	240 CE
•	Disestablished	590 CE
Area		
•	400	3,500,000 km² (1,400,000 sq mi)

Preceded by	Succeeded by
Mahameghavahana dynasty	Later Guptas
Kanva dynasty	Maukhari
Kushan Empire	Maitraka
Bharshiva dynasty	Vardhana dynasty
Western Satraps	Mathara dynasty
	Varman dynasty
	Kalachuris

Today part of	• India • Pakistan • Bangladesh • Nepal

The **Gupta Empire** was an ancient Indian empire, existing from approximately 240 to 590 CE. At its zenith from approximately 319 to 550 CE it covered much of the Indian subcontinent. This period is called the Golden Age of India.[1180,1181]</ref> The ruling dynasty of the empire was founded by Sri Gupta; the most notable rulers of the dynasty were Chandragupta I, Samudragupta, and Chandragupta II. The 5th-century CE Sanskrit poet Kalidasa credits the Guptas with having conquered about twenty-one kingdoms, both in and outside India, including the kingdoms of Parasikas, the Hunas, the Kambojas, tribes located in the west and east Oxus valleys, the Kinnaras, Kiratas, and others.[1182]Wikipedia:No original research#Primary, secondary and tertiary sources

The high points of this period are the great cultural developments which took place during the reign of Chandragupta II. All literary sources, such as Mahabharata and Ramayana, were canonised during this period.[1183] The Gupta period produced scholars such as Kalidasa, Aryabhata, Varahamihira, Vishnu Sharma and Vatsyayana who made great advancements in many academic fields.[1184,1185] Science and political administration reached new heights during the Gupta era. The period gave rise to achievements in architecture, sculpture, and painting that "set standards of form and taste [that] determined the whole subsequent course of art, not only in India but far beyond her borders".[1186] Strong trade ties also made the region an important cultural centre and established the region as a base that would influence nearby kingdoms and regions in Burma, Sri Lanka, and Southeast Asia.[1187] Wikipedia:Identifying reliable sources The Puranas, earlier long poems on a variety of subjects, are also thought to have been committed to written texts around this period.

The empire eventually died out because of many factors such as substantial loss of territory and imperial authority caused by their own erstwhile feudatories, as well as the invasion by the Huna peoples (Kidarites and Alchon Huns) from Central Asia.[1188] After the collapse of the Gupta Empire in the 6th century, India was again ruled by numerous regional kingdoms. A minor line of the Gupta clan continued to rule Magadha after the disintegration of the empire. These Guptas were ultimately ousted by the Vardhana ruler Harsha, who established his empire in the first half of the 7th century.Wikipedia:Citation needed

Origin

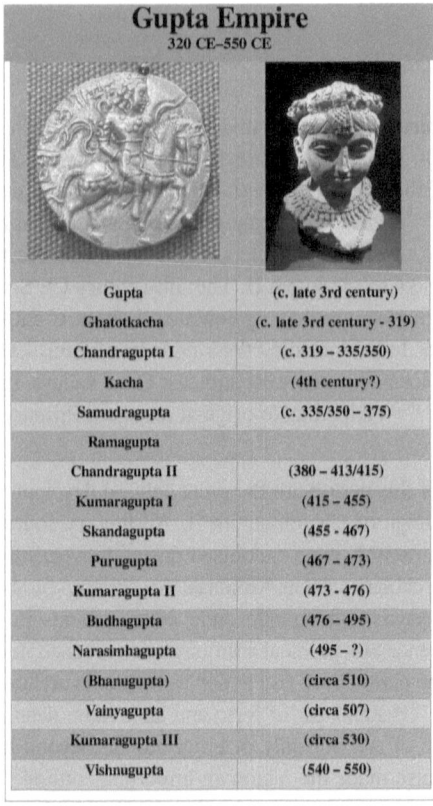

Gupta Empire 320 CE–550 CE	
Gupta	(c. late 3rd century)
Ghatotkacha	(c. late 3rd century - 319)
Chandragupta I	(c. 319 – 335/350)
Kacha	(4th century?)
Samudragupta	(c. 335/350 – 375)
Ramagupta	
Chandragupta II	(380 – 413/415)
Kumaragupta I	(415 – 455)
Skandagupta	(455 - 467)
Purugupta	(467 – 473)
Kumaragupta II	(473 - 476)
Budhagupta	(476 – 495)
Narasimhagupta	(495 – ?)
(Bhanugupta)	(circa 510)
Vainyagupta	(circa 507)
Kumaragupta III	(circa 530)
Vishnugupta	(540 – 550)

- v̲
- t̲
- e̲[1189]

According to many scholars and historians, the Gupta Dynasty was of *Vaishya* origin. Historian Ram Sharan Sharma asserts that the *Vaishya* Guptas "appeared as a reaction against oppressive rulers". A.S. Altekar, a historian and archaeologist, who has written several books on Gupta coinage,[1190] also regarded the caste of the Guptas as Vaishya on the basis of the ancient Indian texts on law, which associate the Gupta name suffix with a member of the *Vaishya* caste. According to historian Michael C. Brannigan, the rise of the Gupta Empire was one of the most prominent violations of the caste system in ancient India.

However Gupta Empire records and Chinese records provided by the later I-Tsing, furnished the names of the first three rulers of the Gupta Dynasty: Maharaja Sri Gupta, Maharaja Sri Ghatotkacha and Ghatotokacha's son, and Maharajadhiraja Sri Chandragupta, who is considered the first Gupta emperor. Recently, the historian Ashvini Agarwal, on the basis of the matrimonial alliances of the Guptas with the Vakataka, assumed that they belong to the Brahmin caste.[1191] Another modern historian, S. Chattopaddhyaya, has put forth a different theory about the ancestry of the Guptas. According to him, in the Panchobh Copper Plate, some kings bearing the title Guptas and related to the imperial Gupta Dynasty, claimed themselves as Vaishyas. Nepalese historian D. R. Regmi says that the imperial Guptas were descendants of Abhira Guptas who had ruled the Kathmandu valley in present-day Nepal.[1192]

Original homeland of the Guptas

There is controversy among scholars about the original homeland of the Guptas. Jayaswal has pointed out that the Guptas were originally inhabitants of Prayaga (Allahabad), Uttar Pradesh, in north India, as the vassal of the Nagas or Bhaarshivas. Thereafter they rose in prominence. Another scholar, Gayal supported the theory of Jayaswal, suggesting that the original home of the Guptas was Antarvedi and embracing the regions of Oudh and Prayag. These historians have derived their theory from several Gupta Dynasty coins found in those regions, and this study of numismatic evidence led to the theory that the Guptas were the original inhabitants of that region of northeastern India. However, another historian of this time in Indian history, D. K. Ganguly, has offered a different view about the original Gupta homeland. According to him the Guptas' homeland is further south, the Murshidabad region of Bengal, and not Magadha in Bihar. He based his theory on the statement of the Chinese Buddhist monk, Yijing (I-Tsing), who visited India during 675 and 695 CE. J.

F. Fleet and other historians, however, criticize Ganguly's theory because Sri Gupta ruled during the end of the 3rd century, but Yijing placed him at the end of the 2nd century. Hence the theory of historians, who have provided their views based on the accounts of Yijing, are considered less valid than theories based on other sources such as coinage.

From these theories, several conflicting opinions about the original homeland and the Empire of the Guptas are available. According to John Allan and a few other scholars, the Guptas were initially concentrated in the region of Magadha and from there they extended their sway to Bengal. According to other groups, the original homeland of the Guptas was Varendri or the Varendra Bhumi in Bengal, wherefrom they extended their Empire to Magadha. Whatever the theory is, the rule of the Guptas initiated the Golden Age in history of ancient India and with passage of time they became the sole authority of entire Northern India.

Bengali historians like HC Raychoudhuri the Guptas originated from the Varendri region which is now part of Rangpur and Rajshahi Division of modern-day Bangladesh. D.C. Ganguly, on the other hand, considers the surrounding region of Murshidabad as the original home of the Guptas.

History

Srigupta and Ghatotkacha

The most likely time for the reign of Sri Gupta is c. 240–280.[1193] The Murundas, who were feudal lords of Kushans, provided or granted land to Sri Gupta. He can be considered the first person of Gupta's empire, but not the founder of the empire. His son and successor Ghatotkacha ruled presumably from c. 280–319. He challenged other feudal lords and conquered their lands. In contrast to his successor, Chandragupta I, who is mentioned as *Maharajadhiraja*, he and his son Ghatotkacha are referred to in inscriptions as *Maharaja*.[1194] At the beginning of the 4th century, the Guptas established and ruled a few small Hindu kingdoms in Magadha and around modern-day Bihar.

Yijing also mentioned Sri Gupta in his writings. He was succeeded by his son Ghatotkacha.

Figure 305: *Queen Kumaradevi and King Chandragupta I, depicted on a coin of their son Samudragupta, 335–380.*

Chandragupta I

Ghatotkacha reigned from about 280 CE to 319 CE, and had a son named Chandragupta (reigned c. 320–335 CE) His son is not to be confused with Chandragupta Maurya (322–298 BCE), founder of the Mauryan Empire. In a breakthrough deal, Chandragupta was married to Kumaradevi, a Licchhavi princess—the main power in Magadha. With a dowry of the kingdom of Magadha (capital Pataliputra) and an alliance with the Licchavis of Nepal, Chandragupta set about expanding his power, conquering much of Magadha, Prayaga, and Saketa. Unlike most other classical empires, Gupta India failed to build fortresses to shore up these vulnerable regions, which led in part to letting them fall out of Guptan hands. He established a realm stretching from the Ganges River to Prayaga (modern-day Allahabad) by 321. He assumed the imperial title of *Maharajadhiraja*. He expanded his empire through marriage alliances.

Figure 306: *Coin of Samudragupta, with Garuda pillar. British Museum.*

Samudragupta

Samudragupta, *Parakramanka* succeeded his father in 335, and ruled for about 45 years, until his death in 380. He took the kingdoms of Ahichchhatra and Padmavati early in his reign. He then attacked the Malwas, the Yaudheyas, the Arjunayanas, the Maduras and the Abhiras, all of which were tribes in the area. By his death in 380, he had incorporated over twenty kingdoms into his realm and his rule extended from the Himalayas to the river Narmada and from the Brahmaputra to the Yamuna. He gave himself the titles *King of Kings* and *World Monarch*. Historian Vincent Smith described him as the "Indian Napoleon". He performed Ashwamedha Yajna in which a horse with an army is sent to all the nearby territories of friends and foes. These territorial kings on arrival either accept the king's alliance, who is performing this Yajna, or fight if they do not. The stone replica of the horse, then prepared, is in the Lucknow Museum. The Samudragupta Prashasti inscribed on the Ashokan Pillar, now in Akbar's Fort at Allahabad, is an authentic record of his exploits and his sway over most of the continent.

Samudragupta was not only a talented military leader but also a great patron of art and literature. He conquered what is now Kashmir and Afghanistan, enlarging the empire.[1195] The critical scholars present in his court were Harishena, Vasubandhu, and Asanga. He was a poet and musician himself. He was

Figure 307: *Head of Tirthankara, Mathura Museum*

a firm believer in Hinduism and is known to have worshipped Lord Vishnu. He was considerate of other religions and allowed Sri Lanka's Buddhist king Sirimeghvanna to build a monastery at Bodh Gaya. That monastery was called by Xuanzang as the *Mahabodhi Sangharama*.[1196]Wikipedia:Identifying reliable sources He provided a gold railing around the Bodhi Tree.

Ramagupta

Although, the narrative of the *Devichandragupta* is not supported by any contemporary epigraphical evidence, the historicity of Rama Gupta is proved by his Durjanpur inscriptions on three Jaina images, where he is mentioned as the *Maharajadhiraja*. A large number of his copper coins also have been found from the Eran-Vidisha region and classified in five distinct types, which include the *Garuda, Garudadhvaja, lion* and *border legend* types. The Brahmi legends on these coins are written in the early Gupta style. In the opinion of art historian Dr. R. A. Agarawala, D. Litt., Rama Gupta may be the eldest son of Samudragupta. He became king because of being the eldest. It is possible that he was dethroned because of being considered unfit to rule, and his younger brother Chandragupta II took over.

Figure 308: *Krishna fighting the horse demon Keshi, 5th century*

Chandragupta II "Vikramaditya"

According to the Gupta records, amongst his sons, Samudragupta nominated prince Chandragupta II, born of queen Dattadevi, as his successor. Chandragupta II, *Vikramaditya* (the Sun of Power), ruled from 375 until 415. He married a Kadamba princess of Kuntala and of Naga lineage (*Nāgakulotpannnā*), Kuberanaga. His daughter Prabhavatigupta from this Naga queen was married to Rudrasena II, the Vakataka ruler of Deccan.[1197] His son Kumaragupta I was married to a Kadamba princess of the Karnataka region. Chandragupta II expanded his realm westwards, defeating the Saka Western Kshatrapas of Malwa, Gujarat and Saurashtra in a campaign lasting until 409. His main opponent Rudrasimha III was defeated by 395, and he crushed the Bengal chiefdoms. This extended his control from coast to coast, established a second capital at Ujjain and was the high point of the empire.

Despite the creation of the empire through war, the reign is remembered for its very influential style of Hindu art, literature, culture and science, especially during the reign of Chandragupta II. Some excellent works of Hindu art such as the panels at the Dashavatara Temple in Deogarh serve to illustrate the magnificence of Gupta art. Above all it was the synthesis of elements that gave Gupta art its distinctive flavour. During this period, the Guptas were supportive of thriving Buddhist and Jain cultures as well, and for this reason there is

Figure 309: *Gold coins of Chandragupta II.*

also a long history of non-Hindu Gupta period art. In particular, Gupta period Buddhist art was to be influential in most of East and Southeast Asia. Many advances were recorded by the Chinese scholar and traveller Faxian (Fa-hien) in his diary and published afterwards.

The court of Chandragupta was made even more illustrious by the fact that it was graced by the *Navaratna* (Nine Jewels), a group of nine who excelled in the literary arts. Amongst these men was the immortal Kālidāsa whose works dwarfed the works of many other literary geniuses, not only in his own age but in the years to come. Kalidasa was mainly known for his subtle exploitation of the *shringara* (romantic) element in his verse.

Chandragupta II's Campaigns against Foreign Tribes

The 4th century Sanskrit poet Kalidasa credits Chandragupta Vikramaditya with conquering about twenty one kingdoms, both in and outside India. After finishing his campaign in East and West India, Vikramaditya (Chandragupta II) proceeded northwards, subjugated the Parasikas, then the Hunas and the Kambojas tribes located in the west and east Oxus valleys respectively. Thereafter, the king proceeded into the Himalaya mountains to reduce the mountain tribes of the Kinnaras, Kiratas, as well as India proper.Wikipedia:No original research#Primary, secondary and tertiary sources

The *Brihatkathamanjari* of the Kashmiri writer Kshemendra states, King Vikramaditya (Chandragupta II) had "unburdened the sacred earth of the Barbarians like the Sakas, Mlecchas, Kambojas, Yavanas, Tusharas, Parasikas, Hunas, and others, by annihilating these sinful Mlecchas completely".[1198]Wikipedia:No original research#Primary, secondary and tertiary sources[1199,1200]Wikipedia:Identifying reliable sources

Figure 310: *Silver coin of the Gupta King Kumaragupta I (Coin of his Western territories, design derived from the Western Satraps). Obv: Bust of king with crescents, with traces of corrupt Greek script.*[1201] *Rev: Garuda standing facing with spread wings. Brahmi legend: Parama-bhagavata rajadhiraja Sri Kumaragupta Mahendraditya.*

Faxian

Faxian (or Fa Hsien etc.), a Chinese Buddhist, was one of the pilgrims who visited India during the reign of the Gupta emperor Chandragupta II. He started his journey from China in 399 and reached India in 405. During his stay in India up to 411, he went on a pilgrimage to Mathura, Kannauj, Kapilavastu, Kushinagar, Vaishali, Pataliputra, Kashi, and Rajagriha, and made careful observations about the empire's conditions. Faxian was pleased with the mildness of administration. The Penal Code was mild and offenses were punished by fines only. From his accounts, the Gupta Empire was a prosperous period. And until the Rome-China trade axis was broken with the fall of the Han dynasty, the Guptas did indeed prosper. His writings form one of the most important sources for the history of this period.

Kumaragupta I

Chandragupta II was succeeded by his second son Kumaragupta I, born of *Mahadevi* Dhruvasvamini. Kumaragupta I assumed the title, *Mahendraditya*.[1202] He ruled until 455. Towards the end of his reign a tribe in the Narmada valley, the Pushyamitras, rose in power to threaten the empire. The Kidarites as well probably confronted the Gupta Empire towards the end of the rule of Kumaragupta I, as his son Skandagupta mentions in the Bhitari pillar inscription his efforts at reshaping a country in disarray, through reorganization and military victories over the Pushyamitras and the Hunas.[1203]

Figure 311: *The Alchon Huns under Toramana and his son Mihirakula (here depicted) gravely weakened the Gupta Empire.*

He was the founder of Nalanda University which on July 15, 2016 was declared as a UNESCO world heritage site.

Skandagupta

Skandagupta, son and successor of Kumaragupta I is generally considered to be the last of the great Gupta rulers. He assumed the titles of *Vikramaditya* and *Kramaditya*.[1204] He defeated the Pushyamitra threat, but then was faced with invading Kidarites (sometimes described as the Hephthalites or "White Huns", known in India as the Sweta Huna), from the northwest.

He repelled a *Huna* attack around 455 CE, but the expense of the wars drained the empire's resources and contributed to its decline. The Bhitari Pillar inscription of Skandagupta, the successor of Chandragupta, recalls the near-annihilation of the Gupta Empire following the attacks of the Kidarites.[1205] The Kidarites seem to have retained the western part of the Gupta Empire.

Skandagupta died in 467 and was succeeded by his agnate brother Purugupta.[1206]

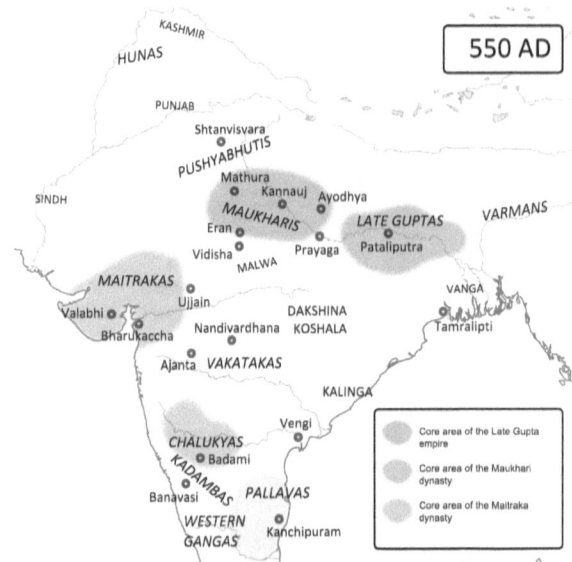

Figure 312: *The much-weakened Late Guptas, circa 550 CE.*

Decline of the empire

Following Skandagupta's death, the empire was clearly in decline.[1207] He was followed by Purugupta (467–473), Kumaragupta II (473–476), Budhagupta (476–495), Narasimhagupta (495—?), Kumaragupta III (530—540), Vishnugupta (540—550), two lesser known kings namely, Vainyagupta and Bhanugupta.

In the 480's the Alchon Huns under Toramana and Mihirakula broke through the Gupta defenses in the northwest, and much of the empire in the northwest was overrun by the Huns by 500. The empire disintegrated under the attacks of Toramana and his successor Mihirakula. It appears from inscriptions that the Guptas, although their power was much diminished, continued to resist the Huns. The Hun invader Toramana was defeated by Bhanugupta in 510.[1208,1209] The Huns were defeated and driven out of India in 528 by king Yashodharman from Malwa, and possibly Gupta emperor Narasimhagupta.[1210]

These invasions, although only spanning a few decades, had long term effects on India, and in a sense brought an end to Classical Indian civilization.[1211] Soon after the invasions, the Gupta Empire, already weakened by these invasions and the rise of local rulers such as Yashodharman, ended as well.[1212] Following the invasions, northern India was left in disarray, with numerous smaller Indian powers emerging after the crumbling of the Guptas.[1213] The

Huna invasions are said to have seriously damaged India's trade with Europe and Central Asia. In particular, Indo-Roman trade relations, which the Gupta Empire had greatly benefited from. The Guptas had been exporting numerous luxury products such as silk, leather goods, fur, iron products, ivory, pearl, and pepper from centres such as Nasik, Paithan, Pataliputra, and Benares. The Huna invasion probably disrupted these trade relations and the tax revenues that came with them.[1214]

Furthermore, Indian urban culture was left in decline, and Buddhism, gravely weakened by the destruction of monasteries and the killing of monks by the hand of the vehemently anti-Buddhist Shaivist Mihirakula, started to collapse. Great centres of learning were destroyed, such as the city of Taxila, bringing cultural regression. During their rule of 60 years, the Alchons are said to have altered the hierarchy of ruling families and the Indian cast system. For example, the Hunas are often said to have become the precursors of the Rajputs.

The succession of the 6th-century Guptas is not entirely clear, but the tail end recognized ruler of the dynasty's main line was king Vishnugupta, reigning from 540 to 550. In addition to the Hun invasion, the factors, which contribute to the decline of the empire include competition from the Vakatakas and the rise of Yashodharman in Malwa.

The last known inscription by a Gupta emperor is from the reign of Vishnugupta (the Damodarpur copper-plate inscription),[1215] in which he makes a land grant in the area of Kotivarsha (Bangarh in West Bengal) in 542/543 CE.[1216] This follows the occupation of most of northern and central India by the Aulikara ruler Yashodharman circa 532 CE.

Military organization

The Imperial Guptas couldn't have achieved their successes through force of arms without an efficient martial system. Historically, the best accounts of this not only come from Indian sources themselves but from Chinese and Western observers. However, a contemporary Indian document, regarded as a military classic of the time, the *Siva-Dhanur-veda*, offers some insight into the military system of the Guptas.Wikipedia:Citation needed

The Guptas seem to have relied heavily on infantry archers, and the bow was one of the dominant weapons of their army. The Indian version of the longbow was composed of metal, or more typically bamboo, and fired a long bamboo cane arrow with a metal head.Wikipedia:Citation needed Unlike the composite bows of Western and Central Asian foes, bows of this design would be less prone to warping in the damp and moist conditions often prevalent to the region. The Indian longbow was reputedly a powerful weapon capable of

Figure 313: *Gold coin of Gupta era, depicting Gupta king Kumaragupta holding a bow.*

Figure 314: *Sculpture of Vishnu (red sandstone), 5th century CE*

great range and penetration and provided an effective counter to invading horse archers. Iron shafts were used against armored elephants and fire arrows were not part of the bowmen's arsenal, contrary to popular belief. India historically has had a prominent reputation for its steel weapons. One of these was the steel bow. Because of its high tensility, the steel bow was capable of long range and penetration of exceptionally thick armor. These were less common weapons than the bamboo design and found in the hands of noblemen rather than in the ranks. Archers were frequently protected by infantry equipped with shields, javelins, and longswords. The Guptas also had knowledge of siegecraft, catapults, and other sophisticated war machines.Wikipedia:Citation needed

The Guptas apparently showed little predilection for using horse archers, despite the fact these warriors were a primary component in the ranks of their Scythian, Parthian, and Hepthalite (Huna) enemies. However, the Gupta armies were probably better disciplined. Able commanders such as Samudragupta and Chandragupta II would have likely understood the need for combined armed tactics and proper logistical organization. Gupta military success likely stemmed from the concerted use of elephants, armored cavalry, steel bow and foot archers in tandem against both Hindu kingdoms and foreign armies invading from the Northwest. The Guptas also maintained a navy, allowing them to control regional waters.Wikipedia:Citation needed

The collapse of the Gupta Empire in the face of the Huna onslaught was due not directly to the inherent defects of the Gupta army, which after all had initially defeated these people under Skandagupta. More likely, internal dissolution sapped the ability of the Guptas to resist foreign invasion, as was simultaneously occurring in Western Europe and China.Wikipedia:Citation needed

During the reign of Chandragupta II, Gupta Empire maintained a large army consisting of 500,000 infantry, 50,000 cavalry, 20,000 charioteers and 10,000 elephantsWikipedia:Citation needed along with a powerful navy with more than 1200 shipsWikipedia:Citation needed. Chandragupta II controlled the whole of the Indian subcontinent; the Gupta empire was the most powerful empire in the world during his reign, at a time when the Roman Empire in the West was in decline.Wikipedia:Citation needed

Religion

The Guptas were traditionally a Hindu dynasty.[1217] They were orthodox Hindus, but did not force their beliefs on the rest of the population, as Buddhism and Jainism also were encouraged.[1218] Sanchi remained an important centre of Buddhism. Kumaragupta I (c. 414 – c. 455 CE) is said to have founded Nalanda.

Figure 315: *Meditating Buddha from the Gupta era, 5th century CE.*

Some later rulers however seem to have especially favoured Buddhism. Narasimhagupta Baladitya (c. 495-?), according to contemporary writer Paramartha, was brought up under the influence of the Mahayanist philosopher, Vasubandhu. He built a sangharama at Nalanda and also a 300 ft (91 m) high vihara with a Buddha statue within which, according to Xuanzang, resembled the "great Vihara built under the Bodhi tree". According to the *Manjushrimulakalpa* (c. 800 CE), king Narasimhsagupta became a Buddhist monk, and left the world through meditation (Dhyana). The Chinese monk Xuanzang also noted that Narasimhagupta Baladitya's son, Vajra, who commissioned a sangharama as well, "possessed a heart firm in faith".:45:330

Gupta administration

A study of the epigraphical records of the Gupta empire shows that there was a hierarchy of administrative divisions from top to bottom. The empire was called by various names such as *Rajya*, *Rashtra*, *Desha*, *Mandala*, *Prithvi* and *Avani*. It was divided into 26 provinces, which were styled as *Bhukti*, *Pradesha* and *Bhoga*. Provinces were also divided into *Vishayas* and put under the control of the *Vishayapati*s. A *Vishayapati* administered the *Vishaya* with the help of the *Adhikarana* (council of representatives), which comprised four representatives: *Nagarasreshesthi*, *Sarthavaha*, *Prathamakulike* and *Prathama*

Figure 316: *Later image of Krishna and Radha playing chaturanga on an 8 × 8 Ashtāpada*

Kayastha. A part of the *Vishaya* was called *Vithi*.[1219] There were also trade links of Gupta business with the Roman empire.

Legacy of the Gupta Empire

Scholars of this period include Varahamihira and Aryabhata, who is believed to be the first to come up with the concept of zero, postulated the theory that the Earth moves round the Sun, and studied solar and lunar eclipses. Kalidasa, who was a great playwright, who wrote plays such as Shakuntala, and marked the highest point of Sanskrit literature is also said to have belonged to this period. The Sushruta Samhita, which is a Sanskrit redaction text on all of the major concepts of ayurvedic medicine with innovative chapters on surgery, dates to the Gupta period.

Chess is said to have originated in this period, where its early form in the 6th century was known as *caturaṅga*, which translates as "four divisions [of the military]" – infantry, cavalry, elephantry, and chariotry – represented by the pieces that would evolve into the modern pawn, knight, bishop, and rook, respectively. Doctors also invented several medical instruments, and even performed operations. The Indian numerals which were the first positional base 10 numeral systems in the world originated from Gupta India. The ancient Gupta text Kama Sutra by the Indian scholar Vatsyayana is widely considered to be the standard work on human sexual behavior in Sanskrit literature.

Figure 317: *A tetrastyle prostyle Gupta period temple at Sanchi besides the Apsidal hall with Maurya foundation, an example of Buddhist architecture. 5th century CE.*

Aryabhata, a noted mathematician-astronomer of the Gupta period proposed that the earth is round and rotates about its own axis. He also discovered that the Moon and planets shine by reflected sunlight. Instead of the prevailing cosmogony in which eclipses were caused by pseudo-planetary nodes Rahu and Ketu, he explained eclipses in terms of shadows cast by and falling on Earth.[1220]

Art and architecture

The Gupta period is generally regarded as a classic peak of North Indian art for all the major religious groups. Although painting was evidently widespread, the surviving works are almost all religious sculpture. The period saw the emergence of the iconic carved stone deity in Hindu art, as well as the Buddha figure and Jain *tirthankara* figures, the latter often on a very large scale. The two great centres of sculpture were Mathura and Gandhara, the latter the centre of Greco-Buddhist art. Both exported sculpture to other parts of northern India. Unlike the preceding Kushan Empire there was no artistic depiction of the monarchs, even in the very fine Guptan coinage,[1221] with the exception of some coins of the Western Satraps, or influenced by them.

The most famous remaining monuments in a broadly Gupta style, the caves at Ajanta, Elephanta, and Ellora (respectively Buddhist, Hindu, and mixed including Jain) were in fact produced under later dynasties, but primarily reflect

Figure 318: *The current structure of the Mahabodhi Temple dates to the Gupta era, 5th century CE. Marking the location where the Buddha is said to have attained enlightenment.*

the monumentality and balance of Guptan style. Ajanta contains by far the most significant survivals of painting from this and the surrounding periods, showing a mature form which had probably had a long development, mainly in painting palaces.[1222] The Hindu Udayagiri Caves actually record connections with the dynasty and its ministers,[1223] and the Dashavatara Temple at Deogarh is a major temple, one of the earliest to survive, with important sculpture.[1224]

Figure 319: *Vishnu reclining on the serpent Shesha (Ananta), Dashavatara Temple 5th century*

Figure 320: *Buddha from Sarnath, 5–6th century CE*

Figure 321: *The Colossal trimurti at the Elephanta Caves*

Figure 322: *Rock-cut temples at Ellora*

Figure 323: *Painting of Padmapani Cave 1 at Ajanta*

References

 Wikisource has the text of the 1911 *Encyclopædia Britannica* article ***Gupta***.

<templatestyles src="Template:Refbegin/styles.css" />

- Harle, J.C. (1994). *The Art and Architecture of the Indian Subcontinent*, 2nd ed., Yale University Press Pelican History of Art, ISBN 0300062176
- Keay, John, *India, a History*, 2000, HarperCollins, ISBN 0002557177
- Majumdar, R.C. (1977). *Ancient India*, New Delhi: Motilal Banarsidass, ISBN 81-208-0436-8
- Mahajan, Vidya Dhar, *A History of India*, 1990, State Mutual Book & Periodical Service, ISBN 0785511911, 9780785511915
- Raychaudhuri, H.C. (1972). Political History of Ancient India[1225], Calcutta: University of Calcutta, ISBN 1-4400-5272-7
- Tej Ram Sharma (1978). *Personal and geographical names in the Gupta inscriptions*[1226]. Concept Publishing Co., Delhi.

External links

 Wikiquote has quotations related to: ***Gupta Empire***

 Wikimedia Commons has media related to ***Gupta Empire***.

- Coins of Gupta Empire[1227]
- Photo Feature on Gupta Period Art[1228]

Preceded by **Kanva dynasty**	**Magadha dynasties** CE 240–550	Succeeded by **possibly Pala dynasty**

Vakataka dynasty

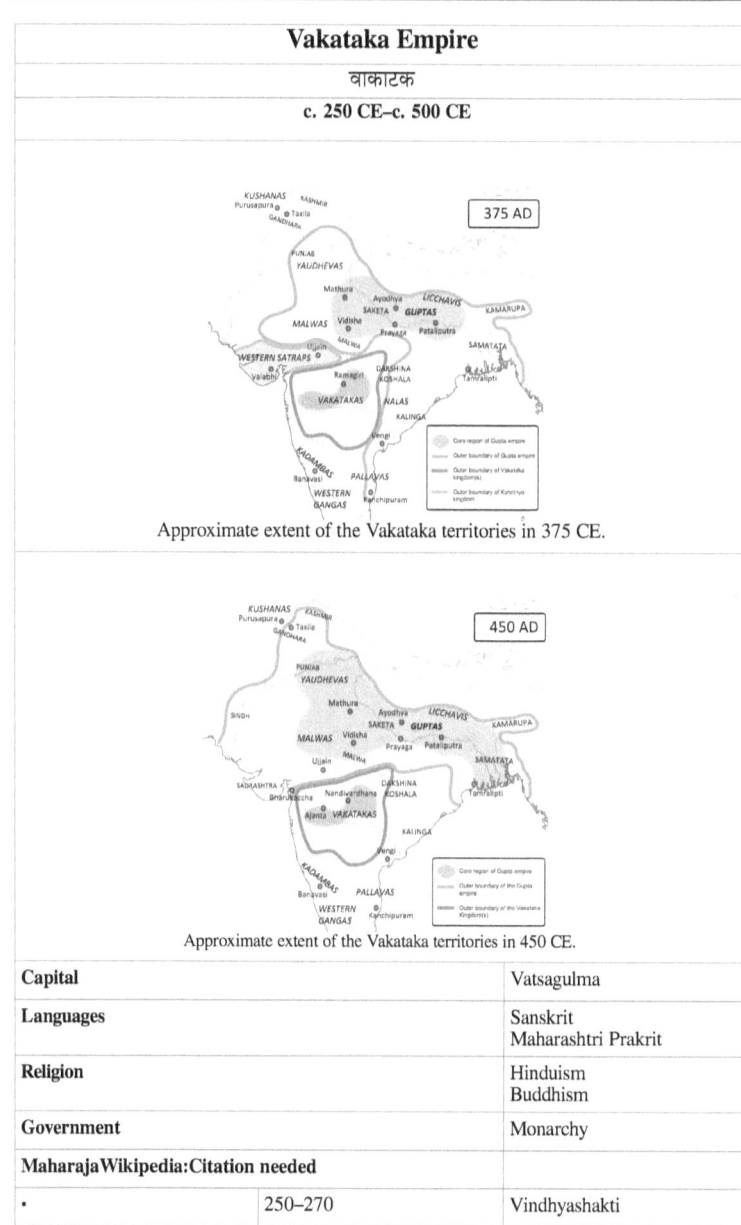

Vakataka Empire	
वाकाटक	
c. 250 CE–c. 500 CE	
Approximate extent of the Vakataka territories in 375 CE.	
Approximate extent of the Vakataka territories in 450 CE.	
Capital	Vatsagulma
Languages	Sanskrit Maharashtri Prakrit
Religion	Hinduism Buddhism
Government	Monarchy
Maharaja Wikipedia:Citation needed	
•	250–270	Vindhyashakti
•	270–330	Pravarasena I
•	475–500	Harishena

Historical era		Classical India
•	Established	c. 250 CE
•	Disestablished	c. 500 CE
Preceded by		Succeeded by
Satavahana dynasty		Vishnukundina
Today part of		India

Vakataka dynasty 250 CE–500 CE	
Vindhyashakti	(250–270)
Pravarasena I	(270–330)
Pravarapura–Nandivardhana branch	
Rudrasena I	(330–355)
Prithivishena I	(355–380)
Rudrasena II	(380–385)
Prabhavatigupta (regent)	(385–405)
Divakarasena	(385–400)
Damodarasena	(400–440)
Narendrasena	(440–460)
Prithivishena II	(460–480)
Vatsagulma branch	
Sarvasena	(330–355)
Vindhyasena	(355–400)
Pravarasena II	(400–415)
Unknown	(415–450)
Devasena	(450–475)
Harishena	(475–500)

The **Vakataka Empire** (IAST: *Vākāṭaka*) was a dynasty from the Indian subcontinent that originated from the Deccan in the mid-3rd century CE. Their state is believed to have extended from the southern edges of Malwa and Gujarat in the north to the Tungabhadra River in the south as well as from the Arabian Sea in the west to the edges of Chhattisgarh in the east. They were the most important successors of the Satavahanas in the Deccan and contemporaneous with the Guptas in northern India.

The Vakataka dynasty was a Brahmin dynasty.[1229,1230,1231] Little is known about Vindhyashakti (c. 250 – c. 270 CE), the founder of the family. Territorial expansion began in the reign of his son Pravarasena I. It is generally believed that the Vakataka dynasty was divided into four branches after Pravarasena I. Two branches are known and two are unknown. The known branches are the Pravarapura-Nandivardhana branch and the Vatsagulma branch. The Gupta emperor Chandragupta II married his daughter into Vakataka royal family and with their support annexed Gujarat from the Saka Satraps in 4th century CE. The Vakataka power was followed by that of the Chalukyas of Badami in Deccan.[1232]

The Vakatakas are noted for having been patrons of the arts, architecture and literature. They led public works and their monuments are a visible legacy. The rock-cut Buddhist viharas and chaityas of Ajanta Caves (a UNESCO World Heritage Site) were built under the patronage of Vakataka emperor, Harishena.

Vindhyashakti

The founder of the dynasty was Vindhyashakti (250-270), whose name is derived from the name of the goddess Vindhya. The dynasty may be originated there. Almost nothing is known about Vindhyashakti, the founder of the Vakatakas. In the Cave XVI inscription of Ajanta he was described as the *banner of the Vakataka family* and a *Dvija*. It is stated in this inscription that he added to his power by fighting great battles and he had a large cavalry. But no regal title is prefixed to his name in this inscription. The Puranas say that he ruled for 96 years. He was placed variously at south Deccan, Madhya Pradesh and Malwa. K.P. Jayaswal attributes Bagat, a village in the Jhansi district as the home of Vakatakas. But after refuting the theory regarding the northern home of the Vakatakas, V.V. Mirashi points out that the earliest mention of the name Vakataka occurs in an inscription found on a fragment of a pillar at Amravati which records the gift of a *Grihapati* (householder) Vakataka and his two wives. This Grihapati in all probability was the progenitor of Vidhyashakti. It appears from the Puranas that Vindhyasakti was a ruler of Vidisha (in the present day Madhya Pradesh state) but that is not considered to be correct.[1233] Wikipedia:Identifying reliable sources

As per Dr Mirashi, who has rejected the identification of Rudra deva in the Allahabad pillar inscription of Samudra Gupta with Rudra sena I. He has also pointed out there are no coins of Vakataka and there are no inscriptions of them in the north of Vindhyas. Hence, a south home of Vakatakas is correct. However, it is true that they have ruled on some of these places, since the epigraphs were available in MP etc.Wikipedia:Citation needed

Pravarasena I

The next ruler was Pravarasena I (270-330), who maintained the realm as a great power, he was the first Vakataka ruler, who called himself a *Samrat* (universal ruler) and conducted wars with the Naga kings. He has become an emperor in his own right, perhaps the only emperor in the dynasty, with his kingdom embracing a good portion of North India and whole of Deccan. He carried his arms to the Narmada in the north and annexed the kingdom of Purika which was being ruled by a king named Sisuka. In any case, he certainly ruled from Bundelkhand in the north (though Dr Mirashi does not accept that he has crossed the Narmada) to the present Andhra Pradesh in the south. The puranas assign him a reign of 60 years.

As per V.V. Mirashi, it is unlikely that he made any conquest in Northern Maharashtra, Gujarat or Konkan. But, he may have conquered parts of North Kuntala comprising Kolhapur, Satara and Solapur districts of Maharashtra. In the east, he may have carried his arms to Dakshina Kosala, Kalinga and Andhra. He was a follower of Vedic religion and performed several *Yajnas* (sacrifices) which include Agnishtoma, Aptoryama, Ukthya, Shodasin, Atiratra, Vajapeya, Brihaspatisava, Sadyaskra and four Asvamedhas. He heavily donated to the Brahmins during the Vajapeya sacrifice as per the Puranas. He also took up the title of *Dharmamaharaja* in addition to *Samrat*. He called himself as *Haritiputra*. His prime minister Deva was a very pious and learned Brahmin. The Puranas say that Pravarasena I has four sons. He married his son Gautamiputra to a daughter of King Bhavanaga of the powerful Bharashiva family, which might have proved to be helpful. However, Gautamiputra predeceased him and he was succeeded by his grandson Rudrasena I, the son of Gautamiputra. His second son, Sarvasena set up his capital at Vatsagulma (the present day Washim). Nothing is known about the dynasties set up by the other two sons.[1234]Wikipedia:Identifying reliable sources

Branches of Vakataka dynasty

It is generally believed that the Vakataka ruling family was divided into four branches after Pravarasena I. Two branches are known and two are unknown. The known branches are the Pravarpura-Nandivardhana branch and the Vatsagulma branch.

Figure 324: *Ruins of Nandivardhana fort*

Pravarapura-Nandivardhana branch

The Pravarapura-Nandivardhana branch ruled from various sites like Pravarapura (Paunar) in Wardha district and Mansar and Nandivardhan (Nagardhan) in Nagpur district. This branch maintained matrimonial relations with the Imperial Guptas.

Rudrasena I

Not much is known about Rudrasena I, the son of Gautamiputra, who ruled from Nandivardhana, near Ramtek hill, about 30 km from Nagpur. There is a mention of Rudradeva in the Allahabad pillar inscription, bundled along with the other rulers of Aryavarta. A number of scholars, like A.S. Altekar do not agree that Rudradeva is Rudrasena I, since if Rudrasena I had been exterminated by Samudragupta, it is extremely unlikely that his son Prithivishena I would accept a Gupta princess (Prabhavatigupta) as his daughter-in-law. Secondly, no inscription of Rudrasena I has been found north of the Narmada. The only stone inscription of Rudrasena I's reign discovered so far was found at Deotek in the present-day Chandrapur district, so he can not be equated with Rudradeva of the Allahabad pillar inscription, who belonged to the Aryavarta.

Figure 325: *Remains of the Pravareshvara Shiva temple built by Pravarasena II at Mansar*

Prithivishena I

Rudrasena I was succeeded by his named Prithivishena I (355-380), and Prithivishena I was succeeded by his son named Rudrasena II.

Rudrasena II, Divakarasena and Pravarasena II

Rudrasena II (380–385) is said to have married Prabhavatigupta, the daughter of the Gupta King Chandragupta II (375-413/15). Rudrasena II died fortuitously after a very short reign in 385 CE, following which Prabhavatigupta (385 - 405) ruled as a regent on behalf of her two sons, Divakarasena and Damodarasena (Pravarasena II) for 20 years. During this period the Vakataka realm was practically a part of the Gupta Empire. Many historians refer to this period as the Vakataka-Gupta age. While this has been widely accepted more than 30 years ago, this line of argument has no proper evidence. Prabhavati Gupta's inscription mentions about one "Deva Gupta" who is her father and the historians equated him with Chandra Gupta II. However, there is no other source to prove that Deva Gupta is really Chandra Gupta II. This is questionable more since the dating of Vakatakas is more or less established while that of Guptas is sometimes predated to that of Greek invasion of Alexander by the Indeginists.Wikipedia:Please clarifyWikipedia:Citation needed

Pravarasena II composed the *Setubandha* in Maharashtri Prakrit. A few verses of the *Gaha Sattasai* are also attributed to him. He shifted the capital from Nandivardhana to Pravarapura, a new city of founded by him. He built a temple dedicated to Rama in his new capital.[1235] Wikipedia:Identifying reliable sources

The highest number of so far discovered copperplate inscriptions of the Vakataka dynasty (in all 17) pertain to Pravarasena II. He is perhaps the most recorded ruler of ancient India after Ashoka the Great. See: Shreenand L. Bapat, A Second Jamb (Khandvi) Copperplate Grant of Vakataka Ruler Pravarasena II (Shravana Shuddha 13, Regnal Year 21), Annals of the Bhandarkar Oriental Research Institute, Vol. 91, pp. 1–31

Narendrasena and Prithivishena II

Pravarasena II was succeeded by Narendrasena (440-460), under whom the Vakataka influence spread to some central Indian states. Prithivishena II, the last known king of the line, succeeded his father Narendrasena in c. 460. After his death in 480, his kingdom was probably annexed by Harishena of the Vatsagulma branch.

Vatsagulma branch

Ajanta Caves

Figure 326: *The rock-cut Buddhist viharas and chaityas of Ajanta Caves, built under the patronage of the Vatsagulma branch of the Vakataka rulers.*

Figure 327: *Bird's Eye View of Ajanta Caves.*

Figure 328: *Entrance of cave no. 9.*

Figure 329: *Lord Buddha statue at Ajanta.*

The Vatsagulma branch was founded by Sarvasena, the second son of Pravarasena I after his death. King Sarvasena made Vatsagulma, the present day Washim in Washim district of Maharashtra his capital.[1236]Wikipedia:Identifying reliable sources The territory ruled by this branch was between the Sahydri Range and the Godavari River. They patronized some of the Buddhist caves at Ajanta.

Painting of Padmapani and Vajrapani from Cave No. 1 at Ajanta Caves.

Sarvasena

Sarvasena (c. 330 - 355) took the title of *Dharmamaharaja*. He is also known as the author of *Harivijaya* in Prakrit which is based on the story of bringing the *parijat* tree from heaven by Krishna. This work, praised by later writers is lost. He is also known as the author of many verses of the Prakrit *Gaha Sattasai*. One of his minister's name was Ravi. He was succeeded by his son Vindhyasena.Wikipedia:Identifying reliable sources

Vindhyasena

Vindhysena (c. 355 - 400) was also known as Vindhyashakti II. He is known from the well-known Washim plates which recorded the grant of a village situated in the northern marga (sub-division) of Nandikata (presently Nanded) in his 37th regnal year. The genealogical portion of the grant is written in Sanskrit and the formal portion in Prakrit. This is the first known land grant by any Vakataka ruler. He also took the title of *Dharmamaharaja*.[1237]Wikipedia:Identifying reliable sources Vindhyasena defeated the ruler of Kuntala, his southern neighbour. One of his minister's name was Pravara. He was succeeded by his son Pravarasena II.Wikipedia:Identifying reliable sources

Pravarasena II

Pravarasena II (c. 400 - 415) was the next ruler of whom very little is known except from the Cave XVI inscription of Ajanta, which says that he became exalted by his excellent, powerful and liberal rule. He died after a very short rule and succeeded by his minor son, who was only 8 years old when his father died. Name of this ruler is lost from the Cave XVI inscription.Wikipedia:Identifying reliable sources

Devasena

This unknown ruler was succeeded by his son Devasena (c. 450 - 475). His administration was actually run by his minister Hastibhoja.Wikipedia:Identifying reliable sources During his reign, one of his servant Svaminadeva excavated a tank named *Sudarshana* near Washim in c. 458-59.Wikipedia:Identifying reliable sources

Harishena

Harishena (c. 475 - 500) succeeded his father Devasena. He was a great patron of Buddhist architecture, art and culture. The World Heritage monument Ajanta Caves is surviving example of his works. The rock cut architectural cell-XVI inscription of Ajanta states that he conquered Avanti (Malwa) in the north, Kosala (Chhattisgarh), Kalinga and Andhra in the east, Lata (Central and Southern Gujarat) and Trikuta (Nasik district) in the west and Kuntala (Southern Maharashtra) in the south.Wikipedia:Identifying reliable sources Varahadeva, a minister of Harishena and the son of Hastibhoja, excavated the rock-cut vihara of Cave XVI of Ajanta.Wikipedia:Identifying reliable sources Three of the Buddhist caves at Ajanta, two viharas - caves XVI and XVII and a chaitya - cave XIX were excavated and decorated with painting and sculptures during the reign of Harishena. According to an art historian, Walter M. Spink, all the rock-cut monuments of Ajanta excluding caves nos. 9,10,12,13 and 15A (Ref: Page No. 4, Ajanta-A Brief History and Guide - Walter M. Spink) were built during Harishena's reign[1238] though his view is not universally accepted.

Harishena was succeeded by two rulers whose names are not known. The end of the dynasty is unknown. They were probably defeated by the Kalachuri of Mahismati.Wikipedia:Identifying reliable sources

The *Dashakumaracharita* version of the end

According to the eighth *ucchvāsaḥ* of the *Dashakumaracharita* of Dandin, which was written probably around 125 years after the fall of the Vakataka dynasty, Harishena's son, though intelligent and accomplished in all arts, neglected the study of the *Dandaniti* (Political Science) and gave himself up to the enjoyment of pleasures and indulged in all sorts of vices. His subjects also followed him and led a vicious and dissolute life. Finding this a suitable opportunity, the ruler of the neighbouring *Ashmaka* sent his minister's son to the court of the Vakatakas. The latter ingratiated himself with the king and egged him on in his dissolute life. He also decimated his forces by various means. Ultimately, when the country was thoroughly disorganised, the ruler of Ashmaka instigated the ruler of Vanavasi (in the North Kanara district) to invade

Figure 330: *Foreign dignitary in Persian dress drinking wine, on ceiling of Cave 1, at Ajanta Caves, either depicting the Sasanian embassy to Pulakesin II (610-642 CE), or simply a genre scene during the Vakataka Dynasty if the 460-480 CE dating is retained (photograph and drawing).*[1239]

the Vakataka territory. The king called all his feudatories and decided to fight his enemy on the bank of the Varada (Wardha). While fighting with the forces of the enemy, he was treacherously attacked in the rear by some of his own feudatories and killed. The Vakataka dynasty ended with his death.

Coinage

Although the Vakatakas replaced the Satavahanas, it does not seem that they continued their coin-minting tradition. As of today, no Vakataka coins have ever been identified.[1240]

References

<templatestyles src="Template:Refbegin/styles.css" />
- Altekar, Anant Sadashiv; Majumdar, Ramesh Chandra, eds. (1986) [1967]. *Vākāṭaka-Gupta age : circa 200-550 A.D.*[1241] (1st ed.). Delhi: Motilal Banarsidass. ISBN 81-208-0026-5.

External links

- History of Maharashtra[1242]
- Vakataka Rule In Telangana[1243]

Harsha

Harsha	
Maharajadhiraja	
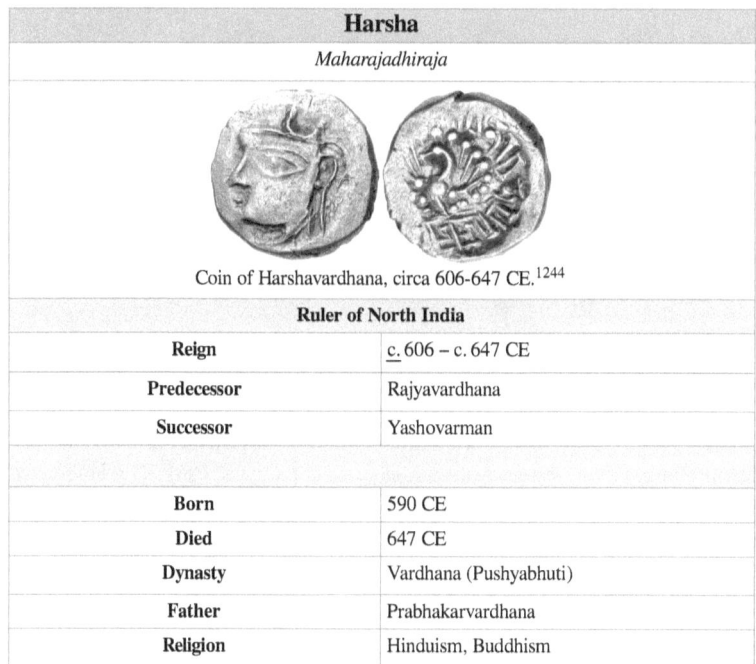	
Coin of Harshavardhana, circa 606-647 CE.[1244]	
Ruler of North India	
Reign	c. 606 – c. 647 CE
Predecessor	Rajyavardhana
Successor	Yashovarman
Born	590 CE
Died	647 CE
Dynasty	Vardhana (Pushyabhuti)
Father	Prabhakarvardhana
Religion	Hinduism, Buddhism

Harsha (c. 590–647 CE), also known as **Harshavardhana**, was an Indian emperor who ruled North India from 606 to 647 CE. He was a member of the Vardhana dynasty; and was the son of Prabhakarvardhana who defeated the Alchon Huna invaders,[1245] and the younger brother of Rajyavardhana, a king of Thanesar, present-day Haryana. At the height of Harsha's power, his Empire covered much of North and Northwestern India, extended East till Kamarupa, and South until Narmada River; and eventually made Kannauj (in present Uttar Pradesh state) his capital, and ruled till 647 CE.[1246] Harsha was defeated by the south Indian Emperor Pulakeshin II of the Chalukya dynasty, when Harsha tried to expand his Empire into the southern peninsula of India.[1247]

The peace and prosperity that prevailed made his court a centre of cosmopolitanism, attracting scholars, artists and religious visitors from far and wide.

Figure 331: *Palace ruins at "Harsh ka tila" mound area spread over 1 km*

The Chinese traveller Xuanzang visited the court of Harsha and wrote a very favourable account of him, praising his justice and generosity. His biography *Harshacharita* ("Deeds of Harsha") written by Sanskrit poet Banabhatta, describes his association with Thanesar, besides mentioning the defence wall, a moat and the palace with a two-storied *Dhavalagriha* (white mansion).

Origins

After the downfall of the Gupta Empire in the middle of the 6th century, North India was split into several independent kingdoms. The northern and western regions of India passed into the hands of a dozen or more feudatory states. Prabhakara Vardhana, the ruler of Sthanvisvara, who belonged to the Vardhana family, extended his control over neighbouring states. Prabhakar Vardhana was the first king of the Vardhana dynasty with his capital at Thaneswar. After Prabhakar Vardhana's death in 605, his eldest son, Rajya Vardhana, ascended the throne. Harsha Vardhana was Rajya Vardhana's younger brother. This period of kings from the same line has been referred to as the Vardhana dynasty in many publications.[1248,1249,1250,1251]

According to major evidences, Harsha, like the Guptas, was of the *Vaishya* Varna. The Chinese traveler Xuanzang mentions an emperor named Shiladitya, who had been claimed to be Harsha. Xuanzang mentions that this king

Figure 332: *Territorial reach of Harsha.*

belonged to "Fei-she". This word is generally restored as "Vaishya" (a varna or social class).

Ascension

Rajya Vardhana's and Harsha's sister Rajyashri had been married to the Maukhari king, Grahavarman. This king, some years later, had been defeated and killed by king Devagupta of Malwa and after his death Rajyashri had been cast into prison by the victor. Harsha's brother, Rajya Vardhana, then the king at Thanesar, could not stand this affront on his family, marched against Devagupta and defeated him. But it so happened at this moment that Shashanka, king of Gauda in Eastern Bengal, entered Magadha as a friend of Rajyavardhana, but in secret alliance with the Malwa king. Accordingly, Shashanka treacherously murdered Rajyavardhana. On hearing about the murder of his brother, Harsha resolved at once to march against the treacherous king of Gauda and killed Shashanka in a battle. Harsha ascended the throne at the age of 16.

Reign

As North India reverted to small republics and small monarchical states ruled by Gupta rulers after the fall of the prior Gupta Empire, Harsha united the small republics from Punjab to central India, and their representatives crowned him king at an assembly in April 606 giving him the title of Maharaja. Harsha established an empire that brought all of northern India under his control.[1246] The peace and prosperity that prevailed made his court a center of cosmopolitanism, attracting scholars, artists and religious visitors from far and wide. The Chinese traveler Xuanzang visited the court of Harsha, and wrote a very favourable account of him, praising his justice and generosity.

Pulakeshin II defeated Harsha on the banks of Narmada in the winter of 618-619 CE. Pulakeshin entered into a treaty with Harsha, with the Narmada River designated as the border between the Chalukya Empire and that of Harshavardhana.

Xuanzang describes the event thus:

> "Shiladityaraja (i.e., Harsha), filled with confidence, himself marched at the head of his troops to contend with this prince (i.e., Pulakeshin); but he was unable to prevail upon or subjugate him".

In 648, Tang dynasty emperor Tang Taizong sent Wang Xuance to India in response to Harsha sending an ambassador to China. However once in India he discovered Harsha had died and the new king attacked Wang and his 30 mounted subordinates. This led to Wang Xuance escaping to Tibet and then, mounting a joint force of over 7,000 Nepalese mounted infantry and 1,200 Tibetan infantry attacked the Indian state on June 16. The success of this attack brought Wang Xuance the prestigious title of the "Grand Master for the Closing Court." He also secured a reported Buddhist relic for China.

Religion

Like many other ancient Indian rulers, Harsha was eclectic in his religious views and practices. His seals describe his ancestors as sun-worshippers, his elder brother as a Buddhist, and himself as a Shaivite. His land grant inscriptions describe him as *Parama-maheshvara* (supreme devotee of Shiva), and his play *Nagananda* is dedicated to Shiva's consort Gauri. His court poet Bana also describes him as a Shaivite.

According to the Chinese Buddhist traveler Xuanzang, Harsha became a devout Buddhist at some point in his life. Xuanzang states that Harsha banned animal slaughter for food, and built monasteries at the places visited by Gautama Buddha. He erected several thousand 100-feet high stupas on the banks of the Ganges river, and built well-maintained hospices for travelers and poor people on highways across India. He organized an annual assembly of global scholars, and bestowed charitable alms on them. Every five years, he held a great assembly called Moksha. Xuanzang also describes a 21-day religious festival organized by Harsha in Kannauj; during this festival, Harsha and his subordinate kings performed daily rituals before a life-sized golden statue of the Buddha.

Since Harsha's own records describe him as Shaivite, his conversion to Buddhism would have happened, if at all, in the later part of his life. Even Xuanzang states that Harsha patronized scholars of all religions, not just Buddhist monks.

Author

Harsha is widely believed to be the author of three Sanskrit plays Ratnavali, Nagananda and Priyadarsika. While some believe (e.g., Mammata in Kavyaprakasha) that it was Bana, Harsha's court poet who wrote the plays as a paid commission, Wendy Doniger is "persuaded, however, that king Harsha really wrote the plays ... himself."

Further reading

Wikisourcehas the text of the 1911 *Encyclopædia Britannica*article ***Harsha***.

- Reddy, Krishna (2011), Indian History[1252], Tata McGraw-Hill Education Private Limited, New Delhi
- Price, Pamela (2007), Early Medieval India, HIS2172 - Periodic Evaluation[1253], University of Oslo
- "Conquests of Siladitya in the south"[1254] by S. Srikanta Sastri

Gurjar

<indicator name="pp-default"> 🔒 </indicator>

Gurjar / Gujjar

Regions with significant populations
India • Pakistan • Afghanistan
Languages
Gujari
Religion
Hinduism • Islam • Sikhism

Gurjar or **Gujjar** are a pastoral agricultural ethnic group with populations in India, Nepal, Pakistan, and a small number in northeastern Afghanistan. Alternative spellings include *Gurjara*, *Gurjjar*, *Gojar* and *Gūjar*.

Gurjars are linguistically and religiously diverse. Although they are able to speak the language of the region and country where they live, Gurjars have their own language, known as Gujari. They variously follow Hinduism, Islam, and Sikhism.The Hindu Gurjars are mostly found in Indian states of Rajasthan, Haryana, Madhya Pradesh, Punjab Plains and Maharashtra , while the Muslim Gujjars are mostly found in Pakistan, Afghanistan and Indian Himalayan regions such as Jammu & Kashmir, Himachal Pradesh and Garhwal and Kummaon divisons of Uttarakhand.

The Gurjars are classified as Other Backward Class (OBC) in twelve of India's thirty-six States and UTs; however, only Gujjars in Jammu and Kashmir and some parts of Himachal Pradesh are categorised as a Scheduled Tribe. Hindu Gurjars were assimilated into various varnas in the medieval period.

History

Origin

Historians and anthropologists differ on issue of Gurjar origin. According to one view, the ancient ancestors of Gurjars came from central Asia via Georgia from near the Caspian Sea; that Sea's alternate name of the Bahr-e-Khizar caused the tribe to be known as Khizar, Guzar, Gujur, Gurjara, or Gujjar. According to this view, between 1 BCE and 1 CE, the ancient ancestors of Gurjars came in multiple waves of migration and they were initially accorded status as high-caste warriors in the Hindu fold in the North-Western regions (modern Rajasthan and Gujarat). Aydogdy Kurbanov states that some Gurjars, along with people from northwestern India, merged with the Hephthalites to become the Rajput clan.

According to scholars such as Baij Nath Puri, the Mount Abu (ancient Arbuda Mountain) region of present-day Rajasthan had been abode of the Gurjars during medieval period. The association of the Gurjars with the mountain is noticed in many inscriptions and epigraphs including *Tilakamanjari of Dhanpala*. These Gurjars migrated from the Arbuda mountain region and as early as in the 6th century A.D., they set up one or more principalities in Rajasthan and Gujarat. The whole or a larger part of Rajasthan and Gujarat had been long known as *Gurjaratra* (country ruled or protected by the Gurjars) or *Gurjarabhumi* (land of the Gurjars) for centuries prior to the Mughal period.

In Sanskrit texts, the ethnonym has sometimes been interpreted as "destroyer of the enemy": *gur* meaning "enemy" and *ujjar* meaning "destroyer").

In its survey of *The People of India*, the Anthropological Survey of India (AnSI) – a government-sponsored organisation – noted that

> *The Gurjars/Gujjars were no doubt a remarkable people spread from Kashmir to Gujarat and Maharashtra, who gave an identity to Gujarat, established kingdoms, entered the Rajput groups as the dominant lineage of Badgujar, and survive today as a pastoral and a tribal group with both Hindu and Muslim segments.*

Irawati Karve, the Indologist and historian, believed that the Gurjars position in society and the caste system generally varied from one linguistic area of India to another. In Maharashtra, Karve thought that they were probably absorbed by the Rajputs and Marathas but retained some of their distinct identity. She based her theories on analysis of clan names and tradition, noting that while most Rajputs claim their origins to lie in the mythological Chandravansh or Suryavansh dynasties, at least two of the communities in the region claimed instead to be descended from the Agnivansh.[1255]

A 2009 study conducted by Tribal Research and Cultural Foundation, under the supervision of Gurjar scholar Javaid Rahi, claimed that the word "Gojar" has a Central Asian Turkic origin, written in romanized Turkish as Göçer. The study claimed that according to the new research, the Gurjar race "remained one of the most vibrant identity of Central Asia in BC era and later ruled over many princely states in northern India for hundred of years."

Gurjar rulers

After the collapse of the ancient Gupta empire in 6 CE, greater parts of northern India were eventually reunited under an empire known as the Gurjara Pratihara or Pratihara Gurjara (730 - 1027 CE) This period is roughly associated with the Late Classical period of the Indian subcontinent.

The question of identity and origin of this empire remains largely unanswered. According to one school of thought, Gurjara was the name of the territory (see Gurjara-desha) originally ruled by the Pratiharas; gradually, the term came to denote the people of this territory. An opposing theory is that Gurjara was the name of the tribe to which the dynasty belonged, and Pratihara was a clan of this tribe.

According to Pemble, these were Gurjaras originally a migrant community associated with or originating from the Huns who arrived in 5 CE. Some suggest that the Gurjars were descendents of the Scythians (Sakas) or the Yue Chi (Kushans) who arrived between 1 BCE and 1 CE. D. B. Bhandarkar believed that Gurjara-Pratiharas were a clan of Gurjars. Dasrath Sharma believed that although some sections of the Pratiharas (i.e., the one to which Mathanadeva belonged) were Gurjars by caste, the Pratiharas of Kannauj were not Gurjars and there was no Gurjara empire in Northern India in 8th and 9th century.

The Gurjara Pratihara empire existed in Northern India from the mid-7th to the 11th century. This empire reached its peak of prosperity and power under Mihira Bhoja and his successor Mahendrapala I. By the time of Mahendrapala, the extent of its territory rivalled that of the Gupta Empire stretching from the border of Sindh in the west to Bengal in the east and from the Himalayas in the north to areas past the Narmada in the south. The expansion triggered a tripartite power struggle with the Rashtrakuta and Pala empires for control of the Indian Subcontinent. During this period, Imperial Pratihara took the title of *Maharajadhiraja of Āryāvarta* (*Great King of Kings of India*). The power of the Pratiharas was gradually weakened by dynastic strife, raids led by parallel empires within the Indian subcontinent, increasing powers of their feudatories, and eventually by the end of the 10th century, they controlled little more than the Gangetic Doab. The last king, Rajyapala, was driven from Kannauj by Mahmud of Ghazni in 1018.

Gurjara-Pratihara are known for their sculptures, carved panels and open pavilion style temples. The greatest development of their style of temple building was at Khajuraho, now a UNESCO World Heritage Site.

British rule

In the 18th century, several Gurjar chieftains and small kings were in power. During the reign of Rohilla Nawab Najib-ul-Daula, Dargahi Singh, the Gurjar chieftain of Dadri possessed 133 villages at a fixed revenue of Rs.29,000. A fort at Parlchhatgarh in Meerut District, also known as Qila Parikishatgarh, is ascribed to a Gurjar Raja Nain Singh.

During the colonial period, upward mobility characterised a small section of the north Indian peasantry including Jats who benefited from the East Yamuna canal but most peasant castes and western Jat factions faced an increasingly desperate situation under pressure of high revenue assessment, famines, and growing indebtedness. Gangs of Gurjar, Meena, Mewati raiders had come into being in the late 18th century and become active in the early 19th century feeding into a colonial discourse of para-criminality that led to the making of the infamous Criminal Tribes Act of 1870-71. The unrest among peasant-pastoral groups such as the Gurjars and Mewatis fed into the making of the Revolt of 1857.

Gurjar turbulence owed a lot to their nomadic status and the British attempt to settle them as peaceful land revenue paying peasantry. During the Mughal era, Gurjars were known for their entrepreneurial role — they not only exchanged milk and other commodities but also guarded the trade routes of North India. The colonial-British State, keen to turn every rural element into a peasant, did not understand the community's entrepreneurial role. So after the revolt of 1857, the British classified the Gurjars (and around 150 other Indian communities) as 'criminal tribes' through the Criminal Tribes Act, 1871. In this move, communities that had fought for Bahadur Shah Zafar in 1857 were openly targeted.

During the revolt of 1857, the Gurjars of Chundrowli rose against the British, under the leadership of Damar Ram. The Gurjars of Shunkuri village, numbering around three thousand, joined the rebel sepoys. According to British records, the Gurjars plundered gunpowder and ammunition from the British and their allies. In Delhi, the Metcalfe House was sacked by Gurjar villagers from whom the land was taken to erect the building. The British records claim that the Gurjars carried out several robberies. Twenty Gurjars were reported to have been beheaded by Rao Tula Ram for committing dacoities in July 1857. In September 1857, the British were able to enlist the support of many Gurjars at Meerut. The colonial authors always used the code word "turbulent" for the castes who were generally hostile to British rule. They cited proverbs that appear to evaluate the caste in an unfavorable light. A British administrator, William Crooke, described that Gurjars seriously impeded the operations of the British Army before Delhi.[1256] Reporter Meena Radhakrishna believe

Figure 333: *Gurjar children in Afghanistan, 1984*

that the British classified the Gurjars along with others as "criminal tribes" because of their active participation in the revolt of 1857, and also because, they considered these tribes to be prone to criminality in the absence of legitimate means of livelihood.

Culture

Afghanistan

Small pockets of Gurjars are found in Afghanistan's northeastern region, particularly in and around the Nuristan province.

India

The Gujjars, estimated to number 1.6 crore nationwide, are internally differentiated in terms of religion, occupation, and socio-economic status. Historically, they have comprised a hugely heterogeneous group ranging from the Gurjar-Pratihara rulers of north India to the Gujjar and Bakarwal nomads of Jammu and the Kashmir valley who are today mostly Sunni Muslim. There is said to have been a migration from Gujarat, Kathiawad, and Rajasthan to Kashmir in the 6th-7th century and an earlier one from Georgia via Central Asia, Iraq, Iran, and Afghanistan. In Uttarakhand, they comprise forest communities called Van Gujjars and in Rajasthan Gujjar villages are in the Aravalli

Gurjar

Figure 334: *Fairs of Shri Devnarayan Bhagwan are organized two times in a year at Demali, Maalasheri, Asind and Jodhpuriya*

forests and they have been sought to be "rehabilitated" (read displaced) from the National Parks of Sariska and Ranthambhor.

Today, the Gurjars are classified under the Other Backward Class category in some states in India. However, in Jammu and Kashmir and parts of Himachal Pradesh, they are designated as a Scheduled Tribe under the Indian government's reservation program of positive discrimination. Hindu Gurjars were assimilated into several varnas.

Haryana

The Gurjar community in Haryana has set elaborate guidelines for solemnizing marriages and holding other functions. In a *mahapanchayat* ("the great panchayat"), the Gurjar community decided that those who sought dowry would be excommunicated from the society.

Rajasthan

Songs pertaining to Krishna and Gurjars were documented in Gurjar-inhabited areas during the British Raj, the connection being that Nand Mihir, the foster-father of Krishna, is claimed to be a Gurjar. Radha, the consort of Krishna, was also a Gurjar.

Figure 335: *Statue of Sri Sawai Bhoj Bagaravat, one of the 24 Gurjar brothers collectively known as Bagaravats, at Dev Dham Jodhpuriya temple.*

The Rajasthani Gurjars worship the Sun God, Devnarayan (an avatar of Vishnu), Shiva and Bhavani.

In Rajasthan, some members of the Gurjar community resorted to violent protests over the issue of reservation in 2006 and 2007. During the 2003 election to the Rajasthan assembly, the Bharatiya Janata Party (BJP) promised them ST status. However, the party failed to keep its promise after coming to the power, resulting in protests by the Gurjars in September 2006.

In May 2007, during violent protests over the reservation issue, the members of the Gurjar community clashed with the police twenty six people (including two policemen). Subsequently, the Gurjars protested violently, under various groups including the Gurjar Sangarsh Samiti, Gurjar Mahasabha and the Gurjar Action Committee. The protestors blocked roads and set fire to two police stations and some vehicles. Presently, the Gurjars in Rajasthan are classified as Other Backward Classes.

On 5 June 2007, Gurjars rioted over their desire to be added to the central list of tribes who are given preference in India government job selection as well as placement in the schools sponsored by the states of India. This preference is given under a system designed to help India's poor and disadvantaged citizens. However, other tribes on the list oppose this request as it would make it harder to obtain the few positions already set aside.

In December 2007, the Akhil Bhartiya Gurjar Mahasabha ("All-India Gurjar Council") stated that the community would boycott BJP, which is in power in Rajasthan. But now in 2009 all Gurjars were supporting BJP so that they can be politically benefitted.Kirori Singh Bainsla fought and lost at BJP ticket. In early 2000s (decade), the Gurjar community in Dang region of Rajasthan was also in news for the falling sex ratio, unavailability of brides, and the resulting polyandry.

Madhya Pradesh

As of 2007[1257], the Gurjars in Madhya Pradesh are classified as Other Backward Classes.

Maharashtra

Dode Gujars and Dore Gujars are listed as Other Backward Classes in Maharashtra.

Gujarat

Gurjars are one of the 6 main carpenter (Suthar) castes of Gujarat, and are believed to be of Central Asian descent. They are listed among the Other Backward Classes of Gujarat.

The Kutch Gurjar Kshatriya (also known as Mistri) and Gurjar Kshatriya Kadia are minority communities of Gujarat which are listed among the Other Backward Classes of Gujarat.

A few scholars believe that the Leva Kunbis (or Kambis) of Gujarat, a section of the Patidars, are possibly of Gurjar origin. However, several others state that the Patidars are Kurmis or Kunbis (Kanbis); Gurjars are included in the OBC list in Gujarat but Patidars are not.

The Gurjars are a subtype of Kumhar and Prajapati community of Gujarat and are listed among the Other Backward Classes of Gujarat.

Gurjars of North Gujarat, along with those of Western Rajasthan and Punjab, worship Sitala and Bhavani.

Himachal Pradesh

As of 2001[1257], the Gurjars in parts of Himachal Pradesh were classified as a Scheduled Tribe.[1258]

Jammu and Kashmir

In the Indian state of Jammu and Kashmir, the concentration of Muslim Gurjars is observed in the districts of Rajouri and Poonch, followed by, Ananatnag, Udhampur and Doda districts. It is believed that Gurjars migrated to Jammu and Kashmir from Gujarat (via Rajasthan) and Hazara district of Khyber Pakhtunkhwa.

As of 2001[1257], the Gurjars and the Bakarwals in Jammu and Kashmir were classified as Scheduled Tribes. According to the 2001 Census of India, Gurjar is the most populous scheduled tribe in J&K, having a population of 763,806. Around 99.3 per cent population of Gurjar and Bakarwal in J&K follow Islam.

The Gurjars of Jammu and Kashmir in 2007 demanded to treat this tribal community as a linguistic minority in the State and provide constitutional safeguards to their language Gojri. They also impressed upon the state government to take up the matter with Delhi for inclusion of Gojri in the list of official languages of India.

In 2002, some Gurjars and Bakarwals in J&K demanded a separate state (Gujaristan) for Gurjar and Bakarwal communities, under the banner of All India Gurjar Parishad.

Uttarakhand - Van Gurjars

The Van Gurjars ("forest Gurjars") are found in the Shivalik hills area of North India. The Van Gurjars follow Islam, and they have their own clans, similar to the Hindu gotras. They are a pastoral semi-nomadic community, practising transhumance. In the winter season, the Van Gurjars migrate with their herds to the Shiwalik foothills, and in summer, they migrate to pastures high up in the mountains. The Van Gurjars have had conflicts with the forest authorities, who prohibited human and livestock populations inside a reserved park, and blamed the Van Gurjar community for poaching and timber smuggling. After the creation of the Rajaji National Park (RNP), the Van Gurjars in Deharadun were asked to shift to a resettlement colony at Pathari near Hardwar. In 1992, when they returned to the foothills, the RNP authorities tried to block them from the park area. The community fought back and finally the forest authorities had to relent.

References

Notes

Citations

Further reading

- Rawat, Ajay Singh (1993), *Man and Forests: The Khatta and Gujjar Settlements of Sub-Himalayan Tarai*[1259], Indus Publishing, ISBN 978-81-85182-97-1
- Singh, David Emmanuel (2012), *Islamization in Modern South Asia: Deobandi Reform and the Gujjar Response*[1260], Walter de Gruyter, ISBN 978-1-61451-246-2
- Hāṇḍā, Omacanda (1998), *Textiles, Costumes, and Ornaments of the Western Himalaya*[1261], Indus Publishing, pp. 257–, ISBN 978-81-7387-076-7

External links

 Wikimedia Commons has media related to *Gurjar*.

- Report of NDTV on Baisoya Gurjars of Kalka Garhi (a village in central Delhi) and their traditions including their ruling monarchs[1262]

Vishnukundina dynasty

Vishnukundina dynasty	
420–624	
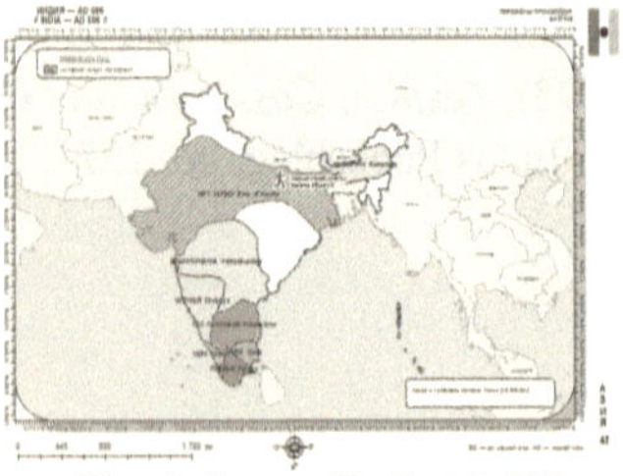 Historical map of India AD 606	
Capital	Nalgonda, Eluru, Amaravati
Languages	Sanskrit, Telugu
Religion	Hinduism
Government	Monarchy
Janasraya	Govinda Varma I
	Vikramendra Varma II
	Govinda Varma II
Historical era	Classical India
•	Established	420
•	Disestablished	624
Preceded by	Succeeded by
Vakataka dynasty	Eastern Chalukyas Pallava Dynasty

Part of a series on

Andhra Pradesh and Telangana

Chronology of the Telugu people, Andhra Pradesh, and Telangana history

• Geography • Political history
History and Kingdoms
• v • t • e [1263]

The **Vishnukundina dynasty** (IAST: Viṣṇukundina) was an Indian imperial power controlling the Deccan, Orissa and parts of South India during the 5th and 6th centuries, carving land out from the Vakataka Empire. It played an important role in the history of the Deccan during the 5th and 6th centuries.

The area north of the Godavari, Kalinga, became independent. The area south of the Krishna River fell to the Pallavas. The Vishnukundin reign came to an end with the conquest of the eastern Deccan by the Chalukya, Pulakeshin II. Pulakeshin appointed his brother Kubja Vishnuvardhana as Viceroy to rule over the conquered lands. Eventually Vishnuvardhana declared his independence and started the Eastern Chalukya dynasty.

Origin

"Vishnukundina" is a Sanskritised name for *Vinukonda*. The early rulers of the dynasty migrated to the west in search of employment and under the Vakatakas they might have attained feudatory status.

During the reign of Madhava Varma, they became independent and conquered coastal Andhra from the Salankayanas and established their capital at Denduluru near Eluru, West Godavari district.

Chronology

The Vishnukundin reign might be fixed between the end of the Salankayana and the rise of the Eastern Chalukyan power in 624. Some historians mention Vishnukundins reign was from 420 to 624, while some other historian say there reign was from early 5th century to the 7th century.

Govinda Varma I

Govinda Varma I took the imperial title of Maharaja and his son Madhav Varma I was the founder of the power based on grants from Sriparvata (Nagarjunakonda) and Indrapalagutta.

Madhav Varma I

The reign of Madhav Varma (c. 420 – c. 455). He was the founder of the Vishnukundina power.

Madhav Varma II

By the middle of the 5th century, the dynasty began its imperial expansion under its most efficient ruler Madhav Varma II who ruled for nearly half a century. The reign of Madhav Varma (c. 440 – c. 460) was a golden age in the history of the Vishnukundins. It was during this period, the small Vishnukundin dynasty rose to imperial heights. A princess of the then powerful ruling family of the Deccan the Vakatakas was given in marriage to Madhav Varma's son, Vikramendra Varma.

This alliance gave them great power and made it easy for them to extend their influence to the east coast and vanquishing the petty chieftains lingering on in that area. Madhav Varma II led his arms against Ananda Gotrikas who were ruling over Guntur, Tenali and Ongole, probably enjoying subordinate position under the Pallavas of Kanchipuram.

After occupying these areas from the Ananda Gotrikas, Madhav Varma II made Amarapura (modern Amaravati) his capital. Keeping in view the constant threat from the Pallavas, he created an out-post to check their activities and appointed his son, Deva Varma and after his death the grandson Madhav Varma III as its Viceroy.

Madhav Varma II next turned his attention against the Vengi kingdom which was under the Salankayanas. The Vengi region was annexed. The Godavari tract became part of the Vishnukundin territory. After these conquests the capital might have been shifted to Bezwada (Vijayawada), a more central location than Amarapura. These extensive conquests entitle him to the title of the lord of Dakshinapatha (southern country). After these various conquests Madhav Varma performed many Asvamedha, Rajasuya and other Vedic sacrifices.

Successors of Madhav Varma II

The fortunes of the Vishnukundins were at a low point during the reign of next ruler Vikramendra Varma I (508–528). The next two and half decades also experienced the constant strife and dynastic struggles during the reign of Indra Bhattaraka Varma (528–555). Though Indra Bhattaraka could not withstand the hostile Kalinga subordinate, Indra Varma and lost his life in battle. The Vishnukundins lost their Kalinga possessions north of the Godavari.

Vikramendra Varma II

With the accession of Vikramendra Varma II (555–569), the fortunes of the Vishnukundin family were restored. To have an immediate access to the Kalinga region, he shifted his capital from Bezwada to Lenduluru (modem Denduluru in the West Godavari district). He repulsed the attack of the Pallava ruler Simhavarman. He was successful enough to restore the fortunes of the Vishnukundins in the Kalinga region. His son Govinda Varma II enjoyed a comparatively short period of rule (569–573).

Govinda Varma II

The Vishnukundin empire set about again to imperial expansion and cultural prosperity under its able ruler Janssraya Madhav Varma IV (573-621). This prudent king spent his early years of rule in consolidating his position in Vengi. The later part of his reign is marked by wars and annexations. In his 37th regnal year, he suppressed the revolt of his subordinate chief the Durjaya Prithvi Maharaja in Guddadivishya (modern Ramachandrapuram in the East Godavari district).

Madhav Varma IV had to face the Chalukyan onslaught in his last years of rule. By about 616, Pulakeshin II and his brother Kubja Vishnuvardhana conquered Vengi from the Vishnukundins and the Pithapuram area from their subordinate Durjayas. In 621 in his 48th regnal year, Madhava crossed the Godavari probably to oust the Chalukyas from his territories. However he lost his life on the battlefield. His son Manchana Bhattaraka also might have been expelled by the Chalukyas. Thus the Vishnukundin rule was brought to a close by 624.

Vishnukundin country

They had three important cities, near Eluru, Amaravati and Puranisangam.

Administration

For administrative convenience, the empire was divided into a number of *Rashtras* and *Vishayas*. Inscriptions refer to Palki Rashtra, Karma rashtra, Guddadi Vishaya, etc.

Madhav Varma III appointed members of the royal family as Viceroys for various areas of the kingdom.

The king was the highest court of appeal in the administrator of justice. The Vishnukundin rulers established various kinds of punishments for various crimes. They were known for their impartial judgment and high sense of justice.

Army

Their army consisted of traditional fourfold divisions:

- Elephants
- Chariots
- Cavalry
- Infantry

The Hastikosa was the officer-in charge of elephant forces and the Virakosa was the officer-in-charge of land forces. These officers issued even grants on behalf of the kings.

Taxes

There may have been well-organised administrative machinery for collection of land revenue.Wikipedia:Citation needed Agrahara villages enjoyed tax exemptions. Sixteen types of coins of the Vishnukundin rulers have been found by archaeologists.

Religion

All the records of the Vishnukundins and the kings prior to the Madhav Varma II seem to be patrons of Hinduism.

From the time of accession of Madhav Varma II, an aggressive self-assertion of the Vedic Brahmanism occurred. Elaborate Vedic ceremonies like Rajasuya, Purushamedha,Wikipedia:Citation needed Sarvamedha and Aswamedha were undertaken. The celebration of all these sacrifices represents the traditional spirit of the brahmanical revival. Some of the rulers referred to themselves as 'Parama Mahesvaras'. The inscriptions refer to their family deity Sri Parvata Swami.

The names of rulers like Madhav Varma and Govinda Varma show their Vaishnavite leanings. Thus both the Hindu sects of Saivism and Vaishnavism might have received equal patronage from them.

Figure 336: *Vishnukundina Empire, 420-674 AD, Cast Copper, 4.65g, Vidarbha (Maharashtra), Bull type*

Literature

The Vishnukundins were also great patrons of learning. They established colleges for vedic learning. Learned Brahmins were encouraged by gifts of lands and colleges were established for the propagation of Vedic studies. Indra Bhattaraka established many schools for imparting education on Vedic literature. Performance of several elaborate Vedic ceremonies by Madhav Varma is evidence of the faith of the rulers in Brahmanism and popularity of Vedic learning with the people during this period.

Some of the Vishnukundin kings were credited with authorship of several books. Vikramendra Varma I was described as *Mahakavi* – great poet in a record. Further, an incomplete work on Sanskrit poetics called 'Janasraya Chando Vichiti', was attributed to Madhav Varma IV who bore the title of 'Janasraya'. Sanskrit enjoyed royal patronage.

Art and Architecture

Being great devotees of Siva, the Vishnukundins seem to have been responsible for construction of a number of cave temples dedicated to Siva. The cave structures at Bezwada (Vijayawada), Mogalrajapuram, Undavalli caves and Bhairavakonda were dated to this period. Though some of these cave temples were attributed to the Pallava Mahendra Varman I, the emblems found on the caves and the areas being under the rule of the Vishnukundins during this period clearly show that these were contributions of the Vishnukundins. The big four-storeyed cave at Undavalli and the 8 cave temples in Bhairavakonda in Nellore district show however clear resemblances with the architecture of Pallava Mahendra Varman's period.

Figure 337: *Vishnukundina Empire, 420-674 AD, Cast Copper, 7.80g, Vidarbha (Maharashtra), Lion type*

References

Bibliography

<templatestyles src="Template:Refbegin/styles.css" />

- Durga Prasad, History of the Andhras up to 1565 A. D., P. G. PUBLISHERS, GUNTUR (1988)
- South Indian Inscriptions[1264]
- Nilakanta Sastri, K.A. (1955). A History of South India, OUP, New Delhi (Reprinted 2002).

External links

- Map of find-spots of inscriptions[1265] issued by Vishnukundinas and other neighbouring dynasties
- Media related to Vishnukundina Empire at Wikimedia Commons

Maitraka dynasty

Maitraka of Valabhi	
c. 493 AD–c. 776 AD	
Maitrakas and their contemporaries in India in 590 AD	
Capital	Vallabhi
Languages	Sanskrit Prakrit Sauraseni Apabhramsa
Religion	Shaivism Buddhism Jainism Sun-worship
Government	Monarchy
Paramabhataraka	
• c. 475 - c. 493 AD	Bhatarka
• c. 762 - c. 776 AD	Siladitya VI
History	
• Established	c. 493 AD
• Disestablished	c. 776 AD
Preceded by	Succeeded by
Gupta Empire	Vardhana dynasty Chavda dynasty

History of Gujarat
• v • t • e[1266]

The **Maitraka dynasty** ruled western India (now Gujarat) from approximately 475 to approximately 776 AD from their capital at Vallabhi. With the sole exception of Dharapatta (the fifth king in the dynasty), who followed the Mithraic mysteries[1267], they were followers of Shaivism. Their origin is uncertain but they were probably Chandravanshi Kshatriyas.

Following decline of the Gupta Empire, Maitraka dynasty was founded by *Senapati* (general) Bhatarka, who was a military governor of Saurashtra under Gupta Empire, who had established himself as the independent around 475 AD. The first two Maitraka rulers Bhatarka and Dharasena I used only the title of *Senapati* (general). The third ruler Dronasimha declared himself as the *Maharaja*. During the reign Dhruvasena I, Jain council at Vallabhi was probably held. The next ruler Dharapatta is the only ruler considered as a sun-worshipper. King Guhasena stopped using the term *Paramabhattaraka Padanudhyata* along his name like his predecessors, which denotes the cessation of displaying of the nominal allegiance to the Gupta overlords. He was succeeded by his son Dharasena II, who used the title of *Mahadhiraja*. His son, the next ruler Siladitya I Dharmaditya was described by Hiuen Tsang, visited in 640 CE, as a "monarch of great administrative ability and of rare kindness and compassion". Siladitya I was succeeded by his younger brother Kharagraha I.[1268] Virdi copperplate grant (616 CE) of Kharagraha I proves that his territories included Ujjain. During the reign of the next ruler, Dharasena III, north Gujarat was included in this kingdom. Dharasena II was succeeded by another son of Kharagraha I, Dhruvasena II, Baladitya. He married the daughter of Harshavardhana. His son Dharasena IV assumed the imperial titles of *Paramabhattaraka Mahrajadhiraja Parameshvara Chakravartin*. Sanskrit poet Bhatti was his court poet. The next powerful ruler of this dynasty was Siladitya II. During the reign of Siladitya V, Arabs probably invaded this kingdom. The last known ruler of this dynasty was Siladitya VI.

Maitrakas set up a Vallabhi University which came to be known far and wide for its scholastic pursuits and was compared with the Nalanda University. They came under the rule of Harsha of Vardhana dynasty in the mid-seventh century, but retained local autonomy, and regained their independence after Harsha's death. After repeated attacks by Arabs from sea, the kingdom had weakened considerably. The dynasty ended by 783 AD. Apart from legendary accounts which connects fall of Vallabi with the Tajjika (Arab) invasions, no historical source mention how the dynasty ended.

More than hundred temples of this period are known, mostly located along the western coast of Saurashtra.

Origin

Early scholars like Fleet had misread copperplate grant and considered Maitrakas as some foreign tribe defeated by Bhatarka. Bhagwanlal Indraji believed that Maitrakas were foreign tribe while Bhatarka, who defeated them, belonged to indigenous dynasty. Later readings corrected that Bhatarka was himself Maitraka who had succeeded in many battles. The earlier scholars had suggested the name Maitraka is derived from Mithra, the Sun or solar deity, and their supposed connection to Mihira and their sun-worshiping inclination.[1269,1270,1271,1272,1273,1274,1275]

Though Mitra and Mihira are synonyms for the sun, the Sanskrit literature do not use it in sense of sun-worshipers. Dharapatta is the fifth and the only king of all Maitraka kings connected with sun-worship. All other kings were followers of Shaivism.[1267]

The copperplate grants do not help in identifying their origin, they describe only that the dynasty was born from war-like tribe whose capital was at Vallabhi and they were Shaivas. Chinese traveler Hieun-Tsang visited Vallabhi during second quarter of 7th century had described the ruler as a Kshatriya. Later Mahayana Buddhist work *Manju-Shri-Mula-Kalpa* had described them as Varavatya Yadava. The late Jain traditional work *Shatrunjaya-Mahatmaya* of Dhaneshwara describes Shiladitya as the Yadavas of Lunar race.[1276]

Virji concludes that Maitrakas were a Kshatriya of Lunar race and their origin was probably from Mitra dynasty which once ruled region around Mathura (now in Uttar Pradesh, India). Several scholars like Benerjee, D. Shastri, D. R. Bhandarkar agree with her conclusion.[1276]

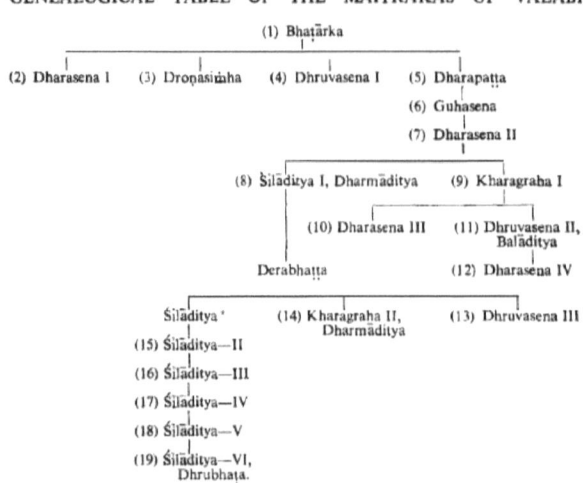

Figure 338: *Genealogical Tree of Maitrakas*

Vallabhi

The Maitrakas ruled from their capital at Vallabhi. They came under the rule of Harsha in the mid-7th century, but retained local autonomy, and regained their independence after Harsha's death.[1277]

When I-Tsing, another Chinese traveller, visited Vallabhi in the last quarter of seventh century, he found Vallabhi as a great center of learning including Buddhism. Gunamati and Sthiramati were two famous Buddhist scholars of Vallabhi at the middle of seventh century. Vallabhi was famous for its catholicity and the students from all over the country, including the Brahmana boys, visited it to have higher education in secular and religious subjects. We are told that the graduates of Valabhi were given higher executive posts.

History

Bhatarka

The *Senapati* (general) Bhatarka, was a military governor of Saurashtra peninsula under Gupta Empire, who had established himself as the independent ruler of Gujarat approximately in the last quarter of 5th century when the Gupta empire weakened. He continued to use the title of *Senapati* (general). Apart from

Figure 339: *The Eran stone pillar inscription of Bhanugupta mentions a "very big and famous battle" between the Guptas and the Maitrakas.*

his military accomplishments, not much is known from the copper-plates. He was Shaiva according to the title *Parama-Maheshwara* used for him in grants by his descendants. It seems that he transferred the capital from Girinagar (Girnar) to Vallabhi. The legends of all Valabhi coins are marked with *Sri-Bhatarka*. Almost all the Maitraka inscriptions start with his name. He is known only from the copperplate inscriptions of descendants.[1278]

Dharasena I

Bhatarka was succeeded by his eldest son Dharasena I who also used only the title of *Senapati* (general). He reigned approximately from 174 to 180 Valabhi Era (VE) (c. 493 - c. 499 CE). It seems that he further consolidated power in weakening Gupta Empire. the Maitrkas had marriage alliance with Harisena, the Vakataka king of Avanti who had himself captured many region formerly under Guptas. Chandralekha, who is described in *Dharasanasara* of Devasena as the daughter of the king of Ujjayani and the queen of Dhruvasena I.[1279]

Dronasimha

Dronasimha (c. 499 - c. 519 CE) was younger brother of Dharasena I. He had declared himself as the *Maharaja* known from his copperplate dated 183 VE (502 CE). It is known that his coronation was attended by some higher authority, probably Vakataka as they had a marriage alliance.[1280,1281]

According to the Eran inscription of Gupta Empire ruler Bhanugupta (new revised translation published in 1981), Bhanugupta and his chieftain or noble

Goparaja participated in a battle against the "Maittras" in 510 CE, thought to be the Maitrakas (the reading being without full certainty, but "as good as certain" according to the authors). This would directly allude to conflict between the Maitrakas and the Guptas during the reign of Dronasimha. The inscription reads:

- *(Verses 3-4) (There is) the glorious Bhanugupta, a distinguished hero on earth, a mighty ruler, brave being equal to Partha. And along with him Goparaja, following (him) without fear, having overtaken the Maittras and having fought a very big and famous battle, went to heaven, becoming equal to Indra, the best of the gods; and (his) devoted, attached, beloved, and beauteous wife, clinging (to him), entered into the mass of fire (funeral pyre).*

—*Eran inscription of Bhanugupta, 510 CE.*[1282]

It is also around this time, or soon after, that the Alchon Huns king Toramana invaded Malwa, leading to his mention as "ruler of the earth" in the Eran boar inscription of Toramana.

Dhruvasena I

Dhruvasena I was the third son of Bhatarka and the younger brother of Dronasimha. He reigned c. 519 - c. 549 CE. During his rule, Yashodharman of Malwa had defeated Harisena of the Vakataka dynasty, as well as the Huna king Mihirakula (in 528 CE). Dhruvasena probably had to acknowledge to overlord-ship of Yashodharman. It is known that they had regained their glory as Yashodharman's rule was short lived and was supplanted by the Guptas.[1283]

In these grants Dhruvasena's father Bhaṭárka and his elder brothers are described as 'great Máheśvaras' that is followers of Śiva, while Dhruvasena himself is called 'Paramabhágavata', the great Vaishṇava. He must be liberal in religious beliefs. In the 535 CE grant, he had made an arrangement for a Buddhist monastery at Valabhi built by his Buddhist niece Duḍḍá (or Lulá?). He had made several grants to Brahmanas of Vadnagar. The Jain council at Vallabhi was probably held during his rule which was arranged by his wife Chandralekha. During these days, he had lost his son as the Vallabhi council has condoled on loss.[1284] Kalpa Sutra, the Jain text, was compiled probably during the reign of Dhruvasena, 980 or 993 years after the death (*Nirvana*) of Mahavira. Kalpa Sutra mentions that the public reading of it started at Anandapura (Vadnagar) to relieve Dhruvasena from the grief of death of his son.[1285] Based on his grants, it known that his kingdom extended from Dwarika to Valabhi, whole Saurashtra paninsula and as far as Vadnagar in the north.[1286]

During his rule, the Garulakas or Garudakas had accepted the Maitrkas as their overlord. The Garulaka had captured Dwarika probably with help of the Maitrakas. They probably has an emblem of the Garuda and it his clear from their grants that they were Vaishnavas. They had made grants to Brahmanas and Buddhists alike.[1284]

Dharapatta

Dhruvasena I was succeeded by his younger brother Dharapatta who reigned for very short period, c. 549 to c. 553. He must be old when he ascended to throne as his elder brothers ruled before him and thus his reign may has been short. He is the only ruler described as *Paramaditya-Bhakta*, the devotee of the sun god. He is known by the copperplate grants of his grandson.[1287]

Guhasena

Dharapatta was succeeded by Guhasena who reigned from c. 553 to c. 569 CE. He must be grest king as the all later ruler from Shiladitya I to last ruler records his name in grants.[1288]

Guhasena stopped using the term *Paramabhattaraka Padanudhyata* along his name like his predecessors, which denotes the cessation of displaying of the nominal allegiance to the Gupta overlords. He had assumed title of *Maharajadhiraja*. During his early rule, the Maitraka kingdom was invaded by Maukhara or Maukhari king Ishwaravarman. The Raivataka (Girnar) hill is mentioned in his Jaunpur stone inscription but who won the war is unclear as the inscription is fragmentary. It is assumed that Guhasena must have repelled the attack.[1289]

All his copper-plates record donations to Buddhist monasteries. He was devotee of Shiva as mentioned in his grants and the copperplate bore the symbol of the Nandi, the vehicle of Shiva. He was interested in Buddhism in his last years of reign which is known from his grants. Guhasena wrote poems in Panskrit, Prakrit and Saurseni Apabhramsa.[1289]

Early historians had considered Gahlots (Gohil) of Mewar (Guhilas of Medapata) as his descendants. James Tod had recorded one such legend but epigraph evidences do not support the assumption. Virji also makes the point that Gahlots were Brahmanas as per their inscriptions while the Maitrakas were Kshatriyas.[1289]

Figure 340: *Maliya inscription of Dharasena II of the year 252 (571 CE).*[1290]

Dharasena II

Gahasena was succeeded by his son Dharasena II, who used the title of *Samanta* in his early grants and later readopts the title of *Maharaja* and later again as *Mahasamanta*. He reigned from 569 to 589–90 CE. It is considered that he had become subordinate to Maukhari ruler Ishanavarman for sometime between which reflect in the changes in titles. From Haraha inscription it known that Ishanavarman held sway over several rulers and Dharasena may have had to submit to him.[1291]

He had made land grants to Brahmanas noted in his copperplate grants. One of his grants of 254 or 257 VE mentions solar eclipse which had helped in establish the dating of the Valabhi Era (VE). His one grant mentions Sthiramati, the Buddhist monk mentioned by Chinese traveler Hiuen Tsang. One independent grant dated 574 CE made by Garulaka king Simhaditya is also found at Palitana along with him.[1291]

Śīlāditya I

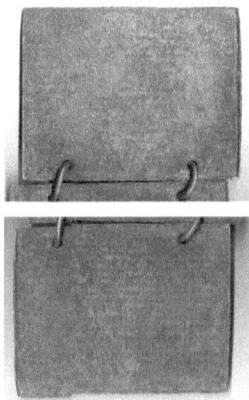

Copper plate grant issued by Śīlāditya I, dated year 290 [?] aśvayuja badi 10 recording a donation of villages and lands.

Dharasena II was succeeded by Śīlāditya I who is also called Dharmaditya, the "sun of Dharma". He reigned from c. 590 - 615 CE. *Manju-Sri-Mula-Kalpa* assigns him thirty years. The *Śatruñjaya Máhátmya* has a prophetic account of one Śīláditya who will be a propagator of religion in Vikrama Saṃvat 477 (420 CE). The work is comparatively modern and do not correspond to chronology and dating of Maitraka kingdom. Although no reliance can be placed on the date still his second name Dharmáditya gives support to his identification with the Śīláditya of the Máhátmya.[1292] Based on *Manju-Sri-Mula-Kalpa* and his grants, it is known that his rule extended from Malwa to the oceans of Kutch in western India.[1293]

He was Shaiva. The one of his grant, to a temple of Śiva, has for its Dútaka the illustrious Kharagraha apparently the brother and successor of the king. He had made grants to sun temple and Buddhist monks shows that he tolerated and respected Buddhism also. The writer of one of the grants is mentioned as the minister of peace and war Chandrabhaṭṭi; the Dútaka or causer of the gift in two of the Buddhist grants is Bhaṭṭa Ádityayaśas apparently some military officer. The Jain work *Śatruñjaya Máhátmya* mentions that hits author of the his preceptor. His equal treatment to all religions justifies his title *Dharmaditya*. The *Śatruñjaya Máhátmya*, though exaggerated, mentions that he had expelled some Buddhists from his kingdom sympathetic to his rival Harsha. He is praised in accounts of Hiuen Tsang as a "monarch of great administrative ability and of rare kindness and compassion".[1294,1268]

He had a son named Derabhatta. He was succeeded by his younger brother Kharagraha I. It seems that there must have been contest between his elder brother Upendra and him but finally Kharagraha I had succeeded. Derabhatta is mentioned to had helped Siladitya is conquering some region between Sahya and Vindhya. He probably had helped Pulakeshin in war against Kalachuris and may gained the region as a result. He may have ruled the region independently till his death. His son and successor Siladitya may have ruled the region as an arrangement with his brother Karagraha. A queen named Janjika is mentioned in one of copperplates which may be wife of Siladitya I.[1295]

Kharagraha I

Siladitya I was succeeded by his younger brother Kharagraha I, also known as Ishwaragraha.[1296] Virdi copperplate grant (616 CE) of Kharagraha I proves that his territories included Ujjain which is mentioned as "victorious camp". He was probably in continued struggle with Harsha started during reign of his brother. He was Shaiva and reigned c. 615 - 621 CE.[1296]

Dharasena III

Kharagraha was succeeded by his son Dharasena III. He reigned from c. 621 to 627 CE. His only grant is made from military camp at Khetaka (Kheda). Chapala mentioned in *Manju-Sri-Mula-Kalpa* as a successor of Siladitya must be Dharasena III according to Virji while Jayaswal consider him as Kharagraha. He was Shaiva too. He had some gain in north Gujarat. He must have lost some power as his neighbouring kingdoms; Chalukya and Harshvardhan were in constant struggle.[1297]

Dhruvasena II Baladitya

After death of Dharasena III, he was succeeded by his younger brother Dhruvasena II also known as Baladitya, the "rising son". He reigned from c. 627-641 CE. He was well versed in grammar and the science of polity. Hiuen Tsang had wrote "a livey and hasty disposition and his wisdom and statecraft were shallow". He further adds that "he had attached himself to the precious three recently", viz. the Buddha, Dhamma and Sangha of Buddhism. he had made grants to Buddhist Viharas and Hindu temples alike. He used title of *Paramamaheshwara*, thus Shaiva.He had renewed the grant to the Kottammhikadevi, aHindu temple, by his ancestor Dronasimha. Dadda II, the Gurjara king of Lata had mentioned that he had given refuge to the Maitraka ruler in struggle with Harsha. But it is unclear that he was Dhruvasena II or Dharasena IV. Huien Tsang had mentioned that he had married the daughter of Harshavardhan of Kanauj, probably as the marriage allegiance.[1298]

His rule extended to Ratlam, a town west of Ujjain so whole modern central and north Gujarat were under the Maitrakas.[1298]

Dharasena IV

Dharasena IV succeeded Dhruvasena II and reigned from c. 641 to 650 CE. He had subdued Gurjaras of Lata (south Gujarat) as he has issued copperplate grants from Bharuch. he had assumed the imperial titles of *Paramabhattaraka Mahrajadhiraja Parameshvara Chakravartin*. He had made grants to Buddhist Viharas and Brahmanas. He was petron of scholars and the master archer. Probably during his reign, the Bhatti, the author of *Bhattikavya* or *Ravanavadha*, flourished. It is a grammatical poem.[1299]

As Dharasena IV had no son, the succession transferred to the elder branch, Derabhatta lineage. He was succeeded by Dhruvasena III.[1300]

Dhruvasena III

Dhruvasena III was son of Derabhatta. He reigned from c. 650 to 654-655 CE. He had dropped the title of *Chakravartin* and was Shaiva. He may have lost his sway on Lata region to Chalukyas.[1301]

Kharagraha II

Kharagraha II Dharamaditya was successor of his younger brother Dhruvasena II. He had made agrant from military camp at Pulindaka which suggest that he was in continued struggle with Chalukyas. He reigned from c. 655 to 658. He had no son.[1302]

Siladitya II

Siladitya was son of Siladitya, the elder brother of Kharagraha II. As Kharagraha II had no son, he assumed the throne. He reigned from c. 658 to 685 CE. He has mentioned his father Derabhatta in his grants. He had probably recovered the Lata region from the Sendraka governor under the Chalukyas. The Chalukyas recovered the region under Vikramaditya I and placed his son Dharashraya Jayasimha as its governor. The region was still rulerd by Gurjaras of Lata and Dadda III was probably in the constant struggle with the Maitrakas.[1303]

Arab historians mentions that the Arab commander Ismail had attacked the Ghogha in 677 CE (AH 57) but gives no details. He must be defeated by Siladitya II.[1304]

Siladitya III

Siladitya was son and the successor of Siladitya II. He reigned from c. 690 - 710 CE. Probably during this period, Panchasar held by Jayasekhara of Chavda dynasty was attacked.[1305]

Siladitya IV

Siladitya IV was son of Siladitya III who probably had Dharasena as his personal name. He ruled from c. 710 to 740 CE. Chalukya king Vikramaditya II had captured the Khetaka region from the Maitrakas with presumed help of Jayabhatta IV, the Gurjara king of Lata. Sanjan plate of 733 CE informs that Rashtrakuta Indra I had forcefully married Chalukya princess Bhvanaga at Kaira (Kheda) so the region must be under them then.[1306]

Biladuri, the Arab historian informs that the Maitraka kingdom was invaded by the Arabs under Junaid during the Caliphate of Hasham (724-743 CE). The invasion must be carried out in 735-736 CE mentioned by the Gurjaras of Lata. They had invaded all Gurjara region of north and south. The Navsari plate of Avanijanashraya Pulakeshin mentions that the Tajjika (Arabs) had destroyed the Kachchelas (of Kutch), Saindhavas, Surastra, Chavotkata (Chavdas), Mauryas and Gurjaras (of Lata) and proceeded towards the Deccan. Jayabhatta had helped the Maitrakas in battle at Valabhi at which they had defeated the Arabs but eventually lost. Finally at Navsari, the confederate army led by Chalukya troops routed the Arabs. Pulakeshin was awarded the titles of *Dakshinapatha Svadharna*, the solid pillar of the Deccan, *Amvarta Kanivartayitr*, the Repeller of the Unrepellable and *Avanijanashraya*, the refuge of the people.[1307]

Siladitya V

After the Arab invasion, the fragmented western states were organised under Siladitya V. Malwa was lost to Gurjara-Pratiharas before the invasion. He probably had tried to recover Malwa as one of his grant (760 CE) is made from military camp at Godraka (Godhra). He must have failed to recover Malwa but nonetheless recovered the Khetaka (Kheda) region. He had to face another invasion of the Tajjika (Arabs) from sea in 759 CE fighting for Umayyad Caliphate. The naval fleet under Amarubin Jamal was sent by Hasham, the governor of Sindh to the coast of Barda (the Barda hills near Porbandar). The invasion was defeated by the naval fleet the Saindhava dynasty which were in allegiance with the Maitrakas. He reigned from c. 740 -762 CE.[1308]

Siladitya VI

Siladitya VI, also known as Dhrubhata, reigned c. 762 to c. 776 CE. As he had issued a grant from Anandpura (Vadnagar), it is assumed that he was on expansion again taking advantage of prevailing situation in Rastrakutas and was in struggle with the Gurjara-Pratiharas. Saurashtra was again invaded by the Tajjikas (Arabs) in 776 CE (AH 159). They captured the township of Barada but the epidemic broke out. The Arabs had to return and the Caliph had decided to stop further attempt to enter India. Agguka I of the Saindhava dynasty had claimed in his inscription a victory thus they had to withdraw. The Maitraka dynasty ended by c. 783 CE.[1309] Apart from legendary accounts which connects fall of Vallabi with the Tajjika (Arab) invasions, no historical source mention how the dynasty ended.[1310]

The governors of Girinagar (Girnar) and Vamanasthali (Vanthli) became independent and established their own dynasty on the fall of Vallabhi.[1311]

Religion

The Maitrakas were follower of the Shiva except Dhruvasena I who was Vaishnava and Dharapatta who was sun-worshiper. They all used title of *paramamaheshwara* before the names of king except those two. It is evident from the use of symbols like Nandi, the Bull and Trishula, the trident in their coins and inscriptions. There were presence of Vaishnavism and Goddess worship under their rule. There were large number of Buddhist Viharas in the Maitraka kingdom. Jains held their important Valabhi council here. The Maitrakas were tolerant to all religions and made donations and grants to all of them without partiality.[1312]

Administration

There were administrative divisions managed by head of the division and helped by his subordinates. The highest division *Vishaya* were headed by Rashtrapati or Amatya and the lowest division *Grama* (equivalent to village) was headed by Gramakuta.[1313]

Maitrakas set up a Vallabhi University which came to be known far and wide for its scholastic pursuits and was compared with the Nalanda University.

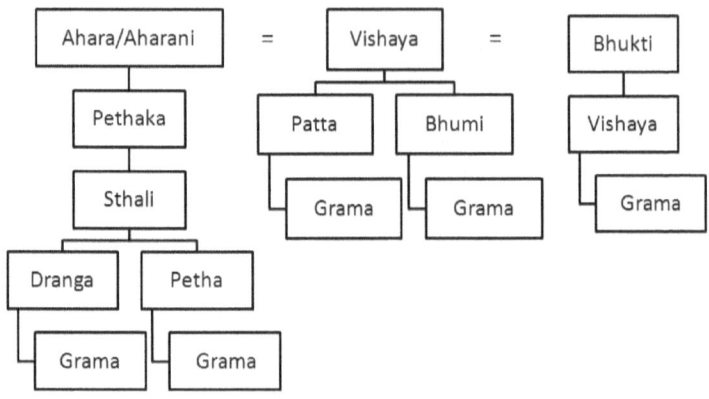

Figure 341: *Administrative divisions in the Maitraka kingdom*

Architecture

Temples and monuments

Mentioned in the literary sources

The copper plate inscriptions of Maitrakas mentions religious edifices, Brahmanical as well as Buddhist. Some Buddhist monuments were constructed by the Maitrakas themselves. Some Brahmanical shrines includes Shiva temple at Vatapadra in Saurashtra (before 609 CE), Bhartishwara temple (extant in 631 CE), Goddess Kotammahika temple at Trisangamaka (extant in 639 CE, built during or before reign of Dronasimha), Pandurarya temple at Hathab in Saurashtra (502 CE inscription). Other temples include Saptamatrika temple at Madasara-sthali (extant in 676 CE), Sun temple at Vatapadra (609 CE) and Bhadreniyaka (611 CE); all in Saurashtra.

Several Buddhist monuments were built by Maitrakas. Majority of them were built in and around Vallabhi. Bhataraka probably the Bhataraka-vihara. Princess Dudda, sister of Dhruvasena I, built Dudda-vihara around the onset of the sixth century. Before 605 CE, Shiladitya I built Shiladitya-vihara Vamsakata in Saurashtra. Abhyantarika-vihara (before 567 CE) was built by a lady Mimma. Kakka Mankila added Kakka-vihara to Dudda-vihara mandala before 589 CE and another Gohaka-vihara was built there before 629 CE. The Yakshasura-vihara for nuns at Vallabhi was built around middle of the sixth century. Before 549 CE, Ajita, a merchant, built Ajita-vihara, probably besides the Yakshasura-vihara. Purnabhatta-vihara was built by Purnabhatta before 638 CE to the later group. Skandabhatta II, grandson of Mahasandhivigrahaka Sandabhatta I, built a Sandabhatta-vihara at Yodhavaka.

Literary sources also mention some temples dedicated to the Jinas. Around 601 CE, Shantinatha temple at Vallabhi existed. At the time of destruction of Vallabhi, the images of Chandraprabha, Adinatha, Parshwanatha and Mahavira were transferred to safer places. The temples of Parshwanatha and Shantinatha existed at Vardhamana (Wadhwan) and Dostatika as well as probably the temple of Yakshi Ambika on the summit of Mount Girnar.

Most of the constructions in this period were made of non-durable materials like bricks and wood. None of them survives now.

Extant temples

Figure 342: *Gop Temple*

Figure 343: *Firangi Deval at Kalsar*

Figure 344: *Magderu, Dhrasanvel, Okhamandal*

Figure 345: *Ruined temples at Sonkansari, Ghumli*

Figure 346: *Temple at Sonkansari, Ghumli*

The architecture is in continuum of earlier Gupta period architecture found in caves at Uparkot and Khambhalida. More than hundred temples of this period is known. Almost all of them are located along the coastal belt of the western Saurashtra region except the one at Kalsar and few temples in the Barda hills region. Several temples of them are located in the territories controlled by the Saindhavas.

The extant temples of this period are the temple at Gop, Sonkansari (Ghumli), Pachtar, Prachi, Firangi Deval at Kalsar, group of temples at Vasai near Dwarka, Kadvar, Bileshwar, Sutrapada, Visavada, Kinderkheda, Pata, Miyani, Pindara, Khimrana, two temples at Dhrasanvel (Magderu and Kalika Temple), two temples near Dhrewad (Kalika Mata Temple), Gayatri temple and Naga temple and Sun temple at Pasnavada, early temples at Junagadh, Gosa, Boricha, Prabhas Patan, Savri, Navadra, Suvarnatieth temple at Dwarka, Jhamra, Degam near Porbandar, Sarma near Ghed. Other extant temples include the temple groups at Khimeshwara, Shrinagar, Nandeshwara, Balej, Bhansara, Odadar; and the shrines at Bokhira, Chhaya, Visavada, Kuchadi, Ranavav, Tukada, Akhodar, Kalavad, Bhanvad, Pasthar, and Porbandar.

Two *kund*s are known of this period, at Kadvar and Bhansara. The Shaivaite monastery at the Khimeshwara Group of temples is the oldest known Brahminical monastery of India, preceding three centuries to that in central India.

These temples are austere in their design and simple in decoration. They are important in architectural study to know the origin of Nagara-style *shikhara* and the beginning of their complex designs in temple architecture. These temples also point to the second of the two early Gujarat temple architecture schools; the north Gujarat early Nagara style and the Saurashtra style which initially influenced and ultimately ousted by the evolving Nagara style. The Saurashtra style disappeared by the tenth century.

Coinage

The Maitrakas continued coinage styles established by their predecessors; the Guptas and the Western Kshatrapas. Large number of copper and silver coins are found in Vallabhi and elsewhere. There are two types of coins found. The first were 6" in diametre and weighted 29 grains. They were perhaps earlier coins modeled after the Western Kshatrapa coins. Later coins were similar to the Gupta coins in shape, size and legends. Like Gupta coins, they were not made of pure silver but silver-coated.[1314]

The obverse of coin had the head of the kings facing right, as in Kshatrapa coins, but no legends or date. The reverse had Trishula, the trident, the emblem of Shiva. An axe (*parashu*) is added in reverse of some later coins. These symbols are surrounded by the legend in debased characters of Brahmi script.[1314] It reads,

> "
> *Rájño Mahákshatrapasa Bhatárakasa Mahesara–Śrī Bhaṭṭárakasa*
> or
> *Rájño, Mahákshatrapasa Bhatarakasa Mahesara Śrī Śarvva Bhaṭṭárakasa*
> Translation: "[This is a coin] of the illustrious the Shaivaite, Bhattaraka, the great king; the great Kshtrapa; the Lord and the devotee of Maheshwara.[1314]

List of rulers

The list as follows:

- Bhatarka (c. 470-c. 492)
- Dharasena I (c. 493-c. 499)
- Dronasinha (also known as Maharaja) (c. 500-c. 520)
- Dhruvasena I (c. 520-c. 550)
- Dharapatta (c. 550-c. 556)
- Guhasena (c. 556-c. 570)
- Dharasena II (c. 570-c. 595)
- Śīlāditya I (also known as Dharmaditya) (c. 595-c. 615)
- Kharagraha I (c. 615-c. 626)
- Dharasena III (c. 626-c. 640)
- Dhruvasena II (also known as Baladitya) (c. 640-c. 644)
- Chakravarti king Dharasena IV (also known with the titles Param Bhatarka, Maharajadhiraja, Parameshwara) (c. 644-c. 651)
- Dhruvasena III (c. 650-c. 654-655)
- Kharagraha II (c. 655-c. 658)
- Śīlāditya II (c. 658- c. 685)
- Śīlāditya III (c. 690- c. 710)
- Śīlāditya IV (c. 710- c. 740)
- Śīlāditya V (c. 740- c. 762)
- Śīlāditya VI Dhrubhatta (c. 762- c. 776)

References

Bibliography

- Virji, Krishnakumari Jethabhai (1955). *Ancient history of Saurashtra: being a study of the Maitrakas of Valabhi V to VIII centuries A. D.*[1315] Indian History and Culture Series. Konkan Institute of Arts and Sciences.
- Jain, Kailash Chand (1991), *Lord Mahāvīra and His Times*[1316], Motilal Banarsidass, ISBN 978-81-208-0805-8

Gurjara-Pratihara dynasty

Gurjara-Pratihara dynasty	
mid-8th century CE–1036 CE	
Extent of the Pratihara Empire shown in green	
Capital	Kannauj
Languages	Sanskrit, Prakrit
Religion	Hinduism
Government	Monarchy
Historical era	Late Classical India
• Established	mid-8th century CE
• Conquest of Kannauj by Mahmud of Ghazni	1008 CE
• Disestablished	1036 CE
Preceded by	**Succeeded by**
Empire of Harsha	Chandela
	Paramara dynasty
	Kalachuris of Tripuri
	Ghurid Sultanate
	Chavda dynasty
	Chahamanas of Shakambhari
Today part of	India

The **Gurjara-Pratihara dynasty**, also known as the **Pratihara Empire**, was an imperial power during the Late Classical period on the Indian subcontinent, that ruled much of Northern India from the mid-8th to the 11th century. They ruled first at Ujjain and later at Kannauj.[1318]

The Gurjara-Pratiharas were instrumental in containing Arab armies moving east of the Indus River. Nagabhata I defeated the Arab army under Junaid and Tamin during the Caliphate campaigns in India. Under Nagabhata II, the Gurjara-Pratiharas became the most powerful dynasty in northern India. He was succeeded by his son Ramabhadra, who ruled briefly before being succeeded by his son, Mihira Bhoja. Under Bhoja and his successor Mahendrapala I, the Pratihara Empire reached its peak of prosperity and power. By the time of Mahendrapala, the extent of its territory rivalled that of the Gupta Empire stretching from the border of Sindh in the west to Bengal in the east and from the Himalayas in the north to areas past the Narmada in the south.[1319,1320] The expansion triggered a tripartite power struggle with the Rashtrakuta and Pala empires for control of the Indian Subcontinent. During this period, Imperial Pratihara took the title of *Maharajadhiraja of Āryāvarta* (*Great King of Kings of India*).

Figure 347: *Nilgund inscription (866) of Amoghavarsha mentions that his father Govinda III subjugated the Gurjaras of Chitrakuta*

Gurjara-Pratihara are known for their sculptures, carved panels and open pavilion style temples. The greatest development of their style of temple building was at Khajuraho, now a UNESCO World Heritage Site.[1321]

The power of the Pratiharas was weakened by dynastic strife. It was further diminished as a result of a great raid led by the Rashtrakuta ruler Indra III who, in about 916, sacked Kannauj. Under a succession of rather obscure rulers, the Pratiharas never regained their former influence. Their feudatories became more and more powerful, one by one throwing off their allegiance until, by the end of the 10th century, the Pratiharas controlled little more than the Gangetic Doab. Their last important king, Rajyapala, was driven from Kannauj by Mahmud of Ghazni in 1018.[1320]

Etymology and origin

The origin of the dynasty and the meaning of the term "Gurjara" in its name is a topic of debate among historians. The rulers of this dynasty used the self-designation "Pratihara" for their clan, and never referred to themselves as Gurjaras.[1322] The *Imperial* Pratiharas could have emphasized their Kshatriya, instead of Gurjara, identity for political reasons. However, at local levels *Pratiharas* were not wary of projecting their tribal (Gurjara) identity.[1323] They claimed descent from the legendary hero Lakshmana, who is said to have acted as a *pratihara* ("door-keeper") for his brother Rama.[1324,1325] K. A. Nilakanta

Sastri theorized that the ancestors of the Pratiharas served the Rashtrakutas, and the term "Pratihara" derives from the title of their office in the Rashtrakuta court.

Multiple inscriptions of their neighbouring dynasties describe the Pratiharas as "Gurjara".[1326] The term "Gurjara-Pratihara" occurs only in the Rajor inscription of a feudatory ruler named Mathanadeva, who describes himself as a "Gurjara-Pratihara". Another Pratihara king named Hariraja is also mentioned as a "ferocious Gurjara" (garjjad gurjjara meghacanda) in the Kadwaha inscription.[1327] According to one school of thought, Gurjara was the name of the territory (see Gurjara-desha) originally ruled by the Pratiharas; gradually, the term came to denote the people of this territory. An opposing theory is that Gurjara was the name of the tribe to which the dynasty belonged, and Pratihara was a clan of this tribe.[1328] Several historians consider Gurjaras to be the ancestors of the modern Gurjar or Gujjar tribe.[1329] The proponents of the tribal designation theory argue that the Rajor inscription mentions the phrase: "all the fields cultivated by the Gurjaras". Here, the term "Gurjara" obviously refers to a group of people rather than a region.[1330,1331] The *Pampa Bharata* refers the Gurjara-Pratihara king Mahipala as a Gurjara king. Rama Shankar Tripathi argues that here Gurjara can only refer to the king's ethnicity, and not territory, since the Pratiharas ruled a much larger area of which Gurjara-desha was only a small part.[1330] Critics of this theory, such as D. C. Ganguly, argue that the term "Gurjara" is used as a demonym in the phrase "cultivated by the Gurjaras".[1332] Several ancient sources including inscriptions clearly mention "Gurjara" as the name of a country.[1333,1334,1335] Shanta Rani Sharma notes that an inscription of Gallaka in 795 CE states that Nagabhata I, the founder of the Imperial Pratihara dynasty, conquered the "invincible Gurjaras," which makes it unlikely that the Pratiharas were themselves Gurjaras.[1336] However, she does concede that Imperial Pratiharas were indeed known as Gurjaras, on account of their nationality. She mentions two groups of people who were known as Gurjaras, and draws a line between them; i.e. Gurjaras who were an *ethnic* people and Gurjaras who were *nationals* of Gurjaradesa (Gurjara Country).[1337] According to her, Gujjars are the descendants of ethnic Gurjaras, and have nothing to do with imperial Pratiharas and Chalukyas who were also known as Gurjaras (due to their Gurjara nationality).[1336]

Among those who believe that the term Gurjara was originally a tribal designation, there are disagreements over whether they were native Indians or foreigners.[1338] The proponents of the foreign origin theory point out that the Gurjara-Pratiharas suddenly emerged as a political power in north India around 6th century CE, shortly after the Huna invasion of that region.[1339] Critics of the foreign origin theory argue that there is no conclusive evidence of their foreign origin: they were well-assimilated in the Indian culture. Moreover, if they invaded Indian through the north-west, it is inexplicable why would they choose to settle in the semi-arid area of present-day Rajasthan, rather than the fertile Indo-Gangetic Plain.[1340]

According to the Agnivansha legend given in the later manuscripts of *Prithviraj Raso*, the Pratiharas and three other Rajput dynasties originated from a sacrificial fire-pit (agnikunda) at Mount Abu. Some colonial-era historians interpreted this myth to suggest a foreign origin for these dynasties. According to this theory, the foreigners were admitted in the Hindu caste system after performing a fire ritual.[1341] However, this legend is not found in the earliest available copies of *Prithviraj Raso*. It is based on a Paramara legend; the 16th century Rajput bards probably extended the original legend to include other dynasties including the Pratiharas, in order to foster Rajput unity against the Mughals.[1342]

History

The original centre of Pratihara power is a matter of controversy. R. C. Majumdar, on the basis of a verse in the Harivamsha-Purana, AD 783, the interpretation of which he conceded was not free from difficulty, held that Vatsaraja ruled at Ujjain. Dasharatha Sharma, interpreting it differently located the original capital in the Bhinmala Jalor area. M. W. Meister and Shanta Rani Sharma concur with his conclusion in view of the fact that the writer of the Jaina narrative Kuvalayamala states that it was composed at Jalor in the time of Vatsaraja in AD 778, which is five years before the composition of Harivamsha-Purana.

Early rulers

Nagabhata I (730–756) extended his control east and south from Mandor, conquering Malwa as far as Gwalior and the port of Bharuch in Gujarat. He established his capital at Avanti in Malwa, and checked the expansion of the Arabs, who had established themselves in Sind. In this battle (738 CE) Nagabhata led a confederacy of Gurjara-Pratiharas to defeat the Muslim Arabs who had till then been pressing on victorious through West Asia and Iran. Nagabhata I was followed by two weak successors, who were in turn succeeded by Vatsraja (775–805).

Conquest of Kannauj and further expansion

The metropolis of Kannauj had suffered a power vacuum following the death of Harsha without an heir, which resulted in the disintegration of the Empire of Harsha. This space was eventually filled by Yashovarman around a century later but his position was dependent upon an alliance with Lalitaditya Muktapida. When Muktapida undermined Yashovarman, a tri-partite struggle for

Gurjara-Pratihara dynasty

Figure 348: *Varaha (the boar-headed Vishnu avatar), on a Gurjara-Pratihara coin. 850–900 CE. British Museum.*

control of the city developed, involving the Pratiharas, whose territory was at that time to the west and north, the Palas of Bengal in the east and the Rashtrakutas, whose base lay at the south in the Deccan. Vatsraja successfully challenged and defeated the Pala ruler Dharmapala and Dantidurga, the Rashtrakuta king, for control of Kannauj.

Around 786, the Rashtrakuta ruler Dhruva (c. 780–793) crossed the Narmada River into Malwa, and from there tried to capture Kannauj. Vatsraja was defeated by the Dhruva Dharavarsha of the Rashtrakuta dynasty around 800. Vatsraja was succeeded by Nagabhata II (805–833), who was initially defeated by the Rashtrakuta ruler Govinda III (793–814), but later recovered Malwa from the Rashtrakutas, conquered Kannauj and the Indo-Gangetic Plain as far as Bihar from the Palas, and again checked the Muslims in the west. He rebuilt the great Shiva temple at Somnath in Gujarat, which had been demolished in an Arab raid from Sindh. Kannauj became the center of the Gurjara-Pratihara state, which covered much of northern India during the peak of their power, c. 836–910.Wikipedia:Citation needed

Rambhadra (833-c. 836) briefly succeeded Nagabhata II. Mihira Bhoja (c. 836–886) expanded the Pratihara dominions west to the border of Sind, east to Bengal, and south to the Narmada. His son, Mahenderpal I (890–910), expanded further eastwards in Magadha, Bengal, and Assam.Wikipedia:Citation needed

Decline

Bhoj II (910–912) was overthrown by Mahipala I (912–944). Several feudatories of the empire took advantage of the temporary weakness of the Gurjara-Pratiharas to declare their independence, notably the Paramaras of Malwa, the Chandelas of Bundelkhand, the Kalachuris of Mahakoshal, the Tomaras of Haryana, and the Chauhans of Rajputana. The south Indian Emperor Indra III (c. 914–928) of the Rashtrakuta dynasty briefly captured Kannauj in 916, and although the Pratiharas regained the city, their position continued to weaken in the 10th century, partly as a result of the drain of simultaneously fighting off Turkic attacks from the west, the attacks from the Rashtrakuta dynasty from the south and the Pala advances in the east. The Gurjara-Pratiharas lost control of Rajasthan to their feudatories, and the Chandelas captured the strategic fortress of Gwalior in central India around 950. By the end of the 10th century the Gurjara-Pratihara domains had dwindled to a small state centered on Kannauj.Wikipedia:Citation needed

Mahmud of Ghazni captured Kannauj in 1018, and the Pratihara ruler Rajapala fled. He was subsequently captured and killed by the Chandela ruler Vidyadhara. The Chandela ruler then placed Rajapala's son Trilochanpala on the throne as a proxy. Jasapala, the last Gurjara-Pratihara ruler of Kannauj, died in 1036.Wikipedia:Citation needed

Gurjara-Pratihara art

Vishnu Trivikrama, an 11th-century Pratihara stone sculpture from Kashipur, kept at the National Museum, New Delhi.

Teli ka Mandir is a 8-9th century Hindu Temple built by the Pratihara emperor Mihira Bhoja.

There are notable examples of architecture from the Gurjara-Pratihara era, including sculptures and carved panels. Their temples, constructed in an open pavilion style, were particularly impressive at Khajuraho.

Māru-Gurjara architecture

Māru-Gurjara architecture was developed during Gurjara Pratihara Empire.

Bateshwar Hindu temples complex

Bateshwar Hindu temples, Madhya Pradesh was constructed during the Gurjara-Pratihara Empire between 8th to 11th century.[1343]

Caliphate campaigns in India

Junaid, the successor of Qasim, finally subdued the Hindu resistance within Sindh. Taking advantage of the conditions in Western India, which at that time was covered with several small states, Junaid led a large army into the region in early 738 CE. Dividing this force into two he plundered several cities in southern Rajasthan, western Malwa, and Gujarat.

Indian inscriptions confirm this invasion but record the Arab success only against the smaller states in Gujarat. They also record the defeat of the Arabs at two places. The southern army moving south into Gujarat was repulsed at Navsari by the south Indian Emperor Vikramaditya II of the Chalukya dynasty and Rashtrakutas. The army that went east, after sacking several places, reached Avanti whose ruler Nagabhata (Gurjara-Pratihara) trounced the invaders and forced them to flee. After his victory Nagabhata took advantage of the disturbed conditions to acquire control over the numerous small states up to the border of Sindh.

Junaid probably died from the wounds inflicted in the battle with the Gurjara-Pratihara. His successor Tamin organized a fresh army and attempted to avenge Junaid's defeat towards the close of the year 738 CE. But this time Nagabhata, with his Chauhan and Guhilot feudatories, met the Muslim army before it could leave the borders of Sindh. The battle resulted in the complete rout of the Arabs who fled broken into Sindh with the Gurjara-Pratihara close behind them.

The Arabs crossed over to the other side of the Indus River, abandoning all their lands to the victorious Hindus. The local chieftains took advantage of these conditions to re-establish their independence. Subsequently, the Arabs constructed the city of Mansurah on the other side of the wide and deep Indus, which was safe from attack. This became their new capital in Sindh. Thus began the reign of the imperial Gurjara-Pratiharas.

In the Gwalior inscription, it is recorded that Gurjara-Pratihara emperor Nagabhata "crushed the large army of the powerful Mlechcha king." This large army consisted of cavalry, infantry, siege artillery, and probably a force of camels. Since Tamin was a new governor he had a force of Syrian cavalry from Damascus, local Arab contingents, converted Hindus of Sindh, and foreign mercenaries like the Turkics. All together the invading army may have had anywhere between 10–15,000 cavalry, 5000 infantry, and 2000 camels.Wikipedia:Citation needed

The Arab chronicler Sulaiman describes the army of the Pratiharas as it stood in 851 CE, "The ruler of Gurjars maintains numerous forces and no other Indian prince has so fine a cavalry. He is unfriendly to the Arabs, still he acknowledges that the king of the Arabs is the greatest of rulers. Among the princes of India there is no greater foe of the Islamic faith than he. He has got riches, and his camels and horses are numerous."

Legacy

Historians of India, since the days of Elphinstone, have wondered at the slow progress of Muslim invaders in India, as compared with their rapid advance in other parts of the world. The Arabs possibly only stationed small invasions independent of the Caliph. Arguments of doubtful validity have often been put forward to explain this unique phenomenon. Currently it is believed that it was the power of the Gurjara-Pratihara army that effectively barred the progress of the Muslims beyond the confines of Sindh, their first conquest for nearly three hundred years. In the light of later events this might be regarded as the "Chief contribution of the Gurjara Pratiharas to the history of India".

List of rulers

- Nagabhata I (730–760)
- Kakustha and Devaraja (760–780)
- Vatsaraja (780–800)
- Nagabhata II (800–833)
- Ramabhadra (833–836)
- Mihira Bhoja or Bhoja I (836–885)
- Mahendrapala I (885–910)
- Bhoja II (910–913)
- Mahipala I (913–944)
- Mahendrapala II (944–948)
- Devapala (948–954)
- Vinayakapala (954–955)
- Mahipala II (955–956)
- Vijayapala II (956–960)
- Rajapala (960–1018)
- Trilochanapala (1018–1027)
- Yasahpala (1024–1036)

References

Bibliography

<templatestyles src="Template:Refbegin/styles.css" />

- Avari, Burjor (2007). *India: The Ancient Past. A History of the Indian-Subcontinent from 7000 BC to AD 1200*[1344]. New York: Routledge. ISBN 978-0-203-08850-0.
- Sircar, Dineschandra (1971). *Studies in the Geography of Ancient and Medieval India*[1345]. Motilal Banarsidass Publ. ISBN 9788120806900.
- Ganguly, D. C. (1935), Narendra Nath Law, ed., "Origin of the Pratihara Dynasty", *The Indian Historical Quarterly*, Caxton, **XI**: 167–168
- Majumdar, R. C. (1981), "The Gurjara-Pratiharas", in R. S. Sharma and K. K. Dasgupta, *A Comprehensive history of India: A.D. 985-1206*[1346], 3 (Part 1), Indian History Congress / People's Publishing House, ISBN 978-81-7007-121-1
- Majumdar, R.C. (1955). The Age of Imperial Kanauj (First ed.). Bombay: Bharatiya Vidya Bhavan.
- Mishra, V. B. (1954), "Who were the Gurjara-Pratīhāras?", *Annals of the Bhandarkar Oriental Research Institute*, **35** (¼): 42–53, JSTOR 41784918[1347]

- Meister, M.W (1991). Encyclopaedia of Indian Temple Architecture, Vol. 2, pt.2, North India: Period of Early Maturity, c. AD 700-900 (first ed.). Delhi: American Institute of Indian Studies. p. 153. ISBN 0195629213
- Puri, Baij Nath (1957), *The history of the Gurjara-Pratihāras*[1348], Munshiram Manoharlal
  - Puri, Baij Nath (1986) [first published 1957], *The History of the Gurjara-Pratiharas*, Delhi: Munshiram Manoharlal
- Sharma, Dasharatha (1966). Rajasthan through the Ages. Bikaner: Rajasthan State Archives
- Sharma, Sanjay (2006), "Negotiating Identity and Status Legitimation and Patronage under the Gurjara-Pratīhāras of Kanauj", *Studies in History*, **22** (22): 181–220, doi: 10.1177/025764300602200202[1349]
- Sharma, Shanta Rani (2012), "Exploding the Myth of the Gūjara Identity of the Imperial Pratihāras", *Indian Historical Review*, **39** (1): 1–10, doi: 10.1177/0376983612449525[1350]
- Singh, R. B. (1964), *History of the Chāhamānas*[1351], N. Kishore
- Sharma, Shanta Rani (2017). Origin and Rise of the Imperial Pratihāras of Rajasthan: Transitions, Trajectories and Historical Change (First ed.). Jaipur: University of Rajasthan. p. 77-78. ISBN 978-93-85593-18-5.
- Tripathi, Rama Shankar (1959). *History of Kanauj: To the Moslem Conquest*[1352]. Motilal Banarsidass. ISBN 978-81-208-0478-4.
- Yadava, Ganga Prasad (1982), *Dhanapāla and His Times: A Sociocultural Study Based Upon His Works*[1353], Concept

 Wikimedia Commons has media related to *Gurjara-Pratihara dynasty*.

 Wikiquote has quotations related to: *Gurjara-Pratihara dynasty*

Rajput

<indicator name="pp-default"> 🔒 </indicator>

Rajput
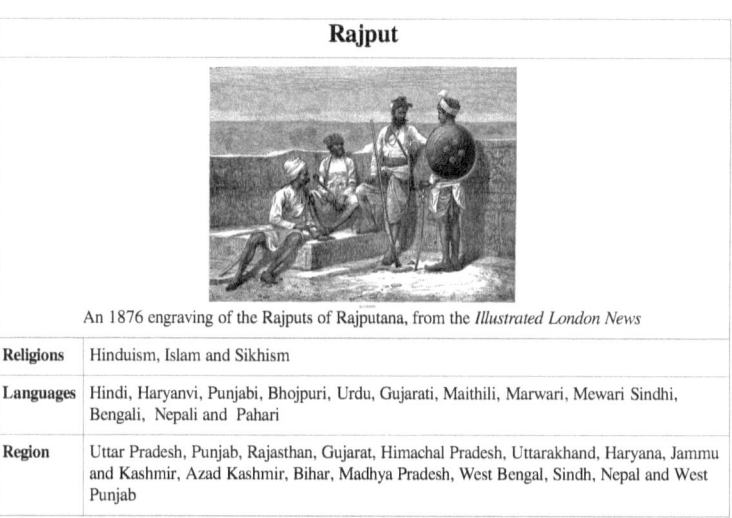
An 1876 engraving of the Rajputs of Rajputana, from the *Illustrated London News*
Religions Hinduism, Islam and Sikhism
Languages Hindi, Haryanvi, Punjabi, Bhojpuri, Urdu, Gujarati, Maithili, Marwari, Mewari Sindhi, Bengali, Nepali and Pahari
Region Uttar Pradesh, Punjab, Rajasthan, Gujarat, Himachal Pradesh, Uttarakhand, Haryana, Jammu and Kashmir, Azad Kashmir, Bihar, Madhya Pradesh, West Bengal, Sindh, Nepal and West Punjab

Rajput (from Sanskrit *raja-putra*, "son of a king") is a large multi-component cluster of castes, kin bodies, and local groups, sharing social status and ideology of genealogical descent originating from the Indian subcontinent. The term Rajput covers various patrilineal clans historically associated with warriorhood: several clans claim Rajput status, although not all claims are universally accepted.

The term "Rajput" acquired its present meaning only in the 16th century, although it is also anachronistically used to describe the earlier lineages that emerged in northern India from 6th century onwards. In the 11th century, the term "*rajaputra*" appeared as a non-hereditary designation for royal officials. Gradually, the Rajputs emerged as a social class comprising people from a variety of ethnic and geographical backgrounds. During the 16th and 17th centuries, the membership of this class became largely hereditary, although new claims to Rajput status continued to be made in the later centuries. Several Rajput-ruled kingdoms played a significant role in many regions of central and northern India until the 20th century.

The Rajput population and the former Rajput states are found in north, west and central India. These areas include Rajasthan, Gujarat, Uttar Pradesh, Himachal Pradesh, Haryana, Jammu, Punjab, Uttarakhand, Madhya Pradesh, West Bengal and Bihar. In Pakistan they are found on the eastern parts of the country, Punjab and Sindh.

History

Origins

The origin of the Rajputs has been a much-debated topic among the historians. Colonial-era writers characterised them as descendants of the foreign invaders such as the Scythians or the Hunas, and believed that the Agnikula myth was invented to conceal their foreign origin.[1354] According to this theory, the Rajputs originated when these invaders were assimilated into the Kshatriya category during the 6th or 7th century, following the collapse of the Gupta Empire.[1355,1356] While many of these colonial writers propagated this foreign-origin theory in order to legitimise the colonial rule, the theory was also supported by some Indian scholars, such as D. R. Bhandarkar.[1354] The Indian nationalist historians, such as C. V. Vaidya, believed the Rajputs to be descendants of the ancient Vedic Aryan Kshatriyas.[1357] A third group of historians, which includes Jai Narayan Asopa, theorized that the Rajputs were Brahmins who became rulers.[1358]

However, recent research suggests that the Rajputs came from a variety of ethnic and geographical backgrounds.[1359] The root word "*rajaputra*" (literally "son of a king") first appears as a designation for royal officials in the 11th century Sanskrit inscriptions. According to some scholars, it was reserved for the immediate relatives of a king; others believe that it was used by a larger group of high-ranking men.[1360] Over time, the derivative term "Rajput" came to denote a hereditary political status, which was not necessarily very high: the term could denote a wide range of rank-holders, from an actual son of a king to the lowest-ranked landholder.[1361] Before the 15th century, the term "Rajput" was associated with people of mixed-caste origin, and was therefore considered inferior in rank to "Kshatriya".[1362]

Gradually, the term Rajput came to denote a social class, which was formed when the various tribal and nomadic groups became landed aristocrats, and transformed into the ruling class.[1363] These groups assumed the title "Rajput" as part of their claim to higher social positions and ranks.[1364] The early medieval literature suggests that this newly formed Rajput class comprised people from multiple castes.[1365] Thus, the Rajput identity is not the result of a shared ancestry. Rather, it emerged when different social groups of medieval India sought to legitimize their newly acquired political power by claiming Kshatriya status. These groups started identifying as Rajput at different times, in different ways.[1366]

Figure 349: *Chandramahal in City Palace, Jaipur, built by Kachwaha Rajputs*

Emergence as a community

Scholarly opinions differ on when the term Rajput acquired hereditary connotations and came to denote a clan-based community. Historian Brajadulal Chattopadhyaya, based on his analysis of inscriptions (primarily from Rajasthan), believed that by the 12th century, the term *"rajaputra"* was associated with fortified settlements, kin-based landholding, and other features that later became indicative of the Rajput status.[1360] According to Chattopadhyaya, the title acquired "an element of heredity" from c. 1300.[1367] A later study by of 11th-14th century inscriptions from western and central India, by Michael B. Bednar, concludes that the designations such as *"rajaputra"*, *"thakkura"* and *"rauta"* were not necessarily hereditary during this period.[1367]

During its formative stages, the Rajput class was quite assimilative and absorbed people from a wide range of lineages.[1363] However, by the late 16th century, it had become genealogically rigid, based on the ideas of blood purity.[1368] The membership of the Rajput class was now largely inherited rather than acquired through military achievements.[1367] A major factor behind this development was the consolidation of the Mughal Empire, whose rulers had great interest in genealogy. As the various Rajput chiefs became Mughal feduatories, they no longer engaged in major conflicts with each other. This decreased the possibility of achieving prestige through military action, and made hereditary prestige more important.[1369]

The word "Rajput" thus acquired its present-day meaning in the 16th century.[1370,1371] During 16th and 17th centuries, the Rajput rulers and their bards (*charans*) sought to legitimize the Rajput socio-political status on the basis of descent and kinship.[1372] They fabricated genealogies linking the Rajput families to the ancient dynasties, and associated them with myths of origins that established their Kshatriya status.[1367,1373] This led to the emergence of what Indologist Dirk Kolff calls the "Rajput Great Tradition", which accepted only hereditary claims to the Rajput identity, and fostered a notion of eliteness and exclusivity.[1374] The legendary epic poem *Prithviraj Raso*, which depicts warriors from several different Rajput clans as associates of Prithviraj Chauhan, fostered a sense of unity among these clans.[1375] The text thus contributed to the consolidation of the Rajput identity by offering these clans a shared history.[1360]

Despite these developments, migrant soldiers made new claims to the Rajput status until as late as the 19th century.[1368] In the 19th century, the colonial administrators of India re-imagined the Rajputs as similar to the Anglo-Saxon knights. They compiled the Rajput genealogies in the process of settling land disputes, surveying castes and tribes, and writing history. These genealogies became the basis of distinguishing between the "genuine" and the "spurious" Rajput clans.[1376]

Rajput kingdoms

The Rajput kingdoms were disparate: loyalty to a clan was more important than allegiance to the wider Rajput social grouping, meaning that one clan would fight another. This and the internecine jostling for position that took place when a clan leader (raja) died meant that Rajput politics were fluid and prevented the formation of a coherent Rajput empire.[1377]

The first major Rajput kingdom was the Sisodia-ruled kingdom of Mewar.[1359] However, the term "Rajput" has also been used as an anachronistic designation for the earlier Hindu dynasties that succeeded the Gurjara-Pratiharas, such as the Chahamanas (of Shakambhari, Nadol and Jalor), the Tomaras, the Chaulukyas, the Paramaras, the Gahadavalas, and the Chandelas.[1378,1379] These dynasties confronted the Ghaznavid and Ghurid invaders during the 11th and 12th centuries. Although the Rajput identity did not exist at this time, these lineages were classified as aristocratic Rajput clans in the later times.[1380]

In the 15th century, the Muslim sultans of Malwa and Gujarat put a joint effort to overcome the Mewar ruler Rana Kumbha but both the sultans were defeated. Subsequently, in 1518 the Rajput Mewar Kingdom under Rana Sanga achieved

Figure 350: *During their centuries-long rule, the Rajputs constructed several palaces. Shown here is the Junagarh Fort in Bikaner, Rajasthan, which was built by the Rathore Rajputs.*

Figure 351: *Amarkot Fort built by Rana Amar Singh in present-day Sindh, Pakistan*

Figure 352: *Chittor Fort, built by a dynasty of Sisodia Rajputs, is one of the largest forts in India.*

a major victory over Sultan Ibrahim Lodhi of Delhi Sultanate and afterwards Rana's influence extended up to the striking distance of Pilia Khar in Agra. Accordingly, Rana Sanga came to be the most distinguished indigenous contender for supremacy but was defeated by the Mughal invader Babur at Battle of Khanwa in 1527.[1381]

From as early as the 16th century, Purbiya Rajput soldiers from the eastern regions of Bihar and Awadh, were recruited as mercenaries for Rajputs in the west, particularly in the Malwa region.

Mughal period

Akbar's policy (Akbar - Shah Jahan)

After the mid-16th century, many Rajput rulers formed close relationships with the Mughal emperors and served them in different capacities. It was due to the support of the Rajputs that Akbar was able to lay the foundations of the Mughal empire in India. Some Rajput nobles gave away their daughters in marriage to Mughal emperors and princes for political motives.[1382] For example, Akbar accomplished 40 marriages for him, his sons and grandsons, out of which 17 were Rajput-Mughal alliances. Akbar's successors as Mogul emperors, his son Jahangir and grandson Shah Jahan had Rajput mothers. The ruling Sisodia Rajput family of Mewar made it a point of honour not to engage in matrimonial

Figure 353: *Mayo College was established by the British government in 1875 at Ajmer, Rajputana to educate Rajput princes and other nobles.*

relationships with Mughals and thus claimed to stand apart from those Rajput clans who did so.[1383]

Aurangzeb's policy

Akbar's diplomatic policy regarding the Rajputs was later damaged by the intolerant rules introduced by his great-grandson Aurangzeb. A prominent example of these rules included the re-imposition of Jaziya, which had been abolished by Akbar. However, despite imposition of Jaziya Aurangzeb's army had a high proportion of Rajput officers in the upper ranks of the imperial army and they were all exempted from paying Jaziya The Rajputs then revolted against the Mughal empire. Aurangzeb's conflicts with the Rajputs, which commenced in the early 1680s, henceforth became a contributing factor towards the downfall of the Mughal empire.

In the 18th century, the Rajputs came under influence of the Maratha empire.[1384] By the late 18th century, the Rajput rulers begin negotiations with the East India Company and by 1818 all the Rajput states had formed an alliance with the company.

Figure 354: *The Derawar Fort built by a Hindu dynasty of Bhatti Rajputs, in modern-day Bahawalpur, Pakistan*

British colonial period

The medieval bardic chronicles (*kavya* and *masnavi*) glorified the Rajput past, presenting warriorhood and honour as Rajput ideals. This later became the basis of the British reconstruction of the Rajput history and the nationalist interpretations of Rajputs' struggles with the Muslim invaders.[1385] James Tod, a British colonial official, was impressed by the military qualities of the Rajputs but is today considered to have been unusually enamoured of them. Although the group venerate him to this day, he is viewed by many historians since the late nineteenth century as being a not particularly reliable commentator. Jason Freitag, his only significant biographer, has said that Tod is "manifestly biased".

The Rajput practices of female infanticide and *sati* (widow immolation) were other matters of concern to the British. It was believed that the Rajputs were the primary adherents to these practices, which the British Raj considered savage and which provided the initial impetus for British ethnographic studies of the subcontinent that eventually manifested itself as a much wider exercise in social engineering.

In reference to the role of the Rajput soldiers serving under the British banner, Captain A. H. Bingley wrote:

Rajputs have served in our ranks from Plassey to the present day (1899). They have taken part in almost every campaign undertaken by the Indian armies. Under Forde they defeated the French at Condore. Under Monro at Buxar they routed the forces of the Nawab of Oudh. Under Lake they took part in the brilliant series of victories which destroyed the power of the Marathas.

Independent India

On India's independence in 1947, the princely states, including those of the Rajput, were given three choices: join either India or Pakistan, or remain independent. Rajput rulers of the 22 princely states of Rajputana acceded to newly independent India, amalgamated into the new state of Rajasthan in 1949–1950. Initially the maharajas were granted funding from the Privy purse in exchange for their acquiescence, but a series of land reforms over the following decades weakened their power, and their privy purse was cut off during Indira Gandhi's administration under the 1971 Constitution 26th Amendment Act. The estates, treasures, and practices of the old Rajput rulers now form a key part of Rajasthan's tourist trade and cultural memory.

In 1951, the Rajput Rana dynasty of Nepal came to an end, having been the power behind the throne of the Shah dynasty figureheads since 1846.

The Rajput Dogra dynasty of Kashmir and Jammu also came to an end in 1947. though title was retained until monarchy was abolished in 1971 by the 26th amendment to the Constitution of India.

The Rajputs, in states such as Madhya Pradesh are today considered to be a Forward Caste in India's system of positive discrimination. This means that they have no access to reservations here. But they are classified as an Other Backward Class by the National Commission for Backward Classes in the state of Karnataka. However, some Rajputs too like other agricultural castes demand reservations in Government jobs, which so far is not heeded to by the Government of India.

Subdivisions

"Rajput" is a vaguely-defined term, and there is no universal consensus on which clans make up the Rajput community.[1386] In medieval Rajasthan (the historical Rajputana) and its neighbouring areas, the word Rajput came to be restricted to certain specific clans, based on patrilineal descent and intermarriages. On the other hand, the Rajput communities living in the region to the east of Rajasthan had a fluid and inclusive nature. The Rajputs of Rajasthan eventually refused to acknowledge the Rajput identity claimed by their

Figure 355: *A contingent of the Rajput Regiment of the Indian Army, during the Republic day parade*

eastern counterparts,[1387] such as the Bundelas.[1388] The Rajputs claim to be Kshatriyas or descendants of Kshatriyas, but their actual status varies greatly, ranging from princely lineages to common cultivators.

There are several major subdivisions of Rajputs, known as *vansh* or *vamsha*, the step below the super-division jāti[1389] These *vansh* delineate claimed descent from various sources, and the Rajput are generally considered to be divided into three primary vansh: Suryavanshi denotes descent from the solar deity Surya, Chandravanshi (Somavanshi) from the lunar deity Chandra, and Agnivanshi from the fire deity Agni. The Agnivanshi clans include Parmar, Chaulukya (Solanki), Parihar and Chauhan.

Lesser-noted *vansh* include Udayvanshi, Rajvanshi, and Rishivanshi Wikipedia:Citation needed. The histories of the various *vansh*s were later recorded in documents known as *vamshāavalīis*; André Wink counts these among the "status-legitimizing texts".

Beneath the *vansh* division are smaller and smaller subdivisions: *kul*, *shakh* ("branch"), *khamp* or *khanp* ("twig"), and *nak* ("twig tip").[1389] Marriages within a *kul* are generally disallowed (with some flexibility for kul-mates of different *gotra* lineages). The *kul* serves as the primary identity for many of the Rajput clans, and each *kul* is protected by a family goddess, the *kuldevi*. Lindsey Harlan notes that in some cases, *shakh*s have become powerful enough to be functionally *kul*s in their own right.[1390]

Figure 356: *The Rajput bride, illustration in The Oriental Annual, or Scenes of India (1835)*

Culture and ethos

The Rajputs were designated as a Martial Race in the period of the British Raj. This was a designation created by administrators that classified each ethnic group as either "martial" or "non-martial": a "martial race" was typically considered brave and well built for fighting, whilst the remainder were those whom the British believed to be unfit for battle because of their sedentary lifestyles.

Rajput lifestyle

The double-edged scimitar known as the khanda was a popular weapon among the Rajputs of that era. On special occasions, a primary chief would break up a meeting of his vassal chiefs with *khanda nariyal*, the distribution of daggers and coconuts. Another affirmation of the Rajput's reverence for his sword was the *Karga Shapna* ("adoration of the sword") ritual, performed during the annual Navaratri festival, after which a Rajput is considered "free to indulge his passion for rapine and revenge". The Rajput of Rajasthan also offer a sacrifice of water buffalo or goat to their family Goddess (Kuldevta) during Navaratri. The ritual requires slaying of the animal with a single stroke. In the past this ritual was considered a rite of passage for young Rajput men.[1391]

Figure 357: *A royal Rajput procession, depicted on a mural at the Mehrangarh Fort in Jodhpur*[1393]

Rajputs generally have adopted the custom of purdah (seclusion of women).

By the late 19th century, there was a shift of focus among Rajputs from politics to a concern with kinship. Many Rajputs of Rajasthan are nostalgic about their past and keenly conscious of their genealogy, emphasising a Rajput ethos that is martial in spirit, with a fierce pride in lineage and tradition.[1392]

Rajput diet

Rajputs are 'by and large' non-vegetarians, eating wild boar, regular drinkers of alcohol, and also smoke and chew betel leaves.Wikipedia:Citing sources#What information to include

Rajput politics

Rajput politics refers to the role played by the Rajput community in the electoral politics of India. In states such as Rajasthan, Uttar Pradesh, Madhya Pradesh, Bihar, Uttrakhand, Jammu, Himachal Pradesh, and Gujarat, the large populations of Rajputs gives them a decisive role.

Arts

The term Rajput painting refers to works of art created at the Rajput-ruled courts of Rajasthan, Central India, and the Punjab Hills. The term is also used to describe the style of these paintings, distinct from the Mughal painting style.[1394]

According to Ananda Coomaraswamy, Rajput painting symbolised the divide between Muslims and Hindus during Mughal rule. The styles of Mughal and Rajput painting are oppositional in character. He characterised Rajput painting as "popular, universal and mystic".

Rajput painting varied geographically, corresponding to each of the various Rajput kingdoms and regions. The Delhi area, Punjab, Rajasthan, and Central India each had its own variant.Wikipedia:Verifiability

References

Bibliography

<templatestyles src="Template:Refbegin/styles.css" />

- Alf Hiltebeitel (1999). *Rethinking India's Oral and Classical Epics: Draupadi among Rajputs, Muslims, and Dalits*[1395]. University of Chicago Press. ISBN 978-0-226-34055-5.
- André Wink (1990). *Al- Hind: The slave kings and the Islamic conquest*[1396]. **1**. BRILL. p. 269. ISBN 9789004095090.
- Ayan Shome (2014). *Dialogue & Daggers: Notion of Authority and Legitimacy in the Early Delhi Sultanate (1192 C.E. – 1316 C.E.)*[1397]. Vij Books. ISBN 978-93-84318-46-8.
- Barbara N. Ramusack (2004). *The Indian Princes and their States*[1398]. Cambridge University Press. ISBN 9781139449083.
- Brajadulal Chattopadhyaya (1994). "Origin of the Rajputs: The Political, Economic and Social Processes in Early Medieval Rajasthan". *The Making of Early Medieval India*[1399]. Oxford University Press. ISBN 9780195634150.
- Bhrigupati Singh (2015). *Poverty and the Quest for Life*[1400]. University of Chicago Press. ISBN 978-0-226-19468-4.
- Catherine B. Asher; Cynthia Talbot (2006). *India Before Europe*[1401]. Cambridge University Press. ISBN 978-0-521-80904-7.
- Cynthia Talbot (2015). *The Last Hindu Emperor: Prithviraj Cauhan and the Indian Past, 1200–2000*[1402]. Cambridge University Press. ISBN 9781107118560.
- David Ludden (1999). *An Agrarian History of South Asia*[1403]. Cambridge University Press. p. 4. ISBN 978-0-521-36424-9.

- Dirk H. A. Kolff (2002). *Naukar, Rajput, and Sepoy*[1404]. Cambridge University Press. ISBN 978-0-521-52305-9.
- Irfan Habib (2002). *Essays in Indian History*[1405]. Anthem Press. p. 90. ISBN 978-1-84331-061-7.
- Karine Schomer (1994). *Idea of Rajasthan: Constructions*[1406]. South Asia Publications. ISBN 978-0-945921-25-7.
- Lindsey Harlan (1992). *Religion and Rajput Women: The Ethic of Protection in Contemporary Narratives*[1407]. Berkeley, California: University of California Press. ISBN 978-0-520-07339-5.
- Pradeep Barua (2005). *The State at War in South Asia*[1408]. University of Nebraska Press. ISBN 0-8032-1344-1.
- Peter Jackson (2003). *The Delhi Sultanate: A Political and Military History*[1409]. Cambridge University Press. ISBN 978-0-521-54329-3.
- Richard Gabriel Fox (1971). *Kin, Clan, Raja, and Rule: Statehinterland Relations in Preindustrial India*[1410]. University of California Press. ISBN 9780520018075.
- Satish Chandra (1982). *Medieval India: Society, the Jagirdari Crisis, and the Village*[1411]. Macmillan.
- Shail Mayaram (2013). *Against History, Against State: Counterperspectives from the Margins*[1412]. Columbia University Press. ISBN 978-0-231-52951-8.
- Tanuja Kothiyal (2016). *Nomadic Narratives: A History of Mobility and Identity in the Great Indian Desert*[1413]. Cambridge University Press. ISBN 9781107080317.

External links

Media related to Rajput people at Wikimedia Commons

 Wikiquote has quotations related to: *Rajput*

Katoch

Katoch is a Rajput clan of the Chandravanshi lineage. Their traditional area of residence was in the Trigarta Kingdom, based at Jalandhar and at Kangra Fort. The members of the Katoch clan claim the dynasty to be the oldest surviving royal dynasty in India.[1414,1415]</ref>

Etymology

There are two possible origins for the word *Katoch*. Members of the clan say it comes from the words *Kat* (army) and *uch* (upper class) but other sources say that it comes from *kot* (fort). The Kangra fort was known as Nagarkot or Kot Kangra, and since the administrators/rulers resided within that particular *kot* they were vernacularly called "Kot'ch" or कोटच, which means *those within the fort*. This over time became Katoch.

History

The main branch of the Katoch clan were the rulers of the Kangra State, which was, by some accounts, the most prominent kingdom between the Ravi and Sutlej in the pre-modern period. The Kangra State was also known as *Trigadh*, a name derived from the ancient Trigarta Kingdom mentioned in the *Mahabharata*. The tradition holds that the Katoch were the rulers of Kangra from the times of *Mahabharata* till the pre-independence era.

They defeated the army of Muhammad bin Tughluq which was not able to fight in the hills. Nearly all his 10,000 soldiers perished in 1333 AD and he was forced to retreat.[1416]

In the pre-modern period, the hill states of the modern Himachal Pradesh are said to have constantly warred with each other, despite relations of kinship and intermarriage. Then they were brought under the Mughal suzerainty by the emperor Akbar. The Mughal control was limited, however. The rulers of the states retained a fair degree of independence. Emperor Jahangir captured the Kangra fort in 1610, annexing the surrounding area and reducing the Katoch rajas to the status of vassals.

After the decline of the Mughal power, Raja Ghamand Chand (r. 1751–1823) recovered most of the territory earlier ceded to the Mughals. Raja Sansar Chand (r. 1775–1823) established the supremacy of Kangra over all the surrounding hill states. During his reign, Kangra became a major centre for the arts and several palaces were built.

In the year 1805, the neighbouring hill states rebelled, with the aid of the Gurkha army. Raja Sansar Chand was forced to seek the help of Maharaja

Figure 358: *The strategic Kangra fort commanded the respect of the region.*

Ranjit Singh of Lahore. The Gurkha army was expelled but Ranjit Singh also annexed the most fertile party of the Kangra valley, reducing the Katochs of Kangra as well as the neighbouring rajas to the status of vassals. After the First Anglo-Sikh War of 1846, the whole area was ceded to the British East India Company, eventually integrated into the Punjab province. The Katochs and the surrounding hill rajas were assigned small *jagirs* over which they had the rights of revenue and magisterial authority.

Clans and surnames

The Katoch clan has four branches: the Jaswal, Guleria, Sibaia and Dadwal. Dadwal stems from Dada, a place in Siba. Sibaia also stems from Siba. Guleria stems from Guler region. The four branches came into existence after the 11th century CE.

Each sub-clan has several subordinate surnames, which number 24 in total. Katochs suffixed 'Chandra' to their names until the rise of the Sikh dynasty in Punjab, after which some clan members started suffixing 'Singh' also. However, most clan members today, including in the sub-clans, suffix Chand.

Until the reforms of 1930s, the Katoch women were only married westward, generally to the Pathania and Jamwal/Jamuwal men. The higher the sub-clan rated its own status, the farther away towards the west they tended to marry.

Regions ruled by the clan

In past centuries, the clan and its branches ruled several princely states in the region of Trigarta. Trigarta refers to the land between three rivers, namely, Beas, Sutlej, and Ravi. However, the clan lost lands and by the 17th century had been reduced to a small hill state. The originator of the clan was Rajanaka Bhumi Chand. Their rulers include Sansar Chand II and Rajanaka Bhumi Chand, the latter being the founder of the Jwalamukhi temple in Himachal Pradesh.

Chauhan

<indicator name="pp-default"> </indicator> **Chauhan**, **Chouhan**, **Chohan**, or **Chohhan**, is a Rajput caste from northern and western India.

Myths of origin

The word *Chauhan* is the vernacular form of the Sanskrit term *Chahamana*. Several Chauhan inscriptions name a legendary hero called Chahamana as their ancestor, but none of them state the period in which he lived.[1417]

The earliest extant inscription that describes the origin of the Chauhans is the 1119 CE Sevadi inscription of Ratnapala, a ruler of the Naddula Chahamana dynasty. According to this inscription, the ancestor of the Chahamanas was born from the eye of Indra.[1418]

The 1170 CE Bijolia rock inscription of the Shakambhari Chahamana king Someshvara states that his ancestor Samantaraja was born at Ahichchhatrapura (possibly modern Nagaur[1419]) in the gotra of sage Vatsa. The 1262 CE Sundha hill inscription of the Jalor Chahamana king Chachiga-deva states that the dynasty's ancestor Chahamana was "a source of joy" to the Vatsa. The 1320 Mount Abu (Achaleshwar temple) inscription of the Deora Chauhan ruler Lumbha states that Vatsa created the Chahamanas as a new lineage of warriors, after the solar dynasty and the lunar dynasty had ceased to exist.[1420]

The Ajmer inscription of the Shakambhari Chahamana ruler Vigraharaja IV (c. 1150–64 CE) claims that Chahamana belonged to the solar dynasty, descending from Ikshavaku and Rama. The 12th-century *Prithviraja Vijaya* mahakavya, composed by Prithviraja III's court poet Jayanaka, also claims a solar dynasty origin for the ruling dynasty. According to this text, Chahamana came to earth from *Arkamandal* (the orbit of the sun).[1421]

The 15th-century *Hammira Mahakavya* of Nayachandra Suri, which describes the life of the Ranthambore branch ruler Hammira, gives the following account: Once Brahma was wandering in search of an auspicious place to conduct a ritual sacrifice. He ultimately chose the place where a lotus from his hand fell; this place came to be known as Pushkara. Brahma wanted to protect his sacrificial ceremony against interference from danavas (miscreant beings). Therefore, he remembered the Sun, and a hero came into being from the sun's orb. This hero was Chohan, the ancestor of the Hammira's dynasty.[1422] The earliest extant recension of *Prithviraj Raso* of Chand Bardai, dated to 15th or 16th century, states that the first Chauhan king – Manikya Rai – was born from Brahma's sacrifice.[1422] The 16th-century *Surjana-Charita*, composed by the Bengali poet Chandra Shekhara under patronage of the Ranthambore ruler Rao Surjana, contains a similar account. It states that Brahma created the first Chahamana from the Sun's disc during a sacrificial ceremony at Pushkara.[1423]

Despite these earlier myths, it was the Agnivanshi (or Agnikula) myth that became most popular among the Chauhans and other Rajput clans. According to this myth, some of the Rajput clans originated from Agni, in a sacrificial fire pit. This legend was probably invented by the 10th-century Paramara court poet Padmagupta, whose *Nava-Sahasanka-Charita* mentions only the Paramaras as fire-born.[1424] The inclusion of Chauhans in the Agnivanshi myth can be traced back to the later recensions of *Prithviraj Raso*. In this version of the legend, once Vashistha and other great sages begin a major sacrificial ceremony on Mount Abu. The ritual was interrupted by miscreant daityas (demons). To get rid of these demons, Vashistha created progenitors of three Rajput dynasties from the sacrificial fire pit. These were Parihar (Pratiharas), Chaluk (Chaulukya or Solanki), and Parmar (Paramara). These heroes were unable to defeat the demons. So, the sages prayed again, and this time a fourth warrior appeared: Chahuvana (Chauhan). This fourth hero slayed the demons.[1425,1426]

The earliest available copies of *Prithviraj Raso* do not mention the Agnivanshi legend.[1427] It is possible that the 16th-century bards came up with the legend to foster Rajput unity against the Mughal emperor Akbar.[1428] Adaptions of the *Prithviraj Raso* occur in several later works. The *Hammira Raso* (1728 CE) by Jodharaja, a court poet of prince Chandrabhana of Neemrana, states that once the Kshatriyas (warriors) became extinct. So, the great sages assembled at Mount Abu and created three heroes. When these three heroes could not defeat the demons, they created Chahuvanaji.[1429] A slight variation occurs in the writings of Surya Malla Mishrana, the court poet of Bundi. In this version, the various gods create the four heroes on Vashistha's request.[1430] According to the bardic tale of the Khichi clan of Chauhans, the Parwar (Paramara) was born from Shiva's essence; the Solankhi (Solanki) or Chaluk Rao (Chalukya) was born from Brahma's essence; the Pariyar (Parihar) was born from Devi's essence; and the Chahuvan (Chauhan) was born from Agni, the fire.[1431]

Ethnographic status

Denzil Ibbetson, an administrator of the British Raj, classified the Chauhans as a tribe rather than as a caste. He believed, like John Nesfield, that the society of the Northwest Frontier Provinces and Punjab in British India did not permit the rigid imposition of an administratively defined caste construct as his colleague, H. H. Risley preferred. According to Ibbetson, society in Punjab was less governed by Brahmanical ideas of caste, based on varna, and instead was more open and fluid. Tribes, which he considered to be kin-based groups that dominated small areas, were the dominant feature of rural life. Caste designators, such as Jat and Rajput, were status-based titles to which any tribe that rose to social prominence could lay a claim, and which could be dismissed by their peers if they declined. Susan Bayly, a modern anthropologist, considers him to have had "a high degree of accuracy in his observations of Punjab society ... [I]n his writings we really do see the beginnings of modern, regionally based Indian anthropology."

History

The Chauhans were historically a powerful group in the region now known as Rajasthan. For around 400 years from the 7th century CE their strength in Sambhar was a threat to the power-base of the Guhilots in the south-west of the area, as also was the strength of their fellow Agnivanshi clans.[1432] They suffered a set-back in 1192 when their leader, Prithviraj Chauhan, was defeated at the Battle of Tarain but this did not signify their demise.[1433] The kingdom broke into the Satyapura and Devda branches after the invasion of Qutbu l-Din Aibak in 1197.

The earliest Chauhan inscription is a copper-plate inscription found at Hansot.[1434]

Dynasties

The ruling dynasties belonging to the Chauhan clan included:

- Chahamanas of Shakambhari (Chauhans of Ajmer)
- Chahamanas of Naddula (Chauhans of Nadol)
- Chahamanas of Lata[1435]
- Chahamanas of Dholpur[1436]
- Chahamanas of Partabgarh[1437]
- Chahamanas of Jalor (Chauhans of Jalore); branched off from the Chahamanas of Naddula
- Chahamanas of Ranastambhapura (Chauhans of Ranthambore); branched off from the Chahamanas of Shakambhari

The princely states ruled by families claiming Chauhan descent include:

- Bundi State
- Changbhakar State
- Korea State
- Kota State
- Sirohi State
- Sonepur State
- Ambliara State

Notable people

- Prithviraj (1178–1192 AD) fought the Chandellas, Chaulukyas of Gujarat and the Gahadavalas, besides Muhammad Ghori in the Battles of Tarain.
- Gugga, a warrior, minor king and Nāga demigod
- Hammir Dev Chauhan, ruler of Ranathambore

References

Citations

Bibliography

<templatestyles src="Template:Refbegin/styles.css" />

- Gupta, R. K.; Bakshi, S. R., eds. (2008). *Studies In Indian History: Rajasthan Through The Ages: The Heritage of Rajputs*[1438]. **1**. Sarup & Sons. ISBN 978-8-17625-841-8.
- Majumdar, Asoke Kumar (1956). *Chaulukyas of Gujarat: A Survey of the History and Culture of Gujarat from the Middle of the Tenth to the End of the Thirteenth Century*[1439]. Bharatiya Vidya Bhavan.
- Seth, Krishna Narain (1978). *The Growth of the Paramara Power in Malwa*[1440]. Progress.
- Singh, R. B. (1964). *History of the Chāhamānas*[1441]. N. Kishore.

Chahamanas of Shakambhari

Chahamanas of Shakambhari	
7th century–12th century	
Capital	Shakambhari
Religion	Hinduism
Government	Monarchy
History	
• Established	7th century
• Disestablished	12th century
Preceded by	Succeeded by
Gurjara-Pratihara, Tomara dynasty	Ghurid dynasty
Today part of	India

The **Chahamanas of Shakambhari** (IAST: Cāhamāna), colloquially known as the **Chauhans of Sambhar**, were an Indian dynasty that ruled parts of the present-day Rajasthan and its neighbouring areas between 7th to 12th centuries. The territory ruled by them was known as Sapadalaksha. They were the most prominent ruling family of the Chahamana (Chauhan) clan, and were categorized among Agnivanshi Rajputs in the later medieval legends.

The Chahamanas originally had their capital at Shakambhari (present-day Sambhar). Until the 10th century, they ruled as Gurjara-Pratihara vassals. When the Pratihara power declined after the Tripartite Struggle, the Chahamana ruler Simharaja assumed the title Maharajadhiraja. In the early 12th century, Ajayaraja II moved the kingdom's capital to Ajayameru (modern Ajmer). For this reason, the Chahamana rulers are also known as the **Chauhans of Ajmer**.

The Chahamanas fought several wars with their neighbours, including the Chaulukyas of Gujarat, the Tomaras of Delhi, and the Paramaras of Malwa. From 11th century onwards, they started facing Muslim invasions, first by the Ghaznavids, and then by the Ghurids. The Chahamana kingdom reached its zenith under Vigraharaja IV in the mid-12th century. The dynasty's power effectively ended in 1192 CE, when the Ghurids defeated his nephew Prithviraja III.

Figure 359: *Coin of the Chahamana ruler Vigraharaja IV, circa 1150-1164.*

Origin

According to the 1170 CE Bijolia rock inscription of Someshvara, the early Chahamana king Samantaraja was born at Ahichchhatrapura in the gotra of sage Vatsa .[1442] Historian R. . Singh theorizes that the Chahamanas probably started out as petty rulers of Ahichchhatrapura (identified with Nagaur), and moved their capital to Shakambhari (Sambhar) as their kingdom grew. Later, they became the vassals of the imperial Gurjara-Pratiharas.[1443]

Several mythical accounts of the dynasty's origin also exist. The earliest of the dynasty's inscriptions and literary works state that the dynasty's progenitor was a legendary hero named Chahamana. They variously state that this hero was born from Indra's eye, in the lineage of the sage Vatsa , in the solar dynasty and/or during a ritual sacrifice performed by Brahma.[1444]

In the later period, the Chahamanas were categorized as one of the Rajput clans, although the Rajput identity did not exist during their time.[1445] A popular medieval account classifies the dynasty among the four Agnivanshi Rajput clans, whose ancestors are said to have come out of sacrificial fire pit. The earliest source to mention this legend are the 16th century recensions of *Prithviraj Raso*. Some colonial-era historians interpreted this myth to suggest a foreign origin of the dynasty, speculating that the foreign warriors were initiated into the Hindu society through a fire ritual.[1446] However, the earliest extant copy of *Prithviraj Raso* does not mention this legend at all. Instead, it states that the first ruler of the dynasty was Manikya Rai, who is said to have been born from Brahma's sacrifice.[1447]

Territory

<mapframe text="[[Find spot]]s of the inscriptions issued during the Shakambhari Chahamana reign.{{sfn|Anita Sudan|1989|pp=312-316}}" width="400" height="400" zoom="5" latitude="26.45" longitude="74.62"> { "type": "FeatureCollection", "features": [{ "type": "Feature", "properties": { "marker-symbol": "star", "marker-color": "302060", "title": "Ajmer", "description": "Adhai Din Ka Jhonpra" }, "geometry": { "type": "Point", "coordinates": [74.6251327, 26.4552512] } }, { "type": "Feature", "properties": { "marker-symbol": "monument", "title": "Amalda", "description": "Also known as Anvalda" }, "geometry": { "type": "Point", "coordinates": [75.1487007, 25.4840273] } }, { "type": "Feature", "properties": { "marker-symbol": "monument", "title": "Bajta" }, "geometry": { "type": "Point", "coordinates": [75.2770721, 25.8440912] } }, { "type": "Feature", "properties": { "marker-symbol": "monument", "title": "Barla" }, "geometry": { "type": "Point", "coordinates": [72.8382547, 26.6120892] } }, { "type": "Feature", "properties": { "marker-symbol": "monument", "title": "Bassi" }, "geometry": { "type": "Point", "coordinates": [76.050499, 26.8391525] } }, { "type": "Feature", "properties": { "marker-symbol": "monument", "title": "Bijolia" }, "geometry": { "type": "Point", "coordinates": [75.3266416, 25.1635904] } }, { "type": "Feature", "properties": { "marker-symbol": "monument", "title": "Bisaldeo temple", "description": "At Bisalpur or Visalapur" }, "geometry": { "type": "Point", "coordinates": [75.4571403, 25.9271197] } }, { "type": "Feature", "properties": { "marker-symbol": "monument", "title": "Charla", "description": "Also known as Charlu, in Churu district" }, "geometry": { "type": "Point", "coordinates": [74.3000878, 27.7084401] } }, { "type": "Feature", "properties": { "marker-symbol": "monument", "title": "Chittorgarh" }, "geometry": { "type": "Point", "coordinates": [74.6269216, 24.8887435] } }, { "type": "Feature", "properties": { "marker-symbol": "monument", "title": "Dhod" }, "geometry": { "type": "Point", "coordinates": [74.9862056, 27.4923745] } }, { "type": "Feature", "properties": { "marker-symbol": "monument", "title": "Harsh", "description": "Harshnath temple" }, "geometry": { "type": "Point", "coordinates": [75.172475, 27.4999733] } }, { "type": "Feature", "properties": { "marker-symbol": "monument", "title": "Jodhpur" }, "geometry": { "type": "Point", "coordinates": [73.0243094, 26.2389469] } }, { "type": "Feature", "properties": { "marker-symbol": "monument", "title": "Kinsariya" }, "geometry": { "type": "Point", "coordinates": [74.7044425, 26.9350885] } }, { "type": "Feature", "properties": { "marker-symbol": "monument", "title": "Ladnu", "description": "Also known as Ladnun" }, "geometry": { "type": "Point", "coordinates": [74.3880699, 27.6442908] } }

}, { "type": "Feature", "properties": { "marker-symbol": "monument", "title": "Lohari", "description": "in Bhilwara district" }, "geometry": { "type": "Point", "coordinates": [75.4, 25.65] } }, { "type": "Feature", "properties": { "marker-symbol": "monument", "title": "Madanpur", "description": "Issued during Prithviraja III's raid against the Chandelas" }, "geometry": { "type": "Point", "coordinates": [78.6951795, 24.2510993] } }, { "type": "Feature", "properties": { "marker-symbol": "monument", "title": "Narhar", "description": "Also known as Narhada or Narhad" }, "geometry": { "type": "Point", "coordinates": [75.5960745, 28.2944746] } }, { "type": "Feature", "properties": { "marker-symbol": "monument", "title": "Phalodi" }, "geometry": { "type": "Point", "coordinates": [72.3589284, 27.1312346] } }, { "type": "Feature", "properties": { "marker-symbol": "monument", "title": "Pushkar" }, "geometry": { "type": "Point", "coordinates": [74.5510856, 26.489749] } },

{ "type": "Feature", "properties": { "marker-symbol": "monument", "title": "Rewasa", "description": "Also known as Revasa" }, "geometry": { "type": "Point", "coordinates": [76.5191968, 27.0925499] } }, { "type": "Feature", "properties": { "marker-symbol": "monument", "title": "Sewari", "description": "Also known as Sevadi" }, "geometry": { "type": "Point", "coordinates": [73.297175, 25.0944987] } }, { "type": "Feature", "properties": { "marker-symbol": "monument", "title": "Tantoti" }, "geometry": { "type": "Point", "coordinates": [74.8170822, 26.1405014] } }, { "type": "Feature", "properties": { "marker-symbol": "monument", "title": "Thanwala", "description": "Thanvala" }, "geometry": { "type": "Point", "coordinates": [74.4649512, 26.557162] } }, { "type": "Feature", "properties": { "marker-symbol": "monument", "title": "Topra", "description": "Issued during Vigraharaja IV's northern campaign. Now at Delhi." }, "geometry": { "type": "Point", "coordinates": [77.1623852, 30.1252841] } }, { "type": "Feature", "properties": { "marker-symbol": "monument", "title": "Udaipur" }, "geometry": { "type": "Point", "coordinates": [73.712479, 24.585445] } }, { "type": "Feature", "properties": { "marker-symbol": "monument", "title": "Jeenmata temple", "comment": "Source: Har Bilas Sarda (1941). *Ajmer: historical and descriptive*, p. 451" }, "geometry": { "type": "Point", "coordinates": [75.194225, 27.4442969] } }] } </mapframe> The core territory of the Chahamanas was located in present-day Rajasthan. It was known as *Sapadalaksha* (IAST: Sapādalakṣa) or *Jangala-desha* (IAST: Jangaladeśa).[1448]

The term Jangladesha ("rough and arid country") appears to be older, as it mentioned in the *Mahabharata*.[1449] The text does not mention the exact location of the region. The later Sanskrit texts, such as *Bhava-Prakasha* and *Shabdakalpadruma-Kosha* suggest that it was a hot, arid region, where trees requiring little water grew. The region is identified with the area around Bikaner.[1450]

The term Sapadalaksha (literally "one and a quarter lakhs" or 125,000) refers to the large number of villages in the area.[1451] It became prominent during the Chahamana reign. It appears that the term originally referred to the area around modern Nagaur near Bikaner. This area was known as *Savalak* (vernacular form of Sapadalaksha) in as late as 20th century.[1449] The early Chahamana king Samantaraja was based in Ahichchhatrapura, which can be identified with modern Nagaur. The ancient name of Nagaur was Nagapura, which means "the city of the serpent". Ahichchhatrapura has a similar meaning: "the city whose *chhatra* or protector is serpent".[1452]

As the Chahamana territory expanded, the entire region ruled by them came to be known as Sapadalaksha.[1449] This included the later Chahamana capitals Ajayameru (Ajmer) and Shakambhari (Sambhar).[1453] The term also came to be applied to the larger area captured by the Chahamanas. The early medieval Indian inscriptions and the writings of the contemporary Muslim historians suggest that the following cities were also included in Sapadalaksha: Hansi (now in Haryana), Mandore (now in Marwar region), and Mandalgarh (now in Mewar region).[1454]

History

The earliest historical Chahamana king is the 6th century ruler Vasudeva. According to a mythical account in *Prithviraja Vijaya*, he received the Sambhar Salt Lake as a gift from a vidyadhara (a supernatural being).[1455] Little is known about his immediate successors. The 8th century Chahamana ruler Durlabharaja I and his successors are known to have served the Gurjara-Pratiharas as vassals. In 10th century, Vakpatiraja I made an attempt to overthrow the Gurjara-Pratihara suzerainty, and assumed the title Maharaja ("great king").[1456] His younger son Lakshmana established the Naddula Chahamana branch. Vakpatiraja's elder son and successor Simharaja assumed the title Maharajadhiraja ("king of great kings"), which suggests that he was a sovereign ruler.[1457]

Simharaja's successors consolidated the Chahamana power by engaging in wars with their neighbours, including the Chaulukyas of Gujarat and the Tomaras of Delhi. The dynasty's earliest extant inscription (973 CE) is from the reign of Vigraharaja II.[1451] During the reign of Viryarama (r. c. 1040 CE), the Paramara king Bhoja invaded the Chahamana kingdom, and probably occupied their capital Shakambhari for a brief period.[1458] Chamundaraja restored the Chahamana power, possibly with the help of the Naddula Chahamanas.[1458]

Figure 360: *The Ana Sagar lake in Ajmer was commissioned by the Chahamana ruler Arnoraja alias Ana*

The subsequent Chahamana kings faced several Ghaznavid raids. Ajayaraja II (r. c. 1110-1135 CE) repulsed a Ghaznavid attack, and also defeated the Paramara king Naravarman. He moved the kingdom's capital from Shakambhari to Ajayameru (Ajmer), a city that he either established or greatly expanded.[1459,1460] His successor Arnoraja raided the Tomara territory, and also repulsed a Ghaznavid invasion. However, he suffered setbacks against the Gujarat Chaulukya kings Jayasimha Siddharaja and Kumarapala, and was killed by his own son Jagaddeva.[1461]

Arnoraja's younger son Vigraharaja IV greatly expanded the Chahamana territories, and captured Delhi from the Tomaras. His kingdom included parts of the present-day Rajasthan, Haryana, and Delhi. It probably also included a part of Punjab (to the south-east of Sutlej river) and a portion of the northern Gangetic plain (to the west of Yamuna).[1462] His 1164 CE Delhi-Shivalik pillar inscription claims that he conquered the region between the Himalayas and the Vindhyas, and thus restored the rule of Aryans in Aryavarta. While this is an exaggeration, it is not completely baseless. The inscription was originally found in Topra village, near the Shivalik Hills (Himalayan foothills). Also, the exiled ruler of Malwa (Vindhyan region) possibly acknowledged his suzerainty. Thus Vigraharaja's influence extended from the Himalayas to the Vindhyas, at least in name.[1463]

Figure 361: *Bisaldeo temple commissioned by Vigraharaja IV*

Vigraharaja was succeeded by his son Amaragangeya, and then his nephew Prithviraja II. Subsequently, his younger brother Someshvara ascended the throne.[1464]

The most celebrated ruler of the dynasty was Someshvara's son Prithviraja III, better known as Prithviraj Chauhan. He defeated several neighbouring kings, including the Chandela ruler Paramardi in 1182-83, although he could not annex the Chandela territory to his kingdom.[1465] In 1191, he defeated the Ghurid king Muhammad of Ghor at the first Battle of Tarain. However, the next year, he was defeated at the second Battle of Tarain, and subsequently killed.[1466]

Muhammad of Ghor appointed Prithviraja's son Govindaraja IV as a vassal. Prithviraja's brother Hariraja dethroned him, and regained control of a part of his ancestral kingdom. Hariraja was defeated by the Ghurids in 1194 CE. Govindaraja was granted the fief of Ranthambore by the Ghurids. There, he established a new branch of the dynasty.[1467]

Cultural activities

The Chahamanas commissioned a number of Hindu temples, several of which were destroyed by the Ghurid invaders after the defeat of Prithviraja III.[1468]

Figure 362: *The Harshnath temple was commissioned by the Chahamana rulers*

Multiple Chahamana rulers contributed to the construction of the Harshanatha temple, which was probably commissioned by Govindaraja I.[1469] According to *Prithviraja Vijaya*:

- Simharaja commissioned a large Shiva temple at Pushkar[1470]
- Chamundaraja commissioned a Vishnu temple at Narapura (modern Narwar in Ajmer district)[1471]
- Prithviraja I built a food distribution centre (*anna-satra*) on the road to Somnath temple for pilgrims.[1472]
- Someshvara commissioned a number of temples, including five temples in Ajmer.[1473,1474]

Vigraharaja IV was known for his patronage to arts and literature, and himself composed the play *Harikeli Nataka*. The structure that was later converted into the Adhai Din Ka Jhonpra mosque was constructed during his reign.[1475]

The Chahamana rulers also patronized Jainism. Vijayasimha Suri's *Upadeśāmālavritti* (1134 CE) and Chandra Suri's *Munisuvrata-Charita* (1136 CE) state that Prithviraja I donated golden kalashas (cupolas) for the Jain temples at Ranthambore.[1476] The *Kharatara-Gachchha-Pattavali* states that Ajayaraja II allowed the Jains to build their temples in his capital Ajayameru (Ajmer), and also donated a golden kalasha to a Parshvanatha temple.[1477] Someshvara granted the Revna village to a Parshvanatha temple.[1473]

Figure 363: *Prithviraja III, the most celebrated ruler of the dynasty*

List of rulers

Following is a list of Chahmana rulers of Shakambhari and Ajmer, with approximate period of reign, as estimated by R. B. Singh:[1478]

- Chahamana (possibly mythical)
- Vasu-deva (c. 6th century CE)
- Samanta-raja (c. 684-709 CE); identified as the legendary Manik Rai by R. B. Singh
- Nara-deva (c. 709-721 CE)
- Ajaya-raja I (c. 721-734 CE), alias Jayaraja or Ajayapala
- Vigraha-raja I (c. 734-759 CE)
- Chandra-raja I (c. 759-771 CE)
- Gopendra-raja (c. 771-784 CE)
- Durlabha-raja I (c. 784-809 CE)
- Govinda-raja I (c. 809-836 CE), alias Guvaka I
- Chandra-raja II (c. 836-863 CE)
- Govindaraja II (c. 863-890 CE), alias Guvaka II
- Chandana-raja (c. 890-917 CE)
- Vakpati-raja (c. 917-944 CE); his younger son established the Naddula Chahamana branch
- Simha-raja (c. 944-971 CE)

- Vigraha-raja II (c. 971-998 CE)
- Durlabha-raja II (c. 998-1012 CE)
- Govinda-raja III (c. 1012-1026 CE)
- Vakpati-raja II (c. 1026-1040 CE)
- Viryarama (c. 1040 CE)
- Chamunda-raja (c. 1040-1065 CE)
- Durlabha-raja III (c. 1065-1070 CE), alias Duśala
- Vigraha-raja III (c. 1070-1090 CE), alias Visala
- Prithvi-raja I (c. 1090-1110 CE)
- Ajaya-raja II (c. 1110-1135 CE), moved the capital to Ajayameru (Ajmer)
- Arno-raja (c. 1135-1150 CE), alias Ana
- Jagad-deva (c. 1150 CE)
- Vigraha-raja IV (c. 1150-1164 CE), alias Visaladeva
- Apara-gangeya (c. 1164-1165 CE)
- Prithvi-raja II (c. 1165-1169 CE)
- Someshvara (c. 1169-1178 CE)
- Prithvi-raja III (c. 1178-1192 CE), better known as Prithviraj Chauhan
- Govinda-raja IV (c. 1192 CE); banished by Hari-raja for accepting Muslim suzerainty; established the Chahamana branch of Ranastambhapura
- Hari-raja (c. 1193-1194 CE)

References

Bibliography

<templatestyles src="Template:Refbegin/styles.css" />

- Alf Hiltebeitel (1999). *Rethinking India's Oral and Classical Epics: Draupadi among Rajputs, Muslims, and Dalits*[1479]. University of Chicago Press. ISBN 978-0-226-34055-5.
- Anita Sudan (1989). *A study of the Cahamana inscriptions of Rajasthan*[1480]. Research. OCLC 20754525[1481].
- Cynthia Talbot (2015). *The Last Hindu Emperor: Prithviraj Cauhan and the Indian Past, 1200–2000*[1482]. Cambridge University Press. ISBN 9781107118560.
- Dasharatha Sharma (1959). *Early Chauhān Dynasties*[1483]. S. Chand / Motilal Banarsidass. ISBN 9780842606189.
- Har Bilas Sarda (1935). *Speeches And Writings Har Bilas Sarda*[1484]. Ajmer: Vedic Yantralaya.
- Iqtidar Alam Khan (2008). *Historical Dictionary of Medieval India*[1485]. Scarecrow Press. ISBN 9780810864016.
- R. B. Singh (1964). *History of the Chāhamānas*[1486]. N. Kishore. OCLC 11038728[1487].

> Wikiquote has quotations related to: *Chahamanas of Shakambhari*

Kachwaha

<indicator name="pp-default"> 🔒 </indicator>

The **Kachwaha** are a caste group with origins in India. Traditionally they were peasants involved in agriculture but in the 20th century they began to make claims of being a Rajput clan. Some families within the caste did rule a number of kingdoms and princely states, such as Alwar, Amber (later called Jaipur) and Maihar.

The Kachwaha are sometimes referred to as Kushwaha. This umbrella term is used to represent at least four communities with similar occupational backgrounds, all of whom claim descent from the mythological Suryavansh (Solar) dynasty via Kusha, who was one of the twin sons of Rama and Sita. Previously, they had worshipped Shiva and Shakta.

Origins

The modern-day Kushwaha community, of which the Kachwaha form a part, generally claim descent from Kusha, a son of the mythological avatar of Vishnu, Rama. This enables their claim to be of the Suryavansh dynasty but it is a myth of origin developed in the twentieth century. Prior to that time, the various branches that form the Kushwah community - the Kachwahas, Kachhis, Koeris, and Muraos - favoured a connection with Shiva and Shakta.

Ganga Prasad Gupta claimed in the 1920s that Kushwah families worshiped Hanuman - described by Pinch as "the embodiment of true devotion to Ram and Sita" - during Kartika, a month in the Hindu lunar calendar.

Rulers

A Kachwaha family ruled at Amber, which later became known as the Jaipur State, and this branch is sometimes referred to as being Rajput. They were chiefs at Amber and in 1561 sought support from Akbar, the Mughal emperor. The then chief, Bharamail Kachwaha, was formally recognised as a Raja and was invested into the Mughal nobility in return for him giving his daughter to Akbar's harem. A governor was appointed to oversee Bharamail's territory and a tribute arrangement saw Bharamail given a salaried rank, paid for from a share of the area's revenue. The Rajput practice of giving daughters

Figure 364: *The Pachrang flag of the former Jaipur state. Prior to the adoption of the Pachrang (five coloured) flag by Raja Man Singh I of Amber, the original flag of the Kachwahas was known as the "Jharshahi (tree-marked) flag".*

to the Mughal emperors in return for recognition as nobility and the honour of fighting on behalf of the Empire originated in this arrangement and thus the Mughals were often able to assert their dominance over Rajput chiefs in north India without needing to physically intimidate them, especially after their rout of rulers in Gondwana.

Classification

The Kushwaha were traditionally a peasant community and considered to be of the stigmatised Shudra varna. Pinch describes them as "skilled agriculturalists". The traditional perception of Shudra status was increasingly challenged during the later decades of British Raj rule, although various castes had made claims of a higher status well before the British administration instituted its first census.[1488]</ref> Pinch describes that "The concern with personal dignity, community identity, and caste status reached a peak among Kurmi, Yadav, and Kushvaha peasants in the first four decades of the twentieth century."

From around 1910, the Kachhis and the Koeris, both of whom for much of the preceding century had close links with the British as a consequence of their favoured role in the cultivation of the opium poppy, began to identify themselves as Kushwaha Kshatriya. An organisation claiming to represent those two groups and the Muraos petitioned for official recognition as being of the Kshatriya varna in 1928. This action by the All India Kushwaha Kshatriya Mahasabha (AIKKM) reflected the general trend for social upliftment by communities that had traditionally been classified as being Shudra. The process, which M. N. Srinivas called sanskritisation, was a feature of late nineteenth- and early twentieth-century caste politics.

The position of the AIKKM was based on the concept of Vaishnavism, which promoted the worship and claims of descent from Rama or Krishna as a means to assume the trappings of Kshatriya symbolism and thus permit the wearing of the sacred thread even though the physical labour inherent in their cultivator occupations intrinsically defined them as Shudra. The movement caused them to abandon their claims to be descended from Shiva in favour of the alternate myth that claimed descent from Rama. In 1921, Ganga Prasad Gupta, a proponent of Kushwaha reform, had published a book offering a proof of the Kshatriya status of the Koeri, Kachhi, Murao and Kachwaha. His reconstructed history argued that the Kushwaha were Hindu descendants of Kush and that in the twelfth century they had served Raja Jaichand in a military capacity during the period of Muslim consolidation of the Delhi Sultanate. Subsequent persecution by the victorious Muslims caused the Kushwaha kshatryia to disperse and disguise their identity, foregoing the sacred thread and thereby becoming degraded and taking on various localised community names. Gupta's attempt to prove Kshatriya status, in common with similar attempts by others to establish histories of various castes, was spread via the caste associations, which Dipankar Gupta describes as providing a link between the "urban, politically literate elite" and the "less literate villagers". Some communities also constructed temples in support of these claims as, for example, did the Muraos in Ayodhya.

Some Kushwaha reformers also argued, in a similar vein to the Kurmi reformer Devi Prasad Sinha Chaudhari, that since Brahmans and also Kshatriya Rajputs and Bhumihars worked the fields in some areas, there was no rational basis for assertions that such labour marked a community as being of the Shudra varna.

Notable people

- Pajawan
- Jai Singh I
- Ramsingh I
- Maharaja Sawai Jai Singh II
- Maharaj Sawai Madhosingh I
- Maharaja Sawai Pratapsingh
- Maharaja Sawai Man Singh II
- Maharaja Sawai Bhawani Singh
- Rao Shekha

References

Notes

Citations

Further reading

- Bayley C. (1894) *Chiefs and Leading Families In Rajputana*
- Henige, David (2004). *Princely states of India;A guide to chronology and rulers*
- Jyoti J. (2001) *Royal Jaipur*
- Krishnadatta Kavi, Gopalnarayan Bahura(editor) (1983) *Pratapa Prakasa, a contemporary account of life in the court at Jaipur in the late 18th century*
- Khangarot, R.S., and P.S. Nathawat (1990). *Jaigarh- The invincible Fort of Amber*
- Topsfield, A. (1994). *Indian paintings from Oxford collections*
- Tillotson, G. (2006). *Jaipur Nama*, Penguin books

Paramara dynasty

Paramaras of Malwa	
9th or 10th century CE–1305 CE	
Map of Asia in 1200 CE. Paramara kingdom is shown in central India.	
Capital	Dhar
Languages	Sanskrit, Prakrit
Religion	Shaivism
Government	Monarchy
King	
•	possibly 9th century CE	Upendra
•	c. 1010-1055 CE	Bhoja
•	died 1305 CE	Mahlakadeva
Historical era		Classical India
•	Established	9th or 10th century CE
•	Disestablished	1305 CE
Preceded by	Succeeded by
Gurjara-Pratihara	Delhi Sultanate
Today part of	India

The **Paramara dynasty** (IAST: Paramāra) was an Indian dynasty that ruled Malwa and surrounding areas in west-central India between 9th and 14th centuries. The medieval bardic literature classifies them among the Agnivanshi Rajput dynasties.

The Paramara dynasty was established in either 9th or 10th century. The earliest extant Paramara inscriptions, issued by the 10th century ruler Siyaka, have been found in Gujarat and suggest that he was a vassal of the Rashtrakutas of Manyakheta. Around 972 CE, Siyaka sacked the Rashtrakuta capital Manyakheta, and established the Paramaras as a sovereign power. By the time of his successor Munja, the Malwa region in present-day Madhya Pradesh had become the core Paramara territory, with Dhara (now Dhar) as their capital. The dynasty reached its zenith under Munja's nephew Bhoja, whose kingdom extended from Chittor in the north to Konkan in the south, and from the Sabarmati River in the west to Vidisha in the east.

The Paramara power rose and declined several times as a result of their struggles with the Chaulukyas of Gujarat, the Chalukyas of Kalyani, the Kalachuris of Tripuri and other neighbouring kingdoms. The later Paramara rulers moved their capital to Mandapa-Durga (now Mandu) after Dhara was sacked multiple times by their enemies. Mahalakadeva, the last known Paramara king, was defeated and killed by the forces of Alauddin Khalji of Delhi in 1305 CE, although epigraphic evidence suggests that the Paramara rule continued for a few years after his death.

Malwa enjoyed a great level of political and cultural prestige under the Paramaras. The Paramaras were well known for their patronage to Sanskrit poets and scholars, and Bhoja was himself a renowned scholar. Most of the Paramara kings were Shaivites and commissioned several Shiva temples, although they also patronized Jain scholars.

Origin

Ancestry

The Harsola copper plates (949 CE) issued by the Paramara king Siyaka II establish that the early Paramara rulers were the feudatories of the Rashtrakutas of Manyakheta. This inscription mentions a king called Akalavarsha (identified with the Rashtrakuta ruler Krishna III), followed by the expression *tasmin kule* ("in that family"), and then followed by the name "Vappairaja" (identified with the Paramara king Vakpati I).[1489] Based on the Harsola inscription, some historians such as D. C. Ganguly theorized that the Paramaras were descended from the Rashtrakutas. Ganguly also tried to find support for his theory in *Ain-i-Akbari*, whose variation of the Agnikula myth (see below) states that the founder of the Paramara kingdom came to Malwa from Deccan,[1490] and that "Aditya Ponwar" was the first sovereign ruler of the dynasty.[1491] Moreover, Siyaka's successor Munja (Vakpati II) assumed titles such as Amoghavarsha, Sri-vallabha and Prithvi-vallabha: these are distinctively Rashtrakuta titles.[1492]

Several historians have been critical of this theory. Dasharatha Sharma notes that the Agnikula myth about the Paramara origin had come into being by the time of Siyaka's son Sindhuraja. Sharma argues that the Rashtrakuta royal origin of the Paramaras could not have been forgotten within a generation.[1492] K. C. Jain theorizes that Vappairaja's mother was related to the Rashtrakuta family, because the other Paramara records do not boast of the Rashtrakuta royals

Figure 365: *Harsola copper plates*

as their ancestors.[1490] Siyaka and other Paramara kings before Munja did not adopt any Rashtrakuta titles: Munja may have adopted these titles to commemorate his predecessor's victory over the Rashtrakutas, and to strengthen his claim over the former Rashtrakuta territories.[1493,1490]

The later Paramara kings claimed to be members of the Agnikula or Agnivansha ("fire clan"). The Agnikula myth of origin, which appears in several of their inscriptions and literary works, goes like this: The sage Vishvamitra forcibly took a wish-granting cow from another sage Vashistha on the Arbuda mountain (Mount Abu). Vashistha then conjured a hero from a sacrificial fire pit (*agni-kunda*), who defeated Vashistha's enemies and brought back the cow. Vashistha then gave the hero the title Paramara ("enemy killer").[1494] The earliest known source to mention this story is the *Nava-sahasanka-charita* of Padmagupta Parimala, who was a court-poet of the Paramara king Sindhuraja (ca. 997-1010).[1495] The legend is not mentioned in earlier Paramara-era inscriptions or literary works. By this time, all the neighbouring dynasties claimed divine or heroic origin, which might have motivated the Paramaras to invent a legend of their own.[1496]

In the later period, the Paramaras were categorized as one of the Rajput clans, although the Rajput identity did not exist during their time.[1497] A legend mentioned in a recension of *Prithviraj Raso* extended their Agnikula legend to describe other dynasties as fire-born Rajputs. The earliest extant copies of *Prithviraj Raso* do not contain this legend; this version might have been invented by the 16th century poets who wanted to foster Rajput unity against the Mughal emperor Akbar.[1498] Some colonial-era historians interpreted this mythical account to suggest a foreign origin for the Paramaras. According to this theory, the ancestors of the Paramaras and other Agnivanshi Rajputs came to India after the decline of the Gupta Empire around the 5th century CE. They were admitted in the Hindu caste system after performing a fire ritual.[1499] However, this theory is weakened by the fact that the legend is not mentioned in the earliest of the Paramara records, and even the earliest Paramara-era account does not mention the other dynasties as Agnivanshi.[1500]

Some historians, such as Dasharatha Sharma and Pratipal Bhatia, have argued that the Paramaras were originally Brahmins from the Vashistha gotra.[1490] This theory is based on the fact that Halayudha, who was patronized by Munja, describes the king as "Brahma-Kshtra" in *Pingala-Sutra-Vritti*. According to Bhatia this expression means that Munja came from a family of Brahmins who became Kshatriyas.[1501] In addition, the Patanarayana temple inscription states that the Paramaras were of Vashistha gotra, which is a gotra among Brahmins claiming descent from the sage Vashistha.[1502]

D. C. Sircar theorized that the dynasty descended from the Malavas. However, there is no evidence of the early Paramara rulers being called Malava; the Paramaras began to be called Malavas only after they began ruling the Malwa region.[1490]

Original homeland

File:India Gujarat location map.svg

Places in Gujarat where the earliest Paramara inscriptions (of Siyaka II) have been discovered

Based on the Agnikula legend, some scholars such as C. V. Vaidya and V. A. Smith speculated that Mount Abu was the original home of the Paramaras. Based on the Harsola copper plates and *Ain-i-Akbari*, D. C. Ganguly believed they came from the Deccan region.[1503]

The earliest of the Paramara inscriptions (that of Siyaka II) have all been discovered in Gujarat, and concern land grants in that region. Based on this, D. B. Diskalkar and H. V. Trivedi theorized that the Paramaras were associated with Gujarat during their early days.[1504]

Early rulers

Historical evidence suggests that between 808-812 CE, the Rashtrakutas of Manyakheta expelled the Gurjara-Pratiharas from the Malwa region. The Rashtrakuta king Govinda III placed Malwa under the protection of Karkaraja, the Rashtrakuta chief of Lata (a region bordering Malwa, in present-day Gujarat). Malwa was subsequently ruled by a vassal of the Rashtrakutas. This vassal could have been a member of the Paramara dynasty, but there is no definitive proof of this. The start of the Paramara rule in Malwa cannot be dated with certainty, but it is incontestable that they did not rule the Malwa before the 9th century CE.[1505]

Siyaka is the earliest known Paramara king attested by his own inscriptions. His Harsola copper plate inscription (949 CE) is the earliest available Paramara inscription: it suggests that he was a vassal of the Rashtrakutas.[1489] The list of his predecessors varies between accounts:[1506,1489]

List of early Paramara rulers according to different sources

Harsola copper plates (949 CE)	Nava-Sahasanka-Charita (early 11th century)	Udaipur Prashasti inscription (11th century)	Nagpur Prashasti inscription (1104 CE)	Other land grants
	Paramara	Paramara	Paramara	Paramara
	Upendra	Upendra		Krishna
	"Other kings"	Vairisimha (I)		
		Siyaka (I)		
Vappairaja	Vakpati (I)	Vakpati (I)		
Vairisimha	Vairisimha	Vairisimha (II)	Vairisimha	Vairisimha
Siyaka	Siyaka alias Harsha	Harsha	Siyaka	Siyaka

Paramara is the dynasty's mythical progenitor, according to the Agnikula legend. Whether the other early kings mentioned in the *Udaipur Prashasti* are historical or fictional is a topic of debate among historians.[1507]

According to C. V. Vaidya and K. A. Nilakantha Sastri, the Paramara dynasty was founded only in the 10th century CE. Vaidya believes that the kings such as Vairisimha I and Siyaka I are imaginary, duplicated from the names of later historical kings in order to push back the dynasty's age.[1507] The 1274 CE Mandhata copper-plate inscription of Jayavarman II similarly names eight successors of Paramara as Kamandaludhara, Dhumraja, Devasimhapala, Kanakasimha, Shriharsha, Jagaddeva, Sthirakaya and Voshari: these do not appear to be historical figures.[1508] HV Trivedi states that there is a possibility that Vairisimha I and Siyaka I of the *Udaipur Prashasti* are same as Vairisimha II and Siyaka II; the names might have been repeated by mistake. Alternatively, he theorizes that these names have been omitted in other inscriptions because these rulers were not independent sovereigns.[1489]

Several other historians believe that the early Paramara rulers mentioned in the *Udaipur Prashasti* are not fictional, and the Paramaras started ruling Malwa in the 9th century (as Rashtrakuta vassals). K. N. Seth argues that even some of the later Paramara inscriptions mention only 3-4 predecessors of the king who issued the inscription. Therefore, the absence of certain names from the genealogy provided in the early inscriptions does not mean that these were imaginary rulers. According to him, the mention of Upendra in *Nava-Sahasanka-Charitra* (composed by the court poet of the later king Sindhuraja) proves that Upendra is not a fictional king.[1509] Historians such as Georg Bühler and James Burgess identify Upendra and Krishnaraja as one person, because these are synonyms (Upendra being another name of Krishna). However, an inscription of Siyaka's successor Munja names the preceding kings as Krishnaraja, Vairisimha, and Siyaka. Based on this, Seth however identifies Krishnaraja with Vappairaja or Vakpati I mentioned in the Harsola plates (Vappairaja appears to be the Prakrit form of Vakpati-raja). In his support, Seth points out that Vairisimha has been called *Krishna-padanudhyata* in the inscription of Munja i.e. Vakpati II. He theorizes that Vakpati II used the name "Krishnaraja" instead of Vakpati I to identify his ancestor, in order to avoid confusion with his own name.[1509]

The imperial Paramaras

The first independent sovereign of the Paramara dynasty was Siyaka (sometimes called Siyaka II to distinguish him from the earlier Siyaka mentioned in the *Udaipur Prashasti*). The Harsola copper plates (949 CE) suggest that

Figure 366: *The Bhojeshwar Temple, Bhojpur*

Figure 367: *Detail of the masonry of the northern dam at Bhojpur*

Siyaka was a feudatory of the Rashtrakuta ruler Krishna III in his early days. However, the same inscription also mentions the high-sounding *Maharajadhirajapati* as one of Siyaka's titles. Based on this, K. N. Seth believes that Siyaka's acceptance of the Rashtrakuta lordship was nominal.[1510]

As a Rashtrakuta feudatory, Siyaka participated in their campaigns against the Pratiharas. He also defeated some Huna chiefs ruling to the north of Malwa.[1511] He might have suffered setbacks against the Chandela king Yashovarman.[1512] After the death of Krishna III, Siyaka defeated his successor Khottiga in a battle fought on the banks of the Narmada River. He then pursued Khottiga's retreating army to the Rashtrakuta capital Manyakheta, and sacked that city in 972 CE. His victory ultimately led to the decline of the Rashtrakutas, and the establishment of the Paramaras as an independent sovereign power in Malwa.[1513]

Siyaka's successor Munja achieved military successes against the Chahamanas of Shakambari, the Chahamanas of Naddula, the Guhilas of Mewar, the Hunas, the Kalachuris of Tripuri, and the ruler of Gurjara region (possibly a Gujarat Chaulukya or Pratihara ruler).[1514] He also achieved some early successes against the Western Chalukya king Tailapa II, but was ultimately defeated and killed by Tailapa some time between 994 CE and 998 CE.[1515,1516]

As a result of this defeat, the Paramaras lost their southern territories (possibly the ones beyond the Narmada river) to the Chalukyas.[1517] Munja was reputed as a patron of scholars, and his rule attracted scholars from different parts of India to Malwa.[1518] He was also a poet himself, although only a few stanzas composed by him now survive.[1519]

Munja's brother Sindhuraja (ruled c. 990s CE) defeated the Western Chalukya king Satyashraya, and recovered the territories lost to Tailapa II.[1520] He also achieved military successes against a Huna chief, the Somavanshi of south Kosala, the Shilaharas of Konkana, and the ruler of Lata (southern Gujarat).[1520] His court poet Padmagupta wrote his biography *Nava-Sahasanka-Charita*, which credits him with several other victories, although these appear to be poetic exaggerations.[1521]

Sindhuraja's son Bhoja is the most celebrated ruler of the Paramara dynasty. He made several attempts to expand the Paramara kingdom varying results. Around 1018 CE, he defeated the Chalukyas of Lata in present-day Gujarat.[1522] Between 1018 CE and 1020 CE, he gained control of the northern Konkan, whose Shilahara rulers probably served as his feudatories for a brief period.[1523,1524] Bhoja also formed an alliance against the Kalyani Chalukya king Jayasimha II, with Rajendra Chola and Gangeya-deva Kalachuri. The extent of Bhoja's success in this campaign is not certain, as both Chalukya and Paramara panegyrics claimed victory.[1525] During the last years of Bhoja's reign, sometime after 1042 CE, Jayasimha's son and successor Someshvara I invaded Malwa, and sacked his capital Dhara.[1520] Bhoja re-established his control over Malwa soon after the departure of the Chalukya army, but the defeat pushed back the southern boundary of his kingdom from Godavari to Narmada.[1526,1527]

Bhoja's attempt to expand his kingdom eastwards was foiled by the Chandela king Vidyadhara.[1528] However, Bhoja was able to extend his influence among the Chandela feudatories, the Kachchhapaghatas of Dubkund.[1529] Bhoja also launched a campaign against the Kachchhapaghatas of Gwalior, possibly with the ultimate goal of capturing Kannauj, but his attacks were repulsed by their ruler Kirtiraja.[1530] Bhoja also defeated the Chahamanas of Shakambhari, killing their ruler Viryarama. However, he was forced to retreat by the Chahamanas of Naddula.[1531] According to medieval Muslim historians, after sacking Somnath, Mahmud of Ghazni changed his route to avoid confrontation with a Hindu king named Param Dev. Modern historians identify Param Dev as Bhoja: the name may be a corruption of Paramara-Deva or of Bhoja's title *Parameshvara-Paramabhattaraka*.[1532,1533] Bhoja may have also contributed troops to support the Kabul Shahi ruler Anandapala's fight against the Ghaznavids.[1534] He may have also been a part of the Hindu alliance that expelled Mahmud's governors from Hansi, Thanesar and other areas around 1043 CE.[1535,1520] During the last year of Bhoja's reign, or shortly after his death, the Chaulukya king Bhima I and the Kalachuri king Karna attacked his kingdom. According to the 14th century author Merutunga, Bhoja died of a disease at the same time the allied army attacked his kingdom.[1536,1537]

At its zenith, Bhoja's kingdom extended from Chittor in the north to upper Konkan in the south, and from the Sabarmati River in the west to Vidisha in the east.[1538] He was recognized as a capable military leader, but his territorial conquests were short-lived. His major claim to fame was his reputation as a scholar-king, who patronized arts, literature and sciences. Noted poets and writers of his time sought his sponsorship.[1539] Bhoja was himself a polymath, whose writings cover a wide variety of topics include grammar, poetry, architecture, yoga, and chemistry. Bhoja established the Bhoj Shala which was a centre for Sanskrit studies and a temple of Sarasvati in present-day Dhar. He is said to have founded the city of Bhojpur, a belief supported by historical evidence. Besides the Bhojeshwar Temple there, the construction of three now-breached dams in that area is attributed to him.[1540] Because of his patronage to literary figures, several legends written after his death featured him as a righteous scholar-king.[1541] In terms of the number of legends centered around him, Bhoja is comparable to the fabled Vikramaditya.[1542]

Figure 368: *Pillar in the Bijamaṇḍal, Vidisha with an inscription of Naravarman*

Decline

Bhoja's successor Jayasimha I, who was probably his son,[1543] faced the joint Kalachuri-Chaulukya invasion immediately after Bhoja's death.[1544] Bilhana's writings suggest that he sought help from the Chalukyas of Kalyani.[1545] Jayasimha's successor and Bhoja's brother Udayaditya was defeated by Chamundaraja, his vassal at Vagada. He repulsed an invasion by the Chaulukya ruler Karna, with help from his allies. Udayaditya's eldest son Lakshmadeva has been credited with extensive military conquests in the *Nagpur Prashasti* inscription of 1104-05 CE. However, these appear to be poetic exaggerations. At best, he might have defeated the Kalachuris of Tripuri.[1546] Udayaditya's younger son Naravarman faced several defeats, losing to the Chandelas of Jejakabhukti and the Chaulukya king Jayasimha Siddharaja. By the end of his reign, one Vijayapala had carved out an independent kingdom to the north-east of Ujjain.[1547]

Yashovarman lost control of the Paramara capital Dhara to Jayasimha Siddharaja. His successor Jayavarman I regained control of Dhara, but soon lost it to an usurper named Ballala.[1548] The Chaulukya king Kumarapala defeated Ballala around 1150 CE, supported by his feudatories the Naddula Chahamana ruler Alhana and the Abu Paramara chief Yashodhavala. Malwa

Figure 369: *Fragments of the Dhar iron pillar attributed to the Paramaras*

then became a province of the Chaulukyas. A minor branch of the Paramaras, who styled themselves as *Mahakumara*s, ruled the area around Bhopal during this time.[1549] Nearly two decades later, Jayavarman's son Vindhyavarman defeated the Chaulukya king Mularaja II, and re-established the Paramara sovereignty in Malwa.[1550] During his reign, Malwa faced repeated invasions from the Hoysalas and the Yadavas of Devagiri.[1551] He was also defeated by the Chaulukya general Kumara.[1552] Despite these setbacks, he was able to restore the Paramara power in Malwa before his death.[1553]

Vindhyavarman's son Subhatavarman invaded Gujarat, and plundered the Chaulukya territories. But he was ultimately forced to retreat by the Chaulukya feudatory Lavana-Prasada.[1554] His son Arjunavarman I also invaded Gujarat, and defeated Jayanta-simha (or Jaya-simha), who had usurped the Chaulukya throne for a brief period.[1555] He was defeated by Yadava general Kholeshvara in Lata.[1556]

Arjunavarman was succeeded by Devapala, who was the son of Harishchandra, a *Mahakumara* (chief of a Paramara branch).[1556] He continued to face struggles against the Chaulukyas and the Yadavas. The Sultan of Delhi Iltutmish captured Bhilsa during 1233-34 CE, but Devapala defeated the Sultanate's governor and regained control of Bhilsa.[1557,1558] According to the *Hammira Mahakavya*, he was killed by Vagabhata of Ranthambhor, who suspected him of plotting his murder in connivance with the Delhi Sultan.[1559]

During the reign of Devapala's son Jaitugideva, the power of the Paramaras greatly declined because of invasions from the Yadava king Krishna, the Delhi Sultan Balban, and the Vaghela prince Visala-deva.[1560] Devapala's younger son Jayavarman II also faced attacks from these three powers. Either Jaitugi or Jayavarman II moved the Paramara capital from Dhara to the hilly Mandapa-Durga (present-day Mandu), which offered a better defensive position.[1561]

Arjunavarman II, the successor of Jayavarman II, proved to be a weak ruler. He faced rebellion from his minister.[1562] In the 1270s, the Yadava ruler Ramachandra invaded Malwa,[1563] and in the 1280s, the Ranthambhor Chahamana ruler Hammira also raided Malwa.[1564] Arjuna's successor Bhoja II also faced an invasion from Hammira. Bhoja II was either a titular ruler controlled by his minister, or his minister had usurped a part of the Paramara kingdom.[1565]

Mahalakadeva, the last known Paramara king, was defeated and killed by the army of Alauddin Khalji in 1305 CE.[1566]

Rulers

<mapframe text="[[Find spot]]s of the inscriptions from the reigns of Paramara monarchs of Malwa{{sfn|Harihar Vitthal Trivedi|1991|pp=v-vi}}" width="350" height="350" zoom="5" longitude="76.15" latitude="22.25">
{ "type": "FeatureCollection", "features": [{ "type": "Feature", "properties": { "marker-symbol": "monument", "title": "Atru" }, "geometry": { "type": "Point", "coordinates": [76.6701, 24.8768] } }, { "type": "Feature", "properties": { "marker-symbol": "monument", "title": "Banswara" }, "geometry": { "type": "Point", "coordinates": [74.4350, 23.5461] } }, { "type": "Feature", "properties": { "marker-symbol": "monument", "title": "Betma" }, "geometry": { "type": "Point", "coordinates": [75.6143, 22.6854] } }, { "type": "Feature", "properties": { "marker-symbol": "monument", "title": "Bhojpur" }, "geometry": { "type": "Point", "coordinates": [77.5784, 23.0092] } }, { "type": "Feature", "properties": { "marker-symbol": "monument", "title": "Depalpur" }, "geometry": { "type": "Point", "coordinates": [75.5422, 22.8514] } }, { "type": "Feature", "properties": { "marker-symbol": "monument", "title": "Dewas" }, "geometry": { "type": "Point", "coordinates": [76.0508, 22.9623] } }, { "type": "Feature", "properties": { "marker-symbol": "star", "marker-color": "000080", "title": "Dhar" }, "geometry": { "type": "Point", "coordinates": [75.3025, 22.6013] } }, { "type": "Feature", "properties": { "marker-symbol": "monument", "title": "Dharampuri" }, "geometry": { "type": "Point", "coordinates": [75.3500, 22.1562] } }, { "type": "Feature", "properties": { "marker-symbol": "monument", "title": "Gaowdi", "description": "Also known as Gaonri" }, "geometry":

{ "type": "Point", "coordinates": [75.9666, 23.0975] } }, { "type": "Feature", "properties": { "marker-symbol": "monument", "title": "Gyaraspur" }, "geometry": { "type": "Point", "coordinates": [78.1222, 23.6727] } }, { "type": "Feature", "properties": { "marker-symbol": "monument", "title": "Harsud", "description": "Also known as Harsauda" }, "geometry": { "type": "Point", "coordinates": [76.7365, 22.1014] } }, { "type": "Feature", "properties": { "marker-symbol": "monument", "title": "Harsol", "description": "Also known as Harsola" }, "geometry": { "type": "Point", "coordinates": [73.0140, 23.3628] } }, { "type": "Feature", "properties": { "marker-symbol": "monument", "title": "Jhalrapatan" }, "geometry": { "type": "Point", "coordinates": [76.1726, 24.5403] } }, { "type": "Feature", "properties": { "marker-symbol": "monument", "title": "Kheda", "description": "Also known as Kaira" }, "geometry": { "type": "Point", "coordinates": [72.9933, 22.9251] } }, { "type": "Feature", "properties": { "marker-symbol": "monument", "title": "Kalwan" }, "geometry": { "type": "Point", "coordinates": [74.0271, 20.4891] } }, { "type": "Feature", "properties": { "marker-symbol": "monument", "title": "Kamed" }, "geometry": { "type": "Point", "coordinates": [75.7924, 23.2273] } }, { "type": "Feature", "properties": { "marker-symbol": "monument", "title": "Jivapur Mahodia", "description": "Also known as Mahaudi" }, "geometry": { "type": "Point", "coordinates": [76.5084, 23.0666] } }, { "type": "Feature", "properties": { "marker-symbol": "monument", "title": "Mandhata" }, "geometry": { "type": "Point", "coordinates": [76.1523, 22.2508] } }, { "type": "Feature", "properties": { "marker-symbol": "monument", "title": "Modasa" }, "geometry": { "type": "Point", "coordinates": [73.2999, 23.4629] } }, { "type": "Feature", "properties": { "marker-symbol": "monument", "title": "Modi" }, "geometry": { "type": "Point", "coordinates": [76.2030, 23.9974] } }, { "type": "Feature", "properties": { "marker-symbol": "monument", "title": "Pathari" }, "geometry": { "type": "Point", "coordinates": [78.2220, 23.9353] } }, { "type": "Feature", "properties": { "marker-symbol": "monument", "title": "Pipliya Nagar", "description": "Also known as Piplianagar" }, "geometry": { "type": "Point", "coordinates": [76.9816, 23.2939] } }, { "type": "Feature", "properties": { "marker-symbol": "monument", "title": "Rahatgarh" }, "geometry": { "type": "Point", "coordinates": [78.3984, 23.7905] } }, { "type": "Feature", "properties": { "marker-symbol": "monument", "title": "Sehore" }, "geometry": { "type": "Point", "coordinates": [77.0851, 23.2050] } }, { "type": "Feature", "properties": { "marker-symbol": "monument", "title": "Shergarh", "description": "Also known as Shergadh" }, "geometry": { "type": "Point", "coordinates": [76.5416, 24.7169] } }, { "type": "Feature", "properties": { "marker-symbol": "monument", "title": "Tilakvada", "description": "Also known as Tilakwada" }, "geometry": { "type": "Point", "coordinates": [73.5903, 21.9526] } },

{ "type": "Feature", "properties": { "marker-symbol": "monument", "title": "Udaipur" }, "geometry": { "type": "Point", "coordinates": [78.0709, 23.8737] } }, { "type": "Feature", "properties": { "marker-symbol": "monument", "title": "Ujjain" }, "geometry": { "type": "Point", "coordinates": [75.7849, 23.1793] } }, { "type": "Feature", "properties": { "marker-symbol": "monument", "title": "Un" }, "geometry": { "type": "Point", "coordinates": [75.4566, 21.8227] } }, { "type": "Feature", "properties": { "marker-symbol": "monument", "title": "Vidisha" }, "geometry": { "type": "Point", "coordinates": [77.8081, 23.5251] } }] } </mapframe> The Paramara rulers mentioned in the various inscriptions and literary sources are as follows. The rulers are sons of their predecessors, unless otherwise specified.[1567,1568]

- Paramara, mythical ancestor mentioned in the Agnikula legend
- Upendra, 9th century
- Vairisimha (I), 9th century; considered fictional by some historians
- Siyaka (I), 9th century; considered fictional by some historians
- Vakpati (I), 9th-10th century; called Vappairaja or Bappiraja in Harsola copper plates
- Vairisimha (II), 10th century
- Siyaka (II) alias Harsha, 948-972
- Vakpati (II) alias Munja, 972-990s; Siyaka's elder son
- Sindhuraja, 990s-1010; Siyaka's younger son
- Bhoja, 1010-1055
- Jayasimha (I), 1055-1070
- Udayaditya, 1070-1086; Bhoja's brother
- Lakshma-deva, 1086-1094; Udayaditya's elder son
- Naravarman, 1094-1130; Udayaditya's younger son
- Yashovarman, 1133-1142
- Jayavarman (I), 1142-1143
- *Interregnum*, 1144-1174: An usurper named Ballala captured power in Malwa. He was defeated by the Chaulukyas of Gujarat. The Paramara kingdom remained under Chaulukya suzerainty during this period.
- Vindhyavarman, 1175-1194
- Subhatavarman, 1194-1209
- Arjunavarman I, 1210-1215
- Devapala, 1218-1239; Son of *Mahakumara* Harishchandra
- Jaitugideva, 1239-1255; Devapala's elder son
- Jayavarman II, 1255-1274; Devapala's younger son
- Arjunavarman II, 13th century
- Bhoja II, 13th century
- Mahlakadeva, died 1305

An inscription from Udaipur indicates that the Paramara dynasty survived until 1310, at least in the north-eastern part of Malwa. A later inscription shows that the area had been captured by the Delhi Sultanate by 1338.[1569]

Branches and claimed descendants

Besides the Paramara sovereigns of Malwa, several branches of the dynasties ruled as feudatories at various places. These include:

- Paramaras of Bhinmal (also known as the Paramaras of Kiradu)
  - Branched off from the Paramaras of Chandravati[1570]
- Paramaras of Chandravati (also known as Paramaras of Abu)
  - Became feudatories of the Chaulukyas of Gujarat by the 12th century[1571]
- Paramaras of Vagada
  - Ruled at Arthuna as feudatories of the Paramaras of Malwa[1572]
- Paramaras of Jalor
  - Supplanted by the Chahamanas of Jalor[1573]

The rulers of several princely states claimed connection with the Paramaras. These include:

- Baghal State: It is said to have been founded by Ajab Dev Parmar, who came to present-day Himachal Pradesh from Ujjain in the 14th century.[1574]
- Danta State: Its rulers claimed membership of the Parmar clan and descent from the legendary king Vikramaditya of Ujjain[1575]
- Dewas State (Senior and Junior): The Maratha Puar rulers of these states claimed descent from the Paramara dynasty.[1576]
- Dhar State: Its founder Anand Rao Puar, who claimed Paramara descent, received a fief from Peshwa Baji Rao I in the 18th century.[1577]
- Gangpur State: Its rulers claimed Paramara ancestry. According to David Henige, this claim is doubtful.[1578]
- Muli State: Its rulers claimed Paramara descent, and are said to have started out as feudatories of the Vaghelas.[1579]
- Narsinghgarh State
- Jagdishpur and Dumraon: The Rajputs of Bhojpur district in present-day Bihar, who styled themselves as Ujjainiya Panwar Rajputs, started claiming descent from the royal family of Ujjain in the 17th century. The Rajas of Jagdishpur and Dumraon in Bihar claimed descent from the Ujjainia branch of Paramaras.
- The Gandhawaria Rajputs of Mithila and the Ujjainiyas of Bhojpur also claim descent from the Paramara dynasty.

- Bijolia: Located in present day Rajasthan. It is the Head House of Rajput Parmars. It was taken over by Rao Ashok Parmar of Jagner (present day Uttar Pradesh) from the Hada and Chouhan rulers of Bundi State. During the 13-14 Century Afghan Invasion on Dhar State,main ruling took refuge here and settled here.Wikipedia:Citation needed

References

Bibliography

<templatestyles src="Template:Refbegin/styles.css" />

- Alf Hiltebeitel (2009). *Rethinking India's Oral and Classical Epics*[1580]. University of Chicago Press. ISBN 9780226340555.
- Asoke Kumar Majumdar (1956). *Chaulukyas of Gujarat*[1581]. Bharatiya Vidya Bhavan. OCLC 4413150[1582].
- Asoke Kumar Majumdar (1977). *Concise History of Ancient India: Political history*[1583]. Munshiram Manoharlal. OCLC 5311157[1584].
- Anthony Kennedy Warder (1992). "XLVI: The Vikramaditya Legend". *Indian Kāvya Literature: The art of storytelling*[1585]. Motilal Banarsidass. ISBN 978-81-208-0615-3.
- Cynthia Talbot (2015). *The Last Hindu Emperor: Prithviraj Cauhan and the Indian Past, 1200–2000*[1586]. Cambridge University Press. ISBN 9781107118560.
- Dasharatha Sharma (1975). *Early Chauhān Dynasties: A Study of Chauhān Political History, Chauhān Political Institutions, and Life in the Chauhān Dominions, from 800 to 1316 A.D.*[1587] Motilal Banarsidass. ISBN 978-0-8426-0618-9.
- David P. Henige (2004). *Princely States of India: A Guide to Chronology and Rulers*[1588]. Orchid. ISBN 978-974-524-049-0.
- Ganga Prasad Yadava (1982). *Dhanapāla and His Times: A Sociocultural Study Based Upon His Works*[1589]. Concept.
- Georg Bühler (1892). "The Udepur Prasasti of the Kings of Malva". *Epigraphia Indica*[1590]. **1**. Archaeological Survey of India.
- Harihar Vitthal Trivedi (1991). *Inscriptions of the Paramāras, Chandēllas, Kachchapaghātas, and two minor dynasties*[1591]. Archaeological Survey of India.
- John Middleton (2015). *World Monarchies and Dynasties*[1592]. Routledge. ISBN 978-1-317-45158-7.
- Kailash Chand Jain (1972). *Malwa Through the Ages, from the Earliest Times to 1305 A.D*[1593]. Motilal Banarsidass Publ. ISBN 978-81-208-0824-9.

- Kirit Mankodi (1987). "Scholar-Emperor and a Funerary Temple: Eleventh Century Bhojpur"[1594]. *Marg*. National Centre for the Performing Arts. **39** (2): 61–72.
- Krishna Narain Seth (1978). *The Growth of the Paramara Power in Malwa*[1595]. Progress. OCLC 8931757[1596].
- M. Srinivasachariar (1974). *History of Classical Sanskrit Literature*[1597]. Motilal Banarsidass. ISBN 9788120802841.
- Mahesh Singh (1984). *Bhoja Paramāra and His Times*[1598]. Bharatiya Vidya Prakashan. OCLC 11786897[1599].
- Poonam Minhas (1998). *Traditional Trade & Trading Centres in Himachal Pradesh: With Trade-routes and Trading Communities*[1600]. Indus Publishing. ISBN 978-81-7387-080-4.
- Prabhakar Narayan Kawthekar (1995). *Bilhana*[1601]. Sahitya Akademi. ISBN 9788172017798.
- Peter Jackson (2003). *The Delhi Sultanate: A Political and Military History*[1602]. Cambridge University Press. ISBN 978-0-521-54329-3.
- Pratipal Bhatia (1970). *The Paramāras, c. 800-1305 A.D.*[1603] Munshiram Manoharlal. OCLC 199886[1604].
- R. B. Singh (1964). *History of the Chāhamānas*[1605]. N. Kishore. OCLC 11038728[1606].
- R. C. Majumdar (1977). *Ancient India*[1607]. Motilal Banarsidass. ISBN 9788120804364.
- Saikat K. Bose (2015). *Boot, Hooves and Wheels: And the Social Dynamics behind South Asian Warfare*[1608]. Vij. ISBN 978-9-38446-454-7.
- Sailendra Nath Sen (1999). *Ancient Indian History and Civilization*[1609]. New Age International. ISBN 9788122411980.
- Sheldon Pollock (2003). *The Language of the Gods in the World of Men: Sanskrit, Culture, and Power in Premodern India*[1610]. University of California Press. ISBN 0-5202-4500-8.
- Tony McClenaghan (1996). *Indian Princely Medals*[1611]. Lancer. ISBN 978-1-897829-19-6.
- Virbhadra Singhji (1994). *The Rajputs of Saurashtra*[1612]. Popular Prakashan. ISBN 978-81-7154-546-9.

Chaulukya dynasty

Chaulukyas of Gujarat	
c. 940 CE–1244 CE	
Capital	Anahilavada (modern Patan)
Religion	Shaivism, Jainism
Government	Monarchy
King	
• c. 940 – c. 995	Mularaja
• c. 1240 – c. 1244	Tribhuvanapala
History	
• Established	c. 940 CE
• Disestablished	1244 CE
Preceded by	Succeeded by
Chavda dynasty	Vaghela dynasty
Chalukyas of Lata	Cutch State
Today part of	India

History of Gujarat
• v
• t
• e[1613]

<mapframe text="[[Find spot]]s of inscriptions issued during the Chaulukya rule.{{sfn|Asoke Kumar Majumdar|1956|pp=498-502}}" width="350" height="350" zoom="5" longitude="75.13" latitude="23.64"> { "type": "FeatureCollection", "features": [{ "type": "Feature", "properties": { "marker-symbol": "monument", "marker-size": "small", "title": "Abu" }, "geometry": { "type": "Point", "coordinates": [72.7156274, 24.5925909] } }, { "type": "Feature", "properties": { "marker-symbol": "monument", "marker-size": "small", "title": "Ahada", "description": "Also known as

Ahad, near Udaipur in Rajasthan" }, "geometry": { "type": "Point", "coordinates": [73.7158921, 24.5878896] } }, { "type": "Feature", "properties": { "marker-symbol": "monument", "marker-size": "small", "title": "Balera", "description": "in Jalore district" }, "geometry": { "type": "Point", "coordinates": [71.475945, 24.7287792] } }, { "type": "Feature", "properties": { "marker-symbol": "monument", "marker-size": "small", "title": "Bali" }, "geometry": { "type": "Point", "coordinates": [73.2853816, 25.1909176] } }, { "type": "Feature", "properties": { "marker-symbol": "monument", "marker-size": "small", "title": "Vadodara", "description": "Also known as Baroda" }, "geometry": { "type": "Point", "coordinates": [73.1812187, 22.3071588] } }, { "type": "Feature", "properties": { "marker-symbol": "monument", "marker-size": "small", "title": "Bhadresar", "description": "Also known as Bhadresvar" }, "geometry": { "type": "Point", "coordinates": [69.903889, 22.911944] } }, { "type": "Feature", "properties": { "marker-symbol": "monument", "marker-size": "small", "title": "Bhatund", "description": "Also known as Bhatunda" }, "geometry": { "type": "Point", "coordinates": [73.2316, 25.0402] } }, { "type": "Feature", "properties": { "marker-symbol": "monument", "marker-size": "small", "title": "Bhinmal" }, "geometry": { "type": "Point", "coordinates": [72.2624706, 25.0085128] } }, { "type": "Feature", "properties": { "marker-symbol": "monument", "marker-size": "small", "title": "Brahmanwada" }, "geometry": { "type": "Point", "coordinates": [72.3636704, 23.864246] } }, { "type": "Feature", "properties": { "marker-symbol": "monument", "marker-size": "small", "title": "Chittorgarh" }, "geometry": { "type": "Point", "coordinates": [74.6269, 24.8887] } }, { "type": "Feature", "properties": { "marker-symbol": "monument", "marker-size": "small", "title": "Dahod", "description": "Also known as Dohad" }, "geometry": { "type": "Point", "coordinates": [74.123996, 22.8596159] } }, { "type": "Feature", "properties": { "marker-symbol": "monument", "marker-size": "small", "title": "Gala" }, "geometry": { "type": "Point", "coordinates": [70.841725, 22.9657613] } }, { "type": "Feature", "properties": { "marker-symbol": "monument", "marker-size": "small", "title": "Girnar", "description": "including Neminatha Temple" }, "geometry": { "type": "Point", "coordinates": [70.5502916, 21.5178869] } }, { "type": "Feature", "properties": { "marker-symbol": "monument", "marker-size": "small", "title": "Junagadh" }, "geometry": { "type": "Point", "coordinates": [70.4579, 21.5222] } }, { "type": "Feature", "properties": { "marker-symbol": "monument", "marker-size": "small", "title": "Kadi" }, "geometry": { "type": "Point", "coordinates": [72.3310025, 23.2978500] } }, { "type": "Feature", "properties": { "marker-symbol": "monument", "marker-size": "small", "title": "Kiradu" }, "geometry": { "type": "Point", "coordinates": [71.097715, 25.7528219] } }, { "type": "Feature", "properties": { "marker-symbol": "monument", "marker-size": "small", "title": "Ladol" }, "geometry": { "type": "Point", "coordinates": [72.7289768, 23.6176825] } }, { "type": "Feature", "properties": { "marker-symbol": "monument", "marker-size": "small", "title": "Mangrol" }, "geometry": { "type": "Point", "coordinates": [70.1158, 21.1172] } }, { "type": "Feature", "properties": { "marker-symbol": "monument", "marker-size": "small", "title": "Narlai", "description": "Nadlai" }, "geometry": { "type": "Point", "coordinates": [73.5344, 25.3159] } }, { "type": "Feature", "properties": { "marker-symbol": "monument", "marker-size": "small", "title": "Nadol" }, "geometry": { "type": "Point", "coordinates": [73.4552, 25.3699] } }, { "type": "Feature", "properties": { "marker-symbol": "monument", "marker-size": "small", "title": "Nana" }, "geometry": { "type": "Point", "coordinates": [71.9034947, 23.7893157] } }, { "type": "Feature", "properties": { "marker-symbol": "monument", "marker-size": "small", "title": "Nanana" }, "geometry": { "type": "Point", "coordinates": [74.1680, 26.1542] } }, { "type": "Feature", "properties": { "marker-symbol": "monument", "marker-size": "small", "title": "Navsari" }, "geometry": { "type": "Point", "coordinates": [73.1349605, 20.7694591] } }, { "type": "Feature", "properties": { "marker-symbol": "monument", "marker-size": "small", "title": "Palanpur" }, "geometry": { "type": "Point", "coordinates": [72.4330989, 24.1740510] } }, { "type": "Feature", "properties": { "marker-symbol": "monument", "marker-size": "small", "title": "Pali" }, "geometry": { "type": "Point", "coordinates": [73.3234, 25.7711] } }, { "type": "Feature", "properties": { "marker-symbol": "star", "marker-color": "000080", "marker-size": "small", "title": "Patan" }, "geometry": { "type": "Point", "coordinates": [72.1266255, 23.8493246] } }, { "type": "Feature", "properties": { "marker-symbol": "monument", "marker-size": "small", "title": "Prachi" }, "geometry": { "type": "Point", "coordinates": [70.6075, 20.9208] } }, { "type": "Feature", "properties": { "marker-symbol": "monument", "marker-size": "small", "title": "Radhanpur" }, "geometry": { "type": "Point", "coordinates": [71.6139348, 23.8286354] } }, { "type": "Feature", "properties": { "marker-symbol": "monument", "marker-size": "small", "title": "Ratnapura" }, "geometry": { "type": "Point", "coordinates": [73.4460, 23.7640] } }, { "type": "Feature", "properties": { "marker-symbol": "monument", "marker-size": "small", "title": "Sambhar" }, "geometry": { "type": "Point", "coordinates": [75.1859476, 26.9095549] } }, { "type": "Feature", "properties": { "marker-symbol": "monument", "marker-size": "small", "title": "Siddhpur", "description": "Kirtistambha" }, "geometry": { "type": "Point", "coordinates": [72.3668366, 23.9196207] } }, { "type": "Feature", "properties": { "marker-symbol": "monument", "marker-size": "small", "title": "Somnath", "description": "Also known as Somanatha or Devapattana" }, "geometry": { "type": "Point", "coordinates": [70.3843721, 20.9060022] } }, { "type": "Feature", "properties": { "marker-symbol": "monument", "marker-size": "small", "title": "Sunak" }, "geometry": { "type": "Point", "coordinates": [72.3222331, 23.8018886] } }, { "type": "Feature", "properties": { "marker-symbol": "monument", "marker-size": "small", "title": "Talwara" }, "geometry": { "type": "Point", "coordinates": [74.321437, 23.5664512] } }, { "type": "Feature", "properties": { "marker-symbol": "monument", "marker-size": "small", "title": "Timana" }, "geometry": { "type": "Point", "coordinates": [71.9949616, 21.4282827] } }, { "type": "Feature", "properties": { "marker-symbol": "monument", "marker-size": "small", "title": "Udaipur", "description": "Also known as Udayapur; located in Madhya Pradesh" }, "geometry": { "type": "Point", "coordinates": [78.0708985, 23.8737373] } }, { "type": "Feature", "properties": { "marker-symbol": "monument", "marker-size": "small", "title": "Ujjain" }, "geometry": { "type": "Point", "coordinates": [75.7849097, 23.1793013] } }, { "type": "Feature", "properties": { "marker-symbol": "monument", "marker-size": "small", "title": "Unjha" }, "geometry": { "type": "Point", "coordinates": [72.3843867, 23.8063156] } }, { "type": "Feature", "properties": { "marker-symbol": "monument", "marker-size": "small", "title": "Vadasma", "description": "Varunasarmaka" }, "geometry": { "type": "Point", "coordinates": [72.4894235, 23.4115366] } }, { "type": "Feature", "properties": { "marker-symbol": "monument", "marker-size": "small", "title": "Vadnagar" }, "geometry": { "type": "Point", "coordinates": [72.6166, 23.7757] } }, { "type": "Feature", "properties": { "marker-symbol": "monument", "marker-size": "small", "title": "Veraval" }, "geometry": { "type": "Point", "coordinates": [70.3629, 20.9159] } }, { "type": "Feature", "properties": { "marker-symbol": "monument", "marker-size": "small", "title": "Virapura" }, "geometry": { "type": "Point", "coordinates": [73.6212417, 22.5097341] } }] } </mapframe> The **Chaulukya dynasty** (IAST: *Caulukya*), also known as the **Chalukyas of Gujarat**, ruled parts of what are now Gujarat and Rajasthan in north-western India, between c. 940 CE and c. 1244 CE. Their capital was located at Anahilavada (modern Patan). At times, their rule extended to the Malwa region in present-day Madhya Pradesh. The medieval legends describe them as Agnivanshi Rajputs, and they are also known as the **Solanki dynasty** in the vernacular literature.

Mularaja, the founder of the dynasty, supplanted the last ruler of the Chapotkata dynasty (Chavda) around 940 CE. His successors fought several battles with the neighbouring rulers such as the Chudasamas, the Paramaras and the Chahamanas of Shakambhari. During the reign of Bhima I, the Ghaznavid ruler Mahmud invaded the kingdom and raided the Somnath temple during 1024-1025 CE. The Chaulukyas soon recovered, and the kingdom reached its zenith under the rule of Jayasimha Siddharaja and Kumarapala in the 12th century. Several minor dynasties, such as the Chahamanas of Jalor and the Chahamanas of Naddula, served as Chaulukya vassals during this period. After Kumarapala's death, the kingdom was gradually weakened by internal rebellions; uprisings by feudatories; and invasions by the Paramaras, the Ghurids, the Yadavas and others. Taking advantage of this, the Vaghelas, who had earlier served as Chaulukya generals, usurped the power and established a new dynasty in the 1240s.

Several princely state rulers of the Solanki clan claimed descent from the Chaulukyas.

Name

The dynasty used the self-designation "Chaulukya" in all but four of its records.[1614] The four exceptions are:[1615]

- "Chaulukika" in the Kadi grant of Mularaja
- "Saulkika" in a grant of Chamundaraja
- "Chaulakya" in the Sambhar inscription of Jayasimha
- "Chaullakya" in the Jalor inscription of Kumarapala

Hemachandra, a Jain scholar in the Chaulukya court, generally used the terms "Chaulukya" and "Chulukya".[1615] His *Dvyasraya Mahakavya* mentions the variants "Chulakya", "Chalukka", and "Chulukka"; his *Kumarapala-Charita* mentions another variant "Chuluga". The Chaulukya court poet Someshvara describes the dynasty as "Chaulukya" (in *Kirti-Kaumudi*) and "Chulukya" (in the Abu inscription of Vastupala Tejapala).[1616]

"Solanki" or "Solankhi" is a vernacular form of the term.[1617]

Origins

The word "Chaulukya" is thought to be a variant of the word "Chalukya". Several other dynasties were known by the name "Chalukya", including the Chalukyas of Vatapi, Navasarika, Vemulavada, Kalyani, Vengi and Lata. These dynasties are sometimes thought to be branches of the same family, but the relationship between all of them is not certain. Unlike the Chalukyas of Kalyani and Vengi, the Chaulukyas of Gujarat never claimed a shared descent or any other association with the earliest Chalukya dynasty — the Chalukyas of Vatapi. Moreover, they never used the term "Chalukya" to describe themselves.[1614]

However, the Chaulukyas of Gujarat shared a myth of origin with the Chalukyas of Kalyani and Vengi. According to this legend, the progenitor

Figure 370: *A Chaulukya-Paramara coin, circa 950-1050 CE. Stylized rendition of Chavda dynasty coins: Indo-Sassanian style bust right; pellets and ornaments around / Stylised fire altar; pellets around.*[1620]

of the dynasty was created by Brahma.[1614] The version of the legend mentioned in the Vadnagar *prashasti* inscription of Kumarapala is as follows: the deities once asked the creator god Brahma to protect them from the danavas (demons). Brahma then created a hero from his *chuluka* (pot or folded palm), which was filled with Ganges water. This hero was named "Chulukya", and became the progenitor of the dynasty. A variation of this legend is mentioned by Abhayatilaka Gani in his commentary on Hemachandra's *Dvyashraya-Kavya*. According to this version, Brahma produced the hero to support the earth, after his other creations disappointed him. These stories are of no historical value, as it was customary for contemporary royal houses to claim mythical and heroic origins. The *Kumarapala-Bhupala-Charita* of Jayasimha Suri presents Chulukya as a historical warrior, whose capital was Madhupadma. Mularaja was his descendant, with nearly a hundred generations separating the two.[1618] This account may be partly historical: Madhupadma has been identified variously as a location outside Gujarat, including present-day Mathura.[1619]

C. V. Vaidya theorized that the Chaulukyas were different from the Chalukyas. G. H. Ojha opposed this theory, pointing out that an inscription of the Lata Chalukya ruler Kirtiraja describes his family as "Chalukya", while an inscription of his grandson Trilochanapala describes the family as "Chaulukya".[1616] According to Asoke Majumdar, while these similar-sounding names suggest a common origin for all these dynasties, there is no concrete evidence to draw any definitive conclusion.[1614] Majumdar theorized that the Chaulukyas were connected to the Sulikas or the Chulikas, a tribe mentioned in several ancient records. This tribe is described as living on the northern frontier of ancient India. However, Majumdar admitted that there is not enough evidence to regard

Figure 371: *Coin of the Chaulukyas of Anahillapataka, King Kumarapala, c. 1145 – c. 1171.*[1621]

this theory as conclusive.[1622]

In the later period, the Chaulukyas were categorized as one of the Rajput clans, although the Rajput identity did not exist during their time.[1623] According to the Agnikula myth mentioned in a 16th century recension of the legendary text *Prithviraj Raso*, four Rajput clans including the Chaulukyas were born from a fire-pit on Mount Abu. A section of colonial-era historians interpreted this mythical account to suggest that these clans were foreigners who came to India after the decline of the Gupta Empire around the 5th century CE, and were admitted in the Hindu caste system after performing a fire ritual.[1624,1625] In addition, the Chaulukya rulers have been called "*Gurjararāja*" and "*Gurjareśvara*" ("ruler of Gurjara").[1626] Based on this legend, D. R. Bhandarkar and others theorized that the Chaulukyas were a branch of Gurjaras, whom they believed to be a tribe of foreign origin.[1627] Bhandarkar and Augustus Hoernle also believed that the name of the "Lata" region changed to "Gurjaratra" (later Gujarat) during the Chaulukya reign, presumably because they were Gurjaras.[1628]

However, this foreign-origin theory is weakened by a number of factors. The Chaulukyas did not claim an Agnikula origin for themselves:[1629] it was the neighbouring Paramara rulers who used the legend to explain their own origin.[1630] The inscriptions from the reign of Bhima II prove that the Chaulukyas knew about the Agnikula legend, but associated it with the Paramaras, not themselves.[1631] The earliest copies of *Prithviraj Raso* do not mention this legend either.[1631] The legend that includes the Chaulukyas among the fire-born clans is first mentioned by the 16th century poets, who may have extended the Paramara legend to include other dynasties, in order to foster

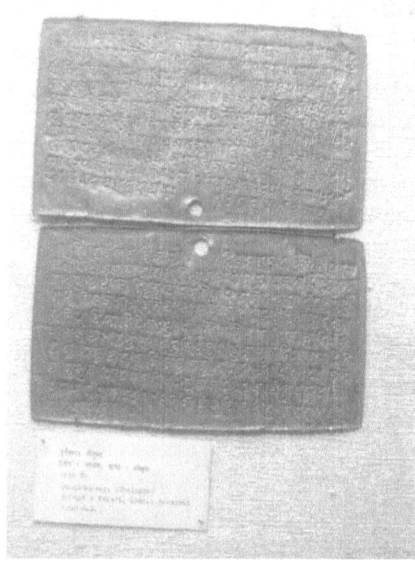

Figure 372: *A 1010 CE copper-plate inscription from the reign of Durlabharaja*

Rajput unity against the Mughals.[1632] Moreover, there is no evidence that the Chaulukya territory area came to be known as "Gurjaratra" during the Chaulukya reign.[1628] "Gurjara" and "Lata" were two distinct historical regions in northern and southern parts of present-day Gujarat respectively, and the term "Lata" was never used to describe the whole of Gujarat.[1633] The Chaulukya kings were called *"Gurjararāja"* and *"Gurjareśvara"* because they ruled the territory which was already called Gurjara by their time.[1626,1634] Several other kings who held similar epithets had earlier ruled this territory: these include the Gurjara-Pratiharas and the Gurjaras of Nandipuri.[1635] Historian Asoke Kumar Majumdar points out that even the southern Ganga chief Marasimha II assumed the title "king of Gurjaras" after defeating a northern king on behalf of the Rashtrakutas.[1634]

History

Early rulers

In the mid-tenth century CE, the dynasty's founder Mularaja supplanted Samantasimha, the last Chapotkata (Chavda) king.[1636] According to legends, he was a nephew of Samantasimha.[1637] According to the 12th century chronicler Hemachandra, Mularaja defeated Graharipu, the king of Saurashtra.[1638] He also defeated the Lata Chalukya chief Barapa, aided by his son Chamundaraja.[1639]

Chamundaraja succeeded Mularaja around 996 CE. During his reign, the Paramara king Sindhuraja appears to have invaded the Lata region, which was under Chaulukya suzerainty. Mularaja forced Sindhuraja to retreat; the 14th century chronicler Jayasimha Suri claims that Chamundaraja killed Sindhuraja in a battle, but this claim appears to be doubtful, as it does not appear in any earlier source.[1640] Sometime before 1007 CE, the Lata region was captured by the Chalukyas of Kalyani led by Satyashraya.[1641]

Around 1008 CE, Chamundaraja retired after appointing his son Vallabharaja as the next king. Legendary accounts state that he set out for a pilgrimage to Varanasi. During this journey, he was insulted by a ruler whose kingdom lay on the way to Varanasi. He returned to the Chaulukya capital, and asked his son to avenge his insult. Vallabharaja died of smallpox during a march to the enemy kingdom, which is identified as the Paramara kingdom of Malwa by some chroniclers.[1642]

Chamundaraja's other son Durlabharaja became the next king in c. 1008 CE. He invaded the Lata region, and defeated the Lata Chalukya ruler Kirtiraja (or Kirtipala), who was a vassal of the Kalyani Chalukyas. However, Kirtiraja regained control of the region within a short time, before being defeated by the Paramara king Bhoja.[1643]

Neighbouring rivalries

Durlabharaja was succeeded by his nephew Bhima I, who faced an invasion from the Ghaznavid ruler Mahmud during 1024-1025 CE. Bhima fled to Kanthkot, as Mahmud entered the Chaulukya territory unopposed and sacked the Somnath temple.[1644] After Mahmud's departure, Bhima restored the Chaulukya rule. He crushed revolts by the Paramara chiefs of Arbuda, who used to serve as Chaulukya vassals.[1645] Bhima also defeated and imprisoned Krishnadeva, a ruler of the Paramara branch of Bhinmal. He unsuccessfully fought against the Naddula Chahamana ruler Anahilla. Anahilla's sons Balaprasada and Jendraraja defeated Bhima and forced him to release Krishnadeva.[1646] Later legendary accounts credit Bhima with a victory against Hammuka, a ruler of Sindh, although the accuracy of this claim is not certain.[1647]

Semi-legendary accounts suggest that Bhima formed an alliance with the Kalachuri king Lakshmi-Karna, and the two played an important role in the downfall of the Paramara king Bhoja around 1055 CE. According to the 14th century chronicler Merutunga, Bhoja and Lakshmi-Karna invaded Bhoja's

Figure 373: *Ruins of the Somnath temple, 1869*

kingdom of Malwa from two opposite directions, and Bhoja died of a disease during this invasion.[1648] Some Chaulukya chroniclers boast that Bhima annexed Bhoja's capital Dhara or that he captured Bhoja alive, but these claims are not corroborated by historical evidence.[1649] After Bhoja's death, a rivalry developed between the Bhima and Lakshmi-Karna over sharing the spoils of their victory.[1650]

Bhima's son Karna succeeded him around 1064 CE. Bhoja's brother Udayaditya, supported by the Shakambhari Chahamana king Vigraharaja III, forced Karna to retreat from Malwa.[1651,1652] Meanwhile, the Kalachuris managed to capture the Lata region. By 1074 CE, Karna evicted the Kalachuris from Lata, and annexed the region to the Chaulukya kingdom, before losing it to one Trivikramapala within three years.[1653]

The Naddula Chahamana ruler Prithvipala defeated Karna, and his successor Jojalladeva occupied the Chaulukya capital Anahilapataka, possibly when Karna was busy at another place.[1654] The Shakambhari Chahamana king Durlabharaja III also appears to have achieved some military success against Karna, although the Chahamana descriptions of this victory are highly exaggerated.[1655] According to legendary chronicles, Karna also defeated Bhil and Koli tribals, who used to raid the Chaulukya territories. He established a city called Karnavati after defeating a Bhil chief named Asha (Āśā). Karnavati is identified with modern Ahmedabad by some, but this is not certain.[1656]

Figure 374: *Jain Shvetambara Tirthankara in Meditation, Chaulukya period now in Metropolitan Museum of Art, c. 1000 – c. 1050*

Imperial expansion

Karna's son Jayasimha Siddharaja (r. c. 1092–1142 CE) greatly expanded the Chaulukya power. He defeated Khangara alias Navaghana, the Chudasama king of Saurashtra.[1657] The Naddula Chahamana ruler Asharaja, who had been dethroned by his rival Ratnapala, became a vassal of Jayasimha sometime before 1143 CE.[1658]

Jayasimha defeated the Shakambhari Chahamana ruler Arnoraja.[1659] Later, however, Jayasimha accepted Arnoraja as an ally, and the Chahamana ruler married Jayasimha's daughter Kanchanadevi.[1660] The couple's son (and thus Jayasimha's grandson) Someshvara, was brought up at the Chaulukya court.[1661] Someshvara's sons Prithviraja III (better known as Prithviraj Chauhan) and Hariraja were also born in Gujarat.[1662]

During the 1135-1136 CE, Jayasimha annexed the Paramara kingdom of Malwa, with support from Asharaja and Arnoraja. The Paramara kings defeated by him were Naravarman and his successor Yashovarman.[1663] Jayasimha continued his eastward march, and reached as far as the Chandela kingdom ruled by Madanavarman. The Chaulukya-Chandela conflict was inconclusive, with both the sides claiming victory.[1664] Jayasimha also defeated several minor rulers, including Sindhuraja, who was probably a Soomra king of Sindh.[1665]

Jayasimha was succeeded by his relative Kumarapala, who spent his early life in exile to avoid persecution by Jayasimha.[1666] After Jayasimha's death, Kumarapala came back to the Chaulukya capital and ascended the throne in 1043 CE, with help of his brother-in-law Kanhadadeva.[1667] Arnoraja opposed Kumarapala's ascension to the throne, but Kumarapala defeated him decisively.[1668] Kumarapala seems to have helped Asharaja's son Katukaraja capture the throne of Naddula.[1669] Katukaraja's younger brother and successor Alhanadeva continued to rule as Kumarapala's vassal.[1670] Arnoraja's son Vigraharaja IV subdued Kumarapala's Chahamana feudatories at Naddula.[1671] The Shakambhari Chahamana-Chaulukya relations seem to have become more cordial when Arnoraja's son (and Jayasimha's grandson) Someshvara became the Chahamana king in later years, possibly with support from Kumarapala.[1672]

After Jayasimha's death, the Paramara king Jayavarman I regained control of Malwa, but he was soon dethroned by an usurper named Ballala. Kumarapala captured Malwa from Ballala, who was killed by Kumarapala's Arbuda Paramara feudatory Yashodhavala in a battle.[1673] Kumarapala subdued a rebellion by his vassal Vikramasimha, a Paramara chief of Arbuda.[1674] The Paramara branch at Kiradu continued to acknowledge Kumarapala's suzerainty.[1675]

In the early 1160s, Kumarapala sent an army against Mallikarjuna, the Shilahara king of northern Konkana. This campaign was probably triggered by a Shilahara raid in southern Gujarat, and ended with Mallikarjuna's death.[1676] Kumarapala's Naddula Chahamana feudatory Alhana put down disturbances in Saurashtra at Kumarapala's request.[1677]

Historical evidence suggests that Kumarapala's empire extended from Chittor and Jaisalmer in the north to the Vindhyas and the Tapti river in the south (ignoring his raid of the Shilahara kingdom of northern Konkana). In the west, it included Kachchha and Saurashtra; in the east, it extended up to at least Vidisha (Bhilsa).[1678]

Kumarapala was succeeded by Ajayapala, who retained Kumarapala's territories, but died after a short reign.[1679] Ajayapala's young sons Mularaja II and Bhima II succeeded him one after other. During this period, the Ghurid king Muhammad of Ghor invaded the Chaulukya kingdom in 1178 CE. In the ensuing battle at Kasahrada (or Kayadara), Muhammad was defeated by a large army, which included loyal Chaulukya feudatories such as the Naddula Chahamana ruler Kelhanadeva, the Jalor Chahamana ruler Kirtipala, and the Arbuda Paramara ruler Dharavarsha.[1680,1681]

Decline

Taking advantage of the young age of Bhima II, some provincial governors rebelled against him in order to establish independent states. His loyal Vaghela feudatory Arnoraja came to his rescue, and died fighting the rebels. Arnoraja's descendants Lavanaprasada and Viradhavala became powerful during Bhima's reign.[1682]

During Bhima's reign, the Hoysala ruler Veera Ballala II seems to have raided the Lata region.[1683] The Yadava ruler Bhillama V also invaded Gujarat, but was forced to retreat by Bhima's feudatory Kelhanadeva.[1683] The Shakambhari Chahamana king Prithviraja III also fought with the Chaulukyas, but Bhima's general Jagaddeva managed to conclude a peace treaty with Prithviraja sometime before 1187 CE.[1684]

By the mid-1190s CE, the Ghurids defeated the Prithviraja and the other major Hindu kings of northern India. On 4 February 1197 CE, the Ghurid general Qutb al-Din Aibak invaded Bhima's capital Anahilapataka, and inflicted a massive defeat on the Chaulukyas.[1685] Bhima's generals Lavanaprasada and Shridhara later forced the Ghurids to retreat, and the capital was back under the Chaulukya rule by 1201 CE.[1686]

Subhatavarman, the Paramara king of Malwa, invaded the Lata region around 1204 CE, taking advantage of the turmoil caused by the Ghurid invasions. He probably also sacked the Chaulukya capital Anahilapataka.[1687] Once again, Lavanaprasada and Shridhara saved the kingdom by forcing Subhatavarman to retreat.[1688] During 1205-1210 CE, Bhima's relative Jayantasimha (or Jayasimha) usurped the throne. In the early 1210s, Subhatavarman's successor Arjunavarman defeated Jayantasimha, and later established a matrimonial alliance with him.[1688] Bhima managed to regain control of the throne during 1223-1226 CE.[1689]

Meanwhile, the Yadavas invaded the southern part of the Chaulukya kingdom, led by Bhillama's successors Jaitugi and Simhana. During these invasions, the Chaulukya feudatories in the northern region of Marwar rebelled. Lavanaprasada and Viradhavala warded off the Yadava invasions, and also subdued the rebellions.[1690] The Guhilas of Medapata (Guhilots of Mewar) also rebelled against Bhima sometime between 1207-1227 CE, and declared their independence.[1691]

By the end of Bhima's reign, Lavanaprasada and Viradhavala assumed regal titles such as *Maharajadhiraja* ("king of great kings") and *Maharaja* ("great king"). However, the two continued to nominally acknowledge Bhima (and his successor Tribhuvanapala) as their overlord. After Tribhuvanapala, they seized the throne, establishing the Vaghela dynasty.[1692]

Claimed descendants

The Vaghela dynasty, which succeeded the Chaulukyas, claimed descent from a sister of Kumarapala.[1693]

Various princely state dynasties calling themselves Solanki (the vernacular form of Chaulukya) claimed descent from the Chaulukyas as well. These included the rulers of the Lunavada State, which was a tributatry to the Marathas before coming under the British rule.[1694]

Several of the Bohra Walis and Da'i al-Mutlaqs claimed descent from Jayasimha Siddharaja.[1695] These included Syedna Ismail, the 34th Da'i al-Mutlaq.[1696]

List of rulers

The Chalukya rulers of Gujarat, with approximate dates of reign, are as follows:[1697,1698]

- Mularaja (c. 940 – c. 995)
- Chamundaraja (c. 996 – c. 1008)
- Vallabharaja (c. 1008)
- Durlabharaja (c. 1008 – c. 1022)
- Bhima I (c. 1022 – c. 1064)
- Karna (c. 1064 – c. 1092)
- Jayasimha Siddharaja (c. 1092 – c. 1142)
- Kumarapala (c. 1142 – c. 1171)
- Ajayapala (c. 1171 – c. 1175)
- Mularaja II (c. 1175 – c. 1178)
- Bhima II (c. 1178 – c. 1240)
- Tribhuvanapala (c. 1240 – c. 1244)

Religion

Most of the dynasty's rulers were Shaivaite, although they also patronized Jainism. The dynasty's founder Mularaja is said to have built Mulavasatika temple for Digambara Jains and the Mulanatha-Jinadeva temple for the Svetambara Jains.[1636] The earliest of the Dilwara Temples and the Modhera Sun Temple were constructed during the reign of Bhima I. According to popular tradition, his queen Udayamati also commissioned the Queen's step-well.[1699] Kumarapala started patronizing Jainism at some point in his life, and the subsequent Jain accounts portray him as the last great royal patron of Jainism.[1678] The Chaulukya rulers also endowed mosques to maintain good relationship with the Muslim traders.[1700]

References

Bibliography

<templatestyles src="Template:Refbegin/styles.css" />

- Asoke Kumar Majumdar (1956). *Chaulukyas of Gujarat*[1701]. Bharatiya Vidya Bhavan. OCLC 4413150[1702].
- Cynthia Talbot (2015). *The Last Hindu Emperor: Prithviraj Cauhan and the Indian Past, 1200–2000*[1703]. Cambridge University Press. ISBN 9781107118560.
- Dasharatha Sharma (1959). *Early Chauhān Dynasties*[1704]. S. Chand / Motilal Banarsidass. ISBN 9780842606189.
- David P. Henige (2004). *Princely States of India: A Guide to Chronology and Rulers*[1705]. Orchid. ISBN 978-974-524-049-0.
- Durga Prasad Dikshit (1980). *Political History of the Chālukyas of Badami*[1706]. Abhinav Publications. ISBN 9780836406450.
- Edward A. Alpers (2014). *The Indian Ocean in World History*[1707]. Oxford University Press USA. ISBN 978-0-19-533787-7.
- Ganga Prasad Yadava (1982). *Dhanapāla and His Times: A Socio-cultural Study Based Upon His Works*[1708]. Concept.
- Jai Narayan Asopa (1976). *Origin of the Rajputs*[1709]. Bharatiya. OCLC 483180949[1710].
- John E. Cort, ed. (1998). *Open Boundaries: Jain Communities and Cultures in Indian History*[1711]. SUNY Press. ISBN 0-7914-3785-X.
- Jonah Blank (2001). *Mullahs on the Mainframe: Islam and Modernity Among the Daudi Bohras*[1712]. University of Chicago Press. p. 44. ISBN 978-0-226-05676-0.
- Krishna Narain Seth (1978). *The Growth of the Paramara Power in Malwa*[1713]. Progress. OCLC 8931757[1714].
- N. Jayapalan (2001). *History of India*[1715]. Atlantic Publishers & Distri. ISBN 978-81-7156-928-1.
- P.B. Udgaonkar (1986). *Political Institutions & Administration*[1716]. Motilal Banarsidass. ISBN 978-81-208-2087-6.
- Romila Thapar (2008). *Somanatha*[1717]. Penguin. ISBN 9780143064688.
- R. B. Singh (1964). *History of the Chāhamānas*[1718]. N. Kishore. OCLC 11038728[1719].
- R. K. Dikshit (1976). *The Candellas of Jejākabhukti*[1720]. Abhinav. ISBN 9788170170464.
- Shanta Rani Sharma (2012). "Exploding the Myth of the Gūjara Identity of the Imperial Pratihāras"[1721]. *Indian Historical Review*. ICHR. **39** (1). doi: 10.1177/0376983612449525[1722].
- Tommaso Bobbio (2015). *Urbanisation, Citizenship and Conflict in India: Ahmedabad 1900-2000*[1723]. Routledge. ISBN 978-1-317-51400-8.

- Vinod Chandra Srivastava (2008). *History of Agriculture in India, Up to C. 1200 A.D.*[1724] Concept. p. 857. ISBN 978-81-8069-521-6.

External links

- ⓘ Media related to Chaulukya dynasty at Wikimedia Commons

Tomara dynasty

Tomara dynasty	
9th century–12th century	
Capital	Delhi
Government	Monarchy
History	
• Established	9th century
• Disestablished	12th century
Preceded by	Succeeded by
Gurjara-Pratihara	Chahamanas of Shakambhari
Today part of	India

The **Tomara** (also called **Tomar** in modern vernaculars because of schwa deletion) were an Indian dynasty who ruled parts of present-day Delhi and Haryana during 9th-12th century. Their rule over this region is attested to by multiple inscriptions and coins. In addition, much of the information about them comes from medieval bardic legends, which are not historically reliable. They were displaced by the Chahamanas of Shakambhari in 12th century.

Territory

The Tomara territory included parts of the present-day Delhi and Haryana.[1725] A 13th century inscription states that the Tomaras ruled the Hariyanaka (Haryana) country before the Chahamanas and the Shakas (Muslims in this context). A 14th century inscription states that they built the Dhillika (Delhi) city in the Hariyana (Haryana) country, and that their rule was followed by that of the Chahamanas and the mlechchha Sahavadina (Shihab ad-Din).[1726]

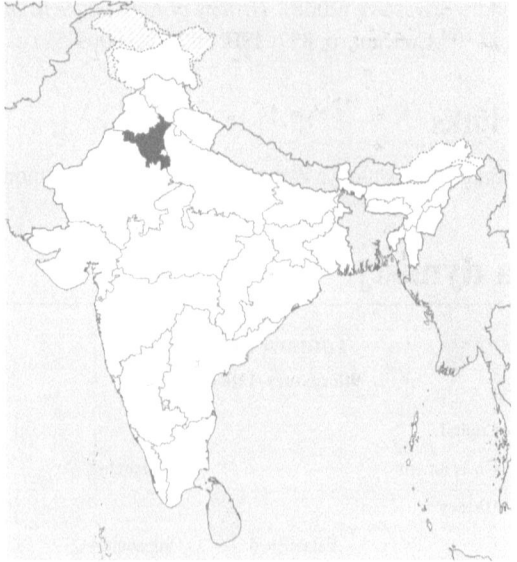

Figure 375: *Location of Haryana in present-day India*

History

The Tomaras are known from some inscriptions and coins. However, much of the information about the dynasty comes from medieval bardic legends, which are not historically reliable. Because of this, the reconstruction of the Tomara history is difficult.[1726]

As feudatories

The earliest extant historical reference to the Tomaras occurs in the Pehowa inscription issued during the reign of the Gurjara-Pratihara king Mahendrapala I (r. c. 885-910 CE).[1727] This undated inscription states that Jaula of the Tomara family became prosperous by serving an unnamed king. His descendants included Vajrata, Jajjuka, and Gogga. The inscription suggests that Gogga was a vassal of Mahendrapala I. It records the construction of three Vishnu temples by Gogga and his step-brothers Purna-raja and Deva-raja. The temples were located at Prithudaka (IAST: Pṛthūdaka; Pehowa), on the banks of the river Sarasvati.[1728]

No information is available about the immediate successors of Gogga.[1729] The Pehowa inscription suggests that this particular Tomara family was settled around the Karnal area. However, F. Kielhorn suggested that this Tomara family actually resided in Delhi: they may have visited Pehowa on pilgrimage, and built a temple there.[1730]

As sovereigns

As the Pratihara power declined, the Tomaras established a sovereign principality around Delhi by the 10th century.[1731] The medieval bardic literature names the dynasty as "Tuar", and classifies them as one of the 36 Rajput clans.[1726] According to the bardic tradition, the dynasty's founder Anangapal Tuar (that is Anangapala I Tomara) founded Delhi in 736 CE.[1727] However, the authenticity of this claim is doubtful.[1726] A 1526 CE source names the successors of Anangapala as Tejapala, Madanapala, Kritapala, Lakhanapala and Prithvipala. The *Dravya-Pariksha* (1318 CE) of Thakkura Pheru mentions the coins of Madanapala, Prithvipala and another ruler, Chahadapala.[1732]

Soon after gaining independence, the Tomaras became involved in conflicts with their neighbours, the Chahamanas of Shakambhari. According to a 973 CE inscription of the Chahamana king Vigraharaja II, his ancestor Chandana (c. 900 CE) killed the Tomara chief Rudrena (or Rudra) in a battle.[1731] The Harsha stone inscription states that Chandana's descendant Simharaja (c. 944-971 CE) defeated a Tomara leader called Lavana or Salavana. Historian R. B. Singh identifies the defeated ruler as Tejapala.[1733] Another fragmentary Chahamana *prashasti* (eulogistic inscription), now at the Ajmer museum, mentions that the Chahamana king Arnoraja invaded the Haritanaka country. This country is identified with the Tomara territory. According to the inscription, Arnoraja's army rendered the waters of the Kalindi river (Yamuna) muddy and the women of Hartinaka tearful.[1734]

The writings of the medieval Muslim historians suggest that a king named Mahipala was ruling Delhi in the 11th century. Although these medieval historians do not mention the dynasty of this king, he is identified as a Tomara ruler by some modern historians. Some coins featuring crude depictions of a horseman and a bull, and bearing the name "Mahipala", have been attributed to this king. These coins are similar to those of Mawdud of Ghazni (r. 1041-50 CE), confirming that Mahipala must have ruled in the 11th century. The horseman-and-bull were a characteristic of the Kabul Shahi coinage; Mawdud probably adopted this style after capturing the Shahi territories. Mahipala probably imitated the same style after capturing Hansi and Thaneshvara regions from Mawdud. Some fragmentary Tomara inscriptions have been discovered from Mahipalpur near Delhi. Historian Y. D. Sharma theorizes that Mahipala established a new capital at Mahipalapura (now Mahipialpur).[1735]

The Suraj Kund reservoir is said to have been commissioned by a Tomara king named Surajpala.[1736]

Figure 376: *The construction of the Suraj Kund is attributed to a Tomara king*

Multiple Tomara kings seem to have shared the name "Anangapala" (IAST: Anaṅgapāla). One of these is said to have established the Lal Kot citadel in the Mehrauli area. The construction of the Anang Tal tank and the Anangpur Dam is also attributed to him.[1736] His coins also feature the horseman-and-bull figure, and bear the title "Shri Samanta-deva". These coins are very similar to those of the Shakambhari Chahamana kings Someshvara and Prithviraja III, indicating that Anangapala was a contemporary of these 12th century kings.[1737] One of the several inscriptions on the Iron Pillar of Delhi mentions Anangapala. A medieval legend mentioned in a copy of *Prithviraj Raso* mentions a legend about the pillar: a Brahmin once told Anangapala (alias Bilan Deo) that the base of the pillar rested on the head of the Vasuki serpent, and that his rule would last as long as the pillar stood upright. Out of curiosity, Anangapala dug out the pillar, only to find it smeared with the blood of Vasuki. Realizing his mistake, the king ordered it to be re-instated, but it remained loose ("dhili"). Because of this, the area came to be known as "Dhilli" (modern Delhi). This legend is obviously a myth.[1736]

Decline

The bardic legends state that the last Tomara king, Anangpal Tomar (also known as Anangapala), handed over the throne of Delhi to his son-in-law Prithviraj Chauhan (Prithviraja III of the Chahamana dynasty of Shakambhari; r. c. 1179-1192 CE). However, this claim is not correct: the historical evidence shows that Prithviraj inherited Delhi from his father Someshvara.[1726]

According to the Bijolia inscription of Someshvara, his brother Vigraharaja IV had captured Dhillika (Delhi) and Ashika (Hansi). He probably defeated the Tomara ruler Anangapala III.[1730]

List of rulers

Various historical texts provide different lists of the Tomara kings:[1738]

- Khadag Rai's history of Gwalior (*Gopācala ākhyāna*) names 18 Tomara kings, plus Prithvi Pala (who is probably the Chahamana king Prithviraja III). According to Khadag Rai, Delhi was originally ruled by the legendary king Vikramaditya. It was deserted for 792 years after his death, until Bilan Dev of Tomara dynasty re-established the city (in 736 CE).
- The Kumaon-Garhwal manuscript names only 15 rulers of "Toar" dynasty, and dates the beginning of their rule to 789 CE (846 Vikram Samvat).
- Abul Fazl's *Ain-i-Akbari* (Bikaner manuscript, edited by Syed Ahmad Khan) names 19 Tomara kings. It places the first Tomara king in 372 CE (429 Vikram Samvat). It might be possible that the era mentioned in the original source used by Abul Fazl was Gupta era, which starts from 318-319 CE; Abul Fazl might have mistaken this era to be Vikrama Samvat. If this is true, then the first Tomara king can be dated to 747 CE (429+318), which is better aligned with the other sources.

As stated earlier, the historians doubt the claim that the Tomaras established Delhi in 736 CE.[1726]

List of Tomara rulers according to various sources[1739,1740]

#	Abul Fazl's *Ain-i-Akbari* / Bikaner manuscript	Gwalior manuscript of Khadag Rai	Kumaon-Garhwal manuscript	Ascension year in CE (according to Gwalior manuscript)	Length of reign		
					Years	Months	Days
1	Ananga Pāla	Bilan Dev		736	18	0	0
2	Vasu Deva			754	19	1	18
3	Gangya	Ganggeva		773	21	3	28
4	Prithivi Pāla (or Prithivi Malla)	Prathama	Mahi Pāla	794	19	6	19
5	Jaya Deva	Saha Deva	Jadu Pāla	814	20	7	28
6	Nīra Pāla or Hira Pāla	Indrajita (I)	Nai Pāla	834	14	4	9
7	Udiraj (or Adereh)	Nara Pāla	Jaya Deva Pāla	849	26	7	11

8	Vijaya (or Vacha)	Indrajita (II)	Chamra Pāla	875	21	2	13
9	Biksha (or Anek)	Vacha Raja	Bibasa Pāla	897	22	3	16
10	Rīksha Pāla	Vira Pāla	Sukla Pāla	919	21	6	5
11	Sukh Pāla (or Nek Pāla)	Go-Pāla	Teja Pāla	940	20	4	4
12	Go-Pāla	Tillan Dev	Mahi Pāla	961	18	3	15
13	Sallakshana Pāla	Suvari	Sursen	979	25	10	10
14	Jaya Pāla	Osa Pāla	Jaik Pāla	1005	16	4	3
15	Kunwar Pāla	Kumara Pāla		1021	29	9	18
16	Ananga Pāla (or Anek Pāla)	Ananga Pāla	Anek Pāla	1051	29	6	18
17	Vijaya Pāla (or Vijaya Sah)	Teja Pāla	Teja Pāla	1081	24	1	6
18	Mahi Pāla (or Mahatsal)	Mahi Pāla	Jyūn Pāla	1105	25	2	23
19	Akr Pāla (or Akhsal)	Mukund Pāla	Ane Pāla	1130	21	2	15
	Prithivi Raja (Chahamana)	Prithvi Pala		1151			

References

Bibliography

<templatestyles src="Template:Refbegin/styles.css" />

- Alexander Cunningham, ed. (1871). *Archaeological Survey of India: Reports 1862-1884*[1741]. I. Archaeological Survey of India. OCLC 421335527[1742].
- Buddha Prakash (1965). *Aspects of Indian History and Civilization*[1743]. Shiva Lal Agarwala. OCLC 6388337[1744].
- D. C. Ganguly (1981). R. S. Sharma, ed. *A Comprehensive History of India (A. D. 300-985)*[1745]. 3, Part 1. Indian History Congress / Orient Longmans.
- Dilip Kumar Ganguly (1984). *History and Historians in Ancient India*[1746]. Abhinav. ISBN 978-0-391-03250-7.
- H. A. Phadke (1990). *Haryana, Ancient and Medieval*[1747]. Harman. ISBN 978-81-85151-34-2.
- Jagbir Singh (2002). *The Jat Rulers of Upper Doab: Three Centuries of Aligarh Jat Nobility*[1748]. Aavishkar. ISBN 9788179100165.

- P. C. Roy (1980). *The Coinage of Northern India*[1749]. Abhinav. ISBN 9788170171225.
- R. B. Singh (1964). *History of the Chāhamānas*[1750]. N. Kishore. OCLC 11038728[1751].
- Sailendra Nath Sen (1999). *Ancient Indian History and Civilization*[1752]. New Age. ISBN 9788122411980.
- Swati Datta (1989). *Migrant Brāhmaṇas in Northern India*[1753]. Motilal Banarsidass. ISBN 978-81-208-0067-0.
- Upinder Singh (2008). *A History of Ancient and Early Medieval India: From the Stone Age to the 12th Century*[1754]. Pearson Education India. ISBN 978-81-317-1120-0.

Pala Empire

Pala Empire	
8th century–12th century	
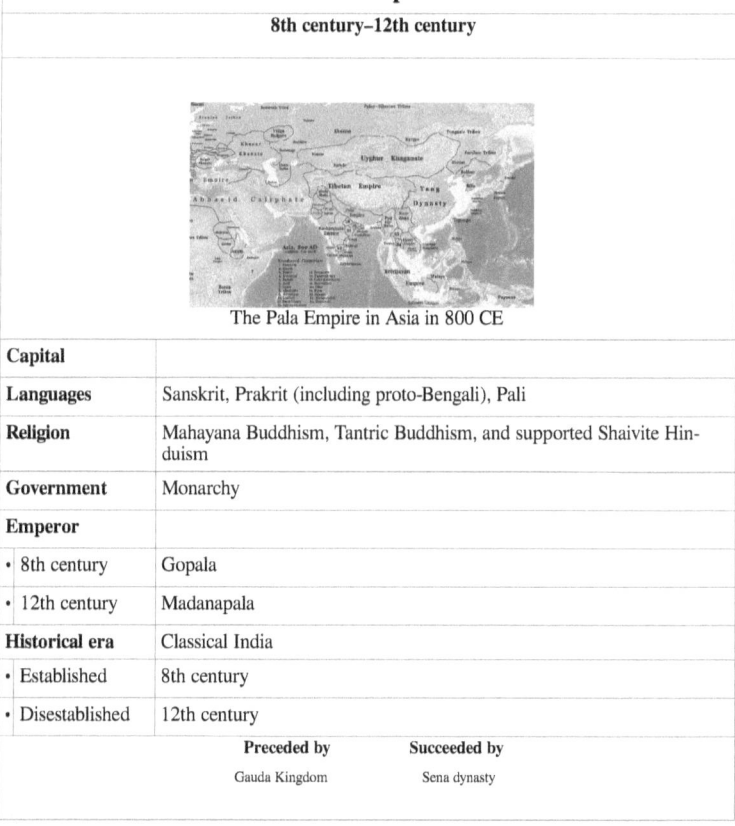 The Pala Empire in Asia in 800 CE	
Capital	
Languages	Sanskrit, Prakrit (including proto-Bengali), Pali
Religion	Mahayana Buddhism, Tantric Buddhism, and supported Shaivite Hinduism
Government	Monarchy
Emperor	
• 8th century	Gopala
• 12th century	Madanapala
Historical era	Classical India
• Established	8th century
• Disestablished	12th century
Preceded by	Succeeded by
Gauda Kingdom	Sena dynasty

| Today part of | Bangladesh
India
Nepal
Pakistan |

The **Pala Empire** was an imperial power during the Late Classical period on the Indian subcontinent, which originated in the region of Bengal. It is named after its ruling dynasty, whose rulers bore names ending with the suffix of *Pala* ("protector" in Sanskrit). They were followers of the Mahayana and Tantric schools of Buddhism. The empire was founded with the election of Gopala as the emperor of Gauda in 750 CE. The Pala stronghold was located in Bengal and Bihar, which included the major cities of Vikrampura, Pataliputra, Gauda, Monghyr, Somapura, Ramvati (Varendra), Tamralipta and Jaggadala.

The Palas were astute diplomats and military conquerors. Their army was noted for its vast war elephant corps. Their navy performed both mercantile and defensive roles in the Bay of Bengal. The Palas were important promoters of classical Indian philosophy, literature, painting and sculpture. They built grand temples and monasteries, including the Somapura Mahavihara, and patronised the great universities of Nalanda and Vikramashila. The Proto-Bengali language developed under Pala rule. The empire enjoyed relations with the Srivijaya Empire, the Tibetan Empire and the Arab Abbasid Caliphate. Islam first appeared in Bengal during Pala rule, as a result of increased trade between Bengal and the Middle East. Abbasid coinage found in Pala archaeological sites, as well as records of Arab historians, point to flourishing mercantile and intellectual contacts. The House of Wisdom in Baghdad absorbed the mathematical and astronomical achievements of Indian civilisation during this period.

At its height in the early 9th century, the Pala Empire was the dominant power in the northern subcontinent, with its territory stretching across parts of modern-day eastern Pakistan, northern and northeastern India, Nepal and Bangladesh. The empire reached its peak under Emperors Dharmapala and Devapala. The Palas also exerted a strong cultural influence under Atisa in Tibet, as well as in Southeast Asia. Pala control of North India was ultimately ephemeral, as they struggled with the Gurjara-Pratiharas and the Rashtrakutas for the control of Kannauj and were defeated. After a short lived decline, Emperor Mahipala I defended imperial bastions in Bengal and Bihar against South Indian Chola invasions. Emperor Ramapala was the last strong Pala ruler, who gained control of Kamarupa and Kalinga. The empire was considerably weakened by the 11th century, with many areas engulfed in rebellion.

The resurgent Hindu Sena dynasty dethroned the Pala Empire in the 12th century, ending the reign of the last major Buddhist imperial power in the subcontinent. The Pala period is considered one of the golden eras of Bengali history.[1756] The Palas brought stability and prosperity to Bengal after centuries of civil war between warring divisions. They advanced the achievements of previous Bengali civilisations and created outstanding works of art and architecture. They laid the basis for the Bengali language, including its first literary work, the *Charyapada*. The Pala legacy is still reflected in Tibetan Buddhism.

History

Origins

According to the Khalimpur copper plate inscription, the first Pala king Gopala was the son of a warrior named Vapyata. The *Ramacharitam* attests that Varendra (North Bengal) was the fatherland (*Janakabhu*) of the Palas. The ethnic origins of the dynasty are unknown, although the later records claim that Gopala was a Kshatriya belonging to the legendary Solar dynasty. The *Ballala-Carita* states that the Palas were Kshatriyas, a claim reiterated by Taranatha in his *History of Buddhism in India* as well as Ghanaram Chakrabarty in his *Dharmamangala* (both written in the 16th century CE). The *Ramacharitam* also attests the fifteenth Pala emperor, Ramapala, as a Kshatriya. Claims of belonging to the legendary Solar dynasty are unreliable and clearly appear to be an attempt to cover up the humble origins of the dynasty.[1756] The Pala dynasty has also been branded as Śudra in some sources such as *Manjushri-Mulakalpa*; this might be because of their Buddhist leanings.[1757,1758] According to Abu'l-Fazl ibn Mubarak (in Ain-i-Akbari), the Palas were Kayasthas. There are even accounts that claim Gopala may have been from a Brahmin lineage.

Establishment

After the fall of Shashanka's kingdom, the Bengal region was in a state of anarchy. There was no central authority, and there was constant struggle between petty chieftains. The contemporary writings describe this situation as *matsya nyaya* ("fish justice" i.e. a situation where the big fish eat the small fish). Gopala ascended the throne as the first Pala king during these times. The Khalimpur copper plate suggests that the *prakriti* (people) of the region made him the king.[1756] Taranatha, writing nearly 800 years later, also writes that he was democratically elected by the people of Bengal. However, his account is in form of a legend, and is considered historically unreliable. The legend mentions that after a period of anarchy, the people elected several kings in succession, all of whom were consumed by the Naga queen of an earlier king on the night following their election. Gopal, however managed to kill the queen

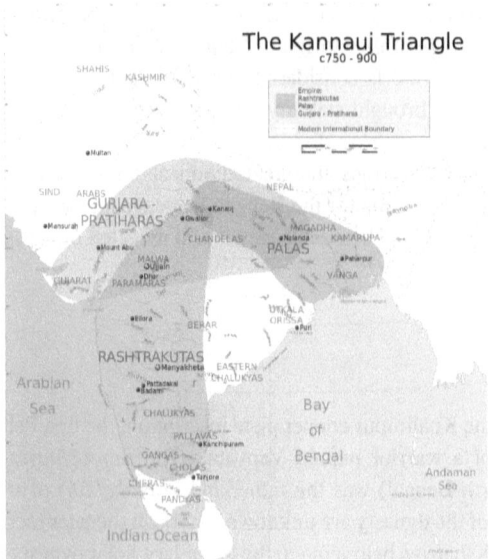

Figure 377: *An illustration of the Kannauj triangle*

and remained on the throne. The historical evidence indicates that Gopala was not elected directly by his citizens, but by a group of feudal chieftains. Such elections were quite common in contemporary societies of the region.[1756]

Gopala's ascension was a significant political event as the several independent chiefs recognised his political authority without any struggle.

Expansion under Dharmapala and Devapala

Gopala's empire was greatly expanded by his son Dharmapala and his grandson Devapala. Dharmapala was initially defeated by the Pratihara ruler Vatsaraja. Later, the Rashtrakuta king Dhruva defeated both Dharmapala and Vatsaraja. After Dhruva left for the Deccan region, Dharmapala built a mighty empire in the northern India. He defeated Indrayudha of Kannauj, and installed his own nominee Chakrayudha on the throne of Kannauj. Several other smaller states in North India also acknowledged his suzerainty. Soon, his expansion was checked by Vatsaraja's son Nagabhata II, who conquered Kannauj and drove away Chakrayudha. Nagabhata II then advanced up to Munger and defeated Dharmapala in a pitched battle. Dharmapala was forced to surrender and to seek alliance with the Rashtrakuta emperor Govinda III, who then intervened by invading northern India and defeating Nagabhata II. The Rashtrakuta records show that both Chakrayudha and Dharmapala recognised the

Rashtrakuta suzerainty. In practice, Dharmapala gained control over North India after Govinda III left for the Deccan. He adopted the title *Paramesvara Paramabhattaraka Maharajadhiraja*.

Dharmapala was succeeded by his son Devapala, who is regarded as the most powerful Pala ruler. His expeditions resulted in the invasion of Pragjyotisha (present-day Assam) where the king submitted without giving a fight and the Utkala (present-day Orissa) whose king fled from his capital city.[1759] The inscriptions of his successors also claim several other territorial conquests by him, but these are highly exaggerated (see the Geography section below).[1756]

First period of decline

Following the death of Devapala, the Pala empire gradually started disintegrating. Vigrahapala, who was Devapala's nephew, abdicated the throne after a brief rule, and became an ascetic. Vigrahapala's son and successor Narayanapala proved to be a weak ruler. During his reign, the Rashtrakuta king Amoghavarsha defeated the Palas. Encouraged by the Pala decline, the King Harjara of Assam assumed imperial titles and the Sailodbhavas established their power in Orissa.

Naryanapala's son Rajyapala ruled for at least 12 years, and constructed several public utilities and lofty temples. His son Gopala II lost Bengal after a few years of rule, and then ruled only Bihar. The next king, Vigrahapala II, had to bear the invasions from the Chandelas and the Kalachuris. During his reign, the Pala empire disintegrated into smaller kingdoms like Gauda, Radha, Anga and Vanga. Kantideva of Harikela (eastern and southern Bengal) also assumed the title *Maharajadhiraja*, and established a separate kingdom, later ruled by the Chandra dynasty. The Gauda state (West and North Bengal) was ruled by the Kamboja Pala dynasty. The rulers of this dynasty also bore names ending in the suffix -pala (e.g. Rajyapala, Narayanapala and Nayapala). However, their origin is uncertain, and the most plausible view is that they originated from a Pala official who usurped a major part of the Pala kingdom along with its capital.[1756]

Revival under Mahipala I

Mahipala I recovered northern and eastern Bengal within three years of ascending the throne in 988 CE. He also recovered the northern part of the present-day Burdwan division. During his reign, Rajendra Chola I of the Chola Empire frequently invaded Bengal from 1021 to 1023 CE to get Ganges water and in the process, succeeded to humble the rulers, acquiring considerable booty. The rulers of Bengal who were defeated by Rajendra Chola were Dharmapal, Ranasur and Govindachandra, who might have been feudatories under Mahipala I of the Pala Dynasty.[1760] Rajendra Chola I also defeated Mahipala, and obtained from the Pala king "elephants of rare strength, women and treasure". Mahipala also gained control of north and south Bihar, probably aided by the invasions of Mahmud of Ghazni, which exhausted the strength of other rulers of North India. He may have also conquered Varanasi and surrounding area, as his brothers Sthirapala and Vasantapala undertook construction and repairs of several sacred structures at Varanasi. Later, the Kalachuri king Gangeyadeva annexed Varanasi after defeating the ruler of Anga, which could have been Mahipala I.

Second period of decline

Nayapala, the son of Mahipala I, defeated the Kalachuri king Karna (son of Ganggeyadeva) after a long struggle. The two later signed a peace treaty at the mediation of the Buddhist scholar Atiśa. During the reign of Nayapala's son Vigrahapala III, Karna once again invaded Bengal but was defeated. The conflict ended with a peace treaty, and Vigrahapala III married Karna's daughter Yauvanasri. Vigrahapala III was later defeated by the invading Chalukya king Vikramaditya VI. The invasion of Vikramaditya VI saw several soldiers from South India into Bengal, which explains the southern origin of the Sena Dynasty. Vigrahapala III also faced another invasion led by the Somavamsi king Mahasivagupta Yayati of Orissa. Subsequently, a series of invasions considerably reduced the power of the Palas. The Varmans occupied eastern Bengal during his reign.[1756]

Mahipala II, the successor of Vigrahapala III, brought a short-lived reign of military glory. His reign is well-documented by Sandhyakar Nandi in *Ramacharitam*. Mahipala II imprisoned his brothers Ramapala and Surapala II, on the suspicion that they were conspiring against him. Soon afterwards, he faced a rebellion of vassal chiefs from the Kaibarta (fishermen). A chief named Divya (or Divvoka) killed him and occupied the Varendra region. The region remained under the control of his successors Rudak and Bhima. Surapala II escaped to Magadha and died after a short reign. He was succeeded by his brother Ramapala, who launched a major offensive against Divya's grandson Bhima. He was supported by his maternal uncle Mathana of the Rashtrakuta dynasty, as well as several feudatory chiefs of south Bihar and south-west Bengal. Ramapala conclusively defeated Bhima, and killing him and his family in a cruel manner.[1756]

Revival under Ramapala

After gaining control of Varendra, Ramapala tried to revive the Pala empire with limited success. He ruled from a new capital at Ramavati, which remained the Pala capital until the dynasty's end. He reduced taxation, promoted cultivation and constructed public utilities. He brought Kamarupa and Rar under his control, and forced the Varman king of east Bengal to accept his suzerainty. He also struggled with the Ganga king for control of present-day Orissa; the Gangas managed to annexe the region only after his death. Ramapala maintained friendly relations with the Chola king Kulottunga to secure support against the common enemies: the Ganas and the Chalukyas. He kept the Senas in check, but lost Mithila to a Karnataka chief named Nanyuadeva. He also held back the aggressive design of the Gahadavala ruler Govindacharndra through a matrimonial alliance.[1756]

Final decline

Ramapala was the last strong Pala ruler. After his death, a rebellion broke out in Kamarupa during his son Kumarapala's reign. The rebellion was crushed by Vaidyadeva, but after Kumarapala's death, Vaidyadeva practically created a separate kingdom. According to *Ramacharitam*, Kumarapala's son Gopala III was murdered by his uncle Mandapala. During Madanapala's rule, the Varmans in east Bengal declared independence, and the Eastern Gangas renewed the conflict in Orissa. Madanapala captured Munger from the Gahadavalas, but was defeated by Vijayasena, who gained control of southern and eastern Bengal. A ruler named Govindapala ruled over the Gaya district around 1162 CE, but there is no concrete evidence about his relationship to the imperial Palas. The Pala dynasty was replaced by the Sena dynasty.[1756]

Geography

The borders of the Pala Empire kept fluctuating throughout its existence. Though the Palas conquered a vast region in North India at one time, they could not retain it for long due to constant hostility from the Gurjara-Pratiharas, the Rashtrakutas and other less powerful kings.[1761]

No records are available about the exact boundaries of original kingdom established by Gopala, but it might have included almost all of the Bengal region. The Pala empire extended substantially under Dharmapala's rule. Apart from Bengal, he directly ruled the present-day Bihar. The kingdom of Kannauj (present-day Uttar Pradesh) was a Pala dependency at times, ruled by his nominee Chakrayudha. While installing his nominee on the Kannauj throne, Dharmapala organised an imperial court. According to the Khalimpur copper plate issued by Dharmapala, this court was attended by the rulers of Bhoja (possibly Vidarbha), Matsya (Jaipur region), Madra (East Punjab), Kuru (Delhi region), Yadu (possibly Mathura, Dwarka or Simhapura in the Punjab), Yavana, Avanti, Gandhara and Kira (Kangra Valley).[1756] These kings accepted the installation of Chakrayudha on the Kannauj throne, while "bowing down respectfully with their diadems trembling".[1762] This indicates that his position as a sovereign was accepted by most rulers, although this was a loose arrangement unlike the empire of the Mauryas or the Guptas. The other rulers acknowledged the military and political supremacy of Dharmapala, but maintained their own territories.[1756] The poet Soddhala of Gujarat calls Dharmapala an *Uttarapathasvamin* ("Lord of the North") for his suzerainty over North India.[1763]

The epigraphic records credit Devapala with extensive conquests in hyperbolic language. The Badal pillar inscription of his successor Narayana Pala states that by the wise counsel and policy of his Brahmin minister Darbhapani, Devapala became the suzerain monarch or Chakravarti of the whole tract of Northern India bounded by the Vindhyas and the Himalayas. It also states that his empire extended up to the two oceans (presumably the Arabian Sea and the Bay of Bengal). It also claims that Devpala defeated Utkala (present-day Orissa), the Hunas, the Kambojas, the Dravidas, the Kamarupa (present-day Assam), and the Gurjaras:

- The Gurjara adversary may have been Mihira Bhoja, whose eastward expansion was checked by Devapala
- The identity of the Huna king is uncertain.
- The identity of the Kamboja prince is also uncertain. While an ancient country with the name Kamboja was located in what is now Afghanistan, there is no evidence that Devapala's empire extended that far. Kamboja, in this inscription, could refer to the Kamboja tribe that had entered North India (see Kamboja Pala dynasty).
- The Dravida king is usually identified with the Rashtrakuta king Amoghavarsha. Some scholars believe that the Dravida king could have been the Pandya ruler Shri Mara Shri Vallabha, since "Dravida" usually refers to the territory south of the Krishna river. According to this theory, Devapala could have been helped in his southern expedition by the Chandela king Vijaya. In any case, Devapala's gains in the south, if any, were temporary.

The claims about Devapala's victories are exaggerated, but cannot be dismissed entirely: there is no reason to doubt his conquest of Utkala and Kamarupa. Besides, the neighbouring kingdoms of Rashtrakutas and the Gurjara-Pratiharas were weak at the time, which might have helped him extend his empire. Devapala is also believed to have led an army up to the Indus river in

Punjab.

The empire started disintegrated after the death of Devapala, and his successor Narayanapala lost control of Assam and Orissa. He also briefly lost control over Magadha and north Bengal. Gopala II lost control of Bengal, and ruled only from a part of Bihar. The Pala empire disintegrated into smaller kingdoms during the reign of Vigrahapala II. Mahipala recovered parts of Bengal and Bihar. His successors lost Bengal again. The last strong Pala ruler, Ramapala, gained control of Bengal, Bihar, Assam and parts of Orissa. By the time of Madanapala's death, the Pala kingdom was confined to parts of central and east Bihar along with northern Bengal.

Administration

The Pala rule was monarchial. The king was the centre of all power. Pala kings would adopt imperial titles like *Parameshwara*, *Paramvattaraka*, *Maharajadhiraja*. Pala kings appointed Prime Ministers. The **Line of Garga** served as the Prime Ministers of the Palas for 100 years.

- Garga
- Darvapani (or Darbhapani)
- Someshwar
- Kedarmisra
- Bhatta Guravmisra

Pala Empire was divided into separate *Bhukti*s (Provinces). Bhuktis were divided into *Vishaya*s (Divisions) and *Mandala*s (Districts). Smaller units were *Khandala*, *Bhaga*, *Avritti*, *Chaturaka*, and Pattaka. Administration covered widespread area from the grass root level to the imperial court.[1764]

The Pala copperplates mention following administrative posts:[1765]

- *Raja*
- *Rajanyaka*
- *Ranaka* (possibly subordinate chiefs)
- *Samanta* and *Mahasamanta* (Vassal kings)
- *Mahasandhi-vigrahika* (Foreign minister)
- *Duta* (Head Ambassador)
- *Rajasthaniya* (Deputy)
- *Aggaraksa* (Chief guard)
- *Sasthadhikrta* (Tax collector)
- *Chauroddharanika* (Police tax)
- *Shaulkaka* (Trade tax)
- *Dashaparadhika* (Collector of penalties)
- *Tarika* (Toll collector for river crossings)

- *Mahaksapatalika* (Accountant)
- *Jyesthakayastha* (Dealing documents)
- *Ksetrapa* (Head of land use division) and *Pramatr* (Head of land measurements)
- *Mahadandanayaka* or *Dharmadhikara* (Chief justice)
- *Mahapratihara*
- *Dandika*
- *Dandapashika*
- *Dandashakti* (Police forces)
- *Khola* (Secret service). Agricultural posts like *Gavadhakshya* (Head of dairy farms)
- *Chhagadhyakshya* (Head of goat farms)
- *Meshadyakshya* (Head of sheep farms)
- *Mahishadyakshya* (Head of Buffalo farms) and many other like *Vogpati*
- *Vishayapati*
- *Shashtadhikruta*
- *Dauhshashadhanika*
- *Nakadhyakshya*

Culture

Religion

The Palas were patrons of Mahayana Buddhism. A few sources written much after Gopala's death mention him as a Buddhist, but it is not known if this is true.[1766] The subsequent Pala kings were definitely Buddhists. Taranatha states that Gopala was a staunch Buddhist, who had built the famous monastery at Odantapuri.Wikipedia:Verifiability Dharmapala made the Buddhist philosopher Haribhadra his spiritual preceptor. He established the Vikramashila monastery and the Somapura Mahavihara. Taranatha also credits him with establishing 50 religious institutions and patronising the Buddhist author Haribhadra. Devapala restored and enlarged the structures at Somapura Mahavihara, which also features several themes from the epics *Ramayana* and *Mahabharata*. Mahipala I also ordered construction and repairs of several sacred structures at Saranath, Nalanda and Bodh Gaya. The *Mahipala geet* ("songs of Mahipala"), a set of folk songs about him, are still popular in the rural areas of Bengal.

The Palas developed the Buddhist centres of learnings, such as the Vikramashila and the Nalanda universities. Nalanda, considered one of the first great universities in recorded history, reached its height under the patronage of

Figure 378: *Nalanda is considered one of the first great universities in recorded history. It reached its height under the Palas.*

Figure 379: *Atisha was a Buddhist teacher, who helped establish the Sarma lineages of Tibetan Buddhism.*

the Palas. Noted Buddhist scholars from the Pala period include Atisha, Santaraksita, Saraha, Tilopa, Bimalamitra, Dansheel, Dansree, Jinamitra, Jnanasrimitra, Manjughosh, Muktimitra, Padmanava, Sambhogabajra, Shantarakshit, Silabhadra, Sugatasree and Virachan.

As the rulers of Gautama Buddha's land, the Palas acquired great reputation in the Buddhist world. Balaputradeva, the Sailendra king of Java, sent an ambassador to him, asking for a grant of five villages for the construction of a monastery at Nalanda. The request was granted by Devapala. He appointed the Brahmin Viradeva (of Nagarahara, present-day Jalalabad) as the head of the Nalanda monastery. The Budhdist poet Vajradatta (the author of Lokesvarashataka), was in his court. The Buddhist scholars from the Pala empire travelled from Bengal to other regions to propagate Buddhism. Atisha, for example, preached in Tibet and Sumatra, and is seen as one of the major figures in the spread of 11th-century Mahayana Buddhism.

The Palas also supported the Saiva ascetics, typically the ones associated with the Golagi-Math.[1767] Narayana Pala himself established a temple of Shiva, and was present at the place of sacrifice by his Brahmin minister.[1768] Queen of King Madanapaladeva, namely Chitramatika, made a gift of land to a Brahmin named Bateswara Swami as his remuneration for chanting the Mahabharata at her request, according to the principle of the Bhumichhidranyaya.Wikipedia:Citation needed Besides the images of the Buddhist deities, the images of Vishnu, Siva and Sarasvati were also constructed during the Pala dynasty rule.

Literature

The Palas patronised several Sanskrit scholars, some of whom were their officials. The *Gauda riti* style of composition was developed during the Pala rule. Many Buddhist Tantric works were authored and translated during the Pala rule. Besides the Buddhist scholars mentioned in the Religion section above, Jimutavahana, Sandhyakar Nandi, Madhava-kara, Suresvara and Chakrapani Datta are some of the other notable scholars from the Pala period.

The notable Pala texts on philosophy include *Agama Shastra* by Gaudapada, *Nyaya Kundali* by Sridhar Bhatta and *Karmanushthan Paddhati* by Bhatta Bhavadeva. The texts on medicine include

- *Chikitsa Samgraha, Ayurveda Dipika, Bhanumati, Shabda Chandrika* and *Dravya Gunasangraha* by Chakrapani Datta
- *Shabda-Pradipa, Vrikkhayurveda* and *Lohpaddhati* by Sureshwara
- *Chikitsa Sarsamgraha* by Vangasena
- *Sushrata* by Gadadhara Vaidya
- *Dayabhaga, Vyavohara Matrika* and *Kalaviveka* by Jimutavahana

Sandhyakar Nandi's semi-fictional epic *Ramacharitam* (12th century) is an important source of Pala history.

A form of the proto-Bengali language can be seen in the *Charyapada*s composed during the Pala rule.

Art and architecture

The Pala school of sculptural art is recognised as a distinct phase of the Indian art, and is noted for the artistic genius of the Bengal sculptors. It is influenced by the Gupta art.

Figure 380: *A basalt statue of Lalita flanked by Gaṇeśa and Kārttikeya*

Figure 381: *Carved shankhas*

Figure 382: *Sculpture of Khasarpana Lokesvara from Nalanda*

Figure 383: *Sculpture of Varaha avatar of Lord Vishnu*

As noted earlier, the Palas built a number of monasteries and other sacred structures. The Somapura Mahavihara in present-day Bangladesh is a World Heritage Site. It is a monastery with 21 acre (85,000 m²) complex has 177 cells, numerous stupas, temples and a number of other ancillary buildings. The gigantic structures of other Viharas, including Vikramashila, Odantapuri, and Jagaddala are the other masterpieces of the Palas. These mammoth structures were mistaken by the forces of Bakhtiyar Khalji as fortified castles and were demolished.Wikipedia:Citation needed The art of Bihar and Bengal during the Pala and Sena dynasties influenced the art of Nepal, Burma, Sri Lanka and Java.

Figure 384: *Somapura Mahavihara, a World Heritage Site, was built by Dharmapala*

Figure 385: *Central shrine decor at Somapura*

Figure 386: *A model of the Somapura Mahavihara by Ali Naqi*

Figure 387: *Ruins of Vikramashila*

List of Pala rulers

Most of the Pala inscriptions mention only the regnal year as the date of issue, without any well-known calendar era. Because of this, the chronology of the Pala kings is hard to determine. Based on their different interpretations of the various epigraphs and historical records, different historians estimate the Pala chronology as follows:

	RC Majumdar (1971)	AM Chowdhury (1967)	BP Sinha (1977)	DC Sircar (1975–76)	D. K. Ganguly (1994)
Gopala I	750–770	756–781	755–783	750–775	750–774
Dharmapala	770–810	781–821	783–820	775–812	774–806
Devapala	810–c. 850	821–861	820–860	812–850	806–845
Mahendrapala	NA (Mahendrapala's existence was conclusively established through a copper-plate charter discovered later.)				845–860
Shurapala I	850–853	861–866	860–865	850–858	860–872
Vigrahapala I				858–60	872–873
Narayanapala	854–908	866–920	865–920	860–917	873–927
Rajyapala	908–940	920–952	920–952	917–952	927–959
Gopala II	940–957	952–969	952–967	952–972	959–976
Vigrahapala II	960–c. 986	969–995	967–980	972–977	976–977
Mahipala I	988–c. 1036	995–1043	980–1035	977–1027	977–1027
Nayapala	1038–1053	1043–1058	1035–1050	1027–1043	1027–1043
Vigrahapala III	1054–1072	1058–1075	1050–1076	1043–1070	1043–1070
Mahipala II	1072–1075	1075–1080	1076–1078/9	1070–1071	1070–1071
Shurapala	1075–1077	1080–1082		1071–1072	1071–1072
Ramapala	1077–1130	1082–1124	1078/9–1132	1072–1126	1072–1126
Kumarapala	1130–1125	1124–1129	1132–1136	1126–1128	1126–1128
Gopala III	1140–1144	1129–1143	1136–1144	1128–1143	1128–1143
Madanapala	1144–1162	1143–1162	1144–1161/62	1143–1161	1143–1161
Govindapala	1155–1159	NA	1162–1176 or 1158–1162	1161–1165	1161–1165
Palapala	NA	NA	NA	1165–1199	1165–1200

Note:

- Earlier historians believed that Vigrahapala I and Shurapala I were the two names of the same person. Now, it is known that these two were cousins; they either ruled simultaneously (perhaps over different territories) or in rapid succession.
- AM Chowdhury rejects Govindapala and his successor Palapala as the members of the imperial Pala dynasty.
- According to BP Sinha, the Gaya inscription can be read as either the "14th year of Govindapala's reign" or "14th year after Govindapala's reign". Thus, two sets of dates are possible.

Military

The highest military officer in the Pala empire was the *Mahasenapati* (commander-in-chief). The Palas recruited mercenary soldiers from a number of kingdoms, including Malava, Khasa, Huna, Kulika, Kanrata, Lata, Odra and Manahali. According to the contemporary accounts, the Rashtrakutas had the best infantry, the Gurjara-Pratiharas had the finest cavalry and the Palas had the largest elephant force. The Arab merchant Sulaiman states that the Palas had an army bigger than those of the Balhara (possibly the Rashtrakutas) and the king of Jurz (possibly the Gurjara-Pratiharas). He also states that the Pala army employed 10,000–15,000 men for fuelling and washing clothes. He further claims that during the battles, the Pala king would lead 50,000 war elephants. Sulaiman's accounts seem to be based on exaggerated reports; Ibn Khaldun mentions the number of elephants as 5,000.[1769]

Since Bengal did not have a good native breed of horses, the Palas imported their cavalry horses from the foreigners, including the Kambojas. They also had a navy, used for both mercantile and defence purposes.[1770]

Sources

The main sources of information about the Pala empire include:[1771]

Pala accounts

- Various epigraphs, coins, sculptures and architecture
- *Ramacharita*, a Sanskrit work by Abhinanda (9th century)
- *Ramacharitam*, a Sanskrit epic by Sandhyakar Nandi (12th century)
- *Subhasita Ratnakosa*, a Sanskrit compilation by Vidyakara (towards the end of the Pala rule)

Other accounts

- *Silsiltut-Tauarikh* by the Arab merchant Suleiman (951 CE), who referred to the Pala kingdom as *Ruhmi* or *Rahma*
- *Dpal dus khyi 'khor lo'i chos bskor gyi byung khungs nyer mkh* (History of Buddhism in India) by Taranatha (1608), contains a few traditional legends and hearsays about the Pala rule
- *Ain-i-Akbari* by Abu'l-Fazl (16th-century)

References

Bibliography

- Bagchi, Jhunu (1993). *The History and Culture of the Pālas of Bengal and Bihar, Cir. 750 A.D.-cir. 1200 A.D.*[1772] Abhinav Publications. ISBN 978-81-7017-301-4.
- Huntington, Susan L. (1984). *The "Pāala-Sena" Schools of Sculpture*[1773]. Brill Archive. ISBN 90-04-06856-2.
- Paul, Pramode Lal (1939). *The Early History of Bengal*[1774]. Indian History. 1. Indian Research Institute. Archived from the original[1775] on 17 August 2016. Retrieved 28 March 2014.
- Sengupta, Nitish K. (2011). *Land of Two Rivers: A History of Bengal from the Mahabharata to Mujib*[1776]. Penguin Books India. pp. 39–49. ISBN 978-0-14-341678-4.

Chandra dynasty

Part of a series on the
History of Bengal

- v
- t
- e[1777]

The **Chandra dynasty** were a family who ruled over the kingdom of Harikela in eastern Bengal (comprising the ancient lands of Harikela, Vanga and Samatala) for roughly 150 years from the beginning of the 10th century CE. Their empire also encompassed Vanga and Samatala, with Srichandra expanding his domain to include parts of Kamarupa. Their empire was ruled from their capital, Vikrampur (modern Munshiganj) and was powerful enough to militarily withstand the Pala Empire to the north-west.

They were replaced later by the Varman dynasty as rulers of Harikela.

Rulers

The five Chandra rulers were:
- Traillokyachandra (900–930 CE)
- Srichandra (930–975 CE)
- Kalyanachandra (975–1000 CE)
- Ladahachandra (1000–1020 CE)
- Govindachandra (1020–1050 CE)

Bibliography

- Singh, Nagendra Kr. (2003). *Encyclopaedia of Bangladesh*. Anmol Publications Pvt Ltd. pp. 7–21. ISBN 81-261-1390-1.
- Majumdar, Ramesh Chandra (1943). *The History of Bengal*. Dacca: B.R. Publishing. pp. 134–135, 192–197. ISBN 81-7646-237-3.
- Chowdhury, Abdul Momin (1967). *Dynastic History of Bengal*. Dacca: The Asiatic Society of Pakistan.
- Chowdhury, AM (2012). "Chandra Dynasty, The"[1778]. In Islam, Sirajul; Jamal, Ahmed A. *Banglapedia: National Encyclopedia of Bangladesh* (Second ed.). Asiatic Society of Bangladesh.

Eastern Ganga dynasty

Eastern Ganga Empire	
1078–1434	
Capital	Dantapura Kalinganagara Kataka
Religion	Hinduism
Government	Monarchy
Tri-Kalingadhipati	
• 1078–1147	Anantavarman Chodagangadeva
• 1178–1198	Ananga Bhima Deva II
• 1238–1264	Narasimha Deva I
• 1414–1434	Bhanu Deva IV
Historical era	Classical India
• Established	1078
• Disestablished	1434
Succeeded by	
Gajapati Kingdom	

The **Eastern Ganga dynasty** or **Chodaganga dynasty**[1779] was a medieval Indian dynasty that reigned from Kalinga from the 11th century to the early 15th century. Their rule consisted of the whole of the modern-day Indian state of Odisha as well as parts of West Bengal, Andhra Pradesh and Chhattisgarh.[1780] The early rulers of the dynasty ruled from Dantapura; the capital was later moved to Kalinganagara (modern Mukhalingam), and ultimately to Kataka (modern Cuttack). Today, they are most remembered as the builders of the Konark Sun Temple, a UNESCO World Heritage site at Konark, Odisha.

The dynasty was founded by King Anantavarman Chodaganga, descendants of the Western Ganga Dynasty that rule southern parts of modern Karnataka and the Chola dynasty. The Eastern Ganga rulers were matrimonially related to the Cholas and Eastern Chalukyas. Their currency was called Ganga fanams and was greatly influenced by the Cholas and Eastern Chalukyas of southern India. Anantavarman was a religious person as well as a patron of art and literature. He is credited for having built the famous Jagannath Temple of Puri in Odisha.[1781] King Anantavarman Chodagangadeva was succeeded by a long line of illustrious rulers such as Narasimha Deva I (1238–1264).

The rulers of Eastern Ganga dynasty defended their kingdom from the constant attacks of the Muslim rulers. This kingdom prospered through trade and commerce and the wealth was mostly used in the construction of temples. The rule of the dynasty came to an end under the reign of King Bhanudeva IV (1414–34), in the early 15th century.

Background

After the fall of Mahameghavahana dynasty, Kalinga was divided into different kingdoms under feudatory chiefs. Each of these chiefs bore the title Kalingadhipathi (Lord of Kalinga). The beginnings of what became the Eastern Ganga dynasty came about when Indravarma I defeated the Vishnukundin king, Indrabhattaraka and established his rule over the region with Kalinganagara (or Mukhalingam) as his capital, and Dantapura as a secondary capital. The Ganga kings assumed various titles viz. *Trikalingadhipathi* or *Sakala Kalingadhipathi* (Lord of three Kalinga or all three Kalingas namely Kalinga proper (South), Utkal (North), and Kosal (West)).

Mukhalingam near Srikakulam of Andhra Pradesh bordering Odisha has been identified as Kalinganagara, the capital of the early Eastern Gangas.

After the decline of the early Eastern Gangas reign, the Chalukyas of Vengi took control of the region. Vajrahastha I, a descendant of the early Eastern Ganga dynasty took advantage of the internal strife and revived the power of the Ganga dynasty. It was during their rule that Shaivism took precedence over Buddhism and Jainism. The magnificent Srimukhalingam Temple at Mukhalingam was built during this period.

In the 11th century, the Cholas brought the Ganga Kingdom under their rule.

Figure 388: *Jagannath Temple at Puri, built by Maharaja Anantavarman Chodaganga Deva.*

Intermarriage

The Eastern Gangas were known to have intermarried with the Cholas as well as Chalukyas. The early state of the dynasty may have started from the early 8th century.

Anantavarman Chodaganga

The dynastic founding started with Anantavarman Chodaganga. He is believed to have ruled from the Ganges River in the north to the Godavari River in the south. This laying the foundation of the Eastern Ganga Dynasty. Also during his rule, the great Jagannath Temple at Puri was being built. He assumed the title of Trikalingadhipathi (ruler of the three Kalingas which comprise Kalinga proper, Utkal north and Koshal west) in 1076. Resulting in him being the first to rule all three divisions of Kalinga.

Intrudes

Rajaraja III ascended the throne in 1198 and did nothing to resist the Muslims of Bengal, who invaded Orissa in 1206. Rajaraja's son Anangabhima III, however, repulsed the Muslims and built the temple of Megheshvara at Bhuvaneshvara. Narasimhadeva I, the son of Anangabhima, invaded southern Bengal in 1243, defeated its Muslim ruler, captured the capital (Gauda), and built the Sun Temple at Konark to commemorate his victory. With the death of Narasimha in 1264, the Eastern Gangas began to decline; the sultan of Delhi invaded Odisha in 1324, and Musunuri NayaksWikipedia:Citation needed defeated the Odishan powers in 1356. Narasimha IV, the last known king of the Eastern Ganga dynasty, ruled until 1425. The "mad king," Bhanudeva IV, who succeeded him, left no inscriptions; his minister Kapilendra usurped the throne and founded the Suryavamsha dynasty in 1434–35.

Legacy

The Eastern Gangas were great patrons of religion and the arts, and the temples of the Ganga period rank among the masterpieces of Hindu architecture.[1782]

Rulers

1. Indravarman (496–535)
2. Devendravarman IV (893-?)
3. Vajrahasta Anantavarman (1038-?)
4. Rajaraja I (?-1078)
5. Anantavarman Chodaganga (1078–1150)
6. Ananga Bhima Deva II (1178–1198)
7. Rajaraja II (1198–1211)
8. Ananga Bhima Deva III (1211–1238)
9. Narasimha Deva I (1238–1264)
10. Bhanu Deva I (1264–1279)
11. Narasimha Deva II (1279–1306)
12. Bhanu Deva II (1306–1328)
13. Narasimha Deva III (1328–1352)
14. Bhanu Deva III (1352–1378)
15. Narasimha Deva IV (1379–1424)
16. Bhanu Deva IV (1424–1434)

Gallery

Figure 389: *A Temple in Sri Mukhalingam temple complex*

Figure 390: *Konark Sun Temple at Konark, Orissa, built by King Narasimhadeva I (1238–1264),*[1783] *it is now a World Heritage Site.*

Figure 391: *A Stone carved throne at Simhachalam temple*

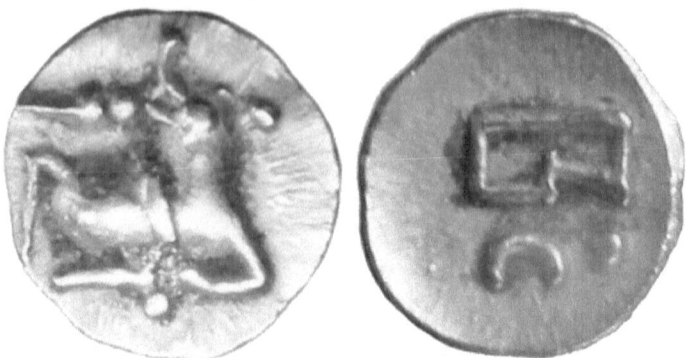

Figure 392: *A Fanam (Coin) of Eastern Ganga Dynasty*[1784]

External links

 Wikimedia Commons has media related to *Eastern Ganga Dynasty*.

- History of *Srikakulam* (Kalinga)[1785]
- Coins of the Eastern Gangas[1786]

Sena dynasty

Sena Empire	
সেন সাম্রাজ্য *Shen Shamrajjo*	
CE 1070–CE 1230	
Capital	Nabadwip
Languages	Sanskrit
Religion	Hinduism Buddhism
Government	Monarchy
King	
• 1070–1096 AD	Hemanta Sena
• 1159–1179 AD	Ballala Sena
• 1225–1230 AD	Keshava Sena
Historical era	Classical India
• Established	CE 1070
• Disestablished	CE 1230
Preceded by	**Succeeded by**
Pala Empire	Deva dynasty

Part of a series on the
History of Bengal

- v
- t
- e[1787]

The **Sena Empire** (Bengali: সেন সাম্রাজ্য, *Shen Shamrajjo*) was a Hindu dynasty during the Late Classical period on the Indian subcontinent, that ruled from Bengal through the 11th and 12th centuries. The empire at its peak covered much of the north-eastern region of the Indian subcontinent. The rulers of the Sena Dynasty traced their origin to the south Indian region of Karnataka.[1788]

The dynasty's founder was Samanta Sena. After him came Hemanta Sena who usurped power and styled himself king in 1095 AD. His successor Vijaya Sena (ruled from 1096 AD to 1159 AD) helped lay the foundations of the dynasty, and had an unusually long reign of over 60 years. Ballala Sena conquered Gaur from the Pala, became the ruler of the Bengal Delta, and made Nabadwip the capital as well. Ballala Sena married Ramadevi a princess of the Western Chalukya Empire which indicates that the Sena rulers maintained close social contact with south India.[1789] Lakshmana Sena succeeded Ballala Sena in 1179, ruled Bengal for approximately 20 years, and expanded the Sena Empire to Assam, Odisha, Bihar and probably to Varanasi. In 1203–1204 AD, the Turkic general Bakhtiyar Khalji attacked Nabadwip. Khalji defeated Lakshman Sen and captured northwest Bengal – although Eastern Bengal remained under Sena control.

Origins

The political space after the decline of the Pala power in Bengal was occupied by the Senas whose king Vijayasena succeeded in conquering a large part of Pala territory. The Senas were the supporters of orthodox Hinduism. The dynasty traces its origin to the South, to the Western Chalukya Empire of southern India.[1790] Theres is a record of a Western Chalukya invasion during the reign of Someshvara I led by his son Vikramaditya VI who defeated the kings of Gauda and Kamarupa.[1791,1792] This invasion of the Kannada ruler brought bodies of his countrymen from Karnataka into Bengal which explains the origin of the Sena Dynasty.

The founder of the Sena rule was Samantasena who described himself as a Kshatriya of Karnata (Karnataka). He himself stated that he fought the outlaws of Karnata and later turned an ascetic.wikipedia:Citation needed The inscriptions of the Sena kings mention them as Brahma-Kshatriyas or Kshatriyas. Otherwise, sources have identified them with the Vaidya as well as the Ambashtha caste or sub-caste, considered as a mixed caste, being born of Brahmin father and Vaishya mother, and they married with and were identified with the Bengali Vaidyas (commonly known as Baidyas in Bengal) in Vaidya *Kula-panjikas* (family-tree accounts).

Sena Dynasty had ruled Bengal for little over a century (c 1097–1225). The emergence of the dynasty, which supplanted the Palas in Bengal towards the close of 11th century A.D., had constituted a significant epoch in the history of ancient India. Taking advantage of the revolt of Samantachakra in Varendra during the reign of Mahipala II, Vijayasena, founder of the Sena dynasty, gradually consolidated his position in western Bengal and ultimately assumed an independent position during the reign of Madanapala. One important aspect of Sena rule in Bengal is that the whole territory of Bengal was brought under a single rule for the first time. It is likely impossible to provide definite information to the question as to how the family entered Bengal. The Sena records also are amazingly silent about this.

The Sena kings claim in their own inscriptions that they are Brahma-Kshatriyas. Their remote ancestor was one Virasena, whose name was supposed to have been mentioned in Puranas. The "Deopara Inscription" of the Senas also traces the Sena ancestry from Virasena. Since there are no authentic records available still, a keen controversy prevails among scholars regarding origin of the Senas.Wikipedia:Citation needed

Like the origin of the Senas, their early history or circumstances, which led them to concentrate in Bengal is also still unknown. It has been presumed by historians that the Senas came to Bengal on the eve of the invading army led by the Chalukya kings Vikramaditya VI and Someswara III. Some scholars have also suggested that when Rajendra Chola's army had invaded Bengal, the Senas had accompanied them. According to some other historians, a few Karnataka officials, who were subordinate to the Pala kings, had established their independent kingdom in the region of Radha, taking advantage of the weakness of the Pala powers. Those Karnataka chiefs might have arrived in Bengal in wake of the Chalukya invasion and had settled into a kingdom of

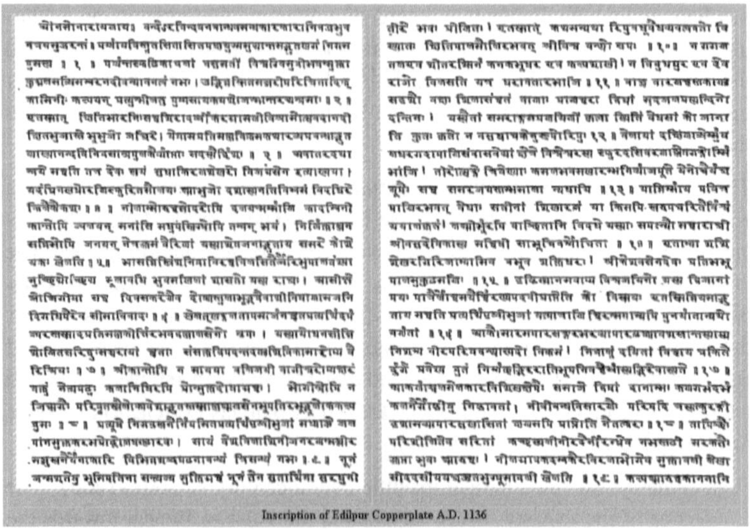

Figure 393: *Edilpur Copperplate*

their own. According to historians Samantasena was such a chief who had established his independent kingdom in the Radha region of Bengal.

Samantasena was a scion of the Sena family, who had distinguished himself through various warfares in South India. He had settled in Radha in Bengal, at an old age. He had also laid the foundation of the Sena family in Bengal. His son Hemantasena carved out an important kingdom in Radha, taking advantage of the decline of the Pala Empire. From their base in Radha, the Senas ultimately extended their powers over the whole of Bengal.

Inscriptions

Sena dynasty 1070 CE–1230 CE	
Samanta Sena	–
Hemanta Sena	(1070 – 1096)
Vijaya Sena	(1095 – 1158)
Ballala Sena	(1158 – 1179)
Lakshmana Sena	(1179 – 1206)
Vishvarupa Sena	(1206 – 1225)
Keshava Sena	(1225 – 1230)

Sena dynasty 577

- v
- t
- e[1793]

A copperplate was found in the Adilpur or Edilpur pargana of Faridpur District in 1838 A.D. and was acquired by the Asiatic Society of Bengal, but now the copperplate is missing from collection. An account of the copperplate was published in the *Dacca Review* and *Epigraphic Indica*. The copperplate inscription is written in Sanskrit and in Ganda character, and dated 3rd jyaistha of 1136 samval, or 1079 A.D. In the Asiatic Society's proceeding for January 1838, an account of the copperplate states that three villages were given to a Brahman in the third year of Keshava Sena. The grant was given with the landlord rights, which include the power of punishing the chandrabhandas or Sundarbans, a race that lived in the forest. The land was granted in the village of Leliya in the Kumaratalaka mandala, which is situated in shatata-padamavati-visaya. The copperplate of Keshava Sena records that the king Vallala Sena carried away, from the enemies, the goddesses of fortune on palanquins (Shivaka), which elephant tusk staff supported; and also states that Vallala Sena's son, Lakshmana Sena (1179–1205), erected pillars of victory and sacrificial posts at Varanasi, Allahabad, and Adon Coast of the South Sea. The copperplate also describes the villages with smooth fields growing excellent paddy, the dancing and music in ancient Bengal, and ladies adorned with blooming flowers. The Edilpur copperplate of Keshava Sena records that the king made a grant in favour of Nitipathaka Isvaradeva Sarman for the inscae of the subhavarsha.

The Deopara Prashasti is a stone inscription eulogising the Sena kings, particularly Vijaya Sena, composed by the court poet Umapati Dhara.

Society

The Sena rulers consolidated the caste system in Bengal. Although Bengal borrowed from the caste system of Mithila, caste was not so strong in Bengal as in Mithila.[1794]

Architecture

The Sena dynasty is famous for building Hindu temples and monasteries, which include the renowned Dhakeshwari Temple in what is now Dhaka, Bangladesh.

In Kashmir, the dynasty also likely built a temple knows as Sankara Gaureshwara.

Literature

The Sena rulers were also great patrons of literature. During the Pala dynasty and the Sena dynasty, major growth in Bengali was witnessed. Some Bengali authors believe that Jayadeva, the famous Sanskrit poet and author of Gita Govinda, was one of the *Pancharatnas* (five gems) in the court of Lakshmana Sena. Dhoyin – himself an eminent court poet of Sena dynasty – mentions nine gems (ratna) in the court of Lakshmana Sena, among whom were:

- Govardhana
- Sarana
- Jayadeva
- Umapati
- Dhoyi/ Dhoyin Kaviraja

Legacy

After the Sena dynasty, the Deva dynasty ruled in eastern Bengal. The Deva dynasty was probably the last independent Hindu dynasty of Bengal.

References

Sources <templatestyles src="Template:Refbegin/styles.css" />

- Early History of India 3rd and revised edition by Vincent A Smith

External links

- Chowdhury, AM (2012). "Sena Dynasty"[1795]. In Islam, Sirajul; Jamal, Ahmed A. *Banglapedia: National Encyclopedia of Bangladesh* (Second ed.). Asiatic Society of Bangladesh.

Preceded by **Pala dynasty**	**Bengal dynasty**	Succeeded by **Deva dynasty**

Varman dynasty

Kamarupa Kingdom	
Varman dynasty	
350 CE–655 CE	
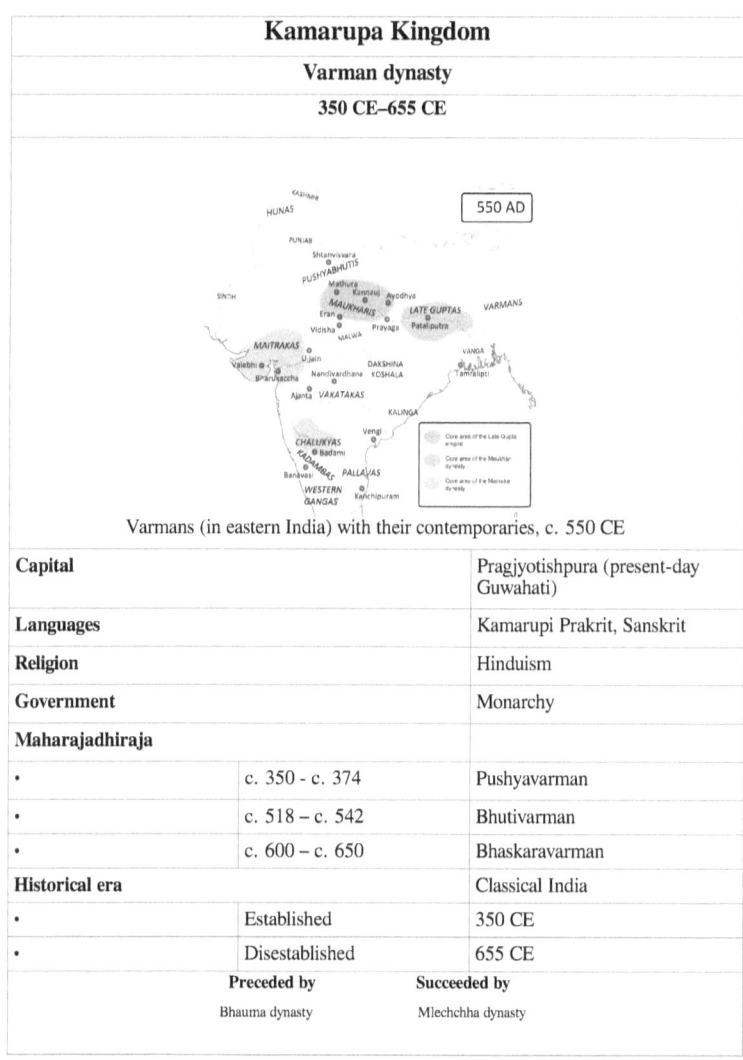 Varmans (in eastern India) with their contemporaries, c. 550 CE	
Capital	Pragjyotishpura (present-day Guwahati)
Languages	Kamarupi Prakrit, Sanskrit
Religion	Hinduism
Government	Monarchy
Maharajadhiraja	
•	c. 350 - c. 374	Pushyavarman
•	c. 518 – c. 542	Bhutivarman
•	c. 600 – c. 650	Bhaskaravarman
Historical era	Classical India
•	Established	350 CE
•	Disestablished	655 CE
Preceded by	Succeeded by
Bhauma dynasty	Mlechchha dynasty

The **Varman dynasty** (350-650) is the first historical dynasty of the Kamarupa kingdom. It was established by Pushyavarman, a contemporary of Samudragupta.[1796,1797] This dynasty became vassals of the Gupta Empire, but as the power of the Guptas waned, Mahendravarman (470-494) performed two horse sacrifices and threw off the imperial yoke.[1798] The first of the three Kamarupa dynasties, the Varmans were followed by the Mlechchha and then the Pala dynasties.

Genealogy

The genealogy of the Varman dynasty appears most fully in the Dubi and Nidhanpur copperplate inscription of the last Varman king, Bhaskaravarman (600-650), where Pushyavarman is named the founder. The Dubi copper plate inscription of Bhaskaravarman asserts that Pushyavarman was born in the family of Naraka, Bhagadatta and Vajradatta (as did the other two Kamarupa dynasties)[1799] three thousand years after these mythical ancestors.[1800] The middle or Mlechha (Mech) dynasty, though claim same descent, are native tribal rulers.[1801] K.L. Barua opines that there was a Mlechha (i.e., Mech) revolt in Kamarupa and Salastambha, the leader or governor of the Mlecchas usurped the throne by deposing Bhaskaravarman's immediate successor Avantivarman.

Ethnic origins

The dynasty traces its lineage from Naraka.

The exact ethnic genealogy of Naraka is in dispute, with authors such as N N Vasu and K L Barua claiming he was Dravidian, whereas authors like P C Choudhury consider him to be of Alpine origin. Since the claim to Naraka's lineage was made at the end of the Varman dynasty (Bhaskarvarman); and since it was natural for the ruling house to fabricate a respectable lineage,[1802] authors like Sircar refuse to give much importance to these claims.

Historical documents and legends are contradictory on the ethnicity of this dynasty. Naraka, according to an early account was the son of an *asura* named Hiranksha and Bhumi (Earth).[1803] In the late 10th-century Kalika Purana, Naraka is said to be the son of Vishnu in his Varaha form and Bhumi, who grew up in household of Janaka. The Kalika Purana goes on to describe two Narakas: one who was religious and the other who was hostile to Brahminism.[1804]

The relationship of Bhagadatta, also mentioned as an ancestor of the Varmans, with Naraka is not clear from legendary sources either: Bhagadatta is called a grandson (Kalika Purana), a son (Bhagavata Purana) or not specified at all (Mahabharata, Harivamsha and Vishnu Purana). In the Mahabharata, a much earlier text, Bhagadatta, the son of Naraka is mentioned as *Mleccha*,[1805] an appellation used sometimes for degraded Aryans,[1806] non-Aryans and also foreigners, such as Hunas. All three Kamarupa dynasties draw their lineage from Naraka and Bhagadatta and Vajradatta.

Xuanzang, a Chinese traveller who stayed in Kamarupa for three months termed Bhaskaravarman a Brahmana king who originated with Narayana Deva.[1807]

Figure 394:
Pragjyotishpura, Varmana capital

Lévi Sylvain wrote, when Bhaskaravarman had business with others than Indians, the same prince boasted of another origin altogether. Bhaskaravarman told *She-Kia-Fang-Che* that his ancestors hailed from China, four thousand years ago, flying through air as holy spirit. As though he would show sympathy for China, he asked the envoy to get him a portrait of Lao-tseu and a Sanskrit translation of the Tao-to-king.[1808,1809]

Many scholars have opined that the Varman dynasty are probably of Indo-Aryan descent, that was overthrown by Salastambha of Mongoloid origin, who then made himself the king of Kamarupa.[1810,1811,1812]

Suniti Kumar Chatterjee calls Bhaskaravarman a mleccha king,[1813] Mukunda Madhava Sharma considers all the dynasties of Kamarupa as of Aryan origin.[1814] Urban terms all kings of Brahmaputra Valley as non-Aryans.[1815]

Kanak Lal Barua asserts Bhaskaravarman was a kshatriya not a hinduised Koch.[1816]

Politics and diplomacy

The most illustrious of this dynasty was the last, Bhaskaravarman, who claimed be a descendant from god Vishnu and referred to as "lord of eastern India". He accompanied King Harshavardhana to religious processions from Pataliputra to Kannauj.Wikipedia:Citation needed

Kings of Varman dynasty maintained both diplomatic and matrimonial relations with other countries of Aryavarta. Pushyavarman who himself named after king Pushyamitra Shunga, named his son Samudravarman after king Samudragupta in appreciations of kings of Aryavarta.Wikipedia:Citation needed

King Balavarman organised Swayamvara for his daughter Amrita Prabha; which was attended by princes of different countries. Princess eventually chosen prince of Kashmir Meghavahana as her groom. The alliance between king Harsha of Thanesar and Bhaskaravarman lead to spread of political influence of later to entire eastern India.Wikipedia:Citation needed

The dynasty

In the Nidhanpur plate of Bhaskaravarman the genealogy of all rulers of dynasty mentioned therein is traced from Naraka, Bhagadatta and Vajradatta. Chinese traveller (Xuanzang) designated the rulers of this dynasty as Brahmins.

	Reign	Name	succession	Queen
1	350-374	Pushyavarman	claimed descent from Bhagadatta	(unknown)
2	374-398	Samudravarman	son of Pushyavarman	Dattadevi
3	398-422	Balavarman	son of Samudravarman	Ratnavati
4	422-446	Kalyanavarman	son of Balavarman	Gandharavati
5	446-470	Ganapativarman	son of Kalyanavarman	Yajnavati
6	470-494	Mahendravarman	son of Ganapativarman	Suvrata
7	494-518	Narayanavarman	son of Mahendravarman	Devavati
8	518-542	Bhutivarman	son of Narayanavarman	Vijnayavati
9	542-566	Chandramukhavarman	son of Bhutivarman	Bhogavati
10	566-590	Sthitavarman	son of Chandramukhavarman	Nayanadevi
11	590-595	Susthitavarman	son of Sthitavarman	Syamadevi
12	595-600	Supratisthitavarman	son of Susthitavarman	(Bachelor)
13	600-650	Bhaskaravarman	brother of Supratisthitavarman	(Bachelor)

| 14 | 650-655 | Avantivarman[1817] | (unknown) | (unknown) |

Bibliography

<templatestyles src="Template:Refbegin/styles.css" />

- Barua, Kanak Lal (1933). *Early History Of Kamarupa*.
- Beal, Samuel (1884). *Si-Yu-Ki. Buddhist Records of the Western World*[1818]. **II**. Ludgate Hill: Trubner & Co. Retrieved February 17, 2013.
- Chatterji, S. K. (1974). *Kirata-Jana-Krt*. Calcutta: The Asiatic Society.
- Chattopadhyaya, S (1990), "Social Life", in Barpujari, H K, *The Comprehensive History of Assam*, **I**, Guwahati: Publication Board, Assam, pp. 195–232
- Choudhury, P. C. (1966). *The History of the Civilisation of the People of Assam to the Twelfth Century AD*. Gauhati: Department of Historical and Antiquarian Studies of Assam.
- Sharma, Mukunda Madhava (1978). *Inscriptions of Ancient Assam*. Gauhati University, Assam.
- Sircar, D C (1990), "Political History", in Barpujari, H K, *The Comprehensive History of Assam*, **I**, Guwahati: Publication Board, Assam, pp. 94–171
- Sylvain, Lévi (1929). *Pre-Aryan and Pre-Dravidian in India*[1819]. Calcutta: University of Calcutta. Retrieved February 25, 2013.
- Urban, Hugh B. (2011). "The Womb of Tantra: Goddesses, Tribals, and Kings in Assam". *The Journal of Hindu Studies*. **4**: 231–247. doi: 10.1093/jhs/hir034[1820].

The Northeast

Kamarupa

Kamarupa Kingdom	
350–1140	

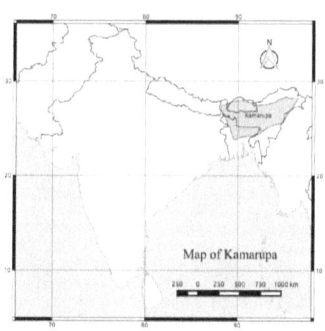

Map of Kamarupa

The 7th and 8th century extent of Kamarupa kingdom, located on the eastern region of the Indian subcontinent, what is today modern-day Assam, Bengal and Bhutan.[1821] Kamarupa at its height covered the entire Brahmaputra Valley, North Bengal, Bhutan and northern part of Bangladesh, and at times portions of West Bengal and Bihar.[1822]

Capital		Pragjyotishpura Haruppeswara Durjaya
Government		Absolute monarchy, unitary state
Historical era		Classical India
•	Established	350
•	Disestablished	1140

Succeeded by	
Ahom kingdom	
Kachari kingdom	
Kamata kingdom	
Chutiya Kingdom	
Sylhet_Division	
Baro Bhuyans	
Bhutanese Kingdom	
Today part of	India Bhutan Bangladesh Myanmar

Part of a series on the
Culture of Assam

Religion

- Assam portal
- $\underline{v}$
- $\underline{t}$
- $\underline{e}$[1823]

Kāmarūpa (/ˈkɑːməˌruːpə/; also called **Pragjyotisha**), was a power during the Classical period on the Indian subcontinent; and along with Davaka, the first historical kingdom of Assam.[1825] Though Kamarupa existed from 350 CE to 1140 CE, Davaka was absorbed by Kamarupa in the 5th century CE.[1826,1827]

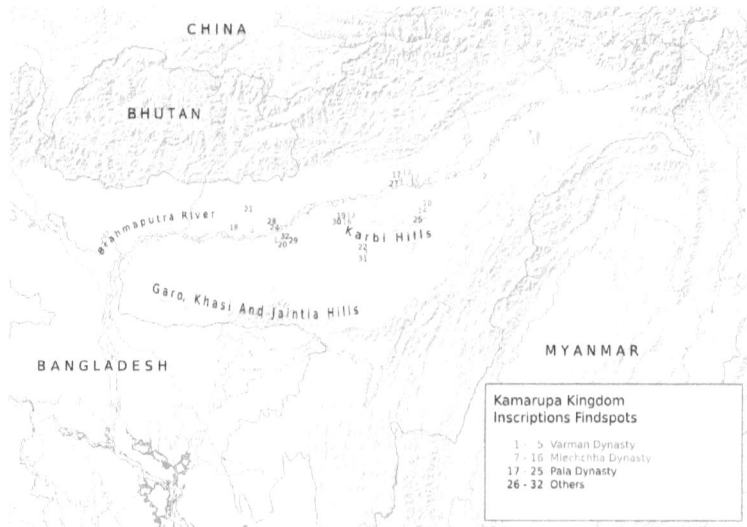

Figure 395: *The findspots of inscriptions*[1824] *associated with the Kamarupa kingdom give an estimate of its geographical location and extent.*

Ruled by three dynasties from their capitals in present-day Guwahati, North Guwahati and Tezpur, Kamarupa at its height covered the entire Brahmaputra Valley, North Bengal,[1828] Bhutan and northern part of Bangladesh, and at times portions of West Bengal and Bihar.[1822]

Though the historical kingdom disappeared by the 12th century to be replaced by smaller political entities, the notion of Kamarupa persisted and ancient and medieval chroniclers continued to call this region by this name.[1829] In the 16th century the Ahom kingdom came into prominence and assumed for itself the political and territorial legacy of the Kamarupa kingdom.[1830]

Etymology

The kingdom derived its name from the region it constitutes. The origin of the name is attributed to be of Austric origin.

Antecedents

Kamarupa and the northeast Indian region find no mention in the Ashokan records (3rd century BCE). The first dated mention comes from the *Periplus of the Erythraean Sea* (1st century) where it describes a people called Sêsatai,[1831] and the second mention comes from Ptolemy's Geographia (2nd century) calls the region *Kirrhadia* after the Kirata population.[1832] Arthashastra (early centuries of the Christian era[1833]) mentions "Lauhitya",[1834] which is identified with Brahmaptra valley by a later commentator.[1835]

The earliest mention of a kingdom comes from the 4th-century Allahabad inscription of Samudragupta that calls the kings of Kamarupa (Western Assam) and Davaka (now in Nagaon district) frontier rulers (*pratyanta nripati*). The Chinese traveler Xuanzang visited the kingdom in the 7th century, then ruled by Bhaskaravarman.[1836] The corpus of Kamarupa inscriptions left by the rulers of Kamarupa, including Bhaskaravarman, at various places in Assam and present-day Bangladesh are important sources of information. Nevertheless, local grants completely eschew the name Kamarupa; instead they use the name Pragjyotisha, with the kings called *Pragjyotishadhipati*.[1837]

Boundaries

The kingdom in the fourth century was small, located to the west of Nagaon that soon engulfed the entire Brahmaputra valley and beyond.[1838] According to the 10th century Kalika Purana and the 7th century Xuanzang, the western boundary was the historical Karatoya River. The eastern border was the temple of the goddess Tamreshvari (*Pūrvāte Kāmarūpasya devī Dikkaravasini*, given in Kalika Purana) near present-day Sadiya,[1839] in the eastern most corner of Assam, which too agrees with Xuanzang.[1840] The people of Kamarupa were aware of Sichuan which lay two months' journey away from its eastern borders.[1841]

The southern boundary was near the border between the Dhaka and Mymensingh districts in Bangladesh. Thus it spanned the entire Brahmaputra valley and at various times included present-day Bhutan and parts of Bangladesh. This is supported by the various epigraphic records found scattered over these regions. The kingdom appears to have broken up entirely by the 13th century into smaller kingdoms and from among them rose the Kamata kingdom, Dimasa kingdom and the Chutiya kingdom as the main successors. The Shans who entered Assam in 1228 later took power and ruled over Assam, while the rest was absorbed by the Mughals

State

The extent of state structures can be culled from the numerous Kamarupa inscriptions left behind by the Kamarupa kings as well as accounts left by travellers such as those from Xuanzang.[1842] Governance followed the classical *saptanga* structure of state.[1843]

Kings and courts: The king was considered to be of divine origin. Succession was primogeniture, but two major breaks resulted in different dynasties. In the second, the high officials of the state elected a king, Brahmapala, after the previous king died without leaving an heir. The royal court consisted of a *Rajaguru*, poets, learned men and physicians. Different epigraphic records mention different officials of the palace: *Mahavaradhipati, Mahapratihara, Mahallakapraudhika*, etc.

Council of Ministers: The king was advised by a council of ministers (*Mantriparisada*), and Xuanzang mentions a meeting Bhaskaravarman had with his ministers. According to the Kamauli grant, these positions were filled by Brahmanas and were hereditary. State functions were specialized and there were different groups of officers looking after different departments.

Revenue: Land revenue (*kara*) was collected by special tax-collectors from cultivators. Cultivators who had no proprietary rights on the lands they tilled paid *uparikara*. Duties (*sulka*) were collected by toll collectors (*Keot(Kaivarta)* an indigenous fishermen community) from merchants who plied keeled boats. The state maintained a monopoly on copper mines (*kamalakara*). The state maintained its stores and treasury via officials: *Bhandagaradhikrita* and *Koshthagarika*.

Grants: The king occasionally gave Brahmanas grants (*brahmadeya*), which consisted generally of villages, water resources, wastelands etc. (*agraharas*). Such grants conferred on the donee the right to collect revenue and the right to be free of any regular tax himself and immunity from other harassments. Sometimes, the Brahmanas were relocated from North India, with a view to establish *varnashramdharma*. Nevertheless, the existence of donees indicate the existence of a feudal class. Grants made to temples and religious institutions were called *dharmottara* and *devottara* respectively.

Land survey: The land was surveyed and classified. Arable lands (*kshetra*) were held individually or by families, whereas wastelands (*khila*) and forests were held collectively. There were lands called *bhucchidranyaya* that were left unsurveyed by the state on which no tax was levied.

Administration: The entire kingdom was divided into a hierarchy of administrative divisions. From the highest to the lowest, they were *bhukti, mandala, vishaya, pura* (towns), *agrahara* (collection of villages) and *grama* (village). These units were administered by headed by *rajanya, rajavallabha, vishayapati* etc.[1843] Some other offices were *nyayakaranika, vyavaharika, kayastha* etc., led by the *adhikara*. They dispensed judicial duties too, though the ultimate authority lay with the king. Law enforcement and punishments were made by officers called *dandika*, (magistrate) and *dandapashika* (one who executed the orders of a *dandika*).

Political history

Part of a series on the
History of Kamarupa

Ruling dynasties

- v
- t
- e[1844]

Kamarupa, first mentioned on Samudragupta's Allahabad rock pillar as a frontier kingdom, began as a subordinate but sovereign ally of the Gupta empire around present-day Guwahati in the 4th century. It finds mention along with Davaka, a kingdom to the east of Kamarupa in the Kapili river valley in present-day Nagaon district, but which is never mentioned again as an independent political entity in later historical records. Kamarupa, which was probably one among many such state structures, grew territorially to encompass the entire Brahmaputra valley and beyond. The kingdom was ruled by three major dynasties, all of which drew their lineage from the legendary aboriginal king Naraka, who is said to have established his line by defeating another aboriginal king Ghatakasura of the Danava dynasty.

Varman dynasty (c. 350 – c. 650)

Pushyavarman (350–374) established the Varman Dynasty, by fighting many enemies from within and without his kingdom; but his son Samudravarman (374–398), named after Samudragupta, was accepted as an overlord by many local rulers.[1845] Nevertheless, subsequent kings continued their attempts to stabilise and expand the kingdom.[1846] The Nagajari Khanikargaon rock inscription of 5th century found in Sarupathar in Golaghat district of Assam adduces the fact that the kingdom spread to the east very quickly. Kalyanavarman (422–446) occupied Davaka and Mahendravarman (470–494) further eastern areas. Narayanavarma (494–518) and his son Bhutivarman (518–542) offered the *ashwamedha* (horse sacrifice); and as the Nidhanpur inscription of Bhaskarvarman avers, these expansions included the region of Chandrapuri *visaya*, identified with present-day Sylhet division. Thus, the small but powerful kingdom that Pushyavarman established grew in fits and starts over many generations of kings and expanded to include adjoining possibly smaller kingdoms and parts of Bangladesh.

After the initial expansion till the beginning of Bhutivarman's reign, the kingdom came under attack from Yasodharman (525–535) of Malwa, the first major assault from the west.[1847] Though it is unclear what the effect of this invasion was on the kingdom; that Bhutivarman's grandson, Sthitavarman (566–590), enjoyed victories over the Gauda of Karnasuvarna and performed two aswamedha ceremonies suggests that the Kamarupa kingdom had recovered nearly in full. His son, Susthitavarman (590–600) came under the attack of Mahasenagupta of East Malwa. These back and forth invasions were a result of a system of alliances that pitted the Kamarupa kings (allied to the Maukharis) against the Gaur kings (allied with the East Malwa kings). Susthitavarman died as the Gaur invasion was on, and his two sons, Suprathisthitavarman and Bhaskarvarman fought against an elephant force and were captured and taken to Gaur. They were able to regain their kingdom due probably to a promise of allegiance. Suprathisthitavarman's reign is given as 595–600, a very short period, at the end of which he died without an heir.

Supratisthitavarman was succeeded by his brother, Bhaskarvarman (600–650), the most illustrious of the Varman kings who succeeded in turning his kingdom and invading the very kingdom that had taken him captive. Bhaskarvarman had become strong enough to offer his alliance with Harshavardhana just as the Thanesar king ascended the throne in 606 after the murder of his brother, the previous king, by Shashanka of Gaur. Harshavardhana finally took control over the kingless Maukhari kingdom and moved his capital to Kanauj. The alliance between Harshavardhana and Bhaskarvarman squeezed Shashanka from either side and reduced his kingdom, though it is unclear whether this alliance resulted in his complete defeat. Nevertheless, Bhaskarvarman did issue the Nidhanpur copper-plate inscription from his victory camp in the Gaur capital Karnasuvarna (present-day Murshidabad, West Bengal) to replace a grant issued earlier by Bhutivarman for a settlement in the Sylhet region of present-day Bangladesh.[1848]

Mlechchha dynasty (c. 655 – c. 900 CE)

After Bhaskaravarman's death without an heir, the kingdom passed into the hands of Salasthambha (655–670), an erstwhile local governor and a member of an aboriginal group called Mlechchha (or Mech), after a period of civil and political strife. This dynasty too drew its lineage from the Naraka dynasty, though it had no dynastic relationship with the previous Varman dynasty. The capital of this dynasty was Haruppeshvara, now identified with modern Dah Parbatiya near Tezpur. The kingdom took on feudal characteristics[1849] with political power shared between the king and second and third tier rulers called *mahasamanta* and *samanta* who enjoyed considerable autonomy.[1850] The last ruler in this line was Tyāga Singha (890–900).

Pala dynasty (c. 900 – c. 1100)

After the death of Tyāgasimha without an heir, a member of the Bhauma family, Brahmapala (900–920), was elected as king by the ruling chieftains, just as Gopala of the Pala dynasty of Bengal was elected. The original capital of this dynasty was Hadapeshvara, and was shifted to Durjaya built by Ratnapala (920–960), near modern Guwahati. The greatest of the Pala kings, Dharmapala (1035–1060) had his capital at Kamarupanagara, now identified with North Guwahati. The last Pala king was Jayapala (1075–1100). Around this time, Kamarupa was attacked and the western portion was conquered by the Pala king Ramapala.

Non-dynastic Independent Kings

The Gaur king could not hold Kamarupa for long, and Timgyadeva (1110–1126) ruled Kamarupa independently for some time. Vaidyadeva, a minister of the Gaur king Kumarapala (the son of Ramapala) began an expedition against Timgyadeva and installed himself as a ruler at Hamshkonchi in the Kamrup region. Though he maintained friendly relationships with Kumarapala, he styled himself after the Kamarupa kings issuing grants under the elephant seal of erstwhile Kamarupa kings and assuming the title of *Maharajadhiraja*.

Lunar dynasty

Not much is known about dynastic kings from this period. Nevertheless, a single inscription (1185) gives a list of four rulers that have been called the Lunar dynasty—Bhaskara, Rayarideva, Udayakarna and Vallabhadeva, dated to 1120–1200.

The period saw a waning of the Kamarupa kingdom, and in 1206 the Afghan Muhammad-i-Bakhtiyar passed through Kamarupa against Tibet which ended in disaster, the first of many Turko-Afghan invasions. The ruler of Kamarupa at this point was Prithu (d. 1228, called Britu in Tabaqat-i Nasiri), who is sometimes identified with Visvasundara, the son of Vallabhadeva of the Lunar dynasty, mentioned in the Gachtal inscription of 1232 A.D.[1851] Prithu withstood invasions (1226–27) from Ghiyasuddin Iwaj Shah of Gauda who retreated, but was killed in the subsequent invasion by Nasir ud din Mahmud in 1228. Nasir-ud-din installed a tributary king but after his death in 1229 there was much civil strife.

End of Kamarupa kingdom and the beginning of Kamata

There emerged a strong ruler named Sandhya (c. 1250 – 1270), the *Rai of Kamrup*, with his capital at Kamarupanagara in present-day North Guwahati. Malik Ikhtiyaruddin Iuzbak, a governor of Gaur for the Mameluk rulers of Delhi, attempted an invasive attack on Sandhya's domain in 1257; and Sandhya, with the help of the spring floods that same year, captured and killed the Sultan. Subsequent to this attack, Sandhya moved his capital from Kamarupanagara to Kamatapur (North Bengal) and established a new kingdom, that came to be called Kamata.[1852] At that time, western Kamarupa was being ruled by the chiefs of the Bodo people, Koch and Mech tribes. In parts of the erstwhile Kamarupa the Kachari kingdom (central Assam, South bank), Baro Bhuyans (central Assam, North bank), and the Chutiya kingdom (east) were emerging. The Ahoms, who would establish a strong and independent kingdom later, began building their state structures in the region between the Kachari and the Chutiya kingdoms in 1228.

References

 Wikimedia Commons has media related to *Kamarupa Kingdom*.

<templatestyles src="Template:Refbegin/styles.css" />

- Acharya, N. N. (1968), Asama Aitihashik Bhuchitravali *(Maps of Ancient Assam)*, Bina Library, Gauhati, Assam
- Casson, Lionel (1989). *The Periplus Maris Erythraei: Text With Introduction, Translation, and Commentary*[1853]. Princeton University Press. ISBN 0-691-04060-5.
- Choudhury, P. C. (1959), *The History of Civilization of the People of Assam to the Twelfth Century AD*, Department of History and Antiquarian Studies, Gauhati, Assam

- Dutta, Anima (2008). *Political geography of Pragjyotisa Kamarupa*[1854] (Ph.D.). Gauhati University.
- Guha, Amalendu (December 1983), "The Ahom Political System: An Enquiry into the State Formation Process in Medieval Assam (1228–1714)", *Social Scientist*, **11** (12): 3–34, doi: 10.2307/3516963[1855]
- Guha, Amalendu (1984). "Pre-Ahom Roots and the Medieval State in Assam: A Reply". *Social Scientist*. Social Scientist. **12** (6): 70–77. JSTOR 3517005[1856].
- Lahiri, Nayanjot (1991), *Pre-Ahom Assam: Studies in the Inscriptions of Assam between the Fifth and the Thirteenth Centuries AD*, Munshiram Manoharlal Publishers Pvt Ltd
- Puri, Baij Nath (1968), *Studies in Early History and Administration in Assam*, Gauhati University
- Saikia, Nagen (1997). "Medieval Assamese Literature". In Ayyappa Panicker, K. *Medieval Indian Literature: Assamese, Bengali and Dogri*[1857]. **1**. New Delhi: Sahitya Akademi. pp. 3–20.
- Sarkar, J N (1990), "Koch Bihar, Kamrup and the Mughals, 1576–1613", in Barpujari, H K, *The Comprehensive History of Assam: Mediebal Period, Political*, **II**, Guwahati: Publication Board, Assam, pp. 92–103
- Sarkar, J. N. (1992), "Chapter II The Turko-Afghan Invasions", in Barpujari, H. K., *The Comprehensive History of Assam*, **2**, Guwahati: Assam Publication Board, pp. 35–48
- Sircar, D C (1990a), "Pragjyotisha-Kamarupa", in Barpujari, H K, *The Comprehensive History of Assam*, **I**, Guwahati: Publication Board, Assam, pp. 59–78
- Sircar, D C (1990b), "Political History", in Barpujari, H K, *The Comprehensive History of Assam*, **I**, Guwahati: Publication Board, Assam, pp. 94–171
- Sharma, Mukunda Madhava (1978), *Inscriptions of Ancient Assam*, Gauhati University, Assam
- Watters, Thomas (1905). Davids, T. W. Rhys; Bushell, S. W, eds. *On Yuan Chwang's Travels in India*[1858]. **2**. London: Royal Asiatic Society. Retrieved January 29, 2013.

Mlechchha dynasty

For the ancient pejorative term for foreign people in India, see Mleccha

Kamarupa Kingdom	
Mlechchha dynasty	
650 CE–900 CE	
Capital	Hadapeshvar (present-day Tezpur)
Religion	Polytheism
Government	Monarchy
Maharajadhiraja	
• c. 650 - c. 670	Salasthamba
• c. 815 – c. 832	Harjjaravarman
• c. 890 – c. 900	Tyagasimha
Historical era	Classical India
• Established	650 CE
• Disestablished	900 CE
Preceded by	Succeeded by
Varman dynasty	Pala dynasty (Kamarupa)

The **Mlechchha dynasty**[1859] (c. 650 - 900) ruled Kamarupa from their capital at Hadapeshvar in the present-day Tezpur, Assam, after the fall of the Varman dynasty. The rulers were aboriginals (local clan, genetically non-diverse), and like all other claimed lineages, their lineage from Narakasura was constructed to accord legitimacy to their rule. According to historical records, there were twenty one rulers in this dynasty but the line is obscure and the names of some intervening rulers are not known. The Mlechchha dynasty in Kamarupa was followed by the Pala kings.

According to some historians, the remnant of the Mlechchha kingdom formed the later Kachari kingdom based in Dimapur after being driven south and east by Brahmapala of the Pala dynasty.

Rulers

Part of a series on the
History of Kamarupa

Ruling dynasties

- v
- t
- e[1860]

- Salasthamba (650-670)
- Vijaya alias Vigrahastambha
- Palaka
- Kumara
- Vajradeva
- Harshadeva alias Harshavarman (725-745)
- Balavarman II
- Salambha[1861]
- Harjjaravarman (815-832)
- Vanamalavarmadeva (832-855)
- Jayamala alias Virabahu (855-860)
- Balavarman III (860-880)
- Tyagasimha (890-900)

References

<templatestyles src="Template:Refbegin/styles.css" />

- Bhattacharjee, J. B. (1992), "The Kachari (Dimasa) state formation", in Barpujari, H. K., *The Comprehensive History of Assam*, **2**, Guwahati: Assam Publication Board, pp. 391–397

- Sharma, M M (1978), *Inscriptions of Ancient Assam*, Guwahati: Gauhati University
- Sircar, D. C. (1990), "The Mlechchha Dynasty of Salasthambha", in Barpujari, H. K., *The Comprehensive History of Assam*, **1**, Guwahati: Assam Publication Board

Pala dynasty (Kamarupa)

Kamarupa Kingdom		
900 CE–1100 CE		
Capital	Durjaya (present-day North Guwahati), Kamarupanagara (present-day North Guwahati)	
Religion	Hinduism	
Government	Monarchy	
Maharajadhiraja		
•	c. 900 - c. 920	Brahma Pala
•	c. 920 – c. 960	Ratna Pala
•	c. 960 – c. 990	Indra Pala
•	c. 990 – 1015	Go Pala
•	c. 1015 – c. 1035	Harsha Pala
•	c. 1035 – c. 1060	Dharma Pala
•	c. 1075 – c. 1100	Jaya Pala
Historical era	Classical India	
•	Established	900 CE
•	Disestablished	1100 CE
Preceded by		Succeeded by
Mlechchha dynasty		Kachari kingdom
		Chutiya kingdom
		Khen dynasty
		Ahom dynasty

Part of a series on the
History of Kamarupa

Ruling dynasties

- v
- t
- e¹⁸⁶²

The **Pala dynasty** of Kamarupa kingdom ruled from 900. Like the Pala dynasty of Bengal, the first ruler in this dynasty was elected, which probably explains the name of this dynasty "Pala". But unlike the Palas of Bengal, who were Buddhists, the Palas of Kamarupa were Hindus. The Hindu orthodoxy drew their lineage from the earlier Varman dynasty and thus ultimately from Narakasura.

The Pala dynasty came to an end when Kamarupa was invaded by the Gaur king Ramapala (c. 1072-1126). Timgyadeva was made the governor of Kamarupa who ruled between 1110 and 1126. Timgyadeva threw off the yoke of the Pala king and ruled independently for some years when he was attacked and replaced by Vaidyadeva under Ramapala's son Kumarapala. Vaidyadeva, who ruled between 1126 and 1140, declared independence within four years of his rule after the death of Kumarapala. Both Timgyadeva and Vaidyadeva issued grants in the style of the Kamarupa kings (three copper plates attached to the seal of the Kamarupa kings by a ring).

Rulers

- Brahma Pala (900-920)
- Ratna Pala (920-960)
- Indra Pala (960-990)

- Go Pala (990-1015)
- Harsha Pala (1015-1035)
- Dharma Pala (1035-1060)
- Jaya Pala (1075-1100).

References

- Sircar, D. C. *The Bhauma-Naraka or the Pala Dynasty of Brahmapala*, The Comprehensive History of Assam, ed H. K. Barpujari, Guwahati, 1990.

Twipra Kingdom

Kingdom of Tripura	
Part of History of Tripura	
Kings of Tripura	
Dhanya Manikya	1463-1515
Dharma Manikya II	1714-1733
Vijay Manikya II	1743-1760
Krishna Manikya	1760-1761
Rajdhar Manikya	1783-1804
Ramgana Manikya	1804-1809
Durga Manikya	1809-1813
Kashi Chandra	1826-1830
Krishna Kishore	1830-1849
Ishan Chandra	1849-1862
Bir Chandra	1862-1896
Radha Kishore	1896-1909
Birendra Kishore	1909-1923
Bir Bikram Kishore	1923–1947
Kirit Bikram Kishore	1947-1949
Kirit Pradyot Deb Barman	1978-
Tripura monarchy data	
Manikya dynasty (Royal family)	
Agartala (Capital of the kingdom)	
Ujjayanta Palace (Royal residence)	

Neermahal (Royal residence)
Rajmala (Royal chronicle)
Tripura Buranji (Chronicle)
• v • t • e¹⁸⁶³

Twipra Kingdom (Sanskrit: **Tripura**, Anglicized: **Tippera**) was one of the largest historical kingdoms of the Twipra people in the North-east India.

The Twipra Kingdom was established around the confluence of the Brahmaputra river (*Twima*Wikipedia:Please clarify) with the Meghna and Surma rivers in today's Central Bangladesh area. The capital was called Khorongma (Kholongma) and was along the Meghna river in the Sylhet Division of present-day Bangladesh.

Geography

The present political areas which were part of the Tipra Kingdom are:

- Sylhet, Dhaka and Chittagong Divisions of Bangladesh
- Cachar Valley of Assam
- Mizoram and Tripura states of India

The Tipra Kingdom in all its various ages comprised the areas with the borders:

1. Khasi Hills in the North
2. Manipur Hills in the North-East
3. Arakan Hills of Burma in the East
4. The Bay of Bengal to the South
5. The Brahmaputra river to the West

History

Early history

A list of legendary Tripuri kings is given in the Rajmala chronicle, a 15th-century chronicle in Bengali verse written by the court pandits of Dharma Manikya (r. 1431). The chronicle traces the king's ancestry to the mythological Lunar Dynasty. In the 8th century, the Kingdom shifted its capital eastwards along the Surma river in Sylhet near present Kailasahar town of North Tripura.Wikipedia:Citation needed

The religion of the Tipra had 14 deities known as "Chibrwi Mwtai" (in Kokborok language) and is still preserved in the Chibrwi Mwtai nok in Old Agartala, which is maintained by the Tipra priests known as Chontai/Ochai's, who oversee the festivals of the Kharchi and Ker according to traditions. It was similar to the Chinese folk religions.

Islamic Era

The earliest historical records concerning the Twipra kingdom concern the 13th century, when it first came under pressure from the Islamic conquests in India. This is also the time of origin of the Manikya Dynasty, started when Ratna Fa adopted the title *Manikya*, which was held by all Kings of Tripura until the death of Bir Bikram Kishore Manikya in 1947. Ratna Fa shifted the capital to Rangamati on the banks of the river Gumti, now in South Tripura.

Twipra was first overrun by the Muslims under Tughril in 1279, but it managed to maintain its independence during the 14th through 19th centuries, until the British arrived. Tripura was one of the states that pushed back successive waves of invasions from Turks, Ethipian Muslims, Afghans, and Mughals. On many occasions, Tripurans also pushed back Burmese and Arakanese invasions from the East. The Hill territories of Tripura, comprising present day Tripura state, Sylhet hills of Assam state, Cachar hills of Assam state, Mizoram state, and Chittagong Hill Tracts, remained free and independent before the British takeover. The plains of Tripura, however, fell to the attacks from Mughals. The plains territories comprise today's South East Dhaka and Comilla areas. While the plains areas were thus Islamized, the Hills of Tripura served as a continuous bulwark against penetration to the East. The Tripura Hill Kings were major sponsors of Hindu traditions and customs. In the modern age they are remembered as one of the longest and most stable dynasties from the Indian East.

Dhanya Manikya (r. 1463 to 1515) expanded Twipra's territorial domain well into Eastern Bengal. Rangamati was renamed Udaipur after Udai Manikya. The kingdom flourished in the 16th and 17th centuries, Kings such as Govinda Manikya putting up a defense against the pressure of the Muslim kingdoms to the west, until the final conquest of the plains areas by a renegade Tripuri prince backed by Mughal governors of Eastern Bengal plains. After this, plains Twipra was a Mughal client kingdom, with the Mughal rulers taking influence on the appointment of its kings.However the Mughals could never penetrate the Hill territories to the East.The plains,on the other hand were Islamized through conversion of the Bengali people living there.[*citation not found*]

British India

In British India, the kings retained an estate in British India, known as Tippera district or Chakla Roshnabad (now the greater Comilla region of Bangladesh), in addition to the independent area known as *Hill Tippera*, the present-day state of Tripura. Bir Chandra Manikya (1862–1896) modelled his administration on the pattern of British India, and enacted reforms including the formation of Agartala Municipal Corporation. The last king was Kirit Bikram Kishore, son of Bir Bikram Kishore Debbarma, who ruled for two years, 1947-1949. In 1949, Tripura became part of the Republic of India. The Tripuri "heir apparent" is Kirit Pradyot Deb Barma (born 1978), the son of the last king, who is sometimes given the courtesy title of "Maharaja".

References

- *Tripura Buranji* 17th Century Ahom Chronicle.
- *Progressive Tripura*, 1930
- *Rajmala*, royal chronicle of Tripura Kings.
- Hill Tippera - History[1864] *The Imperial Gazetteer of India*, 1909, v. 13, p. 118.

External links

- Information on the kingdom of Tripura at the University of Queensland[1865]
- Tripura kingdom at Royal ark[1866]
- About Tippera District[1867] Present day Comilla District of Bangladesh

The Deccan plateau and South

Sangam period

Sangam period (Tamil: சங்ககாலம், *Sangakālam* ?) is the period of history of ancient Tamil Nadu and Kerala (known as Tamilakam) spanning from c. 3rd century BC to c. 3rd century AD. It is named after the famous Sangam academies of poets and scholars centered in the city of Madurai.

In Old Tamil language, the term Tamilakam (*Tamiḻakam* தமிழகம், *Purananuru* 168. 18) referred to the whole of the ancient Tamil-speaking area, corresponding roughly to the area known as southern India today, consisting of the territories of the present-day Indian states of Tamil Nadu, Kerala, parts of Andhra Pradesh, parts of Karnataka and northern Sri Lanka also known as Eelam.[1868]

History

According to Tamil legends, there were three Sangam periods, namely Head Sangam, Middle Sangam and Last Sangam period. Historians use the term Sangam period to refer the last of these, with the first two being legendary. So it is also called **Last Sangam period** (Tamil: கடைச்சங்க பருவம், *Kaṭaissanka paruvam* ?), or **Third Sangam period** (Tamil: மூன்றாம் சங்க பருவம், *Mūnṟām sanka paruvam* ?). The Sangam literature is thought to have been produced in three Sangam academies of each period. The evidence on the early history of the Tamil kingdoms consists of the epigraphs of the region, the Sangam literature, and archaeological data.

The period between 600 BC to AD 200, Tamilakam was ruled by the three Tamil dynasties of Pandya, Chola and Chera, and a few independent chieftains, the Velir.

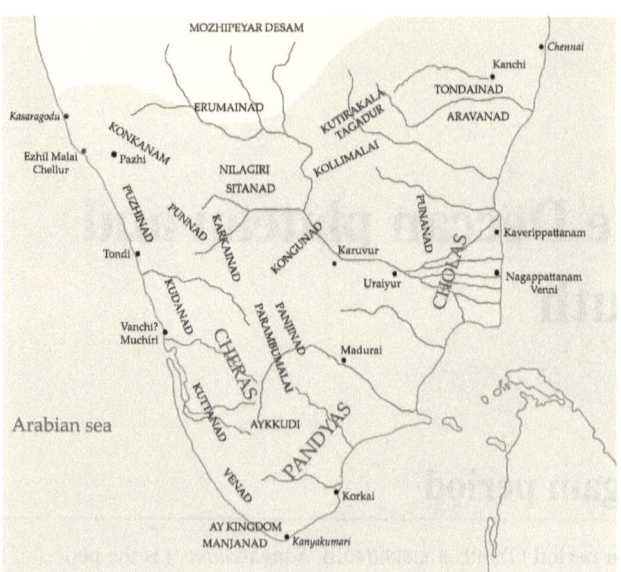

Figure 396: *Tamilakam, located in the tip of South India during the Sangam Period, ruled by Chera dynasty, Chola dynasty and the Pandyan dynasty.*

Literary sources

There is a wealth of sources detailing the history, socio-political environment and cultural practices of ancient Tamilakam, including volumes of literature and epigraphy.

Tamilakam's history is split into three periods; prehistoric, classical (see Sangam period) and medieval. A vast array of literary, epigraphical and inscribed sources from around the world provide insight into the socio-political and cultural occurrences in the Tamil region. The ancient Tamil literature consists of the grammatical work Tolkappiyam, the anthology of ten mid-length books collection Pathupattu, the eight anthologies of poetic work Ettuthogai, the eighteen minor works Patiṉeṇkīḻkaṇakku; and there are The Five Great Epics of Tamil Literature composed in classical Tamil language — *Manimegalai, Cīvaka Cintāmaṇi, Silappadikaram, Valayapathi* and *Kundalakesi* as well as five lesser Tamil epics, *Ainchirukappiyangal*, which are *Neelakesi, Naga kumara kaviyam, Udhyana kumara Kaviyam, Yasodhara Kaviyam* and *Soolamani*.

Figure 397: *Ilango Adigal is the author of Silappatikaram, one of the five great epics of Tamil literature.*

Culture

Religion

The religion of the ancient Tamils closely follow roots of nature worship and some elements of it can also be found in Tamil Shaiva Siddhanta traditions. In the ancient Sangam literature, Sivan was the supreme God, and Murugan was the one celebrated by the masses; both of them were sung as deified Tamil poets ascending the Koodal academy. The Tamil landscape was classified into five categories, *thinais*, based on the mood, the season and the land. *Tolkappiyam*, one of the oldest grammatical works in Tamil mentions that each of these *thinai* had an associated deity such as Kottravai (Mother goddess i.e. Kali) and Sevvael (Murugan) in Kurinji (the hills), Thirumal (Maayon) in Mullai (the forests), Vendhan (Wanji-ko or Seyyon i.e. Indra) in Marutham (the plains i.e. Vayu), and Kadaloan (Varuna) in the Neithal (the coasts and the seas). Other ancient works refer to Maayon (Maal) and Vaali.

The most popular deity was Murugan, who has from a very early date been identified with Karthikeya, the son of Siva. Kannagi, the heroine of the *Silappatikaram*, was worshiped as Pathini (பத்தினி) by many Tamilians, particularly in Sri Lanka. There were also many temples and devotees of Thirumal, Siva, Ganapathi, and the other common Hindu deities.

Calendar

The ancient Tamil calendar was based on the sidereal year similar to the ancient Hindu solar calendar, except that months were from solar calculations, and originally there was no 60-year cycle as seen in Sanskrit calendar. The year was made up of twelve months and every two months constituted a season. With the popularity of Mazhai vizhavu, traditionally commencement of Tamil year was clubbed on April 14, deviating from the astronomical date of *vadavazhi vizhavu*.

Festivals

- *Pongal* (பொங்கல்) the festival of harvest and spring, thanking Lord **El** (the sun), comes on January 14/15 (*Thai 1*).
- *Peru Vaenil Kadavizha*, the festival for wishing quick and easy passage of the mid-summer months, on the day when the Sun or El stands directly above the head at noon (the start of Agni Natchaththiram) at the southern tip of ancient Tamil land. This day comes on April 14/15 (*Chithirai 1*).
- *Mazhai Vizhavu*, aka *Indhira Vizha*, the festival for want of rain, celebrated for one full month starting from the full moon in *Ootrai* (later name-Cittirai) சித்திரை and completed on the full moon in *Puyaazhi* (Vaikaasi) (which coincides with Buddhapurnima). It is epitomised in the epic Cilapatikaram in detail.
- *Puyaazhi (Vaikaasi) visaagam* and *Thai poosam*, தைப்பூசம் the festivals of Tamil God [Muruga]'s birth and accession to the *Thirupparankundram Koodal* Academy, coming on the day before the full moons of *Puyaazhi* and *Thai* respectively.
- *Soornavai Vizha*, the slaying of legendary Kadamba Asura king Surabadma, by Lord [Muruga], comes on the sixth day after new moon in *Itrai* (Kaarthigai). It is sung about in *Thirumurugatrupadai* and *Purananuru* anthology.
- *Vaadai Vizha* or *Vadavazhi Vizha*, the festival of welcoming the Lord Surya back to home, as He turns northward, celebrated on December 21/22 (Winter Solstice) (the sixth day of *Panmizh*[Maargazhi]). It is sung about in *Akanauru* anthology.
- *Semmeen Ezhumin Vizhavu (Aathi-Iṟai Darisanam) or Aruthra Darishanam*, the occasion of Lord *Siva* coming down from the *ThiruCitrambalam* திருச்சிற்றம்பலம் and taking a look at the *Vaigarai Thiru Aathirai* star in the early morning on the day before the full moon in *Panmizh*. Aathi Irai min means *the star of the God (Siva) on the Bull (Nandi)*.
- *Thiruonam or Onam*, the birthday of Mayon (Lord Vishnu), thiruonam is a group of stars which are bright together and resemble like an eagle.

Lord Vishnu's mount is Garuda (eagle), so the day was considered as the birthday of Lord Vishnu by the people of Pandya kingdom and was celebrated for 10 days. That was mentioned in '[Maduraikanji]' one of the 'Pathupaatu' book, 'Thirupallandu' by Periyazhwar and from the song of Thirugnanasambandhar in Thevaram. On this day, Keralites celebrate Onam as the state's harvest festival. Onam is observed for 10 days, ending in Thiruvonam (or Thirounam).

Arts

Musicians, stage artists, and performers entertained the kings, the nobility, the rich and the general population. Groups of performers included:

- *Thudian*, players of the *thuda*, a small percussion instrument
- *Paraiyan*, who beat *maylam* (drums) and performed *kooththu*, a stage drama in dance form, as well as proclaiming the king's announcements
- *Muzhavan*, who blew into a *muzhavu*, a wind instrument, with the army indicating the start and end of the day and battlefield victories. They also performed in *kooththu* alongside other artists.
- *Kadamban* who beat a large bass-like drum, the *kadamparai*, and blew a long bamboo, *kuzhal*, the *cerioothuthi* (similar to the present *naagasuram*).
- *PaaNan*, who sang songs in all *pann* tunes (tunes that are specific for each landscape) and were masters of the *yaazh*, a stringed instrument with a wide frequency range.

Together with the poets (*pulavar*) and the academic scholars (*saandror*), these people of talent appeared to originate from all walks of life, irrespective of their native profession.

People

The people were divided into five different clans ("kudes") based on their profession. They were:

- Mallars: the farmers.
- Malavars: the hill people who gather hill products, and the traders.
- Nagars: people in charge of border security, who guarded the city walls and distant fortresses.
- Kadambars: people who thrive in forests.
- Thiraiyars: the seafarers.
- maravars : the warriors

Figure 398: *Political map of South India, 210 B.C.E.*

All the five kudes constituted a typical settlement, which was called an "uru". Later each clan spread across the land, formed individual settlements of their own and concentrated into towns, cities, and countries. Thus the Mallars settled in Tamil Nadu and Sri Lanka, while the Malavars came to live in Kerala, western Tamil Nadu, eastern Andhra Pradesh and southern Sri Lanka. The Nagars inhabited southern and eastern Tamil Nadu, and northern Sri Lanka, while the Kadambars settled in central Tamil Nadu first and later moved to western Karnataka. The Thiraiyars inhabited throughout the coastal regions. Later various subsects were formed based on more specific professions in each of the five landscapes (Kurinji, Mullai, Marutam, Neithal and Palai).

- Poruppas (the soldiers), Verpans (the leaders of the tribe or weapon-ists), Silambans (the masters of martial arts or the arts of fighting), Kuravar (the hunters and the gatherers, the people of foothills) and Kanavars (the people of the mountainous forests) in Kurinji.
- Kurumporai Nadan-kizhaththis (the landlords of the small towns amidst the forests in the valleys), Thonral-manaivi (the ministers and other noble couples), Idaiyars (the milkmaids and their families), Aiyars (the cattle-rearers) in Mullai.
- Mallar or Pallar (the farmers),Maravars (the warriors) Vendans (Chera, Chola and Pandya kings were called as "Vendans"), Urans (small landlords), Magizhnans (successful small scale farmers), Uzhavars (the farm

workers), Kadaiyars (the merchants) in Marutham.[1869]
- Saerppans (the seafood vendors and traders), Pulampans (the vegetarians who thrive on coconut and palm products), Parathars or Paravas (people who lived near the seas-the rulers, sea warriors, merchants and the pirates), Nulaiyars (the wealthy people who both do fishing and grow palm farms) and Alavars (the salt cultivators) in Neithal.
- Palai symbolises the dry arid lands and scorching deserts of Tamil country where nothing except for the hardy and war-like perseverant tribes native to those lands can survive. It is also the only land among all five lands of the Sangam landscape that a female God, fierce mother goddess, Kotravai was worshipped which is synonymous with the common belief that all the other lands of Tamil country emerged from these original dry arid lands. The tribes existed in these lands were the ruthless and fearsome Maravars (Noble Warriors, Hunters and Bandits) and Eyinars (Warriors and Bandits). They actively seek out for wars, knowledge, invade far and distant lands and engage in banditry.
- people were known on the basis of their occupation they followed such as artisans, merchants etc.
- warriors occupied a special position in society and memorial stones called "Nadukan" were raised in honour of those who died in fighting and they were worshiped.[1870]

References

Bibliography

 Wikimedia Commons has media related to *Sangam period*.

- A. L. Basham, *The Wonder that was India*, Picador (1995) ISBN 0-330-43909-X
- P. T. Srinivasa Iyengar, *History of the Tamils from the earliest times to 600 AD*[1871], Madras, 1929; Chennai, Asian Educational Svcs. (2001) ISBN 81-206-0145-9.
- "History of Mallars"[1872]

Chera dynasty

Chera	
Monarchy	
c. 3rd century BCE–12th century CE	
Capital	• Vanchi • Mahodayapuram • Kollam • Karuvur
Languages	Tamil Malayalam
Political structure	Monarchy
History	
• Established	c. 3rd century BCE
• Disestablished	12th century CE
Succeeded by	
Kingdom of Travancore	
Kingdom of Cochin	
Venad	
Today part of	India

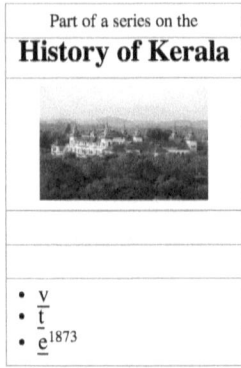

Part of a series on the
History of Kerala

- v
- t
- e[1873]

Part of a series on
History of Tamil Nadu

- v
- t
- e[1874]

The **Cheras** were a line of rulers in present-day state of Tamil Nadu and Kerala in southern India. Together with the Cholas and the Pandyas, they were also known as one of the three major political powers of ancient Tamilakam ("the abode of the Tamils") in the early centuries of the Christian Era.

The age and antiquity of the Cheras is difficult to establish.[1875] The Cheras of Karur-Vanchi (near Trichinopoly, in modern-day central Tamil Nadu) can be dated as far back as c. 3rd century BCE. The Kongu Cheras controlled central Tamil Nadu in the middle ages. The Chera Perumals of Makotai (modern Cranganore, Kerala), formerly known in literature as the Kulasekharas, were in power between c. 8th and 12th century in Kerala. The exact nature of the relation between the three lines of rulers is unclear.[1876]

Inscriptions and traveller's accounts suggest that the Cheras were existing during the 4th century BCE. Most of their history is reconstructed from a body of literature known as the Sangam literature written in Old Tamil around the 3rd century CE. Sangam literature records the names of a long line of Chera kings, princes, and the court poets who extolled them. The internal chronology of this literature is still far from settled and a connected account of the history of the period is an area of active research. Uthiyan Cheralathan, Nedum Cheralathan and Senguttuvan are some of the rulers referred to in the Sangam poems. Senguttuvan, the most celebrated of the Chera kings, is famous for the legends surrounding Kannagi, the heroine of the epic *Silapathikaram*.WP:NOTRS

The exact location of the Chera homeland has been subject to some speculation. The Chera capital has been called, 'Vanchi' and 'Karur' in several works.

This has led to several theories identifying the Chera capital in places named Karur in both Kerala and Tamil Nadu. However, it is fairly clear that the capital was near the famous port known as Muziris, now identified to be near modern-day Kodungallur. Pliny refers to Muziris as the Chera capital, while the author of the Periplus identifies the capital to be a couple of miles away from the mouth of the river at Muziris. Ptolemy who identifies the capital as 'Karoura' gives a geographical location that is very close to Muziris as well. The capital of the Cheras and the port of Muziris were very close and almost indistinguishable.[1877]

It is understood that the early Cheras started their imperial expansion from the Kuttanad region. Sangam era notion Kuttanad included not only present day Kuttanad Taluk but also a vast area around Vembanad lake which comprises present day districts of Alappuzha, Ernakulam and Kottayam. Various other regions such as Tyndis and Kongunad have been gained or lost at various times during the continuous conflicts with the neighbouring kingdoms.[1877] The Cheras also seem to have fought battles with other neighbouring dynasties such as the Pallavas, the Rashtrakutas, the Kadambas and even with the Yavanas (the Greeks) on the South Indian coast. After the end of the Sangam era, around the 5th century CE, there seems to be a period where the Cheras' power declined and is, in many ways, a dark period in Chera history.

The Chera kingdom owed its importance to trade with the Middle East, North Africa, Greece, Rome and China. Its geographical advantages, like the navigability of the rivers connecting the Ghat mountains with the Arabian sea, the favourable Monsoon winds which carried sailing ships directly from the Arabian coast to Chera kingdom as well as the abundance of exotic spices combined to make the Chera empire a major power in foreign trade.[1878]WP:NOTRS

The Later Cheras (the Kulasekharas) ruled from Mahodayapuram (now Kodungallur) on the banks of River Periyar and fought numerous wars with their powerful neighbours such as the Cholas and Rashtrakutas. During these battles, they were forced to moved their capital further south to Quilon (now Kollam) and this formed the beginning of the Venad kingdom.[1879] The rulers of Venad, based out of the port of Quilon in southern Kerala, traced their ancestry to the Later Cheras. Ravi Varma Kulasekhara, their most ambitious ruler, set out to expand his kingdom by annexing the ruins of the other southern kingdoms.[1880]

Etymology

Early writers on the region have used the words *Kerala* and *Chera* almost synonymously and their etymology is still a matter of considerable speculation. One approach proposes that the word *Chera* is derived from *Cheral*, a corruption of *Charal* meaning "declivity of a mountain" in Tamil, suggesting a connection with the mountainous geography of Kerala. Another links the words to *Kera*, a root word for the coconut, one of the primary products of the land. Another theory argues that the *Keralam* and *Cheralam* are derived from *cher* (sand) and *alam* (region), literally meaning, "the slushy land".[1881]</ref> This compound could also be interpreted to mean "the land which was added on" (to the existing mountainous or hilly country) as *Cher* or *Chernta* means "added".[1882]</ref>

In other sources, the Cheras are referred to by various names. The Cheras are referred as *Kedalaputa* ("Kerala Putra") in the Ashoka's edicts (3rd century BCE).[1883] While Pliny and Ptolemy refer to the Cheras as *Calobotras*, the Graeco-Roman trade map *Periplus Maris Erythraei* refers to the Cheras as *Keprobotras*.[1884]

The term *Ceralamdivu* or *Ceran tivu* and its cognates, meaning the "island of the Ceran kings", is a Classical Tamil name of Sri Lanka that takes root from the term Chera, from which the dynasty name is derived.[1885]

History

Early Cheras

The earliest traveller's accounts referring to the Cheras are by the Greek ambassador Megasthenes (4th century BCE), Pliny in the 1st century CE, in the Periplus of the 1st century CE, and by Ptolemy in the 2nd century CE. While Pliny names the ruler of the land as *Calobotras*, the Periplus names him *Keprobotras*.[1886]

One of the earliest Sanskrit works which refers to Kerala is probably the Aitareya Aranyaka in which the *Cherapadah* are noted as one of the three peoples who did not follow some ancient injunctions. There are also brief references by Katyayana (4th century BCE), Edicts of Ashoka (2nd century BCE), Patanjali (2nd century BCE) and Kautilya (c. 4th century BCE) though Pāṇini (5th century BCE) does not mention the land. However, it is the Tamil works collectively known as the Sangam literature that form the most important sources for a more detailed history of the Cheras and ancient Kerala. These works roughly span the period 100 CE to 300 CE. Among them, the most important sources for the Cheras are the *Pattittupattu*, the *Agananuru*, the *Purananuru* and the *Silappatikaram*.[1887]

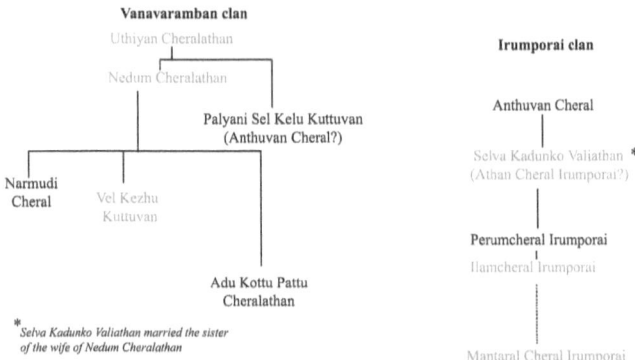

Figure 399: *Family tree of the kings of the Chera dynasty based on Sangam literature. The monarchs ruled in the first two centuries of the Common Era.*

In Sangam literature

While there are several mentions in literary works of Sanskrit and Greek, the primary literary sources giving detailed accounts of the early Chera Kings are the anthologies of Sangam literature, created between c. 1st and the 4th centuries CE.[1888,1889] They are rich in descriptions about a number of Chera kings and princes, along with the poets who extolled them. However, these are not worked into connected history and settled chronology so far. A chronological device, known as Gajabahu synchronism, is used by historians to help date early Tamil history. Despite its dependency on numerous conjectures, Gajabahu synchronism has wide acceptance among modern scholars and is considered as the *sheet anchor* for the purpose of dating ancient Tamil literature.[1890] The method depends on an event depicted in *Silappatikaram*, which describes the visit of *Kayavaku*, the king of Ilankai (Sri Lanka), in the Chera kingdom during the reign of the Chera king, Senguttuvan. The Gajabahu method considers this *Kayavaku* as Gajabahu, who according *Mahavamsa*, a historical poem written in Pali language on the kings of Sri Lanka, lived in the latter half of the 2nd century CE. This, in turn, has been used to fix the period Senguttuvan, who ruled his kingdom for 55 years (according to the *Pathitrupathu*), in the 2nd century CE.[1891]

Among the Sangam works, the most important sources for the Cheras are the Pathitrupathu, the Agananuru, the Purananuru and the Silappatikaram. The *Pathitrupathu*, the fourth book in the *Ettuthokai* anthology of Sangam poems, mentions a number of rulers and heirs-apparent of the Chera dynasty. Each ruler is praised in ten songs sung by the court poet.Wikipedia:Identifying reliable sources

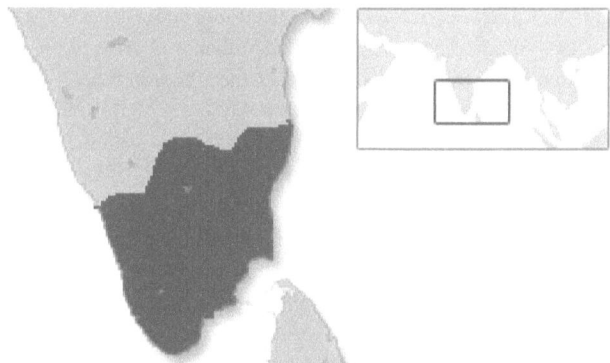

Figure 400: *Kalabhras controlled large parts of southern India in the 5th and 6th centuries CE*

Decline of early Cheras

The Chera empire enters a period of "historical darkness" in the 6th, 7th and 8th centuries. Little is known for certain about the Cheras during this period. Kerala seems to have been affected by the Kalabhra upheaval in the 5th and 6th centuries CE. Though there is no authentic information about them, some Buddhist records mention that the Kalabhra ruler Achuta Vikkanta managed to extend his influence over a large part of Southern India. Tradition tells that he kept the Chera, Chola and Pandya rulers in his confinement. The Kalabhras were defeated around the 6th century by the rise of the Chalukyas, Pallavas and Pandyas.[1876]

The main sources of knowledge of the period are through the inscriptions of other South Indian kingdoms such as the Chalukyas, Pallavas, Pandyas and the Rashtrakutas. They all claim to have overrun Kerala or at least parts of it. The Chalukyas of Badami must have conducted temporary conquests of parts of North Kerala. An inscription of Pulakeshin I claims that he conquered the Chera ruler. A number of other inscriptions mentions their victories over the kings of Chera kingdom and Ezhil Malai rulers. Pulakeshin II (610–642) is also said to have conquered Chera, Pandya and Chola kingdoms. Soon the three rulers made an alliance and marched against the Chalukyas. But the Chalukyas defeated the confederation. Vinayaditya also claims to have subjugated the Chera king and made him pay tribute to the Chalukyas. King Vikramaditya II (734-745) also claims to have defeated the Cheras. An inscription to this effect was found in Adur (Kasargod district of Kerala), perhaps testifying to their dominance in the region. Their influence came to an end in 755 CE with the rise of the Rashtrakutas.[1892]

Around the same period, the Pallavas also claim conquest over the Chera kingdoms. King Simhavishnu (560-580) and Mahendra Varman (580–630) are the first Pallava rulers to claim victories over the Chera kingdom. Narasimhavarman (630–668) also claims victories over the Cheras and the Pandya ruler Sendan (654–670). King Nandivarman II of the Pallavas allied with the Cheras in a fight against the Pandya king Varaguna I. Among the other dynasties, Sendan also claims a victory over Kerala. The Rashtrakutas also claimed control over Cheras. Dantidurga (752–756) and Govinda III (792–814) are said to have had victories over the Kerala kings. In this manner, the post-Sangam era was in many ways a 'dark period' in Kerala history where it was invaded by outside powers in rapid succession. However, the claims of most of these dynasties to have established sway over Kerala at this time is not supported by any tangible evidence with the exception of the Pandyas.[1893]

The Pandyan kingdom established control over Chera territories by repeated attacks on the Ays who were located on the southern border of the Cheras. The Ay kingdom, long functioned as an effective buffer state between the Chera and Pandya kingdoms. But with the decline of the Ays, the Chera kingdoms were exposed to direct conflict with the Pandyas, and later with the Cholas.[1894] The Pandyas conquered the Ays and a made it a tributary state. As late as 788 CE, the Pandyas under Maranjadayan or Jatilavarman Parantaka invaded the Ay kingdom and captured the port city of Vizhinjam. However, the Ays did not seem to have submitted to the Pandyas easily, as the Ay king Karunandan, appears to have been still fighting after a decade.[1895] This seems to offer proof that conquered lands in South India, such as Vizhinjam in this case, were not settled permanently but used to assert their independence at the first available opportunity.[1896] Shortly thereafter, the Ay kingdom appears to have merged with Venad kingdom and there are almost no mentions of them.[1897]

Later Cheras

After a period of relative obscurity between the 6th to 8th centuries CE, Chera power was revived under Kulasekhara Varman who ruled from 800 to 820 CE. The illustrious line of kings who followed were called the **Kulasekharas** and are also known as the *Second Cheras*. They ruled large parts of Kerala between 800 and 1102 CE. They ruled from their capital Mahodayapuram (also called Makotai or Mahodayapattanam), near the present day Kodungalloor, Kerala.[1899] The Kulasekhara kings were also known as **Perumals** (Kulasekhara Perumals or Cheraman Perumals).[1900] Wikipedia:Identifying reliable sources

Conflicts and Aftermath

The second part of the Kulasekhara empire in the 10th and 11th centuries was characterised by a series of great conflicts with the Cholas in what became known as the "Hundred Years War". It is believed that Raja Raja Chola

Chera dynasty 617

Figure 401: *The Chera kingdom and chieftaincies, c. 11th century.*[1898]

(985–1016 CE) wanted to recapture some territory which had asserted independence with the rest of Tamizhakam.[1901] In c. 989, he mounted a probing attack which reached Kandalur Salai before returning. In 999, he was able to inflict a major defeat on the Cheras, defeating Chera strongholds in Kandalur and Vizhinjam. By the end of his reign, much of South Travancore came under Chola control. The wars continued into the reign of Rajendra Chola (1012–1044 CE) who also won battles at Kandalur and Vizhinjam in 1019 which had been taken back by the Cheras in the interim. The capital of the Kulasekharas, Mahodayapuram was sacked in a decisive battle when the Chola armies attacked via the Palakkad gap and this battle led to the deaths of several important chieftains and generals.[1902] However, the Cheras once again regrouped and by 1070 CE, Chera territories were back under their control. Kulottunga Chola I (1070–1122) CE had to fight once again to gain Kandalur and Vizhinjam and is known to have proceeded further north and destroyed Kollam in 1096 CE. This defeat led to a major reorganisation and mobilisation of the Chera forces under the rule of Rama Varma Kulasekhara who rallied them under his banner with the primary objective of throwing out the Chola imperialists. A large body of fighters called the *Chavers* was raised who were styled as suicide squads. In c. 1100, the Chavers played a decisive part in the defeat of Kulottunga Chola I, inflicting heavy casualties on the Cholas and forcing them to retreat to Kottar. The Cholas were never able to conquer the Chera regions again and withdrew from the region.[1903]

After the sack of Mahodayapuram and Kollam, the Chera king Rama Varma Kulasekhara moved a majority of the Chera forces further south to Kollam in order to ensure the continued protection of the southern regions of Kerala. A new capital was set up at Kollam and was called *Ten Vanchi* (literally the new Vanchi). The Cheras under Rama Varma Kulasekhara then seems to have merged with the existing house of Venad and this forms the next phase of the dynasty, in the form of the Venad empire. The subsequent kings of Venad take the title of "Kulasekhara" or "Kulasekhara Perumal" that used to be assumed by the Chera kings of Mahodayapuram.[1904]

The prolonged series of wars with the Cholas had led to a significant weakening of the Chera ruler's control over various parts of Kerala. Some of the *naduvazhis* (local cheftians) tried to take advantage and assert their independence. The movement of the capital of the later Cheras further south to Kollam meant that the northern houses asserted their independence. Northern kingdoms such as Polanad (Kozhikode area), Kolathunad (North Malabar region) formed semi-independent kingdoms from their existing royal houses. Kochi, comprising the area of the old Chera capital of Mahodayapuram, formed its own *Swaroopam* (state) later in the 14th century CE.[1905]

Government

Chera dynasty
Early Cheras
• Uthiyan Cheralathan • Nedum Cheralathan • Selva Kadumko Valiathan • Senguttuvan Chera • Illam Cheral Irumporai • Mantaran Cheral
Later Cheras

Kulashekhara Varma	800–820
Rajashekhara Varma	820–844
Sthanu Ravi Varma	844–885
Rama Varma Kulashekhara	885–917
Goda Ravi Varma	917–944
Indu Kotha Varma	944–962
Bhaskara Ravi Varma I	962–1019
Bhaskara Ravi Varma II	1019–1021
Vira Kerala	1021–1028
Rajasimha	1028–1043
Bhaskara Ravi Varma III	1043–1082
Ravi Rama Varma	1082–1090
Rama Varma Kulashekhara	1090–1102

- v
- t
- e[1906]

Monarchy was the most important political institution of the Chera kingdom. There was a high degree of pomp and pageantry associated with the person of the king. The king wore a gold crown studded with precious stones. The king was an autocrat, but his powers were limited by the counsel of ministers and scholars. The king held daily *durbar* to hear the problems of the common men and to redress them on the spot. The royal queen had a very important and privileged status and she took her seat by the side of the king in all religious ceremonies.[1907]

Another important institution was the *manram* which functioned in each village of the Chera kingdom. Its meetings were usually held by the village elders under a banyan tree, and helped in the local settlement disputes. The manrams were the venues for the village festivals as well.[1908] In the course of the imperial expansion of the Cheras, the members of the royal family set up residence at several places of the kingdom. They followed the collateral system of succession according to which the eldest member of the family, wherever he lived, ascended the throne. Junior princes and heir-apparents (crown princes) helped the ruling king in the administration.[1909]

Revenue was accrued through a combination of taxes on land and trade. It is unclear as to the share of the agricultural produce that was accrued by the state. Taxes were imposed on internal trade as well articles for exports and imports and this brought in a lot of revenue. Smuggling was heavily cracked down upon and elaborate arrangements were made for security in the kingdom. Roads were patrolled at night by watchmen with torches. The Cheras had a well-equipped army which consisted of infantry, cavalry, elephants and chariots. They were also in possession of an impressive navy fleet which was regarded as one of the most powerful in the Sangam era.[1907] The Chera soldiers made

Figure 402: *A depiction of Cheraman Perumal, from "A History of Travancore from the Earliest Times" (1878) by Peshkar. Shankhunni Menon*

offering to the war goddess Kottavai before any military operation. It was traditional when the Chera rulers were victorious in a battle to wear anklets made out of the crowns of the defeated rulers.[1910]

Rulers

Chera rulers according to the Sangam poems

Utiyan Cheralathan - The first of the known rulers of the Chera entity, he was also known as "Vanavaramban" Perumchettutiyan Cheralathan. His capital was at Kuzhumur in Kuttanad. Uthiyan Cheralathan was a contemporary of the Chola ruler Karikala Chola. Mamulanar credits him with having conducted a feast in honour of his ancestors. In a battle at Venni, Uthiyan Cheralathan was wounded on the back by Karikala Chola. Unable to bear the disgrace, the Chera committed suicide by starvation.[1911]

Nedum Cheralathan - Nedum Cheralathan is the hero of the second decad of *Pathirruppaththu* which was composed by the poet, Kannanar. In it, he is praised for having subdued seven crowned kings to achieve the title of *Adhiraja*. With characteristic exaggeration, Kannanar also lauds the king for conquering foes from Kumari to the Himalayas. Cheralathan, famous for his hospitality, gifted Kannanar with a part of Umbarkkattu (Anamalai). The greatest of his enemies were the Kadambas of Banavasi whom he defeated. The contemporaneity with the Kadambas tentatively dates Cheralathan to around the 4th century. He also won another victory over the Yavanas (westerners) on the coast. Nedum Cheralathan was killed in a battle with a Chola ruler. The Chola is also said to have been killed by a spear thrown at him by Cheralathan.[1911]

Senguttuvan - Vel Kelu Kuttuvan, son of Nedum Cheralathan, ascended to the Chera throne after the death of his father. He is often identified with the legendary Kadal Pirakottiya "Senguttuvan Chera", the most illustrious ruler of the early Cheras. Under his reign, the Chera kingdom extended from Kollimalai in the east to Tondi and Mantai on the western coast. The queen of Senguttuvan was Illango Venmal (the daughter of a Velir chief).[1912]Wikipedia:Citing sources In the early years of his rule, Senguttuvan successfully intervened in a civil war in the Chola Kingdom. The war was among the Chola princes and the Cheras stood on the side of their relative Killi. The rivals of Prince Killi were defeated in a battle at Neriyavil, Uraiyur and he firmly established the Chola throne. The land and naval expedition against the Kadambas was also successful. The Kadambas had the support of the Yavanas, who were routed in the Battle of Idumbil and Valyur. The Fort Kodukur in which the Kadamba army took shelter was stormed and the Kadambas was beaten. In the following naval expedition the Yavana-supported Kadamba army was crushed. He is said to have defeated the Kongu people and a warrior called Mogur Mannan. Ilango Adigal wrote the legendary Tamil epic *Silappatikaram*, which describes his brother Senguttuvan Chera's decision to propitiate a temple (*Virakkallu*) for the goddess Pattini (Kannagi) at Vanchi.Wikipedia:Citation needed

Senguttuvan Chera was perhaps a contemporary of Gajabahu, king of Sri Lanka. Gajabahu, according to the Sangam poems, visited the Chera country during the Pattini festival at Vanchi.[1913]Wikipedia:Identifying reliable sources He is mentioned in the context of Gajabahu's rule in Sri Lanka, which can be dated to either the first or last quarter of the 2nd century CE, depending on whether he was the earlier or the later Gajabahu.

Selvakadumko Valiathan - Selvakadumko Valiathan was the son of Anthuvan Cheral and the hero of the 7th set of poems composed by Kapilar. His residence was at the city of Tondi. He married the sister of the wife of Nedum Cheralathan. Selva Kadumko defeated the combined armies of the Pandyas and the Cholas. He is sometimes identified as the Athan Cheral Irumporai mentioned in the Aranattar-malai inscription of Pugalur.[1914]

Perum Cheral Irumporai - "Tagadur Erinta" Perum Cheral Irumporai defeated the combined armies of the Pandyas, Cholas and that of the chief of Tagadur(now called as Dharmapuri). He destroyed the famous city of Tagadur which was ruled by the powerful ruler Adigaman Ezhni. He is also called "the lord of Puzhinad and Kollimala" and "the lord of Puhar". Puhar was the Chola capital. Perum Cheral Irumporai also annexed the territories of a minor chief called Kaluval.[1915]

Illam Cheral Irumporai - Illam Cheral Irumporai defeated the Pandyas and the Cholas and brought immense wealth to his capital at a city called Vanchi. He is said to have distributed these treasures among the Pana poets.[1915]

Yanaikatchai Mantaran Cheral Irumporai - King Yanaikatchai Mantaran Cheral Irumporai preserved the territorial integrity of the Chera Kingdom under his rule. However, by the time of Mantaran Cheral the decline of the kingdom had begun. The Chera ruled from Kollimalai in the east to Tondi and Mantai on the western coast. He defeated his enemies in a battle at Vilamkil. The famous Pandya ruler Nedum Chezhian captured Mantaran Cheral as a prisoner. However, he managed to escape and regain the lost kingdom.[1916]

Kanaikkal Irumporai - Kanaikkal Irumporai is said to have defeated a local chief called Muvan. The Chera then brutally pulled out the teeth of his prisoner and planted them on the gates of the city of Tondi. Kanaikkal Irumporai was later captured by the Chola ruler Sengannan and he committed suicide by starvation.[1916]

Archaeological sources

Archaeology has found epigraphic evidence of the early Cheras.[1917] Wikipedia:Identifying reliable sources Wikipedia:Link rot Two identical inscriptions near Tiruchirappalli, dated to the 2nd century CE, describe three generations of Chera rulers of the Irumporai clan. They record the construction of a rock shelter for Jains on the occasion of the investiture of the crown prince Ilam Kadungo, son of Perum Kadungo, and the grandson of Athan Cheral Irumporai.

Later Chera or Kulasekhara rulers

Elamkulam Kunjan Pillai[1918]	M. G. S. Narayanan[1919]
• Kulashekhara Varman (800–820 CE)	• Rama Rajasekhara (800–844 CE)
• Rajashekhara Varman (820–844 CE)	• Sthanu Ravi Kulasekhara (844–883 CE)
• Sthanu Ravi Varman (844–885 CE)	• Kota Ravi Vijayaraga (883–913)
• Rama Varma Kulashekhara (885–917 CE)	• Kota Kota Kerala Kesari (913–943 CE)
• Goda Ravi Varma (917–944 CE)	• Indu Kota (943–962 CE)
• Indu Kotha Varma (944–962 CE)	• Bhaskara Ravi Manukuladilya (962–1021)
• Bhaskara Ravi Varman I (962–1019 CE)	• Ravi Kota Rajasimha (1021–1036 CE)
• Bhaskara Ravi Varman II (1019–1021 CE)	• Raja Raja (1036–1089 CE)
• Vira Kerala (1021–1028 CE)	• Ravi Rama Rajaditya (1036–1089 CE)
• Rajasimha (1028–1043 CE)	• Aditya Kota Ranaditya (1036–1089 CE)

• Bhaskara Ravi Varman III (1043–1082 CE) • Ravi Rama Varma (1082–1090 CE) • Rama Varma Kulashekhara (1090–1102 CE)	• Rama Kulasekhara (1089–1122 CE)

Administration

Mahodayapuram, *Mahodayapattanam* or *Makotai* was the capital city of Chera dynasty between 8th and 12th centuries CE. It was spread around present-day Kodungallur.[1920]

The city was built around Tiruvanchikkulam temple and was protected by high fortresses on all sides and had extensive pathways and palaces. The temple was a centre of Shaivism in the early years of the later Chera age. The royal palace was at Gotramalleswaram, now known as Cheraman Parambu. The city administration was controlled by a special representative body, the *Kuttam*. Mahodayaouram was also called *Vanchi* by the later Chera rulers after their former capital.[1912]Wikipedia:Citing sources

The Chera rulers shifted their capital to Mahodayapuram from Vanchi. Chera ruler Kulashekhara Varman (9th century) styles himself in his works as the "Lord of Mahodayapuram". The famous Jewish Copper Plate grant (1000 CE) was issued by Muyirikkode (Mahodayapuram).[1912]Wikipedia:Citing sources

Mahodayapuram was famous throughout South India in the 9th and 10th centuries as great centre of learning and science. A well-equipped observatory functioned there under the charge of Sankaranarayana (c. 840 – c. 900), the Chera court astronomer. It functioned in accordance with the rules of astronomy laid down by Aryabhata. The Chera ruler, Sthanu Ravi, equipped a section of the observatory with some special yantras (Rasi Chakra, Jalesa Sutra, Golayantra etc.) and hence it came to be called *Ravi Varma Yantra Valayam*. It seems that arrangements had been made in the city for recording correct time and announcing it to the public from different centres by the tolling of bells at regular intervals of a *Ghatika* (25 minutes). This practice (*Nazhikakkottu*) continued until the early 15th century.[1921]

The localities within the city included:[1920]

- Senamugham
- Kottakkakam
- Gotramalleswaram
- Kodungallur
- Balakrideswaram

Figure 403: *Ilango Adigal, author of the epic Silappatikaram*

Economy

Foreign trade

Chera trade with foreign countries around the Mediterranean sea can be traced back to before the Common Era and was substantially consolidated in the early years of the Common Era.[1922]Wikipedia:Identifying reliable sources[1923]Wikipedia:Identifying reliable sources In the 1st century of the Common Era, the Romans conquered Egypt, which helped them to establish dominance in the Arabian sea trade. The *Periplus of the Erythraean Sea* portrays the trade in the kingdom of *Cerobothras* in detail. Muziris was the most important port in the Malabar coast, which according to the *Periplus*, abounded with large ships of Romans, Arabs and Greeks. Bulk spices, ivory, timber, pearls and gems were exported from the Chera ports to Mesopotamia, Egypt, Greece, Rome, Phoenicia and Arabia.[1924] The Romans brought vast amounts of gold in exchange for pepper.[1925]Wikipedia:Identifying reliable sourcesWikipedia:Link rotWikipedia:Identifying reliable sources[1926]Wikipedia:Citing sources This is testified by the large number of Roman coins that have been found in various parts of Kerala. Pliny, in the 1st century CE, laments about the drain of Roman gold into India and China for unproductive luxuries such as spices, silk

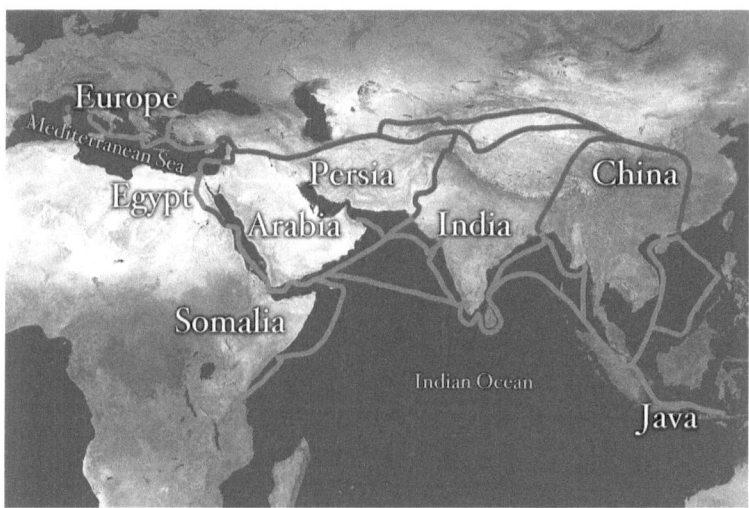

Figure 404: *Silk Road map showing ancient trade routes*

and muslin. This trade declined with the decline of the Roman empire in the 3rd-4th centuries CE.Wikipedia:Citation needed

There were also extensive trade contacts with the Chinese and this is confirmedWikipedia:Citation needed by the discovery of Chinese coins from the 1st century CE. It is speculated by some authorsWikipedia:Manual of Style/Words to watch#Unsupported attributions that the trade with China is older and lasted longer than the trade with the Greeks and the Phoenicians. Kollam was an important port of trade with the Chinese and Marco Polo, in the 15th century CE, discovers extensive trade ties between Kerala and China, mainly in the trade of pepper.Wikipedia:Citation needed

Society and culture

Early Cheras

Most of the Chera population followed native Dravidian practices. The worship of departed heroes was a common practice in the Chera kingdom along with tree worship and other kinds of ancestor worship. The war goddess Kottavai was propitiated with elaborate offerings of meat and toddy. The Cheras probably worshipped this mother goddess. It is theorised that Kottavai was assimilated into the present-day form of the goddess Durga. There is no evidence of snake worship in the Chera realms during the Sangam Age.[1927] It is thought that the first wave of Brahmin migration came to the Chera kingdom

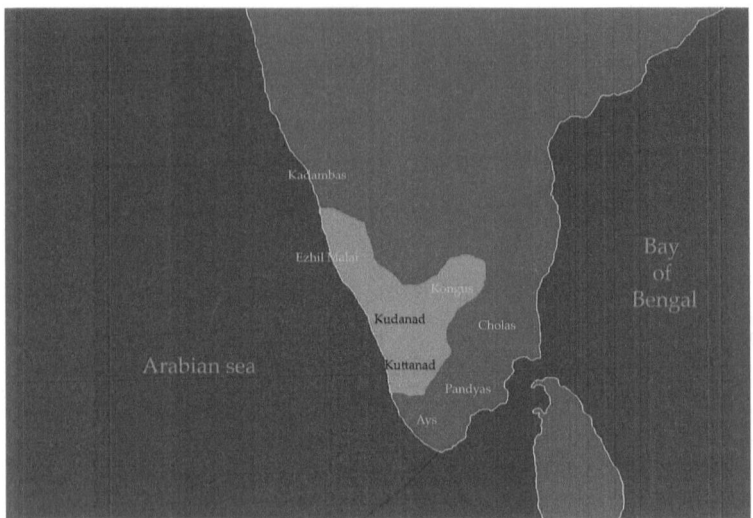

Figure 405: *Chera kingdom in the Sangam Period*

around the 3rd century BCE behind the Jain and Buddhist missionaries. It was only in the 8th century CE that the Aryanisation of the Chera country reached its climax.[1928]

Though the vast majority of the population followed native Dravidian practices, a small percentage of the population followed Jainism, Buddhism and Brahmanism. These three philosophies came from regions in northern India to the Chera kingdom.[1927] Populations of Jews and Christians were also known to have lived in these territories.[1929,1930,1931]

The division of the society into castes and communities was conspicuously absent and practices of untouchability and exclusiveness were unknown. There was dignity of labour accorded to all work and no one was looked down upon due to their work or occupation.[1908] A striking feature of the social life of the Cheras in the Sangam age is the high status accorded to women. Women enjoyed freedom of movement as well as the right to full education. Child marriage was unknown in the early Sangam era and adult marriage was the general rule. The practice of 'bride-price', where the groom would pay the girl's parents, appears to be prevalent in the time. Women were free to follow any occupation though most of them were involved in weaving or the sale of goods.[1932] A martial spirit was pervasive and women even went to the battlefield along with the men, largely playing a key role in keeping up the morale of the fighting forces.Wikipedia:Citation needed

Agriculture was the primary occupation of the people and rice was the main staple of the people. Various agricultural occupations such as harvesting, threshing and drying are described. Fish and meat were also eaten liberally. There is a mention of *ney-ven choru* or butter-laden rice with meat of the best quality being served to guests assembled for a wedding (mentioned in *Agam 136*). Liquor, mainly wines, that were brought by the *Yavanas* (or Westerners) was quite popular. However, the local population was partial to palm-wine or Toddy. Music, poetry and dancing provided entertainment for the people. And poets and musicians were held in high regard in society. Sangam literature is full of references about the lavish patronage extended to court poets. There were professional poets and poetesses who composed poems praising their patrons and were generously rewarded for this. Musical instruments such as drums, pipes and flutes were also known in the time.[1933]

Later Cheras

The early period of the Kulasekharas i.e. the period of the 9th and 10th centuries constitutes a "golden period" in the history of Kerala. There was great patronage of the arts, literature and science and several important contributions in these fields were made during this period. At its height, the Kulasekhara empire comprised almost all of modern-day Kerala, some parts of the Nilgiri hills and parts of the Salem-Coimbatore regions. Political administration was distributed federally and the various areas were divided into various administrative provinces called *nadus*. The southern-most region was the Venad, comprising regions of modern-day Thiruvananthapuram and Kollam, while the northern-most was called the Kolathunadu and comprised areas of Kannur and Kasaragod. The administration of these *nadus* was carried out by feudatory local chieftains also known as *naduvazhis*. These chieftains were overseen by royal representatives named *koyiladhikarikal* who were usually selected from the blood relations of the Kulasekhara's family.Each of these *nadus* or provinces were sub-divided into smaller *Desams*. These *desams* were governed by *desavazhis* who were usually selected by the local representative bodies named *kuttams*.[1934]

The Chera state had extensive trade relations with countries of the outside world. The most important ports of this period were Kandalur (near Vizhinjam), Kollam and Kodungallur. Sulaiman and al-Mas'udi, the Arab travellers who visited the Malabar Coast during the period, have testified to the high degree of economic prosperity achieved by the state from its foreign trade. Sulaiman makes specific mention of the brisk trade with China. A number of copper-plates and inscriptions testify to the high importance given to trade corporations and merchant guilds.[1935]

Figure 406: *Vazhappally script*

The Kulasekhara period is characterised by a great flowering of the arts and literature. Several notable works in Sanskrit and Tamil were written during this period under the patronage of the Kulasekharas who themselves indulged in authoring several works. Malayalam emerged with its own distinct script around this period, around the Kollam era (early 9th century). Hinduism as a religion, became more prominent around this period and was accompanied by a corresponding decline in Buddhism and Jainism. There was an increase in the number of Vedic schools called *salais* and an increase in their prestige with the widespread prominence of the Advaita philosopher, Adi Shankara, who was born at Kaladi on the banks of the river Periyar.[1936] The Kulasekhara empire was characterised by eclectic beliefs and religious harmony that was free from sectarian conflict evidenced by the simultaneous existence of several religions. This is also evidenced in the form of grants given to Christians as well as copper-plate grants given to the Jews of Kochi.[1937]

Copper-plate grants

The Vazhapally Plates are a set of copper-plate grants issued by Kulasekhara Mahodayapuram king, Rajashekhara Varman (820–844).[1938]

The Tharisapalli plates are a set of copper-plate grants issued to Mar Sapir Iso, the leader of the Saint Thomas Christians by Ayyan Atikal Thiruvatikal in 849, conferring on the Palli and Palliyar a large number of privileges, including the 72 royal rights. These copper-plates are still present at Devalokam Aramana Kottayam, the headquarters of Malankara Orthodox Syrian Church (successor to the Saint Thomas Christians).[1938,1939]Wikipedia:Citing sources[1940]Wikipedia:Citing sources

The Jewish copper plate was given to the Cochin Jews by the Kulasekhara king, Bhaskara Ravi Varman I (962–1019 CE). This inscription conferred on a Jewish leader, Joseph Rabban, the rights of the Anjuvannam and 72 other proprietary rights.[1941,1942]

Chera dynasty

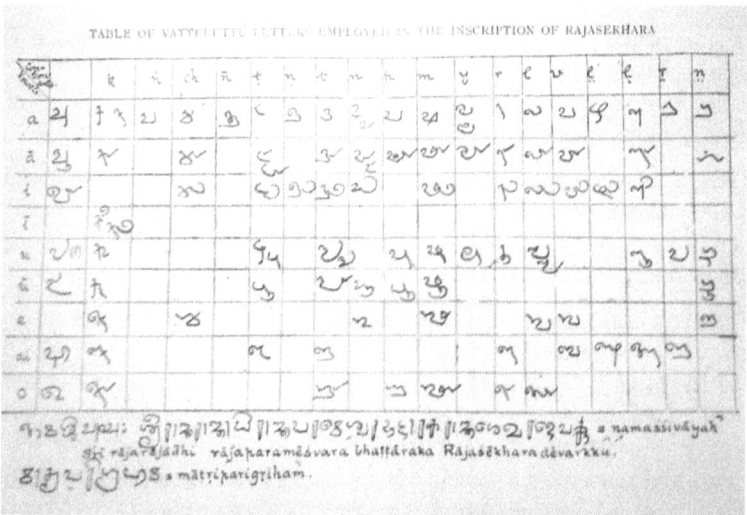

Figure 407: *Vazhappally plates (detail)*

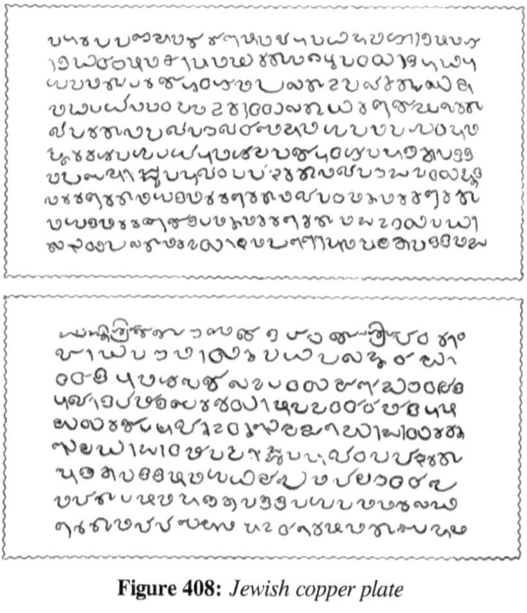

Figure 408: *Jewish copper plate*

Cheras of Venadu

In the absence of a central power at Makkotai, the divisions of the Chera kingdom soon emerged as principalities under separate chieftains. The post-Chera period witnessed a gradual decadence of the Nambudiri-Brahmans and rise of the Nairs.Wikipedia:Citation needed

The original Chera dynasty migrated to Kollam (Quilon) and merged with the Ay kingdom. Ramavarma Kulasekhara, the last Chera King of Makotaiya Puram (Kodungaloor), became the first ruler of the Chera-Ai Dynasty and was called Ramar Thiruvadi.Wikipedia:Citation needed

The rulers of the kingdom of Venadu, based at port Quilon in southern Kerala, trace their relations to the Perumals of Makkotai. Venadu ruler Kotha Varma (1102–1125) probably conquered Kottar and portions of Nanjanadu from the Pandyas. Under the reign of Vira Ravi Varma the system of government became very efficient, and village assemblies functioned vigorously. Udaya Marthanda Varma's tenure was noted for the close relationship between the Venadu and Pandyas. By the time of Ravi Kerala Varma (1215–1240), Odanadu kingdom had acknowledged the authority of the Venadu rulers. The next Venadu ruler Padmanabha Marthanda Varma is alleged to have been killed by Vikrama Pandya in 1264 CE.[1912]Wikipedia:Citing sources

The Pandyas probably led a successful military expedition to Venadu and captured the capital city of Quilon between 1250 and 1300 CE. The records of Jatavarman Sundara Pandya and Maravarman Kulasekhara Pandya testify to the establishment of Pandya rule over Venadu Cheras.[1943]

Ravi Varma Kulasekhara

Ravi Varma Kulasekhara, the last of the Venadu kings, ruled Venadu as a vassal of the Pandyas till the death of king Maravarman Kulasekhara. After the death of the king he became independent and even claimed the throne of the Pandyas (Ravi Varma had married the daughter of the deceased Pandya ruler). He later annexed large parts of southern India and raised Venadu Cheras to the position of a powerful military state for a short time. The chaotic succession battles in the Pandya kingdom helped his conquests. The Venadu ruler invaded the Pandya kingdom and defeated the forces of Vira Pandya. After annexing the entire Pandya state, he was crowned as "Emperor of South India" in 1312 at Madurai. He later annexed Tiruvati and Kanchi (the Chola kingdom). Under Ravi Varma Venadu attained a high degree of economic prosperity.[1944]

The success of Ravi Varma was short lived and soon after his death the region became a conglomeration of warring states. Venadu itself transformed into one these states. The line of Venadu kings after Ravi Varma continued through the law of matrilineal succession.Wikipedia:Citation needed

Aditya Varma Sarvanganatha (1376–1383) is known have defeated the Muslim raiders of the south and checked the tide of Islamic advance. Under the rule of Chera Udaya Marthanda Varma, the Venadu gradually extended their sway over the Tirunelveli region. Vira Ravi Ravi Varma (1484–1503) was the ruler of Venad during the arrival of the Portuguese in India.[1912]Wikipedia:Citing sources

References

Sources

- Menon, A. Sreedhara (2007). *A survey of Kerala history*[1945] (2007 ed.). Kerala, India: D C Books. ISBN 8126415789.
- Menon, A. Sreedhara (1967). *A Survey of Kerala History*[1946]. Sahitya Pravarthaka Co-operative Society. OCLC 555508146[1947].
- Kulke, Hermann; Rothermund, Dietmar (2004). *A History of India*[1948] (Fourth ed.). Routledge. ISBN 9780415329200.
- Thapar, Romila (2004). *Early India : from the origins to AD 1300*[1949]. Berkeley [u.a.]: University of California Press. ISBN 9780520242258.
- Karashima, Noboru (2014). *A Concise History of South India: Issues and Interpretations*[1950]. Oxford University Press. ISBN 9780198099772.
- Kamil Zvelebil (1975). *Tamil Literature*[1951]. BRILL. ISBN 978-90-04-04190-5.
- Zvelebil, Kamil (1973). *The smile of Murugan: On Tamil literature of south India*[1952]. Brill Academic Publishers. ISBN 90-04-03591-5.
- Robert Caldwell (1998) [1913]. *A Comparative Grammar of the Dravidian Or South-Indian Family of Languages*[1953] (3rd ed.). Asian Educational Services. ISBN 978-81-206-0117-8.
- Fischel, Walter J. (1967). "The Exploration of the Jewish Antiquities of Cochin on the Malabar Coast". *Journal of the American Oriental Society.* **87** (3): 230–248. doi: 10.2307/597717[1954]. JSTOR 597717[1955].
- Narayanan, M.G.S. (2013). *Perumāḷs of Kerala : Brahmin oligarchy and ritual monarchy : political and social conditions of Kerala under the Cēra Perumāḷs of Makōtai (c. AD 800-AD 1124)*[1956]. Thrissur: CosmoBooks. ISBN 9788188765072.

External links

 Wikimedia Commons has media related to *Chera Dynasty*.

- *Tamil Coins*, R. Nagasamy[1957]

Kalabhra dynasty

Kalabhra Empire	
250–600	
Kalabhra territories	
Capital	Kaveripumpattinam, Madurai
Languages	Prakrit, Tamil
Religion	Hinduism Buddhism Jainism Christianity
Government	Monarchy
Maharaja Wikipedia:Citation needed	
•	5th century	Achyutavikranta
		Tiraiyan of Pavattiri
		Pulli of Vengadam Tirupati
Historical era		Classical India
•	3rd century	c. 250
•	7th century	c. 600
Preceded by	Succeeded by
Ancient Tamil country	Pallava dynasty Pandyan dynasty

The **Kalabhra dynasty** (Tamil: களப்பிரர் *Kalappirar*) ruled over the entire ancient Tamil country between the 3rd and the 7th century in an era of South Indian history called the *Kalabhra interregnum*. The Kalabhras, possibly Jain, displaced the kingdoms of the early Cholas, early Pandyas and Chera dynasties by a revolt.

Information about the origin and reign of the Kalabhras is scarce. They left neither artefacts nor monuments, and the only sources of information are scattered mentions in Sangam, Buddhist and Jain literature. The Kalabhras were defeated by the joint efforts of the Pallavas, Pandyas and Chalukyas of Badami. Pancha Gowda Brahmins arrived in Tamilnadu during Kalabhras regime.Wikipedia:Citation needed

Identification

The origin and identity of the Kalabhras is uncertain. They are generally believed to have been hill tribes that rose out of obscurity to become a power in South India. Their kings were likely followers of Buddhism and Jainism. Some of their coins feature images such as a seated Jain monk, the Buddhist Bodhisattva Manjushri, or the Swastika symbol, with Prakrit inscriptions in Brahmi script on the other side. Later specimens dating towards the 6th century employ both Prakrit and Tamil in their inscriptions and feature images of Hindu gods and goddesses.

A number of theories have been advanced for the identity of the Kalabhras. T. A. Gopinath Rao equates them with the Muttaraiyars and an inscription in the Vaikunta Perumal temple at Kanchi mentions a Muttaraiyar named as *Kalavara-Kalvan*. The word *Kalabhra* might possibly be a Sanskrit derivation of the Tamil *Kalvan*. M. Raghava Iyengar, on the other hand, identifies the Kalabhras with the Vellala Kalappalars. The c. 770 Velvikudi plates of the Pandyan king Parantaka Nedunjadaiyan mention the Kalabhras and R. Narasimhacharya and V. Venkayya believe them to have been *Karnatas*. K. R. Venkatarama Iyer suggests that the Kalabhras might have settled in the Bangalore-Chittoor region early in the 5th century.

Evidence from literature

The history of Cholas of Uraiyur (Tiruchirappalli) is exceedingly obscure from 4th to the 9th century, chiefly owing to the occupation of their country by the Kalabhras. Buddhadatta, the great writer in Pali, belonged to Uraiyur. He mentions his contemporary, King Achyutavikranta of the Kalabharakula, as ruling over the Chola country from Kaveripumpattinam. He was a Buddhist. Tamil literary tradition refers to an Achyuta who kept the Chera, Chola and Pandya rulers in captivity. On the basis of the contemporaneity of Buddhadatta with Buddhaghosha, Achyuta may be assigned to the 5th century. Thus, after the Sangam age, the Cholas were forced into obscurity by the Kalabhras, who disturbed the placid political conditions of the Tamil country.Wikipedia:Citation needed The Kalabhras are mentioned in Cāḷukya, Pallava and Pāṇḍyan copper-plates, indicating Kalabhras presence from the sixth to the eight century. These records suggest that the Kalabrha Dynasty was overcome and never ruled in South India.

Reasons for the unpopularity

Kalabhras, by ruling the Tamil country, disturbed the prevailing order. The Velvikudi inscription from the third regnal year of Pandya ruler Nedunjadaiyan (c. 765 – c. 815) say that Pandya ruler Mudukudumi Peruvaludi gave the village of Velvikudi as *Brahmadeya* (gift to the Brahmins). They enjoyed it for a long time. Then a Kali king named Kalabhran took possession of the extensive earth, driving away numberless great kings.Wikipedia:Citation needed

Patrons of literature

The period of Kalabhras was marked by the ascendancy of Buddhism, and probably also of Jainism. It was characterized by considerable literary activity in Tamil. Most of the works grouped under the head, "*The Eighteen Minor works*" might have been written during this period as also the Silappadhikaram, Manimegalai and other works. Many of the authors were characterised as belonging to the "heretical" sects (meaning Buddhists and Jains). However, the great Tamil lexicographer Vaiyapuri Pillai had ascribed later dates to many of these works. This theory would undermine the link between the Kalabhras and the "*Eighteen Minor works*".Wikipedia:Identifying reliable sources

Religion

It is known that the Kalabhras patronised Buddhism and Jainism.[1958,1959] The late Kalabhras appear to have been Shaivite and Vaishnavite. Scholar F. E. Hardy traced the palace ceremony to a Vishnu or Mayon temple to the rule of the Kalabhras.[1960] They are known for patronising the Hindu god, Skanda or Subramanya. They imprinted his image on their 5th-century coins, especially those of the Kaveripumpattinam rulers.[1961] King Achyuta worshipped Vaishnava Tirumal.[1962]

Fall of the Kalabhras

The rule of the Kalabhras of South India was ended by the counter-invasions of Pandyas, Chalukyas and Pallavas. There are other references to the Kalabhras in Pallava and Chalukya inscriptions. They were conquered by Pallava, Simhavishnu and Pandya, Kadungon.Wikipedia:Citation needed

Further reading

- Arunachalam, M. (1979). *The Kalabhras in the Pandiya Country and Their Impact on the Life and Letters There*[1963]. University of Madras.

References

- Cort, John E., ed. (1998), *Open Boundaries: Jain Communities and Cultures in Indian History*[1964], SUNY Press, ISBN 0-7914-3785-X

Kadamba dynasty

Kadambas of Banavasi		
Banavasi Kadambaru		
Empire (Subordinate to Pallava until 345)		
345–525		
Extent of Kadamba Empire, 500 CE		
Capital	Banavasi	
Languages	Kannada Sanskrit	
Religion	Hinduism Jainism	
Government	Monarchy	
Maharaja		
•	345–365	Mayurasharma
		Krishna Varma II
History		
•	Earliest Kadamba records	450
•	Established	345
•	Disestablished	525
Preceded by Pallava dynasty	Succeeded by Chalukya dynasty	
Today part of	India	

Kadamba Kings (345–525)

(Banavasi Kings)	
Mayurasharma	(345–365)
Kangavarma	(365–390)
Bagitarha	(390–415)
Raghu	(415–435)
Kakusthavarma	(435–455)
Santivarma	(455–460)
Mrigeshavarma	(460–480)
Shivamandhativarma	(480–485)
Ravivarma	(485–519)
Harivarma	(519–525)
(Triparvatha Branch)	
Krishna Varma I	(455)
Vishnuvarma	
Simhavarma	
Krishna Varma II	
Pulakeshin I (*Chalukya*)	(543–566)

The **Kadambas** (Kannada: ಕದಂಬರು) (345–525 CE) were an ancient royal family of Karnataka, India, that ruled northern Karnataka and the Konkan from Banavasi in present-day Uttara Kannada district. At the peak of their power under King Kakushtavarma, they ruled large parts of modern Karnataka state.

The dynasty was founded by Mayurasharma in 345 CE which at later times showed the potential of developing into imperial proportions, an indication to which is provided by the titles and epithets assumed by its rulers. King Mayurasharma defeated the armies of the Pallavas of Kanchi possibly with help of some native tribes. The Kadamba fame reached its peak during the rule of Kakusthavarma, a notable ruler with whom even the kings of Gupta Dynasty of northern India cultivated marital alliances. Tiring of the endless battles and bloodshed, one of the later descendants, King Shivakoti adopted Jainism. The Kadambas were contemporaries of the Western Ganga Dynasty and together they formed the earliest native kingdoms to rule the land with absolute autonomy. The dynasty later continued to rule as a feudatory of larger Kannada empires, the Chalukya and the Rashtrakuta empires, for over five hundred years during which time they branched into minor dynasties known as the Kadambas of Goa, Kadambas of Halasi and Kadambas of Hangal.

During the pre-Kadamba era the ruling families that controlled the Karnataka region, the Mauryas, and the Satavahanas were not natives of the region and the nucleus of power resided outside present-day Karnataka. The Kadambas were the first indigenous dynasty to use Kannada, the language of the soil, at an administrative level. In the history of Karnataka, this era serves as a broad based historical starting point in the study of the development of region as an enduring geo-political entity and Kannada as an important regional language. Their legacy was so impressive that even the Vijayanagara rulers who fought the Deccan sultanates hired descendants of the Kadambas to manage their Goan military naval fleet.[1965]

History

There is no shortage of myths about the origin of the Kadambas. According to one account the dynasty was founded by one Trilochana Kadamba also known from the Halsi and Degamve records as *Jayanta* who had three eyes and four arms.[1966] He was born out of the sweat of Shiva, which had fallen under a Kadamba tree and hence his name Kadamba. According to another myth, Mayurasharma himself was born to Lord Shiva and mother earth and had three eyes.[1967] Most of the inscriptions of the Kadambas mention Skanda and his *Matrs* (mothers). According to the Talagunda inscription, the founder Mayurasharma was annointed by *the six-faced god of war*, that is Skanda or Kartikeya. According to *Grama Paddhati*, a Kannada work dealing with the history of the Tulu Brahmanas, Mayurasharma was born to Lord Shiva and goddess Parvathi under a Kadamba tree in the Sahyadri mountains and hence the name Kadamba. An inscription of the Nagarakhanda Kadambas, a later descendent dynasty, gives a legendary account and traces their lineage back to the Nandas. According to the inscription, King Nanda who had no heir prayed to Lord Shiva in the Kailash mountains when a heavenly voice advised him that two sons would be born to him, would bear the name of Kadamba *Kula* (family) and they should be instructed in the use of weapons.

There are two theories to the origin of the Kadamba dynasty, a native Kannadiga origin and the other a north Indian origin. Mention of the north Indian origin of the Kadambas are only found in their later records of their offshoot descendent dynasty and is considered legendary. The earliest record making this claim is the 1053 and 1055 inscriptions of Harikesari Deva which are copied in inscriptions thereafter, describing Mayurasharma as the progenitor of the kingdom who established his might on the summit of Mount Himavat. But this theory has not found popularity as there is no indication of this account in any of their early records.[1968] On the contrary, the family derives its name from the Kadamba tree that is common only to the South India region.[1969]

Historians are divided on the issue of the caste of the Kadamba family, whether the founders of the kingdom belonged to the Brahmin caste as claimed by the Talagunda inscription, or were of tribal origin. A claim has been made that the Kadambas were none other than a tribe called the Kadambu, who were in conflict with the Chera kingdom (of modern Kerala). The 'Kadambus' find mention in the Sangam literature as totemic worshippers of the Kadambu tree and the Hindu god Subramanya.[1970] While some historians have argued that they being of Brahmin descent made Mayurasharma's ancestors natives of northern India, the counter argument is that it was common for Dravidian peoples to be received into the Brahmanic caste during early and later medieval times. Being native Kannadigas, the Kadambas promptly gave administrative and political importance to their language, Kannada, after coming to power.[1971] It is thus claimed that the family of the Kadambas were undoubtedly of Kanarese descent and may have been admitted into the Brahminical caste.[1972,1973] The Naga descent of the Kadambas has been stated in early inscriptions of King Krishna Varma I too, which confirms the family was from present day Karnataka.

Inscriptions in Sanskrit and Kannada are the main sources of the Kadamba history. The Talagunda, Gundanur, Chandravalli, Halasi and Halmidi inscription are some of the important inscriptions that throw light on this ancient ruling family of Karnataka.[1974] They belonged to the *Manavya Gotra* and were *Haritiputras* (lineage), which connects them to the native Chutus of Banavasi, a feudatory of the Satavahana empire.[1975] Inscriptions of the Kadambas in Kannada and Sanskrit ascribed to the main dynasty and branch kingdoms have been published by historians.[1976] The Kadambas minted coins with Nagari, Kannada and Grantha legends which provide additional numismatic evidence of their history.[1977]

Kadambas were the first rulers to use Kannada as an additional official administrative language, as evidenced by the Halmidi inscription of 450.[1978,1979,1980] Three Kannada inscriptions from their early rule from Banavasi have been discovered.[1981] Several early Kadamba dynasty coins bearing the Kannada inscription *Vira* and *Skandha* was found in Satara collectorate.[1982] A gold coin of King Bhagiratha (390–415 CE) bearing the old Kannada legend *Sri* and *Bhagi* also exists.[1983] Recent discovery of 5th century Kadamba copper coin in Banavasi with Kannada script inscription *Srimanaragi* on it proves the usage of Kannada at the administrative level further.

One of their earliest inscriptions, the Talagunda inscription of Santivarma (450) gives what may be the most possible cause for the emergence of the Kadamba kingdom. It states that Mayurasharma was a native of Talagunda, (in present-day Shimoga district) and his family got its name from the Kadamba tree that grew near his home.[1984,1985] The inscription narrates how Mayurasharma proceeded to Kanchi in 345 along with his guru and grandfather Veerasarma to pursue his Vedic studies at a Ghatika (school). There, owing to some misunderstanding between him and a Pallava guard or at an *Ashvasanstha* (a place of horse sacrifice), a quarrel arose in which Mayurasharma was humiliated. In high rage, the Brahmana discontinued his studies, left Kanchi, swearing vengeance on the impudent Pallavas, and took to arms. He collected a faithful group of followers and routed the Pallava armies near Srisilam region. After a prolonged period of low intensity warfare against the Pallavas and other smaller kings such as the Brihad-Banas of Kolar region, he proclaimed independence. Unable to contain him, the Pallavas had to accept his sovereignty.[1986,1987] Thus in an act of righteous indignation was born the first native kingdom of Karnataka, the Pallava King Skandavarman condescending to recognise the growing might of the Kadambas south of the Malaprabha river as a sovereign power.[1988] Scholars such as Mores and Sastry opine that Mayurasharma availed himself of the confusion that was created by the invasion of Samudragupta who in his Allahabad Inscription claims to have defeated Vishnugopa of Kanchi. Taking advantage of the weakening of the Pallava power, Mayura appears to have succeeded in establishing a new kingdom."[1989] The fact that Mayurasharma had to travel to distant Kanchi for Vedic studies gives an indication that Vedic lore was quite rudimentary in the region at that time. The recently discovered Gudnapur inscription states that Mauryasharma's grandfather and preceptor was Virasarma and his father Bandhushena developed the character of a Kshatriya.[1990]

Mayurasharma's successor was his son Kangavarma in 365 who had to fight the Vakataka might to protect *Kuntala*. He was defeated by Vakataka Prithvisena but managed to maintain his freedom.[1991] His son Bhagiratha is said to have retrieved his fathers losses but Vakataka inscriptions do not attest to this.[1992] His son Raghu died fighting the Pallavas. He was succeeded by his brother Kakusthavarma who was the most powerful ruler of the dynasty.[1993] He maintained marital relations with even the imperial Guptas of the north, according to the Talagunda inscription. One of his daughters was married to Kumara Gupta's son Skanda Gupta. His other daughter was married to a Vakataka king Narendrasena.[1994] He maintained similar relations with the Bhatari, the Alupas of South Canara and the Western Ganga Dynasty of Gangavadi according to the Talagunda inscription. The great poet Kalidasa had visited his court.[1995]

After Kakusthavarma only Ravivarma who came to the throne in 485 was able to build upon the kingdom. His rule was marked by a series of clashes within the family, and also against the Pallavas and the Gangas. He is also credited with a victory against the Vakatakas, which helped extend his Kingdom as far north as the river Narmada. The crux of their kingdom essentially consisted of large areas of Karnataka, Goa and southern areas of present-day Maharashtra. After his death, the kingdom went into decline due to family feuds. The Birur plates of Kadamba Vishnuvarman call Shantivarman "The master of the entire Karnataka region". The Triparvatha branch that broke away in 455 ruled from Murod in Belagavi for some time and merged with the main Banavasi kingdom during rule of Harivarma. Finally the kingdom fell to the power of the Badami Chalukyas. The Kadambas thereafter became feudatories of the Badami Chalukyas and later the Rashtrakutas and Kalyani Chalukyas. The successors of Mayurasharma took to the name "varma" to indicate their Kshatriya status.

Part of a series on the
History of Karnataka
• Political history of medieval Karnataka • Origin of Karnataka's name • Kadambas and Gangas • Chalukya Empire • Rashtrakuta Empire • Western Chalukya Empire • Southern Kalachuri • Hoysala Empire • Vijayanagara Empire • Bahmani Sultanate • Bijapur Sultanate • Kingdom of Mysore • Nayakas of Keladi • Nayakas of Chitradurga • Haleri Kingdom • Unification of Karnataka
Categories
• Architecture • Forts • Economies • Societies

- $\underline{v}$
- $\underline{t}$
- $\underline{e}$[1996]

Coins

Kadamba coins were one the heaviest and perhaps purest of all medieval Indian gold coinage. They issued 2 types of gold coins, those which were punch-marked and others which were die-struck. During 1075-1094 CE, Shanti Varma, issued gold punch-marked coins and in 1065 CE, Toyimadeva, issued die-struck gold coins.

Punch-marked gold coins

- Kadamba punch-marked gold coin issued in name of *Jaysimha II* Jagadekamalla (Chalukya).
- Coin consists of a central punch mark of Hanuman, and 4 retrospectant lions.
- 2 prominent punch marks create 2 Shri alphabets depicts goddess Laxmi in Kadamba script Kannada script.

Die struck gold coins (Pagoda)

- In 1065 AD Kadambas *Toyimadeva* issued *first die struck gold coins*.
- The gold coin of Kadambas depict god Hanuman, inside lined circle and dotted circle, flanked by two chouries and conch. Also include the figures of sun and moon. Below is the legend Nakara (Nagara, the deity of Bankapura, Nagareshwara) in Kannada script.

They have been definitively attributed to the Kadambas because they not only have various Kadamba symbols, such as conches and chakras, but one of the epithets on the coins, *sri dosharashi*, is known from inscriptions to have been used by the Kadamba king Krishnavarma II (ruled 516–540).[1997] Other coins with the legend *sri manarashi* were also found, along with anepigraphic coins (that is, coins without any legends) featuring flowers, *chakras*, and conches. The lotus, *chakra* (discus), and conch are all symbols of the god Vishnu. Kadamba inscriptions frequently invoke Vishnu, indicating they must have been devotees of this deity. The identity of the king named *sri manarashi* has still not been determined.

The coins are perhaps the earliest ones to use Kannada letters, a confirmation that the Kadambas were the first ruling dynasty native to Karnataka.

Kadamba dynasty

Figure 409: *Early coin of Shanthivarma or Mrigeshavarma. Obverse shows the 5th century Kannada legend "Sri Manarashi", an epithet of the king.*

Figure 410: *Early coin of Krishnavarma ( ), who has an epithet "sri dosharashi. The reverse of the coin has the legend Shri shashankaha. Shashanka means "moon" in Sanskrit.*

Figure 411: *Gold coins issued by King Toyimadeva of Kadamba Dynasty, 1048–1075 CE*

Kadamba Coins and the earliest Kannada inscription

The Halmidi inscription was the earliest known epigraph that showed the early usage of Kannada script (Kadamba script). The stone inscription found at Halmidi has been assigned to C. 450 CE. and belongs to Kadamba ruler *Kakusthavarma*, whose reign is estimated to be between 435 CE to 455 CE.

In the year 2006, the Jalagars, the sand sievers family, from Tamil Nadu, yielded around 6 Kannada inscribed potin coins from the riverbed of Varada in Sirsi Taluk, which is in Uttara Kannada district. The legends could not be satisfactorily deciphered by Sri MM Prabhu of Mangalore due to the poor chipped condition of coins, and was read Sri Manaragi. Later, when more coins came to limelight, the next year, he managed to attribute it to the Kadambas of Banavasi. The Banavasi village, which is 22 miles (35 km) away from the Sirsi town was the ancient capital of the Kadambas of Banavasi. Banavasi was also known as "Jaldurga" in the *Aihole inscription of Pulakeshin II*. The Varada river encompassed the Banavasi town in all the four directions to form a natural water port and hence the name Jal (water) durga (port).

For the next two years (2007–2008), the Jalagars made a headway and yielded Satavahana Potin coins bearing Elephant/quadri-directional symbol in quantity above 5000 pieecs along with few hundreds of Kura Potin coins bearing Bull/Bow-and-Arrow symbols. Most of the elephant Satavahana coins were of rulers Siri, Satakarni and Pudumavi. The Satavahaha fractions of up to 50 mg weight, with similar elephant motiff and illegible legend were also obtained. The Bull/Discus Potin coins were issued mainly by Rajno Vishnurudra though other rulers name such as Vishnurudra Putra, Vasithi Putra, Satakarni etc. exist. Third of the series, the inscribed Kadamba Potin coins were found too, but in small quantities, estimated to be around 100 pieces with four unique legend types. Only the coins bearing the legend Sri-Manarashi and Sr-Dhosharashi have been published yet. There exist around 10 die variations of the same. Other coins such as Bull/Trident-Goad coins in bell metal of tetradrachm standard bearing legend Vinukhata Brahmananda were found in 5 to 6 numbers, Copper and Lead coins of Chutukulananda, Mulananda and Sivalananda etc. are seen seldom in those river beds but in too lesser numbers. Copper coins of Chutus were not known hitherto. Since Banavasi was an important religious site of sanctity, the site attracted old-age piigrims from distant places who spent their last days in the holy site. They offered coins such as Guptas, Kushan, Roman, Western Kshatrapas, Vijayanagaras and Hoysalas etc., which stands evidence to this.

As far as the chronology of these Banavasi Kadamba coins concerned, Sri-Dhosharashi coins follow Sri-Manarashi coins as evidenced by the script style.

Since Dhosharashi epithet was adorned by Ravivarma, the Manarashi coins are either issued by the predecessors Shanthivarma or Mrigeshavarma. This is understood by the script style of Manarashi coins that resembled more that of Halmidi inscription. Moreover, Halmidi inscription is assigned to Kakkushthavarman. These potin coins are observed in varied weights such as 200 mg to 400 mg stanadard. The fractional coins weighed around 100 mg and contained religious symbols such as Discus, Conch and Lotus, which are the icons of Lord Vishnu.

Their Talagunda inscription had an invocation of Lord Shiva while the Halmidi and Banavasi inscriptions started with an invocation of Lord Vishnu. Moreover, their temple, the Madukeshwara, also seem to have undergone several changes over a period. The initial statue is believed to be of Lord Vishnu while Siva Linga is currently worshipped. Another tale about this place involves the slaying of demon Madhu by Lord Vishnu at the behest of Lord Shiva. This tale is mentioned in the Puranas. So, the religious symbol such as Conch, Discuss and Lotus only signifies the fractional value of coin, which is seen evenin the Hanas and Hagas of the Alupas and Gangas, who were the contemporaries and also in time, the feudatories of the Kadambas of Banavasi.

It is impressive to see the shift of script usage to Kannada, from the Satavahana Brahmi. Satavahana Brahmi was used by the Chutus, Satavahanas and the Kuras respectively as the official script. It is quite possible that Kannada was in use prior to the rule of the Chutus but Brahmi was the script. The usage of Kannada script in coins and inscriptions is the gift of the Kadambas and trend continued in the whole of then Karnataka. The stone tablets recently found in Parkala, Udupi taluk, attests the usage of Kannada around the same period (5th century CE).

Figure 412: *The Halmidi inscription at Halmidi village, dated 450 CE. is the earliest Kannada inscription issued by the Kadamba Dynasty*

Figure 413: *Old Kannada inscriptions of Kadamba king Kamadeva (c.1180) and Hoysala king Veera Ballala II (c.1196) in the open mantapa of the Tarakeshwara temple at Hangal*

Figure 414: *Old Kannada inscription (1200 AD) of King Kamadeva of the Kadamba dynasty of the Hangal branch*

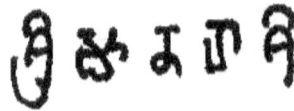

Figure 415: *Kannada legend sri manarashi*

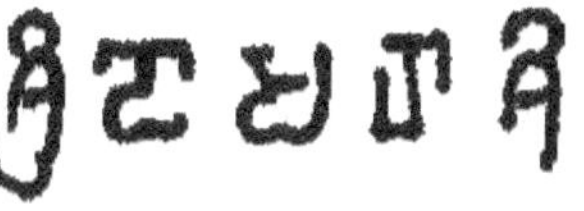

Figure 416: *Kannada legend sri dosharashi*

Administration

The Kadamba kings called themselves *Dharmamaharajas* like the Satavahana kings. Dr. Mores has identified various cabinet and other positions in the kingdom from inscriptions. The prime minister (*Pradhana*), Steward (*Manevergade*), secretary of council (*Tantrapala* or *Sabhakarya Sachiva*), scholarly elders (*Vidyavriddhas*), physician (*Deshamatya*), private secretary (*Rahasyadhikritha*), chief secretary (*Sarvakaryakarta*), chief justice (*Dharmadhyaksha*) and other officials (*Bhojaka* and *Ayukta*). The army consisted of officers like *Jagadala, Dandanayaka* and *Senapathi*.

A crown prince from the royal family helped the king in administration. Princesses of the royal family were appointed as governors of various provinces. King Kakusthavarma had appointed his son Krishna as viceroy of Thriparvatha region. This later proved detrimental to the kingdom as it gave opportunity for break away factions in the kingdom.

The kingdom was divided into *Mandalas* (provinces) or *Desha*. Under a *Mandala* was *Vishayas* (districts). A total of nine *Vishaya* have been identified.[1998] Under a *Vishaya* were *Mahagramas* (Taluk) and *Dashagramas* (Hobli). *Mahagrama* had more villages than *Dashagramas*. One sixth of land produce was collected as tax. Taxes were collected as *Perjunka* (levy on load), *Vaddaravula* (social security tax for royal family), *Bilkoda* (sales tax), *Kirukula* (land tax), *Pannaya* (betel tax) and other professional taxes on traders etc.

Culture

Religious condition

The Kadambas were followers of Vedic Hinduism. The founder, Mayurasharma was a Brahmin by birth but later his successors changed their surname to *Varma* to indicate their Kshatriya status but they used to marry brahmins only. Some Kadamba kings like Krishna Varma performed the *Ashwamedha* (horse sacrifice). Their Talagunda inscription starts with an invocation of Lord Shiva while the Halmidi and Banavasi inscriptions start with an invocation of Lord Vishnu. They built the Madhukesvara temple which is considered their family deity. Many records like the Kudalur, Sirsi records

Figure 417: *Kadamba shikara (tower) with Kalasa (pinnacle) on top, Doddagaddavalli*

speak of grants made by them to scholarly Brahmins. Grants were also made to Buddhist viharas.

The Kadambas also patronised Jainism; several of the latter kings adopted the religion, and built numerous Jain *Basadis* (temples) that are scattered around Banavasi, Belagavi, Mangaluru and Goa. Kings and Queens of the dynasty were renowned for their support of literature, arts and liberal grants to temples and educational institutions.

Several descendants are scattered around present day Goa, Belagavi, Mangaluru and Bengaluru. Adikavi Pampa highly spoke of this kingdom in his writings. Following are his famous quotes on Banavasi: *Aaramkushamittodam nenevudenna manam banavasi deshamam* (*I shall cherish the sweet memories of Banavasi even when tortured*), *Maridumbiyagi mEN Kogileyagi puttuvudu nandanadol Banavasi deshadol* (*As a bee or as nightingale should one born here in this beautiful country of Banavasi*).

Architecture

The contribution of the Kadambas to the architectural heritage of Karnataka is certainly worthy of recognition. The Kadamba style can be identified and that it has a few things in common with the Chalukya and the Pallava styles. The most prominent feature of their architecture, basic as it was is their *Shikara* called *Kadamba Shikara*. The *Shikara* is pyramid shaped and rises in steps without any decoration with a *Stupika* or *Kalasha* at the top. This style of *Shikara* are used several centuries later in the Doddagaddavalli Hoysala temple and the Mahakuta temples in Hampi. Some of their temples also use perforated screen windows. It has also been pointed out that in architecture and sculpture, the Kadambas contributed to the foundation of the later Chalukya-Hoysala style.[1999]

The *Madhukeshwara* (Lord Shiva) temple built by them still exists in Banavasi. Built in the 10th century and renovated many times, the temple is a very good piece of art. The stone cot with wonderful carvings is one of the main tourist attractions in the temple.

Impact

Kadambotsava ("The festival of Kadamba") a festival is celebrated every year by Government of Karnataka in honour of this kingdom.[2000] A popular Kannada film, *Mayura* starring Dr. Raj Kumar based on a novel of the same name by Devudu Narasimha Sastri celebrates the creation of the first Kannada kingdom.

On 31 May 2005 Defence minister Pranab Mukherjee commissioned India's most advanced and first dedicated military naval base named INS Kadamba after the Kadamba dynasty, in Karwar.[2001]

References

<templatestyles src="Template:Refbegin/styles.css" />

- George M. Moraes (1931), The Kadamba Kula, A History of Ancient and Medieval Karnataka, Asian Educational Services, New Delhi, Madras, 1990 ISBN 81-206-0595-0
- Encyclopaedia of Indian literature vol. 2, (1988) Sahitya Akademi, ISBN 81-260-1194-7
- Dr. Suryanath U. Kamath, A Concise history of Karnataka from prehistoric times to the present, Jupiter books, 2001, MCC, Bangalore (Reprint 2002) LCCN 80-95179[2002], OCLC 7796041[2003]
- K.V. Ramesh, Chalukyas of Vatapi, 1984, Agam Kala Prakashan, Delhi OCLC 13869730[2004] OL 3007052M[2005] LCCN 84-900575[2006] ASIN B0006EHSP0[2007]
- Chopra P.N., Ravindran T.K., Subrahmanian N. (2003), History of South India (Ancient, Medieval and Modern), Part 1, Chand publications, New Delhi ISBN 81-219-0153-7

- Rice, B.L. (2001) [1897]. *Mysore Gazetteer Compiled for Government-vol 1*. New Delhi, Madras: Asian Educational Services. ISBN 81-206-0977-8.
- "Kadambas of Banavasi, Dr. Jyotsna Kamat"[2008]. *Kamat's Potpourri*. Retrieved 2006-11-28.
- "History of Karnataka – Kadambas of Banavasi, Arthikaje"[2009]. OurKarnataka.Com. Retrieved 2006-11-28.
- "Indian Inscriptions"[2010]. *Archaeological Survey of India*. Retrieved 2006-11-28.
- "5th century copper coin discovered at Banavasi"[2011]. *Deccan Herald*. February 7, 2006. Archived from the original[2012] on 6 October 2006. Retrieved 2006-11-28.
- "Halmidi village finally on the road to recognition"[2013]. *The Hindu*. Chennai, India. 3 November 2003. Retrieved 2006-11-28.
- Heche karnataka One of the village falling under kadamba empire.
- "Indian Coins, Dynasties of South India, Govindayara Prabhu"[2014]. *G.S Prabhu*. 1 November 2001. Archived from the original[2015] on 6 January 2004. Retrieved 13 November 2006.

 Wikimedia Commons has media related to *Kadamba Dynasty*.

External links

- Coins of the Kadambas of Banavasi[2016]

Western Ganga dynasty

Western Ganga dynasty	
Kingdom (Subordinate to Pallava until 350)	
350–1000	
Core Western Ganga Territory	
Capital	Kolar Talakad
Languages	Kannada Sanskrit
Religion	Jainism Hinduism
Government	Monarchy
Maharaja	
•	350–370	Konganivarma Madhava
•	986–999	Rachamalla V
History		
•	Earliest Ganga records	400
•	Established	350
•	Disestablished	1000
Preceded by	**Succeeded by**
Pallava dynasty	Chola dynasty
Today part of	India

Western Ganga kings

(350–999)

Konganivarman Madhava	(350–370)
Madhava	(370–390)
Harivarman	(390–410)
Vishnugopa	(410–430)
Madhava III Tandangala	(430–469)
Avinita	(469–529)
Durvinita	(529–579)
Mushkara	(579–604)
Polavira	(604–629)
Srivikrama	(629–654)
Bhuvikarma	(654–679)
Shivamara I	(679–726)
Sripurusha	(726–788)
Shivamara II	(788–816)
Rachamalla I	(816–843)
Ereganga Neetimarga	(843–870)
Rachamalla II	(870–907)
Ereganga Neetimarga II	(907–921)
Narasimha	(921–933)
Rachamalla III	(933–938)
Butuga II	(938–961)
Marulaganga Neetimarga	(961–963)
Marasimha II Satyavakya	(963–975)
Rachamalla IV Satyavakya	(975–986)
Rachamalla V (Rakkasaganga)	(986–999)
Neetimarga Permanadi	(999)

- v
- t
- e^{2017}

Western Ganga was an important ruling dynasty of ancient Karnataka in India which lasted from about 350 to 1000 CE. They are known as 'Western Gangas' to distinguish them from the Eastern Gangas who in later centuries ruled over Kalinga (modern Odisha). The general belief is that the Western Gangas began their rule during a time when multiple native clans asserted their freedom due to the weakening of the Pallava empire in South India, a geo-political

Western Ganga dynasty

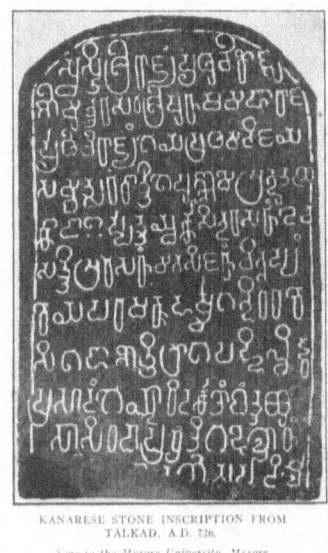

Figure 418: *Old Kannada inscription of c. 726 CE, discovered in Talakad, from the rule of King Shivamara I or Sripurusha*

Figure 419: *Ganga Dynasty emblem on a 10th-century copper plate*

event sometimes attributed to the southern conquests of Samudra Gupta. The Western Ganga sovereignty lasted from about 350 to 550 CE, initially ruling from Kolar and later, moving their capital to Talakadu on the banks of the Kaveri River in modern Mysore district.

After the rise of the imperial Chalukyas of Badami, the Gangas accepted Chalukya overlordship and fought for the cause of their overlords against the Pallavas of Kanchi. The Chalukyas were replaced by the Rashtrakutas of Manyakheta in 753 CE as the dominant power in the Deccan. After a century of struggle for autonomy, the Western Gangas finally accepted Rashtrakuta overlordship and successfully fought alongside them against their foes, the Chola Dynasty of Tanjavur. In the late 10th century, north of Tungabhadra river, the Rashtrakutas were replaced by the emerging Western Chalukya Empire and the Chola Dynasty saw renewed power south of the Kaveri river. The defeat of the Western Gangas by Cholas around 1000 resulted in the end of the Ganga influence over the region.

Though territorially a small kingdom, the Western Ganga contribution to polity, culture and literature of the modern south Karnataka region is considered important. The Western Ganga kings showed benevolent tolerance to all faiths but are most famous for their patronage toward Jainism resulting in the construction of monuments in places such as Shravanabelagola and Kambadahalli. The kings of this dynasty encouraged the fine arts due to which literature in Kannada and Sanskrit flourished. Chavundaraya's writing, *Chavundaraya Purana* of 978 CE, is an important work in Kannada prose. Many classics were written on various subjects ranging from religion to elephant management.

History

Multiple theories have been proposed regarding the ancestry of the founders of the Western Ganga dynasty (prior to the 4th century). Some mythical accounts point to a northern origin,[2018] while theories based on epigraphy suggest a southern origin. Historians who propose the southern origin have further debated whether the early petty chieftains of the clan (prior to their rise to power) were natives of the southern districts of modern Karnataka,[2019,2020,2021] the Kongu region in modern Tamil Nadu[2022] or of the southern districts of modern Andhra Pradesh.[2023,2024] These regions encompass an area of the southern Deccan where the three modern states merge geographically. It is theorised that the Gangas may have taken advantage of the confusion caused by the invasion of southern India by the northern king Samudra Gupta prior to 350, and carved out a kingdom for themselves. The area they controlled was called Gangavadi and included regions of the modern districts of Mysore, Hassan Chamarajanagar, Tumkur, Kolar, Mandya and Bangalore in Karnataka state.[2025] At times, they also controlled some areas in modern Tamil Nadu (Kongu region starting from the 6th century rule of King Avinita) and Andhra Pradesh (Ananthpur region starting from the middle of the 5th century). The founding king of the dynasty was Konganivarma Madhava who made Kolar his capital around 350 and ruled for about twenty years.

By the time of Harivarma in 390, the Gangas had consolidated their kingdom with Talakad as their capital. Their move from the early capital Kolar may have been a strategic one with the intention of containing the growing Kadamba power.[2026] By 430 they had consolidated their eastern territories comprising modern Bangalore, Kolar and Tumkur districts and by 470 they had gained control over Kongu region in modern Tamil Nadu, Sendraka (modern Chikkamagaluru and Belur), Punnata and Pannada regions (comprising modern Heggadadevanakote and Nanjangud) in modern Karnataka.[2027,2028] In 529, King Durvinita ascended the throne after waging a war with his younger brother who was favoured by his father, King Avinita.[2029] Some accounts suggest that in this power struggle, the Pallavas of Kanchi supported Avinita's choice of heir and the Badami Chalukya King Vijayaditya supported his father-in-law, Durvinita.[2030] From the inscriptions it is known that these battles were fought in Tondaimandalam and Kongu regions (northern Tamil Nadu) prompting historians to suggest that Durvinita fought the Pallavas successfully.[2031] Considered the most successful of the Ganga kings, Durvinita was well versed in arts such as music, dance, ayurveda and taming wild elephants. Some inscriptions sing paeans to him by comparing him to Yudhishthira and Manu – figures from Hindu mythology known for their wisdom and fairness.[2032,2033]

Politically, the Gangas were feudatories and close allies who also shared matrimonial relations with the Chalukyas. This is attested by inscriptions which describe their joint campaigns against their arch enemy, the Pallavas of Kanchi.[2034] From the year 725 onwards, the Gangavadi territories came to be called as the "Gangavadi-96000" (*Shannavati Sahasra Vishaya*) comprising the eastern and western provinces of modern south Karnataka.[2035] King Sripurusha fought the Pallava King Nandivarman Pallavamalla successfully, bringing Penkulikottai in north Arcot under his control temporarily for which he earned the title *Permanadi*.[2036,2037] A contest with the Pandyas of Madurai over control of Kongu region ended in a Ganga defeat, but a matrimony between a Ganga princess and Rajasimha Pandya's son brought peace helping the Gangas retain control over the contested region.[2038,2039]

In 753, when the Rashtrakutas replaced the Badami Chalukyas as the dominant force in the Deccan, the Gangas offered stiff resistance for about a century.[2040,2041] King Shivamara II is mostly known for his wars with the Rashtrakuta Dhruva Dharavarsha, his subsequent defeat and imprisonment, his release from prison and eventually his death on the battle field. The Ganga re-

Figure 420: *Saint Bharatha at Shravanabelagola temple complex*

sistance continued through the reign of Rashtrakuta Govinda III and by 819, a Ganga resurgence gained them partial control over Gangavadi under King Rachamalla.[2042] Seeing the futility of waging war with the Western Ganga, Rashtrakuta Amoghavarsha I gave his daughter Chandrabbalabbe in marriage to Ganga prince Butuga I, son of King Ereganga Neetimarga. The Gangas thereafter became staunch allies of the Rashtrakutas, a position they maintained till the end of the Rashtrakuta dynasty of Manyakheta.[2043,2044,2045]

After an uneventful period, Butuga II ascended the throne in 938 with the help of Rashtrakuta Amoghavarsha III (whose daughter he married).[2046] He helped the Rashtrakutas win decisive victories in Tamilakam in the battle of Takkolam against the Chola Dynasty. With this victory, the Rashtrakutas took control of modern northern Tamil Nadu.[2047,2048,2049] In return for their valour, the Gangas were awarded extensive territories in the Tungabhadra river valley.[2050] King Marasimha II who came to power in 963 aided the Rashtrakutas in victories against the Gurjara Pratihara King Lalla and the Paramara kings of Malwa in Central India.[2051,2052] Chavundaraya, a minister in the Western Ganga court was a valiant commander, able administrator and an accomplished poet in Kannada and Sanskrit.[2053,2054] He served King Marasimha II and his successors ably and helped King Rachamalla IV suppress a civil war in 975. Towards the end of the 10th century, the Rashtrakutas had been supplanted by the Western Chalukya Empire in Manyakheta. In the south, the Chola Dynasty who were seeing a resurgence of power under Rajaraja Chola I conquered Gangavadi around the year 1000, bringing the Western Ganga dynasty to an end. Thereafter, large areas of south Karnataka region came under Chola control for about a century.[2055]

Administration

The Western Ganga administration was influenced by principles stated in the ancient text *arthashastra*. The *praje gavundas* mentioned in the Ganga records held responsibilities similar to those of the village elders (*gramavriddhas*) mentioned by Kautilya. Succession to the throne was hereditary but there were instances when this was overlooked.[2056] The kingdom was divided into *Rashtra* (district) and further into *Visaya* (consisting of possibly 1000 villages) and *Desa*. From the 8th century, the Sanskrit term *Visaya* was replaced by the Kannada term *Nadu*. Examples of this change are Sindanadu-8000 and Punnadu-6000,[2057] with scholars differing about the significance of the numerical suffix. They opine that it was either the revenue yield of the division computed in cash terms[2058] or the number of fighting men in that division or the number of revenue paying hamlets in that division[2059] or the number of villages included in that territory.

Inscriptions have revealed several important administrative designations such as prime minister (*sarvadhikari*), treasurer (*shribhandari*), foreign minister (*sandhivirgrahi*) and chief minister (*mahapradhana*). All of these positions came with an additional title of commander (*dandanayaka*). Other designations were royal steward (*manevergade*), master of robes (*mahapasayita*), commander of elephant corps (*gajasahani*), commander of cavalry (*thuragasahani*) etc.[2060] In the royal house, *Niyogis* oversaw palace administration, royal clothing and jewellery etc. and the *Padiyara* were responsible for court ceremonies including door keeping and protocol.[2061]

Officials at the local level were the *pergade, nadabova, nalagamiga, prabhu* and *gavunda*.[2062] The *pergades* were superintendents from all social classes such as artisans, gold smiths, black smiths etc. The *pergades* dealing with the royal household were called *manepergade* (house superintendent) and those who collected tolls were called *Sunka vergades*.[2063] The *nadabovas* were accountants and tax collectors at the *Nadu* level and sometimes functioned as scribes.[2064] The *nalagamigas* were officers who organized and maintained defence at the *Nadu* level.[2065] The *prabhu* constituted a group of elite people drawn together to witness land grants and demarcation of land boundaries.[2066] The *gavundas* who appear most often in inscriptions were the backbone of medieval polity of the southern Karnataka region. They were landlords and local elite whom the state utilized their services to collect taxes, maintain records of landownership, bear witness to grants and transactions and even raise militia when required.[2067]

Inscriptions that specify land grants, rights and ownership were descriptive of the boundaries of demarcation using natural features such as rivers, streams, water channels, hillocks, large boulders, layout of the village, location of forts

Figure 421: *The Panchakuta Basadi in Kambadahalli was an important center of Jainism during the Ganga period.*

(*kote*) if any in the proximity, irrigation canals, temples, tanks and even shrubs and large trees. Also included was the type of soil, the crops meant to be grown and tanks or wells to be excavated for irrigation.[2068,2069] Inscriptions mention wet land, cultivable land, forest and waste land.[2070] There are numerous references to hamlets (*palli*) belonging to the hunter communities who resided in them (*bedapalli*).[2071] From the 6th century onwards, the inscriptions refer to feudal lords by the title *arasa*. The *arasas* were either brahmins or from tribal background who controlled hereditary territories paying periodic tribute to the king.[2072] The *velavali* who were loyal bodyguards of the royalty were fierce warriors under oath (*vele*). They moved with the royal family and were expected to fight for the master and be willing to lay down their lives in the process. If the king died, the *velavali* were required to self immolate on the funeral pyre of the master.[2073]

Economy

The Gangavadi region consisted of the malnad region, the plains (Bayaluseemae) and the semi-malnad with lower elevation and rolling hills. The main crops of the malnad region were paddy, betel leaves, cardamom and pepper and the semi-malnad region with its lower altitude produced rice, millets

Figure 422: *The famous Begur inscription in old Kannada, dated to c. 908–938 CE, from the rule of Western Ganga dynasty King Ereyappa.*

such as ragi and corn, pulses, oilseeds and it was also the base for cattle farming.[2074] The plains to the east were the flat lands fed by Kaveri, Tungabhadra and Vedavati rivers where cultivations of sugarcane, paddy, coconut, areca nut (*adeka totta*), betel leaves, plantain and flowers (*vara vana*) were common.[2075] Sources of irrigation were excavated tanks, wells, natural ponds and water bodies in the catchment area of dams (*Katta*).[2076] Inscriptions attesting to irrigation of previously uncultivated lands seem to indicate an expanding agrarian community.[2077]

Soil types mentioned in records are black soil (*Karimaniya*) in the Sinda-8000 territory and to red soil (*Kebbayya mannu*)[2078,2079] Cultivated land was of three types; wet land, dry land and to a lesser extent garden land with paddy being the dominant crop of the region. Wet lands were called *kalani, galde, nir mannu* or *nir panya* and was specifically used to denote paddy land requiring standing water.[2080] The fact that pastoral economies were spread throughout Gangavadi region comes from references to cowherds in many inscriptions. The terms *gosahasra* (a thousand cows), *gasara* (owner of cows), *gosasi* (donor of cows), *goyiti* (cowherdess), *gosasa* (protector of cows) attest to this.[2081] Inscriptions indicate ownership of cows may have been as important as cultivable land and that there may have existed a social hierarchy based on this.[2082] Inscriptions mention cattle raids attesting to the importance of the pastoral economy, destructive raids, assaults on women (*pendir-udeyulcal*), abduction of women by *bedas* (hunter tribes); all of which indicate the existing militarism of the age.[2083]

Lands that were exempt from taxes were called *manya* and sometimes consisted of several villages. They were granted by local chieftains without any reference to the overlord, indicating a de-centralised economy. These lands, often given to heroes who perished in the line of duty were called *bilavritti* or *kalnad*.[2084] When such a grant was made for the maintenance of temples at the time of consecration, it was called *Talavritti*.[2085] Some types of taxes on income were *kara* or *anthakara* (internal taxes), *utkota* (gifts due to the king), *hiranya* (cash payments) and *sulika* (tolls and duties on imported items). Taxes were collected from those who held the right to cultivate land; even if the land was not actually cultivated.[2086,2087]

Siddhaya was a local tax levied on agriculture and *pottondi* was a tax levied on merchandise by the local feudal ruler. Based on context, *pottondi* also meant 1/10, *aydalavi* meant 1/5 and *elalavi* meant 1/7.[2088] *Mannadare* literally meant land tax and was levied together with shepherds tax (*Kurimbadere*) payable to the chief of shepherds. *Bhaga* meant a portion or share of the produce from land or the land area itself. Minor taxes such as *Kirudere* (due to the landlords) and *samathadere* (raised by the army officers or *samantha*) are mentioned. In addition to taxes for maintenance of the local officer's retinue, villages were obligated to feed armies on the march to and from battles.[2089] *Bittuvatta* or *niravari* taxes comprised usually of a percentage of the produce and was collected for constructing irrigation tanks.[2090]

Culture

Religion

The Western Gangas gave patronage to all the major religions of the time; Jainism and the Hindu sects of Shaivism, Vedic Brahminism and Vaishnavism. However scholars have argued that not all Gangas kings may have given equal priority to all the faiths. Some historians believe that the Gangas were ardent Jains.[2091] However, inscriptions contradict this by providing references to *kalamukhas* (staunch Shaiva ascetics), *pasupatas* and *lokayatas* (followers of *Pasupatha* doctrine) who flourished in Gangavadi, indicating that Shaivism was also popular. King Madhava and Harivarma were devoted to cows and brahmins, King Vishnugopa was a devout Vaishnava,[2092] Madhava III's and Avinita's inscriptions describe lavish endowments to Jain orders and temples[2093] and King Durvinita performed Vedic sacrifices prompting historians to claim he was a Hindu.[2094]

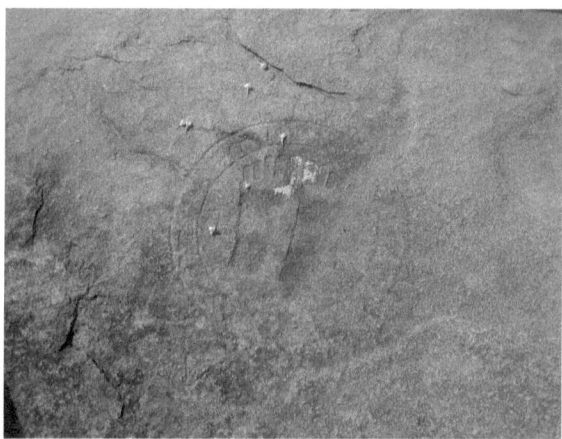

Figure 423: *Footprint worship at Shravanabelagola*

Figure 424: *A mantapa (hall) at the Jain Panchakuta basadi of 9th–10th century at Kambadahalli*

Figure 425: *Gommateshwara at Shravanabelagola (982–983) C.E.*

Jainism became popular in the dynasty in the 8th century when the ruler King Shivamara I constructed numerous Jain *basadis*.[2095] King Butuga II and minister Chavundaraya were staunch Jains which is evident from the construction of the Gommateshwara monolith.[2096] Jains worshipped the twenty four *tirthankars* (*Jinas*) whose images were consecrated in their temples. The worship of the footprint of spiritual leaders such as those of Bhadrabahu in Shravanabelagola from the 10th century is considered a parallel to Buddhism.[2097] Some brahminical influences are seen in the consecration of the Gomateshwara monolith which is the statue of Bahubali, the son of *Tirthankar Adinatha* (just as Hindus worshipped the sons of Shiva).[2098] The worship of subordinate deities such as *yaksa* and *yaksi*, earlier considered as mere attendants of the *tirthankars* was seen from the 7th century to the 12th century.[2099]

Vedic Brahminism was popular in the 6th and 7th centuries when inscriptions refer to grants made to *Srotriya* Brahmins.[2100] These inscriptions also describe the *gotra* (lineage) affiliation to royal families and their adherence of such Vedic rituals as *asvamedha* (horse sacrifice) and *hiranyagarbha*.[2101] Brahmins and kings enjoyed a mutually beneficial relationship; rituals performed by the brahmins gave legitimacy to kings and the land grants made by kings to brahmins elevated them in society to the level of wealthy landowners.[2102] Vaishnavism however maintained a low profile and not many inscriptions describe grants towards its cause.[2103] Some Vaishnava temples were built by the

Figure 426: *Kalleshwara Temple Complex, built in the 10th century by the Nolambas, a Western Ganga feudatory, at Aralaguppe in the Tumkur district*

Gangas such as the *Narayanaswami* temples at Nanjangud, Sattur and Hangala in modern Mysore district.[2104] The deity Vishnu was depicted with four arms holding a conch (*sanka*), discus (*cakra*), mace (*gada*) and lotus (*padma*).[2105] From the beginning of the 8th century, patronage to Shaivism increased in every section of the society; the landed elite, landlords, assemblies (*samaya*), schools of learning (*aghraharas*)[2106] and minor ruling families such as the Bana, Nolamba and Chalukya clans.[2107,2108] The Shaiva temples contained a Shiva *linga* (phallus) in the sanctum sanctorum along with images of the mother goddess, Surya (Sun god)[2109] and Nandi (a bull and attendant of Shiva) which was normally enshrined in a separate pavilion facing the sanctum.[2110,2111] The *linga* was man made and in some cases had etchings of Ganapati (son of Shiva) and Parvati (consort and wife of Shiva) on it. Due to the vigorous efforts of priests and ascetics, Shaiva monastic orders flourished in many places such as Nandi Hills, Avani and Hebbata in modern Kolar district.[2112]

Society

The Western Ganga society in many ways reflected the emerging religious, political and cultural developments of those times. Women became active in local administration because Ganga kings distributed territorial responsibility to their queens such as the feudal queen Parabbaya-arasi of Kundattur[2113] and the queens of King Sripurusha, Butuga II and feudal king Permadi.[2114] Inheritance of fiscal and administrative responsibility by the son-in-law, the wife or

Figure 427: *Hero stone (870–906 A.D.) with old Kannada inscription at Kalleshvara temple in Aralaguppe*

by the daughter is evident. The position of prime minister of King Ereganga II and position of *nalgavunda* (local landlord) bestowed upon Jakkiabbe, the wife of a fallen hero are examples. When Jakkiabbe took to asceticism, her daughter inherited the position.[2115,2116]

The devadasi system (*sule* or courtesan) in temples was prevalent and was modelled after the structures in the royal palace.[2117] Contemporaneous literature such a *Vaddaradhane* makes a mention of the chief queen (*Dharani Mahadevi*) accompanied by lower ranking queens (*arasiyargal*) and courtesans of the women's royal quarter (*pendarasada suleyargal*). Some of the courtesans and concubines employed in the harem of the kings and chieftains were well respected, examples being Nandavva at whose instance a local chief made land grant to a Jain temple.[2118] Education in the royal family was closely supervised and included such subjects as political science, elephant and horse riding, archery, medicine, poetry, grammar, drama, literature, dance, singing and use of musical instruments. Brahmins enjoyed an influential position in society and were exempt from certain taxes and customs due on land. In turn they managed public affairs such as teaching, local judiciary, functioned as trustees and bankers, managed schools, temples, irrigation tanks, rest houses, collected taxes due from villages and raised money from public subscriptions.[2119]

By virtue of a Hindu belief that killing of a brahmin (*Bramhatya*) was a sin, capital punishment was not applicable to them.[2120] Upper caste kshatriyas (*satkshatriya*) were also exempt from capital punishment due to their higher position in the caste system. Severe crimes committed were punishable by the severing of a foot or hand.[2121] Contemporary literary sources reveal up to ten castes in the Hindu caste system; three among kshatriya, three among brahmin, two among vaishya and two among shudras.[2122] Family laws permitted a wife or daughter or surviving relatives of a deceased person to claim properties such as his home, land, grain, money etc. if there were no male heirs. If no claimants to the property existed, the state took possession of these properties as *Dharmadeya* (charitable asset).[2123] Intercaste marriage, child marriage, marriage of a boy to maternal uncles daughter, *Svayamvara* marriage (where the bride garlands her choice of a groom from among many aspirants) were all in vogue.[2124] Memorials containing hero stones (*virkal*) were erected for fallen heroes and the concerned family received monetary aid for maintenance of the memorial.[2125]

The presence of numerous *Mahasatikals* (or *Mastikal* – hero stones for a woman who accepted ritual death upon the demise of her husband) indicates the popularity of Sati among royalty.[2126] Ritual death by *sallekhana* and by *jalasamadhi* (drowning in water) were also practiced.[2127] Popular clothing among men was the use of two unrestricted garments, a Dhoti as a lower garment and a plain cloth as upper garment while women wore Saris with stitched petticoats. Turbans were popular with men of higher standing and people used umbrellas made with bamboo or reeds.[2128] Ornaments were popular among men and women and even elephants and horses were decorated. Men wore finger rings, necklaces (*honnasara* and *honnagala sara*), bracelets (*Kaduga*) and wristlets (*Kaftkina*). Women wore a nose jewel (*bottu*), nose ring (*mugutti*), bangles (*bale* or *kankana*) and various types of necklaces (*honna gante sara* and *kati sutra*). During leisure, men amused themselves with horse riding, watching wrestling bouts, cock fights and ram fights.[2129] There existed a large and well organised network of schools for imparting higher education and these schools were known by various names such as *agraharas*, *ghatikas*, *brahmapura* or *matha*.[2130] Inscriptions mention schools of higher education at Salotgi, Balligavi, Talagunda, Aihole, Arasikere and other places.

Literature

The Western Ganga rule was a period of brisk literary activity in Sanskrit and Kannada, though many of the writings are now considered extinct and are known only from references made to them. Chavundaraya's writing, *Chavundaraya Purana* (or *Trishashtilakshana mahapurana*) of 978 CE, is an early

Figure 428: *The famous Atakur inscription (949 C.E.), a classical Kannada composition pertaining to the Western Ganga-Rashtrakuta victory over the Chola dynasty of Tanjore in the famous battle of Takkolam*

existing work in prose style in Kannada and contains a summary of the Sanskrit writings, *Adipurana* and *Uttarapurana* which were written a century earlier by Jinasena and Gunabhadra during the rule of Rashtrakuta Amoghavarsha I.[2131] The prose, composed in lucid Kannada, was mainly meant for the common man and avoided any reference to complicated elements of Jain doctrines and philosophy. His writings seem to be influenced by the writings of his predecessor Adikavi Pampa and contemporary Ranna. The work narrates the legends of a total of 63 Jain proponents including twenty-four Jain *Tirthankar*, twelve *Chakravartis*, nine *Balabhadras*, nine *Narayanas* and nine *Pratinarayanas*.[2132,2133]

The earliest postulated Kannada writer from this dynasty is King Durvinita of the 6th century. Kavirajamarga of 850 CE, refers to a Durvinita as an early writer of Kannada prose.[2134,2135] Around 900 CE, Gunavarma I authored the Kannada works, *Shudraka* and *Harivamsha*. His writings are considered extinct but references to these writings are found in later years. He is known to have been patronised by King Ereganga Neetimarga II. In *Shudraka*, he has favourably compared his patron to King Shudraka of ancient times.[2136,2137] The great Kannada poet Ranna was patronised by Chavundaraya in his early

Figure 429: *Mahasthambha (pillar) and Chandragupta Basadi at Chandragiri Hill in Shravanabelagola*

literary days.[2138] Ranna's classic *Parashurama charite* is considered a eulogy of his patron who held such titles as *Samara Parashurama*.

Nagavarma I, a brahmin scholar who came from Vengi in modern Andhra Pradesh (late 10th century) was also patronised by Chavundaraya. He wrote *Chandombudhi* (ocean of prosody) addressed to his wife. This is considered the earliest available Kannada writing in prosody. He also wrote one of the earliest available romance classics in Kannada called *Karnataka Kadambari* in sweet and flowing *champu* (mixed verse and prose) style. It is based on an earlier romantic work in Sanskrit by poet Bana and is popular among critics. *Gajashtaka* (hundred verses on elephants), a rare Kannada work on elephant management was written by King Shivamara II around 800 CE but this work is now considered extinct.[2139] Other writers such as Manasiga and Chandrabhatta were known to be popular in the 10th century.[2140]

In an age of classical Sanskrit literature, Madhava II (brother of King Vishnugopa) wrote a treatise *Dattaka Sutravritti* which was based on an earlier work on erotics by a writer called Dattaka. A Sanskrit version of *Vaddakatha*, a commentary on Pāṇini's grammar called *Sabdavathara* and a commentary on the 15th chapter of a Sanskrit work called *Kiratarjunneya* by poet Bharavi (who was in Durvinita's court) are ascribed to Durvinita.[2141] King Shivamara II is known to have written *Gajamata Kalpana*. Hemasena, also known as Vidya Dhananjaya authored *Raghavapandaviya*, a narration of the stories of Rama and the Pandavas simultaneously through puns.[2142] *Gayachintamani* and *Kshatrachudamini* which were based on poet Bana's work *Kadambari* were written by Hemasena's pupil Vadeebhasimha in prose style. and Chavundaraya wrote *Charitarasara*.

Figure 430: *Chandragiri hill temple complex at Shravanabelagola*

Architecture

The Western Ganga style of architecture was influenced by the Pallava and Badami Chalukya architectural features, in addition to indigenous Jain features.[2143] The Ganga pillars with a conventional lion at the base and a circular shaft of the pillar on its head, the stepped *Vimana* of the shrine with horizontal mouldings and square pillars were features inherited from the Pallavas. These features are also found in structures built by their subordinates, the Banas and Nolambas.

The monolith of Gomateshwara commissioned by Chavundaraya is considered the high point of the Ganga sculptural contribution in ancient Karnataka. Carved from fine-grained white granite, the image stands on a lotus. It has no support up to the thighs and is 60 feet (18 m) tall with the face measuring 6.5 feet (2.0 m). With the serene expression on the face of the image, its curled hair with graceful locks, its proportional anatomy, the monolith size, and the combination of its artistry and craftsmanship have led it to be called the mightiest achievement in sculptural art in medieval Karnataka.[2144] It is the largest monolithic statue in the world. Their free standing pillars called *Mahasthambha* or *Bhrahmasthambha* are also considered unique, examples of which are the Brahmadeva pillar and Tyagada Brahmadeva Pillar.[2145,2146] At the top of the pillar whose shaft (cylindrical or octagonal) is decorated with creepers and other floral motifs is the seated *Brahma* and the base of the pillar normally has engravings of important Jain personalities and inscriptions.[2147]

Other important contributions are the Jain basadis' whose towers have gradually receding stories (*talas*) ornamented with small models of temples. These tiny shrines have in them engravings of tirthankars (Jain saints). Semicircular windows connect the shrines and decorative Kirtimukha (demon faces) are

Figure 431: *Ceiling sculpture, Panchakuta Basadi, Kambadahalli*

used at the top. The Chavundaraya basadi built in the 10th or 11th century, Chandragupta basadi built in the 6th century and the monolithic of Gomateshwara of 982 are the most important monuments at Shravanabelagola.[2148] Some features were added to the Chandragupta basadi by famous Hoysala sculptor Dasoja in the 12th century. The decorative doorjambs and perforated screen windows which depict scenes from the life of King Chandragupta Maurya are known to be his creation.[2149] The Panchakuta Basadi at Kambadahalli (five towered Jan temple) of about 900 with a Brahmadeva pillar is an excellent example of Dravidian art.[2150] The wall niches here are surmounted by *torana* (lintel) with carvings of floral motifs, flying divine creatures (*gandharva*) and imaginary monsters (*makara*) ridden by *Yaksas* (attendants of saints) while the niches are occupied by images of tirthankars themselves.[2151]

The Gangas built many Hindu temples with impressive Dravidian gopuras containing stucco figures from the Hindu pantheon, decorated pierced screen windows which are featured in the *mantapa* (hall) along with *saptamatrika* carvings (seven heavenly mothers).[2152] Some well known examples are the Arakeshvara Temple at Hole Alur,[2153] Kapileswara temple at Manne, Kolaramma temple at Kolar, Rameshvara temple at Narasamangala,[2154] Nagareshvara temple at Begur[2155] and the Kallesvara temple at Aralaguppe.[2156] At Talakad they built the Maralesvara temple, the Arakesvara temple and the Patalesvara temple. Unlike the Jain temples where floral frieze decoration is

Figure 432: *Chavundaraya basadi on Chandragiri hill in Shravanabelagola temple complex*

common, Hindu temples were distinguished by friezes (slab of stone with decorative sculptures) illustrating episodes from the epics and puranas. Another unique legacy of the Gangas are the number of *virgal* (hero stones) they have left behind; memorials containing sculptural details in relief of war scenes, Hindu deities, *saptamatrikas*, Jain tirthankars and ritual death (such as the Doddahundi hero stone).[2157]

Language

Part of a series on the
History of Karnataka

- Political history of medieval Karnataka
- Origin of Karnataka's name
- Kadambas and Gangas
- Chalukya Empire
- Rashtrakuta Empire
- Western Chalukya Empire
- Southern Kalachuri
- Hoysala Empire

- Vijayanagara Empire
- Bahmani Sultanate
- Bijapur Sultanate
- Kingdom of Mysore
- Nayakas of Keladi
- Nayakas of Chitradurga
- Haleri Kingdom
- Unification of Karnataka

Categories

- Architecture
- Forts
- Economies
- Societies

- $\underline{v}$
- $\underline{t}$
- $\underline{e}^{2158}$

The Western Gangas used Kannada and Sanskrit extensively as their language of administration. Some of their inscriptions are also bilingual in these languages. In bilingual inscriptions the formulaic passages stating origin myths, genealogies, titles of Kings and benedictions tended to be in Sanskrit, while the actual terms of the grant such as information on the land or village granted, its boundaries, participation of local authorities, rights and obligations of the grantee, taxes and dues and other local concerns were in the local language.[2159] The usage of these two languages showed important changes over the centuries. During the first phase (350–725), Sanskrit copper plates dominated, indicating the initial ascendancy of the local language as a language of administration and the fact that majority of the records from this phase were *brahmadeya* grants (grants to Brahmin temples).[2160] In the second phase (725–1000), lithic inscriptions in Kannada outnumbered Sanskrit copper plates, consistent with the patronage Kannada received from rich and literate Jains who used Kannada as their medium to spread the Jain faith.[2161] Recent excavations at Tumbula near Mysore have revealed a set of early copper plate bilingual inscriptions dated 444. The genealogy of the kings of the dynasty is described in Sanskrit while Kannada was used to describe the boundary of the village. An interesting inscription discovered at Beguru near modern Bangalore that deserves mention is the epigraph dated 890 that refers to a *Bengaluru* war. This is in *Hale Kannada* (old Kannada) language and is the earliest mention of the name of Bangalore city. The Western Gangas minted coins with Kannada and Nagari legends,[2162] the most common feature on their coins was the image of an elephant on the obverse and floral petal symbols on the reverse. The Kannada legend *Bhadr*, a royal umbrella or a conch shell appeared on top of the elephant image. The denominations are the *pagoda* (weighing 52 grains), the

Figure 433: *Old Kannada inscription at the base of Gomateshwara monolith in Shravanabelagola (981 CE.)*

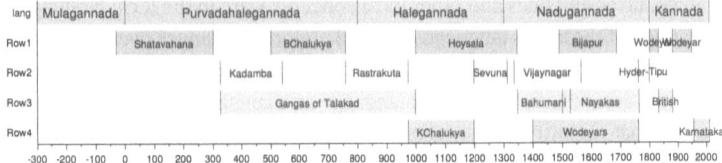

fanam weighting one tenth or one half of the *pagoda* and the quarter *fanams*.

Timeline

The template below shows the Timeline of Karnataka. Note the extent of time (around 700 years) the Ganga kingdom flourished.

Bibliography

 Wikimedia Commons has media related to ***Western Ganga Dynasty***.

Books <templatestyles src="Template:Refbegin/styles.css" />
- Adiga, Malini (2006) [2006]. *The Making of Southern Karnataka: Society, Polity and Culture in the early medieval period, AD 400–1030.* Chennai: Orient Longman. ISBN 81-250-2912-5.
- Altekar, Anant Sadashiv (1934) [1934]. *The Rashtrakutas And Their Times; being a political, administrative, religious, social, economic and literary history of the Deccan during C. 750 A.D. to C. 1000 A.D.* Poona: Oriental Book Agency. OCLC 3793499[2163].
- Chopra, Ravindran, Subrahmanian, P.N., T.K., N. (2003) [2003]. *History of South India (Ancient, Medieval and Modern) Part I.* New Delhi: Chand publications. ISBN 81-219-0153-7.
- Kamath, Suryanath U. (2001) [1980]. *A concise history of Karnataka : from pre-historic times to the present.* Bangalore: Jupiter books. LCCN 80905179[2164]. OCLC 7796041[2165].
- Karmarkar, A.P. (1947) [1947]. *Cultural history of Karnataka : ancient and medieval.* Dharwar: Karnataka Vidyavardhaka Sangha. OCLC 8221605[2166].
- Keay, John (2000) [2000]. *India: A History.* New York: Grove Publications. ISBN 0-8021-3797-0.
- Narasimhacharya, R (1988) [1988]. *History of Kannada Literature.* New Delhi, Madras: Asian Educational Services. ISBN 81-206-0303-6.
- Prabhu, Govindaraya S (2009). *The Nolambas Coinage and History.* Govindraya Prabhu S. ISBN 81-8465-141-4.
- Ramesh, K.V. (1984) [1984]. *Chalukyas of Vatapi.* Delhi: Agam Kala Prakashan. ASIN B0006EHSP0[2167]. LCCN 84900575[2168]. OCLC 13869730[2169]. OL 3007052M[2170].
- Sarma, I.K. (1992) [1992]. *Temples of the Gangas of Karnataka.* New Delhi: Archaeological Survey of India. ISBN 0-19-560686-8.
- Sastri, Nilakanta K.A. (2002) [1955]. *A history of South India from prehistoric times to the fall of Vijayanagar.* New Delhi: Indian Branch, Oxford University Press. ISBN 0-19-560686-8.
- Thapar, Romila (2003) [2003]. *Penguin History of Early India: From origins to AD 1300.* New Delhi: Penguin. ISBN 0-14-302989-4.

Web <templatestyles src="Template:Refbegin/styles.css" />
- "Gangas of Talakad" by [[S. Srikanta Sastri[2171]]]
- Arthikaje. "History of Karnataka: The Gangas of Talakad"[2172]. OurKarnataka.Com. Archived from the original[2173] on 15 December 2006. Retrieved 2006-12-31.
- Havalaiah, N (January 2004). "Ancient inscriptions"[2174]. *The Hindu*. Chennai, India. Retrieved 2007-05-30.

- Kamat, Jyotsna. "The Ganga Dynasty"[2175]. *Kamat's Potpourri*. Retrieved 2007-05-30.
- Khajane, Muralidhara (February 2006). "An ancient site connected with Jainism"[2176]. *The Hindu*. Chennai, India. Retrieved 2007-06-30.
- Prabhu, Govindaraya S. "Coins of Gangas"[2177]. *Indian Coins*. Prabhu's web page on Indian coinage. Archived from the original[2178] on 2007-07-10. Retrieved 2007-06-30.
- Staff Reporter (August 20, 2004). "Inscription reveals Bangalore is over 1,000 years old"[2179]. *The Hindu*. Chennai, India. Retrieved 2007-06-30.

<indicator name="featured-star"> ⭐ </indicator>

Chalukya dynasty

Chalukya dynasty	
Empire (Subordinate to Kadamba Dynasty until 543)	
543–753	
Extent of Badami Chalukya Empire, 636 CE, 740 CE	
Capital	Badami
Languages	Kannada Sanskrit
Religion	Hinduism Buddhism[2180] Jainism
Government	Monarchy
Maharaja	
• 543–566	Pulakeshin I
• 746–753	Kirtivarman II

Chalukya dynasty

History		
•	Earliest records	543
•	Established	543
•	Disestablished	753
	Preceded by	**Succeeded by**
	Kadamba dynasty	Rashtrakuta dynasty Eastern Chalukyas

Today part of	India

The **Chalukya dynasty** ([tʃaːlukjə]) was an Indian royal dynasty that ruled large parts of southern and central India between the 6th and the 12th centuries. During this period, they ruled as three related yet individual dynasties. The earliest dynasty, known as the "Badami Chalukyas", ruled from Vatapi (modern Badami) from the middle of the 6th century. The Badami Chalukyas began to assert their independence at the decline of the Kadamba kingdom of Banavasi and rapidly rose to prominence during the reign of Pulakeshin II. After the death of Pulakeshin II, the Eastern Chalukyas became an independent kingdom in the eastern Deccan. They ruled from Vengi until about the 11th century. In the western Deccan, the rise of the Rashtrakutas in the middle of the 8th century eclipsed the Chalukyas of Badami before being revived by their descendants, the Western Chalukyas, in the late 10th century. These Western Chalukyas ruled from Kalyani (modern Basavakalyan) until the end of the 12th century.

The rule of the Chalukyas marks an important milestone in the history of South India and a golden age in the history of Karnataka. The political atmosphere in South India shifted from smaller kingdoms to large empires with the ascendancy of Badami Chalukyas. A Southern India-based kingdom took control and consolidated the entire region between the Kaveri and the Narmada rivers. The rise of this empire saw the birth of efficient administration, overseas trade and commerce and the development of new style of architecture called "Chalukyan architecture". Kannada literature, which had enjoyed royal support in the 9th century Rashtrakuta court found eager patronage from the Western Chalukyas in the Jain and Veerashaiva traditions. The 11th century saw the birth of Telugu literature under the patronage of the Eastern Chalukyas.

Figure 434: *Old Kannada inscription of Chalukya King Mangalesha dated 578 CE at Badami cave temple no.3*

Origins

Natives of Karnataka

While opinions vary regarding the early origins of the Chalukyas, the consensus among noted historians such as John Keay, D.C. Sircar, Hans Raj, S. Sen, Kamath, K. V. Ramesh and Karmarkar is the founders of the empire at Badami were native to the modern Karnataka region.[2181,2182,2183,2184,2185,2186,2187,2188,2189,2190]

A theory that they were descendants of a 2nd-century chieftain called Kandachaliki Remmanaka, a feudatory of the Andhra Ikshvaku (from an Ikshvaku inscription of the 2nd century) was put forward. This according to Kamath has failed to explain the difference in lineage. The Kandachaliki feudatory call themselves *Vashisthiputras* of the *Hiranyakagotra*. The Chalukyas, however, address themselves as *Harithiputras* of *Manavyasagotra* in their inscriptions, which is the same lineage as their early overlords, the Kadambas of Banavasi. This makes them descendants of the Kadambas. The Chalukyas took control of the territory formerly ruled by the Kadambas.[2191]

A later record of Eastern Chalukyas mentions the northern origin theory and claims one ruler of Ayodhya came south, defeated the Pallavas and married a Pallava princess. She had a child called Vijayaditya who is claimed

Figure 435: *Old Kannada inscription on victory pillar, Virupaksha Temple, Pattadakal, 733–745 CE*

to be the Pulakeshin I's father. However, according to the historians K. V. Ramesh, Chopra and Sastri, there are Badami Chalukya inscriptions that confirm Jayasimha was Pulakeshin I's grandfather and Ranaraga, his father.[2192,2193,2194,2195] Kamath and Moraes claim it was a popular practice in the 11th century to link South Indian royal family lineage to a Northern kingdom. The Badami Chalukya records themselves are silent with regards to the Ayodhya origin.[2196,2197]

While the northern origin theory has been dismissed by many historians, the epigraphist K. V. Ramesh has suggested that an earlier southern migration is a distinct possibility which needs examination.[2198] According to him, the complete absence of any inscriptional reference of their family connections to Ayodhya, and their subsequent Kannadiga identity may have been due to their earlier migration into present day Karnataka region where they achieved success as chieftains and kings. Hence, the place of origin of their ancestors may have been of no significance to the kings of the empire who may have considered themselves natives of the Kannada speaking region.[2199] The writing of 12th century Kashmiri poet Bilhana suggests the Chalukya family belonged to the Shudra caste while other sources claim they were Kshatriyas.[2200]

The historians Jan Houben and Kamath, and the epigraphist D.C. Sircar note the Badami Chalukya inscriptions are in Kannada and Sanskrit.[2201,2202,2203]

According to the historian N. L. Rao, their inscriptions call them *Karnatas* and their names use indigenous Kannada titles such as *Priyagallam* and *Noduttagelvom*. The names of some Chalukya princes end with the pure Kannada term *arasa* (meaning "king" or "chief").[2204,2205] The Rashtrakuta inscriptions call the Chalukyas of Badami *Karnatabala* ("Power of Karnata"). It has been proposed by the historian S. C. Nandinath that the word "Chalukya" originated from *Salki* or *Chalki* which is a Kannada word for an agricultural implement.[2206,2207]

Historical sources

Inscriptions in Sanskrit and Kannada are the main source of information about Badami Chalukya history. Among them, the Badami cave inscriptions of Mangalesha (578), Kappe Arabhatta record of c. 700, Peddavaduguru inscription of Pulakeshin II, the Kanchi Kailasanatha Temple inscription and Pattadakal Virupaksha Temple inscription of Vikramaditya II (all in Kannada language) provide more evidence of the Chalukya language.[2208,2209] The Badami cliff inscription of Pulakeshin I (543), the Mahakuta Pillar inscription of Mangalesha (595) and the Aihole inscription of Pulakeshin II (634) are examples of important Sanskrit inscriptions written in old Kannada script.[2210] The reign of the Chalukyas saw the arrival of Kannada as the predominant language of inscriptions along with Sanskrit, in areas of the Indian peninsula outside what is known as Tamilaham (Tamil country).[2211] Several coins of the Badami Chalukyas with Kannada legends have been found. All this indicates that Kannada language flourished during this period.[2212]

Travelogues of contemporary foreign travellers have provided useful information about the Chalukyan empire. The Chinese traveller Xuanzang had visited the court of Pulakeshin II. At the time of this visit, as mentioned in the Aihole record, Pulakeshin II had divided his empire into three *Maharashtrakas* or great provinces comprising 99,000 villages each. This empire possibly covered present day Karnataka, Maharashtra and coastal Konkan.[2213,2214] Xuanzang, impressed with the governance of the empire observed that the benefits of the king's efficient administration was felt far and wide. Later, Persian emperor Khosrau II exchanged ambassadors with Pulakeshin II.[2215,2216,2217]

Legends

Court poets of the Western Chalukya dynasty of Kalyani narrate:

"Once when Brahma, the creator, was engaged in the performance of the *sandhya* (twilight) rituals, Indra approached and beseeched him to create a hero who could put to an end the increasing evil on earth. On being thus requested, Brahma looked steadily into the *Chuluka-jala* (the water of oblation in his palm) and out sprang thence a great warrior, the progenitor of the Chalukyas".[2218] The Chalukyas claimed to have been nursed by the *Sapta Matrikas* ("seven divine mothers") and were worshippers of many gods including Siva, Vishnu, Chamundi, Surya, Kubera, Parvati, Vinayaka and Kartikeya.

Some scholars connect the Chalukyas with the Chaulukyas (Solankis) of Gujarat. According to a myth mentioned in latter manuscripts of Prithviraj Raso, Chaulukyas were born out of fire-pit (Agnikund) at Mount Abu. However it has been reported that the story of Agnikula is not mentioned at all in the original version of the Prithviraj Raso preserved in the Fort Library at Bikaner.

According to the Nilagunda inscription of King Vikramaditya VI (11th century or later), the Chalukyas originally hailed from Ayodhya where fifty-nine kings ruled, and later, sixteen more of this family ruled from South India where they had migrated. This is repeated by his court poet Bilhana, who claims that the first member of the family, "Chalukya", was so named as he was born in the "hollow of the hands" of God Brahma.[2219,2220]

According to a theory put forward by Lewis, the Chalukya were descendants of the "Seleukia" tribe of Iraq and that their conflict with the Pallava of Kanchi was, but a continuation of the conflict between ancient Seleukia and "Parthians", the proposed ancestors of Pallavas. However, this theory has been rejected by Kamath as it seeks to build lineages based simply on similar-sounding clan names.[2221]

Periods in Chalukya history

Chalukya dynasties
• $\frac{v}{t}$ • $\frac{-}{e}$[2222]

The Chalukyas ruled over the Deccan plateau in India for over 600 years. During this period, they ruled as three closely related, but individual dynasties. These are the "Chalukyas of Badami" (also called "Early Chalukyas"), who ruled between the 6th and the 8th century, and the two sibling dynasties, the "Chalukyas of Kalyani" (also called Western Chalukyas or "Later Chalukyas") and the "Chalukyas of Vengi" (also called Eastern Chalukyas).

Figure 436: *Bhutanatha temple complex, at Badami*

Chalukyas of Badami

In the 6th century, with the decline of the Gupta dynasty and their immediate successors in northern India, major changes began to happen in the area south of the Vindhyas – the Deccan and Tamilaham. The age of small kingdoms had given way to large empires in this region.[2223] The Chalukya dynasty was established by Pulakeshin I in 543.[2224,2225,2226] Pulakeshin I took Vatapi (modern Badami in Bagalkot district, Karnataka) under his control and made it his capital. Pulakeshin I and his descendants are referred to as "Chalukyas of Badami". They ruled over an empire that comprised the entire state of Karnataka and most of Andhra Pradesh in the Deccan.

Pulakeshin II, whose pre-coronation name was Ereya,[2227] commanded control over the entire Deccan and is perhaps the most well-known emperor of the Badami dynasty.[2228,2229] He is considered one of the notable kings in Indian history.[2230,2231,2232] His queens were princess from the Alupa Dynasty of South Canara and the Western Ganga Dynasty of Talakad, clans with whom the Chalukyas maintained close family and marital relationships.[2233,2234] Pulakeshin II extended the Chalukya Empire up to the northern extents of the Pallava kingdom and halted the southward march of Harsha by defeating him on the banks of the river Narmada. He then defeated the Vishnukundins in the south-eastern Deccan.[2235,2236,2237,2238] Pallava Narasimhavarman however reversed this victory in 642 by attacking and occupying Badami temporarily. It is presumed Pulakeshin II, "the great hero", died fighting.[2239]

The Badami Chalukya dynasty went into a brief decline following the death of Pulakeshin II due to internal feuds when Badami was occupied by the Pallavas for a period of thirteen years.[2240,2241] It recovered during the reign of Vikramaditya I, who succeeded in pushing the Pallavas out of Badami and restoring order to the empire. Vikramaditya I took the title "Rajamalla" (*lit* "Sovereign of the *Mallas*" or Pallavas).[2242] The thirty-seven year rule of Vijayaditya (696–733) was a prosperous one and is known for prolific temple building activity.[2243,2244]

The empire was its peak again during the rule of the illustrious Vikramaditya II (733–744) who is known not only for his repeated invasions of the territory of Tondaimandalam and his subsequent victories over Pallava Nandivarman II, but also for his benevolence towards the people and the monuments of Kanchipuram, the Pallava capital.[2245,2246] He thus avenged the earlier humiliation of the Chalukyas by the Pallavas and engraved a Kannada inscription on the victory pillar at the Kailasanatha Temple.[2247,2248] During his reign Arab intruders of the Umayyad Caliphate invaded southern Gujarat which was under Chalukya rule but the Arabs were defeated and driven out by Pulakesi, a Chalukya governor of Navsari.[2249] He later overran the other traditional kingdoms of Tamil country, the Pandyas, the Cholas and the Cheras in addition to subduing a Kalabhra ruler.[2250] The last Chalukya king, Kirtivarman II, was overthrown by the Rashtrakuta King Dantidurga in 753.[2251] At their peak, the Chalukyas ruled a vast empire stretching from the Kaveri in the south to the Narmada in the north.

Chalukyas of Kalyani

The Chalukyas revived their fortunes in 973 after over 200 years of dormancy when much of the Deccan was under the rule of the Rashtrakutas. The genealogy of the kings of this empire is still debated. One theory, based on contemporary literary and inscriptional evidence plus the finding that the Western Chalukyas employed titles and names commonly used by the early Chalukyas, suggests that the Western Chalukya kings belonged to the same family line as the illustrious Badami Chalukya dynasty of the 6th century[2252,2253] while other Western Chalukya inscriptional evidence indicates they were a distinct line unrelated to the Early Chalukyas.[2254]

Tailapa II, a Rashtrakuta feudatory ruling from Tardavadi – 1000 (Bijapur district) overthrew Karka II, re-established the Chalukya rule in the western Deccan and recovered most of the Chalukya empire.[2255,2256] The Western Chalukyas ruled for over 200 years and were in constant conflict with the Cholas, and with their cousins, the Eastern Chalukyas of Vengi. Vikramaditya VI is widely considered the most notable ruler of the dynasty.[2257,2258]

Starting from the very beginning of his reign, which lasted fifty years, he abolished the original *Saka* era and established the *Vikrama Era*. Most subsequent Chalukya inscriptions are dated in this new era.[2259,2260] Vikramaditya VI was an ambitious and skilled military leader. Under his leadership the Western Chalukyas were able to end the Chola influence over Vengi (coastal Andhra) and become the dominant power in the Deccan.[2261,2262] The Western Chalukya period was an important age in the development of Kannada literature and Sanskrit literature.[2263,2264] They went into their final dissolution towards the end of the 12th century with the rise of the Hoysala Empire, the Pandyas, the Kakatiya and the Seuna Yadavas of Devagiri.[2265]

Chalukyas of Vengi

Pulakeshin II conquered the eastern Deccan, corresponding to the coastal districts of modern Andhra Pradesh in 616, defeating the remnants of the Vishnukundina kingdom. He appointed his brother Kubja Vishnuvardhana as Viceroy in 621.[2266,2267] Thus the Eastern Chalukyas were originally of Kannada stock.[2268] After the death of Pulakeshin II, the Vengi Viceroyalty developed into an independent kingdom and included the region between Nellore and Visakhapatnam.[2269]

After the decline of the Badami Chalukya empire in the mid-8th century, territorial disputes flared up between the Rashtrakutas, the new rulers of the western deccan, and the Eastern Chalukyas. For much of the next two centuries, the Eastern Chalukyas had to accept subordination towards the Rashtrakutas.[2270] Apart from a rare military success, such as the one by Vijayaditya II(c.808–847), it was only during the rule of Bhima I (c.892–921) that these Chalukyas were able to celebrate a measure of independence. After the death of Bhima I, the Andhra region once again saw succession disputes and interference in Vengi affairs by the Rashtrakutas.

The fortunes of the Eastern Chalukyas took a turn around 1000. Danarnava, their king, was killed in battle in 973 by the Telugu Choda King Bhima who then imposed his rule over the region for twenty-seven years. During this time, Danarnava's two sons took refuge in the Chola kingdom. Choda Bhima's invasion of Tondaimandalam, a Chola territory, and his subsequent death on the battlefield opened up a new era in Chola–Chalukya relations. Saktivarman I, the elder son of Danarnava was crowned as the ruler of Vengi in 1000, though under the control of king Rajaraja Chola I.[2271] This new relationship between the Cholas and the coastal Andhra kingdom was unacceptable to the Western Chalukyas, who had by then replaced the Rashtrakutas as the main power in the western Deccan. The Western Chalukyas sought to brook the growing Chola influence in the Vengi region but were unsuccessful.[2272]

Figure 437: *Virupaksha temple in Dravidian style at Pattadakal, built 740 CE*

Initially, the Eastern Chalukyas had encouraged Kannada language and literature, though, after a period of time, local factors took over and they gave importance to Telugu language.[2273,2274] Telugu literature owes its growth to the Eastern Chalukyas.[2275]

Architecture

The Badami Chalukya era was an important period in the development of South Indian architecture. The kings of this dynasty were called *Umapati Varlabdh* and built many temples for the Hindu god Shiva.[2276] Their style of architecture is called "Chalukyan architecture" or "Karnata Dravida architecture".[2277,2278] Nearly a hundred monuments built by them, rock cut (cave) and structural, are found in the Malaprabha river basin in modern Bagalkot district of northern Karnataka.[2279] The building material they used was a reddish-golden Sandstone found locally. These cave temples are basically excavations, cut out of the living rock sites they occupy. They were not built as their structural counterparts were, rather created by a special technique known as "subtraction" and are basically sculptural.[2280] Though they ruled a vast empire, the Chalukyan workshops concentrated most of their temple building activity in a relatively small area within the Chalukyan heartland – Aihole, Badami, Pattadakal and Mahakuta in modern Karnataka state.[2281]

Their temple building activity can be categorised into three phases. The early phase began in the last quarter of the 6th century and resulted in many cave temples, prominent among which are three elementary cave temples at Aihole (one Vedic, one Jain and one Buddhist which is incomplete), followed by four developed cave temples at Badami (of which cave 3, a Vaishnava temple, is dated accurately to 578 CE). These cave temples at Badami are similar, in that, each has a plain exterior but an exceptionally well finished interior consisting of a pillared verandah, a columned hall (*mantapa*) and a cella (shrine, cut deep into rock) which contains the deity of worship.[2282] In Badami, three caves temples are Vedic and one in Jain. The Vedic temples contain large well sculpted images of Harihara, Mahishasuramardhini, Varaha, Narasimha, Trivikrama, Vishnu seated on Anantha (the snake) and Nataraja (dancing Shiva).[2283]

The second phase of temple building was at Aihole (where some seventy structures exist and has been called "one of the cradles of Indian temple architecture"[2284]) and Badami. Though the exact dating of these temples has been debated, there is consensus that the beginnings of these constructions are from c. 600.[2285,2286,2287] These are the Lad Khan Temple (dated by some to c. 450 but more accurately to 620) with its interesting perforated stone windows and sculptures of river goddesses; the Meguti Jain Temple (634) which shows progress in structural design; the Durga Temple with its northern Indian style tower (8th century) and experiments to adapt a Buddhist *Chaitya* design to a brahminical one (its stylistic framework is overall a hybrid of north and south Indian styles.); the Huccimalli Gudi Temple with a new inclusion, a vestibule, connecting the sanctum to the hall.[2288] Other *dravida* style temples from this period are the Naganatha Temple at Nagaral; the Banantigudi Temple, the Mahakutesvara Temple and the Mallikarjuna Temple at Mahakuta; and the Lower Sivalaya Temple, the Malegitti Sivalaya Temple (upper) and the Jambulingesvara Temple at Badami. Located outside the Chalukyan architectural heartland, 140 km south-east of Badami, with a structure related to the Early Chalukya style is the unusual Parvati Temple at Sanduru which dates to the late 7th century. It is medium-sized, 48 ft long and 37 ft wide. It has a *nagara* (north Indian) style *vimana* (tower) and *dravida* (south Indian) style parts, has no mantapa (hall) and consists of an *antarala* (vestibule) crowned with a barrel-vaulted tower (*sukhanasi*). The "staggered" base plan of the temple became popular much later, in the 11th century.[2289,2290]

The structural temples at Pattadakal, built in the 8th century and now a UNESCO World Heritage Site, marks the culmination and mature phase of Badami Chalukyan architecture. The Bhutanatha group of temples at Badami are also from this period. There are ten temples at Pattadakal, six in southern *dravida* style and four in the northern *nagara* style. Well known among these are the Sangamesvara Temple (725), the Virupaksha Temple (740–745) and the Mallikarjuna Temple (740–745) in the southern style. The Papanatha temple (680) and Galaganatha Temple (740) are early attempts in the *nagara – dravida* fusion style.[2291] Inscriptional evidence suggests that the Virupaksha and the Mallikarjuna Temples were commissioned by the two queens of King Vikramaditya II after his military success over the Pallavas of Kanchipuram. Some well known names of Chalukyan architects are Revadi Ovajja, Narasobba and Anivarita Gunda.[2292]

The reign of Western Chalukyas was an important period in the development of Deccan architecture. Their architecture served as a conceptual link between the Badami Chalukya architecture of the 8th century and the Hoysala architecture popularised in the 13th century.[2293,2294] The centre of their cultural and temple-building activity lay in the Tungabhadra region of modern Karnataka state, encompassing the present-day Dharwad district; it included areas of present-day Haveri and Gadag districts.[2295,2296] Here, large medieval workshops built numerous monuments.[2297] These monuments, regional variants of pre-existing dravida temples, defined the *Karnata dravida* tradition.[2298]

The most notable of the many buildings dating from this period are the Mahadeva Temple at Itagi in the Koppal district,[2299,2300] the Kasivisvesvara Temple at Lakkundi in the Gadag district,[2301,2302] the Mallikarjuna Temple at Kuruvatti, and the Kallesvara Temple at Bagali,[2303] both in the Davangere district.[2304] Other notable constructions are the Dodda Basappa Temple at Dambal (Gadag district),[2305,2306] the Siddhesvara Temple at Haveri (Haveri district),[2307,2308] and the Amrtesvara Temple at Annigeri (Dharwad district).[2309,2310] The Eastern Chalukyas built some fine temples at Alampur, in modern eastern Andhra Pradesh.[2311,2312]

Figure 438: *Bahubali at Jain Cave temple No. 4 at Badami, 6th century*

Figure 439: *Vishnu image in Cave temple No. 3*

Figure 440: *Bhutanatha group of temples facing the Badami tank*

Figure 441: *The Parvati Temple, located about 140 km southeast to the Badami*

Figure 442: *Aihole – Durga Temple Front View*

Figure 443: *Aihole – Meguti Jain Temple*

Figure 444: *Mallikarjuna temple in dravidian style and Kashi Vishwanatha temple in nagara style at Pattadakal, built 740 CE*

Figure 445: *Dancing Shiva in cave no. 1 in Badami*

Figure 446: *Papanatha temple at Pattadakal – fusion of southern and northern Indian styles, 680 CE*

Literature

The Aihole inscription of Pulakeshin II (634) written by his court poet Ravikirti in Sanskrit language and Kannada script is considered as a classical piece of poetry.[2313] A few verses of a poet named Vijayanaka who describes herself as the "dark Sarasvati" have been preserved. It is possible that she may have been a queen of prince Chandraditya (a son of Pulakeshin II).[2314] Famous writers in Sanskrit from the Western Chalukya period are Vijnaneshwara who achieved fame by writing Mitakshara, a book on Hindu law, and King Someshvara III,

Figure 447: *Poetry on stone at the Meguti temple (Aihole inscription) dated 634 CE, in Sanskrit language and old Kannada script, with a Kannada language endorsement of about the same date at the bottom.*

a noted scholar, who compiled an encyclopedia of all arts and sciences called *Manasollasa*.[2315]

From the period of the Badami Chalukyas, references are made to the existence of Kannada literature, though not much has survived.[2316] Inscriptions however refer to Kannada as the "natural language".[2317] The Kappe Arabhatta record of c. 700 in *tripadi* (three line) metre is the earliest available work in Kannada poetics.[2318] *Karnateshwara Katha*, which was quoted later by Jayakirti, is believed to be a eulogy of Pulakeshin II and to have belonged to this period.[2319] Other probable Kannada writers, whose works are not extant now but titles of which are known from independent references[2320] are Syamakundacharya (650), who is said to have authored the *Prabhrita*, and Srivaradhadeva (also called Tumubuluracharya, 650 or earlier), the possible author of the *Chudamani* ("Crest Jewel"), a lengthy commentary on logic.[2321,2322,2323]

The rule of the Western and Eastern Chalukyas, however, is a major event in the history of Kannada and Telugu literatures respectively. By the 9th–10th centuries, Kannada language had already seen some of its most notable writers. The "three gems" of Kannada literature, Adikavi Pampa, Sri Ponna and Ranna belonged to this period.[2324,2325] In the 11th century, Telugu literature was born under the patronage of the Eastern Chalukyas with Nannaya Bhatta as its first writer.[2326]

Badami Chalukya country

Army

The army was well organised and this was the reason for Pulakeshin II's success beyond the Vindyas.[2327] It consisted of an infantry, a cavalry, an elephant corps and a powerful navy. The Chinese traveller Hiuen-Tsiang wrote that the Chalukyan army had hundreds of elephants which were intoxicated with liquor prior to battle.[2328] It was with their navy that they conquered *Revatidvipa* (Goa), and Puri on east coast of India. Rashtrakuta inscriptions use the term *Karnatabala* when referring to the powerful Chalukya armies.[2329]

Land governance

The government, at higher levels, was closely modelled after the Magadhan and Satavahana administrative machinery. The empire was divided into *Maharashtrakas* (provinces), then into smaller *Rashtrakas* (*Mandala*), *Vishaya* (district), *Bhoga* (group of 10 villages) which is similar to the *Dasagrama* unit used by the Kadambas. At the lower levels of administration, the Kadamba style prevailed fully. The Sanjan plates of Vikramaditya I even mentions a land unit called *Dasagrama*.[2330] In addition to imperial provinces, there were autonomous regions ruled by feudatories such as the Alupas, the Gangas, the Banas and the Sendrakas.[2331] Local assemblies and guilds looked after local issues. Groups of *mahajanas* (learned brahmins) looked after *agraharas* (called *ghatika* or "place of higher learning") such as at Badami which was served by 2000 *mahajans* and Aihole which was served by 500 *mahajanas*. Taxes were levied and were called the *herjunka* – tax on loads, the *kirukula* – tax on retail goods in transit, the *bilkode* – sales tax, the *pannaya* – betel tax, *siddaya* – land tax and the *vaddaravula* – tax levied to support royalty.

Coinage

The Badami Chalukyas minted coins that were of a different standard compared to the coins of the northern kingdoms.[2332] The coins had *Nagari* and Kannada legends. The coins of Mangalesha had the symbol of a temple on the obverse and a 'sceptre between lamps' or a temple on the reverse. Pulakeshin II's coins had a caparisoned lion facing right on the obverse and a temple on the reverse. The coins weighed 4 grams and were called, in old-Kannada, *hun* (or *honnu*) and had fractions such as *fana* (or *fanam*) and the *quarter fana* (the modern day Kannada equivalent being *hana* – which literally means "money"). A gold coin called *gadyana* is mentioned in a record at the Vijayeshwara Temple at Pattadakal, which later came to be known as *varaha* (their royal emblem).

Figure 448: *Vaishnava Cave temple No. 3 at Badami, 578 CE*

Religion

Part of a series on the
History of Karnataka

- Political history of medieval Karnataka
- Origin of Karnataka's name
- Kadambas and Gangas
- Chalukya Empire
- Rashtrakuta Empire
- Western Chalukya Empire
- Southern Kalachuri
- Hoysala Empire
- Vijayanagara Empire
- Bahmani Sultanate

- Bijapur Sultanate
- Kingdom of Mysore
- Nayakas of Keladi
- Nayakas of Chitradurga
- Haleri Kingdom
- Unification of Karnataka

Categories

- Architecture
- Forts
- Economies
- Societies

- v
- t
- e[2333]

Both Shaivism and Vaishnavism flourished during the Badami Chalukya period, though it seems the former was more popular.[2334] Famous temples were built in places such as Pattadakal, Aihole and Mahakuta, and priests (*archakas*) were invited from northern India. Vedic sacrifices, religious vows (*vrata*) and the giving of gifts (*dana*) was important.[2335] The Badami kings were followers of Vedic Hinduism and dedicated temples to popular Hindu deities in Aihole. Sculptures of deities testify to the popularity of Hindu Gods such as Vishnu, Shiva, Kartikeya, Ganapathi, Shakti, Surya and *Sapta Matrikas* ("seven mothers"). The Badami kings also performed the Ashwamedha ("horse sacrifice").[2336] The worship of Lajja Gauri, a fertility goddess is known. Jainism too was a prominent religion during this period. The kings of the dynasty were however secular and actively encouraged Jainism. One of the Badami Cave temples is dedicated to the Jain faith. Jain temples were also erected in the Aihole complex, the temple at Maguti being one such example.[2337] Ravikirti, the court poet of Pulakeshin II was a Jain. Queen Vinayavati consecrated a temple for the Trimurti ("Hindu trinity") at Badami. Sculptures of the Trimurti, Harihara (half Vishnu, half Shiva) and *Ardhanarishwara* (half Shiva, half woman) provide ample evidence of their tolerance. Buddhism was on a decline, having made its ingress into Southeast Asia. This is confirmed by the writings of Hiuen-Tsiang. Badami, Aihole, Kurtukoti and Puligere (modern Lakshmeshwar in the Gadag district) were primary places of learning.

Society

The Hindu caste system was present and devadasis were recognised by the government. Some kings had concubines (*ganikas*) who were given much respect,[2338] and Sati was perhaps absent since widows like Vinayavathi and

Vijayanka are mentioned in records. Devadasis were however present in temples. Sage Bharata's *Natyashastra*, the precursor to Bharatanatyam, the classical dance of South India, was popular and is seen in many sculptures and is mentioned in inscriptions.[2339] Some women from the royal family enjoyed political power in administration. Queen Vijayanka was a noted Sanskrit poet, Kumkumadevi, the younger sister of Vijayaditya (and queen of Alupa King Chitravahana) made several grants and had a Jain basadi called Anesajjebasadi constructed at Puligere,[2340] and the queens of Vikramaditya II, Lokamahadevi and Trailokyamahadevi made grants and possibly consecrated the Lokesvara Temple (now called Virupaksha temple) but also and the Mallikarjuna temple respectively at Pattadakal.[2341]

In popular culture

The Chalukya era may be seen as the beginning of the fusion of cultures of northern and southern India, making way for the transmission of ideas between the two regions. This is seen clearly in the field of architecture. The Chalukyas spawned the *Vesara* style of architecture which includes elements of the northern *nagara* and southern *dravida* styles. During this period, the expanding Sanskritic culture mingled with local Dravidian vernaculars which were already popular. Dravidian languages maintain these influences even today. This influence helped to enrich literature in these languages.[2342] The Hindu legal system owes much to the Sanskrit work *Mitakshara* by Vijnaneshwara in the court of Western Chalukya King Vikramaditya VI. Perhaps the greatest work in legal literature, *Mitakshara* is a commentary on *Yajnavalkya* and is a treatise on law based on earlier writings and has found acceptance in most parts of India. Englishman Henry Thomas Colebrooke later translated into English the section on inheritance, giving it currency in the British Indian court system.[2343] It was during the Western Chalukya rule that the Bhakti movement gained momentum in South India, in the form of Ramanujacharya and Basavanna, later spreading into northern India.

A celebration called *Chalukya utsava*, a three-day festival of music and dance, organised by the Government of Karnataka, is held every year at Pattadakal, Badami and Aihole. The event is a celebration of the achievements of the Chalukyas in the realm of art, craft, music and dance. The program, which starts at Pattadakal and ends in Aihole, is inaugurated by the Chief Minister of Karnataka. Singers, dancers, poets and other artists from all over the country take part in this event. In the 26 February 2006 celebration, 400 art troupes took part in the festivities. Colorful cutouts of the *Varaha* the Chalukya emblem, *Satyashraya* Pulakeshin (Pulakeshin II), famous sculptural masterpieces such as Durga, Mahishasuramardhini (Durga killing demon Mahishasura) were present everywhere. The program at Pattadakal is named *Anivaritacharigund vedike* after the famous architect of the Virupaksha temple, Gundan Anivaritachari. At Badami it is called *Chalukya Vijayambika Vedike* and at Aihole, *Ravikirti Vedike* after the famous poet and minister (Ravikirti) in the court of Pulakeshin II. *Immadi Pulakeshi*, a Kannada movie of the 1960s starring Dr. Rajkumar celebrates the life and times of the great king.

References

Books <templatestyles src="Template:Refbegin/styles.css" />

- Bolon, Carol Radcliffe (1 January 1979). "The Mahākuṭa Pillar and Its Temples". **41** (2/3): 253–268. doi: 10.2307/3249519[2344]. JSTOR 3249519[2345].
- Chopra, P.N.; Ravindran, T.K.; Subrahmanian, N (2003) [2003]. *History of South India (Ancient, Medieval and Modern) Part 1*. New Delhi: Chand Publications. ISBN 81-219-0153-7.
- Cousens, Henry (1996) [1926]. *The Chalukyan Architecture of Kanarese Districts*. New Delhi: Archaeological Survey of India. OCLC 37526233[2346].
- Foekema, Gerard (1996). *Complete Guide to Hoysala Temples*. New Delhi: Abhinav. ISBN 81-7017-345-0.
- Foekema, Gerard (2003) [2003]. *Architecture decorated with architecture: Later medieval temples of Karnataka, 1000–1300 AD*. New Delhi: Munshiram Manoharlal Publishers Pvt. Ltd. ISBN 81-215-1089-9.
- Hardy, Adam (1995) [1995]. *Indian Temple Architecture: Form and Transformation-The Karnata Dravida Tradition 7th to 13th Centuries*. Abhinav Publications. ISBN 81-7017-312-4.
- Houben, Jan E.M. (1996) [1996]. *Ideology and Status of Sanskrit: Contributions to the History of the Sanskrit language*. Brill. ISBN 90-04-10613-8.
- Kamath, Suryanath U. (2001) [1980]. *A concise history of Karnataka: from pre-historic times to the present*. Bangalore: Jupiter books. LCCN 80905179[2347]. OCLC 7796041[2348].
- Karmarkar, A.P. (1947) [1947]. *Cultural history of Karnataka: ancient and medieval*. Dharwad: Karnataka Vidyavardhaka Sangha. OCLC 8221605[2349].
- Keay, John (2000) [2000]. *India: A History*. New York: Grove Publications. ISBN 0-8021-3797-0.
- Michell, George (2002) [2002]. *Pattadakal – Monumental Legacy*. Oxford University Press. ISBN 0-19-566057-9.
- Moraes, George M. (1990) [1931]. *The Kadamba Kula, A History of Ancient and Medieval Karnataka*. New Delhi, Madras: Asian Educational Services. ISBN 81-206-0595-0.

- Mugali, R.S. (1975) [1975]. *History of Kannada literature*. Sahitya Akademi. OCLC 24924061[2350].
- Narasimhacharya, R (1988) [1988]. *History of Kannada Literature*. New Delhi, Madras: Asian Educational Services. ISBN 81-206-0303-6.
- Ramesh, K.V. (1984). *Chalukyas of Vatapi*. Delhi: Agam Kala Prakashan. OCLC 567370037[2351]. 3987-10333.
- Sastri, Nilakanta K.A. (2002) [1955]. *A history of South India from prehistoric times to the fall of Vijayanagar*. New Delhi: Indian Branch, Oxford University Press. ISBN 0-19-560686-8.
- Sen, Sailendra Nath (1999). *Ancient Indian History and Civilization*. New Age Publishers. ISBN 81-224-1198-3.
- Thapar, Romila (2003) [2003]. *The Penguin History of Early India*. New Delhi: Penguin Books. ISBN 0-14-302989-4.
- Vaidya, C.V. *History of Mediaeval Hindu India (Being a History of India from 600 to 1200 A.D.)*. Poona: Oriental Book Supply Agency. OCLC 6814734[2352].
- Various (1988) [1988]. *Encyclopaedia of Indian literature – vol 2*. Sahitya Akademi. ISBN 81-260-1194-7.

Web <templatestyles src="Template:Refbegin/styles.css" />

- "APOnline – History of Andhra Pradesh-ancient period-Eastern Chalukyas by Tata Consultancy Services"[2353]. Archived from the original[2354] on 6 December 2006. Retrieved 12 November 2006.
- "Architecture of Indian Subcontinent, Takeyo Kamiya, 20 September 1996, Published by Gerard da Cunha-Architecture Autonomous, Bardez, Goa, India"[2355]. Retrieved 2006-11-12.
- "Badami Chalukyans' magical transformation, an article by Azmathulla Shariff in Deccan Herald, Spectrum, 26 July 2005"[2356]. Archived from the original[2357] on 2007-02-10. Retrieved 2006-11-12.

<indicator name="featured-star"> </indicator>

External links

> Wikimedia Commons has media related to *Chalukya dynasty*.

- "Chalukyan Art by Dr. Jyotsna Kamat, Kamat's Potpourri, 4 November 2006"[2358]. Retrieved 2006-11-10.
- "History of the Kannada Literature, Dr. Jyotsna Kamat, on Kamat's Potpourri, Timeless Theater-Karnataka-History of Kannada, 4 November 2006"[2359]. Retrieved 2006-11-12.

- "Aihole Temples, Photographs by Michael D. Gunther, 2002"[2360]. Retrieved 2006-11-10.
- "Badami Cave Temples, Photographs by Michael D. Gunther, 2002"[2361]. Retrieved 2006-11-10.
- "Pattadakal Temples, Photographs by Michael D. Gunther, 2002"[2362]. Retrieved 2006-11-10.
- Chalukyas of Kalyana (973–1198 CE)[2363] by Dr. Jyotsna Kamat
- "Coins of Alupas"[2364]. Archived from the original[2365] on 2006-08-15. Retrieved 2006-11-10.

Pallava dynasty

Pallava Empire	
Dynasty	
275 CE–897 CE	
Pallava territories during Narasimhavarman I c. 645. This includes the Chalukya territories occupied by the Pallavas.	
Capital	Kanchipuram
Languages	Prakrit, Sanskrit, Tamil, Telugu
Religion	Hinduism
Government	Monarchy
King	
• 275–300	Simhavarman I
• 882–897	Aparajitavarman
Historical era	Classical India
• Established	275 CE
• Disestablished	897 CE
Preceded by	Succeeded by
Andhra Ikshvaku	Chola dynasty
Kalabhra dynasty	Eastern Chalukyas

Today part of	India Sri Lanka[2366]

Pallava Kings (200s–800s)

Vishnugopa II	
Simhavarman III	
Simhavishnu	
Mahendravarman I	(600-630)
Narasimhavarman I	(630–668)
Mahendravarman II	(668–670)
Paramesvaravarman I	(670–695)
Narasimhavarman II	(700-728)
Paramesvaravarman II	(728–731)
Nandivarman II	(731–795)
Dantivarman	(795–846)
Nandivarman III	(846-869)
Aparajitavarman	(880-897)
Aditya I (*Chola Empire*)	(870-907)

The **Pallava dynasty** was a South Indian dynasty that existed from 275 CE to 897 CE, ruling a portion of southern India. They gained prominence after the eclipse of the Satavahana dynasty, whom the Pallavas served as feudatories.[2367,2368]

Pallavas became a major power during the reign of Mahendravarman I (571 – 630 CE) and Narasimhavarman I (630 – 668 CE) and dominated the Telugu and northern parts of the Tamil region for about 600 years until the end of the 9th century. Throughout their reign they were in constant conflict with both Chalukyas of Badami in the north and the Tamil kingdoms of Chola and Pandyas in the south and were finally defeated by the Chola kings in the 9th century CE.Wikipedia:Citation needed

Pallavas are most noted for their patronage of architecture, the finest example being the Shore Temple, a UNESCO World Heritage Site in Mahabalipuram. The Pallavas, who left behind magnificent sculptures and temples, established the foundations of medieval South Indian architecture. They developed the Pallava script from which Grantha ultimately descended. The Pallava script gave rise to several other southeast Asian scripts. Chinese traveller Xuanzang visited Kanchipuram during Pallava rule and extolled their benign rule.

Figure 449: *Kailasanathar Temple, Kanchipuram, Tamil Nadu, 685-705*

Origins

Inner court or the circumambulatory passage with 58 subshrines. Kailasanathar Temple, Kanchipuram

Pillar with multi-headed lions. Kailasanathar Temple, Kanchipuram

Kailasanathar Temple, Kanchipuram

A Sangam Period classic, *Manimekalai*, attributes the origin of the first Pallava King from a liaison between the daughter of a Naga king of Manipallava named Pilli Valai (Pilivalai) with a Chola king, Killivalavan, out of which union was born a prince, who was lost in ship wreck and found with a twig (*pallava*) of Cephalandra Indica (*Tondai*) around his ankle and hence named *Tondai-man*. Another version states that "Pallava" was born from the union of the Brahmin Ashvatthama with a Naga Princess also supposedly supported in the sixth verse of the Bahur plates which states "From Ashvatthama was born the king named Pallava". The Pallavas themselves claimed to descend from Brahma and Ashvatthama.

Though *Manimekalai* posits Ilam Tiriyan as a Chola, not a Pallava, the Velurpalaiyam plates dated to 852, do not mention the Cholas. Instead, they credit the Naga liaison episode, and creation of the Pallava line, to a different Pallava king named Virakurcha, while preserving its legitimising significance:

> ...*from him (Aśvatthāman) in order (came) Pallava, the lord of the whole earth, whose fame was bewildering. Thence, came into existence the race of Pallavas...* [*including the son of Chūtapallava*] *Vīrakūrcha, of celebrated name, who simultaneously with (the hand of) the daughter of the chief of serpents grasped also the complete insignia of royalty and became famous.*

Historically, early relations between Nagas and Pallavas became well-established before the myth of Pallava's birth to Ashvatthama took root. A *prashasti* (literally "praise"), composed in 753 on the dynastic eulogy in the Kasakadi (Kasakudi) plates, by the Pallava Trivikrama, traces the Pallava lineage from creation through a series of mythic progenitors, and then praises the dynasty in terms of two similes hinged together by triple use of the word avatara ("descent"), as below:

> *From* [*them*] *descended the powerful, spotless Pallava dynasty* [*vaṁśāvatāra*], *which resembled a partial incarnation* [*aṁśāvatāra*] *of Visnu, as it displayed unbroken courage in conquering the circle of the world...and which resembled the descent of the Ganges* [*gaṅgāvatāra*] *as it purified the whole world.*

The *Proceedings of the First Annual Conference* of South Indian History Congress also notes: The word *Tondai* means a creeper and the term *Pallava* conveys a similar meaning. Since the Pallavas ruled in the territory extending from Bellary to Bezwada, it led to the theory that they were a northern dynasty who contracted marriages with princesses of the Andhra Dynasty and so inherited a portion of southern Andhra Pradesh.

Historian K. R. Subramanian says the Pallavas were originally a Telugu power rather than a Tamil one. Telugu sources know of a Trilochana Pallava as the earliest Telugu king and they are confirmed by later inscriptions.[2369] The first Chalukya king is said to have been met, repulsed and killed by the same Trilochana near Mudivemu (Cuddappah district). A Buddhist story describes Kala the Nagaraja, resembling the Pallava Kalabhartar as a king of the region near Krishna district. The Pallava Bogga may be identified with the kingdom of Kala in Andhra which had close and early maritime and cultural relations with Ceylon.

K. A. Nilakanta Sastri postulated that Pallavas were descendants of a North Indian dynasty who moved southwards, adopted local traditions to their own use, and named themselves as Tondaiyar after the land called Tondai. K. P. Jayaswal also proposed a North Indian origin, putting forward the theory that the Pallavas were a branch of the Vakatakas.

The earliest inscriptions of the Pallavas were found in the districts of Bellary, Guntur and Nellore and all the inscriptions of the dynasty till the rise of Simhavishnu were found in the latter two of those.[2370]

Rivalries

With Cholas

The Pallavas captured Kanchi from the Cholas as recorded in the Velurpalaiyam Plates, around the reign of the fifth king of the Pallava line Kumaravishnu I. Thereafter Kanchi figures in inscriptions as the capital of the Pallavas. The Cholas drove the Pallavas away from Kanchi in the mid-4th century, in the reign of Vishugopa, the tenth king of the Pallava line. The Pallavas re-captured Kanchi in the mid-6th century, possibly in the reign of Simhavishnu, the fourteenth king of the Pallava line, whom the Kasakudi plates state as "the lion of the earth". Thereafter the Pallavas held on to Kanchi until the 9th century, until the reign of their last king, Vijaya-Nripatungavarman.[2371]

With Kadambas

The Pallavas were in conflict with major kingdoms at various periods of time. A contest for political supremacy existed between the early Pallavas and the Kadambas. Numerous Kadamba inscriptions provide details of Pallava-Kadamba hostilities.[2372]

Figure 450: *Coin of the Pallavas of Coromandel, king Narasimhavarman I. (630-668 AD).**Obv** Lion left **Rev** Name of Narasimhavarman with solar and lunar symbols around.*

With Kalabhras

During the reign of Vishnugopavarman II (approx. 500-525), political convulsion engulfed the Pallavas due to the Kalabhra invasion of the Tamil country. Towards the close of the 6th century, the Pallava Simhavishnu stuck a blow against the Kalabhras. The Pandyas followed suit. Thereafter the Tamil country was divided between the Pallavas in the north with Kanchipuram as their capital, and Pandyas in the south with Madurai as their capital.

Birudas

The royal custom of using a series of descriptive honorific titles, *Birudas*, was particularly prevalent among the Pallavas. The birudas of Mahendravarman I are in Sanskrit, Tamil and Telugu. The Telugu birudas show Mahendravarman's involvement with the Andhra region continued to be strong at the time he was creating his cave-temples in the Tamil region. The suffix "Malla" was used by the Pallava rulers.[2373] Mahendravarman I used the biruda, *Satrumalla*, "a warrior who overthrows his enemies", and his grandson Paramesvara I was called *Ekamalla* "the sole warrior or wrestler". Pallava kings, presumably exalted ones, were known by the title *Mahamalla* ("great wrestler").

Languages used

All the early Pallava royal inscriptions are either in Sanskrit or in Prakrit language, considered the official languages of the dynasty while the official scripts were Pallava script and later Grantha. Similarly, inscriptions found in Andhra Pradesh and Karnataka State are in Sanskrit and Prakrit.[2374] The phenomenon of using Prakrit as official languages in which rulers left their inscriptions and epigraphies continued till the 6th century. It would have been in the interest of the ruling elite to protect their privileges by perpetuating their hegemony of Prakrit in order to exclude the common people from sharing power (Mahadevan 1995a: 173–188). The Pallavas in their Tamil country used Tamil and Sanskrit in their inscriptions.[2375]

Tamil came to be the main language used by the Pallavas in their inscriptions, though a few records continued to be in Sanskrit. This language was first adopted by Mahendravarman I himself in a few records of his; but from the time of Paramesvaravarman I, the practice came into vogue of inscribing a part of the record in Sanskrit and the rest in Tamil. Almost all the copper plate records, viz., Kasakudi, Tandantottam, Pattattalmangalm, Udayendiram and Velurpalaiyam are composed both in Sanskrit and Tamil.

Writing system

Under the Pallava dynasty, a unique form of Grantha script, a descendant of Pallava script which is a type of Brahmic script, was used. Around the 6th century, it was exported eastwards and influenced the genesis of almost all Southeast Asian scripts.

Religion

Pallavas were followers of Hinduism and made gifts of land to gods and Brahmins. In line with the prevalent customs, some of the rulers performed the *Aswamedha* and other Vedic sacrifices. They were, however, tolerant of other faiths. The Chinese monk Xuanzang who visited Kanchipuram during the reign of Narasimhavarman I reported that there were 100 Buddhist monasteries, and 80 temples in Kanchipuram.[2376]

Pallava architecture

The Pallavas were instrumental in the transition from rock-cut architecture to stone temples. The earliest examples of Pallava constructions are rock-cut temples dating from 610–690 and structural temples between 690–900. A number of rock-cut cave temples bear the inscription of the Pallava king, Mahendravarman I and his successors.[2377]

Among the accomplishments of the Pallava architecture are the rock-cut temples at Mahabalipuram. There are excavated pillared halls and monolithic

Figure 451: *The Shore Temple at Mahabalipuram built by Narasimhavarman II*

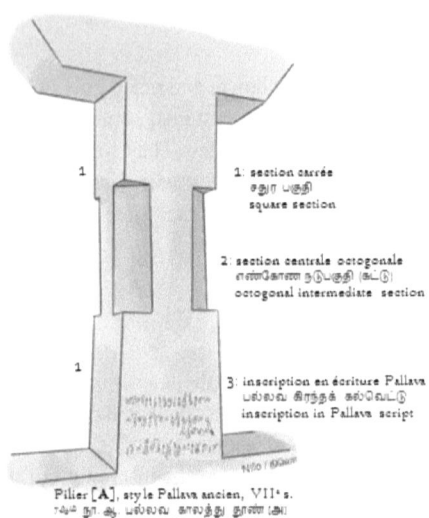

shrines known as *Rathas* in Mahabalipuram. Early temples were mostly dedicated to Shiva. The Kailasanatha temple in Kanchipuram and the Shore Temple built by Narasimhavarman II, rock cut temple in Mahendravadi by Mahendravarman are fine examples of the Pallava style temples.[2378] The temple of Nalanda Gedige in Kandy, Sri Lanka is another. The famous Tondeswaram temple of Tenavarai and the ancient Koneswaram temple of Trincomalee were patronized and structurally developed by the Pallavas in the 7th century.Wikipedia:Citation needed

Pallava society

The Pallava period beginning with Simhavishnu (575 AD – 900 AD) was a transitional stage in southern Indian society with monument building, foundation of devotional (bhakti) sects of Alvars and Nayanars, the flowering of rural brahmanical institutions of Sanskrit learning, and the establishment of *chakravartin* model of kingship over a territory of diverse people; which ended the pre-Pallavan era of territorially segmented people, each with their culture, under a tribal chieftain. While a system of ranked relationship among groups existed in the classical period, the Pallava period extolled ranked relationships based on ritual purity as enjoined by the *shastras*. Burton distinguishes between the *chakravatin* model and the *kshatriya* model, and likens kshatriyas to locally based warriors with ritual status sufficiently high enough to share with Brahmins; and states that in south India the kshatriya model did not emerge. As per Burton, south India was aware of the Indo-Aryan *varna* organized society in which decisive secular authority was vested in the *kshatriyas*; but apart from the Pallava, Chola and Vijayanagar line of warriors which claimed *chakravartin* status, only few locality warrior families achieved the prestigious kin-linked organization of northern warrior groups.

Chronology

Sastri chronology

The earliest documentation on the Pallavas is the three copper-plate grants, now referred to as the *Mayidavolu*, *Hirahadagalli* and the *British Museum* plates (Durga Prasad, 1988) belonging to Skandavarman I and written in Prakrit.[2379] Skandavarman appears to have been the first great ruler of the early Pallavas, though there are references to other early Pallavas who were probably predecessors of Skandavarman.[2380] Skandavarman extended his dominions from the Krishna in the north to the Pennar in the south and to the Bellary district in the West. He performed the *Aswamedha* and other Vedic sacrifices and bore the title of "Supreme King of Kings devoted to dharma".

In the reign of Simhavarman IV, who ascended the throne in 436, the territories lost to the Vishnukundins in the north up to the mouth of the Krishna were recovered.Wikipedia:Citation needed The early Pallava history from this period onwards is furnished by a dozen or so copper-plate grants in Sanskrit. They are all dated in the regnal years of the kings.[2381]

The following chronology was composed from these charters by Nilakanta Sastri in his *A History of South India*:

Early Pallavas

- Simhavarman I (275–300)
- Skandavarman (unknown)
- Visnugopa (350–355)
- Kumaravishnu I (350–370)
- Skandavarman II (370–385)
- Viravarman (385–400)
- Skandavarman III (400–436)
- Simhavarman II (436–460)
- Skandavarman IV (460–480)
- Nandivarman I (480–510)
- Kumaravishnu II (510–530)
- Buddhavarman (530–540)
- Kumaravishnu III (540–550)
- Simhavarman III (550–560)

Later Pallavas

The incursion of the Kalabhras and the confusion in the Tamil country was broken by the Pandya Kadungon and the Pallava Simhavishnu.[2382] Mahendravarman I extended the Pallava Kingdom and was one of the greatest sovereigns. Some of the most ornate monuments and temples in southern India, carved out of solid rock, were introduced under his rule. He also wrote the play *Mattavilasa Prahasana*.

The Pallava kingdom began to gain both in territory and influence and were a regional power by the end of the 6th century, defeating kings of Ceylon and mainland Tamilakkam.[2383] Narasimhavarman I and Paramesvaravarman I stand out for their achievements in both military and architectural spheres. Narasimhavarman II built the Shore Temple.

- Simhavishnu (575–600)
- Mahendravarman I (600–630)
- Narasimhavarman I (Mamalla) (630–668)
- Mahendravarman II (668–672)
- Paramesvaravarman I (670–695)

Figure 452: *The rock-cut temples at Mamallapuram constructed during the reign of Narasimhavarman I*

Figure 453: *Elephant carved out of a single-stone*

- Narasimhavarman II (Raja Simha) (695–722)
- Paramesvaravarman II (705–710)
- Nandivarman II (Pallavamalla) (730–795)
- Dantivarman (795–846)
- Nandivarman III (846–869)
- Aparajitavarman (879–897)

Aiyangar chronology

According to the available inscriptions of the Pallavas, historian S. Krishnaswami Aiyangar proposes the Pallavas could be divided into four separate families or dynasties; some of whose connections are known and some unknown.[2384] Aiyangar states

> We have a certain number of charters in Prakrit of which three are important ones. Then follows a dynasty which issued their charters in Sanskrit; following this came the family of the great Pallavas beginning with Simha Vishnu; this was followed by a dynasty of the usurper Nandi Varman, another great Pallava. We are overlooking for the present the dynasty of the Ganga-Pallavas postulated by the Epigraphists. The earliest of these Pallava charters is the one known as the Mayidavolu 1 (Guntur district) copper-plates.

Based on a combination of dynastic plates and grants from the period, Aiyangar proposed their rule thus:

Early Pallavas

- Bappadevan (250-275) – married a Naga of Mavilanga (Kanchi) - *The Great Founder of a Pallava lineage*
- Shivaskandavarman I (275–300)
- Simhavarman (300-320)
- Bhuddavarman (320-335)
- Bhuddyankuran (335-340)

Middle Pallavas

- Visnugopa (340–355) (*Yuvamaharaja Vishnugopa*)
- Kumaravisnu I (355–370)
- Skanda Varman II (370–385)
- Vira Varman (385–400)
- Skanda Varman III (400–435)
- Simha Varman II (435–460)
- Skanda Varman IV (460–480)
- Nandi Varman I (480–500)

- Kumaravisnu II (c. 500–510)
- Buddha Varman (c. 510–520)
- Kumaravisnu III (c. 520–530)
- Simha Varman III (c. 530–537)

Later Pallavas

- Simhavishnu (537-570)
- Mahendravarman I (571–630)
- Narasimhavarman I (Mamalla) (630–668)
- Mahendravarman II (668–672)
- Paramesvaravarman I (672–700)
- Narasimhavarman II (Raja Simha) (700–727)
- Paramesvaravarman II (705–710)
- Nandivarman II (Pallavamalla) (732–796)
- Dantivarman (775–825)
- Nandivarman III (825–869)
- Nirupathungan (869–882)
- Aparajitavarman (882–896)

Genealogy

The genealogy of Pallavas mentioned in the *Māmallapuram Praśasti* is as follows:

- Vishnu
- Brahma
- Unknown / undecipherable
- Unknown / undecipherable
- Bharadvaja
- Drona
- Ashvatthaman
- Pallava
- Unknown / undecipherable
- Unknown / undecipherable
- Simhavarman I (c. 275)
- Unknown / undecipherable
- Unknown / undecipherable
- Simhavarman IV (436 — c. 460)
- Unknown / undecipherable
- Unknown / undecipherable
- Skandashishya
- Unknown / undecipherable

- Unknown / undecipherable
- Simhavisnu (c. 550-585)
- Mahendravarman I (c. 571-630)
- Maha-malla Narasimhavarman I (630-668)
- Unknown / undecipherable
- Paramesvaravarman I (669-690)
- Rajasimha Narasimhavaram II (690-728)
- Unknown / undecipherable
- Pallavamalla Nandivarman II (731-796)
- Unknown / undecipherable
- Nandivarman III (846-69)

Other relationships

Pallava royal lineages were influential in the old kingdom of Kedah of the Malay Peninsula under Rudravarman I, Champa under Bhadravarman I and the Kingdom of the Funan in Cambodia.

References

<templatestyles src="Template:Refbegin/styles.css" />

- Avari, Burjor (2007). *India: The Ancient Past*. New York: Routledge.
- Hermann, Kulke; Rothermund D (2001) [2000]. *A History of India*. Routledge. ISBN 0-415-32920-5.
- Minakshi, Cadambi (1938). *Administration and Social Life Under the Pallavas*. Madras: University of Madras.
- Prasad, Durga (1988). *History of the Andhras up to 1565 A.D.* Guntur, India: P.G. Publishers.
- Raghava Iyengar, R (1949). *Perumbanarruppatai, a commentary*. Chidambaram, India: Annamalai University Press.

External links

- Media related to Pallava at Wikimedia Commons

Eastern Chalukyas

Chalukyas of Vengi	
624–1189	
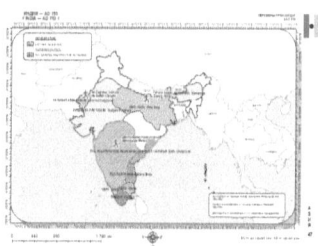	
Map of India c. 753 CE. The Eastern Chalukya kingdom is shown on the eastern coast.	
Capital	Vengi Rajahmundry
Languages	• Sanskrit • Telugu, Kannada
Religion	Hinduism
Government	Monarchy
Maharaja		
•	624–641	Kubja Vishnuvardhana (brother of Pulakeshin II)
•	1018–1061	Rajaraja Narendra
History		
•	Established	624
•	Disestablished	1189
Preceded by	Succeeded by
Chalukyas of Badami	Cholas

Part of a series on
Andhra Pradesh and Telangana

Chronology of the Telugu people, Andhra Pradesh, and Telangana history

- Geography
- Political history

History and Kingdoms

- v
- t
- e[2385]

Eastern Chalukyas, also known as the **Chalukyas of Vengi**, were a dynasty that ruled parts of South India between the 7th and 12th centuries. They started out as governors of the Chalukyas of Badami in the Deccan region. Subsequently, they became a sovereign power, and ruled the Vengi region of present-day Andhra Pradesh until c. 1130 CE. They continued ruling the region as feudatories of the Cholas until 1189 CE.

Originally, the capital of the Eastern Chalukyas was located at the Vengi city (modern Pedavegi near Eluru). It was subsequently moved to Rajamahendravaram (modern Rajahmundry). Throughout their history the Eastern Chalukyas were the cause of many wars between the more powerful Cholas and Western Chalukyas over the control of the strategic Vengi country. The five centuries of the Eastern Chalukya rule of Vengi saw not only the consolidation of this region into a unified whole, but also saw the efflorescence of Telugu culture, literature, poetry and art during the later half of their rule.[2386]

Origin

The Chalukyas of Vengi branched off from the Chalukyas of Badami. The Badami ruler Pulakeshin II (608–644 C.E) conquered the Vengi region in eastern Deccan, after defeating the remnants of the Vishnukundina dynasty. He appointed his brother Kubja Vishnuvardhana the governor of this newly acquired territory in 624 CE.[2387] Vishnuvardhana's viceroyalty subsequently developed into an independent kingdom, possibly after Pulakeshin died fighting the Pallavas in the Battle of Vatapi.[2388]

From the 11th century onward, the dynasty started claiming legendary lunar dynasty origins. According to this legend, the dynasty descended from the Moon, via Budha, Pururava, the Pandavas, Satanika and Udayana. 59 unnamed descendants of Udayana ruled at Ayodhya. Their descendant Vijayaditya was killed in a battle with Trilochana Pallava, during an expedition in Dakshinapatha (Deccan). His pregnant widow was given shelter by Vishnubhatta Somayaji of Mudivemu (modern Jammalamadugu). She named her son Vishnuvardhana after her benefactor. When the boy grew up, he became the ruler of Dakshinapatha by the grace of the goddess Nanda Bhagavati.[2389]

History

Between 641 CE and 705 CE some kings, except Jayasimha I and Mangi Yuvaraja, ruled for very short durations. Then followed a period of unrest characterised by family feuds and weak rulers. Meanwhile, the Rashtrakutas of Malkhed ousted Western Chalukyas of Badami. The weak rulers of Vengi had to meet the challenge of the Rashtrakutas, who overran their kingdom more than once. There was no Eastern Chalukya ruler who could check them until Gunaga Vijayaditya III came to power in 848 CE. The then Rashtrakuta ruler Amoghavarsha treated him as his ally and after Amoghavarsha's death, Vijayaditya proclaimed independence.[2390]

Administration

In its early life, the Eastern Chalukya court was essentially a republic of Badami, and as generations passed, local factors gained in strength and the Vengi monarchy developed features of its own. External influences still continued to be present as the Eastern Chalukyas had long and intimate contact, either friendly or hostile, with the Pallavas, the Rashtrakutas, the Cholas and the Chalukyas of Kalyani.[2391]

Type of Government

The Eastern Chalukyan government was a monarchy based on the Hindu philosophy. The inscriptions refer to the traditional seven components of the state (Saptanga), and the eighteen Tirthas (Offices), such as:[2392]

- Mantri (Minister)
- Purohita (Chaplain)
- Senapati (Commander)
- Yuvaraja (Heir-apparent)
- Dauvarika (Door keeper)
- Pradhana (Chief)
- Adhyaksha (Head of department) and so on.

No information is available as to how the work of administration was carried out. The *Vishaya* and *Kottam* were the administrative subdivisions known from records. The *Karmarashtra* and the *Boya-Kottams* are examples of these. The royal edicts (recording gifts of lands or villages) are addressed to all *Naiyogi Kavallabhas*, a general term containing no indication of their duties, as well as to the *Grameyakas*, the residents of the village granted. The *Manneyas* are also occasionally referred in inscriptions. They held assignments of land or revenue in different villages.[2393]

Fratricidal wars and foreign invasions frequently disturbed the land. The territory was parcelled out into many small principalities (estates) held by the nobility consisting of collateral branches of the ruling house such as those of Elamanchili, Pithapuram and Mudigonda, and a few other families such as the Kona Haihayas (Heheya, Kalachuris, Kolanu Saronathas, Chagis, Parichedas, Kota Vamsas, Velanadus and Kondapadamatis, closely connected by marriage ties with the Eastern Chalukyas and families who were raised to high position for their loyal services. When the Vengi ruler was strong, the nobility paid allegiance and tribute to him, but when the weakness was apparent, they were ready to join hands with the enemies against the royal house.[2394]

Society

The population in the Vengi country was heterogeneous in character. Xuanzang, who travelled in the Andhra country after the establishment of the Eastern Chalukya kingdom, noted that the people were of a violent character, were of a dark complexion and were fond of arts. The society was based on hereditary caste system. Even the Buddhists and Jains who originally disregarded caste, adopted it. Besides the four traditional castes, minor communities like Boyas and Savaras (Tribal groups) also existed.[2395]

The Brahmins were held in high esteem in the society. They were proficient in Vedas and Shastras and were given gifts of land and money. They held lucrative posts such as councillors, ministers and members of civil service. They even entered the army and some of them rose to positions of high command. The Kshatriyas were the ruling class. Their love of intrigue and fighting was responsible for civil war for two centuries. The Komatis (Vaishyas) were a flourishing trading community. Their organisation into a powerful guild (Nakaram) which had its headquarters in Penugonda (West Godavari) and branches in seventeen other centres had its beginnings in this period. It seems there used to be a minister for communal affairs (Samaya Mantri) in the government. The Shudras constituted the bulk of the population and there were several sub-castes among them. The army furnished a career for most of them and some of them acquired the status of Samanta Raju and Mandalika.[2396]

Religion

Hinduism was the prominent religion of the Eastern Chalukya kingdom, with Shaivism being more popular than Vaishnavism. The Mahasena temple at Chebrolu became famous for its annual Jatra, which involved a procession of the deity's idol from Chebrolu to Vijayawada and back.[2397] Some of the rulers,

Figure 454: *Eastern Chalukya coin. Central punchmark depicting lion standing left. Incuse of punchmarks.*

declared themselves as *Parama Maheswaras* (Emperors). The Buddhist religious centres eventually attained great celebrity as Siva pilgrim centres. Eastern Chalukya rulers like Vijayaditya II, Yuddhamalla I, Vijayaditya III and Bhima I took active interest in the construction of many temples. The temple establishments like dancers and musicians show that during this period, temples were not only a centre of religious worship but a fostering ground for fine arts.[2398]

Buddhism, which was dominant during the Satavahanas was in decline.[2397] Its monasteries were practically deserted. Due to their love of sacred relics in stupas, a few might have lingered on, Xuanzang noticed some twenty or more Buddhist monasteries in which more than three thousand monks lived.[2395]

Jainism, unlike Buddhism, continued to enjoy some support from the people.[2397] This is evident from the several deserted images in ruined villages all over Andhra. The inscriptions also record the construction of Jain temples and grants of land for their support from the monarchs and the people. The rulers like Kubja Vishnuvardhana, Vishnuvardhana III and Amma II patronised Jainism. Vimaladitya even became a declared follower of the doctrine of Mahavira. Vijayawada, Jenupadu, Penugonda (West Godavari) and Munugodu were the famous Jain centres of the period.[2396]

Literature

Telugu literature owes its origin to the Eastern Chalukyas. Poetry makes its first appearance in the Addanki, Kandukur and Dharmavaram inscriptions of Pandaranga, Army Chief of Vijayaditya III, in the later half of the 9th century. However, literary compositions dating earlier than 11th century CE are

Figure 455: *c. 10th century Sanskrit copper plates of Amma II written in Telugu-Kannada script.*

not clearly known. Nannaya was the poet-laureate of Rajaraja Narendra in the middle of the 11th century. An erudite scholar, he was well-versed in the Vedas, Shastras and the ancient epics, and undertook the translation of the Mahabharata into Telugu. Narayana Bhatta who was proficient in eight languages assisted him in his endeavour. Though incomplete, his work is acclaimed as a masterpiece of Telugu literature.[2399]

Connection between Kannada and Telugu literature

Kubja Vishnuvardhana, the founder of the Eastern Chalukya dynasty, was the brother of the Chalukya king, Pulakeshin II. The Chalukyas therefore governed both the Karnata and Andhra countries and patronised Kannada as well as Telugu. This very likely led to a close connection between Telugu and Kannada literature. A number of Telugu authors of the age also wrote in Kannada and vice versa. Nannaya-Bhatta's *Bharata* in Telugu includes the *Akkara*, a metre considered unique to Kannada works. The same metre is also found in Yudhamalla's Bezwada inscription. Another inscription notes that Narayana-Bhatta, who assisted Nannaya-Bhatta in composing the *Bharata*, was also a Kannada poet and was granted a village by Rajaraja Narendra in 1053 for his contribution. Later Kannada poets, Pampa I and Nagavarma I, also hailed from families originally from Vengi.

Figure 456: *The Bhimeshvara temple at Draksharama*

Architecture

Due to the widely spread Shiva devotional cult in the kingdom, the Eastern Chalukyan kings undertook construction of temples on a large scale. Vijayaditya II is credited with the construction of 108 temples. Yuddhamalla I erected a temple to Kartikeya at Vijayawada. Bhima I constructed the famous Draksharama and Chalukya Bhimavaram (Samalkot) temples. Rajaraja Narendra erected three memorial shrines at Kalidindi (West Godavari). The Eastern Chalukyas, following the Pallava and Chalukya traditions, developed their own independent style of architecture, which is visible in the Pancharama shrines (especially the Draksharama temple) and Biccavolu temples. The Golingeshvara temple at Biccavolu contains some richly carved out sculptures of deities like Ardhanarishvara, Shiva, Vishnu, Agni, Chamundi and Surya.[2400]

Rulers

Chalukya dynasties
- $\underline{v}$ - $\underline{t}$ - $\underline{e}^{2401}$

- Kubja Vishnuvardhana (624 – 641 CE)
- Jayasimha I (641 – 673 CE)
- Indra Bhattaraka (673 CE, seven days)
- Vishnuvardhana II (673 – 682 CE)
- Mangi Yuvaraja (682 – 706 CE)
- Jayasimha II (706 – 718 CE)
- Kokkili (718–719 CE, six months)
- Vishnuvardhana III (719 – 755 CE)
- Vijayaditya I (755 – 772 CE)
- Vishnuvardhana IV (772 – 808 CE)
- Vijayaditya II (808 – 847 CE)
- Vishnuvardhana V (847– 849 CE)
- Vijayaditya III (849 – 892 CE) with his two brothers : Vikramaditya I and Yuddhamalla I
- Chalukya Bhima I (892 – 921 CE)
- Vijay Aditya IV (921 CE, six months)
- Amma I and Vishnuvardhana VI (921 – 927 CE)
- Vijayaditya V (927 CE, fifteen days)
- Tadapa (927 CE, one month)
- Vikramaditya II (927 – 928 CE)
- Chalukya Bhima II (928 – 929 CE)
- Yuddha Malla II (929 – 935 CE)
- Chalukya Bhima III and Vishnuvardhana VII (935 – 947 CE)
- Amma II (947 – 970 CE)
- Danarnava (970 – 973 CE)
- Jata Choda Bhima (973 – 999 CE)
- Shaktivarman I (999 – 1011 CE)
- Vimaladitya (1011–1018 CE)
- Rajaraja Narendra (1018–1061 CE)
- Shaktivarman II (1062 CE)
- Vijayaditya VI (1063–1068 CE, 1072–1075 CE)
- Raja Raja II (1075–1079)

- Vira Chola Vishnuvardhana IX (1079–1102)

References

Bibliography

<templatestyles src="Template:Refbegin/styles.css" />

- K. A. Nilakanta Sastri; N Venkataramanayya (1960). Ghulam Yazdani, ed. *The Early History of the Deccan Parts*[2402]. VII: The Eastern Chāḷukyas. Oxford University Press. OCLC 59001459[2403].
- N. Ramesan (1975). *The Eastern Chalukyas of Vengi*[2404]. Andhra Pradesh Sahithya Akademi. OCLC 4885004[2405].
- Durga Prasad, History of the Andhras up to 1565 A. D., P. G. Publishers, Guntur (1988)
- Nilakanta Sastri, K.A. (1955). A History of South India, OUP, New Delhi (Reprinted 2002).
- Rao, P. Raghunatha (1994), *History And Culture Of Andhra Pradesh: From The Earliest Times To The Present Day*, Sterling Publishers, ISBN 81-207-1719-8
- Nagabhusanasarma (2008), *History and culture of the Andhras*[2406], Komarraju Venkata Lakshmana Rau Vijnana Sarvaswa Sakha, Telugu University, 1995
- Yazdani (2009), *The Early History of the Deccan, Volume 2*[2407], Published under the authority of the Government of Andhra Pradesh by the Oxford University Press, 1961
- Kumari (2008), *Rule Of The Chalukya-Cholas In Andhradesa*[2408], B.R. Pub. Corp., 1985

External links

- Media related to Eastern Chalukyas at Wikimedia Commons

Pandyan dynasty

Pandyan Empire	
300 BCE–1650 CE	
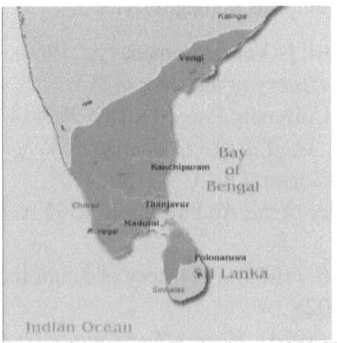 Extent of the Pandya Territories c. 1250 CE	
Capital	Korkai Madurai (3rd century BCE – 1345 CE) Tenkasi (1345 – 1630 CE), Tirunelveli (1345 – 1650 CE), Vizhinjam (Thiruvananthapuram) (Earlier Ay kingdom)Wikipedia:Citation needed
Languages	Tamil, Sanskrit
Religion	Jainism, Hinduism, Buddhism
Government	Monarchy
King	
• 560–590 CE	Kadungon
• 1309–1345 CE	Vira Pandyan IV
• 1422–1463 CE	Jatavarman Parakrama Pandyan
Historical era	Iron Age to Renaissance
• Established	300 BCE
• Disestablished	1650 CE
Succeeded by	
Delhi Sultanate	
Madurai Nayak dynasty	
Jaffna kingdom	
Sambuvaraya	
Today part of	India Sri Lanka

Part of a series on
History of Tamil Nadu

- v
- t
- e[2409]

The **Pandyan dynasty** was an ancient Tamil dynasty, one of the three Tamil dynasties, the other two being the Chola and the Chera. The kings of the three dynasties were referred to as the Three Crowned Kings of Tamilakam.

The Early Pandyans ruled parts of Southern India from at least 4th century BCE. Pandyan rule ended in the first half of the 16th century CE. They initially ruled their country *Pandya Nadu* from Korkai, a seaport on the southernmost tip of the Indian Peninsula, and in later times moved to Madurai. Fish being their flag, Pandyas were experts in water management, agriculture(mostly near river banks) and fisheries and they were eminent sailors and sea traders too. *Pandyan* was well known since ancient times, with contacts, even diplomatic, reaching the Roman Empire. The Pandyan empire was home to temples including Meenakshi Amman Temple in Madurai, and Nellaiappar Temple built on the bank of the river Thamirabarani in Tirunelveli.

The Pandya kings were called either Jatavarman or Maravarman. They were Jains in their early ages but later became Shaivaites. Strabo states that an Indian king called Pandion sent Augustus Caesar "presents and gifts of honour".[2410] The country of the Pandyans was described as *Pandyas* by Megasthenes, *Pandi Mandala* in the Periplus of the Erythraean Sea and described as *Pandyan Mediterranea* and *Modura Regia Pandionis* by Ptolemy.

Traditionally, the legendary Sangams were held in Madurai under their patronage, and some of the Pandya Kings were poets themselves. The early Pandyan Dynasty of the Sangam Literature faded into obscurity upon the invasion of the Kalabhras. The dynasty revived under Kadungon in the early 6th century, pushed the Kalabhras out of the Tamil country and ruled from Madurai. They again went into decline with the rise of the Cholas in the 9th century and were in constant conflict with them. The Pandyas allied themselves with the Sinhalese and the Cheras in harassing the Chola empire until they found an opportunity for reviving their fortunes during the late 13th century. The Later Pandyas (1216–1345) entered their golden age under Maravarman Sundara Pandyan and Jatavarman Sundara Pandyan (c. 1251), who expanded the empire into Telugu country, conquered Kalinga (Orissa) and invaded and conquered Sri Lanka. They also had extensive trade links with the Southeast Asian maritime empires of Srivijaya and their successors. The Pandyas excelled in both trade and literature. They controlled the pearl fisheries along the South Indian coast between Sri Lanka and India which produced some of the finest pearls in the known ancient world.

During their history, the Pandyas were repeatedly in conflict with the Pallavas, Cholas, Hoysalas and finally the Muslim invaders from the Delhi Sultanate. The Islamic invasion led to the end of Pandyan supremacy in South India and in 1323, the Jaffna Kingdom of Sri Lanka declared its independence from the crumbling Pandyan Empire.[2411,2412] The Pandyans lost their capital city Madurai to Madurai Sultanate in 1335. However, they shifted their capital to Tenkasi and continued to rule the Tirulnelveli, Tuticorin, Ramanad, Sivagangai regions. Meanwhile, Madurai sultanate was replaced by Nayaka governors of Vijayanagara in 1378. In 1529 Nayaka governors declared independence and established Madurai Nayak dynasty.

Etymology

The word Pandya is derived from the Tamil word "Pandu" meaning very old. Another theory is that the word "Pandya" is derived from the Tamil word "Pandi" meaning bull. Ancient Tamils, considered the bull as a sign of masculinity and valor. Robert Caldwell derives the word *Pandya* from Pandu, the father of the Pandavas from Mahabharata, whose descendants Pandyans claim.

Another theory suggests that in Sangam Tamil lexicon the word Pandya means *old country* in contrast with Chola meaning *new country*, Chera meaning *hill country* and Pallava meaning *branch* in Sanskrit. The Chera, Chola and Pandya are the traditional Tamil siblings and together with the Pallavas are the major Kings that ruled ancient Tamilakam.

Historians have used several sources to identify the origins of the early Pandyan dynasty with the pre-Christian Era and also to piece together the names of the Pandyan kings. The Pandyans were one of the longest ruling dynasty of Indian history.

Figure 457: *Four-armed Vishnu, Pandya Dynasty, 8th–9th century CE.*

Mythology

According to the Epic Mahabharatha the legendary Malayadwaja Pandya, who sided with the Pandavas and took part in the Kurukshetra War of the Mahabharata, is described as follows in Karna Parva (verse 20.25):[2413,2414]

"Although knowing that the shafts (arrows) of the high souled son of Drona employed in shooting were really inexhaustible, yet Pandya, that bull among men, cut them all into pieces".

Malayadwaja Pandya and his queen Kanchanamala had one daughter Thataathagai alias Meenakshi who succeeded her father and reigned the kingdom successfully. The Madurai Meenakshi Amman Temple was built after her. The city of Madurai was built around this temple. It is also notable that the etymology of the name Meenakshi or *Meenatchi*, is derived from either the Tamil *Meen* (fish) and Sanskrit *akshi* (eyes) which collectively means the one with "Fish-shaped eyes", or the Tamil words *Meen* (fish) and *aatchi* (rule), literally meaning "Rule of the Fish".

Sources

Sangam literature

Pandya kings find mention in a number of poems in the Sangam Literature. Among them Nedunjeliyan, 'the victor of Talaiyalanganam', and Mudukudimi Peruvaludi 'of several sacrifices' deserve special mention. Beside several short poems found in the *Akananuru* and the *Purananuru* collections, there are two major works – *Mathuraikkanci* and the *Netunalvatai* (in the collection of *Pattupattu*) – which give a glimpse into the society and commercial activities in the Pandyan kingdom during the Sangam age.

It is difficult to estimate the exact dates of these Sangam age Pandyas. The period covered by the extant literature of the Sangam is unfortunately not easy to determine with any measure of certainty. Except the longer epics *Silapathikaram* and *Manimekalai*, which by common consent belong to an age later than the Sangam age, the poems have reached us in the forms of systematic anthologies. Each individual poem has generally attached to it a colophon on the authorship and subject matter of the poem. The name of the king or chieftain to whom the poem relates and the occasion which called forth the eulogy are also found.Wikipedia:Citation needed

It is from these colophons, and rarely from the texts of the poems themselves, that we gather the names of many kings and chieftains and the poets patronised by them. The task of reducing these names to an ordered scheme in which the different generations of contemporaries can be marked off one another has not been easy. To add to the confusions, some historians have even denounced these colophons as later additions and untrustworthy as historical documents.Wikipedia:Citation needed

Any attempt at extracting a systematic chronology from these poems should take into consideration the casual nature of these poems and the wide differences between the purposes of the anthologist who collected these poems and the historian's attempts to arrive at a continuous history.

Pandyas are also mentioned by Greek Megesthenes where he writes about southern kingdom being ruled by women.

Epigraphy

The earliest Pandyan king to be found in epigraph is Nedunjeliyan, figuring in the Tamil-Brahmi Mangulam inscription assigned from the 2nd to the 1st centuries BCE.The record documents a gift of rock-cut beds, to a Jain ascetic. Silver Punch-marked coins with the fish symbol in the Pandya country dating from around the same time have also been found.

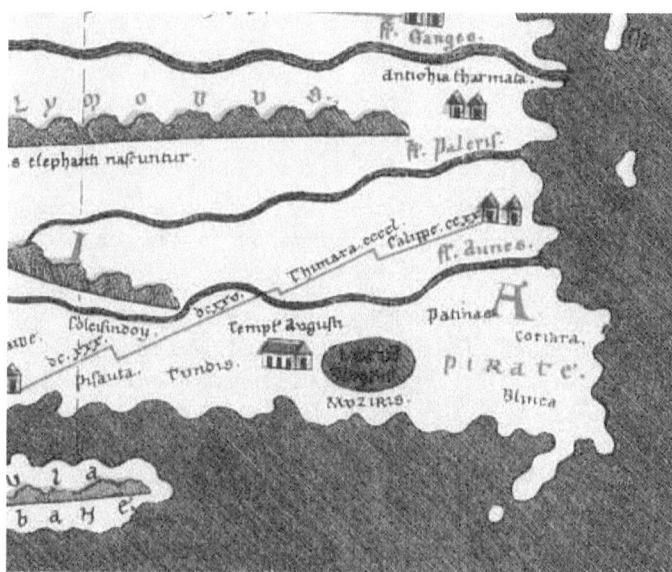

Figure 458: *Muziris, as shown in the Tabula Peutingeriana, with a "Templum Augusti".*

Pandyas are also mentioned in the Pillars of Ashoka (inscribed 273 – 232 BCE). In his inscriptions Ashoka refers to the peoples of south India – the Cholas, Cheras, Pandyas and Satiyaputras – as recipients of his Buddhist proselytism.[2415,2416] These kingdoms, although not part of the Mauryan Empire, were on friendly terms with Ashoka:

> *The conquest by Dharma has been won here, on the borders, and even six hundred yojanas (5,400–9,600 km) away, where the Greek king Antiochos rules, beyond there where the four kings named Ptolemy, Antigonos, Magas and Alexander rule, likewise in the south among the Cholas, the Pandyas, and as far as Tamraparni river.*[2417]

Kharavela, the Kalinga king who ruled during the 2nd century BCE, in his Hathigumpha inscription, claims to have destroyed a confederacy of Tamil states (*Tamiradesasanghatam*) which had lasted 132 years, and to have acquired a large quantity of pearls from the Pandyas.

Foreign sources

Megasthenes knew of the Pandyan kingdom around 300 BCE. He described it in *Indika* as *occupying the portion of India which lies southward and extends to the sea*. According to his account, it had 365 villages, each of which was expected to meet the needs of the royal household for one day in the year. He described the Pandyan queen at the time, *Pandaia* as a daughter of Heracles.[2418]

The Periplus of the Erythraean Sea (c. 60 – c. 100 CE) describes the riches of a 'Pandian Kingdom':

> ...*Nelcynda is distant from Muziris by river and sea about five hundred stadia, and is of another Kingdom, the Pandian. This place also is situated on a river, about one hundred and twenty stadia from the sea*....[2419]

The Chinese historian Yu Huan in his 3rd-century text, the *Weiliie*, mentions the Panyue kingdom: ...*The kingdom of Panyue is also called* Hanyuewang. *It is several thousand li to the southeast of Tianzhu (Northern India)...The inhabitants are small; they are the same height as the Chinese....* John E. Hill identified Panyue as Pandya kingdom.[2420] However, others have identified it with an ancient state located in modern Burma or Assam.

The Roman emperor Julian received an embassy from a Pandya about 361. A Roman trading centre was located on the Pandyan coast at the mouth of the Vaigai river, southeast of Madurai.

Pandyas also had trade contacts with Ptolemaic Egypt and, through Egypt, with Rome by the 1st century, and with China by the 3rd century. The 1st-century Greek historian Nicolaus of Damascus met, at Antioch, the ambassador sent by a king from India "named Pandion or, according to others, Porus" to Caesar Augustus around 13 CE (Strabo XV.4 and 73).[2421,2422]

The Chinese traveler Xuanzang mentions a kingdom further south from Kanchipuram, a kingdom named *Malakutta*, identified with Madurai described by his Buddhist friends at Kanchipuram.

In the later part of the 13th century Venetian traveller Marco Polo visited the Pandyan kingdom and left a vivid description of the land and its people.[2423,2424] Polo exclaimed that:

> *The darkest man is here the most highly esteemed and considered better than the others who are not so dark. Let me add that in very truth these people portray and depict their gods and their idols black and their devils white as snow. For they say that God and all the saints are black and the devils are all white. That is why they portray them as I have described.*[2425]

History

Literary sources

Although there are many instances of the Pandyas being referred to in surviving ancient Hindu texts including the Mahabharata, we currently have no way of determining a cogent genealogy of these ancient kings. We have a connected history of the Pandyas from the fall of Kalabhras during the middle of the 6th century.

Tamil literary sources

Several Tamil literary works, such as Iraiyanar Agapporul, mention the legend of three separate Tamil Sangams lasting several centuries before the Christian Era and ascribe their patronage to the Pandyas.

The Sangam poem *Maduraikkanci* by Mankudi Maruthanaar contains a full-length description of Madurai and the Pandyan country under the rule of Neduncheliyan III. The *Nedunalvadai* by Nakkirar contains a description of the king's palace. The *Purananuru* and *Agananuru* collections of the 3rd century BCE contain poems sung in praise of various Pandyan kings and also poems that were composed by the kings themselves.

Sanskrit literary sources

The *Ramayana* makes a few references to the Pandyas. For instance, when Sugriva sends his monkey warriors to search Sita, he mentions Chera, Chola and Pandya of the Southern region.[2426] Kalidasa's *Raghuvamsha*, an epic poem about Rama's dynasty, states that Ravana signed a peace treaty with a Pandya king.

The *Mahabharata* mentions the Pandyas a number of times. It states that the Pandya country was located on the sea shore, and supplied troops to the Pandava king Yudhishthira during the war (5:19). The Pandya king Sarangadhwaja commanded 140,000 warriors (7.23). Pandya warrior Malayadhwaja had a one-to-one fight with Drona's son Ashwatthama (8:20). *Mahabharata* mentions that *tirtha*s (sacred places) of Agastya, Varuna and Kumari were located in the Pandya country.

Figure 459: *Sculpture of Lord Rama*

Early Pandyas (3rd century BCE – 3rd century CE)

The following is a partial list of Pandyan emperors who ruled during the Sangam age:

- Koon Pandyan
- Nedunjeliyan I (Aariyap Padai Kadantha Nedunj Cheliyan)
- Pudappandyan
- Mudukudumi Peruvaludhi
- Nedunjeliyan II
- Nan Maran
- Nedunj Cheliyan III (Talaiyaalanganathu Seruvendra Nedunj Cheliyan)
- Maran Valudi
- Kadalan valuthi
- Musiri Mutriya Cheliyan
- Ukkirap Peruvaludi

First Pandyan Empire (6th – 10th centuries CE)

After the close of the Sangam age, the first Pandyan empire was established by Kadungon in the 6th century by defeating the Kalabhras. The following chronological list of the Pandya emperors is based on an inscription found on the Vaigai riverbeds. Succeeding kings assumed the titles of "Maravarman"

Figure 460: *Manikkavacakar, Minister of Pandya king Varagunavarman II (c. 862 – 885)*

and "Sadayavarman" alternately, where Sadayavarman denotes themselves as followers of Lord Sadaiyan ("The one with Jata", referring to Siva).

After the defeat of the Kalabhras, the Pandya kingdom grew steadily in power and territory. With the Cholas in obscurity, the Tamil country was divided between the Pallavas and the Pandyas, the river Kaveri being the frontier between them.

After Vijayalaya Chola conquered Thanjavur by defeating the Muttarayar chieftains who were part of Pandya family tree around 850, the Pandyas went into a period of decline. They were constantly harassing their Chola overlords by occupying their territories. Parantaka I invaded the Pandya territories and defeated Rajasimha III. However, the Pandyas did not wholly submit to the Cholas despite loss of power, territory and prestige. They tried to forge various alliances with the Cheras and the Kings of Lanka and tried to engage the Cholas in war to free themselves from Chola supremacy. But right from the times of Parantaka I to the early 12th century up to the times of Kulottunga Chola I the Pandyas could not overpower the Cholas who right from 880–1215 remained the most powerful empire spread over South India, Deccan and the Eastern and Western Coast of India during this period.

List of kings with dates as estimated by K. A. Nilakanta Sastri:[2427]

Figure 461: *Jatavarman Veera Pandyan II's double fish carp black granite bas-relief of the Koneswaram temple in Trincomalee, reminiscent of the dynasty's coinage symbols found on the island from the pre-modern era, installed after defeating the usurper Chandrabhanu of Tambralinga. Pandyan affairs in Northern Sri Lanka grew stronger following the intervention of Srimara Srivallabha in 815*

- Kadungon (r. c. 590–620 CE)
- Maravarman Avani Sulamani (r. c. 620-645 CE)
- Jayantavarman alias Seliyan Sendan (r. c. 645-670 CE)
- Arikesari Maravarman (r. c. 670–700 CE)
- Kochadaiyan Ranadhiran (r. c. 700–730 CE)
- Maravarman Rajasimha I (r. c. 735–765 CE)
- Jatila Parantaka Nedunjadayan (r. c. 765–815 CE)
- Maravarman Rajasimha II (r. c. 815-817 CE)
- Varaguna I (r. c. 817–835 CE)
- Srimara Srivallabha (r. c. 815–862 CE)
- Varaguna II (r. c. 862–885 CE)
- Parantaka Viranarayanan (r. c. 880–905 CE)
- Maravarman Rajasimha II (r. c. 905–920 CE)

Under Chola Influence (10th – 13th centuries)

The Chola domination of the Tamil country began in earnest during the reign of Parantaka Chola II. Chola armies led by Aditya Karikala, son of Parantaka Chola II defeated Vira Pandya in battle. The Pandyas were assisted by the Sinhalese forces of Mahinda IV. Pandyas were driven out of their territories and had to seek refuge on the island of Sri Lanka. This was the start of the long exile of the Pandyas. They were replaced by a series of Chola viceroys with the title *Chola Pandyas* who ruled from Madurai from c. 1020. Rajadhiraja III aided the Kulesekhara III by defeating the Sinhalese army and crowning him as king of Madurai. The "Chola yoke" started from about 920 and lasted until the start of the 13th century. The following list gives the names of the Pandya kings who were active during the 10th century and the first half of 11th century.

- Sundara Pandya I
- Vira Pandya I
- Vira Pandya II
- Amarabhujanga Tivrakopa
- Jatavarman Sundara Chola Pandya
- Maravarman Vikrama Chola Pandya
- Maravarman Parakrama Chola Pandya
- Jatavarman Chola Pandya
- Seervallabha Manakulachala (1101–1124)
- Maaravarman Seervallaban (1132–1161)
- Parakrama Pandyan I (1161–1162)
- Kulasekara Pandyan III
- Vira Pandyan III
- Jatavarman Srivallaban (1175–1180)
- Jatavarman Kulasekaran I (1190–1216)

Second Pandyan Empire (13th and 14th centuries)

Part of **a series** on the
History of India

- v
- t
- e[2428]

The 13th century is the greatest period in the history of the Pandyan Empire. This period saw the rise of seven prime Lord Emperors (*Ellarkku Nayanar – Lord of All*) of Pandyan, who ruled the kingdom alongside Pandyan princes. Their power reached its zenith under Jatavarman Sundara Pandyan in the middle of the 13th century. The foundation for such a great empire was laid by Maravarman Sundara Pandyan early in the 13th century.

- Parakrama Pandyan II (king of Polonnaruwa) (1212–1215)
- Maravarman Sundara Pandyan(1216–1238)
- Sundaravarman Kulasekaran II (1238–1240)
- Maravarman Sundara Pandyan II (1238–1251)
- Jatavarman Sundara Pandyan (1251–1268)
- Maravarman Kulasekara Pandyan I (1268–1310)
- Sundara Pandyan IV (1309–1327)
- Vira Pandyan IV (1309–1345)

The Pandyan kingdom was replaced by the Chola princes who assumed the title as Chola Pandyas in the 11th century. After being overshadowed by the Pallavas and Cholas for centuries, Pandyan glory was briefly revived by the much celebrated Jatavarman Sundara Pandyan I in 1251 AD.

Pandyan power extended from the Telugu countries on banks of the Godavari river to Sri Lanka, which was invaded by Jatavarman Sundara Pandyan I in

Figure 462: *A Pandya StyleWikipedia:Citation needed sculpture*

1258 and on his behalf by his younger brother Jatavarman Vira Pandyan II from 1262 to 1264. They ruled the whole peninsula and reduced the power of the Cholas and the Hoysala, also making Chera Nadu and Sri Lanka Pandyan provinces. Later Jatavarman Sundara Pandyan appointed his brother to rule Kongu country, Chola country and Hoysala country.

The marital alliance of Kulothunga Chola III and one of his successors, Rajaraja Chola III, with the Hoysalas did not yield any advantage in countering the Pandyan resurgence, who got defeated by Maravarman Sundara Pandyan I, who after the victory burnt down Uraiyur and Thanjavur. The Cholas renewed their control with the help of the Hoysalas under Hoysala king Vira Someshwara. The later successor of Maravarman Sundara Pandyan I, Maravarman Sundara Pandyan II got defeated by Rajendra Chola III around 1250.

Jatavarman Sundara Pandyan I subdued Rajendra Chola III in around 1258–1260 and was an equal antagonist of the Hoysalas whose presence he absolutely disliked in the Tamil country. He first vanquished the Kadava Pallavas under Kopperunchinga II, who had challenged the Hoysala army stationed in and around Kanchipuram and killed a few of their commanders.

Around 1260 dragged Jatavarman I first the Hoysalas into war by routing Vira Someshwara's son Ramanatha out of Tiruchirappalli. Vira Someshwara

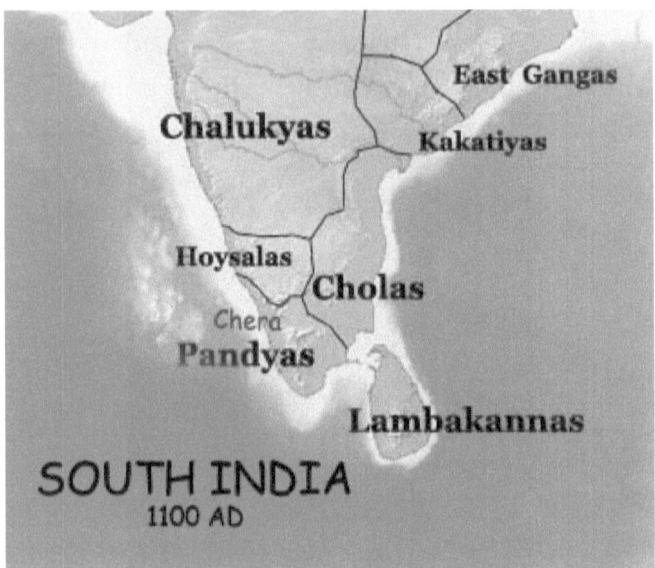

Figure 463: *Pandya power in South India*

Hoysala, who had given the control of the empire to his sons tried to challenge Jatavarman. Between Samayapuram and Tiruchy, the armies of Vira Someshwara were routed with Vira Someshwara losing his life in this battle to Jatavarman Sundara Pandyan I in Kannanur.

Next concentrated Jatavarman I on completely wiping out the Chola empire. Rajendra Chola III had been counting on Hoysala assistance in case he was challenged by the Pandyans, keeping in mind the earlier marital alliance of the Cholas with the Hoysalas. Initially, Jatavarman consolidated the Pandyan hold on Tiruchirappalli and Thiruvarangam and marched towards Thanjavur and Kumbakonam. The Hoysala king Narasimha III joined hands with the Pandyans, opposing alliance with the Cholas. When challenged by Jatavarman Sundara Pandyan, Rajendra III marched against the Pandyans between Tanjore and Tiruchy, hoping for assistance and participation in war from the Hoysalas. However, the already vanquished Hoysalas were in a defensive position. They did not want to go to war and risk yet another defeat by the resurgent Pandyans. Jatavarman Sundara Pandyan who defeated the Kadava Pallavas, Hoysalas and also the Telugu Choda, forced Rajendra III to become his tributary vassal.

Jatavarman Sundara Pandiyan invaded Sri Lanka in 1258 and took control over Jaffna Kingdom by defeating the Javaka king Chandrabhanu, making the Javaka king paying tribute to him. Chandrabhanu and two Sinhalese princes revolted against the Pandyans in 1270, and got his final defeat in 1270 by the brother of Jatavarman Sundara Pandyan I, Jatavarman Vira Pandyan II.

Around 1279 was the combined force of Hoysala Ramanatha and Rajendra Chola III defeated by Maravarman Kulasekara Pandyan I, giving an ultimate end on the Chola dynasty.

Pandyan Civil War (AD 1308 to 1311)

After the death of the king Maravarman Kulashekhara, his sons Vira and Sundara fought a war of succession for control of the kingdom. Taking advantage of this situation, the neighbouring Hoysala king Ballala III invaded the Pandya territory. However, Ballala had to retreat to his capital, when Malik Kafur, a general of the Muslim Delhi Sultanate, invaded his kingdom at the same time.[2429] After subjugating Ballala, Malik Kafur marched to the Pandya territory in March 1311.[2430] His army raided a number of places in the kingdom, massacring people and destroying temples. The Pandya brothers fled their headquarters, and Kafur pursued them unsuccessfully, hoping to make one of them a tributary to the Delhi Sultan Alauddin Khalji. Nevertheless, the invaders obtained a large number of treasures, elephants and horses.[2431,2432]

According to the 14th century Sanskrit treatise *Lilatilakam*, a general named Vikrama Pandya defeated the Muslims. Some historians have identified Vikrama as an uncle of Vira and Sundara, and believe that he defeated Malik Kafur. However, this identification is not supported by historical evidence: Vikrama Pandya mentioned in *Leelathilakam* appears to have defeated a later Muslim army during 1365-70.[2433] By late April 1311, the rains had obstructed the operations of the Delhi forces, and the invading generals received the news that the defenders had assembled a large army against them.[2434] Kafur gave up his plans to pursue the Pandya brothers, and returned to Delhi with the plunder.[2435]

After Kafur's departure, Vira and Sundara resumed their conflict. Sundara Pandya was defeated, and sought help from the Delhi Sultanate. With their help, he regained control of the South Arcot region by 1314.[2434]

Decline and fall

Subsequently, this there were two other expeditions from the Khalji Sultanate in 1314 led by Khusro Khan (later Sultan Nasir-ud-din) and in 1323 by Ulugh Khan (Muhammad bin Tughluq) under Sultan Ghiyath al-Din Tughluq. These invasions shattered the Pandyan empire beyond revival. While the previous invasions were content with plunder, Ulugh Khan annexed the former Pandyan dominions to the Delhi Sultanate as the province of Ma'bar. Most of South India came under the Delhi's rule and was divided into five provinces – Devagiri, Tiling, Kampili, Dorasamudra and Ma'bar.[2436] Jalaluddin Ahsan Khan

Figure 464: *An aerial view of Madurai city from atop the Meenakshi Amman temple*

was appointed governor of the newly created southern-most Ma'bar province of the Delhi Sultanate by Muhammad bin Tughluq. In 1333, Sayyid Jalaluddin Ahsan Khan declared his independence and created Madurai Sultanate, a short lived independent Muslim kingdom based in the city of Madurai. Hoysala king Veera Ballala III, from his capital in Tiruvannamalai, challenged the Madurai Sultans at Kannanur Kuppam near Srirangam and died fighting them in 1343. Bukkaraya I of Vijayanagara Empire conquered the city of Madurai in 1371, imprisoned the Sultan, released and restored Arcot's Tamil prince Sambuva Raya to the throne. Bukka I appointed his son Veera Kumara Kampana as the viceroy of the Tamil region. Later, Nayaka governors were appointed.Wikipedia:Identifying reliable sources who would continue ruling till 1736.

Architecture

Rock cut and structural temples are significant part of pandyan architecture. The Vimana and mandapa are some of the features of the early Pandyan temples.

Groups of small temples are seen at Tiruchirappalli district of Tamil Nadu. The Shiva temples have a Nandi bull sculpture in front of the *maha mandapa*. In the later stages of Pandyas rule, finely sculptured idols, gopurams on the vimanas were developed. Gopurams are the rectangular entrance and portals of the temples.

Meenakshi Amman Temple in Madurai and Nellaiappar Temple in Tirunelveli were built during the reign of the Pandyas.

Figure 465: *The Gopuram of Nellaiappar Temple*

Figure 466: *One of the early coins of the Pandyans showing their emblem of the two fishes.*

Figure 467: *Temple between hill symbols and elephant coin of the Pandyas Sri Lanka 1st century CE.*

Coinage

The early coins of Tamilakam bore the symbols of the Three Crowned Kings, the tiger, the fish and the bow, representing the symbols of the Cholas, Pandyas and Cheras. Coins of Pandyas bear the legend of different Pandya ruler in different times. The Pandyas had issued silver punch-marked and die struck copper coins in the early period. A few gold coins were attributed to the Pandya rulers of this period. These coins bore the image of fish, singly or in pairs, which where their emblem.

Some of the coins had the names Sundara, Sundara Pandya or merely the letter 'Su' were etched. Some of the coins bore a boar with the legend of 'Vira-Pandya. It had been said that those coins were issued by the Pandyas and the feudatories of the Cholas but could not be attributed to any particular king.

The coins of Pandyas were basically square. Those coins were etched with elephant on one side and the other side remained blank. The inscription on the silver and gold coins during the Pandyas, were in Tamil-Brahmi and the copper coins bore the Tamil legends.

The coins of the Pandyas, which bore the fish symbols, were termed as 'Kodandaraman' and 'Kanchi' Valangum Perumal'. Apart from these, 'Ellamthalaiyanam' was seen on coins which had the standing king on one side and the

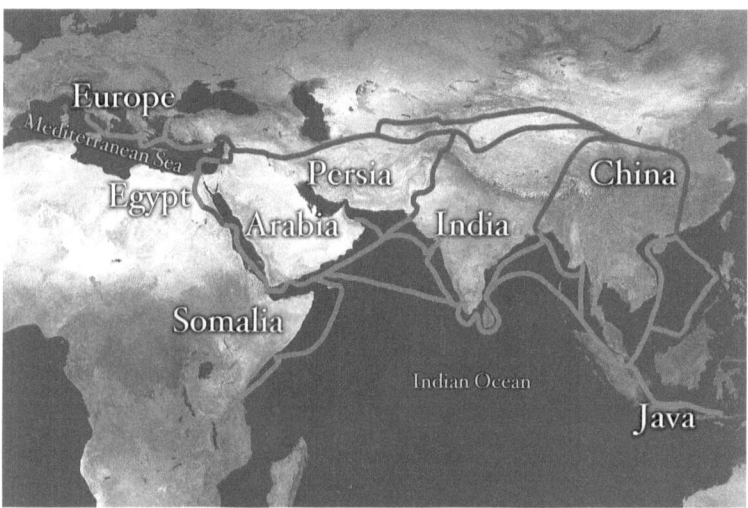

Figure 468: *Silk Road map showing ancient trade routes.*

fish on the other. 'Samarakolahalam' and 'Bhuvanekaviram' were found on the coins having a Garuda, 'Konerirayan' on coins having a bull and 'Kaliyugaraman' on coins that depict a pair of feet.

Government and Society

Trade

Roman and Greek traders frequented the ancient Tamil country, present day Southern India and Sri Lanka, securing trade with the seafaring Tamil states of the Pandyan, Chola and Chera dynasties and establishing trading settlements which secured trade with South Asia by the Greco-Roman world since the time of the Ptolemaic dynasty[2437] a few decades before the start of the Common Era and remained long after the fall of the Western Roman Empire.[2438] As recorded by Strabo, Emperor Augustus of Rome received at Antioch an ambassador from a South Indian King called **Pandyan**. The country of the Pandyas, Pandi Mandala, was described as *Pandyan Mediterranea* in the *Periplus* and *Modura Regia Pandyan* by Ptolemy.[2439] They also outlasted Byzantium's loss of the ports of Egypt and the Red Sea[2440] (c. 639-645) under the pressure of the Muslim conquests. Sometime after the sundering of communications between the Axum and Eastern Roman Empire in the 7th century, the Christian kingdom of Axum fell into a slow decline, fading into obscurity in western sources. It survived, despite pressure from Islamic forces, until the 11th century, when it was reconfigured in a dynastic squabble.

Figure 469: *Pearl fishing was an important industry in ancient Tamilakam*

Pearl fishing

Pearl fishing was another industry that flourished during the Sangam age. The Pandyan port city of Korkai was the center of pearl trade. Written records from Greek and Egyptian voyagers give details about the pearl fisheries off the Pandyan coast. The Periplus of the Erythraean Sea mentions that "Pearls inferior to the Indian sort are exported in great quantity from the marts of Apologas and Omana". The inferior variety of pearls that the Tamils did not require for their use was in very great demand in the foreign markets. Pearls were woven along with nice muslin cloth, before being exported. The most expensive animal product that was imported from India by the Roman Empire was the pearl from the Gulf of Mannar.[2441]

The pearls from the Pandyan Kingdom were also in demand in the kingdoms of north India. Several Vedic mantras refer to the wide use of the pearls. The royal chariots were decked with pearls, as were the horses that dragged them. The use of pearls was so high that the supply of pearls from the Ganges could not meet the demand. Literary references of the pearl fishing mention how the fishermen, who dive into the sea, avoid attacks from sharks, bring up the right-whorled chank and blow on the sounding shell. Convicts were according to the Periplus of the Erythraean Sea used as pearl divers in Korkai.

Megasthenes reported about the pearl fisheries of the Pandyas, indicating that the Pandyas derived great wealth from the pearl trade.[2442]

Religion

Historical Madurai was a stronghold of Shaivism. Following the invasion of Kalabhras, Jainism gained a foothold in the Pandyan kingdom. With the advent of Bhakti movements, Shaivism and Vaishnavism resurfaced. The latter-day Pandyas after 600 CE were Saivites who claimed to descend from Lord Shiva and Goddess Parvati. Pandyan Nedumchadayan was a staunch Vaishnavite.

References

 Wikimedia Commons has media related to *Pandyan Dynasty*.

<templatestyles src="Template:Refbegin/styles.css" />

- Balambal, V. (1998). *Studies in the History of the Sangam Age*. Kalinga Publications. ISBN 978-81-85163-87-1.
- Carswell, John. 1991. "The Port of Mantai, Sri Lanka." *RAI*, pp. 197–203.
- Curtin, Philip D. (1984). *Cross-Cultural Trade in World History*. Cambridge University Press. ISBN 978-0-521-26931-5.
- Hill, John E. 2004. *The Peoples of the West from the Weilüe* 魏略 *by Yu Huan* 魚豢 *: A Third Century Chinese Account Composed between 239 and 265 CE*. Draft annotated English translation.[2443]
- Holl, Augustin (2003). *Ethnoarchaeology of Shuwa-Arab Settlements*. Lexington Books. ISBN 978-0-7391-0407-1.
- Husaini, A.Q. (1972). *History of The Pandya Country*.
- Keay, John (2000) [2001]. *India: A history*. India: Grove Press. ISBN 0-8021-3797-0.
- Kulke, Hermann; Dietmar Rothermund (2004). *A History of India* (4 ed.).
- Lindsay, W S (2006). *History of Merchant Shipping and Ancient Commerce*. Adamant Media Corporation. ISBN 0-543-94253-8.
- Nagasamy, R (1981). *Tamil Coins – A study*. Institute of Epigraphy, Tamil Nadu State Dept. of Archaeology.
- Purushottam, Vi. Pi. (1989). *Cankakala Mannar Kalanilai Varalaru*.

- Ray, Himanshu Prabha, ed. 1996. *Tradition and Archaeology: Early Maritime Contacts in the Indian Ocean.* Proceedings of the International Seminar Techno-Archaeological Perspectives of Seafaring in the Indian Ocean 4th cent. BC – 15th cent. AD New Delhi, 28 February – 4 March 1994. New Delhi, and Jean-François SALLES, Lyon. First published 1996. Reprinted 1998. Manohar Publishers & Distributors, New Delhi.
- Reddy, P. Krishna Mohan. 2001. "Maritime Trade of Early South India: New Archaeological Evidences from Motupalli, Andhra Pradesh." *East and West* Vol. 51 – Nos. 1–2 (June 2001), pp. 143–156.
- Tripathi, Rama Sankar (1967). *History of Ancient India.* India: Motilal Banarsidass Publications. ISBN 81-208-0018-4.
- Sastri, K. A. Nilakanta. *The Pandyan Kingdom: From the Earliest Times to the Sixteenth Century.*
- Shaffer, Lynda (1996). *Maritime Southeast Asia to 1500 (Sources and Studies in World History).* Armonk, N.Y: M.E. Sharpe. ISBN 1-56324-144-7.
- N. Subrahmanian (1962). *History of Tamilnad (To A. D. 1336)*[2444]. Madurai: Koodal. OCLC 43502446[2445]. Archived from the original[2446] on 23 November 2016.
- Venkata Subramanian, T. K. (1988). *Environment and Urbanisation in Early Tamilakam*[2447]. *Issue 92 of Tamil_p Palkalaik Kal_aka ve?iyi?u.* Tamil University. p. 55. ISBN 978-81-7090-110-5.
- Banarsi Prasad Saksena (1992). "The Khaljis: Alauddin Khalji". In Mohammad Habib and Khaliq Ahmad Nizami. *A Comprehensive History of India: The Delhi Sultanat (A.D. 1206-1526)*[2448]. **5** (Second ed.). The Indian History Congress / People's Publishing House. OCLC 31870180[2449].
- K.K.R. Nair (1987). "Venad: Its Early History"[2450]. *Journal of Kerala Studies.* University of Kerala. **14** (1): 1–34. ISSN 0377-0443[2451].
- Kishori Saran Lal (1950). *History of the Khaljis (1290-1320)*[2452]. Allahabad: The Indian Press. OCLC 685167335[2453].
- Peter Jackson (2003). *The Delhi Sultanate: A Political and Military History*[2454]. Cambridge University Press. ISBN 978-0-521-54329-3.

Rashtrakuta dynasty

Rashtrakutas of Manyakheta	
Empire	
753–982	
Extent of Rashtrakuta Empire, 800 CE, 915 CE	
Capital	Manyakheta
Languages	Kannada Sanskrit
Religion	Hinduism Jainism Buddhism[2455]
Government	Monarchy
Maharaja	
• 735–756	Dantidurga
• 973–982	Indra IV
History	
• Earliest Rashtrakuta records	753
• Established	753
• Disestablished	982
Preceded by	Succeeded by
Chalukya dynasty	Western Chalukya Empire
Today part of	India

Rashtrakuta Emperors (753-982)	
Dantidurga	(735 - 756)
Krishna I	(756 - 774)
Govinda II	(774 - 780)
Dhruva Dharavarsha	(780 - 793)
Govinda III	(793 - 814)
Amoghavarsha	(814 - 878)
Krishna II	(878 - 914)
Indra III	(914 -929)
Amoghavarsha II	(929 - 930)
Govinda IV	(930 – 936)
Amoghavarsha III	(936 – 939)
Krishna III	(939 – 967)
Khottiga	(967 – 972)
Karka II	(972 – 973)
Indra IV	(973 – 982)
Tailapa II (*Western Chalukyas*)	(973-997)

Rashtrakuta (IAST: *rāṣṭrakūṭa*) was a royal dynasty ruling large parts of the Indian subcontinent between the sixth and 10th centuries. The earliest known Rashtrakuta inscription is a 7th-century copper plate grant detailing their rule from Manapura, a city in Central or West India. Other ruling Rashtrakuta clans from the same period mentioned in inscriptions were the kings of Achalapur (modern Elichpur in Maharashtra) and the rulers of Kannauj. Several controversies exist regarding the origin of these early Rashtrakutas, their native home and their language.

The Elichpur clan was a feudatory of the Badami Chalukyas, and during the rule of Dantidurga, it overthrew Chalukya Kirtivarman II and went on to build an empire with the Gulbarga region in modern Karnataka as its base. This clan came to be known as the Rashtrakutas of Manyakheta, rising to power in South India in 753. At the same time the Pala dynasty of Bengal and the Prathihara dynasty of Malwa were gaining force in eastern and northwestern India respectively. An Arabic text, *Silsilat al-Tawarikh* (851), called the Rashtrakutas one of the four principal empires of the world.[2456]

This period, between the eighth and the 10th centuries, saw a tripartite struggle for the resources of the rich Gangetic plains, each of these three empires annexing the seat of power at Kannauj for short periods of time. At their

Figure 470: *Shiva sculpture in Kailasanath Temple, Ellora Caves*

peak the Rashtrakutas of Manyakheta ruled a vast empire stretching from the Ganges River and Yamuna River doab in the north to Cape Comorin in the south, a fruitful time of political expansion, architectural achievements and famous literary contributions. The early kings of this dynasty were influenced by Hinduism and the later kings by Jainism.

During their rule, Jain mathematicians and scholars contributed important works in Kannada and Sanskrit. Amoghavarsha I, the most famous king of this dynasty wrote *Kavirajamarga*, a landmark literary work in the Kannada language. Architecture reached a milestone in the Dravidian style, the finest example of which is seen in the Kailasanath Temple at Ellora in modern Maharashtra. Other important contributions are the Kashivishvanatha temple and the Jain Narayana temple at Pattadakal in modern Karnataka, both of which are UNESCO World Heritage Sites.

History

The origin of the Rashtrakuta dynasty has been a controversial topic of Indian history. These issues pertain to the origin of the earliest ancestors of the Rashtrakutas during the time of Emperor Ashoka in the 2nd century BCE,[2457] and the connection between the several Rashtrakuta dynasties that ruled small kingdoms in northern and central India and the Deccan between the 6th and

Figure 471: *Three-storied monolithic Jain cave temple at Ellora*

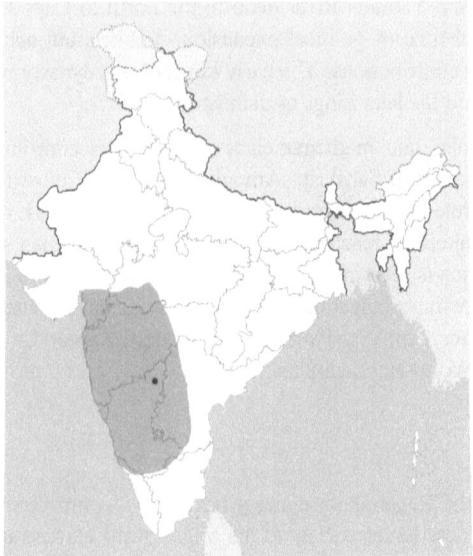

Figure 472: *Core territory of the empire of Manyakheta*

7th centuries. The relationship of these medieval Rashtrakutas to the most famous later dynasty, the Rashtrakutas of Manyakheta (present day Malkhed in the Gulbarga district, Karnataka state), who ruled between the 8th and 10th centuries has also been debated.[2458,2459]

The sources for Rashtrakuta history include medieval inscriptions, ancient literature in the Pali language,[2460] contemporaneous literature in Sanskrit and Kannada and the notes of the Arab travellers.[2461] Theories about the dynastic lineage (*Surya Vamsa*—Solar line and *Chandra Vamsa*—Lunar line), the native region and the ancestral home have been proposed, based on information gleaned from inscriptions, royal emblems, the ancient clan names such as "Rashtrika", epithets (*Ratta, Rashtrakuta, Lattalura Puravaradhiswara*), the names of princes and princesses of the dynasty, and clues from relics such as coins.[2462,2463] Scholars debate over which ethnic/linguistic groups can claim the early Rashtrakutas. Possibilities include the north western ethnic groups of India,[2464] the Kannadiga,[2465,2466] Reddi,[2467] the Maratha,[2468,2469] or the tribes from the Punjab region.[2470]

Scholars however concur that the rulers of the imperial dynasty in the 8th to 10th century made the Kannada language as important as Sanskrit. Rashtrakuta inscriptions use both Kannada and Sanskrit (historians Sheldon Pollock and Jan Houben claim they are mostly in Kannada),[2471,2472,2473,2474,2475] and the rulers encouraged literature in both languages. The earliest existing Kannada literary writings are credited to their court poets and royalty.[2476,2477,2478,2479] Though these Rashtrakutas were Kannadigas,[2480,2481,2482,2483] they were conversant in a northern Deccan language as well.

The heart of the Rashtrakuta empire included nearly all of Karnataka, Maharashtra and parts of Andhra Pradesh, an area which the Rashtrakutas ruled for over two centuries. The Samangadh copper plate grant (753) confirms that the feudatory King Dantidurga, who probably ruled from Achalapura in Berar (modern Elichpur in Maharashtra), defeated the great Karnatic army (referring to the army of the Badami Chalukyas) of Kirtivarman II of Badami in 753 and took control of the northern regions of the Chalukya empire.[2484,2485,2486] He then helped his father-in-law, Pallava King Nandivarman regain Kanchi from the Chalukyas and defeated the Gurjaras of Malwa, and the rulers of Kalinga, Kosala and Srisailam.[2487,2488]

Dantidurga's successor Krishna I brought major portions of present-day Karnataka and Konkan under his control.[2489,2490] During the rule of Dhruva Dharavarsha who took control in 780, the kingdom expanded into an empire that encompassed all of the territory between the Kaveri River and Central India.[2491,2492,2493] He led successful expeditions to Kannauj, the seat of northern

Indian power where he defeated the Gurjara Pratiharas and the Palas of Bengal, gaining him fame and vast booty but not more territory. He also brought the Eastern Chalukyas and Gangas of Talakad under his control.[2494] According to Altekar and Sen, the Rashtrakutas became a pan-India power during his rule.[2495]

Expansion

The ascent of Dhruva Dharavarsha's third son, Govinda III, to the throne heralded an era of success like never before.[2496] There is uncertainty about the location of the early capital of the Rashtrakutas at this time.[2497,2498,2499] During his rule there was a three way conflict between the Rashtrakutas, the Palas and the Pratiharas for control over the Gangetic plains. Describing his victories over the Pratihara Emperor Nagabhatta II and the Pala Emperor Dharmapala, the Sanjan inscription states the horses of Govinda III drank from the icy waters of the Himalayan streams and his war elephants tasted the sacred waters of the Ganges.[2500,2501] His military exploits have been compared to those of Alexander the Great and Arjuna of Mahabharata.[2502] Having conquered Kannauj, he travelled south, took firm hold over Gujarat, Kosala (Kaushal), Gangavadi, humbled the Pallavas of Kanchi, installed a ruler of his choice in Vengi and received two statues as an act of submission from the king of Ceylon (one statue of the king and another of his minister). The Cholas, the Pandyas and the Cheras all paid him tribute.[2503,2504,2505] As one historian puts it, the drums of the Deccan were heard from the Himalayan caves to the shores of the Malabar. The Rashtrakutas empire now spread over the areas from Cape Comorin to Kannauj and from Banaras to Bharuch.[2506,2507]

The successor of Govinda III, Amoghavarsha I made Manyakheta his capital and ruled a large empire. Manyakheta remained the Rashtrakutas' regal capital until the end of the empire.[2508,2509,2510] He came to the throne in 814 but it was not until 821 that he had suppressed revolts from feudatories and ministers. Amoghavarsha I made peace with the Western Ganga dynasty by giving them his two daughters in marriage, and then defeated the invading Eastern Chalukyas at Vingavalli and assumed the title *Viranarayana*.[2511,2512] His rule was not as militant as that of Govinda III as he preferred to maintain friendly relations with his neighbours, the Gangas, the Eastern Chalukyas and the Pallavas with whom he also cultivated marital ties. His era was an enriching one for the arts, literature and religion. Widely seen as the most famous of the Rashtrakuta Emperors, Amoghavarsha I was an accomplished scholar in Kannada and Sanskrit.[2513] His *Kavirajamarga* is considered an important landmark in Kannada poetics and *Prashnottara Ratnamalika* in Sanskrit is a writing of high merit and was later translated into the Tibetan language.[2514] Because of his religious temperament, his interest in the arts and literature and his peace-loving nature, he has been compared to the emperor Ashoka and called "Ashoka of the South".[2515]

During the rule of Krishna II, the empire faced a revolt from the Eastern Chalukyas and its size decreased to the area including most of the Western Deccan and Gujarat.[2516] Krishna II ended the independent status of the Gujarat branch and brought it under direct control from Manyakheta. Indra III recovered the dynasty's fortunes in central India by defeating the Paramara and then invaded the doab region of the Ganges and Jamuna rivers. He also defeated the dynasty's traditional enemies, the Pratiharas and the Palas, while maintaining his influence over Vengi.[2517,2518] The effect of his victories in Kannauj lasted several years according to the 930 copper plate inscription of Emperor Govinda IV.[2519,2520] After a succession of weak kings during whose reigns the empire lost control of territories in the north and east, Krishna III the last great ruler consolidated the empire so that it stretched from the Narmada River to Kaveri River and included the northern Tamil country (Tondaimandalam) while levying tribute on the king of Ceylon.[2521,2522,2523,2524,2525]

Decline

In 972 A.D., during the rule of Khottiga Amoghavarsha, the Paramara King Siyaka Harsha attacked the empire and plundered Manyakheta, the capital of the Rashtrakutas. This seriously undermined the reputation of the Rastrakuta Empire and consequently led to its downfall. The final decline was sudden as Tailapa II, a feudatory of the Rashtrakuta ruling from Tardavadi province in modern Bijapur district, declared himself independent by taking advantage of this defeat.[2526,2527] Indra IV, the last emperor, committed Sallekhana (fasting unto death practised by Jain monks) at Shravanabelagola. With the fall of the Rashtrakutas, their feudatories and related clans in the Deccan and northern India declared independence. The Western Chalukyas annexed Manyakheta and made it their capital until 1015 and built an impressive empire in the Rashtrakuta heartland during the 11th century. The focus of dominance shifted to the Krishna River – Godavari River doab called Vengi. The former feudatories of the Rashtrakutas in western Deccan were brought under control of the Chalukyas, and the hitherto-suppressed Cholas of Tanjore became their arch enemies in the south.[2528]

In conclusion, the rise of Rashtrakutas of Manyakheta had a great impact on India, even on India's north. Sulaiman (851), Al Masudi (944) and Ibn Khurdadba (912) wrote that their empire was the largest in contemporary India and Sulaiman further called it one among the four great contemporary empires of the world.[2529,2530,2531] According to the travelogues of the Arabs Al

Masudi and Ibn Khordidbih of the 10th century, "most of the kings of Hindustan turned their faces towards the Rashtrakuta king while they were praying, and they prostrated themselves before his ambassadors. The Rashtrakuta king was known as the "King of kings" (*Rajadhiraja*) who possessed the mightiest of armies and whose domains extended from Konkan to Sind."[2532] Some historians have called these times an "Age of Imperial Kannauj". Since the Rashtrakutas successfully captured Kannauj, levied tribute on its rulers and presented themselves as masters of North India, the era could also be called the "Age of Imperial Karnataka". During their political expansion into central and northern India in the 8th to the 10th centuries, the Rashtrakutas or their relatives created several kingdoms that either ruled during the reign of the parent empire or continued to rule for centuries after its fall or came to power much later. Well-known among these were the Rashtrakutas of Gujarat (757–888),[2533] the Rattas of Saundatti (875–1230) in modern Karnataka,[2534] the Gahadavalas of Kannauj (1068–1223),[2535] the Rashtrakutas of Rajasthan (known as Rajputana) and ruling from Hastikundi or Hathundi (893–996),[2536] Dahal (near Jabalpur),[2537] Mandore (near Jodhpur), the Rathores of Dhanop,[2538] Rashtraudha dynasty of Mayuragiri in modern Maharashtra[2539] and Rashtrakutas of Kannauj.[2540] Rajadhiraja Chola's conquest of the island of Ceylon in the early 11th century CE led to the fall of four kings there. According to historian K. Pillay, one of them, King Madavarajah of the Jaffna kingdom, was an usurper from the Rashtrakuta Dynasty.

Administration

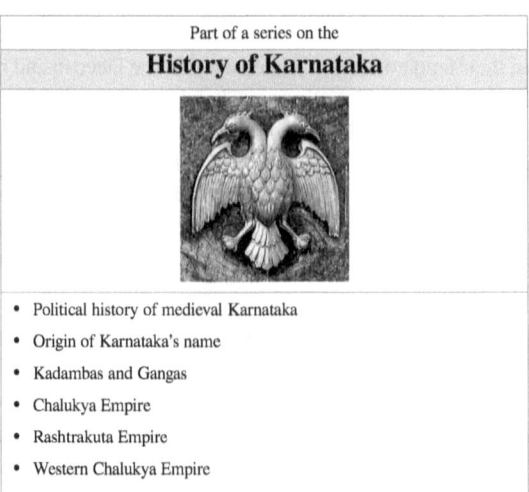

Part of a series on the
History of Karnataka

- Political history of medieval Karnataka
- Origin of Karnataka's name
- Kadambas and Gangas
- Chalukya Empire
- Rashtrakuta Empire
- Western Chalukya Empire
- Southern Kalachuri
- Hoysala Empire

- Vijayanagara Empire
- Bahmani Sultanate
- Bijapur Sultanate
- Kingdom of Mysore
- Nayakas of Keladi
- Nayakas of Chitradurga
- Haleri Kingdom
- Unification of Karnataka

Categories
• Architecture • Forts • Economies • Societies
• $\underline{v}$ • $\underline{t}$ • $\underline{e}^{2541}$

Inscriptions and other literary records indicate the Rashtrakutas selected the crown prince based on heredity. The crown did not always pass on to the eldest son. Abilities were considered more important than age and chronology of birth, as exemplified by the crowning of Govinda III who was the third son of king Dhruva Dharavarsha. The most important position under the king was the Chief Minister (*Mahasandhivigrahi*) whose position came with five insignia commensurate with his position namely, a flag, a conch, a fan, a white umbrella, a large drum and five musical instruments called *Panchamahashabdas*. Under him was the commander (*Dandanayaka*), the foreign minister (*Mahakshapataladhikrita*) and a prime minister (*Mahamatya* or *Purnamathya*), all of whom were usually associated with one of the feudatory kings and must have held a position in government equivalent to a premier.[2542] A *Mahasamantha* was a feudatory or higher ranking regal officer. All cabinet ministers were well versed in political science (*Rajneeti*) and possessed military training. There were cases where women supervised significant areas as when Revakanimaddi, daughter of Amoghavarsha I, administered Edathore *Vishaya*.

The kingdom was divided into *Mandala* or *Rashtras* (provinces). A *Rashtra* was ruled by a Rashtrapathi who on occasion was the emperor himself. Amoghavarsha I's empire had sixteen *Rashtras*. Under a *Rashtra* was a *Vishaya* (district) overseen by a Vishayapathi. Trusted ministers sometimes ruled more than a *Rashtra*. For example, Bankesha, a commander of Amoghavarsha I headed Banavasi-12000, Belvola-300, Puligere-300, Kunduru-500 and Kundarge-70, the suffix designating the number of villages in that territory. Below the *Vishaya* was the *Nadu* looked after by the Nadugowda or Nadugavunda; sometimes there were two such officials, one assuming the position through heredity and another appointed centrally. The

Figure 473: *Kashivishvanatha temple at Pattadakal, Karnataka*

lowest division was a *Grama* or village administered by a *Gramapathi* or *Prabhu Gavunda*.[2543]

The Rashtrakuta army consisted of large contingents of infantry, horsemen, and elephants. A standing army was always ready for war in a cantonment (*Sthirabhuta Kataka*) in the regal capital of Manyakheta. Large armies were also maintained by the feudatory kings who were expected to contribute to the defense of the empire in case of war. Chieftains and all the officials also served as commanders whose postings were transferable if the need arose.[2544]

The Rashtrakutas issued coins (minted in an *Akkashale*) such as *Suvarna*, *Drammas* in silver and gold weighing 65 grains, *Kalanju* weighing 48 grains, *Gadyanaka* weighing 96 grains, *Kasu* weighing 15 grains, *Manjati* with 2.5 grains and *Akkam* of 1.25 grain.[2545]

Economy

The Rashtrakuta economy was sustained by its natural and agricultural produce, its manufacturing revenues and moneys gained from its conquests. Cotton was the chief crop of the regions of southern Gujarat, Khandesh and Berar. Minnagar, Gujarat, Ujjain, Paithan and Tagara were important centres of textile industry. Muslin cloth were manufactured in Paithan and Warangal. The cotton yarn and cloth was exported from Bharoch. White calicos were manufactured in Burhanpur and Berar and exported to Persia, Turkey, Poland, Arabia and Egypt.[2546] The Konkan region, ruled by the feudatory Silharas, produced large quantities of betel leaves, coconut and rice while the lush forests of Mysore, ruled by the feudatory Gangas, produced such woods as sandal, timber, teak and ebony. Incense and perfumes were exported from the ports of Thana and Saimur.

The Deccan was rich in minerals, though its soil was not as fertile as that of the Gangetic plains. The copper mines of Cudappah, Bellary, Chanda, Buldhana, Narsingpur, Ahmadnagar, Bijapur and Dharwar were an important source of income and played an important role in the economy.[2547] Diamonds were mined in Cudappah, Bellary, Kurnool and Golconda; the capital Manyakheta and Devagiri were important diamond and jewellery trading centres. The leather industry and tanning flourished in Gujarat and some regions of northern Maharashtra. Mysore with its vast elephant herds was important for the ivory industry.[2548]

The Rashtrakuta empire controlled most of the western sea board of the subcontinent which facilitated its maritime trade.[2549] The Gujarat branch of the empire earned a significant income from the port of Bharoch, one of the most prominent ports in the world at that time.[2550] The empire's chief exports were cotton yarn, cotton cloth, muslins, hides, mats, indigo, incense, perfumes, betel nuts, coconuts, sandal, teak, timber, sesame oil and ivory. Its major imports were pearls, gold, dates from Arabia, slaves, Italian wines, tin, lead, topaz, storax, sweet clover, flint glass, antimony, gold and silver coins, singing boys and girls (for the entertainment of the royalty) from other lands. Trading in horses was an important and profitable business, monopolised by the Arabs and some local merchants.[2551] The Rashtrakuta government levied a shipping tax of one golden *Gadyanaka* on all foreign vessels embarking to any other ports and a fee of one silver *Ctharna* (a coin) on vessels travelling locally.

Artists and craftsman operated as corporations (guilds) rather than as individual business. Inscriptions mention guilds of weavers, oilmen, artisans, basket and mat makers and fruit sellers. A Saundatti inscription refers to an assemblage of all the people of a district headed by the guilds of the region.[2552] Some guilds were considered superior to others, just as some corporations were, and received royal charters determining their powers and privileges. Inscriptions suggest these guilds had their own militia to protect goods in transit and, like village assemblies, they operated banks that lent money to traders and businesses.[2553]

The government's income came from five principal sources: regular taxes, occasional taxes, fines, income taxes, miscellaneous taxes and tributes from feudatories.²⁵⁵⁴ An emergency tax was imposed occasionally and were applicable when the kingdom was under duress, such as when it faced natural calamities, or was preparing for war or overcoming war's ravages. Income tax included taxes on crown land, wasteland, specific types of trees considered valuable to the economy, mines, salt, treasures unearthed by prospectors.²⁵⁵⁵ Additionally, customary presents were given to the king or royal officers on such festive occasions as marriage or the birth of a son.²⁵⁵⁶

The king determined the tax levels based on need and circumstances in the kingdom while ensuring that an undue burden was not placed on the peasants.²⁵⁵⁷ The land owner or tenant paid a variety of taxes, including land taxes, produce taxes and payment of the overhead for maintenance of the Gavunda (village head). Land taxes were varied, based on type of land, its produce and situation and ranged from 8% to 16%. A Banavasi inscription of 941 mentions reassessment of land tax due to the drying up of an old irrigation canal in the region. The land tax may have been as high as 20% to pay for expenses of a military frequently at war.²⁵⁵⁸ In most of the kingdom, land taxes were paid in goods and services and rarely was cash accepted.²⁵⁵⁹ A portion of all taxes earned by the government (usually 15%) was returned to the villages for maintenance.²⁵⁶⁰

Taxes were levied on artisans such as potters, sheep herders, weavers, oilmen, shopkeepers, stall owners, brewers and gardeners. Taxes on perishable items such as fish, meat, honey, medicine, fruits and essentials like fuel was as high as 16%.²⁵⁶¹ Taxes on salt and minerals were mandatory although the empire did not claim sole ownership of mines, implying that private mineral prospecting and the quarrying business may have been active.²⁵⁶² The state claimed all such properties whose deceased legal owner had no immediate family to make an inheritance claim.²⁵⁶³ Other miscellaneous taxes included ferry and house taxes. Only Brahmins and their temple institutions were taxed at a lower rate.²⁵⁶⁴

Culture

Religion

The Rashtrakuta kings supported the popular religions of the day in the traditional spirit of religious tolerance.²⁵⁶⁵ Scholars have offered various arguments regarding which specific religion the Rashtrakutas favoured, basing their evidence on inscriptions, coins and contemporary literature. Some claim the Rashtrakutas were inclined towards Jainism since many of the scholars who flourished in their courts and wrote in Sanskrit, Kannada and a few in Apabhramsha and Prakrit were Jains.²⁵⁶⁶ The Rashtrakutas built well-known

Figure 474: *Kailasanatha Temple*

Jain temples at locations such as Lokapura in Bagalkot district and their loyal feudatory, the Western Ganga Dynasty, built Jain monuments at Shravanabelagola and Kambadahalli. Scholars have suggested that Jainism was a principal religion at the very heart of the empire, modern Karnataka, accounting for more than 30% of the population and dominating the culture of the region.[2567] King Amoghavarsha I was a disciple of the Jain acharya Jinasena and wrote in his religious writing, *Prashnottara Ratnamalika*, "having bowed to Varaddhamana (Mahavira), I write Prashnottara Ratnamalika". The mathematician Mahaviracharya wrote in his *Ganita Sarasangraha*, "The subjects under Amoghavarsha are happy and the land yields plenty of grain. May the kingdom of King Nripatunga Amoghavarsha, follower of Jainism ever increase far and wide." Amoghavarsha may have taken up Jainism in his old age.[2568,2569]

However, the Rashtrakuta kings also patronized Hinduism's followers of the Shaiva, Vaishnava and Shakta faiths. Almost all of their inscriptions begin with an invocation to god Vishnu or god Shiva. The Sanjan inscriptions tell of King Amoghavarsha I sacrificing a finger from his left hand at the Lakshmi temple at Kolhapur to avert a calamity in his kingdom. King Dantidurga performed the *Hiranyagarbha* (horse sacrifice) and the Sanjan and Cambay plates of King Govinda IV mention Brahmins performing such rituals as *Rajasuya*, *Vajapeya* and *Agnishtoma*.[2570] An early copper plate grant of King Dantidurga (753) shows an image of god Shiva and the coins of his successor, King Krishna

I (768), bear the legend *Parama Maheshwara* (another name for Shiva). The kings' titles such as *Veeranarayana* showed their Vaishnava leanings. Their flag had the sign of the Ganges and Yamuna rivers, perhaps copied from the Badami Chalukyas.[2571] The famous Kailasnatha temple at Ellora and other rock-cut caves attributed to them show that the Hinduism was flourishing. Their family deity was a goddess by name *Latana* (also known as *Rashtrashyena, Manasa Vindyavasini*) who took the form of a falcon to save the kingdom.[2572] They built temples with icons and ornamentation that satisfied the needs of different faiths. The temple at Salotgi was meant for followers of Shiva and Vishnu and the temple at Kargudri was meant for worshipers of Shiva, Vishnu and Bhaskara (Surya, the sun god).

In short, the Rashtrakuta rule was tolerant to multiple popular religions, Jainism, Vaishnavaism and Shaivism. Buddhism too found support and was popular in places such as Dambal and Balligavi, although it had declined significantly by this time.[2455] The decline of Buddhism in South India began in the 8th century with the spread of Adi Shankara's Advaita philosophy.[2573] Islamic contact with South India began as early as the 7th century, a result of trade between the Southern kingdoms and Arab lands. Jumma Masjids existed in the Rashtrakuta empire by the 10th century[2574] and many Muslims lived and mosques flourished on the coasts, specifically in towns such as Kayalpattanam and Nagore. Muslim settlers married local women; their children were known as Mappilas (*Moplahs*) and were actively involved in horse trading and manning shipping fleets.[2575]

Society

Chronicles mention more castes than the four commonly known castes in the Hindu social system, some as many as seven castes.[2576] One traveller's account mentions sixteen castes including the four basic castes of Brahmins, Kshatriya, Vaishya and Sudras.[2577] The *Zakaya* or *Lahud* caste consisted of communities specialising in dance and acrobatics.[2578] People in the professions of sailing, hunting, weaving, cobblery, basket making and fishing belonged to specific castes or subcastes. The *Antyajas* caste provided many menial services to the wealthy. Brahmins enjoyed the highest status in Rashtrakuta society; only those Kshatriyas in the *Sat-Kshatriya* sub-caste (noble Kshatriyas) were higher in status.[2579,2580]

The careers of Brahmins usually related to education, the judiciary, astrology, mathematics, poetry and philosophy[2581] or the occupation of hereditary administrative posts.[2582] Also Brahmins increasingly practiced non-Brahminical professions (agriculture, trade in betel nuts and martial posts).[2583] Capital punishment, although widespread, was not given to the royal Kshatriya sub-castes or to Brahmins found guilty of heinous crimes (as the killing of a Brahmin in medieval Hindu India was itself considered a heinous crime). As an alternate punishment to enforce the law a Brahmin's right hand and left foot was severed, leaving that person disabled.[2584]

By the 9th century, kings from all the four castes had occupied the highest seat in the monarchical system in Hindu India.[2585] Admitting Kshatriyas to Vedic schools along with Brahmins was customary, but the children of the Vaishya and Shudra castes were not allowed. Landownership by people of all castes is recorded in inscriptions[2586] Intercaste marriages in the higher castes were only between highly placed Kshatriya girls and Brahmin boys,[2587] but was relatively frequent among other castes.[2588] Intercaste functions were rare and dining together between people of various castes was avoided.[2589]

Joint families were the norm but legal separations between brothers and even father and son have been recorded in inscriptions.[2590] Women and daughters had rights over property and land as there are inscriptions recording the sale of land by women.[2591] The arranged marriage system followed a strict policy of early marriage for women. Among Brahmins, boys married at or below 16 years of age and the brides chosen for them were 12 or younger. This age policy was not strictly followed by other castes.[2592] Sati (a custom in which a dead man's widow would immolate herself on her husband's funeral pyre) was practiced but the few examples noted in inscriptions were mostly in the royal families.[2593] The system of shaving the heads of widows was infrequent as epigraphs note that widows were allowed to grow their hair but decorating it was discouraged.[2594] The remarriage of a widow was rare among the upper castes and more accepted among the lower castes.[2595]

In the general population men wore two simple pieces of cloth, a loose garment on top and a garment worn like a *dhoti* for the lower part of the body. Only kings could wear turbans, a practice that spread to the masses much later.[2596] Dancing was a popular entertainment and inscriptions speak of royal women being charmed by dancers, both male and female, in the king's palace. Devadasis (girls were "married" to a deity or temple) were often present in temples.[2597] Other recreational activities included attending animal fights of the same or different species. The Atakur inscription (hero stone, *virgal*) was made for the favourite hound of the feudatory Western Ganga King Butuga II that died fighting a wild boar in a hunt.[2598] There are records of game preserves for hunting by royalty. Astronomy and astrology were well developed as subjects of study, and there were many superstitious beliefs such as catching a snake alive proved a woman's chastity. Old persons suffering from incurable diseases preferred to end their lives by drowning in the sacred waters of a pilgrim site or by a ritual burning.[2599]

Figure 475: *Jain Narayana temple at Pattadakal, Karnataka*

Literature

Kannada became more prominent as a literary language during the Rashtrakuta rule with its script and literature showing remarkable growth, dignity and productivity. This period effectively marked the end of the classical Prakrit and Sanskrit era. Court poets and royalty created eminent works in Kannada and Sanskrit that spanned such literary forms as prose, poetry, rhetoric, the Hindu epics and the life history of Jain tirthankars. Bilingual writers such as Asaga gained fame,[2600] and noted scholars such as the Mahaviracharya wrote on pure mathematics in the court of King Amoghavarsha I.[2601,2602]

Kavirajamarga (850) by King Amoghavarsha I is the earliest available book on rhetoric and poetics in Kannada,[2603] though it is evident from this book that native styles of Kannada composition had already existed in previous centuries.[2604] *Kavirajamarga* is a guide to poets (*Kavishiksha*) that aims to standardize these various styles. The book refers to early Kannada prose and poetry writers such as Durvinita, perhaps the 6th-century monarch of Western Ganga Dynasty.[2605,2606,2607]

The Jain writer Adikavi Pampa, widely regarded as one of the most influential Kannada writers, became famous for *Adipurana* (941). Written in champu (mixed prose-verse style) style, it is the life history of the first Jain *tirthankara* Rishabhadeva. Pampa's other notable work was *Vikramarjuna*

ಪದನಱಿದು ನುಡಿಯಲುಂ ನುಡಿದುದ
ನಱಿಯಲುಮಾರ್ಪರಾ ನಾಡವರ್ಗಳ್
ಚದುರರ್ ನಿಜದಿಂ ಕುರಿತೋದದೆಯುಂ
ಕಾವ್ಯಪ್ರಯೋಗ ಪರಿಣತಮತಿಗಳ್

Figure 476: *A stanza from the 9th century Kannada classic Kavirajamarga, praising the people for their literary skills*

Vijaya (941), the author's version of the Hindu epic, Mahabharata, with Arjuna as the hero.[2608] Also called *Pampa Bharata*, it is a eulogy of the writer's patron, King Chalukya Arikeseri of Vemulawada (a Rashtrakuta feudatory), comparing the king's virtues favorably to those of Arjuna. Pampa demonstrates such a command of classical Kannada that scholars over the centuries have written many interpretations of his work.[2609]

Another notable Jain writer in Kannada was Sri Ponna, patronised by King Krishna III and famed for *Shantipurana*, his account of the life of Shantinatha, the 16th Jain tirthankara. He earned the title *Ubhaya Kavichakravathi* (supreme poet in two languages) for his command over both Kannada and Sanskrit. His other writings in Kannada were *Bhuvanaika-ramaabhyudaya*, *Jinaksharamale* and *Gatapratyagata*.[2610] Adikavi Pampa and Sri Ponna are called "gems of Kannada literature".

Prose works in Sanskrit was prolific during this era as well. Important mathematical theories and axioms were postulated by Mahaviracharya, a native of Gulbarga, who belonged to the Karnataka mathematical tradition and was patronised by King Amoghavarsha I. His greatest contribution was *Ganitasarasangraha*, a writing in 9 chapters. Somadevasuri of 950 wrote in the court of Arikesari II, a feudatory of Rashtrakuta Krishna III in Vemulavada. He was the author of *Yasastilaka champu*, *Nitivakyamrita* and other writings. The main aim of the *champu* writing was to propagate Jain tenets and ethics. The second writing reviews the subject matter of *Arthashastra* from the standpoint of Jain morals in a clear and pithy manner.[2611] Ugraditya, a Jain ascetic from Hanasoge in the modern Mysore district wrote a medical treatise called *Kalyanakaraka*. He delivered a discourse in the court of Amoghavarsha I encouraging abstinence from animal products and alcohol in medicine.[2612,2613]

Trivikrama was a noted scholar in the court of King Indra III. His classics were *Nalachampu* (915), the earliest in champu style in Sanskrit, *Damayanti Katha*,

Figure 477: *Kailasanath Temple at Ellora, Maharashtra*

Madalasachampu and Begumra plates. Legend has it that Goddess Saraswati helped him in his effort to compete with a rival in the king's court. Jinasena was the spiritual preceptor and guru of Amoghavarsha I. A theologian, his contributions are *Dhavala* and *Jayadhavala* (written with another theologian Virasena). These writings are named after their patron king who was also called Athishayadhavala. Other contributions from Jinasena were *Adipurana*, later completed by his disciple Gunabhadra, *Harivamsha* and *Parshvabhyudaya*.

Architecture

The Rashtrakutas contributed much to the architectural heritage of the Deccan. Art historian Adam Hardy categorizes their building activity into three schools: Ellora, around Badami, Aihole and Pattadakal, and at Sirval near Gulbarga.[2614] The Rashtrakuta contributions to art and architecture are reflected in the splendid rock-cut cave temples at Ellora and Elephanta, areas also occupied by Jain monks, located in present-day Maharashtra. The Ellora site was originally part of a complex of 34 Buddhist caves probably created in the first half of the 6th century whose structural details show Pandyan influence. Cave temples occupied by Hindus are from later periods.

The Rashtrakutas renovated these Buddhist caves and re-dedicated the rock-cut shrines. Amoghavarsha I espoused Jainism and there are five Jain cave

Figure 478: *Dravidian style architecture. Top view of Navalinga Temples at Kuknur, Karnataka*

temples at Ellora ascribed to his period. The most extensive and sumptuous of the Rashtrakuta works at Ellora is their creation of the monolithic Kailasanath Temple, a splendid achievement confirming the "Balhara" status as "one among the four principal Kings of the world". The walls of the temple have marvellous sculptures from Hindu mythology including Ravana, Shiva and Parvathi while the ceilings have paintings.

The Kailasanath Temple project was commissioned by King Krishna I after the Rashtrakuta rule had spread into South India from the Deccan. The architectural style used is *Karnata Dravida* according to Adam Hardy. It does not contain any of the *Shikharas* common to the *Nagara* style and was built on the same lines as the Virupaksha temple at Pattadakal in Karnataka.[2615] According to art historian Vincent Smith, the achievement at the Kailasanath temple is considered an architectural consummation of the monolithic rock-cut temple and deserves to be considered one of the wonders of the world.[2616] According to art historian Percy Brown, as an accomplishment of art, the Kailasanath temple is considered an unrivalled work of rock architecture, a monument that has always excited and astonished travellers.[2617]

While some scholars have claimed the architecture at Elephanta is attributable to the Kalachuri, others claim that it was built during the Rashtrakuta period.[2618] Some of the sculptures such as *Nataraja* and *Sadashiva* excel in beauty and craftsmanship even that of the Ellora sculptures.[2619] Famous sculptures at Elephanta include *Ardhanarishvara* and *Maheshamurthy*. The latter, a three faced bust of Lord Shiva, is 25 feet (8 m) tall and considered one of the finest pieces of sculpture in India. It is said that, in the world of sculpture, few works of art depicting a divinity are as balanced.[2620] Other famous rock-cut temples in the Maharashtra region are the Dhumer Lena and Dashvatara cave temples in Ellora (famous for its sculptures of Vishnu and Shivaleela) and the Jogeshvari temple near Mumbai. In Karnataka their most famous temples are the *Kashivishvanatha* temple and the Jain Narayana temple at Pattadakal, a UNESCO World Heritage site.[2621] Other well-known temples are the Parameshwara temple at Konnur, Brahmadeva temple at Savadi, the Settavva, Kontigudi II, Jadaragudi and Ambigeragudi temples at Aihole, Mallikarjuna temple at Ron, Andhakeshwara temple at Huli (Hooli), Someshwara temple at Sogal, Jain temples at Lokapura, Navalinga temple at Kuknur, Kumaraswamy temple at Sandur, numerous temples at Shirival in Gulbarga,[2622] and the *Trikuteshwara* temple at Gadag which was later expanded by Kalyani Chalukyas. Archeological study of these temples show some have the stellar (multigonal) plan later to be used profusely by the Hoysalas at Belur and Halebidu.[2623] One of the richest traditions in Indian architecture took shape in the Deccan during this time which Adam Hardy calls *Karnata dravida* style as opposed to traditional Dravida style.[2624]

Language

With the ending of the Gupta Dynasty in northern India in the early 6th century, major changes began taking place in the Deccan south of the Vindyas and in the southern regions of India. These changes were not only political but also linguistic and cultural. The royal courts of peninsular India (outside of Tamilakam) interfaced between the increasing use of the local Kannada language and the expanding Sanskritic culture. Inscriptions, including those that were bilingual, demonstrate the use of Kannada as the primary administrative language in conjunction with Sanskrit. Government archives used Kannada for recording pragmatic information relating to grants of land.[2625] The local language formed the *desi* (popular) literature while literature in Sanskrit was more *marga* (formal). Educational institutions and places of higher learning (*ghatikas*) taught in Sanskrit, the language of the learned Brahmins, while Kannada increasingly became the speech of personal expression of devotional closeness of a worshipper to a private deity. The patronage Kannada received from rich and literate Jains eventually led to its use in the devotional movements of later centuries.[2626]

Contemporaneous literature and inscriptions show that Kannada was not only popular in the modern Karnataka region but had spread further north into

Figure 479: *9th century Old Kannada inscription at Navalinga temple in Kuknur, Karnataka*

present day southern Maharashtra and to the northern Deccan by the 8th century.[2627] Kavirajamarga, the work on poetics, refers to the entire region between the Kaveri River and the Godavari River as "Kannada country".[2628,2629,2630] Higher education in Sanskrit included the subjects of Veda, *Vyakarana* (grammar), *Jyotisha* (astronomy and astrology), *Sahitya* (literature), *Mimansa* (Exegesis), *Dharmashastra* (law), *Puranas* (ritual), and *Nyaya* (logic). An examination of inscriptions from this period shows that the *Kavya* (classical) style of writing was popular. The awareness of the merits and defects in inscriptions by the archivists indicates that even they, though mediocre poets, had studied standard classical literature in Sanskrit.[2631] An inscription in Kannada by King Krishna III, written in a poetic Kanda metre, has been found as far away as Jabalpur in modern Madhya Pradesh. Kavirajamarga, a work on poetics in Kannada by Amoghavarsha I, shows that the study of poetry was popular in the Deccan during this time. Trivikrama's Sanskrit writing, *Nalachampu*, is perhaps the earliest in the *champu* style from the Deccan.[2632]

References

Books <templatestyles src="Template:Refbegin/styles.css" />

- Altekar, Anant Sadashiv (1934) [1934]. *The Rashtrakutas And Their Times; being a political, administrative, religious, social, economic and literary history of the Deccan during C. 750 A.D. to C. 1000 A.D.* Poona: Oriental Book Agency. OCLC 3793499[2633].
- Chopra, P.N.; Ravindran, T.K.; Subrahmanian, N (2003) [2003]. *History of South India (Ancient, Medieval and Modern) Part 1*. New Delhi: Chand Publications. ISBN 81-219-0153-7.
- De Bruyne, J.L. (1968) [1968]. *Rudrakavis Great Poem of the Dynasty of Rastraudha*. EJ Brill.
- Dalby, Andrew (2004) [1998]. *Dictionary of Languages: The Definitive Reference to More Than 400 Languages*. New York: Columbia University Press. ISBN 0-231-11569-5.
- Hardy, Adam (1995) [1995]. *Indian Temple Architecture: Form and Transformation-The Karnata Dravida Tradition 7th to 13th Centuries*. Abhinav Publications. ISBN 81-7017-312-4.
- Houben, Jan E.M. (1996) [1996]. *Ideology and Status of Sanskrit: Contributions to the History of the Sanskrit language*. Brill. ISBN 90-04-10613-8.
- Jain, K.C. (2001) [2001]. *Bharatiya Digambar Jain Abhilekh*. Madhya Pradesh: Digambar Jain Sahitya Samrakshan Samiti.
- Kamath, Suryanath U. (2001) [1980]. *A concise history of Karnataka : from pre-historic times to the present*. Bangalore: Jupiter books. LCCN 80905179[2634]. OCLC 7796041[2635].
- Karmarkar, A.P. (1947) [1947]. *Cultural history of Karnataka : ancient and medieval*. Dharwar: Karnataka Vidyavardhaka Sangha. OCLC 8221605[2636].
- Keay, John (2000) [2000]. *India: A History*. New York: Grove Publications. ISBN 0-8021-3797-0.
- Majumdar, R.C. (1966) [1966]. *The Struggle for Empire*. Bharatiya Vidya Bhavan.
- Masica, Colin P. (1991) [1991]. *The Indo-Aryan Languages*. Cambridge: Cambridge University Press. ISBN 0-521-29944-6.
- Narasimhacharya, R (1988) [1988]. *History of Kannada Literature*. New Delhi, Madras: Asian Educational Services. ISBN 81-206-0303-6.
- Reu, Pandit Bisheshwar Nath (1997) [1933]. *History of the Rashtrakutas (Rathodas)*. Jaipur: Publication Scheme. ISBN 81-86782-12-5.
- Pollock, Sheldon (2006) [2006]. *The Language of the Gods in the World of Men: Sanskrit, Culture, and Power in Premodern India*. Berkeley: University of California Press. ISBN 0-520-24500-8.

- Rao, Seshagiri, L.S (1988) [1988]. "Epic (Kannada)". In Amaresh Datta. *Encyclopaedia of Indian literature – vol 2*. Sahitya Akademi. ISBN 81-260-1194-7.
- Rice, E.P. (1982) [1921]. *Kannada Literature*. New Delhi: Asian Educational Services. ISBN 81-206-0063-0.
- Rice, B.L. (2001) [1897]. *Mysore Gazetteer Compiled for Government-vol 1*. New Delhi, Madras: Asian Educational Services. ISBN 81-206-0977-8.
- Sastri, Nilakanta K.A. (2002) [1955]. *A history of South India from prehistoric times to the fall of Vijayanagar*. New Delhi: Indian Branch, Oxford University Press. ISBN 0-19-560686-8.
- Sen, Sailendra Nath (1999) [1999]. *Ancient Indian History and Civilization*. New Age Publishers. ISBN 81-224-1198-3.
- Thapar, Romila (2003) [2003]. *Penguin History of Early India: From origins to AD 1300*. New Delhi: Penguin. ISBN 0-14-302989-4.
- Vaidya, C.V. (1979) [1924]. *History of Mediaeval Hindu India (Being a History of India from 600 to 1200 A.D.)*. Poona: Oriental Book Supply Agency. OCLC 6814734[2637].
- Warder, A.K. (1988) [1988]. *Indian Kavya Literature*. Motilal Banarsidass. ISBN 81-208-0450-3.

Web <templatestyles src="Template:Refbegin/styles.css" />

- Arthikaje. "The Rashtrakutas"[2638]. *History of karnataka*. OurKarnataka.Com. Archived from the original[2639] on 2006-11-04. Retrieved 2006-12-31.
- Kamat, Jyotsna. "The Rashtrakutas"[2640]. *Dynasties of the Deccan*. Retrieved 2007-02-03.
- Sastri & Rao, Shama & Lakshminarayan. "South Indian Inscriptions-Miscellaneous Inscriptions in Kannada"[2641]. *Rashtrakutas*. Retrieved 2007-02-03.

External links

 Wikimedia Commons has media related to *Rashtrakuta Dynasty*.

Wikisource has the text of the 1911 *Encyclopædia Britannica* article **Rashtrakuta**.

- Archaeological Survey of India[2642]

<indicator name="featured-star"> ⭐ </indicator>

Western Chalukya Empire

Western Chalukya Empire		
Empire (Subordinate to Rashtrakuta until 973)		
973–1189		
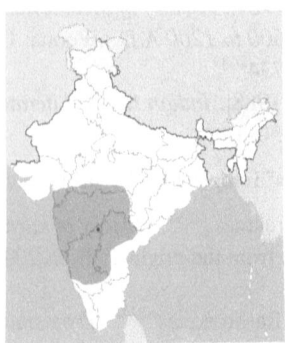 Extent of Western Chalukya Empire, 1121 CE		
Capital		Manyakheta, Basavakalyan
Languages		Kannada, Sanskrit
Religion		Hinduism Jainism
Government		Monarchy
King		
•	957 – 997	Tailapa II
•	1184 – 1189	Someshvara IV
History		
•	Earliest records	957
•	Established	973
•	Disestablished	1189

Preceded by	Succeeded by
 Rashtrakuta dynasty	Hoysala Empire
	Kakatiya dynasty
	Seuna (Yadava) dynasty

The **Western Chalukya Empire** ruled most of the western Deccan, South India, between the 10th and 12th centuries. This Kannadiga dynasty is sometimes called the *Kalyani Chalukya* after its regal capital at Kalyani, today's Basavakalyan in the modern Bidar District of Karnataka state, and alternatively the *Later Chalukya* from its theoretical relationship to the 6th-century Chalukya dynasty of Badami. The dynasty is called Western Chalukyas to differentiate from the contemporaneous Eastern Chalukyas of Vengi, a separate dynasty. Prior to the rise of these Chalukyas, the Rashtrakuta empire of Manyakheta controlled most of Deccan and Central India for over two centuries. In 973, seeing confusion in the Rashtrakuta empire after a successful invasion of their capital by the ruler of the Paramara dynasty of Malwa, Tailapa II, a feudatory of the Rashtrakuta Dynasty ruling from Bijapur region defeated his overlords and made Manyakheta his capital. The dynasty quickly rose to power and grew into an empire under Someshvara I who moved the capital to Kalyani.

For over a century, the two empires of Southern India, the Western Chalukyas and the Chola dynasty of Tanjore fought many fierce wars to control the fertile region of Vengi. During these conflicts, the Eastern Chalukyas of Vengi, distant cousins of the Western Chalukyas but related to the Cholas by marriage took sides with the Cholas further complicating the situation. During the rule of Vikramaditya VI, in the late 11th and early 12th centuries, the Western Chalukyas convincingly contended with the Cholas and reached a peak ruling territories that spread over most of the Deccan, between the Narmada River in the north and Kaveri River in the south. His exploits were not limited to the south for even as a prince, during the rule of Someshvara I, he had led successful military campaigns as far east as modern Bihar and Bengal. During this period the other major ruling families of the Deccan, the Hoysalas, the Seuna Yadavas of Devagiri, the Kakatiya dynasty and the Southern Kalachuris of Kalyani, were subordinates of the Western Chalukyas and gained their independence only when the power of the Chalukya waned during the later half of the 12th century.

The Western Chalukyas developed an architectural style known today as a transitional style, an architectural link between the style of the early Chalukya dynasty and that of the later Hoysala empire. Most of its monuments are in the districts bordering the Tungabhadra River in central Karnataka. Well known

Figure 480: *Old Kannada inscription dated 1028 AD from the rule of King Jayasimha II at the Praneshvara temple in Talagunda, Shivamogga district*

examples are the Kasivisvesvara Temple at Lakkundi, the Mallikarjuna Temple at Kuruvatti, the Kallesvara Temple at Bagali and the Mahadeva Temple at Itagi. This was an important period in the development of fine arts in Southern India, especially in literature as the Western Chalukya kings encouraged writers in the native language Kannada, and Sanskrit.

History

Knowledge of Western Chalukya history has come through examination of the numerous Kannada language inscriptions left by the kings (scholars Sheldon Pollock and Jan Houben have claimed 90 percent of the Chalukyan royal inscriptions are in Kannada),[2643,2644] and from the study of important contemporary literary documents in Western Chalukya literature such as *Gada Yuddha* (982) in Kannada by Ranna and *Vikramankadeva Charitam* (1120) in Sanskrit by Bilhana.[2645] The earliest record is dated 957, during the rule of Tailapa II when the Western Chalukyas were still a feudatory of the Rashtrakutas and Tailapa II governed from Tardavadi in present-day Bijapur district, Karnataka.[2646,2647] The genealogy of the kings of this empire is still debated. One theory, based on contemporary literary and inscriptional evidence

Figure 481: *Old Kannada inscription dated 1057 AD of King Someshvara I at Kalleshwara Temple, Hire Hadagali in Bellary district*

Figure 482: *Mahadeva Temple at Itagi in Koppal district, Karnataka*

plus the finding that the Western Chalukyas employed titles and names commonly used by the early Chalukyas, suggests that the Western Chalukya kings belonged to the same family line as the illustrious Badami Chalukya dynasty of 6th-century,[2648,2649] while other Western Chalukya inscriptional evidence indicates they were a distinct line unrelated to the early Chalukyas.[2650]

The records suggests a possible rebellion by a local Chalukya King, Chattigadeva of Banavasi-12000 province (c. 967), in alliance with local Kadamba chieftains. This rebellion however was unfruitful but paved the way for his successor Tailapa II.[2651] A few years later, Tailapa II re-established Chalukya rule and defeated the Rashtrakutas during the reign of Karka II by timing his rebellion to coincide with the confusion caused in the Rashtrakuta capital of Manyakheta by the invading Paramaras of Central India in 973.[2652,2653] After overpowering the Rashtrakutas, Tailapa II moved his capital to Manyakheta and consolidated the Chalukya empire in the western Deccan by subjugating the Paramara and other aggressive rivals and extending his control over the land between the Narmada River and Tungabhadra River.[2654] However, some inscriptions indicate that Balagamve in Mysore territory may have been a power centre up to the rule of Someshvara I in 1042.[2655]

The intense competition between the kingdom of the western Deccan and those of the Tamil country came to the fore in the 11th century over the acutely contested fertile river valleys in the doab region of the Krishna and Godavari River called Vengi (modern coastal Andhra Pradesh). The Western Chalukyas and the Chola Dynasty fought many bitter wars over control of this strategic resource. The imperial Cholas gained power during the time of the famous king Rajaraja Chola I and the crown prince Rajendra Chola I.[2656] The Eastern Chalukyas of Vengi were cousins of the Western Chalukyas but became increasingly influenced by the Cholas through their marital ties with the Tamil kingdom. As this was against the interests of the Western Chalukyas, they wasted no time in involving themselves politically and militarily in Vengi. When King Satyashraya succeeded Tailapa II to the throne, he was able to protect his kingdom from Chola aggression as well as his northern territories in Konkan and Gujarat although his control over Vengi was shaky.[2657,2658] His successor, Jayasimha II, fought many battles with the Cholas in the south around c. 1020–21 when both these powerful kingdoms struggled to choose the Vengi king.[2659] Shortly thereafter in c. 1024, Jayasimha II subdued the Paramara of central India and the rebellious Yadava King Bhillama.

Chalukya dynasties

- v
- t
- e[2660]

It is known from records that Jayasimha's son Someshvara I, whose rule historian Sen considers a brilliant period in the Western Chalukya rule, moved the Chalukya capital to Kalyani in c. 1042.[2661,2662] Hostilities with the Cholas continued while both sides won and lost battles, though neither lost significant territory[2663,2664] during the ongoing struggle to install a puppet on the Vengi throne.[2662,2665,2666] In 1068 Someshvara I, suffering from an incurable illness, drowned himself in the Tungabhadra River (*Paramayoga*).[2667,2668,2669] Despite many conflicts with the Cholas in the south, Someshvara I had managed to maintain control over the northern territories in Konkan, Gujarat, Malwa and Kalinga during his rule. His successor, his eldest son Someshvara II, feuded with his younger brother, Vikramaditya VI, an ambitious warrior who had initially been governor of Gangavadi in the southern Deccan when Someshvara II was the king. Before 1068, even as a prince, Vikramaditya VI had invaded Bengal, weakening the ruling Pala Empire. These incursions led to the establishment of *Karnata* dynasties such as the Sena dynasty and Varman dynasty in Bengal, and the Nayanadeva dynasty in Bihar.,[2670,2671,2672] Married to a Chola princess (a daughter of Vira Rajendra Chola), Vikramaditya VI maintained a friendly alliance with them. After the death of the Chola king in 1070, Vikramaditya VI invaded the Tamil kingdom and installed his brother-in-law, Adhirajendra, on the throne creating conflict with Kulothunga Chola I, the powerful ruler of Vengi who sought the Chola throne for himself.[2673] At the same time Vikramaditya VI undermined his brother, Someshvara II, by winning the loyalty of the Chalukya feudatories: the Hoysala, the Seuna and the Kadambas of Hangal. Anticipating a civil war, Someshvara II sought help from Vikramaditya VI's enemies, Kulothunga Chola I and the Kadambas of Goa. In the ensuing conflict of 1076, Vikramaditya VI emerged victorious and proclaimed himself king of the Chalukya empire.[2674,2675]

The fifty-year reign of Vikramaditya VI, the most successful of the later Chalukya rulers, was an important period in Karnataka's history and is referred to by historians as the "Chalukya Vikrama era".[2676,2677,2678] Not only was he successful in controlling his powerful feudatories in the north (Kadamba Jayakesi II of Goa, Silhara Bhoja and the Yadava King) and south (Hoysala Vishnuvardhana), he successfully dealt with the imperial Cholas whom he defeated in the battle of Vengi in 1093 and again in 1118. He

Figure 483: *Western Chalukyas of Kalyana, coin of King Somesvara I Trailokyamalla (1043-1068). Temple façade / Ornate floral ornament.*[2689]

retained this territory for many years despite ongoing hostilities with the Cholas.[2679,2680,2681,2682] This victory in Vengi reduced the Chola influence in the eastern Deccan and made him emperor of territories stretching from the Kaveri River in the south to the Narmada River in the north, earning him the titles *Permadideva* and *Tribhuvanamalla* (lord of three worlds). The scholars of his time paid him glowing tributes for his military leadership, interest in fine arts and religious tolerance.[2683,2684] Literature proliferated and scholars in Kannada and Sanskrit adorned his court. Poet Bilhana, who immigrated from far away Kashmir, eulogised the king in his well-known work *Vikramankadeva Charita*.[2685,2686] Vikramaditya VI was not only an able warrior but also a devout king as indicated by his numerous inscriptions that record grants made to scholars and centers of religion.[2687,2688]

The continual warring with the Cholas exhausted both empires, giving their subordinates the opportunity to rebel.[2691] In the decades after Vikramaditya VI's death in 1126, the empire steadily decreased in size as their powerful feudatories expanded in autonomy and territorial command.[2692] The time period between 1150 and 1200 saw many hard fought battles between the Chalukyas and their feudatories who were also at war with each other. By the time of Jagadhekamalla II, the Chalukyas had lost control of Vengi and his successor, Tailapa III, was defeated by the Kakatiya king Prola in 1149. Tailapa III was taken captive and later released bringing down the prestige of the Western Chalukyas. Seeing decadence and uncertainty seeping into Chalukya rule, the Hoysalas and Seunas also encroached upon the empire. Hoysala Narasimha I defeated and killed Tailapa III but was unable to overcome the Kalachuris who were vying for control of the same region. In 1157 the Kalachuris of Kalyanis under Bijjala II captured Kalyani and occupied it for the next twenty

Figure 484: *Coin of the Chalukyas of Kalyana (Western Chalukyas). King Somesvara IV (1181-4/1189). Garuda, with prominent beak, running right / "Dapaga dapasa Murari(?)" in Kannada in three lines divided by pelleted lines.*[2690]

years, forcing the Chalukyas to move their capital to Annigeri in the present day Dharwad district.[2693]

The Kalachuris were originally immigrants into the southern Deccan from central India and called themselves *Kalanjarapuravaradhisavaras*.[2694] Bijjala II and his ancestors had governed as Chalukya commanders (*Mahamandaleshwar*) over the Karhad-4000 and Tardavadi-1000 provinces (overlapping region in present-day Karnataka and Maharashtra) with Mangalavada or Annigeri[2695] as their capital. Bijjala II's Chikkalagi record of 1157 calls him *Mahabhujabala Chakravarti* ("emperor with powerful shoulders and arms") indicating he no longer was a subordinate of the Chalukyas.[2696] However the successors of Bijjala II were unable to hold on to Kalyani and their rule ended in 1183 when the last Chalukya scion, Someshvara IV made a final bid to regain the empire by recapturing Kalyani. Kalachuri King Sankama was killed by Chalukya general Narasimha in this conflict.[2697,2698] During this time, Hoysala Veera Ballala II was growing ambitious and clashed on several occasions with the Chalukyas and the other claimants over their empire. He defeated Chalukya Someshvara IV and Seuna Bhillama V bringing large regions in the Krishna River valley under the Hoysala domains, but was unsuccessful against Kalachuris.[2699] The Seunas under Bhillama V were on an imperialistic expansion too when the Chalukyas regained Kalyani. Their ambitions were temporarily stemmed by their defeat against Chalukya general Barma in 1183 but they later had their vengeance in 1189.[2700]

The overall effort by Someshvara IV to rebuild the Chalukya empire failed and the dynasty was ended by the Seuna rulers who drove Someshvara IV

Figure 485: *Mallikarjuna group of temples at Badami in Bagalkot district, Karnataka*

into exile in Banavasi 1189. After the fall of the Chalukyas, the Seunas and Hoysalas continued warring over the Krishna River region in 1191, each inflicting a defeat on the other at various points in time.[2701] This period saw the fall of two great empires, the Chalukyas of the western Deccan and the Cholas of Tamilakam. On the ruins of these two empires were built the Kingdoms of their feudatories whose mutual antagonisms filled the annals of Deccan history for over a hundred years, the Pandyas taking control over some regions of the erstwhile Chola empire.[2702]

Administration

The Western Chalukya kingship was hereditary, passing to the king's brother if the king did not have a male heir. The administration was highly decentralised and feudatory clans such as the Alupas, the Hoysalas, the Kakatiya, the Seuna, the southern Kalachuri and others were allowed to rule their autonomous provinces, paying an annual tribute to the Chalukya emperor.[2703] Excavated inscriptions record titles such as *Mahapradhana* (Chief minister), *Sandhivigrahika*, and *Dharmadhikari* (chief justice). Some positions such as *Tadeyadandanayaka* (commander of reserve army) were specialised in function while all ministerial positions included the role of *Dandanayaka* (commander), showing that cabinet members were trained as army commanders as well as in general administrative skills.[2704]

The kingdom was divided into provinces such as *Banavasi-12000*, *Nolambavadi-32000*, *Gangavadi-96000*, each name including the number of villages under its jurisdiction. The large provinces were divided into smaller provinces containing a lesser number of villages, as in *Belavola-300*. The big provinces were called *Mandala* and under them were *Nadu* further divided into *Kampanas* (groups of villages) and finally a *Bada* (village). A *Mandala* was under a member of the royal family, a trusted feudatory or a senior official. Tailapa II himself was in charge of Tardavadi province during the Rashtrakuta rule. Chiefs of *Mandalas* were transferable based on political developments. For example, an official named Bammanayya administered Banavasi-12000 under King Someshvara III but was later transferred to Halasige-12000. Women from the royal family also administered *Nadus* and *Kampanas*. Army commanders were titled *Mahamandaleshwaras* and those who headed a *Nadu* were entitled *Nadugouvnda*.[2705]

The Western Chalukyas minted punch-marked gold pagodas with Kannada and Nagari legends[2706] which were large, thin gold coins with several varying punch marks on the obverse side. They usually carried multiple punches of symbols such as a stylised lion, *Sri* in Kannada, a spearhead, the king's title, a lotus and others. Jayasimha II used the legend *Sri Jaya*, Someshvara I issued coins with *Sri Tre lo ka malla*, Someshvara II used *Bhuvaneka malla*, Lakshmideva's coin carried *Sri Lasha*, and Jagadhekamalla II coinage had the legend *Sri Jagade*. The Alupas, a feudatory, minted coins with the Kannada and *Nagari* legend *Sri Pandya Dhanamjaya*. Lakkundi in Gadag district and Sudi in Dharwad district were the main mints (*Tankhashaley*). Their heaviest gold coin was Gadyanaka weighting 96 grains, Dramma weighted 65 grains, Kalanju 48 grains, Kasu 15 grains, Manjadi 2.5 grains, Akkam 1.25 grains and Pana 9.6 grain.[2707]

Economy

Agriculture was the empire's main source of income through taxes on land and produce. The majority of the people lived in villages and worked farming the staple crops of rice, pulses, and cotton in the dry areas and sugarcane in areas having sufficient rainfall, with areca and betel being the chief cash crops. The living conditions of the labourers who farmed the land must have been bearable as there are no records of revolts by the landless against wealthy landlords. If peasants were disgruntled the common practice was to migrate in large numbers out of the jurisdiction of the ruler who was mistreating them, thereby depriving him of revenue from their labor.[2708]

Taxes were levied on mining and forest products, and additional income was raised through tolls for the use of transportation facilities. The state also collected fees from customs, professional licenses, and judicial fines.[2709] Records

Figure 486: *Ornate mantapa at Kalleshvara Temple (987 CE) in Bagali, Davanagere district*

show horses and salt were taxed as well as commodities (gold, textiles, perfumes) and agricultural produce (black pepper, paddy, spices, betel leaves, palm leaves, coconuts and sugar). Land tax assessment was based on frequent surveys evaluating the quality of land and the type of produce. Chalukya records specifically mention black soil and red soil lands in addition to wetland, dry land and wasteland in determining taxation rates.[2710]

Part of a series on the
History of Karnataka
• Political history of medieval Karnataka • Origin of Karnataka's name • Kadambas and Gangas • Chalukya Empire • Rashtrakuta Empire • Western Chalukya Empire

- Southern Kalachuri
- Hoysala Empire
- Vijayanagara Empire
- Bahmani Sultanate
- Bijapur Sultanate
- Kingdom of Mysore
- Nayakas of Keladi
- Nayakas of Chitradurga
- Haleri Kingdom
- Unification of Karnataka

Categories

- Architecture
- Forts
- Economies
- Societies

- v
- t
- e[2711]

Key figures mentioned in inscriptions from rural areas were the Gavundas (officials) or Goudas. The Gavundas belonged to two levels of economic strata, the *Praja Gavunda* (people's Gavunda) and the *Prabhu Gavunda* (lord of Gavundas). They served the dual purpose of representing the people before the rulers as well as functioning as state appointees for tax collection and the raising of militias. They are mentioned in inscriptions related to land transactions, irrigation maintenance, village tax collection and village council duties.[2712]

The organisation of corporate enterprises became common in the 11th century.[2713] Almost all arts and crafts were organised into guilds and work was done on a corporate basis; records do not mention individual artists, sculptors and craftsman. Only in the regions ruled by the Hoysala did individual sculptors etched their names below their creations.[2714] Merchants organised themselves into powerful guilds that transcended political divisions, allowing their operations to be largely unaffected by wars and revolutions. Their only threat was the possibility of theft from brigands when their ships and caravans traveled to distant lands. Powerful South Indian merchant guilds included the *Manigramam*, the *Nagarattar* and the *Anjuvannam*. Local guilds were called *nagaram*, while the *Nanadesis* were traders from neighbouring kingdoms who perhaps mixed business with pleasure. The wealthiest and most influential and celebrated of all South Indian merchant guilds was the self-styled *Ainnurruvar*, also known as the 500 *Svamis* of Ayyavolepura (Brahmins and *Mahajanas* of present-day Aihole),[2715,2716] who conducted extensive land and sea trade and thereby contributed significantly to the total foreign trade of the empire. It fiercely protected its trade obligations (*Vira Bananjudharma* or law of the noble merchants) and its members often recorded their achievements in inscriptions (*prasasti*). Five hundred such excavated *Prasasti* inscriptions, with their own flag and emblem, the bull, record their pride in their business.

Rich traders contributed significantly to the king's treasury through paying import and export taxes. The edicts of the Aihole *Svamis* mention trade ties with foreign kingdoms such as Chera, Pandya, Maleya (Malaysia), Magadh, Kaushal, Saurashtra, Kurumba, Kambhoja (Cambodia), Lata (Gujarat), Parasa (Persia) and Nepal. Travelling both land and sea routes, these merchants traded mostly in precious stones, spices and perfumes, and other specialty items such as camphor. Business flourished in precious stones such as diamonds, lapis lazuli, onyx, topaz, carbuncles and emeralds. Commonly traded spices were cardamom, saffron, and cloves, while perfumes included the by-products of sandalwood, bdellium, musk, civet and rose. These items were sold either in bulk or hawked on streets by local merchants in towns.[2717] The Western Chalukyas controlled most of South India's west coast and by the 10th century they had established extensive trade ties with the Tang Empire of China, the empires of Southeast Asia and the Abbasid Caliphate in Bhagdad, and by the 12th century Chinese fleets were frequenting Indian ports. Exports to Song Dynasty China included textiles, spices, medicinal plants, jewels, ivory, rhino horn, ebony and camphor. The same products also reached ports in the west such as Dhofar and Aden. The final destinations for those trading with the west were Persia, Arabia and Egypt.[2718] The thriving trade center of Siraf, a port on the eastern coast of the Persian Gulf, served an international clientele of merchants including those from the Chalukya empire who were feasted by wealthy local merchants during business visits. An indicator of the Indian merchants' importance in Siraf comes from records describing dining plates reserved for them.[2719] In addition to this, Siraf received aloe wood, perfumes, sandalwood and condiments. The most expensive import to South India were Arabian horse shipments, this trade being monopolised by Arabs and local Brahmin merchants. Traveller Marco Polo, in the 13th century, recorded that the breeding of horses never succeeded in India due to differing climatic, soil and grassland conditions.

Figure 487: *Basavanna Statue*

Culture

Religion

The fall of the Rashtrakuta empire to the Western Chalukyas in the 10th century, coinciding with the defeat of the Western Ganga Dynasty by the Cholas in Gangavadi, was a setback to Jainism. The growth of Virashaivism in the Chalukya territory and Vaishnava Hinduism in the Hoysala region paralleled a general decreased interest in Jainism, although the succeeding kingdoms continued to be religiously tolerant.[2720] Two locations of Jain worship in the Hoysala territory continued to be patronaged, Shravanabelagola and Kambadahalli. The decline of Buddhism in South India had begun in the 8th century with the spread of Adi Shankara's Advaita philosophy.[2721] The only places of Buddhist worship that remained during the Western Chalukya rule were at Dambal and Balligavi.[2722] There is no mention of religious conflict in the writings and inscriptions of the time which suggest the religious transition was smooth.

Although the origin of the Virashaiva faith has been debated, the movement grew through its association with Basavanna in the 12th century.[2723,2724] Basavanna and other Virashaiva saints preached of a faith without a caste system. In his Vachanas (a form of poetry), Basavanna appealed to the masses in simple

Figure 488: *A Hero stone with old Kannada inscription (1115 AD) during the rule of Vikarmaditya VI at the Kedareshvara temple in Balligavi*

Kannada and wrote "work is worship" (Kayakave Kailasa). Also known as the Lingayats (worshipers of the *Linga*, the universal symbol of Shiva), these Virashaivas questioned many of the established norms of society such as the belief in rituals and the theory of rebirth and supported the remarriage of widows and the marriage of unwed older women.[2725] This gave more social freedom to women but they were not accepted into the priesthood. Ramanujacharya, the head of the Vaishnava monastery in Srirangam, traveled to the Hoysala territory and preached the way of devotion (bhakti marga). He later wrote *Sribhashya*, a commentary on Badarayana Brahmasutra, a critique on the Advaita philosophy of Adi Shankara.[2726] Ramanujacharya's stay in Melkote resulted in the Hoysala King Vishnuvardhana converting to Vaishnavism, a faith that his successors also followed.

The impact of these religious developments on the culture, literature, and architecture in South India was profound. Important works of metaphysics and poetry based on the teachings of these philosophers were written over the next centuries. Akka Mahadevi, Allama Prabhu, and a host of Basavanna's followers, including Chenna Basava, Prabhudeva, Siddharama, and Kondaguli Kesiraja wrote hundreds of poems called Vachanas in praise of Lord Shiva.[2727] The esteemed scholars in the Hoysala court, Harihara and

Figure 489: *Kirtimukha relief at Kedareswara Temple in Balligavi, Shimoga district*

Raghavanka, were Virashaivas.[2728] This tradition continued into the Vijayanagar empire with such well-known scholars as Singiraja, Mallanarya, Lakkana Dandesa and other prolific writers of Virashaiva literature.[2729,2730] The Saluva, Tuluva and Aravidu dynasties of the Vijayanagar empire were followers of Vaishnavism and a Vaishnava temple with an image of Ramanujacharya exists today in the Vitthalapura area of Vijayanagara.[2731] Scholars in the succeeding Mysore Kingdom wrote Vaishnavite works supporting the teachings of Ramanujacharya.[2732] King Vishnuvardhana built many temples after his conversion from Jainism to Vaishnavism.

Society

The rise of Veerashaivaism was revolutionary and challenged the prevailing Hindu caste system which retained royal support. The social role of women largely depended on their economic status and level of education in this relatively liberal period. Freedom was more available to women in the royal and affluent urban families. Records describe the participation of women in the fine arts, such as Chalukya queen Chandala Devi's and Kalachuris of Kalyani queen Sovala Devi's skill in dance and music. The compositions of thirty Vachana women poets included the work of the 12th-century Virashaiva mystic Akka Mahadevi whose devotion to the *bhakti* movement is well known.[2733]

Contemporary records indicate some royal women were involved in administrative and martial affairs such as princess Akkadevi, (sister of King Jayasimha II) who fought and defeated rebellious feudals.[2734,2735] Inscriptions emphasise public acceptance of widowhood indicating that Sati (a custom in which a dead man's widow used to immolate herself on her husband's funeral pyre) though present was on a voluntary basis.[2736] Ritual deaths to achieve salvation were seen among the Jains who preferred to fast to death (Sallekhana), while people of some other communities chose to jump on spikes (*Shoolabrahma*) or walking into fire on an eclipse.

In a Hindu caste system that was conspicuously present, Brahmins enjoyed a privileged position as providers of knowledge and local justice. These Brahmins were normally involved in careers that revolved around religion and learning with the exception of a few who achieved success in martial affairs. They were patronised by kings, nobles and wealthy aristocrats who persuaded learned Brahmins to settle in specific towns and villages by making them grants of land and houses. The relocation of Brahmin scholars was calculated to be in the interest of the kingdom as they were viewed as persons detached from wealth and power and their knowledge was a useful tool to educate and teach ethical conduct and discipline in local communities. Brahmins were also actively involved in solving local problems by functioning as neutral arbiters (*Panchayat*).[2737]

Regarding eating habits, Brahmins, Jains, Buddhists and Shaivas were strictly vegetarian while the partaking of different kinds of meat was popular among other communities. Marketplace vendors sold meat from domesticated animals such as goats, sheep, pigs and fowl as well as exotic meat including partridge, hare, wild fowl and boar.[2738] People found indoor amusement by attending wrestling matches (*Kusti*) or watching animals fight such as cock fights and ram fights or by gambling. Horse racing was a popular outdoor past time.[2739] In addition to these leisurely activities, festivals and fairs were frequent and entertainment by traveling troupes of acrobats, dancers, dramatists and musicians was often provided.[2740]

Schools and hospitals are mentioned in records and these were built in the vicinity of temples. Marketplaces served as open air town halls where people gathered to discuss and ponder local issues. Choirs, whose main function was to sing devotional hymns, were maintained at temple expense. Young men were trained to sing in choirs in schools attached to monasteries such as Hindu *Matha*, Jain *Palli* and Buddhist *Vihara*.[2741] These institutions provided advanced education in religion and ethics and were well equipped with libraries (*Saraswati Bhandara*). Learning was imparted in the local language and in Sanskrit. Schools of higher learning were called *Brahmapuri* (or *Ghatika* or *Agrahara*). Teaching Sanskrit was a near monopoly of Brahmins who received

Figure 490: *Grill work at Tripurantkesvara temple in Balligavi, Shimoga district*

royal endowments for their cause. Inscriptions record that the number of subjects taught varied from four to eighteen.[2742] The four most popular subjects with royal students were Economics (*Vartta*), Political Science (*Dandaniti*), Veda (*trayi*) and Philosophy (*Anvikshiki*), subjects that are mentioned as early as Kautilyas Arthashastra.

Literature

The Western Chalukya era was one of substantial literary activity in the native Kannada, and Sanskrit.[2743] In a golden age of Kannada literature,[2744] Jain scholars wrote about the life of Tirthankaras and Virashaiva poets expressed their closeness to God through pithy poems called Vachanas. Nearly three hundred contemporary *Vachanakaras* (*Vachana* poets) including thirty women poets have been recorded.[2745,2746] Early works by Brahmin writers were on the epics, Ramayana, Mahabharata, Bhagavata, Puranas and Vedas. In the field of secular literature, subjects such as romance, erotics, medicine, lexicon, mathematics, astrology, encyclopedia etc. were written for the first time.[2747]

Most notable among Kannada scholars were Ranna, grammarian Nagavarma II, minister Durgasimha and the Virashaiva saint and social reformer Basavanna. Ranna who was patronised by king Tailapa II and Satyashraya is one

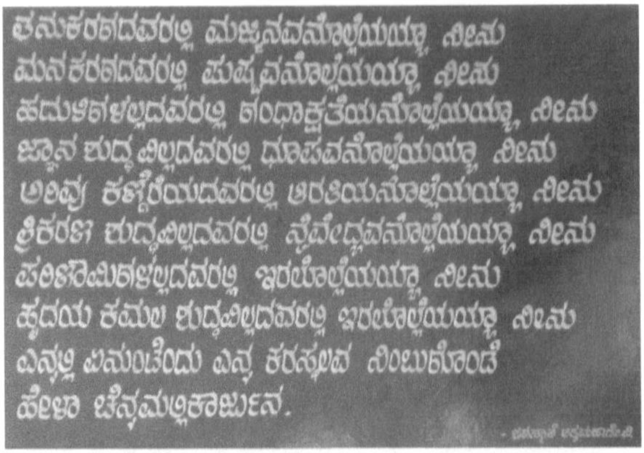

Figure 491: *A popular Vachana poem in the Kannada language by Akka Mahadevi*

among the "three gems of Kannada literature".[2748] He was bestowed the title "Emperor among poets" (*Kavi Chakravathi*) by King Tailapa II and has five major works to his credit. Of these, *Saahasabheema Vijayam* (or *Gada yuddha*) of 982 in *Champu* style is a eulogy of his patron King Satyashraya whom he compares to Bhima in valour and achievements and narrates the duel between Bhima and Duryodhana using clubs on the eighteenth day of the Mahabharata war.[2749] He wrote *Ajitha purana* in 993 describing the life of the second Tirthankara, Ajitanatha.[2750,2751]

Nagavarma II, poet laureate (*Katakacharya*) of King Jagadhekamalla II made contributions to Kannada literature in various subjects.[2752,2753] His works in poetry, prosody, grammar and vocabulary are standard authorities and their importance to the study of Kannada language is well acknowledged. *Kavyavalokana* in poetics, *Karnataka-Bhashabhushana* on grammar and *Vastukosa* a lexicon (with Kannada equivalents for Sanskrit words) are some of his comprehensive contributions.[2754] Several works on medicine were produced during this period. Notable among them were Jagaddala Somanatha's *Karnataka Kalyana Karaka*.[2755]

A unique and native form of poetic literature in Kannada called Vachanas developed during this time. They were written by mystics, who expressed their devotion to God in simple poems that could appeal to the masses. Basavanna, Akka Mahadevi, Allama Prabhu, Channabasavanna and Siddharama are the best known among them.[2756]

In Sanskrit, a well-known poem (*Mahakavya*) in 18 cantos called *Vikramankadeva Charita* by Kashmiri poet Bilhana recounts in epic style the life and achievements of his patron king Vikramaditya VI. The work narrates the episode of Vikramaditya VI's accession to the Chalukya throne after overthrowing his elder brother Someshvara II.[2757] The great Indian mathematician Bhāskara II (born c.1114) flourished during this time. From his own account in his famous work *Siddhanta Siromani* (c. 1150, comprising the *Lilavati*, *Bijaganita* on algebra, *Goladhaya* on the celestial globe and *Grahaganita* on planets) Bijjada Bida (modern Bijapur) was his native place.[2758]

Manasollasa or *Abhilashitartha Chintamani* by king Someshvara III (1129) was a Sanskrit work intended for all sections of society. This is an example of an early encyclopedia in Sanskrit covering many subjects including medicine, magic, veterinary science, valuing of precious stones and pearls, fortifications, painting, music, games, amusements etc.[2759] While the book does not give any of dealt topics particular hierarchy of importance, it serves as a landmark in understanding the state of knowledge in those subjects at that time.[2760] Someshwara III also authored a biography of his famous father Vikramaditya VI called Vikraman-Kabhyudaya. The text is a historical prose narrative which also includes a graphic description of the geography and people of Karnataka.[2761]

A Sanskrit scholar Vijnaneshwara became famous in the field of legal literature for his *Mitakshara*, in the court of Vikramaditya VI. Perhaps the most acknowledged work in that field, Mitakshara is a treatise on law (commentary on *Yajnavalkya*) based on earlier writings and has found acceptance in most parts of modern India. An Englishman Colebrooke later translated into English the section on inheritance giving it currency in the British Indian court system.[2762] Some important literary works of the time related to music and musical instruments were *Sangita Chudamani*, *Sangita Samayasara* and *Sangita Ratnakara*.[2763]

Architecture

The reign of Western Chalukya dynasty was an important period in the development of Deccan architecture. The architecture designed during this time served as a conceptual link between the Badami Chalukya Architecture of the 8th century and the Hoysala architecture popularised in the 13th century.[2764,2765] The art of the Western Chalukyas is sometimes called the "Gadag style" after the number of ornate temples they built in the Tungabhadra River-Krishna River doab region of present-day Gadag district in Karnataka. The dynasty's temple building activity reached its maturity and culmination in the 12th century with over a hundred temples built across the Deccan, more than half of them in present-day central Karnataka.[2766,2767] Apart from temples, the dynasty's architecture is well known for the ornate stepped wells (*Pushkarni*) which served as ritual bathing places, a few of which are well preserved in Lakkundi. These stepped well designs were later incorporated by the Hoysalas and the Vijayanagara empire in the coming centuries.[2768]

Figure 492: *Typical Western Chalukya dravida Vimana at Siddesvara temple in Haveri, Karnataka*

Figure 493: *Ornate pillars at Saraswati temple in Gadag city, Karnataka*

Figure 494: *Brahma Jinalaya at Lakkundi dates to the mid-late 11th century*

The Kasivisvesvara Temple at Lakkundi (Gadag district),[2769,2770] the Dodda Basappa Temple at Dambal (Gadag district),[2771,2772] the Mallikarjuna Temple at Kuruvatti (Bellary district),[2773] the Kallesvara Temple at Bagali (Davangere district),[2774] the Siddhesvara Temple at Haveri (Haveri district),[2775,2776] the Amrtesvara Temple at Annigeri (Dharwad district),[2777] the Mahadeva Temple at Itagi (Koppal district),[2778,2779] the Kaitabheshvara Temple at Kubatur,[2780] and the Kedareshvara Temple at Balligavi are the finest examples produced by the later Chalukya architects.[2781] The 12th-century Mahadeva Temple with its well executed sculptures is an exquisite example of decorative detail. The intricate, finely crafted carvings on walls, pillars and towers speak volumes about Chalukya taste and culture. An inscription outside the temple calls it "Emperor of Temples" (*devalaya chakravarti*) and relates that it was built by Mahadeva, a commander in the army of king Vikramaditya VI.[2782] The Kedareswara Temple (1060) at Balligavi is an example of a transitional Chalukya-Hoysala architectural style.[2783] The Western Chalukyas built temples in Badami and Aihole during their early phase of temple building activity, such as Mallikarjuna Temple, the Yellamma Temple and the Bhutanatha group of Temples.[2784]

The *vimana* of their temples (tower over the shrine) is a compromise in detail between the plain stepped style of the early Chalukyas and the decorative finish of the Hoysalas. To the credit of the Western Chalukya architects is the development of the lathe turned (tuned) pillars and use of Soapstone (Chloritic

Figure 495: *Old Kannada inscription ascribed to King Vikramaditya VI, dated 1112 CE at Mahadeva Temple in Itagi, Karnataka*

Schist) as basic building and sculptural material, a very popular idiom in later Hoysala temples. They popularised the use of decorative *Kirtimukha* (demon faces) in their sculptures. Famous architects in the Hoysala kingdom included Chalukyan architects who were natives of places such as Balligavi.[2785] The artistic wall decor and the general sculptural idiom was dravidian architecture. This style is sometimes called *Karnata dravida*, one of the notable traditions in Indian architecture.[2786]

Language

The local language Kannada was mostly used in Western (Kalyani) Chalukya inscriptions and epigraphs. Some historians assert that ninety percent of their inscriptions are in the Kannada language while the remaining are in Sanskrit language.[2787,2788] More inscriptions in Kannada are attributed to Vikramaditya VI than any other king prior to the 12th century,[2789] many of which have been deciphered and translated by historians of the Archaeological Survey of India. Inscriptions were generally either on stone (*Shilashasana*) or copper plates (*Tamarashasana*). This period saw the growth of Kannada as a language of literature and poetry, impetus to which came from the devotional movement of the Virashaivas (called Lingayatism) who expressed their closeness to their deity in the form of simple lyrics called Vachanas.[2790] At an administrative level, the regional language was used to record locations and rights related to land grants. When bilingual inscriptions were written, the section stating the title, genealogy, origin myths of the king and benedictions were generally done in Sanskrit. Kannada was used to state terms of the grants, including information on the land, its boundaries, the participation of local authorities, rights and obligations of the grantee, taxes and dues, and witnesses. This ensured the content was clearly understood by the local people without any ambiguity.[2791]

In addition to inscriptions, chronicles called *Vamshavalis* were written to provide historical details of dynasties. Writings in Sanskrit included poetry, grammar, lexicon, manuals, rhetoric, commentaries on older works, prose fiction and drama. In Kannada, writings on secular subjects became popular. Some well-known works are *Chandombudhi*, a prosody, and *Karnataka Kadambari*, a romance, both written by Nagavarma I, a lexicon called *Rannakanda* by Ranna (993), a book on medicine called *Karnataka-Kalyanakaraka* by Jagaddala Somanatha, the earliest writing on astrology called *Jatakatilaka* by Sridharacharya (1049), a writing on erotics called *Madanakatilaka* by Chandraraja, and an encyclopedia called *Lokapakara* by Chavundaraya II (1025).[2792,2793]

References

Book <templatestyles src="Template:Refbegin/styles.css" />

- Chopra, P.N.; Ravindran, T.K.; Subrahmanian, N (2003) [2003]. *History of South India (Ancient, Medieval and Modern) Part 1*. New Delhi: Chand Publications. ISBN 81-219-0153-7.
- Cousens, Henry (1996) [1926]. *The Chalukyan Architecture of Kanarese Districts*. New Delhi: Archaeological Survey of India. OCLC 37526233[2794].
- Davison-Jenkins, Dominic J. (2001). "Hydraulic works". In John M. Fritz and George Michell (editors). *New Light on Hampi : Recent Research at Vijayanagara*. Mumbai: MARG. ISBN 81-85026-53-X.
- Foekema, Gerard (1996). *A Complete Guide To Hoysala Temples*. New Delhi: Abhinav. ISBN 81-7017-345-0.
- Hardy, Adam (1995) [1995]. *Indian Temple Architecture: Form and Transformation-The Karnata Dravida Tradition 7th to 13th Centuries*. Abhinav Publications. ISBN 81-7017-312-4.
- Houben, Jan E.M. (1996) [1996]. *Ideology and Status of Sanskrit: Contributions to the History of the Sanskrit language*. Brill. ISBN 90-04-10613-8.
- Kamath, Suryanath U. (2001) [1980]. *A concise history of Karnataka : from pre-historic times to the present*. Bangalore: Jupiter books. LCCN 80905179[2795]. OCLC 7796041[2796].

- Mack, Alexandra (2001). "The temple district of Vitthalapura". In John M. Fritz and George Michell (editors). *New Light on Hampi : Recent Research at Vijayanagara*. Mumbai: MARG. ISBN 81-85026-53-X.
- Moraes, George M. (1990) [1931]. *The Kadamba Kula, A History of Ancient and Medieval Karnataka*. New Delhi, Madras: Asian Educational Services. ISBN 81-206-0595-0.
- Narasimhacharya, R (1988) [1988]. *History of Kannada Literature*. New Delhi: Penguin Books. ISBN 81-206-0303-6.
- Pollock, Sheldon (2006) [2006]. *The Language of the Gods in the World of Men: Sanskrit, Culture, and Power in Premodern India*. Berkeley: University of California Press. ISBN 0-520-24500-8.
- Puranik, Siddya (1992). "Vachana literature (Kannada)". In Mohal Lal. *Encyclopaedia of Indian Literature: sasay to zorgot*. New Delhi: Sahitya Akademi. ISBN 81-260-1221-8.
- Rice, E.P. (1982) [1921]. *Kannada Literature*. New Delhi: Asian Educational Services. ISBN 81-206-0063-0.
- Sastri, Nilakanta K.A. (2002) [1955]. *A history of South India from prehistoric times to the fall of Vijayanagar*. New Delhi: Indian Branch, Oxford University Press. ISBN 0-19-560686-8.
- Sen, Sailendra Nath (1999) [1999]. *Ancient Indian History and Civilization*. New Age Publishers. ISBN 81-224-1198-3.
- Thapar, Romila (2003) [2003]. *The Penguin History of Early India*. New Delhi: Penguin Books. ISBN 0-14-302989-4.

Web

 Wikimedia Commons has media related to *Western Chalukya Empire*.

<templatestyles src="Template:Refbegin/styles.css" />

- Kamiya, Takeyo. "Architecture of Indian subcontinent"[2797]. *Indian Architecture*. Gerard da Cunha. Retrieved 2006-12-31.
- Kamat, Jyotsna. "The Chalukyas of Kalyani"[2798]. *Dynasties of Deccan*. Kamat's Potpourri. Retrieved 2006-12-31.
- "Indian Inscriptions, Vol 9,11,15,17,18,20"[2799]. *Archaeological Survey of India*. What Is India Publishers (P) Ltd. Retrieved 2006-11-10.
- Githa U.B. "Balligavi - An important seat of learning"[2800]. *History of Indian Art*. Chitralakshana.com 2002. Archived from the original[2801] on 2006-10-06. Retrieved 2006-12-31.
- Gunther, Michael D. "Index IV, Late Chalukya"[2802]. *Monuments of India*. Retrieved 2006-11-10.

- Kannikeswaran, K. "Kalyani Chalukyan temples"[2803]. *TempleNet*. webmaster@templenet.com. Retrieved 2006-11-10.
- Prabhu, Govindaraya S. "Alupa Dynasty-catalogue"[2804]. *Prabhu's web page on Indian Coins*. Archived from the original[2805] on 2006-08-15. Retrieved 2006-11-10.
- Prabhu, Govindaraya S. "Chalukya Dynasty-catalogue"[2806]. *Prabhu's web page on Indian Coins*. Retrieved 2006-11-10.
- Rao, Kishan. "Emperor among Temples crying for attention"[2807]. *Southern States - Karnataka*. The Hindu. Retrieved 2006-11-10.

<indicator name="featured-star"> ⭐ </indicator>

Seuna (Yadava) dynasty

Seuna (Yadava) dynasty	
c. 850–1334	
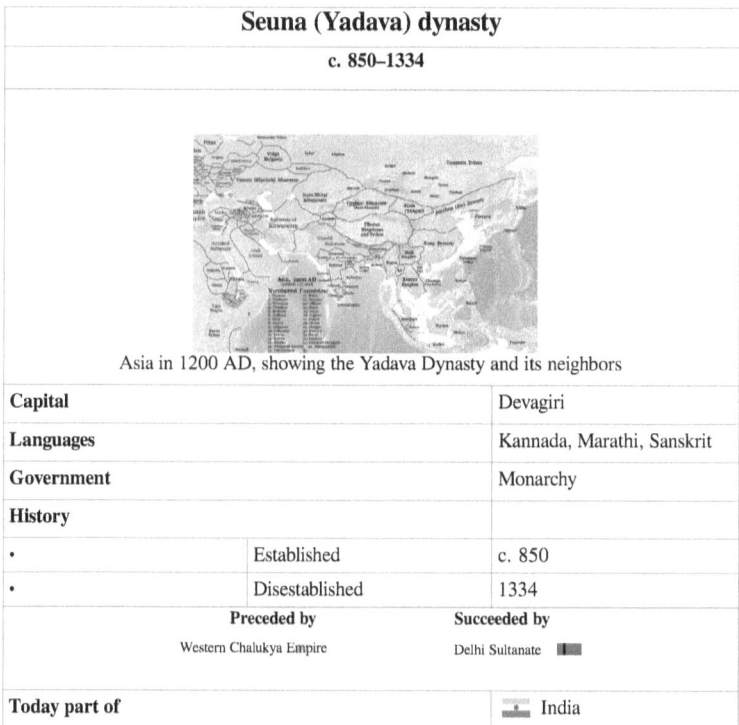 Asia in 1200 AD, showing the Yadava Dynasty and its neighbors	
Capital	Devagiri
Languages	Kannada, Marathi, Sanskrit
Government	Monarchy
History	
• Established	c. 850
• Disestablished	1334
Preceded by	Succeeded by
Western Chalukya Empire	Delhi Sultanate
Today part of	India

The **Seuna**, **Sevuna** or **Yadavas of Devagiri** (c. 850–1334) was an Indian dynasty, which at its peak ruled a kingdom stretching from the Tungabhadra to the Narmada rivers, including present-day Maharashtra, north Karnataka and parts of Madhya Pradesh, from its capital at Devagiri (present-day Daulatabad in modern Maharashtra).

The Yadavas initially ruled as feudatories of the Western Chalukyas. Around the middle of the 12th century, as the Chalukya power waned, the Yadava king Bhillama V declared independence. The Yadava kingdom reached its peak under Simhana II, and flourished until the early 14th century, when it was annexed by the Delhi Sultanate.

Etymology

The Seuna dynasty claimed descent from the Yadavas and therefore, its kings are often referred to as the "Yadavas of Devagiri". The correct name of the dynasty, however, is Seuna or Sevuna.[2808] The inscriptions of this dynasty, as well as those of contemporary kingdoms, the Hoysala, Kakatiya dynasty and Western Chalukyas call them *Seunas*.[2809] The name is probably derived from the name of their second ruler, "Seunachandra".

The "Sevuna" (or Seuna) name was brought back into use by John Faithfull Fleet in his book *The dynasties of the Kanarese districts of the Bombay Presidency from the earliest historical times to the Musalman conquest of A.D. 1318*.[2810,2811]

Origin

The earliest historical ruler of the Seuna/Yadava dynasty can be dated to the mid-9th century, but the origin of the dynasty is uncertain.[2812] Little is known about their early history: their 13th century court poet Hemadri records the names of the family's early rulers, but his information about the pre-12th century rulers is often incomplete and inaccurate.[2813]

The dynasty claimed descent from Yadu, a hero mentioned in the Puranic legends.[2813] According to this account, found in Hemadri's *Vratakhanda* as well as several inscriptions,[2812] their ancestors originally resided at Mathura, and then migrated to Dvaraka (Dvaravati) in present-day Gujarat. A Jain mythological legend states that the Jain saint Jainaprabhasuri saved the pregnant mother of the dynasty's founder Dridhaprahara from a great fire that destroyed Dvaraka. A family feudatory to the Yadavas migrated from Vallabhi (also in present-day Gujarat) to Khandesh. But otherwise, no historical evidence corroborates their connection to Dvaraka. The dynasty never tried to conquer Dvaraka, or establish any political or cultural connections with that region.[2813] Its rulers started claiming to be descendants of Yadu and migrants from Dvaraka after becoming politically prominent.[2814] Dvaraka was associated with Yadu's descendants, and the dynasty's claim of connection with that

Seuna (Yadava) dynasty

Figure 496: *Hero stone (Virgal) with Old Kannada inscription dated 1286. from the rule of Yadava King Ramachandra in Kedareshvara temple at Balligavi in Shimoga district, Karnataka state*

city may simply be a result of their claim of descent from Yadu rather than their actual geographic origin.[2815] The Hoysalas, the southern neighbours of the dynasty, similarly claimed descent from Yadu and claimed to be the former lords of Dvaraka.[2814]

The territory of the early Yadava rulers was located in present-day Maharashtra,[2814] and several scholars (especially Maharashtrian historians[2816]) have claimed a "Maratha" origin for the dynasty.[2817] However, Marathi, the language of present-day Maharashtra, began to appear as the dominant language in the dynasty's inscriptions only in the 14th century, before which Kannada and Sanskrit were the primary language of their inscriptions.[2818,2816] Marathi appears in around two hundred Yadava inscriptions, but usually as translation of or addition to Kannada and Sanskrit text. During the last half century of the dynasty's rule, it became the dominant language of epigraphy, which may have been a result of the Yadava attempts to connect with their Marathi-speaking subjects, and to distinguish themselves from the Kannada-speaking Hoysalas.[2816] The earliest instance of the Yadavas using the term *"marathe"* as a self-designation appears in a 1311 inscription recording a donation to the Pandharpur temple,[2819] towards the end of the dynasty's rule.[2817]

Figure 497: *Hero stone with old Kannada inscription dated 1235. from the rule of Yadava King Simhana II at Kubetur, Soraba Taluk, Shimoga district, Karnataka state*

Epigraphic evidence suggests that the dynasty likely emerged from a Kannada-speaking background.[2820] Around five hundred Yadava inscriptions have been discovered, and Kannada is the most common language of these inscriptions, followed by Sanskrit.[2816] Of the inscriptions found in present-day Karnataka (the oldest being from the reign of Bhillama II), most are in Kannada language and script; others are in the Kannada language but use Devanagari script.[2809] Older inscriptions from Karnataka also attest to the existence of Yadava feudatories (such as Seunas of Masavadi) ruling in the Dharwad region in the 9th century, although these feudatories cannot be connected to the main line of the dynasty with certainty.[2812,2814] Many of the dynasty's rulers had Kannada names and titles such as "Dhadiyappa", "Bhillama", "Rajugi", "Vadugi" and "Vasugi", and "Kaliya Ballala". Some kings had names like "Simhana" (or "Singhana") and "Mallugi", which were also used by the Kalachuris of Kalyani, who ruled in present-day Karnataka. Records show that one of the early rulers, Seunachandra II, had a Kannada title, *Sellavidega*. The rulers had very close matrimonial relationships with Kannada-speaking royal families throughout their rule. Bhillama II was married to Lachchiyavve, who was from a Rashtrakuta descendant family in Karnataka. Vaddiga was married to Vaddiyavve, daughter of Rashtrakuta chieftain Dhorappa. Wives of Vesugi

Figure 498: *The hill of Devagiri, the capital of Yadavas*

and Bhillama III were Chalukya princesess. The early Seuna coins also had Kannada legends engraved on them indicating it was a court language.[2809] The early Yadavas may have migrated northwards owing to the political situation in the Deccan region,[2821] or may have been dispatched by their Rashtrakuta overlords to rule the northern regions.[2811]

Political history

As feudatories

The earliest historically attested ruler of the dynasty is Dridhaprahara (c. 860-880), who is said to have established the city of Chandradityapura (modern Chandor).[2814,2812] He probably rose to prominence by protecting the people of Khandesh region from enemy raiders, amid the instability brought by the Pratihara-Rashtrakuta war.[2814]

Dridhaprahara son and successor was Seunachandra (c. 880-900), after whom the dynasty was called Seuṇa-vaṃśa and their territory was called Seuna-desha.[2823,2814] He probably became a Rashtrakuta feudatory after helping the Rashtrakutas against their northern neighbours, the Paramaras.[2823] He established a new town called Seunapura (possibly modern Sinnar).[2814]

Not much information is available about Seunachandra's successors — Dhadiyappa (or Dadhiyappa), Bhillama I, and Rajugi (or Rajiga) — who ruled

Figure 499: *The Indra Sabha, one of the Jain caves inside Ellora Caves complex. The Jain caves of were built by Yadava dynasty*[2822] *Wikipedia:Verifiability*

during c. 900-950.[2823,2824] The next ruler Vandugi (also Vaddiga I or Baddiga) raised the family's political status by marrying into the imperial Rashtrakuta family. He married Vohivayya, a daughter of Dhorappa, who was a younger brother of the Rashtrakuta emperor Krishna III. Vandugi participated in Krishna's military campaigns, which may have resulted in an increase in his fief, although this cannot be said with certainty.[2824]

Little is known about the next ruler, Dhadiyasa (c. 970-985).[2824] His son Bhillama II acknowledged the suzerainty of the Kalyani Chalukya ruler Tailapa II, who overthrew the Rashtrakutas. As a Chalukya feudatory, he played an important role in Tailapa's victory over the Paramara king Munja.[2823] Bhillama II was succeeded by Vesugi I (r. c. 1005-1025), who married Nayilladevi, the daughter of a Chalukya feudatory of Gujarat. The next ruler Bhillama III is known from his Kalas Budruk grant inscription.[2825] He married Avalladevi, a daughter of the Chalukya king Jayasimha II, as attested by a Vasai (Bassein) inscription. He may have helped his father-in-law Jayasimha and his brother-in-law Someshvara I in their campaigns against the Paramara king Bhoja.[2823,2825]

The Yadava power seems to have declined over the next decade, during the reigns of Vesugi II (alias Vaddiga or Yadugi) and Bhillama IV, for unknown reasons. The next ruler was Seunachandra II, who, according to the Yadava records, restored the family's fortunes just like the god Hari had restored the earth's fortunes with his varaha incarnation. Seunachandra II appears to have ascended the throne around 1050, as he is attested by the 1052 Deolali inscription. He bore the title *Maha-mandaleshvara* and became the overlord of several sub-feudatories, including a family of Khandesh. A 1069 inscription indicates that he had a ministry of seven officers, all of whom bore high-sounding titles.[2825] During his tenure, the Chalukya kingdom saw a war of succession between the brothers Someshvara II and Vikramaditya VI. Seunachandra II supported Vikramaditya (who ultimately succeeded), and rose to the position of *Maha-mandaleshvara*.[2823] His son Airammadeva (or Erammadeva, r. c. 1085-1105), who helped him against Someshvara II, succeeded him. Airammadeva's queen was Yogalla, but little else is known about his reign.[2826] The Asvi inscription credits him with helping place Vikramaditya on the Chalukya throne.[2825]

Airammadeva was succeeded by his brother Simhana I (r. c. 1105-1120).[2827] The Yadava records state that he helped his overlord Vikramaditya VI complete the *Karpura-vrata* ritual, by getting him a *karpura* elephant. A 1124 inscription mentions that he was ruling the Paliyanda-4000 province (identified as the area around modern Paranda).[2826] The dynasty's history over the next fifty years is obscure. The 1142 Anjaneri inscription attests the rule of a person named Seunachandra, but Hemadri's records of the dynasty do not mention any Seunachandra III; historian R. G. Bhandarkar theorized that this Seunachandra may have been a Yadava sub-feudatory.[2828]

The next known ruler Mallugi (r. c. 1145-1160) was a loyal feudatory to the Chalukya king Tailapa III. His general Dada and Dada's son Mahidhara fought with Tailapa's rebellious Kalachuri feudatory Bijjala II. He extended his territory by capturing Parnakheta (modern Patkhed in Akola district).[2828] The Yadava records claim that he seized the elephants of the king of Utkala, but do not provide any details.[2826] He also raided the kingdom of the Kakatiya ruler Rudra, but this campaign did not result in any territorial gains for him.[2828] Mallugi was succeeded by his elder son Amara-gangeya, who was succeeded by his son Amara-mallugi (alias Mallugi II). The next ruler Kaliya-ballala, whose relationship to Mallugi is unknown, was probably an usurper. He was succeeded by Bhillama V around 1175.[2828]

Rise as a sovereign power

At the time of Bhillama V's ascension in c. 1175, his nominal overlords — the Chalukyas — were busy fighting their former feudatories, such as the Hoysalas and the Kalachuris.[2829] Bhillama raided the northern Gujarat Chaulukya and

Paramara territories, although these invasions did not result in any territorial annexations. The Naddula Chahamana ruler Kelhana, who was a Gujarat Chaulukya feudatory, forced him to retreat.[2830] Meanwhile, the Hoysala ruler Ballala II invaded the Chalukya capital Kalyani, forcing Bhillama's overlord Someshvara to flee. Around 1187, Bhillama forced Ballala to retreat, conquered the former Chalukya capital Kalyani, and declared himself a sovereign ruler.[2831]

According to Hemadri, he then established the Devagiri city, which became the new Yadava capital.[2832]

In the late 1180s, Ballala launched a campaign against Bhillama, and decisively defeated his army at Soratur.[2833] The Yadavas were driven to the north of the Malaprabha and Krishna rivers, which formed the Yadava-Hoysala border for the next two decades.[2833]

Imperial expansion

Bhillama's son Jaitugi successfully invaded the Kakatiya kingdom around 1194, and forced them to accept the Yadava suzerainty.[2834,2835]

Jaitugi's son Simhana, who succeeded him around either 1200[2836] or 1210,[2837] is regarded as the dynasty's greatest ruler.[2836] At its height, his kingdom probably extended from the Narmada River in the north to the Tungabhadra River in the south, and from the Arabian Sea in the west to the western part of the present-day Andhra in the east.[2838] He launched a military campaign against the Hoysalas (who were engaged in a war with the Pandyas), and captured a substantial part of their territory.[2839,2840] The Rattas of Saundatti, who formerly acknowledged the Hoysala suzerainty, became his feudatories, and helped him expand the Yadava power southwards.[2840] In 1215, Simhana successfully invaded the northern Paramara kingdom. According to Hemadri, this invasion resulted in the death of the Paramara king Arjunavarman, although this claim is of doubtful veracity.[2841] Around 1216, Simhana defeated the Kohalpur Shilahara king Bhoja II, a former feudatory, who had asserted his sovereignty. The Shilahara kingdom, including its capital Kolhapur, was annexed to the Yadava kingdom as a result of this victory.[2842,2840]

In 1220, Simhana sent an army to the Lata region in present-day Gujarat, whose rulers kept shifting his allegiance between the Yadavas, the Paramaras, and the Chaulukyas.[2843] Simhana's general Kholeshvara killed the defending ruler Simha, and captured Lata.[2844] Simhana then appointed Simha's son Shankha as a Yadava vassal in Lata.[2845] Sometime later, the Chaulukya general Lavanaprasada invaded Lata, and captured the important port city of Khambhat. Simhana's feudatory Shankha invaded Chaulukya-controlled territory twice, with his help, but was forced to retreat.[2846] The Chaulukya-Yadava conflict came to end in c. 1232 with a peace treaty.[2847] In the 1240s, Lavanaprasada's grandson Visaladeva usurped the power in Gujarat, and became the first Vagehla monarch. During his reign, Simhana's forces invaded Gujarat unsuccessfully, and the Yadava general Rama (a son of Kholeshvara) was killed in a battle.[2848]

Several Yadava feudatories kept shifting their allegiance between the Yadavas and the Hoysalas, and tried to assert their independence whenever presented with an opportunity. Simhana's general Bichana subdued several such chiefs, including the Rattas, the Guttas of Dharwad, the Kadambas of Hangal, and the Kadambas of Goa.[2849] The Kakatiya king Ganapati served him as a feudatory for several years, but assumed independence towards the end of his reign. However, Ganapati did not adopt an aggressive attitude towards the Yadavas, so no major conflict happened between the two dynasties during Simhana's reign.[2850]

Simhana was succeeded by his grandson Krishna (alias Kannara), who defeated the invaded the Paramara kingdom, which had weakened because of invasions from the Delhi Sultanate. He defeated the Paramara king sometime before 1250, although this victory did not result in any teritorial annexation.[2851] Krishna also attempted an invasion of the Vaghela-ruled Gujarat, but this conflict was inconclusive, with both sides claiming victory.[2851,2852] He also fought against the Hoysalas; again, both sides claim victory in this conflict.[2852]

Krishna's younger brother and successor Mahadeva curbed a rebellion by the Shilaharas of northern Konkan, whose ruler Someshvara had attempted to assert his sovereignty.[2853] He invaded the eastern Kakatiya kingdom, taking advantage of rebellions against the Kakatiya queen Rudrama,[2854] but this invasion appears to have been repulsed.[2855] He also invaded the southern Hoysala kingdom, but this invasion was repulsed by the Hoysala king Narasimha II.[2854] Mahadeva's Kadamba feudatories rebelled against him, but this rebellion was suppressed by his general Balige-deva around 1268.[2854]

Mahadeva was succeeded by his son Ammana, who was dethroned by Krishna's son Ramachandra after a short reign in 1270.[2856,2857] During the first half of his reign, Ramachandra adopted an aggressive policy against his neighbours. In the 1270s, he invaded the northern Paramara kingdom, which had been weakened by internal strife, and easily defeated the Paramara army.[2858] The Yadava army was also involved in skirmishes against their north-western neighbours, the Vaghelas, with both sides claiming victory.[2858,2859] In 1275, he sent a powerful army led by Tikkama to the southern Hoysala kingdom. Tikkama gathered a large plunder from this invasion, although ultimately, his army was forced to retreat in 1276.[2860] Ramachandra lost some of his territories, including Raichur, to the Kakatiyas.[2859]

The Purushottamapuri inscription of Ramachandra suggests that he expanded the Yadava kingdom at its north-east frontier. First, he subjugated the rulers of Vajrakara (probably modern Vairagarh) and Bhandagara (modern Bhandara).[2861] Next, he marched to the defunct Kalachuri kingdom, and occupied the former Kalachuri capital Tripuri (modern Tewar near Jabalpur). He also constructed a temple at Varanasi, which suggests that he may have occupied Varanasi for 2-3 years, amid the confusion caused by the Delhi Sultanate's invasion of the local Gahadavala kingdom.[2861] He crushed a rebellion by the Yadava feudatories at Khed and Sangameshwar in Konkan.[2861]

Decline

In 1278, Ramachandra appears to have defeated the Turkic invaders from the Delhi Sultanate, as a Sanskrit royal inscription of that year glorifies him as a "Great Boar in securing the earth from the oppression of the Turks".[2862] However, in 1294, Ala-ud-din Khalji of the Delhi Sultanate successfully raided Devagiri. Khalji restored it to Ramachandra in return for his promise of payment of a high ransom and an annual tribute.[2863] However, this was not paid and the Seuna kingdom's arrears to Khalji kept mounting. In 1307, Khalji sent an army commanded by Malik Kafur, accompanied by Khwaja Haji, to Devagiri. The Muslim governors of Malwa and Gujarat were ordered to help Malik Kafur. Their huge army conquered the weakened and defeated forces of Devagiri almost without a battle. Ramachandra was taken to Delhi. Khalji reinstated Ramachandra as governor in return for a promise to help him subdue the Hindu kingdoms in South India. In 1310, Malik Kafur mounted an assault on the Kakatiya kingdom from Devagiri.

Ramachandra's successor Simhana III challenged the supremacy of Khalji, who sent Malik Kafur to recapture Devagiri in 1313. Simhana III was killed in the ensuing battle and Khalji's army occupied Devagiri. The kingdom was annexed by the Khalji sultanate in 1317. Many years later, Muhammad Tughluq of the Tughluq dynasty of the Delhi Sultanate subsequently renamed the city Daulatabad.[2864]

Rulers

The rulers of the Seuna / Yadava dynasty include:[2865,2866]

Feudatories

- Dridhaprahara, r. c. 860-880
- Seunachandra, r. c. 880-900
- Dhadiyappa I, r. c. 900-?
- Bhillama I, r. c. 925

- Rajugi, r. c. ?-950
- Vaddiga, r. c. 950-970
- Dhadiyasa, r. c. 970-985
- Bhillama II, r. c. 985-1005
- Vesugi I, r. c. 1005–1025
- Bhillama III, r. c. 1025–?
- Vesugi II alias Vaddiga or Yadugi, r. c. ?-1050
- Seunachandra II, r. c. 1050-1085
- Airammadeva or Erammadeva, r. c. 1085-1105
- Simhana I (also transliterated as Singhana I) alias Simharaja, r. c. 1105-1120
- Obscure rulers, r. c. 1120-1145
- Mallugi I, r. c. 1145-1160
- Amaragangeya
- Amara-mallugi alias Mallugi II
- Kaliya-ballala, r. c. ?-1175
- Bhillama V, r. c. 1175–1187

Sovereigns

- Bhillama V, r. c. 1187–1191
- Jaitugi I, r. c. 1191-1200 or 1191-1210
- Simhana II, r. c. 1200-1246 or 1210-1246
- Krishna alias Kannara, r. c. 1246–1261
- Mahadeva, r.c. 1261–1270
- Ammana, r. c. 1270
- Ramachandra alias Ramadeva, r. c. 1271–1308

Khalji tributaries

- Ramachandra, r. c. 1308–1311
- Simhana III alias Shankaradeva, r. c. 1311-1313
- Harapaladeva, r. c. 1313–1317

Literature

Marathi

The Yadavas were the first major dynasty to use Marathi as an official language.[2867] Earlier, both Sanskrit and Kannada had been used in present-day Maharashtra; subsequently, at least partly due to the efforts of the Yadava rulers, Marathi became the dominant language of the region.[2868] Even if they were not of Marathi origin, towards the end of their reign, they certainly identified with the Marathi language.[2817] The early Marathi literature emerged during the Yadava rule, because of which some scholars have theorized that it was produced with support from the Yadava rulers.[2869] However, there is no evidence that the Yadava royal court directly supported the production of Marathi literature with state funds, although it regarded Marathi as a significant language for connecting with the general public.[2870]

Hemadri, a minister in the Yadava court, attempted to formalize Marathi with Sanskrit expressions to boost its status as a court language.[2871] Saint-poet Dnyaneshwar wrote *Dnyaneshwari* (c. 1290), a Marathi-language commentary on the *Bhagavad Gita*, during Ramachandra's rule. He also composed devotional songs called *abhanga*s. Dnyaneshwar gave a higher status to Marathi by translating the sacred Geeta from Sanskrit. Mukundaraja wrote the Marathi-language philosophical treatises *Paramamrita* and *Vivekasindhu* during the Yadava period.[2872] The Mahanubhava religious sect, which became prominent in present-day Maharshtra during the late Yadava period, boosted the status of Marathi as a literary language.[2872] Mahimabhatta wrote *Lilacharita*, a biography of the sect's founder Chakradhara. The text claims that Hemadri (who was a Brahmanist) was jealous of Chakradhara's popularity, and the Yadava king Ramachandra ordered killing of Chakradhara, who escaped with his yogic powers. The claim is of doubtful historicity.[2811]

Kannada

Kannada was one of the court languages during early Seuna times, as is evident from a number of Kannada-language inscriptions (see Origin section). Kamalabhava, patronised by Bhillama V, wrote *Santhishwarapurana*. Achanna composed *Varadhamanapurana* in 1198. Amugideva, patronised by Simhana II, composed many *Vachanas* or devotional songs. Chaundarasa of Pandharapur wrote *Dashakumara Charite* around 1300.[2873,2874,2875]

Simhana patronized Changadeva and the Kannada poet Kamalabhava.

Sanskrit

Simhana was a great patron of learning and literature. He established the college of astronomy to study the work of celebrated astronomer Bhaskaracharya. The Sangita Ratnakara, an authoritative Sanskrit work on Indian music was written by Śārṅgadeva (or Shrangadeva) during Simhana's reign.

Hemadri compiled the encyclopedic Sanskrit work *Chaturvarga Chintamani*. He is said to have built many temples in a style known after him – *Hemadapanti*. He wrote many books on *vaidhyakshastra* (medical science) and he introduced and supported bajra cultivation.[2876]

Other Sanskrit literary works created during the Seuna period include:

- *Suktimuktavali* by Jalhana

- *Hammiramadhana* by Jayasimha SuriWikipedia:Citation needed
- *Karnakutuhala* and *Siddhanta Shiromani* by Bhaskaracharya
- Anantadeva's commentaries on Varahamihira's *Brijajjataka* and Brahmagupta's *Brihatsputa siddhanta*
- Haripaladeva's *Sangeetasudhakara*, a treatise on Indian Classical Music, which bifurcates Indian classical music as Hindustani Music and Carnatic Music for the first time, acknowledging the Muslim influence on Indian music.Wikipedia:Verifiability

References

Bibliography

<templatestyles src="Template:Refbegin/styles.css" />

- A. S. Altekar (1960). Ghulam Yazdani, ed. *The Early History of the Deccan Parts*[2877]. VIII: Yādavas of Seuṇadeśa. Oxford University Press. OCLC 59001459[2878].
- A. V. Narasimha Murthy (1971). *The Sevunas of Devagiri*[2879]. Rao and Raghavan.
- Christian Lee Novetzke (2016). *The Quotidian Revolution: Vernacularization, Religion, and the Premodern Public Sphere in India*[2880]. Columbia University Press. ISBN 978-0-231-54241-8.
- Cynthia Talbot (2001). *Precolonial India in Practice: Society, Region, and Identity in Medieval Andhra*[2881]. Oxford University Press. ISBN 978-0-19-803123-9.
- Colin P. Masica (1993). "Subsequent spread of Indo-Aryan in the subcontinent and beyond". *The Indo-Aryan Languages*[2882]. Cambridge University Press. ISBN 978-0-521-29944-2.
- Onkar Prasad Verma (1970). *The Yādavas and Their Times*[2883]. Vidarbha Samshodhan Mandal. OCLC 138387[2884].
- Shrinivas Ritti (1973). *The Seunas: The Yadavas of Devagiri*[2885]. Department of Ancient Indian History and Epigraphy, Karnatak University.
- Suryanath Kamat (1980). *A Concise History of Karnataka*[2886]. Archana Prakashana.
- T. V. Mahalingam (1957). "The Seunas of Devagiri". In R. S. Sharma. *A Comprehensive history of India: A.D. 985-1206*[2887]. 4 (Part 1). Indian History Congress / People's Publishing House. ISBN 978-81-7007-121-1.

External links

 Wikimedia Commons has media related to *Seuna (Yadava) dynasty*.

- Miscellaneous inscriptions in Kannada from Yadava period[2888]
- Bombay-Karnataka inscriptions: The Yadavas[2889]
- Bombay-Karnataka inscriptions (volume III): The Yadavas[2890]

Kakatiya dynasty

<indicator name="pp-default"> 🔒 </indicator>

Kakatiya dynasty	
Empire (Subordinate to Western Chalukyas until 1163)	
1163[2891]–1323	
Capital	Orugallu (Warangal)
Languages	Telugu
Religion	Hinduism
Government	Monarchy
History	
• Earliest rulers	c. 800
• Established	1163[2891]
• Disestablished	1323
Preceded by	Succeeded by
Western Chalukya Empire Eastern Chalukyas Velanati Chodas	Musunuri Nayaks Bahmani Sultanate Reddy dynasty Vijayanagara Empire
Today part of	India

Kakatiya dynasty

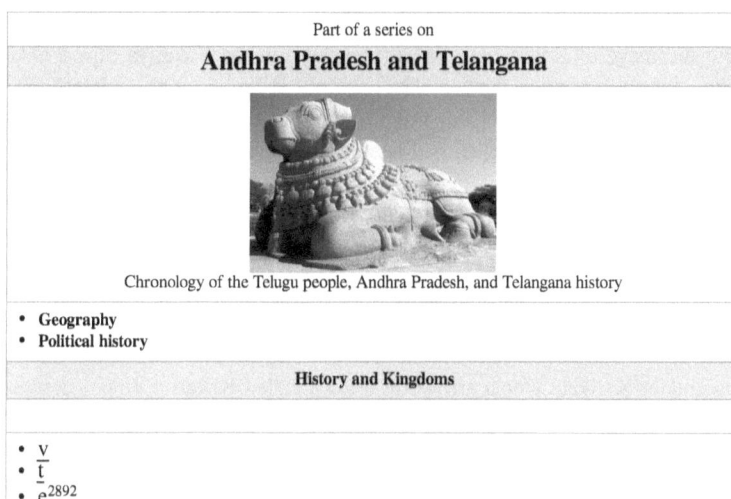

Part of a series on
Andhra Pradesh and Telangana

Chronology of the Telugu people, Andhra Pradesh, and Telangana history

- **Geography**
- **Political history**

History and Kingdoms

- v
- t
- e[2892]

The **Kakatiya dynasty** was a South Indian dynasty whose capital was Orugallu, now known as Warangal. It was eventually conquered by the Delhi Sultanate.

The demise of Kakatiya dynasty resulted in confusion and anarchy under alien rulers for sometime, before the Musunuri Nayaks brought stability to the region.[2893]

Etymology and names

Studies of the inscriptions and coinage by the historian Dineshchandra Sircar reveal that there was no contemporary standard spelling of the family name. Variants include *Kakatiya*, *Kakatiyya*, *Kakita*, *Kakati* and *Kakatya*. The family name was often prefixed to the name of the monarch, giving constructs such as *Kakatiya-Prataparudra*. Some of the monarchs also had alternate names; for example, *Venkata* and *Venkataraya* may have been alternate names of Prataparuda I, with the former appearing on a coin in the form *Venkata-Kakatiya*.[2894,2895]

The dynasty's name derives from the word "Kakati", which is variously thought to be the name of a goddess or a place. It is possible that Kakati was the name of a deity worshipped by the early Kakatiya chiefs, and also the name of the place where they resided.[2896]

Kumarasvami Somapithin, a 15th-century writer who wrote a commentary on Vidyanatha's *Prataparudriya*, states that the dynasty was named after Kakati, a form of goddess Durga. Although the Hindu mythological texts do not mention any such form of Durga, the worship of a goddess named Kakati is attested by several other sources. For example, Vallabharaya's *Krida-bhiramamu* mentions an image of Kakatamma (Mother Kakati) in the Kakatiya capital Orugallu. the 16th century Shitap Khan inscription mentions the reinstallation of the image of goddess Jaganmatrika (mother of the universe) and the lotus seat of the Kakatirajya, which had been destroyed by the Turushkas (Turkic people).[2897] According to one theory, Kakati was originally a Jain Goddess (possibly Padmavati), and later came to be regarded as a form of Durga.[2898]

The Bayyaram tank inscription from the reign of Ganapati-deva names the family's founder as Venna, and states that he resided at Kakati, because of which his descendants came to be known as Kakatishas.[2897] Ganapati-deva's Garavapadu charter names the family's founder as Durjaya, and states that his descendant Karikala Chola arrived at a town called Kakati during a hunting expedition, and set up his camp there.[2896] The modern identity of Kakati is uncertain: different historians have variously attempted to identify it with modern Kakati village in Karnataka and Kanker in Chhattisgarh. *Siddeshvara Charitra*, a later literary work, states that the ancestors of the Kakatiya family lived at Kandarapura (identified with modern Kandhar in Maharashtra). However, no other evidence supports this tradition.[2899]

Sources

Much of the information about the Kakatiya period comes from inscriptions, including around 1,000 stone inscriptions, and 12 copper-plate inscriptions.[2900] Most of these inscriptions document matters relating to religion, such as donations to Hindu temples. They are particularly abundant for the period 1175–1324 CE, which is the period when the dynasty most flourished and are a reflection of that. The probability is that many inscriptions have been lost due to buildings falling into disuse and also the ravages of subsequent rulers, most notably the Muslim Mughal Empire in the Telangana region. Inscriptions are still being discovered today but governmental agencies tend to concentrate on recording those that are already known rather than searching for new examples.[2901] According to a 1978 book, written bby P.V.P. Sastry's 1978 book on the history of the Kakatiyas, published by the Government of Andhra Pradesh

Information about the Kakatiya period also comes from Sanskrit and Telugu literary works written during Kakatiya and post-Kakatiya period. The most notable among these works include *Prataparudriyam*, *Krida-bhiramamu*, *Panditaradhya-charitamu*, *Sivayogasaramu*, *Nitisara*, *Niti-shastra-muktavali*, *Nritta-ratnavali*, *Pratapa-charita*, *Siddheshvara-charita*, *Somadeva-rajiyamu*, *Palnativira-charitra*, *Velugotivari-vamsavali*, and *Velugotivari-vamsacharitra*.[2902] Chronicles by Muslim authors such as

Isami and Firishta describe Prataparudra's defeats against the Muslim armies. The Kannada text *Kumara-Ramana-charita* also provides information about Prataparudra's relations with the Kampili kingdom.[2903]

Besides epigraphs and literature, the forts, temples and tanks constructed during the Kakatiya period are an important source of information about the contemporary society, art and architecture.[2904]

Origin

The Kakatiya rulers traced their ancestry to a legendary chief or ruler named Durjaya. Many other ruling dynasties of Andhra also claimed descent from Durjaya. Nothing further is known about this chief.[2905]

Most of the Kakatiya records do not mention the varna (social class) of the family, but the majority of the ones that do, proudly describe them as Shudra.[2906] Examples include the Bothpur and Vaddamanu inscriptions of Ganapati's general Malyala Gunda *senani*. The Kakatiyas also maintained marital relations with other Shudra families, such as the Kotas and the Natavadi chiefs. All these evidences indicate that the Kakatiyas were of Shudra origin.[2907]

A few copper-plate inscriptions of the Kakatiya family describe them as belonging to the Kshatriya (warrior) varna. These inscriptions primarily document grants to brahmans, and appear to be inspired by the genealogies of the imperial Cholas.[2906] For example, the Motupalli inscription of Ganapati counts legendary solar dynasty kings such as Rama among the ancestors of Durjaya, the progenitor of the Kakatiya family. The Malkapuram inscription of Vishveshvara Shivacharya, the preceptor of Kakatiya rulers Ganapatideva and Rudrama-devi, also connects the Kakatiyas to the solar dynasty (Sūryavaṃsa).[2908] The term "Kshatriya" in these panegyric records appears to signify the family's warrior-like qualities rather than their actual varna.[2909]

Early feudatory chiefs

The regnal years of the early members of the Kakatiya family are not certain. Venna, said to have been born in the family of Durjaya, is the earliest known Kakatiya chief. The Bayyaram tank inscription names his successors as Gunda I, Gunda II, and Gunda III, comparing them to the three Ramas (Parashurama, Dasharatha-Rama, and Balarama). Gunda III was succeeded by Erra, who ruled Kurravadi and other regions. The inscription states that Erra's successor Gunda IV alias Pindi-Gunda (c. 955-995) beheaded all his enemies.[2910] Gunda IV is also mentioned in the Mangallu grant of the Eastern Chalukya ruler Dānārnava in 956 CE.[2911]

Gunda IV was succeeded by Beta I (c. 996-1051), who was succeeded by Prola I (c. 1052-1076), called *ari-gaja-kesari* ("lion to the elephant-like enemies") in the Bayyaram inscription.[2910] The succeeding chiefs included Beta II (c. 1076–1108), Tribhuvanamalla Durgaraja (c. 1108–1116) and then Prola II (c. 1116–1157).[2912]

The early Kakatiya rulers used the title "Reddi"[2913,2914] (derived from "Redu," meaning king in Telugu[2915]). However, after they became sovereigns they were addressed as "deva" (Lord or deity) and "devi" (Lady or deity). There appears to be a significant element of "sanskritisation" in this transition.

Relationship to the Rashtrakutas

Early members of Kakatiya family appear to have served as military generals of the Rashtrakutas, as indicated by a 956 inscription of the Vengi Chalukya prince Dānārnava.[2916] The inscription suggests that an attack by the Rashtrakuta king Krishna III forced the Vengi Chalukya king Amma II to flee his kingdom, after which Dānārnava (titled Vijayaditya) ruled the kingdom as a Rashtrakuta vassal. It records Dānārnava's grant of Mangallu village to a brahmana named Dommana, at the request of Kakatiya Gundyana. Dommana had performed a religious ceremony called *Karpati-vrata* for Gundyana, for which he received the village as an *agrahara*.[2917] The inscription names Gundyana's ancestors as Gundiya-Rashtrakuta and Eriya-Rashtrakuta.[2918] This suggests that Gundyana was a Rashtrakuta general, and not a Vengi Chalukya subordinate, as assumed by some earlier historians.[2918]

The Bayyaram tank inscription, which records the construction of *Dharmakirti-samudra* tank by Ganapati's sister Mailama (or Mailamba), provides another genealogical list.[2910] The similarities of names mentioned in the Mangallu and Bayyaram inscriptions lists suggest that both of these refer to the same family:[2919]

Genealogical list of early Kakatiyas[2920]

Mangallu grant inscription	Bayyaram tank inscription
Kakatiya family	Durjaya family
	Venna-*nripa*
Gundiya Rashtrakuta	Gunda I
	Gunda II
	Gunda III
Eriya Rashtrakuta	Erra
Betiya (married Vandyanamba)	
Kakartya Gundyana	Pindi-Gunda (Gunda IV)

Historian P.V.P. Sastry theorizes that Betiya was the son of Eriya (alias Erra) and father of Gundyana (alias Pindi-Gunda), but may have become too insignificant to be mentioned by his descendants, because of a premature death or another reason.[2921]

The significance of the suffix "Rashtrakuta" in the names of the early Kakatiya chiefs is debated. According to one theory, the suffix implies that these chiefs were Rashtrakuta subordinates. This theory is based on the fact that the phrase *Rashtrakuta-kutumbinah* appears in several Rashtrakuta-era copper-plate inscriptions, and refers to the officers and subjects of the Rashtrakuta kingdom.[2922]

According to another theory, the suffix implies that the Kakatiyas were a branch of the Rashtrakuta family, because the term *Rashtrakuta-kutumbinah* was used for officers employed by the Rashtrakuta administration, not feudatory chiefs: the early records of the Kakatiya chiefs describe them as *samantas* (feudatory chiefs).[2923] The Kazipet Darga inscription of Tribhuvanamalla Durgaraja states that the Kakatiya chief Beta was born in the family of Samanta Viṣṭi.[2924] Historian P.V.P. Sastry theorises that "Viṣṭi" is a corruption of Vrishni, the name of a clan from which some Rashtrakutas claimed descent. He notes that some chiefs of Rashtrakuta origin adopted the title "Viṭṭi-narayana", which means "as great as Narayana (Krishna) of the Vitti (Vrishni) family.[2925] Sastry further proposes that the term "Voddi", which appears in the phrase *Voddi-kula* ("Voddi family") in the Mangallu inscription may be same as "Viṣṭi".[2926] Sastry also believes that the early Kakatiya chiefs followed Jainism, which was also patronized by the Rashtrakutas, thus strengthening the view that the two dynasties were connected (see Religion section below).[2898]

The Kakatiyas seemed to have adopted the mythical bird Garuda as their royal insignia, as attested by the Ekamranatha temple inscription of Ganapatideva, the Palampet inscription of the Kakatiya general Recharla Rudra, and Vidyanatha's *Prataparudriya*.[2924] The Bayyaram tank inscription calls the Kakatiya chief Beta I (son of Gunda IV) *Garudamka*-Beta, and "Garuda" here appears to refer to the family's emblem.[2927] In Hindu mythology, Garuda is the vahana of god Vishnu. The Rashtrakutas and some other dynsaties of Deccan claimed descent from the Vrishni clan (associated with Vishnu's avatar Krishna), and had adopted Garuda as their royal insignia.[2923] According to Sastry, this corroborates the theory that the Kakatiyas were associated with the Rashtrakuta family.[2928] Sastry further speculates that the Kakatiyas may have adopted the Garuda symbol because of Jain influence: the yaksha of the Jain tirthankara Shantinatha is represented by the Garuda symbol.[2928]

Based on Ganapati-deva's Garavapadu inscription, which names Karikala Chola among the family's ancestors, epigraphist C.R.K. Charlu theorised that the Kakatiyas were a branch of the Telugu Cholas. However, no other Kakatiya record mentions Karikala, and unlike the Telugu Cholas, the Kakatiyas did not claim to belong to the Kashyapa-gotra. Therefore, Sastry dismisses Charlu's theory as untenable.[2926]

After the decline of the Rashtrakuta power, the Kakatiyas served as vassals of the Kalyani Chalukyas. After the decline of the Chalukya power in the 12th century, they assumed sovereignty by suppressing other Chalukya subordinates in the Telangana region.[2929]

As sovereigns

Prataparudra I

The 1149 Sanigaram inscription of Prola II is the last known record of the Kakatiyas as vassals. The 1163 Anumakonda inscription of Prataparudra I is the earliest known record that describes the Kakatiyas as a sovereign power.[2916]

According to Sastry, Prataparudra I reigned between around 1158 – 1195,[2912] while Sircar gives the dates 1163–1195. He was also known as Rudra Deva, Kakatiya Rudradeva, Venkata, and Venkataraya[2894,2930] He was the son of Prola II, who had made efforts to assert greater Kakatiya influence on territories in the western parts of the declining Western Chalukyan empire and who died in a battle fought against the Velanati Choda ruler Gonka II around 1157/1158 while doing so.[2931,2932] It was during Prataparudra's reign, in 1163, that the Kakatiyas declared an end to their status as feudatory chiefs of the Chalukyas.[2933] It is notable that inscriptions were henceforth written using the Kakatiya chiefs' vernacular Telugu rather than the Kannada language that had prevailed until that point.[2934]

Mahadeva succeeded Prataparudra I as king, reigning probably from 1195 to 1199.[2912]

Ganapati

Just as the Seuna and Hoysala dynasties took control of linguistically related areas during the 13th century, so too did the Kakatiyas under the rule of Ganapati.[2934] He is also known as Ganapathi Deva and, according to Sastry, reigned between 1199–1262; Sircar gives regnal dates of 1199–1260.[2912,2930] He significantly expanded Kakatiya lands during the 1230s when he launched a series of attacks outside the dynasty's traditional Telangana region and thus brought under Kakatiya control the Telugu-speaking lowland delta areas around the Godavari and Krishna rivers. The outcome in the case of all three dynasties, says historian Richard Eaton, was that they "catalysed processes of supralocal identity formation and community building".[2934]

Figure 500: *Ramappa Temple.*

The Kakatiya capital at Orugallu, established in 1195, was not forgotten while Ganapati expanded his territory. He organised the building of a massive granite wall around the city, complete with ramps designed for ease of access to its ramparts from within. A moat and numerous bastions were also constructed.[2935]

Ganapati was keen to bolster the dynasty's economy. He encouraged merchants to trade abroad, abolishing all taxes except for a fixed duty and supporting those who risked their lives to travel afar.[2936] He created the man-made Pakhal Lake.

Rudrama Devi

Rudrama Devi, also known as Rudramadevi, reigned around 1262–1289 CE (alternative dates: 1261–1295 CE) and is one of the few queens in Indian history.[2912,2937] Sources disagree regarding whether she was the widow of Ganapati or his daughter.[2938]

Marco Polo, who visited India probably some time around 1289–1293, made note of Rudrama Devi's rule and nature in flattering terms.[2939,2940] She continued the planned fortification of the capital, raising the height of Ganapati's wall as well as adding a second earthen curtain wall 1.5 miles (2.4 km) in diameter and with an additional 150 feet (46 m)-wide moat.[2935]

Figure 501: *Statue of Rudrama Devi.*

Rudrama was married to Virabhadra, an Eastern Chalukyan prince of Nidadavolu who had been selected for that purpose by her father.[2941] Having no son as an heir,[2935] Rudrama abdicated in favour of her grandson when it became apparent that the expansionist sultan Alauddin Khalji was encroaching on the Deccan and might in due course attack the Kakatiyas.[2938]

Prataparudra II

The earliest biography of Rudrama Devi's successor, Prataparudra II, is the *Prataparudra Caritramu*, dating from the 16th century.[2942] His reign began in 1289 (alternative date: 1295) and ended with the demise of the dynasty in 1323.[2912] It is described by Eaton as the "first chapter in a larger story" that saw the style of polity in the Deccan change from being regional kingdoms to transregional sultanates that survived until the arrival of the British East India Company in the 18th century.[2943]

Decline

The Kakatiya kingdom attracted the attention of the Delhi Sultanate ruler Alauddin Khalji because of the possibility for plunder.[2944] The first foray into the Kakatiya kingdom was made in 1303 and was a disaster due to the

Kakatiya dynasty 813

Figure 502: *A replica of the Koh-i-Noor diamond. The diamond was originally owned by the Kakatiya dynasty.*

resistance of the Kakatiya army in the battle at Upparapalli.[2945,2946] In 1309 Alauddin sent a general, Malik Kafur, in an attempt to force Prataparudra into acceptance of a position subordinate to the sultanate at Delhi. Kafur organised a month-long siege of Orugallu that ended with success in February 1310. Prataparudra was forced to make various symbolic acts of obeisance designed to demonstrate his new position as a subordinate but, as was Alauddin's plan, he was not removed as ruler of the area but rather forced thereafter to pay annual tribute to Delhi.[2947] It was probably at this time that the Koh-i-Noor diamond passed from Kakatiya ownership to that of Alauddin, along with 20,000 horses and 100 elephants.[2944]

In 1311, Prataparudra formed a part of the sultanate forces that attacked the Pandyan empire in the south, and he took advantage of that situation to quell some of his vassals in Nellore who had seen his reduced status as an opportunity for independence. Later, though, in 1318, he failed to provide the annual tribute to Delhi, claiming that the potential for being attacked on the journey made it impossible. Alauddin's son Mubarak Shah responded by sending another of his generals, Khusrau Khan, to Orugallu with a force that bristled with technology previously unknown in the area, including trebuchet-like machines. Prataparudra had to submit once more, with his obeisance on this occasion being arranged by the sultanate to include a very public display whereby he bowed towards Delhi from the ramparts of Orugallu. The amount of his annual tribute was changed, becoming 100 elephants and 12,000 horses.[2948]

The new arrangements did not last long. Taking advantage of a revolution in Delhi that saw the Khalji dynasty removed and Ghiyasuddin Tughlaq installed as sultan, Prataparudra again asserted his independence in 1320. Tughlaq sent his son, Ulugh Khan, to defeat the defiant Kakatiya king in 1321. Khan's army was riven with internal dissension due to its containing factions from the Khalji and Tughluq camps. This caused the siege on this occasion to last much longer — six months, rather than the few weeks that had previously been the case. The attackers were initially repulsed and Khan's forces retreated to regroup in Devagiri. Prataparudra celebrated the apparent victory by opening up his grain stores for public feasting. Khan returned in 1323 with his revitalised and reinforced army and, with few supplies left, Prataparudra was forced into submission after a five-month siege. The unprepared and battle-weary army of Orugallu was finally defeated, and Orugallu was renamed as Sultanpur. It seems probable, from combining various contemporary and near-contemporary accounts, that Prataparudra committed suicide near to the Narmada River while being taken as a prisoner to Delhi.[2949,2950]

Characterization

Geography

The Kakatiya base was the city of Orugallu[2951] in the dry uplands of northern Telangana on the Deccan Plateau. From there they expanded their influence into Coastal Andhra, the delta between the Godavari and Krishna rivers that feed into the Bay of Bengal. According to Rao and Shulman, the latter contained a high proportion of Brahmins while the former was the haunt of "peasants, artisans and warriors".[2952] Under the Kakatiyas, cultural innovation often began in the uplands, was refined in the lowlands and then recycled back into the Deccan. This bi-directional flow of cultural influences brought into being a feeling of cultural affinity between those who spoke the Telugu language where nothing of that nature had previously existed.[2953] The unification of the distinct upland and lowland cultures was their most significant political achievement, achieved through a process of binding many locally powerful figures in allegiance to the empire.[2951]

The area of land under Kakatiya control reached its zenith around the 13th century CE during the rule of Ganapati Deva. By this time, South India and the Deccan was essentially under the aegis of four Hindu monarchies, of which the Kakatiyas were one.[2954] The four dynasties were in a constant state of warfare with each other, with the Kakatiyas eventually exercising control from close to Anagondi in the west to Kalyani in the north-east, and down to Kanei and Ganjam district in southern Orissa.[2955]

Architecture

A notable trend during the dynastic period was the construction of reservoirs for irrigation in the uplands, around 5000 of which were built by warrior families subordinate to the Kakatiyas. The dramatically altered the possibilities for development in the sparsely populated dry areas. Many of these edifices, often called "tanks", including the large examples at Pakala and Ramappa, are still used today.[2956]

Another notable architectural feature of the dynasty relates to temples. Even before the arrival of the dynasty, there were large, well-established and well-endowed Hindu places of worship in the relatively populous delta areas; however, the temples of the uplands, which were smaller and less cosmopolitan in origin and funding, did not exist until the Kakatiya period. In the lowlands, where Brahmins were numerous, the temples had long benefited from a desire to build social networks for the purposes of domestic and foreign trade, as well as for obtaining grazing rights in the face of competition; in the uplands, the endowment of the buildings was often associated with the construction and continued maintenance of reservoirs and enabled a different type of networking based on political hierarchies. The strengthening of those hierarchies, which was achieved in part by donating land for the temples and then attending worship, was necessary as the inland agrarian society grew rapidly in number and location.[2957]

Society

There is a disparity between analysis of inscriptions, of which the work of Cynthia Talbot has been in the vanguard, and the traditional works of Vedic Hinduism that described pre-colonial India in terms of a reverent and static society that was subject to the strictures of the caste system. Colonial British administrators found much that appealed to them in the latter works but the Kakatiya inscriptions of Andhra Pradesh, which depict a far wider range of society and events, suggest that the reality was far more fluid and very different from the idealised image.[2958]

Caste itself seems to have been of low importance as a social identifier.[2959] Even the Kakatiya kings, with one exception, considered themselves to be Shudras (in the ritual varna system).[2960] They were egalitarian in nature and promoted their subordinate warrior-chiefs who were similarly egalitarian and spurned the Kshatriya rank. Anyone, regardless of birth, could acquire the *nayaka* title to denote warrior status, and this they did. There is also little evidence that Kakatiya society paid much regard to caste identities, in the sense of *jāti*. Although occupation does appear to have been an important designator of social position, the inscriptions suggest that people were not bound to an occupation by birth.[2961,2962]

The population became more settled in geographic terms. The growth of an agricultural peasant class subsumed many tribal people who previously had been nomadic. The nexus of politics and military was a significant feature of the era, and the Kakatiya recruitment of peasants into the military did much to create a new warrior class, to develop social mobility and to extend the influence of the dynasty into areas of its kingdom that previously would have been untouched.[2963] The Kakatiya kings, and in particular the last two, encouraged an egalitarian ethos. The entrenched landed nobility that had existed prior to the dynasty found its power to be on the wane; the royal gifting of lands formerly in the possession of nobles to people of lesser status did much to effect this dilution.[2942]

Religion

Historian P.V.P. Sastry theorises that the early Kakatiya chiefs were followers of Jainism. A story in the *Siddheshvara-charita* states that Madhavavarman, an ancestor of the Kakatiyas, obtained military strength by the grace of goddess Padmakshi. The 1123 Govindapuram Jain inscription of Polavasa, another family of feudatory chiefs, contains a similar account of how their ancestor Madhavavarman obtained military strength by the grace of the Jain goddess Yaksheshvari.[2964]

According to tradition, Prola II was initiated into Shaivism by the Kalamukha preceptor Rameshvara Pandita, and established Shaivism as his family's religion. The Shaivism-affiliated personal names of the later Kakatiya kings (such as Rudra, Mahadeva, Harihara, and Ganapati) also indicate a shift towards Shaivism. This, according to Sastry, strengthens the theory that the early Kakatiya chiefs were Jains.[2928]

Genealogy

The following members of the Kakatiya family are known from epigraphic evidence. The rulers are children of their predecessors, unless otherwise specified.[2965]

Feudatory chiefs

- *Nripa* Venna, born in the family of Durjaya (r. c. 800-815)
- Gunda I (r. c. 815-?)
- Gunda II (r. c. ?-865)
- Gunda III (died before 900)
- *Nripati* Erra
- Betiya
- *Nripati* Gunda IV alias Pindi-Gunda (r. c. 955-995)
- *Nripati* Beta I alias Garuda Beta (r. c. 996-1051)
- Prola I (r. c. 1052-1076)
- Beta II alias Tribhuvanamalla (r. c. 1076-1108)
- Tribhuvanamalla Durgaraja (r. c. 1108-1116), son of Beta II
- Prola II (r. c. 1116-1157), son of Beta II, married Muppama
  - His children included Rudra, Mahadeva, Harihara, Ganapati and Repolla Durga

Sovereign rulers

- Rudra (r. c. 1158-1195), son of Prolla II, became a sovereign 1163
- Mahadeva (r. c. 1196-1199), son of Prolla II, married Bayyama
  - Had three children, including Ganapati-deva, Mailamba, and Kundamba
- Ganapati-deva (r. c. 1199-1262), married Somala-devi
  - Had two children, including Ganapamba (married Kota Beta) and Rudrama-devi
- Rudrama-devi (r. c. 1262-1289), married Chalukya Virabhadra
  - Had three children, including Mummadamba (married Kakati Mahadeva), Rudrama (married Yadava prince Ellana-deva), and Ruyyama (married Induluri Annaya-mantri)
- Prataparudra-deva (r. c. 1289-1323), son of Mummadamba, tributary to the Delhi Sultanate at times

Legacy

Tughlaq control of the area lasted only for around a decade.[2966] The fall of the Kakatiya dynasty resulted in both political and cultural disarray because of both disparate resistance to the sultanate and dissension within it.[2950] The structure of the Kakatiya polity disintegrated and their lands soon fell under the control of numerous families from communities such as the Reddies and Velamas.[2967] As early as 1330,[2968] Musunuri Nayaks who served as army chiefs for Kakatiya kingdom united the various Telugu clans and recovered Warangal from the Delhi Sultanate and ruled for half a century.[2969] Surrounded by more

Figure 503: *Ruins of the Kakatiya Kala Thoranam (Warangal Gate).*

significant states,[2967] by the 15th century these new entities had ceded to the Bahamani Sultanate and the Sangama dynasty, the latter of which evolved to become the Vijayanagara empire.[2970]

A brother of Prataparudra II, Annamaraja, has been associated with ruling what eventually became the princely state of Bastar during the British Raj period. This appears likely to be historical revisionism, dating from a genealogy published by the ruling family in 1703, because it records only eight generations spanning almost four centuries of rule. Such revisionism and tenuous claims of connection to the Kakatiyas was not uncommon because it was perceived as legitimising the right to rule and a warrior status. Talbot notes that there is a record of a brother called Annamadeva and that:

> He is said to have left [*Orugallu*] for the northeast after anointing Prataparudra's son as king. Thus, the founder of the family fortunes in Bastar may very well have been a Telugu warrior from Telangana who was familiar with the prevalent legends about the Kakatiyas.[2971]

According to Talbot and Eaton, a revisionist interpretation of Prataparudra II himself appeared much sooner, within a few years of his death, and for broadly similar reasons. A stone inscription dated 1330 mentions a Prolaya Nayaka, who was said to have restored order, as in Prataparudra days. He presented himself as a legitimate successor to Prataparudra, by portraying both of them as righteous monarchs, meanwhile reconstructing Prataparudra's life and career in a favorable way.[2972,2973] By 1420, Muslim rulers had become accommodated to the Deccan society, and strong dichotomies between Hindus and Muslims were no longer useful. Muslim rulers were no longer conceived as diametrically opposed to the figure of Prataparudra, but rather as rulers of equal status.[2974]

This type of revisionism, which Talbot describes as "social memories" and which persist to the present day,[2975] reappeared in the 16th century with the *Prataparudra Caritramu* hagiography, which claimed him to be the founder of the *padmanayaka* class of Telugu warrior and provided the elite of the Vijayanagara empire with what Talbot has described as a "charter of legitimacy". This work claimed, contrary to all reasonable evidence, that he did not die after being taken prisoner but instead met with the sultan, was recognised as being an avatar of Shiva, and allowed to return to Orugallu. Once back home, the *Prataparudra Caritamu* says, he released the *padmanayakas* from their allegiance to him and told them to become independent kings. The work also claims Vijayanagara to be an ally of Prataparudra, which is clearly anachronistic but served the purpose of elevating the role of the *padmanayakas*, whom it claimed to be ultimately subordinate to Vijayanagara during his time.[2976]

References

Footnotes

Citations

Bibliography <templatestyles src="Template:Refbegin/styles.css" />

- Asher, Catherine B.; Talbot, Cynthia, eds. (2006), "The expansion of Turkic power, 1180–1350", *India before Europe*[2977], Cambridge University Press, ISBN 978-0-52180-904-7
- Chakravarti, Ranabir (1991), "Horse Trade and Piracy at Tana (Thana, Maharashtra, India): Gleanings from Marco Polo", *Journal of the Economic and Social History of the Orient*, **34** (3): 159–182, doi:10.2307/3632243[2978], JSTOR 3632243[2979], (Subscription required (help))
- Chattopadhyaya, B. D. (1998), *Representing the Other? Sanskrit Sources and the Muslims*, New Delhi: Manohar, ISBN 8173042527
- Desai, V. R. M. (1962), "Savings in Ancient Hindu Polity", *The Indian Journal of Political Science*, **23** (1/4): 268–276, JSTOR 41853935[2980], (Subscription required (help))
- Eaton, Richard M. (2005), *A Social History of the Deccan: 1300–1761*[2981], Cambridge University Press, ISBN 978-0-52125-484-7
- Jackson, Peter (2003), *The Delhi Sultanate: A Political and Military History*[2982] (Reprinted ed.), Cambridge University Press, ISBN 978-0-52154-329-3

- Kalia, Ravi (1994), *Bhubaneswar: From a Temple Town to a Capital City*[2983], Southern Illinois University Press – via Questia, (Subscription required (help))
- Kulke, Hermann; Rothermund, Dietmar, eds. (2004) [1986], *A History of India* (4th ed.), Routledge, ISBN 978-0-41532-920-0
- Prasad, G. Durga (1988), *History of the Andhras up to 1565 A. D.*[2984] (PDF), Guntur: P. G. Publishers
- Rao, P. (1994), *History and Culture of Andhra Pradesh*, Sterling
- Rao, Velcheru Narayana (2003), "Court, Temple, and Public", in Pollock, Sheldon, *Literary Cultures in History: Reconstructions from South Asia*[2985], University of California Press – via Questia, (Subscription required (help))
- Rao, Velcheru Narayana; Shulman, David, eds. (2002), *Classical Telugu Poetry: An Anthology*[2986], University of California Press – via Questia, (Subscription required (help))
- Rao, Velcheru Narayana; Shulman, David (2012), *Srinatha: The Poet Who Made Gods and Kings*[2987], Oxford University Press – via Questia, (Subscription required (help))
- Rubiés, Joan-Pau (2000), *Travel and Ethnology in the Renaissance: South India through European Eyes, 1250–1625*[2988], Cambridge University Press – via Questia, (Subscription required (help))
- Sastry, P. V. Parabhrama (1978). N. Ramesan, ed. *The Kākatiyas of Warangal*[2989]. Hyderabad: Government of Andhra Pradesh. OCLC 252341228[2990].
- Sharma, R. S. (1992). *A Comprehensive History of India*[2991]. Orient Longmans. p. 234. ISBN 978-81-7007-121-1.
- Sircar, D. C. (1979), *Some Epigraphical Records of the Medieval Period from Eastern India*[2992], Abhinav Publications, ISBN 978-8-17017-096-9
- Sircar, D. C. (2008) [1968], *Studies in Indian Coins*[2993] (Reprinted ed.), Motilal Banarsidass, ISBN 978-8-12082-973-2
- Subrahmanyam, Sanjay (1998), "Hearing Voices: Vignettes of Early Modernity in South Asia, 1400–1750", *Daedalus*, **127** (3): 75–104, JSTOR 20027508[2994], (Subscription required (help))
- Suryanarayana, Kolluru (1986), *History of the Minor Chaḷukya Families in Medieval Andhradesa*[2995], B. R. Publishing, ISBN 978-8-17018-330-3
- Talbot, Austin Cynthia (2001), *Pre-colonial India in Practice: Society, Region, and Identity in Medieval Andhra*[2996], Oxford University Press, ISBN 978-0-19803-123-9
- Ventakaramanayya, N. (1942), *The Early Muslim Expansion in South India*, University of Madras

Further reading

 Wikimedia Commons has media related to *Kakatiya dynasty*.

- Talbot, Cynthia (May 1991). "Temples, Donors, and Gifts: Patterns of Patronage in Thirteenth-Century South India". *The Journal of Asian Studies*. **50** (2): 308–340. doi: 10.2307/2057210[2997]. JSTOR 2057210[2998]. (Subscription required (help)).

Kalachuri dynasty

Kalachuris of Mahishmati	
6th century–7th century	
Capital	Mahishmati
Languages	Sanskrit
Religion	Hinduism JainismWikipedia:Citation needed
Government	monarchy
History	
• Established	6th century
• Disestablished	7th century
Preceded by	Succeeded by
Vakataka dynasty Vishnukundina Traikutaka dynasty	Chalukya dynasty
Today part of	India

<mapframe text="[[Find spot]]s of the inscriptions issued by the Kalachuris of Mahishmati (map of India){{sfn|Om Prakash Misra|2003|p=13}}{{sfn| Charles Dillard Collins|1988|p=6}}" width="350" height="350" zoom="5" longitude="74.91" latitude="22.03"> { "type": "FeatureCollection", "features": [{ "type": "Feature", "properties": { "marker-symbol": "monument", "title": "Abhona" }, "geometry": { "type": "Point", "coordinates": [73.9271644, 20.4796816] } }, { "type": "Feature", "properties": { "marker-symbol": "monument", "title": "Sankheda", "description": "Also known as Sankhera" }, "geometry": { "type": "Point", "coordinates": [73.5814967, 22.1715494] } }, { "type": "Feature", "properties": { "marker-symbol": "monument", "title": "Sarsavani", "description": "Also known as Sarsavni"

}, "geometry": { "type": "Point", "coordinates": [73.2352525, 20.7275464] } }, { "type": "Feature", "properties": { "marker-symbol": "monument", "title": "Ujjain" }, "geometry": { "type": "Point", "coordinates": [75.7849097, 23.1793013] } }, { "type": "Feature", "properties": { "marker-symbol": "monument", "title": "Vadnagar", "description": "Also known as Anandapura" }, "geometry": { "type": "Point", "coordinates": [72.6165643, 23.7757259] } }, { "type": "Feature", "properties": { "marker-symbol": "monument", "title": "Vadner" }, "geometry": { "type": "Point", "coordinates": [74.5170319, 19.4478632] } }, { "type": "Feature", "properties": { "marker-symbol": "monument", "title": "Vidisha" }, "geometry": { "type": "Point", "coordinates": [77.8081363, 23.5251102] } }, { "type": "Feature", "properties": { "marker-symbol": "star", "title": "Mahishmati", "description": "No Kalachuri inscriptions have been found at Mahishmati, but literary evidence suggests that it was the dynasty's capital.", "comment": "Mandhata; Maheshwar is fairly close", "marker-color": "000080" }, "geometry": { "type": "Point", "coordinates": [76.1522879, 22.2507773] } }] } </mapframe> The **Kalachuris** (IAST: Kalacuri) were an Indian dynasty that ruled in west-central India between 6th and 7th centuries. They are also known as the Haihayas or as the "early Kalachuris" to distinguish them from their later namesakes.

The Kalachuri territory included parts of present-day Gujarat, Madhya Pradesh, and Maharashtra. Their capital was probably located at Mahishmati. Epigraphic and numismatic evidence suggests that the earliest of the Ellora and Elephanta cave monuments were built during the Kalachuri rule.

The origin of the dynasty is uncertain. In the 6th century, the Kalachuris gained control of the territories formerly ruled by the Guptas, the Vakatakas and the Vishnukundinas. Only three Kalachuri kings are known from inscriptional evidence: Shankaragana, Krishnaraja, and Buddharaja. The Kalachuris lost their power to the Chalukyas of Vatapi in the 7th century. One theory connects the later Kalachuri dynasties of Tripuri and Kalyani to the Kalachuris of Mahishmati.

Territory

According to the Kalachuri inscriptions, the dynasty controlled Ujjayini, Vidisha and Anandapura. Literary references suggest that their capital was located at Mahishmati in the Malwa region.[2999]

The dynasty also controlled Vidarbha, where they succeeded the Vakataka and the Vishnukundina dynasties.[2999]

In addition, the Kalachuris conquered northern Konkan (around Elephanta) by the mid-6th century. Here, they succeeded the Traikutaka dynasty.[2999]

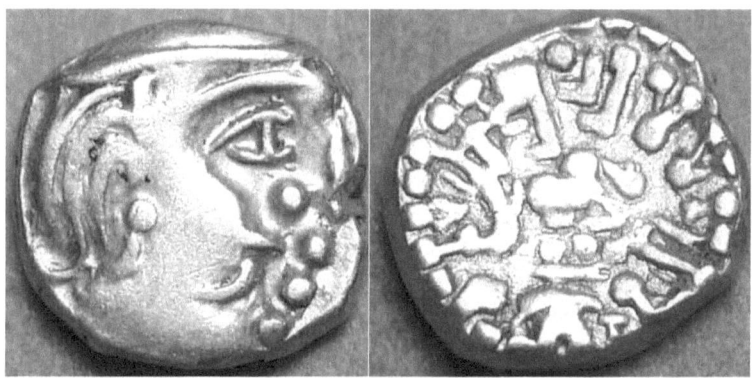

Figure 504: *Silver coin of Krishnaraja*

Figure 505: *Coin of King Kalahasila, a Kalachuri feudatory. Circa (575-610).*

History

Krishnaraja

The origin of the Kalachuris is uncertain.[2999] Krishnaraja (r. c. 550-575) is the earliest known ruler of the dynasty. He issued coins featuring Brahmi script legends, imitating the design of earlier coins issued by the Traikutaka and the Gupta kings. His coins featuring a bull are based on the coins issued by Skandagupta. His silver coins were circulated widely for around 150 years after his reign.[2999]

Krishnaraja's coins describe him as *Parama-Maheshvara* (devotee of Shiva). An inscription of his son Shankaragana states that he was devoted to Pashupati (Shiva) since his birth.[2999] Historical evidence suggests that he may have commissioned the Shaivite monuments at the Elephanta Caves and the earliest of the Brahmanical caves at Ellora, where his coins have been discovered.[3000,3001,2999]

Shankaragana

Shankaragana (r. c. 575-600) is the earliest ruler of the dynasty to be attested by his own inscriptions, which were issued from Ujjain and Nirgundipadraka. His Ujjain grant is the earliest epigraphic record of the dynasty.[3002]

Shakaragana's adopted the titles of the Gupta emperor Skandagupta. This suggests that he conquered western Malwa, which was formerly under the Gupta authority. His kingdom probably also included parts of the present-day Gujarat.[3002]

Like his father, Shankaragana described himself as a *Parama-Maheshvara* (devotee of Shiva).[3002]

Buddharaja

Buddharaja is the last known ruler of the early Kalachuri dyansty. He was a son of Shankaragana.[3002]

Buddharaja conquered eastern Malwa, but he probably lost western Malwa to the ruler of Vallabhi. During his reign, the Chalukya king Mangalesha attacked the Kalachuri kingdom from the south, sometime after 600 CE. The invasion did not result in a complete conquest, as evident by Buddharaja's 609-610 CE (360 KE) Vidisha and 610-611 CE (361 KE) Anandapura grants. Buddharaja probably lost his sovereignty to Mangalesha's nephew Pulakeshin II.[3002]

Like his father and grand-father, Buddharaja described himself as a *Parama-Maheshvara* (devotee of Shiva). His queen Ananta-Mahayi belonged to the Pashupata sect.[3002]

Descendants

No concrete information is available about the successors of Buddharaja, but it is known that by 687 CE, the Kalachuris had become feudatories of the Chalukyas.[3002]

An inscription issued by a prince named Taralasvamin was found at Sankheda (where one of Shankaragana's grants was also found). This inscription describes Taralasvamin as a devotee of Shiva, and his father Maharaja Nanna as a member of the "Katachchuri" family. The inscription is dated to the year 346 of an unspecified era. Assuming the era as Kalachuri era, Taralasvamin would have been a contemporary of Shankaragana. However, Taralasvamin and Nanna are not mentioned in other Kalachuri records. Also, unlike

Figure 506: *Elephanta Caves*

other Kalachuri inscriptions, the date in this inscription is mentioned in decimal numbers. Moreover, some expressions in the inscription appear to have been borrowed from the 7th century Sendraka inscriptions. Because of these evidences, V. V. Mirashi considered Taralasvamin's inscription as a spurious one.[3003]

V. V. Mirashi connected the Kalachuris of Tripuri to the early Kalachuri dynasty. He theorizes that the early Kalachuris moved their capital from Mahishmati to Kalanjara, and from there to Tripuri.[3004]

Cultural contributions

Elephanta

The Elephanta Caves which contain Shaivite monuments are located along the Konkan coast, on the Elephanta Island near Mumbai. Historical evidence suggests that these monuments are associated with Krishnaraja, who was also a Shaivite.[3001]

The Kalachuris appear to have been the rulers of the Konkan coast, when some of the Elephanta monuments were built.[3001] Silver coins of Krishnaraja have been found along the Konkan coast, on the Salsette Island (now part of Mumbai) and in the Nashik district.[3001] Around 31 of his copper coins have been found on the Elephanta Island, which suggests that he was the patron of the main cave temple on the island.[3000] According to numismatist Shobhana Gokhale, these low-value coins may have been used to pay the wages of the workers involved in the cave excavation.[3002]

Figure 507: *Ellora Cave No. 29*

Ellora

The earliest of the Brahmanical caves at Ellora appear to have been built during the Kalachuri reign, and possibly under Kalachuri patronage. For example, the Ellora Cave No. 29 shows architectural and iconographic similarities with the Elephanta Caves.[3001] The earliest coin found at Ellora, in front of Cave No. 21 (Rameshvara), was issued by Krishnaraja.[2999]

Rulers

The following are the known rulers of the Kalachuri dynasty of Malwa with their estimated reigns (IAST names in brackets):[3005]

- Krishnaraja (Kṛṣṇarāja), r. c. 550-575 CE
- Shankaragana (Śaṃkaragaṇa), r. c. 575-600 CE
- Buddharaja (Buddharāja), r. c. 600-625 CE

References

Bibliography

<templatestyles src="Template:Refbegin/styles.css" />

- Charles Dillard Collins (1988). *The Iconography and Ritual of Siva at Elephanta*[3006]. SUNY Press. ISBN 9780887067730.

- Geri Hockfield Malandra (1993). *Unfolding A Mandala: The Buddhist Cave Temples at Ellora*[3007]. SUNY Press. ISBN 9780791413555.
- Ronald M. Davidson (2012). *Indian Esoteric Buddhism: A Social History of the Tantric Movement*[3008]. Columbia University Press. ISBN 9780231501026.
- V. V. Mirashi (1974). *Bhavabhuti*[3009]. Motilal Banarsidass. ISBN 9788120811805.

External links

 Wikimedia Commons has media related to ***Kalachuri Empire***.

- Coins of the Early Kalachuris[3010]

Hoysala Empire

Hoysala Empire	
Empire (Subordinate to the Western Chalukya Empire until 1187)	
1026–1343	
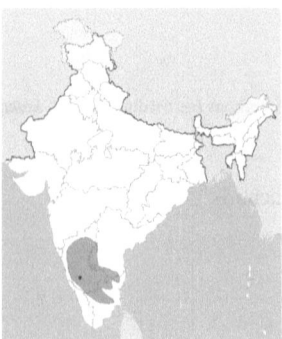 Extent of Hoysala Empire, 1200 CE	
Capital	Halebidu Belur
Languages	Kannada, Sanskrit
Religion	Hinduism, Jainism
Government	Monarchy
King	
•	1026–1047	Nripa Kama II
•	1292–1343	Veera Ballala III
History	
•	Earliest Hoysala records	950
•	Established	1026
•	Disestablished	1343
Preceded by	Succeeded by
Western Chalukya Empire	Vijayanagara Empire

Hoysala Kings (1026–1343)	
Nripa Kama II	(1026–1047)
Vinayaditya	(1047–1098)
Ereyanga	(1098–1102)
Veera Ballala I	(1102–1108)
Vishnuvardhana	(1108–1152)
Narasimha I	(1152–1173)
Veera Ballala II	(1173–1220)
Vira Narasimha II	(1220–1235)
Vira Someshwara	(1235–1263)
Narasimha III	(1263–1292)
Veera Ballala III	(1292–1343)
Harihara Raya (*Vijayanagara Empire*)	(1342–1355)

Part of a series on the
History of Karnataka

- Political history of medieval Karnataka
- Origin of Karnataka's name
- Kadambas and Gangas
- Chalukya Empire
- Rashtrakuta Empire
- Western Chalukya Empire
- Southern Kalachuri
- Hoysala Empire
- Vijayanagara Empire
- Bahmani Sultanate
- Bijapur Sultanate
- Kingdom of Mysore
- Nayakas of Keladi
- Nayakas of Chitradurga
- Haleri Kingdom

• Unification of Karnataka
Categories
• Architecture • Forts • Economies • Societies
• v • t • e[3011]

The **Hoysala Empire** was a Kannadiga power originating from the Indian subcontinent, that ruled most of the what is now Karnataka, India between the 10th and the 14th centuries. The capital of the Hoysalas was initially located at Belur but was later moved to Halebidu.

The Hoysala rulers were originally from Malenadu, an elevated region in the Western Ghats. In the 12th century, taking advantage of the internecine warfare between the Western Chalukya Empire and Kalachuris of Kalyani, they annexed areas of present-day Karnataka and the fertile areas north of the Kaveri delta in present-day Tamil Nadu. By the 13th century, they governed most of Karnataka, minor parts of Tamil Nadu and parts of western Andhra Pradesh and Telangana in the Deccan Plateau.

The Hoysala era was an important period in the development of art, architecture, and religion in South India. The empire is remembered today primarily for Hoysala architecture. Over a hundred surviving temples are scattered across Karnataka.

Well known temples "which exhibit an amazing display of sculptural exuberance" include the Chennakeshava Temple, Belur, the Hoysaleswara Temple, Halebidu, and the Chennakesava Temple, Somanathapura. The Hoysala rulers also patronised the fine arts, encouraging literature to flourish in Kannada and Sanskrit.

History

Kannada folklore tells a tale of a young man, Sala, who saved his Jain guru, Sudatta, by striking dead a tiger he encountered near the temple of the goddess Vasantika at Angadi, now called Sosevuru. The word "strike" literally translates to "hoy" in Old Kannada, hence the name "Hoy-sala". This legend first appeared in the Belur inscription of Vishnuvardhana (1117), but owing to several inconsistencies in the Sala story it remains in the realm of folklore.[3012,3013]

Figure 508: *Sala fighting the Lion, the emblem of the Hoysala Empire at Belur, Karnataka.*

The legend may have come into existence or gained popularity after King Vishnuvardhana's victory over the Cholas at Talakadu as the Hoysala emblem depicts the fight between the mythical warrior Sala and a tiger, the tiger being the emblem of the Cholas.[3014]

Early inscriptions, dated 1078 and 1090, have implied that the Hoysalas were descendants of the Yadava by referring to the Yadava *vamsa* (clan) as the "Hoysala *vamsa*". But there are no early records directly linking the Hoysalas to the Yadavas of North India.[3015,3016]

Historians refer to the founders of the dynasty as natives of Malenadu based on numerous inscriptions calling them *Maleparolganda* or "Lord of the Male (hills) chiefs" (*Malepas*).[3017,3018,3019,3020,3021,3022,3023,3024] This title in the Kannada language was proudly used by the Hoysala kings as their royal signature in their inscriptions. Literary sources from that time in Kannada (*Jatakatilaka*) and Sanskrit (*Gadyakarnamrita*) have also helped confirm they were natives of the region known today as Karnataka.[3025,3026]

The first Hoysala family record is dated 950 and names Arekalla as the chieftain, followed by Maruga and Nripa Kama I (976). The next ruler, Munda (1006–1026), was succeeded by Nripa Kama II who held such titles as *Permanadi* that show an early alliance with the Western Ganga dynasty.[3027] From these modest beginnings, the Hoysala dynasty began its transformation into a strong subordinate of the Western Chalukya Empire.[3028,3029] Through Vishnuvardhana's expansive military conquests, the Hoysalas achieved the status of a real kingdom for the first time.[3030,3031] He wrested Gangavadi from the Cholas in 1116 and moved the capital from Belur to Halebidu.[3032,3033,3034,3035]

Vishnuvardhana's ambition of creating an independent empire was fulfilled by his grandson Veera Ballala II, who freed the Hoysalas from subordination in 1187–1193.[3036,3037,3038] Thus the Hoysalas began as subordinates of the Western Chalukya Empire and gradually established their own empire in Karnataka with such strong Hoysala kings as Vishnuvardhana, Veera Ballala II and later Veera Ballala III. During this time, the Deccan Plateau saw a four-way struggle for hegemony – Pandyan, Kakatiya and Seuna being the other kingdoms.[3039] Veera Ballala II defeated the aggressive Pandya when they invaded the Chola kingdom.[3040,3041,3042,3043] He assumed the title "Establisher of the Chola Kingdom" (*Cholarajyapratishtacharya*), "Emperor of the south" (*Dakshina Chakravarthi*) and "Hoysala emperor" (*Hoysala Chakravarthi*).[3044] He founded the city of Bangalore according to Kannada folklore.

The Hoysalas extended their foothold in areas known today as Tamil Nadu around 1225, making the city of Kannanur Kuppam near Srirangam a provincial capital and giving them control over South Indian politics that began a period of Hoysala hegemony in the southern Deccan.[3045,3046,3047,3048] Vira Narasimha II's son Vira Someshwara earned the honorific "uncle" (*Mamadi*) from the Pandyas and Cholas. The Hoysala influence spread over Pandya kingdom also.[3049] Toward the end of the 13th century, Veera Ballala III recaptured territory in the Tamil country which had been lost to the Pandya uprising, thus uniting the northern and southern portions of the kingdom.[3050,3051,3052,3053]

Major political changes were taking place in the Deccan region in the early 14th century when significant areas of northern India were under Muslim rule. Alauddin Khalji, the Sultan of Delhi, was determined to bring South India under his domain and sent his commander, Malik Kafur, on a southern expedition to plunder the Seuna capital Devagiri in 1311.[3054] The Seuna empire was subjugated by 1318 and the Hoysala capital Halebidu was sacked twice, in 1311 and 1327.

By 1336, the Sultan had conquered the Pandyas of Madurai, the Kakatiyas of Warangal and the tiny kingdom of Kampili. The Hoysalas were the only remaining Hindu empire who resisted the invading armies.[3055] Veera Ballala III stationed himself at Tiruvannamalai and offered stiff resistance to invasions from the north and the Madurai Sultanate to the south.[3056] Then, after nearly three decades of resistance, Veera Ballala III was killed at the battle of Madurai in 1343, and the sovereign territories of the Hoysala empire were merged with the areas administered by Harihara I in the Tungabhadra River

Figure 509: *Gajapati pagoda, ca. 10th–13th century CE.*

region.[3057,3058] This new Hindu kingdom resisted the northern invasions and would later prosper and come to be known as the Vijayanagara Empire.[3059]

Economy

The Hoysala administration supported itself through revenues from an agrarian economy.[3060] The kings gave grants of land as rewards for service to beneficiaries who then became landlords to tenants producing agricultural goods and forest products. There were two types of landlords (*gavunda*); *gavunda* of people (*praja gavunda*) was lower in status than the wealthy lord of *gavundas* (*prabhu gavunda*).[3061] The highlands (*malnad* regions) with its temperate climate was suitable for raising cattle and the planting of orchards and spices. Paddy and corn were staple crops in the tropical plains (*Bailnad*). The Hoysalas collected taxes on irrigation systems including tanks, reservoirs with sluices, canals and wells which were built and maintained at the expense of local villagers. Irrigation tanks such as *Vishnusagara, Shantisagara, Ballalarayasagara* were created at the expense of the state.

Importing horses for use as general transportation and in army cavalries of Indian kingdoms was a flourishing business on the western seaboard.[3062] The forests were harvested for rich woods such as teak which was exported through ports located in the area of present-day Kerala. Song dynasty records from China mention the presence of Indian merchants in ports of South China, indicating active trade with overseas kingdoms.[3063] South India exported textiles, spices, medicinal plants, precious stones, pottery, salt made from salt

Figure 510: *Garuda pillar hero stone (virgal) at Halebidu with old Kannada inscription of about 1220 CE.*

pans, jewels, gold, ivory, rhino horn, ebony, aloe wood, perfumes, sandalwood, camphor and condiments to China, Dhofar, Aden, and Siraf (the entry-port to Egypt, Arabia and Persia).[3064] Architects (*Vishwakarmas*), sculptors, quarry workers, goldsmiths and other skilled craftsmen whose trade directly or indirectly related to temple construction were also prosperous due to the vigorous temple building activities.[3065,3066]

The village assembly was responsible for collecting government land taxes. Land revenue was called *Siddhaya* and included the original assessment (*Kula*) plus various cesses. Taxes were levied on professions, marriages, goods in transit on chariots or carriages, and domesticated animals. Taxes on commodities (gold, precious stones, perfumes, sandalwood, ropes, yarn, housing, hearths, shops, cattle pans, sugarcane presses) as well as produce (black pepper, betel leaves, ghee, paddy, spices, palm leaves, coconuts, sugar) are noted in village records. The village assembly could levy a tax for a specific purpose such as construction of a water tank.

Administration

In its administrative practices, the Hoysala Empire followed some of the well-established and proven methods of its predecessors covering administrative

Hoysala Empire 835

Figure 511: *Hoysala king Vishnuvardhana*

functions such as cabinet organisation and command, the structure of local governing bodies and the division of territory.[3067] Records show the names of many high-ranking positions reporting directly to the king. Senior ministers were called *Pancha Pradhanas*, ministers responsible for foreign affairs were designated *Sandhivigrahi* and the chief treasurer was *Mahabhandari* or *Hiranyabhandari*. *Dandanayakas* were in charge of armies and the chief justice of the Hoysala court was the *Dharmadhikari*.

The kingdom was divided into provinces named *Nadu*, *Vishaya*, *Kampana* and *Desha*, listed in descending order of geographical size.[3068] Each province had a local governing body consisting of a minister (*Mahapradhana*) and a treasurer (*Bhandari*) that reported to the ruler of that province (*Dandanayaka*). Under this local ruler were officials called *Heggaddes* and *Gavundas* who hired and supervised the local farmers and labourers recruited to till the land. Subordinate ruling clans such as Alupas continued to govern their respective territories while following the policies set by the empire.[3069]

An elite and well-trained force of bodyguards known as *Garudas* protected the members of the royal family at all times. These servants moved closely yet inconspicuously by the side of their master, their loyalty being so complete that they committed suicide after his death.[3070] Hero stones (*virgal*) erected in memory of these bodyguards are called Garuda pillars. The Garuda pillar at

Figure 512: *Chennakesava Temple, Somanathapura, built 1268 CE.*

the Hoysaleswara temple in Halebidu was erected in honor of Kuvara Lakshma, a minister and bodyguard of King Veera Ballala II.

King Vishnuvardhana's coins had the legends "victor at Nolambavadi" (*Nolambavadigonda*), "victor at Talakad" (*Talakadugonda*), "chief of the Malepas" (*Maleparolganda*), "Brave of Malepa" (*malapavira*) in Hoysala style Kannada script.[3071] Their gold coin was called *Honnu* or *Gadyana* and weighed 62 grains of gold. *Pana* or *Hana* was a tenth of the *Honnu*, *Haga* was a fourth of the *Pana* and *Visa* was fourth of *Haga*. There were other coins called *Bele* and *Kani*.

Culture

Religion

The defeat of the Jain Western Gangas by the Cholas in the early 11th century and the rising numbers of followers of Vaishnavism and Lingayatism in the 12th century was mirrored by a decreased interest in Jainism.[3072] Two notable locations of Jain worship in the Hoysala territory were Shravanabelagola and Panchakuta Basadi, Kambadahalli. The decline of Buddhism in South India began in the eighth century with the spread of Adi Shankara's Advaita Vedanta.[3073] The only places of Buddhist worship during the Hoysala time were at Dambal and Balligavi. Shantala Devi, queen of Vishnuvardhana, was a Jain but nevertheless commissioned the Hindu Kappe Chennigaraya temple in Belur, evidence that the royal family was tolerant of all religions.

During the rule of the Hoysalas, three important religious developments took place in present-day Karnataka inspired by three philosophers, Basava, Madhvacharya and Ramanuja.

While the origin of Lingayatism is debated, the movement grew through its association with Basava in the 12th century.[3074] Madhvacharya was critical of the teachings of Adi Shankara and argued the world is real and not an illusion.[3075] His Dvaita Vedanta gained popularity, enabling him to establish eight mathas in Udupi. Ramanuja, head of the Vaishnava monastery in Srirangam, preached the way of devotion (*bhakti marga*) and wrote *Sribhashya*, a critique on Adi Shankara's Advaita.[3076]

The effect of these religious developments on culture, literature, poetry and architecture in South India was profound. Important works of literature and poetry based on the teachings of these philosophers were written during the coming centuries. The Saluva, Tuluva and Aravidu dynasties of Vijayanagar empire were followers of Vaishnavism and a Vaishnava temple with an image of Ramanuja exists in the Vitthalapura area of Vijayanagara.[3077] Scholars in the later Kingdom of Mysore wrote Vaishnavite works upholding the teachings of Ramanuja.[3078] King Vishnuvardhana built many temples after his conversion from Jainism to Vaishnavism. The later saints of Madhvacharya's order, Jayatirtha, Vyasatirtha, Sripadaraja, Vadiraja Tirtha and devotees (*dasa*) such as Vijaya Dasa, Gopaladasa and others from the Karnataka region spread his teachings far and wide.[3079] His teachings inspired later philosophers like Vallabha in Gujarat and Chaitanya Mahaprabhu in Bengal.[3080] Another wave of devotion (*bhakti*) in the 17th century–18th century found inspiration in his teachings.[3081]

Society

Hoysala society in many ways reflected the emerging religious, political and cultural developments of those times. During this period, the society became increasingly sophisticated. The status of women was varied. Some royal women were involved in administrative matters as shown in contemporary records describing Queen Umadevi's administration of Halebidu in the absence of Veera Ballala II during his long military campaigns in northern territories. She also fought and defeated some antagonistic feudal rebels.[3082] Records describe the participation of women in the fine arts, such as Queen Shantala Devi's skill in dance and music, and the 12th century vachana sahitya poet and Lingayati mystic Akka Mahadevi's devotion to the *bhakti* movement is well known.[3083] Temple dancers (*Devadasi*) were common and some were well educated and accomplished in the arts. These qualifications gave them more freedom than other urban and rural women who were restricted to daily mundane tasks.[3084] The practice of sati in a voluntary form was prevalent and prostitution was socially acceptable. As in most of India, a caste system was conspicuously present.

Trade on the west coast brought many foreigners to India including Arabs, Jews, Persians, Han Chinese and people from the Malay Peninsula.[3085] Migration of people within Southern India as a result of the expansion of the empire produced an influx of new cultures and skills.[3086] In South India, towns were called *Pattana* or *Pattanam* and the marketplace, *Nagara* or *Nagaram*, the marketplace serving as the nuclei of a city. Some towns such as Shravanabelagola developed from a religious settlement in the 7th century to an important trading center by the 12th century with the arrival of rich traders, while towns like Belur attained the atmosphere of a regal city when King Vishnuvardhana built the Chennakesava Temple there. Large temples supported by royal patronage served religious, social, and judiciary purposes, elevating the king to the level of "God on earth".

Temple building served a commercial as well as a religious function and was not limited to any particular sect of Hinduism. Shaiva merchants of Halebidu financed the construction of the Hoysaleswara temple to compete with the Chennakesava temple built at Belur, elevating Halebidu to an important city as well. Hoysala temples however were secular and encouraged pilgrims of all Hindu sects, the Kesava temple at Somanathapura being an exception with strictly Vaishnava sculptural depictions. Temples built by rich landlords in rural areas fulfilled fiscal, political, cultural and religious needs of the agrarian communities. Irrespective of patronage, large temples served as establishments that provided employment to hundreds of people of various guilds and professions sustaining local communities as Hindu temples began to take on the shape of wealthy Buddhist monasteries.[3087]

Literature

Although Sanskrit literature remained popular during the Hoysala rule, royal patronage of local Kannada scholars increased.[3088,3089] In the 12th century some works were written in the *Champu* style,[3090] but distinctive Kannada metres became more widely accepted. The *Sangatya* metre used in compositions,[3091] *Shatpadi* (six line), *tripadi* (three line) metres in verses and *ragale* (lyrical poems) became fashionable. Jain works continued to extol the virtues of Tirthankaras (Jain saviour figures).[3092]

Figure 513: *Old Kannada inscription dated to 1182 of King Veera Ballala II at Akkana Basadi, Shravanabelagola.*

The Hoysala court supported scholars such as Janna, Rudrabhatta, Harihara and his nephew Raghavanka, whose works are enduring masterpieces in Kannada. In 1209, the Jain scholar Janna wrote *Yashodharacharite*, the story of a king who intends to perform a ritual sacrifice of two young boys to a local deity, Mariamma. Taking pity on the boys, the king releases them and gives up the practice of human sacrifice.[3093,3094] In honour of this work, Janna received the title "Emperor among poets" (*Kavichakravarthi*) from King Veera Ballala II.[3095]

Rudrabhatta, a Smarta Brahmin, was the earliest well-known Brahminical writer. HIs patron was Chandramouli, a minister of King Veera Ballala II.[3096] Based on the earlier work *Vishnu Purana*, he wrote *Jagannatha Vijaya* in the *Champu* style relating the life of Krishna leading up to his fight with the demon Banasura.

Harihara, (also known as Harisvara) a Lingayati writer and the patron of King Narasimha I, wrote the *Girijakalyana* in the old Jain *Champu* style which describes the marriage of Shiva and Parvati in ten sections.[3097,3098] He was one of the earliest Virashaiva writers who was not part of the *vachana* literary tradition. He came from a family of accountants (*Karanikas*) from Halebidu and spent many years in Hampi writing more than one hundred *ragales* (poems in

Figure 514: *"Darpanasundari" (lady with a mirror), one of the many madanakai decorating the Chennakeshava Temple, Belur.*

blank verse) in praise of Virupaksha (a form of Shiva).[3099] Raghavanka was the first to introduce the *Shatpadi* metre into Kannada literature in his *Harishchandra kavya* which is considered a classic even though it occasionally violates strict rules of Kannada grammar.

In Sanskrit, the philosopher Madhvacharya wrote the *Rigbhshya* on the Brahma Sutras (a logical explanation of Hindu scriptures, the Vedas) as well as many polemical works rebutting the doctrines of other schools. He relied more on the Puranas than the Vedas for logical proof of his philosophy.[3100] Another famous writing was *Rudraprshnabhashya* by Vidyatirtha.

Architecture

The modern interest in the Hoysalas is due to their patronage of art and architecture rather than their military conquests. The brisk temple building throughout the kingdom was accomplished despite constant threats from the Pandyas to the south and the Seunas Yadavas to the north. Their architectural style, an offshoot of the Western Chalukya style,[3101,3102] shows distinct Dravidian influences.[3103] The Hoysala architecture style is described as *Karnata Dravida* as distinguished from the traditional *Dravida*,[3104] and is considered an independent architectural tradition with many unique features.[3105,3106]

A feature of Hoysala temple architecture is its attention to exquisite detail and skilled craftsmanship.[3107] The tower over the temple shrine (*vimana*) is delicately finished with intricate carvings, showing attention to the ornate and elaborately detailed rather than to a tower form and height.[3108,3109] The stellate design of the base of the shrine with its rhythmic projections and recesses is carried through the tower in an orderly succession of decorated tiers.[3110,3111] Hoysala temple sculpture replicates this emphasis on delicacy and craftsmanship in its focus on depicting feminine beauty, grace and physique.[3112] The Hoysala artists achieved this with the use of Soapstone (Chloritic schist), a soft stone as basic building and sculptural material.[3113,3114]

The Chennakesava Temple at Belur (1117),[3115,3116] the Hoysaleswara temple at Halebidu (1121),[3117,3118] the Chennakesava Temple at Somanathapura (1279),[3119,3120] the temples at Arasikere (1220),[3121,3122] Amruthapura (1196),[3123,3124] Belavadi (1200),[3125,3126] Nuggehalli (1246),[3127,3128] Hosaholalu (1250),[3129,3130] Aralaguppe (1250),[3131] Korvangla (1173),[3132,3133] Haranhalli (1235),[3134] Mosale[3135,3136] and Basaralu (1234)[3137] are some of the notable examples of Hoysala art. While the temples at Belur and Halebidu are the best known because of the beauty of their sculptures, the Hoysala art finds more complete expression in the smaller and lesser known temples.[3138] The outer walls of all these temples contain an intricate array of stone sculptures and horizontal friezes (decorative mouldings) that depict the Hindu epics. These depictions are generally clockwise in the traditional direction of circumambulation (*pradakshina*). The temple of Halebidu has been described as an outstanding example of Hindu architecture[3139] and an important milestone in Indian architecture.[3140] The temples of Belur and Halebidu are a proposed UNESCO world heritage sites.

Figure 515: *Akkana Basadi, Shravanabelagola*

Figure 516: *Vesara style Vimana of the Lakshmi Narasimha temple at Nuggehalli (1246 CE)*

Figure 517: *Stellate Vimana, at Ishvara Temple (Arasikere) built in 1220 CE*

Figure 518: *Jain temple at Halebidu*

Figure 519: *Twin temples (1200 CE) at Mosale, the Nageshvara (near) and Chennakeshava temple (far)*

Figure 520: *A sculpture of a dancer on pillar bracket, 1117 CE, (Shilabaalika or Madanika) in the Chennakeshava temple at Belur*

Language

The support of the Hoysala rulers for the Kannada language was strong, and this is seen even in their epigraphs, often written in polished and poetic language, rather than prose, with illustrations of floral designs in the margins.[3141] According to historian Sheldon Pollock, the Hoysala era saw the complete displacement of Sanskrit, with Kannada dominating as the courtly language.[3142] Temples served as local schools where learned Brahmins taught in Sanskrit, while Jain and Buddhist monasteries educated novice monks. Schools of higher learning were called *Ghatikas*. The local Kannada language was widely used in the rising number of devotional movements to express the ecstatic experience of closeness to the deity (*vachanas* and *devaranama*). Literary works were written in it on palm leaves which were tied together. While in past centuries Jain works had dominated Kannada literature, Shaiva and early Brahminical works became popular during the Hoysala reign.[3143] Writings in Sanskrit included poetry, grammar, lexicon, manuals, rhetoric, commentaries on older works, prose fiction and drama.[3144] Inscriptions on stone (*Shilashasana*) and copper plates (*Tamarashasana*) were written mostly in Kannada but some were in Sanskrit or were bilingual. The sections of bilingual inscriptions stating the title, genealogy, origin myths of the king and benedictions were generally done in Sanskrit. Kannada was used to state terms of the

Figure 521: *Old Kannada inscription (1270 CE) of King Narasimha III at Keshava Temple, Somanathapura.*

grants, including information on the land, its boundaries, the participation of local authorities, rights and obligations of the grantee, taxes and dues, and witnesses. This ensured the content was clearly understood by the local people without ambiguity.[3145]

References

Books

<templatestyles src="Template:Refbegin/styles.css" />

- Ayyar, P. V. Jagadisa (1993) [1993]. *South Indian Shrines*. Asian Educational Services. ISBN 81-206-0151-3.
- Chopra, P.N.; Ravindran, T.K.; Subrahmanian, N (2003) [2003]. *History of South India (Ancient, Medieval and Modern) Part 1*. New Delhi: Chand Publications. ISBN 81-219-0153-7.
- Foekema, Gerard (1996) [1996]. *A Complete Guide To Hoysala Temples*. New Delhi: Abhinav. ISBN 81-7017-345-0.
- Foekema, Gerard (2003) [2003]. *Architecture decorated with architecture: Later medieval temples of Karnataka, 1000–1300 AD*. New Delhi: Munshiram Manoharlal Publishers Pvt. Ltd. ISBN 81-215-1089-9.

- Fritz, John M. and George Michell (editors) (2001). *New Light on Hampi: Recent Research at Vijayanagar*. Mumbai: MARG. ISBN 81-85026-53-X.
- Hardy, Adam (1995) [1995]. *Indian Temple Architecture: Form and Transformation-The Karnata Dravida Tradition 7th to 13th Centuries*. Abhinav Publications. ISBN 81-7017-312-4.
- Kamath, Suryanath U. (2001) [1980]. *A concise history of Karnataka: from pre-historic times to the present*. Bangalore: Jupiter books. LCCN 80905179[3146]. OCLC 7796041[3147].
- Keay, John (2000) [2000]. *India: A History*. New York: Grove Publications. ISBN 0-8021-3797-0.
- Moraes, George M. (1990) [1931]. *The Kadamba Kula, A History of Ancient and Medieval Karnataka*. New Delhi, Madras: Asian Educational Services. ISBN 81-206-0595-0.
- Narasimhacharya, R (1988) [1988]. *History of Kannada Literature*. New Delhi, Madras: Asian Educational Services. ISBN 81-206-0303-6.
- Pollock, Sheldon (2006). *The Language of Gods in the World of Men: Sanskrit, Culture and Power in Pre-modern India*. Berkeley and London: University of California Press. ISBN 0-520-24500-8.
- Rice, B.L. (2001) [1897]. *Mysore Gazetteer Compiled for Government-vol 1*. New Delhi, Madras: Asian Educational Services. ISBN 81-206-0977-8.
- Rice, E.P. (1982) [1921]. *Kannada Literature*. New Delhi: Asian Educational Services. ISBN 81-206-0063-0.
- Sastri, K.A. Nilakanta (2002) [1955]. *A history of South India from prehistoric times to the fall of Vijayanagar*. New Delhi: Indian Branch, Oxford University Press. ISBN 0-19-560686-8.
- Sen, Sailendra Nath (1999) [1999]. *Ancient Indian History and Civilization*. New Age Publishers. ISBN 81-224-1198-3.
- Shiva Prakash, H.S. (1997). "Kannada". In Ayyappapanicker. *Medieval Indian Literature:An Anthology*. Sahitya Akademi. ISBN 81-260-0365-0.
- Stien, Burton (1989) [1989]. *Vijayanagara*. Wiltshire: Cambridge University Press. ISBN 0-521-26693-9.
- Thapar, Romila (2003) [2003]. *The Penguin History of Early India*. New Delhi: Penguin Books. ISBN 0-14-302989-4.

Web

<templatestyles src="Template:Refbegin/styles.css" />

- Arthikaje, Mangalore. "Kannada, Kannadiga and Karnataka"[3148]. 1998–00 OurKarnataka.Com, Inc. Archived from the original[3149] on 4 November 2006. Retrieved 17 November 2006.

- Govindaraya Prabhu (1 November 2001). "Hoysala Coinage - Southern India"[3150]. Archived from the original[3151] on 19 January 2007. Retrieved 17 November 2006.
- "Hoysala Heritage, Prof. Settar"[3152]. *Frontline, Volume 20 – Issue 08, 12–25 April 2003*. Retrieved 17 November 2006.
- "The City of Boiled Beans"[3153]. *The Hindu, Thursday, 25 July 2002*. Chennai, India. 25 July 2002. Retrieved 17 November 2006.
- "Belur proposal for World Heritage Status"[3154]. *The Hindu, Sunday 25 July 2004*. Chennai, India. 25 July 2004. Retrieved 17 November 2006.
- "Hoysala Temples of Belur, by K. L. Kamat, 04 November 2006"[3155]. © *1996–2006 Kamat's Potpourri*. Retrieved 3 December 2006.

External links

 Wikimedia Commons has media related to *Hoysala Empire*.

- "Hoysala Dynasty, Jyothsna Kamat"[3156]. © *1996–2006 Kamat's Potpourri*. Retrieved 17 November 2006.
- "Indian Inscriptions-South Indian Inscriptions, (vols 9, 15,17,18)"[3157]. *What Is India Publishers (P) Ltd, Saturday, 18 November 2006*. Retrieved 17 November 2006.

<indicator name="featured-star"> ⭐ </indicator>

Chola dynasty

<indicator name="pp-default"> 🔒 </indicator>

Chola dynasty	
300s BCE–1279 CE	
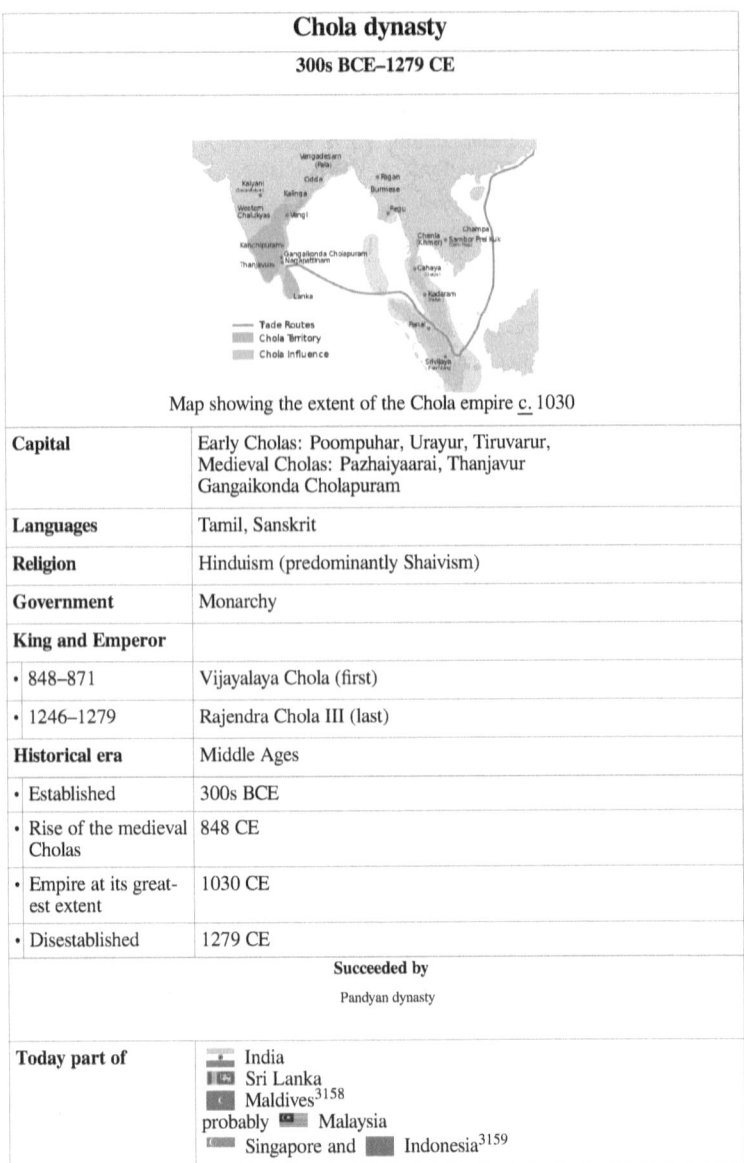 Map showing the extent of the Chola empire c. 1030	
Capital	Early Cholas: Poompuhar, Urayur, Tiruvarur, Medieval Cholas: Pazhaiyaarai, Thanjavur Gangaikonda Cholapuram
Languages	Tamil, Sanskrit
Religion	Hinduism (predominantly Shaivism)
Government	Monarchy
King and Emperor	
• 848–871	Vijayalaya Chola (first)
• 1246–1279	Rajendra Chola III (last)
Historical era	Middle Ages
• Established	300s BCE
• Rise of the medieval Cholas	848 CE
• Empire at its greatest extent	1030 CE
• Disestablished	1279 CE
Succeeded by	
Pandyan dynasty	
Today part of	🇮🇳 India 🇱🇰 Sri Lanka 🇲🇻 Maldives[3158] probably 🇲🇾 Malaysia 🇸🇬 Singapore and 🇮🇩 Indonesia[3159]

Chola dynasty

List of Chola kings and emperors

Early Cholas

- Ellalan
- Kulakkottan
- Ilamchetchenni
- Karikala
- Nedunkilli
- Nalankilli
- Killivalavan
- Kopperuncholan
- Kochchenganan
- Perunarkilli

Interregnum (c. 200 – c. 848)

Medieval Cholas

Vijayalaya	848–891(?)
Aditya I	891–907
Parantaka I	907–950
Gandaraditya	950–957
Arinjaya	956–957
Sundara (Parantaka II)	957–970
Aditya II	(co-regent)
Uttama	970–985
Rajaraja I	985–1014
Rajendra I	1012–1044
Rajadhiraja	1044–1054
Rajendra II	1054–1063
Virarajendra	1063–1070
Athirajendra	1070–1070

Later Cholas

Kulothunga I	1070–1120
Vikrama	1118–1135
Kulothunga II	1133–1150
Rajaraja II	1146–1173
Rajadhiraja II	1166–1178
Kulothunga III	1178–1218
Rajaraja III	1216–1256
Rajendra III	1246–1279

Related dynasties

Telugu Cholas of Andhra
Chodagangas of Kalinga
Rajahnate of Cebu

Chola society
• Chola government • Chola military • Chola Navy • Chola art • Chola literature • Flag of Chola • Great Living Chola Temples • Solesvara Temples • Poompuhar • Uraiyur • Melakadambur • Gangaikonda Cholapuram • Thanjavur • Tiruvarur
• v • t • e[3160]

Part of a series on
History of Tamil Nadu

- v
- t
- e[3161]

The **Chola dynasty** was one of the longest-ruling dynasties in the history of southern India. The earliest datable references to this Tamil dynasty are in inscriptions from the 3rd century BCE left by Ashoka, of the Maurya Empire (Ashoka Major Rock Edict No.13). As one of the Three Crowned Kings of Tamilakam, the dynasty continued to govern over varying territory until the 13th century CE.

The heartland of the Cholas was the fertile valley of the Kaveri River, but they ruled a significantly larger area at the height of their power from the later half of the 9th century till the beginning of the 13th century. The whole country south of the Tungabhadra was united and held as one state for a period of two centuries and more.[3162] Under Rajaraja Chola I and his successors Rajendra Chola I, Rajadhiraja Chola, Virarajendra Chola and Kulothunga Chola I the dynasty became a military, economic and cultural power in South Asia and South-East Asia.[3163] The power of the new empire was proclaimed to the eastern world by the expedition to the Ganges which Rajendra Chola I undertook and by the naval raids on cities of the maritime empire of Srivijaya, as well as by the repeated embassies to China.[3164] The Chola fleet represented the zenith of ancient Indian sea power.

During the period 1010–1153, the Chola territories stretched from the islands of the Maldives in the south to as far north as the banks of the Godavari River in Andhra Pradesh.[3165] Rajaraja Chola conquered peninsular South India, annexed parts of which is now Sri Lanka and occupied the islands of the Maldives. Rajendra Chola sent a victorious expedition to North India that touched the river Ganges and defeated the Pala ruler of Pataliputra, Mahipala. He also successfully invaded cities of Srivijaya of Malaysia and Indonesia.[3166] The Chola dynasty went into decline at the beginning of the 13th century with the rise of the Pandyan Dynasty, which ultimately caused their downfall.[3167,3168]

The Cholas left a lasting legacy. Their patronage of Tamil literature and their zeal in the building of temples has resulted in some great works of Tamil literature and architecture. The Chola kings were avid builders and envisioned the temples in their kingdoms not only as places of worship but also as centres of economic activity.[3169,3170] They pioneered a centralised form of government and established a disciplined bureaucracy. The Chola school of art spread to Southeast Asia and influenced the architecture and art of Southeast Asia.[3171,3172]

Origins

The Cholas are also known as the *Choda*.³¹⁷³ There is very little information available in regarding their origin. Its antiquity is evident from the mentions in ancient Tamil literature and in inscriptions. Later medieval Cholas also claimed a long and ancient lineage. Mentions in the early Sangam literature (c. 150 CE)³¹⁷⁴ indicate that the earliest kings of the dynasty antedated 100 CE. Cholas were mentioned in Ashokan Edicts of 3rd Century BCE as one of the neighboring countries existing in the South.Wikipedia:Citation needed

A commonly held view is that *Chola* is, like *Chera* and *Pandya*, the name of the ruling family or clan of immemorial antiquity. The annotator Parimelazhagar said: "The charity of people with ancient lineage (such as the Cholas, the Pandyas and the Cheras) are forever generous in spite of their reduced means". Other names in common use for the Cholas are *Killi* (கிள்ளி), *Valavan* (வளவன்) and *Sembiyan* (செம்பியன்). *Killi* perhaps comes from the Tamil *kil* (கிள்) meaning dig or cleave and conveys the idea of a digger or a worker of the land. This word often forms an integral part of early Chola names like Nedunkilli, Nalankilli and so on, but almost drops out of use in later times. *Valavan* is most probably connected with "*valam*" (வளம்) – fertility and means owner or ruler of a fertile country. *Sembiyan* is generally taken to mean a descendant of Shibi – a legendary hero whose self-sacrifice in saving a dove from the pursuit of a falcon figures among the early Chola legends and forms the subject matter of the Sibi Jataka among the Jataka stories of Buddhism.³¹⁷⁵ In Tamil lexicon *Chola* means *Soazhi* or *Saei* denoting a newly formed kingdom, in the lines of *Pandya* or the old country.³¹⁷⁶

There is very little written evidence available of the Cholas prior to the 7th century. Historic records exist thereafter, including inscriptions on temples. During the past 150 years, historians have gleaned significant knowledge on the subject from a variety of sources such as ancient Tamil Sangam literature, oral traditions, religious texts, temple and copperplate inscriptions. The main source for the available information of the early Cholas is the early Tamil literature of the Sangam Period.³¹⁷⁷</ref> There are also brief notices on the Chola country and its towns, ports and commerce furnished by the *Periplus of the Erythraean Sea* (*Periplus Maris Erythraei*), and in the slightly later work of the geographer Ptolemy. *Mahavamsa*, a Buddhist text written down during the 5th century CE, recounts a number of conflicts between the inhabitants of Ceylon and Cholas in the 1st century BCE.³¹⁷⁸ Cholas are mentioned in the Pillars of Ashoka (inscribed 273 BCE–232 BCE) inscriptions, where they are mentioned among the kingdoms which, though not subject to Ashoka, were on friendly terms with him.³¹⁷⁹</ref>

History

The history of the Cholas falls into four periods: the Early Cholas of the Sangam literature, the interregnum between the fall of the Sangam Cholas and the rise of the Imperial medieval Cholas under Vijayalaya (c. 848), the dynasty of Vijayalaya, and finally the Later Chola dynasty of Kulothunga Chola I from the third quarter of the 11th century.[3180]</ref>

Early Cholas

The earliest Chola kings for whom there is tangible evidence are mentioned in the Sangam literature. Scholars generally agree that this literature belongs to the second or first few centuries of the common era. The internal chronology of this literature is still far from settled, and at present a connected account of the history of the period cannot be derived. It records the names of the kings and the princes, and of the poets who extolled them.[3181]

The Sangam literature also records legends about mythical Chola kings.[3182] These myths speak of the Chola king Kantaman, a supposed contemporary of the sage Agastya, whose devotion brought the river Kaveri into existence.Wikipedia:Citation needed Two names are prominent among those Chola kings known to have existed who feature in Sangam literature: Karikala Chola and Kocengannan.[3183,3184,3185,3186] There are no sure means of settling the order of succession, of fixing their relations with one another and with many other princelings of around the same period.[3187,3188] Urayur (now a part of Thiruchirapalli) was their oldest capital.[3182] Kaveripattinam also served as an early Chola capital.[3189] The *Mahavamsa* mentions that an ethnic Tamil adventurer, a Chola prince known as Ellalan, invaded the island Sri Lanka and conquered it around 235 BCE with the help of a Mysore army.[3182]

Interregnum

There is not much information about the transition period of around three centuries from the end of the Sangam age (c. 300) to that in which the Pandyas and Pallavas dominated the Tamil country. An obscure dynasty, the Kalabhras invaded Tamil country, displaced the existing kingdoms and ruled during that time.[3190,3191,3192] They were displaced by the Pallava dynasty and the Pandyan dynasty in the 6th century.[3184,3193] Little is known of the fate of the Cholas during the succeeding three centuries until the accession of Vijayalaya in the second quarter of the 9th century.[3194] As per inscriptions found in and around Thanjavur shows that the kingdom was ruled by Mutharaiyars for three centuries which was ended by Vijayalaya chola by Capturing Thanjavur from Ilango Mutharaiyar somewhere between 848-851.

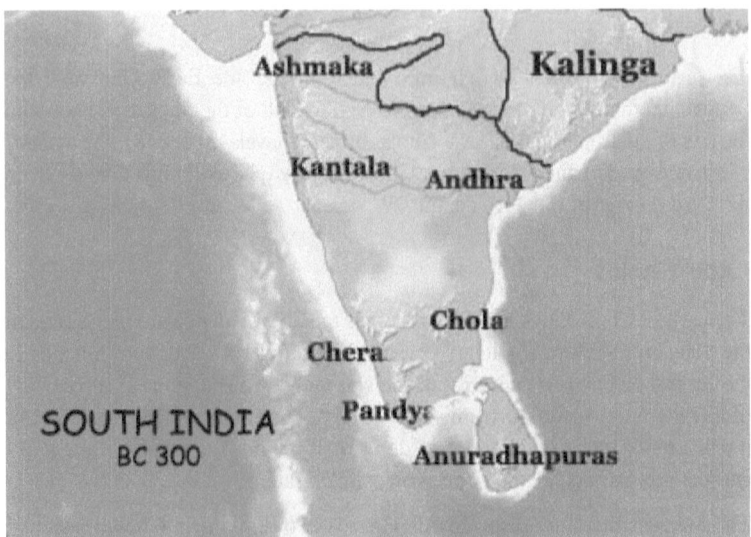

Figure 522: *South India in BC 300, showing the Chera, Pandya and Chola Kingdoms*

Epigraphy and literature provide few glimpses of the transformations that came over this line of kings during this long interval. It is certain that when the power of the Cholas fell to its lowest ebb and that of the Pandyas and Pallavas rose to the north and south of them,[3185,3195] this dynasty was compelled to seek refuge and patronage under their more successful rivals.[3196,3197]</ref> The Cholas continued to rule over a diminished territory in the neighbourhood of Uraiyur, but only in a minor capacity. In spite of their reduced powers, the Pandayas and Pallavas accepted Chola princesses in marriage, possibly out of regard for their reputation.[3198]</ref> Numerous Pallava inscriptions of this period mention their having fought rulers of the Chola country.[3199] Simhavishnu (575–600) is also stated to have seized the Chola country. Mahendravarman I was called the "crown of the Chola country" in his inscriptions.Wikipedia:Citation needed</ref> Despite this loss in influence and power, it is unlikely that the Cholas lost total grip of the territory around Uraiyur, their old capital, as Vijayalaya, when he rose to prominence hailed from that area.[3200,3201]

Around the 7th century, a Chola kingdom flourished in present-day Andhra Pradesh.[3200] These Telugu Cholas traced their descent to the early Sangam Cholas. However, it is not known if they had any relation to the early Cholas.[3203] It is possible that a branch of the Tamil Cholas migrated north during the time of the Pallavas to establish a kingdom of their own, away from

Figure 523: *An early silver coin of Uttama Chola found in Sri Lanka showing the tiger emblem of the Chola and in Nagari script.*[3202]

the dominating influences of the Pandyas and Pallavas.[3204]</ref> The Chinese pilgrim Xuanzang, who spent several months in Kanchipuram during 639–640 writes about the "kingdom of Culi-ya", in an apparent reference to these Telugu Cholas.[3194,3205]

Imperial Cholas

Vijayalaya was the founder of the Imperial Chola dynasty which was the beginning of one of the most splendid empires in Indian history.[3206] Vijayalaya, possibly a feudatory of the Pallava dynasty, took an opportunity arising out of a conflict between the Pandya dynasty and Pallava dynasty in c. 850, captured Thanjavur from Muttarayar, and established the imperial line of the medieval Chola Dynasty.[3207,3208] Thanjavur became the capital of the Imperial Chola Dynasty.[3209]

The Chola dynasty was at the peak of its influence and power during the medieval period.[3210] Through their leadership and vision, Chola kings expanded their territory and influence. The second Chola King, Aditya I, caused the demise of the Pallava dynasty and defeated the Pandyan dynasty of Madurai in 885, occupied large parts of the Kannada country, and had marital ties with the Western Ganga dynasty. In 925, his son Parantaka I conquered Sri Lanka (known as Ilangai). Parantaka I also defeated the Rashtrakuta dynasty under Krishna II in the battle of Vallala.[3211]

Rajaraja Chola I and Rajendra Chola I were the greatest rulers of the Chola dynasty, extending it beyond the traditional limits of a Tamil kingdom.[3196] At its peak, the Chola Empire stretched from the island of Sri Lanka in the south

Figure 524: *Detail of the statue of Rajaraja Chola at Brihadisvara Temple at Thanjavur.*

to the Godavari-Krishna river basin in the north, up to the Konkan coast in Bhatkal, the entire Malabar Coast in addition to Lakshadweep, Maldives, and vast areas of Chera country. Rajaraja Chola I was a ruler with inexhaustible energy, and he applied himself to the task of governance with the same zeal that he had shown in waging wars. He integrated his empire into a tight administrative grid under royal control, and at the same time strengthened local self-government. Therefore, he conducted a land survey in 1000 CE to effectively marshall the resources of his empire.[3212] He also built the Brihadeeswarar Temple in 1010 CE.

Rajendra Chola I conquered Odisha and his armies continued to march further north and defeated the forces of the Pala Dynasty of Bengal and reached the Ganges river in north India.[3213] Rajendra Chola I built a new capital called Gangaikonda Cholapuram to celebrate his victories in northern India.[3214] Rajendra Chola I successfully invaded the Srivijaya kingdom in Southeast Asia which led to the decline of the empire there.[3215] This expedition had such a great impression to the Malay people of the medieval period that his name was mentioned in the corrupted form as Raja Chulan in the medieval Malay chronicle *Sejarah Melayu*.[3216,3217,3218] He also completed the conquest of the island of Sri Lanka and took the Sinhala king Mahinda V as a prisoner, in addition to his conquests of Rattapadi (territories of the Rashtrakutas, Chalukya country,

Figure 525: *Gopuram Corner View of Thanjavur Brihadeeswara Temple.*

Talakkad, and Kolar, where the Kolaramma temple still has his portrait statue) in Kannada country.[3219] Rajendra's territories included the area falling on the Ganges-Hooghly-Damodar basin,[3220] as well as Sri Lanka and Maldives.[3207] The kingdoms along the east coast of India up to the river Ganges acknowledged Chola suzerainty.[3221] Three diplomatic missions were sent to China in 1016, 1033, and 1077.[3207]

The Western Chalukya Empire under Satyashraya and Someshvara I tried to wriggle out of Chola domination from time to time, primarily due to the Chola influence in the Vengi kingdom.[3222] The Western Chalukyas mounted several unsuccessful attempts to engage the Chola emperors in war, and except for a brief occupation of Vengi territories between 1118–1126, all their other attempts ended in failure with successive Chola emperors routing the armies of the Chalukyas at various places in many wars. Virarajendra Chola defeated Someshvara II of the Western Chalukya Empire and made an alliance with Prince Vikramaditya VI.[3223] Cholas always successfully controlled the Chalukyas in the western Deccan by defeating them in war and levying tribute on them.[3224] Even under the emperors of the Cholas like Kulothunga I and Vikrama Chola, the wars against the Chalukyas were mainly fought in Chalukya territories in Karnataka or in the Telugu country like Vengi, Kakinada, Anantapur, or Gutti. Then the former feudatories like the Hoysalas, Yadvas, and Kakatiyas steadily increased their power and finally replaced the

Figure 526: *Brihadeeswara Temple Entrance Gopurams, Thanjavur*

Figure 527: *Model of a Chola's ship's hull (200—848 CE), built by the ASI, based on a wreck 19 miles off the coast of Poombuhar, displayed in a Museum in Tirunelveli.*

Figure 528: *Airavateswara Temple, Darasuram in Thanjavur District.*

Chalukyas.[3225] With the occupation of Dharwar in North Central Karnataka by the Hoysalas under Vishnuvardhana, where he based himself with his son Narasimha I in-charge at the Hoysala capital Dwarasamudra around 1149, and with the Kalachuris occupying the Chalukyan capital for over 35 years from around 1150–1151, the Chalukya kingdom was already starting to dissolve.[3226]

The Cholas under Kulothunga Chola III collaborated to the herald the dissolution of the Chalukyas by aiding Hoysalas under Veera Ballala II, the son-in-law of the Chola monarch, and defeated the Western Chalukyas in a series of wars with Someshvara IV between 1185–1190. The last Chalukya king's territories did not even include the erstwhile Chalukyan capitals Badami, Manyakheta or Kalyani. That was the final dissolution of Chalukyan power though the Chalukyas existed only in name since 1135–1140. But the Cholas remained stable until 1215, were absorbed by the Pandyan empire and ceased to exist by 1279.[3227]

On the other hand, throughout the period from 1150–1280, the staunchest opponents of the Cholas were Pandya princes who tried to win independence for their traditional territories. This period saw constant warfare between the Cholas and the Pandyas. The Cholas also fought regular wars with the Eastern Gangas of Kalinga, protected Vengi though it remained largely independent under Chola control, and had domination of the entire eastern coast with their feudatories the Telugu Cholas, Velananti Cholas, Renandu Cholas etc. who also always aided the Cholas in their successful campaigns against the

Chalukyas and levying tribute on the Kannada kingdoms and fought constantly with the Sinhalas, who attempted to overthrow the Chola occupation of Lanka, but until the time of the Later Chola king Kulottunga I the Cholas had firm control over Lanka. A Later Chola king, Rajadhiraja Chola II, was strong enough to prevail over a confederation of five Pandya princes who were aided by their traditional friend, the king of Lanka, this once again gave control of Lanka to the Cholas despite the fact that they were not strong under the resolute Rajadhiraja Chola II. However, his successor, the last great Chola monarch Kulottunga Chola III reinforced the hold of the Cholas by quelling rebellion and disturbances in Lanka and Madurai, defeated Hoysala generals under Veera Ballala II in Karuvur, in addition to holding on to his traditional territories in Tamil country, Eastern Gangavadi, Draksharama, Vengi and Kalinga. After this, he entered into a marital alliance with Veera Ballala II (with Ballala's marriage to a Chola princess) and his relationship with Hoysalas seems to have become friendlier.[3224,3228]</ref>

Overseas conquests

During the reign of Rajaraja Chola I and his successors Rajendra Chola I, Virarajendra Chola and Kulothunga Chola I the Chola armies invaded Sri Lanka, the Maldives and parts of Southeast Asia like Malaysia, Indonesia and Southern Thailand[3229] of the Srivijaya Empire in the 11th century. Rajaraja Chola I launched several naval campaigns that resulted in the capture of Sri Lanka, Maldives and the Malabar Coast.[3230] In 1025, Rajendra Chola launched naval raids on ports of Srivijaya and against the Burmese kingdom of Pegu.[3231] A Chola inscription states that he captured or plundered 14 places, which have been identified with Palembang, Tambralinga and Kedah among others.[3232] A second invasion was led by Virarajendra Chola, who conquered Kedah in Malaysia of Srivijaya in the late 11th century.[3233]

Later Cholas (1070–1279)

Marital and political alliances between the Eastern Chalukyas began during the reign of Rajaraja following his invasion of Vengi. Rajaraja Chola's daughter married Chalukya prince Vimaladitya[3234] and Rajendra Chola's daughter Ammanga Devi was married to the Eastern Chalukya prince Rajaraja Narendra.[3235] Virarajendra Chola's son, Athirajendra Chola, was assassinated in a civil disturbance in 1070, and Kulothunga Chola I, the son of Ammanga Devi and Rajaraja Narendra, ascended the Chola throne. Thus began the Later Chola dynasty.[3236]

The Later Chola dynasty was led by capable rulers such as Kulothunga Chola I, his son Vikrama Chola, other successors like Rajaraja Chola II, Rajadhiraja Chola II, and Kulothunga Chola III, who conquered Kalinga, Ilam, and

Chola dynasty

Figure 529: *Portrait of Rajaraja Chola and his guru Karuvurar at Brihadeeswarar Temple*

Kataha. However, the rule of the later Cholas between 1218, starting with Rajaraja Chola II, to the last emperor Rajendra Chola III was not as strong as those of the emperors between 850–1215. Around 1118, they lost control of Vengi to the Western Chalukya and Gangavadi (southern Mysore districts) to the Hoysala Empire. However, these were only temporary setbacks, because immediately following the accession of king Vikrama Chola, the son and successor of Kulothunga Chola I, the Cholas lost no time in recovering the province of Vengi by defeating Chalukya Someshvara III and also recovering Gangavadi from the Hoysalas. The Chola Empire, though not as strong as between 850–1150, was still largely territorially intact under Rajaraja Chola II (1146–1175) a fact attested by the construction and completion of the third grand Chola architectural marvel, the chariot-shaped Airavatesvara Temple at Dharasuram on the outskirts of modern Kumbakonam. Chola administration and territorial integrity until the rule of Kulothunga Chola III was stable and very prosperous up to 1215, but during his rule itself, the decline of the Chola power started following his defeat by Maravarman Sundara Pandiyan II in 1215–16.[3237] Subsequently, the Cholas also lost control of the island of Lanka and were driven out by the revival of Sinhala power.Wikipedia:Citation needed

In continuation of the decline, also marked by the resurgence of the Pandyan dynasty as the most powerful rulers in South India, a lack of a controlling central administration in its erstwhile-Pandyan territories prompted a number of claimants to the Pandya throne to cause a civil war in which the Sinhalas and the Cholas were involved by proxy. Details of the Pandyan civil war and the role played by the Cholas and Sinhalas, are present in the *Mahavamsa* as well as the Pallavarayanpettai Inscriptions.[3238,3239]

The Cholas, under Rajaraja Chola III and later, his successor Rajendra Chola III, were quite weak and therefore, experienced continuous trouble. One feudatory, the Kadava chieftain Kopperunchinga I, even held Rajaraja Chola III as hostage for sometime.[3240,3241] At the close of the 12th century, the growing influence of the Hoysalas replaced the declining Chalukyas as the main player in the Kannada country, but they too faced constant trouble from the Seunas and the Kalachuris, who were occupying Chalukya capital because those empires were their new rivals. So naturally, the Hoysalas found it convenient to have friendly relations with the Cholas from the time of Kulothunga Chola III, who had defeated Hoysala Veera Ballala II, who had subsequent marital relations with the Chola monarch. This continued during the time of Rajaraja Chola III the son and successor of Kulothunga Chola III[3237,3242]

The Pandyas in the south had risen to the rank of a great power who ultimately banished the Hoysalas from Malanadu or Kannada country, who were allies of the Cholas from Tamil country and the demise of the Cholas themselves ultimately was caused by the Pandyas in 1279. The Pandyas first steadily gained control of the Tamil country as well as territories in Sri Lanka, Chera country, Telugu country under Maravarman Sundara Pandiyan II and his able successor Jatavarman Sundara Pandyan before inflicting several defeats on the joint forces of the Cholas under Rajaraja Chola III, his successor Rajendra Chola III and the Hoysalas under Someshwara, his son Ramanatha[3237] Rajendra III tried to survive by aligning with the Kadava Pallavas and the Hoysalas in turn in order to counter the constantly rising power of the Pandyans who were the major players in the Tamil country from 1215 and had intelligently consolidated their position in Madurai-Rameswaram-Ilam-Cheranadu and Kanyakumari belt, and had been steadily increasing their territories in the Kaveri belt between Dindigul-Tiruchy-Karur-Satyamangalam as well as in the Kaveri Delta i.e., Thanjavur-Mayuram-Chidambaram-Vriddhachalam-Kanchi, finally marching all the way up to Arcot—Tirumalai-Nellore-Visayawadai-Vengi-Kalingam belt by 1250.[3243]

The Pandyas steadily routed both the Hoysalas and the Cholas.[3244] They also dispossessed the Hoysalas, by defeating them under Jatavarman Sundara Pandiyan at Kannanur Kuppam.[3245] At the close of Rajendra's reign, the Pandyan empire was at the height of prosperity and had taken the place of the Chola empire in the eyes of the foreign observers.[3246] The last recorded date of Rajendra III is 1279. There is no evidence that Rajendra was followed immediately by another Chola prince.[3247,3248] The Hoysalas were routed from Kannanur Kuppam around 1279 by Kulasekhara Pandiyan and in the same war the last Chola emperor Rajendra III was routed and the Chola empire ceased to exist thereafter. Thus the Chola empire was completely overshadowed by the Pandyan empire and sank into obscurity and ceased to exist by the end of the 13th century.[3241,3248]

Administration and society

Chola territory

According to Tamil tradition, the Chola country comprised the region that includes the modern-day Tiruchirapalli District, Tiruvarur District, Nagapattinam District, Ariyalur District, Perambalur district, Pudukkottai district, Thanjavur District in Tamil Nadu and Karaikal District. The river Kaveri and its tributaries dominate this landscape of generally flat country that gradually slopes towards the sea, unbroken by major hills or valleys. The river, which is also known as the *Ponni* (*Golden*) river, had a special place in the culture of Cholas. The annual floods in the Kaveri marked an occasion for celebration, known as *Adiperukku*, in which the whole nation took part.Wikipedia:Citation needed

Kaveripoompattinam on the coast near the Kaveri delta was a major port town.[3182] Ptolemy knew of this, which he called Khaberis, and the other port town of Nagappattinam as the most important centres of Cholas.[3249] These two towns became hubs of trade and commerce and attracted many religious faiths, including Buddhism.[3250]</ref> Roman ships found their way into these ports. Roman coins dating from the early centuries of the common era have been found near the Kaveri delta.[3251] Wikipedia:Citing sources[3252]

The other major towns were Thanjavur, Uraiyur and Kudanthai, now known as Kumbakonam.[3182] After Rajendra Chola moved his capital to Gangaikonda Cholapuram, Thanjavur lost its importance.[3253]

Government

In the age of the Cholas, the whole of South India was for the first time brought under a single government.[3255]

The Cholas' system of government was monarchical, as in the Sangam age.[3184] However, there was little in common between the local chiefdoms of the earlier period and the imperial-like states of Rajaraja Chola and his successors.[3256] Aside from the early capital at Thanjavur and the later on at Gangaikonda

Figure 530: *The mandalams of the Chola empire, c. 11th century.*[3254]

Cholapuram, Kanchipuram and Madurai were considered to be regional capitals in which occasional courts were held. The king was the supreme leader and a benevolent authoritarian. His administrative role consisted of issuing oral commands to responsible officers when representations were made to him. Due to the lack of a legislature or a legislative system in the modern sense, the fairness of king's orders dependent on his morality and belief in *Dharma*. The Chola kings built temples and endowed them with great wealth. The temples acted not only as places of worship but also as centres of economic activity, benefiting the community as a whole.[3257] Some of the output of villages throughout the kingdom was given to temples that reinvested some of the wealth accumulated as loans to the settlements.[3258] The Chola Dynasty was divided into several provinces called Mandalams which were further divided into Valanadus and these Valanadus were sub-divided into units called Kottams or Kutrams.[3259] According to Kathleen Gough, during the Chola period the Vellalar were the "dominant secular aristocratic caste ... providing the courtiers, most of the army officers, the lower ranks of the kingdom's bureaucracy, and the upper layer of the peasantry".[3260]

Before the reign of Rajaraja Chola I huge parts of the Chola territory were ruled by hereditary lords and local princes who were in a loose alliance with the Chola rulers. Thereafter, until the reign of Vikrama Chola in 1133 CE when the Chola power was at its peak, these hereditary lords and local princes virtually vanished from the Chola records and were either replaced or turned into dependent officials. Through these dependent officials the administration was improved and the Chola kings were able to exercise a closer control over the different parts of the empire.[3261] There was an expansion of the administrative structure, particularly from the reign of Rajaraja Chola I onwards. The government at this time had a large land revenue department, consisting of several tiers, which was largely concerned with maintaining accounts. The assessment and collection of revenue were undertaken by corporate bodies such as the ur, nadu, sabha, nagaram and sometimes by local chieftains who passed the revenue to the centre. During the reign of Rajaraja Chola I, the state initiated a massive project of land survey and assessment and there was a reorganisation of the empire into units known as valanadus.[3262]

The order of the King was first communicated by the executive officer to the local authorities. Afterwards the records of the transaction was drawn up and attested by a number of witnesses who were either local magnates or government officers.[3263]

At local government level, every village was a self-governing unit. A number of villages constituted a larger entity known as a *Kurram, Nadu* or *Kottam*, depending on the area.[3264,3265,3266] A number of *Kurrams* constituted a *valanadu*.[3267] These structures underwent constant change and refinement throughout the Chola period.[3268]

Justice was mostly a local matter in the Chola Empire; minor disputes were settled at the village level.[3266] Punishment for minor crimes were in the form of fines or a direction for the offender to donate to some charitable endowment. Even crimes such as manslaughter or murder were punished with fines. Crimes of the state, such as treason, were heard and decided by the king himself; the typical punishment in these cases was either execution or confiscation of property.[3269]

Military

The Chola dynasty had a professional military, of which the king was the supreme commander. It had four elements, comprising the cavalry, the elephant corps, several divisions of infantry and a navy.[3270] There were regiments of bowmen and swordsmen while the swordsmen were the most permanent and dependable troops. The Chola army was spread all over the country and was stationed in local garrisons or military camps known as *Kodagams*. The elephants played a major role in the army and the dynasty had numerous war elephants. These carried houses or huge Howdahs on their backs, full of soldiers who shot arrows at long range and who fought with spears at close quarters.[3271]

The Chola rulers built several palaces and fortifications to protect their cities. The fortifications were mostly made up of bricks but other materials like stone, wood and mud were also used.[3272,3273] According to the ancient Tamil text *Silappadikaram*, the Tamil kings defended their forts with catapults that threw stones, huge cauldrons of boiling water or molten lead, and hooks, chains and traps.[3274,3275] Wikipedia:Verifiability

The soldiers of the Chola dynasty used weapons such as swords, bows, javelins, spears and shields which were made up of steel.[3276] Particularly the famous Wootz steel, which has a long history in south India dating back to the period before the Christian era, seems also be used to produce weapons.[3277] The army consisted of people from different castes but the warriors of the Kaikolar and Vellalar castes played a prominent role.[3278,3279]

The Chola navy was the zenith of ancient India sea power.[3271] It played a vital role in the expansion of the empire, including the conquest of the Ceylon islands and naval raids on Srivijaya.[3280] The navy grew both in size and status during the medieval Cholas reign. The Chola admirals commanded much respect and prestige. The navy commanders also acted as diplomats in some instances. From 900 to 1100, the navy had grown from a small backwater entity to that of a potent power projection and diplomatic symbol in all of Asia, but was gradually reduced in significance when the Cholas fought land battles subjugating the Chalukyas of the Andhra-Kannada area in South India.[3281]

A martial art called *Silambam* was patronised by the Chola rulers. Ancient and medieval Tamil texts mention different forms of martial traditions but the ultimate expression of the loyalty of the warrior to his commander was a form of martial suicide called *Navakandam*. The medieval *Kalingathu Parani* text, which celebrates the victory of Kulothunga Chola I and his general in the battle for Kalinga, describes the practice in detail.

Economy

Land revenue and trade tax were the main source of income.[3282] The Chola rulers issued their coins in gold, silver and copper.[3283] The Chola economy was based on three tiers—at the local level, agricultural settlements formed the foundation to commercial towns nagaram, which acted as redistribution centres for externally produced items bound for consumption in the local economy and as sources of products made by nagaram artisans for the international trade. At the top of this economic pyramid were the elite merchant groups (*samayam*) who organised and dominated the regions international maritime trade.[3284] Wikipedia:Please clarify

One of the main articles which were exported to foreign countries were cotton cloth.[3285] Uraiyur, the capital of the early Chola rulers, was a famous centre for cotton textiles which were praised by Tamil poets.[3286,3287] The Chola rulers actively encouraged the weaving industry and derived revenue from it.[3288] During this period the weavers started to organise themselves into guilds.[3289] The weavers had their own residential sector in all towns. The most important weaving communities in early medieval times were the Saliyar and Kaikolar.[3288] During the Chola period silk weaving attained a high degree and Kanchipuram became one of the main centres for silk.[3290,3291]

Metal crafts reached its zenith during the 10th to 11th centuries because the Chola rulers like Chembian Maadevi extended their patronage to metal craftsmen.[3292] Wootz steel was a major export item.[3293]

The farmers occupied one of the highest positions in society.[3294] These were the Vellalar community who formed the nobility or the landed aristocracy of the country and who were economically a powerful group.[3295] Agriculture was the principal occupation for many people. Besides the landowners, there were others dependent on agriculture.[3296] The Vellalar community was the dominant secular aristocratic caste under the Chola rulers, providing the courtiers, most of the army officers, the lower ranks of the bureaucracy and the upper layer of the peasantry.[3260]

In almost all villages the distinction between persons paying the land-tax (iraikudigal) and those who did not was clearly established. There was a class of hired day-labourers who assisted in agricultural operations on the estates of other people and received a daily wage. All cultivable land was held in one of the three broad classes of tenure which can be distinguished as peasant proprietorship called vellan-vagai, service tenure and eleemosynary tenure resulting from charitable gifts.[3297] The vellan-vagai was the ordinary ryotwari village of modern times, having direct relations with the government and paying a land-tax liable to revision from time to time.[3284] The vellan-vagai villages fell into two broad classes- one directly remitting a variable annual revenue to the state and the other paying dues of a more or less fixed character to the public institutions like temples to which they were assigned.[3298] The prosperity of an agricultural country depends to a large extent on the facilities provided for irrigation. Apart from sinking wells and excavating tanks, the Chola rulers threw mighty stone dams across the Kaveri and other rivers, and cut out channels to distribute water over large tracts of land.[3299] Rajendra Chola I dug near his capital an artificial lake, which was filled with water from the Kolerun and the Vellar rivers.[3298]

There existed a brisk internal trade in several articles carried on by the organised mercantile corporations in various parts of the country. The metal industries and the jewellers art had reached a high degree of excellence. The manufacture of sea-salt was carried on under government supervision and control. Trade was carried on by merchants organised in guilds. The guilds described sometimes by the terms nanadesis were a powerful autonomous corporation of merchants which visited different countries in the course of their trade. They had their own mercenary army for the protection of their merchandise. There were also local organisations of merchants called *"nagaram"* in big centres of trade like Kanchipuram and Mamallapuram.[3300,3298]

Hospitals

Hospitals were maintained by the Chola kings, whose government gave lands for that purpose. The Tirumukkudal inscription shows that a hospital was named after Vira Chola. Many diseases were cured by the doctors of the hospital, which was under the control of a chief physician who was paid annually 80 Kalams of paddy, 8 Kasus and a grant of land. Apart from the doctors, other remunerated staff included a nurse, barber (who performed minor operations) and a waterman.[3301]

The Chola queen Kundavai also established a hospital at Tanjavur and gave land for the perpetual maintenance of it.[3302,3303]

Society

During the Chola period several guilds, communities and castes emerged. The guild was one of the most significant institutions of south India and merchants organised themselves into guilds. The best known of these were the Manigramam and Ayyavole guilds though other guilds such as Anjuvannam and Valanjiyar were also in existence.[3304] The farmers occupied one of the highest positions in society. These were the Vellalar community who formed the nobility or the landed aristocracy of the country and who were economically a powerful group.[3295] The Vellalar community was the dominant secular aristocratic caste under the Chola rulers, providing the courtiers, most of the army officers, the lower ranks of the bureaucracy and the upper layer of the peasantry.[3260] The Vellalar were also sent to northern Sri Lanka by the Chola rulers as settlers.[3305] The Ulavar community were working in the field which was associated with agriculture and the peasants were known as Kalamar.

The Kaikolar community were weavers and merchants but they also maintained armies. During the Chola period they had predominant trading and military roles.[3306] During the reign of the Imperial Chola rulers (10th-13th century) there were major changes in the temple administration and land ownership. There was more involvement of non-Brahmin elements in the temple administration. This can be attributed to the shift in money power. Skilled classes like the weavers and the merchant-class had become prosperous. Land ownership was no longer a privilege of the Brahmins (priest caste) and the Vellalar land owners.[3307]

Figure 531: *This is the Anchor of an Unknown LOLA class Chola ship, excavated by the Indian Navy divers off the coast of Poombuhar.*

There is little information on the size and the density of the population during the Chola reign[3308] The stability in the core Chola region enabled the people to lead a productive and contented life. However, there were reports of widespread famine caused by natural calamities.[3309]

The quality of the inscriptions of the regime indicates a high level of literacy and education. The text in these inscriptions was written by court poets and engraved by talented artisans. Education in the contemporary sense was not considered important; there is circumstantial evidence to suggest that some village councils organised schools to teach the basics of reading and writing to children,[3310] although there is no evidence of systematic educational system for the masses.[3311] Vocational education was through hereditary training in which the father passed on his skills to his sons. Tamil was the medium of education for the masses; Religious monasteries (*matha* or *gatika*) were centres of learning and received government support.[3312]

Foreign trade

The Cholas excelled in foreign trade and maritime activity, extending their influence overseas to China and Southeast Asia.[3313] Towards the end of the 9th century, southern India had developed extensive maritime and commercial activity.[3314] The south Indian guilds played a major role in interregional and overseas trade. The best known of these were the Manigramam and Ayyavole guilds who followed the conquering Chola armies.[3304] The encouragement by the Chola court furthered the expansion of Tamil merchant associations such as the Ayyavole and Manigramam guilds into Southeast Asia and China.[3315] The Cholas, being in possession of parts of both the west and the east coasts of peninsular India, were at the forefront of these ventures.[3316,3317] The Tang dynasty of China, the Srivijaya empire under the Sailendras, and the Abbasid Kalifat at Baghdad were the main trading partners.[3318]

Some credit for the emergence of a world market must also go to the dynasty. It played a significant role in linking the markets of China to the rest of the world. The market structure and economic policies of the Chola dynasty were more conducive to a large-scale, cross-regional market trade than those enacted by the Chinese Song Dynasty. A Chola record gives their rationale for engagement in foreign trade: "Make the merchants of distant foreign countries who import elephants and good horses attach to yourself by providing them with villages and decent dwellings in the city, by affording them daily audience, presents and allowing them profits. Then those articles will never go to your enemies."[3319]

Song dynasty reports record that an embassy from *Chulian* (Chola) reached the Chinese court in 1077,[3320,3321] and that the king of the Chulian at the time, Kulothunga I, was called *Ti-hua-kia-lo*. This embassy was a trading venture and was highly profitable to the visitors, who returned with copper coins in exchange for articles of tribute, including glass and spices.[3322] Probably, the motive behind Rajendra's expedition to Srivijaya was the protection of the merchants' interests.[3323]

Canals and water tanks

There was tremendous agrarian expansion during the rule of the imperial Chola Dynasty (c. 900-1270 AD) all over Tamil Nadu and particularly in the Kaveri Basin. Most of the canals of the Kaveri River belongs to this period e.g., Uyyakondan canal, Rajendran vaykkal, Sembian Mahadegvi vaykkal. There was a well-developed and highly efficient system of water management from the village level upwards. The increase in the royal patronage and also the number of devadana and bramadeya lands which increased the role of the temples and village assemblies in the field. Committees like eri-variyam(tank-committee) and totta-variam(garden committees) were active as also the temples with their vast resources in land, men and money. The water tanks that came up during the Chola period are too many to be listed here. But a few most outstanding may be briefly mentioned. Rajendra Chola built a huge tank named Solagangam in his capital city Gangaikonda Solapuram and was described as the liquid pillar of victory. About 16 miles long, it was provided with sluices and canals for irrigating the lands in the neighbouring areas. Another very large lake of this period, which even today seems an important source

Figure 532: *Detail of the main vimanam (tower) of the Thanjavur Temple*

of irrigation was the Viranameri near Kattumannarkoil in South Arcot district founded by Parantaka Chola. Other famous lakes of this period are Madurantakam, Sundra-cholapereri, Kundavai-Pereri (after a Chola queen).[3324]

Cultural contributions

Under the Cholas, the Tamil country reached new heights of excellence in art, religion, music and literature.[3325] In all of these spheres, the Chola period marked the culmination of movements that had begun in an earlier age under the Pallavas.[3326] Monumental architecture in the form of majestic temples and sculpture in stone and bronze reached a finesse never before achieved in India.[3327]

The Chola conquest of Kadaram (Kedah) and Srivijaya, and their continued commercial contacts with the Chinese Empire, enabled them to influence the local cultures.[3328] Examples of the Hindu cultural influence found today throughout the Southeast Asia owe much to the legacy of the Cholas. For example, the great temple complex at Prambanan in Indonesia exhibit a number of similarities with the South Indian architecture.[3329,3330]

According to the Malay chronicle *Sejarah Melayu*, the rulers of the Malacca sultanate claimed to be descendants of the kings of the Chola

Figure 533: *With heavily ornamented pillars accurate in detail and richly sculpted walls, the Airavateswara temple at Darasuram is a classic example of Chola art and architecture*

Empire.[3331] Wikipedia:Citing sources#What information to include Chola rule is remembered in Malaysia today as many princes there have names ending with Cholan or Chulan, one such being Raja Chulan, the Raja of Perak.[3332] Wikipedia:Citing sources#What information to include[3333] Wikipedia:Citing sources#What information to include

Art

The Cholas continued the temple-building traditions of the Pallava dynasty and contributed significantly to the Dravidian temple design.[3334] They built a number of Shiva temples along the banks of the river Kaveri. The template for these and future temples was formulated by Aditya I and Parantaka.[3335,3336,3337] The Chola temple architecture has been appreciated for its magnificence as well as delicate workmanship, ostensibly following the rich traditions of the past bequeathed to them by the Pallava Dynasty.[3338] Architectural historian James Fergusson says that "the Chola artists conceived like giants and finished like jewelers". A new development in Chola art that characterised the Dravidian architecture in later times was the addition of a huge gateway called gopuram to the enclosure of the temple, which had gradually taken its form and attained maturity under the Pandya Dynasty. The Chola school of art also spread to Southeast Asia and influenced the architecture and art of Southeast Asia.[3339,3340]

Temple building received great impetus from the conquests and the genius of Rajaraja Chola and his son Rajendra Chola I.[3341] The maturity and grandeur to which the Chola architecture had evolved found expression in the two temples of Thanjavur and Gangaikondacholapuram. The magnificent Shiva temple of Thanjavur, completed around 1009, is a fitting memorial to the material achievements of the time of Rajaraja. The largest and tallest of all Indian temples of its time, it is at the apex of South Indian architecture. The temple of Gangaidacholisvaram at Gangaikondacholapuram, the creation of Rajendra Chola, was intended to excel its predecessor. Completed around 1030, only two decades after the temple at Thanjavur and in the same style, the greater elaboration in its appearance attests the more affluent state of the Chola Empire under Rajendra.[3334,3342] Wikipedia:Citing sources The Brihadisvara Temple, the temple of Gangaikondacholisvaram and the Airavatesvara Temple at Darasuram were declared as World Heritage Sites by the UNESCO and are referred to as the Great living Chola temples.

The Chola period is also remarkable for its sculptures and bronzes.[3343,3344,3345] Among the existing specimens in museums around the world and in the temples of South India may be seen many fine figures of Shiva in various forms, such as Vishnu and his consort Lakshmi, and the Shaivite saints.[3334] Though conforming generally to the iconographic conventions established by long tradition, the sculptors worked with great freedom in the 11th and the 12th centuries to achieve a classic grace and grandeur. The best example of this can be seen in the form of Nataraja the Divine Dancer.[3346,3347] </ref>

Literature

The Imperial Chola era was the golden age of Tamil culture, marked by the importance of literature. Chola records cite many works, including the *Rajarajesvara Natakam*, *Viranukkaviyam* and *Kannivana Puranam*.[3348]

The revival of Hinduism from its nadir during the Kalabhras spurred the construction of numerous temples and these in turn generated Shaiva and Vaishnava devotional literature.[3349] Jain and Buddhist authors flourished as well, although in fewer numbers than in previous centuries.[3350] *Jivaka-chintamani* by Tirutakkatevar and *Sulamani* by Tolamoli are among notable works by non-Hindu authors.[3351,3352,3353] The grammarian Buddhamitra wrote a text on Tamil grammar called *Virasoliyam*.[3354] Commentaries were written on the great text *Tolkāppiyam* which deals with grammar but which also mentions ethics of warfare.[3355,3356,3357] *Periapuranam* was another remarkable literary

Figure 534: *Chola bronze from the Ulster Museum*

piece of this period. This work is in a sense a national epic of the Tamil people because it treats of the lives of the saints who lived in all parts of Tamil Nadu and belonged to all classes of society, men and women, high and low, educated and uneducated.[3358]

Kamban flourished during the reign of Kulothunga Chola III. His *Ramavataram* (also referred to as *Kambaramayanam*) is an epic of Tamil literature, and although the author states that he followed Valmiki's *Ramayana*, it is generally accepted that his work is not a simple translation or adaptation of the Sanskrit epic.[3359] Wikipedia:Citing sources He imports into his narration the colour and landscape of his own time; his description of Kosala is an idealised account of the features of the Chola country.[3353,3360] Wikipedia:Citing sources[3361]

Jayamkondar's masterpiece, *Kalingattuparani*, is an example of narrative poetry that draws a clear boundary between history and fictitious conventions. This describes the events during Kulothunga Chola I's war in Kalinga and depicts not only the pomp and circumstance of war, but the gruesome details of the field.[3361,3362] The Tamil poet Ottakuttan was a contemporary of Kulothunga Chola I and served at the courts of three of Kulothunga's successors.[3363,3364] Ottakuttan wrote *Kulothunga Cholan Ula*, a poem extolling the virtues of the Chola king.[3365]

Nannul is a Chola era work on Tamil grammar. It discusses all five branches of grammar and, according to Berthold Spuler, is still relevant today and is one of the most distinguished normative grammars of literary Tamil.[3366]

Of the devotional literature, the arrangement of the Shaivite canon into eleven books was the work of Nambi Andar Nambi, who lived close to the end of the 10th century.[3367,3368] However, relatively few Vaishnavite works were composed during the Later Chola period, possibly because of the rulers' apparent animosity towards them.[3369]

Cultural centres

Chola rulers took an active interest in the development of temple centres and used the temples to widen the sphere of their royal authority. They established educational institutions and hospitals around the temple, enhanced the beneficial aspects of the role of the temple, and projected the royalty as a very powerful and genial presence.[3370] A record of Virarajendra Chola's reign relates to the maintenance of a school in the Jananamandapa within the temple for the study of the Vedas, Sastras, Grammar, and Rupavatara, as well as a hostel for students. The students were provided with food, bathing oil on Saturdays, and oil for pups.Wikipedia:Please clarify A hospital named Virasolan was provided with fifteen beds for sick people. The items of expense set apart for their comforts are rice, a doctor, a surgeon, two maid servants for nursing the patients, and a general servant for the hospital.[3371]

Religion

In general, Cholas were followers of Hinduism. They were not swayed by the rise of Buddhism and Jainism as were the kings of the Pallava and Pandya dynasties. Kocengannan, an Early Chola, was celebrated in both Sangam literature and in the Shaivite canon as a Hindu saint.[3186]

While the Cholas did build their largest and most important temple dedicated to Shiva, it can be by no means concluded that either they were followers of Shaivism only or that they were not favourably disposed to other faiths. This is borne out by the fact that the second Chola king, Aditya I (871–903 CE), built temples for Shiva and also for Vishnu. Inscriptions of 890 refer to his contributions to the construction of the Ranganatha Temple at Srirangapatnam in the country of the Western Gangas, who were both his feudatories and had connections by marriage with him. He also pronounced that the great temples of Shiva and the Ranganatha temple were to be the *Kuladhanam* of the Chola emperors.[3372]

Parantaka II was a devotee of the reclining Vishnu (Vadivu Azhagiya Nambi) at Anbil, on the banks of the Kaveri river on the outskirts of Tiruchy, to whom

Figure 535: *Bronze Chola Statue of Nataraja at the Metropolitan Museum of Art, New York City*

he gave numerous gifts and embellishments. He also prayed before him before his embarking on war to regain the territories in and around Kanchi and Arcot from the waning Rashtrakutas and while leading expeditions against both Madurai and Ilam (Sri Lanka).[3373] Parantaka I and Parantaka Chola II endowed and built temples for Shiva and Vishnu.[3374] Rajaraja Chola I patronised Buddhists and provided for the construction of the Chudamani Vihara, a Buddhist monastery in Nagapattinam, at the request of Sri Chulamanivarman, the Srivijaya Sailendra king.[3375,3376]

During the period of the Later Cholas, there are alleged to have been instances of intolerance towards Vaishnavites[3377] especially towards their acharya, Ramanuja.[3378] Kulothunga Chola II, a staunch Shaivite, is said to have removed a statue of Vishnu from the Shiva temple at Chidambaram, though there are no epigraphical evidences to support this theory. There is an inscription from 1160 that the custodians of Shiva temples who had social intercourses with Vaishnavites would forfeit their property. However, this is more of a direction to the Shaivite community by its religious heads than any kind of dictat by a Chola emperor. While Chola kings built their largest temples for Shiva and even while emperors like Rajaraja Chola I held titles like *Sivapadasekharan*, in none of their inscriptions did the Chola emperors proclaim that their clan only

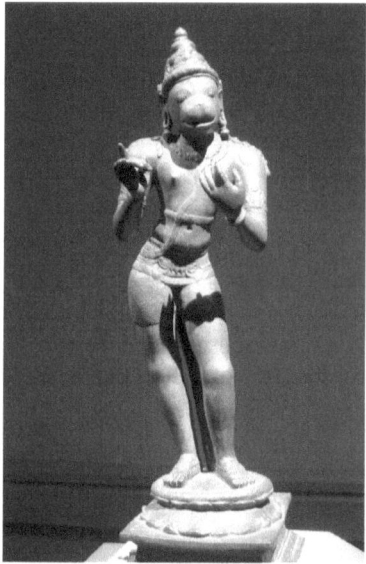

Figure 536: *Standing Hanuman, Chola Dynasty, 11th century.*

and solely followed Shaivism or that Shaivism was the state religion during their rule.[3379,3380,3381]

In popular culture

The Chola dynasty has inspired many Tamil authors.[3382] The most important work of this genre is the popular *Ponniyin Selvan* (The son of *Ponni*), a historical novel in Tamil written by Kalki Krishnamurthy. Written in five volumes, this narrates the story of Rajaraja Chola, dealing with the events leading up to the ascension of Uttama Chola to the Chola throne. Kalki had used the confusion in the succession to the Chola throne after the demise of Parantaka Chola II.[3383] The book was serialised in the Tamil periodical *Kalki* during the mid-1950s. The serialisation lasted for nearly five years and every week its publication was awaited with great interest.

Kalki's earlier historical romance, *Parthiban Kanavu*, deals with the fortunes of the imaginary Chola prince Vikraman, who was supposed to have lived as a feudatory of the Pallava king Narasimhavarman I during the 7th century. The period of the story lies within the interregnum during which the Cholas were in decline before Vijayalaya Chola revived their fortunes.[3384] *Parthiban Kanavu* was also serialised in the *Kalki* weekly during the early 1950s.Wikipedia:Citation needed

Sandilyan, another popular Tamil novelist, wrote *Kadal Pura* in the 1960s. It was serialised in the Tamil weekly *Kumudam*. *Kadal Pura* is set during the period when Kulothunga Chola I was in exile from the Vengi kingdom after he was denied the throne. It speculates the whereabouts of Kulothunga during this period. Sandilyan's earlier work, *Yavana Rani*, written in the early 1960s, is based on the life of Karikala Chola.[3385] More recently, Balakumaran wrote the novel *Udaiyar*, which is based on the circumstances surrounding Rajaraja Chola's construction of the Brihadisvara Temple in Thanjavur.

There were stage productions based on the life of Rajaraja Chola during the 1950s and in 1973 Sivaji Ganesan acted in a screen adaptation of a play titled *Rajaraja Cholan*. The Cholas are featured in the History of the World board game, produced by Avalon Hill.Wikipedia:Citation needed

The Cholas were the subject of the 2010 Tamil-language movie *Aayirathil Oruvan*.

References

Notes

Citations

Bibliography <templatestyles src="Template:Refbegin/styles.css" />

- Barua, Pradeep (2005), *The State at War in South Asia*, University of Nebraska Press, ISBN 978-0-80321-344-9
- Chopra, P. N.; Ravindran, T. K.; Subrahmanian, N. (2003), *History of South India: Ancient, Medieval and Modern*, S. Chand & Company Ltd, ISBN 81-219-0153-7
- Das, Sisir Kumar (1995), *History of Indian Literature (1911–1956): Struggle for Freedom – Triumph and Tragedy*, Sahitya Akademi, ISBN 81-7201-798-7
- Dehejia, Vidya (1990), *The Art of the Imperial Cholas*, Columbia University Press
- Devare, Hema (2009), "Cultural Implications of the Chola Maritime Fabric Trade with Southeast Asia", in Kulke, Hermann; Kesavapany, K.; Sakhuja, Vijay, *Nagapattinam to Suvarnadwipa: Reflections on the Chola Naval Expeditions to Southeast Asia*, Institute of Southeast Asian Studies, ISBN 978-9-81230-937-2
- Eraly, Abraham (2011), *The First Spring: The Golden Age of India*, Penguin Books, ISBN 978-0-67008-478-4
- Gough, Kathleen (2008), *Rural Society in Southeast India*, Cambridge University Press, ISBN 978-0-52104-019-8

- Harle, J. C. (1994), *The art and architecture of the Indian Subcontinent*, Yale University Press, ISBN 0-300-06217-6
- Hellmann-Rajanayagam, Dagmar (2004), "From Differences to Ethnic Solidarity Among the Tamils", in Hasbullah, S. H.; Morrison, Barrie M., *Sri Lankan Society in an Era of Globalization: Struggling To Create A New Social Order*, SAGE, ISBN 978-8-13210-320-2
- Jermsawatdi, Promsak (1979), *Thai Art with Indian Influences*, Abhinav Publications, ISBN 978-8-17017-090-7
- Kulke, Hermann; Rothermund, Dietmar (2001), *A History of India*, Routledge, ISBN 0-415-32920-5
- Lucassen, Jan; Lucassen, Leo (2014), *Globalising Migration History: The Eurasian Experience*, BRILL, ISBN 978-9-00427-136-4
- Majumdar, R. C. (1987) [1952], *Ancient India*, Motilal Banarsidass Publications, ISBN 81-208-0436-8
- John N. Miksic (2013). *Singapore and the Silk Road of the Sea, 1300_1800*[3386]. NUS Press. ISBN 978-9971-69-558-3.
- Mitter, Partha (2001), *Indian art*, Oxford University Press, ISBN 0-19-284221-8
- Mukherjee, Rila (2011), *Pelagic Passageways: The Northern Bay of Bengal Before Colonialism*, Primus Books, ISBN 978-9-38060-720-7
- Mukund, Kanakalatha (1999), *The Trading World of the Tamil Merchant: Evolution of Merchant Capitalism in the Coromandel*, Orient Blackswan, ISBN 978-8-12501-661-8
- Mukund, Kanakalatha (2012), *Merchants of Tamilakam: Pioneers of International Trade*, Penguin Books India, ISBN 978-0-67008-521-7
- Nagasamy, R. (1970), *Gangaikondacholapuram*, State Department of Archaeology, Government of Tamil Nadu
- Nagasamy, R. (1981), *Tamil Coins – A study*, Institute of Epigraphy, Tamil Nadu State Dept. of Archaeology
- Paine, Lincoln (2014), *The Sea and Civilization: A Maritime History of the World*, Atlantic Books, ISBN 978-1-78239-357-3
- Prasad, G. Durga (1988), *History of the Andhras up to 1565 A. D.*, P. G. Publishers
- Rajasuriar, G. K. (1998), *The history of the Tamils and the Sinhalese of Sri Lanka*
- Ramaswamy, Vijaya (2007), *Historical Dictionary of the Tamils*, Scarecrow Press, ISBN 978-0-81086-445-0
- Rothermund, Dietmar (1993), *An Economic History of India: From Pre-colonial Times to 1991* (Reprinted ed.), Routledge, ISBN 978-0-41508-871-8
- Sadarangani, Neeti M. (2004), *Bhakti Poetry in Medieval India: Its Inception, Cultural Encounter and Impact*, Sarup & Sons, ISBN 978-8-

17625-436-6
- Sakhuja, Vijay; Sakhuja, Sangeeta (2009), "Rajendra Chola I's Naval Expedition to South-East Asia: A Nautical Perspective", in Kulke, Hermann; Kesavapany, K.; Sakhuja, Vijay, *Nagapattinam to Suvarnadwipa: Reflections on the Chola Naval Expeditions to Southeast Asia*, Institute of Southeast Asian Studies, ISBN 978-9-81230-937-2
- Sastri, K. A. N. (1984) [1935], *The Cōḷas*, University of Madras
- Sastri, K. A. N. (2002) [1955], *A History of South India: From Prehistoric Times to the Fall of Vijayanagar*, Oxford University Press
- Scharfe, Hartmut (2002), *Education in Ancient India*, Brill Academic Publishers, ISBN 90-04-12556-6
- Schmidt, Karl J. (1995), *An Atlas and Survey of South Asian History*, M.E. Sharpe, ISBN 978-0-76563-757-4
- Sen, Sailendra Nath (1999), *Ancient Indian History and Civilization*, New Age International, ISBN 978-8-12241-198-0
- Sen, Tansen (2009), "The Military Campaigns of Rajendra Chola and the Chola-Srivija-China Triangle", in Kulke, Hermann; Kesavapany, K.; Sakhuja, Vijay, *Nagapattinam to Suvarnadwipa: Reflections on the Chola Naval Expeditions to Southeast Asia*, Institute of Southeast Asian Studies, ISBN 978-9-81230-937-2
- Singh, Upinder (2008), *A History of Ancient and Early Medieval India: From the Stone Age to the 12th Century*, Pearson Education India, ISBN 978-8-13171-120-0
- "South Indian Inscriptions"[3387], *Archaeological Survey of India*, What Is India Publishers (P) Ltd, retrieved 2008-05-30
- Spuler, Bertold (1975), *Handbook of Oriental Studies, Part 2*, BRILL, ISBN 978-9-00404-190-5
- Stein, Burton (1980), *Peasant state and society in medieval South India*, Oxford University Press
- Stein, Burton (1998), *A history of India*, Blackwell Publishers, ISBN 0-631-20546-2
- Subbarayalu, Y. (2009), "A Note on the Navy of the Chola State", in Kulke, Hermann; Kesavapany, K.; Sakhuja, Vijay, *Nagapattinam to Suvarnadwipa: Reflections on the Chola Naval Expeditions to Southeast Asia*, Institute of Southeast Asian Studies, ISBN 978-9-81230-937-2
- Thapar, Romila (1995), *Recent Perspectives of Early Indian History*, South Asia Books, ISBN 81-7154-556-4
- Tripathi, Rama Sankar (1967), *History of Ancient India*, Motilal Banarsidass, ISBN 81-208-0018-4
- Talbot, Austin Cynthia (2001), *Pre-colonial India in Practice: Society, Region, and Identity in Medieval Andhra*, Oxford University Press, ISBN 978-0-19803-123-9

- Vasudevan, Geeta (2003), *Royal Temple of Rajaraja: An Instrument of Imperial Cola Power*, Abhinav Publications, ISBN 81-7017-383-3
- Wolpert, Stanley A (1999), *India*, University of California Press, ISBN 0-520-22172-9

External links

 Wikimedia Commons has media related to *Chola dynasty*.

- UNESCO World Heritage sites – Chola temples[3388]
- Art of Cholas[3389]
- Chola coins of Sri Lanka[3390]

Appendix

References

[1] //en.wikipedia.org/w/index.php?title=Template:Human_history&action=edit
[2] Cunningham, (1888) p. 33.
[3] Cunningham (1888), p. 33.
[4] Barstow (1928), reprint 1985, pp. 105-135, 63, 155, 152, 145.
[5] Latif (1984), p. 56.
[6] Mortimer Wheeler *Flames over Persepolis* (London, 1968). Pp. 112 ff. It is unclear whether the Hellenistic street plan found by John Marshall's excavations dates from the Indo-Greeks or from the Kushans, who would have encountered it in Bactria; Tarn (1951, pp. 137, 179) ascribes the initial move of Taxila to the hill of Sirkap to Demetrius I, but sees this as "not a Greek city but an Indian one"; not a *polis* or with a Hippodamian plan.
[7] "Menander had his capital in Sagala" Bopearachchi, "Monnaies", p.83. McEvilley supports Tarn on both points, citing Woodcock: "Menander was a Bactrian Greek king of the Euthydemid dynasty. His capital (was) at Sagala (Sialkot) in the Punjab, "in the country of the Yonakas (Greeks)"." McEvilley, p.377. However, "Even if Sagala proves to be Sialkot, it does not seem to be Menander's capital for the Milindapanha states that Menander came down to Sagala to meet Nagasena, just as the Ganges flows to the sea."
[8] 11.34 http://www.perseus.tufts.edu/cgi-bin/ptext?lookup=Plb.+11.34
[9] Polybius 11.34 http://www.perseus.tufts.edu/cgi-bin/ptext?lookup=Plb.+11.34
[10] "Notes on Hellenism in Bactria and India". https://www.jstor.org/stable/623931 W. W. Tarn. *Journal of Hellenic Studies*, Vol. 22 (1902), pages 268–293
[11] "A vast hoard of coins, with a mixture of Greek profiles and Indian symbols, along with interesting sculptures and some monumental remains from Taxila, Sirkap and Sirsukh, point to a rich fusion of Indian and Hellenistic influences", *India, the Ancient Past*, Burjor Avari, p.130
[12] "When the Greeks of Bactria and India lost their kingdom they were not all killed, nor did they return to Greece. They merged with the people of the area and worked for the new masters; contributing considerably to the culture and civilization in southern and central Asia." Narain, "The Indo-Greeks" 2003, p. 278.
[13] See: Notes on the Races, Tribes, and Castes inhabiting the Province of Oudh, Lucknow, Oudh Government Press 1868, p 4; The Geographical Data in Early Puranas, a Critical Studies, 1972, p 135, Dr M. R. Singh; Sacred Books of the East, XXV, Intr. p cxv, Rapson, Coins of Ancient India, p 37, n.2.
[14] The Geographical Data in Early Puranas, a Critical Studies, 1972, p 135, M. R. Singh; Sacred Books of the East, XXV, Intr. p cxv; Rapson, Coins of Ancient India, p 37, n.2.
[15] Agarwala (1954), p. 444.
[16] Kharapallana and Vanaspara are known from an inscription discovered in Sarnath, and dated to the 3rd year of Kanishka, in which they were paying allegiance to the Kushanas. Source: "A Catalogue of the Indian Coins in the British Museum. Andhras etc..." Rapson, p ciii
[17] Ptolemy, *Geographia*, Chap 7
[18] Hill (2009), pp. 29, 31.
[19] Hill (2004)
[20] Chadurah, 1991 & 45.
[21] Hasan 1959, pp. 54.
[22] Singh 2008, p. 571.
[23] Majumdar 1977, pp. 260–3.
[24] Wink, 1991 & 72-74.
[25] Shahi Family. Encyclopædia Britannica. 2006. Encyclopædia Britannica Online. 16 October 2006 http://www.britannica.com/eb/article-9067075.
[26] Sehrai, Fidaullah (1979). Hund: *The Forgotten City of Gandhara*, p. 2. Peshawar Museum Publications New Series, Peshawar.
[27] Darius used titles like "Kshayathiya, Kshayathiya Kshayathiyanam" etc.

883

[28] The Shahi Afghanistan and Punjab, 1973, pp 1, 45-46, 48, 80, Dr D. B. Pandey; The Úakas in India and Their Impact on Indian Life and Culture, 1976, p 80, Vishwa Mitra Mohan - Indo-Scythians; Country, Culture and Political life in early and medieval India, 2004, p 34, Daud Ali.
[29] Journal of the Royal Asiatic Society, 1954, pp 112 ff; The Shahis of Afghanistan and Punjab, 1973, p 46, Dr D. B. Pandey; The Úakas in India and Their Impact on Indian Life and Culture, 1976, p 80, Vishwa Mitra Mohan - Indo-Scythians.
[30] India, A History, 2001, p 203, John Keay.
[31] Agrawal, Sadananda (2000): Śrī Khāravela, Sri Digambar Jain Samaj, Cuttack, Odisha
[32] Keling_English Version http://www.visvacomplex.com/Keling_English_Version.html . Visvacomplex.com. Retrieved on 2013-07-12.
[33] Shashi Kant (2000): The Hathigumpha Inscription of Kharavela and the Bhabru Edict of Ashoka, D K Printworld Pvt. Ltd.
[34] A Panorama of Indian Culture: Professor A. Sreedhara Menon Felicitation Volume edited by K. K. Kusuman, Page no 153
[35] India - Historical Setting - The Classical Age - Gupta and Harsha http://historymedren.about.com/library/text/bltxtindia7.htm
[36] The Age of the Guptas and After http://www.wsu.edu:8001/~dee/ANCINDIA/GUPTA.HTM
[37] Gupta dynasty (Indian dynasty) - Britannica Online Encyclopedia http://www.britannica.com/EBchecked/topic/249590/Gupta-dynasty
[38] Encyclopedia - Britannica Online Encyclopedia http://www.britannica.com/EBchecked/topic-art/285248/1960/The-Gupta-empire-at-the-end-of-the-4th-century
[39] The Gupta Empire of India | Chandragupta I | Samudragupta http://www.historybits.com/gupta.htm
[40] Trade | The Story of India - Photo Gallery | PBS https://www.pbs.org/thestoryofindia/gallery/photos/8.html
[41] The Gurjaras of Rajputana and Kannauj, Vincent A. Smith, The Journal of the Royal Asiatic Society of Great Britain and Ireland, (Jan., 1909), pp. 53-75
[42] Roychaudhuri, H.C. (1972). *Political History of Ancient India*, University of Calcutta, Calcutta, pp.553-4
[43] Mahajan V.D. (1960, reprint 2007). *Ancient India*, S. Chand & Company, New Delhi, , pp. 594-6
[44] Gurjara-Pratihara dynasty definition of Gurjara-Pratihara dynasty in the Free Online Encyclopedia http://encyclopedia2.thefreedictionary.com/Gurjara-Pratihara+dynasty
[45] Dharam Prakash Gupta, "Seminar on Katoch dynasty trail". *Himachal Plus*. On line. http://www.tribuneindia.com/2009/20091104/himplus.htm#8
[46] Medieval India: From Sultanat to the Mughals (1206-1526) - I By Satish Chandra https//books.google.com
[47] *A History of India* by August Friedrich Rudolf Hoernle, Herbert Alick Stark
[48] Stella Snead - Guardian Lion http://www.archipelago.org/vol3-4/snead3.htm
[49] Agnivansha: Paramara Dynasty http://agnivanshi.blogspot.com/2008/05/paramara-dynasty.html
[50] Upinder Singh 2008, p. 571.
[51] D. C. Ganguly 1981, p. 704.
[52] Sailendra Nath Sen 1999, p. 339.
[53] Dilip Kumar Ganguly 1984, p. 117.
[54] Ganga Dynasty http://www.britannica.com/eb/topic-225335/Ganga-dynasty www.britannica.com.
[55] Suresh Kant Sharma, Usha Sharma - 2005,"Discovery of North-East India: Geography, History, Culture, ... - Volume 3", Page 248, Davaka (Nowgong) and Kamarupa as separate and submissive friendly kingdoms.
[56] Arun Bhattacharjee (1993), *Assam in Indian Independence*, Page 143 While Pushyavarman was the contemporary of the Gupta Emperor Samudra Gupta, Bhaskaravarman was the contemporary of Harshavardhana of Kanauj.

[57] "Three thousand years after these mythical ancestors (Naraka, Bhagadatta and Vajradatta) there occurred Pushyavarman as the first historical king, after whom we have an uninterrupted line of rulers up to Bhaskarvarman."

[58] "According to him (D C Sircar) Narayanavarma, the father of Bhutivarman, was the first Kamarupa king to perform horse-sacrifices and thus for the first time since the days of Pusyavarman freedom from the Gupta political supremacy was declared by Narayanavarma. But a careful study or even a casual perusal of the seal attached to the Dubi C.P. and of the nalanda seals should show that it is Sri Mahendra, the father of Narayanavarma himself, who is described as the performer of two horse-sacrifices."

[59] N. Laxminarayana Rao and S. C. Nandinath in Kamath 2001, p57

[60] Keay (2000), p168

[61] Jayasimha and Ranaraga, ancestors of Pulakeshin I, were administrative officers in the Badami province under the Kadambas (Fleet in Kanarese Dynasties, p343), (Moraes 1931, p51)

[62] Thapar (2003), p328

[63] Quote:"They belonged to the Karnataka country and their mother tongue was Kannada" (Sen 1999, p360); Kamath (2001), p58,

[64] Considerable number of their records are in Kannada (Kamath 2001, p67)

[65] 7th century Chalukya inscriptions call Kannada the natural language (Thapar 2003, p345)

[66] Sen (1999), p360

[67] In this composition, the poet deems himself an equal to Sanskrit scholars of lore like Bharavi and Kalidasa (Sastri 1955, p312

[68] Kamath (2001), p59

[69] Keay (2000), p169

[70] Sen (1999), pp361–362

[71] Kamath (2001), pp59–60

[72] Some of these kingdoms may have submitted out of fear of Harshavardhana of Kannauj (Majumdar in Kamat 2001, p59)

[73] The rulers of Kosala were the Panduvamshis of South Kosala (Sircar in Kamath 2001, pp59)

[74] Keay (2000), p170

[75] Kamath (2001), pp58

[76] Ramesh 1984, p76

[77] From the notes of Arab traveller Tabari (Kamath 2001, p60)

[78] Sen (1999), p362

[79] Thapar (2003), p331, p345

[80] Sastri (1955) p140

[81] Ramesh (1984), pp159–160

[82] Sen (1999), p364

[83] Ramesh (1984), p159

[84] Hardy (1995), p65–66

[85] Over 125 temples exist in Aihole alone,

[86] The Badami Chalukya introduced in the western Deccan a glorious chapter alike in heroism in battle and cultural magnificence in peace (K.V. Sounderrajan in Kamath 2001, p68

[87] Kamath (2001), p68

[88] K.A.N. Sastri, *A History of South India* pp 91–92

[89] Durga Prasad, *History of the Andhras up to 1565 A. D.*, pp 68

[90] Kamil V. Zvelebil (1987). "The Sound of the One Hand", *Journal of the American Oriental Society*, Vol. 107, No. 1, p. 125-126.

[91] 'Advanced History of India', K.A. Nilakanta Sastri (1970)p. 181-182, Allied Publishers Pvt. Ltd., New Delhi

[92] http://www.whatsindia.org

[93] From the Rashtrakuta inscriptions (Kamath 2001, p57, p64)

[94] The Samangadh copper plate grant (753) confirms that feudatory Dantidurga defeated the Chalukyas and humbled their great *Karnatik* army (referring to the army of the Badami Chalukyas) (Reu 1933, p54)

[95] A capital which could put to shame even the capital of gods-From Karda plates (Altekar 1934, p47)

[96] A capital city built to excel that of Indra (Sastri, 1955, p4, p132, p146)
[97] Altekar (1934), pp411–413
[98] Chopra (2003), p87, part1; Literature in Kannada and Sanskrit flowered during the Rashtrakuta rule (Kamath 2001, p73, pp 88–89)
[99] Even royalty of the empire took part in poetic and literary activities (Thapar 2003, p334)
[100] Reu (1933), pp37–38
[101] Chopra (2003), p89, part1; His victories were a "digvijaya" gaining only fame and booty in that region (Altekar in Kamath 2001, p75)
[102] Chopra (2003), p90, part1
[103] Keay (2000), p199)
[104] Kamath 2001, p76
[105] Kavirajamarga in Kannada and *Prashnottara Ratnamalika* in Sanskrit (Reu 1933, p38)
[106] Kamath (2001), p90
[107]
[108] Panchamukhi in Kamath (2001), p80
[109] Chopra (2003), p92, part1; Altekar in Kamath 2001, p81
[110] Chopra (2003), p92–93, part1
[111] Reu (1933), p39
[112] *Murujul Zahab* by Al Masudi (944), *Kitabul Akalim* by Al Istakhri (951), *Ashkal-ul-Bilad* by Ibn Haukal (976) (Reu 1933, p41–42)
[113] From the Sanjan inscriptions,
[114] Keay (2000), p200
[115] Chopra (2003), p137, part1
[116] Fleet, Bhandarkar and Altekar and Gopal B.R. in (Kamath 2001, p100)
[117]
[118] Sen (1999), p. 393
[119] Sastri (1955), pp356–358; Kamath (2001), p114
[120] More inscriptions in Kannada are attributed to the Chalukya King Vikramaditya VI than to any other king prior to the 12th century,
[121] From the 957 and 965 records (Kamath 2001, p101)
[122] Sastri 1955, p162
[123] Tailapa II was helped in this campaign by the Kadambas of Hanagal (Moraes 1931, pp 93–94)
[124] Ganguli in Kamath 2001, p103
[125] Sastri (1955), p167–168
[126] Kamath (2001), p104
[127] Sastri (1955), p164, p174; The Cholas occupied Gangavadi from 1004–1114 (Kamath 2001, p118)
[128] Chopra (2003), p139, part1
[129] Thapar, 2003, pp 468–469
[130] Chopra (2003), p139, part 1
[131] Poet Bilhana in his Sanskrit work wrote "Rama Rajya" regarding his rule, poet Vijnaneshwara called him "A king like none other" (Kamath 2001, p106)
[132] Sastri (1955), p6
[133] Sastri (1955), pp 427–428; Quote:"Their creations have the pride of place in Indian art tradition" (Kamath 2001, p115)
[134] Quote:"Of the city of Kalyana, situated in the north of Karnataka nothing is left, but a fabulous revival in temple building during the 11th century in central Karnataka testifies to the wealth during Kalyan Chalukya rule"(Foekema (1996), p14)
[135] Kamath (2001), p107
[136] From the 1142 and 1147 records, Kamath (2001), p108
[137] Chopra (2003), p139, part1; From the Chikkalagi records (Kamath 2001, p108)
[138] Chopra (2003), p140, part1; Kamath (2001) p109
[139] Students' Britannica India By Dale Hoiberg, Indu Ramchandani.
[140] Sen (1999), p498
[141] Sen (1999), p499

[142] Vishnuvardhana made many military conquests later to be further expanded by his successors into one of the most powerful empires of South India—William Coelho. He was the true maker of the Hoysala kingdom—B.S.K. Iyengar in Kamath (2001), p124–126
[143] B.L. Rice in Kamath (2001), p123
[144] Keay (2000), p251
[145] Thapar (2003), p367
[146] Kamath (2001), p123
[147] Natives of south Karnataka (Chopra, 2003, p150 Part1)
[148] Shiva Prakash in Ayyappapanicker (1997), pp164, 203; Rice E. P. (1921), p59
[149] Kamath (2001), pp132–134
[150] Sastri (1955), p359, p361
[151] Sastri (1955), p427
[152] Sen (1999), pp500–501
[153] Foekema (1996), p14
[154] Kamath (2001), p124
[155] The most outstanding of the Hoysala kings according to Barrett and William Coelho in Kamath (2001), p126
[156] B.S.K. Iyengar in Kamath (2001), p126
[157] Keay (2000), p252
[158] Sen (1999), p500
[159] Two theories exist about the origin of Harihara I and his brother Bukka Raya I. One states that they were Kannadiga commanders of the Hoysala army and another that they were Telugu speakers and commanders of the earlier Kakatiya Kingdom (Kamath 2001, pp 159–160)
[160] Great Living Chola Temples http://whc.unesco.org/en/list/250.
[161] https://books.google.com/books?id=kXtDAAAAYAAJ
[162] https://books.google.com/books?id=7v76i0eF9tQC&pg=PA117
[163] http://depts.washington.edu/silkroad/texts/weilue/weilue.html#section7
[164] https://books.google.com/books?id=nTFuAAAAMAAJ
[165] https://books.google.com/?id=EUlwmXjE9DQC&pg=PA2
[166] https://books.google.com/books?id=Wk4_ICH_g1EC&pg=PA172
[167] https://books.google.com/books?id=H3lUIIYxWkEC&pg=PA383
[168] http://lcweb2.loc.gov/frd/cs/
[169] http://lcweb2.loc.gov/frd/cs/intoc.html
[170] Kharapallana and Vanaspara are known from an inscription discovered in Sarnath, and dated to the 3rd year of Kanishka, in which they were paying allegiance to the Kushanas. Source: "A Catalogue of the Indian Coins in the British Museum. Andhras etc." Rapson, p ciii
[171] "The titles "Kshatrap" and "Mahakshatrapa" certainly show that the Western Kshatrapas were originally feudatories" in Rapson, "Coins of the British Museum", p.cv
[172] World history from early times to A D 2000 by B .V. Rao: p.97
[173] A Brief History of India, by Alain Daniélou p.136
[174] India in a Globalised World, by Sagarika Dutt p.24
[175] Ancient India, by Ramesh Chandra Majumdar p. 234
[176] http://sourcebooks.fordham.edu/halsall/ancient/arrian-bookVIII-India.asp, Section V.
[177] Ptolemy vi, xiii (1932), p. 143.
[178] Ronca (1971), pp. 39, 102, 108.
[179] Millward (2007), p. 13.
[180] Mallory, J. P.; Mair, Victor H. (2000), The Tarim Mummies: Ancient China and the Mystery of the Earliest Peoples from the West, London: Thames & Hudson, pp. 77–81
[181] *Shiji*, chap. 123 translated in: Burton Watson (1993), p. 234.
[182] *Han Shu* 61 4B Original tex: 西擊塞王。塞王南走遠徙，月氏居其地。
[183] Justin XL.II.2
[184] *Isodor of Charax, Sathmoi Parthikoi*, 18.
[185] *Political History of Ancient India*, 1996, p 693.
[186] *The dynastic art of the Kushans*, John Rosenfield, p 130
[187] *Kshatrapasa pra Kharaostasa Artasa putrasa*. See: *Political History of Ancient India*, 1996, p 398, H. C. Raychaudhury, B. N. Mukerjee; *Ancient India*, 1956, pp 220–221, R. K. Mukerjee

[188] *Ancient India*, pp 220–221, R. k. Mukerjee; *Corpus Inscriptionum Indicarum*, Vol II, Part 1, p 36, D S Konow

[189] Source: "A Catalogue of the Indian Coins in the British Museum. Andhras etc..." Rapson, p ciii

[190] Francine Tissot "Gandhara", p74

[191] Wilcox and McBride (1986), p. 12.

[192] "Let us remind that in Sirkap, stone palettes were found at all excavated levels. On the contrary, neither Bhir-Mound, the Maurya city preceding Sirkap on the Taxila site, nor Sirsukh, the Kushan city succeeding her, did deliver any stone palettes during their excavations", in "Les palettes du Gandhara", p89. "The terminal point after which such palettes are not manufactured anymore is probably located during the Kushan period. In effect, neither Mathura nor Taxila (although the Sirsukh had only been little excavated), nor Begram, nor Surkh Kotal, neither the great Kushan archaeological sites of Soviet Central Asia or Afghanistan have yielded such objects. Only four palettes have been found in Kushan-period archaeological sites. They come from secondary sites, such as Garav Kala and Ajvadz in Soviet Tajikistan and Jhukar, in the Indus Valley, and Dalverzin Tepe. They are rather roughly made." In "Les Palettes du Gandhara", Henri-Paul Francfort, p 91. (in French in the original)

[193] Metropolitan Museum of Art notice http://www.metmuseum.org/art/collection/search/38111

[194] Ahmad Hasan Dani et al., *History of Civilizations of Central Asia*, 1999, p 201, Unesco

[195] Richard Salomon, "An Inscribed Silver Buddhist Reliquary of the Time of King Kharaosta and Prince Indravarman", *Journal of the American Oriental Society*, Vol. 116, No. 3 (July - September 1996), pp. 418-452

[196] "Afghanistan, carrefour en l'Est et l'Ouest" p.373. Also Senior 2003

[197] Des Indo-Grecs aux Sassanides, Rika Gyselen, Peeters Publishers, 2007, p.103 https://books.google.com/books?id=_TIU_jp93xUC&pg=PA103

[198] Source:"Butkara I", Faccena

[199] "Gandhara" Francine Tissot

[200] The Turin City Museum of Ancient Art Text and photographic reference: Terre Lontane O2 http://www.palazzomadamatorino.it/nuovo3/mostre/index.php?lang=2

[201] For the pilaster showing a man in Greek dress File:ButkaraPilaster.jpg.

[202] Facenna, "Sculptures from the sacred area of Butkara I", plate CCCLXXI. The relief is this one, showing Indo-Scythians dancing and reveling, with on the back side a relief of a standing Buddha (not shown).

[203] Serindia, Vol I, 1980 Edition, p 8, M. A. Stein

[204] H. C. Raychaudhury, B. N. Mukerjee; Early History of North India, p 3, S. Chattopadhyava; India and Central Asia, p 126, P. C. Bagchi

[205] *Epigraphia Indiaca* XIV, p 291 S Konow; *Greeks in Bactria and India*, p 473, fn, W. W. Tarn; Yuan Chwang I, pp 259–60, Watters; *Comprehensive History of India*, Vol I, p 189, N. K. Sastri; *History and Culture of Indian People, The Age of Imperial Unity*, 122; *History and Culture of Indian People, Classical Age*, p 617, R. C. Majumdar, A. D. Pusalkar.

[206] Scholars like E. J. Rapson, L. Petech etc. also connect Kipin with Kapisha. Levi holds that prior to AD 600, Kipin denoted Kashmir, but after this it implied Kapisha See Discussion in The Classical Age, p 671.

[207] Corpus Inscriptionum Indicarum, II. 1. XX f; cf: *Early History of North India*, pp 54, S Chattopadhyaya.

[208] *India and Central Asia*, 1955, p 124, P. C. Bagchi; *Geographical Data in Early Puranas*, 1972, p 47, M. R. Singh.

[209] See: Political History of Ancient India, 1996, p fn 13, B. N. Mukerjee; Chilas, Islamabad, 1983, no 72, 78, 85, pp 98, 102, A. H. Dani

[210] *Political History of Ancient India*, 1996, pp 3–4.

[211]
> viparite tada loke purvarupa.n kshayasya tat || 34 ||
> bahavo mechchha rajanah prithivyam manujadhipa |
> mithyanushasinah papa mrishavadaparayanah || 35 ||
> Andhrah Shakah Pulindashcha **Yavanashcha naradhipah** |
> Kamboja Bahlikah Shudrastath abhira narottama || **36** ||
> — *(MBH 3.188.34–36)*.

[212] *History and Culture of Indian People, The Vedic Age*, pp 286–87, 313–14.
[213] Intercourse Between India and the Western World https//books.google.com, pp 75–93, H. G. Rawlinson
[214] e.g.: *Aspa.bhrata.putrasa*. See: An Inscribed Silver Buddhist Reliquary of the Time of King Kharaosta and Prince Indravarman, Jounranal of the American Oriental Society, Vol 116, No 3, 1996, p 448, Richard Saloman.
[215] An Inscribed Silver Buddhist Reliquary of the Time of King Kharaosta and Prince Indravarman, Jounranal of the American Oriental Society, Vol 116, No 3, 1996, p 448, Richard Saloman.
[216] http://people.bu.edu/ptandon/Paratarajas2.pdf Further Light on the Paratarajas
[217] Indian Institute of Romani Studies http://rishi.anantdutta.in/obituary.html
[218] http://depts.washington.edu/silkroad/texts/weilue/weilue.html
[219] http://sanskrit.inria.fr/Dico.pdf
[220] http://muse.jhu.edu/journals/jwh/
[221] https://web.archive.org/web/20071015203904/http://iranica.com/newsite/articles/ot_grp8/ot_indoscyth_20050802.html
[222] https://web.archive.org/web/20040809235721/http://www.grifterrec.com/coins/indoscythian/indoscythian.html
[223] http://www.clevelandart.org/explore/work.asp?searchText=Buner&x=4&y=7&recNo=0&tab=2&display=
[224] http://sites.google.com/site/grecoindian/Home/history-of-greco-india
[225] //en.wikipedia.org/w/index.php?title=Template:Indo-European_topics&action=edit
[226] "Scythian, also called Scyth, Saka, and Sacae, member of a nomadic people, originally of Iranian stock." Scythian-Saka https://global.britannica.com/topic/Scythian
[227] "The ethnonym Saka appears in ancient Iranian and Indian sources as the name of the large family of Iranian nomads called Scythians by the Classical Western sources and Sai by the Chinese (Gk. Sacae; OPers. Sakā)."
[228] "The territory of Yārkand is for the first time mentioned in the Hanshu (1st century BCE), under the name Shache (Old Chinese, approximately, *s³a(j)-ka), which is probably related to the name of the Iranian Saka tribes."
[229] Herodotus Book VII, 64
[230] Naturalis Historia, VI, 19, 50
[231] Kuz'mina, Elena E. (2007). *The Origin of the Indo Iranians*. Edited by J.P. Mallory. Leiden, Boston: Brill, pp 381-382.
[232] "The sons of Gomer were Ashkenaz, Riphath,[a] and Togarmah." See also the entry for Ashkenaz in
[233] George Rawlinson, noted in his translation of *History of Herodotus*, Book VII, p. 378
[234] Journal of the Royal Asiatic Society of Great Britain & Ireland By Royal Asiatic Society of Great Britain and Ireland-page-323
[235] Torday, Laszlo. (1997). *Mounted Archers: The Beginnings of Central Asian History*. Durham: The Durham Academic Press, pp 80-81, .
[236] Yü, Ying-shih. (1986). "Han Foreign Relations," in *The Cambridge History of China: Volume I: the Ch'in and Han Empires, 221 B.C. – A.D. 220*, 377-462. Edited by Denis Twitchett and Michael Loewe. Cambridge: Cambridge University Press, pp 377-388, 391, .
[237] Chang, Chun-shu. (2007). The Rise of the Chinese Empire: Volume II; Frontier, Immigration, & Empire in Han China, 130 B.C. – A.D. 157. Ann Arbor: University of Michigan Press, pp 5-8 .
[238] Di Cosmo, Nicola. (2002). *Ancient China and Its Enemies: The Rise of Nomadic Power in East Asian History*. Cambridge: Cambridge University Press, pp. 174-189, 196-198, 241-242 .
[239] Yu Taishan (June 2010), "The Earliest Tocharians in China" in Victor H. Mair (ed), *Sino-Platonic Papers*, Chinese Academy of Social Sciences, University of Pennsylvania Department of East Asian Languages and Civilizations, pp. 13-14, 21-22.
[240]
[241] Bernard, P. (1994). "The Greek Kingdoms of Central Asia". In Harmatta, János. *History of civilizations of Central Asia, Volume II. The development of sedentary and nomadic civilizations: 700 B.C. to A.D. 250*. Paris: UNESCO. pp. 96–126.

[242] Ulrich Theobald. (26 November 2011). " Chinese History - Sai 塞 The Saka People or Soghdians http://www.chinaknowledge.de/History/Altera/sakas.html." *ChinaKnowledge.de*. Accessed 2 September 2016.
[243] Yaroslav Lebedynsky, P. 84
[244] Loewe, Michael. (1986). "The Former Han Dynasty," in The Cambridge History of China: Volume I: the Ch'in and Han Empires, 221 B.C. – A.D. 220, 103–222. Edited by Denis Twitchett and Michael Loewe. Cambridge: Cambridge University Press, pp 197-198.
[245] Yü, Ying-shih. (1986). "Han Foreign Relations," in *The Cambridge History of China: Volume I: the Ch'in and Han Empires, 221 B.C. – A.D. 220*, 377-462. Edited by Denis Twitchett and Michael Loewe. Cambridge: Cambridge University Press, pp 410-411.
[246] Xue, Zongzheng (薛宗正). (1992). History of the Turks (突厥史). Beijing: Zhongguo shehui kexue chubanshe, p. 596-598. ; OCLC 28622013
[247] Beckwith, Christopher. (1987). The Tibetan Empire in Central Asia. Princeton, NJ: Princeton University Press, pp 36, 146.
[248] Wechsler, Howard J.; Twitchett, Dennis C. (1979). Denis C. Twitchett; John K. Fairbank, eds. *The Cambridge History of China, Volume 3: Sui and T'ang China, 589–906, Part I*. Cambridge University Press. pp. 225–227.
[249] Ulrich Theobald. (16 October 2011). " City-states Along the Silk Road http://www.chinaknowledge.de/History/Altera/citystates.html#yutian." *ChinaKnowledge.de*. Accessed 2 September 2016.
[250] Xavier Tremblay, "The Spread of Buddhism in Serindia: Buddhism Among Iranians, Tocharians and Turks before the 13th Century", in *The Spread of Buddhism*, eds Ann Heirman and Stephan Peter Bumbacker, Leiden: Koninklijke Brill, 2007, p. 77.
[251] Whitfield 2004, p. 47.
[252] Wechsler, Howard J.; Twitchett, Dennis C. (1979). Denis C. Twitchett; John K. Fairbank, eds. The Cambridge History of China, Volume 3: Sui and T'ang China, 589–906, Part I. Cambridge University Press. pp. 225–228.
[253] Sarah Iles Johnston, Religions of the Ancient World: A Guide, Harvard University Press, 2004. pg 197
[254] Edward A Allworth,*Central Asia: A Historical Overview*,Duke University Press, 1994. pp 86.
[255] http://depts.washington.edu/silkroad/texts/weilue/weilue.html
[256] http://www.chinaknowledge.de/History/Altera/sakas.html
[257] https://books.google.com/books?id=pCiNqFj3MQsC
[258] http://www.livius.org/sao-sd/scythians/scythians.html
[259] http://evolutsioon.ut.ee/publications/Kivisild2003b.pdf
[260] http://boole.cs.iastate.edu/book/3-%CA%B7(%C0%FA%CA%B7)/3-%CA%C0%BD%E7%C0%FA%CA%B7/www.friesian.com/sangoku.htm#saka,
[261] //en.wikipedia.org/w/index.php?title=Template:Indo-Greeks&action=edit
[262] //en.wikipedia.org/w/index.php?title=Template:Indo-Greek_articles&action=edit
[263] As in other compounds such as "African-American", "Asian-American", "French-Canadian" and so on, the nationality or race of the newcomers usually comes first, and the area of arrival comes second, so that "Greco-Indian" is normally a more accurate nomenclature than "Indo-Greek". The latter however has become the general usage, especially since the publication of Narain's book *The Indo-Greeks*. In Thomas McEvilley 2002 "The Shape of Ancient Greek Thought" p.395 Note 52
[264] Mortimer Wheeler *Flames over Persepolis* (London, 1968). Pp. 112 *ff*. It is unclear whether the Hellenistic street plan found by Sir John Marshall's excavations dates from the Indo-Greeks or from the Kushans, who would have encountered it in Bactria; Tarn (1951, pp. 137, 179) ascribes the initial move of Taxila to the hill of Sirkap to Demetrius I, but sees this as "not a Greek city but an Indian one"; not a *polis* or with a Hippodamian plan.
[265] "Menander had his capital in Sagala" Bopearachchi, "Monnaies", p.83. McEvilley supports Tarn on both points, citing Woodcock: "Menander was a Bactrian Greek king of the Euthydemid dynasty. His capital (was) at Sagala (Sialkot) in the Punjab, "in the country of the Yonakas (Greeks)"." McEvilley, p.377. However, "Even if Sagala proves to be Sialkot, it does not seem to be Menander's capital for the Milindapanha states that Menander came down to Sagala to meet Nagasena, just as the Ganges flows to the sea."

[266] "A vast hoard of coins, with a mixture of Greek profiles and Indian symbols, along with interesting sculptures and some monumental remains from Taxila, Sirkap and Sirsukh, point to a rich fusion of Indian and Hellenistic influences", *India, the Ancient Past*, Burjor Avari, p.130

[267] Ghose, Sanujit (2011). "Cultural links between India and the Greco-Roman world" http://www.ancient.eu.com/article/208/. Ancient History Encyclopedia

[268] 11.34 http://www.perseus.tufts.edu/cgi-bin/ptext?lookup=Plb.+11.34

[269] ("Notes on Hellenism in Bactria and India". https://www.jstor.org/discover/10.2307/623931?uid=3739616&uid=2&uid=4&uid=3739256&sid=21102674788243 W. W. Tarn. *Journal of Hellenic Studies*, Vol. 22 (1902), pp. 268–293).

[270] Osmund Bopearachchi Was Indo-Greek Artemidoros the son of Indo-Sctythian Maues https://www.academia.edu/14260604/Was_Indo-Greek_Artemidoros_the_son_of_Indo-Sctythian_Maues

[271] "Most of the people east of the Ravi already noticed as within Menander's empire -Audumbaras, Trigartas, Kunindas, Yaudheyas, Arjunayanas- began to coins in the first century BC, which means that they had become independent kingdoms or republics.", Tarn, The Greeks in Bactria and India

[272] https://books.google.com/books?id=-HeJS3nE9cAC&pg=PA324#v=onepage&q&f=false

[273] "When the Greeks of Bactria and India lost their kingdom they were not all killed, nor did they return to Greece. They merged with the people of the area and worked for the new masters; contributing considerably to the culture and civilization in southern and central Asia." Narain, "The Indo-Greeks" 2003, p.278

[274] *India, the Ancient Past*, Burjor Avari, p. 92-93

[275] :"To the colonies settled in India, Python, the son of Agenor, was sent." Justin XIII.4 http://www.forumromanum.org/literature/justin/english/trans13.html

[276] Chandragupta Maurya and His Times, Radhakumud Mookerji, Motilal Banarsidass Publ., 1966, p.26-27 https://books.google.com/books?id=i-y6ZUheQH8C&pg=PA27

[277] Chandragupta Maurya and His Times, Radhakumud Mookerji, Motilal Banarsidass Publ., 1966, p.27 https://books.google.com/books?id=i-y6ZUheQH8C&pg=PA27

[278] History Of The Chamar Dynasty, Raj Kumar, Gyan Publishing House, 2008, p.51 https://books.google.com/books?id=eEJ-sXBmBIkC&pg=PA51

[279] "Kusumapura was besieged from every direction by the forces of Parvata and Chandragupta: Shakas, Yavanas, Kiratas, Kambojas, Parasikas, Bahlikas and others, assembled on the advice of Chanakya" in Mudrarakshasa 2. Sanskrit original: "asti tava Shaka-Yavana-Kirata-Kamboja-Parasika-Bahlika parbhutibhih Chankyamatipragrahittaishcha Chandergupta Parvateshvara balairudidhibhiriva parchalitsalilaih samantaad uprudham Kusumpurama". From the French translation, in "Le Ministre et la marque de l'anneau",

[280] *India, the Ancient Past*, Burjor Avari, p. 106-107

[281] Barua, Pradeep. The State at War in South Asia https://muse.jhu.edu/book/11919. Vol. 2. U of Nebraska Press, 2005. pp13-15 via Project MUSE

[282] Foreign Influence on Ancient India, Krishna Chandra Sagar, Northern Book Centre, 1992, p.83 https://books.google.com/books?id=0UA4rkm9MgkC&pg=PA83

[283] Pratisarga Parva p.18 http://mandhataglobal.com/wp-content/custom/articles/Puranas.pdf. Original Sanskrit of the first two verses: "Chandragupta Sutah Paursadhipateh Sutam. Suluvasya Tathodwahya Yavani Baudhtatapar".

[284] "A minor rock edict, recently discovered at Kandahar, was inscribed in two scripts, Greek and Aramaic", *India, the Ancient Past*, Burjor Avari, p. 112

[285] *India, the Ancient Past*, Burjor Avari, p.108-109

[286] "Three Greek ambassadors are known by name: Megasthenes, ambassador to Chandragupta; Deimachus, ambassador to Chandragupta's son Bindusara; and Dyonisius, whom Ptolemy Philadelphus sent to the court of Ashoka, Bindusara's son", McEvilley, p.367

[287] Classical sources have recorded that following their treaty, Chandragupta and Seleucus exchanged presents, such as when Chandragupta sent various aphrodisiacs to Seleucus: "And Theophrastus says that some contrivances are of wondrous efficacy in such matters as to make people more amorous. And Phylarchus confirms him, by reference to some of the presents which Sandrakottus, the king of the Indians, sent to Seleucus; which were to act like charms in producing a wonderful degree of affection, while some, on the contrary, were to

banish love" Athenaeus of Naucratis, "The deipnosophists" Book I, chapter 32 Ath. Deip. I.32 http://digicoll.library.wisc.edu/cgi-bin/Literature/Literature-idx?type=turn&entity= Literature000701860036&isize=M&pview=hide. Mentioned in McEvilley, p.367

[288] "The very fact that both Megasthenes and Kautilya refer to a state department run and maintained specifically for the purpose of looking after foreigners, who were mostly Yavanas and Persians, testifies to the impact created by these contacts.", Narain, "The Indo-Greeks", p.363

[289] "It also explains (...) random finds from the Sarnath, Basarth, and Patna regions of terra-cotta pieces of distinctive Hellenistic or with definite Hellenistic motifs and designs", Narain, "The Indo-Greeks" 2003, p. 363

[290] "The second Kandahar edict (the purely Greek one) of Ashoka is a part of the "corpus" known as the "Fourteen-Rock-Edicts"" Narain, "The Indo-Greeks" 2003, p.452

[291] "It is also in Kandahar that were found the fragments of a Greek translation of Edicts XII and XIII, as well as the Aramean translation of another edict of Ashoka", Bussagli, p.89

[292] "Within Ashoka's domain Greeks may have had special privileges, perhaps ones established by the terms of the Seleucid alliance. Rock Edict Thirteen indicates the existence of a Greek principality in the northwest of Ashoka's empire -perhaps Kandahar, or Alexandria-of-the-Arachosians- which was not ruled by him and for which he troubled to send Buddhist missionaries and published at least some of his edicts in Greek", McEvilley, p. 368

[293] "Thirteen, the longest and most important of the edicts, contains the claim, seemingly outlandish t first glance, that Ashoka had sent missions to the lands of the Greek monarchs -not only those of Asia, such as the Seleucids, but those back in the Mediterranean also", McEvilley, p.368

[294] "When Ashoka was converted to Buddhism, his first thought was to despatch missionaries to his friends, the Greek monarchs of Egypt, Syria, and Macedonia", Rawlinson, *Intercourse between India and the Western world*, p.39, quoted in McEvilley, p.368

[295] "In Rock Edict Two Ashoka even claims to have established hospitals for men and beasts in the Hellenistic kingdoms", McEvilley, p. 368

[296] "One of the most famous of these emissaries, Dharmaraksita, who was said to have converted thousands, was a Greek (Mhv.XII.5 and 34)", McEvilley, p.370

[297] "The Mahavamsa tells that "the celebrated Greek teacher Mahadharmaraksita in the second century BC led a delegation of 30,000 monks from Alexandria-of-the-Caucasus (Alexandra-of-the-Yonas, or of-the-Greeks, the Ceylonese text actually says) to the opening of the great Ruanvalli Stupa at Anuradhapura"", McEvilley, p. 370, quoting Woodcock, "The Greeks in India", p.55

[298] Full text of the Mahavamsa Click chapter XII http://lakdiva.org/mahavamsa/chapters.html

[299] "The finest of the pillars were executed by Greek or Perso-Greek sculptors; others by local craftsmen, with or without foreign supervision" Marshall, "The Buddhist art of Gandhara", p4

[300] "A number of foreign artisans, such as the Persians or even the Greeks, worked alongside the local craftsmen, and some of their skills were copied with avidity" Burjor Avari, "India, The ancient past", p. 118

[301] Foreign Influence on Ancient India by Krishna Chandra Sagar p.138 https://books.google.com/books?id=0UA4rkm9MgkC&pg=PA138

[302] The Idea of Ancient India: Essays on Religion, Politics, and Archaeology by Upinder Singh p.18 https://books.google.com/books?id=KIWTCwAAQBAJ&pg=PA18

[303] "Antiochos III, after having made peace with Euthydemus I after the aborted siege of Bactra, renewed with Sophagasenus the alliance concluded by his ancestor Seleucos I", Bopearachchi, *Monnaies*, p.52

[304] J. D. Lerner, The Impact of Seleucid Decline on the Eastern Iranian Plateau: The Foundations of Arsacid Parthia and Graeco-Bactria, (Stuttgart 1999)

[305] F. L. Holt, Thundering Zeus (Berkeley 1999)

[306] Justin XLI, paragraph 4 http://www.forumromanum.org/literature/justin/texte41.html

[307] Justin XLI, paragraph 1 http://www.forumromanum.org/literature/justin/texte41.html

[308] Strabo XI.XI.I http://www.perseus.tufts.edu/cgi-bin/ptext?lookup=Strab.+11.11.1

[309] Justin XLI http://www.forumromanum.org/literature/justin/texte41.html

[310]

[311] Strabo 11.11.2 http://www.perseus.tufts.edu/cgi-bin/ptext?lookup=Strab.+11.11.2

[312] Polybius 10.49, Battle of the Arius http://www.perseus.tufts.edu/cgi-bin/ptext?lookup=Plb. +10.49

[313] Polybius 11.34 Siege of Bactra http://www.perseus.tufts.edu/cgi-bin/ptext?lookup=Plb.+11.34

[314] On the image of the Greek kneeling warrior: "A bronze figurine of a kneeling warrior, not Greek work, but wearing a version of the Greek Phrygian helmet.. From a burial, said to be of the 4th century BC, just north of the Tien Shan range". Ürümqi Xinjiang Museum. (Boardman "The diffusion of Classical Art in Antiquity")

[315] Notice of the British Museum on the Zhou vase (2005, attached image): "Red earthenware bowl, decorated with a slip and inlaid with glass paste. Eastern Zhou period, 4th–3rd century BC. This bowl was probably intended to copy a more precious and possibly foreign vessel in bronze or even silver. Glass was little used in China. Its popularity at the end of the Eastern Zhou period was probably due to foreign influence."

[316] "The things which China received from the Graeco-Iranian world-the pomegranate and other "Chang-Kien" plants, the heavy equipment of the cataphract, the traces of Greeks influence on Han art (such as) the famous white bronze mirror of the Han period with Graeco-Bactrian designs (...) in the Victoria and Albert Museum" (Tarn, *The Greeks in Bactria and India*, pp. 363–364)

[317] Copper-Nickel coinage in Greco-Bactria. http://dougsmith.ancients.info/feac58bak.html

[318] Ancient Chinese weapons http://www.chinatoday.com.cn/English/e20026/sunzi1.htm A halberd of copper-nickel alloy, from the Warring States Period. https://web.archive.org/web/20051016180908/http://www.chinatoday.com.cn/English/e20026/images/t20026/p581.jpg

[319] A.A. Moss pp317-318 *Numismatic Chronicle* 1950

[320] C.Michael Hogan, *Silk Road, North China*, Megalithic Portal, ed. A. Burnham http://www.megalithic.co.uk/article.php?sid=18006

[321] Clement of Alexandria "The Stromata, or Miscellanies" Book I, Chapter XV http://www.earlychristianwritings.com/text/clement-stromata-book1.html

[322] "General Pushyamitra, who is at the origin of the Shunga dynasty. He was supported by the Brahmins and even became the symbol of the Brahmanical turnover against the Buddhism of the Mauryas. The capital was then transferred to Pataliputra (today's Patna)", Bussagli, p.99

[323] Pushyamitra is described as a "senapati" (Commander-in-chief) of Brihadratha in the Puranas

[324] E. Lamotte: History of Indian Buddhism, Institut Orientaliste, Louvain-la-Neuve 1988 (1958), p. 109.

[325] Aśoka and the Decline of the Mauryas by Romila Thapar, Oxford University Press,1960 p. 200

[326] Encyclopaedia of Indian Traditions and Cultural Heritage, Anmol Publications, 2009, p.18

[327] Pratisarga Parva p.18 http://mandhataglobal.com/wp-content/custom/articles/Puranas.pdf

[328] See Polybius, Arrian, Livy, Cassius Dio, and Diodorus. Justin, who will be discussed shortly, provides a summary of the histories of Hellenistic Macedonia, Egypt, Asia, and Parthia.

[329] For the date of Trogus, see the *OCD* on "Trogus" and Yardley/Develin, p. 2; since Trogus' father was in charge of Julius Caesar's diplomatic missions before the history was written (Justin 43.5.11), Senior's date in the following quotation is too early: "The Western sources for accounts of Bactrian and Indo-Greek history are: Polybius, a Greek born c.200 BC; Strabo, a Roman who drew on the lost history of Apollodoros of Artemita (c. 130–87 BC), and Justin, who drew on Trogus, a post 87 BC writer", Senior, *Indo-Scythian coins IV*, p.x; the extent to which Strabo is citing Apollodorus is disputed, beyond the three places he names Apollodorus (and he may have those through Eratosthenes). Polybius speaks of Bactria, not of India.

[330] Strabo, *Geographia* 11.11.1 p.516 *Casaubon*. 15.1.2, p. 686 *Casaubon*, "tribes" is Jones' version of *ethne* (Loeb)

[331] For a list of classical testimonia, see Tarn's Index II; but this covers India, Bactria, and several sources for the Hellenstic East as a whole.

[332] Tarn, App. 20; Narain (1957) pp. 136, 156 *et alii*.

[333] Demetrius is said to have founded Taxila (archaeological excavations), and also Sagala in the Punjab, which he seemed to have called Euthydemia, after his father ("the city of Sagala, also called Euthydemia" (Ptolemy, Geographia, VII 1))

[334] A Journey Through India's Past Chandra Mauli Mani, Northern Book Centre, 2005, p.39 https://books.google.com/books?id=HSoE8qR-5BgC&pg=PA39

[335] Polybius 11.34

[336] The first conquests of Demetrius have usually been held to be during his father's lifetime; the difference has been over the actual date. Tarn and Narain agreed on having them begin around 180; Bopearachchi moved this back to 200, and has been followed by much of the more recent literature, but see *Brill's New Pauly: Encyclopaedia of the Ancient World* (Boston, 2006) "Demetrius" §10, which places the invasion "probably in 184". D.H. MacDowell, "The Role of Demetrius in Arachosia and the Kabul Valley", published in the volume: O. Bopearachchi, Landes (ed), *Afghanistan Ancien Carrefour Entre L'Est Et L'Ouest*, (Brepols 2005) discusses an inscription dedicated to Euthydemus, "Greatest of all kings" and his son Demetrius, who is not called king but "Victorious" (Kallinikos). This is taken to indicate that Demetrius was his father's general during the first conquests. It is uncertain whether the Kabul valley or Arachosia were conquered first, and whether the latter province was taken from the Seleucids after their defeat by the Romans in 190 BC. Peculiar enough, more coins of Euthydemus I than of Demetrius I have been found in the mentioned provinces. The calendar of the "Yonas" is proven by an inscription giving a triple synchronism to have begun in 186/5 BC; what event is commemorated is itself uncertain. Richard Salomon "The Indo-Greek era of 186/5 B.C. in a Buddhist reliquary inscription", in *Afghanistan, Ancien Carrefour* cited.

[337] "Demetrius occupied a large part of the Indus delta, Saurashtra and Kutch", Burjor Avari, p.130

[338] "It would be impossible to explain otherwise why in all his portraits Demetrios is crowned with an elephant scalp", Bopearachchi, *Monnaies*, p.53

[339] "We think that the conquests of these regions south of the Hindu Kush brought to Demetrius I the title of "King of India" given to him by Apollodorus of Artemita." Bopearachchi, p.52

[340] For Heracles, see Lillian B. Lawler " Orchesis Kallinikos https://www.jstor.org/stable/283364" *Transactions and Proceedings of the American Philological Association*, Vol. 79. (1948), pp. 254–267, p. 262; for Artemidorus, see K. Walton Dobbins " The Commerce of Kapisene and Gandhāra after the Fall of Indo-Greek Rule https://www.jstor.org/stable/3596097" *Journal of the Economic and Social History of the Orient*, Vol. 14, No. 3. (Dec., 1971), pp. 286–302 (Both JSTOR). Tarn, p.132, argues that Alexander did not assume as a title, but was only hailed by it, but see Peter Green, *The Hellenistic Age*, p.7; see also Senior, Indo-Scythian coins, p.xii. No undisputed coins of Demetrius I himself use this title, but it is employed on one of the pedigree coins issued by Agathocles, which bear on the reverse the classical profile of Demetrius crowned by the elephant scalp, with the legend DEMETRIOS ANIKETOS, and on the reverse Herakles crowning himself, with the legend "Of king Agathocles" (Boppearachchi, "Monnaies", p.179 and Pl 8). Tarn, The Greeks in Bactria and India, Chap IV.

[341] "It now seems most likely that Demetrios was the founder of the newly discovered Greek Era of 186/5", Senior, *Indo-Scythian coins IV*

[342] MacDowall, 2004

[343] "The only thing that seems reasonably sure is that Taxila was part of the domain of Agathocles", Bopearachchi, *Monnaies*, p.59

[344] Iconography of Balarāma, Nilakanth Purushottam Joshi, Abhinav Publications, 1979, p.22 https://books.google.com/books?id=5vd-1KzyFg0C&pg=PA22

[345] Bopearachchi, *Monnaies*, p.63

[346] Reh Inscription Of Menander And The Indo-Greek Invasion Of The Ganga Valley, Sharma, G.R., 1980 p.ix-x, 10-11 https://archive.org/details/in.ernet.dli.2015.119433, Quote: "The archaeological evidence of unprecedented devastation of cities and towns from Delhi Hastinapur to Patna neatly corroborates (...)"

[347] "There is certainly some truth in Apollodorus and Strabo when they attribute to Menander the advances made by the Greeks of Bactria beyond the Hypanis and even as far as the Ganges and Palibothra (...) That the Yavanas advanced even beyond in the east, to the Ganges-Jamuna valley, about the middle of the second century BC is supported by the cumulative evidence provided by Indian sources", Narain, "The Indo-Greeks" p.267.

[348] "The Greeks... took possession, not only of Patalena, but also, on the rest of the coast, of what is called the kingdom of Saraostus and Sigerdis." Strabo 11.11.1 (Strabo 11.11.1 http://www.perseus.tufts.edu/cgi-bin/ptext?lookup=Strab.+11.11.1)

[349] *The Geography of India: Sacred and Historic Places* Educational Britannica Educational p.156 https://books.google.com/books?id=xPUvqtdfjyAC&pg=PA156

[350] Shane Wallace Greek Culture in Afghanistan and India: Old Evidence and New Discoveries https://www.academia.edu/25638818 2016, p.210

[351] Rocher, Ludo (1986), *The Puranas* https://books.google.com/books?id=n0-4RJh5FgoC&pg=PA254#v=onepage&q&f=false, p.254: "The Yuga [Purana] is important primarily as a historical document. It is a matter-of-fact chronicle [...] of the Magadha empire, down to the breakdown of the Sungas and the arrival of the Sakas. It is unique in its description of the invasion and retirement of the Yavanas in Magadha."

[352] "Numismats and historians all consider that Menander was one of the greatest, if not the greatest, and the most illustrious of the Indo-Greek kings", Bopearachchi, "Monnaies", p.76

[353] "Justin refers to an incident in which Eucratides with a small force of 300 was besieged for four months by "Demetrius, king of the Indians" with a large army of 60,000. The numbers are obviously an exaggeration. Eucratides managed to break out and went on to conquer India." It is uncertain who this Demetrius was, and when the siege happened. Some scholars believe that it was Demetrius I."(Demetrius I) was probably the Demetrius who besieged Eucratides for four months", D.W. Mac Dowall, p.201-202, *Afghanistan, ancien carrefour entre l'est et l'ouest*. This analysis goes against Bopearachchi, who has suggested that Demetrius I died long before Eucratides came to power.

[354] Bopearachchi, p.72

[355] "As Bopearachchi has shown, Menander was able to regroup and take back the territory that Eucratides I had conquered, perhaps after Eucratides had died (1991, pp. 84–6). Bopearachchi demonstrates that the transition in Menander's coin designs were in response to changes introduced by Eucratides".

[356] "Numismats and historians are unanimous in considering that Menander was one of the greatest, if not the greatest, and the most famous of the Indo-Greek kings. The coins to the name of Menander are incomparably more abundant than those of any other Indo-Greek king" Bopearachchi, "Monnaies Gréco-Bactriennes et Indo-Grecques", p. 76.

[357] "(In the Milindapanha) Menander is declared an arhat", McEvilley, p. 378.

[358] "Plutarch, who talks of the burial of Menander's relics under monuments or stupas, had obviously read or heard some Buddhist account of the Greek king's death", McEvilley, p. 377.

[359] "The statement of Plutarch that when Menander died "the cities celebrated (...) agreeing that they should divide ashes equally and go away and should erect monuments to him in all their cities", is significant and reminds one of the story of the Buddha", Narain, "The Indo-Greeks" 2003, p. 123, "This is unmistakably Buddhist and recalls the similar situation at the time of the Buddha's passing away", Narain, "The Indo-Greeks" 2003, p. 269.

[360] Bopearachchi, "Monnaies", p. 86.

[361] https://books.google.com/books?id=-HeJS3nE9cAC&pg=PA324#v=onepage&q&f=false

[362] Rudradaman (...) who by force destroyed the Yaudheyas who were loath to submit, rendered proud as they were by having manifested their' title of' heroes among all Kshatriyas.
— Junagadh rock inscription

[363] "By about 130 BC nomadic people from the Jaxartes region had overrun the northern boundary of Bactria itself", McEvilley, p. 372.

[364] Senior, *Indo-Scythian coins and history IV*, p.xxxiii

[365] In the 1st century BC, the geographer Isidorus of Charax mentions Parthians ruling over Greek populations and cities in Arachosia: "Beyond is Arachosia. And the Parthians call this White India; there are the city of Biyt and the city of Pharsana and the city of Chorochoad and the city of Demetrias; then Alexandropolis, the metropolis of Arachosia; it is Greek, and by it flows the river Arachotus. As far as this place the land is under the rule of the Parthians." "Parthians stations", 1st century BC. Mentioned in Bopearachchi, "Monnaies Greco-Bactriennes et Indo-Grecques", p52. Original text in paragraph 19 of Parthian stations http://www.parthia.com/parthian_stations.htm#PARTHIAN_STATIONS

[366] Pompeius Trogus, Prologue to Book XLI.

[367] "When Strabo mentions that "Those who after Alexander advanced beyond the Hypanis to the Ganges and Polibothra (Pataliputra)" this can only refer to the conquests of Menander.", Senior, *Indo-Scythian coins and history*, p.XIV

[368] Mitchener, *The Yuga Purana*, 2000, p.65: "In line with the above discussion, therefore, we may infer that such an event (the incursions to Pataliputra) took place, after the reign of Shalishuka

Maurya (c.200 BC) and before that of Pushyamitra Shunga (187 BC). This would accordingly place the Yavana incursions during the reign of the Indo-Greek kings Euthydemus (c.230–190 BC) or Demetrios (c.205-190 as co-regent, and 190–171 BC as supreme ruler".

[369] According to Tarn, the word used for "advance" (Proelonthes) can only mean a military expedition. The word generally means "going forward"; according to the LSJ this can, but need not, imply a military expedition. See LSJ, sub προέρχομαι. Strabo 15-1-27 http://www.perseus.tufts.edu/cgi-bin/ptext?doc=Perseus%3Atext%3A1999.01.0239&query=head%3D%23118

[370] A.K. Narain and Keay 2000

[371] "Menander became the ruler of a kingdom extending along the coast of western India, including the whole of Saurashtra and the harbour Barukaccha. His territory also included Mathura, the Punjab, Gandhara and the Kabul Valley", Bussagli p101)

[372] Tarn, p.147-149

[373] Strabo on the extent of the conquests of the Greco-Bactrians/Indo-Greeks: "They took possession, not only of Patalena, but also, on the rest of the coast, of what is called the kingdom of Saraostus and Sigerdis. In short, Apollodorus says that Bactriana is the ornament of Ariana as a whole; and, more than that, they extended their empire even as far as the Seres and the Phryni." Strabo 11.11.1 (Strabo 11.11.1 http://www.perseus.tufts.edu/cgi-bin/ptext?lookup=Strab.+11.11.1)

[374] Full text, Schoff's 1912 translation http://www.fordham.edu/halsall/ancient/periplus.html

[375] "the account of the Periplus is just a sailor's story", Narain (p.118-119)

[376] "A distinctive series of Indo-Greek coins has been found at several places in central India: including at Dewas, some 22 miles to the east of Ujjain. These therefore add further definite support to the likelihood of an Indo-Greek presence in Malwa" Mitchener, "The Yuga Purana", p.64

[377] "Coin-moulds of the Indo-Greeks have also been recovered from Ghuram and Naurangabad." Punjab History Conference, Punjabi University, 1990, Proceedings, Volume 23, p.45

[378] History and Historians in Ancient India, Dilip Kumar Ganguly, Abhinav Publications, 1984 p. 108 https://books.google.com/books?id=7v76i0eF9tQC&pg=PA108

[379] Encyclopaedia of Tourism Resources in India, Volume 1, Manohar Sajnani, Gyan Publishing House, 2001 p.93 https://books.google.com/books?id=vdMNBxOsvrUC&pg=PA93

[380] The Art and Architecture of the Indian Subcontinent, James C. Harle, Yale University Press, 1994 p.67 https://books.google.com/books?id=LwcBVvdqyBkC&pg=PA67

[381] Published in "L'Indo-Grec Menandre ou Paul Demieville revisite," Journal Asiatique 281 (1993) p.113

[382]

[383] Ancient Indian History and Civilization, Sailendra Nath Sen, New Age International, 1999, p. 169 https://books.google.com/books?id=Wk4_ICH_g1EC&pg=PA169

[384] History of Early Stone Sculpture at Mathura: Ca. 150 BCE - 100 CE, Sonya Rhie Quintanilla, BRILL, 2007, p.170

[385] "Because the Ionians were either the first or the most dominant group among the Greeks with whom people in the east came in contact, the Persians called all of them *Yauna*, and the Indians used *Yona* and *Yavana* for them", Narain, *The Indo-Greeks*, p.249

[386] "The term (Yavana) had a precise meaning until well into the Christian era, when gradually its original meaning was lost and, like the word Mleccha, it degenerated into a general term for a foreigner" Narain, p.18

[387] "Indo-Greek, Indo-Scythian and Indo-Parthian coins in the Smithsonian institution", Bopearachchi, p16.

[388] Tarn, p.145-146

[389] "But the real story of the Indo-Greek invasion becomes clear only on the analysis of the material contained in the historical section of the Gargi Samhita, the Yuga Purana" Narain, p110, *The Indo-Greeks*. Also "The text of the Yuga Purana, as we have shown, gives an explicit clue to the period and nature of the invasion of Pataliputra in which the Indo-Greeks took part, for it says that the Pancalas and the Mathuras were the other powers who attacked Saketa and destroyed Pataliputra", Narain, p.112

[390] "For any scholar engaged in the study of the presence of the Indo-Greeks or Indo-Scythians before the Christian Era, the *Yuga Purana* is an important source material" Dilip Coomer Ghose, General Secretary, The Asiatic Society, Kolkata, 2002

[391] "..further weight to the likelihood that this account of a Yavana incursion to Saketa and Pataliputra-in alliance with the Pancalas and the Mathuras- is indeed historical" Mitchener, *The Yuga Purana*, p. 65.

[392] "The advance of the Greek to Pataliputra is recorded from the Indian side in the Yuga-purana", Tarn, p.145

[393] "The greatest city in India is that which is called Palimbothra, in the dominions of the Prasians ... Megasthenes informs us that this city stretched in the inhabited quarters to an extreme length on each side of eighty stadia, and that its breadth was fifteen stadia, and that a ditch encompassed it all round, which was six hundred feet in breadth and thirty cubits in depth, and that the wall was crowned with 570 towers and had four-and-sixty gates." Arr. Ind. 10. "Of Pataliputra and the Manners of the Indians.", quoting Megasthenes Text http://www.mssu.edu/projectsouthasia/history/primarydocs/Foreign_Views/GreekRoman/Megasthenes-Indika.htm

[394] "The text of the Yuga Purana, as we have shown, gives an explicit clue to the period and nature of the invasion of Pataliputra in which the Indo-Greeks took part, for it says that the Pancalas and the Mathuras were the other powers who attacked Saketa and destroyed Pataliputra", Narain, *The Indo-Greeks*, p. 112.

[395] The Sungas, Kanvas, Republican Kingdoms and Monarchies, Mahameghavahanas, Dilip Kumar Chakrabarti, p.6 https://www.academia.edu/7469349/I.1._The_Sungas_Kanvas_Republican_Kingdoms_and_Monarchies_Mahameghavahanas

[396]

[397] "The taut posture and location at the entrance of the cave (Rani Gumpha) suggests that the male figure is a guard or dvarapala. The aggressive stance of the figure and its western dress (short kilt and boots) indicates that the sculpture may be that of a Yavana, foreigner from the Graeco-Roman world." in Early Sculptural Art in the Indian Coastlands: A Study in Cultural Transmission and Syncretism (300 BCE-CE 500), by Sunil Gupta, D K Printworld (P) Limited, 2008, p.85

[398] "Indo-Greek, Indo-Scythian and Indo-Parthian coins in the Smithsonian institution", Bopearachchi, p16. Also: "Kalidasa recounts in his Mālavikāgnimitra (5.15.14–24) that Puspamitra appointed his grandson Vasumitra to guard his sacrificial horse, which wandered on the right bank of the Sindhu river and was seized by Yavana cavalrymen- the later being thereafter defeated by Vasumitra. The "Sindhu" referred to in this context may refer the river Indus: but such an extension of Shunga power seems unlikely, and it is more probable that it denotes one of two rivers in central India -either the Sindhu river which is a tributary of the Yamuna, or the Kali-Sindhu river which is a tributary of the Chambal." The Yuga Purana, Mitchener, 2002.)"

[399] Tarn, pp. 132–133.

[400] "The name Dimita is almost certainly an adaptation of "Demetrios", and the inscription thus indicates a Yavana presence in Magadha, probably around the middle of the 1st century BC." Mitchener, *The Yuga Purana*, p. 65.

[401] "The Hathigumpha inscription seems to have nothing to do with the history of the Indo-Greeks; certainly it has nothing to do with Demetrius I", Narain, *The Indo-Greeks*, p. 50.

[402] Translation in Epigraphia Indica 1920 p.87 https://archive.org/details/epigrahiaindicav014769mbp

[403] P.L.Gupta: Kushâna Coins and History, D.K.Printworld, 1994, p.184, note 5

[404] "Numismats and historians all consider that Menander was one of the greatest, if not the greatest, and the most illustrious of the Indo-Greek kings", Bopearachchi, "Monnaies", p.76

[405] "Justin refers to an incident in which Eucratides with a small force of 300 was besieged for four months by "Demetrius, king of the Indians" with a large army of 60,000. The numbers are obviously an exaggeration. Eucratides managed to break out and went on to conquer India." It is uncertain who this Demetrius was, and when the siege happened. Some scholars believe that it was Demetrius I."(Demetrius I) was probably the Demetrius who besieged Eucratides for four months", D.W. Mac Dowall, p.201-202, *Afghanistan, ancien carrefour entre l'est et l'ouest*. This analysis goes against Bopearachchi, who has suggested that Demetrius I died long before Eucratides came to power.

[406] Bopearachchi, p.72

[407] "As Bopearachchi has shown, Menander was able to regroup and take back the territory that Eucratides I had conquered, perhaps after Eucratides had died (1991, pp. 84–6). Bopearachchi demonstrates that the transition in Menander's coin designs were in response to changes introduced by Eucratides".

[408] "Numismats and historians are unanimous in considering that Menander was one of the greatest, if not the greatest, and the most famous of the Indo-Greek kings. The coins to the name of Menander are incomparably more abundant than those of any other Indo-Greek king" Bopearachchi, "Monnaies Gréco-Bactriennes et Indo-Grecques", p. 76.

[409] "Menander, the probable conqueror of Pataliputra, seems to have been a Buddhist, and his name belongs in the list of important royal patrons of Buddhism along with Ashoka and Kanishka", McEvilley, p. 375.

[410] "(In the Milindapanha) Menander is declared an arhat", McEvilley, p. 378.

[411] "Plutarch, who talks of the burial of Menander's relics under monuments or stupas, had obviously read or heard some Buddhist account of the Greek king's death", McEvilley, p. 377.

[412] "The statement of Plutarch that when Menander died "the cities celebrated (...) agreeing that they should divide ashes equally and go away and should erect monuments to him in all their cities", is significant and reminds one of the story of the Buddha", Narain, "The Indo-Greeks" 2003, p. 123, "This is unmistakably Buddhist and recalls the similar situation at the time of the Buddha's passing away", Narain, "The Indo-Greeks" 2003, p. 269.

[413] Bopearachchi, "Monnaies", p. 86.

[414] "By about 130 BC nomadic people from the Jaxartes region had overrun the northern boundary of Bactria itself", McEvilley, p. 372.

[415] Boot, Hooves and Wheels: And the Social Dynamics behind South Asian Warfare, Saikat K Bose, Vij Books India Pvt Ltd, 2015, p.226 https://books.google.com/books?id=ywfsCgAAQBAJ&pg=PT226

[416] On the Cusp of an Era: Art in the Pre-Kuṣāṇa World, Doris Srinivasan, BRILL, 2007, p.101 https://books.google.com/books?id=ZuevCQAAQBAJ&pg=PA101

[417] Osmund Bopearachchi Was Indo-Greek Artemidoros the son of Indo-Sctythian Maues https://www.academia.edu/14260604/Was_Indo-Greek_Artemidoros_the_son_of_Indo-Sctythian_Maues

[418] Bopearachchi, *Monnaies*, p.88

[419] Senior, *Indo-Scythian coins and history IV*, p.xi

[420] Boot, Hooves and Wheels: And the Social Dynamics behind South Asian Warfare, Saikat K Bose, Vij Books India Pvt Ltd, 2015, p.226 https://books.google.com/books?id=ywfsCgAAQBAJ&pg=PT226

[421] On the Cusp of an Era: Art in the Pre-Kuṣāṇa World, Doris Srinivasan, BRILL, 2007, p.101 https://books.google.com/books?id=ZuevCQAAQBAJ&pg=PA101

[422] Osmund Bopearachchi Was Indo-Greek Artemidoros the son of Indo-Sctythian Maues https://www.academia.edu/14260604/Was_Indo-Greek_Artemidoros_the_son_of_Indo-Sctythian_Maues

[423] "P.Bernard thinks that these emissions were destined to commercial exchanges with Bactria, then controlled by the Yuezhi, and were post-Greek coins remained faithful to Greco-Bactrian coinage. In a slightly different perspective (...) G. Le Rider considers that these emission were used to pay tribute to the nomads of the north, who were thus incentivized not to pursue their forays in the direction of the Indo-Greek realm", Bopearachchi, "Monnaies", p.76.

[424] Osmund Bopearachchi, 2016, Emergence of Viṣṇu and Śiva Images in India: Numismatic and Sculptural Evidence https://www.academia.edu/25807197/Emergence_of_Vi%E1%B9%A3%E1%B9%87u_and_%C5%9Aiva_Images_in_India_Numismatic_and_Sculptural_Evidence

[425] Ancient Indian History and Civilization, Sailendra Nath Sen, New Age International, 1999 p. 170 https://books.google.com/books?id=Wk4_ICH_g1EC&pg=PA170

[426]

[427] Buddhist Landscapes in Central India: Sanchi Hill and Archaeologies of Religious and Social Change, C. Third Century BC to Fifth Century AD, by Julia Shaw, Left Coast Press, 2013 p.90 https://books.google.com/books?id=jzkyBgAAQBAJ&pg=PA90

[428] "The railing of Sanchi Stupa No.2, which represents the oldest extensive stupa decoration in existence, (and) dates from about the second century B.C.E" Constituting Communities: Theravada Buddhism and the Religious Cultures of South and Southeast Asia, John Clifford Holt, Jacob N. Kinnard , Jonathan S. Walters, SUNY Press, 2012 p.197 https://books.google.com/books?id=PnnG8sclrdYC&pg=PA197

[429] Didactic Narration: Jataka Iconography in Dunhuang with a Catalogue of Jataka Representations in China, Alexander Peter Bell, LIT Verlag Münster, 2000 p.15ff https://books.google.com/books?id=77hHrXX4COgC&pg=PA15

[430] Buddhist Landscapes in Central India: Sanchi Hill and Archaeologies of Religious and Social Change, C. Third Century BC to Fifth Century AD, Julia Shaw, Left Coast Press, 2013 p.88ff https://books.google.com/books?id=jzkyBgAAQBAJ&pg=PA88

[431] As in other compounds such as "African-American", "Asian-American", "French-Canadian" and so on, the nationality or race of the newcomers usually comes first, and the area of arrival comes second, so that "Greco-Indian" is normally a more accurate nomenclature than "Indo-Greek". The latter however has become the general usage, especially since the publication of Narain's book *The Indo-Greeks*. In Thomas McEvilley 2002 "The Shape of Ancient Greek Thought" p.395 Note 52

[432] Faces of Power: Alexander's Image and Hellenistic Politics, Andrew Stewart, University of California Press, 1993 p.180 https://books.google.com/books?id=1SUw29Q_SeMC&pg=PA180

[433] Popular Controversies in World History: Investigating History's Intriguing Questions [4 volumes]: Investigating History's Intriguing Questions, Steven L. Danver, ABC-CLIO, 2010 p.91 https://books.google.com/books?id=slVobUjdzGMC&pg=RA1-PA91

[434] Buddhist Art & Antiquities of Himachal Pradesh, Up to 8th Century A.D., Omacanda Hāṇḍā, Indus Publishing, 1994 p.48 https://books.google.com/books?id=6Cqgb9pL3L4C&pg=PA48

[435] Didactic Narration: Jataka Iconography in Dunhuang with a Catalogue of Jataka Representations in China, Alexander Peter Bell, LIT Verlag Münster, 2000 p.18 https://books.google.com/books?id=77hHrXX4COgC&pg=PA18

[436]

[437] Buddhist Architecture, Huu Phuoc Le, Grafikol, 2010 p.149ff https://books.google.com/books?id=9jb364g4BvoC&pg=PA149

[438]

[439] "There is evidence of Hellensitic sculptors being in touch with Sanchi and Bharhut" in The Buddha Image: Its Origin and Development, Yuvraj Krishan, Bharatiya Vidya Bhavan, 1996, p. 9 https://books.google.com/books?id=kDyJh--iaL0C&pg=PA9

[440] Buddhist Architecture by Huu Phuoc Le p.161 https://books.google.com/books?id=9jb364g4BvoC&pg=PA161

[441]

[442] These "Greek-looking foreigners" are also described in Susan Huntington, "The art of ancient India", p. 100

[443] "The Greeks evidently introduced the himation and the chiton seen in the terracottas from Taxila and the short kilt worn by the soldier on the Sanchi relief." in Foreign influence on Indian culture: from c. 600 B.C. to 320 A.D., Manjari Ukil Originals, 2006, p.162

[444] "The scene shows musicians playing a variety of instruments, some of them quite extraordinary such as the Greek double flute and wind instruments with dragon head from West Asia" in The Archaeology of Seafaring in Ancient South Asia, Himanshu Prabha Ray, Cambridge University Press, 2003 p.255 https://books.google.com/books?id=iHHzP4uVpn4C&pg=PA255

[445] Epigraphia Indica Vol.2 p.395 inscription 364 https://archive.org/stream/in.ernet.dli.2015.100320/2015.100320.Archaeological-Survey-Of-India-Epigraphia-Indica-Vol-2

[446] John Mashall, The Monuments of Sanchi p.348 inscription No.475 https://archive.org/stream/in.ernet.dli.2015.532798

[447] The Idea of Ancient India: Essays on Religion, Politics, and Archaeology, Sage Publications India, Upinder Singh, 2016 p.18 https://books.google.com/books?id=KIWTCwAAQBAJ&pg=PA18

[448] John Mashall, The Monuments of Sanchi p.308 inscription No.89 https://archive.org/stream/in.ernet.dli.2015.532798

[449] John Mashall, The Monuments of Sanchi p.345 inscription No.433 https://archive.org/stream/in.ernet.dli.2015.532798

[450] "During the century that followed Menander more than twenty rulers are known to have struck coins", Narain, "The Indo-Greeks" 2003, p.270
[451] Bernard (1994), p. 126.
[452] "Kujula Kadphises, founder of the Kushan Empire, succeeded there (in the Paropamisadae) to the nomads who minted imitations of Hermaeus" Bopearachchi, "Monnaies", p.117
[453] "Maues himself issued joint coins with Machene, (...) probably a daughter of one of the Indo-Greek houses" Senior, *Indo-Scythians*, p.xxxvi
[454] G.K. Jenkins, using overstrikes and monograms, showed that, contrary to what Narai would write two years later, Apollodotus II and Hippostratus were posterior, by far, to Maues. (...) He reveals an overstike if Azes I over Hippostratus. (...) Apollodotus and Hippostratus are thus posterior to Maues and anterior to Azes I, whose era we now starts in 57 BC." Bopearachchi, p. 126-127.
[455] "It is curious that on his copper Zoilos used a bow and quiver as a type. A quiver was a badge used by the Parthians (Scythians) and had been used previously by Diodotos, who we know had made a treaty with them. Did Zoilos use Scythian mercenaries in his quest against Menander perhaps?" Senior, *Indo-Scythian coins*, p.xxvii
[456] "The Indo-Scythian conquerors, who, also they adopted the Greek types, minted money with their own names". Bopearachchci, "Monnaies", p.121
[457] Described in R. C. Senior "The Decline of the Indo-Greeks" http://www.onsnumis.org/news/0499newrecpubl.shtml. See also this source http://www.iranica.com/newsite/articles/ot_grp8/ot_indoscyth_20050802.html .
[458] "We get two Greeks of the Parthian period, the first half of the first century AD, who used the Indian form of their names, King Theodamas on his signet-ring found in Bajaur, and Thedorus son of Theoros on two silver bowls from Taxila." Tarn, p. 389.
[459] "Most of the people east of the Ravi already noticed as within Menander's empire -Audumbaras, Trigartas, Kunindas, Yaudheyas, Arjunayanas- began to coins in the first century BC, which means that they had become independent kingdoms or republics.", Tarn, p. 324.
[460] "The coinage of the former (the Audumbaras) to whom their trade was of importance, starts somewhere in the first century BC; they occasionally imitate the types of Demetrius and Apollodotus I", Tarn, p. 325.
[461] The Kunindas must have been included in the Greek empire, not only because of their geographical position, but because they started coining at the time which saw the end of Greek rule and the establishment of their independence", Tarn, p. 238.
[462] "Further evidence of the commercial success of the Greek drachms is seen in the fact that they influenced the coinage of the Audumbaras and the Kunindas", Narain *The Indo-Greeks*, p.114
[463] "The wealthy Audumbaras (...) some of their coins after Greek rule ended imitated Greek types", Tarn, p. 239.
[464] "Later, in the first century a ruler of the Kunindas, Amogabhuti, issued a silver coinage "which would compete in the market with the later Indo-Greek silver"", Tarn, p. 325.
[465] The Sanskrit inscription reads "Yavanarajyasya sodasuttare varsasate 100 10 6". R.Salomon, "The Indo-Greek era of 186/5 B.C. in a Buddhist reliquary inscription", in "Afghanistan, ancien carrefour entre l'est et l'ouest", p373
[466] History of Early Stone Sculpture at Mathura: Ca. 150 BCE - 100 CE, Sonya Rhie Quintanilla, BRILL, 2007, p.170
[467] "Around 10 AD, with the joint rule of Straton II and his son Straton in the area of Sagala, the last Greek kingdom succumbed to the attacks of Rajuvula, the Indo-Scythian satrap of Mathura.", Bopearachchi, "Monnaies", p.125
[468] Epigraphia Indica Vol.18 p.328 Inscription No10 https://archive.org/stream/in.ernet.dli.2015.367557
[469] Mc Evilley "The shape of ancient thought", p385 ("The Yavanajataka is the earliest surviving Sanskrit text in astrology, and constitute the basis of all later Indian developments in horoscopy", himself quoting David Pingree "The Yavanajataka of Sphujidhvaja" p5)
[470] Buddhist architecture, Lee Huu Phuoc, Grafikol 2009, p.98-99 https://books.google.com/books?id=9jb364g4BvoC&pg=PA99&lpg=PA99

[471] World Heritage Monuments and Related Edifices in India, Volume 1 'Alī Jāvīd, Tabassum Javeed, Algora Publishing, 2008 p.42 https://books.google.com/books?id=fg-lGID3WpQC&pg=PA42

[472] * Inscription no.7: "(This) pillar (is) the gift of the Yavana Sihadhaya from Dhenukataka" in Problems of Ancient Indian History: New Perspectives and Perceptions, Shankar Goyal - 2001, p.104
* Inscription no.4: "(This) pillar (is) the gift of the Yavana Dhammadhya from Dhenukataka" Description in Hellenism in Ancient India by Gauranga Nath Banerjee p.20 https://books.google.fr/books?id=3P8YNA-bbGIC&pg=PA20

[473] Epigraphia Indica Vol.18 p.326-328 https://archive.org/stream/in.ernet.dli.2015.367557 and Epigraphia Indica Vol.7 [Epigraphia Indica Vol.7 p.53-54 https://archive.org/details/epigraphiaindica014351mbp

[474] The Greek-Indians of Western India: A Study of the Yavana and Yonaka Buddhist Cave Temple Inscriptions, 'The Indian International Journal of Buddhist Studies', NS 1 (1999-2000) S._1_1999-2000_pp._83-109 https//www.academia.edu

[475] Epigraphia Indica p.90ff https://archive.org/stream/EpigraphiaIndica/Epigraphia_Indica

[476] Hellenism in Ancient India, Gauranga Nath Banerjee p.20

[477] The Roman Empire and the Indian Ocean: The Ancient World Economy and the Kingdoms of Africa, Arabia and India, Raoul McLaughlin, Pen and Sword, 2014 p.170 https://books.google.com/books?id=WmZtBQAAQBAJ&pg=PA170

[478]

[479] Upinder Singh (2008). A History of Ancient and Early Medieval India: From the Stone Age to the 12th Century. Pearson Education India. p.383

[480] Nasik cave inscription No 1. "(Of him) the Kshatriya , who flaming like the god of love, subdued the Sakas, Yavavas and Palhavas" in Parsis of ancient India by Hodivala, Shapurji Kavasji p.16 https://archive.org/stream/parsisofancienti00hodiiala

[481] Epigraphia Indica p.61-62 https://archive.org/stream/EpigraphiaIndica/Epigraphia_Indica

[482] Osmund Bopearachchi "Monnaies Gréco-Bactriennes et Indo-Grecques" Bibliothèque Nationale 1991,

[483]

[484] P. Bernard, Revue Numismatique 1974 http://www.persee.fr/doc/numi_0484-8942_1974_num_6_16_1062

[485] P. Bernard, Revue Numismatique 1974 http://www.persee.fr/doc/numi_0484-8942_1974_num_6_16_1062

[486] Marital alliances: • Discussion on the dynastic alliance in Tarn, pp. 152–153: "It has been recently suggested that Ashoka was grandson of the Seleucid princess, whom Seleucus gave in marriage to Chandragupta. Should this far-reaching suggestion be well founded, it would not only throw light on the good relations between the Seleucid and Maurya dynasties, but would mean that the Maurya dynasty was descended from, or anyhow connected with, Seleucus... when the Mauryan line became extinct, he (Demetrius) may well have regarded himself, if not as the next heir, at any rate as the heir nearest at hand". Also: "The Seleucid and Maurya lines were connected by the marriage of Seleucus' daughter (or niece) either to Chandragupta or his son Bindusara" John Marshall, Taxila, p20. This thesis originally appeared in "The Cambridge Shorter History of India": "If the usual oriental practice was followed and if we regard Chandragupta as the victor, then it would mean that a daughter or other female relative of Seleucus was given to the Indian ruler or to one of his sons, so that Ashoka may have had Greek blood in his veins." The Cambridge Shorter History of India, J. Allan, H. H. Dodwell, T. Wolseley Haig, p33 Source https://www.questia.com/PM.qst?a=o&d=88816404. • Description of the 302 BC marital alliance in Strabo 15.2.1(9) http://www.perseus.tufts.edu/cgi-bin/ptext?doc=Perseus%3Atext%3A1999.01.0239&query=head%3D%23120: "The Indians occupy in part some of the countries situated along the Indus, which formerly belonged to the Persians: Alexander deprived the Ariani of them, and established there settlements of his own. But Seleucus Nicator gave them to Sandrocottus in consequence of a marriage contract, and received in return five hundred elephants." The ambassador Megasthenes was also sent to the Mauryan court on this occasion.

[487] Exchange of presents: • Classical sources have recorded that Chandragupta sent various aphrodisiacs to Seleucus: "And Theophrastus says that some contrivances are of wondrous efficacy in such matters as to make people more amorous. And Phylarchus confirms him, by reference to some of the presents which Sandrakottus, the king of the Indians, sent to Seleucus; which were to act like charms in producing a wonderful degree of affection, while some, on the contrary, were to banish love" Athenaeus of Naucratis, "The deipnosophists" Book I, chapter 32 Ath. Deip. I.32 http://digicoll.library.wisc.edu/cgi-bin/Literature/Literature-idx?type=turn&entity=Literature000701860036&isize=M&pview=hide • Ashoka claims he introduced herbal medicine in the territories of the Greeks, for the welfare of humans and animals (Edict No2). • Bindusara asked Antiochus I to send him some sweet wine, dried figs and a sophist: "But dried figs were so very much sought after by all men (for really, as Aristophanes says, "There's really nothing nicer than dried figs"), that even Amitrochates, the king of the Indians, wrote to Antiochus, entreating him (it is Hegesander who tells this story) to buy and send him some sweet wine, and some dried figs, and a sophist; and that Antiochus wrote to him in answer, "The dry figs and the sweet wine we will send you; but it is not lawful for a sophist to be sold in Greece" Athenaeus, "Deipnosophistae" XIV.67 Athenaeus, "Deipnosophistae" XIV.67 http://digicoll.library.wisc.edu/cgi-bin/Literature/Literature-idx?type=goto&id=Literature.AthV3&isize=M&page=1044

[488] Treaties of friendship: • When Antiochos III, after having made peace with Euthydemus, went to India in 209 BC, he is said to have renewed his friendship with the Indian king there and received presents from him: "He crossed the Caucasus (Hindu Kush) and descended into India; renewed his friendship with Sophagasenus the king of the Indians; received more elephants, until he had a hundred and fifty altogether; and having once more provisioned his troops, set out again personally with his army: leaving Androsthenes of Cyzicus the duty of taking home the treasure which this king had agreed to hand over to him." Polybius 11.39 http://www.perseus.tufts.edu/cgi-bin/ptext?lookup=Plb.+11.39

[489] Ambassadors: • Known ambassadors to India are Megasthenes, Deimakos and Dionysius.

[490] Religious missions: • In the Edicts of Ashoka, king Ashoka claims to have sent Buddhist emissaries to the Hellenistic west around 250 BC.

[491] The historian Diodorus wrote that the king of Pataliputra, apparently a Mauryan king, "loved the Greeks": "Iambulus, having found his way to a certain village, was then brought by the natives into the presence of the king of Palibothra, a city which was distant a journey of many days from the sea. And since the king loved the Greeks ("Philhellenos") and devoted to learning he considered Iambulus worthy of cordial welcome; and at length, upon receiving a permission of safe-conduct, he passed over first of all into Persia and later arrived safe in Greece" Diodorus ii,60.

[492] "Diodorus testifies to the great love of the king of Palibothra, apparently a Mauryan king, for the Greeks" Narain, "The Indo-Greeks", p. 362.

[493] "Obviously, for the Greeks who survived in India and suffered from the oppression of the Shunga (for whom they were aliens and heretics), Demetrios must have appeared as a saviour" Mario Bussagli, p. 101

[494] "We can now, I think, see what the Greek 'conquest' meant and how the Greeks were able to traverse such extraordinary distances. To parts of India, perhaps to large parts, they came, not as conquerors, but as friends or 'saviours'; to the Buddhist world in particular they appeared to be its champions" (Tarn, p. 180)

[495] Tarn p. 175. Also: "The people to be 'saved' were in fact usually Buddhists, and the common enmity of Greek and Buddhists to the Shunga king threw them into each other's arms", Tarn p. 175. "Menander was coming to save them from the oppression of the Sunga kings", Tarn p. 178.

[496] Whitehead, "Indo-Greek coins", p 3-8

[497] Bopearachchi p. 138

[498] Whitehead, p. vi.

[499] "These Indo-Greeks were called Yavanas in ancient Indian literature" p.9 + note 1 "The term had a precise meaning until well into the Christian era, when gradually its original meaning was lost and, like the word *Mleccha*, it degenerated into a general term for a foreigner" p.18, Narain "The Indo-Greeks"

500 "All Greeks in India were however known as Yavanas", Burjor Avari, "India, the ancient past", p.130
501 "The term Yavana may well have been first applied by the Indians to the Greeks of various cities of Asia Minor who were settled in the areas contiguous to north-west India" Narain "The Indo-Greeks", p.227
502 "Of the Sanskrit Yavana, there are other forms and derivatives, viz. Yona, Yonaka, Javana, Yavana, Jonon or Jononka, Ya-ba-na etc... Yona is a normal Prakrit form from Yavana", Narain "The Indo-Greeks", p.228
503 Hinüber (2000), pp. 83-86, para. 173-179.
504 The coins of the Greek and Scythic kings of Bactria and India in the British Museum, P.50 and Pl. XII-7 https://archive.org/details/cu31924022932382
505 "De l'Indus à l'Oxus: archéologie de l'Asie Centrale", Pierfrancesco Callieri, p212: "The diffusion, from the second century BC, of Hellenistic influences in the architecture of Swat is also attested by the archaeological searches at the sanctuary of Butkara I, which saw its stupa "monumentalized" at that exact time by basal elements and decorative alcoves derived from Hellenistic architecture".
506 Tarn, p. 391: "Somewhere I have met with the zhole-hearted statement that every Greek in India ended by becoming a Buddhist (...) Heliodorus the ambassador was a Bhagavatta, a worshiper of Vshnu-Krishna as the supreme deity (...) Theodorus the meridrarch, who established some relics of the Buddha "for the purpose of the security of many people", was undoubtedly Buddhist". Images of the Zoroastrian divinity Mithra – depicted with a radiated phrygian cap – appear extensively on the Indo-Greek coinage of the Western kings. This Zeus-Mithra is also the one represented seated (with the gloriole around the head, and a small protrusion on the top of the head representing the cap) on many coins of Hermaeus, Antialcidas or Heliokles II.
507 The Contribution of the Emperor Asoka Maurya to the Development of the Humanitarian Ideal in Warfare 30-04-1995 Article, International Review of the Red Cross, No. 305, by Gerald Draper
508 Rock Edict Nb13 (S. Dhammika)
509 Lahiri, Bela (1974). Indigenous states of northern India, circa 200 B.C. to 320 A.D. University of Calcutta
510 Strong, John S. (1989). The Legend of King Aśoka : a study and translation of the Aśokāvadāna. Princeton: Princeton University Press. ISBN 0-691-01459-0.
511 "It is not unlikely that "Dikaios", which is translated Dhramaika in the Kharosthi legend, may be connected with his adoption of the Buddhist faith." Narain, "The Indo-Greeks" 2003, p.124
512 "It is probable that the wheel on some coins of Menander is connected with Buddhism", Narain, The Indo-Greeks, p.122
513 Stupavadana, Chapter 57, v15. Quotes in E.Seldeslachts.
514 McEvilley, p.377
515 Plutarch "Political precepts", p147–148
516 Handbuch der Orientalistik, Kurt A. Behrendt, BRILL, 2004, p.49 sig https://books.google.com/books?id=C9_vbgkzUSkC&pg=PA49
517 "King Menander, who built the penultimate layer of the Butkara stupa in the first century BCE, was an Indo-Greek."in Empires of the Indus: The Story of a River, Alice Albinia – 2012
518 Foreign Impact on Indian Life and Culture (c. 326 B.C. to C. 300 A.D.) Satyendra Nath Naskar, Abhinav Publications, 1996, p.69 https://books.google.com/books?id=SuEBGgRHHuIC&pg=PA69
519 The Crossroads of Asia, Elizabeth Errington, Ancient India and Iran Trust, Fitzwilliam Museum, Ancient India and Iran Trust, 1992, p.16
520 Mentioned throughout "Monnaies Greco-Bactriennes et Indo-Grecques", Osmund Bopearachchi, Bibliotheque Nationale, 1991
521 Cultural Sociology of the Middle East, Asia, and Africa: An Encyclopedia, Andrea L. Stanton, Edward Ramsamy, Peter J. Seybolt, Carolyn M. Elliott, SAGE Publications, 2012 p.28 https://books.google.com/books?id=nVN2AwAAQBAJ&pg=RA3-PA28
522 "The extraordinary realism of their portraiture. The portraits of Demetrius, Antimachus and of Eucratides are among the most remarkable that have come down to us from antiquity" Hellenism in Ancient India, Banerjee, p134

[523] "Just as the Frank Clovis had no part in the development of Gallo-Roman art, the Indo-Scythian Kanishka had no direct influence on that of Indo-Greek Art; and besides, we have now the certain proofs that during his reign this art was already stereotyped, of not decadent" Hellenism in Ancient India, Banerjee, p147

[524] "The survival into the 1st century AD of a Greek administration and presumably some elements of Greek culture in the Punjab has now to be taken into account in any discussion of the role of Greek influence in the development of Gandharan sculpture", The Crossroads of Asia, p14

[525] On the Indo-Greeks and the Gandhara school: • 1) "It is necessary to considerably push back the start of Gandharan art, to the first half of the first century BC, or even, very probably, to the preceding century.(...) The origins of Gandharan art... go back to the Greek presence. (...) Gandharan iconography was already fully formed before, or at least at the very beginning of our era" Mario Bussagli "L'art du Gandhara", p331–332 • 2) "The beginnings of the Gandhara school have been dated everywhere from the first century B.C. (which was M.Foucher's view) to the Kushan period and even after it" (Tarn, p. 394). Foucher's views can be found in "La vieille route de l'Inde, de Bactres a Taxila", pp340–341). The view is also supported by Sir John Marshall ("The Buddhist art of Gandhara", pp5–6). • 3) Also the recent discoveries at Ai-Khanoum confirm that "Gandharan art descended directly from Hellenized Bactrian art" (Chaibi Nustamandy, "Crossroads of Asia", 1992). • 4) On the Indo-Greeks and Greco-Buddhist art: "It was about this time (100 BC) that something took place which is without parallel in Hellenistic history: Greeks of themselves placed their artistic skill at the service of a foreign religion, and created for it a new form of expression in art" (Tarn, p. 393). "We have to look for the beginnings of Gandharan Buddhist art in the residual Indo-Greek tradition, and in the early Buddhist stone sculpture to the South (Bharhut etc...)" (Boardman, 1993, p. 124). "Depending on how the dates are worked out, the spread of Gandhari Buddhism to the north may have been stimulated by Menander's royal patronage, as may the development and spread of the Gandharan sculpture, which seems to have accompanied it" McEvilley, 2002, "The shape of ancient thought", p. 378.

[526] Benjamin Rowland JR, foreword to "The Dyasntic art of the Kushan", John Rosenfield, 1967

[527] Boardman, p. 141

[528] Boardman, p. 143.

[529] "Others, dating the work to the first two centuries A.D., after the waning of Greek autonomy on the Northwest, connect it instead with the Roman Imperial trade, which was just then getting a foothold at sites like Barbaricum (modern Karachi) at the Indus-mouth. It has been proposed that one of the embassies from Indian kings to Roman emperors may have brought back a master sculptorto oversee work in the emerging Mahayana Buddhist sensibility (in which the Buddha came to be seen as a kind of deity), and that "bands of foreign workmen from the eastern centres of the Roman Empire" were brought to India" (Mc Evilley "The shape of ancient thought", quoting Benjamin Rowland "The art and architecture of India" p121 and A.C. Soper "The Roman Style in Gandhara" American Journal of Archaeology 55 (1951) pp. 301–319)

[530] Boardman, p.115

[531] McEvilley, p.388-390

[532] Boardman, 109–153

[533] "It is noteworthy that the dress of the Gandharan Bodhisattva statues has no resemblance whatever to that of the Kushan royal portrait statues, which has many affiliations with Parthian costume. The finery of the Gandhara images must be modeled on the dress of local native nobility, princes of Indian or Indo-Greek race, who had no blood connection with the Scythian rulers. It is also evident that the facial types are unrelated to the features of the Kushans as we know them from their coins and fragmentary portrait statues.", Benjamin Rowland JR, foreword to "The Dyasntic art of the Kushan", John Rosenfield, 1967.

[534] "Those tiny territories of the Indo-Greek kings must have been lively and commercially flourishing places", *India: The ancient past*, Burjor Avari, p.130

[535] "No doubt the Greeks of Bactria and India presided over a flourishing economy. This is clearly indicated by their coinage and the monetary exchange they had established with other currencies." Narain, "The Indo-Greeks" 2003, p. 275.

[536] Bopearachchi, "Monnaies", p.27

[537] Rapson, clxxxvi-

538 Bopearachchi, "Monnaies", p. 75.
539 Fussman, JA 1993, p. 127 and Bopearachchi, "Graeco-Bactrian issues of the later Indo-Greek kings", Num. Chron. 1990, pp. 79–104)
540
541 "Since the merchants of Alexandria are already sailing with fleets by way of the Nile and of the Persian Gulf as far as India, these regions also have become far better known to us of today than to our predecessors. At any rate, when Gallus was prefect of Egypt, I accompanied him and ascended the Nile as far as Syene and the frontiers of Ethiopia, and I learned that as many as one hundred and twenty vessels were sailing from Myos Hormos for India, whereas formerly, under the Ptolemies, only a very few ventured to undertake the voyage and to carry on traffic in Indian merchandise." Strabo II.5.12 http://penelope.uchicago.edu/Thayer/E/Roman/Texts/Strabo/2E1*.html
542 "It is curious that on his copper Zoilos used a Bow and quiver as a type. A quiver was a badge used by the Parthians (Scythians) and had been used previously by Diodotos, who we know had made a treaty with them. Did Zoilos use Scythian mercenaries in his quest against Menander perhaps?" Senior, Indo-Scythian coins, p.xxvii
543 Translation in Epigraphia Indica 1920 p.87 https://archive.org/details/epigrahiaindicav014769mbp
544 PL Gupta 1994
545 Tarn, p. 494.
546 "Though the Indo-Greek monarchies seem to have ended in the first century BC, the Greek presence in India and Bactria remained strong", McEvilley, p.379
547 "The use of the Greek months by the Sakas and later rulers points to the conclusion that they employed a system of dating started by their predecessors." Narain, "Indo-Greeks" 2003, p.190
548 "Evidence of the conquest of Saurastra during the reign of Chandragupta II is to be seen in his rare silver coins which are more directly imitated from those of the Western Satraps... they retain some traces of the old inscriptions in Greek characters, while on the reverse, they substitute the Gupta type (a peacock) for the chaitya with crescent and star." in Rapson "A catalogue of Indian coins in the British Museum. The Andhras etc...", p.cli
549 "Parthians stations", 1st century AD. Original text in paragraph 19 of Parthian stations http://www.parthia.com/doc/parthian_stations.htm#PARTHIAN_STATIONS
550 McEvilley, "The Shape of Ancient Thought", p503.
551 Under each king, information from Bopearachchi is taken from *Monnaies Gréco-Bactriennes et Indo-Grecques, Catalogue Raisonné* (1991) or occasionally *SNG9* (1998). Senior's chronology is from *The Indo-Greek and Indo-Scythian king sequences in the second and first centuries BC*, ONS179 Supplement (2004), whereas the comments (down to the time of Hippostratos) are from *The decline of the Indo-Greeks* (1998).
552 O. Bopearachchi, "Monnaies gréco-bactriennes et indo-grecques, Catalogue raisonné", Bibliothèque Nationale, Paris, 1991, p.453
553 History of Early Stone Sculpture at Mathura: Ca. 150 BCE – 100 CE, Sonya Rhie Quintanilla, BRILL, 2007, p.9 https://books.google.com/books?id=X7Cb8IkZVSMC&pg=PA9
554 //www.worldcat.org/oclc/36240864
555 http://poj.peeters-leuven.be/content.php?url=issue&journal_code=IA&issue=0&vol=39
556 http://coinindia.com/index-greek.html
557 http://www.wildwinds.com/coins/greece/baktria/i.html
558 https://web.archive.org/web/20070610192252/http://www.gengo.l.u-tokyo.ac.jp/~hkum/bactrian.html
559 http://www.dbaol.com/armies/army_50_figure_1.htm
560 https://groups.yahoo.com/group/Hellenistica/files/
561 http://sites.google.com/site/grecoindian
562 http://www.ancientopedia.com/article/164/
563 http://www.ancientopedia.com/article/163/
564 The Greeks in Bactria and India by William Woodthorpe Tarn p.257 https://books.google.com/books?id=-HeJS3nE9cAC&pg=PA257
565 *(Mahavamsa XII)* http://lakdiva.org/mahavamsa/chap012.html
566 *(Mahavamsa X)* http://lakdiva.org/mahavamsa/chap010.html

567 *(Mahawamsa XXIX)* http://lakdiva.org/mahavamsa/chap029.html
568 Mahabharata 3.188.34-36.
569 The Śakas in India, 1981, p 12, Satya Shrava; Journal, 1920, p 175, University of Calcutta. Department of Letters; India & Russia: Linguistic & Cultural Affinity, 1982, p 100, Weer Rajendra Rishi; Indological Studies, 1950, p 32, Dr B. C. Law; Political History of India from the Accession of Parikshit to the Coronation of Bimbisara, 1923, Page iii, Hemchandra Raychaudhuri; Political History of Ancient India, 1996, p 4, Raychaudhury; Indological Studies, 1950, p 4, Dr B. C. Law.
570 Political History of Ancient India, 1996, pp 3-4.
571 Gargi-Samhita Paragraph 5, Yuga Purana.
572 Gargi-Samhita, Yuga Purana Chapter, No 7.
573 "A guide to Sanchi" John Marshall. These "Greek-looking foreigners" are also described in Susan Huntington, "The art of ancient India", p. 100
574 Epigraphia Indica Vol.18 p.328 Inscription No10 https://archive.org/stream/in.ernet.dli.2015.367557
575 World Heritage Monuments and Related Edifices in India, Volume 1 'Alī Jāvīd, Tabassum Javeed, Algora Publishing, 2008 p.42 https://books.google.com/books?id=fg-lGID3WpQC&pg=PA42
576 Some Early Dynasties of South India, by Sudhakar Chattopadhyaya p.83 https://books.google.com/books?id=78I5IDHU2jQC&pg=PA83
577 Epigraphia Indica Vol.18 p.326-328 https://archive.org/stream/in.ernet.dli.2015.367557 and Epigraphia Indica Vol.7 [Epigraphia Indica Vol.7 p.53-54 https://archive.org/details/epigraphiaindica014351mbp
578 Epigraphia Indica Vol.7 p.53-54 Inscription No.7 https://archive.org/details/epigraphiaindica014351mbp
579 Problems of Ancient Indian History: New Perspectives and Perceptions, Shankar Goyal - 2001, p.104
580 Epigraphia Indica Vol.7 p.55-56 Inscription No.10 https://archive.org/details/epigraphiaindica014351mbp and Epigraphia Indica Vol.18 p.327 Inscription No.7 https://archive.org/stream/in.ernet.dli.2015.367557 differ on the content of this inscription. Here, Epigraphia Indica Vol.7 was chosen, as Epigraphia Indica Vol.18 only mentions an inscription similar to that of pillar No.3, a possible mixup.
581 Epigraphia Indica Vol.18 p.328 Inscription No10 https://archive.org/stream/in.ernet.dli.2015.367557
582 Epigraphia Indica Vol.18 p.326 Inscription No1 https://archive.org/stream/in.ernet.dli.2015.367557
583 Epigraphia Indica Vol.18 p.326 Inscription No 4 https://archive.org/stream/in.ernet.dli.2015.367557
584 Epigraphia Indica Vol.18 p.327 Inscription No6 https://archive.org/stream/in.ernet.dli.2015.367557
585 Faces of Power: Alexander's Image and Hellenistic Politics by Andrew Stewart p.180 https://books.google.com/books?id=1SUw29Q_SeMC&pg=PA180
586 D.N. Jha,"Early India: A Concise History"p.150, plate 17
587 Mahabharata 5.19.21-23.
588 Ramayana 55.2-3.
589 Ramayana 43.12.
590 See: Mudrarakshas, Act II.
591 Manusmriti X.43-44.
592 Mahabharata 13.33.23.
593 Mahabhasya II.4.10.
594 Gautama-Dharmasutra IV.21.
595 Brihat-Katha-Manjari 10.1.285-86.
596 Brahmanda Purana, Upodghatapada, 16-17.
597 Mahaniddesa, pp 155, 415.

[598] Religions and Trade: Religious Formation, Transformation and Cross-Cultural Exchange between East and West, BRILL, 2013 p.97 Note 97 https://books.google.com/books?id= AXdfAgAAQBAJ&pg=PA97
[599] http://www.palikanon.com/english/pali_names/y/yonaa.htm
[600] http://www.britannica.com/topic/Yavana
[601] Photographic reference: "The dynastic art of the Kushans", Rosenfield, figures 278–279
[602] The chronology of the Gondopharid kings has long been uncertain, predominantly based on coins. This reconstruction is based on "Indo-Scythian Coins and History IV" by Robert Senior, CNG 2006, as the four volumes of Senior's work provide an almost complete catalogue of the coinage of the period. Senior's chronology is based on the existence of only one king Azes, a theory that was vindicated when it was shown that a coin of the so-called Azes II was overstruck with a type attributed to Azes I (see Senior, "The final nail in the coffin of Azes II", Journal of the Oriental Numismatic Society 197, 2008).
[603] Rosenfield, p129
[604] https://web.archive.org/web/20051001231141/http://www.grifterrec.com/coins/par_rel/print/i_ubouzanes.jpg
[605] A votive inscription of the 26th year of Gudavhara or Gondophares, is reported to have been found on a stone at Takht-i-Bahi, northeast of Peshawar with a date in the year 103 of an unspecified era reckoning. This era is likely to have been the Malva or Vikrama era, founded in 57 BCE, this would give a date of 20 CE for this king's ascension (see Hindu calendar). The stone was formerly in the museum at Lahore. The point is especially important for those Christians who consider that a germ of history is embedded in the *Acts of Thomas*.
[606] https://web.archive.org/web/20040411002040/http://www.grifterrec.com/coins/par_rel/print/i_abdagases.jpg
[607] https://web.archive.org/web/20051001231145/http://www.grifterrec.com/coins/par_rel/print/i_satavastres.jpg
[608] Pacores is not dated by Senior in Indo-Scythian Coins and History, but as Senior's chronology generally antedates the Indo-Parthian kings by a few decades, it follows that Pacores is probably also earlier than the date 100-130 AD, that was previously suggested.
[609] see Senior, "The final nail in the coffin of Azes II".
[610] Description of the Hellenistic urbanism of Taxila: • "Taxila, they tell us, is about as big as Nineveh, and was fortified fairly well after the manner of Greek cities" (Life of Apollonius Tyana, II 20) http://www.livius.org/ap-ark/apollonius/life/va_2_16.html#§20 • "I have already described the way in which the city is walled, but they say that it was divided up into narrow streets in the same irregular manner as in Athens, and that the houses were built in such a way that if you look at them from outside they had only one story, while if you went into one of them, you at once found subterranean chambers extending as far below the level of the earth as did the chambers above." (Life of Apollonius Tyana, II 23) http://www.livius.org/ap-ark/apollonius/life/va_2_21.html#§23
[611] (Life of Apollonius Tyana, II 29) http://www.livius.org/ap-ark/apollonius/life/va_2_26.html#§29
[612] (Life of Apollonius Tyana, II 31) http://www.livius.org/ap-ark/apollonius/life/va_2_31.html#§31
[613] Periplus of the Erythraean Sea, Chap 38 http://www.fordham.edu/halsall/ancient/periplus.html
[614] Rosenfield, p130.
[615] Described in "Rome's enemies, Parthians and Sassanid Persians",
[616] "Parthians, from about the 1st century AD, seem to have preferred to show off their carefully tonsured hair, usually only wearing a fillet of thick ribbon; before then, the Scythian cap or bashlyk was worn more frequently". In "Parthians and Sassanid Parthians" Peter Willcox , p12
[617] Pierfrancesco Gallieri, in "Crossroads of Asia": "The parallels are so striking that it is not excluded that the objects discovered in Taxila and dated to between the 1st century BCE and the 1st century CE were in reality produced earlier, maybe by artisans who had followed the Greeks kings during their retreat from Bactria to India" p211 (in French in the original)
[618] "Let us remind that in Sirkap, stone palettes were found at all excavated levels. On the contrary, neither Bhir-Mound, the Maurya city preceding Sirkap on the Taxila site, nor Sirsukh, the Kushan city succeeding her, did deliver any stone palettes during their excavations", in "Les

palettes du Gandhara", p89. "The terminal point after which such palettes are not manufactured anymore is probably located during the Kushan period. In effect, neither Mathura nor Taxila (although the Sirsukh had only been little excavated), nor Begram, nor Surkh Kotal, neither the great Kushan archaeological sites of Soviet Central Asia or Afghanistan have yielded such objects. Only four palettes have been found in Kushan-period archaeological sites. They come from secondary sites, such as Garav Kala and Ajvadz in Soviet Tajikistan and Jhukar, in the Indus Valley, and Dalverzin Tepe. They are rather roughly made." In "Les Palettes du Gandhara", Henri-Paul Francfort, p91. (in French in the original)

[619] https://web.archive.org/web/20051001231146/http://www.grifterrec.com/coins/par_rel/print/i_gondopharesI.jpg

[620] https://web.archive.org/web/20051001231140/http://www.grifterrec.com/coins/par_rel/print/i_sarpedones.jpg

[621] https://web.archive.org/web/20051001231147/http://www.grifterrec.com/coins/indoparthian/i_ipr_abdagases_o.jpg

[622] https://web.archive.org/web/20051001231149/http://www.grifterrec.com/coins/indoparthian/i_ipr_pakores_o5.jpg

[623] https://web.archive.org/web/20050206140303/http://www.grifterrec.com/coins/indoparthian/indoparthian.html

[624] http://sites.google.com/site/grecoindian/Home/history-of-greco-india

[625] See: Notes on the Races, Tribes, and Castes inhabiting the Province of Oudh, Lucknow, Oudh Government Press 1868, p 4; The Geographical Data in Early Puranas, a Critical Studies, 1972, p 135, Dr M. R. Singh; Sacred Books of the East, XXV, Intr. p cxv, Rapson, Coins of Ancient India, p 37, n.2.

[626] The Geographical Data in Early Puranas, a Critical Studies, 1972, p 135, Dr M. R. Singh; Sacred Books of the East, XXV, Intr. p cxv; Rapson, Coins of Ancient India, p 37, n.2.

[627] India as Known to Panini, 1954, p 444, Dr V. S. Agarwala.

[628]
(From Kirfel's Text of Bhuvanakosha).

[629] Markendeya Purana 57.35.

[630] See also: Geographical Data in the Early Puranas, 1972, p 134-135, Dr M. R. Singh.

[631] Vayu Purana I.58.78-83.

[632] Ramayana, 55/2-3

[633] Ramayana Kisk. Kanda, 43-12.

[634] Mahabharata 5.4.15.

[635] Mahabharata Bhishma Parva, Ch. 20.

[636] Since the armies of the Sakas, Yavanas, Tukharas, Khasas, Daradas had fought under the supreme command of Sudakshin Kamboja (See ref: The Nations of India at the Battle Between the Pandavas and Kauravas, Journal of the Royal Asiatic Society of Great Britain and Ireland, 1908, pp 313, 331, Dr F. E. Pargiter, (Royal Asiatic Society of Great Britain and Ireland), it is highly likely that the Pahlavas too fought under Sudakshina Kamboj.

[637] Manu Samhita, X.43-44.

[638] Mudrarakshas, II.

[639] Brihat-Katha-Manjari 10/1/285-86.

[640] Chapter 17.

[641] World history from early times to A D 2000 by B .V. Rao: p.97

[642] Ancient India by Ramesh Chandra Majumdar p. 234

[643] Kharapallana and Vanaspara are known from an inscription discovered in Sarnath, and dated to the 3rd year of Kanishka, in which they were paying allegiance to the Kushanas. Source: "A Catalogue of the Indian Coins in the British Museum. Andhras etc." Rapson, p ciii

[644] Ptolemy, "Geographia", Chap 7

[645] Rapson, p. CVII

[646] "Kharoshthi inscription, Taxila copper plate of Patika", Sten Konow, p25

[647] "The Satavahanas did not hold the western Deccan for long. They were gradually pushed out of the west by the Sakas (Western Khatrapas). The Kshaharata Nahapana's coins in the Nasik area indicate that the Western Kshatrapas controlled this region by the 1st century CE. By becoming master of wide regions including Malwa, Southern Gujarat, and Northern Konkan, from Broach

to Sopara and the Nasik and Poona districts, Nahapana rose from the status of a mere Kshatrapa in the year 41 (58 AD) to that of Mahakshatrapa in the year 46 (63 AD)." in "History of the Andhras"

[648] "Catalogue of Indian coins of the British Museum. Andhras etc." Rapson. p. LVII

[649] Ancient Indian History and Civilization by Sailendra Nath Sen p.188 https://books.google.com/books?id=Wk4_ICH_g1EC&pg=PA188

[650] Epigraphia Indica Vol.8 p.78-79 https://archive.org/details/EpigraphiaIndica

[651] Epigraphia Indica Vol.7, Hultzsch, E. p.58 https://archive.org/details/epigraphiaindica014351mbp

[652] Foreign Influence on Ancient India, Krishna Chandra Sagar, Northern Book Centre, 1992 p.150 https://books.google.com/books?id=0UA4rkm9MgkC&pg=PA150

[653] Cultural and Religious Heritage of India: Zoroastrianism, Suresh K. Sharma, Usha Sharma, Mittal Publications, 2004 p.112 https://books.google.com/books?id=bmu3vZOSp_IC&pg=PA112

[654] The Dynastic Arts of the Kushans, John M. Rosenfield p.131 https://books.google.com/books?id=udnBkQhzHH4C&pg=PA131

[655] Southern India: A Guide to Monuments Sites & Museums, by George Michell, Roli Books Private Limited, 1 mai 2013 p.72 https://books.google.com/books?id=GdBbBAAAQBAJ&pg=PT72

[656] "This hall is assigned to the brief period of Kshatrapas rule in the western Deccan during the 1st century." in Guide to Monuments of India 1: Buddhist, Jain, Hindu - by George Michell, Philip H. Davies, Viking - 1989 Page 374

[657] Ushavadata also presents himself as a Saka in inscription 14a of Cave No.10 of the Pandavleni Caves: "[Success !] By permanent charities of Ushavadata, the Saka, [son of Dinika], son-in-law of king Nahapana, the [Kshahara]ta Kshatrapa...." in Epigraphia Indica p.85-86 https://archive.org/stream/EpigraphiaIndica/Epigraphia_Indica

[658] Epigraphia Indica p.78-79 https://archive.org/stream/EpigraphiaIndica/Epigraphia_Indica

[659] Epigraphia Indica p.82-83 https://archive.org/stream/EpigraphiaIndica/Epigraphia_Indica

[660] Cultural and Religious Heritage of India: Zoroastrianism, by Suresh K. Sharma,Usha Sharma p.114 https://books.google.com/books?id=bmu3vZOSp_IC&pg=PA114

[661] "History of the Andhras", Durga Prasad Source https://web.archive.org/web/20060422120411/http://202.41.85.234:8000/gw_44_5/hi-res/hcu_images/G2.pdf

[662] Source http://www.fordham.edu/halsall/ancient/periplus.html

[663] Source http://depts.washington.edu/silkroad/texts/periplus/periplus.html

[664]

[665] A. Jha and D. Rajgor: *Studies in the Coinage of the Western Ksatraps*, Nashik: Indian Institute of Research in Numismatic Studies, 1992, p. 7.

[666] The Dynastic Art of the Kushans, John Rosenfield, University of California Press, xxxiv

[667] Artefacts of History: Archaeology, Historiography and Indian Pasts, Sudeshna Guha, SAGE Publications India, 2015 p.50 https://books.google.com/books?id=jhqJCwAAQBAJ&pg=PA50

[668] Source http://projectsouthasia.sdstate.edu/Docs/HISTORY/PRIMARYDOCS/EPIGRAPHY/JunagadhRockInscription.htm

[669] Rapson, "Indian coins of the British Museum" p.lx

[670] Junagadh Rock Inscription of Rudradaman I http://projectsouthasia.sdstate.edu/Docs/HISTORY/PRIMARYDOCS/EPIGRAPHY/JunagadhRockInscription.htm , accessed on 23 March 2007.

[671] Rosenfield, "The dynastic art of the Kushans", p132

[672] Rapson, "A catalogue of the Indian coins in the British Museum", p.lx

[673] "Vidarbha also was under the rule of another Mahakshatrapa named Rupiamma, whose pillar inscription was recently discovered at Pavni in the Bhandara district [Mirashi, Studies in Indology, Vol. IV, p. 109 f.]. It records the erection of a chhaya-stambha or sculptured pillar at the place. The Satavahanas had, Therefore, to leave Western Maharashtra and Vidarbha. They seem to have repaired to their capital Pratishthana where they continued to abide waiting for a favourable opportunity to oust the Shaka invaders." Source http://www.maharashtra.gov.in/english/gazetteer/nasik/005%20History/001%20AncientPeriod.htm

[674] Mc Evilley "The shape of ancient thought", p385 ("The Yavanajataka is the earliest surviving Sanskrit text in astrology, and constitute the basis of all later Indian developments in horoscopy", himself quoting David Pingree "The Yavanajataka of Sphujidhvaja" p5)
[675] Rapson, p.cxxiv https://archive.org/stream/catalogueofcoins00brit#page/82/mode/2up
[676] "later Satavahana named Yajna Satakarni seems to have conquered the Southern Dominions of the Western Satraps. His coins contain figures of ships, probably indicating the naval power of the Andras. He not only ruled Aparanta, but probably also the eastern part of the Central Provinces". Majumdar, p. 135
[677] CNG Coins Coin image https://www.cngcoins.com/Coin.aspx?CoinID=322826
[678] Los Angeles County Museum of Art description http://collections.lacma.org/node/242276
[679] Catalogue of the coins of the Andhra dynasty, the Western Ksatrapas, the Traikutaka dynasty, and the "Bodhi" dynasty, by British Museum. Dept. of Coins and Medals; Rapson, E. J. (Edward James) p.170 https://archive.org/details/catalogueofcoins00brit
[680] Marshall, The Monuments of Sanchi p.392 https://archive.org/stream/in.ernet.dli.2015.532798
[681]
[682]
[683] Marshall, The Monuments of India p.388 https://archive.org/stream/in.ernet.dli.2015.532798
[684] Marshall, The Monuments of India p.388 inscription 833 https://archive.org/stream/in.ernet.dli.2015.532798
[685] Rapson CCVIII
[686] Rapson p. CIV
[687] Rapson, "A Catalogue of Indian coins in the British Museum. Andhras etc.", p.cxcii
[688] "Evidence of the conquest of Saurastra during the reign of Chandragupta II is to be seen in his rare silver coins which are more directly imitated from those of the Western Satraps... they retain some traces of the old inscriptions in Greek characters, while on the reverse, they substitute the Gupta type ... for the chaitya with crescent and star." in Rapson "A catalogue of Indian coins in the British Museum. The Andhras etc.", p.cli
[689] "The titles "Kshatrap" and "Mahakshatrapa" certainly show that the Western Kshatrapas were originally feudatories" in Rapson, "Coins of the British Museum", p.cv
[690] //en.wikipedia.org/w/index.php?title=Template:History_of_Gujarat&action=edit
[691] http://www.katragadda.com/articles/HistoryOfTheAndhras.pdf
[692] http://coinindia.com/galleries-kshatrapas.html
[693] https://web.archive.org/web/20051224062028/http://www.grifterrec.com/coins/india/ancientindia3.html
[694] https://web.archive.org/web/20061209050033/http://www.maharashtra.gov.in/english/gazetteer/nasik/005%20History/001%20AncientPeriod.htm
[695] https://www.academia.edu/1563408/The_Origins_of_the_Indian_Coinage_Tradition
[696] "The Rabatak inscription claims that in the year 1 Kanishka I's authority was proclaimed in India, in all the satrapies and in different cities like Koonadeano (Kundina), Ozeno (Ujjain), Kozambo (Kausambi), Zagedo (Saketa), Palabotro (Pataliputra), and Ziri-Tambo (Janjgir-Champa). These cities lay to the east and south of Mathura, up to which locality Wima had already carried his victorious arm. Therefore they must have been captured or subdued by Kanishka I himself." "Ancient Indian Inscriptions", S. R. Goyal, p. 93. See also the analysis of Sims-Williams and J.Cribb, who had a central role in the decipherment: "A new Bactrian inscription of Kanishka the Great", in "Silk Road Art and Archaeology" No4, 1995–1996. Also Mukherjee B.N. "The Great Kushanan Testament", Indian Museum Bulletin.
[697] The Kushans at first retained the Greek language for administrative purposes but soon began to use Bactrian. The Bactrian Rabatak inscription (discovered in 1993 and deciphered in 2000) records that the Kushan king Kanishka the Great (c. 127 AD), discarded Greek (Ionian) as the language of administration and adopted Bactrian ("Arya language"), from Falk (2001): "The yuga of Sphujiddhvaja and the era of the Kuṣâṇas." Harry Falk. Silk Road Art and Archaeology VII, p. 133.
[698] The Bactrian Rabatak inscription (discovered in 1993 and deciphered in 2000) records that the Kushan king Kanishka the Great (c. 127 AD), discarded Greek (Ionian) as the language of administration and adopted Bactrian ("Arya language"), from Falk (2001): "The yuga of Sphujiddhvaja and the era of the Kuṣâṇas." Harry Falk. Silk Road Art and Archaeology VII, p. 133.

[699] André Wink, *Al-Hind, the Making of the Indo-Islamic World: The Slavic Kings and the Islamic conquest, 11th-13th centuries*, (Oxford University Press, 1997), 57.
[700] The Silk Road in World History By Xinru Liu, Pg.61 https//books.google.co.in
[701] Golden 1992, p. 56.
[702] *The Dynasty Arts of the Kushans*, University of California Press, 1967, p. 5 https://books.google.com/books?id=udnBkQhzHH4C&pg=PA7
[703] http://www.kushan.org/general/other/part1.htm and Si-Yu-Ki, Buddhist Records of the Western World, (Tr. Samuel Beal: Travels of Fa-Hian, The Mission of Sung-Yun and Hwei-S?ng, Books 1–5), Kegan Paul, Trench, Trubner & Co. Ltd. London. 1906 and Hill (2009), pp. 29, 318–350
[704] which began about 127 CE. "Falk 2001, pp. 121–136", Falk (2001), pp. 121–136, Falk, Harry (2004), pp. 167–176 and Hill (2009), pp. 29, 33, 368–371.
[705] Mallory & Mair (2000), pp. 270–297.
[706] "They are, by almost unanimous opinion, Indo-Europeans, probably the most oriental of those who occupied the steppes." Roux, p.90
[707] Hill (2009), p. 36 and notes.
[708] Hill (2009), p. 311.
[709] pp. 23–24.
[710] Lebedynsky, p. 62.
[711] Lebedynsky, p. 15.
[712] Hill (2009), p. 29.
[713] Chavannes (1907), pp. 190–192.
[714] S. Frederick Starr, *Lost Enlightenment: Central Asia's Golden Age from the Arab Conquest to Tamerlane*. Princeton, NJ: Princeton University Press, 2013, p. 53
[715] Starr, p. 53
[716] Rosenfield, p. 41.
[717] For "Malwa and Maharashtra, for which it is speculated that the Kushans had an alliance with the Western Kshatrapas", see: Rosenfield, p. 41.
[718] For a translation of the full text of the Rabatak inscription see: Mukherjee, B.N., "The Great Kushana Testament", Indian Museum Bulletin, Calcutta, 1995. This translation is quoted in: Goyal (2005), p.88.
[719] For quotation: "The Rabatak inscription claims that in the year 1 Kanishka I's authority was proclaimed in India, in all the satrapies and in different cities like Koonadeano (Kundina), Ozeno (Ujjain), Kozambo (Kausambi), Zagedo (Saketa), Palabotro (Pataliputra) and Ziri-Tambo (Janjgir-Champa). These cities lay to the east and south of Mathura, up to which locality Wima had already carried his victorious arm. Therefore they must have been captured or subdued by Kanishka I himself." see: Goyal, p. 93.
[720] See also the analysis of Sims-Williams and J. Cribb, specialists of the field, who had a central role in the decipherment: "A new Bactrian inscription of Kanishka the Great", in *Silk Road Art and Archaeology* No. 4, 1995–1996. pp.75–142.
[721] British Museum display, Asian Art room.
[722] The Sino-Kharosthi coins of Khotan part 2, Numismatic Chronicle (1984), pp.129-152., by Joe Cribb https://www.academia.edu/33275660/The_Sino-Kharosthi_coins_of_Khotan_part_2_Numismatic_Chronicle_1984_pp.129-152
[723] Falk (2001), pp. 121–136.
[724] Falk (2004), pp. 167–176.
[725] Xinru Liu, *The Silk Road in World History* (New York: Oxford University Press, 2010), 47.
[726] Sivaramamurti, p. 56-59.
[727] Loeschner, Hans (2012) The Stūpa of the Kushan Emperor Kanishka the Great http://www.sino-platonic.org/complete/spp227_kanishka_stupa_casket.pdf Sino-Platonic Papers, No. 227 (July 2012); page 11
[728] Bopearachchi, O. (2007). Some observations on the chronology of the early Kushans. Res Orientales, 17, 41-53
[729] H. Humbach, 1975, p.402-408. K.Tanabe, 1997, p.277, M.Carter, 1995, p.152. J.Cribb, 1997, p.40. References cited in "De l'Indus à l'Oxus".
[730] Metropolitan Museum of Art exhibition

[731] Perkins, J. (2007). Three-headed Śiva on the Reverse of Vima Kadphises's Copper Coinage. South Asian Studies, 23(1), 31-37
[732] Xinru Liu, *The Silk Road in World History* (New York: Oxford University Press, 2010), 42.
[733] Xinru Liu, *The Silk Road in World History* (New York: Oxford University Press, 2010), 58.
[734] Neelis, Jason. *Early Buddhist Transmission and Trade Networks*. 2010. p. 141
[735] Hill (2009), p. 31.
[736] de Crespigny, Rafe. (2007). *A Biographical Dictionary of Later Han to the Three Kingdoms (23-220 AD)*. Leiden: Koninklijke Brill. page 5-6.
[737] Torday, Laszlo. (1997). *Mounted Archers: The Beginnings of Central Asian History*. Durham: The Durham Academic Press. page 393.
[738] Joe Cribb, 1974, "Chinese lead ingots with barbarous Greek inscriptions in Coin Hoards" pp. 76-8 https://www.academia.edu/33859218/Chinese_lead_ingots_with_barbarous_Greek_inscriptions_in_Coin_Hoards_vol.IV_London_1978_pp.76-8?auto=download
[739]
[740] //en.wikipedia.org/w/index.php?title=Template:Part_of_History_of_India&action=edit
[741] //en.wikipedia.org/w/index.php?title=Template:History_of_Afghanistan&action=edit
[742] //en.wikipedia.org/w/index.php?title=Template:History_of_Tajikistan&action=edit
[743] https://books.google.com/books?id=9U6RlVVjpakC
[744] http://depts.washington.edu/silkroad/texts/weilue/weilue.html
[745] https://books.google.com/books?id=cHA7Ey0-pbEC
[746] https://books.google.com/books?id=wLeYkgEACAAJ
[747] https://books.google.com/books?id=tzU3RIV2BWIC
[748] https://books.google.com/books?id=EOytGwAACAAJ
[749] https://books.google.com/books?id=pCiNqFj3MQsC
[750] https://books.google.com/books?id=VT1uAAAAMAAJ
[751] http://chrisdorneich.tumblr.com/
[752] http://libmma.contentdm.oclc.org/cdm/compoundobject/collection/p15324coll10/id/105494
[753] http://muse.jhu.edu/journals/jwh/
[754] http://www.britannica.com/EBchecked/topic/325483/Kushan-dynasty
[755] http://www.metmuseum.org/toah/hd/kush/hd_kush.htm
[756] https://web.archive.org/web/20050204064550/http://www.grifterrec.com/coins/kushan/kushan.html
[757] http://www.wildwinds.com/coins/greece/indo_scythians/i.html
[758] http://webarchive.loc.gov/all/20130207084302/http://home.comcast.net/~pankajtandon/home.html
[759] http://www.kushan.org/
[760] http://coinindia.com/galleries-kushan.html
[761] The Cambridge Companion to the Age of Attila, Michael Maas, Cambridge University Press, 2014 p.284 ff https://books.google.com/books?id=e0dcBAAAQBAJ&pg=PA284
[762] Sasanian Seals and Sealings, Rika Gyselen, Peeters Publishers, 2007, p.1 https://books.google.com/books?id=RjWAXVYNIzkC&pg=PA1
[763]
[764]
[765] CNG Coins https://www.cngcoins.com/Coin.aspx?CoinID=76467
[766] The Buddhist Caves at Aurangabad: Transformations in Art and Religion, Pia Brancaccio, BRILL, 2010 p.82 https://books.google.com/books?id=m_4pXm7dD78C&pg=PA82
[767] The ancient & classical world, 600 B.C.-A.D. 650 by Michael Mitchiner http//books.google.co.in
[768] Richard Foltz, *Religions of the Silk Road*, New York: Palgrave Macmillan, 2010
[769] History of Civilizations of Central Asia, Ahmad Hasan Dani, B. A. Litvinsky, Unesco p.105 https://books.google.com/books?id=883OZBe2sMYC&pg=PA105
[770] Numismatic Evidence for Kushano-Sasanian Chronology Joe Cribb 1990 p.171 https://www.academia.edu/542387/Numismatic_Evidence_for_Kushano-Sasanian_Chronology_St_Ir_1990_pp._151-93_plates_I-VIII
[771] CNG Coins https://www.cngcoins.com/Coin.aspx?CoinID=134399
[772] http://www.iranicaonline.org/articles/kushanshahs-01

[773] https://books.google.nl/books?id=B5BHDAAAQBAJ&dq=sasanians+rhodes&hl=nl&source=gbs_navlinks_s
[774] https://web.archive.org/web/20050828050211/http://grifterrec.com/coins/kushanshah/kushanshah.html
[775] Hans Bakker 24th Gonda lecture https://zenodo.org/record/377032/files/Bakker%202016.pdf
[776] India: A History by John Keay p.158
[777] Sumpa Yeshe Peljor's 18th century work *Dpag-bsam-ljon-bzah* (Tibetan title) may be translated as "The Excellent Kalpavriksha"): "Tho-gar yul dań yabana dań Kambodza dań Khasa [sic] dań Huna dań Darta dań..."
[778] Pag-Sam-Jon-Zang (1908), I.9, Sarat Chandra Das; Ancient Kamboja, 1971, p 66, H. W. Bailey.
[779] Hyun Jin Kim, *The Huns*, Abingdon, Routledge, *passim*.
[780] British Museum notice http://www.britishmuseum.org/research/collection_online/collection_object_details.aspx?objectId=247021&partId=1
[781] Procopius of Caesarea: Tyranny, History, and Philosophy at the End of Antiquity, Anthony Kaldellis, University of Pennsylvania Press, 2012, p.70 https://books.google.com/books?id=Ag0mUQiLb7kC&pg=PA70
[782] Staying Roman: Conquest and Identity in Africa and the Mediterranean, 439–700, Jonathan Conant Cambridge University Press, 2012 p.259 https://books.google.com/books?id=wJEgAwAAQBAJ&pg=PA259
[783] Procopius, *History of the Wars*. Book I, Ch. III, "The Persian War"
[784] History of Civilizations of Central Asia, Ahmad Hasan Dani, B. A. Litvinsky, Unesco p.119 sq https://books.google.com/books?id=883OZBe2sMYC&pg=PA119
[785] Sardonyx seal
[786] The Cambridge Companion to the Age of Attila, Michael Maas p.287 https://books.google.com/books?id=e0dcBAAAQBAJ&pg=PA287
[787] Ancient History of Central Asia by Adesh Katariya p.169 https://books.google.com/books?id=ihFUDAAAQBAJ&pg=RA1-PA169
[788] CNG Coins https://www.cngcoins.com/Coin.aspx?CoinID=246722
[789] Kurbanov, p164; Merv p167.
[790] CNG Coins https://www.cngcoins.com/Coin.aspx?CoinID=103669
[791] History of Civilizations of Central Asia, Ahmad Hasan Dani, B. A. Litvinsky, Unesco p.38ff https://books.google.com/books?id=883OZBe2sMYC&pg=PA38
[792] Zeimal 1996, p. 130.
[793]
[794] Iaroslav Lebedynsky, "Les Nomades", p172.
[795] British Museum notice http://www.britishmuseum.org/research/collection_online/collection_object_details.aspx?objectId=247021&partId=1
[796] The war is variously dated. 560–565 (Gumilyov, 1967); 555 (Stark, 2008, Altturkenzeit, 210); 557 (Iranica, Khosrow ii); 558–561 (Iranica.hephthalites); 557–563 (Baumer, Hist. Cent. Asia, 2, 174); 557–561 (Sinor, 1990, Hist. Inner Asia, 301); 560–563 (UNESCO, Hist. Civs. C. A., iii, 143); 562–565 (Christian, Hist. Russia, Mongolia, C. A., 252); c. 565 (Grousset,Empire Steppes, 1970, p. 82); 567 (Chavannes, 1903, Documents, 236 and 229)
[797] The Cambridge Companion to the Age of Attila, Michael Maas, Cambridge University Press, 2014 p.284sq https://books.google.com/books?id=e0dcBAAAQBAJ&pg=PA284
[798] CNG Coins https://www.cngcoins.com/Coin.aspx?CoinID=76476
[799]
[800] The Huns by Hyun Jin Kim, Routledge p.56 https://books.google.fr/books?id=bnv4CgAAQBAJ&pg=PA56
[801] Enoki, K. "The Liang shih-kung-t'u on the origin and migration of the Hua or Ephthalites," *Journal of the Oriental Society of Australia* 7:1–2 (December 1970):37–45
[802] History of Buddhism in Afghanistan http://studybuddhism.com/en/advanced-studies/history-culture/buddhism-in-mongolia-central-asia/history-of-buddhism-in-afghanistan, Alexander Berzin, Study Buddhism
[803] CNG Coins https://www.cngcoins.com/Coin.aspx?CoinID=169495

[804] M. A. Shaban, "Khurasan at the Time of the Arab Conquest", in *Iran and Islam*, in memory of Vlademir Minorsky, Edinburgh University Press, (1971), p481; .

[805] "The White Huns – The Hephthalites" http://www.silk-road.com/artl/heph.shtml, Silk Road

[806] Enoki Kazuo, *"On the nationality of White Huns"*, 1955

[807] David Christian *A History of Russia, Inner Asia and Mongolia* (Oxford: Basil Blackwell) 1998 p248

[808] "White Huns" http://columbia.thefreedictionary.com/White+Huns, *Columbia Electronic Encyclopedia*

[809] Enoki, Kazuo: "On the Nationality of the White Huns", *Memoirs of the Research Department of the Tokyo Bunko*, 1959, No. 18, p. 56. Quote: "Let me recapitulate the foregoing. The grounds upon which the White Huns are assigned an Iranian tribe are: (1) that their original home was on the east frontier of Tokharestan; and (2) that their culture contained some Iranian elements. Naturally, the White Huns were sometimes regarded as another branch of the Kao-ch'e tribe by their contemporaries, and their manners and customs are represented as identical with those of the T'u-chueh, and it is a fact that they had several cultural elements in common with those of the nomadic Turkish tribes. Nevertheless, such similarity of manners and customs is an inevitable phenomenon arising from similarity of their environments. The White Huns could not be assigned as a Turkish tribe on account of this. The White Huns were considered by some scholars as an Aryanized tribe, but I would like to go further and acknowledge them as an Iranian tribe. Though my grounds, as stated above, are rather scarce, it is expected that the historical and linguistic materials concerning the White Huns are to be increased in the future and most of the newly-discovered materials seem to confirm my Iranian-tribe theory." here or "Hephtalites" http://www.azargoshnasp.net/history/Hephtalites/Hephtalites.htm or "On the Nationality of the Hephtalites" https://archive.org/details/OnTheNationalityOfTheEphthalites.

[810] Xavier Tremblay, *Pour une histoire de la Sérinde. Le manichéisme parmi les peoples et religions d'Asie Centrale d'aprés les sources primaire*, Vienna: 2001, Appendix D «Notes Sur L'Origine Des Hephtalites», pp. 183–88 «Malgré tous les auteurs qui, depuis KLAPROTH jusqu' ALTHEIM in SuC, p113 sq et HAUSSIG, *Die Geschichte Zentralasiens und der Seidenstrasse in vorislamischer Zeit*, Darmstadt, 1983 (cf. n.7), ont vu dans les White Huns des Turcs, l'explication de leurs noms par le turc ne s'impose jamais, est parfois impossible et n'est appuyée par aucun fait historique (aucune trace de la religion turque ancienne), celle par l'iranien est toujours possible, parfois évidente, surtout dans les noms longs comme *Mihirakula, Toramana* ou *γοβοζοκο* qui sont bien plus probants qu' αλ- en Αλχαννο. Or l'iranien des noms des White Huns n'est pas du bactrien et n'est donc pas imputable à leur installation en Bactriane [...] Une telle accumulation de probabilités suffit à conclure que, jusqu'à preuve du contraire, les Hepthalites étaient des Iraniens orientaux, mais non des Sogdiens.» Available here or here http://www.azargoshnasp.net/history/Hephtalites/Hephtalites.htm

[811] Denis Sinor, "The establishment and dissolution of the Türk empire" in Denis Sinor, "The Cambridge history of early Inner Asia, Volume 1", Cambridge University Press, 1990. p. 300:"There is no consensus concerning the Hephthalite language, though most scholars seem to think that it was Iranian."

[812] Jacques Duchesne-Guillemin, Congrès International d&Etud. *Études mithriaques: actes du 2e Congrès International, Téhéran, du 1er au 8 september 1975* https://books.google.com.pk/books?id=_MoUAAAAIAAJ. p 293. Retrieved 2012-9-5.

[813] Janos Harmatta, "The Rise of the Old Persian Empire: Cyrus the Great," AAASH (Acta Antiqua Acadamie Scientiarum Hungaricae 19, 197, pp. 4–15.

[814] R. Frye, "Central Asia in pre-Islamic Times" http//www.iranica.com , *Encyclopaedia Iranica*

[815] G. Ambros/P.A. Andrews/L. Bazin/A. Gökalp/B. Flemming and others, "Turks", in *Encyclopaedia of Islam*, Online Edition 2006

[816] A.D.H. Bivar, " Hephthalites https://web.archive.org/web/20080415095919/http://www.encyclopediairanica.com/articles/v12f2/v12f2036.html", in *Encyclopaedia Iranica*, Online Edition.

[817] M. Schottky, " Iranian Huns https://web.archive.org/web/20080424000230/http://www.iranica.com/newsite/articles/v12f6/v12f6008.html", in *Encyclopaedia Iranica*, Online Edition

[818] Robert L. Canfield, *Turko-Persia in Historical Perspective*, Cambridge University Press, 1991, p. 49
[819] Procopius, *History of the Wars*. Book I, Ch. III, "The Persian War"
[820] Kurbanov pp2-32
[821] *Columbia Encyclopedia*
[822] "Ephtalites" http://www.1911encyclopedia.org/Ephthalites, *Classic Encyclopædia Britannica*, 1911
[823] Grousset (1970), p. 67.
[824]
[825] Litvinsky, pp144-47
[826]
[827] *Ancient India: History and Culture* by Balkrishna Govind Gokhale, p.69
[828] *Ancient Indian History and Civilization* by Sailendra Nath Sen, p.220
[829] *Encyclopaedia of Indian Events and Dates* by S. B. Bhattacherje, p.A15
[830] *India: A History* by John Keay, p.158
[831] *History of India, in Nine Volumes: Vol. II* by Vincent A. Smith, p.290
[832] Kurbanov pp238-243
[833] Gankovsky, Yu. V., et al. *A History of Afghanistan*, Moscow: Progress Publishers, 1982, p. 382
[834] http://www.diss.fu-berlin.de/diss/servlets/MCRFileNodeServlet/FUDISS_derivate_000000007165/01_Text.pdf
[835] https://books.google.com/books?id=pCiNqFj3MQsC
[836] https://books.google.dk/books?id=883OZBe2sMYC&dq=false
[837] http://www.transoxiana.org/Eran/Articles/Tezcan_Apar.pdf
[838] http://www.historicalchina.net/admin/WebEdit/UploadFile/AfrasiabXH.pdf
[839] https://www.webcitation.org/query?url=http://www.geocities.com/pak_history/hephthalites.html&date=2009-10-26+00:09:20
[840] http://columbia.thefreedictionary.com/Hephthalite
[841] http://www.anythinganywhere.com/commerce/coins/coinpics/indi-heph.htm
[842] https://web.archive.org/web/20091027002731/http://geocities.com/ziadnumis/home
[843] http://rick-heli.info/silkroad/eph.html
[844] https://web.archive.org/web/20050209163941/http://depts.washington.edu/uwch/silkroad/exhibit/hephthalites/essay.html
[845] http://www.iranicaonline.org/articles/hephthalites
[846] *Harsha and His Times: A Glimpse of Political History During the Seventh Century A.D.*, Page 78 https://books.google.com/books?id=m68BAAAAMAAJ& by Bireshwar Nath Srivastava (Chowkhamba Sanskrit Series Office, 1976)
[847] Peter Crawford, *The War of the Three Gods: Romans, Persians and the Rise of Islam*, (Pen & Sword, 2013), 192.https://books.google.com/books?id=ZPAHBAAAQBAJ&pg=PA192&dq=raja+rasil&hl=en&sa=X&ei=aOwYVd23ONWhugS-_IHIDg&ved=0CCAQ6AEwAQ
[848] André Wink, *Al-hind: The Making of the Indo-islamic World*, Vol. I, (E.J. Brill, 1990), 133.https://books.google.com/books?id=U7Q3AAAAIAAJ&pg=PA133&lpg=PA133&focus=viewport&vq=Chach&output=html_text
[849] Mirchandani, B. D.; *Glimpses of Ancient Sind*
[850] *The Chachnamah: an ancient history of Sind*. Translated from the Persian by Mirza Kalichbeg Fredunbeg. Commissioner's Press (1900).
[851] "Chach Nama - The queen falls in love with Chach who becomes the Ruler through her love" http://persian.packhum.org/persian/pf?file=12701030&ct=8, Packhum.org
[852] "Chach fights with Maha-rat and kills him by a strategem" http://persian.packhum.org/persian/main?url=pf%3Ffile%3D12701030%26ct%3D8, Packhum.org
[853] //en.wikipedia.org/w/index.php?title=Template:History_of_Pakistan&action=edit
[854] Puṣkalavati meaning "Lotus City" in Sanskrit
[855] Sanskrit Puruṣapura, literally meaning "city of men", from *puruṣa*, "(primordial) man" and *pura*, "city".
[856] "UW Press: Ancient Buddhist Scrolls from Gandhara" http://www.washington.edu/uwpress/search/books/SALANC.html. Retrieved April 2018.

[857] • Schmidt, Karl J. (1995). *An Atlas and Survey of South Asian History* https://books.google.com/books?id=BqdzCQAAQBAJ, p.120: "In addition to being a center of religion for Buddhists, as well as Hindus, Taxila was a thriving center for art, culture, and learning."
• Srinivasan, Doris Meth (2008). "Hindu Deities in Gandharan art," in *Gandhara, The Buddhist Heritage of Pakistan: Legends, Monasteries, and Paradise* https://books.google.com/books?id=lHBEAQAAIAAJ, pp.130-143: "Gandhara was not cut off from the heartland of early Hinduism in the Gangetic Valley. The two regions shared cultural and political connections and trade relations and this facilitated the adoption and exchange of religious ideas. [...] It is during the Kushan Era that a flowering of religious imagery occurred. [...] Gandhara often introduced its own idiosyncratic expression upon the Buddhist and Hindu imagery it had initially come in contact with." • Blurton, T. Richard (1993). *Hindu Art* https://books.google.com/books?id=xJ-lzU_nj_MC, Harvard University Press: "The earliest figures of Shiva which show him in purely human form come from the area of ancient Gandhara" (p.84) and "Coins from Gandhara of the first century BC show Lakshmi [...] four-armed, on a lotus." (p.176)
[858] Kurt A. Behrendt (2007), The Art of Gandhara in the Metropolitan Museum of Art https://books.google.com/books?id=MJ3eCZVlT48C, pp.4-5,91
[859] Kalhana Rajatarangini referred to them as simply *Shahi* and inscriptions refer to them as *sahi*. (Wink, pg 125)
[860] Al Biruni refers to the subsequent rulers as "Brahman kings"; however, most other references such as Kalahan refer to them as kshatriyas. (Wink, pg 125)
[861] Kabul Shahi
[862] At Google Books.
[863] At the Internet Archive.
[864] At Google Books.
[865] http://www.livius.org/articles/place/gandara/?
[866] At the Perseus Project.
[867] At the Perseus Project.
[868] https://archive.org/details/catalogueofcoins01lahoiala
[869] H. C. Raychaudhuri, *Political History of Ancient India* (1996), p.77
[870] UNESCO World Heritage Centre: Taxila http://whc.unesco.org/en/list/139
[871] Histories, epigraphy and authority: Achaemenid and indigenous control in Pakistan in the 1st millennium BC http://www.arch.cam.ac.uk/bannu-archaeological-project/petrie2007_02.pd
[872] Rafi U. Samad, *The Grandeur of Gandhara: The Ancient Buddhist Civilization of the Swat, Peshawar, Kabul and Indus Valleys.* https://books.google.com/books?id=pNUwBYGYgxsC&pg=PA33 Algora Publishing, 2011, p. 32
[873] Marshall, John (1975) [1951]. Taxila: Volume I. Delhi: Motilal Banarsidass. pp. 83.
[874] Curtius in McCrindle, p. 192, J. W. McCrindle; *History of Punjab*, Vol I, 1997, p 229, Punjabi University, Patiala (editors): Fauja Singh, L. M. Joshi; *Kambojas Through the Ages*, 2005, p. 134, Kirpal Singh.
[875] Revue des etudes grecques 1973, p 131, Ch-Em Ruelle, Association pour l'encouragement des etudes grecques en France.
[876] Early Indian Economic History, 1973, pp 237, 324, Rajaram Narayan Saletore.
[877] Myths of the Dog-man, 199, p 119, David Gordon White; Journal of the Oriental Institute, 1919, p 200; Journal of Indian Museums, 1973, p 2, Museums Association of India; The Pāradas: A Study in Their Coinage and History, 1972, p 52, Dr B. N. Mukherjee – Pāradas; Journal of the Department of Sanskrit, 1989, p 50, Rabindra Bharati University, Dept. of Sanskrit- Sanskrit literature; The Journal of Academy of Indian Numismatics & Sigillography, 1988, p 58, Academy of Indian Numismatics and Sigillography – Numismatics; Cf: Rivers of Life: Or Sources and Streams of the Faiths of Man in All Lands, 2002, p 114, J. G. R. Forlong.
[878] Journal of the Oriental Institute, 1919, p 265, Oriental Institute (Vadodara, India) – Oriental studies; For Kuru-Kamboja connections, see Dr Chandra Chakraberty's views in: Literary history of ancient India in relation to its racial and linguistic affiliations, pp 14,37, Vedas; The Racial History of India, 1944, p 153, Chandra Chakraberty – Ethnology; Paradise of Gods, 1966, p 330, Qamarud Din Ahmed – Pakistan.

[879] Ancient India, History of India for 1000 years, four Volumes, Vol I, 1938, pp 38, 98 Dr T. L. Shah.
[880] *NOTE*: See long discussion under Mahajanapada from the Ancient Buddhist text Anguttara Nikaya's list of Mahajanapadas.
[881] Rowland, Benjamin 1945 'Ganhdara and Early Christian Art: Buddha Palliatus', *American Journal of Archaeology* 49.4, 445–8 https://www.jstor.org/stable/499859
[882] Bracey, R 'Pilgrims Progress' Brief Guide to Kushan History http://www.kushan.org/sources/thomasandapollonius.htm
[883] *Alberuni's India*. (c. 1030 AD). Translated and annotated by Edward C. Sachau in two volumes. Kegana Paul, Trench, Trübner, London. (1910). Vol. I, p. 22.
[884] http://factsanddetails.com/asian/cat62/sub406/item2566.html
[885] Mukherjee, Bratindra Nath. *India in Early Central Asia.* 1996. p. 15
[886] Williams, Paul. *Mahāyāna Buddhism: The Doctrinal Foundations.* 2008. p. 30
[887] Nakamura, Hajime. *Indian Buddhism: A Survey With Biographical Notes.* 1999. p. 205
[888] Williams, Paul. *Mahāyāna Buddhism: The Doctrinal Foundations.* 2008. p. 239
[889] Ray, Reginald. *Buddhist Saints in India: A Study in Buddhist Values and Orientations.* 1999. p. 410
[890] Ray, Reginald. *Buddhist Saints in India: A Study in Buddhist Values and Orientations.* 1999. p. 426
[891] Bakshi, S.R. *Kashmir: History and People.* 1998. p. 194
[892] http://www.perseus.tufts.edu/hopper/text?doc=Hdt.+1.1.0&fromdoc=Perseus%3Atext%3A1999.01.0125
[893] http://depts.washington.edu/silkroad/texts/hhshu/hou_han_shu.html
[894] http://libmma.contentdm.oclc.org/cdm/compoundobject/collection/p15324coll10/id/105494
[895] http://www.livius.org/ga-gh/gandara/gandara.html
[896] https://web.archive.org/web/20040626090537/http://www.washington.edu/research/showcase/1996a.html
[897] https://web.archive.org/web/20040405065830/http://www.washington.edu/newsroom/news/2002archive/08-02archive/k082002a.html
[898] https://web.archive.org/web/20070222024000/http://home.comcast.net/~pankajtandon/galleries-gandhara.html
[899] http://heritage.gov.pk/html_Pages/gandhara.html
[900] //tools.wmflabs.org/geohack/geohack.php?pagename=Gandhara&params=33.7560_N_72.8291_E_type:landmark_region:PK
[901] Dwivedi 1977: 287 "The Kambojas were probably the descendants of the Indo-Iranians popularly known later on as the Sassanians and Parthians who occupied parts of north-western India in the first and second centuries of the Christian era."
[902] Mishra 1987
[903] Ramesh Chandra Majumdar, Achut Dattatrya Pusalker, A. K. Majumdar, Dilip Kumar Ghose, Bharatiya Vidya Bhavan, Vishvanath Govind Dighe. *The History and Culture of the Indian People*, 1962, p 264,
[904] "Political History of Ancient India", H. C. Raychaudhuri, B. N. Mukerjee, University of Calcutta, 1996.
[905] See: Vedic Index of names & subjects by Arthur Anthony Macdonnel, Arthur. B Keath, I.84, p 138.
[906] See more Refs: Ethnology of Ancient Bhārata, 1970, p 107, Ram Chandra Jain; The Journal of Asian Studies, 1956, p 384, Association for Asian Studies, Far Eastern Association (U.S.)
[907] *India as Known to Pāṇini: A Study of the Cultural Material in the Ashṭādhyāyī*, 1953, p 49, Vasudeva Sharana Agrawala; *Afghanistan*, p 58, W. K. Fraser, M. C. Gillet; *Afghanistan, its People, its Society, its Culture*, Donal N. Wilber, 1962, p 80, 311
[908] Walker and Tapp 2001
[909] *Encyclopedia of the Peoples of Asia and Oceania*, Barbara A. West, Infobase Publishing (2009), p. 359
[910] Encyclopaedia Indica, "The Kambojas: Land and its Identification", First Edition, 1998 New Delhi, page 528
[911] Sethna, K. D. (2000) *Problems of Ancient India*, New Delhi: Aditya Prakashan.

[912] Numerous scholars now locate the Kamboja realm on the southern side of the Hindu Kush ranges (in the Kabul, Swat, and Kunar valleys) and the Parama-Kambojas in the territories on the north side of the Hindu Kush. See: Geographical and Economic Studies in the Mahābhārata: Upāyana Parva, 1945, p 11-13, Moti Chandra - India; *Geographical Data in the Early Purāṇas: A Critical Study*, 1972, p 165/66, M. R. Singh

[913] *Purana*, Vol VI, No 1, January 1964, p 207 sqq; *Inscriptions of Asoka: Translation and Glossary*, 1990, p 86, Beni Madhab Barua, Binayendra Nath Chaudhury - Inscriptions, Prakrit).

[914] The Peoples of Pakistan: An Ethnic History, 1971, pp 64-67, Yuri Vladimirovich Gankovski - Ethnology.

[915] History of the Pathans, 2002, p 11, Haroon Rashid - Pushtuns.

[916] Michael Witzel Persica-9, p 92, fn 81.

[917] Asoka and His Inscriptions, 1968, pp 93-96, Beni Madhab Barua, Ishwar Nath Topa.

[918] See: *Proceedings and Transactions of the All-India Oriental Conference*, 1930, p 118, J. C. Vidyalankara

[919] *The Deeds of Harsha: Being a Cultural Study of Bāṇa's Harshacharita*, 1969, p 199, Vasudeva Sharana Agrawala

[920] *Central Asiatic Provinces of the Mauryan Empire*, p 403, H. C. Seth; See also: *Indian Historical Quarterly*, Vol. XIII, 1937, No 3, p. 400; *Journal of the Asiatic Society*, 1940, p 37, (India) Asiatic Society (Calcutta, Royal Asiatic Society of Bengal - Asia; cf: *History and Archaeology of India's Contacts with Other Countries, from Earliest Times to 300 B.C.*, 176, p 152, Shashi P. Asthana; *Mahabharata Myth and Reality*, 1976, p 232, Swarajya Prakash Gupta, K. S. Ramachandran. Cf also: *India and Central Asia*, p 25 etc, P. C. Bagchi.

[921] *Indian Historical Quarterly*, 1963, p 403; Central Asiatic provinces of the Maurya Empire, p403, H.C. Seth

[922] *History and Archaeology of India's Contacts with Other Countries, from Earliest Times to 300 B.C.*, 1976, p 152, Shashi Asthana; *Mahabharata Myth and Reality*, 1976, p 232, Swarajya Prakash Gupta, K. S. Ramachandran.

[923] "The Town of Darwaz in Badakshan is still called Khum (Kum) or Kala-i-Khum. It stands for the valley of Basht. The name Khum or Kum conceals the relics of ancient Kamboja" (*Journal of the Asiatic Society*, 1956, p 256, Buddha Prakash [Asiatic Society (Calcutta, India), Asiatic Society of Bengal]).

[924] *India and the World*, p 71, Buddha Prakash; also see: *Central Asiatic Provinces of Maurya Empire*, p 403, H. C. Seth; *India and Central Asia*, p 25, P. C. Bagchi

[925] *Journal of the Asiatic Society*, 1956, p 256, Asiatic Society (Calcutta, India), Asiatic Society of Bengal.

[926] Talbert 2000, p. 99

[927] For Tambyzoi=Kamboja, see refs: Pre Aryan and Pre Dravidian in India, 1993, p 122, Sylvain Lévi, Jean Przyluski, Jules Bloch, Asian Educational Services; Cities and Civilization, 1962, p 172, Govind Sadashiv Ghurye

[928] For Ambautai=Kamboja, see Witzel 1999a

[929] Patton and Bryant 2005, p. 257

[930] Histoire Auguste: Pt. 2. Vies des deux Valérines et des deux Galliens, 2000, p 90, Ammn Marcellin, Jean Pierre Callu, O. Desbordes (*Les hydronymes de Transcaucasie, en question ici, auraient pu, dès lors, aussi dériver aussi de ces ethniques, lors de l'extension des tribus iraniennes vers le Nord de la Médie, et non pas de ces souverains achéménides — dont la présente légende répond mieux à l'ingéniosité «heurématique» des Grecs*)

[931] See: Problems of Ancient India, 2000, p 5-6; cf: Geographical Data in the Early Puranas, p 168.

[932] *Hindu Polity: A Constitutional History of India in Hindu Times*, Parts I and II., 1955, p 52, Dr Kashi Prasad Jayaswal - Constitutional history; Prācīna Kamboja, jana aura janapada =: Ancient Kamboja, people and country, 1981, Dr Jiyālāla Kāmboja - Kamboja (Pakistan).

[933] Studies in Skanda Purana, 1978, p 59, A. B. L. Awasthi.

[934] The Indian Historical Quarterly, 1963, p 103

[935] Hindu Polity, 1978, pp 121, 140, K. P. Jayswal.

[936] War in Ancient India, 1944, p 178, V. R. Ramachandra Dikshitar - Military art and science.

[937] The Indian Historical Quarterly, 1963, p 103; The Achaemenids in India, 1950, p 47, Sudhakar Chattopadhyaya; Poona Orientalist: A Quarterly Journal Devoted to Oriental Studies, 1945, P i, (edi) Har Dutt Sharma; The Poona Orientalist, 1936, p 13, Sanskrit philology

[938] "Par ailleurs le Kamboja est régulièrement mentionné comme la "patrie des chevaux" (Asvanam ayatanam), et cette reputation bien etablie gagné peut-etre aux eleveurs de chevaux du Bajaur et du Swat l'appellation d'Aspasioi (du v.-p. aspa) et d'assakenoi (du skt asva "cheval")". E. Lamotte, Historie du Bouddhisme Indien, p. 110. (WP translation. Quotation should be taken from the published English translation: Lamotte 1988, p. 100)

[939] Panjab Past and Present, pp 9-10; also see: History of Porus, pp 12, 38, Buddha Parkash

[940] Proceedings, 1965, p 39, by Punjabi University. Dept. of Punjab Historical Studies - History.

[941] De Sélincourt, A., & Hamilton, J. (1971, 2003). Arrian: The Campaigns of Alexander. Harmondsworth: Penguin. Book IV, pp. 244

[942] History of Punjab, 1997, Editors: Fauja Singh, L. M. Joshi

[943] Acharya 2001, p 91

[944] Geographical Data in the Early Purāṇas: A Critical Study, 1972, p 168, M. R. Singh - India.

[945] History of Ceylon, 1959, p 91, Ceylon University, University of Ceylon, Peradeniya, Hem Chandra Ray, K. M. De Silva.

[946] Pande (R.) 1984, p. 93

[947] Shrava 1981, p. 12

[948] Rishi, 1982, p. 100

[949] See: Corpus Inscriptionum Indicarum, Vol II, Part I, p xxxvi; see also p 36, Sten Konow; Indian Culture, 1934, p 193, Indian Research Institute; Cf: Journal of the Royal Asiatic Society of Great Britain and Ireland, 1990, p 142, Royal Asiatic Society of Great Britain and Ireland - Middle East.

[950] Indian Historical Quarterly, 1963, p 127

[951] Shastri and Choudhury 1982, p. 112

[952] B. C. Sen, Some Historical Aspects of the Inscriptions of Bengal, p. 342, fn 1

[953] M. R. Singh, A Critical Study of the Geographical Data in the Early Puranas, p. 168

[954] Ganguly 1994, p. 72, fn 168

[955] H. C. Ray, The Dynastic History of Northern India, I, p. 309

[956] A. D. Pusalkar, R. C. Majumdar et al., History and Culture of Indian People, Imperial Kanauj, p. 323,

[957] R. R. Diwarkar (ed.), Bihar Through the Ages, 1958, p. 312

[958] Ancient Indian History and Civilization by Sailendra Nath Sen p.281

[959] The Cambridge Shorter History of India p.145

[960] H. C. Raychaudhury, B. N. Mukerjee; Asoka and His Inscriptions, 3d Ed, 1968, p 149, Beni Madhab Barua, Ishwar Nath Topa.

[961] Hindu Polity, A Constitutional History of India in Hindu Times, 1978, p 117-121, K. P. Jayswal; Ancient India, 2003, pp 839-40, V. D. Mahajan; Northern India, p 42, Mehta Vasisitha Dev Mohan etc

[962] Bimbisāra to Aśoka: With an Appendix on the Later Mauryas, 1977, p 123, Sudhakar Chattopadhyaya.

[963] The North-west India of the Second Century B.C., 1974, p 40, Mehta Vasishtha Dev Mohan - India; Tribes in Ancient India, 1973, p 7

[964] Yar-Shater 1983, p. 951

[965] http://www.kambojsociety.com/kamboja-ancient-kamboj-country.html

[966] //en.wikipedia.org/w/index.php?title=Template:Part_of_History_of_India&action=edit

[967] Kalhana (1147-1149); Rajatarangini.

[968] Wink 2002, p. 243.

[969] Chadurah 1991, p. 45.

[970] Hasan 1959, p. 54.

[971] https://books.google.com/books?id=g2m7_R5P2oAC&pg=PA243

[972] https://books.google.com/books?id=nTFuAAAAMAAJ

[973] https://books.google.com/books?id=EUlwmXjE9DQC&&pg=PA2

[974] André Wink, Early Medieval India and the Expansion of Islam: 7th-11th Centuries, (Brill, 2002), 125.

[975] as in: Rajatarangini, IV, 140-43, Kalahana.
[976] as in inscriptions: See: Hindu Sahis of Afghanistan and the Punjab, 1972, p 111, Yogendra Mishra.
[977] as in: Tarikh-al-Hind, trans. E. C. Sachau, 1888/1910, vol ii, pp 10, Abu Rihan Alberuni; Sehrai, Fidaullah (1979). Hund: *The Forgotten City of Gandhara*, p. 1. Peshawar Museum Publications New Series, Peshawar.
[978] Sehrai, Fidaullah (1979). Hund: *The Forgotten City of Gandhara*, p. 2. Peshawar Museum Publications New Series, Peshawar.
[979] Kohzad, Ahmad Ali, "Kabul Shāhāni Berahmanī", 1944, Kabul
[980] The Pathans, 1958, p 108, 109, Olaf Caroe.
[981] Abu Rihan Alberuni *Tarikh-al-Hind*, trans. E. C. Sachau, 1888/1910, vol ii, pp. 10–14.
[982] Charles Frederick Oldham *The Sun and the Serpent: A Contribution to the History of Serpent-worship*, 1905, pp. 113-126, — Serpent worship.
[983] Important Note: Urasa, Rajauri/Poonch and Abhisara were off-shoots of ancient Kamboja (see: *Political History of Ancient India*, 1996, p 133, 219/220, Dr H. C. Raychaudhury, Dr B. N. Mukerjee; A History of India, p 269-71, N. R. Ray, N. K. Sinha; *Journal of Indian History*, 1921, P 304, University of Allahabad, Department of Modern Indian History, University of Kerala).
[984] Chintaman Vinayak Vaidya *History of Mediaeval Hindu India*, 1979, p 200.
[985] *Si-Yu-KI VI: Buddhist Records of the Western World*, Edition 2006, pp. 54-55, Hsuen Tsang; *The Sun and the Serpent: A Contribution to the History of Serpent-worship*, 1905, p. 120, Charles Frederick Oldham – *Serpent worship; The Shahis of Afghanistan and the Punjab*, 1973, p 17, Deena Bandhu Pandey; *The History and Culture of the Indian People*, 1977, p 165, Dr Ramesh Chandra Majumdar, Dr A. D. Pusalkar — India.
[986] Dr Ramesh Chandra Majumdar, Dr A. D. Pusalkar *The History and Culture of the Indian People*, 1977, p. 165.
[987] *History of Mediaeval Hindu India*, 1979, p. 200, Chintaman Vinayak Vaidya — India.
[988] "The view that Nepali Traditions apply name Kamboja Desha to Tibet is based on the statement made by Foucher (Ref: Étude sur l'Iconographie bouddhique de l'Inde, pp 134–135, A. Foucher) on the authority of Ranga Nath, Pandit to B. H. Hodgson. But it is also supported by two manuscripts [No 7768 & 7777] described in the Catalogue of Sanskrit and Prakrit Mss in the library of India Office, Vol II, Part II." (Refs: *History of Bengal*, I, 191, Dr R. C. Majumdar; Dist. Gazetteer [Rajashahi], 1915, p 26; Some Historical Aspects of the Inscriptions of Bengal, Dr B. C. Sen, p 342, fn 1.)
[989] "The Pal Kings of Bengal" in *Calcutta Review*, June 1874, pp 74, 95, 96, E. Vesey Westmacott, Bengal Civil Service, Bengal Asiatic Society of Royal Asiatic Society, F.R.G.S.).
[990] "The Pal Kings of Bengal" in *Calcutta Review*, June 1874, pp 74, 95, 96, E. Vesey Westmacott, Bengal Civil Service, Bengal Asiatic Society of Royal Asiatic Society, F.R.G.S.
[991] *The Kafirs of the Hindukush*, 1896, pp 75–85; A Passage to Nurestan explaining the mysteries of Afghan Hinterland, 2006, p 80, I. B. Tauris, Nicholas Barrington, Joseph T. Kenderick, Reinhard Schlangitweit, Sardy Gall.
[992] *The Káfirs of the Hindu-Kush*, 1896, pp 71–77, George Scott Robertson — Nuristani (Asian people).
[993] NOTE: According to Persiacs-9, in the 7th century, the Kabol area (i.e Kabol, Kapisa, Lamghan, etc.) was the stronghold of the Iranian cis-Hindkush Kambojas whose influence extended as far as Arachosia/Kandhahar (See: Early East Iran and Arthaveda, 1981, p 92 sqq, Dr Michael Witzel).
[994] For example: King Ashoka's Rock Edicts at Shahbazgarhi and Mansehra list the Kambojas among the Yonas and Gandharas as the most eminent clan of this region, i.e., Kabul/Kapisa/Swat.
[995] According to *Sata-pañcāśaddesa-vibhaga* of *Saktisamgma Tantra*, Book III, Ch VII, v 24–28 (a medieval era Tantra text), the Kambojas are said to be located to west of South-west Kashmir (Pir-pañcāla), to South of Bactria, and to east of Maha-Mlechcha-desa (Mohammadan countries i.e Khorasan/Iran). Likewise verse 42–44 of the same reference locates the medieval Huna-desa to the north of Maru-desa (Rajputana) and to the south of Kama-giri (*Kama hills*) (See Ref: Geography of Ancient and Medieval India, 1971, p 100-102, 108, Dr D. C. Sircar). The Kama/

kamma is the name of hilly territory of eastern Afghanistan, lying between Jalalabad and Khyber pass. Hence, the general location of Huna-desa may indeed have comprised south-western Punjab and parts of Southern and Central Afghanistan which territory again was same as the Zabulistan of Arab writers.

[996] *Proceedings and Transactions of the All-India Oriental Conference*, 1930, p 108, Dr J. C. Vidyalankar (All-India Oriental Conference); The Cultural Heritage of India: Sri Ramakrishna Centenary Memorial, 1936, p 135, Dr S. K. Chatterjee, Sri Ramakrishna Centenary Committee.

[997] Bhartya Itihaas ki Ruprekha, p 534, Dr J. C. Vidyalankar; *Ancient Kamboja, People and the Country*, 1981, pp 129, 300, Dr J. L. Kamboj.

[998] Cf: *The History and Culture of the Indian People*, 1977, pp 165 sqq, Dr Ramesh Chandra Majumdar, Dr A. D. Pusalkar — India.

[999] *History and Culture of Indian People*, Vol II, and several other noted authorities identify Kapisa kingdom a part of ancient cis-Hindukush Kamboja (See: *The History and Culture of the Indian People*, Vol II, 1977, p 122, Dr Ramesh Chandra Majumdar, Dr Achut Dattatraya Pusalker, Dr Asoke Kumar Majumdar — India.

[1000] Si-yu-ki: Buddhist Records of the Western World, 1906 edition, pp 50, 54, Samuel Beal.

[1001] Rajatarangini 4.164–166.

[1002] For identification of Kumijis with Kambojas, see: India and Central Asia, p 25, Dr P. C. Bagchi; Prācīna Kamboja, Jana aur Janapada =: Ancient Kamboja, People and Country, 1981, pp 300, 401, Jiyālāla Kāmboja, Satyavrat Śāstrī. The tribal name Kumiji may also be compared to Camoji/Caumojee or Kamoje Kafir tribes of the Hindukush as referred to by Elphinstone (*An Account of the Kingdom of Caubul*) and Kams/Kamoz as mentioned by George Scott Robertson (*The Kafirs of the Hindukush*). The Kafir tribes Kamojis/Kamozis of the Hindukush represent the relics of the ancient Kambojas. For Kamoj/Kamoji people of Hindukush and their relations with ancient Kambojas, See: Wishnu Purana, p 374, fn, H. H. Wilson; *The Sun and the Serpent: A Contribution to the History of Serpent-worship*, 1905, p 127, Charles Frederick Oldham; Peter Weiss: *Von existentialistischen Drama zum marxistischen Weltheater ...*, 1971, Otto F. Best; *Geographical and Economic Studies in the Mahābhārata*: Upāyana Parva, 1945, p 131, Moti Chandra; *The Living Age*, 1873, p 781; Mountstuart Elphinstone, "An account of the kingdom of Caubol", fn p 619; *Journal of the Royal Asiatic Society*, 1843, p 140; *Journal of Asiatic Society of Bengal*, 1874, p 260 fn; *Die altpersischen Keilinschriften: Im Grundtexte mit Uebersetzung, Grammatik und Glossar*, 1881, p 86, Friedrich Spiegel; *Political History of Ancient India*, 1996, p 133, fn, Dr H. C. Raychaudhury, Dr B. N. Banerjee; *The Achaemenids and India*, 1974, p 13, Dr S Chattopadhyaya.

[1003] Quoted in: *India and Central Asia*, p 25, Dr P. C. Bagchi; *The Achamenids in India*, p 7 by Dr S. Chattopadhya, where the author identifies the Kambojas as of Turko-Iranian stock; cf also: *The Indian Historical Quarterly*, 1963, p 192, India; Cf: Annals of the Bhandarkar Oriental Research Institute, Poona, 1928, pp 130,138, Bhandarkar Oriental Research Institute, which connects the Kambhojas with Tartar ethnics.

[1004] Some writers have gone to the extent of designating these 11th-century Pamirian Kumijis (the remnants of ancient Kambojas of Pamirs/Hindukush) as extractions from the Hephthalites (See: History of Civilizations of Central Asia, 1999, p 102, Dr Ahmad Hasan Dani, Vadim Mikhaĭlovich Masson, János Harmatta, Boris Abramovich Litvinovskiĭ, Clifford Edmund Bosworth, Unesco — Asia, Central.

[1005] There are numerous references to Kambojas and Tukharas (Turukshakas) being bracketed together as allied tribes or as neighboring tribes located in Central Asia. See: Tukhara Kingdom. The Tukharas/Tusharas had also joined the Kamboja army and fought the Kurukshetra war under the supreme command of Kamboja Sudakshina (MBH 5.19.21–23; The Nations of India at the Battle Between the Pandavas and Kauravas, Journal of the Royal Asiatic Society of Great Britain and Ireland, 1908, pp 313, 331, Dr F. E. Pargiter; (See: Royal Asiatic Society of Great Britain and Ireland). As noted above, as late as the 8th century AD, the Kambojas and Tukharas are attested to be immediate neighbors in around Oxus (Rajatarangini 4.164–166).

[1006] IMPORTANT COMMENT: As noted above, the Kambojas and the Tukharas/Turukshakas, for long time, had co-existed in the former Kamboja/Tukharistan country and thus, their culture, customs, mannerism and dress had become shared over the time. Thus, it is but natural that some writers make mistakes in identifying these remnants of ancient Kambojas of the Pamirs/ Hindukush with the Turks or the Hephthalites.

[1007] There are even some noted scholars who identify the Kambojas as a branch of the Tukharas (See for example: *Buddhism in Central Asia, 1987, p 90, Dr B. N. Puri — Buddhism*).

[1008] See: Si-yu-ki, Buddhist Records of the Western World, 1906, p c (Introduction), Samuel Beal.

[1009] *The Pathans*, 1958, p 101, Olaf Caroe.

[1010] See: *The Maha-Bodhi*, p 181, Maha Bodhi Society, Calcutta — Buddhism; *Ancient Indian History and Culture*, 1974, p 149, Shripad Rama Sharma — India; *Journal of the Royal Asiatic Society*, April 1903, p 369, M Anesaki; *The Sun and the Serpent: A Contribution to the History of Serpent-worship*, 1905, p 125, Charles Frederick Oldham — Serpent worship.

[1011] See entry *Varman* in Monier Williams, Sanskrit-English Dictionary; see also entry Varman in: *Cologne Digital Sanskrit English Dictionary*)

[1012] "Varman" is the virtual name ending of a Kshatriya in India (See: *Some Aspects of Asian History and Culture*, 1986, p 17, Upendra Thakur.

[1013] For "Varman" being a Kshatriya surname, see also: *Inscriptions of Orissa*, 1997, p 25, Snigdha Tripathy, Indian Council of Historical Research, Indian council of historical research).

[1014] Cf: Surname Sarman always indicated a Brahmana and Varman a Kshatriya (See: *Concise History of Ancient India*, 1977, p 43, Asoke Kumar Majumdar).

[1015] For Chinese Buddhist records referencing Guna Varman, see reference: J.R.A.S., April 1903, p 369, M. Anesaki. From the account of Guna Varman as referenced in Chinese Buddhist Records, there were Hindu (*Kshatriya*) kings in Kabul/Kapisa more than two centuries before Xuanzang's arrival in AD 631 (644/45 in Kapis) when he found a *Kshatriya* king upon the throne of Afghanistan (See: The Sun and the Serpent: A Contribution to the History of Serpent-worship, 1905, p 125, Charles Frederick Oldham).

[1016] *Mudrarakshasa* act II; History of Poros, 1967, p 89, Dr Buddha Prakash.

[1017] *A History of Zoroastrianism*, 1991, p 136, Mary Boyce, Frantz Grenet; *Mauryan Samrajya Ka Itihaas*, Hindi, 1927, p 665-67 by Dr Sataketu Vidyalankar; *Hindu Polity, A Constitutional History of India in Hindu Times*, 1978, p 117-121, Dr K. P. Jayswal; *Ancient India*, 2003, pp 839–40, Dr V. D. Mahajan; Northern India, p 42, Dr Mehta Vasisitha Dev Mohan etc.

[1018] *History of Punjab*, Vol I, 1997, p 225, Dr Buddha Prakash; *Raja Poros*, 1990, p 9, Publication Bureau, Punjabi University Patiala.

[1019] Raghuvamsa, 4.67–70, Kalidasa.

[1020] The *Bhishma Parva* of the *Mahabharata*, which is supposed to have been edited around the 4th or 5th century AD, in one of its verses mentions the Hunas with the Parasikas and other *Mlechha tribes* of the northwest including the Kambojas, Yavanas, Chinas, Darunas, Sukritvahas, Kulatthas, etc.

HrishIvidarbhah kantikasta∼Nganah parata∼Nganah. |
uttarashchapare mlechchhA jana bharatasattama. || 63 ||
YavanAshcha sa Kamboja Daruna mlechchha jatayah. |
Sakahaddruhah Kuntalashcha Hunah Parasikas saha.|| 64 ||
Tathaiva maradhAahchinastathaiva dasha malikah. |
Kshatriyopaniveshashcha vaishyashudra kulani cha.|| 65 ||
(Mahabharata 6.9.63–65) .

[1021] Early History of India, p 339, Dr V. A. Smith; See also Early Empire of Central Asia (1939), W. M. McGovern.

[1022] Book III, Ch VII, v 24–28.

[1023] Book III, Ch VII, v 42–44.

[1024] Raj Shekhar Chapter 17, Kavy Mimansa.

[1025] Cf: *The Sun and the Serpent: A Contribution to the History of Serpent-worship*, 1905, p 125, Charles Frederick Olmsted.

[1026] Sakas used titles like "Sahi and Sahanusahi".

[1027] Kushanas used the grandiloquent title like "daivaputra-sahi.sahanu.sahi", "Shaonano shao", and "Shao".

[1028] The Hunas had the title "Shāhī".

[1029] The title "Shahi" appears on Indo-Bactrian coins.

[1030] "Shahi of Kalhana's Rajatrangini, Shahiya of Alberuni and Sahi of the inscriptions".

[1031] *The Shahi Afghanistan and Punjab*, 1973, pp 1, 45–46, 48, 80, Dr D. B. Pandey; *The Śakas in India and Their Impact on Indian Life and Culture*, 1976, p 80, Vishwa Mitra Mohan – *Indo-Scythians; Country, Culture and Political life in early and medieval India*, 2004, p 34, Daud Ali.

[1032] *Journal of the Royal Asiatic Society*, 1954, pp 112 ff; *The Shahis of Afghanistan and Punjab*, 1973, p 46, Dr D. B. Pandey; *The Śakas in India and Their Impact on Indian Life and Culture*, 1976, p 80, Vishwa Mitra Mohan — Indo-Scythians.

[1033] India, A History, 2001, p 203, John Keay.

[1034] J.B.B.R.A.S., 139ff; J.B.O.R.S, xvi, 233, 293; *Political History of Ancient India*, 1996, p 383, Dr H. C. Raychaudhury; Zeitschrift der deutschen morgenlandischen Gesellschaft 34, pp 247ff, 262; *Indian Antiquary*, X, 222; *Jaina Journal*, V-22, 1987–88, p 107; *The Śakas in India*, 1981, p 23, Satya Shrava; *Mālwa in Post-Maurya Period*, 1981, p 41, Manika Chakrabarti — Malwa (Madhya Pradesh and Rajasthan, India).

[1035] The Shahis of Afghanistan and the Punjab, 1973, p 1, Dr Deena Bandhu Pandey.

[1036] The former Kafirs like Aspins of Chitral and Ashkuns or Yashkuns of Gilgit are identified as the modern representatives of the Pāṇinian Aśvakayanas (*Greek: Assakenoi*); and the Asip/Isap or Yusufzai (from *Aspa.zai*) in the Kabul valley (between river Kabul and Indus) are believed to be modern representatives of the Pāṇinian Aśvayanas (*Greek: Aspasioi*) respectively (See: *The Quarterly Review*, 1873, p 537, William Gifford, George Walter Prothero, John Gibson Lockhart, John Murray, Whitwell Elwin, John Taylor Coleridge, Rowland Edmund Prothero Ernle, William Macpherson, William Smith; *An Inquiry Into the Ethnography of Afghanistan*, 1893, p 75, Henry Walter Bellew; *Journal of the Royal Asiatic Society of Great Britain and Ireland*, 1864, p 681, by Royal Asiatic Society of Great Britain and Ireland; *The Invasion of India by Alexander the Great*, 1896, p 334, John Watson M'Crindle; *Evolution of Heroic Tradition in Ancient Panjab*, 1971, p 72; History of Punjab, Publication Bureau Punjabi University Patiala, 1997, p 225, Dr Buddha Prakash; *A Comprehensive History of India*, Vol II, p 118, Dr Nilkantha Shastri; See also: Ancient Kamboja, People & the Country, 1981, p 278, These Kamboj People, 1979, pp 119–20, K. S. Dardi etc.

[1037] NOTE: The Aspasios and Assaekoi clans of Kunar/Swat valleys are stated to be sub-sections of the Kambojas who were especially engaged in horse-culture and were expert horsemen (*Asva.yuddhah-kushalah*). See: Ashvakas. See also: Mahabharata 12.101.5, Kumbhakonam Ed.; See also: Hindu Polity, 1955, p 140, Dr K. P. Jayswal).

[1038] See: *Glossary of Tribes and Castes of Punjab and North West Frontier Province*, 1910, Vol III, p 524, H. A. Rose.

[1039] Note: *No systematic excavation of the area has so far been made in the Kabul Shahi realm, but the sporadic finds made in the region affirm the spread of Hindu influence at the cost of Buddhism during the period spanning AD 600–900. The replacement of Buddhist kingship with Hindu kingship around AD 870 seems to symbolize the Brahmanization of the so-called Turk kings as well as the population south of the Hindukush. A Brahmanised king named Kallar started the Hindu Shahi dynasty of Gandhara* (Cf: *The Afghans*, 2002, p 183, W. Vogelsang; See also: "The Pal Kings of Bengal" in *Calcutta Review*, June 1874, p 96, E. Vesey Westmacott, Bengal Civil Service, Bengal Asiatic Society of Royal Asiatic Society, F.R.G.S.).

[1040] http://www.thewalt.de/afghanistan/69d10/pages/69d10-04.html

[1041] See Gilgit Manuscripts http://www.the-south-asian.com/Aug2004/Gilgit_manuscript.htm

[1042] *The Sun and the Serpent: A Contribution to the History of Serpent-worship*, 1905, p 126, Charles Frederick Oldham — Serpent worship.

[1043] Comments Charles Frederick Oldham: "Whether this king of Kabul was same Kshatriya chief who had entertained Chinese pilgrim is uncertain; but he too must have been a Kshatriya, or the warriors (Kshatriyas) of Hind would have taken little notice of his appeal for assistance (op cit, p 126, Charles Frederick Oldham.

[1044] See: *The Geography of Ancient and Medieval India*, 1971, p 292-93, Dr D. C. Sircar. Dr Sircar continues: "The fact that Kalhana speaks of the Shahis with reference to the period earlier than that of king Lalitaditya (c 730–66 AD) and of Udabhanda as the capital of the Shahis at least from the time of king Lalliya of Kashmir (c 875–90 AD) and that Chinese evidence refers to the city as the residence of the emperor of Kapisa about 645 AD would indicate that Xuanzang's king of Kapisa was a Shahi ruler. It is very interesting that this king has been called by Hsuen

Tsang as a Kshatriya." (See: "Udabhanda" in *The Geography of Ancient and Medieval India*, 1971, p 293, Dr D. C. Sircar).

[1045] Modern day Hund, also called *Waihind* by Al Biruni (Wink p 125).

[1046] *Tarikh-al-Hind*, trans Sachau, 1910, vol ii, p 13, Abu Rihan Alberuni.

[1047] *The Pathans*, 1958, pp 108–09, Olaf Caroe; cf: *Evolution of Heroic Tradition in Ancient Punjab*, 1971, p 135, Dr Buddha Prakash.

[1048] NOTE: Alberuni also records in "Tarikh-al-Hind" that the Kabul Shahi rulers claimed descent from Kanik (believed by some to be Kanishka of Kushana dynasty) and further also boast of their Tibetan origin (sic) (Alberuni's *Indica, A Record of the Cultural History of South Asia*, 1973, p 38, Ahmad Hasan Dani, Muḥammad ibn Aḥmad Bīrūnī, Eduard Sachau; *History of Mediaeval Hindu India*, 1979, p 199, Chintaman Vinayak Vaidya; *The Shahis of Afghanistan and the Punjab*, 1973, p 51, D. B. Pandey). *There is abundant evidence that a branch of Kambojas was living in Tibet around the 4th or 5th century AD as is evidenced by Brahma Purana (53.19). Many scholars like Charles Elliot, Dr Foucher, Dr G. G. Gokhale, V.A. Smith etc locate the Kambojas in Tibet. Nepalese traditions also apply name Kamboja-desa to Tibet (See refs:* Iconographie bouddhique, p 132); History of the Koch Kingdom, C. 1515–1615, 1989, P 10, D. Nath. Even otherwise also, the ancient Kambojas of Kafiristan are said to have extended as far as little Tibet and Ladak (See Refs: Peter weiss: *Von existentialistischen Drama zum marxistischen Welttheater ...*, 1971, Otto F. Best; *The Devi Bhagavatam*, Vol. 2 of 3, p 117, Swami Vijnanannanda; *Historical Mahākāvyas in Sanskrit, Eleventh to Fifteenth Century A.D.*, 1976, 373, Chandra Prabha; *Kāmarūpaśāsanāvalī*, 1981, p 137, Dimbeswar Sarma, P. D. Chowdhury, R. K. Deva *Sarma — Assam* (India; Cf: *The Early History of India*, 1904, p 165, Vincent A. Smith*); The Khamba province of Tibet still carries the vestiges of ancient Kamboja in it. The above tradition recorded by Alberuni may also go in favor of "Shahi origin from Tibetan Kambojas" rather than from Kushanas, Hunas or Turks.*

[1049] Kalhana Rajatarangini referred to them as simply *Shahi* and inscriptions refer to them as *sahi*(Wink, p 125).

[1050] Al Biruni refers to the subsequent rulers as "Brahman kings" however most other references such as Kalahan refer to them as kshatriyas (Wink, p 125).

[1051] (*Journal of the Pakistan Historical Society*, xxxvi, Dr N Ahmad, 1988, i, NWF *Regions of Pakistan, Geographical Tribes and Historical Perspective*, p 53).

[1052] Refs: *Studies in the Geography of Ancient and Medieval India*, 1971, p 291, Dr D. C. Sircar; *Hindu Sahis of Afghanistan and the Punjab*, 1972, p 5, Yogendra Mishra. Furthermore, Kalhana makes the dynasty of the ancestors of the Hindu Shahi rulers Lallya (Kallar), Kamala Toramana, Bhimadeva, Jaipala, Anandapala, Trilochanpala, Bhimapala. NOTE: Some scholars arbitrarily assume, without presenting any evidence, that the line of Shahi princes with names ending in -pala represents a change-over in royal dynasty. But this view is refuted by well-known examples of similar changes in royal names in the same family (See ref: The History and Culture of the Indian People, 1977, p 114, Dr Ramesh Chandra Majumdar, Dr Achut Dattatrya Pusalker, Dr A. K. Majumdar — India). For instance, in the Pratihara dynasty of Kanauj, king Nagabhata I was followed by kings Kakkuka, Devaraja, Vatsaraja, Nagabhata II, Ramabhadra, Mihirbhoja, Mahendrapala, Bhoja II, Mahipala, Devapala, Vijayapala, Rajyapala etc. There was no change-over of dynasty here and all kings belonged to the same Pratihara royal family though there have been frequent changes in name endings.

[1053] Cf: Rajatrangini, IV, 140-43, Kalhana; Studies in the Geography of Ancient and Medieval India, 1971, p 292, 293, Dr D. C. Sircar.

[1054]

    Adyapi dyotate sahevahvayena digantare,
    Tatsantana bhavonantah samuhah Ksatrajanamanam ||
    (Kalahana's Rajatrangini, New Delhi, 1960, VIII, 3230, M. A. Stein (Editor).

[1055] *The Hindu Sahis of Afghanistan and the Punjab, A.D. 865–1026: A phase of Islamic advance into India*, 1972, p 3, Yogendra Mishra; Cf: *Al-Hind: The Making of the Indo-Islamic World*, 2002, p 125-26, André Wink.

[1056] Dr D. C. Sircar: "It will be seen that the Kashmirian who knew the Shahis from before 730 AD down to the 12th century AD regarded them as Kshatriyas, although Alberuni refers to the

Hindu Shahis of Tibetan origin and their successors of Brahmana origin. That the early Shahis were regarded as Kshatriyas in India is also indicated by another evidence."

[1057] *The system of naming the kings of the so-called Turki Shahi dynasty and the Hindu Shahi dynasty is also similar for which reason it is very likely that the caste of the two might also have been same, i.e., Kshatriya*, Hindu Sahis of Afghanistan and the Punjab, 1972, p 5, Yogendra Mishra. Thus, if we follow Kalhana, then the ancestors of Shahi kings Lallya, Toramana, Kamalu, Bhimadeva, Jaipala, Anandapala, Trilochanapala etc may be traced back to the Kshatriya ruler of Kapisa/Kabul (AD 644–45) mentioned by Xuanzang and also probably to prince Guna Varman (AD 424), a princely scion of the Kshatriya rulers ruling at the start of the 5th century in Kapisa (*Ki-pin*) as mentioned in the Chinese Buddhist records.

[1058] The Ghaznavids or *Turushkas* by Kalhana.

[1059] Wink, pp 125–126

[1060] This was the westernmost extent of the Hindu Shahi, and last foothold in the Kabul/Gandhara region. (Wink, pp 125–126.)

[1061] Al-Idrisi, p 67, Maqbul Ahmed; *Al-Hind, the Making of the Indo-Islamic World*, 1991, p 127, Andre Wink.

[1062] Kalhana's Rajatangini, VIII, 3230; Evolution of Heroic Tradition in Ancient Punjab, 1971, p 147, Dr Buddha Prakash.

[1063] *Coins of Medieval India*, A. Cunningham, London, 1894, pp 56, 62; *The Last Two Dynasties of The Sahis*, A. Rehman, 1988, Delhi, pp 131, 48, 49, 3001

[1064] H. G. Raverty's trans., Vol.1, p.82.

[1065] *Indian Resistance to Early Muslim Invaders Up to 1206 AD*, R.G. Misra, Anu Books, repr. 1992.

[1066] *Coins of Medieval India*, A.Cunningham, London, 1894, p56, p62

[1067] *The Last Two Dynasties of The Sahis*, A. Rehman, 1988, Delhi, pp 131, 48, 49)(*Gazetteer of the Jhelum District*, Lahore, 1904, p93.

[1068] https://www.webcitation.org/query?url=http://www.geocities.com/ziadnumis3/Shahi.htm&date=2009-10-26+00:34:30

[1069] //tools.wmflabs.org/geohack/geohack.php?pagename=Kabul_Shahi&params=28_33_00_N_79_19_12_E_region:IN_type:city_source:kolossus-viwiki

[1070] Carla M. Sinopoli 2001, p. 163.

[1071] Carla M. Sinopoli 2001, p. 168.

[1072] Ajay Mitra Shastri 1998, pp. 20-21.

[1073] I. K. Sarma 1980, p. 3.

[1074] Sailendra Nath Sen 1999, pp. 172–176.

[1075] Damodar Dharmanand Kosambi 1975, p. 243.

[1076] Carla M. Sinopoli 2001, p. 166.

[1077] Carla M. Sinopoli 2001, p. 167.

[1078] Himanshu Prabha Ray 1986, p. 43.

[1079] Ajay Mitra Shastri 1999, p. 306.

[1080] G. Mannepalli 2013, p. 107-113.

[1081] P. Raghunadha Rao 1993, p. 5.

[1082] Carla M. Sinopoli 2001, p. 169.

[1083] I. K. Sarma 1980, pp. 126-130.

[1084] Akira Shimada 2012, p. 45.

[1085] B. S. L. Hanumantha Rao 1976, p. 8.

[1086] Singh 2008, pp. 381–382.

[1087] Carla M. Sinopoli 2001, p. 168-170.

[1088] Sudhakar Chattopadhyaya 1974, pp. 17-56.

[1089] Carla M. Sinopoli 2001, pp. 167-168.

[1090] Sailendra Nath Sen 1999, p. 172.

[1091] Hemchandra Raychaudhuri 2006, pp. 342, 360, 363–364.

[1092] Akira Shimada 2012, p. 43.

[1093] Carla M. Sinopoli 2001, pp. 162-163.

[1094] M. K. Dhavalikar 1996, p. 133.

[1095] Ajay Mitra Shastri 1998, p. 42.

[1096] Upinder Singh 2008, pp. 381–384.
[1097] Sudhakar Chattopadhyaya 1974, pp. 17–56.
[1098] Charles Higham 2009, p. 299.
[1099] Upinder Singh 2008, p. 382.
[1100] Sailendra Nath Sen 1999, pp. 176–177.
[1101] Sudhakar Chattopadhyaya 1974, pp. 44–50.
[1102] R.C.C. Fynes 1995, p. 43.
[1103] R.C.C. Fynes 1995, p. 44.
[1104] Inscription of Queen Mother Gautami Balashri at Cave No.3 of the Pandavleni Caves in Nashik
[1105] Mala Dutta 1990, pp. 52.
[1106] ""The different branches of the Satavahana family, which ruled in different parts of the kingdom after the decline in central authority, weres soon ousted by new powers some of which were probably feudatories at the outset."
[1107] Carla M. Sinopoli 2001, p. 170.
[1108] Carla M. Sinopoli 2001, p. 439.
[1109] Carla M. Sinopoli 2001, p. 171.
[1110] Carla M. Sinopoli 2001, p. 173.
[1111] Carla M. Sinopoli 2001, p. 177.
[1112] Carla M. Sinopoli 2001, p. 178.
[1113] Carla M. Sinopoli 2001, p. 172.
[1114] Carla M. Sinopoli 2001, p. 176.
[1115] Carla M. Sinopoli 2001, p. 175.
[1116] Carla M. Sinopoli 2001, pp. 175-176.
[1117] Sen 1999, pp. 173–174.
[1118] John Marshall, "A guide to Sanchi", p.48 https://archive.org/stream/in.ernet.dli.2015.459148
[1119] M. K. Dhavalikar 2004, p. 57: "The Satavahana sculptures unfortunately has never been recognized as an independent school in spite of the fact it has its own distinctive characteristic features. The earliest in point of time is that in the Bhaja Vihara cave which marks the beginning of sculptural art in the Satavahana dominion around 200BC. It is profusely decorated with carvings, and even pillars have a lotus capital crowned with sphinx-like mythic animals."
[1120] M. K. Dhavalikar 2004, p. 63: "...the panel occurring on the west pillar of Northern Gateway portrays a very important event in Buddha's life. It depicts votaries, two each on either side of what looks like a ladder which actually is the promenade which Buddha is supposed to have walked. It is said that Buddha, after attaining Enlightment, spent four weeks near the Bodhi tree. Of these, the third week he spent walking along the promenade (chankama) to and fro."
[1121] These sculptures are mentioned in Satavahana Art by M.K Dhavalikar. Only names have been mentioned.
[1122] M. K. Dhavalikar 2004, pp. 77, 81, 84.
[1123] Satavahana Art by M.K. Dhavalikar, p.19
[1124] Original text "L1: Rano Siri Satakarnisa L2: avesanisa Vasithiputasa L3: Anamdasa danam",
[1125] Rao 1994, p. 20.
[1126] Carla M. Sinopoli 2001, pp. 166-168.
[1127] M. K. Dhavalikar 1996, p. 134.
[1128] M. K. Dhavalikar 1996, p. 139.
[1129] https://books.google.com/books?id=LRpuAAAAMAAJ
[1130] https://books.google.com/books?id=S0puAAAAMAAJ
[1131] https://books.google.com/books?id=YweEJsuLNCUC&pg=PA43
[1132] https://books.google.com/books?id=Ppc8AAAAMAAJ
[1133] https://books.google.com/books?id=MBuPx1rdGYIC&pg=PA155
[1134] https://books.google.com/books?id=H1c1UIEVH9gC&pg=PA299
[1135] https://books.google.com/books?id=fTvQiXVFB0gC&pg=PA243
[1136] http://iasir.net/AIJRHASSpapers/AIJRHASS13-351.pdf
[1137] http://booksandjournals.brillonline.com/content/journals/10.1163/001972409x445924
[1138] //doi.org/10.1163/001972409X445924
[1139] //www.worldcat.org/issn/0019-7246
[1140] https://books.google.com/books?id=h1KObc_qaXYC

[1141] https://books.google.com/books?id=3zVGAAAAMAAJ
[1142] https://books.google.com/books?id=ilBmAAAAMAAJ
[1143] https://books.google.com/books?id=Io8aAAAAYAAJ
[1144] //www.jstor.org/stable/41702166
[1145] https://books.google.com/books?id=wENuAAAAMAAJ
[1146] http://www.tandfonline.com/doi/abs/10.1080/02666030.1995.9628494?journalCode=rsas20
[1147] https://books.google.com/books?id=Wk4_ICH_g1EC&pg=PA172
[1148] https://books.google.com/books?id=78I5lDHU2jQC&pg=PA37
[1149] https://books.google.com/books?id=H3lUIIYxWkEC&pg=PA383
[1150] http://dsal.uchicago.edu/reference/schwartzberg/fullscreen.html?object=057
[1151] R. K. Sharma 2001, p. 156.
[1152] Ashvini Agrawal 1989, p. 53.
[1153] R. K. Sharma 2001, p. 143.
[1154] R. K. Sharma 2001, p. 157.
[1155] H. V. Trivedi 1957, p. vi.
[1156] Ashvini Agrawal 1989, p. 55.
[1157] H. V. Trivedi 1957, pp. ix-xiii.
[1158] H. V. Trivedi 1957, p. i.
[1159] R. K. Sharma 2001, p. 148.
[1160] R. K. Sharma 2001, pp. 152-155.
[1161] R. K. Sharma 2001, p. 154.
[1162] H. V. Trivedi 1957, pp. xxxiii-xxxvi.
[1163] Ashvini Agrawal 1989, p. 54.
[1164] Dilip Kumar Ganguly 1984, p. 28.
[1165] Ashvini Agrawal 1989, pp. 53-55.
[1166] R. K. Sharma 2001, p. 149.
[1167] R. K. Sharma 2001, p. 150.
[1168] R. K. Sharma 2001, p. 152.
[1169] R. K. Sharma 2001, p. 151.
[1170] H. V. Trivedi 1957, p. ii.
[1171] H. V. Trivedi 1957, p. iv.
[1172] H. V. Trivedi 1957, pp. v, ix.
[1173] H. V. Trivedi 1957, p. vii.
[1174] H. V. Trivedi 1957, p. ix.
[1175] https://books.google.com/books?id=hRjC5IaJ2zcC&pg=PA315
[1176] https://books.google.com/books?id=7v76i0eF9tQC&pg=PA28
[1177] https://archive.org/details/in.ernet.dli.2015.104095
[1178] https://books.google.com/books?id=jUwFL3IipK0C&pg=PA143
[1179] https://books.google.com/books?id=fWVZWjNAcAgC&pg=PA54
[1180] N. Jayapalan, *History of India*, Vol. I, (Atlantic Publishers, 2001), 130.
[1181] An idea contested by D. N. Jha.<ref>
[1182] Raghu Vamsa v 4.60–75
[1183] Gupta dynasty (Indian dynasty) http://www.britannica.com/EBchecked/topic/249590/Gupta-dynasty . Britannica Online Encyclopedia. Retrieved on 2011-11-21.
[1184] Mahajan, p. 540; Keay, 132, 145-154
[1185] Gupta dynasty: empire in 4th century http://www.britannica.com/EBchecked/topic-art/285248/1960/The-Gupta-empire-at-the-end-of-the-4th-century . Britannica Online Encyclopedia. Retrieved on 2011-11-21.
[1186] Harle, 87
[1187] Trade | The Story of India – Photo Gallery https://www.pbs.org/thestoryofindia/gallery/photos/8.html . PBS. Retrieved on 2011-11-21.
[1188] Agarwal, Ashvini (1989). *Rise and Fall of the Imperial Guptas*, Delhi:Motilal Banarsidass, , pp. 264–9
[1189] //en.wikipedia.org/w/index.php?title=Template:Gupta_Empire&action=edit
[1190] List of Altekar's publications http://openlibrary.org/a/OL9771A/Anant-Sadashiv-Altekar in the Open Library.

[1191] Agarwal, Ashvini (1989). *Rise and Fall of the Imperial Guptas*, Delhi:Motilal Banarsidass, , pp. 82-4
[1192] Human rights in the Hindu-Buddhist tradition By Lal Deosa Rai, Page no.155 https://books.google.com/books?id=ahrXAAAAMAAJ&q=gupta+dynasty+abhira+origin&dq=gupta+dynasty+abhira+origin&lr=&ei=S7FxS6foNpX6lQTmi5X5DA&cd=46
[1193] Agarwal, Ashvini (1989). *Rise and Fall of the Imperial Guptas*, Delhi:Motilal Banarsidass, , pp. 84–7
[1194] Majumdar, p. 474
[1195] The Gupta Polity, pp.199
[1196] Mahajan, p. 487
[1197] Raychaudhuri, p. 489
[1198] ata shrivikramadityo helya nirjitakhilah Mlechchana Kamboja. Yavanan neechan Hunan Sabar-bran Tushara. Parsikaanshcha tayakatacharan vishrankhalan hatya bhrubhangamatreyanah bhuvo bharamavarayate (Brahata Katha, 10/1/285-86, Kshmendra).
[1199] Kathasritsagara 18.1.76–78
[1200] Cf:"In the story contained in Kathasarit-sagara, king Vikarmaditya is said to have destroyed all the barbarous tribes such as the Kambojas, Yavanas, Hunas, Tokharas and the, National Council of Teachers of English Committee on Recreational Reading – Sanskrit language.
[1201] "Evidence of the conquest of Saurastra during the reign of Chandragupta II is to be seen in his rare silver coins which are more directly imitated from those of the Western Satraps... they retain some traces of the old inscriptions in Greek characters, while on the reverse, they substitute the Gupta type (a peacock) for the chaitya with crescent and star." in Rapson "A catalogue of Indian coins in the British Museum. The Andhras etc...", p.cli
[1202] Agarwal, Ashvini (1989). *Rise and Fall of the Imperial Guptas*, Delhi:Motilal Banarsidass, , pp. 191–200
[1203] History of Civilizations of Central Asia, Ahmad Hasan Dani, B. A. Litvinsky, Unesco p.119 sq https://books.google.com/books?id=883OZBe2sMYC&pg=PA119
[1204] Raychaudhuri, p. 510
[1205] The Huns, Hyun Jin Kim, Routledge, 2015 p.50 sq https://books.google.com/books?id=mcf4CgAAQBAJ&pg=PT50
[1206] Raychaudhuri, p. 516
[1207] Sachchidananda Bhattacharya, *Gupta dynasty, A dictionary of Indian history*, (George Braziller, Inc., 1967), 393.
[1208] Ancient Indian History and Civilization by Sailendra Nath Sen p.220
[1209] Encyclopaedia of Indian Events & Dates by S. B. Bhattacherje p.A15
[1210] *Columbia Encyclopedia*
[1211] The First Spring: The Golden Age of India by Abraham Eraly p.48 sq https://books.google.com/books?id=te1sqTzTxD8C&pg=PA48
[1212] Ancient Indian History and Civilization by Sailendra Nath Sen p.221 https://books.google.com/books?id=Wk4_ICH_g1EC&pg=PA221
[1213] A Comprehensive History Of Ancient India p.174 https://books.google.com/books?id=gE7udqBkACwC&pg=PA174
[1214] Longman History & Civics ICSE 9 by Singh p.81 https://books.google.com/books?id=EXPouL4BYTMC&pg=PA81
[1215] Corpus Inscriptionum Indicarum Vol.3 (inscriptions Of The Early Gupta Kings) p.362 https://archive.org/details/in.ernet.dli.2015.108395
[1216] Indian Esoteric Buddhism: Social History of the Tantric Movement by Ronald M. Davidson p. 31 https://books.google.com/books?id=n_VquVQvnBwC&pg=PA31
[1217] A History of Ancient and Early Medieval India by Upinder Singh p.521 https://books.google.com/books?id=H3lUIIYxWkEC&pg=PA521
[1218] The Gupta Empire by Radhakumud Mookerji p.133 sq https://books.google.com/books?id=uYXDB2gIYbwC&pg=PA133
[1219] Mahajan, pp. 530–1
[1220] Thomas Khoshy, Elementary Number Theory with Applications, Academic Press, 2002, p. 567.
[1221] Harle, 87-89
[1222] Harle, respectively 118-122, 123-126, 129-135

[1223] Harle, 92-97
[1224] Harle, 113-114
[1225] https://books.google.com/books?id=pGwjFsqwF0YC&printsec=frontcover
[1226] https://archive.org/stream/personalgeograph00sharuoft#page/n5/mode/2up
[1227] http://coinindia.com/galleries-gupta.html
[1228] http://www.frontline.in/navigation/?type=static&page=flonnet&rdurl=fl2920/stories/20121019292006100.htm
[1229] I Indian Costume By Govind Sadashiv Ghurye, Popular Prakashan Publications, Page 43 https://books.google.co.in/books?id=irh9dvlLz3MC&dq
[1230] I Dynastic History of Magadha, Cir. 450-1200 A.D. By Bindeshwari Prasad Sinha, Page 28 https://books.google.co.in/books?id=V3KDaZY85wYC&dq
[1231] I Rabindranath Tagore: The Poet of India By A. K. Basu Majumdar, Indus Publishing, Page 50(Vakatakas and Chalukyas-both of [[Brahmin https://books.google.co.in/books?id=s5Up306hrBIC&dq] origin)]
[1232] Ancient India, A History Textbook for Class XI, Ram Sharan Sharma, National Council of Educational Research and Training, India, pp 211
[1233] Mahajan V.D. (1960, reprint 2007) *Ancient India*, New Delhi: S.Chand, , pp.587-8
[1234] Mahajan V.D. (1960, reprint 2007) *Ancient India*, New Delhi: S. Chand, , p.588
[1235] Mahajan V.D. (1960, reprint 2007) *Ancient India*, New Delhi: S. Chand, , p.589
[1236] Mahajan V.D. (1960, reprint 2007) *Ancient India*, New Delhi: S. Chand, , pp.590-91
[1237] Nashik district e-gazetteer - History, ancient period http://www.maharashtra.gov.in/english/gazetteer/nasik/005%20History/001%20AncientPeriod.htm
[1238] Spink, Walter, M. (2009). *Ajanta: Defining Features*, in *Indica*, Vol.46, No.1, Mumbai: Heras Institute of Indian History and Culture, pp.3-38
[1239] The Buddhist Caves at Aurangabad: Transformations in Art and Religion, Pia Brancaccio, BRILL, 2010 p.82 https://books.google.com/books?id=m_4pXm7dD78C&pg=PA82
[1240] Vakataka - Gupta Age Circa 200-550 A.D.by Ramesh Chandra Majumdar p.301 https://books.google.com/books?id=OswUZtL1_CUC&pg=PA301
[1241] https://books.google.co.in/books?id=OswUZtL1_CUC
[1242] https://web.archive.org/web/20060603010304/http://www.maharashtra.gov.in/english/gazetteer/FINAL_GAZETTEE/his1.html
[1243] http://www.tspscportal.in/telangana-history-vakataka-dynasty/102/
[1244] CNG Coins https://www.cngcoins.com/Coin.aspx?CoinID=261204
[1245] India: History, Religion, Vision and Contribution to the World, by Alexander P. Varghese p.26
[1246] International Dictionary of Historic Places: Asia and Oceania by Trudy Ring, Robert M. Salkin, Sharon La Boda p.507
[1247] Ancient India by Ramesh Chandra Majumdar p.274
[1248] Harsha Charitra by Banabhatt https://books.google.com/boo.../about/The_Harshacharita.html...
[1249] *Legislative Elite in India: A Study in Political Socialization* by Prabhu Datta Sharma, Publ. Legislators 1984, p32
[1250] *Revival of Buddhism in Modern India* by Deodas Liluji Ramteke, Publ Deep & Deep, 1983, p19
[1251] *Some Aspects of Ancient Indian History and Culture* by Upendra Thakur, Publ. Abhinav Publications, 1974,
[1252] https://books.google.com/books/about/Indian_History.html?id=X4j7Nf_MU24C
[1253] http://www.uio.no/studier/emner/hf/iakh/HIS2172/h07/
[1254] http://www.srikanta-sastri.org/conquests-siladitya-in-south/4584992949
[1255] AnSI cites I. Karve's *Hindu Society – An Interpretation," page 64. UNIQ-ref-0-8c889858087207e6-QINU*
[1256] Everyday life in South Asia By Diane P. Mines, Sarah Lamb, Published by Indiana University Press, 2002, pp.206
[1257] //en.wikipedia.org/w/index.php?title=Gurjar&action=edit
[1258] http://www.peoplegroupsindia.com/profiles/gujjar/
[1259] https://books.google.com/books?id=XvNQU4VFrbgC
[1260] https://books.google.com/books?id=upk5AgAAQBAJ
[1261] https://books.google.com/books?id=JFPnh9B5zncC&pg=PA257

[1262] http://www.ndtv.com/news/videos/video_player.php?id=150460
[1263] //en.wikipedia.org/w/index.php?title=Template:History_of_Andhra_Pradesh&action=edit
[1264] http://www.whatisindia.com/inscriptions/
[1265] https://www.google.com/maps/d/embed?mid=1f4m674MGwDo7pQ1IhTgA-CxAi7w&ll=15.884755024376066%2C81.27649050000002&z=7
[1266] //en.wikipedia.org/w/index.php?title=Template:History_of_Gujarat&action=edit
[1267] Virji 1955, p. 17–18.
[1268] Mahajan V.D. (1960, reprint 2007). *Ancient India*, S.Chand & Company, New Delhi, , pp. 594-6
[1269] Journal of the Asiatic Society of Bombay, p 245, Bhau Daji (by Asiatic Society of Bombay, Royal Asiatic Society of Great Britain and Ireland, Bombay Branch).
[1270] Gazetteer of the Bombay Presidency, 1904, p 142, 476, by Bombay (India : State); A Concise History of the Indian People, 1950, p 106, H. G. (Hugh George) Rawlinson.
[1271] Advanced History of India, 1971, p 198, G. Srinivasachari; History of India, 1952, p 140.
[1272] Views of Dr Fleet, Dr V. A. Smith, H. A. Rose, Peter N. Stearns and other scholars
[1273] See: The Oxford History of India: From the Earliest Times to the End of 1911, p 164, Dr Vincent Arthur Smith
[1274] History of India, 1907, 284 A. V. Williams Jackson, Romesh Chunder Dutt, Vincent Arthur Smith, Stanley Lane-Poole, H. M. (Henry Miers) Elliot, William Wilson Hunter, Alfred Comyn Lyall.
[1275] Also: Journal of the United Service Institution of India, United Service Institution of India, p331.
[1276] Virji 1955, p. 19.
[1277] History and Culture of Indian People, Classical age, p 150, (Ed) Dr A. D. Pusalkar, Dr R. C. Majumdar.
[1278] Virji 1955, p. 21–25.
[1279] Virji 1955, p. 26–27.
[1280] Roychaudhuri, H.C. (1972). *Political History of Ancient India*, University of Calcutta, Calcutta, pp.553-4
[1281] Virji 1955, p. 28–30.
[1282]
[1283] Virji 1955, p. 31–33.
[1284] Virji 1955, p. 33–34.
[1285] Kailash Chand Jain 1991, p. 75.
[1286] Virji 1955, p. 34.
[1287] Virji 1955, p. 35–37.
[1288] Virji 1955, p. 38.
[1289] Virji 1955, p. 38–42.
[1290] Corpus Inscriptionum Indicarum Vol 3 p.164ff https://archive.org/stream/in.ernet.dli.2015.358795
[1291] Virji 1955, p. 42–45.
[1292] Virji 1955, p. 46–47.
[1293] Virji 1955, p. 47.
[1294] Virji 1955, p. 58–59.
[1295] Virji 1955, p. 59–61.
[1296] Virji 1955, p. 63–64.
[1297] Virji 1955, p. 65–69.
[1298] Virji 1955, p. 71–75.
[1299] Virji 1955, p. 71–80.
[1300] Virji 1955, p. 80.
[1301] Virji 1955, p. 81–82.
[1302] Virji 1955, p. 83–84.
[1303] Virji 1955, p. 85–88.
[1304] Virji 1955, p. 88.
[1305] Virji 1955, p. 90–93.
[1306] Virji 1955, p. 94.

[1307] Virji 1955, p. 94–96.
[1308] Virji 1955, p. 97–100.
[1309] Virji 1955, p. 101–102.
[1310] Virji 1955, p. 102–105.
[1311] Virji 1955, p. 105.
[1312] Virji 1955, p. 165–186.
[1313] Virji 1955, p. 230–247.
[1314] Virji 1955, p. 225–229.
[1315] https://archive.org/details/in.ernet.dli.2015.57287
[1316] https://books.google.com/books?id=8-TxcO9dfrcC
[1317] //en.wikipedia.org/w/index.php?title=Template:Part_of_History_of_India&action=edit
[1318] Avari 2007, pp. 204–205: Madhyadesha became the ambition of two particular clans among a tribal people in Rajasthan, known as Gurjara and Pratihara. They were both part of a larger federation of tribes, some of which later came to be known as the Rajputs
[1319] Avari 2007, p. 303.
[1320] Sircar 1971, p. 146.
[1321] Partha Mitter, Indian art, Oxford University Press, 2001 pp.66
[1322] Sanjay Sharma 2006, p. 188.
[1323] Sanjay Sharma 2006, p. 190.
[1324] Tripathi 1959, p. 223.
[1325] Puri 1957, p. 7.
[1326] Puri 1957, p. 9-13.
[1327] Sanjay Sharma 2006, p. 189.
[1328] Majumdar 1981, pp. 612-613.
[1329] Puri 1957, p. 1-18.
[1330] Tripathi 1959, p. 222.
[1331] Ganguly 1935, p. 167.
[1332] Ganguly 1935, pp. 167-168.
[1333] Ganguly 1935, p. 168.
[1334] Puri 1986, pp. 9-10.
[1335] Mishra 1954, pp. 50-51.
[1336] Shanta Rani Sharma 2012, p. 8.
[1337] Shanta Rani Sharma 2012, p. 7.
[1338] Puri 1957, p. 1-2.
[1339] Puri 1957, p. 2.
[1340] Puri 1957, pp. 4-6.
[1341] Yadava 1982, p. 35.
[1342] Singh 1964, pp. 17-18.
[1343] {{cite web | url=https://m.hindustantimes.com/india-news/asi-to-resume-restoration-of-bateshwar-temple-complex-in-chambal/story-kBaxGfcRWVsrNbw3Vw8dLN.html
[1344] https://books.google.com/books?id=DmB_AgAAQBAJ&pg=PT204
[1345] https://books.google.com/books?id=AqKw1Mn8WcwC
[1346] https://books.google.com/books?id=ahFuAAAAMAAJ
[1347] //www.jstor.org/stable/41784918
[1348] https://books.google.com/books?id=szkhAAAAMAAJ
[1349] //doi.org/10.1177/025764300602200202
[1350] //doi.org/10.1177/0376983612449525
[1351] https://books.google.com/books?id=TKs9AAAAIAAJ
[1352] https://books.google.com/books?id=U8GPENMw_psC&pg=PA231
[1353] https://books.google.com/books?id=aY_I3zgxfpsC&pg=PA32
[1354] Alf Hiltebeitel 1999, pp. 439-440.
[1355] Bhrigupati Singh 2015, p. 38.
[1356] Pradeep Barua 2005, p. 24.
[1357] Alf Hiltebeitel 1999, pp. 440-441.
[1358] Alf Hiltebeitel 1999, pp. 441-442.
[1359] Catherine B. Asher & Cynthia Talbot 2006, p. 99.

[1360] Cynthia Talbot 2015, p. 119.
[1361] Brajadulal Chattopadhyaya 1994, pp. 79-80.
[1362] Satish Chandra 1982, p. 92.
[1363] Tanuja Kothiyal 2016, p. 8.
[1364] Richard Gabriel Fox 1971, p. 16.
[1365] Brajadulal Chattopadhyaya 1994, p. 60.
[1366] Brajadulal Chattopadhyaya 1994, p. 59.
[1367] Cynthia Talbot 2015, p. 120.
[1368] Tanuja Kothiyal 2016, pp. 8-9.
[1369] Cynthia Talbot 2015, p. 121.
[1370] Irfan Habib 2002, p. 90.
[1371] David Ludden 1999, p. 4.
[1372] Barbara N. Ramusack 2004, p. 13.
[1373] André Wink 1990, p. 282.
[1374] Cynthia Talbot 2015, pp. 121-122.
[1375] Cynthia Talbot 2015, pp. 121-125.
[1376] Tanuja Kothiyal 2016, p. 11.
[1377] Pradeep Barua 2005, p. 25.
[1378] Peter Jackson 2003, p. 9.
[1379] Cynthia Talbot 2015, p. 33.
[1380] Cynthia Talbot 2015, pp. 33-35.
[1381] Pradeep Barua 2005, pp. 33-34.
[1382] Dirk H. A. Kolff 2002, p. 132.
[1383] Barbara N. Ramusack 2004, pp. 18-19.
[1384] Sir Jadunath Sarkar (1994). A History of Jaipur 1503–1938. Orient Longman.
[1385] Tanuja Kothiyal 2016, pp. 9-10.
[1386] Ayan Shome 2014, p. 196.
[1387] Catherine B. Asher & Cynthia Talbot 2006, p. 99 (Para 3): "...Rajput did not originally indicate a hereditary status but rather an occupational one: that is, it was used in reference to men from diverse ethnic and geographical backgrounds, who fought on horseback. In Rajasthan and its vicinity, the word Rajput came to have a more restricted and aristocratic meaning, as exclusive networks of warriors related by patrilineal descent and intermarriage became dominant in the fifteenth century. The Rajputs of Rajasthan eventually refused to acknowledge the Rajput identity of the warriors who lived farther to the east and retained the fluid and inclusive nature of their communities far longer than did the warriors of Rajasthan."
[1388] Cynthia Talbot 2015, p. 120 (Para 4): "Kolff's provocative thesis certainly applies to more peripheral groups like the Bundelas of Cenral India, whose claims to be Rajput were ignored by the Rajput clans of Mughal-era Rajasthan, and to other such lower-status martial communities."
[1389] Shail Mayaram 2013, p. 269.
[1390] Lindsey Harlan 1992, p. 31.
[1391] Lindsey Harlan 1992, p. 88.
[1392] Lindsey Harlan 1992, p. 27.
[1393] Rajput procession, Encyclopædia Britannica http://www.britannica.com/media/full/147427
[1394] Karine Schomer 1994, p. 338.
[1395] https://books.google.com/books?id=MMFdosx0PokC&pg=PR1
[1396] https://books.google.com/books?id=bCVyhH5VDjAC&pg=PA279
[1397] https://books.google.com/books?id=6Q2qCQAAQBAJ&pg=PA196
[1398] https://books.google.com/books?id=Kz1-mtazYqEC&pg=PA13
[1399] https://books.google.ca/books?id=AmVuAAAAMAAJ
[1400] https://books.google.com/books?id=FhnRBgAAQBAJ&pg=PA38
[1401] https://books.google.com/books?id=ZvaGuaJIJgoC&pg=PA99
[1402] https://books.google.com/books?id=m3DjCgAAQBAJ
[1403] https://books.google.com/books?id=eHi62S7vZlsC&pg=PA4
[1404] https://books.google.com/books?id=SrdiVPsFRYIC
[1405] https://books.google.com/books?id=jUcu6uD5bU4C&pg=PA90
[1406] https://books.google.com/books?id=eFJuAAAAMAAJ

[1407] https://books.google.com/books?id=7HLrPYOe38gC&pg=PA88
[1408] https://books.google.com/books?id=FIIQhuAOGaIC&pg=PA33
[1409] https://books.google.com/books?id=lt2tqOpVRKgC&pg=PA221
[1410] https://books.google.com/books?id=FHEcBTmxlOEC&pg=PA16
[1411] https://books.google.com/books?id=vRM1AAAAIAAJ
[1412] https://books.google.com/books?id=TyUtKfcjzG4C&pg=PA269
[1413] https://books.google.com/books?id=be-7CwAAQBAJ&pg=PA8
[1414] Dharam Prakash Gupta, "Seminar on Katoch dynasty trail". *Himachal Plus*. On line. http://www.tribuneindia.com/2009/20091104/himplus.htm#8, Chandigarh Tribune, 3 November 2009
[1415] Royalty and its associated titles were legally abolished after India became a republic.<ref>**1.** , "Through a constitutional amendment passed in 1971, Indira Gandhi stripped the princes of the titles, privy purses and regal privileges which her father's government had granted." **2.** Quote: "The princes of India – their number and variety reflecting to a large extent the chaos that had come to the country with the break up of the Mughal empire – had lost real power in the British time. Through generations of idle servitude they had grown to specialize only in style. A bogus, extinguishable glamour: in 1947, with Independence, they had lost their state, and Mrs. Gandhi in 1971 had, without much public outcry, abolished their privy purses and titles.".
[1416] Chandra, Satish (1997). Medieval India: From Sultanate to the Mughals. New Delhi, India: Har-Anand Publications. pp. 101–102.
[1417] Singh 1964, p. 10.
[1418] Singh 1964, pp. 10-11.
[1419] Singh 1964, p. 89.
[1420] Singh 1964, p. 11.
[1421] Singh 1964, p. 12.
[1422] Singh 1964, p. 13.
[1423] Singh 1964, pp. 13-14.
[1424] Seth 1978, p. 10-13.
[1425] Seth 1978, p. 5.
[1426] Singh 1964, pp. 14-15.
[1427] Majumdar 1956, p. 9.
[1428] Singh 1964, pp. 17-18.
[1429] Singh 1964, p. 15.
[1430] Singh 1964, p. 16.
[1431] Seth 1978, p. 6.
[1432] Gupta & Bakshi 2008, p. 95.
[1433] Gupta & Bakshi 2008, p. 100.
[1434] Sharma, Dasharatha : " Early Chauhan Dynasties https://books.google.com/books/about/Early_Chauh%C4%81n_Dynasties.html?id=A86fAAAACAAJ&hl=en" (1959) by S.Chand & Co. Page 14.
[1435] Singh 1964, p. 105.
[1436] Singh 1964, p. 114.
[1437] Singh 1964, p. 115.
[1438] https://books.google.com/books?id=gHNoU2zcDnIC
[1439] https://books.google.ca/books?id=ffAdAAAAMAAJ
[1440] https://books.google.ca/books?id=-Q4dAAAAMAAJ
[1441] https://books.google.com/books?id=TKs9AAAAIAAJ
[1442] R. B. Singh 1964, p. 11.
[1443] R. B. Singh 1964, p. 89.
[1444] R. B. Singh 1964, pp. 10-12.
[1445] Cynthia Talbot 2015, pp. 33-35.
[1446] R. B. Singh 1964, p. 25-26.
[1447] Hiltebeitel 1999, p. 447.
[1448] Har Bilas Sarda 1935, pp. 220-221.
[1449] Har Bilas Sarda 1935, p. 217.
[1450] Har Bilas Sarda 1935, p. 214.

[1451] Cynthia Talbot 2015, p. 33.
[1452] Har Bilas Sarda 1935, p. 223.
[1453] Har Bilas Sarda 1935, p. 224.
[1454] Har Bilas Sarda 1935, p. 225.
[1455] Dasharatha Sharma 1959, p. 23.
[1456] R. B. Singh 1964, p. 100.
[1457] R. B. Singh 1964, p. 103.
[1458] Dasharatha Sharma 1959, pp. 34-35.
[1459] R. B. Singh 1964, pp. 131-132.
[1460] Dasharatha Sharma 1959, p. 40.
[1461] R. B. Singh 1964, p. 140-141.
[1462] R. B. Singh 1964, p. 150.
[1463] Dasharatha Sharma 1959, p. 62.
[1464] R. B. Singh 1964, p. 156.
[1465] Cynthia Talbot 2015, pp. 39.
[1466] Iqtidar Alam Khan 2008, p. xvii.
[1467] R. B. Singh 1964, p. 221.
[1468] Dasharatha Sharma 1959, p. 87.
[1469] Dasharatha Sharma 1959, p. 26.
[1470] R. B. Singh 1964, p. 104.
[1471] R. B. Singh 1964, p. 124.
[1472] R. B. Singh 1964, p. 128.
[1473] Dasharatha Sharma 1959, pp. 69-70.
[1474] R. B. Singh 1964, p. 159.
[1475] Cynthia Talbot 2015, pp. 37-38.
[1476] Dasharatha Sharma 1959, p. 38.
[1477] Dasharatha Sharma 1959, p. 41.
[1478] R. B. Singh 1964, pp. 51-70.
[1479] https://books.google.com/books?id=MMFdosx0PokC&pg=PR1
[1480] https://books.google.com/books?id=X7VHAAAAMAAJ
[1481] //www.worldcat.org/oclc/20754525
[1482] https://books.google.com/books?id=m3DjCgAAQBAJ
[1483] https://books.google.com/books?id=n4gcAAAAMAAJ
[1484] https://archive.org/stream/speechesandwriti030754mbp#page/n272/mode/1up
[1485] https://books.google.com/books?id=iGSKTttoa3IC&pg=PR17
[1486] https://books.google.com/books?id=TKs9AAAAIAAJ
[1487] //www.worldcat.org/oclc/11038728
[1488] William Pinch records that, "... a popular concern with status predated the rise of an imperial census apparatus and the colonial obsession with caste. ... [C]laims to personal and community dignity appeared to be part of a longer discourse that did not require European political and administrative structures."<ref>
[1489] Harihar Vitthal Trivedi 1991, p. 4.
[1490] Kailash Chand Jain 1972, p. 327.
[1491] Pratipal Bhatia 1970, p. 18.
[1492] Ganga Prasad Yadava 1982, p. 36.
[1493] Krishna Narain Seth 1978, p. 87.
[1494] Ganga Prasad Yadava 1982, p. 32.
[1495] Alf Hiltebeitel 2009, p. 444.
[1496] Krishna Narain Seth 1978, pp. 10-13.
[1497] Cynthia Talbot 2015, pp. 33-35.
[1498] R. B. Singh 1964, pp. 17-18.
[1499] Ganga Prasad Yadava 1982, p. 35.
[1500] Krishna Narain Seth 1978, p. 16.
[1501] Ganga Prasad Yadava 1982, p. 37.
[1502] Krishna Narain Seth 1978, p. 29.
[1503] Krishna Narain Seth 1978, p. 30.

[1504] Harihar Vitthal Trivedi 1991, p. 9.
[1505] Krishna Narain Seth 1978, pp. 44-47.
[1506] Mahesh Singh 1984, pp. 3-4.
[1507] Krishna Narain Seth 1978, pp. 48-49.
[1508] Harihar Vitthal Trivedi 1991, p. 212.
[1509] Krishna Narain Seth 1978, pp. 48-51.
[1510] Krishna Narain Seth 1978, pp. 76-77.
[1511] Krishna Narain Seth 1978, p. 79.
[1512] Kailash Chand Jain 1972, p. 334.
[1513] Krishna Narain Seth 1978, pp. 81-84.
[1514] Kailash Chand Jain 1972, p. 336-338.
[1515] Krishna Narain Seth 1978, pp. 102-104.
[1516] M. Srinivasachariar 1974, p. 502.
[1517] Kailash Chand Jain 1972, pp. 339-340.
[1518] Kailash Chand Jain 1972, pp. 340-341.
[1519] Krishna Narain Seth 1978, p. 105.
[1520] Sailendra Nath Sen 1999, p. 320.
[1521] Kailash Chand Jain 1972, p. 341.
[1522] Krishna Narain Seth 1978, p. 137.
[1523] Krishna Narain Seth 1978, pp. 140-141.
[1524] Mahesh Singh 1984, p. 46.
[1525] Saikat K. Bose 2015, p. 27.
[1526] Krishna Narain Seth 1978, p. 154.
[1527] Mahesh Singh 1984, p. 56.
[1528] Mahesh Singh 1984, p. 69.
[1529] Mahesh Singh 1984, pp. 172-173.
[1530] Mahesh Singh 1984, pp. 173.
[1531] Krishna Narain Seth 1978, p. 177.
[1532] Krishna Narain Seth 1978, pp. 163-165.
[1533] Mahesh Singh 1984, pp. 61-62.
[1534] Krishna Narain Seth 1978, p. 158.
[1535] Krishna Narain Seth 1978, p. 166.
[1536] Krishna Narain Seth 1978, p. 182.
[1537] Mahesh Singh 1984, pp. 66-67.
[1538] Kirit Mankodi 1987, p. 62.
[1539] Sheldon Pollock 2003, p. 179.
[1540] Kirit Mankodi 1987, p. 71.
[1541] Sheldon Pollock 2003, pp. 179-180.
[1542] Anthony Kennedy Warder 1992, pp. 176.
[1543] Anthony Kennedy Warder 1992, pp. 177.
[1544] Krishna Narain Seth 1978, pp. 182-184.
[1545] Prabhakar Narayan Kawthekar 1995, p. 72.
[1546] Harihar Vitthal Trivedi 1991, p. 110.
[1547] Pratipal Bhatia 1970, p. 115-122.
[1548] Kailash Chand Jain 1972, pp. 362-363.
[1549] Kailash Chand Jain 1972, pp. 363-364.
[1550] R. C. Majumdar 1977, p. 328.
[1551] Harihar Vitthal Trivedi 1991, p. 162.
[1552] Pratipal Bhatia 1970, p. 137.
[1553] Sailendra Nath Sen 1999, p. 322.
[1554] Kailash Chand Jain 1972, p. 370.
[1555] Asoke Kumar Majumdar 1956, p. 148.
[1556] Kailash Chand Jain 1972, p. 371.
[1557] Harihar Vitthal Trivedi 1991, pp. 188.
[1558] Sircar 1966, pp. 187-188.
[1559] Kailash Chand Jain 1972, p. 372.

[1560] Kailash Chand Jain 1972, p. 373.
[1561] Harihar Vitthal Trivedi 1991, p. 203.
[1562] Asoke Kumar Majumdar 1977, p. 445.
[1563] Pratipal Bhatia 1970, p. 158.
[1564] Dasharatha Sharma 1975, p. 124.
[1565] Pratipal Bhatia 1970, p. 160.
[1566] Sailendra Nath Sen 1999, p. 25.
[1567] Georg Bühler 1892, p. 222.
[1568] Kailash Chand Jain 1972, p. 327-375.
[1569] Peter Jackson 2003, p. 199.
[1570] Harihar Vitthal Trivedi 1991, p. 321.
[1571] Harihar Vitthal Trivedi 1991, p. 244.
[1572] Harihar Vitthal Trivedi 1991, p. 280.
[1573] Harihar Vitthal Trivedi 1991, p. 333.
[1574] Poonam Minhas 1998, p. 49.
[1575] Tony McClenaghan 1996, p. 115.
[1576] John Middleton 2015, p. 236.
[1577] Tony McClenaghan 1996, p. 122.
[1578] David P. Henige 2004, p. 66.
[1579] Virbhadra Singhji 1994, p. 44.
[1580] https://books.google.com/books?id=MMFdosx0PokC&pg=PA444
[1581] https://books.google.ca/books?id=ffAdAAAAMAAJ
[1582] //www.worldcat.org/oclc/4413150
[1583] https://books.google.com/books?id=F3VDAAAAYAAJ
[1584] //www.worldcat.org/oclc/5311157
[1585] https://books.google.com/books?id=Fl0l5ZTkNxIC&pg=PA176
[1586] https://books.google.com/books?id=m3DjCgAAQBAJ
[1587] https://books.google.com/books?id=n4gcAAAAMAAJ
[1588] https://books.google.com/books?id=fqDpAAAAMAAJ
[1589] https://books.google.com/books?id=aY_I3zgxfpsC&pg=PA32
[1590] https://archive.org/stream/EpigraphiaIndicaVol1/Epigraphia%20Indica_vol%201#page/n255/mode/2up
[1591] https://books.google.com/books?id=0ybQrQEACAAJ
[1592] https://books.google.com/books?id=R63ACQAAQBAJ&pg=PA236
[1593] https://books.google.com/books?id=_3O7q7cU7k0C&pg=PA158
[1594] http://vmis.in/Resources/digital_publication_popup?id=140#page/2
[1595] https://books.google.com/books?id=-Q4dAAAAMAAJ
[1596] //www.worldcat.org/oclc/8931757
[1597] https://books.google.ca/books?id=4dVRvVyHaiQC&pg=PA502
[1598] https://books.google.com/books?id=uPsgAAAAMAAJ
[1599] //www.worldcat.org/oclc/11786897
[1600] https://books.google.com/books?id=_52-WyPfLG0C&pg=PA49
[1601] https://books.google.com/books?id=Bq5rT0yXGC0C&pg=PA72
[1602] https://books.google.com/books?id=lt2tqOpVRKgC&pg=PA198
[1603] https://books.google.com/books?id=a5gcAAAAMAAJ
[1604] //www.worldcat.org/oclc/199886
[1605] https://books.google.com/books?id=TKs9AAAAIAAJ
[1606] //www.worldcat.org/oclc/11038728
[1607] https://books.google.com/books?id=XNxiN5tzKOgC&pg=PA327
[1608] https://books.google.co.in/books?id=ywfsCgAAQBAJ&pg=PT281
[1609] https://books.google.com/books?id=Wk4_ICH_g1EC&pg=PA172
[1610] https://books.google.com/books?id=0UCh7r2TjQIC&pg=PA179
[1611] https://books.google.com/books?id=YQdZlHJ2WTAC&pg=PA115
[1612] https://books.google.com/books?id=NYK7ZSpPzkUC&pg=PA44
[1613] //en.wikipedia.org/w/index.php?title=Template:History_of_Gujarat&action=edit
[1614] Asoke Kumar Majumdar 1956, p. 5.

[1615] Asoke Kumar Majumdar 1956, p. 421.
[1616] Jai Narayan Asopa 1976, p. 43.
[1617] Jai Narayan Asopa 1976, p. 42.
[1618] Asoke Kumar Majumdar 1956, pp. 6-7.
[1619] Asoke Kumar Majumdar 1956, p. 22.
[1620] Post-Gupta (Chaulukya-Paramara) coin https://www.cngcoins.com/Coin.aspx?CoinID=261205, Classical Numismatic Group.
[1621] Coin of Chaulukyas of Anahillapataka - Kumarapala https://www.cngcoins.com/Coin.aspx?CoinID=55245, Classical Numismatic Group
[1622] Asoke Kumar Majumdar 1956, p. 13-17.
[1623] Cynthia Talbot 2015, pp. 33-35.
[1624] Ganga Prasad Yadava 1982, p. 35.
[1625] N. Jayapalan 2001, p. 146.
[1626] Shanta Rani Sharma 2012, pp. 7-8.
[1627] Asoke Kumar Majumdar 1956, p. 8.
[1628] Durga Prasad Dikshit 1980, p. 21.
[1629] Asoke Kumar Majumdar 1956, p. 8-9.
[1630] Dasharatha Sharma 1959, p. 4.
[1631] Asoke Kumar Majumdar 1956, p. 9.
[1632] R. B. Singh 1964, pp. 17-18.
[1633] Asoke Kumar Majumdar 1956, p. 12.
[1634] Asoke Kumar Majumdar 1956, p. 13.
[1635] Asoke Kumar Majumdar 1956, pp. 10-12.
[1636] John E. Cort 1998, p. 87.
[1637] Asoke Kumar Majumdar 1956, pp. 23-24.
[1638] Asoke Kumar Majumdar 1956, p. 25.
[1639] Asoke Kumar Majumdar 1956, p. 34.
[1640] Asoke Kumar Majumdar 1956, pp. 34-35.
[1641] Asoke Kumar Majumdar 1956, p. 35.
[1642] Asoke Kumar Majumdar 1956, pp. 36-39.
[1643] Krishna Narain Seth 1978, pp. 136-137.
[1644] Asoke Kumar Majumdar 1956, pp. 43-45.
[1645] Asoke Kumar Majumdar 1956, pp. 49-50.
[1646] Asoke Kumar Majumdar 1956, pp. 50-51.
[1647] Asoke Kumar Majumdar 1956, pp. 48-49.
[1648] Asoke Kumar Majumdar 1956, pp. 52-53.
[1649] Krishna Narain Seth 1978, p. 184.
[1650] Asoke Kumar Majumdar 1956, p. 54-55.
[1651] R. B. Singh 1964, p. 127.
[1652] Asoke Kumar Majumdar 1956, pp. 57-58.
[1653] Asoke Kumar Majumdar 1956, pp. 59-60.
[1654] Asoke Kumar Majumdar 1956, p. 60.
[1655] R. B. Singh 1964, p. 125.
[1656] Tommaso Bobbio 2015, p. 164.
[1657] Asoke Kumar Majumdar 1956, p. 69.
[1658] Asoke Kumar Majumdar 1956, p. 70.
[1659] Dasharatha Sharma 1959, p. 47.
[1660] Asoke Kumar Majumdar 1956, p. 71.
[1661] R. B. Singh 1964, p. 156.
[1662] Dasharatha Sharma 1959, p. 69.
[1663] Asoke Kumar Majumdar 1956, pp. 74-75.
[1664] R. K. Dikshit 1976, p. 133.
[1665] Asoke Kumar Majumdar 1956, pp. 80-81.
[1666] Asoke Kumar Majumdar 1956, p. 92.
[1667] Asoke Kumar Majumdar 1956, pp. 99-103.
[1668] Asoke Kumar Majumdar 1956, pp. 106-108.

[1669] R. B. Singh 1964, p. 253.
[1670] R. B. Singh 1964, p. 254.
[1671] R. B. Singh 1964, p. 149.
[1672] Asoke Kumar Majumdar 1956, p. 109.
[1673] Asoke Kumar Majumdar 1956, p. 112.
[1674] Asoke Kumar Majumdar 1956, pp. 109-110.
[1675] Asoke Kumar Majumdar 1956, p. 111.
[1676] Asoke Kumar Majumdar 1956, p. 113-114.
[1677] Asoke Kumar Majumdar 1956, p. 116.
[1678] Asoke Kumar Majumdar 1956, p. 119.
[1679] Asoke Kumar Majumdar 1956, pp. 130-131.
[1680] Dasharatha Sharma 1959, p. 138.
[1681] R. B. Singh 1964, p. 259.
[1682] Asoke Kumar Majumdar 1956, p. 139.
[1683] Asoke Kumar Majumdar 1956, p. 140.
[1684] Asoke Kumar Majumdar 1956, p. 141.
[1685] Asoke Kumar Majumdar 1956, p. 143.
[1686] Asoke Kumar Majumdar 1956, p. 145-146.
[1687] Asoke Kumar Majumdar 1956, p. 146.
[1688] Asoke Kumar Majumdar 1956, p. 148.
[1689] Asoke Kumar Majumdar 1956, p. 160-161.
[1690] Asoke Kumar Majumdar 1956, pp. 149-155.
[1691] Asoke Kumar Majumdar 1956, p. 156.
[1692] Asoke Kumar Majumdar 1956, p. 163-164.
[1693] P.B. Udgaonkar 1986, p. 215.
[1694] David P. Henige 2004, p. 125.
[1695] Jonah Blank 2001, p. 38.
[1696] Jonah Blank 2001, p. 44.
[1697] Romila Thapar 2008, p. 236.
[1698] Asoke Kumar Majumdar 1956, p. 199.
[1699] Vinod Chandra Srivastava 2008, p. 857.
[1700] Edward A. Alpers 2014, p. 57.
[1701] http://www.new.dli.ernet.in/handle/2015/219763
[1702] //www.worldcat.org/oclc/4413150
[1703] https://books.google.com/books?id=m3DjCgAAQBAJ
[1704] https://books.google.com/books?id=n4gcAAAAMAAJ
[1705] https://books.google.com/books?id=fqDpAAAAMAAJ
[1706] https://books.google.com/books?id=lEB11tKmCgcC&pg=PA21
[1707] https://books.google.com/books?id=pjsfAQAAQBAJ&pg=PA57
[1708] https://books.google.com/books?id=aY_I3zgxfpsC&pg=PA32
[1709] https://books.google.com/books?id=BTxuAAAAMAAJ
[1710] //www.worldcat.org/oclc/483180949
[1711] https://books.google.co.in/books?id=yoHfm7BgqTgC
[1712] https://books.google.com/books?id=r_FExBRnC3YC&pg=PA44
[1713] https://books.google.ca/books?id=-Q4dAAAAMAAJ
[1714] //www.worldcat.org/oclc/8931757
[1715] https://books.google.com/books?id=tU1yDpYlu38C&pg=PA146
[1716] https://books.google.com/books?id=Jdoym34QydQC&pg=PA215
[1717] https://books.google.com/books?id=3ZZ8T8tZc4YC&pg=PA236
[1718] https://books.google.com/books?id=TKs9AAAAIAAJ
[1719] //www.worldcat.org/oclc/11038728
[1720] https://books.google.com/books?id=a9j9ZJGJOV0C&pg=PA130
[1721] http://journals.sagepub.com/doi/abs/10.1177/0376983612449525
[1722] //doi.org/10.1177/0376983612449525
[1723] https://books.google.com/books?id=-5vwCQAAQBAJ&pg=PA164
[1724] https://books.google.com/books?id=FvjZVwYVmNcC&pg=PA857

[1725] Upinder Singh 2008, p. 571.
[1726] D. C. Ganguly 1981, p. 704.
[1727] Sailendra Nath Sen 1999, p. 339.
[1728] Dilip Kumar Ganguly 1984, pp. 116-117.
[1729] D. C. Ganguly 1981, p. 705.
[1730] Dilip Kumar Ganguly 1984, p. 117.
[1731] Swati Datta 1989, p. 102.
[1732] Buddha Prakash 1965, p. 182.
[1733] R. B. Singh 1964, pp. 100-102.
[1734] H. A. Phadke 1990, p. 87.
[1735] P. C. Roy 1980, pp. 93-94.
[1736] Upinder Singh 2008, p. 570.
[1737] P. C. Roy 1980, p. 95.
[1738] Alexander Cunningham 1871, p. 141-145.
[1739] Alexander Cunningham 1871, p. 149.
[1740] Jagbir Singh 2002, p. 28.
[1741] https://books.google.com/books?id=SmgSvB5B9I4C&pg=PA149
[1742] //www.worldcat.org/oclc/421335527
[1743] https://books.google.com/books?id=lKg5AQAAIAAJ
[1744] //www.worldcat.org/oclc/6388337
[1745] https://books.google.com/books?id=kXtDAAAAYAAJ
[1746] https://books.google.com/books?id=7v76i0eF9tQC&pg=PA117
[1747] https://books.google.com/books?id=HxlIAAAAIAAJ
[1748] https://books.google.ca/books?id=9H9uAAAAMAAJ
[1749] https://books.google.com/books?id=f2Et2zZGJPUC&pg=PA69
[1750] https://books.google.com/books?id=TKs9AAAAIAAJ
[1751] //www.worldcat.org/oclc/11038728
[1752] https://books.google.com/books?id=Wk4_ICH_g1EC&pg=PA172
[1753] https://books.google.com/books?id=pKAb9DPUCCcC&pg=PA28
[1754] https://books.google.com/books?id=H3lUIIYxWkEC&pg=PA383
[1755] Huntington 1984, p. 56.
[1756] Sengupta 2011, pp. 39–49.
[1757] Bagchi 1993, p. 37.
[1758] The Caste of the Palas, The Indian Culture, Vol IV, 1939, pp 113–14, B Chatterji
[1759] Bhagalpur Charter of Narayanapala, year 17, verse 6, *The Indian Antiquary*, XV p 304.
[1760] Sengupta 2011, p. 45.
[1761] Bagchi 1993, p. 4.
[1762] Paul 1939, p. 38.
[1763] Bagchi 1993, p. 39–40.
[1764] Paul 1939, p. 122–124.
[1765] Paul 1939, p. 111–122.
[1766] Huntington 1984, p. 39.
[1767] Bagchi 1993, p. 19.
[1768] Bagchi 1993, p. 100.
[1769] Paul 1939, p. 139–143.
[1770] Paul 1939, p. 143–144.
[1771] Bagchi 1993, pp. 2–3.
[1772] https://books.google.com/books?id=J7RKoMeAtpUC&pg=PA2
[1773] https://books.google.com/books?id=xLA3AAAAIAAJ&pg=PA32
[1774] https://web.archive.org/web/20160817073236/http://dli.ernet.in/handle/2015/503174
[1775] http://dli.ernet.in/handle/2015/503174
[1776] https://books.google.com/books?id=kVSh_TyJ0YoC&pg=PA40
[1777] //en.wikipedia.org/w/index.php?title=Template:History_of_Bengal&action=edit
[1778] http://en.banglapedia.org/index.php?title=Chandra_Dynasty,_The
[1779] The Second Pandyan empire, A.D. 1190–1312 by A.J. Thinakaran, 1987, p.63
[1780] Ganga Dynasty http://www.britannica.com/eb/topic-225335/Ganga-dynasty britannica.com.

[1781] Eastern Ganga Dynasty in India http://www.india9.com/i9show/Eastern-Ganga-Dynasty-50611.htm. India9.com (2005-06-07). Retrieved on 2013-07-12.
[1782] Ganga dynasty (Indian dynasties) - Encyclopædia Britannica http://www.britannica.com/EBchecked/topic/225335/Ganga-dynasty. Britannica.com. Retrieved on 2013-07-12.
[1783] The Second Pandyan empire, A.D. 1190–1312 by A.J. Thinakaran, 1987, p.63
[1784] Ganga Dynasty http://www.britannica.com/eb/topic-225335/Ganga-dynasty britannica.com.
[1785] https://web.archive.org/web/20090410024222/http://srikakulam.ap.nic.in/intach/story_on_stone/1.1.htm
[1786] http://coinindia.com/galleries-eastern-gangas.html
[1787] //en.wikipedia.org/w/index.php?title=Template:History_of_Bengal&action=edit
[1788] The History of the Bengali Language by Bijay Chandra Mazumdar p.50
[1789] Land of Two Rivers: A History of Bengal from the Mahabharata to Mujib by Nitish K. Sengupta p.51
[1790] Ancient India by Ramesh Chandra Majumdar p.320
[1791] The Cambridge Shorter History of India p.10
[1792] B.P. Sinha in George E. Somers, Dynastic History of Magadha, p.214, Abhinav Publications, 1977, New Delhi,
[1793] //en.wikipedia.org/w/index.php?title=Template:Sena_dynasty&action=edit
[1794] Momtazur Rahman Tarafdar, "Itihas O Aitihasik", Bangla Academy Dhaka, 1995
[1795] http://en.banglapedia.org/index.php?title=Sena_Dynasty
[1796] Arun Bhattacharjee (1993), *Assam in Indian Independence*, Page 143 While Pushyavarman was the contemporary of the Gupta Emperor Samudra Gupta, Bhaskaravarman was the contemporary of Harshavardhana of Kanauj.
[1797] "Three thousand years after these mythical ancestors (Naraka, Bhagadatta and Vajradatta) there occurred Pushyavarman as the first historical king, after whom we have an uninterrupted line of rulers up to Bhaskarvarman."
[1798] "According to him (D C Sircar) Narayanavarma, the father of Bhutivarman, was the first Kamarupa king to perform horse-sacrifices and thus for the first time since the days of Pusyavarman freedom from the Gupta political supremacy was declared by Narayanavarma. But a careful study or even a casual perusal of the seal attached to the Dubi C.P. and of the nalanda seals should show that it is Sri Mahendra, the father of Narayanavarma himself, who is described as the performer of two horse-sacrifices."
[1799] "(I)t is significant that like the kings of the Bhauma-Naraka family they also claim descent from Naraka or Bhagadatta, and this descent is acknowledged outside also outside their own kingdom when the Pashupatinath temple inscription of Nepal described Rajyamati, the daughter of Sri Harsha of the family of Salasthambha as *bhagadatta-raja-kulaja*.
[1800] "The mythical ancestors of this line of rulers were Naraka, Bhagadatta and Vajradatta. Three thousand years after these mythical ancestors there occurred Pushyavarman..." In the Nidhanpur copperplate inscription, it is mentioned: "When the kings of his (Vajradatta's) family having enjoyed the position (of rulers) for three thousand years had (all) attained the state of gods, Pushyavarman became the lord of the world."
[1801] George van Driem (2001), *India - Volume 2; Volume 10*, Page 506 Although Kamarupa was at times ruled by Indo-Aryan dynasties and at times by native Mleccha dynasties
[1802] "Since the Epico-Pauranic myths associated Pragjyotisha with Naraka and his descendants, it was quite natural for the kings of ancient Assam to fabricate the story of descent from Naraka's family"
[1803] Dalal, Roshen (2011) "Narakasura" in *Hinduism: An Alphabetical Guide* p274
[1804] B M Barua *Common Ancestry of Pre-Ahom rulers and some problems of early History of Assam* in "Discovery of Northeast India" (ed Sharma S. K et al.) p277.
[1805] B M Barua *Common Ancestry of Pre-Ahom rulers and some problems of early History of Assam* in "Discovery of Northeast India" (ed Sharma S. K et al.) p277. "In some sections of the *Great Epic*, Bhagadatta is represented as Yavana or Mleccha ruler, although a friend of Indra."
[1806] Vishveshvaranand Vedic Research Institute, India (1983),*Vishveshvaranand Indological Series - Issue 77*, P 26 tribes designated as Yavanas, Mlecchas or Dasyus were degraded Aryans is also indicated by the story in the Mahabharata

[1807] "The present king belongs to the old line (*tso yari*) of Narayana-deva. He is of the Brahman caste. His name is Bhaskaravarman, and his title Kumara (Keu-mo-lo)."

[1808] "But the She-Kia-Fang-Che records that Bhaskarvarman was a Kshatriya (and not a Brahmin) and his ancestors hailed from China (=Han) itself having nothing to do with Narayana Deva"

[1809] At the time of Hiuan-tsang's visit King Bhaskaravarman, was "a descendant of the God Narayana" ; he was "of the caste of the Brahman, as," and had the title of " Kumara." "Since the possession of the kingdom by his family up to his time, the succession of princes covers a space of a thousand generations" (Mem.II,77.)The evidence of his contemporary Bana (Harsacarita, chap. VII) confirms almost all these details. Finally we possess since a few years ago an inscription of King Bhaskaravarman (Nidhanpur plates,Ep.Ind.,XII,65), which takes back the genealogy up to King Bhagadatta, the famous adversary of the by a long list of ancestors. However, when he had business with others than Indians, the same prince boasted of another origin altogether. When the envoy of the T'ang dynasty, Li Yi-piao, paid him a visit during the course of his mission (643-646) the king in a private conversation told him: "the royal family has handed down its power for 4,000 years. The first was a holy spirit which came from China (*Han-ti*) flying through the air." (*She-kia fang tche*, ed. Tok. XXXV, 1, 94b, *col. ult.*) As though he would show sympathy for China, he asked the envoy to get him a portrait of Lao-tseu and a Sanskrit translation of the Tao-to-king. (*She-kia fang tche*, ed. Tok. XXXV, 1, 94b, *col. ult.*).

[1810] Kāmarūpa Anusandhāna Samiti, *Readings in the history & culture of Assam - Page 179*, 1984 "The Varman dynasty, which was probably the first Indo-Aryan dynasty in Assam was overthrown by Salastambha, a man of Mleccha or non-Aryan (Mongolian) origin."

[1811] Niśipada Caudhurī, *Historical archaeology of central Assam - Page 83*, 1985 "K.N. Dutta seems to be right in concluding that the Varman dynasty, which was probably the first Indo-Aryan dynasty in Assam, was overthrown by Salastambha, (Mongoloid) origin, who then made himself the king of Kamarupa."

[1812] Suresh Kant Sharma, Usha Sharma, *Discovery of North-East India: Geography, History, Culture ..., Volume 3 - Page 275*, 2005 "One may go perhaps a step further and suggest that Pusyavarman was the first Indo-Aryan ruler set up by Samudragupta over the two territories of Kamarupa and Davaka unified into a single kingdom. None can or should deny it as a fact if Bhattasali simply means to say that the process leading to the assertion of independence by the Varmans of Kamarupa commenced earlier, ie., before Bhutivarman, even without specifically bringing Mahendravarman into play. The above suggestion, that the first Indo-Aryan rule favourable to Brahmanism was founded in Kamarupa with Pusyavarman as the first ruler under Samudragupta, received its support from these two facts: (1) that Bhagadatta the great legendary ancestor of the Varmans, is described in the Nidhanpur grant of Bhaskaravarman as Indrasakhah, "The friend of Indra (the heavenly prototype of the earthly Indo-Aryan monarch)", and his father and predecessor Naraka as one begotten of the Varaha form of vishnu, and (2) the descent claimed, as known to Hwen Thsang, by the Varmans from "the god Narayana." If thus the earlier rulers of the Varmans line were Vaisnavas, at least up till Bhutivarman."

[1813] "Hiuen Ts'ang by mistake described Bhaskara-varman as a Brahman, but he was just a neo-Kshatriya, a member of a Hinduised mleccha or non-Hindu Indo-Mongoloid family which had been accepted within the fold of Hindu orthodoxy"

[1814] Sharma, Mukunda Madhava (1978), Inscriptions of Ancient Assam

[1815] "Virtually all of Assam's kings, from the fourth-century Varmans down to the eighteenth-century Ahoms, came from non-Aryan tribes that were only gradually Sanskritised."

[1816] "Suffice is to say that he (Bhaskaravarman) was Hindu by religion spreading light of Arya Dharma though he has great preverence for learned Buddhist priests and professors of his time and was distinctly inclined towards Buddhism. The text of his message to Silabhadra leave no doubt in this point. The very high functions allotted to him during the famous religious assembly at Kanauj by the Hindu emperor Sri Harsha proves that he was not a Hindu of despised low caste. He was undoubtedly looked upon as a good Kshatriya, as his surname Varma indicates, whatever might have been his origin. In any case he was certainly not a Hinduized Koch. All the kings of his dynasty beginning from Pushyavarman were Kshatriya monarchs. When Xuanzang visited the kingdom he found hundreds of Hindu temples there and evidently there were large numbers of Brahmans and other high caste Hindus living within the kingdom which was a seat of learning that people of other countries came there for study."

1817 Though there exists no direct evidence, there are indirect evidence of a king who ruled for a short period after Bhaskaravarman, but was ousted by Salasthamba .
1818 https://archive.org/details/siyukibuddhistre02hsuoft
1819 https://archive.org/details/prearyanandpredr035083mbp
1820 //doi.org/10.1093/jhs/hir034
1821 , reproduced from .
1822 Sircar (1990a), pp. 63–68.
1823 //en.wikipedia.org/w/index.php?title=Template:Culture_of_Assam&action=edit
1824 Lahiri (1991), pp. 26–28.
1825 Suresh Kant Sharma, Usha Sharma - 2005,"Discovery of North-East India: Geography, History, Culture, ... - Volume 3", Page 248, Davaka (Nowgong) and Kamarupa as separate and submissive friendly kingdoms.
1826 "As regards the eastern limits of the kingdom, Davaka was absorbed within Kamarupa under Kalyanavarman and the outlying regions were brought under subjugation by Mahendravarman."
1827 "It is presumed that (Kalyanavarman) conquered Davaka, incorporating it within the kingdom of Kamarupa"
1828 "According to the *Kalika Purana* and the *Yogonitantra*, the ancient Kamarupa included, besides the districts of modern Assam, Cooch-Behar, Rang-pura, Jalpaiguri and Dinajpur within its territory."
1829 In the medieval times the region between the Sankosh river and the Barnadi river on the northern bank of the Brahmaputra river was defined as Kamrup (or Koch Hajo in Persian chronicles)
1830 "They also looked upon themselves as the heirs of the glory that was ancient Kamarupa by right of conquest, and they long cherished infructuously their unfulfilled hopes of expanding up to that frontier." . 'An Ahom force reached the banks of the Karatoya in hot pursuit of an invading Truko-Afghan army in the 1530's. Since then "the washing of the sword in the Karatoya" became a symbol of the Assamese aspirations, repeatedly evoked in the *Bar-Mels* and mentioned in the chronicles."
1831 *Besatae* in the Schoff translation and also sometimes used by Ptolemy, they are a people similar to Kirradai and they lived in the region between "Assam and Sichuan"
1832 "The *Periplus of the Erythraen Sea* (last quarter of the first century A.D)and Ptolemy's *Geography* (middle of the second century A.D) appear to call the land including Assam Kirrhadia after its Kirata population."
1833 "...the Arthashastra in its present form has to be assigned to the early centuries of the Christian era and the commentaries to much later dates."
1834 Niśipada Caudhurī (1985), Historical archaeology of central Assam, p.2
1835 "If we go by Bhattaswamin's commentary on *Arthashastra* Magadha was already importing certain items of trade from this [Brahmaputra] Valley in Kautilya's days"
1836 Bhushan 2005, p. 21.
1837 "The name Kamarupa does not appear in local grants where Pragjyotisha alone figures with the local rulers called Pragjyotishadhipati."
1838 Sailendra Nath Sen (1999), *Ancient Indian History and Civilization*, p.303 Kamarupa at that time did not comprise the whole of the Assam valley as Davaka mentioned along with Kamarupa in the Allahabad Inscription, has been located in modern Nowgong district.
1839 "...the temple of the goddess Tameshwari (Dikkaravasini) is now located at modern Sadiya about 100 miles to the northeast of Sibsagar"
1840 "To the east of Kamarupa, the description continues, the country was a series of hills and hillocks without any principal city, and it reached the to the southwest Barbarians [of China]" Therefore, the hills to the east of Kamarupa could not have been the Karbi Hills because they do not reach to the southwest of China.
1841 "The pilgrim learned from the people [of Kamarupa] that the southwest borders of Szuchuan were distant about 2 months' journey, but the mountains and rivers were hard to pass, there were pestinential vapurs and poisonous snakes and herbs."
1842 Choudhury, P. C., (1959) *The History of Civilization of the People of Assam*, Guwahati
1843 Puri (1968), p. 56.
1844 //en.wikipedia.org/w/index.php?title=Template:Kamarupa&action=edit
1845 Lahiri (1991), p. 68.

[1846] Lahiri (1991), p. 72.
[1847]. Though the first evidence is from the Mansador stone pillar inscription of Yasodharman, there is no reference to this invasion in the Kamarupa inscriptions.
[1848] Sircar (1990b), p. 115.
[1849] Lahiri (1991), pp. 77–79.
[1850] Lahiri (1991), p. 78.
[1851] "Visvasundara (son and successor of Vallabhadeva), (?) was perhaps to be identified with Prithu or Bartu of Minhaj." (Note:11)
[1852] (Kamarupa) was reorganized as a new state, 'Kamata' by name with Kamatapur as capital. The exact time when the change was made is uncertain. But possibly it had been made by Sandhya (c. 1250 – 1270) as a safeguard against mounting dangers from the east and the west. Its control on the eastern regions beyond the Manah (Manas river) was lax."
[1853] https://books.google.com/books?id=qQWYkSs51rEC
[1854] http://shodhganga.inflibnet.ac.in/handle/10603/68309
[1855] //doi.org/10.2307/3516963
[1856] //www.jstor.org/stable/3517005
[1857] https://books.google.com/books?id=KYLpvaKJIMEC&lpg=PP1&pg=PA3
[1858] https://books.google.com/books?id=0VIoAAAAYAAJ
[1859] Though *mlechchha* is a derogatory word, Harjaravarman, a king of this dynasty explains the term (though illegible) in the Hayunthal copper plates .
[1860] //en.wikipedia.org/w/index.php?title=Template:Kamarupa&action=edit
[1861] Pralambha, read from the Tezpur plates, can be corrected to Salambha, in light of the Parbatiya plates,
[1862] //en.wikipedia.org/w/index.php?title=Template:Kamarupa&action=edit
[1863] //en.wikipedia.org/w/index.php?title=Template:Kingdom_of_Tripura&action=edit
[1864] http://dsal.uchicago.edu/reference/gazetteer/pager.html?objectid=DS405.1.I34_V13_124.gif
[1865] http://www.uq.net.au/~zzhsoszy/ips/t/tripura.html
[1866] http://www.4dw.net/royalark/India/tripura.htm
[1867] http://www.theodora.com/encyclopedia/t/tippera.html
[1868] https://books.google.com/books?id=P1naAAAAMAAJ&q=nagadipa+naga+nadu&dq= nagadipa+naga+nadu&hl=en&sa=X&ei=DkuIT8-ZM5OA0AWYhoTtAw&ved= 0CDgQ6AEwAA
[1869] Mannar Uruvana 'Mallar' Varalaru http://www.tamilagaarasiyal.com/ActionPages/Content.aspx?bid=817&rid=43
[1870] https//books.google.com
[1871] https://books.google.com/books?id=ERq-OCn2cloC
[1872] http://www.devendrakulam.org/wst_page5.html
[1873] //en.wikipedia.org/w/index.php?title=Template:Keralahistory&action=edit
[1874] //en.wikipedia.org/w/index.php?title=Template:TNhistory&action=edit
[1875] Karashima 2014, p. 30.
[1876] Menon 2007, p. 81.
[1877] Menon 2007, p. 73.
[1878] Cyclopaedia of India and of Eastern and Southern Asia. https://books.google.com/books?id=eONSAAAAcAAJ&q=Muziris#v=snippet&q=Muziris&f=false Ed. by Edward Balfour (1871), Second Edition. Volume 2. p. 584.
[1879] Menon 2007, p. 118.
[1880] Thapar 2004, p. 368.
[1881] Citing Komattil Achutha Menon, Ancient Kerala, p. 7<ref name="FOOTNOTEMenon200721">Menon 2007, p. 21.
[1882] According to Menon, this etymology of "added" or "reclaimed" land also complements the Parashurama myth about the formation of Kerala. In it, Parashurama, one of the avatars of Vishnu, flung his axe across the sea from Gokarnam towards Kanyakumari (or vice versa) and the water receded up to the spot where it landed, thus creating Kerala.<ref name="FOOTNOTEMenon200720,21">Menon 2007, pp. 20,21.
[1883] Keay, John (2000) [2001]. India: A history. India: Grove Press.
[1884] Caldwell 1998, p. 92.

[1885] M. Ramachandran, Irāmaṉ Mativāṇaṉ (1991). *The spring of the Indus civilisation*. Prasanna Pathippagam, pp. 34. "Srilanka was known as "Cerantivu' (island of the Cera kings) in those days. The seal has two lines. The line above contains three signs in Indus script and the line below contains three alphabets in the ancient Tamil script known as Tamil ...
[1886] Menon 2007, p. 33.
[1887] Menon 2007, pp. 26–29.
[1888] Kamil Veith Zvelebil, *Companion Studies to the History of Tamil Literature*, p.12
[1889] K.A. Nilakanta Sastry, *A History of South India*, OUP (1955) p.105
[1890] Zvelebil 1973, pp. 37–39: The opinion that the Gajabahu Synchronism is an expression of genuine historical tradition is accepted by most scholars today
[1891] Zvelebil 1973, p. 38.
[1892] Menon 2007, pp. 81–82.
[1893] Menon 2007, p. 82.
[1894] Menon 2007, p. 98.
[1895] Menon 2007, p. 99.
[1896] K.A. Nilakanta Sastri (1976) - The Pandyan kingdom, pg 76
[1897] Menon 2007, p. 102.
[1898] Karashima 2014, p. 132.
[1899] Menon 2007, p. 111.
[1900] *Focus on a PhD thesis that threw new light on Perumals* - R. Madhavan Nair [The Hindu], 2 April 2011 http://www.thehindu.com/todays-paper/tp-national/Focus-on-a-PhD-thesis-that-threw-new-light-on-Perumals/article14695237.ece
[1901] Menon 2007, pp. 115.
[1902] Menon 2007, pp. 115–116.
[1903] Menon 2007, pp. 117–118.
[1904] Menon 2007, pp. 118,140–141.
[1905] Menon 2007, pp. 138,147.
[1906] //en.wikipedia.org/w/index.php?title=Template:Chera_Dynasty&action=edit
[1907] Menon 2007, p. 75.
[1908] Menon 2007, p. 77.
[1909] Menon 2007, p. 67.
[1910] Menon 2007, pp. 75–76.
[1911] Menon 2007, pp. 67–68.
[1912] Menon 1967.
[1913] See Mahavamsa – http://lakdiva.org/mahavamsa/. Since Senguttuvan (Kadal Pirakottiya Vel Kezhu Kuttuvan) was a contemporary of Gajabahu I of Sri Lanka he was perhaps the Chera king during the 2nd century CE.
[1914] Menon 2007, p. 70.
[1915] Menon 2007, p. 71.
[1916] Menon 2007, p. 72.
[1917] See report in *Frontline*, June/July 2003 http://www.hinduonnet.com/fline/fl2013/stories/20030704000207100.htm
[1918] Menon 2007, pp. 111–119.
[1919] Menon 2007, p. 122.
[1920] Menon 2007, p. 126.
[1921] Menon 2007, pp. 126,127.
[1922] "Artefacts from the lost Port of Muziris." http://www.thehindu.com/news/cities/Delhi/artefacts-from-the-lost-port-of-muziris/article6657446.ece The Hindu. December 3, 2014.
[1923] "Pattanam richest Indo-Roman site on Indian Ocean rim." http://www.thehindu.com/todays-paper/tp-national/pattanam-richest-indoroman-site-on-indian-ocean-rim/article274715.ece The Hindu. May 3, 2009.
[1924] Kulke & Rothermund 2004, pp. 105–.
[1925] http://www.hinduonnet.com/thehindu/thscrip/print.pl?file=2007012800201800.htm&date=2007/01/28/&prd=th&
[1926] Raoul McLaughlin, Rome and the distant East: trade routes to the ancient lands of Arabia, India and China Continuum International Publishing Group, 6 July 2010

[1927] Menon 2007, p. 83.
[1928] Menon 2007, p. 89.
[1929] *The Jews of India: A Story of Three Communities* https//books.google.com by Orpa Slapak. The Israel Museum, Jerusalem. 2003. p. 27.
[1930] *The Encyclopedia of Christianity, Volume 5* https//books.google.com by Erwin Fahlbusch. Wm. B. Eerdmans Publishing – 2008. p. 285.
[1931] Manimekalai, by Merchant Prince Shattan, Gatha 27
[1932] Menon 2007, p. 78.
[1933] Menon 2007, pp. 79–80.
[1934] Menon 2007, pp. 123–124.
[1935] Menon 2007, p. 127.
[1936] Menon 2007, pp. 128,129.
[1937] Menon 2007, p. 135.
[1938] Menon 2007, p. 112.
[1939] M. G. S. Narayanan (1972), *Cultural Symbiosis*, Kerala Society.
[1940] George Menachery (1998) *Indian Church History Classics, Vol. I, The Nazranies*, SARAS.
[1941] Menon 2007, p. 114.
[1942] Fischel 1967, pp. 230.
[1943] Menon 2007, p. 142.
[1944] Menon 2007, pp. 143–144.
[1945] https://books.google.co.in/books?id=FVsw35oEBv4C
[1946] https://books.google.co.in/books/about/A_Survey_of_Kerala_History.html?id=N7WaZe2PBy8C
[1947] //www.worldcat.org/oclc/555508146
[1948] https://books.google.com/books?id=V73N8js5ZgAC&pg=PA105
[1949] https://books.google.co.in/books?id=-5irrXX0apQC
[1950] https://books.google.co.in/books?id=fpdVoAEACAAJ
[1951] https://books.google.com/books?id=Kx4uqyts2t4C&pg=PA39
[1952] https://books.google.com/?id=VF2VMUoY_okC&pg=PA38&dq=gajabahu+synchronism
[1953] https://books.google.com/books?id=5PPCYBApSnIC&pg=PA92
[1954] //doi.org/10.2307/597717
[1955] //www.jstor.org/stable/597717
[1956] https://books.google.co.in/books?id=0YDCngEACAAJ
[1957] https://web.archive.org/web/20060718060412/http://tamilartsacademy.com/books/coins/chapter01.html
[1958] Cort 1998, p. 166.
[1959] P. 146 *Kerala State gazetteer, Volume 2, Part 1* By Adoor K. K. Ramachandran Nair
[1960] Veermani Pd. Upadhyaya Felicitation Volume by Veermani Prasad Upadhyaya
[1961] P. 150 and P. 152 *The peacock, the national bird of India* By P. Thankappan Nair
[1962] *Buddhism in Tamil Nadu: collected papers* By G. John Samuel, Ār. Es Śivagaṇēśamūrti, M. S. Nagarajan, Institute of Asian Studies (Madras, India)
[1963] https://books.google.com/books?id=dvq1AAAAIAAJ
[1964] https://books.google.co.in/books?id=yoHfm7BgqTgC
[1965] P. 48 *Goa Today, Volume 17* By Goa Publications, 1982 - Goa, Daman and Diu (India)
[1966] George M. Moraes (1931), The Kadamba Kula, A History of Ancient and Medieval Karnataka, Asian Educational Services, 1990, p8
[1967] Yet another legend is that Mayurasarma was born to a sister of Jain Thirtankara Ananda Jinavritindra under a Kadamba tree. All these legends are from the records of the later Hangal Kadambas and Kadambas of Goa, George M. Moraes (1931), The Kadamba Kula, A History of Ancient and Medieval Karnataka, Asian Educational Services, 1990, p7
[1968] Royal families of the Deccan in the 11th century period often concocted northern origin theories according to George M. Moraes (1931), The Kadamba Kula, A History of Ancient and Medieval Karnataka, Asian Educational Services, 1990, p.9
[1969] George M. Moraes (1931), The Kadamba Kula, A History of Ancient and Medieval Karnataka, Asian Educational Services, 1990, p.10
[1970] Chopra et al. (2003), p.161

[1971] Sahitya Akademi (1988), p.1717
[1972] George M. Moraes (1931), The Kadamba Kula, A History of Ancient and Medieval Karnataka, Asian Educational Services, 1990, p.11
[1973] Kadambas were essentially Mysoreans (Rice 1897, pp.296, 335)
[1974] Dr. Suryanath U. Kamath, A Concise history of Karnataka from pre-historic times to the present, Jupiter books, 2001, MCC, Bangalore (Reprint 2002), pp 30–39
[1975] Both the Talagunda and Gundanur inscriptions attest to this-Dr. Suryanath U. Kamath, A Concise history of Karnataka from pre-historic times to the present, Jupiter books, 2001, MCC, Bangalore (Reprint 2002), p30
[1976] 21 Kannada and 2 Sanskrit inscriptions have been deciphered and published by George M. Moraes (1931), The Kadamba Kula, A History of Ancient and Medieval Karnataka, Asian Educational Services, New Delhi, Madras, 1990, pp 387–474
[1977] Coins with Kannada legends have been discovered from the rule of the Kadambas, according to Dr. Suryanath U. Kamath, A Concise history of Karnataka from pre-historic times to the present, Jupiter books, 2001, MCC, Bangalore (Reprint 2002), p12
[1978] A report on Halmidi inscription,
[1979] The Kadamba-Western Ganga Dynasty era is a momentous importance to Kannada language for it was with these rulers that Kannada language first gained official language status-K.V. Ramesh, Chalukyas of Vatapi, 1984, Agam Kala Prakashan, Delhi, p10
[1980] Dr. S.U. Kamath opines that Kannada may have been a local language at this time-Dr. Suryanath U. Kamath, A Concise history of Karnataka from pre-historic times to the present, Jupiter books, 2001, MCC, Bangalore (Reprint 2002), p37
[1981] Dr. Suryanath U. Kamath, A Concise history of Karnataka from pre-historic times to the present, Jupiter books, 2001, MCC, Bangalore (Reprint 2002), p37
[1982] The coins are preserved at the Archaaeological Section, Prince of Wales Museum of Western India, Mumbai – Moraes (1931), p382
[1983] The coin is preserved at the Indian Historical Research Institute, St. Xavier's College, Mumbai – Moraes (1931), p382
[1984] According to Dr. B. L. Rice-Dr. Suryanath U. Kamath, A Concise history of Karnataka from pre-historic times to the present, Jupiter books, 2001, MCC, Bangalore (Reprint 2002), p30
[1985] George M. Moares (1931), The Kadamba Kula, A History of Ancient and Medieval Karnataka, Asian Educational Services, 1990, p10
[1986] The Talagunda inscription of 450 states that Mayurasharma was the progenitor of the kingdom. The inscription gives a graphic description of the happenings at Kanchi, "That the hand dextrous in grasping the Kusha (grass), fuel and stones, ladle, melted butter and the oblation vessel, unsheathed a flaming sword, eager to conquer the earth"-Dr. Suryanath U. Kamath, A Concise history of Karnataka from pre-historic times to the present, Jupiter books, 2001, MCC, Bangalore (Reprint 2002), pp 30–31
[1987] K.V. Ramesh, Chalukyas of Vatapi, 1984, Agam Kala Prakashan, p6
[1988] K.V. Ramesh, Chalukyas of Vatapi, 1984, Agam Kala Prakashan, p3
[1989] A CONCISE HISTORY OF KARNATAKA By Dr.SURYANATH U.KAMATH, page 31.
[1990] The inscription was discovered by Dr. B.R. Gopal,
[1991] According to Prof. Jouveau-Dubreuil-Dr. Suryanath U. Kamath, A Concise history of Karnataka from pre-historic times to the present, Jupiter books, 2001, MCC, Bangalore (Reprint 2002), p32
[1992] The Talagunda inscription describes Bhagiratha as the sole lord of the Kadamba land and the great *Sagara* himself, indicating he may have retrieved their losses against the Vakatakas-Dr. Suryanath U. Kamath, A Concise history of Karnataka from pre-historic times to the present, Jupiter books, 2001, MCC, Bangalore (Reprint 2002), p32
[1993] According to Dr. G. M. Moraes who wrote *Kadamba Kula: A History of Ancient and Medieval Karnataka*, under the rule Kakusthavarma, the kingdom reached its acme of success and the Talagunda record calls him the ornament of the family, the Halsi and Halmidi inscriptions also hold him in high esteem-Dr. Suryanath U. Kamath, A Concise history of Karnataka from pre-historic times to the present, Jupiter books, 2001, MCC, Bangalore (Reprint 2002), p32

[1994] According to Dr. P.B. Desai and the Balaghat inscription of Vakataka Pritvisena-Dr. Suryanath U. Kamath, A Concise history of Karnataka from pre-historic times to the present, Jupiter books, 2001, MCC, Bangalore (Reprint 2002), p33

[1995] The Sanskrit work *Auchitya Vichara* by Kshemendra quotes certain portions of a work by great Poet Kalidasa called *Kunthalesvara Dautya* which discusses his visit to the Kadamba court. Apparently, the Kadamba did not offer the poet a seat to sit on and Kalidasa had to sit on the ground, indicating the Kadambas treated the ambassador from the Gupta kingdom with scant respect. This is also verified from a Sanskrit work by Bhoja called *Shringara Prakasika* which mentions a Gupta ambassador being sent to the court of Kuntala. While Dr. Moraes opines the ambassador went during the time of Kadamba king Bhagiratha, Dr. P.B. Desai, R.S. Panchamukhi feel it was during the rule of king Kakusthavarma-Dr. Suryanath U. Kamath, A Concise history of Karnataka from pre-historic times to the present, Jupiter books, 2001, MCC, Bangalore (Reprint 2002), p33

[1996] //en.wikipedia.org/w/index.php?title=Template:Karnataka_History&action=edit

[1997] K. Ganesh: *Coins of Banavasi*, Bangalore, March 2008.

[1998] Prof. R.S. Panchamukhi has identified nine such Vishaya like the Sendraka Vishaya, Tagare Vishaya etc-Dr. Suryanath U. Kamath, A Concise history of Karnataka from pre-historic times to the present, Jupiter books, 2001, MCC, Bangalore (Reprint 2002), p35

[1999] Dr. G. M. Moraes opines that apart from using some unique features, the Kadambas used many mixed styles in their architecture derived from their predecessors and overlords. The Kadambas were the originators of the Karnataka architecture-Dr. Suryanath U. Kamath, A Concise history of Karnataka from pre-historic times to the present, Jupiter books, 2001, MCC, Bangalore (Reprint 2002), pp 37–38

[2000] *Kadambotsava* is held at Banavasi as it is here that the Kadamba kings organised the spring festival every year.

[2001] Defense Minister Pranab Mukherjee opened the first phase of India's giant western naval base INS Kadamba in Karwar, Karnataka state, on 31 May.

[2002] https://lccn.loc.gov/80095179

[2003] https://www.worldcat.org/oclc/7796041

[2004] https://www.worldcat.org/oclc/13869730

[2005] //openlibrary.org/books/OL3007052M

[2006] https://lccn.loc.gov/84900575

[2007] https://www.amazon.com/dp/B0006EHSP0

[2008] http://www.kamat.com/kalranga/deccan/kadamba.htm

[2009] http://www.ourkarnataka.com/states/history/historyofkarnataka10.htm

[2010] http://inscriptions.whatisindia.com

[2011] https://web.archive.org/web/20061006041816/http://www.deccanherald.com/deccanherald/feb72006/state171017200626.asp

[2012] http://www.deccanherald.com/deccanherald/feb72006/state171017200626.asp

[2013] http://www.hindu.com/2003/11/03/stories/2003110304550500.htm

[2014] https://web.archive.org/web/20040106121800/http://prabhu.50g.com/southind/kadamba/south_kadambagcat.html

[2015] http://prabhu.50g.com/southind/kadamba/south_kadambagcat.html

[2016] http://coinindia.com/galleries-kadambas-banavasi.html

[2017] //en.wikipedia.org/w/index.php?title=Template:Western_Ganga_kings&action=edit

[2018] (Rice in Adiga 2006, p88)

[2019] Adiga and Sheik Ali in Adiga (2006), p89

[2020] Sarma (1992), pp1–3

[2021] Ramesh (1984), pp1–2

[2022] Baji and Arokiaswamy in Adiga (2006), p89

[2023] Kamath (2001), p39

[2024] Krishna Rao in Adiga (2006), p88

[2025] Kamath (2001), pp39–40

[2026]

[2027] Adiga 2006, p97, p100

[2028] From the Cakra-Kedara grant, Kodunjeruvu grant (Adiga 2006, p99

[2029] Kamath (2001), p40
[2030] Sheik Ali and Ramesh in Adiga (2006), p100–101
[2031] Adiga (2006), p101
[2032] from the Nallala grant (Kamath 2001, p41)
[2033] Adiga (2006), p109
[2034] From the Aihole inscriptions and the Jangamarahalli inscription (Adiga 2006, 102)
[2035] (Adiga 2006, p103)
[2036] From the Shimoga records (N.L. Rao in Kamath 2001, p41)
[2037] The title was given to a later Ganga King Rachamalla I (Ramesh in Adiga p115), the Agali grant and Devarahalli inscription calls Sripurusha *Maharajadhiraja Paramamahesvara Bhatara* (Adiga 2006, pp115–116)
[2038] Sastri in Adiga 2006, p115
[2039] From Salem plates of Sripurusha dated 771 and the Koramangala grant (Ramesh in Adiga 2006, p116)
[2040] Kamath (2001), p42
[2041] From several Tumkur inscriptions (Adiga 2006, p117)
[2042] Adiga 2006, p118
[2043] from the Konnur inscriptions of 860 and Rajaramadu inscription (Adiga 2006, p119)
[2044] From the Keregodi Rangapura plates and Chikka Sarangi inscription of 903 (Adiga 2006, p119)
[2045] Kamath (2001), p43
[2046] Kamath (2001), p44
[2047] Tirukkalukkunram and Laksmeshwar inscriptions – Kanchi and Tanjore were annexed by Krishna III who was an incarnation of death for the Chola Dynasty (Reu 1933, p83)
[2048] Thapar 2003, p334
[2049] Sastri 1955, p162
[2050] From the Kudlur inscription of King Marasimha II (Adiga 2006, p120)
[2051] From the Kukkanur inscription (Adiga 2006, p122)
[2052] These victories were recorded in a Kannada inscription of 964 near Jabalpur (Kamath 2001, p83)
[2053] Kamath (2001), p45
[2054] Sastri (1955), pp356–357
[2055] Kamath (2001), p118
[2056] Kamath (2001), p46
[2057] Adiga (2006), p10
[2058] Rice in Adiga (2006), p15)
[2059] Sharma in Adiga (2006), p16
[2060] Kamath (2001), p47
[2061] Adiga (2006), p238
[2062] Adiga (2006), pp161–177
[2063] From the Kanatur inscription (Adiga 2006, p161)
[2064] From the Kanatur inscription (Adiga 2006, p164)
[2065] From the Mavali inscription of the 8th century and Indravalli inscription (Adiga 2006), p165
[2066] Doddakunce inscription, the Karagada and Maruru inscription (Adiga 2006, p167–68)
[2067] Bedirur inscriptions of 635 (Adiga 2006, p168)
[2068] From the Kumsi inscription of 931 and Doddahomma inscription of 977 (Adiga 2006, pp21–22, p27, p29)
[2069] From the Mavali inscription and Indivalli inscription (Adiga 2006, p31)
[2070] From the Devarahalli and Hosur copper plates (Adiga 2006, p33)
[2071] From inscriptions and literary writings such as *Vaddaradhane* (920) and *Pampa Bharata* (940) (Adiga 2006, p36–37)
[2072] Adiga (2006), p208
[2073] Adiga (2006), pp233–234
[2074] Adiga (2006), p6
[2075] from the Melkote copper plates and Mamballi inscriptions, Medutambihalli inscription of the 9th century (Adiga 2006, p53)
[2076] Adiga (2006), p42

[2077] Adiga (2006), p45
[2078] from the Narasimhapura plates (Adiga 2006), p46
[2079] From the Doddahomma inscription of Rachaballa IV of 977 (Adiga 2006, p47)
[2080] Kittel in Adiga (2006), p48
[2081] Belagi inscription of 964, Sasarvalli inscription of 1001 (Krishna and Adiga 2006, p55/56)
[2082] Adiga (2006), p57
[2083] From the Kodagu inscription of the 11th century, Guduve inscription of 1032, Kambadahalli inscription of 979 (Adiga 2006, p59, p60, p63)
[2084] From the Narasimhapura inscription of the 9th century (Sircar and Ramesh in Adiga 2006, pp210–211)
[2085] Indian epigraphical glossary, Hecca inscription pF 939 for SriKanteshvara temple (Adiga 2006, p213)
[2086] From Nonamangala copper plates of the 5th century of King Avinita (Adiga 2006, p216)
[2087] From the Kuppepalya inscription of the 8th century (Adiga 2006, p218)
[2088] Kotutu inscription of the 9th century, Rampura inscription of 905 (Adiga 2006, p219)
[2089] Varuna inscription, (Adiga 2006, p223–224)
[2090] Adiga (2006), p230
[2091] Dr. Lewis Rice, S. R. Sharma and M. V. Krishna Rao
[2092] Srikantha Shastri in Kamath (2001), p49
[2093] Adiga (2006), p249
[2094] Srikanta Sastri in
[2095] From the Kulaganga and Narasimhapura copper plates (Adiga 2006, p255)
[2096] From the Kudlur plates of Butuga II (Adiga 2006, p256)
[2097] P.B. Desai and Jaiswal in Adiga (2006), pp263–264
[2098] Adiga (2006), p264
[2099] Adiga (2006), pp264–265
[2100] Adiga (2006), p253
[2101] From the Bendiganhalli and Bangalore copper plates, the Chaluvanahalli plates, Kutalur grant, Kadagattur and Nallala grants of King Durvinita, Kondunjeruvu grant of King Avinita (Adiga 2006, pp281–282)
[2102] Adiga (2006), p282
[2103] Adiga (2006), p313
[2104] From the Kalkunda inscription (Adiga 2006, pp314–316)
[2105] Adiga (2006), p317
[2106] Adiga (2006), p291
[2107] From the Nandi copper plates of Rashtrakuta Govinda III of 800, Koyattur-12000 grant of King Dodda Naradhipa Bana in 810, the Ganiganur inscription, Nolamba King Mahendradhirajas grant of his house towards a Shaiva temple in 878, Baragur inscription of 914 of King Ayappadeva Nolamba, the Ninneshvaradeva temple built by King Dilipayya Nolamba in 942.
[2108] Among minor Chalukya kings, Narasinga Chalukya of Mysore constructed the Narasingeshwara temple and Kings Goggi and Durga build the Buteshvara temple at Varuna in modern Mysore region – From the Kukkarahalli, Manalevadi, Aragodupalli and Torevalli inscriptions, (Adiga 2006, 294)
[2109] This was popularised by the *kalamukha* monks (Adiga 2006, p292)
[2110] Adiga (2006), p301
[2111] H.V. Stietencron in Adiga 2006, p303
[2112] From Nandi copper plates of 800, Avani pillar inscription, Perbetta hero stones, 878 inscription of Nolamba Mahendradhiraja, Baragur inscription of 919, 942 Tumkur grant and Basavanahalli inscriptions (Adiga 2006, p304–305)
[2113] From the Kuntur inscription of the 10th century (Adiga 2006, p203)
[2114] Karmarkar (1947), p66
[2115] from the Bandalike inscription of 919 (Adiga 2006, p203)
[2116] From the Shravanabelagola inscription (Adiga 2006, p204)
[2117] Adiga (2006), p398
[2118] From the Perur plates (Adiga 2006, p398)
[2119] Karmarkar (1947), pp. 72, 74

[2120] Altekar (1934), p329
[2121] From the notes of Alberuni and Bouchet (Karmarkar 1947, p103)
[2122] From the notes of Yuan Chwang (Karmarkar 1947, p103)
[2123] From a modern Bijapur inscription of 1178 (Karmarkar, 1947, p104)
[2124] The *Svayamvara* marriage of Chalukya King Vikramaditya VI to Chandaladevi in the 11th century being an example (Karmarkar, 1947 p105)
[2125] Karmarkar (1947), p109
[2126] From the writings of Marco Polo, Ibn Batuta, Bernier and Tavernier (Karmarkar 1947, p110)
[2127] Karmarkar (1947), p110
[2128] Karmarkar (1947), p111
[2129] Karmarkar (1947), p112
[2130] Karmarkar (1947), p113
[2131]
[2132] Sastri (1955), p357
[2133] Kulkarni (1975) in Adiga (2006), p256
[2134] Sastri (1955), p355
[2135] Narasimhacharya (1988), p2
[2136] kamath (2001), p50
[2137] Narasimhacharya (1988), p18
[2138] One among the three gems of Kannada literature (Sastri 1955, p356)
[2139] Kamath (2001), p50
[2140] Narasimhacharya (1988), p19
[2141]
[2142] Venkatasubbiah in Kamath (2001), p50
[2143] Reddy, Sharma and Krishna Rao in Kamath (2001), pp 50–52
[2144] Seshadri in Kamath (2001), p51
[2145] If there is one aspect of Indian architecture which has its perfection and weakness, it is these free standing pillars (Fergusson in Kamath 2001, p52)
[2146] Sarma (1992), p153, p206, p208
[2147] In the whole of Indian art, nothing perhaps equals these pillars in good taste, Vincent Smith in Kamath (2001), p52
[2148] Some historians claim the Chavundaraya basadi was built by Chavundaraya himself while others argue it was the work of his on Jinadevana (Gopal et al. in Adiga 2006, p256). Another view holds that the original shrine was consecrated in the 11th century and built in memory of Chavundaraya (Settar in Adiga 2006, 256)
[2149] Adiga 2006, p269
[2150] Sarma (1992), pp153–167
[2151] Adiga 2006, p268
[2152] Kamath (2001), p51
[2153] Sarma (1992), pp.105–111
[2154] Sarma (1992), pp91–102
[2155] Sarma (1992), pp78–83
[2156] Sarma (1992), pp88–91
[2157] Sarma (1992), p17, p202, p204
[2158] //en.wikipedia.org/w/index.php?title=Template:Karnataka_History&action=edit
[2159] Thapar 2003, pp393–394
[2160] Adiga (2006), p110
[2161] Thapar 2003, p396
[2162] Kamath (2001), p12
[2163] //www.worldcat.org/oclc/3793499
[2164] //lccn.loc.gov/80905179
[2165] //www.worldcat.org/oclc/7796041
[2166] //www.worldcat.org/oclc/8221605
[2167] //www.amazon.com/dp/B0006EHSP0
[2168] //lccn.loc.gov/84900575
[2169] //www.worldcat.org/oclc/13869730

[2170] //openlibrary.org/books/OL3007052M
[2171] http://www.srikanta-sastri.org/#/gangas-of-talakad-article/4550857520
[2172] https://web.archive.org/web/20061215103823/http://www.ourkarnataka.com/states/history/historyofkarnataka11.htm
[2173] http://www.ourkarnataka.com/states/history/historyofkarnataka11.htm
[2174] http://www.hindu.com/2004/01/24/stories/2004012407180300.htm
[2175] http://www.kamat.com/kalranga/deccan/gangas.htm
[2176] http://www.hindu.com/2006/02/03/stories/2006020313510400.htm
[2177] https://web.archive.org/web/20070710231517/http://prabhu.50g.com/southind/ganga/south_gangacat.html
[2178] http://prabhu.50g.com/southind/ganga/south_gangacat.html
[2179] http://www.hindu.com/2004/08/20/stories/2004082016400300.htm
[2180] An inscription dated 1095 CE of Vikramaditya VI mentions grants to a *Vihara* of Buddha and Arya-Taradevi (Cousens 1926, p11)
[2181] N. Laxminarayana Rao and Dr. S. C. Nandinath have claimed the Chalukyas were *Kannadigas* (Kannada speakers) and very much the natives of Karnataka (Kamath 2001, p. 57)
[2182] The Chalukyas were Kannadigas (D.C. Sircar in Mahajan V.D., 1960, Reprint 2007, Ancient India, Chand and Company, New Delhi, p. 690,)
[2183] Natives of Karnataka (Hans Raj, 2007, Advanced history of India: From earliest times to present times, Part-1, Surgeet publications, New Delhi, p. 339
[2184] The Chalukyas hailed from Karnataka (John Keay, 2000, p. 168)
[2185] Quote:"They belonged to Karnataka country and their mother tongue was Kannada" (Sen 1999, 360)
[2186] The Chalukyas of Badami seem to be of indigenous origin (Kamath 2001, p. 58)
[2187] Jayasimha and Ranaraga, the first members of the Chalukya family were possibly employees of the Kadambas in the northern part of the Kadamba Kingdom (Fleet [in *Kanarese Dynasties*, p. 343] in Moraes, 1931, pp. 51–52)
[2188] Pulakesi I must have been an administrative official of the northern Kadamba territory centered in Badami (Moraes 1931, pp. 51–52)
[2189] The Chalukya base was Badami and Aihole (Thapar 2003, p. 328)
[2190] Inscriptional evidence proves the Chalukyas were native Kannadigas (Karmarkar, 1947, p. 26)
[2191] Pulakesi I of Badami who was a feudatory of the Kadamba king Krishna Varman II, overpowered his overlord in c. 540 and took control of the Kadamba Kingdom (Kamath 2001, p. 35)
[2192] Jayasimha (Pulakesi I's grandfather) is known from the Kaira inscription of 472–473 CE. Both Jayasimha and Ranaraga (Pulakesi I's father) are known from Mahakuta inscription of 599 CE and Aihole record of 634 CE (Ramesh 1984, pp. 26–27, p. 30)
[2193] From the Badami Cliff inscription of Pulakesi I and from the Hyderabad record of Pulakesi II which states their family ancestry (Kamath 2001, pp. 56–58)
[2194] Sastri (1955), p. 154
[2195] Chopra (2003), p. 73, part 1
[2196] Kamath (2001), p. 56
[2197] Moraes (1931). pp. 10–11
[2198] Ramesh (1984), p. 19
[2199]
[2200] Bilhana, in his Sanskrit work *Vikramanakadevacharitam* claims the Early Chalukya family were born from the feet of Hindu God Brahma, implying they were Shudras by caste, while other sources claim they were born in the arms of Brahma, and hence were Kshatriyas (Ramesh 1984, p. 15)
[2201] Sircar D.C. (1965), p. 48, *Indian Epigraphy*, Motilal Banarsidass Publishers, Delhi,
[2202] Kamath (2001), p. 57
[2203] Houben (1996), p. 215
[2204] Professor N.L. Rao has pointed out that some of their family records in Sanskrit have also named the princes with "arasa", such as Kattiyarasa (Kirtivarman I), Bittarasa (Kubja Vishnuvardhana) and Mangalarasa (Mangalesha, Kamath 2001, pp. 57–60)

[2205] Historians Shafaat Ahmad Khan and S. Krishnasvami Aiyangar clarify that **Arasa** is Kannada word, equivalent to Sanskrit word **Raja** – *Journal of Indian History* p. 102, Published by Department of Modern Indian History, University of Allahabad
[2206] Dr. Hoernle suggests a non-Sanskrit origin of the dynastic name. Dr. S.C. Nandinath feels the Chalukyas were of agricultural background and of Kannada origin who later took up a martial career. He feels the word *Chalki* found in some of their records must have originated from *salki*, an agricultural implement (Kamath 2001, p. 57)
[2207] The word *Chalukya* is derived from a Dravidian root (Kittel in Karmarkar 1947, p. 26)
[2208] Kamath (2001), p. 6, p. 10, p. 57, p. 59, p. 67
[2209] Ramesh (1984), p. 76, p. 159, pp. 161–162
[2210] Kamath (2001), p. 59
[2211] Thapar, (2003), p. 326
[2212] Kamath (2001), pp. 12, 57, 67
[2213] Pulakesi II's *Maharashtra* extended from Nerbudda (Narmada river) in the north to Tungabhadra in the south (Vaidya 1924, p. 171)
[2214] Kamath (2001), p. 60
[2215] From the notes of Arab traveller Tabari (Kamath 2001, p. 60)
[2216] Chopra (2003), p. 75, part 1
[2217] The Buddhist Caves at Aurangabad: Transformations in Art and Religion, Pia Brancaccio, BRILL, 2010 p.82 https://books.google.com/books?id=m_4pXm7dD78C&pg=PA82
[2218] Ramesh (1984), p. 14
[2219] Kamath 2001, pp. 56
[2220] Quote:"Another unhistorical trend met with in the epigraphical records of the 11th and subsequent centuries is the attempt, on the part of the court poets, no doubt, again, with the consent of their masters, to invent mythical genealogies which seek to carry back the antiquity of the royal families not merely to the periods of the epics and the Vedas but to the very moment of their creation in the heavens. As far as the Chalukyas of Vatapi are concerned, the blame of engineering such travesties attaches, once again, to the Western Chalukyas of Kalyani and their Eastern Chalukya contemporaries. The Eastern Chalukyas, for instance, have concocted the following long list of fifty-two names commencing with no less a personage than the divine preserver"(Ramesh 1984, p. 16)
[2221] Dr. Lewis's theory has not found acceptance because the Pallavas were in constant conflict with the Kadambas, prior to the rise of Chalukyas (Kamath 2001, p. 57)
[2222] //en.wikipedia.org/w/index.php?title=Template:Chalukyas&action=edit
[2223] Thapar (2003), p. 326
[2224] Popular theories regarding the name are: *Puli* – "tiger" in Kannada and *Kesin* – "haried" in Sanskrit; *Pole* – "lustrous" in Kannada, from his earliest Badami cliff inscription that literally spells *Polekesi*; *Pole* – from Tamil word *Punai* (to tie a knot; Ramesh 1984, pp. 31–32)
[2225] The name probably meant "the great lion" (Sastri 1955, p. 134)
[2226] The name probably meant "One endowed with the strength of a great lion" (Chopra 2003, p. 73, part 1)
[2227] Kamath (2001), pp. 58–59
[2228] Ramesh (1984), p. 76
[2229] Chopra 2003, p. 74, part 1
[2230] Quote:"His fame spread far and wide even beyond India" (Chopra 2003, p. 75 part 1)
[2231] Quote:"One of the great kings of India". He successfully defied the expansion of king Harshavardhana of Northern India into the deccan. The Aihole inscription by Ravikirti describes how King Harsha lost his *Harsha* or cheerful disposition after his defeat. The Chinese traveller Hiuen Tsiang also confirms Pulakesi II's victory over King Harsha in his travelogue. Pulakesi II took titles such as *Prithvivallabha* and *Dakshinapatha Prithviswamy* (Kamath 2001, pp. 58–60)
[2232] Quote:"Thus began one of the most colourful careers in Indian History" (Ramesh 1984, p. 76)
[2233] Vikramaditya I, who later revived the Chalukya fortunes was born to Pulakesi II and the daughter of Western Ganga monarch Durvinita (Chopra 2003, p. 74, part 1)
[2234] His other queen, an Alupa princess called Kadamba was the daughter of Aluka Maharaja (G.S. Gai in Kamath 2001, p. 94)

[2235] Quote:"The Aihole record gives an impressive list of his military conquests and other achievements. According to the record, he conquered the Kadambas, the Western Gangas, the north Konkan by naval victory, Harsha of Thanesar, the Latas, the Malwas, the Gurjaras (thereby obtaining sovereignty over the Maharashtras), Berar, Maharashtra and Kuntala (with their nine and ninety thousand villages), the Kalingas and the Kosalas, Pishtapura (Pishtapuram in eastern Andhra) and Kanchipuram, whose king had opposed the rise of his power" (Chopra 2003, p. 74 part 1)

[2236] Ramesh (1984), pp. 79–80, pp. 86–87

[2237] According to Dr. R. C. Majumdar, some principalities may have submitted to Pulakesi II out of fear of Harsha of Kanauj (Kamath 2001, p. 59)

[2238] Sastri (1955), pp. 135–136

[2239] Sastri (1955), p. 136

[2240] This is attested to by an inscription behind the Mallikarjuna temple in Badami (Sastri 1955, p. 136)

[2241] Chopra (2003), pp. 75–76, part 1

[2242] From the Gadval plates dated c. 674 of Vikramaditya I (Chopra 2003, p. 76, part 1)

[2243] Chopra (2003), p. 76, part 1

[2244] Sastri (1955), p. 138

[2245] From the Kannada inscription at the Kailasanatha temple in Kanchipuram (Sastri 1955, p. 140)

[2246] Kamath (2001), p. 63

[2247] Thapar (2003), p. 331

[2248] Ramesh (1984), pp. 159–160

[2249] Dikshit, Durga Prasad (1980), p. 166–167, *Political History of the Chālukyas of Badami*, Abhinav Publications, New Delhi, OCLC 831387906

[2250] Ramesh (1984), p. 159

[2251] Ramesh (1984), pp. 173–174

[2252] Poet Bilhanas 12th century Sanskrit work *Vikramadeva Charitam* and Ranna's Kannada work *Gadayuddha* (982) and inscriptions from Nilagunda, Yevvur, Kauthem and Miraj claim Tailapa II was son of Vikramaditya IV, seventh in descent from Bhima, brother of Badami Chalukya Vikramaditya II (Kamath 2001, p. 100)

[2253] Kings of the Chalukya line of Vemulavada, who were certainly from the Badami Chalukya family line used the title "Malla" which is often used by the Western Chalukyas. Names such as "Satyashraya" which were used by the Badami Chalukya are also names of a Western Chalukya king, (Gopal B.R. in Kamath 2001, p. 100)

[2254] Unlike the Badami Chalukyas, the Kalyani Chalukyas did not claim to be *Harithiputhras* of *Manavysya gotra* in lineage. The use of titles like *Tribhuvanamalla* marked them as of a distinct line (Fleet, Bhandarkar and Altekar in Kamath 2001, p. 100)

[2255] Later legends and tradition hailed Tailapa as an incarnation of the God Krishna who fought 108 battles against the race of Ratta (Rashtrakuta) and captured 88 fortresses from them (Sastri 1955, p. 162)

[2256] From his c. 957 and c.965 records (Kamath 2001, p. 101

[2257] Vijnyaneshavara, the Sanskrit scholar in his court, eulogised him as "a king like none other" (Kamath 2001, p. 106)

[2258] The writing *Vikramankadevacharita* by Bilhana is a eulogy of the achievements of the king in 18 cantos (Sastri, 1955 p. 315)

[2259] Cousens 1926, p. 11

[2260] Vikrama–Chalukya era of 1075 CE (Thapar 2003, p. 469)

[2261] Chopra (2003), p. 139, part 1

[2262] Sastri (1955), p. 175

[2263] Kamath (2001), pp. 114–115

[2264] Narasimhacharya (1988), pp. 18–20

[2265] Sastri (1955), p. 192

[2266] Pulakesi II made Vishnuvardhana the *Yuvaraja* or crown prince. Later Vishnuvardhana become the founder of the Eastern Chalukya empire (Sastri 1955, pp. 134–136, p. 312)

[2267] Chopra (2003), p. 132, part 1

[2268] Kamath (2001), p. 8

[2269] Kamath 2001, p. 60
[2270] Chopra (2003), p. 133
[2271] Sastri (1955), pp. 164–165
[2272] Sastri (1955), p. 165
[2273] Narasimhacharya (1988), p. 68
[2274] The Eastern Chalukya inscriptions show a gradual shift towards Telugu with the appearance of Telugu stanzas from the time of king Gunaga Vijayaditya (Vijayaditya III) in the middle of the 9th century,
[2275] The first work of Telugu literature is a translation of *Mahabharata* by Nannaya during the rule of Eastern Chalukya king Rajaraja Narendra (1019–1061; Sastri 1955, p. 367)
[2276] by Tartakov, Gary Michael (1997), *The Durga Temple at Aihole: A Historiographical Study*, Oxford University Press,
[2277] Hardy (1995), p. 5
[2278] Quote"The Badami Chalukyas had introduced a glorious chapter, alike in heroism in battle and cultural magnificence in peace, in the western Deccan" (K.V. Sounder Rajan in Kamath 2001, p. 68)
[2279] Kamath 2001, p. 68
[2280] Tarr, Gary (1970), p.156, *Chronology and Development of the Chāḷukya Cave Temples*, Ars Orientalis, Vol. 8, pp. 155–184
[2281] Hardy (1995), p. 65
[2282] Sastri (1955), p. 406
[2283] Quote:"The Chalukyas cut rock like titans but finished like jewellers"(Sheshadri in Kamath 2001, pp. 68–69)
[2284] Percy Brown in Kamath (2001), p. 68
[2285] Sastri (1955), p. 407
[2286] Hardy (1995), p. 67
[2287] Foekema (2003), p. 11
[2288] Sastri (1955), pp. 407–408
[2289] Carol Radcliffe Bolon, (1980) pp. 303–326, *The Pārvatī Temple, Sandur and Early Images of Agastya*, Artibus Asiae Vol. 42, No. 4
[2290] Hardy (1995), p.342, p.278
[2291] Sastri (1955), p. 408
[2292] Kamath (2001), p. 69
[2293] Quote:"Their creations have the pride of place in Indian art tradition" (Kamath 2001, p. 115)
[2294] Sastri (1955), p. 427
[2295] Cousens (1926, p 17
[2296] Foekema (1996), p. 14
[2297] Hardy (1995), p. 156
[2298] Hardy (1995), pp. 6–7
[2299] Cousens (1926), pp. 100–102
[2300] Hardy (1995), p. 333
[2301] Cousens (1926), pp. 79–82
[2302] Hardy (1995), p. 336
[2303] Hardy (1995), p. 323
[2304] The Mahadeva Temple at Itagi has been called the finest in Kannada country after the Hoysaleswara temple at Halebidu (Cousens in Kamath 2001, p 117)
[2305] Cousens (1926), pp. 114–115
[2306] Hardy (1995), p. 326
[2307] Cousens (1926), pp. 85–87
[2308] Hardy (1995), p. 330
[2309] Foekema (2003), p. 52
[2310] Hardy (1995), p. 321
[2311]
[2312] The Badami Chalukyas influenced the art of the rulers of Vengi and those of Gujarat (Kamath 2001, pp. 68, 69)

[2313] Quote:"He deemed himself the peer of Bharavi and Kalidasa". An earlier inscription in Mahakuta, in prose is comparable to the works of Bana (Sastri, 1955, p. 312)
[2314] Sastri, 1955, p. 312
[2315] The writing is on various topics including traditional medicine, music, precious stones, dance etc. (Kamath 2001, p. 106)
[2316] Sen (1999), p. 366
[2317] Thapar (2003), p. 345
[2318] Sahitya Akademi (1988), p. 1717
[2319]
[2320] Such as Indranandi's *Srutavatara*, Devachandra's *Rajavalikathe* (Narasimhacharya, 1934, pp. 4–5); Bhattakalanka's *Sabdanusasana* of 1604 (Sastri 1955, p. 355)
[2321] Sastri (1955), p. 355
[2322] Mugali (1975), p. 13
[2323] Narasimhacharya (1988), p. 4
[2324] Sastri 1955, p. 356
[2325] Chopra (2003), p. 196, part 1
[2326] Sastri (1955), p. 367
[2327] Chopra (2003), p. 77, part1
[2328] Kamath (2001), p. 64
[2329] Kamath 2001, pp. 57, 65
[2330] The breakup of land into *mandalas*, *vishaya* existed in the Kadamba administrative machinery (Kamath 2001, pp. 36, 65, 66)
[2331] Kamath (2001), p. 65
[2332] However, they issued gold coins that weighed 120 grams, in imitation of the Gupta dynasty (A.V. Narasimha Murthy in Kamath 2001, p. 65)
[2333] //en.wikipedia.org/w/index.php?title=Template:Karnataka_History&action=edit
[2334] Chopra (2003), p. 191, part 1
[2335] Sastri (1955), p. 391
[2336] Kamath 2001, p. 66
[2337] Chopra (2003), p. 78, part 1
[2338] Vinopoti, a concubine of King Vijayaditya is mentioned with due respect in an inscription (Kamath 2001, p. 67)
[2339] One record mentions an artist called Achala who was well versed in *Natyashastra* (Kamath 2001, p. 67)
[2340] From the Shiggaon plates of c. 707 and Gudigeri inscription dated 1076 (Ramesh 1984, pp. 142, 144)
[2341] Cousens (1926), p. 59
[2342] Sastri (1955), p. 309
[2343] Sastri (1955), p. 324
[2344] //doi.org/10.2307/3249519
[2345] //www.jstor.org/stable/3249519
[2346] //www.worldcat.org/oclc/37526233
[2347] //lccn.loc.gov/80905179
[2348] //www.worldcat.org/oclc/7796041
[2349] //www.worldcat.org/oclc/8221605
[2350] //www.worldcat.org/oclc/2492406
[2351] //www.worldcat.org/oclc/567370037
[2352] //www.worldcat.org/oclc/6814734
[2353] https://web.archive.org/web/20061206081329/http://www.aponline.gov.in/Quick%20links/HIST-CULT/history_ancient.html#ChalukyasPart
[2354] http://www.aponline.gov.in/quick%20links/hist-cult/history_ancient.html#ChalukyasPart
[2355] http://www.indoarch.org/place.php?placelink=R%3D5%2BS%3D18%2BP%3D0%2BM%3D0
[2356] https://web.archive.org/web/20070210222449/http://www.deccanherald.com/deccanherald/jul262005/spectrum1422512005725.asp
[2357] http://www.deccanherald.com/deccanherald/jul262005/spectrum1422512005725.asp

[2358] http://www.kamat.com/kalranga/deccan/chalukya/
[2359] http://www.kamat.com/kalranga/kar/literature/history1.htm
[2360] http://www.art-and-archaeology.com/india/aihole/aihplan.html
[2361] http://www.art-and-archaeology.com/india/badami/baplan.html
[2362] http://www.art-and-archaeology.com/india/pattadakal/pat0.html
[2363] http://www.kamat.com/kalranga/deccan/chalukya/kalyani.htm
[2364] https://web.archive.org/web/20060815095514/http://Prabhu.50g.com/southind/alupa/south_alupacat.html
[2365] http://prabhu.50g.com/southind/alupa/south_alupacat.html
[2366] Ancient Jaffna: Being a Research Into the History of Jaffna from Very Early Times to the Portuguese Period, C. Rasanayagam, p.241, Asian Educational Services 1926
[2367] The journal of the Numismatic Society of India, Volume 51, p.109
[2368] Alī Jāvīd and Tabassum Javeed. (2008). World heritage monuments and related edifices in India, p.107 https://books.google.com/books?id=54XBlIF9LFgC&pg=PA107
[2369] KR Subramanian. (1989). Buddhist remains in Āndhra and the history of Āndhra between 224 & 610 A.D, p.71: *The Pallavas were first a Telugu and not a Tamil power. Telugu traditions know a certain Trilochana Pallava as the earliest Telugu King and they are confirmed by later inscriptions.* https://books.google.com/books?id=vnO2BMPdYEoC&pg=PA71
[2370]
[2371] Rev. H Heras, SJ (1931) Pallava Genealogy: An attempt to unify the Pallava Pedigrees of the Inscriptions, Indian Historical Research Institute
[2372] KR Subramanian. (1989). Buddhist remains in Āndhra and the history of Āndhra between 224 & 610 A.D, p.106-109
[2373] Marilyn Hirsh (1987) Mahendravarman I Pallava: Artist and Patron of Māmallapuram, Artibus Asiae, Vol. 48, Number 1/2 (1987), pp. 109-130
[2374] Rajan K. (Jan-Feb 2008). Situating the Beginning of Early Historic Times in Tamil Nadu: Some Issues and Reflections, Social Scientist, Vol. 36, Number 1/2, pp. 40-78
[2375] Heras, p 38
[2376] Kulke and Rothermund, pp121–122
[2377] Nilakanta Sastri, pp412–413
[2378] Nilakanta Sastri, p139
[2379] Nilakanta Sastri, *A History of South India*, p.91
[2380] Nilakanta Sastri, *A History of South India*, p.91–92
[2381]
[2382] Kulke and Rothermund, p.120
[2383] Kulke and Rothermund, p111
[2384] S.Krishnaswami Aiyangar. Some Contributions Of South India To Indian Culture. Early History of the Pallavas http://chestofbooks.com/history/india/South-India-Culture/Chapter-VIII-Early-History-Of-The-Pallavas.html
[2385] //en.wikipedia.org/w/index.php?title=Template:History_of_Andhra_Pradesh&action=edit
[2386] Rao 1994, p. 36.
[2387] K. A. Nilakanta Sastri & N Venkataramanayya 1960, p. 471.
[2388] N. Ramesan 1975, p. 7.
[2389] N. Ramesan 1975, pp. 4-5.
[2390] Nagabhusanasarma 2008, p. 62.
[2391] The Early History of the Deccan, Volume 2 & 2009 498.
[2392] Rao 1994, pp. 53,54.
[2393] Kumari 2008, p. 134.
[2394] Rao 1994, pp. 49,50.
[2395] Rao 1994, p. 55.
[2396] Rao 1994, p. 56.
[2397] N. Ramesan 1975, p. 2.
[2398] Rao 1994, pp. 54,55.
[2399] Rao 1994, p. 48.
[2400] Rao 1994, pp. 42,55.
[2401] //en.wikipedia.org/w/index.php?title=Template:Chalukyas&action=edit

[2402] http://www.dli.ernet.in/handle/2015/531155
[2403] //www.worldcat.org/oclc/59001459
[2404] http://www.dli.ernet.in/handle/2015/175058
[2405] //www.worldcat.org/oclc/4885004
[2406] https//books.google.co.in
[2407] https//books.google.co.in
[2408] https//books.google.co.in
[2409] //en.wikipedia.org/w/index.php?title=Template:TNhistory&action=edit
[2410] The First Spring: The Golden Age of India – Abraham Eraly – Google Books https://books.google.com/books?id=te1sqTzTxD8C&pg=PA72&lpg=PA72. Books.google.co.in. Retrieved on 12 July 2013.
[2411] Sri Lanka and South-East Asia: Political, Religious and Cultural Relations from A.D. C. 1000 to C. 1500, 1978 By W. M. Sirisena, 57 p.
[2412] Politics of Tamil Nationalism in Sri Lanka, South Asian Publishers, 1996 By Ambalavanar Sivarajah, 22 p.
[2413] Mahabharata Book Eight: Karna By Adam Bowles
[2414] The Mahabharata of Krishna-Dwaipayana Vyasa translated into ..., Volume 8 By Kisari Mohan Ganguli
[2415] Kulke and Rothermund, p104
[2416] Keay, p119
[2417] S. Dhammika, *The Edicts of King Ashoka: An English Rendering* http://www.cs.colostate.edu/~malaiya/ashoka.html Buddhist Publication Society, Kandy (1994)
[2418] India By John Keay
[2419] *Periplus* 54. Original Greek: "Ἡ δὲ Νέλκυνδα σταδίους μὲν ἀπὸ Μουζιρέως ἀπέχει σχεδὸν πεντακοσίους, ὁμοίως διά τε ποταμοῦ (καὶ πεζῇ) καὶ διὰ θαλάσσης, βασιλείας δέ ἐστιν ἑτέρας, τῆς Πανδίονος· κεῖται δὲ καὶ αὐτὴ παρὰ ποταμόν, ὡσεὶ ἀπὸ σταδίων ἑκατὸν εἴκοσι τῆς θαλάσσης."
[2420] Hill, John
[2421] Strabo, Geography, BOOK XV., CHAPTER I., section 73 http://www.perseus.tufts.edu/hopper/text?doc=Perseus%3Atext%3A1999.01.0239%3Abook%3D15%3Achapter%3D1%3Asection%3D73. Perseus.tufts.edu. Retrieved on 12 July 2013.
[2422] Keay, p121
[2423] Travel and ethnology in the Renaissance: South India through European eyes, Joan-Pau Rubiés https://books.google.com/books?id=adpkHQ9ScQ0C&pg=PA5
[2424] Muslim identity, print culture, and the Dravidian factor in Tamil Nadu, J. B. Prashant More https://books.google.com/books?id=11FYACaVySoC&pg=PA9
[2425] Layers of blackness: colourism in the African diaspora, Deborah Gabriel https://books.google.com/books?id=0-yEfRP0RwgC&pg=PA110
[2426] The Ramayana, The Great Hindu Epic Translated by R C Dutt, RAMAYANA BOOK VII: KISHKINDHA (Part – VI THE QUEST FOR SITA)
[2427] N. Subrahmanian 1962, pp. 133-136.
[2428] //en.wikipedia.org/w/index.php?title=Template:Part_of_History_of_India&action=edit
[2429] Banarsi Prasad Saksena 1992, p. 412.
[2430] Banarsi Prasad Saksena 1992, p. 414.
[2431] Banarsi Prasad Saksena 1992, pp. 416-417.
[2432] Kishori Saran Lal 1950, pp. 208-213.
[2433] K.K.R. Nair 1987, p. 27.
[2434] Peter Jackson 2003, p. 207.
[2435] Kishori Saran Lal 1950, p. 212.
[2436] Nilakanta Sastri, P.213
[2437] Lindsay (2006) p. 101
[2438] Curtin 1984: 100
[2439] The cyclopædia of India and of Eastern and Southern Asia By Edward Balfour
[2440] Holl 2003: 9
[2441] Venkata Subramanian 1988, p. 55.
[2442] Kulke and Rothermund, p99, p107

[2443] http://depts.washington.edu/silkroad/texts/weilue/weilue.html
[2444] https://archive.is/20161123181101/http://www.dli.ernet.in/handle/2015/462306
[2445] //www.worldcat.org/oclc/43502446
[2446] http://www.dli.ernet.in/handle/2015/462306
[2447] https://books.google.com/books?id=NN4fAAAAIAAJ
[2448] https://books.google.com/books?id=_9cmAQAAMAAJ
[2449] //www.worldcat.org/oclc/31870180
[2450] https://books.google.com/books?id=EgSSAAAAIAAJ
[2451] //www.worldcat.org/issn/0377-0443
[2452] https://books.google.com/books?id=2XXqAQAACAAJ
[2453] //www.worldcat.org/oclc/685167335
[2454] https://books.google.com/books?id=lt2tqOpVRKgC&pg=PA174
[2455] The Rise and Decline of Buddhism in India, K.L. Hazara, Munshiram Manoharlal, 1995, pp288–294
[2456] Reu (1933), p39
[2457] Reu (1933), pp1–5
[2458] Altekar (1934), pp1–32
[2459] Reu (1933), pp6–9, pp47–53
[2460] Reu (1933), p1
[2461] Kamath (2001), p72
[2462]
[2463] Reu (1933), pp1–15
[2464] J. F. Fleet in Reu (1933), p6
[2465] A Kannada dynasty was created in Berar under the rule of Badami Chalukyas (Altekar 1934, p21–26)
[2466] Kamath 2001, p72–3
[2467] A.C. Burnell in Pandit Reu (1933), p4
[2468] C.V. Vaidya (1924), p171
[2469] D.R.Bhandarkar in Reu, (1933), p1, p7
[2470] Hultzsch and Reu in Reu (1933), p2, p4
[2471] Kamath (2001), p73
[2472] Pollock 2006, p332
[2473] Houben(1996), p215
[2474] Altekar (1934), p411–3
[2475] Dalby (1998), p300
[2476] Sen (1999), pp380-381
[2477] During the rule of the Rashtrakutas, literature in Kannada and Sanskrit flowered (Kamath 2001, pp 88–90)
[2478] Even royalty of the empire took part in poetic and literary activities – Thapar (2003), p334
[2479] Narasimhacharya (1988), pp17–18, p68
[2480] Altekar (1934), pp21–24
[2481] Possibly Dravidian Kannada origin (Karmarkar 1947 p26)
[2482] Masica (1991), p45-46
[2483] Rashtrakutas are described as Kannadigas from Lattaluru who encouraged the Kannada language (Chopra, Ravindran, Subrahmanian 2003, p87)
[2484] Reu (1933), p54
[2485] From Rashtrakuta inscriptions call the Badami Chalukya army *Karnatabala* (power of *Karnata*) (Kamath 2001, p57, p65)
[2486] Altekar in Kamath (2001), p72
[2487] Sastri (1955), p141
[2488] Thapar (2003), p333
[2489] Sastri (1955), p143
[2490] Sen (1999), p368
[2491] Desai and Aiyar in Kamath (2001), p75
[2492] Reu (1933), p62
[2493] Sen (1999), p370

[2494] The Rashtrakutas interfered effectively in the politics of Kannauj (Thapar 2003), p333
[2495] From the Karda inscription, a *digvijaya* (Altekar in Kamath 2001, p75)
[2496] The ablest of the Rashtrakuta kings (Altekar in Kamath 2001, p77)
[2497] Modern Morkhandi (Mayurkhandi in Bidar district (Kamath 2001, p76)
[2498] modern Morkhand in Maharashtra (Reu 1933, p65)
[2499] Sooloobunjun near Ellora (Couseris in Altekar 1934, p48). Perhaps Elichpur remained the capital until Amoghavarsha I built Manyakheta. From the Wani-Dmdori, Radhanpur and Kadba plates, Morkhand in Maharashtra was only a military encampment, from the Dhulia and Pimpen plates it seems Nasik was only a seat of a viceroy, and the Paithan plates of Govinda III indicate that neither Latur nor Paithan was the early capital.(Altekar, 1934, pp47–48)
[2500] Kamath 2001, MCC, p76
[2501] From the Sanjan inscriptions,
[2502] Keay (2000), p199
[2503] From the Nesari records (Kamath 2001, p76)
[2504] Reu (1933), p65
[2505] Sastri (1955), p144
[2506] "The victorious march of his armies had literally embraced all the territory between the Himalayas and Cape Comorin" (Altekar in Kamath 2001, p77)
[2507] Sen (1999), p371
[2508] Which could put to shame even the capital of gods-From Karda plates (Altekar 1934, p47)
[2509] A capital city built to excel that of Indra (Sastri, 1955, p4, p132, p146)
[2510] Reu 1933, p71
[2511] from the Cambay and Sangli records. The Bagumra record claims that Amoghavarsha saved the "Ratta" kingdom which was drowned in a "ocean of Chalukyas" (Kamath 2001, p78)
[2512] Sastri (1955), p145
[2513] Narasimhacharya (1988), p1
[2514] Reu (1933), p38
[2515] Panchamukhi in Kamath (2001), p80
[2516] Sastri (1955), p161
[2517] From the writings of Adikavi Pampa (Kamath 2001, p81)
[2518] Sen (1999), pp373-374
[2519] Kamath (2001), p82
[2520] The Rashtrakutas of Manyakheta gained control over Kannauj for a brief period during the early 10th century (Thapar 2003, p333)
[2521] From the Siddalingamadam record of 944 – Krishna III captured Kanchi and Tanjore as well and had full control over northern Tamil regions (Aiyer in Kamath 2001, pp82–83)
[2522] From the Tirukkalukkunram inscription – Kanchi and Tanjore were annexed by Krishna III. From the Deoli inscription – Krishna III had feudatories from Himalayas to Ceylon. From the Laksmeshwar inscription – Krishna III was an incarnation of death for the Chola Dynasty (Reu 1933, p83)
[2523] Conqueror of Kanchi, (Thapar 2003, p334)
[2524] Conqueror of Kanchi and Tanjore (Sastri 1955, p162)
[2525] Sen 1999), pp374-375
[2526] The province of Tardavadi in the very heart of the Rashtrakuta empire was given to Tailapa II as a *fief* (provincial grant) by Rashtrakuta Krishna III for services rendered in war (Sastri 1955, p162)
[2527] Kamath (2001), p101
[2528] Kamath (2001), pp100–103
[2529] Reu (1933), p39–41
[2530] Keay (2000), p200
[2531] Kamath (2001), p94
[2532] Burjor Avari (2007), *India: The Ancient Past:* A History of the Indian Sub-Continent from c. 7000 BC to AD 1200, *pp.207–208, Routledge, New York,*
[2533] Reu (1933), p93
[2534] Reu (1933), p100
[2535] Reu (1933), p113

[2536] Reu (1933), p110
[2537] Jain (2001), pp67–75
[2538] Reu (1933), p112
[2539] De Bruyne (1968)
[2540] Majumdar (1966), pp50–51
[2541] //en.wikipedia.org/w/index.php?title=Template:Karnataka_History&action=edit
[2542] whose main responsibility was to draft and maintain inscriptions or *Shasanas* as would an archivist. (Altekar in Kamath (2001), p85
[2543] Kamath (2001), p86
[2544] From the notes of Al Masudi (Kamath 2001, p88)
[2545] Kamath (2001), p88
[2546] Altekar (1934), p356
[2547] Altekar (1934), p355
[2548] From notes of Periplus, Al Idrisi and Alberuni (Altekar 1934, p357)
[2549]
[2550] Altekar (1934), p358
[2551] Altekar (1934), p358–359
[2552] Altekar (1934), p368
[2553] Altekar (1934), p370–371
[2554] Altekar (1934), p223
[2555] Altekar (1934), p213
[2556] From the Davangere inscription of Santivarma of Banavasi-12000 province (Altekar 1934, p234
[2557] From the writings of Chandesvara (Altekar 1934, p216)
[2558] From the notes of Al Idrisi (Altekar (1934), p223
[2559] From the Begumra plates of Krishna II (Altekar 1934, p227
[2560]
[2561]
[2562] Altekar (1934), p242
[2563] From the writings of Somadeva (Altekar 1934, p244)
[2564] From the Hebbal inscriptions and Torkhede inscriptions of Govinda III (Altekar 1934, p232
[2565] "Wide and sympathetic tolerance" in general characterised the Rashtrakuta rule (Altekar in Kamath 2001, p92)
[2566] Kamath (2001), p92
[2567] Altekar in Kamath (2001), p92
[2568] Reu (1933), p36
[2569] The Vaishnava Rashtrakutas patronised Jainism (Kamath 2001, p92)
[2570] Kamath (2001), p91
[2571] Reu (1933), p34
[2572] Reu (1933, p34
[2573] A 16th-century Buddhist work by Lama Taranatha speaks disparagingly of Shankaracharya as close parallels in some beliefs of Shankaracharya with Buddhist philosophy was not viewed favourably by Buddhist writers (Thapar 2003, pp 349–350, 397)
[2574] From the notes of 10th-century Arab writer Al-Ishtakhri (Sastri 1955, p396)
[2575] From the notes of Masudi (916) (Sastri 1955, p396)
[2576] From the notes of Magasthenesis and Strabo from Greece and Ibn Khurdadba and Al Idrisi from Arabia (Altekar 1934, p317)
[2577] From the notes of Alberuni (Altekar 1934, p317)
[2578] Altekar (1934), p318
[2579] From the notes of Alberuni (Altekar 1934, p324)
[2580] From the notes of Alberuni (Altekar 1934, pp330–331)
[2581] From the notes of Alberuni, Altekar (1934) p325
[2582] From the notes of Abuzaid (Altekar 1934, p325)
[2583] From the notes of Alberuni (Altekar 1934, p326)
[2584] Altekar (1934), p329
[2585] From the notes of Yuan Chwang, Altekar (1934), p331
[2586] From the notes of Alberuni (Altekar 1934, p332, p334)

[2587] From the notes of Ibn Khurdadba (Altekar 1934, p337)
[2588] From the notes of Alberuni (Altekar 1934, p337)
[2589] From the notes of Al Masudi and Al Idrisi (Altekar 1934, p339)
[2590] From the Tarkhede inscription of Govinda III, (Altekar 1934, p339)
[2591] Altekar (1934), p341
[2592] From the notes of Alberuni (Altekar 1934, p342)
[2593] From the notes of Sulaiman and Alberuni (Altekar 1934, p343)
[2594] Altekar (1934), p345
[2595] From the notes of Ibn Khurdadba (Altekar 1934, p346)
[2596] Altekar (1934), p349
[2597] Altekar (1934), p350
[2598] Altekar (1934), p351
[2599] From the notes of Ibn Kurdadba (Altekar 1934, p353)
[2600] Warder A.K. (1988), p. 248
[2601] Kamath (2001), p89
[2602] "Mathematical Achievements of Pre-modern Indian Mathematicians", Putta Swamy T.K., 2012, chapter=Mahavira, p.231, Elsevier Publications, London,
[2603]
[2604] The *Bedande* and *Chattana* type of composition (Narasimhacharya 1988, p12)
[2605] It is said *Kavirajamarga* may have been co-authored by Amoghavarsha I and court poet Sri Vijaya (Sastri 1955, pp355–356)
[2606] Other early writers mentioned in *Kavirajamarga* are Vimala, Udaya, Nagarjuna, Jayabhandu for Kannada prose and Kavisvara, Pandita, Chandra and Lokapala in Kannada poetry (Narasimhacharya 1988, p2)
[2607] Warder A.K. (1988), p240
[2608] Sastri (1955), p356
[2609] L.S. Seshagiri Rao in Amaresh Datta (1988), p1180
[2610] Narasimhacharya (1988, p18
[2611] Sastri (1955), p314
[2612] S.K. Ramachandra Rao, (1985), Encyclopedia of Indian Medicine: Historical perspective, pp100-101, Popular Prakashan, Mumbai,
[2613] Narasimhachar (1988), p11
[2614] Hardy (1995), p111
[2615] Hardy (1995), p327
[2616] Vincent Smith in
[2617] Percy Brown and James Fergusson in
[2618] Kamath (2001), p93
[2619] Arthikaje in
[2620] Grousset in
[2621] Hardy (1995), p.341
[2622] Hardy (1995), p344-345
[2623] Sundara and Rajashekar,
[2624] Hardy (1995), p5 (introduction)
[2625] Thapar (2002), pp393–4
[2626] Thapar (2002), p396
[2627] Vaidya (1924), p170
[2628] Sastri (1955), p355
[2629] Rice, E.P. (1921), p12
[2630] Rice, B.L. (1897), p497
[2631] Altekar (1934), p404
[2632] Altekar (1934), p408
[2633] //www.worldcat.org/oclc/3793499
[2634] //lccn.loc.gov/80905179
[2635] //www.worldcat.org/oclc/7796041
[2636] //www.worldcat.org/oclc/8221605
[2637] //www.worldcat.org/oclc/6814734

[2638] https://web.archive.org/web/20061104123203/http://www.ourkarnataka.com/states/history/historyofkarnataka18.htm
[2639] http://www.ourkarnataka.com/states/history/historyofkarnataka18.htm
[2640] http://www.kamat.com/kalranga/deccan/deckings.htm
[2641] http://www.whatisindia.com/inscriptions/south_indian_inscriptions/volume_9/rashtrakutas.html
[2642] http://archive.wikiwix.com/cache/20110707080339/http://asi.nic.in/
[2643] Pollock (2006), pp. 288–289, 332
[2644] Houben(1996), p. 215
[2645] Kamath (2001), pp10–12, p100
[2646] The province of Tardavadi, lying in the very heart of the Rashtrakuta empire, was given to Tailapa II as a *fief* (provincial grant) by Rashtrakuta Krishna III for services rendered in war (Sastri 1955, p162)
[2647] Kamath (2001), p101
[2648] poet Bilhana's 12th-century Sanskrit work *Vikramadeva Charitam* and Ranna's Kannada work *Gadayuddha* (982) and inscriptions from Nilagunda, Yevvur, Kauthem and Miraj claim Tailapa II was son of Vikramaditya IV, seventh in descent from Bhima, brother of Badami Chalukya Vikramaditya II (Kamath 2001, p100)
[2649] Kings of the Chalukya line of Vemulavada, who were certainly from the Badami Chalukya family line used the title "Malla" which is often used by the Western Chalukyas. Names such as "Satyashraya" which were used by the Badami Chalukya are also name of a Western Chalukya king, (Gopal B.R. in Kamath 2001, p100)
[2650] Unlike the Badami Chalukyas, the Kalyani Chalukyas did not claim to be *Harithiputhras* of *Manavysya gotra* in lineage. The use of titles like *Tribhuvanamalla* marked them of as a distinct line (Fleet, Bhandarkar and Altekar in Kamath 2001, p100)
[2651] Moraes (1931), pp88-93
[2652] Later legends and tradition hailed Tailapa as an incarnation of the God Krishna who fought 108 battles against the race of Ratta (Rashtrakuta) and captured 88 fortresses from them (Sastri 1955, p162)
[2653] According to a 973 inscription, Tailapa II helped by Kadambas of Hangal, destroyed the Rattas (Rashtrakutas), killed the valiant Munja (of the Paramara kingdom), took the head of Panchala (Ganga dynasty) and restored the royal dignity of the Chalukyas (Moraes 1931, pp 93–94)
[2654] Sastri (1955), p164
[2655] A minor capital of Jayasimha II (Cousens 1926, p10, p105)
[2656] King Rajaraja Chola conquered parts of Chalukya territory in present-day South Karnataka by subjugating the Western Ganga Dynasty of Gangavadi (Kamath 2001, p102)
[2657] From the Hottur inscriptions dated 1007 – 1008, Satyashraya was able to defeat crown prince Rajendra Chola (Kamath 2001, p102)
[2658] Sen (1999), p383
[2659] Jayasimha's choice was Vijayaditya VII while the Cholas sought to place Rajaraja Narendra, son-in-law of Rajendra Chola I (Kamath 2001, p102
[2660] //en.wikipedia.org/w/index.php?title=Template:Chalukyas&action=edit
[2661] Quote:"Beautified it so that it surpassed all the other cities of the earth" (Cousens 1926, p10)
[2662] Sen (1999), p384
[2663] Ganguli in Kamath 2001, p103
[2664] Sastri (1955), p166
[2665] Someshvara I supported the cause of Shaktivarman II, son of Vijayaditya II while the Cholas preferred Rajendra, son of the previous king Rajaraja Narendra (Kamath 2001, p103)
[2666] Sastri (1955), p169
[2667] Kamath (2001), p104
[2668] Sastri (1955), p170
[2669] Cousens (1926), pp10–11
[2670]
[2671]
[2672]
[2673] Sastri (1955), p171

[2674] Sastri 1955, p172
[2675] Eulogising Vikramaditya VI, Kashmiri poet Bilhana wrote in his *Vikramanakadeva Charita* that lord Shiva himself advised Chalukya Vikramaditya VI to replace his elder brother from the throne (Thapar 2003, p468)
[2676] Vikramaditya VI abolished the *saka* era and established the *Vikrama-varsha* (Vikrama era). Most Chalukya inscriptions thereafter are dated to this new era (Cousens 1926, p11)
[2677] Vikramaditya's rule is mentioned as an era (*samvat*) along with Satavahana Vikrama era 58 BCE, Shaka era, of 78 CE, Harshavardhana era of 606 CE (Thapar, 2003, pp 468–469)
[2678] Sen (1999), p386
[2679]
[2680]
[2681]
[2682]
[2683] Vijnyaneshavara, his court scholar in Sanskrit, wrote of him as a king like none other (Kamath 2001, p106)
[2684] Cousens (1926), p12
[2685] Bilhana called the reign "Rama Rajya" in his writing that consisted of 18 cantos. The last canto of this work is about the life of author himself who writes that the work was composed by him in gratitude for the great honor bestowed upon him by the ruler of *Karnata* (Sastri 1955, p315)
[2686] Bilhana was made *Vidyapati* (chief pandit) by the king (Cousens 1926, p12)
[2687] No other king prior to the Vijayanagara rulers have left behind so many records as Vikramaditya VI (Kamath 2001, p105)
[2688] Sen (1999), p387
[2689] CNG Coins https://www.cngcoins.com/Coin.aspx?CoinID=302739
[2690] CNG Coins https://www.cngcoins.com/Coin.aspx?CoinID=133198
[2691] Their feudatories, Hoysalas of Mysore region, Kakatiyas of Warangal, Seunas of Devagiri and the Pandyas of Madurai wasted no time in seizing the opportunity, (Sastri 1955,p158)
[2692] Sastri (1955), p176
[2693] Sen (1999), p388
[2694] Kamath (2001), p107
[2695] Cousens (1926), p13
[2696]
[2697] From the Minajagi record of 1184 (Kamath 2001, p109)
[2698] A Kalachuri commander called Barmideva or Brahma is known to have given support to the Chalukyas (Sastri 1955, p179–180)
[2699] Kamath (2001), p127
[2700] Sen (1999), pp388-389
[2701] Sastri (1955), p180
[2702] Sastri (1955), p192
[2703] Kamath (2001), p110
[2704] Kamath (2001), p109
[2705] There was flexibility to the terms used to designate territorial division (Dikshit G.S. in Kamath 2001, p110)
[2706] Coins of Western Chalukyas with Kannada legends have been found (Kamath 2001, p12)
[2707] Kamath (2001), p111
[2708] Thapar (2002), p373
[2709] Thapar (2002), p378
[2710] Sastri (1955), p298
[2711] //en.wikipedia.org/w/index.php?title=Template:Karnataka_History&action=edit
[2712] Thapar (2002), p379
[2713] Thapar (2002), p382
[2714] Sastri (1955), p299
[2715] Sastri (1955), p300
[2716] Thapar (2002), p384
[2717] Sastri (1955), 301
[2718] Thapar (2002), 383

[2719] Sastri (1955), p302
[2720] Kamath (2001), p112, p132
[2721] A 16th-century Buddhist work by Lama Taranatha speaks disparagingly of Shankaracharya as close parallels in some beliefs of Shankaracharya with Buddhist philosophy was not viewed favourably by Buddhist writers (Thapar, 2003, pp 349–350, p397)
[2722] An inscription dated 1095 CE of Vikramaditya VI mentions grants to a *Vihara* of Buddha and Arya-Taradevi (Cousens 1926, p11)
[2723] It is said five earlier saints Renuka, Daruka, Ekorama, Panditharadhya and Vishwaradhya were the original founders of Virashaivism (Kamath 2001, p152)
[2724] However it is argued that these saints were from the same period as Basavanna (Sastri 1955, p393)
[2725] Thapar (2003), p399
[2726] He criticised Adi Shankara as a "Buddhist in disguise" (Kamath 2001, p151)
[2727] Narasimhacharya (1988), p20
[2728] Sastri (1955), p361–362
[2729] Kamath (2001), p182
[2730] Narasimhacharya (1988), p22
[2731] Mack (2001), pp35–36
[2732] Kamath (2001), p152
[2733] She was not only a pioneer in the era of Women's emancipation but also an example of a transcendental world-view (Thapar 2003, p392)
[2734] Sastri (1955), p286
[2735] This is in stark contrast to the literature of the time (like Vikramankadeva Charita of Bilhana) that portrayed women as retiring, overly romantic and unconcerned with affairs of the state (Thapar 2003, p392)
[2736] The Belathur inscription of 1057 describes the end of a widow called Dekabbe who committed Sati despite the requests of her parents not to while some widows such as Chalukya queen Attimabbe long survived their deceased husbands (Kamath 2001, pp 112–113)
[2737] The intellectual qualifications of the Brahmins made them apt to serve as ministers and advisers of Kings(*Rajguru*), (Charles Eliot in Sastri 1955, p289)
[2738] Sastri (1955), p288
[2739] Sastri (1955), p289
[2740] The *Manasollasa* written by King Someshvara III contains significant information of the social life of Western Chalukyan times (Kamath 2001, p112)
[2741] Orchestras were popularised by the Kalamukhas, a cult who worshipped Lord Shiva (Kamath 2001, p115)
[2742] Sastri (1955), p292
[2743] Kamath (2001), p114
[2744] Sen (1999), p. 393
[2745] S.S.Basavanal in Puranik, p4452, (1992)
[2746] Sastri (1955), p361
[2747] Narasimhacharya (1988), pp18–20
[2748] The other two gems are Adikavi Pampa and Sri Ponna (Sastri 1955, p356)
[2749] A composition written in a mixed prose-verse style is called Champu (Narasimhacharya 1988, p12)
[2750] This also is in *Champu* style and was written at the request of Attimabbe, a pious widow of general Nagavarma who promoted the cause of Jainism (Sastri 1955, p356)
[2751] E.P.Rice (1921), p32
[2752] Narasimhacharya (1988), pp64–65,
[2753] E.P.Rice (1921), p34
[2754] Nagavarma II was the teacher (*guru*) of another noteworthy scholar Janna who later adorned the court of Hoysala Empire (Sastri 1955, p358)
[2755] Narasimhachar (1988), p.63
[2756] Vachanas are disconnected paragraphs ending with a name attributed to lord Shiva or one of his forms. The poems teach the valuelessness of riches, rituals and book learning and the spiritual privileges of worshipping Shiva, (B.L. Rice in Sastri 1955, p361)

[2757] Thapar (2003), p394
[2758] "Mathematical Achievements of Pre-modern Indian Mathematicians", Putta Swamy T.K., 2012, chapter=Bhaskara II, p331, Elsevier Publications, London,
[2759] Thapar, (2003), p393
[2760] Sastri (1955), p315
[2761] A Textbook of Historiography, 500 B.C. to A.D. 2000 by E. Sreedharan p.328
[2762] Sastri (1955), p324
[2763] *Sangita Ratnakara* being written in the court of feudatory Seuna kingdom, (Kamath 2001, p115)
[2764] An important period in the development of Indian art (Kamath 2001, p115)
[2765] Sastri (1955), p427
[2766] A fabulous revival of Chalukya temple building in central Karnataka in the 11th century (Foekema (1996), p14)
[2767] Hardy (1995), pp156-157
[2768] Davison-Jenkins (2001), p89
[2769] Cousens (1926), pp79–82
[2770] Hardy (1995), p336
[2771] Cousens (1926), pp114–115
[2772] Hardy (1995), p326
[2773] Kamath (2001), p117
[2774] Hardy (1995), p323
[2775] Cousens (1926), pp85–87
[2776] Hardy (1995), p330
[2777] Hardy (1995), p321
[2778] Cousens (1926), pp100–102
[2779] Hardy (1995), p333
[2780] Hardy (1995), p335
[2781] Hardy (1995), p324
[2782] Quote:"A title it fully deserves, for it is probably the finest temple in Kanarese districts, after Halebidu"(Cousens 1926, p101)
[2783] Cousens (1926), pp105–106
[2784] Hardy (1995), p 157
[2785] Kamath (2001), pp116–118
[2786] Hardy (1995), pp6–7
[2787] Pollock (2006), p332
[2788] Houben(1996), p215
[2789] Thousands of Kannada language inscriptions are ascribed by Vikramaditya VI and pertain to his daily land and charitable grants (*Nityadana*),
[2790] Kannada enjoyed patronage from royalty, influential Jains and the Lingayat movement of Virashaivas (Thapar 2003, p396)
[2791] However by the 14th century, bilingual inscriptions lost favour and inscriptions became mostly in the local language (Thapar, 2003, pp393–95)
[2792]
[2793] E.P.Rice (1921), p33
[2794] //www.worldcat.org/oclc/37526233
[2795] //lccn.loc.gov/80905179
[2796] //www.worldcat.org/oclc/7796041
[2797] http://www.indoarch.org/place.php?placelink=R%3D5%2BS%3D18%2BP%3D0%2BM%3D0
[2798] http://www.kamat.com/kalranga/deccan/deckings.htm
[2799] http://www.whatisindia.com/inscriptions/
[2800] https://web.archive.org/web/20061006025111/http://chitralakshana.com/articles/UB%20githa/balligavi.htm
[2801] https://www.chitralakshana.com/articles/UB%20githa/balligavi.htm
[2802] http://www.art-and-archaeology.com/india/india.html
[2803] http://www.templenet.com/Karnataka/kalyani_chalukya.html

[2804] https://web.archive.org/web/20060815095514/http://prabhu.50g.com/southind/alupa/south_alupacat.html
[2805] http://prabhu.50g.com/southind/alupa/south_alupacat.html
[2806] https://www.forumancientcoins.com/india/southind/chalukya/south_chalcat.html
[2807] http://www.hinduonnet.com/2002/06/10/stories/2002061003760500.htm
[2808] *The quoted pages can be read at Google Book Search https://books.google.com/.*
[2809] Suryanath Kamat 1980, pp. 136-137.
[2810] The Dynasties of the Kanarese Districts of the Bombay Presidency"(1894) J.F.Fleet, Gazetteer of the Bombay Presidency (Vol-1, Part-II, Book-III)
[2811] A. V. Narasimha Murthy 1971, p. 32.
[2812] T. V. Mahalingam 1957, p. 137.
[2813] A. S. Altekar 1960, p. 515.
[2814] A. S. Altekar 1960, p. 516.
[2815] A. S. Altekar 1960, pp. 515-516.
[2816] Christian Lee Novetzke 2016, p. 53.
[2817] Christian Lee Novetzke 2016, p. 316.
[2818] Colin P. Masica 1993, p. 45.
[2819] Christian Lee Novetzke 2016, p. 314.
[2820] Christian Lee Novetzke 2016, pp. 51-54.
[2821] Shrinivas Ritti 1973.
[2822] World Heritage Sites - Ellora Caves http://asi.nic.in/asi_monu_whs_ellora.asp, Archeological Survey of India (2011), Government of India
[2823] T. V. Mahalingam 1957, p. 138.
[2824] A. S. Altekar 1960, p. 517.
[2825] A. S. Altekar 1960, p. 518.
[2826] T. V. Mahalingam 1957, p. 139.
[2827] A. S. Altekar 1960, p. 518-519.
[2828] A. S. Altekar 1960, p. 519.
[2829] A. S. Altekar 1960, p. 522.
[2830] A. S. Altekar 1960, p. 523.
[2831] A. S. Altekar 1960, p. 524.
[2832] T. V. Mahalingam 1957, p. 140.
[2833] A. S. Altekar 1960, p. 525.
[2834] A. S. Altekar 1960, p. 529.
[2835] T. V. Mahalingam 1957, p. 143.
[2836] T. V. Mahalingam 1957, p. 144.
[2837] A. S. Altekar 1960, p. 531.
[2838] T. V. Mahalingam 1957, p. 147.
[2839] A. S. Altekar 1960, p. 532.
[2840] T. V. Mahalingam 1957, p. 145.
[2841] A. S. Altekar 1960, p. 534.
[2842] A. S. Altekar 1960, p. 533.
[2843] A. S. Altekar 1960, p. 535.
[2844] A. S. Altekar 1960, pp. 535-536.
[2845] A. S. Altekar 1960, p. 536.
[2846] A. S. Altekar 1960, pp. 536-537.
[2847] A. S. Altekar 1960, p. 537.
[2848] T. V. Mahalingam 1957, p. 146.
[2849] A. S. Altekar 1960, p. 538.
[2850] A. S. Altekar 1960, pp. 538-539.
[2851] A. S. Altekar 1960, p. 544.
[2852] T. V. Mahalingam 1957, p. 148.
[2853] A. S. Altekar 1960, p. 546.
[2854] A. S. Altekar 1960, p. 547.
[2855] T. V. Mahalingam 1957, p. 150.
[2856] A. S. Altekar 1960, pp. 548-549.

2857 T. V. Mahalingam 1957, p. 151.
2858 A. S. Altekar 1960, p. 549.
2859 T. V. Mahalingam 1957, p. 152.
2860 A. S. Altekar 1960, p. 550.
2861 A. S. Altekar 1960, p. 551.
2862 Eternal Garden: Mysticism, History, and Politics at a South Asian Sufi Center by Carl W. Ernst p.107
2863 . *The quoted pages can be read at Google Book Search https://books.google.com/*.
2864 "Yādava Dynasty" Encyclopædia Britannica. Encyclopædia Britannica 2007 Ultimate Reference Suite
2865 A. S. Altekar 1960, pp. 516-551.
2866 T. V. Mahalingam 1957, pp. 137-152.
2867 Cynthia Talbot 2001, p. 211.
2868 Cynthia Talbot 2001, p. 212.
2869 Christian Lee Novetzke 2016, p. 74,86.
2870 Christian Lee Novetzke 2016, p. x,74.
2871 Cynthia Talbot 2001, pp. 211-212.
2872 Onkar Prasad Verma 1970, p. 266.
2873 R. Narasimhacharya, p. 68, *History of Kannada Literature*, 1988, Asian Educational Services, New Delhi, Madras, 1988
2874 Suryanath Kamat 1980, pp. 143-144.
2875 Sujit Mukherjee, p. 410, p. 247, "Dictionary of Indian Literature One: Beginnings - 1850", 1999, Orient Blackswan, Delhi,
2876 Marathyancha Itihaas by Dr. S.G Kolarkar, p.4, Shri Mangesh Prakashan, Nagpur.
2877 https://books.google.ca/books?id=14DvAQAACAAJ5
2878 //www.worldcat.org/oclc/59001459
2879 https://books.google.com/books?id=jxhY_3vLA_YC
2880 https://books.google.com/books?id=z9kbDQAAQBAJ&pg=PA53
2881 https://books.google.com/books?id=pfAKljlCJq0C&pg=PA212
2882 https://books.google.com/books?id=Itp2twGR6tsC&pg=RA1-PA45
2883 https://books.google.com/books?id=v8ABAAAAMAAJ
2884 //www.worldcat.org/oclc/138387
2885 https://books.google.com/books?id=jYMdAAAAMAAJ
2886 https://books.google.com/books?id=oqY9AAAAMAAJ
2887 https://books.google.com/books?id=ahFuAAAAMAAJ
2888 http://www.whatisindia.com/inscriptions/south_indian_inscriptions/volume_9/yadavas.html
2889 http://www.whatisindia.com/inscriptions/south_indian_inscriptions/volume_15/yadavas.html
2890 http://www.whatisindia.com/inscriptions/south_indian_inscriptions/volume_18/the_yadavas.html
2891 Talbot 2001, p. 26.
2892 //en.wikipedia.org/w/index.php?title=Template:History_of_Andhra_Pradesh&action=edit
2893 ·,·,
2894 Sircar 2008, p. 241.
2895 Kakatiya coins bore the Nandinagari script.(Prasad 1988, p. 9)
2896 Sastry 1978, pp. 22-23.
2897 Sastry 1978, p. 22.
2898 Sastry 1978, pp. 24-25.
2899 Sastry 1978, p. 23.
2900 Sastry 1978, pp. 3-6.
2901 Talbot 2001, pp. 11, 17, 19.
2902 Sastry 1978, pp. 8-12.
2903 Sastry 1978, p. 12.
2904 Sastry 1978, pp. 12-13.
2905 Talbot 2001, p. 53.
2906 Talbot 2001, p. 51.
2907 Sastry 1978, p. 29.

[2908] Sastry 1978, p. 27.
[2909] Sastry 1978, pp. 27-29.
[2910] Sastry 1978, p. 30.
[2911] Quote: "Eriya was succeeded not by his son Beta but by his grandson Gunda IV who, according to the Mangallu grant, in his early career had been deputed by Rashtrakuta Krishna III in 956 to help the Chalukya prince Danarnava in his attempts to oust his step-brother..."
[2912] Sastry 1978, p. 36.
[2913] Quote: "poet named Balasarasvati author of an inscription dated S. 1136 had lived at the court of Prola Reddi, ruler of the same Kakatiya dynasty."
[2914] Quote: "Displacement was rapid as the Reddis with their superior technology swiftly spread over the entire Telangana... and were aided by a stronger political power of Kakatiya Reddi kingdom."
[2915] Quote: "Redu is a king. Reddi is supposed to be another form of Redu.:
[2916] Sastry 1978, p. 2.
[2917] Sastry 1978, p. 15.
[2918] Sastry 1978, p. 16.
[2919] Sastry 1978, pp. 17-18.
[2920] Sastry 1978, p. 17.
[2921] Sastry 1978, p. 18.
[2922] Sastry 1978, pp. 18-19.
[2923] Sastry 1978, p. 19.
[2924] Sastry 1978, p. 20.
[2925] Sastry 1978, pp. 20-21.
[2926] Sastry 1978, p. 21.
[2927] Sastry 1978, p. 19, 25.
[2928] Sastry 1978, p. 25.
[2929] Sastry 1978, p. 6.
[2930] Sircar 1979, p. 130.
[2931] Prasad 1988, pp. 119, 124.
[2932] Talbot 2001, p. 184.
[2933] Talbot (2001, p. 128): "Soon after he came to power, Rudradeva had the Thousand Pillared temple built in Hanumakonda, then the Kakatiya capital. The Sanskrit inscription recording its foundation in 1163 contains an elaborate genealogy of Rudradeva's ancestry... Since it was the earliest of Rudradeva's inscriptions to omit any mention of the Chalukya dynasty of Kalyani, we can assume that the construction of the temple was meant to mark Rudradeva's new status as an overlord in his own right."
[2934] Eaton 2005, p. 13.
[2935] Eaton 2005, p. 17.
[2936] Desai 1962.
[2937] Kalia 1994, p. 21.
[2938] Rubiés 2000, p. 73.
[2939] Rubiés 2000, pp. 50, 73.
[2940] Marco Polo referred to the kingdom as Mutfili, which was the name for the area around a major port of the dynasty, now known as Masulipatnam.(Chakravarti 1991)
[2941] Suryanarayana 1986, p. 163.
[2942] Eaton 2005, p. 16.
[2943] Eaton 2005, pp. 9-11.
[2944] Asher & Talbot 2006, p. 40.
[2945] Kulke & Rothermund 2004, p. 160 "An earlier attack on Warangal in 1304 had been unsuccessful.".
[2946] Sharma (1992, p. 234): "Vennama, the son of Dāma, led his troops in a defeat of the Turks very probably during Ala-ud-din Khalji's first invasion of Telangana in 1303. This success against the Turkish arms took place in the battle of Upparapalli, where Potuganti Maili is said to have put the enemies to flight."
[2947] Eaton 2005, pp. 17–18.
[2948] Eaton 2005, pp. 18–19.

[2949] Eaton 2005, pp. 20-21.
[2950] Talbot 2001, p. 176.
[2951] Rao & Shulman 2012, p. 17.
[2952] Rao & Shulman 2002, p. 4.
[2953] The term *andhra bhasa*, meaning *language of Andhra*, appeared as a synonym for the Telugu language at least as early as 1053 and suggests an emerging correlation of linguistics and geography. (Eaton 2005, p. 13) The linguistic mapping of regions of India continues to the present day and formed a part of the States Reorganisation Act, 1956.
[2954] Aside from the Kakatiyas, the dominant Hindu monarchies in South India and the Deccan around the 13th century CE were the Seunas, the Hoysalas and the Pandyas. The Seunas, Hoysalas and Kakatiyas had carved up what had been the area controlled by the Western Chalukya Empire, while the Pandyas controlled lands formerly under the Chola Empire. (Ventakaramanayya 1942, p. 1)
[2955] Ventakaramanayya 1942, pp. 1–2.
[2956] Eaton 2005, p. 14.
[2957] Eaton 2005, pp. 14–15.
[2958] Eaton 2005, p. 12.
[2959] Subrahmanyam 1998.
[2960] Talbot (2001, p. 51): "An inscription reads: 'The Kakatiya dynasty, praised by the entire world and belonging to the fourth *varna*, then came into existence. In it was born the king named Prola, who was renowned for being exceedingly judicious.'... [In a handful of inscriptions], the Kakatiyas are linked with the solar dynasty of the ancient *kshatriyas*, stemming from Ikshvaku through Dasharatha and Rama... The lack of consistency regarding the *varna* rank of the Kakatiya dynasty is noteworthy, as is the fact that their *kshatriya* claims were put forth primarily in documents associated with gifts to *brahmans*."
[2961] Eaton 2005, pp. 15–16.
[2962] Talbot 2001, pp. 50-52.
[2963] Talbot 2001, p. 174.
[2964] Sastry 1978, p. 24.
[2965] Sastry 1978, pp. 30-36.
[2966] Asher & Talbot 2006, p. 43.
[2967] Rao & Shulman 2012, p. 16.
[2968] Talbot 2001, p. 177.
[2969] Talbot 2001, pp. 177-182.
[2970] Eaton 2005, p. 22.
[2971] Talbot 2001, pp. 192–193.
[2972] Eaton 2005, pp. 26-27.
[2973] Chattopadhyaya (1998, pp. 57–58) quotes from the Vilasa grant of Prolaya Nayaka: "[W]hen Prataparudra of the Kakati family ruled, even such celebrated rulers of the past as *Yayati*, *Nabhaga* and *Bhagiratha* were completely forgotten."... "[W]hen the Sun, *viz.*, Prataparudra set, the world was enveloped in the *Turuska* darkness. The evil (*adharma*), which he had up to that time kept under check, flourished under them, as the conditions were very favourable for its growth."
[2974] Eaton 2005, pp. 27-28.
[2975] Talbot 2001, p. 175.
[2976] Eaton 2005, pp. 28-29.
[2977] https://books.google.com/books?id=ZvaGuaJIJgoC
[2978] //doi.org/10.2307/3632243
[2979] //www.jstor.org/stable/3632243
[2980] //www.jstor.org/stable/41853935
[2981] https://books.google.com/books?id=DNNgdBWoYKoC
[2982] https://books.google.com/books?id=lt2tqOpVRKgC
[2983] https://www.questia.com/read/55271807
[2984] http://www.katragadda.com/articles/HistoryOfTheAndhras.pdf
[2985] https://www.questia.com/read/108156994
[2986] https://www.questia.com/read/105967930

[2987] https://www.questia.com/read/121703743
[2988] https://www.questia.com/read/105026315
[2989] https://books.google.com/books?id=FiRuAAAAMAAJ
[2990] //www.worldcat.org/oclc/252341228
[2991] https://books.google.com/books?id=ucQKAQAAIAAJ
[2992] https://books.google.com/books?id=-O18xhA_BXUC
[2993] https://books.google.com/books?id=m1JYwP5tVQUC
[2994] //www.jstor.org/stable/20027508
[2995] https://books.google.com/books?id=f6seAAAAMAAJ
[2996] https://books.google.com/books?id=pfAKljlCJq0C
[2997] //doi.org/10.2307/2057210
[2998] //www.jstor.org/stable/2057210
[2999] Charles Dillard Collins 1988, p. 9.
[3000] Charles Dillard Collins 1988, pp. 9-10.
[3001] Geri Hockfield Malandra 1993, p. 6.
[3002] Charles Dillard Collins 1988, p. 10.
[3003] Charles Dillard Collins 1988, pp. 10-11.
[3004] V. V. Mirashi 1974, p. 376.
[3005] Ronald M. Davidson 2012, p. 37.
[3006] https://books.google.com/books?id=pQNi6kAGJQ4C
[3007] https://books.google.com/books?id=MU44LPu3mbUC
[3008] https://books.google.com/books?id=nwyeIyWTlEMC
[3009] https://books.google.com/books?id=hLGgZOzTYzsC&pg=PA376
[3010] http://coinindia.com/galleries-kalachuri-mahismati.html
[3011] //en.wikipedia.org/w/index.php?title=Template:Karnataka_History&action=edit
[3012] Historians feel that Sala was a mythical founder of the empire (Kamath 2001, p123)
[3013] Derrett in Chopra, Ravindran and Subrahmanian (2003), p150 Part 1
[3014] The myth and the emblem was a creation of King Vishnuvardhana. Another opinion is the emblem symbolically narrates the wars between the early Hoysala chieftains and the Cholas, (Settar in Kamath 2001, p123)
[3015] Quotation:"There was not even a tradition to back such poetic fancy"(William Coelho in Kamath, 2001, p122). Quotation:"All royal families in South India in the 10th and 11th century deviced puranic genealogies" (Kamath 2001, p122)
[3016] Quotation:"It is therefore clear that there was a craze among the rulers of the south at this time (11th century) to connect their families with dynasties from the north" (Moraes 1931, p10–11)
[3017] Rice B.L. in Kamath (2001), p123
[3018] Quotation:"A purely Karnataka dynasty" (Moraes 1931, p10)
[3019] Keay (2000), p251
[3020] Quotation:"The home of the Hoysalas lay in the hill tracts to the north-west of Gangavadi in Mysore" (Sen 1999, p498)
[3021] Thapar (2003), p367
[3022] Stien (1989), p16
[3023] Rice, B.L. (1897), p335
[3024] Natives of south Karnataka (Chopra 2003, p150 Part 1)
[3025] The Hoysalas originated from Sosevuru, identified as modern Angadi in Mudigere taluk (Kamath 2001, p123)
[3026] An indigenous ruling family of Karnataka from Sosevuru (modern Angadi) (Ayyar 1993, p600)
[3027] Seetharam Jagirdhar, M.N. Prabhakar, B.S. Krishnaswamy Iyengar in Kamath (2001), p123
[3028] During the rule of Vinyaditya (1047–1098), the Hoysalas established themselves as a powerful feudatory (Chopra 2003, p151, part 1)
[3029] Sen (1999), p498
[3030] Sen (1999), pp498–499
[3031] Quotation:"Reign of Vishnuvardhana is packed with glorious military campaigns from start to finish" (Coelho in Kamath 2001, p124). Quotation:"The maker of the Hoysala kingdom" (B.S.K. Iyengar in Kamath p126). Quotation:"In spite of the fact that Vikramaditya VI foiled

his attempt to become independent, the achievements of Vishnuvardhana were not small" (P.B. Desai in Kamath 2001, p126)

3032 Quotation:"He was the real maker of the Hoysala kingdom, corresponding to modern Mysore. He annexed the Chola province of Gangavadi and parts of Nolambavadi" (Sen 1999, pp498–499)

3033 Quotation:"Another campaign carried out in AD 1115 and AD 1116 and recorded in a document at Chamrajnagar is dated 1117. According to that record Vishnuvardhana frightened the Cholas, drove the Gangas underground, entered the Nila mountain and became the master of Kerala. His conquest of the Nilgiris is mentioned in more than one inscription." Quotation:"He captured Talakad which had owed allegiance to the Cholas ever since the days of Rajaraja I". Quotation:"This significant achievement which included Vishnuvardhanas temporary stay in Kanchi is proudly mentioned in Hoysala records".(Chopra 2003, p152–153, part 1)

3034 Quotation:"Vishnuvardhana was the governor of Gangavadi in the days of his brother and he took serious steps to free parts of Gangavadi, still under the control of the Cholas. He captured Talakadu and Kolara in 1116 and assumed the title *Talakadugonda* in memory of his victory" (Kamath 2001, p124)

3035 Quotation:"While still engaged in suppressing the Hoysalas, Vikramaditya renewed his designs against Kulottunga; possibly the success of the Hoysalas against the monarch in Gangavadi encouraged him to do so" (Sastri 1955, p175)

3036 Quotation:"In the first twenty years of his rule, he had to fight hard against the Nolambas and the Kalachuris, the two feudatories of the Chalukya Empire. He entered into a protracted war against the Yadavas and fought successfully against the Kadambas. Emboldened by the decline of the Chalukya empire, he finally declared independence in AD 1193" (Sen 1999, p499)

3037 Quotation:"Ballala vied for glory with his grandfather, and his long and vigorous reign of 47 years saw the achievement of independence which had long been coveted by his forefather" (Prof. Coelho in Kamath 2001, p126)

3038 Quotation:"It was Ballala's achievement to have consolidated his grandfather's conquests. He may be supposed to have been the founder of a sort of Hoysala imperialism" (Chopra 2003, p154, part1)

3039 Their mutual competition and antagonisms were the main feature during this period (Sastri 1955, p192)

3040 Quotation:"He helped the Chola Kulottunga III and Rajaraja III against Sundara Pandya compelling the latter to restore the Chola country to its ruler (AD 1217)" (Sen 1999, p499)

3041 Quotation:"A Hoysala king claimed to have rescued the Chola king who had been captured by a tributary Raja" (Thapar, 2003, p368)

3042 Quotation:"Meanwhile Kulottunga had appealed for aid to Hoysala Ballala II who promptly sent an army under his son Narasimha to Srirangam. Sundara Pandya therefore had to make peace and restore the Chola kingdom to Kulottunga and Rajaraja after they made formal submission at Pon Amaravati and acknowledged him as suzerain" (Sastri 1955, pp193–194)

3043 Quotation:"In response to this request (*by the Cholas*), Ballala II sent his son Vira Narasimha with an army to the Tamil country. The interfering Hoysala forces drove back the invading Pandyas and helped the Cholas, though temporarily to retain status" (Chopra, 2003, p155, part1)

3044 Quotation:"When the Chola was attacked by the Pandya, Ballala sent crown prince Narasimha II to help Kulottunga III. Ballala assumed the title "establisher of the Chola king" after his victory in Tamil Nadu, and he gained some territory in the Chola country too" (Kamath 2001, p127)

3045 Quotation:"To protect the Chola Kingdom from the harassing attacks of the Pandyas, Narasimha's son and successor, Someshvara established himself in the south and built a capital at Kannanur about six or eight kilometers from Srirangam" (Sen 1999, p499)

3046 Quotation:"The Hoysalas were regarded as arbiters of South Indian politics. With the waning of the power of the Pandyas and the Cholas, the Hoysalas had to take up the role of leadership in South India" (B.S.K. Iyengar in Kamath, 2001, p128)

3047 Quotation:"Gloriously if briefly the Hoysalas were paramount throughout most of the Kannada speaking Deccan, and could pose as arbiters in the lusher lands below the Eastern Ghats" (Keay, 2000, p252)

[3048] Quotation:"Thus for a second time the Hoysalas interfered in the politics of the Tamil country and stemmed the tide to Pandyan expansion to the north. Then Vira Narasimha styled himself the 'refounder of the Chola Kingdom.'" Quotation:"But what the Hoysalas lost in the north (*to the Yadavas*) they gained in the south by stabilising themselves near Srirangam at Kannanur (Chopra 2003, p155, part 1)

[3049] Quotation:"..while Hoysala influence over the whole area of the Chola kingdom and even the Pandya country increased steadily from 1220 to 1245, a period that may well be described as that of Hoysala hegemony in the south" (Sastri 1955, p195)

[3050] Thapar (2003), p368

[3051] Chopra 2003, p156, part 1

[3052] Sen (1999), p500

[3053] Kamath (2001), p129

[3054] Sastri (1955), pp206–208

[3055] Sastri (1955), pp212–214

[3056] Quotation:"The greatest hero in the dark political atmosphere of the south" (Kamath 2001, p130)

[3057] Chopra (2003), p156, part 1

[3058] While many theories exist about the origin of Harihara I and his brothers, collectively known as the Sangama brothers, it is well accepted that they administered the northern territories of the Hoysala empire in the 1336–1343 time either as Hoysala commanders or with autonomous powers (Kamath 2001, pp159–160)

[3059] A collaboration between the waning Hoysala kingdom and the emerging Hindu Vijayanagara empire is proven by inscriptions. The queen of Veera Ballala III, Krishnayitayi, made a grant to the Sringeri monastery on the same day as the founder of the Vijayanagara empire, Harihara I in 1346. The Sringeri monastic order was patronised by both Hoysala and Vijayanagara empires (Kamath 2001, p161)

[3060] Kamath (2001), p132

[3061] Thapar (2003), p378

[3062] Marco Polo who claims to have travelled in India at this time wrote of a monopoly in horse trading by the Arabs and merchants of South India. Imported horses became an expensive commodity because horse breeding was never successful in India, perhaps due to the different climatic, soil and pastoral conditions (Thapar 2003, p383)

[3063] Thapar (2003), p382

[3064] Thapar (2003), p383

[3065] Some 1500 monuments were built during these times in about 950 locations-

[3066] More than 1000 monuments built by the Hoysalas creating employment for people of numerous guilds and backgrounds (Kamath 2001, p132)

[3067] Kamath (2001), p130–131

[3068] It is not clear which among *Vishaya* and *Nadu* was bigger in area and that a *Nadu* was under the supervision of the commander (*Dandanayaka*) (Barrett in Kamath 2001, pp 130–31)

[3069] Kamath (2001), p131

[3070] Shadow like, they moved closely with the king, lived near him and disappeared upon the death of their master –

[3071] Many Coins with Kannada legends have been discovered from the rule of the Hoysalas (Kamath 2001, p12, p125)

[3072] Kamath (2001), p112, p132

[3073] A 16th-century Buddhist work by Lama Taranatha speaks disparagingly of Shankaracharya as close parallels in some beliefs of Shankaracharya with Buddhist philosophy was not viewed favorably by Buddhist writers (Thapar 2003, pp 349–350, p397)

[3074] Kamath 2001, p152

[3075] (Kamath 2001, p155)

[3076] He criticised Adi Shankara as a "Buddhist in disguise" (Kamath 2001, p151)

[3077] Fritz and Michell (2001), pp35–36

[3078] Kamath (2001), p152

[3079] Shiva Prakash (1997), pp192–200

[3080] Kamath 2001, p156

[3081] Shiva Prakash (1997), pp200–201
[3082] This is in stark contrast to the literature of the time (like *Vikramankadeva Charita* of Bilhana) that portrayed women as retiring, overly romantic and unconcerned with affairs of the state (Thapar 2003, p392)
[3083] She was not only a pioneer in the era of Women's emancipation but also an example of a transcendental world-view (Thapar 2003, p392)
[3084] Thapar (2003), p391
[3085] Sastri (1955), p286
[3086] Royal patronage of education, arts, architecture, religion and establishment of new forts and military outposts caused the large scale relocation of people (Sastri 1955, p287)
[3087] Thapar (2003), p389
[3088] Ayyar (1993), p600
[3089] Narasimhacharya (1988), p19
[3090] A composition which is written in a mixed prose-verse style is called *Champu*, Narasimhacharya (1988), p12
[3091] A *Sangatya* composition is meant to be sung to the accompaniment of a musical instrument (Sastri 1955), p359
[3092] Sastri(1955), p361
[3093] Sastri (1955), p359
[3094] E.P. Rice (1921), p 43–44
[3095] Narasimhacharya (1988), p20
[3096] Sastri (1955), p364
[3097] Sastri (1955), p362
[3098] Narasimhacharya, (1988), p20
[3099] E.P.Rice (1921), p60
[3100] Sastri (1955), p324,
[3101] Hardy (1995), p215, p243
[3102] Kamath (2001), p115, p118
[3103] Sastri (1955), p429
[3104] Hardy (1995), pp6–7
[3105] Hoysala style has negligible influences of the Indo-Aryan style and owing to its many independent features, it qualifies as an independent school of architecture (Brown in Kamath 2001, p134)
[3106] An independent tradition, according to Havell, Narasimhachar, Sheshadri and Settar –
[3107] Sen (1999), pp500–501
[3108] Foekema (1996), pp27–28
[3109] Though the Hoysala *vimana* have rich texture, yet they are formless and lacks structural strength, according to Brown –
[3110] This is a Hoysala innovation (Brown in Kamath 2001, p135)
[3111] Foekema (1996), pp21–22
[3112] Quotation:"Their sculptured figures, especially the bracket figures, have been objects of praise at the hands of art critics of the whole world. They include *Sukhabhasini*, *Darpanadharini* and other damsels in various dancing poses". (Kamath 2001, p 136)
[3113] Sastri (1955), p428
[3114] Hardy (1995), p37
[3115] Foekema (1996), p47
[3116] Hardy (1995), p325
[3117] Foekema (1996), p59
[3118] Hardy (1995), p329
[3119] Foekema (1996), p87
[3120] Hardy (1995), p346
[3121] Foekema (1996), p41
[3122] Hardy (1995), p321
[3123] Foekema (1996), p37
[3124] Hardy (1995), p320
[3125] Foekema (1996), p53

[3126] Hardy (1995), p324
[3127] Foekema (1996), p83
[3128] Hardy (1995), p340
[3129] Foekema (1996), p71
[3130] Hardy (1995), pp 330–333
[3131] Foekema (1996), p39
[3132] Foekema (1996), p77
[3133] Hardy (1995), p334
[3134] Foekema (1996), p67
[3135] Foekema (1996), p81
[3136] Hardy (1995), p339
[3137] Foekema (1996), p43
[3138] Foekema (1996), preface, p47, p59
[3139] Foekema (1996), p61
[3140] Brown in Kamath (2001), p135
[3141] Ayyar (2006), p. 600
[3142] Pollock (2006), p. 288–289
[3143] Narasimhacharya (1988), p17
[3144] The *Manasollasa* of king Someshvara III is an early encyclopedia in Sanskrit (Thapar 2003, p393)
[3145] However by the 14th century, bilingual inscriptions lost favor and inscriptions were mostly in the local language (Thapar 2003, pp393–95)
[3146] //lccn.loc.gov/80905179
[3147] //www.worldcat.org/oclc/7796041
[3148] https://web.archive.org/web/20061104095148/http://www.ourkarnataka.com/history.htm
[3149] http://www.ourkarnataka.com/history.htm
[3150] https://web.archive.org/web/20070119114119/http://prabhu.50g.com/southind/hoysala/south_hoysalacat.html
[3151] http://prabhu.50g.com/southind/hoysala/south_hoysalacat.html
[3152] http://www.frontline.in/static/html/fl2008/stories/20030425000206700.htm
[3153] http://www.hindu.com/thehindu/mp/2002/07/25/stories/2002072500270200.htm
[3154] http://www.hindu.com/2004/07/25/stories/2004072501490300.htm
[3155] http://www.kamat.com/kalranga/deccan/hoysala/belur.htm
[3156] http://www.kamat.com/kalranga/deccan/hoysala.htm
[3157] http://inscriptions.whatisindia.com/
[3158] A History of Ancient and Early Medieval India: From the Stone Age to the 12th Century (2008), Upinder Singh, p. 559.
[3159] John N. Miksic 2013, p. 79"...the north end of the Straits, from Barus to Kedah and Takuapa, may have been under direct Chola administration; a crown prince of the Chola dynasty probably served as viceroy in Kedah."
[3160] //en.wikipedia.org/w/index.php?title=Template:Chola_history&action=edit
[3161] //en.wikipedia.org/w/index.php?title=Template:TNhistory&action=edit
[3162] K.A. Nilakanta Sastri, *A History of South India*, p 157
[3163] Keay, p 215
[3164] K.A. Nilakanta Sastri, *A History of South India*, p 158
[3165] Majumdar (contains no mention of Maldives)
[3166] Meyer, p 73
[3167] K.A. Nilakanta Sastri, *A History of South India*, p 195
[3168] K.A. Nilakanta Sastri, *A History of South India*, p 196
[3169] Vasudevan, pp 20–22
[3170] Keay, pp 217–218
[3171] Thai Art with Indian Influences by Promsak Jermsawatdi p.57
[3172] Columbia Chronologies of Asian History and Culture by John Stewart Bowman p.335
[3173] Prasad (1988), p. 120

³¹⁷⁴The age of Sangam is established through the correlation between the evidence on foreign trade found in the poems and the writings by ancient Greek and Romans such as *Periplus*. K.A. Nilakanta Sastri, *A History of Cyril and Lulu Charles*, p 106

³¹⁷⁵Sastri (1984), pp. 19-20

³¹⁷⁶Archaeological News A. L. Frothingham, Jr. *The American Journal of Archaeology and of the History of the Fine Arts*, Vol. 4, No. 1 (Mar., 1998), pp. 69–125

³¹⁷⁷The period covered by the Sangam poetry is likely to extend not longer than five or six generations.<ref name="FOOTNOTESastri19843">Sastri (1984), p. 3

³¹⁷⁸Columbia Chronologies of Asian History and Culture by John Bowman p.401

³¹⁷⁹The Ashokan inscriptions speak of the Cholas in plural, implying that, in his time, there were more than one Chola.<ref name="FOOTNOTESastri198420">Sastri (1984), p. 20

³¹⁸⁰The direct line of Cholas of the Vijayalaya dynasty came to an end with the death of Virarajendra Chola and the assassination of his son Athirajendra Chola. Kulothunga Chola I, ascended the throne in 1070.<ref name="FOOTNOTESastri2002170-172">Sastri (2002), pp. 170-172

³¹⁸¹Sastri (2002), pp. 19-20, 104-106

³¹⁸²Tripathi (1967), p. 457

³¹⁸³Majumdar (1987), p. 137

³¹⁸⁴Kulke & Rothermund (2001), p. 104

³¹⁸⁵Tripathi (1967), p. 458

³¹⁸⁶Sastri (2002), p. 116

³¹⁸⁷Sastri (2002), pp. 105-106

³¹⁸⁸The only evidence for the approximate period of these early kings is the Sangam literature and the synchronisation with the history of Sri Lanka as given in the *Mahavamsa*. Gajabahu I who is said to be the contemporary of the Chera Senguttuvan, belonged to the 2nd century and this means the poems mentioning Senguttuvan and his contemporaries date to that period.Wikipedia:Citation needed

³¹⁸⁹Sastri (2002), p. 113

³¹⁹⁰Sastri (2002), pp. 130, 135, 137

³¹⁹¹Majumdar (1987), p. 139

³¹⁹²Thapar (1995), p. 268

³¹⁹³Sastri (2002), p. 135

³¹⁹⁴Sastri (2002), pp. 130, 133Quote:"The Cholas disappeared from the Tamil land almost completely in this debacle, though a branch of them can be traced towards the close of the period in Rayalaseema – the Telugu-Chodas, whose kingdom is mentioned by Yuan Chwang in the seventh century A.D."

³¹⁹⁵Sastri (1984), p. 102

³¹⁹⁶Kulke & Rothermund (2001), p. 115

³¹⁹⁷Pandya Kadungon and Pallava Simhavishnu overthrew the Kalabhras. Acchchutakalaba is likely the last Kalabhra king.<ref name="FOOTNOTESastri1984102">Sastri (1984), p. 102

³¹⁹⁸*Periyapuranam*, a Shaivite religious work of 12th century tells us of the Pandya king Nindrasirnedumaran, who had for his queen a Chola princess.<ref name="FOOTNOTEChopraRavindranSubrahmanian200395">Chopra, Ravindran & Subrahmanian (2003), p. 95

³¹⁹⁹Copperplate grants of the Pallava Buddhavarman (late 4th century) mention that the king as the "underwater fire that destroyed the ocean of the Chola army".<ref name="FOOTNOTESastri1984104-105">Sastri (1984), pp. 104-105

³²⁰⁰Chopra, Ravindran & Subrahmanian (2003), p. 95

³²⁰¹Tripathi (1967), p. 459

³²⁰²Chopra, Ravindran & Subrahmanian (2003), p. 31

³²⁰³Sastri (2002), p. 4Quote:"it is not known what relation, if any, the Telugu-Chodas of the Renadu country in the Ceded District, bore to their namesakes of the Tamil land, though they claimed descent from Karikala, the most celebrated of the early Chola monarchs of the Sangam age."

³²⁰⁴K. A. Nilakanta Sastri postulates that there was a live connection between the early Cholas and the Renandu Cholas of the Andhra country. The northward migration probably took place during the Pallava domination of Simhavishnu. Sastri also categorically rejects the claims that

these were the descendants of Karikala Chola.<ref name="FOOTNOTESastri1984107">Sastri (1984), p. 107
[3205] Tripathi (1967), pp. 458-459
[3206] Sen (1999), pp. 477-478
[3207] Dehejia (1990), p. xiv
[3208] Kulke & Rothermund (2001), pp. 122–123
[3209] Eraly (2011), p. 67
[3210] Sastri (2002), p. 157
[3211] Sen (1999), pp. 373
[3212] Eraly (2011), p. 68
[3213] *The Dancing Girl: A History of Early India* by Balaji Sadasivan p.133
[3214] *A Comprehensive History of Medieval India*, by Farooqui Salma Ahmed, Salma Ahmed Farooqui p.25
[3215] *Power and Plenty: Trade, War, and the World Economy in the Second Millennium* by Ronald Findlay, Kevin H. O'Rourke p.67
[3216] *History Without Borders: The Making of an Asian World Region, 1000-1800* by Geoffrey C. Gunn p.43
[3217] Sen (2009), p. 91
[3218] *Buddhism, Diplomacy, and Trade: The Realignment of Sino-Indian Relations* by Tansen Sen p. 226
[3219] Kalā: The Journal of Indian Art History Congress, The Congress, 1995, p.31
[3220] Sastri (1984), pp. 194-210
[3221] Majumdar (1987), p. 407
[3222] Sastri (2002), p. 158
[3223] *Ancient India: Collected Essays on the Literary and Political History of Southern India* by Sakkottai Krishnaswami Aiyangar p.233
[3224] Chopra, Ravindran & Subrahmanian (2003), pp. 107-109
[3225] ndia: The Most Dangerous Decades by Selig S. Harrison p.31
[3226] Sastri (2002), p. 184
[3227] Mukund (2012), p. xlii
[3228] "After the second Pandya War, Kulottunga undertook a campaign to check to the growth of Hoysala power in that quarter. He re-established Chola suzerainty over the Adigaimans of Tagadur, defeated a Chera ruler in battle and performed a *vijayabhisheka* in Karuvur (1193). His relations with the Hoysala Ballala II seem to have become friendly afterwards, for Ballala married a Chola princess".<ref name="FOOTNOTESastri2002178">Sastri (2002), p. 178
[3229] Between 2 Oceans (2nd Edn): A Military History of Singapore from 1275 to 1971 by Malcolm H. Murfett, John Miksic, Brian Farell, Chiang Ming Shun p.16
[3230] *South India* by Stuart Butler, Jealous p.38
[3231] *Asia: A Concise History* by Arthur Cotterell p.190
[3232] Paine (2014), p. 281
[3233] *History of Asia* by B.V. Rao p.211
[3234] Majumdar (1987), p. 405
[3235] Chopra, Ravindran & Subrahmanian (2003), p. 120
[3236] Majumdar (1987), p. 408
[3237] Tripathi (1967), p. 471
[3238] *South Indian Inscriptions*, Vol. 12
[3239] Chopra, Ravindran & Subrahmanian (2003), pp. 128-129
[3240] Sastri (2002), p. 194
[3241] Tripathi (1967), p. 472
[3242] Majumdar (1987), p. 410
[3243] South India and Her Muhammadan Invaders by S. Krishnaswami Aiyangar p.40-41
[3244] Sastri (2002), pp. 195-196
[3245] Sastri (2002), p. 196
[3246] Tripathi (1967), p. 485
[3247] Sastri (2002), p. 197
[3248] Chopra, Ravindran & Subrahmanian (2003), p. 130

[3249] Proceedings, American Philosophical Society *(1978), vol. 122, No. 6, p 414*
[3250] The Buddhist work *Milinda Panha* dated to the early Christian era, mentions Kolapttna among the best-known sea ports on the Chola coast.<ref name="FOOTNOTESastri198423">Sastri (1984), p. 23
[3251] Nagasamy (1981)
[3252] Sastri (2002), p. 107
[3253] Chopra, Ravindran & Subrahmanian (2003), p. 106
[3254] Karashima 2014, p. 132.
[3255] The only other time when peninsular India would be brought under one umbrella before the independence of India was during the Vijayanagara Empire (1336–1614).Wikipedia:Citation needed
[3256] Stein (1998), p. 26
[3257] Vasudevan (2003), pp. 20-22
[3258] A Global History of Architecture by Francis D. K. Ching, Mark M. Jarzombek, Vikramaditya Prakash p.338
[3259] History of India by N. Jayapalan p.171
[3260] Gough (2008), p. 29
[3261] Talbot (2001), p. 172.
[3262] Singh (2008), p. 590
[3263] *Administrative System in India: Vedic Age to 1947* by U. B. Singh p.77
[3264] Tripathi (1967), pp. 474-475
[3265] Stein (1998), p. 20
[3266] Sastri (2002), p. 185
[3267] Sastri (2002), p. 150
[3268] Sastri (1984), p. 465
[3269] Sastri (1984), p. 477
[3270] Sakhuja & Sakhuja (2009), p. 88
[3271] Barua (2005), p. 18
[3272] Dehejia (1990), p. 79
[3273] Subbarayalu (2009), pp. 97-99
[3274] Eraly (2011), p. 176
[3275] Rajasuriar (1998), p. 15
[3276] Sen (1999), p. 205
[3277] Technology and Society by Menon R.V.G. p.15
[3278] Stein (1980), p. 130
[3279] Lucassen & Lucassen (2014), p. 120
[3280] The State at War in South Asia by Pradeep Barua p.17
[3281] Sastri (2002), p. 175
[3282] *The Pearson General Studies Manual* 2009, 1/e by Showick Thorpe Edgar Thorpe p.59
[3283] Singh (2008), p. 54
[3284] Schmidt (1995), p. 32
[3285] Devare (2009), p. 179
[3286] Eraly (2011), p. 208
[3287] Ramaswamy (2007), p. 20
[3288] Singh (2008), p. 599
[3289] *Trade and Politics on the Coromandel Coast: Seventeenth and Early Eighteenth centuries* by Radhika Seshan p.18
[3290] *Indian Textiles: Past and Present* by G. K. Ghosh, Shukla Ghosh p.123-124
[3291] *Kanchipuram: Land of Legends, Saints and Temples* by P. V. L. Narasimha Rao p.134
[3292] Ramaswamy (2007), p. 51
[3293] Mukherjee (2011), p. 105
[3294] *History of People and Their Environs: Essays in Honour of Prof. B.S. Chandrababu* by S.Ganeshram p.319
[3295] Singh (2008), p. 592
[3296] Sen (1999), pp. 490-492
[3297] Indian History by Reddy p.B57

[3298] Mukund (1999), pp. 30-32
[3299] Ramaswamy (2007), p. 86
[3300] Rothermund (1993), p. 9
[3301] *Economic History of India* by N. Jayapalan p.49
[3302] Temple art under the Chola queens by Balasubrahmanyam Venkataraman p.72
[3303] *Temple Art Under the Chola Queens* by Balasubrahmanyam Venkataraman p.72
[3304] Mukund (1999), p. 29-30
[3305] Hellmann-Rajanayagam (2004), p. 104
[3306] *The Political Economy of Craft Production: Crafting Empire in South India*, by Carla M. Sinopoli p.188
[3307] Sadarangani (2004), p. 16
[3308] Sastri (2002), p. 284
[3309] Chopra, Ravindran & Subrahmanian (2003), pp. 125, 129
[3310] Scharfe (2002), p. 180
[3311] 17th century Italian traveler Pietro Della Valle (1623) has given a vivid account of the village schools in South India. These accounts reflect the system of primary education in existence until the morder times in Tamil Nadu
[3312] Sastri (2002), p. 293
[3313] Kulke & Rothermund (2001), pp. 116-117
[3314] Kulke & Rothermund (2001), pp. 12, 118
[3315] Buddhism, Diplomacy, and Trade: The Realignment of Sino-Indian Relations by Tansen Sen p. 159
[3316] Kulke & Rothermund (2001), p. 124
[3317] Tripathi (1967), pp. 465, 477
[3318] Sastri (1984), p. 604
[3319] *Buddhism, Diplomacy, and Trade: The Realignment of Sino-Indian Relations* by Tansen Sen p. 156
[3320] Kulke & Rothermund (2001), p. 117
[3321] Thapar (1995), p. xv
[3322] Mukund (2012), p. 92
[3323] Mukund (2012), p. 95
[3324] *History of Agriculture in India, Up to c. 1200 A.D.* by Lallanji Gopal p.501
[3325] Mitter (2001), p. 2
[3326] Sastri (2002), p. 418
[3327] Thapar (1995), p. 403 Quote: "It was, however, in bronze sculptures that the Chola craftsmen excelled, producing images rivalling the best anywhere."
[3328] Kulke & Rothermund (2001), p. 159
[3329] Sastri (1984), p. 789
[3330] Kulke & Rothermund (2001), pp. 159-160
[3331] A History of Early Southeast Asia: Maritime Trade and Societal Development by Kenneth R. Hall
[3332] Aryatarangini, the Saga of the Indo-Aryans, by A. Kalyanaraman p.158
[3333] India and Malaya Through the Ages: by S. Durai Raja Singam
[3334] Tripathi (1967), p. 479
[3335] Dehejia (1990), p. 10
[3336] Harle (1994), p. 295
[3337] Mitter (2001), p. 57
[3338] *Temples of South India* by V. V. Subba Reddy p.110
[3339] Jermsawatdi (1979), p. 57
[3340] *Columbia Chronologies of Asian History and Culture* by John Stewart Bowman p.335
[3341] Vasudevan (2003), pp. 21-24
[3342] Nagasamy (1970)
[3343] Chopra, Ravindran & Subrahmanian (2003), p. 186
[3344] Mitter (2001), p. 163
[3345] Thapar (1995), p. 309-310
[3346] Wolpert (1999), p. 174

[3347] By common consent, the finest Chola masterpieces are the bronze images of Siva Nataraja.<ref name="FOOTNOTEMitter200159">Mitter (2001), p. 59
[3348] Sastri (1984), pp. 663-664
[3349] Sastri (2002), p. 333
[3350] Sastri (2002), p. 339
[3351] Chopra, Ravindran & Subrahmanian (2003), p. 188
[3352] Sastri (2002), pp. 339-340
[3353] Ismail (1988), p. 1195
[3354] *Ancient India: Collected Essays on the Literary and Political History of southern India* by Sakkottai Krishnaswami Aiyangar p.127
[3355] *The Princeton Encyclopedia of Poetry and Poetics* by Roland Greene, Stephen Cushman, Clare Cavanagh, Jahan Ramazani, Paul F. Rouzer, Harris Feinsod, David Marno, Alexandra Slessarev p.1410
[3356] Singh (2008), p. 27
[3357] *Portraits of a Nation: History of Ancient India*, by Kamlesh Kapur p.617
[3358] *Concise Encyclopaedia Of India* by Kulwant Rai Gupta, Amita Gupta p.288
[3359] *Legend of Ram* By Sanujit Ghose
[3360] *Rays and Ways of Indian Culture* By D. P. Dubey
[3361] Chopra, Ravindran & Subrahmanian (2003), p. 116
[3362] Sastri (2002), pp. 20, 340-341
[3363] Sastri (2002), pp. 184, 340
[3364] Chopra, Ravindran & Subrahmanian (2003), p. 20
[3365] *Encyclopaedia of Indian literature, vol. 1*, p 307
[3366] Spuler (1975), p. 194
[3367] Sastri (2002), pp. 342-343
[3368] Chopra, Ravindran & Subrahmanian (2003), p. 115
[3369] Sastri (1984), p. 681
[3370] Sadarangani (2004), p. 15
[3371] *South Indian Shrines*, Illustrated by P. V. Jagadisa Ayyar p.23
[3372] Darasuram Temple Inscriptions @ http://www.whatisindia.com/inscriptions/south_indian_inscriptions/darasuram/kulottunga.html. Whatisindia.com (2007-01-29). Retrieved on 2013-07-12.
[3373] Tripathi (1967), p. 480
[3374] Vasudevan (2003), p. 102
[3375] Sastri (1984), p. 214
[3376] Majumdar (1987), p. 4067
[3377] Stein (1998), p. 134
[3378] Vasudevan (2003), p. 104
[3379] Sastri (2002), p. 176
[3380] Sastri (1984), p. 645
[3381] Chopra, Ravindran & Subrahmanian (2003), p. 126
[3382] Das (1995), p. 108
[3383] Das (1995), pp. 108-109
[3384] Das (1995), p. 109
[3385] *Encyclopaedia of Indian Literature, vol. 1*, pp 631–632
[3386] https://books.google.com/books?id=8NJ3BgAAQBAJ&pg=PA79
[3387] http://www.whatisindia.com/inscriptions/
[3388] http://whc.unesco.org/pg.cfm?cid=31&id_site=250
[3389] http://www.indianartcircle.com/arteducation/page_14_artofCholas.shtml
[3390] http://lakdiva.org/coins/medievalindian/rajaraja_chola.html

Article Sources and Contributors

The sources listed for each article provide more detailed licensing information including the copyright status, the copyright owner, and the license conditions.

Middle kingdoms of India *Source:* https://en.wikipedia.org/w/index.php?oldid=847084253 *License:* Creative Commons Attribution-Share Alike 3.0 *Contributors:* 28bytes, Adamgerber80, Againme, Akram0101, Alan, AlanM1, Anadrev, Andres rojas22, Arnavmikel21, Arunsingh16, AtticusX, Aurorion, BD2412, Bender235, Bgwhite, Bhaskarbhagawati, Biscuittin, Blaylockjam10, Bongan, Capankajsmilyo, Cartakes, Chaipau, Charles Matthews, Chewings72, Chhora, Chris the speller, ChrisCork, ChrisGualtieri, Chuniyana, ClueBot NG, Colonies Chris, CommonsDelinker, Compfreak7, CouvGeek, Cpt.a.haddock, Crusoe8181, Cyberbot II, Dbkasar, Dewritech, EWikist, Eddie891, Esszet, Faizhaider, Filippof, Fixer88, FoCuSandLeArN, Fratrep, Frietjes, GDibyendu, Gaius Cornelius, Generalboss3, GermanJoe, Ghatus, Grafen, Greg Grahame, Hebrides, Hmains, HotWinters, Iitkgpatiitk, JLincoln, JaGa, Jayarathina, Jduperra, Jjtanwar, John Hill, John of Reading, Jonathanarpith, Jonesey95, Jonoikobangali, Josh3580, Joshua Jonathan, JzG, Kanashimi, Ketiltrout, Kwamikagami, Kwiki, Kww, Lateg, LilHelpa, Look2See1, LouisAragon, Maestro2016, Manjunath Doddamani Gajendragad, Marcocapelle, Marcus Cyron, Materialscientist, Mbartelsm, Merbabu, Mkrestin, Mogism, MohitSingh, Nayansatya, Nayvik, Neo-Jay, Nick Number, NickTheRipper, Nizamboy, Ogress, Onel5969, PhnomPencil, Pratyya Ghosh, R'n'B, Reahad, Reddi, Rich Farmbrough, Ricky81682, Rjwilmsi, Sanjoydey33, SchreiberBike, SchuminWeb, Seanwal111111, Shreevatsa, Sitush, Solomon7968, Sreenath sree103, Tassedethe, Thapa 75, Thomas.W, Tijfo098, ToonLucas22, Utcursch, Vanished user qwqwijr8hwrkjdnvkanfoh4, Vin09, Wbm1058, Welsh, Wiae, Wikid77, Woohookitty, Xezbeth, 133 anonymous edits 1

Indo-Scythians *Source:* https://en.wikipedia.org/w/index.php?oldid=851698686 *License:* Creative Commons Attribution-Share Alike 3.0 *Contributors:* AScythianSoul, Abdaaal, Abhijeetrana5665, Abstruce, Agaceri, Againme, Agnostos Theos, Akmal94, Anachronist, Ancientcoincollector, Andres rojas22, Artacoana, Aschillez, Astynax, Avantiputra7, Awadhi, Awiseman, BD2412, Baji12, Bender235, Bermicourt, Bgwhite, Biglovinb, Blue Papa Boy, Bodhisattwa, Calluday, CanisRufus, Capankajsmilyo, Carlon, Ceosad, Chris the speller, Colonies Chris, Cpt.a.haddock, Damien2016, Darokrithia, Delljvc, Dev Mor, DevMor, Dominus, Double Plus Ungood, Doug Weller, Ekabhishek, Equinox, Ermahgerd9, Fasi100, Fayenatic london, Fconaway, FlyingOnFloor, Frietjes, Goethean, GoingBatty, HavelockWilltravel, Hind meri jaan, HistoryofIran, Hmains, Hmainsbot1, Hzh, Imeriki al-Shimoni, JesseRafe, John Hill, Joostik, Joshua Jonathan, Just a guy from the KP, Jy1998, Keeby101, Khestwol, Kirananils, Kithira, Krakkos, Kww, KylieTastic, LaHistoria, Laodah, Lateg, LazarozI, Look2See1, Lotje, LouisAragon, Lubossekk, Ludde23, Mabdul, Magioladitis, Mar4d, Marcocapelle, Mark the train, Mojo Hand, Mywikieditbh, Nick Number, Nizil Shah, Oriondown, PAKHIGHWAY, PKT, PR-0927, Paine Ellsworth, Pathare Prabhu, Peeta Singh, Pepper Black, Per Honor et Gloria, Phil wink, PhnomPencil, Pi3.124, Priyadasi, R'n'B, RScheiber, Rani nurmai, Rattans, Ricky81682, Roland zh, Saladin1987, Samee, Sammy22111, Sitush, Solomon7968, Spalagdama, Steliokardam, Stemonitis, Sumitkachroo, Sun Creator, Sushilmishra, Taeyebar, Tahar Jelun, Taromsky, Teishin, TheSuave, Thomas.W, Tribe of Tiger, Utcursch, Vajra Raja, VerifiedCactus, Vsusarla55555, Wachoviadeal, Wario-Man, Willard84, Woudloper, Wrappos, ZxxZxxZ, पाटलिपुत्र, 148 anonymous edits 41

Saka *Source:* https://en.wikipedia.org/w/index.php?oldid=853040223 *License:* Creative Commons Attribution-Share Alike 3.0 *Contributors:* Abstruce, Andrew Gray, Apexpreci, Arjayay, Aymankamelwiki, Bakhytjan, Bamsi2929, Bender235, Benjamin Trovato, Blaylockjam10, Cattus, Cd2014, Chris the speller, ClueBot NG, Corinne, Darokrithia, Davidcannon, Dbachmann, Dmitri Lytov, Dthomsen8, Fayenatic london, Fhjmi54, Franrasyan, Frietjes, Future Perfect at Sunrise, Ged UK, Grant65, HistoryofIran, Hmains, Hzh, IdreamofJeanie, JeoRecep, Kervani, Khiruge, Kind Tennis Fan, Kintetsubuffalo, Kishorekumar 62, Krakkos, Kwamikagami, LilHelpa, LlywelynII, LouisAragon, Lysozym, Marcocapelle, Massagetae, Mazandar, Mean as custard, Milktaco, Moduin, Ogress, PериclesofAthens, Pi3.124, Quinton Feldberg, R'n'B, Roman Sakhan, Saladin1987, SchreiberBike, Sitush, Sjö, Sturanos, Suburbs, Svetlyo.agafonkin, Teishin, The Quixotic Potato, TheSuave, Til Eulenspiegel, Trappist the monk, Trinanjon, User without username, Viktalen, Wario-Man, Wavehunter, Wavelength, Willard84, Writeecrit, Xasin, Yamaha5, Zmflavius, Zoupan, 70 anonymous edits 74

Indo-Greek Kingdom *Source:* https://en.wikipedia.org/w/index.php?oldid=851387008 *License:* Creative Commons Attribution-Share Alike 3.0 *Contributors:* -phaethon, Adavidb, Ancientcoincollector, Anotherclown, Arjayay, Avantiputra7, BD2412, Bagas Chrisara, Beads and reels, Bermicourt, Bgwhite, Ceosad, Chewings72, Cpt.a.haddock, Dewritech, Diannaa, Dr.K., Edward, Eldumpo, Ermahgerd9, Finnusertop, Fixer88, Gereon K., GoingBatty, Goldsmelter, GünniX, Highpeaks35, Ira Leviton, JFG, Jdcomix, JesseRafe, JimRenge, John of Reading, Just a guy from the KP, JzG, Khestwol, Khirurg, Kintetsubuffalo, Lanwi1, LittleWink, LouisAragon, Magioladitis, Marcocapelle, Mark the train, Mifter, Mrflip, Ms Sarah Welch, NadirAli, Numberguy6, Nwbeeson, Peter Gao, Pkbwcgs, Pppery, Priyadasi, Rodw, Serols, ShakespeareFan00, Tahar Jelun, Tahc, Tantpis330, Thanatos666, Thomas.W, Tigercompanion25, Tillya Tepe gold, Trappist the monk, Utcursch, Vajra Raja, Verbum Veritas, WOSlinker, WereSpielChequers, Wienerbund, Willard84, पाटलिपुत्र, 神风 , 75 anonymous edits 87

Yona *Source:* https://en.wikipedia.org/w/index.php?oldid=837468719 *License:* Creative Commons Attribution-Share Alike 3.0 *Contributors:* 3rdAlcove, Aarandir, Adam Keller, Againme, Ahivarn, Aldux, Aristo Class, Awadhi, BCtl, BD2412, Bender235, Bhikkhu Sujato, Biglovinb, Botteville, Brenont, Burpingchickenhockey, CALR, CaliforniaAliBaba, Caltas, CanisRufus, Carlossuarez46, Certes, Charles Matthews, Chris the speller, ClueBot NG, Cminard, Colonies Chris, CommonsDelinker, Corvus cornix, Cpq29gpl, Cpt.a.haddock, Cucumbers610, DabMachine, DanMS, Dangerous-Boy, Dbachmann, Demiurge1000, Deshpandeguy, Edgar181, Enkyklios, Extraordinary, Fixer88, Florian Blaschke, FocalPoint, Fylindfotberserk, Gardar Rurak, Gilgamesh~enwiki, Goethean, Grant65, Grenavitar, Hectorian, Hind meri jaan, Hmains, Hrafn, Insider, JForget, Jagged 85, JesseRafe, Jwy, JzG, K.Nevelsteen, Kaisershatner, Kautilya3, Kuralyov, Kutkut16~enwiki, Legaleagle86, LouisAragon, Macedonian, Magioladitis, Malaiya, Marcocapelle, Materialscientist, Matia.gr, MatthewVanitas, Midas02, Milktaco, Mojo Hand, Ms Sarah Welch, Naniwako, Naraht, NatusRoma, Naveen Sankar, Ogress, Omnipaedista, Paine Ellsworth, Paknur, Paxsimius, Per Honor et Gloria, Phil wink, Pictureuploader, Plrk, Pseudomonas, R'n'B, Randeepa, Reddogsix, Redtigerxyz, Sam Hocevar, Satbir Singh, SchreiberBike, ShelfSkewed, Shenme, Shyamsunder, Siddiqui, Sprocket Crocket, Stemonitis, Steorra, Sundarikasha, Thanatos666, That Guy, From That Show!, Tigercompanion25, Til Eulenspiegel, Tim1357, Tonifer, Torvalu4, Trinanjon, Varanwal, Venu62, Vikimedia, Wikidas, Woohookitty, Wubbabubba, Xdivider, Zsero, पाटलिपुत्र, தென்காசி சுப்பிரமணியன், 118 anonymous edits 158

Indo-Parthian Kingdom *Source:* https://en.wikipedia.org/w/index.php?oldid=847022244 *License:* Creative Commons Attribution-Share Alike 3.0 *Contributors:* 1Tolasona, AdventurousSquirrel, Ahrarara, Aldux, Amir85, Anbu121, Artacoana, Astynax, BD2412, Basil II, Bellatores, Blue Papa Boy, Briangotts, BurritoBazooka, CambridgeBayWeather, Chirag, Chochopk, Chris the speller, Clicketyclack, Colonies Chris, CommonsDelinker, Cpt.a.haddock, Darsie, Dbachmann, Dewan357, Dimadick, Doug Weller, Download, Ducknish, Echuck215, Edwy, Fasi100, Fayenatic london, Frietjes, Fullstop, GB fan, Gaius Cornelius, Gdr, Gilgamesh~enwiki, Good Olfactory, Greenshed, Gurch, HavelockWilltravel, Headbomb, Hertz1888, Highpeaks35, HistoryofIran, Hmains, Hongooi, Intothefire, J04n, JLaTondre, Japanese Searobin, JoaoRicardo, John K, Kashmiri, Kattigara, Khardamagh, Kintetsubuffalo, Kwamikagami, Linguiste, LouisAragon, Macrakis, Mallerd, Marcocapelle, MatthewVanitas, Mike Storm, Narky Blert, Nick Number, Nickzlapeor, Nowhither, Omerlives, Omnipaedista, Panairjdde~enwiki, Pappig, Per Honor et Gloria, Podzemnik, Priyadasi, Rajaashoka, Rama's Arrow, Rich Farmbrough, Ricky81682, Roland zh, Ronhjones, Rurik the Varangian, Shiggy1, Shwudnhchs, Shyamsunder, Siddiqui, SimonP, Sitush, Sparta3, Sponsianus, Sushilmishra, ThanMore, Thomas.W, Tim1357, Tobias Conradi, Tom Radulovich, Toolen, Udimu, Utcursch, WOSlinker, Wario-Man, Wbm1058, WereSpielChequers, Willard84, Woohookitty, Woudloper, Zimthi, Zscout370, ماني, फ़िलप्रो, 神风 , 62 anonymous edits 170

Pahlavas *Source:* https://en.wikipedia.org/w/index.php?oldid=847042940 *License:* Creative Commons Attribution-Share Alike 3.0 *Contributors:* BD2412, Bgwhite, Biglovinb, Braincricket, Charles Matthews, Chris the speller, Ciriii, Cpt.a.haddock, Dewan357, Dewan753, Dpv, Fixer88, Fullstop, Hmains, Igiffin, JLaTondre, JaGa, Jeff3000, Ketiltrout, Khazar2, Khoikhoi, Klbrain, LilHelpa, LouisAragon, Marcocapelle, Natobxl, Nmadhubala, Paxse, Phil wink, Radagast83, Satbir Singh, Siddiqui, Sistan, Solomon7968, Steven J. Anderson, Swarm Internationale, Sze cavalry01, Thomas.W, UsaSatsui, Utcursch, Wiae, Woohookitty, ماني, 39 anonymous edits 183

Western Satraps *Source:* https://en.wikipedia.org/w/index.php?oldid=850673623 *License:* Creative Commons Attribution-Share Alike 3.0 *Contributors:* Againme, Ancientcoinsofindia1, AnsarParacha, Arjayay, Astynax, Atushabharucha, BD2412, Baji12, Bellatores, Bender235, Bermicourt, Bodhisattwa, Brigade Piron, Buddhipriya, Capankajsmilyo, Catalographer, Cbyneorne, Ceosad, Chaoborus, Chris the speller, CoinIndia, Colonies Chris, CommonsDelinker, DanDaMan020, Devanampriya, Dewan357, Dewan753, Dewritech, Fixer88, Frietjes, Fylindfotberserk, Gts-tg, Gulbenk, HavelockWilltravel, HistoryofIran, Hmains, Hmainsbot1, JaGa, John Hill, John of Reading, Joy1963, JustAGal, Kww, Lachs1, Leszek Jańczuk, LilHelpa, LouisAragon, Marcocapelle, Miaow Miaow, Niceguyedc, Nizil Shah, Noah5151, Omnipaedista, Onel5969, Parulsingh1478, Paul S, Paxse, Per Honor et Gloria, Philg88, Podzemnik, Priyadasi, Rani nurmai, Rejectwater, Rich Farmbrough, Ricky81682, Rorkadian, Samee, Saxenasaurabhblr, Shyamsunder, Signalhead, Soetermans, Solomon7968, Sumitkachroo, Sushilmishra, Talessman, Vin09, Vssun, Vultur~enwiki, Wienerbund, Woohookitty, ماني, पाटलिपुत्र, 29 anonymous edits 186

Kushan Empire *Source:* https://en.wikipedia.org/w/index.php?oldid=852869264 *License:* Creative Commons Attribution-Share Alike 3.0 *Contributors:* Agaceri, Ale King, Anandmoorti, Anarchyte, AryamanA, Avantiputra7, Awale-Abdi, Bearcat, Bender235, Bgwhite, Blanche of King's Lynn, Bodhisattwa, Bongwarrior, CAPTAIN RAJU, CambridgeBayWeather, Capankajsmilyo, Ccxlslr98, Chewings72, ClueBot NG, CommonsDelinker, Corinne, Cpt.a.haddock, Csldigicol, Darokrithia, Dimadick, Doug Weller, DrRC, EZpwnage, Ekabhishek, Fanghong, Fayenatic london, Fconaway, Fixer88, Foonarres, FourLights, Frietjes, Fycafterpro, GELongstreet, Grant65, Gurjar vishal tomar, HaeB, Hairy Dude, HavelockWilltravel, Hebrides, HistoryofIran, Hmains, Hydronium Hydroxide, IronGargoyle, Jaggajat, John of Reading, Kamlesh4rmBhopal, Kanguole, Kansas Bear, Kasana the great kushan, Khestwol, Krakkos, KylieTastic, LazarozI, LouisAragon, Lubossekk, Makyen, Marcocapelle, Mark Ironie, Mkrestin, Mogism, Mohd zabbar kasana, Morningstar1814, Muhammadahmad79, Nikhilmn2002, Non-dropframe, OneGreek, Onel5969, PericlesofAthens, Pi3.124, Piledhighandeep, Prashant chaprana, Pratyk321,

Prime541, Quest for Truth, RA0808, Redhat101, Ricky81682, RolandR, SUHdewwwcisx, Saladin1987, Sanjoydey33, Seasonsinthesun, Sitush, Somebody500, Tachs, Tahar Jelun, Tahc, TheOakenshield, Thomas.W, TompaDompa, Tracield, Ulric1313, Uskill, Wario-Man, Wbm1058, Wienerbund, Wikismartaleck, Willard84, Worldciv 2017 kushan, Yamaguchi先生 , ZxxZxxZ, Zyxw, पाटलिपुत्र, 神风 , 163 anonymous edits 215

Kushano-Sasanian Kingdom *Source:* https://en.wikipedia.org/w/index.php?oldid=852066591 *License:* Creative Commons Attribution-Share Alike 3.0 *Contributors:* Alansohn, Amir85, AshishG, Astynax, Bencherlite (AWB), BinKhaye, Bumm13, Cabolitae, Chochopk, Cplakidas, Delljvc, Devanampriya, Dewan357, EagleFan, Edwy, Esnible, Frietjes, Fuhghettaboutit, Fullstop, Grant65, Gwern, Hajji Piruz, Headbomb, Hibernian, HistoryofIran, Hmains, Intothefire, J. Finkelstein, JaGa, Japanese Searobin, Jguk, Kwamikagami, LittleWink, Liverpoolpics, LouisAragon, Manitobamountie, Marcocapelle, Mdmday, Nandesuka, Natg 19, Oliver Lineham, PMLF, Paine Ellsworth, Panairjdde～enwiki, Per Honor et Gloria, PhnomPencil, Qsoothaxial, R'n'B, Rama's Arrow, Rashti, Ravichandar84, STBotD, Samee, Siddiqui, Simone ostini, Stepheng3, Sushilmishra, Talessman, The Anomebot2, The Behnam, TimBentley, Wario-Man, Woohookitty, Zain1987, पाटलिपुत्र, 25 anonymous edits 249

Huna people *Source:* https://en.wikipedia.org/w/index.php?oldid=828250840 *License:* Creative Commons Attribution-Share Alike 3.0 *Contributors:* A.j.roberts, Abstruce, Al Hanvar, Alansohn, Alx bio, Angelo De La Paz, Ankit21694, AroundTheGlobe, Astynax, Backendgaming, Briangotts, Capankajsmilyo, CapitalR, Charles Matthews, Chhora, Chris the speller, Cpt.a.haddock, Danger, Deeptrivia, Devanampriya, Dewan357, Dewritech, E104421, Edwy, Eurodyne, Geoff.powers, Grant65, Gwern, Gwguffey, Hind meri jaan, Hmainsbot1, Iamthecheese44, Imc, Intothefire, J04n, Jagged 85, Jeff3000, Jguk, Joostik, JustAGal, Kansas Bear, KartikMistry, Khazar, Kuralyov, Kww, Lokesh 2000, LouisAragon, MatthewVanitas, Ms Sarah Welch, Nakon, Nandesuka, NeilN, Neo-Jay, NoychoH, Omerlives, PatGallacher, Per Honor et Gloria, Phil wink, Pi3.124, Piyushgujjar, Qatarihistorian, QuartierLatin1968, Qwyrxian, RandomCritic, Regnator, Rejectwater, Richard Keatinge, Rossen4, Saladin1987, Satbir Singh, SchreiberBike, Shan174, Shreevatsa, Shyamsunder, Siddiqui, Sisodia, Sitush, Solomon7968, Sushilkumarmishra, Sushilmishra, Takabeg, Talessman, Tigercompanion25, TimBentley, Tom Radulovich, Tomas e, Updatehelper, Utcursch, Verbum Veritas, WALTHAM2, Zaenon, पाटलिपुत्र, 75 anonymous edits 257

Hephthalite Empire *Source:* https://en.wikipedia.org/w/index.php?oldid=852868948 *License:* Creative Commons Attribution-Share Alike 3.0 *Contributors:* 1sasdasd, A.j.roberts, Adûnâi, AidanP02, Al Hanvar, Alfie Gandon, Alx bio, Ancientsteppe, Anoplocis, Anotherclown, Attilios, BD2412, Badarchiinayurzana, Baji12, Bamsi2929, Bejnar, Bender235, Benjamin Trovato, Bgwhite, Blaylockjam10, Brozozo, Bryanzmason, Buziatov, CV9933, Capankajsmilyo, Cemsentin1, Chewings72, ClueBot NG, Cookieballer, Corvus Park, Cpt.a.haddock, Crovata, Darokrithia, Delljvc, Dewritech, Donner60, Ebizur, Edward321, Erim Turukku, Ermahgerd9, Erminwin, Everyking, Fayenatic london, Fixer88, Florian Blaschke, Flyer22 Reborn, Franrasyan, GoingBatty, Grant65, GünniX, H.Arian, HD86, Hairy Dude, Hibernian, Hind meri jaan, HistoryofIran, Hmains, I dream of horses, Ineuw, Ira Leviton, J8079s, JackintheBox, John of Reading, Johnbod, Jukkuj, Kabasakaloglu, Kansas Bear, Khestwol, Khorichar, KnowledgeAndPeace, Krakkos, Kwamikagami, LilHelpa, Linuxxe, LittleWink, Look2See1, LouisAragon, MRD2014, Maproom, Mar4d, Marcocapelle, Mazandar, Mert soysaç, Narky Blert, Natg 19, Ogress, Paul S, Pavel Stankov, Persia2099, Philg88, Pi3.124, Piledhighandeep, Primaler, Quest for Truth, Rani nurmai, Rjwilmsi, Rossen4, Saladin1987, Shivanshhhg, Sissai, Sleimok12, Slovenski Volk, Sonerbcrc, Srnec, Sweepy, Thomas.W, Tigercompanion25, Timrollpickering, TompaDompa, Ugog Nizdast, Unbuttered Parsnip, Utcursch, VerifiedCactus, Wario-Man, Wikiuser13, Wujastyk, Yakbul, Yamaguchi先生 , Ymblanter, ·1e0nid·, पाटलिपुत्र, 121 anonymous edits 262

Rai dynasty *Source:* https://en.wikipedia.org/w/index.php?oldid=853272375 *License:* Creative Commons Attribution-Share Alike 3.0 *Contributors:* Acabashi, Afipundir, Akhil.bharathan, American55, Anik01, AryamanA, Attilios, Bender235, Bgwhite, Bhavinkundaliya, Bongwarrior, Chris the speller, ChrisHodgesUK, ClueBot NG, Cplakidas, Czeror, DabMachine, Dangerous-Boy, Delljvc, Dewan357, Doug Weller, Enurarfa, Gad 123, Gadre, Gadri, Generalboss3, Green Giant, Gryffindor, Hhitesh2012, Histological, Hmains, Hmainsbot1, HotWinters, Intothefire, Jethwarp, JogiAsad, Jonesey95, Joy1963, KahnJohn27, Kautilya3, LRBurdak, Liberal Humanist, LouisAragon, Madelinejenks, Marcocapelle, Materialscientist, MatthewVanitas, Meegs, Melcous, Misaq Rabab, Mkrestin, Mojo Hand, MonsterHunter32, Mujtaba!, Nick Moyes, Nyttend, Onel5969, PAKHIGHWAY, Rahpal, Rai empire, Rama's Arrow, Ribena786, Rjwilmsi, Rorkadian, Saladin1987, SchreiberBike, ShelfSkewed, Shimlaites, Shyland, Sir Sputnik, Sitush, SkateTier, Stalwart111, Superstar141996, Tigeroo, Utcursch, Vegaswikian, Willard84, Woohookitty, Yamaguchi先生 , Zain1987, ～～(...MA.Tay.CA...)～～, ～～Gadri1～～, مجتبی, کب ا مم, சதீஸ், ☫, 185 anonymous edits 278

Gandhara *Source:* https://en.wikipedia.org/w/index.php?oldid=853521401 *License:* Creative Commons Attribution-Share Alike 3.0 *Contributors:* Abecedare, Ainalhafila, Akmal94, AlexiusHoratius, Anasaitis, Arjayay, AshokSrinath, Avantiputra7, BD2412, Beads and reels, Bender235, Bennv3771, Biografer, Bongan, Cabolitae, Capankajsmilyo, Chewings72, CoolieCoolster, Corinne, Cpt.a.haddock, DawedalRaqqa, DrRC, Dthomsen8, Ebyabe, Erico Tachizawa, Fanghong, Felix Jaegar, Fish and karate, GenQuest, Gilo1969, Glatisant, Gluons12, Gymnophoria, Hedwig in Washington, Hessamnia, Highpeaks35, History of Persia, Hzh, Immcim2c, Informationskampagne, JaconaFrere, Javierfv1212, Jayarava, Jdaloner, JimRenge, John Hill, John of Reading, Joshua Jonathan, Kautilya3, Keith D, Ketiltrout, Khansahib666, Khestwol, KylieTastic, Lemnaminor, Loopy30, LouisAragon, Lubossekk, Magioladitis, Marcocapelle, Materialscientist, Mcc1789, Mild Bill Hiccup, Milktaco, Navops47, NeilN, Nestwiki, Niceguyedc, NickTheRipper, Nicnote, Nizil Shah, Nyttend, Omnipaedista, Onel5969, Oshwah, Out-typer, PAKHIGHWAY, Patelshishil, Pi3.124, Piledhighandeep, Pratham Kailasiya, R'n'B, Rattans, RegentsPark, Ricky81682, Rollingcontributor, SDC, SUM1, Sahara4u, Saladin1987, Samee, Sjlain, Spasage, Sulaimandaud, TheodoreIndiana, Thomas.W, Tigercompanion25, Trappist the monk, Twofingered Typist, Uanfala, Utcursch, Vivek Sarje, Vreswiki, Wario-Man, Willard84, Work number1987, Yamaguchi先生 , Zanhe, Zap guy, ZxxZxxZ, पाटलिपुत्र, 175 anonymous edits 281

Kambojas *Source:* https://en.wikipedia.org/w/index.php?oldid=852627005 *License:* Creative Commons Attribution-Share Alike 3.0 *Contributors:* A. Parrot, Ahivarn, Ambar wiki, AshokSrinath, Aus RichAlex, BD2412, Barthateslisa, Bgpaulus, Biglovinb, Bongan, Cabolitae, Chewings72, Colonies Chris, Cpt.a.haddock, Darokrithia, David Straub, Dbachmann, Deepakkamboj, Dekimasu, Delljvc, Ekabhishek, EllsworthSchmittendorf, Eman2129, Epson Salts, Fconaway, Felix Folio Secundus, Frze, Fyrael, Grant65, Harvinder Chandigarh, Hind meri jaan, Hmains, Indicologist, Itsmejudith, John of Reading, Jonesmith4, Joostik, Krakkos, Kwamikagami, LilHelpa, LlywelynII, LouisAragon, Magioladitis, Marcocapelle, Massagetae, Mazdakabedi, Mccapra, Menchi, Morinae, Narky Blert, Natg 19, Navops47, Niceguyedc, Nick Number, Omnipaedista, Paine Ellsworth, Pawyilee, PhnomPencil, PiCo, R'n'B, Riana, Saladin1987, Salamurai, Sankalpdravid, SchreiberBike, Seair21, Siddhartha Ghai, Sitush, Smommss, Solomon7968, SpacemanSpiff, Sumitkachroo, The Interior, The Mysterious El Willstro, Titodutta, Utcursch, Vazgen Ghazaryan, WOSlinker, Wario-Man, Webclient101, WereSpielChequers, Woohookitty, Worldbruce, 60 anonymous edits 316

Karkoṭa Empire *Source:* https://en.wikipedia.org/w/index.php?oldid=852722338 *License:* Creative Commons Attribution-Share Alike 3.0 *Contributors:* Bender235, Capankajsmilyo, Cpt.a.haddock, Highpeaks35, Kautilya3, Kriteesh, KylieTastic, Magentic Manifestations, Mntzr, Pol098, Shivansh.ganjoo, UserNumber, Utcursch, Xz786, पाटलिपुत्र, 46 anonymous edits 324

Kabul Shahi *Source:* https://en.wikipedia.org/w/index.php?oldid=850805915 *License:* Creative Commons Attribution-Share Alike 3.0 *Contributors:* 1ForTheMoney, Agaceri, Alexius08, Alx bio, AnsarParacha, AnwarInsaan, Areapeaslol, Arjayay, Aymatth2, BD2412, Barkeep, Barthateslisa, Bender235, Bodhisattwa, Brenont, Brigade Piron, Cabolitae, Chewings72, Chris the speller, ClueBot NG, Colonies Chris, Cookiemohnsta, Copperknickers, Cpt.a.haddock, Czeror, DHN-bot～enwiki, Danger, Deacon of Pndapetzim, Delljvc, Dewan357, Dewan753, Dongar Kathorekar, Doug Weller, Dr. Blofeld, Drpickem, EJF, Ekabhishek, Felix Folio Secundus, Frietjes, Generalboss3, Georgejmyersjr, Goldsmiths295, Good Olfactory, Grant65, Highpeaks35, Hind meri jaan, HistoryofIran, Hmains, Intothefire, Irfan shehzad, J04n, JaGa, Jambudveepam, Jethwarp, John of Reading, Julliedon, Jwy, Kansas Bear, Khalid Mahmood, Kingturtle, Kintetsubuffalo, Koavf, Krakkos, Kww, KylieTastic, Liberal Humanist, LouisAragon, MALLUS, Magioladitis, Marcocapelle, MatthewVanitas, Mazdakabedi, Mild Bill Hiccup, Misaq Rabab, Mojo Hand, MonsterHunter32, More random musing, Morinae, Nasir Ghobar, Natg 19, Nick Number, Nikhilmohan17, Nirvana888, NuclearWarfare, Ogress, Ohconfucius, Oshwah, PWilkinson, Per Honor et Gloria, PeterSymonds, Qatarihistorian, R'n'B, RJFJR, Rahulmothiya, RainbowOfLight, RenamedUser01302013, Rickard Vogelberg, Rq88187, RyanCross, Saladin1987, Satbir Singh, SchreiberBike, Scope creep, Seair21, Seantai, Sgnpkd, Sitush, Skyerise, Solomon7968, Spasage, Stevenmitchell, Sze cavalry01, Tajik, Talessman, Terry J. Carter, The Anomebot2, Thingg, Toolen, Topbanana, Updatehelper, Utcursch, VIKRAM.SINGH.VIKRAM.SINGH, Warut, Wikiglobaleditor, Willard84, Woohookitty, Yashasvipratap, Yozer1, Zeshan Mahmmod, पाटलिपुत्र, சதீஸ், Ἀλέξανδρος ὁ Μέγας, 黑暗魔君 , 161 anonymous edits 326

Satavahana dynasty *Source:* https://en.wikipedia.org/w/index.php?oldid=850331460 *License:* Creative Commons Attribution-Share Alike 3.0 *Contributors:* 1989, Arpvr, BAYYAPPANAHALLI, BD2412, Bender235, Bgwhite, Capankajsmilyo, Chan144, Chewings72, ClueBot NG, CommonsDelinker, Cpt.a.haddock, Czeror, Dimadick, Doug Weller, Dueep Eik, Ermahgerd9, Fixer88, HavelockWilltravel, Highpeaks35, Hmains, John of Reading, Jonny555, Jusdafax, Kautilya3, Kautuk1, M.K.Dan, Magioladitis, Marianna251, Materialscientist, Memesfornoobs, Muppavarapu Navya, NitinBhargava2016, Onel5969, PWilkinson, Pppery, Punyaboy, Ramkaanthala, Sipabacus, SpacemanSpiff, Sriyerram, Srkris, Steamerrr, TMahesh naik, The Quixotic Potato, The Untouchables, Tigercompanion25, Tillya Tepe gold, Utcursch, Vibhss, Vitthallaxmankhot, Worldciv 2017 kushan, Worldciv207 satavahanas, पाटलिपुत्र, 90 anonymous edits 343

Mahameghavahana dynasty *Source:* https://en.wikipedia.org/w/index.php?oldid=798637543 *License:* Creative Commons Attribution-Share Alike 3.0 *Contributors:* Againme, Areapeaslol, Beingtastegood, Bender235, Bhagat.bb, Capankajsmilyo, Drmies, Fayenatic london, Good Olfactory, Hmains, Indian Chronicles, Kanashimi, Keeby101, Kenfyre, Kww, Linguisticgeek, Malcolma, Marcocapelle, Ms Sarah Welch, Ogress, PKT, Pratyk321, Primefac, Richard-of-Earth, Sadads, Sambitaadi, Shyamsunder, Srnec, Talessman, Tijfo098, Utcursch, Wikiuser13, 34 anonymous edits 377

Nagas of Padmavati *Source:* https://en.wikipedia.org/w/index.php?oldid=852121870 *License:* Creative Commons Attribution-Share Alike 3.0 *Contributors:* Chuniyana, Cpt.a.haddock, Daranz, Frietjes, Ira Leviton, Linguisticgeek, Malaiya, Sitush, Utcursch, WereSpielChequers, Woodlot, 4 anonymous edits 383

Gupta Empire *Source:* https://en.wikipedia.org/w/index.php?oldid=853238978 *License:* Creative Commons Attribution-Share Alike 3.0 *Contributors:* *thing goes, A.j.roberts, Abc1019, Abhishek0831996, Al Legorhythm, AnvitZero, Arjun singh verma, AryamanA, AshishHJain, Audaciter, Avantiputra7, Beta7, Bitthalns, Bojo1498, Bongan, Callanecc, Capankajsmilyo, Chewings72, Chrissymad, ClickedMoss5, ClueBot NG, Cpt.a.haddock, Dane, David.moreno72, Decan.reporter, DeniedClub, Diannaa, Dimadick, Donner60, Dorintosh, Dorsetonian, Drewmutt, EdwardElric2016, Ermahgerd9,

Excirial, Fayenatic london, Fuortu, Galobtter, Guanaco, Gupta2016-17, Guptaman3, Happysailor, Helwett, Highpeaks35, Hulksar2003, IVORK, Imtushar, IronGargoyle, Jaideepnain123, Jakepaul888, Jennica, Jessicapierce, Jim1138, JimVC3, Johnbod, Johnrameshkhan, Kbseah, Kuber Nayak, Kumar Ripudaman, Kushwahaboy, LawrenceScafuri, Lepsyleon, Maestro2016, Magioladitis, Materialscientist, Maximajorian Viridio, Mild Bill Hiccup, Narayananm1998, Negro69gupta, Nfalceso, Obamachan112604, Ollinilsson, Omnipaedista, Onel5969, Patrick Neylan, PerfumeMarele, Pinnerup, Pratyk321, PratyushSinha101, Prime541, Qerti, Quinton Feldberg, Qzd, R'n'B, RNLockwood, Rishabh78, Risto hot sir, Sahilsarekh, Samee, Serols, Shellwood, Shivck13, Simplexity22, SparklingPessimist, Stewartsoda, SuyashVader, Thapa 75, Theinstantmatrix, ToBeFree, ToMt, TompaDompa, Travelbird, Uday pratap ssiinngghh, Uran00bnotjk, Utcursch, Vedanti sen, Vibhss, WereSpielChequers, White Shadows, Wienerbund, Wikishovel, Worldbruce, Wtmitchell, X. Squire, Zaenon, पाटलिपुत्र, 193 anonymous edits 388

Vakataka dynasty *Source:* https://en.wikipedia.org/w/index.php?oldid=851923330 *License:* Creative Commons Attribution-Share Alike 3.0 *Contributors:* Abhijitsaumitra, Abhiran, Anthony Ivanoff, Asitaram, BD2412, Balu.ji, Bender235, Capankajsmilyo, Capitals00, Chris the speller, Colonies Chris, Cpt.a.haddock, Dbachmann, Dewan357, Dimadick, Douglasfrankfort∼enwiki, Ekabhishek, Fconaway, FeatherPluma, Fraggle81, Frietjes, Gaius Cornelius, Generalboss3, Giraffedata, GoingBatty, Hannabeprakash, Harshabob, Hmains, Holenarasipura, Hororoka, Indianprithvi, J04n, Jacob.jose, Jim1138, Joy1963, Kishorepatnaik, KylieTastic, Leonidaa, Marco polo, MatthewVanitas, More random musing, Narky Blert, Nick Number, Nirvana888, Omnipaedista, Onel5969, PeterSymonds, Rejectwater, Rosiestep, RoverDingbat, Sankalpdravid, Satish-ansingkar, Serols, Shivap, Shivashree, Shreevatsa, Shyamsunder, SpacemanSpiff, StartTerminal, Tabletop, Talessman, Tassedethe, Tigercompanion25, Utcursch, Vijay Singh Suryawanshi, Vishal1976, Zippymarmalade, पाटलिपुत्र, Ἀλέξανδρος ὁ Μέγας, 64 anonymous edits 411

Harsha *Source:* https://en.wikipedia.org/w/index.php?oldid=853533942 *License:* Creative Commons Attribution-Share Alike 3.0 *Contributors:* Aayush18, Abhishek0831996, Againme, Allens, Ambarishatluri, Amitrochates, Anir1uph, Aravind V R, Arunkumararun, AryamanA, Ashokachola, Bender235, Bgwhite, Bkrish68, CLCStudent, Caballero1967, Capankajsmilyo, Cartakes, Chewings72, Chris the speller, ClueBot NG, CommonsDelinker, Cpt.a.haddock, Crazynyancat, DVdm, Derek R Bullamore, Dewritech, Discospinster, DynamoDegsy, Ecsunil92, Ekabhishek, Frietjes, Gilabrand, Gilliam, Gurpreetsingh56, Harshacan, Hebrides, Highpeaks35, Hmains, Hmainsbot1, Jaideepnain123, Jairaj991, John K, Jonesmith4, Kagundu, Kautilya3, Klbrain, Kmg90, Kongugirl, Library Guy, Mahensingha, Materialscientist, MatthewVanitas, Mike Rosoft, Morinae, Mzilikazi1939, Naam Tamilar, Napoleon 100, Nick Number, Nimishv, Niteshgughane, Nizil Shah, NottNott, Ntrikha, Ohconfucius, Oshwah, Padmacharan123, Pinethicket, Pratyya Ghosh, Raghav Sharman, Raghuvanshidude, Ranaharra, Rani nurmai, Rao Ravindra, Reliable88, Roland zh, RoyalBharat, Rsrikanth05, SalariaRajput, Sandeyad, Serols, Shash, Shubhbilam, Sidlivestrong, Sitush, Skinsmoke, Sparta3, StarmanW, Stjohn1970, Strike Eagle, Sumone10154, Team VJ, Thakurjiofficial, TheDevMor, Tigerleapgorge, Timrollpickering, Titodutta, Uday.zaildar, Utcursch, Vijay bramhane, VishalB, Vishnukumar1974, War wizard90, WarriorRaj, Wbm1058, Wiki-uk, Wikiuser13, Woohookitty, Worldbruce, Xiaoxkzh, Yokeesh, पाटलिपुत्र, 221 anonymous edits 423

Gurjar *Source:* https://en.wikipedia.org/w/index.php?oldid=853329687 *License:* Creative Commons Attribution-Share Alike 3.0 *Contributors:* 8XM, A145029, Abrahamic Faiths, Aisteco, Akeel2781, Albaadiankit, Ali rock 1, Ankush 89, Arampha, Arjayay, AsadUK200, Axtramedium, BD2412, BeenAroundAWhile, Bender235, Black Epsilon∼, Chaudharys-3591, ChrisTakey, ClueBot NG, CommonsDelinker, Compassionate727, Cyberbot I, DMacks, DatGuy, Delljvc, DemocraticLuntz, Dev raj gujjar, Dm51c, Dorpater, DpkKumar34, Dr.K., EISIGMA, EISIGMA2, EISIGMA9, Ekdalian, Faiyzaan, Flyer22 Reborn, Future Perfect at Sunrise, Fylindfotberserk, Gareth Griffith-Jones, Gewingewin, Gilo1969, Gurjeshwar, Headbomb, Highpeaks35, Himanshu Gujjar, Hmains, Hunter Arjunsinh, InformavoreSultan, JatDelhi, Javaidrahi1970, Jdcomix, Jo-Jo Eumerus, John811jd, Kashmiri, Kautilya3, King vishal singh, Krisxlowry, Krrish.Viky, Kunal gurjar, Liberal Humanist, LilHelpa, LittleWink, Loopy30, LouisAragon, Magioladitis, Mahensingha, Majidgujjar, Malik Mubashir Awan, Malushahi1, Masterknighted, Mike Rosoft, Mikro Nekros, Mkrestin, Mubarak 647, Muhammadffsh, NeilN, Niceguyedc, Onel5969, POLLO PHONICA, ParaVeet+, Philg88, Pk041, Ptbg, Ravensfire, Rodw, Rubbish computer, Saladin1987, Samad PG, Saqib A. Gujjar, Saqraat, Sitush, Sjö, Skinsmoke, Snori, SpacemanSpiff, Sudomukherjee, Teledildonix314, The Quixotic Potato, Thorwald, Tigercompanion25, Trappist the monk, Tushar Chaudharyy, Uanfala, Utcursch, Vibhss, Wasiq 9320, Winged Blades of Godric, Zardari123, Zhgujjar, דאמ׳זורצם 428

Vishnukundina dynasty *Source:* https://en.wikipedia.org/w/index.php?oldid=852148352 *License:* Creative Commons Attribution-Share Alike 3.0 *Contributors:* Abecedare, Againme, Arudraraju, BD2412, Brown cp, CALR, Capankajsmilyo, Chris the speller, ChrisCork, Cpt.a.haddock, DadaNeem, DavidFarmbrough, Dbachmann, Dewan357, Dewan753, Dreadstar, Edwy, Fayenatic london, Frietjes, Highpeaks35, Hmains, Hmainsbot1, Hohum, Holenarasipura, Indianprithvi, J04n, Jeremy112233, Kamal singh munda, Kww, Leolaursen, Marcocapelle, MarnetteD, Mattisse, Mitresh66, Nagarjuna198, Naveen Uppalapati, Nick Number, Nizil Shah, Onel5969, Pepsidude, Philippe, PhnomPencil, RJFJR, Rama's Arrow, Rockin It Loud, Roland zh, Rubbish computer, Salilb, Shareo2, ShelfSkewed, Shyamsunder, Sitush, SomeFreakOnTheInternet, SpacemanSpiff, Tejas.B, The Anome, Utcursch, Vatasura, Venu62, Vin09, Wiki842, Ziggurat, 48 anonymous edits 438

Maitraka dynasty *Source:* https://en.wikipedia.org/w/index.php?oldid=852725056 *License:* Creative Commons Attribution-Share Alike 3.0 *Contributors:* Akiva.avraham, Alren, Anthony Ivanoff, Areapeaslol, Arjayay, BD2412, Beingtastegood, Blaxthos, Bot-maru, Charles Matthews, DanMS, Dbachmann, Deepakkamboj, Deville, Editorofthewiki, Gaius Cornelius, Generalboss3, Highpeaks35, Hmains, Jodosma, Joy1963, Kww, LilHelpa, MJBurrage, Malaiya, Mboverload, More random musing, Myasuda, Narky Blert, Nick Moyes, Nirvana888, Nizil Shah, Onel5969, Orenburg1, P.K.Niyogi, Paxse, R'n'B, Rachmat04, RandomCritic, Rayc, Satbir Singh, SchreiberBike, Shirazibustan, Shreevatsa, Shyamsunder, Sitush, Solomon7968, Sze cavalry01, The Quixotic Potato, Tiger888, TimBentley, Tom Radulovich, Tormozko, Trappist the monk, Utcursch, Vivek Ray, WereSpielChequers, पाटलिपुत्र, □□□□, 70 anonymous edits 445

Gurjara-Pratihara dynasty *Source:* https://en.wikipedia.org/w/index.php?oldid=853331323 *License:* Creative Commons Attribution-Share Alike 3.0 *Contributors:* Abhisheksingh2001a, Ajayrajposwal, Alpha3031, Arjayay, Axtramedium, Bender235, Biker1985, Bladesmulti, BrownHairedGirl, CAPTAIN RAJU, Capankajsmilyo, Cartakes, Chaudharys-3591, Chewings72, Chief Editor(Apoorv), ClueBot NG, Cpt.a.haddock, Deepaksinghchn, Dewritech, DpkKumar34, Frietjes, Ganganathlal, Gaurav Gurjar Sahab, Gewingewin, Grant65, Gujjar Han, Highpeaks35, Hmains, India culture, Iridescent, IronGargoyle, JediKnight20, Jitendra Singh Gurjar, Jonesey95, KartikMistry, Kautilya3, Kumar aaaditya, KylieTastic, Liz, Lokeshbhati45, Marek69, Mark Ironie, Matt7899, Mayank china, Mewla bhatti, Mohitnagar96, Morinae, Niceguyedc, Nizil Shah, Onel5969, Original thinker, Oshwah, Parthvipulpandya, Pi3.124, PolicyReformer, Prabhat1729, RT Gujar, Rajput Sirdar, Rajputtiger0, Ribena786, Ricky81682, Risto hot sir, Ronneythakur, Sandip tanwar, Saqib A. Gujjar, Sitush, SpacemanSpiff, Utcursch, Virender rakwal, Vishal0soni, WereSpielChequers, Winnan Tirunallur, Wxzapghy, Yadav1985, Yamaguchi先生 , 134 anonymous edits 464

Rajput *Source:* https://en.wikipedia.org/w/index.php?oldid=853212816 *License:* Creative Commons Attribution-Share Alike 3.0 *Contributors:* 8XM, A145029, Abilngeorge, Acharya63, Airkeeper, Anoyet, Arjayay, Ashokharsana, Atrisomkshraj, Awesomehimachali, BD2412, Barthateslisa, Bender235, Bgwhite, Bishonen, Bramhesh Patil, BreadBuddy, Burbak, C1MM, CIA1234, Chrimas1, Chris the speller, Dahiya1208, Damien2016, Divyraj, Doug4, DpkKumar34, Dr. Sroy, Ekdalian, Eric1998, GünniX, Highpeaks35, Histological, Jai Rajput, Jairaj991, Jamesmcardle, JogiAsad, Jonathansammy, Jy1998, Karanduke99, Kautilya3, King vishal singh, Lakhbir87, Lamro, LilHelpa, LocalWorld, Lokeshbhati45, Magioladitis, Mahensingha, Mar4d, Materialscientist, Mohanbhan, Mr Stephen, NadirAli, Narky Blert, Newblog 32, Niceguyedc, NidekUS, Nizil Shah, Nppatil123, Nyttend, Ohnoitsjamie, Onel5969, Prototypehumanoid, Quinton Feldberg, R'n'B, Raghvendra99674010, Raja Hussain Iqbal, Rajavksingh, Rajkumar 1 02, Rajputclann, Rasheed Barsar, Rashkeqamar, RegentsPark, Rich Farmbrough, Risto hot sir, Rmkop, Rodw, Ronneythakur, Rudra1999, SDC, SUM1, Samee, Shimmerr, Shinjoya, Shivammahesh7, Shrikanthv, Shxahxh, Sitush, Sjö, Skbaral484, SpacemanSpiff, Spasage, Stonemountainfox, Tachs, Takafumi1, Taoni, Tikka Rao, Utcursch, Worldbruce, Writereditor009, Yintan, हिंदुस्थान वासी 475

Katoch *Source:* https://en.wikipedia.org/w/index.php?oldid=853571873 *License:* Creative Commons Attribution-Share Alike 3.0 *Contributors:* Aanri, Abhi7777, Bgwhite, Chris the speller, ClueBot NG, Cst17, Del Piero, Diannaa, Digvijaykatoch, Discospinster, Dl2000, Falcon8765, Fconaway, Fraggle81, Gkatoch, Grafen, HMSSolent, Hardscarf, Himmy.20, Hongooi, ImpuMozhi, IndianGeneralist, JaGa, Jairaj991, Jaisingh rathore, Jim1138, John of Reading, Johnuniq, Kangrasp, Kautilya3, Khairaarsh, LRBurdak, Loopman, Mahensingha, Narky Blert, NeilN, NitinMlk, Omnipaedista, Philip Trueman, RAJA DR.ASHOK K.THAKUR, Raj masterjeet, Rajput666, RegentsPark, Rich Farmbrough, Romanaccio999, RonJohnson10, Saksham ahi, SalariaRajput, Samuel Blanning, Scabbers the Rat, Sickmick101, Sitush, SpacemanSpiff, Sugandhaaa, Supeyia, Sushant gupta, Swingoswingo, T Singh, Telex, Tiptoety, Utcursch, Veerjawan22682, Vyom25, WALTHAM2, Wavelength, WereSpielChequers, Widr, Wikibaba1977, Woudloper, Xufanc, Yintan, 222 anonymous edits 489

Chauhan *Source:* https://en.wikipedia.org/w/index.php?oldid=848246452 *License:* Creative Commons Attribution-Share Alike 3.0 *Contributors:* -glove-, 0xF8E8, 78.26, Aadi.00, Adamstraw99, Airkeeper, Ajayrajposwal, Alichauhanrajput, Amanhanda, Apparition11, Arjayay, Arjun127492, Arunchauhan415, Ashokharsana, Atenderachauhangurjar, Bender235, Benzband, Bgwhite, Bhadoriyaofbhind, Bishonen, CIA1234, CambridgeBayWeather, Chaudhary tanuj salar, Chauhan1192, Chndelagujjar, Chris the speller, ClueBot NG, Dcirovic, Delljvc, Dharamraghu, DhruvChauhan The Great, Dhruvrana30, DpkKumar34, Dr.prashant chauhan, Eurpan, Frietjes, Gareth Griffith-Jones, GiantSnowman, Happysailor, Helpsome, Honi02, KahnJohn27, Kajan lakhan, Kamalchauhan067, Kansas Bear, Kggochar, King vishal singh, KrakatoaKatie, L293D, Manit Rana, MarnetteD, Marvellous Spider-Man, Materialscientist, MatthewVanitas, Mewla bhatti, Milansinghaswal, MrBill3, Niceguyedc, Nsinghjadon, Onel5969, Optakeover, Owais Khursheed, Pi3.124, Pilla pilla, Priya.niam, RacIndian, Raghogarh, Rajput Sirdar, Redrose64, ScrapIronIV, Serols, Sitush, SpacemanSpiff, StratMan001, The Quixotic Potato, Tigercompanion25, Tillerh11, Utcursch, Widr, Yamaguchi先生 , Yaris678, Zanhe, 188 anonymous edits 491

Chahamanas of Shakambhari *Source:* https://en.wikipedia.org/w/index.php?oldid=852791571 *License:* Creative Commons Attribution-Share Alike 3.0 *Contributors:* Abhishek0831996, Capankajsmilyo, Chanduking333, Frietjes, Onel5969, Risto hot sir, Utcursch, पाटलिपुत्र, 6 anonymous edits ... 495

Kachwaha *Source:* https://en.wikipedia.org/w/index.php?oldid=842379723 *License:* Creative Commons Attribution-Share Alike 3.0 *Contributors:* 1990satya, 1997kB, 81jsc, Ajraddatz, Akrajput8373, Anand kushwaha maurya, Anna Frodesiak, Arjayay, Babitaarora, Bgwhite, Bishonen, Brajendracseb, Burbak, Chrissymad, ClueBot NG, DadaNeem, Dashrath009, Discospinster, Dl2000, Doug Weller, Ekabhishek, Eyesnore, Felicia777, Flat Out, Flyer22 Reborn, Ginsuloft, Gotra68, Graphium, HiHa1234, Humblewikicontributor, I dream of horses, Illuminatifire1212, Ism schism, Jairaj991, Jethwarp, Jim1138, Jmsrajsaraj22, Joymay1, KNHaw, KUNWAR GAURAV SINGH KALYANWAT, Kushsinghkushwaha, KylieTastic, Luxure, Mahensingha, Mark Arsten, Materialscientist, MatthewVanitas, MusikAnimal, NeilN, Oshwah, Owsert, Pappuverma11, Papsaraj22, Premkoli99, Priyeshsingh2511, Rajkumar 1 02,

Ravishekhaji, Ravisingh2712, Rayaraya, Rijusikri, Rjwilmsi, Rohitcusatmca, SPSKachhwaha, Santoshsingh430, Santoshsinghindia, Ser Amantio di Nicolao, Serols, Siddhapratap, Sir Sher, Sitush, SpacemanSpiff, Strike Eagle, Sunil kshatriya, Surajpratapsinghraj, SurjeetSinghSuryavansi, Tailor jigyasu 12345, TalgoKL, Tbhotch, Trivender singh, Truth only 1, Utcursch, Vdr11, Vensco, Widr, YOGENDRA PRATAP SINGH ARCHAEOLOGIST, Yogeshkushwahathakur, आनंद कुशवाहा कछवाहा, 152 anonymous edits 505

Paramara dynasty *Source:* https://en.wikipedia.org/w/index.php?oldid=853555461 *License:* Creative Commons Attribution-Share Alike 3.0 *Contributors:* 0101vishal, A.amitkumar, Akram0101, Aksaks 09, Arjayay, Avenue X at Cicero, Awais141, Bean 19, Bender235, Bgwhite, BrownHairedGirl, Capankajsmilyo, Chhora, CommonsDelinker, Damien2016, Denisarona, Doug Weller, DpkKumar34, Fayenatic london, Fconaway, Flat Out, G9H, Good Olfactory, Google survey, Harshadityasinh, HistoricalQuest, Histrocity, Hmains, Hmainsbot1, Hymavarma, Imagination.mahen, Iron0037, JanetteDoe, Jattttsingh, Jdcomix, Jjparmar, John of Reading, Jonesmith4, Joy1963, KH-1, Kansas Bear, King vishal singh, Kpowar, Kww, Malaiya, Manannnnn, Materialscientist, Mkrestin, Mrsinghparmar, MusikAnimal, Narky Blert, Onel5969, Orenburg1, Person who formerly started with "216", Pi3.124, Ravindrasinh THAKOR, Ricky81682, RoverDingbat, SJ Defender, Sandeep7422, SchreiberBike, Shyamsunder, Sitush, SpacemanSpiff, Tahc, Utcursch, WOSlinker, Zhgujjar, Zippymarmalade, पाटलिपुत्र, Ἀλέξανδρος ὁ Μέγας, 78 anonymous edits 509

Chaulukya dynasty *Source:* https://en.wikipedia.org/w/index.php?oldid=853643788 *License:* Creative Commons Attribution-Share Alike 3.0 *Contributors:* Abhi.analyst, Ajitsinh, Appi53007, Arihant Brahmane, Baislax, BrownHairedGirl, CAKrutesh, Capankajsmilyo, Chndelagujjar, ClueBot NG, Cpt.a.haddock, Dhraun, Doug Weller, DpkKumar34, Dueep Eik, El cid, el campeador, Fayenatic london, GenuineArt, Good Olfactory, GünniX, HParv Kumar, Hymavarma, Iluvumerijaan, Iridescent, Jairaj991, Jayrajsolanki07, Jethwarp, Jn045, John of Reading, KDTW Flyer, KartikMistry, Kautilya3, Kunal Singh Solanki Nathawat, LiamKasbar, LilHelpa, Mahensingha, Marcocapelle, NeilN, Nizil Shah, Nsinghvns, Ogress, Onel5969, Oshwah, Pi3.124, Pratyk321, Rajput Sirdar, Ricky81682, SOLANKI KISHAN, Sagarsinh jadav, Sawai Solanki, ShamusHarper, Sheopura, Majal, Shyamsunder, Sitush, Smalljim, Solankiabhishek, Solanusa, Tahc, Utcursch, WarriorRaj, Woodlot, World Civ 2017-SOLANKI, Zziccardi, पाटलिपुत्र, 81 anonymous edits ... 526

Tomara dynasty *Source:* https://en.wikipedia.org/w/index.php?oldid=849043778 *License:* Creative Commons Attribution-Share Alike 3.0 *Contributors:* Capankajsmilyo, Cpt.a.haddock, Diannaa, John of Reading, Makert40, Prasannaravi663, Pratyk321, Rudrakshi Kumari, Sitush, Thakur shera, Tony Fox, Utcursch, Vineeta.varshney, 10 anonymous edits 541

Pala Empire *Source:* https://en.wikipedia.org/w/index.php?oldid=851661252 *License:* Creative Commons Attribution-Share Alike 3.0 *Contributors:* Abecedare, Againme, Akib.H, Altes, Arjayay, Ashish-Sharma-Dilli, Astynax, Avanendra psr, BD2412, Bazaan, Bender235, BirBikrom, BrightStarSky, Callanecc, Capankajsmilyo, Cartakes, Chaipau, Chewings72, ClueBot NG, Cpt.a.haddock, DaGizza, Dakinijones, Deepak D'Souza, Diya Titu, Editor2020, Farihashabnam, Fayenatic london, Fylindfotberserk, Gavia immer, GenQuest, Generalboss3, Gyrodoor33, Helpsome, Hibernian, Highpeaks35, Himanshu.raam, Ibrahim Husain Meraj, Iktus, Jagged 85, Jamesx12345, Jayjg, Jim1138, Jodosma, John of Reading, Johnbod, Jonesey95, Jonesmith4, JorisvS, Joy1963, Just4edit, K6ka, Kadamburvijay, Kamlesh4rmBhopal, Koavf, Kww, LilHelpa, Lonely Explorer, Malaiya, Mar4d, Markwiki, Mashupzone, Materialscientist, Mayasandra, Mayasutra, Mdmday, Melakavijay, Mimihitam, Morinae, Musabbir Islam, NadirAli, Niceguyedc, Nick Number, Nikhilmn2002, Nimetapoeg, Niteshgughane, Ohconfucius, Omnipaedista, Osprey39, PIL1987, PKT, Paulrajarshi, Petronis, Pied Hornbill, Proudtobeindian007, Raghuholkar, Rahulwiki1996, Rayaraya, Reahad, Redtigerxyz, Rickjpelleg, Ricky81682, Rjwilmsi, Rockin It Loud, RockyAlley, RockyMasum, Samudrakula, Sanjoydey33, Serols, Shiggy1, Shivamtanwer, Shubh leo5, Shyamsunder, Skinsmoke, Sodabottle, Solomon7968, Tachs, Takafumi1, Titodutta, Utcursch, Vanished user ija0qfr2o3ijfi 4i4tijwci823irnf, Vanished user qwqwijr8hwrkjdnvkanfoh4, Vanished user zm34pq51mz, Vastu, Vikram singh06, WOSlinker, Wieralee, WikHead, Wikipapon, Woohookitty, Worldbruce, Worldciv pala, Xufanc, Zhongguoyingdu, ,ה-זפר বিজয় চক্রবর্তী, 102 anonymous edits .. 547

Chandra dynasty *Source:* https://en.wikipedia.org/w/index.php?oldid=744260972 *License:* Creative Commons Attribution-Share Alike 3.0 *Contributors:* Ajithpr, AkhilKumarPal, Anthony Appleyard, Cpt.a.haddock, Eckertbt, Finetooth, Malcolma, Md.altaf.rahman, Pontificalibus, Reahad, Retired username, Rockin It Loud, Sanjaysahawbpdcl, Sitush, SpacemanSpiff, Takafumi1, Toon05, Tóraí, UltimatePyro, Utcursch, Worldbruce, 2 anonymous edits 566

Eastern Ganga dynasty *Source:* https://en.wikipedia.org/w/index.php?oldid=849483163 *License:* Creative Commons Attribution-Share Alike 3.0 *Contributors:* Adityamadhav83, Akarkera, Astynax, BD2412, Bender235, Bgwhite, Biplab.K.M, CanisRufus, Cartakes, CommonsDelinker, Compfreak7, Cpt.a.haddock, DadaNeem, Dbachmann, Devraj77, Dewan357, Ekabhishek, Fconaway, Fixer88, GSS, GenQuest, Generalboss3, Glumanda7, Grafen, Highpeaks35, Iridescent, Jaivanth, Jim1138, Joy1963, KLBot2, Kahtar, Kenfyre, Kwiki, KylieTastic, L Manju, LeftAire, Life of Riley, Lifebonzza, Lillinan1, MKar, Manjit Keshari Nayak, Mark Ironie, Mayasandra, Mogism, Mr Stephen, Muvendar, Naniwako, Natg 19, Nayansatya, Nehwyn, Niceguyedc, Nirvana888, PeterSymonds, Pharaoh han, Pi3.124, Psr27, Raghu ji, Rajasekhar1961, Rani nurmai, Ravichandar84, Rayaraya, Rich Farmbrough, Richard-of-Earth, Roland zh, Saurabh.vinian, Shiggy1, Shyamsunder, Sidsahu, Sitush, Srimaymohapatra, SteveM123, Subramanya sarma, Sujit kumar, Takafumi1, Tellasitis, Titodutta, Utcursch, Vatasura, Vin09, Wavelength, Whpq, Yaris678, Zenpriyesh1, தென்காசி சுப்பிரமணியன், 79 anonymous edits ... 567

Sena dynasty *Source:* https://en.wikipedia.org/w/index.php?oldid=851471839 *License:* Creative Commons Attribution-Share Alike 3.0 *Contributors:* Anionmission, Astynax, Avanendra, Avanendra psr, Balthazarduju, Bender235, Bongan, BrightStarSky, Cartakes, ClueBot NG, Colonies Chris, Cpt.a.haddock, Dangerous-Boy, Dewan357, Dewan753, Dineshkannambadi, Doug Weller, Dthomsen8, Dwaipayanc, Ekdalian, Frietjes, Garg92, Good Olfactory, Greenshed, Holenarasipura, InedibleHulk, Jacob.jose, Janmejaya09, Je regrette, Jonesmith4, Katharineamy, Kayastha Shiromani, Khoikhoi, Kiranmayi pal, Kww, Le Anh-Huy, Magioladitis, Malaiya, Mayasandra, Mimihitam, Mizan1947, Monster eagle, Nakula Kedar Valsan, Ohconfucius, Pearle, Pi3.124, PiCo, Pied Hornbill, Precision0203, R'n'B, Ragib, Rama's Arrow, Recurring dreams, Rkghadai, Rmky87, Rockin It Loud, RonBeeCNC, Rumpelstiltskin223, STK YATHU, Salilb, SameerKhan, Samudrakula, Shiggy1, Shyamsunder, Skinsmoke, Sminthopsis84, Solomon7968, SpacemanSpiff, Springnuts, Tahmidal Zami, Takafumi1, Tarikur, TheDragonFire300, Tinton5, Utcursch, Varadarajd, WTucker, Wavelength, Windrider24584, Wizardman, Woohookitty, Worldbruce, Xezbeth, ❦, 132 anonymous edits 573

Varman dynasty *Source:* https://en.wikipedia.org/w/index.php?oldid=845414172 *License:* Creative Commons Attribution-Share Alike 3.0 *Contributors:* Abhiran, Arjayay, Bakasuprman, Bender235, Bhaskarbhagawati, CMBJ, Chaipau, Courcelles, Cpt.a.haddock, Dthomsen8, Ettrig, Felicia777, Flyer22 Reborn, FolkTraditionalist, Fram, Good Olfactory, Hmainsbot1, JimCubb, John of Reading, LilHelpa, Magioladitis, Niceguyedc, Night w, Nirongkun bora, OlEnglish, Oshwah, PhnomPencil, Pkbwcgs, PlyrStar93, PurpleHz, Qwertywander, Qwertywander1, Rsrikanth05, Shyamsunder, Sitush, Tabletop, Tom.Reding, Utcursch, 19 anonymous edits 579

Kamarupa *Source:* https://en.wikipedia.org/w/index.php?oldid=852730640 *License:* Creative Commons Attribution-Share Alike 3.0 *Contributors:* 7VIES, Abhiran, Adamgerber80, Aeusoes1, Amartyabag, Anshuman.jrt, Anthony Appleyard, Arjayay, Ash wki, AshokSrinath, Axomiya deka, Bender235, Bhaskarbhagawati, Bijay Dutta, Binod deori, Bongan, CMBJ, Caerwine, Capankajsmilyo, Chaipau, Chao Arunav, Chewings72, ChrisCork, ChrisGualtieri, CommonsDelinker, Cpt.a.haddock, Dangerous-Boy, Delusion23, Dkonwar, Douglasfrankfort∼enwiki, Edwy, Ekabhishek, Faizhaider, Fayenatic london, Finnusertop, Gaius Cornelius, GenQuest, Giraffedata, Gog the Mild, Good Olfactory, Hmains, Hmainsbot1, Ira Leviton, JaGa, Jagged 85, Jamy crock, Jayantanth, Jijithnr, Karthikndr, Kww, LilHelpa, MKar, MapSGV, Maproom, Mark the train, Mattisse, Mild Bill Hiccup, Mohiuddin06, Naniwako, Narky Blert, Necrothesp, Neodymium-142, Niceguyedc, Nirongkun bora, Ogine, P.K.Niyogi, Penguinnumbers, Philg88, Quibitos, Rama's Arrow, Redheylin, Rodw, Roland zh, Shekhar Jyoti Das, Shovon76, Shyamsunder, Sitush, SpacemanSpiff, Taketa, The Black Truth, TheObsidianFriar, Utcursch, Venu62, WereSpielChequers, Worldbruce, Yann, पाटलिपुत्र, 50 anonymous edits 585

Mlechchha dynasty *Source:* https://en.wikipedia.org/w/index.php?oldid=820633553 *License:* Creative Commons Attribution-Share Alike 3.0 *Contributors:* Akashkachari, AroundTheGlobe, Bhadani, CMBJ, Capankajsmilyo, Chaipau, Cpt.a.haddock, Egha95, Fixit1989, Good Olfactory, Hmains, JzG, Karthikndr, LauraGoldstein67, Ogress, Rama's Arrow, Shyamsunder, TabaWala, Tableshakers, Wiki-uk, 13 anonymous edits 595

Pala dynasty (Kamarupa) *Source:* https://en.wikipedia.org/w/index.php?oldid=846884139 *License:* Creative Commons Attribution-Share Alike 3.0 *Contributors:* Agent 78787, Bhaskarbhagawati, CMBJ, Capankajsmilyo, Chaipau, Cpt.a.haddock, Fixit1989, GSS, Good Olfactory, Greenshed, Hmainsbot1, Hugo999, Karthikndr, Narky Blert, Paulrajarshi, Rajarshipaul, Reahad, Shyamsunder, Utcursch, 40 anonymous edits 597

Twipra Kingdom *Source:* https://en.wikipedia.org/w/index.php?oldid=849467540 *License:* Creative Commons Attribution-Share Alike 3.0 *Contributors:* Abhishekjoshi, Aditya Kabir, Ainalhafila, Bdebbarma, Belsabull, Bonnienunisa14, BusanHP, Capankajsmilyo, Chaipau, ChrisGualtieri, Coinmanj, CommonsDelinker, Coolian, Crystallina, Cyfal, David Murasing, Dbachmann, Denisarona, Edcolins, Ekabhishek, Fixit1989, Giraffedata, Hindustan10, Ivysaur, JaGa, LoremIpsumDolorSitAsmet, Magioladitis, Naersjoen, Nick Number, Oshwah, PKT, Penguinnumbers, Qtcomputer, R'n'B, Rjwilmsi, RobNS, SQGibbon, Samudrakula, SchreiberBike, Sephia karta, Shovon76, Skylark2008, Snigbrook, Tabletop, Tameem7320, Titodutta, Titus III, Twipra, Urduboy, Utcursch, Victor D, Wavelength, Wikisopher, Xufanc, 32 anonymous edits 599

Sangam period *Source:* https://en.wikipedia.org/w/index.php?oldid=851928321 *License:* Creative Commons Attribution-Share Alike 3.0 *Contributors:* Aayush18, Antonio Lopez, Arulraja, Auntof6, Avedeus, Aymatth2, Bender235, Benwing, Clubover, ClueBot NG, Cobi, Copperchloride, Cpt.a.haddock, Curb Chain, Cyberbot II, D6, DVdm, Dalit Llama, Dbachmann, Dmol, DocWatson42, Doug Weller, Eeekster, Eletsinger, Enlil Ninlil, Eshwar.om, FROSTOXIC, Facsix, Faizhaider, Fconaway, Finnusertop, Fram, Fratrep, Gingerjoos, Gioto, Gjs238, GreenC, Gthorvey, Headbomb, HenryFaber, Hibernian, Highpeaks35, Hongooi, In2thats12, Itsmejudith, Iwazaki, J04n, Jaggivasudev, Jillball, Jim1138, John of Reading, Joshua Jonathan, Jpkole, JudeBob123, JueLinLi, Kalki361, Kanatonian, Kandarp2007, Kautilya3, Kingpin13, Kongugirl, Lifebonzza, LilHelpa, Limideen, Lotadutt, Lotlil, Lou Sander, Maayan pandithevan, Materialscientist, Michael Hardy, Muvendar, Nagadeepa, Nijgoykar, PONDHEEPANKAR, Pandbar, Pasetu22222, Pavan977, Pearll's sun, Pepper Black, Perumalshankars, Philippe, Pinethicket, Prabahar82, Praveenskpillai, RA0808, RJFJR, Raghith, Rambam rashi, Ravichandar84, Redhome, Ricky81682, Roland zh, Ronz, Sankalpdravid, Sarvagnya, Senthilkumaras, Shasho1, Shyamsunder, Sigma 7, Squids and Chips, SriSuren, Srikrish85, Ssven2, SteveM123, THEN WHO WAS PHONE?, Tamil1988, Tamilan101, The Behnam, Thingg, Tnellalan, Tripping Nambiar, UnsungKing123, Utcursch, Vanished user qwqwijr8hwrkjdnvkanfoh4, Vatasura, Vayalir, Venu62, Wangond, WeedFruits, Widr, Wiki Raja, Wikiality123, Wubbabubba, Xezbeth, Yamaguchi先生 , Zigomer trubahin, தென்காசி சுப்பிரமணியன், 171 anonymous edits 603

Chera dynasty *Source:* https://en.wikipedia.org/w/index.php?oldid=853510661 *License:* Creative Commons Attribution-Share Alike 3.0 *Contributors:* Aashiq Ibn Asim, Akmal Hashim, Akshayacropolis, Azhaganvimalan, Azhaganvimalan96, Blackknight12, CASSIOPEIA, Capankajsmilyo, Certes, Chewings72, ClueBot NG, CommanderOzEvolved, CommonsDelinker, Cpt.a.haddock, Discospinster, Doug Weller, Fr.ta, Galaxplorer4414, GeneralizationsAreBad, Giraffedata, Gluons12, HaeB, Hareeshh, Helwett, Hyper9, IronGargoyle, Jim1138, John of Reading, KGirlTrucker81, Kalki361, Kljunas, Krsmoorthi, Kunlunpenglai, Lsvsiva, MBlaze Lightning, Magioladitis, Materialscientist, Mattoor, MelanieN, Meldort, Mild Bill Hiccup, Muvendar, Narayaniv8, Narky

Blert, Nouz er, RajeshUnuppally, Ranjithsiji, RegentsPark, Robin7013, Rodw, SUM1, Saiwiki95, Sanjoydey33, Senthil k23, Shellwood, Sitush, SpacemanSpiff, Sree lesh191, TJH2018, The Quixotic Potato, Thomas.W, Tigercompanion25, Ullanhun, Utcursch, Vibhss, Vijay Kumar S, VishnuTheTraveller, WIKIVIDYA, Waleed Baqeer, WereSpielChequers, Weybridgeguy, WorldCiv2017 chera, Xenophrenic, 121 anonymous edits 610

Kalabhra dynasty *Source:* https://en.wikipedia.org/w/index.php?oldid=853619476 *License:* Creative Commons Attribution-Share Alike 3.0 *Contributors:* Abecedare, Abhishek0831996, Ajeyaajeya, Akhil.bharathan, Arjayay, Astynax, Balablitz, Bender235, Bladesmulti, Broccoli and Coffee, Capankajsmilyo, Cpt.a.haddock, Danny, Dewan357, Dipendra2007, Ermn, Exclusivly limited, Fayenatic london, Fconaway, Felida97, Gnanapiti, Goldenhawk 0, Gongshow, Grafen, HenryFaber, Hmains, Hongooi, Jim1138, Joaquin008, Kirkkadav, Konguboy, Kww, Luigi Boy, Marcus334, Materialscientist, MatthewVanitas, Meldort, Mr. Credible, Mukkulam, Nat Krause, Nijgoykar, NitinBhargava2016, PKT, Pandian tamil, Pelmeen10, Pratyk321, Pvasque8, Rama's Arrow, Ravichandar84, Rich Farmbrough, Rjwilmsi, SJ Defender, SchreiberBike, Ser Amantio di Nicolao, ShivNarayanan, Shyamsunder, Sitush, Slaggart, Sodabottle, Solomon7968, Sprocket Crocket, Srinath Sridevan, Srkris, SteveM123, Sundar, Suryapradeep88, Sushilmishra, Tan Meifen, TinucherianBot II, Utcursch, Vatasura, Venu62, Vssun, Wangond, Wikiality123, WizOfWords, Woohookitty, Xufanc, Yasirian, Δ, 79 anonymous edits 632

Kadamba dynasty *Source:* https://en.wikipedia.org/w/index.php?oldid=851865627 *License:* Creative Commons Attribution-Share Alike 3.0 *Contributors:* Aaron Schulz, Abecedare, Abhiran, Adimovk5, Aerofighter2010, Ahoerstemeier, Amarrg, Anand.Hegde, Apsubrahmanyam, ArielGold, Astynax, BD2412, Basilicofresco, Bender235, Calidore Chase, Capankajsmilyo, Chewings72, ChrisCork, ChrisGualtieri, Cpt.a.haddock, Decan.reporter, Dewan357, Dineshkannambadi, Doloco, Dppowell, Drmies, F-402, Fayenatic london, Frietjes, Gaius Cornelius, GenQuest, Generalboss3, George D. Watson, Gnanapiti, GoingBatty, Gongshow, Gryffindor, HansHermans, Hemujain, Highpeaks35, Holenarasipura, J04n, John of Reading, Jonathansammy, Jrsanthosh, Just4edit, KNM, Kannadiga, Kardamkas, Karthickbala, Keith D, Khazar, Kngd2007, Kroger2005, LeoFrank, Lightmouse, LilHelpa, Linguisticgeek, Luna Santin, Makyen, Manjunath Doddamani Gajendragad, Mark Ironie, Materialscientist, Mattisse, Mauler90, Mayasandra, Melakavijay, Naveenbm, Nichalp, Nick Number, Nijgoykar, Niri.M, Nishkid64, Nittavinoda, Ohconfucius, Pied Hornbill, Planemad, Prabhupaatil, Pratyk321, Ramk2004, Rani nurmai, Ravichandar84, Redtigerxyz, Rich Farmbrough, Ricky81682, Rjwilmsi, Rockin It Loud, Roland zh, Sanjeev76, Shyamsunder, Simple-man-everyday, Sitush, SpacemanSpiff, Spidermen, Steamerrr, Sushilkumarmishra, Sushilmishra, Tabletop, Talessman, TexasJyotish, The Quixotic Potato, Thumperward, Timawesomeness, Timrollpickering, Utcursch, Vatasura, Victuallers, Vishal1976, Vishu123, Vssun, Welsh, WereSpielChequers, Wikid77, Winston786, Woohookitty, Xufanc, YellowMonkey, Ἀλέξανδρος ὁ Μέγας, 132 anonymous edits 636

Western Ganga dynasty *Source:* https://en.wikipedia.org/w/index.php?oldid=842609428 *License:* Creative Commons Attribution-Share Alike 3.0 *Contributors:* 52 Pickup, 777sms, 83d40m, Adimovk5, Aldo samulo, All Worlds, Altzinn, Amarrg, Anand.Hegde, Another Believer, Anwar saadat, Asenine, BD2412, Bender235, Bobblehead, Bongwarrior, Br'er Rabbit, Brant.merrell, Brederode∼enwiki, Bugs2beatles, Capankajsmilyo, Celebrategoodtimes, Chandru1234, Charlik, Chimino, Chris the speller, ClueBot NG, Colonies Chris, CommonsDelinker, Cor anglais 16, Courcelles, Cpt.a.haddock, DaGizza, Daonguyen95, DashyGames, Dcirovic, Deepak D'Souza, Demiurge1000, Dewan357, Dineshkannambadi, Dirkbb, DrKay, Dudley Miles, Dwaipayanc, Favonian, Fayenatic london, Flubeca, Fratrep, Frietjes, Gimmetrow, Gnanapiti, Gryffindor, Gyrodoor33, Harryboyles, Holenarasipura, Indian Chronicles, Ineck, Iohannes Animosus, Jayapal.hr, Jim1138, John of Reading, Jrsanthosh, Jugaari cross, KNM, Kbdank71, Ketiltrout, Khazar2, Kww, Leolaursen, Lightmouse, Lugia2453, Makyen, Marcus Cyron, Mathighat, Mayasandra, Mayesdan, Meredyth, MorelMWilliam, Mr Stephen, Nishkid64, NuclearWarfare, Onel5969, Paxsimius, PeterSymonds, PhnomPencil, Pied Hornbill, Piledhigheranddeeper, Pinecar, Primefac, Psubhashish, Raul654, Ravichandar84, Razimantv, Redtigerxyz, Rich Farmbrough, Rjwilmsi, Roland zh, Sardanaphalus, Sarvagnya, Shyamsunder, Skinsmoke, Sri Harsha Bhogi, Stemonitis, Sushilkumarmishra, Sushilmishra, Tahc, Tamilyomen, Teammm, Tellasitis, Theonlynitin, Thumperward, Timeshifter, Titodutta, Topbanana, Utcursch, Visor, VoABot II, Wilfredsimon, Woohookitty, World8115, YellowMonkey, Zanhe, आशीष भटनागर, जैन, ರವಿಚಂದ್ರ, Ἀλέξανδρος ὁ Μέγας, 100 anonymous edits 651

Chalukya dynasty *Source:* https://en.wikipedia.org/w/index.php?oldid=851744431 *License:* Creative Commons Attribution-Share Alike 3.0 *Contributors:* AManWithNoPlan, Alan, Anand.Hegde, Ansumang, Begoon, Bender235, Bisasam7, Bob1960evens, CambridgeBayWeather, Capankajsmilyo, CapitalR, Chackerian, Chalukya123, Chewings72, Chhora, Chris the speller, Citation bot 1, Civfanatic, Cpt.a.haddock, Crusoe8181, Dbkasar, DivermanAU, Donner60, DrKay, Dthomsen8, EdwardElric2016, Ekabhishek, Eric-Wester, Ermahgerd9, Fayenatic london, Fconaway, Feminist, Frietjes, Fyyer, GenQuest, Giraffedata, Gnanapiti, Good Olfactory, Gurjar singh, HaeB, Hind meri jaan, Hmains, Holenarasipura, Human3015, IM3847, Ivanpares, Jethwarp, Jim1138, John of Reading, Jonesey95, Kamal singh munda, Kansas Bear, Kautilya3, Khardamagh, Khazar2, Klisz, Kumarrao, Kwamikagami, Kww, Lachs1, Lanet303, Laszlo Panaflex, LilHelpa, MALLUS, MANGOSEEDSDATES, Manju24nath, Manjunath Doddamani Gajendragad, MatthewVanitas, Mayasandra, Mkrestin, Morinae, Mr Stephen, Mx. Granger, NERIUM, NQ, Niceguyedc, Nick Number, Nissar khan234, Nithin bolar k, Nittavinoda, Nizil Shah, O.Koslowski, Onel5969, Pebble101, Pi3.124, Pied Hornbill, Pratyk321, Priyadarshineeraj, Rajaashoka, Ricky81682, Rjwilmsi, RobertG, Roland zh, Rubbish computer, Satdeep Gill, Solomon7968, Sumitkachroo, Sushilkumarmishra, Sushilmishra, Takafumi1, Tangopaso, The Quixotic Potato, Thumperward, Timrollpickering, Tom.Reding, Trivialist, Utcursch, Utkarsh sawale, Vibhss, WOSlinker, Wavelength, Woohookitty, Worldciv2017 Chalukya Empire, पाटलिपुत्र, Ἀλέξανδρος ὁ Μέγας, 122 anonymous edits 674

Pallava dynasty *Source:* https://en.wikipedia.org/w/index.php?oldid=853224060 *License:* Creative Commons Attribution-Share Alike 3.0 *Contributors:* Abbanadu, Aggi007, Alvinraj86, Amarprasad.v, Ambivaidy, ArunGYadhav, Arvind asia, Ashwinrajagopalan85, Awsmsp, Babushan, Balablitz, Banda.krishna, Bender235, Capankajsmilyo, Chewings72, ClueBot NG, Cpt.a.haddock, DMacks, Delan singh, Dewritech, Dharmaputhra, Doncram, Duraish, Eshwar.om, Feanor0, Good Olfactory, Highpeaks35, Hmains, Holenarasipura, Ira Leviton, Iyengar 1960, Javith akram, Jeff G., Joefromrandb, John of Reading, Johnbod, Kbssomnath, L Manju, Last edited by:, Luigi Boy, Mayasutra, Muvendar, Naveen Uppalapati, Navops47, Niceguyedc, Nick Number, Nilo.boss, Nittavinoda, Oshwah, Paul2520, Phanindrabn, Pi3.124, Premthanjavur, Prince raja emperor, Raja.m82, Reddyvx, Ricky81682, Robevans123, Rsrikanth05, Sahrudayan, Sai18021993, Saibala18, Sangitha rani111, Satheeshpukal, Shellwood, Sitush, Soumit ban, SpacemanSpiff, Srksamala, Ssrirammt, Steamerrr, Sundarelsa, Tachs, Takafumi1, Tlroche, Utcursch, Vatasura, Vermont, WikiArasu, Wikiname12345, पाटलिपुत्र, 189 anonymous edits ..697

Eastern Chalukyas *Source:* https://en.wikipedia.org/w/index.php?oldid=851771498 *License:* Creative Commons Attribution-Share Alike 3.0 *Contributors:* Altruism, Bender235, Braincricket, BrownHairedGirl, Bsskchaitanya, CALR, Cpt.a.haddock, Dewan357, Dineshkannambadi, Dl2000, Empirado, Fayenatic london, Foodie 377, Frietjes, Gnanapiti, Gorthian, Headbomb, Hmains, Holenarasipura, Hv1972, J04n, KNM, Kautilya3, Kumarrao, LiamKasbar, Lightmouse, Lilac Soul, Look2See1, Manjunath Doddamani Gajendragad, Mattisse, Mekala Harika, Morinae, Muppavarapu Navya, Niceguyedc, NitinBhargava2016, Onel5969, Panel1, Petrb, Pied Hornbill, Plastikspork, Rayaraya, Ricky81682, Rjwilmsi, Roland zh, Sarvabhaum, Shesha 06, Shyamsunder, Sitush, SpacemanSpiff, Steamerrr, SteveM123, Sumanthk, Tassedethe, Tejas.B, Thegreatgrabber, Thumperward, Utcursch, Vamsi Janga, Venu62, Vin09, Wavelength, Worldciv2017 Chalukya Empire, पाटलिपुत्र, Ἀλέξανδρος ὁ Μέγας, 92 anonymous edits 711

Pandyan dynasty *Source:* https://en.wikipedia.org/w/index.php?oldid=853229246 *License:* Creative Commons Attribution-Share Alike 3.0 *Contributors:* 2016rewind, Abhishek0831996, Aggi007, Ahamed Adnan Bin Alim, Anup Ramakrishnan, ArunGYadhav, Arunnagammal, Azhaganvimalan, Azhaganvimalan96, BD2412, Bender235, CAPTAIN RAJU, Capankajsmilyo, Chewings72, Chris the speller, Classicwiki, ClueBot NG, Cocohead781, CommanderOzEvolved, CommonsDelinker, Cpt.a.haddock, Daniel0Wellby sch, Dewritech, Dharani Maran, Dirkbb, EdmundT, Euryalus, Fort5000, Gilliam, Gurjar singh, HaeB, Helwett, Highpeaks35, I dream of horses, Ira Leviton, JaconaFrere, Jennica, Jtrrs0, JudeBob123, Kansas Bear, Kongugirl, Lakun.patra, Let There Be Sunshine, LiamKasbar, Luigi Boy, Madhu siddharth, Magentic Manifestations, Materialscientist, Mccapra, Menaechmi, Muvendar, Mx. Granger, Natg 19, Navops47, NitinBhargava2016, Nittavinoda, PKT, Pratyk321, Ramanan KL, Ranjithsiji, Redtigerxyz, Rich Farmbrough, Ros1602, Rubbish computer, SA 13 Bro, Saibala18, Sakthisainath, Sandhyanathtiwari, Sarafvpz, Sbrighton, Shkarthikeyan, SirPigwig, SpacemanSpiff, Srirangam99, StanchevFPS, Takafumi1, Timmyshin, UY Scuti, Utcursch, Vatasura, Vijay Kumar S, Vijayakumar Kaushik, Winnan Tirunallur, Xenani, ԱշոտՏՆՂ, தென்காசி சுப்பிரமணியன், 167 anonymous edits 720

Rashtrakuta dynasty *Source:* https://en.wikipedia.org/w/index.php?oldid=851162415 *License:* Creative Commons Attribution-Share Alike 3.0 *Contributors:* Adamgerber80, Altes, Anand.Hegde, Ashokachola, Ashvawiki, BD2412, Bappa3, Bender235, Bgwhite, Biscuittin, Brad101, BrainProgrammers, BudChrSch, Capankajsmilyo, Capitals00, Chewings72, Chris the speller, Classicwiki, ClueBot NG, Cpt.a.haddock, Crisco 1492, Daonguyen95, Discospinster, Donner60, DrKay, Dragonflame1738, Dthomsen8, EdwardElric2016, Ekabhishek, EncyclopediaUpdaticus, Fayenatic london, Feminist, Firebrace, Flegmon12, Frietjes, Gerda Arendt, Good Olfactory, Gryffindor, Holenarasipura, Human3015, I.am.viji, Inikac, John of Reading, Jonesey95, Jonesmith4, Kautilya3, Keith D, Kethrus, Khazar2, Knife-in-the-drawer, Koavf, Kogmaw, Kww, Languagehat, Lifebonzza, Look2See1, Maddiebb77, Magmar3, Malaiya, Manjunath Doddamani Gajendragad, Marcocapelle, Marcus Cyron, Mary Ria, Materialscientist, Mayasandra, Mr Stephen, Natg 19, Niceguyedc, Nick Number, NitinBhargava2016, Onel5969, Pied Hornbill, Pratyk321, R'n'B, Raguks, Redtigerxyz, Richard Keatinge, Ricky81682, Sanjoydey33, Shadowjams, Shhashhi, Shyamsunder, Solomon7968, Srikanth Aviator, Steamerrr, Sushilkumarmishra, Sushilmishra, Takafumi1, Tamilyomen, Thnidu, Thor Dockweiler, Thumperward, Titodutta, Tpbradbury, Ugog Nizdast, Utcursch, Veeresh1209, Vyom25, Wiae, Zcarstvnz, 한번영, 162 anonymous edits 743

Western Chalukya Empire *Source:* https://en.wikipedia.org/w/index.php?oldid=851162202 *License:* Creative Commons Attribution-Share Alike 3.0 *Contributors:* -revi, AManWithNoPlan, Adamgerber80, Adimovk5, Ankush 89, Astynax, BD2412, BDD, Ben Ben, Bender235, BrownHairedGirl, Calliopejen1, Capankajsmilyo, Catlemur, Chewings72, Chris the speller, Cpt.a.haddock, DashyGames, Dcirovic, Dewan357, Dewritech, Dineshkannambadi, Doug Weller, Dppowell, Dr.Radha Mohan Das Agrawal, DrKay, EdwardElric2016, Ermahgerd9, Fayenatic london, Frietjes, Gimmetrow, Good Olfactory, Green Mostaza, Gurjar singh, Holenarasipura, Hugo999, Human3015, J04n, Jonesey95, Jonesmith4, Just4edit, Kbdank71, Krishnachandranvn, Kwamikagami, Kww, LilHelpa, Magioladitis, Manjunath Doddamani Gajendragad, Marcus Cyron, Masterknower, Mayasandra, Mr Stephen, Neelix, Niceguyedc, Nick Number, Nvvchar, Onel5969, Oshwah, Ost316, Papa November, Pi3.124, Pied Hornbill, Pratyk321, Raghith, Rajaashoka, RekishiEJ, Rich Farmbrough, Ricky81682, Rjwilmsi, Roland zh, Sai18021993, SchreiberBike, ShelfSkewed, Shellwood, Shiggy1, Shreevatsa, Shyamsunder, Sitush, Srirangam99, Sun Creator, Sushilkumarmishra, Tabletop, Tahc, Tamilyomen, Thumperward, Tim!, Tiptoety, Titodutta, Topbanana, Ugog Nizdast, Utcursch, Vanished user vjhsduheuiui4t5hjri, Vin09, Vyom25, WOSlinker, Widr, Woohookitty, Worldciv2017 Chalukya Empire, YellowMonkey, पाटलिपुत्र, ರವಿಚಂದ್ರ, 90 anonymous edits 766

Seuna (Yadava) dynasty *Source:* https://en.wikipedia.org/w/index.php?oldid=850086438 *License:* Creative Commons Attribution-Share Alike 3.0 *Contributors:* Adamgstarr, Ancientcoinsofindia1, Areapeaslol, Arnavlamba, Astynax, BD2412, Bender235, Bgwhite, Bhadani, BrownHairedGirl, Buddhipriya, Capankajsmilyo, Chewings72, Cpt.a.haddock, DVdm, DeadEyeArrow, Dewan357, Dineshkannambadi, Donnowin1, Ekabhishek, EscapingLife,

Exactpitchpoint, Fayenatic london, Fconaway, Ged UK, Gnanapiti, Gyrodoor33, Hasiru, Hmainsbot1, Holenarasipura, Hsarpotdar1, Idib, Internet Scholar, Iph, JForget, JaGa, Jayeshbsuryawanshi, Jethwarp, Jugaari cross, Jujill123, KNM, Kedar Borhade, Krishnaa999, Kww, Leujohn, Magmar3, Mahensingha, Manjunath Doddamani Gajendragad, Marcocapelle, Mattisse, Mauler90, Mayasandra, Michael Devore, Natasha singh19, Naveenbm, Nick Number, Nizil Shah, Onel5969, PWilkinson, Pi3.124, Pied Hornbill, Pratyk321, Prometheus.pyrphoros, Proudtobeindian007, R'n'B, RL0919, Raguks, Rayaraya, Ricky81682, Rjwilmsi, Rodw, Sagar R Salvi, Sarvabhaum, Sarvagnya, Sfan00 IMG, ShivNarayanan, Shreewiki, Shyamsunder, Sitush, Sodabottle, Squids and Chips, Sumitkachroo, Talessman, Tamilyomen, Tbhotch, Tej smiles, TheShepherds, Utcursh, Vanished user 39948282, Vitthal.khot, Vivek.cdma, Vontrotta, Woohookitty, Yamamoto Ichiro, YellowMonkey, 128 anonymous edits 791
Kakatiya dynasty Source: https://en.wikipedia.org/w/index.php?oldid=852929702 License: Creative Commons Attribution-Share Alike 3.0 Contributors: 79spirit, Ahendra, Aldis90, Allamsanjeev, BAYYAPPANAHALLI, BD2412, Bender235, Bladesmulti, Capankajsmilyo, Civfanatic, Cpt.a.haddock, Devanampriya, DrNavid, Fastifex, Fauzan, Home Lander, I dream of horses, Iridescent, John of Reading, Joshua Jonathan, Kautilya3, Lakun.patra, Lateraldissonance, LilHelpa, Lillinan1, Maduraj nayak vamsa, Marutheeraja, Memesfornoobs, Mr.Bill3, Narky Blert, NeilN, Niceguyedc, Ohconfucius, Onel5969, Param Mudgal, Pi3.124, Plantdrew, Psuedocode, Rajal naikil, Randhirreddy, Rich Farmbrough, Rjwilmsi, Satishk01, ScitDei, Shashi.Arjula, Sitush, Stesmo, TeeVeeed, The Ajan, The Blade of the Northern Lights, Utcursh, Vijender.sriramoju1, WOSlinker, Warangalite, Weckkrum, Wikiuser13, Woodlot, 97 anonymous edits 804
Kalachuri dynasty Source: https://en.wikipedia.org/w/index.php?oldid=844580311 License: Creative Commons Attribution-Share Alike 3.0 Contributors: Capankajsmilyo, Utcursh, पाटलिपुत्र, 3 anonymous edits 821
Hoysala Empire Source: https://en.wikipedia.org/w/index.php?oldid=853121778 License: Creative Commons Attribution-Share Alike 3.0 Contributors: Adimovk5, Akshaysrinivasan, Alan, Alexf, Andreas Kaganov, Astynax, Bender235, Capankajsmilyo, Chewings72, Chris the speller, ChrysalSnowlax, CommonsDelinker, Cpt.a.haddock, Cybertraker, Dewan357, Dineshkannambadi, Dppowell, DrKay, Edward, El C, Feminist, Frietjes, Friginator, Gaius Cornelius, Ganesha1, Ged UK, Gimmetrow, Gnanapiti, Good Olfactory, HC NATARAJ, Highpeaks35, Holenarasipura, Hosalya, John of Reading, Jonesmith4, Jrsanthosh, Just4edit, Kannadiga, Kbdank71, Ketiltrout, Khazar2, Kintetsubuffalo, Kithira, Kwamikagami, Kww, LeoFrank, LilHelpa, Linguisticgeek, Liontooth, Magioladitis, Malurian123, Marcus Cyron, Martarius, Mathighat, Mayasandra, Michael Devore, Mr Stephen, Nick Number, Ogress, Ohconfucius, Omar35880, Orion90810, Otisjimmy1, PISCOSOUR786, Pevster101, Pi3.124, Pied Hornbill, Plastikspork, Pranavraj007, Prathamgn, Pratyk321, Pulakeshi, Quadell, Rahul.s gowda, Redtigerxyz, Rich Farmbrough, Rjwilmsi, Roland zh, Rubbish computer, Sai18021993, Saibala18, Sballal, Sbblr geervaanee, Shellwood, Shreevatsa, Shrikanthv, Sitush, Spyguy1112, Srirangam99, SteveM123, Sumanthkb, Sushilkumarmishra, Tellasitis, The Jacobin, TheGeneralUser, Thumperward, Tim1357, Tpbradbury, Treisijs, U yousafzai54, Ugog Nizdast, Utcursh, V2Blast, Wavelength, Wilhelmina Will, Woohookitty, YellowMonkey, ಮಲ್ನಾಡಿ, 118 anonymous edits 828
Chola dynasty Source: https://en.wikipedia.org/w/index.php?oldid=849951517 License: Creative Commons Attribution-Share Alike 3.0 Contributors: Abecedare, Abhishek0831996, Aggi007, Ajithnandhini, Amirthalingam ariyalur, Andyjsmith, AntanO, Arcadio Maxwell, BD2412, Babushan, Bender235, Bgwhite, Blackknight12, Capankajsmilyo, Chackerian, Chewings72, ClueBot NG, Cpt.a.haddock, Czeror, Dcirovic, Dharmaputhra, DragoniteLeopard, Drewmutt, Eggishorn, Ermahgerd9, Eshwar.om, Frosty, Furius, Giraffedata, Gunkarta, Gurjar singh, HaeB, Harithvh, Hessamnia, Hugo999, I dream of horses, I enjoy sandwiches, Jessica meena, Jim1138, John of Reading, Karnatamilking, Kbssomnath, KumaranMee86, Letters From Adi, Linguist111, LittleWink, M.K.Dan, Magentic Manifestations, Mark Ironie, Materialscientist, Mayavan murugan, Mish sta, Mx. Granger, Navops47, Neelyadi, Nidafatimashahi, NitinBhargava2016, Notthebestusername, Onel5969, Pearll's sun, Philostratus, Pi3.124, Rahulbigg, Ranjithsiji, Rubbish computer, S9971706h, Sakthiprasanna, Sarafvpz, Serols, Sipabacus, Sitush, Skabe24, Snori, SpacemanSpiff, Srednuas Lenoroc, SrivijayP, Sskmuhil, Stylez995, Tahc, Takafumi1, The Transhumanist, Utcursh, Vatasura, Vibhss, Vijay Kumar S, Waleed Baqeer, WinterVacation, WorldGov, Worldbruce, Worldciv2017 chola, पाटलिपुत्र, फिल्मी, 159 anonymous edits 848

Image Sources, Licenses and Contributors

The sources listed for each image provide more detailed licensing information including the copyright status, the copyright owner, and the license conditions.

Figure 1 *Source:* https://en.wikipedia.org/w/index.php?title=File:DemetriusCoin.jpg *License:* Public Domain *Contributors:* ESnible 3
Figure 2 *Source:* https://en.wikipedia.org/w/index.php?title=File:Kushanmap.jpg *License:* Creative Commons Attribution-ShareAlike 3.0 Unported *Contributors:* PHGCOM 6
Figure 3 *Source:* https://en.wikipedia.org/w/index.php?title=File:HephthaliteCoin.jpg *License:* GNU Free Documentation License *Contributors:* Allforrous, File Upload Bot (Magnus Manske), Howcheng, Leoboudv, MGA73, OgreBot 2, Roland zh, Zaccarias, पाटलिपुत्र 7
Figure 4 *Source:* https://en.wikipedia.org/w/index.php?title=File:Karkota_Empire,_India_(derived).jpg *License:* Creative Commons Attribution-Sharealike 3.0 *Contributors:* Amitrochates, Daderot, Utcursch 8
Figure 5 *Source:* https://en.wikipedia.org/w/index.php?title=File:Silver_Coin_of_Kumaragupta_I.jpg *License:* GNU Free Documentation License *Contributors:* Athenara, Bodhisattwa, Chaoborus, File Upload Bot (Magnus Manske), MGA73bot2, Mhmrodrigues, OgreBot 2 10
Figure 6 *Source:* https://en.wikipedia.org/w/index.php?title=File:Ajanta_(6).jpg *License:* Creative Commons Attribution-ShareAlike 3.0 Unported *Contributors:* User:Soman 12
Figure 7 *Source:* https://en.wikipedia.org/w/index.php?title=File:Prithvi_Raj_Chauhan_(Edited).jpg *License:* GNU Free Documentation License *Contributors:* Prithvi_Raj_Chauhan.JPG: LRBurdak at en.wikipedia derivative work: original uploader was Dhiresh b at en.wikipedia 15
Figure 8 *Source:* https://en.wikipedia.org/w/index.php?title=File:Sun_Temple_Sabha_Mandap.JPG *License:* Creative Commons Attribution 2.5 *Contributors:* Uday Parmar / Parmar uday at en.wikipedia 16
Figure 9 *Source:* https://en.wikipedia.org/w/index.php?title=File:IndianBuddha11.JPG *License:* Public domain *Contributors:* BotMultichill, Ekabhishek, Farm, Gryffindor, Ismoon, Nagy, Podzemnik, Roland zh 17
Figure 10 *Source:* https://en.wikipedia.org/w/index.php?title=File:Konark_Sun_Temple_Front_view.jpg *License:* Public Domain *Contributors:* http://en.wikipedia.org/wiki/User_talk:Vinayreddym 19
Figure 11 *Source:* https://en.wikipedia.org/w/index.php?title=File:Assam_MK_Lion.JPG *License:* Creative Commons Attribution 3.0 *Contributors:* Porikpokh Oxom 21
Figure 12 *Source:* https://en.wikipedia.org/w/index.php?title=File:Doddagaddavalli_Lakshmidevi_temple1_retouched.JPG *License:* GNU Free Documentation License *Contributors:* OgreBot 2, Rehtuber, Roland zh 25
Figure 13 *Source:* https://en.wikipedia.org/w/index.php?title=File:Gometeswara.jpg *License:* Attribution *Contributors:* FSII, Fontema, Guanaco, Hystrix, Jungpionier, Kilom691, MPF, Ranveig, Roland zh, Soerfm, Str4nd, Thureson, Vssun, 8 anonymous edits 26
Figure 14 *Source:* https://en.wikipedia.org/w/index.php?title=File:Relief_of_seated_Vishnu_at_the_Badami_cave_temple_no.3.jpg *License:* Public domain *Contributors:* Original uploader was Dineshkannambadi at en.wikipedia 28
Figure 15 *Source:* https://en.wikipedia.org/w/index.php?title=File:Mamallapuram1a.jpg *License:* Creative Commons Attribution 2.0 *Contributors:* mckaysavage 29
Figure 16 *Source:* https://en.wikipedia.org/w/index.php?title=File:Indian_Rashtrakuta_Empire_map.svg *License:* Creative Commons Attribution-Sharealike 3.0 *Contributors:* AnonMoos, Aschroet, Io Herodotus, Nikotins, Planemad, Roland zh 31
Figure 17 *Source:* https://en.wikipedia.org/w/index.php?title=File:Kailasha_temple_at_ellora.JPG *License:* Creative Commons Attribution-Sharealike 2.5 *Contributors:* Pratheepps 31
Figure 18 *Source:* https://en.wikipedia.org/w/index.php?title=File:Ornate_pillars_in_the_Saraswati_temple_at_Gadag.jpg *License:* GNU Free Documentation License *Contributors:* AnRo0002, Dineshkannambadi, File Upload Bot (Magnus Manske), MGA73bot2, Marcus Cyron, Neithsabes, OgreBot 2, Papa November, Roland zh 34
Figure 19 *Source:* https://en.wikipedia.org/w/index.php?title=File:Kudalasangama.jpg *License:* Public domain *Contributors:* Denniss, File Upload Bot (Magnus Manske), OgreBot 2, Roland zh, Tine 35
Figure 20 *Source:* https://en.wikipedia.org/w/index.php?title=File:Shilabaalika_on_pillar_bracket_in_Chennakeshava_Temple_at_Belur3.jpg *License:* GNU Free Documentation License *Contributors:* Alan, Dineshkannambadi, File Upload Bot (Magnus Manske), MGA73bot2, OgreBot 2, Papa November, Roland zh, Vivek Sarje, Xufanc, 1 anonymous edits 36
Figure 21 *Source:* https://en.wikipedia.org/w/index.php?title=File:Rajendra_map_new.svg *License:* GNU Free Documentation License *Contributors:* Rajendra_map_new.png: derivative work: Gregors (talk) 38
Image *Source:* https://en.wikipedia.org/w/index.php?title=File:PD-icon.svg *License:* Public Domain *Contributors:* Alex.muller, Anomie, Anonymous Dissident, CBM, Jo-Jo Eumerus, MBisanz, PBS, Quadell, Rocket000, Strangerer, Timotheus Canens, 1 anonymous edits 39
Image *Source:* https://en.wikipedia.org/w/index.php?title=File:IndoScythianKingdom.svg *License:* Creative Commons Attribution-Sharealike 3.0 *Contributors:* User:DLommes 41
Image *Source:* https://en.wikipedia.org/w/index.php?title=File:Blank.png *License:* Public Domain *Contributors:* Bastique, Chlewey, ChrisDHDR, Ghouston, It Is Me Here, Jed, Paradoctor, Patrick, Penubag, Perhelion, Rocket000, Roomba, Sarang, Timeroot, Tintazul 42
Figure 22 *Source:* https://en.wikipedia.org/w/index.php?title=File:PazyrikHorseman.JPG *Contributors:* Aphasic, Bontenbal, BotAdventures, Bullenwächter, Clpo13, Dr pda, Ismoon, Joostik, Mattes, Schreiber, Shakko, SunOfErat, Un1c0s bot~commonswiki, Wolfmann, Überraschungsbilder .. 43
Figure 23 *Source:* https://en.wikipedia.org/w/index.php?title=File:MenWithDragons.jpg *License:* Creative Commons Attribution-ShareAlike 3.0 Unported *Contributors:* User:World Imaging 44
Figure 24 *Source:* https://en.wikipedia.org/w/index.php?title=File:ManWithCapProbablyScythianBamiyan3-4thCentury.jpg *License:* Creative Commons Attribution-ShareAlike 3.0 Unported *Contributors:* PHGCOM 44
Figure 25 *Source:* https://en.wikipedia.org/w/index.php?title=File:Orlat_plaque_detail.jpg *License:* Public Domain *Contributors:* पाटलिपुत्र . 45
Figure 26 *Source:* https://en.wikipedia.org/w/index.php?title=File:SakastanMap.jpg *License:* Public Domain *Contributors:* User:World Imaging 47
Figure 27 *Source:* https://en.wikipedia.org/w/index.php?title=File:Asia_001ad.jpg *License:* Creative Commons Attribution 3.0 *Contributors:* Bot-Multichill, Codrinb, Cold Season, File Upload Bot (Magnus Manske), Look2See1, OgreBot 2, Rodhullandemu, Roland zh, Tatmadav, Tulsi Bhagat, Verdy p, Zaccarias, Zykassa, 3 anonymous edits 48
Figure 28 *Source:* https://en.wikipedia.org/w/index.php?title=File:Scythian_devotee_Butkara_I.jpg *License:* Creative Commons Attribution-Sharealike 3.0 *Contributors:* Uploadmo 48
Figure 29 *Source:* https://en.wikipedia.org/w/index.php?title=File:AzesIIFineCoin.jpg *License:* Public Domain *Contributors:* User:World Imaging 49
Figure 30 *Source:* https://en.wikipedia.org/w/index.php?title=File:StonePalette5.JPG *License:* Creative Commons Attribution-ShareAlike 3.0 Unported *Contributors:* User:World Imaging 50
Figure 31 *Source:* https://en.wikipedia.org/w/index.php?title=File:Indo_Scythian_Bronze_Coin_from_reign_of_Azes_I.jpg *Contributors:* User:Ancientcointraders 51
Figure 32 *Source:* https://en.wikipedia.org/w/index.php?title=File:BimaranCasket2.JPG *License:* GNU Free Documentation License *Contributors:* Gryffindor, Ismoon, Jastrow, MGA73bot2, World Imaging, पाटलिपुत्र 51
Figure 33 *Source:* https://en.wikipedia.org/w/index.php?title=File:Rajuvula_coin_Northern_Satrap_with_Greek_legend_and_Athena_Alkidemos.jpg *License:* GNU Free Documentation License *Contributors:* पाटलिपुत्र 52
Figure 34 *Source:* https://en.wikipedia.org/w/index.php?title=File:MathuraLionCapital.JPG *License:* GNU Free Documentation License *Contributors:* User:PHGCOM 53
Figure 35 *Source:* https://en.wikipedia.org/w/index.php?title=File:AzesIITriratna.jpg *License:* Public Domain *Contributors:* User:World Imaging 54
Figure 36 *Source:* https://en.wikipedia.org/w/index.php?title=File:KingAzesIIProfile.JPG *License:* Creative Commons Attribution-ShareAlike 3.0 Unported *Contributors:* User:World Imaging 54
Figure 37 *Source:* https://en.wikipedia.org/w/index.php?title=File:Western_Satrap_Coin_of_Rudrasimha_I_.jpg *License:* GNU Free Documentation License *Contributors:* Bodhisattwa, File Upload Bot (Magnus Manske), Kelly, Nizil Shah, OgreBot 2, Roland zh 55
Figure 38 *Source:* https://en.wikipedia.org/w/index.php?title=File:Coin_of_Maues.jpg *License:* GNU Free Documentation License *Contributors:* Classical Numismatic Group 56
Figure 39 *Source:* https://en.wikipedia.org/w/index.php?title=File:AzilisesWearingTunic.jpg *License:* Public Domain *Contributors:* Whitehead 57
Figure 40 *Source:* https://en.wikipedia.org/w/index.php?title=File:Buner_reliefs_Scythian_bacchanalian_cropped.jpg *Contributors:* Elisfkc, EurekaLott, FlickreviewR 2, पाटलिपुत्र 57
Figure 41 *Source:* https://en.wikipedia.org/w/index.php?title=File:IndoScythiansDyonisos.jpg *License:* Public Domain *Contributors:* User:World Imaging 58

Figure 42 *Source:* https://en.wikipedia.org/w/index.php?title=File:SoldiersBattllingAnimals2.jpg *License:* Creative Commons Attribution-ShareAlike 3.0 Unported *Contributors:* PHGCOM ... 58

Figure 43 *Source:* https://en.wikipedia.org/w/index.php?title=File:SoldiersBattllingAnimals5.jpg *License:* Creative Commons Attribution-ShareAlike 3.0 Unported *Contributors:* PHGCOM ... 59

Figure 44 *Source:* https://en.wikipedia.org/w/index.php?title=File:MET_1987_142_111.jpeg *License:* Creative Commons Zero *Contributors:* BotMultichill, Hilohello, Pharos, पाटलिपुत्र ... 60

Figure 45 *Source:* https://en.wikipedia.org/w/index.php?title=File:BajaurCasket.jpg *License:* Creative Commons Attribution-Sharealike 3.0,2.5,2.0,1.0 *Contributors:* PHGCOM ... 61

Figure 46 *Source:* https://en.wikipedia.org/w/index.php?title=File:Indo-GreekStupaIII.jpg *License:* Creative Commons Attribution-ShareAlike 3.0 Unported *Contributors:* User:World Imaging ... 62

Figure 47 *Source:* https://en.wikipedia.org/w/index.php?title=File:Kushan,_Brahma,_Indra,_Indian.JPG *License:* Creative Commons Attribution-ShareAlike 3.0 Unported *Contributors:* User:World Imaging ... 62

Figure 48 *Source:* https://en.wikipedia.org/w/index.php?title=File:PilarImage4.jpg *License:* Public Domain *Contributors:* User:World Imaging 63

Figure 49 *Source:* https://en.wikipedia.org/w/index.php?title=File:DancingIndoScythians.jpg *License:* Public Domain *Contributors:* User:World Imaging ... 63

Figure 50 *Source:* https://en.wikipedia.org/w/index.php?title=File:ButkaraDoorJamb.jpg *License:* Creative Commons Attribution-Sharealike 2.5 *Contributors:* User:World Imaging ... 64

Figure 51 *Source:* https://en.wikipedia.org/w/index.php?title=File:TabulaPeutingerianaIndo-Scythia.jpg *License:* Public Domain *Contributors:* Kilom691, World Imaging, 1 anonymous edits ... 65

Figure 52 *Source:* https://en.wikipedia.org/w/index.php?title=File:Coin_of_the_Indian-Scythian_king_Azes_I.jpg *License:* Creative Commons Attribution-ShareAlike 3.0 Unported *Contributors:* User:World Imaging ... 66

Figure 53 *Source:* https://en.wikipedia.org/w/index.php?title=File:BalaramaMauesCoin1stCenturyBCE.jpg *License:* Creative Commons Attribution-ShareAlike 3.0 Unported *Contributors:* User:PHGCOM, User:PHGCOM ... 67

Figure 54 *Source:* https://en.wikipedia.org/w/index.php?title=File:Coin_of_Parataraja_Bhimarjuna.jpg *License:* Creative Commons Attribution-Share Alike *Contributors:* PHGCOM ... 69

Image *Source:* https://en.wikipedia.org/w/index.php?title=File:ChastanaCoin.jpg *License:* Public Domain *Contributors:* Alfons Åberg, BotMultichill, Roland zh, World Imaging, पाटलिपुत्र ... 70

Image *Source:* https://en.wikipedia.org/w/index.php?title=File:Coin_of_Rudradaman.jpg *License:* Creative Commons Attribution-ShareAlike 3.0 Unported *Contributors:* User:World Imaging ... 70

Image *Source:* https://en.wikipedia.org/w/index.php?title=File:Coin_of_Rudrasena.jpg *License:* Creative Commons Attribution-ShareAlike 3.0 Unported *Contributors:* User:World Imaging ... 70

Image *Source:* https://en.wikipedia.org/w/index.php?title=File:Coin_of_Rudrasimha_III.jpg *License:* Public Domain *Contributors:* Bodhisattwa, BotMultichill, Deadstar, Nizil Shah, Roland zh, World Imaging, 1 anonymous edits ... 71

Image *Source:* https://en.wikipedia.org/w/index.php?title=File:Commons-logo.svg *License:* logo *Contributors:* Anomie, Callanecc, CambridgeBayWeather, Jo-Jo Eumerus, RHaworth ... 73

Figure 55 *Source:* https://en.wikipedia.org/w/index.php?title=File:Scythia-Parthia_100_BC.png *License:* GNU Free Documentation License *Contributors:* Dbachmann ... 75

Image *Source:* https://en.wikipedia.org/w/index.php?title=File:Indo-European_migrations.gif *Contributors:* User:Joshua Jonathan ... 74

Figure 56 *Source:* https://en.wikipedia.org/w/index.php?title=File:MenWithDragons.jpg *License:* Creative Commons Attribution-ShareAlike 3.0 Unported *Contributors:* User:World Imaging ... 75

Figure 57 *Source:* https://en.wikipedia.org/w/index.php?title=File:Issyk_Golden_Cataphract_Warrior.jpg *License:* Public Domain *Contributors:* Idot ... 76

Figure 58 *Source:* https://en.wikipedia.org/w/index.php?title=File:TilliaTepeReconstitution.jpg *License:* Creative Commons Attribution-ShareAlike 3.0 Unported *Contributors:* PHGCOM ... 78

Figure 59 *Source:* https://en.wikipedia.org/w/index.php?title=File:Behistun.Inscript.Skunkha.jpg *License:* Attribution *Contributors:* Glenn, Gm King, Kurgus, Stifle, Sumerophile∼commonswiki, Themightyquill, Xenophon, ZxxZxxZ, 1 anonymous edits ... 79

Figure 60 *Source:* https://en.wikipedia.org/w/index.php?title=File:KingGurgamoyaKhotan1stCenturyCE.jpg *License:* Creative Commons Attribution-ShareAlike 3.0 Unported *Contributors:* PHGCOM ... 81

Figure 61 *Source:* https://en.wikipedia.org/w/index.php?title=File:Khotanese_animal_zodiac_BLI6_OR11252_1R2_1.jpg *License:* Public Domain *Contributors:* Andrew Gray, Parabolooidal ... 82

Figure 62 *Source:* https://en.wikipedia.org/w/index.php?title=File:Issyk_inscription.png *License:* Public Domain *Contributors:* Diannaa, File Upload Bot (Magnus Manske), Joostik, OgreBot 2 ... 84

Image *Source:* https://en.wikipedia.org/w/index.php?title=File:Indo-Greeks_100bc.jpg *License:* Creative Commons Attribution-Sharealike 3.0 *Contributors:* Thomas Lessman • (Contact!) ... 87

Image *Source:* https://en.wikipedia.org/w/index.php?title=File:Flag_of_Pakistan.svg *License:* Public Domain *Contributors:* User:Zscout370 ... 88

Image *Source:* https://en.wikipedia.org/w/index.php?title=File:Flag_of_Afghanistan.svg *Contributors:* 5ko, Ahmad2099, Alex Great, Alkari, Amateur55, Andres gb.ldc, Ankry, Antonsusi, Avala, Bastique, BotMultichill, BotMultichillT, Cycn, Dancingwombatsrule, Dbenbenn, Denelson83, Denniss, Domhnall, Duduziq, Erlenmeyer, F l a n k e r, Farhod, Frigotoni, Fry1989, Gast32, Golden Bosnian Lily, GoldenRainbow, Happenstance, Henriquebachelor, Herbythyme, Homo lupus, Ilfga, Illegitimate Barrister, Jarekt, Jebulon, JoaoPedro10029, Khwahan, Klemen Kocjancic, Koefbac, Kookaburra, Lokal Profil, Ludger1961, Lumia1234, MPF, Mattes, MrPanyGoff, Myself488, Neq00, Nersy, Nightstallion, O, Orange Tuesday, Palosirkka, Prev, RainbowSilver, Rainforest tropicana, Reisio, Ricordisamoa, Rocket000, Sangjinhwa, Sarang, Sarilho1, SiBr4, Smaug the Golden, Smooth O, Sojah, Solar Police, Stasyan117, SteveGOLD, Stewi101015, Supreme Dragon, TFerenczy, Tabasco∼commonswiki, Tcfc2349, Unma.af, Zscout370, \\'arrior 786, Şêr, ייהלי׳ושמר, 李焜泽 567, 33 anonymous edits ... 88

Image *Source:* https://en.wikipedia.org/w/index.php?title=File:Flag_of_India.svg *License:* Public Domain *Contributors:* Anomie, Jo-Jo Eumerus, Mifter ... 88

Image *Source:* https://en.wikipedia.org/w/index.php?title=File:Flag_of_Turkmenistan.svg *License:* Public Domain *Contributors:* User:Vzb83 . 88

Image *Source:* https://en.wikipedia.org/w/index.php?title=File:King_Hippostratos_circa_100_BCE.jpg *License:* GNU Free Documentation License *Contributors:* Beads and reels, Mhmrodrigues, पाटलिपुत्र ... 88

Image *Source:* https://en.wikipedia.org/w/index.php?title=File:Evolution_of_Zeus_Nikephoros_on_Indo-Greek_coinage.jpg *License:* GNU Free Documentation License *Contributors:* Beads and reels ... 88

Image *Source:* https://en.wikipedia.org/w/index.php?title=File:Coin_of_Antialkidas.jpg *License:* GNU Free Documentation License *Contributors:* Classical Numismatic Group; ... 89

Figure 63 *Source:* https://en.wikipedia.org/w/index.php?title=File:Pataliputra_Palace_capital_by_L_A_Waddell_1895.jpg *Contributors:* Goldsmelter, GreenMeansGo, Wienerbund, ZxxZxxZ, पाटलिपुत्र ... 90

Figure 64 *Source:* https://en.wikipedia.org/w/index.php?title=File:AsokaKandahar.jpg *License:* Public Domain *Contributors:* Abhishekjoshi, Archidamus∼commonswiki, BotAdventures, BotMultichill, Fertejol, Frenezulo, Gryffindor, Iustinus, JMCC1, Jastrow, Jdx, Le Behnam, Mahmudmasri, Man vyi, Mikhail Ryazanov, Mmcannis∼commonswiki, Officer, Ranveig, Roland zh, Sreejithk2000 AWB, Storkk, Tahar Jelun, The Evil IP address, Wieralee, Wiki-uk, World Imaging, Zaccarias, ZxxZxxZ, पाटलिपुत्र, 17 anonymous edits ... 92

Figure 65 *Source:* https://en.wikipedia.org/w/index.php?title=File:Ruvanvelisaya_Dagoba.jpg *License:* Creative Commons Attribution-Sharealike 2.5 *Contributors:* Morgendorfferr ... 93

Figure 66 *Source:* https://en.wikipedia.org/w/index.php?title=File:PhilosopherBust.jpg *License:* Public Domain *Contributors:* User:World Imaging 94

Figure 67 *Source:* https://en.wikipedia.org/w/index.php?title=File:CapitalSharp.jpg *License:* Public Domain *Contributors:* User:World Imaging 96

Figure 68 *Source:* https://en.wikipedia.org/w/index.php?title=File:EuthydemusMedailles.jpg *License:* Creative Commons Attribution-ShareAlike 3.0 Unported *Contributors:* User:World Imaging ... 97

Figure 69 *Source:* https://en.wikipedia.org/w/index.php?title=File:Bronze_Warrior_Statue_without_shade.jpg *Contributors:* User:Goldsmelter 98

Figure 70 *Source:* https://en.wikipedia.org/w/index.php?title=File:AiKhanoumAndIndia.jpg *License:* Creative Commons Attribution-ShareAlike 3.0 Unported *Contributors:* PHGCOM ... 100

Figure 71 *Source:* https://en.wikipedia.org/w/index.php?title=File:Khalsi_rock_edict_of_Ashoka.jpg *License:* Public Domain *Contributors:* पाटलिपुत्र ... 101

Figure 72 *Source:* https://en.wikipedia.org/w/index.php?title=File:Sunga_horseman_Bharhut.jpg *License:* Creative Commons Attribution 2.0 *Contributors:* Bodhisattwa, पाटलिपुत्र ... 102

Figure 73 *Source:* https://en.wikipedia.org/w/index.php?title=File:Apollodotosi.jpg *Contributors:* - ... 104

Figure 74 *Source:* https://en.wikipedia.org/w/index.php?title=File:DemetriusIMet.jpg *License:* Creative Commons Attribution-Sharealike 3.0,2.5,2.0,1.0 *Contributors:* PHGCOM ... 105

Figure 75 *Source:* https://en.wikipedia.org/w/index.php?title=File:Artemidoros_coin_obverse_with_transliteration.jpg *License:* GNU Free Documentation License *Contributors:* Mhmrodrigues, Wienerbund ... 106

Figure 76 *Source:* https://en.wikipedia.org/w/index.php?title=File:Coin_of_the_Bactrian_King_Agathokles.jpg *License:* GNU Free Documentation License *Contributors:* Classical Numismatic Group; Coin ID 57554 107
Figure 77 *Source:* https://en.wikipedia.org/w/index.php?title=File:Menander_Alexandria-Kapisa.jpg *License:* Public Domain *Contributors:* Alfons Åberg, Bodhisattwa, DenghiùComm, Fast track∼commonswiki, Ismoon, Mattes, Schimmelreiter, Tahar Jelun, Umherirrender 107
Image *Source:* https://en.wikipedia.org/w/index.php?title=File:Reh_inscription_of_Menander.jpg *License:* Public Domain *Contributors:* पाटलिपुत्र 108
Image *Source:* https://en.wikipedia.org/w/index.php?title=File:Indo-Greek_arrowheads_from_Kausambi.jpg *License:* Public Domain *Contributors:* Jeff G., पाटलिपुत्र 108
Image *Source:* https://en.wikipedia.org/w/index.php?title=File:MenandrosCoin.jpg *License:* Public Domain *Contributors:* User:World Imaging 109
Image *Source:* https://en.wikipedia.org/w/index.php?title=File:EucratidesStatere.jpg *License:* Creative Commons Attribution-ShareAlike 3.0 Unported *Contributors:* User:World Imaging 109
Figure 78 *Source:* https://en.wikipedia.org/w/index.php?title=File:King_Hippostratos_circa_100_BCE.jpg *License:* GNU Free Documentation License *Contributors:* Beads and reels, Mhmrodrigues, पाटलिपुत्र 110
Figure 79 *Source:* https://en.wikipedia.org/w/index.php?title=File:Yavanarajya_inscription.jpg *License:* Public Domain *Contributors:* Jeff G., Ms Sarah Welch, पाटलिपुत्र 111
Figure 80 *Source:* https://en.wikipedia.org/w/index.php?title=File:Mathura_Herakles.jpg *License:* Public Domain *Contributors:* Bodhisattwa, Kenmayer, पाटलिपुत्र 112
Figure 81 *Source:* https://en.wikipedia.org/w/index.php?title=File:Udayagiri_Yavana_warrior.jpg *Contributors:* User:Saileshpat 114
Figure 82 *Source:* https://en.wikipedia.org/w/index.php?title=File:Heliocles_I_helmetted.jpg *License:* GNU Free Documentation License *Contributors:* Lliura, Priyadasi 116
Figure 83 *Source:* https://en.wikipedia.org/w/index.php?title=File:Coin_of_Antialkidas.jpg *License:* GNU Free Documentation License *Contributors:* Classical Numismatic Group; 117
Figure 84 *Source:* https://en.wikipedia.org/w/index.php?title=File:Coin_of_Philoxenos.jpg *License:* GNU Free Documentation License *Contributors:* Classical Numismatic Group; 117
Figure 85 *Source:* https://en.wikipedia.org/w/index.php?title=File:Zoilos_I_coin_alliance_of_the_Heraklean_club_and_the_Scythian_bow.jpg *License:* GNU Free Documentation License *Contributors:* Beads and reels, Mhmrodrigues 118
Figure 86 *Source:* https://en.wikipedia.org/w/index.php?title=File:Heliodorus_pillar_with_elevation.jpg *Contributors:* User:Dilipkumarftii1977 119
Figure 87 *Source:* https://en.wikipedia.org/w/index.php?title=File:Taxila_Vidisha_Sanchi_Bharut.jpg *License:* Public Domain *Contributors:* पाटलिपुत्र 120
Image *Source:* https://en.wikipedia.org/w/index.php?title=File:Sanchi_Stupa_No2.jpg *Contributors:* पाटलिपुत्र 120
Figure 88 *Source:* https://en.wikipedia.org/w/index.php?title=File:Sanchi_Stupa_2_man_on_horse.jpg *Contributors:* User:Travel Miles With Smiles 121
Figure 89 *Source:* https://en.wikipedia.org/w/index.php?title=File:Lakshmi_Sanchi_Stupa_2.jpg *Contributors:* पाटलिपुत्र 121
Figure 90 *Source:* https://en.wikipedia.org/w/index.php?title=File:Lotus_within_beads_and_reels_motif_Stupa_No2_Sanchi.jpg *Contributors:* User:Travel Miles With Smiles 122
Figure 91 *Source:* https://en.wikipedia.org/w/index.php?title=File:Flower_motif_Stupa_No2_Sanchi.jpg *Contributors:* User:Travel Miles With Smiles 122
Figure 92 *Source:* https://en.wikipedia.org/w/index.php?title=File:Bharhut_Stupa_Yavana_symbolism.jpg *Contributors:* User:G41rn8 123
Figure 93 *Source:* https://en.wikipedia.org/w/index.php?title=File:Bharhut_Eastern_gateway.jpg *License:* Creative Commons Attribution 3.0 *Contributors:* User:Gangulybiswarup 124
Figure 94 *Source:* https://en.wikipedia.org/w/index.php?title=File:Foreigners_at_Sanchi_Stupa_I_North_Gateway.jpg *License:* Creative Commons Attribution 3.0 *Contributors:* Goldsmelter, पाटलिपुत्र, 神风 124
Figure 95 *Source:* https://en.wikipedia.org/w/index.php?title=File:Helmetted_Hermaios.jpg *License:* GNU Free Documentation License *Contributors:* Beads and reels, Mhmrodrigues 126
Figure 96 *Source:* https://en.wikipedia.org/w/index.php?title=File:Hermaios_posthumous_issue_struck_by_Indo-Scythians_near_Kabul,_circa_80-75_BCE.jpg *License:* GNU Free Documentation License *Contributors:* Priyadasi 126
Figure 97 *Source:* https://en.wikipedia.org/w/index.php?title=File:Hippostratos.jpg *Contributors:* - 127
Figure 98 *Source:* https://en.wikipedia.org/w/index.php?title=File:Coin_of_Azes_I.jpg *License:* Creative Commons Attribution-Sharealike 3.0 *Contributors:* Uploadalt 128
Figure 99 *Source:* https://en.wikipedia.org/w/index.php?title=File:Strato_II_East_Punjab_territory_with_capital_in_Sagala.jpg *Contributors:* User:Yug 129
Figure 100 *Source:* https://en.wikipedia.org/w/index.php?title=File:Strato_II_other_coin.jpg *License:* GNU Free Documentation License *Contributors:* Beads and reels, Mhmrodrigues 129
Figure 101 *Source:* https://en.wikipedia.org/w/index.php?title=File:Karla_Caves_Great_Chaitya_Left_pillar_No9.jpg *License:* Creative Commons Attribution 3.0 *Contributors:* User:Sunitaburra 130
Figure 102 *Source:* https://en.wikipedia.org/w/index.php?title=File:Shivneri_Yavana.jpg *License:* Public Domain *Contributors:* पाटलिपुत्र 131
Figure 103 *Source:* https://en.wikipedia.org/w/index.php?title=File:059_Cave_17,_Inscription_(33839378301).jpg *License:* Creative Commons Attribution 2.0 *Contributors:* Photo Dharma from Sadao, Thailand 132
Image *Source:* https://en.wikipedia.org/w/index.php?title=File:Bhutalinga_caves_chaitya.jpg *Contributors:* Beads and reels 132
Image *Source:* https://en.wikipedia.org/w/index.php?title=File:Manmodi_Chaitya_Yavanasa_inscription.jpg *Contributors:* Beads and reels, पाटलिपुत्र 132
Image *Source:* https://en.wikipedia.org/w/index.php?title=File:Brahmi_y_2nd_century_CE.jpg *Contributors:* User:पाटलिपुत्र 132
Image *Source:* https://en.wikipedia.org/w/index.php?title=File:Brahmi_v_2nd_century_CE.gif *Contributors:* User:पाटलिपुत्र 132
Image *Source:* https://en.wikipedia.org/w/index.php?title=File:Brahmi_n.svg *License:* Public Domain *Contributors:* Mhss 132
Image *Source:* https://en.wikipedia.org/w/index.php?title=File:Brahmi_s.svg *License:* Public Domain *Contributors:* Mhss 132
Figure 104 *Source:* https://en.wikipedia.org/w/index.php?title=File:Evolution_of_Zeus_Nikephoros_on_Indo-Greek_coinage.jpg *License:* GNU Free Documentation License *Contributors:* Beads and reels 133
Figure 105 *Source:* https://en.wikipedia.org/w/index.php?title=File:Deities_on_the_coinage_of_Agathokles.jpg *License:* GNU Free Documentation License *Contributors:* पाटलिपुत्र 134
Image *Source:* https://en.wikipedia.org/w/index.php?title=File:Heliodorus_pillar_inscription.jpg *License:* Public Domain *Contributors:* पाटलिपुत्र 135
Figure 106 *Source:* https://en.wikipedia.org/w/index.php?title=File:Capitello_corinzio_con_busti_di_devoti_clarified.jpg *Contributors:* User:Codas 136
Figure 107 *Source:* https://en.wikipedia.org/w/index.php?title=File:Menander_Soter_wheel_coin.jpg *Contributors:* DenghiùComm, Mhmrodrigues, पाटलिपुत्र 136
Figure 108 *Source:* https://en.wikipedia.org/w/index.php?title=File:ButkaraStupa.jpg *License:* Public Domain *Contributors:* User:World Imaging 137
Figure 109 *Source:* https://en.wikipedia.org/w/index.php?title=File:Menander_II_Zeus_and_wheel_reverse.jpg *License:* GNU Free Documentation License *Contributors:* Beads and reels, Mhmrodrigues 139
Figure 110 *Source:* https://en.wikipedia.org/w/index.php?title=File:PhiloxenusCoin2.JPG *License:* Creative Commons Attribution-ShareAlike 3.0 Unported *Contributors:* User:PHGCOM, User:PHGCOM 140
Figure 111 *Source:* https://en.wikipedia.org/w/index.php?title=File:Nicias_in_uniform_making_a_blessing_gesture.jpg *License:* GNU Free Documentation License *Contributors:* पाटलिपुत्र 140
Figure 112 *Source:* https://en.wikipedia.org/w/index.php?title=File:Agathokleia_drachm_king_Strato_in_uniform_circa_100_BCE.jpg *License:* GNU Free Documentation License *Contributors:* Beads and reels, Mhmrodrigues, पाटलिपुत्र 141
Figure 113 *Source:* https://en.wikipedia.org/w/index.php?title=File:IGMudras.jpg *License:* Public Domain *Contributors:* Photos by Osmund Bopearachchi 141
Figure 114 *Source:* https://en.wikipedia.org/w/index.php?title=File:GandharaDonorFrieze2.JPG *License:* Public Domain *Contributors:* BotAdventures, Johnbod, Jonathan Cardy, Ronaldino, Sailko, Talmoryair, World Imaging, Zaccarias, 2 anonymous edits 142
Figure 115 *Source:* https://en.wikipedia.org/w/index.php?title=File:Indo-GreekBanquet.JPG *License:* Public Domain *Contributors:* Daderot, G.dallorto, Gryffindor, Malo, Mats Halldin∼commonswiki, Sailko, Thorguds, Uploadalt, Vassil 143
Figure 116 *Source:* https://en.wikipedia.org/w/index.php?title=File:Standing_Bodhisattva_Gandhara_Musee_Guimet.jpg *License:* Public Domain *Contributors:* Vassil 144
Figure 117 *Source:* https://en.wikipedia.org/w/index.php?title=File:SeatedBuddhaGandhara2ndCenturyOstasiatischeMuseum.jpg *License:* Creative Commons Attribution-Share Alike *Contributors:* PHGCOM 145

Figure 118 *Source:* https://en.wikipedia.org/w/index.php?title=File:StonePaletteMythologicalScene.jpg *License:* Creative Commons Attribution-Sharealike 3.0,2.5,2.0,1.0 *Contributors:* PHGCOM 146
Figure 119 *Source:* https://en.wikipedia.org/w/index.php?title=File:Coin_of_Greco-Baktrian_Kingdom_king_Pantaleon.jpg *License:* GNU Free Documentation License *Contributors:* Classical Numismatic Group; 147
Figure 120 *Source:* https://en.wikipedia.org/w/index.php?title=File:Gandharan_Athena.jpg *License:* Creative Commons Attribution-Sharealike 3.0 *Contributors:* Uploadmo 148
Figure 121 *Source:* https://en.wikipedia.org/w/index.php?title=File:Agathokleia_drachm_king_Strato_in_uniform_circa_100_BCE.jpg *License:* GNU Free Documentation License *Contributors:* Beads and reels, Mhmrodrigues, पाटलिपुत्र 150
Figure 122 *Source:* https://en.wikipedia.org/w/index.php?title=File:TaxilaCopperPlate.JPG *License:* Creative Commons Attribution-ShareAlike 3.0 Unported *Contributors:* PHGCOM 151
Figure 123 *Source:* https://en.wikipedia.org/w/index.php?title=File:Couple_from_Taxila_IV.jpg *License:* Creative Commons Attribution-Sharealike 3.0 *Contributors:* Uploadalt 152
Figure 124 *Source:* https://en.wikipedia.org/w/index.php?title=File:IndoGreeksTrojanHorse.jpg *License:* Public Domain *Contributors:* User:World Imaging 153
Image *Source:* https://en.wikipedia.org/w/index.php?title=File:Alexander_the_Great_India_coin.jpg *License:* Public Domain *Contributors:* User:PHGCOM 154
Image *Source:* https://en.wikipedia.org/w/index.php?title=File:Gold_coin_of_Diodotos_I_of_Bactria.jpg *License:* Creative Commons Attribution-Sharealike 3.0 *Contributors:* Rani nurmai 154
Image *Source:* https://en.wikipedia.org/w/index.php?title=File:Coin_of_Diodotos_II.jpg *License:* GNU Free Documentation License *Contributors:* Classical Numismatic Group; 154
Image *Source:* https://en.wikipedia.org/w/index.php?title=File:EuthydemusIICoin.jpg *Contributors:* CanisRufus, Monkeybait, Per Honor et Gloria, Sfan00 IMG 154
Image *Source:* https://en.wikipedia.org/w/index.php?title=File:Coin_of_the_Bactrian_king_Agathokles.jpg *License:* GNU Free Documentation License *Contributors:* Classical Numismatic Group; 154
Image *Source:* https://en.wikipedia.org/w/index.php?title=File:Coin_of_King_Pantaleon.jpg *License:* Public Domain *Contributors:* Original uploader was User:PHG at en.wikipedia 154
Image *Source:* https://en.wikipedia.org/w/index.php?title=File:AntimachusMedaille.jpg *License:* Creative Commons Attribution-ShareAlike 3.0 Unported *Contributors:* User:World Imaging 154
Image *Source:* https://en.wikipedia.org/w/index.php?title=File:Demetriosii.jpg *Contributors:* - 154
Image *Source:* https://en.wikipedia.org/w/index.php?title=File:Animachusii(2).jpg *Contributors:* - 154
Image *Source:* https://en.wikipedia.org/w/index.php?title=File:Monnaie_de_Bactriane,_Eucratide_I,_2_faces.jpg *License:* Creative Commons Zero *Contributors:* Eucratides I / BnF 154
Image *Source:* https://en.wikipedia.org/w/index.php?title=File:Coin_of_Eukratides_II.jpg *License:* GNU Free Documentation License *Contributors:* Classical Numismatic Group; 154
Image *Source:* https://en.wikipedia.org/w/index.php?title=File:Coin_of_Plato_of_Bactria.jpg *License:* Public Domain *Contributors:* Alfons Åberg, Bodhisattwa, BotAdventures, Butko, Carlomorino, Denniss, G.dallorto, Gveret Tered, Mahagaja, 2 anonymous edits 154
Image *Source:* https://en.wikipedia.org/w/index.php?title=File:HelioclesCoin.jpg *License:* Public Domain *Contributors:* Bodhisattwa, OgreBot 2 154
Image *Source:* https://en.wikipedia.org/w/index.php?title=File:ZoilosI-525.jpg *Contributors:* Monkeybait, Per Honor et Gloria, Sfan00 IMG .. 154
Image *Source:* https://en.wikipedia.org/w/index.php?title=File:Coin_of_Agathokleia.jpg *License:* GNU Free Documentation License *Contributors:* Classical Numismatic Group 154
Image *Source:* https://en.wikipedia.org/w/index.php?title=File:Lysias-150.jpg *Contributors:* Monkeybait, Per Honor et Gloria, Sfan00 IMG ... 154
Image *Source:* https://en.wikipedia.org/w/index.php?title=File:Coin_of_Agathokleia_&_Strato.jpg *License:* Public Domain *Contributors:* Bodhisattwa, BotAdventures, Magog the Ogre 154
Image *Source:* https://en.wikipedia.org/w/index.php?title=File:Antialcidas.JPG *Contributors:* - 155
Image *Source:* https://en.wikipedia.org/w/index.php?title=File:Helioclesii.jpg *Contributors:* - 155
Image *Source:* https://en.wikipedia.org/w/index.php?title=File:Polyxenos.jpg *Contributors:* - 155
Image *Source:* https://en.wikipedia.org/w/index.php?title=File:Demetrius_Aniketou.jpg *Contributors:* Ketiltrout, Monkeybait, Per Honor et Gloria, Sfan00 IMG 155
Image *Source:* https://en.wikipedia.org/w/index.php?title=File:Philoxenos.jpg *Contributors:* - 155
Image *Source:* https://en.wikipedia.org/w/index.php?title=File:Diomedes2.jpg *Contributors:* - 155
Image *Source:* https://en.wikipedia.org/w/index.php?title=File:Coin_of_Amyntas_Nicator.jpg *License:* GNU Free Documentation License *Contributors:* Classical Numismatic Group 155
Image *Source:* https://en.wikipedia.org/w/index.php?title=File:Epander.jpg *Contributors:* - 155
Image *Source:* https://en.wikipedia.org/w/index.php?title=File:Theophilos-634.jpg *Contributors:* Adavidb, Monkeybait, Per Honor et Gloria, Sfan00 IMG 155
Image *Source:* https://en.wikipedia.org/w/index.php?title=File:Peukolaos_coin.jpg *License:* Public Domain *Contributors:* Whitehead 155
Image *Source:* https://en.wikipedia.org/w/index.php?title=File:Thraso_coin_simulation.jpg *License:* GNU Free Documentation License *Contributors:* 神风 155
Image *Source:* https://en.wikipedia.org/w/index.php?title=File:Nikias.jpg *Contributors:* - 155
Image *Source:* https://en.wikipedia.org/w/index.php?title=File:MenanderDikaiou.jpg *Contributors:* - 155
Image *Source:* https://en.wikipedia.org/w/index.php?title=File:Artimedoros.jpg *Contributors:* - 155
Image *Source:* https://en.wikipedia.org/w/index.php?title=File:HermaeusCoin.jpg *License:* Public Domain *Contributors:* PHGCOM 155
Image *Source:* https://en.wikipedia.org/w/index.php?title=File:Coin_of_Indo-Greek_king_Archebios.jpg *License:* Public Domain *Contributors:* Bodhisattwa, BotAdventures, Magog the Ogre 155
Image *Source:* https://en.wikipedia.org/w/index.php?title=File:Telephos.jpg *Contributors:* - 155
Image *Source:* https://en.wikipedia.org/w/index.php?title=File:Appollodotosii.jpg *Contributors:* - 155
Image *Source:* https://en.wikipedia.org/w/index.php?title=File:Dyonisos_coin.jpg *License:* Public Domain *Contributors:* Whitehead 1914 155
Image *Source:* https://en.wikipedia.org/w/index.php?title=File:ZoilosIICoin.JPG *License:* Public Domain *Contributors:* User:World Imaging . 155
Image *Source:* https://en.wikipedia.org/w/index.php?title=File:Coin_of_Apollophanes.jpg *License:* Public Domain *Contributors:* Bodhisattwa, BotAdventures, OgreBot 2 155
Image *Source:* https://en.wikipedia.org/w/index.php?title=File:Stratoii.jpg *Contributors:* - 155
Image *Source:* https://en.wikipedia.org/w/index.php?title=File:Bhadrayasha_coin.jpg *License:* GNU Free Documentation License *Contributors:* Beads and reels 155
Image *Source:* https://en.wikipedia.org/w/index.php?title=File:Front_page_of_Monnaies_Greco-Bactriennes_et_Indo-Grecques_by_Osmund_Bopearachchi.jpg *License:* GNU Free Documentation License *Contributors:* Alfons Åberg, Bodhisattwa, BotAdventures, Linguist Fr, MGA73bot2, Officer 156
Figure 125 *Source:* https://en.wikipedia.org/w/index.php?title=File:MenanderCoinFront.jpg *License:* Public Domain *Contributors:* Alfons Åberg, Bodhisattwa, DenghiùComm, Dorieo, Guanxito~commonswiki, Tuvalkin, 1 anonymous edits 159
Figure 126 *Source:* https://en.wikipedia.org/w/index.php?title=File:Europe_map_220BC.PNG *License:* GNU Free Documentation License *Contributors:* Astrokey44 160
Figure 127 *Source:* https://en.wikipedia.org/w/index.php?title=File:Asoka_Kaart.gif *Contributors:* - 161
Figure 128 *Source:* https://en.wikipedia.org/w/index.php?title=File:Khalsi_rock_edict_of_Ashoka_with_names_of_the_Greek_kings.jpg *License:* Public Domain *Contributors:* पाटलिपुत्र 162
Figure 129 *Source:* https://en.wikipedia.org/w/index.php?title=File:Inscription_Yonakasa_No.18_Cave_No.17_Nasik_caves.jpg *License:* Creative Commons Attribution 2.0 *Contributors:* पाटलिपुत्र 163
Figure 130 *Source:* https://en.wikipedia.org/w/index.php?title=File:Foreigners_at_Sanchi_Stupa_I_North_Gateway.jpg *License:* Creative Commons Attribution 3.0 *Contributors:* Goldsmelter, पाटलिपुत्र, 神风 165
Figure 131 *Source:* https://en.wikipedia.org/w/index.php?title=File:Karla_Caves_Great_Chaitya_Left_pillar_No9.jpg *License:* Creative Commons Attribution 3.0 *Contributors:* User:Sunitaburra 166
Figure 132 *Source:* https://en.wikipedia.org/w/index.php?title=File:Bharhut_Yavana.jpg *Contributors:* User:G41rn8 167
Figure 133 *Source:* https://en.wikipedia.org/w/index.php?title=File:Manmodi_Chaitya_Yavanasa_inscription.jpg *Contributors:* Beads and reels, पाटलिपुत्र 169
Image *Source:* https://en.wikipedia.org/w/index.php?title=File:IndoParthianKingdom.svg *License:* Creative Commons Attribution-Sharealike 3.0 *Contributors:* User:DLommes 170
Figure 134 *Source:* https://en.wikipedia.org/w/index.php?title=File:GondopharesCoin.JPG *License:* Creative Commons Attribution-ShareAlike 3.0 Unported *Contributors:* User:World Imaging 172

Figure 135 *Source:* https://en.wikipedia.org/w/index.php?title=File:StandingAbdagases.jpg *License:* Public Domain *Contributors:* User:World Imaging 173
Figure 136 *Source:* https://en.wikipedia.org/w/index.php?title=File:Takht-e-bahi.jpg *License:* Creative Commons Attribution-Sharealike 3.0 *Contributors:* User:Asifnwz 173
Figure 137 *Source:* https://en.wikipedia.org/w/index.php?title=File:A_picture_Texila_by_Usman_Ghani.jpg *License:* Creative Commons Attribution-Sharealike 3.0 *Contributors:* User:Usman.pg 173
Figure 138 *Source:* https://en.wikipedia.org/w/index.php?title=File:GondopharesOnHorse.jpg *License:* Public Domain *Contributors:* BotMultichill, BurritoBazooka, Giggy, Rocket000, Roland zh, World Imaging 175
Figure 139 *Source:* https://en.wikipedia.org/w/index.php?title=File:GondopharesFinePortrait.jpg *License:* Creative Commons Attribution-ShareAlike 3.0 Unported *Contributors:* User:World Imaging 175
Figure 140 *Source:* https://en.wikipedia.org/w/index.php?title=File:FireAltarWorship.JPG *License:* Creative Commons Attribution-ShareAlike 3.0 Unported *Contributors:* User:World Imaging 177
Figure 141 *Source:* https://en.wikipedia.org/w/index.php?title=File:IndoParthianKing.JPG *License:* Creative Commons Attribution-ShareAlike 3.0 Unported *Contributors:* User:World Imaging 178
Figure 142 *Source:* https://en.wikipedia.org/w/index.php?title=File:IndoParthianHunting.JPG *License:* Creative Commons Attribution-ShareAlike 3.0 Unported *Contributors:* User:World Imaging 179
Figure 143 *Source:* https://en.wikipedia.org/w/index.php?title=File:IndoParthianReveling.JPG *License:* Creative Commons Attribution-ShareAlike 3.0 Unported *Contributors:* User:World Imaging 179
Figure 144 *Source:* https://en.wikipedia.org/w/index.php?title=File:IndoParthianCouple.JPG *License:* Creative Commons Attribution-ShareAlike 3.0 Unported *Contributors:* User:World Imaging 179
Figure 145 *Source:* https://en.wikipedia.org/w/index.php?title=File:BuddhistReliquaryWithContent1stCenturyCE.jpg *License:* Creative Commons Attribution-Share Alike *Contributors:* PHGCOM 180
Figure 146 *Source:* https://en.wikipedia.org/w/index.php?title=File:AbdagasesOnHorse.jpg *License:* Public Domain *Contributors:* User:World Imaging 181
Figure 147 *Source:* https://en.wikipedia.org/w/index.php?title=File:AbdagasesOnHorseFacing.jpg *License:* Creative Commons Attribution-ShareAlike 3.0 Unported *Contributors:* User:World Imaging 182
Image *Source:* https://en.wikipedia.org/w/index.php?title=File:WKshatrapas.jpg *License:* Public Domain *Contributors:* BotMultichill, BotMultichillT, Electionworld, Nizil Shah, Roland zh, Sankalpdravid, Zaccarins 186
Figure 148 *Source:* https://en.wikipedia.org/w/index.php?title=File:Coin_of_Bhumaka.jpg *License:* Public Domain *Contributors:* Alfons Åberg, Bodhisattwa, BotMultichill, Nizil Shah, Roland zh, World Imaging, पाटलिपुत्र, 1 anonymous edits 188
Figure 149 *Source:* https://en.wikipedia.org/w/index.php?title=File:Silver_coin_of_Nahapana_British_Museum.jpg *License:* Creative Commons Attribution-Sharealike 3.0 *Contributors:* Uploadalt 189
Figure 150 *Source:* https://en.wikipedia.org/w/index.php?title=File:Karla_Caves_inscription_13_of_Nahapana.jpg *License:* Public Domain *Contributors:* OgreBot 2, पाटलिपुत्र 190
Figure 151 *Source:* https://en.wikipedia.org/w/index.php?title=File:Karla_Amit_R_Mahadik_01.jpg *License:* Creative Commons Attribution-Sharealike 3.0 *Contributors:* User:Amitmahadik100 191
Figure 152 *Source:* https://en.wikipedia.org/w/index.php?title=File:Caves,_Temple_and_inscription_(Karla_Caves).jpg *Contributors:* User:Vatsalbhawsinka 192
Figure 153 *Source:* https://en.wikipedia.org/w/index.php?title=File:Fine_carvings_2.jpg *Contributors:* User:Suniaburra 192
Figure 154 *Source:* https://en.wikipedia.org/w/index.php?title=File:Karla_Amit_R_Mahadik_02.jpg *License:* Creative Commons Attribution-Sharealike 3.0 *Contributors:* User:Amitmahadik100 192
Figure 155 *Source:* https://en.wikipedia.org/w/index.php?title=File:Nasik_Cave_inscription_No_10.jpg *License:* Public Domain *Contributors:* पाटलिपुत्र 194
Figure 156 *Source:* https://en.wikipedia.org/w/index.php?title=File:Pillar_built_by_Ushavadata_circa_120_CE_Pandavleni_Caves_caves_No10.jpg *License:* Creative Commons Attribution 2.0 *Contributors:* पाटलिपुत्र 194
Figure 157 *Source:* https://en.wikipedia.org/w/index.php?title=File:Nahapana_coin_hoard.jpg *License:* GNU Free Documentation License *Contributors:* Priyadasi 196
Figure 158 *Source:* https://en.wikipedia.org/w/index.php?title=File:Map_of_the_Periplus_of_the_Erythracan_Sea.jpg *License:* Creative Commons Attribution-Share Alike *Contributors:* PHGCOM 197
Figure 159 *Source:* https://en.wikipedia.org/w/index.php?title=File:GautamiputraRestruckOnANahapanaCoin.JPG *License:* Creative Commons Attribution-ShareAlike 3.0 Unported *Contributors:* PHGCOM 198
Figure 160 *Source:* https://en.wikipedia.org/w/index.php?title=File:Coin_of_Chastana.jpg *License:* Public Domain *Contributors:* PHGCOM 199
Figure 161 *Source:* https://en.wikipedia.org/w/index.php?title=File:Chastana_with_costume_details.jpg *License:* Creative Commons Attribution 3.0 *Contributors:* User:Gangulybiswarup 200
Figure 162 *Source:* https://en.wikipedia.org/w/index.php?title=File:Coin_of_Rudradaman.jpg *License:* Creative Commons Attribution-ShareAlike 3.0 Unported *Contributors:* User:World Imaging 201
Figure 163 *Source:* https://en.wikipedia.org/w/index.php?title=File:Ashoka_Rock_Edict_at_Junagadh.jpg *License:* GNU Free Documentation License *Contributors:* Fountain Posters, MGA73bot2, OgreBot 2, Wiki-uk 201
Figure 164 *Source:* https://en.wikipedia.org/w/index.php?title=File:Jivadaman_Saka_Era_100_coin.jpg *License:* Public Domain *Contributors:* पाटलिपुत्र 203
Figure 165 *Source:* https://en.wikipedia.org/w/index.php?title=File:Western_Satrap_Coin_of_Rudrasimha_I_.jpg *License:* GNU Free Documentation License *Contributors:* Bodhisattwa, File Upload Bot (Magnus Manske), Kelly, Nizil Shah, Roland zh 204
Figure 166 *Source:* https://en.wikipedia.org/w/index.php?title=File:Rudrasena_II_Circa_256-278_CE.jpg *License:* GNU Free Documentation License *Contributors:* पाटलिपुत्र 205
Figure 167 *Source:* https://en.wikipedia.org/w/index.php?title=File:Head_of_Buddha_Shakyamuni_LACMA_M.79.8.jpg *Contributors:* A ri gi bod, Fæ, JMCC1 206
Figure 168 *Source:* https://en.wikipedia.org/w/index.php?title=File:Bhadramukhas_ruler_Rudrasimha_III_Circa_385-415_CE.jpg *License:* GNU Free Documentation License *Contributors:* पाटलिपुत्र 207
Figure 169 *Source:* https://en.wikipedia.org/w/index.php?title=File:Western_Satrap_Damasena_year_153.jpg *License:* Public Domain *Contributors:* पाटलिपुत्र 208
Figure 170 *Source:* https://en.wikipedia.org/w/index.php?title=File:Western_Satrap_Coin_of_Rudrasimha_I_.jpg *License:* GNU Free Documentation License *Contributors:* Bodhisattwa, File Upload Bot (Magnus Manske), Kelly, Nizil Shah, Roland zh 209
Figure 171 *Source:* https://en.wikipedia.org/w/index.php?title=File:Silver_Coin_of_Kumaragupta_I.jpg *License:* GNU Free Documentation License *Contributors:* Athaenara, Bodhisattwa, Chaoborus, File Upload Bot (Magnus Manske), MGA73bot2, Mhmrodrigues, OgreBot 2 210
Figure 172 *Source:* https://en.wikipedia.org/w/index.php?title=File:South_Asia_historical_AD375_EN.svg *License:* Creative Commons Attribution-Sharealike 3.0,2.5,2.0,1.0 *Contributors:* Woudloper 211
Figure 173 *Source:* https://en.wikipedia.org *License:* Creative Commons Attribution 3.0 *Contributors:* Biswarup Ganguly 212
Image *Source:* https://en.wikipedia.org/w/index.php?title=File:Jayadaman.jpg *License:* Public Domain *Contributors:* पाटलिपुत्र 213
Image *Source:* https://en.wikipedia.org/w/index.php?title=File:Damajadasri.jpg *License:* Public Domain *Contributors:* पाटलिपुत्र 213
Image *Source:* https://en.wikipedia.org/w/index.php?title=File:Satyadaman.jpg *License:* Public Domain *Contributors:* पाटलिपुत्र 213
Image *Source:* https://en.wikipedia.org/w/index.php?title=File:Coin_of_Jivadaman_119_Shaka_Era_197_CE.jpg *License:* Public Domain *Contributors:* PHGCOM 213
Image *Source:* https://en.wikipedia.org/w/index.php?title=File:Prthivisena.jpg *License:* Public Domain *Contributors:* पाटलिपुत्र 213
Image *Source:* https://en.wikipedia.org/w/index.php?title=File:Samghadaman.jpg *License:* Public Domain *Contributors:* पाटलिपुत्र 213
Image *Source:* https://en.wikipedia.org/w/index.php?title=File:Western_Satrap_Damasena.jpg *License:* Public Domain *Contributors:* पाटलिपुत्र 213
Image *Source:* https://en.wikipedia.org/w/index.php?title=File:Western_Satrap_Damajadasri_II.jpg *License:* Public Domain *Contributors:* पाटलिपुत्र 213
Image *Source:* https://en.wikipedia.org/w/index.php?title=File:Western_Satrap_Viradaman.jpg *License:* Public Domain *Contributors:* पाटलिपुत्र 213
Image *Source:* https://en.wikipedia.org/w/index.php?title=File:Western_Satrap_Isvaradatta.jpg *License:* Public Domain *Contributors:* पाटलिपुत्र 213
Image *Source:* https://en.wikipedia.org/w/index.php?title=File:Western_Satrap_Yasodaman_I.jpg *License:* Public Domain *Contributors:* पाटलिपुत्र 213
Image *Source:* https://en.wikipedia.org/w/index.php?title=File:I85_drachme_Vijayasena_MACW270203_1ar_(8507423804).jpg *License:* Creative Commons Attribution 2.0 *Contributors:* Jean-Michel Moullec from Vern sur Seiche (35, Bretagne), France 213

Image *Source:* https://en.wikipedia.org/w/index.php?title=File:Western_Satrap_Damajadasri_III.jpg *License:* Public Domain *Contributors:* पाटलिपुत्र 213
Image *Source:* https://en.wikipedia.org/w/index.php?title=File:Western_Satrap_Visvasimha.jpg *License:* Public Domain *Contributors:* पाटलिपुत्र 213
Image *Source:* https://en.wikipedia.org/w/index.php?title=File:Silver_coin_of_Bhartrdaman.jpg *License:* Creative Commons Attribution-Sharealike 3.0 *Contributors:* Rani nurmai ... 213
Image *Source:* https://en.wikipedia.org/w/index.php?title=File:Western_Satrap_Visvasena.jpg *License:* Public Domain *Contributors:* पाटलिपुत्र 214
Image *Source:* https://en.wikipedia.org/w/index.php?title=File:Rudrasimha_II_coin.jpg *License:* Public Domain *Contributors:* पाटलिपुत्र ... 214
Image *Source:* https://en.wikipedia.org/w/index.php?title=File:Yasodaman_II.jpg *License:* Public Domain *Contributors:* पाटलिपुत्र ... 214
Image *Source:* https://en.wikipedia.org/w/index.php?title=File:Rudrasena_III.jpg *License:* Public Domain *Contributors:* पाटलिपुत्र ... 214
Image *Source:* https://en.wikipedia.org/w/index.php?title=File:Simhasena.jpg *License:* Public Domain *Contributors:* पाटलिपुत्र ... 214
Image *Source:* https://en.wikipedia.org/w/index.php?title=File:Rudrasena_IV.jpg *License:* Public Domain *Contributors:* पाटलिपुत्र ... 214
Image *Source:* https://en.wikipedia.org/w/index.php?title=File:Derafsh_Kaviani_flag_of_the_late_Sassanid_Empire.svg *License:* Public Domain *Contributors:* User:Oneasy ... 216
Figure 174 *Source:* https://en.wikipedia.org/w/index.php?title=File:KushanHead.jpg *License:* Creative Commons Attribution-ShareAlike 3.0 Unported *Contributors:* PHGCOM ... 218
Figure 175 *Source:* https://en.wikipedia.org/w/index.php?title=File:Heraios_profile.jpg *License:* GNU Free Documentation License *Contributors:* OgreBot 2, पाटलिपुत्र ... 219
Figure 176 *Source:* https://en.wikipedia.org/w/index.php?title=File:Kushan_script.jpg *License:* Public Domain *Contributors:* पाटलिपुत्र ... 220
Figure 177 *Source:* https://en.wikipedia.org/w/index.php?title=File:KushanDevoteeFullLength.jpg *License:* Creative Commons Attribution-Share Alike *Contributors:* PHGCOM ... 220
Figure 178 *Source:* https://en.wikipedia.org/w/index.php?title=File:Sho_uc_lc.svg *License:* Public Domain *Contributors:* Dcoetzee, F l a n k e r 221
Figure 179 *Source:* https://en.wikipedia.org/w/index.php?title=File:Kushan_king_or_prince.jpg *License:* Creative Commons Attribution-Sharealike 3.0 *Contributors:* user:sailko ... 222
Figure 180 *Source:* https://en.wikipedia.org/w/index.php?title=File:A_picture_of_Sirsukh_Texila_by_Usman_Ghani.jpg *License:* Creative Commons Attribution-Sharealike 3.0 *Contributors:* User:Usman.pg ... 223
Figure 181 *Source:* https://en.wikipedia.org/w/index.php?title=File:BodhGayaEnlightmentThroneOfferingAndHuvishkaCoin.jpg *License:* Creative Commons Attribution-ShareAlike 3.0 Unported *Contributors:* PHGCOM ... 224
Figure 182 *Source:* https://en.wikipedia.org/w/index.php?title=File:Kanishka_enhanced.jpg *License:* Creative Commons Attribution-Sharealike 3.0 *Contributors:* User:Gangulybiswarup ... 226
Figure 183 *Source:* https://en.wikipedia.org/w/index.php?title=File:Qila_Mubarak_in_Bathinda.jpg *License:* Public domain *Contributors:* en:User:Guneeta ... 226
Figure 184 *Source:* https://en.wikipedia.org/w/index.php?title=File:Kumara,_The_Divine_General_LACMA_M.85.279.3.jpg *Contributors:* Fæ, JMCC1 ... 228
Figure 185 *Source:* https://en.wikipedia.org/w/index.php?title=File:Gandhara,_omaggio_di_un_re_kushana_al_bodhisattva,_II-III_sec.JPG *License:* GNU Free Documentation License *Contributors:* sailko ... 229
Image *Source:* https://en.wikipedia.org/w/index.php?title=File:ZeusSerapisOhrmazdWithWorshipperBactria3rdCenturyCE.jpg *License:* Creative Commons Attribution-Share Alike *Contributors:* PHGCOM ... 230
Image *Source:* https://en.wikipedia.org/w/index.php?title=File:PharroAndWorshipperBactria3rdCenturyCE.jpg *License:* Creative Commons Attribution-Share Alike *Contributors:* PHGCOM ... 230
Image *Source:* https://en.wikipedia.org/w/index.php?title=File:ShivaOeshoBactria3rdCenturyCE.jpg *License:* Creative Commons Attribution-Share Alike *Contributors:* PHGCOM ... 230
Image *Source:* https://en.wikipedia.org/w/index.php?title=File:MahasenaHuvishka.jpg *License:* Creative Commons Attribution-ShareAlike 3.0 Unported *Contributors:* PHGCOM ... 231
Image *Source:* https://en.wikipedia.org/w/index.php?title=File:CoinOfHuvishkaWithOisho.JPG *License:* Creative Commons Attribution-ShareAlike 3.0 Unported *Contributors:* PHGCOM ... 231
Image *Source:* https://en.wikipedia.org/w/index.php?title=File:CoinOfHuvishkaWithRishtiAsRoma.JPG *License:* Creative Commons Attribution-ShareAlike 3.0 Unported *Contributors:* PHGCOM ... 231
Image *Source:* https://en.wikipedia.org/w/index.php?title=File:Manaobago.JPG *License:* Creative Commons Attribution-ShareAlike 3.0 Unported *Contributors:* PHGCOM ... 231
Image *Source:* https://en.wikipedia.org/w/index.php?title=File:CoinOfHuvishkaWithPharro.JPG *License:* Creative Commons Attribution-ShareAlike 3.0 Unported *Contributors:* PHGCOM ... 231
Image *Source:* https://en.wikipedia.org/w/index.php?title=File:CoinOfHuvishkaWithArdochsho.JPG *License:* Creative Commons Attribution-ShareAlike 3.0 Unported *Contributors:* PHGCOM ... 232
Image *Source:* https://en.wikipedia.org/w/index.php?title=File:KanihkaIOishoShiva.jpg *License:* Creative Commons Attribution-ShareAlike 3.0 Unported *Contributors:* PHGCOM ... 232
Image *Source:* https://en.wikipedia.org/w/index.php?title=File:KanihkaIOishoShivaCoin2.jpg *License:* Creative Commons Attribution-ShareAlike 3.0 Unported *Contributors:* PHGCOM ... 232
Image *Source:* https://en.wikipedia.org/w/index.php?title=File:SkandaAndVisakhaHuvishkaCoin.jpg *License:* Creative Commons Attribution-ShareAlike 3.0 Unported *Contributors:* PHGCOM ... 233
Image *Source:* https://en.wikipedia.org/w/index.php?title=File:Coin_of_Kanishka_I.jpg *License:* GNU Free Documentation License *Contributors:* A ri gi bod, Alfons Åberg, AnonMoos, Bodhisattwa, Dbachmann, Ismoon, MGA73bot2, Solon, Tahar Jelun, TommyBee, Udimu, World Imaging, पाटलिपुत्र 233
Image *Source:* https://en.wikipedia.org/w/index.php?title=File:Dinar,_Kushan_Empire,_Depiction_of_Hercules,_152-192_AD.jpg *License:* GNU Free Documentation License *Contributors:* Gts-tg, Jeff G., पाटलिपुत्र ... 233
Image *Source:* https://en.wikipedia.org/w/index.php?title=File:AdshoCarnelianSeal.jpg *License:* Public Domain *Contributors:* User:World Imaging 234
Image *Source:* https://en.wikipedia.org/w/index.php?title=File:Coin_of_Kujula_Kadphises.jpg *License:* Public Domain *Contributors:* Akinom, Alfons Åberg, Bodhisattwa, BotAdventures, BotMultichill, Gts-tg, JuTa, McZusatz, Mhmrodrigues, Takeaway, World Imaging, 1 anonymous edits ... 234
Figure 186 *Source:* https://en.wikipedia.org/w/index.php?title=File:Four_sets_of_Gold_Coins_of_Vima_Kadphises.jpg *License:* Creative Commons Attribution 2.0 *Contributors:* Ancient Art ... 235
Figure 187 *Source:* https://en.wikipedia.org/w/index.php?title=File:Kanishka-Inaugurates-Mahyana-Buddhism.jpg *License:* Public Domain *Contributors:* Cpt.a.haddock, Mhmrodrigues, Napoleon 100, Roland zh, శ్రీధర్ బాబు ... 235
Figure 188 *Source:* https://en.wikipedia.org/w/index.php?title=File:BuddhistTriad.JPG *License:* Creative Commons Attribution-ShareAlike 3.0 Unported *Contributors:* User:World Imaging ... 236
Figure 189 *Source:* https://en.wikipedia.org/w/index.php?title=File:Taxila._Standing_Female._88.194.jpg *Contributors:* Tracield ... 237
Figure 190 *Source:* https://en.wikipedia.org/w/index.php?title=File:BegramGladiator.JPG *License:* Public Domain *Contributors:* User:Shizhao 238
Figure 191 *Source:* https://en.wikipedia.org/w/index.php?title=File:TrajanCoinAhinposhBuddhistMonasteryAfghanistan.jpg *License:* Creative Commons Attribution-ShareAlike 3.0 Unported *Contributors:* User:PHGCOM, User:PHGCOM ... 238
Figure 192 *Source:* https://en.wikipedia.org/w/index.php?title=File:Eurasia_in_2nd_Century.png *Contributors:* User:Seasonsinthesun ... 239
Figure 193 *Source:* https://en.wikipedia.org/w/index.php?title=File:KanishkaICoinFoundInKhotan.jpg *License:* Creative Commons Attribution-ShareAlike 3.0 Unported *Contributors:* PHGCOM ... 239
Figure 194 *Source:* https://en.wikipedia.org/w/index.php?title=File:Lokaksema.jpg *License:* Public Domain *Contributors:* BotMultichill, BotMultichillT, Pieter Kuiper, Shizhao, Un1c0s bot~commonswiki, Väsk ... 240
Figure 195 *Source:* https://en.wikipedia.org/w/index.php?title=File:Eastern_Han_ingot_imprints_with_barbarous_Greek_inscriptions.jpg *License:* Public Domain *Contributors:* Tahar Jelun, पाटलिपुत्र ... 241
Figure 196 *Source:* https://en.wikipedia.org/w/index.php?title=File:Hormizd_I_Kushanshah_on_the_Naqsh-e_Rustam_Bahram_II_panel.jpg *Contributors:* User:Poco a poco, User:पाटलिपुत्र ... 241
Figure 197 *Source:* https://en.wikipedia.org/w/index.php?title=File:KushanTamgas.gif *License:* Public Domain *Contributors:* Barefact ... 242
Figure 198 *Source:* https://en.wikipedia.org/w/index.php?title=File:Kushan_devotee_Mathura.jpg *License:* Creative Commons Attribution 3.0 *Contributors:* User:Gangulybiswarup ... 245
Image *Source:* https://en.wikipedia.org/w/index.php?title=File:North_Gateway_-_Rear_Side_-_Stupa_1_-_Sanchi_Hill_2013-02-21_4480-4481.JPG *License:* Creative Commons Attribution 3.0 *Contributors:* Biswarup Ganguly ... 243
Image *Source:* https://en.wikipedia.org/w/index.php?title=File:Jam_leaning_minaret_jam_ghor.jpg *License:* Public Domain *Contributors:* david adamec ... 244

Image *Source:* https://en.wikipedia.org/w/index.php?title=File:Symbol_book_class2.svg *License:* Creative Commons Attribution-Sharealike 2.5 *Contributors:* Lokal_Profil 244
Image *Source:* https://en.wikipedia.org/w/index.php?title=File:Folder_Hexagonal_Icon.svg *License:* GNU Free Documentation License *Contributors:* Anomie, Jo-Jo Eumerus, Mifter 244
Image *Source:* https://en.wikipedia.org/w/index.php?title=File:Portal-puzzle.svg *License:* Public Domain *Contributors:* Anomie, Jo-Jo Eumerus, Topbanana 244
Image *Source:* https://en.wikipedia.org/w/index.php?title=File:Tajikistan_crown_and_stars.svg *License:* Public Domain *Contributors:* User:Sangjinhwa 245
Image *Source:* https://en.wikipedia.org/w/index.php?title=File:Flag_of_Tajikistan.svg *License:* Public Domain *Contributors:* Abakan1992, Achim1999, Alex Spade, Anime Addict AA, Antonsusi, Apatomerus, Benzoyl, Bjankuloski06en, Cathy Richards, CemDemirkartal, Cycn, Daphne Lantier, Ecad93, Erlenmeyer, EugeneZelenko, Fred the Oyster, Fry1989, Homo lupus, Johnny Rotten, Khwahan, Klemen Kocjancic, Leonid 2, Ludger1961, MAXXX-309, Mattes, Nameneko∼commonswiki, Neq00, Nightstallion, OAlexander∼commonswiki, Omid Jeyhani, Ricordisamoa, Rinkio, Sarang, SiBr4, SouthSudan, Yeenosaurus, Zscout370, 7 anonymous edits 245
Figure 199 *Source:* https://en.wikipedia.org/w/index.php?title=File:Kushano-Sasanid_realm_based_on_coinage_mint_locations.jpg *License:* Creative Commons Attribution-Sharealike 3.0 *Contributors:* User:Keeby101, User:पाटलिपुत्र 250
Figure 200 *Source:* https://en.wikipedia.org/w/index.php?title=File:Hormizd_I_Kushanshah_portrait.jpg *License:* Creative Commons Attribution-Sharealike 3.0 *Contributors:* User:PHGCOM, User:पाटलिपुत्र 251
Figure 201 *Source:* https://en.wikipedia.org/w/index.php?title=File:Hormizd_I_Kushanshah_on_the_Naqsh-e_Rustam_Bahram_II_panel.jpg *Contributors:* User:Poco a poco, User:पाटलिपुत्र 251
Figure 202 *Source:* https://en.wikipedia.org/w/index.php?title=File:Ajanta_Cave_1_Group_of_foreigners.jpg *Contributors:* पाटलिपुत्र 252
Figure 203 *Source:* https://en.wikipedia.org/w/index.php?title=File:BahramITheIndoSasanian.jpg *License:* GNU Free Documentation License *Contributors:* Classical Numismatic Group; 253
Figure 204 *Source:* https://en.wikipedia.org/w/index.php?title=File:KUSHANO-SASANIANS_Ardashir_I_Kushanshah_Circa_AD_230-250.jpg *License:* GNU Free Documentation License *Contributors:* पाटलिपुत्र 254
Figure 205 *Source:* https://en.wikipedia.org/w/index.php?title=File:Ardashir_I_Kushanshah_in_the_name_of_Vasudeva_circa_230-245_CE.jpg *License:* GNU Free Documentation License *Contributors:* पाटलिपुत्र 255
Figure 206 *Source:* https://en.wikipedia.org/w/index.php?title=File:Indo-SassanianCoinage.jpg *License:* Public Domain *Contributors:* User:World Imaging 255
Figure 207 *Source:* https://en.wikipedia.org/w/index.php?title=File:Indo-SassanianCoin.jpg *License:* Public Domain *Contributors:* User:World Imaging 256
Figure 208 *Source:* https://en.wikipedia.org/w/index.php?title=File:Hormizd_I_Kushanshah_Merv_mint.jpg *License:* GNU Free Documentation License *Contributors:* पाटलिपुत्र 256
Figure 209 *Source:* https://en.wikipedia.org/w/index.php?title=File:Hephthalite_horseman_on_British_Museum_bowl_460-479_CE.jpg *License:* Creative Commons Attribution-Sharealike 3.0 *Contributors:* User:PHGCOM, User:पाटलिपुत्र 258
Figure 210 *Source:* https://en.wikipedia.org/w/index.php?title=File:Sondani.jpg *License:* Creative Commons Attribution-Sharealike 3.0 *Contributors:* LRBurdak 259
Figure 211 *Source:* https://en.wikipedia.org/w/index.php?title=File:Asia_500ad.jpg *License:* Creative Commons Attribution 3.0 *Contributors:* Thomas A. Lessman. 260
Figure 212 *Source:* https://en.wikipedia.org/w/index.php?title=File:HunCoinDerivedFromSassanianDesign5thCE.JPG *License:* Creative Commons Attribution-ShareAlike 3.0 Unported *Contributors:* PHGCOM 260
Figure 213 *Source:* https://en.wikipedia.org/w/index.php?title=File:HunaKing.JPG *License:* Creative Commons Attribution-ShareAlike 3.0 Unported *Contributors:* PHGCOM 260
Figure 214 *Source:* https://en.wikipedia.org/w/index.php?title=File:SilverBowlNFPPakistan5-6thcenturyCE.JPG *License:* Creative Commons Attribution-ShareAlike 3.0 Unported *Contributors:* PHGCOM 261
Image *Source:* https://en.wikipedia.org/w/index.php?title=File:Hephtalites(An-mu-lu-chjen).gif *License:* Public Domain *Contributors:* Barefact 262
Image *Source:* https://en.wikipedia.org/w/index.php?title=File:Hephthalites500.png *License:* Creative Commons Attribution 3.0 *Contributors:* Gabagool 262
Image *Source:* https://en.wikipedia.org/w/index.php?title=File:Kidarite_Tamga.png *Contributors:* User:Alx bio 262
Image *Source:* https://en.wikipedia.org/w/index.php?title=File:Alchon_Tamga.png *Contributors:* User:Alx bio 262
Image *Source:* https://en.wikipedia.org/w/index.php?title=File:Nezak_Crown.png *Contributors:* User:Alx bio 262
Image *Source:* https://en.wikipedia.org/w/index.php?title=File:Gok1.png *License:* Creative Commons Attribution-Sharealike 3.0 *Contributors:* User:Dolatjan 262
Figure 215 *Source:* https://en.wikipedia.org/w/index.php?title=File:Hephthalites_chieftain_circa_484-560.jpg *License:* GNU Free Documentation License *Contributors:* User:पाटलिपुत्र 264
Figure 216 *Source:* https://en.wikipedia.org/w/index.php?title=File:Hephthalites_coinage_imitating_Peroz_I_Late_5th_century_CE.jpg *License:* GNU Free Documentation License *Contributors:* पाटलिपुत्र 265
Figure 217 *Source:* https://en.wikipedia.org/w/index.php?title=File:Hephthalites_coin._Uncertain_ruler._Late_5th_century_CE.jpg *License:* GNU Free Documentation License *Contributors:* पाटलिपुत्र 265
Figure 218 *Source:* https://en.wikipedia.org/w/index.php?title=File:SilverBowlNFPPakistan5-6thcenturyCE.JPG *License:* Creative Commons Attribution-ShareAlike 3.0 Unported *Contributors:* PHGCOM 266
Figure 219 *Source:* https://en.wikipedia.org/w/index.php?title=File:Hephthalites._Anonymous._Before_AD_700._Imitating_Khosrau_II.jpg *License:* GNU Free Documentation License *Contributors:* पाटलिपुत्र 267
Figure 220 *Source:* https://en.wikipedia.org/w/index.php?title=File:Hephthalites_circa_350_CE.jpg *License:* GNU Free Documentation License *Contributors:* पाटलिपुत्र 268
Figure 221 *Source:* https://en.wikipedia.org/w/index.php?title=File:Hephthalites_chieftain_late_5th_century.jpg *License:* GNU Free Documentation License *Contributors:* User:पाटलिपुत्र 269
Figure 222 *Source:* https://en.wikipedia.org/w/index.php?title=File:Hephthalite_wearing_the_crown_of_Peroz_I_Late_5th_century_CE.jpg *License:* GNU Free Documentation License *Contributors:* पाटलिपुत्र 270
Figure 223 *Source:* https://en.wikipedia.org/w/index.php?title=File:Asia_500ad.jpg *License:* Creative Commons Attribution 3.0 *Contributors:* Thomas A. Lessman. 271
Figure 224 *Source:* https://en.wikipedia.org/w/index.php?title=File:Hephthalite_horseman_on_British_Museum_bowl_460-479_CE.jpg *License:* Creative Commons Attribution-Sharealike 3.0 *Contributors:* User:PHGCOM, User:पाटलिपुत्र 272
Figure 225 *Source:* https://en.wikipedia.org/w/index.php?title=File:Kushano-Hephthalites_600ad.jpg *License:* Creative Commons Attribution-Sharealike 3.0 *Contributors:* Thomas Lessman (Contact!) 274
Image *Source:* https://en.wikipedia.org/w/index.php?title=File:Mahajanapadas_(c._500_BCE).png *License:* Creative Commons Attribution-Sharealike 3.0 *Contributors:* User:Avantiputra7 281
Image *Source:* https://en.wikipedia.org/w/index.php?title=File:Gandhara.JPG *License:* Public Domain *Contributors:* BotMultichill, BotMultichillT, Electionworld, Roland zh, Zaccarias, 1 anonymous edits 281
Image *Source:* https://en.wikipedia.org/w/index.php?title=File:Standard_of_Cyrus_the_Great_(Achaemenid_Empire).svg *License:* Creative Commons Attribution-Sharealike 3.0 *Contributors:* Sodacan 281
Image *Source:* https://en.wikipedia.org/w/index.php?title=File:Mohenjo-daro_Priesterkönig.jpeg *License:* Creative Commons world66 *Contributors:* Botev, Daphne Lantier, Gryffindor, Icarusgeek, Jungpionier, Look2See1, Mmcannis∼commonswiki, Oksmith, Roland zh, Themightyquill, 1 anonymous edits 282
Figure 226 *Source:* https://en.wikipedia.org/w/index.php?title=File:GandharaFemale.JPG *License:* GNU Free Documentation License *Contributors:* Abhishekjoshi, BotAdventures, Daderot, Jonathan Cardy, MGA73bot2, Sailko, TommyBee, World Imaging 284
Figure 227 *Source:* https://en.wikipedia.org/w/index.php?title=File:GandharaMotherGoddess.JPG *License:* GNU Free Documentation License *Contributors:* Abhishekjoshi, BotAdventures, Durga, Jonathan Cardy, MGA73bot2, Roland zh, Sailko, TommyBee, World Imaging 285
Figure 228 *Source:* https://en.wikipedia.org/w/index.php?title=File:Gandhara1.JPG *License:* Creative Commons Attribution 2.5 *Contributors:* User:Ancientcoinsofindia1, English Wikipedia 288
Figure 229 *Source:* https://en.wikipedia.org/w/index.php?title=File:I9_18satamana_TaxilaGandhara_1ar_(8482057992).jpg *License:* Creative Commons Attribution 2.0 *Contributors:* Jean-Michel Moullec from Vern sur Seiche (35, Bretagne), France 289
Figure 230 *Source:* https://en.wikipedia.org/w/index.php?title=File:Gandhara_Buddha_(tnm).jpeg *License:* Public domain *Contributors:* User:World Imaging 291
Figure 231 *Source:* https://en.wikipedia.org/w/index.php?title=File:Marine_deities_Gandhara.jpg *Contributors:* Beads and reels 292

Figure 232 *Source:* https://en.wikipedia.org/w/index.php?title=File:KanishkaCasket.JPG *License:* GNU Free Documentation License *Contributors:* Personal photograph ... 293
Figure 233 *Source:* https://en.wikipedia.org/w/index.php?title=File:Gandharan_sculpture_-_head_of_a_bodhisattva.jpg *License:* Public Domain *Contributors:* FlickreviewR 2, Flock, Hedwig in Washington, Hzh, INeverCry, Jacklee, JesseW, Jim.henderson ... 294
Figure 234 *Source:* https://en.wikipedia.org/w/index.php?title=File:SFAAMBuddha.jpg *Contributors:* User:Willard84 ... 294
Figure 235 *Source:* https://en.wikipedia.org/w/index.php?title=File:Gandhara_fortified_city.jpg *License:* Creative Commons Attribution-Sharealike 3.0 *Contributors:* Uploadmo ... 295
Figure 236 *Source:* https://en.wikipedia.org/w/index.php?title=File:Sharing_of_relics_and_Gandhara_fortified_city.jpg *License:* Creative Commons Attribution-Sharealike 3.0 *Contributors:* Uploadmo ... 296
Figure 237 *Source:* https://en.wikipedia.org/w/index.php?title=File:Shingerdar_Stupa1.jpg *License:* Creative Commons Attribution-Sharealike 3.0 *Contributors:* JiriMatejicek, Willard84 ... 298
Figure 238 *Source:* https://en.wikipedia.org/w/index.php?title=File:BuddhistTriad.JPG *License:* Creative Commons Attribution-ShareAlike 3.0 Unported *Contributors:* User:World Imaging ... 300
Figure 239 *Source:* https://en.wikipedia.org/w/index.php?title=File:Avalokitesvara_Gandhara_Musée_Guimet_2418_1.jpg *License:* Public Domain *Contributors:* Vassil ... 301
Figure 240 *Source:* https://en.wikipedia.org/w/index.php?title=File:HaddaTypes.JPG *License:* GNU Free Documentation License *Contributors:* Dodo, Gryffindor, MGA73bot2, Nataraja∼commonswiki, Sailko, Vassil, World Imaging ... 303
Figure 241 *Source:* https://en.wikipedia.org/w/index.php?title=File:Standing_Bodhisattva_Gandhara_Musee_Guimet.jpg *License:* Public Domain *Contributors:* Vassil ... 304
Figure 242 *Source:* https://en.wikipedia.org/w/index.php?title=File:BuddhaHead.JPG *License:* Public Domain *Contributors:* Art-top, Geek3, Gryffindor, Ismoon, Martin H., Mats Halldin∼commonswiki, Phg, Rama, Rocket000, Sailko, Underwaterbuffalo, Uploadalt, Vassil, 1 anonymous edits ... 304
Figure 243 *Source:* https://en.wikipedia.org/w/index.php?title=File:Gandhara_Buddha.jpg *License:* Creative Commons Attribution 2.0 *Contributors:* Wonderlane ... 305
Figure 244 *Source:* https://en.wikipedia.org/w/index.php?title=File:BuddhaAcanthusCapitol.JPG *License:* Public Domain *Contributors:* Kilom691, MM, Man vyi, Phg, Sailko, Satrughna02, Vassil, World Imaging ... 305
Figure 245 *Source:* https://en.wikipedia.org/w/index.php?title=File:GandharanAtlas.JPG *License:* Public Domain *Contributors:* Gryffindor, Ismoon, Mats Halldin∼commonswiki, Ranveig, Ricky81682, Sailko, SolLuna, Vassil, Y-barton, 4 anonymous edits ... 305
Figure 246 *Source:* https://en.wikipedia.org/w/index.php?title=File:KushanMaitreya.JPG *License:* Public domain *Contributors:* BotAdventures, BotMultichill, Daderot, File Upload Bot (Magnus Manske), Jorunn, OgreBot 2, Ranveig, Roland zh, Sailko, Tengu800, Testus, 1 anonymous edits ... 306
Figure 247 *Source:* https://en.wikipedia.org/w/index.php?title=File:Indo-GreekBanquet.JPG *License:* Public Domain *Contributors:* Daderot, G.dallorto, Gryffindor, Malo, Mats Halldin∼commonswiki, Sailko, Thorguds, Uploadalt, Vassil ... 306
Figure 248 *Source:* https://en.wikipedia.org/w/index.php?title=File:MayaDream.jpg *License:* GNU Free Documentation License *Contributors:* User PHG on en.wikipedia ... 307
Figure 249 *Source:* https://en.wikipedia.org/w/index.php?title=File:SiddhartaBirth.jpg *License:* GNU Free Documentation License *Contributors:* BotAdventures, Daderot, Ddalbiez, Gryffindor, MGA73bot2, Podzemnik, Tttrung, 1 anonymous edits ... 307
Figure 250 *Source:* https://en.wikipedia.org/w/index.php?title=File:LeavingPalace.jpg *License:* Public Domain *Contributors:* User PHG on en.wikipedia ... 308
Figure 251 *Source:* https://en.wikipedia.org/w/index.php?title=File:EndAscetism.JPG *License:* Public Domain *Contributors:* Aotake, Daderot, FSII, File Upload Bot (Magnus Manske), Leoboudv, OgreBot 2, Samulili, Shoulder-synth, Soranoch, 1 anonymous edits ... 308
Figure 252 *Source:* https://en.wikipedia.org/w/index.php?title=File:Sarnath3.JPG *License:* Public domain *Contributors:* Daderot, File Upload Bot (Magnus Manske), Jarekt, MGA73bot2, OgreBot 2 ... 309
Figure 253 *Source:* https://en.wikipedia.org/w/index.php?title=File:Gandhara_Buddha_scene.jpg *License:* GNU Free Documentation License *Contributors:* Per Honor et Gloria at en.wikipedia ... 309
Figure 254 *Source:* https://en.wikipedia.org/w/index.php?title=File:Paranirvana.JPG *License:* Public Domain *Contributors:* BotAdventures, BotMultichill, Daderot, Iudexvivorum, Malo, Mistvan, Podzemnik, Shoulder-synth ... 310
Figure 255 *Source:* https://en.wikipedia.org/w/index.php?title=File:HaddaSculpture.jpg *License:* Public Domain *Contributors:* OgreBot 2, Pieter Kuiper, Zaccarias ... 310
Figure 256 *Source:* https://en.wikipedia.org/w/index.php?title=File:HaddaBodhisattva.jpg *License:* Public Domain *Contributors:* OgreBot 2, Zaccarias ... 310
Figure 257 *Source:* https://en.wikipedia.org/w/index.php?title=File:Buddha-Herakles.JPG *License:* GNU Free Documentation License *Contributors:* Clpo13, Magog the Ogre ... 311
Figure 258 *Source:* https://en.wikipedia.org/w/index.php?title=File:GandharaScrolls.JPG *License:* Public Domain *Contributors:* Daderot, Gryffindor, Johnbod, Mats Halldin∼commonswiki, Sailko, Vassil, Zaccarias ... 311
Figure 259 *Source:* https://en.wikipedia.org/w/index.php?title=File:GandharaFrieze.JPG *License:* GNU Free Documentation License *Contributors:* BotAdventures, MGA73bot2, Ronaldino, World Imaging ... 312
Figure 260 *Source:* https://en.wikipedia.org/w/index.php?title=File:StonePalette1.JPG *License:* Creative Commons Attribution-ShareAlike 3.0 Unported *Contributors:* User:World Imaging ... 312
Figure 261 *Source:* https://en.wikipedia.org/w/index.php?title=File:Hadda_laughing_boy_008.jpg *License:* Public Domain *Contributors:* Gryffindor ... 312
Figure 262 *Source:* https://en.wikipedia.org/w/index.php?title=File:Gandhara,_bodhisattva_assiso,_II_sec..JPG *License:* GNU Free Documentation License *Contributors:* sailko ... 313
Figure 263 *Source:* https://en.wikipedia.org/w/index.php?title=File:Map_of_Vedic_India.png *License:* GNU Free Documentation License *Contributors:* Abhishekjoshi, AnonMoos, BotMultichillT, Dbachmann, Fast track∼commonswiki, LX, Mywikicommons, Roland zh, Rosarino, 2 anonymous edits ... 317
Image *Source:* https://en.wikipedia.org/w/index.php?title=File:Flag_of_Bangladesh.svg *License:* Public Domain *Contributors:* User:SKopp ... 324
Image *Source:* https://en.wikipedia.org/w/index.php?title=File:Asia_800ad.jpg *License:* Creative Commons Attribution 3.0 *Contributors:* Artix Kreiger 2, BotMultichill, Denniss, File Upload Bot (Magnus Manske), Gecary, Grendill, Gryffindor, JuTa, Kaba, OgreBot 2, P199, Rocket000, Sreejithk2000, Takeaway, Tatmadav, Unserefahne, Verdy p ... 326
Figure 264 *Source:* https://en.wikipedia.org/w/index.php?title=File:Coins_of_the_Shahis_8th_century.jpg *License:* Creative Commons Attribution-Sharealike 3.0 *Contributors:* Uploadalt ... 328
Figure 265 *Source:* https://en.wikipedia.org/w/index.php?title=File:Coin_of_Samantadeva.jpg *License:* GNU Free Documentation License *Contributors:* User:Ancientcoinsofindia1, English Wikipedia ... 328
Figure 266 *Source:* https://en.wikipedia.org/w/index.php?title=File:AMB_Temple_in_Soon_Sakasar_Valley_by_Usman_Ghani.JPG *License:* Creative Commons Attribution-Sharealike 3.0 *Contributors:* User:Usman.pg ... 329
Figure 267 *Source:* https://en.wikipedia.org/w/index.php?title=File:Kushanshas-Hepthalites_565ad.jpg *License:* Creative Commons Attribution-Sharealike 3.0 *Contributors:* Thomas Lessman (Contact!) ... 331
Figure 268 *Source:* https://en.wikipedia.org/w/index.php?title=File:Mes_Aynak_stupa.jpg *License:* Creative Commons Attribution-Sharealike 2.0 *Contributors:* Jerome Starkey ... 333
Figure 269 *Source:* https://en.wikipedia.org/w/index.php?title=File:Abbasid_Iraq_908_930_Shahi_inspired_coin.jpg *License:* Creative Commons Attribution-Sharealike 3.0 *Contributors:* PHGCOM ... 334
Figure 270 *Source:* https://en.wikipedia.org/w/index.php?title=File:Kabul_ganesh_khingle.jpg *License:* GNU Free Documentation License *Contributors:* Durga, MGA73, MGA73bot2, Officer, OgreBot 2, Roland zh, Teb728, Zaccarias ... 337
Image *Source:* https://en.wikipedia.org/w/index.php?title=File:Padlock-silver.svg *Contributors:* AzaToth, BotMultichill, BotMultichillT, Gurch, Jarekt, Kallerna, Multichill, Perhelion, Rd232, Riana, Sarang, Siebrand, Steinsplitter, 4 anonymous edits ... 343
Image *Source:* https://en.wikipedia.org/w/index.php?title=File:Satvahana.svg *License:* Creative Commons Attribution-Sharealike 3.0 *Contributors:* chetanv ... 343
Figure 271 *Source:* https://en.wikipedia.org/w/index.php?title=File:Nasik_cave_19.jpg *Contributors:* Beads and reels, पाटलिपुत्र ... 346
Figure 272 *Source:* https://en.wikipedia.org/w/index.php?title=File:Inscription_Cave_19_Nasik.jpg *License:* Public Domain *Contributors:* पाटलिपुत्र 346
Figure 273 *Source:* https://en.wikipedia.org/w/index.php?title=File:Complete_view_of_Inscription_in_cave_at_Naneghat.jpg *License:* Creative Commons Attribution-Sharealike 3.0 *Contributors:* User:Karchetan ... 347
Figure 274 *Source:* https://en.wikipedia.org/w/index.php?title=File:City_of_Kusinagara_in_the_War_over_the_Buddha's_Relics,_South_Gate,_Stupa_no._1,_Sanchi.jpg *License:* Creative Commons Attribution 2.0 *Contributors:* Rahul Bott, पाटलिपुत्र ... 349
Figure 275 *Source:* https://en.wikipedia.org/w/index.php?title=File:Gautamiputra_Sri_Satakarni_overstruck_on_a_coin_of_Nahapana.jpg *License:* Creative Commons Attribution-Sharealike 3.0 *Contributors:* Uploadalt ... 351
Figure 276 *Source:* https://en.wikipedia.org/w/index.php?title=File:010_Cave_3,_Exterior_(33156264563).jpg *License:* Creative Commons Attribution 2.0 *Contributors:* Photo Dharma from Sadao, Thailand ... 352

Figure 277 *Source:* https://en.wikipedia.org/w/index.php?title=File:Vashishtiputra_Sri_Satakarni.jpg *License:* Creative Commons Attribution-Sharealike 3.0 *Contributors:* Uploadalt 353
Figure 278 *Source:* https://en.wikipedia.org/w/index.php?title=File:Gautamiputra_Rajni_Shri_Satakarni.jpg *License:* Public Domain *Contributors:* PHGCOM 354
Figure 279 *Source:* https://en.wikipedia.org/w/index.php?title=File:Ashoka_with_his_Queens_at_Sannati-Kanaganahalli_Stupa.jpg *Contributors:* पाटलिपुत्र 356
Figure 280 *Source:* https://en.wikipedia.org/w/index.php?title=File:Indian_ship_on_lead_coin_of_Vashishtiputra_Shri_Pulumavi.jpg *License:* Public Domain *Contributors:* PHGCOM 358
Figure 281 *Source:* https://en.wikipedia.org/w/index.php?title=File:Statuetta_indiana_di_Lakshmi,_avorio,_da_pompei,_1-50_dc_ca.,_149425,_02.JPG *License:* Creative Commons Attribution-Sharealike 3.0 *Contributors:* User:Sailko 359
Figure 282 *Source:* https://en.wikipedia.org/w/index.php?title=File:Siri-Satakani_inscription_Sanchi_Stupa_1_Southern_Gateway_Rear_of_top_architrave.jpg *License:* Creative Commons Attribution 2.0 *Contributors:* पाटलिपुत्र 361
Figure 283 *Source:* https://en.wikipedia.org/w/index.php?title=File:Coin_of_Gautamiputra_Sri_Yajna_Satakarni.jpg *License:* Creative Commons Attribution-Sharealike 3.0 *Contributors:* Bodhisattwa, OgreBot 2, Utcursch 362
Figure 284 *Source:* https://en.wikipedia.org/w/index.php?title=File:Karla_caves_Chaitya.jpg *Contributors:* Beads and reels, Johnbod 363
Figure 285 *Source:* https://en.wikipedia.org/w/index.php?title=File:Andhra_Pradesh_Royal_earrings_1st_Century_BCE.jpg *License:* Creative Commons Attribution-Sharealike 3.0,2.5,2.0,1.0 *Contributors:* PHGCOM 364
Image *Source:* https://en.wikipedia.org/w/index.php?title=File:East_Gateway_-_Stupa_1_-_Sanchi_Hill_2013-02-21_4398.JPG *License:* Creative Commons Attribution 3.0 *Contributors:* Biswarup Ganguly 365
Figure 286 *Source:* https://en.wikipedia.org/w/index.php?title=File:Chankrama_Sanchi_Stupa_1_Eastern_Gateway_Left_pillar_Front_top_panel.jpg *License:* Creative Commons Attribution 3.0 *Contributors:* User:Gangulybiswarup 366
Figure 287 *Source:* https://en.wikipedia.org/w/index.php?title=File:Pipal_tree_temple_of_Bodh_Gaya_depicted_in_Sanchi_Stupa_1_Eastern_Gateway.jpg *License:* Creative Commons Attribution 3.0 *Contributors:* User:Gangulybiswarup 366
Figure 288 *Source:* https//en.wikipedia.org *License:* Creative Commons Attribution 3.0 *Contributors:* User:Gangulybiswarup 366
Figure 289 *Source:* https://en.wikipedia.org/w/index.php?title=File:Bimbisara_with_his_royal_cortege_issuing_from_the_city_of_Rajagriha_to_visit_the_Buddha.jpg *License:* Creative Commons Attribution 3.0 *Contributors:* User:Gangulybiswarup 367
Figure 290 *Source:* https://en.wikipedia.org/w/index.php?title=File:Foreigners_making_a_dedication_to_Stupa_1at_the_Northern_Gateway_of_Stupa_1_Sanchi.jpg *License:* Creative Commons Attribution 3.0 *Contributors:* User:Gangulybiswarup 368
Figure 291 *Source:* https://en.wikipedia.org/w/index.php?title=File:Procession_of_king_Suddhodana_from_Kapilavastu_in_full_Sanchi_Stupa_1_Eastern_Gateway.jpg *License:* Creative Commons Attribution 2.0 *Contributors:* User:Gangulybiswarup 368
Figure 292 *Source:* https://en.wikipedia.org/w/index.php?title=File:Sanchi_6-09.jpg *Contributors:* User:G41rn8 369
Figure 293 *Source:* https://en.wikipedia.org/w/index.php?title=File:Sanchi2_N-MP-220.jpg *License:* Creative Commons Attribution-Sharealike 3.0 *Contributors:* User:Asitjain 369
Figure 294 *Source:* https://en.wikipedia.org/w/index.php?title=File:Yakshini_Sanchi_Stupa_1_Eastern_Gateway.jpg *License:* Creative Commons Attribution 2.0 *Contributors:* पाटलिपुत्र 369
Figure 295 *Source:* https://en.wikipedia.org/w/index.php?title=File:Elephants_Eastern_Gateway_Stupa_1_Sanchi.jpg *License:* Creative Commons Attribution-Sharealike 3.0 *Contributors:* User:Amigo&oscar 370
Figure 296 *Source:* https://en.wikipedia.org/w/index.php?title=File:Sanchi_lion_pillar_with_flame_palmette.jpg *License:* Creative Commons Attribution 3.0 *Contributors:* User:Gangulybiswarup 370
Figure 297 *Source:* https://en.wikipedia.org/w/index.php?title=File:Udayagiri_puri_-_March_2010.jpg *License:* Public domain *Contributors:* Xeteli 378
Figure 298 *Source:* https://en.wikipedia.org/w/index.php?title=File:Udayagiri_Caves_-_Ganesha_Gumpha_04.jpg *License:* Creative Commons Attribution-Sharealike 3.0,2.5,2.0,1.0 *Contributors:* Bernard Gagnon 378
Figure 299 *Source:* https://en.wikipedia.org/w/index.php?title=File:Udayagiri_Caves_-_Hathi_Gumpha.jpg *License:* Creative Commons Attribution-Sharealike 3.0,2.5,2.0,1.0 *Contributors:* Bernard Gagnon 379
Figure 300 *Source:* https://en.wikipedia.org/w/index.php?title=File:Hatigumfa.jpg *License:* Creative Commons Attribution 3.0 *Contributors:* Amitava 379
Figure 301 *Source:* https://en.wikipedia.org/w/index.php?title=File:KU24.jpg *Contributors:* User:Saileshpat 380
Figure 302 *Source:* https://en.wikipedia.org/w/index.php?title=File:Udaygiri_Stone_Caves.JPG *License:* Creative Commons Attribution-Sharealike 3.0 *Contributors:* User:Agbpatro 380
Figure 303 *Source:* https://en.wikipedia.org/w/index.php?title=File:KU17.jpg *Contributors:* User:Saileshpat 381
Figure 304 *Source:* https://en.wikipedia.org/w/index.php?title=File:CAVE_LIKE_SNAKE_MOUTH.jpg *License:* Creative Commons Attribution-Sharealike 3.0 *Contributors:* User:Balajijagadesh 381
Image *Source:* https://en.wikipedia.org/w/index.php?title=File:South_Asia_historical_AD450_EN.svg *Contributors:* User:Woudloper 388
Image *Source:* https://en.wikipedia.org/w/index.php?title=File:ChandraguptaIIOnHorse.jpg *License:* Creative Commons Attribution-ShareAlike 3.0 Unported *Contributors:* PHGCOM 390
Image *Source:* https//en.wikipedia.org *License:* Public Domain *Contributors:* User:Daderot 390
Figure 305 *Source:* https://en.wikipedia.org/w/index.php?title=File:Queen_Kumaradevi_and_King_Chandragupta_I_on_a_coin_of_their_son_Samudragupta_350_380_CE.jpg *License:* Creative Commons Attribution-Sharealike 3.0 *Contributors:* Uploadalt 393
Figure 306 *Source:* https://en.wikipedia.org/w/index.php?title=File:SamudraguptaCoin.jpg *License:* Creative Commons Attribution-ShareAlike 3.0 Unported *Contributors:* PHGCOM 394
Figure 307 *Source:* https//en.wikipedia.org *License:* Creative Commons Attribution 3.0 *Contributors:* Biswarup Ganguly 395
Figure 308 *Source:* https://en.wikipedia.org/w/index.php?title=File:Met,_india_(uttar_pradesh),_gupta_period,_krishna_battling_the_horse_demon_keshi,_5th_century.JPG *License:* GNU Free Documentation License *Contributors:* sailko 396
Figure 309 *Source:* https://en.wikipedia.org/w/index.php?title=File:Two_Gold_coins_of_Chandragupta_II.jpg *License:* Public Domain *Contributors:* User:World Imaging 397
Figure 310 *Source:* https://en.wikipedia.org/w/index.php?title=File:Silver_Coin_of_Kumaragupta_I.jpg *License:* GNU Free Documentation License *Contributors:* Athaenara, Bodhisattwa, Chaoborus, File Upload Bot (Magnus Manske), MGA73bot2, Mhmrodrigues, OgreBot 2 398
Figure 311 *Source:* https://en.wikipedia.org/w/index.php?title=File:Mihirakula_portrait.jpg *License:* GNU Free Documentation License *Contributors:* User:पाटलिपुत्र 399
Figure 312 *Source:* https://en.wikipedia.org/w/index.php?title=File:South_Asia_historical_AD550_EN.svg *Contributors:* User:Woudloper 400
Figure 313 *Source:* https://en.wikipedia.org/w/index.php?title=File:KumaraguptaFightingLion.jpg *License:* Creative Commons Attribution-ShareAlike 3.0 Unported *Contributors:* PHGCOM 402
Figure 314 *Source:* https://en.wikipedia.org/w/index.php?title=File:Vishnu_sculpture.jpg *License:* Creative Commons Attribution-Sharealike 3.0 *Contributors:* Jen 402
Figure 315 *Source:* https://en.wikipedia.org/w/index.php?title=File:Buddha_in_Sarnath_Museum_(Dhammajak_Mutra).jpg *License:* Creative Commons Attribution-Sharealike 3.0 *Contributors:* พระมหาเทวประภาส วชิรญาณเมธี (ผู้ถ่าย-ปล่อยสัญญาอนุญาตภาพให้นำไปใช้ได้เพื่อการศึกษาโดยอยู่ภายใต้ cc-by-sa-3.0) 404
Figure 316 *Source:* https://en.wikipedia.org/w/index.php?title=File:Radha-Krishna_chess.jpg *License:* Public domain *Contributors:* Billinghurst, File Upload Bot (Magnus Manske), Laurens∼commonswiki, MGA73bot2, OgreBot 2, Shonagon, Wiki-uk 405
Figure 317 *Source:* https://en.wikipedia.org/w/index.php?title=File:Sanchi_temple_17.jpg *License:* Creative Commons Attribution 2.0 *Contributors:* Nagarjun Kandukuru 406
Figure 318 *Source:* https://en.wikipedia.org/w/index.php?title=File:Mahabodhitemple.jpg *License:* Creative Commons Attribution-Sharealike 2.5 *Contributors:* Bpilgrim 407
Figure 319 *Source:* https://en.wikipedia.org/w/index.php?title=File:Vishnu_Hood2_Deogarh.jpg *License:* Creative Commons Attribution 2.0 *Contributors:* Bob King 407
Figure 320 *Source:* https://en.wikipedia.org/w/index.php?title=File:Buddha_from_Sarnath.jpg *License:* Creative Commons Attribution-Sharealike 2.0 *Contributors:* Chaoborus, Ddalbiez, Ekabhishek, Gryffindor, Ismoon, Martin H., Mhss, Underwaterbuffalo 408
Figure 321 *Source:* https://en.wikipedia.org/w/index.php?title=File:Elephanta_tourists.jpg *License:* Creative Commons Attribution 2.0 *Contributors:* Paul Morrison 408
Figure 322 *Source:* https://en.wikipedia.org/w/index.php?title=File:Ellora_cave16_001.jpg *License:* Creative Commons Attribution-ShareAlike 3.0 Unported *Contributors:* Y.Shishido 408
Figure 323 *Source:* https://en.wikipedia.org/w/index.php?title=File:Ajanta_Padmapani.jpg *License:* Public Domain *Contributors:* Eurodyne, G41rn8, Gunkarta, Ismoon, Johnbod, Parabolooidal, Redtigerxyz, Roland zh, Túrelio, Viktorianec, Yann, पाटलिपुत्र, 4 anonymous edits 409
Image *Source:* https://en.wikipedia.org/w/index.php?title=File:Wikisource-logo.svg *License:* Creative Commons Attribution-Sharealike 3.0 *Contributors:* ChrisiPK, Guillom, INeverCry, Jarekt, JuTa, Leyo, Lokal Profil, MichaelMaggs, NielsF, Rei-artur, Rocket000, Romaine, Steinsplitter 410
Image *Source:* https://en.wikipedia.org/w/index.php?title=File:Wikiquote-logo.svg *License:* Public Domain *Contributors:* Rei-artur 410

Image *Source:* https://en.wikipedia.org/w/index.php?title=File:Indischer_Maler_des_7._Jahrhunderts_001.jpg *License:* Public Domain *Contributors:* Ekabhishek, File Upload Bot (Eloquence), Gryffindor, Johnbod, Redtigerxyz, Roland zh, 2 anonymous edits 412
Figure 324 *Source:* https://en.wikipedia.org/w/index.php?title=File:Nagardhan_Fort.jpg *License:* Creative Commons Attribution-Sharealike 3.0 *Contributors:* Ganesh Dhamodkar 415
Figure 325 *Source:* https://en.wikipedia.org/w/index.php?title=File:MansarExcavation5.JPG *License:* Creative Commons Zero *Contributors:* Savearth 416
Figure 326 *Source:* https://en.wikipedia.org/w/index.php?title=File:Ajanta_(63).jpg *License:* Creative Commons Attribution-ShareAlike 3.0 Unported *Contributors:* User:Soman 417
Figure 327 *Source:* https://en.wikipedia.org/w/index.php?title=File:Ajanta_Caves,_Aurangabad,_Maharashtra,_INDIA_-_Bird's_Eye_View_of_a_World_Heritage_Site.JPG *License:* Creative Commons Attribution-Sharealike 3.0 *Contributors:* User:Anooljm 418
Figure 328 *Source:* https://en.wikipedia.org/w/index.php?title=File:Ajanta_cave_no._9_2010.jpg *License:* Creative Commons Attribution-Share Alike *Contributors:* Marcin Białek 418
Figure 329 *Source:* https://en.wikipedia.org/w/index.php?title=File:Ajanta_Ellora_buddha_statue_aurangabad_maharastra.jpg *License:* Creative Commons Attribution-Sharealike 3.0 *Contributors:* User:Karthikeyan.pandian 418
Figure 330 *Source:* https://en.wikipedia.org/w/index.php?title=File:Foreigner_on_ceiling_of_Cave_1at_Ajanta_Caves_photograph_and_drawing.jpg *License:* Creative Commons Attribution-Sharealike 3.0 *Contributors:* User:Aadi Maurya 422
Image *Source:* https://en.wikipedia.org/w/index.php?title=File:Harshavardhana_Circa_AD_606-647.jpg *License:* GNU Free Documentation License *Contributors:* पाटलिपुत्र 423
Figure 331 *Source:* https://en.wikipedia.org/w/index.php?title=File:Palace_ruins_2.JPG *License:* Creative Commons Attribution-Sharealike 3.0 *Contributors:* User:Viraat2000 424
Figure 332 *Source:* https://en.wikipedia.org/w/index.php?title=File:Harshabysumchung.jpg *Contributors:* Sum Chung 425
Figure 333 *Source:* https://en.wikipedia.org/w/index.php?title=File:Bakitar_Gujar,_1984.jpg *License:* Creative Commons Attribution 2.0 *Contributors:* Etter Studio 432
Figure 334 *Source:* https://en.wikipedia.org/w/index.php?title=File:Shri_Devnarayan_BhagwanVeerGurjar.JPG *License:* Creative Commons Attribution-Sharealike 3.0 *Contributors:* Chhora 433
Figure 335 *Source:* https://en.wikipedia.org/w/index.php?title=File:SawaibhojGurjar.jpg.JPG *Contributors:* - 434
Image *Source:* https://en.wikipedia.org/w/index.php?title=File:Historical_map_of_India_AD_606.jpg *Contributors:* User:Istkart 438
Image *Source:* https://en.wikipedia.org/w/index.php?title=File:Lepakshi...jpg *License:* Creative Commons Attribution-Sharealike 3.0 *Contributors:* User:Vinay332211 438
Figure 336 *Source:* https://en.wikipedia.org/w/index.php?title=File:VishnukundinCastCpr1.jpg *Contributors:* User:Mitresh66 443
Figure 337 *Source:* https://en.wikipedia.org/w/index.php?title=File:VishnukundinCastCpr2.jpg *Contributors:* User:Mitresh66 444
Image *Source:* https://en.wikipedia.org/w/index.php?title=File:South_Asia_historical_AD590_EN.svg *Contributors:* User:Woudloper 445
Figure 338 *Source:* https://en.wikipedia.org/w/index.php?title=File:Maitrakas_of_Valllabhi_Family_Tree.png *License:* Public Domain *Contributors:* Nizil Shah 448
Figure 339 *Source:* https://en.wikipedia.org/w/index.php?title=File:Bhanugupta_Eran_stone_pillar_inscription.jpg *License:* Public Domain *Contributors:* Ms Sarah Welch, OgreBot 2, पाटलिपुत्र 449
Figure 340 *Source:* https://en.wikipedia.org/w/index.php?title=File:Maliya_inscription_of_Dharasena_II_Year_252.jpg *License:* Public Domain *Contributors:* पाटलिपुत्र 452
Image *Source:* https://en.wikipedia.org/w/index.php?title=File:Maitraka_plate_1.jpg *Contributors:* User:Shirazibustan 453
Image *Source:* https://en.wikipedia.org/w/index.php?title=File:Maitraka_plate_2.jpg *Contributors:* User:Shirazibustan 453
Figure 341 *Source:* https://en.wikipedia.org/w/index.php?title=File:Administrative_divisions_in_the_Maitraka_kingdom.png *Contributors:* User:Nizil Shah 458
Figure 342 *Source:* https://en.wikipedia.org/w/index.php?title=File:Old_temple,_general_view_from_the_north-west,_Gop,_Gujarat.jpg *License:* Public Domain *Contributors:* Johnbod, Malaiya, Nizil Shah, Rachmat04 459
Figure 343 *Source:* https://en.wikipedia.org/w/index.php?title=File:Firangi_Deval,_Bhavnagar_district,_Gujarat,_India.jpg *License:* Creative Commons Attribution-Sharealike 3.0 *Contributors:* User:Sarthak2106 459
Figure 344 *Source:* https://en.wikipedia.org/w/index.php?title=File:Dharashnvel_Temple_(Magderu),_From_East.jpg *Contributors:* User:Phdaveindia 460
Figure 345 *Source:* https://en.wikipedia.org/w/index.php?title=File:General_view_of_ruined_temples_at_Sonkansari_pond,_Ghumli,_Saurashtra.jpg *License:* Public Domain *Contributors:* Jeff G., Nizil Shah 460
Figure 346 *Source:* https://en.wikipedia.org/w/index.php?title=File:Sonkansari_Bhanvad_01.JPG *License:* Creative Commons Attribution-Sharealike 3.0 *Contributors:* User:Nileshbandhiya 461
Image *Source:* https://en.wikipedia.org/w/index.php?title=File:Indian_Kanauj_triangle_map.svg *License:* Creative Commons Attribution-Sharealike 3.0 *Contributors:* Aschroet, Capankajsmilyo, Chhora, Io Herodotus, Nikotins, Pierpao, Planemad, Roland zh, Wieralee, Zykasaa, 1 anonymous edits 464
Figure 347 *Source:* https//en.wikipedia.org *Contributors:* Holenarasipura 466
Figure 348 *Source:* https://en.wikipedia.org/w/index.php?title=File:VarahaVishnuAvatarPratiharaKings850-900CE.jpg *License:* Creative Commons Attribution-ShareAlike 3.0 Unported *Contributors:* User:PHGCOM, User:PHGCOM 469
Image *Source:* https://en.wikipedia.org/w/index.php?title=File:Vishnu_Trivikrama_Delhi_National_Museum_ni02-24.jpg *Contributors:* User:G41rn8 470
Image *Source:* https://en.wikipedia.org/w/index.php?title=File:Teli_ka_mandir_fort_Gwalior_-_panoramio_-_Gyanendrasinghchauha…_(1).jpg *License:* Creative Commons Attribution 3.0 *Contributors:* JiriMatejicek, Kalbbes 471
Image *Source:* https://en.wikipedia.org/w/index.php?title=File:Rajpoots_2.png *License:* Public Domain *Contributors:* VD, ED, CD, and JMP. Victorian engravings can be very difficult to identify the authors of 475
Figure 349 *Source:* https://en.wikipedia.org/w/index.php?title=File:Pritam_niwas_with.jpg *License:* Creative Commons ShareAlike 1.0 Generic *Contributors:* BotMultichill, Dharmadhyaksha, Diggers2004, Ekabhishek, File Upload Bot (Magnus Manske), GermanJoe, OgreBot 2, Palamède, Parabolooidal, Roland zh, Tony Wills, 1 anonymous edits 477
Figure 350 *Source:* https://en.wikipedia.org/w/index.php?title=File:Bikaner_fort_view_08.jpg *License:* Creative Commons Attribution-Sharealike 3.0 *Contributors:* User:Schwiki 479
Figure 351 *Source:* https://en.wikipedia.org/w/index.php?title=File:Umer_Kot_Fort_by_Usman_Ghani.jpg *License:* Creative Commons Attribution-Sharealike 3.0 *Contributors:* User:Usman.pg 479
Figure 352 *Source:* https://en.wikipedia.org/w/index.php?title=File:Chittorgarh_fort.JPG *License:* Creative Commons Attribution-Sharealike 3.0 *Contributors:* User:Ssjoshi111 480
Figure 353 *Source:* https://en.wikipedia.org/w/index.php?title=File:Monitors_Mayo_College_Ajmer.jpg *License:* GNU Free Documentation License *Contributors:* User:Pratap Singh Rajawat 481
Figure 354 *Source:* https://en.wikipedia.org/w/index.php?title=File:Derawar_fort_during_winters_by_Jazib_Saeed_Khan.jpg *Contributors:* User:Jazibsaeed 482
Figure 355 *Source:* https://en.wikipedia.org/w/index.php?title=File:Indian_Army-Rajput_regiment.jpeg *License:* Creative Commons Attribution 3.0 *Contributors:* Antônio Milena 484
Figure 356 *Source:* https://en.wikipedia.org/w/index.php?title=File:The_Rajpootnee_Bride.jpg *License:* Public Domain *Contributors:* Ellin Beltz, Raghvendra99674010 485
Figure 357 *Source:* https://en.wikipedia.org/w/index.php?title=File:A_royal_Rajput_procession.jpg *License:* Public Domain *Contributors:* Simisa, The Pakistan, Xwejnusgozo 486
Figure 358 *Source:* https://en.wikipedia.org/w/index.php?title=File:View_from_top_of_Kangra_Fort_overlooking_river.jpg *License:* Creative Commons Attribution-Sharealike 3.0 *Contributors:* John Hill 490
Figure 359 *Source:* https://en.wikipedia.org/w/index.php?title=File:Vigraha_Raja_IV_of_the_Chauhans_of_Ajmer_Circa_1150-1164.jpg *License:* GNU Free Documentation License *Contributors:* पाटलिपुत्र 496
Figure 360 *Source:* https://en.wikipedia.org/w/index.php?title=File:Anna_sarobar-2-ajmir.jpg *License:* Creative Commons Attribution-Sharealike 3.0 *Contributors:* User:Debabrata Ghosh 500
Figure 361 *Source:* https://en.wikipedia.org/w/index.php?title=File:Bisaldeo_temple_submerged.jpg *Contributors:* User:Siddharth 36 501
Figure 362 *Source:* https://en.wikipedia.org/w/index.php?title=File:Harshnathtemple.jpg *Contributors:* User:Mahaveershekhawat77 502
Figure 363 *Source:* https://en.wikipedia.org/w/index.php?title=File:Prithvi_Raj_Chauhan_(Edited).jpg *License:* GNU Free Documentation License *Contributors:* Prithvi_Raj_Chauhan.JPG: LRBurdak at en.wikipedia derivative work: original uploader was Dhiresh b at en.wikipedia 503
Figure 364 *Source:* https://en.wikipedia.org/w/index.php?title=File:Flag_of_Jaipur.svg *License:* Public Domain *Contributors:* Robert Alfers . 506
Image *Source:* https://en.wikipedia.org/w/index.php?title=File:Asia_1200ad.jpg *License:* Creative Commons Attribution 3.0 *Contributors:* Artix Kreiger 2, Ashitagaarusa, Berillium, Erdaal, Firespeaker, Gryffindor, High Contrast, Infrogmation, Joostik, OgreBot 2, Sarang, Tatmadav, Turzh, Túrelio, Undead warrior, Utcursch, Verdy p, Zaccarias, Zlerman, Zykasaa, 大南層大龍飛圖, 2 anonymous edits 509
Image *Source:* https://en.wikipedia.org/w/index.php?title=File:Delhi_Sultanate_Flag_(catalan_atlas).png *Contributors:* User:History of Persia 509
Figure 365 *Source:* https://en.wikipedia.org/w/index.php?title=File:Siyak_harsola1005ga.jpg *License:* Public Domain *Contributors:* Malaiya 511

Figure 366 *Source:* https://en.wikipedia.org/w/index.php?title=File:Temple_of_Bhojpur.jpg *License:* Creative Commons Attribution-Share Alike *Contributors:* Yann (talk) ... 515

Figure 367 *Source:* https://en.wikipedia.org/w/index.php?title=File:Dam_PP.JPG *License:* Creative Commons Attribution-Sharealike 3.0 *Contributors:* User:Zippymarmalade ... 515

Figure 368 *Source:* https://en.wikipedia.org/w/index.php?title=File:Naravarman_PP.jpg *License:* Creative Commons Attribution-Sharealike 3.0 *Contributors:* Zippymarmalade ... 518

Figure 369 *Source:* https://en.wikipedia.org/w/index.php?title=File:Iron_pillar_Dhar.jpg *License:* Public Domain *Contributors:* User:Zippymarmalade ... 519

Image *Source:* https://en.wikipedia.org/w/index.php?title=File:Kachchhflag.png *License:* Creative Commons Attribution-Sharealike 3.0 *Contributors:* Lommes, OgreBot 2, Xufanc ... 526

Figure 370 *Source:* https://en.wikipedia.org/w/index.php?title=File:Chaulukya-Paramara_coin_circa_AD_950-1050.jpg *License:* GNU Free Documentation License *Contributors:* पाटलिपुत्र ... 531

Figure 371 *Source:* https://en.wikipedia.org/w/index.php?title=File:Chaulukyas_of_Anahillapataka_King_Kumarapala_Circa_1145-1171.jpg *License:* GNU Free Documentation License *Contributors:* Cpt.a.haddock, पाटलिपुत्र ... 532

Figure 372 *Source:* https://en.wikipedia.org/w/index.php?title=File:Copper_plates_NMND-3.JPG *License:* Public Domain *Contributors:* Daderot 533

Figure 373 *Source:* https://en.wikipedia.org/w/index.php?title=File:Somnath_temple_ruins_(1869).jpg *License:* Public Domain *Contributors:* Anhilwara, Hansmuller, Magog the Ogre, Ms Sarah Welch, P199, Razr Nation, Rosarino, 1 anonymous edits ... 535

Figure 374 *Source:* https//en.wikipedia.org *License:* Creative Commons Attribution 3.0 *Contributors:* User:Sailko ... 536

Image *Source:* https://en.wikipedia.org/w/index.php?title=File:Open_Access_logo_PLoS_transparent.svg *License:* Creative Commons Zero *Contributors:* Adrignola, Aloneinthewild, AnonMoos, Closeapple, Ickx6, JakobVoss, Josve05a, Renardo la vulpo, Šturm, Varnent ... 540

Figure 375 *Source:* https://en.wikipedia.org/w/index.php?title=File:Haryana_in_India_(claims_hatched).svg *License:* Creative Commons Attribution-Sharealike 3.0 Germany *Contributors:* Shadowxfox, TUBS ... 542

Figure 376 *Source:* https://en.wikipedia.org/w/index.php?title=File:Suraj_Kund.jpg *License:* Creative Commons Attribution 2.0 *Contributors:* Jyoti Prakash Bhattacharjee ... 544

Image *Source:* https://en.wikipedia.org/w/index.php?title=File:Flag_of_Nepal.svg *License:* Public Domain *Contributors:* Drawn by User:Pumbaa80, User:Achim1999 ... 548

Figure 377 *Source:* https://en.wikipedia.org/w/index.php?title=File:Indian_Kanauj_triangle_map.svg *License:* Creative Commons Attribution-Sharealike 3.0 *Contributors:* Aschroet, Capankajsmilyo, Chhora, Io Herodotus, Nikotins, Pierpao, Planemad, Roland zh, Wieralee, Zykasaa, 1 anonymous edits ... 550

Figure 378 *Source:* https://en.wikipedia.org/w/index.php?title=File:Nalanda.jpg *License:* Creative Commons Attribution-Sharealike 2.5 *Contributors:* myself ... 557

Figure 379 *Source:* https://en.wikipedia.org/w/index.php?title=File:Atisha.jpg *License:* Public Domain *Contributors:* Unknown [Tibet (a Kadampa monastery)] ... 557

Figure 380 *Source:* https://en.wikipedia.org/w/index.php?title=File:Lalita_statue.jpg *License:* Creative Commons Attribution-Sharealike 3.0 *Contributors:* User:Fæ ... 559

Figure 381 *Source:* https://en.wikipedia.org/w/index.php?title=File:Carved_Conch.jpg *License:* Creative Commons Attribution-Sharealike 2.0 *Contributors:* Claire H. ... 559

Figure 382 *Source:* https://en.wikipedia.org/w/index.php?title=File:Khasarpana_Lokesvara.jpg *License:* Creative Commons Attribution-Sharealike 2.0 *Contributors:* Hyougushi ... 560

Figure 383 *Source:* https//en.wikipedia.org *License:* Creative Commons Attribution-ShareAlike 3.0 Unported *Contributors:* User:Sailko, user:sailko 560

Figure 384 *Source:* https://en.wikipedia.org/w/index.php?title=File:Naogaon_Paharpur_11Oct12_IMG_3656.jpg *Contributors:* User:Krabdallah 561

Figure 385 *Source:* https://en.wikipedia.org/w/index.php?title=File:Central_Sherine_deccor-Paharpur.jpg *License:* Public Domain *Contributors:* User:Ori∼ ... 561

Figure 386 *Source:* https://en.wikipedia.org/w/index.php?title=File:Naqi_model.jpg *License:* Creative Commons Attribution 3.0 *Contributors:* Ali Naqi, modified by Hafizur Rahaman ... 562

Figure 387 *Source:* https://en.wikipedia.org/w/index.php?title=File:Vikramshila_2012-08-10-17.48.39.jpg *License:* Creative Commons Attribution-Sharealike 3.0 *Contributors:* User:Prataparya ... 562

Image *Source:* https://en.wikipedia.org/w/index.php?title=File:Royal_Peacock_Barge_LACMA_M.82.154.jpg *Contributors:* Fæ, JMCC1 ... 566

Figure 388 *Source:* https://en.wikipedia.org/w/index.php?title=File:PURI_JAGANATHA_TEMPLE,_PURI,_ORISSA,_INDIA,_ASIA.jpg *License:* Creative Commons Attribution-Sharealike 3.0 *Contributors:* User:RJ Rituraj ... 569

Figure 389 *Source:* https://en.wikipedia.org/w/index.php?title=File:A_Temple_in_Sri_Mukhalingam_temple_complex.jpg *Contributors:* User:Adityamadhav83 ... 571

Figure 390 *Source:* https://en.wikipedia.org/w/index.php?title=File:Konark_Sun_Temple_Front_view.jpg *License:* Public Domain *Contributors:* http://en.wikipedia.org/wiki/User_talk:Vinayreddym ... 571

Figure 391 *Source:* https://en.wikipedia.org/w/index.php?title=File:A_Stone_carved_throne_in_the_backyard_of_Simhachalam_temple.jpg *License:* Creative Commons Attribution-Sharealike 3.0 *Contributors:* User:Adityamadhav83 ... 572

Figure 392 *Source:* https://en.wikipedia.org/w/index.php?title=File:Eastern_Ganga_Fanam.jpg *Contributors:* User:Sujit kumar ... 572

Figure 393 *Source:* https://en.wikipedia.org/w/index.php?title=File:Edilpur_copperplate.jpg *License:* Creative Commons Attribution-Sharealike 3.0 *Contributors:* Mizan1947 ... 576

Figure 394 *Source:* https://en.wikipedia.org/w/index.php?title=File:Ruins_of_Pragjyotishpura_(Guwahati),_Kamarupa_-_Panel_on_Plinth.jpg *License:* Creative Commons Attribution-Sharealike 3.0 *Contributors:* User:Bhaskarbhagawati ... 581

Image *Source:* https://en.wikipedia.org/w/index.php?title=File:Kamarupa_map.png *Contributors:* Chaipau, Kkathis ... 585

Image *Source:* https://en.wikipedia.org/w/index.php?title=File:Ahom_insignia_plain.svg *License:* GNU Free Documentation License *Contributors:* Chaipau (talk) ... 586

Image *Source:* https://en.wikipedia.org/w/index.php?title=File:Sutiyakingdom.jpg *License:* Creative Commons Attribution-Sharealike 3.0 *Contributors:* DalQ95, Sfan00 IMG ... 586

Image *Source:* https://en.wikipedia.org/w/index.php?title=File:Flag_of_Bhutan.svg *License:* Public Domain *Contributors:* (original uploader), the author of xrmap (improved version) ... 586

Image *Source:* https://en.wikipedia.org/w/index.php?title=File:Flag_of_Myanmar.svg *License:* Public Domain *Contributors:* *drew∼commonswiki, AnonMoos, Artix Kreiger, Cathy Richards, CommonsDelinker, Cycn, Daphne Lantier, Dinsdagskind, Duduziq, Fry1989, Garam, Gunkarta, Homo lupus, INeverCry, Josegeographic, Klemen Kocjancic, Legnaw, Mason Decker, Mattes, Neq00, Nightstallion, Pixeltoo, Rfc1394, Rodejong, Sangjinhwa, Sarang, SeNeKa∼commonswiki, SiBr4, Sixflashphoto, Stevanb, TFerenczy, Takahara Osaka, Techman224, ThomasPusch, Túrelio, UnreifeKirsche, Vividuppers, WikipediaMaster, Winzipas, Xiengyod∼commonswiki, Zscout370, 白布飘扬 , 21 anonymous edits 586

Image *Source:* https://en.wikipedia.org/w/index.php?title=File:Montage_of_Asamiya_Cultural_Symbols.png *Contributors:* User:Rex86 ... 586

Image *Source:* https://en.wikipedia.org/w/index.php?title=File:Seal_of_Assam.png *License:* Public Domain *Contributors:* OgreBot 2, Roland zh, Shubhamkanodia, Urdangaray ... 586

Figure 395 *Source:* https://en.wikipedia.org/w/index.php?title=File:Kamarupa-inscriptions-findspots.png *License:* Creative Commons Attribution 3.0 *Contributors:* en:User:Chaipau ... 587

Image *Source:* https://en.wikipedia.org/w/index.php?title=File:Copper_Plate_Seal_of_Kamarupa_Kings.jpg *License:* Creative Commons Attribution-Sharealike 3.0 *Contributors:* User:Bhaskarbhagawati ... 590

Figure 396 *Source:* https://en.wikipedia.org/w/index.php?title=File:South_India_in_Sangam_Period.jpg *License:* Creative Commons Attribution-Sharealike 3.0 *Contributors:* User:Yon Man33 ... 604

Figure 397 *Source:* https://en.wikipedia.org/w/index.php?title=File:Puhar-ILango.jpg *License:* Creative Commons Attribution-Sharealike 3.0 *Contributors:* Kasiarunachalam (talk) ... 605

Figure 398 *Source:* https://en.wikipedia.org/w/index.php?title=File:Map_2bc.jpg *License:* GNU Free Documentation License *Contributors:* Senthil Kumar A.S.User:senthilkumaras ... 608

Image *Source:* https://en.wikipedia.org/w/index.php?title=File:Palace_of_Trivandrum.jpg *License:* Creative Commons Attribution-Sharealike 3.0 *Contributors:* BotMultichill, Durga, File Upload Bot (Magnus Manske), Lower fourth, MGA73bot2, Roland zh, Slashme, Sreejithk2000 ... 610

Image *Source:* https://en.wikipedia.org/w/index.php?title=File:Thanjavur_temple.jpg *License:* Public Domain *Contributors:* AnRo0002, Bgag, Elcobbola, Fransvannes, Maximaximax, OgreBot 2, Roland zh, Woudloper ... 611

Figure 399 *Source:* https://en.wikipedia.org/w/index.php?title=File:Chera_monarchs_family_tree.jpg *License:* Creative Commons Attribution 3.0 *Contributors:* User:Pepper Black ... 614

Figure 400 *Source:* https://en.wikipedia.org/w/index.php?title=File:Kalabhras_territories.png *License:* GNU Free Documentation License *Contributors:* BotMultichill, BotMultichillT, DenghiùComm, Electionworld, Roland zh ... 615

Figure 401 *Source:* https://en.wikipedia.org/w/index.php?title=File:Chera_kingdom,_chieftaincies,_c._11th_century.svg *Contributors:* User:Cpt.a.haddock ... 617
Figure 402 *Source:* https://en.wikipedia.org/w/index.php?title=File:Cheraman_Perumal.png *License:* Public Domain *Contributors:* P. Shungoonny Menon ... 620
Figure 403 *Source:* https://en.wikipedia.org/w/index.php?title=File:Puhar-ILango.jpg *License:* Creative Commons Attribution-Sharealike 3.0 *Contributors:* Kasiarunachalam (talk) ... 624
Figure 404 *Source:* https://en.wikipedia.org/w/index.php?title=File:Silk_route.jpg *License:* Public Domain *Contributors:* User:HighInBC ... 625
Figure 405 *Source:* https://en.wikipedia.org/w/index.php?title=File:Map_of_Chera_Kingdom.jpg *License:* Creative Commons Attribution-Sharealike 3.0 *Contributors:* User:Pepper Black ... 626
Figure 406 *Source:* https://en.wikipedia.org/w/index.php?title=File:Vazhappally_Plates.JPG *License:* Public Domain *Contributors:* RajeshUnuppally ... 628
Figure 407 *Source:* https://en.wikipedia.org/w/index.php?title=File:Vazhappally_Plates_-_Description.JPG *License:* Public Domain *Contributors:* RajeshUnuppally ... 629
Figure 408 *Source:* https://en.wikipedia.org/w/index.php?title=File:JosephRabban_-_sasanam.png *Contributors:* Christophe cagé, Cpt.a.haddock, Jacklee, Magog the Ogre, Roland zh ... 629
Image *Source:* https://en.wikipedia.org/w/index.php?title=File:Indian_Kadamba_Empire_map.svg *License:* Creative Commons Attribution-Sharealike 3.0 *Contributors:* Aschroet, LX, Nikotins, Planemad, Roland zh, Wieralee, 1 anonymous edits ... 636
Image *Source:* https://en.wikipedia.org/w/index.php?title=File:GBerunda.JPG *License:* Creative Commons Attribution-ShareAlike 3.0 Unported *Contributors:* Sarvagnya ... 641
Figure 409 *Source:* https://en.wikipedia.org/w/index.php?title=File:Coin_of_Kadamba_king_Sri_Manarashi.jpg *License:* Creative Commons Attribution-Sharealike 3.0 *Contributors:* Rani nurmai ... 643
Figure 410 *Source:* https://en.wikipedia.org/w/index.php?title=File:Coin_of_Kadamba_king_Sri_Dosharashi.jpg *License:* Creative Commons Attribution-Sharealike 3.0 *Contributors:* Rani nurmai ... 643
Figure 411 *Source:* https://en.wikipedia.org/w/index.php?title=File:□□□□_-_□□□□□□□□.jpg *Contributors:* User:Kannadiga ... 643
Figure 412 *Source:* https://en.wikipedia.org/w/index.php?title=File:Halmidi_OldKannada_inscription.JPG *License:* GNU Free Documentation License *Contributors:* en:User:Dineshkannambadi ... 645
Figure 413 *Source:* https//en.wikipedia.org *Contributors:* User:Dineshkannambadi ... 646
Figure 414 *Source:* https://en.wikipedia.org/w/index.php?title=File:Old_Kannada_inscription_(1200_AD)_of_King_Kamadeva_of_the_Kadamba_dynasty_of_the_Hangal_branch.jpg *Contributors:* Holenarasipura ... 646
Figure 415 *Source:* https://en.wikipedia.org/w/index.php?title=File:Sri-manarashi.jpg *License:* Creative Commons Attribution-Sharealike 3.0 *Contributors:* Rani nurmai ... 646
Figure 416 *Source:* https://en.wikipedia.org/w/index.php?title=File:Kannada_legend_of_Sri-dosharashi.jpg *License:* Creative Commons Attribution-Sharealike 3.0 *Contributors:* Rani nurmai ... 647
Figure 417 *Source:* https://en.wikipedia.org/w/index.php?title=File:Close_up_view_of_shrines_at_Lakshmi_Devi_temple_complex_at_Doddagaddavalli.JPG *License:* Creative Commons Attribution-Sharealike 3.0 *Contributors:* User:Dineshkannambadi ... 648
Image *Source:* https://en.wikipedia.org/w/index.php?title=File:Western-ganga-empire-map.svg *License:* Creative Commons Attribution-ShareAlike 3.0 Unported *Contributors:* Mlpkr ... 651
Figure 418 *Source:* https://en.wikipedia.org/w/index.php?title=File:TalakadInscription.jpg *License:* Public Domain *Contributors:* Edward P Rice 653
Figure 419 *Source:* https://en.wikipedia.org/w/index.php?title=File:Ganga_file.jpg *License:* Creative Commons Attribution-Sharealike 3.0 *Contributors:* Jrsanthosh ... 653
Figure 420 *Source:* https://en.wikipedia.org/w/index.php?title=File:Bharatha.jpg *License:* Creative Commons Attribution 2.5 *Contributors:* Nikhil Varma ... 656
Figure 421 *Source:* https://en.wikipedia.org/w/index.php?title=File:Panchakuta_Basadi_(10th_century_AD)_at_Kambadahalli.JPG *License:* Creative Commons Attribution-Sharealike 3.0 *Contributors:* User:Dineshkannambadi ... 658
Figure 422 *Source:* https://en.wikipedia.org/w/index.php?title=File:Old_Kannada_inscription_(908-938_AD)_of_Western_Ganga_dynasty_King_Ereyappa_on_hero_stone_at_Begur.jpg *Contributors:* Holenarasipura ... 659
Figure 423 *Source:* https://en.wikipedia.org/w/index.php?title=File:Rock_edit_-_inscription.jpg *License:* Creative Commons Attribution 2.5 *Contributors:* Nikhil Varma ... 661
Figure 424 *Source:* https://en.wikipedia.org/w/index.php?title=File:A_mantapa_(hall)_in_Panchakuta_Basadi_at_Kambadahalli.JPG *License:* Creative Commons Attribution-Sharealike 3.0 *Contributors:* User:Dineshkannambadi ... 661
Figure 425 *Source:* https://en.wikipedia.org/w/index.php?title=File:Gomateswara.jpg *License:* Attribution *Contributors:* FSII, Fontema, Guanaco, Hystrix, Jungpionier, Kilom691, MPF, Ranveig, Roland zh, Soerfm, Str4nd, Thuresson, Vssun, 8 anonymous edits ... 662
Figure 426 *Source:* https://en.wikipedia.org/w/index.php?title=File:Kalleshvara_Temple_at_Aralaguppe_(10th_century_AD).JPG *License:* Creative Commons Attribution-Sharealike 3.0 *Contributors:* User:Dineshkannambadi ... 663
Figure 427 *Source:* https://en.wikipedia.org/w/index.php?title=File:Old_Kannada_inscription_Hero_Stone_from_9th_century_AD_in_Kalleshvara_Temple_at_Aralaguppe.jpg *License:* Creative Commons Attribution-Sharealike 3.0 *Contributors:* User:Dineshkannambadi ... 664
Figure 428 *Source:* https://en.wikipedia.org/w/index.php?title=File:Atakur_memorial_stone_with_inscription_in_old_Kannada_(949_C.E.).jpg *License:* Creative Commons Attribution-Sharealike 3.0 *Contributors:* User:Holenarasipura ... 666
Figure 429 *Source:* https://en.wikipedia.org/w/index.php?title=File:View_of_Chandragupta_Basadi_at_Chandragiri_hill_in_Shravanabelagola.jpg *License:* Creative Commons Attribution-Sharealike 3.0 *Contributors:* Dineshkannambadi (talk) 01:06, 21 May 2008 (UTC) ... 667
Figure 430 *Source:* https://en.wikipedia.org/w/index.php?title=File:Chandragiri_hill_temple_complex_at_Shravanabelagola.jpg *License:* Creative Commons Attribution-Sharealike 3.0 *Contributors:* Dineshkannambadi (talk) 00:42, 21 May 2008 (UTC) ... 668
Figure 431 *Source:* https://en.wikipedia.org/w/index.php?title=File:Relief_of_Jain_tirthankara_in_the_Panchakuta_Basadi_at_Kambadahalli.jpg *License:* GNU Free Documentation License *Contributors:* en:User:Dineshkannambadi ... 669
Figure 432 *Source:* https://en.wikipedia.org/w/index.php?title=File:Chavundaraya_Basadi_on_Chandragiri_hill_at_Shravanabelagola.jpg *License:* Creative Commons Attribution-Sharealike 3.0 *Contributors:* Dineshkannambadi (talk) 00:48, 21 May 2008 (UTC) ... 670
Figure 433 *Source:* https://en.wikipedia.org/w/index.php?title=File:Old_Kannada_inscription_dated_981_CE_in_Vindyagiri_hill_at_Shravanabelagola.jpg *License:* GNU Free Documentation License *Contributors:* en:User:Dineshkannambadi ... 672
Image *Source:* https://en.wikipedia.org/w/index.php?title=File:Cscr-featured.svg *License:* GNU Lesser General Public License *Contributors:* Anomie ... 674
Image *Source:* https://en.wikipedia.org/w/index.php?title=File:Badami-chalukya-empire-map.svg *License:* Creative Commons Attribution-ShareAlike 3.0 Unported *Contributors:* Mlpkr ... 674
Figure 434 *Source:* https://en.wikipedia.org/w/index.php?title=File:6th_century_Kannada_inscription_in_cave_temple_number_3_at_Badami.jpg *License:* Creative Commons Attribution-Sharealike 3.0 *Contributors:* Dineshkannambadi (talk) 22:48, 30 July 2008 (UTC) ... 676
Figure 435 *Source:* https://en.wikipedia.org/w/index.php?title=File:8th_century_Kannada_inscription_on_victory_pillar_at_Pattadakal.jpg *License:* Creative Commons Attribution-Sharealike 3.0 *Contributors:* Dineshkannambadi (talk) 22:39, 30 July 2008 (UTC) ... 677
Figure 436 *Source:* https://en.wikipedia.org/w/index.php?title=File:Bhutanatha_temple_in_Badami,_Karnataka,_India.jpg *License:* Creative Commons Attribution-Sharealike 3.0 *Contributors:* User:Gs9here ... 680
Figure 437 *Source:* https://en.wikipedia.org/w/index.php?title=File:Virupaksha_temple_at_Pattadakal.jpg *License:* Creative Commons Attribution-Sharealike 3.0 *Contributors:* Dineshkannambadi (talk) 23:05, 1 August 2008 (UTC) ... 683
Figure 438 *Source:* https://en.wikipedia.org/w/index.php?title=File:Badami,_Höhle_4,_Bahubali_(1999).jpg *License:* Public domain *Contributors:* ArnoldBetten ... 685
Figure 439 *Source:* https://en.wikipedia.org/w/index.php?title=File:Vishnu_image_inside_cave_number_3_in_Badami.jpg *License:* Creative Commons Attribution-Sharealike 3.0 *Contributors:* Dineshkannambadi (talk) 03:35, 13 August 2008 (UTC) ... 686
Figure 440 *Source:* https://en.wikipedia.org/w/index.php?title=File:Bhutanatha_temple_complex_in_Badami.jpg *License:* Creative Commons Attribution-Sharealike 3.0 *Contributors:* Dineshkannambadi (talk) 22:33, 1 August 2008 (UTC) ... 686
Figure 441 *Source:* https://en.wikipedia.org/w/index.php?title=File:Parvati_temple_at_Krauncha_Giri_near_Sandur,_Ballary_district.jpg *Contributors:* User:Shreyasu ... 686
Figure 442 *Source:* https://en.wikipedia.org/w/index.php?title=File:Durga_Temple.jpg *License:* Creative Commons Attribution-Sharealike 3.0 *Contributors:* User:Nag4pl ... 687
Figure 443 *Source:* https://en.wikipedia.org/w/index.php?title=File:Jain_basadi.JPG *License:* Creative Commons Attribution-Sharealike 3.0 *Contributors:* User:Shishir jain ... 687
Figure 444 *Source:* https://en.wikipedia.org/w/index.php?title=File:Mallikarjuna_and_Kasivisvanatha_temples_at_Pattadakal.jpg *License:* Creative Commons Attribution-Sharealike 3.0 *Contributors:* Dineshkannambadi (talk) 22:46, 1 August 2008 (UTC) ... 688
Figure 445 *Source:* https://en.wikipedia.org/w/index.php?title=File:Badami-shiva.JPG *License:* Public domain *Contributors:* Original uploader was Ashwatham at en.wikipedia ... 688
Figure 446 *Source:* https://en.wikipedia.org/w/index.php?title=File:Papanatha_temple_at_Pattadakal.jpg *License:* Creative Commons Attribution-Sharealike 3.0 *Contributors:* 23:09, 1 August 2008 (UTC ... 689

Figure 447 *Source:* https://en.wikipedia.org/w/index.php?title=File:Aihole_inscription_of_Ravi_Kirti.jpg *License:* Creative Commons Attribution-Sharealike 3.0 *Contributors:* Dineshkannambadi (talk) 12:36, 1 August 2008 (UTC) 690
Figure 448 *Source:* https://en.wikipedia.org/w/index.php?title=File:Cave_temple_number_3_at_Badami.jpg *License:* Creative Commons Attribution-Sharealike 3.0 *Contributors:* Dineshkannambadi (talk) 03:32, 13 August 2008 (UTC) 692
Image *Source:* https://en.wikipedia.org/w/index.php?title=File:Pallava_territories.png *License:* GNU Free Documentation License *Contributors:* BotMultichill, BotMultichillT, Discanto, Electionworld, Roland zh 697
Image *Source:* https://en.wikipedia.org/w/index.php?title=File:Flag_of_Sri_Lanka.svg *License:* Public Domain *Contributors:* Zscout370 698
Figure 449 *Source:* https://en.wikipedia.org/w/index.php?title=File:Kailasanathar_Temple.jpg *License:* Creative Commons Attribution 2.0 *Contributors:* Keshav Mukund Kandhadai 699
Image *Source:* https://en.wikipedia.org/w/index.php?title=File:Kailasawaathar_innercourt.jpg *License:* Public Domain *Contributors:* R. Mayooranathan 699
Image *Source:* https://en.wikipedia.org/w/index.php?title=File:01Kailasanathar_Temple_Rich_Architecture_in_Sculptures_Design.jpg *License:* Creative Commons Attribution 2.0 *Contributors:* FlickreviewR, INeverCry, Ismoon, Keyan20, Parabolooidal, Roland zh 699
Image *Source:* https://en.wikipedia.org/w/index.php?title=File:Kailayanathar2.jpg *License:* Creative Commons Attribution-Sharealike 3.0 *Contributors:* User:Ssriram mt 699
Figure 450 *Source:* https://en.wikipedia.org/w/index.php?title=File:Pallavas_of_Coromandel.jpg *License:* GNU Free Documentation License *Contributors:* Balajijagadesh, DenghiùComm, Jeff G., Nizil Shah, पाटलिपुत्र 702
Figure 451 *Source:* https://en.wikipedia.org/w/index.php?title=File:Shore_Temple_(Detail_of_North_Face,_2011-05-28).jpg *License:* Creative Commons Attribution-Sharealike 3.0 *Contributors:* User:Pratyeka 704
Image *Source:* https://en.wikipedia.org/w/index.php?title=File:Pallava_Pillar_Mandagappattu.png *Contributors:* User:Nilo.boss 704
Figure 452 *Source:* https://en.wikipedia.org/w/index.php?title=File:Mamallapuram_Five_Rathas.jpg *License:* GNU Free Documentation License *Contributors:* Venu62 707
Figure 453 *Source:* https://en.wikipedia.org/w/index.php?title=File:Elephant_mpuram.jpg *License:* Public Domain *Contributors:* Vrraghy ... 707
Image *Source:* https://en.wikipedia.org/w/index.php?title=File:Historical_map_of_India_AD_753.jpg *Contributors:* User:Istkart 711
Figure 454 *Source:* https://en.wikipedia.org/w/index.php?title=File:Eastern_Chalukya_coin.jpg *License:* GNU Free Documentation License *Contributors:* पाटलिपुत्र 715
Figure 455 *Source:* https://en.wikipedia.org/w/index.php?title=File:Copper_plates_NMND-9.JPG *License:* Public Domain *Contributors:* Daderot 716
Figure 456 *Source:* https://en.wikipedia.org/w/index.php?title=File:Draksharama_temple_-_Main_entrance.jpg *License:* Public domain *Contributors:* Twooars 717
Image *Source:* https://en.wikipedia.org/w/index.php?title=File:Pandya_territories.png *License:* GNU Free Documentation License *Contributors:* Blackknight12, BotMultichill, BotMultichillT, Electionworld, Roland zh, 4 anonymous edits 720
Figure 457 *Source:* https://en.wikipedia.org/w/index.php?title=File:FourArmedVishnuPandyaDynasty8-9thCentury.jpg *License:* Creative Commons Attribution-Sharealike 3.0,2.5,2.0,1.0 *Contributors:* PHGCOM 723
Figure 458 *Source:* https://en.wikipedia.org/w/index.php?title=File:TabulaPeutingerianaMuziris.jpg *License:* Public Domain *Contributors:* Aschroet, Challiyan, Kilom691, Roland zh, World Imaging 725
Figure 459 *Source:* https://en.wikipedia.org/w/index.php?title=File:Rama_at_Srivaikundam.jpg *Contributors:* - 728
Figure 460 *Source:* https://en.wikipedia.org/w/index.php?title=File:The_Hindu_Saint_Manikkavacakar_LACMA_AC1997.16.1_(1_of_12).jpg *Contributors:* Fæ, Redtigerxyz 729
Figure 461 *Source:* https://en.wikipedia.org/w/index.php?title=File:Double_fish_Pandyan_relief,_Koneswaram.jpg *License:* Creative Commons Zero *Contributors:* User:RuperDoc 730
Figure 462 *Source:* https://en.wikipedia.org/w/index.php?title=File:Srivaikundam_Temple_Structure,_Thirunelveli4.jpg *License:* Creative Commons Attribution 2.0 *Contributors:* sowrirajan s 733
Figure 463 *Source:* https://en.wikipedia.org/w/index.php?title=File:South_India_in_AD_1100.jpg *License:* Creative Commons Attribution-Sharealike 3.0 *Contributors:* User:Yon Man33 734
Figure 464 *Source:* https://en.wikipedia.org/w/index.php?title=File:An_aerial_view_of_Madurai_city_from_atop_of_Meenakshi_Amman_temple.jpg *License:* Creative Commons Attribution 3.0 *Contributors:* எஸ்ஸார் 736
Figure 465 *Source:* https://en.wikipedia.org/w/index.php?title=File:Tirunelveli_Nellaiappar_Temple_1.jpg *License:* Creative Commons Attribution 2.0 *Contributors:* arunpnair 737
Figure 466 *Source:* https://en.wikipedia.org/w/index.php?title=File:Coin_Pandya_Bull_Obv_2.jpg *License:* Public Domain *Contributors:* User:Jnumis, User:JnumisJnumis 737
Figure 467 *Source:* https://en.wikipedia.org/w/index.php?title=File:Temple_between_hill_symbols_and_elephant_coin_of_the_Pandyas_Sri_Lanka_1st_century_CE.jpg *License:* Creative Commons Attribution-Sharealike 3.0 *Contributors:* Uploadalt 738
Figure 468 *Source:* https://en.wikipedia.org/w/index.php?title=File:Silk_route.jpg *License:* Public Domain *Contributors:* User:HighInBC ... 739
Figure 469 *Source:* https://en.wikipedia.org/w/index.php?title=File:White_pearl_necklace.jpg *License:* Creative Commons Attribution 2.0 *Contributors:* Flickr.com user "tanakawho" 740
Figure 470 *Source:* https://en.wikipedia.org/w/index.php?title=File:Ellora_Kailash_temple_Shiva_panel.jpg *License:* Creative Commons Attribution 2.5 *Contributors:* User:QuartierLatin1968, User:QuartierLatin1968 745
Figure 471 *Source:* https://en.wikipedia.org/w/index.php?title=File:Ellora-Jain-cave.jpg *License:* GNU Free Documentation License *Contributors:* KRS(talk). Original uploader was KRS at en.wikipedia 746
Figure 472 *Source:* https://en.wikipedia.org/w/index.php?title=File:Rashtrakuta-empire-map.svg *License:* Creative Commons Attribution-ShareAlike 3.0 Unported *Contributors:* Mlpkr 746
Figure 473 *Source:* https://en.wikipedia.org/w/index.php?title=File:Kasivisvanatha_temple_at_Pattadakal.jpg *License:* Creative Commons Attribution-Sharealike 3.0 *Contributors:* Dineshkannambadi (talk) 23:13, 30 July 2008 (UTC) 752
Figure 474 *Source:* https://en.wikipedia.org/w/index.php?title=File:Ellora-Kailasanatha-5.jpg *License:* GNU Free Documentation License *Contributors:* KRS(talk) 755
Figure 475 *Source:* https://en.wikipedia.org/w/index.php?title=File:Jain_Narayana_temple1_at_Pattadakal.jpg *License:* Creative Commons Attribution-Sharealike 3.0 *Contributors:* Dineshkannambadi (talk) 02:46, 13 August 2008 (UTC) 758
Figure 476 *Source:* https://en.wikipedia.org/w/index.php?title=File:Kavi_file2.jpg *License:* Creative Commons Attribution-Sharealike 3.0 *Contributors:* Jrsanthosh (talk) 759
Figure 477 *Source:* https://en.wikipedia.org/w/index.php?title=File:Kailasha_temple_at_ellora.JPG *License:* Creative Commons Attribution-Sharealike 2.5 *Contributors:* Pratheepps 760
Figure 478 *Source:* https://en.wikipedia.org/w/index.php?title=File:Kuknur_Navalinga_temples.JPG *License:* GNU Free Documentation License *Contributors:* en:User:Dineshkannambadi 761
Figure 479 *Source:* https://en.wikipedia.org/w/index.php?title=File:Old_Kannada_inscription_in_the_mantapa_of_Navalinga_temple_at_Kuknur.jpg *License:* GNU Free Documentation License *Contributors:* en:User:Dineshkannambadi 763
Image *Source:* https://en.wikipedia.org/w/index.php?title=File:Western-chalukya-empire-map.svg *License:* Creative Commons Attribution-ShareAlike 3.0 Unported *Contributors:* Mlpkr 766
Figure 480 *Source:* https://en.wikipedia.org/w/index.php?title=File:Virgal_(hero_stone)_in_Praneshvara_temple_at_Talagunda.JPG *License:* Creative Commons Attribution-Sharealike 3.0 *Contributors:* User:Dineshkannambadi 768
Figure 481 *Source:* https://en.wikipedia.org/w/index.php?title=File:Old_Kannada_inscription_(c.1057)_in_Kalleshvara_temple_at_Hire_Hadagali.jpg *License:* Creative Commons Attribution-Sharealike 3.0 *Contributors:* User:Dineshkannambadi 769
Figure 482 *Source:* https://en.wikipedia.org/w/index.php?title=File:Itagi_Mahadeva_temple.JPG *License:* GNU Free Documentation License *Contributors:* Dinesh Kannambadi (User:Dineshkannambadi) 769
Figure 483 *Source:* https://en.wikipedia.org/w/index.php?title=File:Western_Chalukyas_of_Kalyana_King_Somesvara_I_Trailokyamalla_1043-1068.jpg *License:* GNU Free Documentation License *Contributors:* पाटलिपुत्र 772
Figure 484 *Source:* https://en.wikipedia.org/w/index.php?title=File:Chalukyas_of_Kalyana_(Western_Chalukyas)_Possibly_King_Somesvara_IV_Chalukya._1181-4_1189.jpg *License:* GNU Free Documentation License *Contributors:* पाटलिपुत्र 773
Figure 485 *Source:* https://en.wikipedia.org/w/index.php?title=File:Mallikarjuna_group_of_temples_at_Badami.jpg *License:* Creative Commons Attribution-Sharealike 3.0 *Contributors:* Dineshkannambadi (talk) 23:11, 7 August 2008 (UTC) 774
Figure 486 *Source:* https://en.wikipedia.org/w/index.php?title=File:Open_mantapa_(hall)_in_Kalleshvara_temple_at_Bagali_1.JPG *License:* Creative Commons Attribution-Sharealike 3.0 *Contributors:* User:Dineshkannambadi 776
Figure 487 *Source:* https://en.wikipedia.org/w/index.php?title=File:Basava_statue.jpg *License:* GNU Free Documentation License *Contributors:* Kajasudhakarababu~commonswiki, MGA73bot2, OgreBot 2, Roland zh, TeleComNasSprVen 779
Figure 488 *Source:* https://en.wikipedia.org/w/index.php?title=File:Virgal_(hero_stone)_in_Kedareshvara_temple_at_Balligavi4.JPG *License:* Creative Commons Attribution-Sharealike 3.0 *Contributors:* User:Dineshkannambadi 780

Figure 489 *Source:* https://en.wikipedia.org/w/index.php?title=File:Kirtimukha_(gargoyle)_sculpture_on_vesara_tower_in_the_Kedareshvara_temple_at_Balligavi.jpg *License:* GNU Free Documentation License *Contributors:* -revi, Dineshkannambadi, File Upload Bot (Magnus Manske), MGA73bot2, MathewTownsend, OgreBot 2, Papa November, Roland zh, Xufanc ... 781

Figure 490 *Source:* https://en.wikipedia.org/w/index.php?title=File:Tripurantakesvara_Temple_Sculpture_and_Grill_work_at_Balligavi.jpg *License:* GNU Free Documentation License *Contributors:* File Upload Bot (Magnus Manske), MGA73bot2, OgreBot 2, Papa November, Roland zh 783

Figure 491 *Source:* https://en.wikipedia.org/w/index.php?title=File:Akkamahadevi_Vachana2.JPG *License:* GNU Free Documentation License *Contributors:* Amarrg ... 784

Figure 492 *Source:* https://en.wikipedia.org/w/index.php?title=File:Siddesvara_Temple_Shrine_at_Haveri.JPG *License:* GNU Free Documentation License *Contributors:* File Upload Bot (Magnus Manske), MGA73bot2, OgreBot 2, Papa November, Roland zh ... 786

Figure 493 *Source:* https://en.wikipedia.org/w/index.php?title=File:Ornate_pillars_in_the_Saraswati_temple_at_Gadag.jpg *License:* GNU Free Documentation License *Contributors:* AnRo0002, Dineshkannambadi, File Upload Bot (Magnus Manske), MGA73bot2, Marcus Cyron, Neithsabes, OgreBot 2, Papa November, Roland zh ... 786

Figure 494 *Source:* https://en.wikipedia.org/w/index.php?title=File:Jain_temple_at_Lakkundi.jpg *License:* Creative Commons Attribution-Sharealike 3.0 *Contributors:* User:Rkiran josh ... 787

Figure 495 *Source:* https://en.wikipedia.org/w/index.php?title=File:Old_Kannada_inscription_(1112_CE)_of_King_Vikramaditya_VI_in_the_Mahadeva_temple_at_Itagi.jpg *License:* GNU Free Documentation License *Contributors:* Abhishekjoshi, Cpt.a.haddock, Dineshkannambadi, File Upload Bot (Magnus Manske), Green Mostaza, MGA73bot2, Mhmrodrigues, OgreBot 2, Papa November, Roland zh ... 788

Figure 496 *Source:* https://en.wikipedia.org/w/index.php?title=File:Virgal_(hero_stone)_in_Kedareshvara_temple_at_Balligavi_3.JPG *License:* Creative Commons Attribution-Sharealike 3.0 *Contributors:* User:Dineshkannambadi ... 793

Figure 497 *Source:* https://en.wikipedia.org/w/index.php?title=File:A_virgal_(herostone)_in_Kaitabhesvara_temple_at_Kubatur.JPG *License:* Creative Commons Attribution-Sharealike 3.0 *Contributors:* User:Dineshkannambadi ... 794

Figure 498 *Source:* https://en.wikipedia.org/w/index.php?title=File:Daulatabad_Fort_Geography.jpg *Contributors:* User:VA Photography ... 795

Figure 499 *Source:* https://en.wikipedia.org/w/index.php?title=File:Indra_Sabha_Ellora_Temple_Maharashtra_India.jpg *License:* Creative Commons Attribution 2.0 *Contributors:* Jean-Pierre Dalbéra from Paris, France ... 796

Image *Source:* https://en.wikipedia.org/w/index.php?title=File:Flag_of_vijaynagara.jpg *Contributors:* User:Vydya.areyur ... 804

Figure 500 *Source:* https://en.wikipedia.org/w/index.php?title=File:Ramappa1.jpg *License:* Creative Commons Attribution-Sharealike 3.0 *Contributors:* Ravichandrae ... 811

Figure 501 *Source:* https://en.wikipedia.org/w/index.php?title=File:Rudrama_devi_vigraham.JPG *License:* Creative Commons Attribution-Sharealike 3.0 *Contributors:* User:Bhaskaranaidu ... 812

Figure 502 *Source:* https://en.wikipedia.org/w/index.php?title=File:Koh-i-Noor_old_version_copy.jpg *License:* GNU Free Documentation License *Contributors:* Borvan53, Chris 73, Kluka, Ra'ike ... 813

Figure 503 *Source:* https://en.wikipedia.org/w/index.php?title=File:Kakatiya_Kala_Thoranam_(Warangal_Gate)_and_Ruins.jpg *License:* Creative Commons Attribution-Sharealike 3.0 *Contributors:* User:Sridhar Raju ... 818

Figure 504 *Source:* https://en.wikipedia.org/w/index.php?title=File:Silver_coin_of_Krishnaraja_Kalachuri.jpg *License:* Creative Commons Attribution-Sharealike 3.0 *Contributors:* User:Rani nurmai ... 823

Figure 505 *Source:* https://en.wikipedia.org/w/index.php?title=File:Kalachuri_Feudatories_in_Malwa_and_Vidarbha_King_Kalahasila_Circa_AD_575-610.jpg *License:* GNU Free Documentation License *Contributors:* पाटलिपुत्र ... 823

Figure 506 *Source:* https://en.wikipedia.org/w/index.php?title=File:Elephanta_Caves_(27737333312).jpg *License:* Creative Commons Attribution-Sharealike 2.0 *Contributors:* Ashwin Kumar from Bangalore, India ... 825

Figure 507 *Source:* https://en.wikipedia.org/w/index.php?title=File:Ellora,_cave_29,_Ravana_shaking_Mount_Kailasa_(9841650413).jpg *License:* Creative Commons Attribution 2.0 *Contributors:* Arian Zwegers from Brussels, Belgium ... 826

Image *Source:* https://en.wikipedia.org/w/index.php?title=File:Hoysala_Empire_extent.svg *License:* Creative Commons Attribution-Sharealike 2.5 *Contributors:* Nicholas (Nichalp) ... 828

Figure 508 *Source:* https://en.wikipedia.org/w/index.php?title=File:Hoysala_emblem.JPG *License:* GNU Free Documentation License *Contributors:* Original uploader was Dineshkannambadi at en.wikipedia ... 831

Figure 509 *Source:* https://en.wikipedia.org/w/index.php?title=File:□□□□□_□□□□.jpg *Contributors:* User:Kannadiga ... 833

Figure 510 *Source:* https//en.wikipedia.org *License:* GNU Free Documentation License *Contributors:* Original uploader was Dineshkannambadi at en.wikipedia ... 834

Figure 511 *Source:* https://en.wikipedia.org/w/index.php?title=File:Vishnuvardhana.JPG *License:* Creative Commons Attribution-Sharealike 3.0 *Contributors:* User:Kannadiga ... 835

Figure 512 *Source:* https://en.wikipedia.org/w/index.php?title=File:Somanathapura_Keshava_temple_altered.JPG *License:* GNU Free Documentation License *Contributors:* MGA73bot2, Roland zh ... 836

Figure 513 *Source:* https://en.wikipedia.org/w/index.php?title=File:Old_Kannada_inscription_dated_1182_A.D._at_the_Akkana_Basadi_in_Shravanebelagola.jpg *License:* Creative Commons Attribution-Sharealike 3.0 *Contributors:* User:Anks.manuja ... 839

Figure 514 *Source:* https://en.wikipedia.org/w/index.php?title=File:Belur_Temple_Apsara_with_Mirror.JPG *Contributors:* User:Nithin bolar k 840

Figure 515 *Source:* https://en.wikipedia.org/w/index.php?title=File:View_of_Akkana_Basadi_from_northeastern_side_at_Shravanabelagola.jpg *License:* Creative Commons Attribution-Sharealike 3.0 *Contributors:* User:HoysalaPhotos ... 841

Figure 516 *Source:* https://en.wikipedia.org/w/index.php?title=File:Vesara_style_shrine_and_superstructure_in_Lakshmi_Narasimha_temple_at_Nuggehalli.JPG *License:* Creative Commons Attribution-Sharealike 3.0 *Contributors:* User:Dineshkannambadi ... 842

Figure 517 *Source:* https://en.wikipedia.org/w/index.php?title=File:Rear_view_of_stellate_shrine_in_the_Ishvara_temple_at_Arasikere_1.JPG *License:* Creative Commons Attribution-Sharealike 3.0 *Contributors:* User:Dineshkannambadi ... 842

Figure 518 *Source:* https://en.wikipedia.org/w/index.php?title=File:Jain_Temple_at_Halebidu.jpg *License:* Creative Commons Attribution-Sharealike 3.0 *Contributors:* MGA73bot2, Magog the Ogre, OgreBot 2, Pratyk321, Roland zh, Sreejithk2000 ... 843

Figure 519 *Source:* https://en.wikipedia.org/w/index.php?title=File:Nageshvara_(near)_and_Chennakeshava_(far)_temples_at_Mosale.JPG *License:* Creative Commons Attribution-Sharealike 3.0 *Contributors:* User:Dineshkannambadi ... 843

Figure 520 *Source:* https://en.wikipedia.org/w/index.php?title=File:Shilabaalika_on_pillar_bracket_in_Chennakeshava_Temple_at_Belur2.jpg *License:* GNU Free Documentation License *Contributors:* Alan, Dineshkannambadi, File Upload Bot (Magnus Manske), MGA73bot2, OgreBot 2, Papa November, Roland zh, Vivek Sarje, Xufanc, 1 anonymous edits ... 843

Figure 521 *Source:* https://en.wikipedia.org/w/index.php?title=File:Shasana_(Inscription)_at_Keshava_Temple,_Somanathapura.jpg *License:* Creative Commons Attribution-Sharealike 3.0 *Contributors:* User:HPNadig ... 845

Image *Source:* https://en.wikipedia.org/w/index.php?title=File:Flag_of_Maldives.svg *License:* Public Domain *Contributors:* user:Nightstallion 848

Image *Source:* https://en.wikipedia.org/w/index.php?title=File:Flag_of_Malaysia.svg *Contributors:* , and ... 848

Image *Source:* https://en.wikipedia.org/w/index.php?title=File:Flag_of_Singapore.svg *License:* Public Domain *Contributors:* Various ... 848

Image *Source:* https://en.wikipedia.org/w/index.php?title=File:Flag_of_Indonesia.svg *License:* Public Domain *Contributors:* Drawn by User:SKopp 848

Figure 522 *Source:* https://en.wikipedia.org/w/index.php?title=File:South_India_in_BC_300.jpg *License:* Creative Commons Attribution-Sharealike 3.0 *Contributors:* User:Yon Man33 ... 854

Figure 523 *Source:* https://en.wikipedia.org/w/index.php?title=File:Uttama_coin.png *License:* Creative Commons Attribution-Sharealike 2.5 *Contributors:* Marcus334, Mhmrodrigues, Mindmatrix, Roland zh, Tetraktys, Venu62～commonswiki, 3 anonymous edits ... 855

Figure 524 *Source:* https://en.wikipedia.org/w/index.php?title=File:Raraja_detail.png *License:* Public Domain *Contributors:* User:Venu62～commonswiki ... 856

Figure 525 *Source:* https://en.wikipedia.org/w/index.php?title=File:Gopuram_Corner_View_of_Thanjavur_Brihadeeswara_Temple..JPG *Contributors:* User:KARTY JazZ ... 857

Figure 526 *Source:* https://en.wikipedia.org/w/index.php?title=File:Brihadeeswara_Temple_Entrance_Gopurams,_Thanjavur.JPG *Contributors:* User:KARTY JazZ ... 858

Figure 527 *Source:* https://en.wikipedia.org/w/index.php?title=File:Ship_compartments.jpg *License:* GNU Free Documentation License *Contributors:* AntanO, OgreBot 2, Speravir ... 858

Figure 528 *Source:* https://en.wikipedia.org/w/index.php?title=File:Airavateswara_Temple,Darasuram_in_Thanjavur_District..JPG *Contributors:* User:KARTY JazZ ... 859

Figure 529 *Source:* https://en.wikipedia.org/w/index.php?title=File:Rajaraja_mural-2.jpg *License:* Public Domain *Contributors:* Rajaraja_mural.jpg: Original uploader was Venu62 at en.wikipedia derivative work: Keyan20 (talk) ... 861

Figure 530 *Source:* https://en.wikipedia.org/w/index.php?title=File:Chera_kingdom,_chieftaincies,_and_Chola_mandalams_c._11th_century_(zoom).svg *Contributors:* User:Cpt.a.haddock ... 864

Figure 531 *Source:* https://en.wikipedia.org/w/index.php?title=File:Anchor_of_an_unknown_Lola(ship).jpg *License:* Creative Commons Attribution 3.0 *Contributors:* Everdawn, Onel5969 ... 869

Figure 532 *Source:* https://en.wikipedia.org/w/index.php?title=File:Thanjavur_temple.jpg *License:* Public Domain *Contributors:* AnRo0002, Bgag, Elcobbola, Fransvannes, Maximaximax, OgreBot 2, Roland zh, Woudloper ... 871

Figure 533 *Source:* https://en.wikipedia.org/w/index.php?title=File:Ornamented_pillar_Darasuram.jpg *License:* Creative Commons Attribution 3.0 *Contributors:* RavichandarMy coffee shop. Ravichandar84 at en.wikipedia 872
Figure 534 *Source:* https://en.wikipedia.org/w/index.php?title=File:Cholacrop.jpg *License:* Creative Commons Attribution-Sharealike 2.5 *Contributors:* Robert Nash 874
Figure 535 *Source:* https://en.wikipedia.org/w/index.php?title=File:NatarajaMET.JPG *License:* Creative Commons Attribution-Sharealike 2.5 *Contributors:* User Kaysov on en.wikipedia 876
Figure 536 *Source:* https://en.wikipedia.org/w/index.php?title=File:StandingHanumanCholaDynasty11thCentury.jpg *License:* Creative Commons Attribution-Sharealike 3.0,2.5,2.0,1.0 *Contributors:* PHGCOM 877

License
Creative Commons Attribution-Share Alike 3.0
//creativecommons.org/licenses/by-sa/3.0/

www.ingramcontent.com/pod-product-compliance
Lightning Source LLC
Chambersburg PA
CBHW031931290426
44108CB00011B/522